ENCYCLOPEDIA OF SOCIAL AND CULTURAL ANTHROPOLOGY

ENCYCLOPEDIA OF
SOCIAL AND CULTURAL
ANTHROPOLOGY

Edited by

Alan Barnard
Jonathan Spencer

London & New York

First published 1996
by Routledge
11 New Fetter Lane, London EC4P 4EE
29 West 35th Street, New York, NY 10001

© Routledge 1996

Typeset in Baskerville and Optima by Florencetype Ltd, Stoodleigh, Devon
Printed and bound in Great Britain by TJ Press (Padstow Ltd), Padstow, Cornwall

British Library Cataloguing in Publication Data
A catalogue record for this book is available from the British Library

Library of Congress Cataloguing in Publication Data
A catalogue record for this book has been requested

ISBN 0-415-09996-X

To the memory of
Julia Swannell
(1952–92)

Editorial board

Contents

Acknowledgements   ix

Introduction   x

How to use this book   xiii

List of entries   xiv

List of contributors   xvi

Analytical table of contents   xx

Contributions by author   xxii

Entries   1

Biographical appendix   568

Glossary   594

Name index   629

People and places index   642

Subject index   647

Acknowledgements

Many people have helped the editors to bring this volume to completion. The project itself was first suggested by Mark Barragry of Routledge and, at different times, we have been ably supported by Michelle Darraugh, Robert Potts and Samantha Parkinson of the Routledge Reference Section. Friends and colleagues too numerous to mention have withstood our many casual requests for advice and support, not to mention contributions – some of which have been provided under heroic pressures of time and space. Our editorial board has also been a source of sound advice and ideas. The Department of Social Anthropology in Edinburgh has provided space, calm and, in the final stages of the work, a smoking laser-printer. At different times we have been helped there by Francis Watkins, Colin Millard, Sandra Brown and especially Joni Wilson – all past or present PhD students in the department. Colin Millard and Robert Gibb, together with the editors, translated contributions from the French. We have been especially fortunate to work with Alan McIntosh who has brought a rare combination of skill, patience and good advice to the copy-editing and indexing of this book

The editors have other, more personal debts to acknowledge. For Spencer, Janet Carsten has been a source of amused tolerance as the project drifted out of control, while Jessica Spencer gleefully set it all back a few months. Spencer learnt a great deal of what he knows about lexicography from John Simpson, Yvonne Warburton and Edmund Weiner of the *Oxford English Dictionary*. He learnt most, though, about the pleasure of words and food and many other things, from Julia Swannell.

Barnard would like to thank Joy Barnard for putting up with his mild obsession for the biographical details of long-dead anthropologists, and for providing strength and the voice of common sense throughout the long hours the project has required. Corrie and Buster added the calm atmosphere that only cats can create, while Jake the labrador was as long-suffering as he was bemused by it all. Barnard has benefited much from discussions with his students too, especially those in 'Anthropological Theory'. Their repeated request for a work of this kind has, we both hope, now been met with a source that both embodies their inspirations and serves their intellectual desires.

ALAN BARNARD and JONATHAN SPENCER
Edinburgh, January 1996

Introduction

The very idea of an encyclopedia seems eminently anthropological – in at least two different ways. In its earliest use in classical Rome the term 'encyclopedia' referred to the 'circle of learning', that broad knowledge of the world which was a necessary part of any proper education. In its employment in post–Renaissance Europe it has come to refer more narrowly to attempts to map out systematically all that is known about the world. Anthropology likes to think of itself as the great encyclopedic discipline, provoking, criticizing, stimulating, and occasionally chastening its students by exposure to the extraordinary variety of ways in which people in different places and times have gone about the business of being human. But anthropology, through most of its 150-year history as an academic discipline, has also been alternately seduced and repulsed by the lure of great taxonomic projects to pin down and catalogue human differences.

If anthropology is indeed the most encyclopedic of disciplines, it is not especially well–served with reference works of its own. This book aims to meet some of the need for an accessible and provocative guide to the many things that anthropologists have had to say. It focuses on the biggest and most influential area of anthropology, generally known as cultural anthropology in North America and social anthropology (or ethnology) in Europe. By combining 'social' and 'cultural', the American and the European, in our title we have tried to indicate our desire to produce a volume that reflects the diversity of anthropology as a genuinely global discipline. That desire is also shown in the topics we have covered, from nutrition to postmodernism, incest to essentialism, and above all in the specialists we have invited to contribute. Inside this book you will find a Brazilian anthropologist charting the anthropological history of the idea of society, an Indian reflecting on inequality, a Russian discussing ethnicity and an Australian writing on colonialism, as well as a systematic set of entries on what anthropologists have had to say about the lives and cultures of people living in different regions of the world.

The great encyclopedic projects of the eighteenth and nineteenth centuries are, with grand theories of all kinds, rather out of fashion in contemporary anthropology. Classification, it is widely argued in the humanities and social sciences, is but one form of 'normalization', and even Murray's great *Oxford English Dictionary* has been deconstructed to reveal a meaner project of imperial hegemony lurking beneath its elaborate Victorian structure. What the world does not need, it seems, is an encyclopedia which promises the last word and the complete truth on all that anthropologists know. (And what teachers of anthropology do not need, it might be added, is the prospect of endless course papers made up of apparently authoritative quotations from such a work.) Instead of attempting the impossible task of fitting all that our colleagues do into some final Procrustean schema, we have worked with more modest aims – to help our readers find their way around a discipline which is far too interesting and important to be left in the hands of academic specialists.

Since the Second World War, anthropology has grown enormously, and its concerns are far wider than popular preconceptions about the study of 'primitive peoples'. There is, now, an anthropology of capitalism and global consumerism, an anthropology of gender, an anthropology of war and an anthropology of peace; there is a lot of anthropology *in* museums but more and more anthropology *of* museums; anthropologists are still interested in the political life of people who live on the margins of the modern state, but they are also increasingly interested in nationalism and ethnicity and the rituals and symbols employed by modern politicians at the centre of modern states; anthropologists are often now employed to advise on development projects, but they have also started to look at the very idea of 'development' as a product of a particular culture and history, one more way to imagine what it is to be human. Even the idea of the 'primitive', it has lately been discovered, tells us rather more about the people who use the term to describe other people, than it does about the people so described.

Readers should think of this book, then, as a guide and an introduction, a map which will help them find their way around the anthropological landscape rather than an authority set up to police what counts as anthropologically correct knowledge about the world. The readers we have imagined as we worked on the volume include, of course, students and colleagues in university departments of anthropology around the world; but they also include students and teachers in other disciplines – history, archaeology, sociology, psychology, cultural studies among many others – who may feel the need to come to terms with particular areas of anthropological work. Above all we hope we also reach all sorts of people who are plain curious about who anthropologists are, what they do, and what we can learn from them. We hope that all these different kinds of reader will find material here which stimulates and provokes as well as informs.

Coverage and contributors

In drawing up our headword list we tried to balance a number of considerations. Obviously we wanted to cover as broad a spectrum of contemporary social and cultural anthropology as we could, but we were also aware that anthropology is oddly self-conscious about its own past. Arguments in the present are frequently couched in the form of revisionist versions of familiar charter myths, and controversies between contemporaries ritually re-enact the great arguments of the ancestors. Students, in particular, often find this confusing, knowing little about the collective memory of the discipline and wondering why they should worry so much about the ancestors. When they read the ancestors, there is often further confusion – key terms like 'culture' or 'structure' have shifted meaning over time, while much of the argument at any one time has been about what exactly we *should* mean by these terms.

We have, therefore, tried as far as possible to represent the past as well as the present, both in our choice of headwords for entries, and in our instructions to contributors. But we have also tried to reflect the fact that anthropology is, as it has always been, a pluralistic and occasionally fractious discipline. We have not tried to impose an editorial orthodoxy on our contributors, and we have encouraged all our authors to be explicit about their own opinions and arguments. The balance in our coverage comes from combining *different* points of view, rather than hiding behind some pretence of editorial distance. (Dismayed students may, at this point, realize that this means they should never read a single entry; the safe minimum is always to read two on related subjects, but by different authors.) This makes the choice of contributors as important as the original choice of headwords. Again we have tried to achieve balance by combining difference: European, North American, Asian and Australasian; women and men; seasoned scholars and (we believe) rising stars. Our minimal criteria were simple: each contributor should be able to write with clarity and authority on the topic in question; and taken together, the contributors should reflect the different contexts in which anthropology can be found today.

There was one other important editorial decision that had to be made. Anthropology involves two kinds of academic work: detailed study of the lives of people in different social and cultural contexts, based on long–term fieldwork and resulting in that curious genre known as ethnography; and theoretical and comparative work which draws upon ethnographic knowledge but seeks to move beyond its particularity. This book, we felt, needed to give due weight to both sides of the discipline, but this presented us with two difficulties. Drawing up a list of entries on particular 'peoples', 'tribes', or 'ethnic groups' seemed inappropriate for all sorts of reasons, even though casual references to 'Nuer-type' political organization, or 'Kachin-style equilibrium' abound in the literature. And writing a set of abstract theoretical entries with no reference to the particular knowledge of particular people on which the discipline is based would be both dull and misleading. We therefore decided to deal with the first problem by commissioning a set of entries surveying the regional traditions of ethnographic writing – writing on Southern Africa, Lowland South America, Southern Europe, and so on. And we decided to supplement this by encouraging individual authors to use detailed, and sometimes extended, ethnographic examples wherever appropriate in all the entries.

Other editorial decisions can be discerned in the list of entries. The history of the discipline is covered in entries on topics like diffusionism and evolutionism, as well as separate entries on the main national traditions of anthropology – British, French, American, as well as Indian and East European, divisions which are now beginning to crumble but which have been important in shaping modern anthropology. There is also an entry covering writing *about* the history of anthropology. We have tried to systematically cover anthropology's relations with our neighbours in the humanities and social sciences – linguistics, archaeology, biological anthropology (with cultural anthopology, the 'four fields' of American anthropology), sociology, history, classical studies. After four years of planning, commissioning, editing and writing, we recognize how dangerous it would be to claim that this book is complete. We hope, though, that what is here is enough.

How to use this book

There are three kinds of entry in this encyclopedia.

- The main text is taken up with 231 substantial entries, organized alphabetically, on important areas of anthropological work. Each of these entries includes a guide to further reading and cross-references to other related entries.

- At the end of the main text there is a separate section containing short biographical entries on leading figures who have been important in the development of anthropology.

- Finally, there is a glossary providing definitions and explanations of technical terms used in the encyclopedia itself and elsewhere in anthropology.

The choice of headwords is inevitably rather arbitrary – should we look for information on theories of ritual, or rituals of power under ritual itself, under religion, under the names of the more important theorists, or even under politics or kingship? We have tried to make the index as full and explicit as possible, and this is where most readers should start their search for what they want to know. When they have found the entry that seems most relevant they should also pay attention to the cross-references to other entries: at the end of each main entry there is a list of other entries which touch on similar subject matter; within the text of each entry cross-references are indicated by either an asterisk or a dagger symbol:

* indicates another main entry

† indicates a name or a term in the biographical appendix or the glossary

In the list of further reading at the end of each entry we encouraged our contributors to err on the side of economy. Our readers, we felt, did not need a list of *everything* that had been written on a particular topic; they needed a selective list of those books and articles most helpful as an introduction to the topic.

List of entries

Aboriginal Australia
adoption and fostering
aesthetics
Africa: East
Africa: Nilotic
Africa: Southern
Africa: West
age
alliance
American anthropology
Americas: Central
Americas: Latin America
Americas: Native North
    America
Americas: Native South
    America (Highland)
Americas: Native South
    America (Lowland)
ancestors
anthropological societies
archaeology
Arctic
art
Asia: East
Asia: South
Asia: Southeast
avunculate

belief
Big Man
biological anthropology
Boas, Franz
body
British anthropology
Buddhism

cannibalism
capitalism
cargo cult
Caribbean
caste
cattle complex
childhood

Chinese anthropology
Christianity
class
classical studies
classification
cognatic society
cognition
colonialism
community
compadrazgo
comparative method
complementary filiation
complex society
componential analysis
conception, theories of
consumption
cosmology
Crow–Omaha systems
cultural materialism
cultural studies
culture
culture and personality

dance
death
descent
development
diffusionism
discourse
divination
dreams
dual organization
Dutch anthropology

ecological anthropology
economic anthropology
education
emic and etic
Enlightenment anthropology
environment
essentialism
ethnicity
ethnography

ethnopsychiatry
ethnoscience
Europe: Central and Eastern
Europe: Northern
Europe: Southern
evolution and evolutionism
exchange

factions
family
feudalism
fieldwork
film
fishing
folklore
food
formalism and substantivism
French anthropology
friendship
functionalism

gender
genealogical method
German and Austrian
    anthropology
ghost dance
gossip
great and little traditions
Gypsies

Hinduism
history and anthropology
history of anthropology
honour and shame
house
household
hunting and gathering

identity
ideology
incest
Indian anthropology
individualism
inequality

Islam

Japan
joking and avoidance

kingship
kinship
kula

land tenure
landscape
language and linguistics
law
Lévi-Strauss, Claude
literacy

magic
Malinowski, Bronislaw
mana
markets
marriage
Marxism and anthropology
mass media
medical anthropology
memory
menstruation
methodology
Middle East and North Africa
migration
millennial movements,
    millenarianism
missionaries
mode of production
modernism, modernity and
    modernization
money
Morgan, Lewis Henry
museums
music
myth and mythology

names and naming
nationalism
nature and culture

network analysis
nomadism
number
nutrition

Occidentalism
oral literature
oratory
Orientalism

Pacific: Melanesia
Pacific: Polynesia
pastoralists
patrons and clients
peasants
person
pilgrimage
play
plural society
poetics
political anthropology
political economy
pollution and purity
possession
postmodernism
potlatch
power
preference and prescription
primitive communism
primitive mentality
property
psychoanalysis
psychological anthropology

race
Radcliffe-Brown, A.R.
rationality
reflexivity
refugees
regional analysis and regional
    comparison
relationship terminology
relativism

religion
reproductive technologies
resistance
rite of passage
ritual
Russian and Soviet anthro-
    pology

sacred and profane
sacrifice
Sapir–Whorf hypothesis
scandals, anthropological
science
settlement patterns
shamanism
sharecropping
slavery
social structure and social
    organization
socialization
society
sociobiology
sociology
state
structuralism
symbolic anthropology
syncretism

taboo
technology
time and space
totemism
tourism
transhumance
translation

urban anthropology

violence

war, warfare
witchcraft
work
world system

List of contributors

Prof. Marc Abélès
Laboratory of Social Anthropology
CNRS, Paris, France

Prof. Joseph Agassi
Department of Philosophy
York University, Ontario, Canada

Prof. W. Arens
Department of Anthropology
State University of New York, Stony
    Brook, USA

Prof. Donald W. Attwood
Department of Anthropology
McGill University, Montreal, Canada

Prof. Lawrence Babb
Department of Anthropology and Sociology
Amherst College, MA, USA

Dr Marcus Banks
Institute of Social and Cultural Anthropology
University of Oxford, UK

Dr Alan Barnard
Department of Social Anthropology
University of Edinburgh, UK

Dr Gerd Baumann
Research Centre Religion and Society
University of Amsterdam, Netherlands

Dr Paul Baxter
Manchester, UK

Dr Barbara Bender
Department of Anthropology
University College London, UK

Prof. Bernardo Bernardi
Rome, Italy

Prof. André Béteille
Department of Sociology
Delhi School of Economics, India

Prof. Maurice Bloch
Department of Anthropology
London School of Economics, UK

Prof. Reginald Byron
Department of Sociology and Anthropology
University College Swansea, UK

Dr Jeanne Cannizzo
Department of Social Anthropology
University of Edinburgh, UK

Dr James G. Carrier
Department of Anthropology
University of Durham, UK

Prof. Michael Carrithers
Department of Anthropology
University of Durham, UK

Dr Paul Cartledge
Clare College
University of Cambridge, UK

Prof. H.J.M. Claessen
Department of Anthropology
University of Leiden, Netherlands

Dr Elisabeth Copet-Rougier
Laboratory of Social Anthropology
CNRS, Paris, France

Prof. Thomas Crump
Amsterdam, Netherlands

Prof. Frederick H. Damon
Dept of Anthropology
University of Virginia, USA

Prof. Michael Dietler
Department of Anthropology
University of Chicago, USA

Dr Roy Dilley
Department of Social Anthropology
University of St Andrews, UK

Dr Walter Dostal
Institut für Völkerkunde
University of Vienna, Austria

Prof. Dale F. Eickelman
Department of Anthropology
Dartmouth College, Hanover, USA

Prof. Roy Ellen
Eliot College
University of Kent, UK

Dr Richard Fardon
Department of Anthropology and Sociology
School of Oriental and African Studies,
London, UK

Prof. James Ferguson
Department of Anthropology
University of California, Irvine, USA

Prof. Ruth Finnegan
Faculty of Social Sciences
The Open University, UK

Prof. Robin Fox
Department of Anthroplogy
Rutgers University, New Brunswick, USA

Dr Sarah Franklin
Department of Sociology
University of Lancaster, UK

Prof. C.J. Fuller
Department of Anthropology
London School of Economics, UK

Prof. John G. Galaty
Department of Anthropology
McGill University, Montreal, Canada

Dr David N. Gellner
Department of Human Sciences
Brunel University, Uxbridge, UK

Prof. Thomas Gibson
Department of Anthropology
University of Rochester, USA

Dr Lisa Gilad
Immigration and Refugee Board
St John's, Newfoundland, Canada

Prof. André Gingrich
Institut für Völkerkunde
University of Vienna, Austria

Dr Anthony Good
Department of Social Anthropology
University of Edinburgh, UK

Prof. Ralph Grillo
AFRAS
University of Sussex, UK

Prof. Stephen Gudeman
Department of Anthropology
University of Minnesota, USA

Prof. Ørnulf Gulbrandson
Department of Social Anthropology
University of Bergen, Norway

Prof. C.M. Hann
Eliot College
University of Kent, UK

Prof. Judith Lynne Hanna
University of Maryland, USA

Prof. Ulf Hannerz
Department of Social Anthropology
Stockholm University, Sweden

Dr Simon Harrison
Department of Sociology and Social
    Anthropology
University of Ulster, UK

Dr Penelope Harvey
Department of Social Anthropology
University of Manchester, UK

Prof. Michael Herzfeld
Department of Anthropology
Harvard University, Cambridge, USA

Prof. Signe Howell
Department and Museum of Anthropology
University of Oslo, Norway

Dr Mary Tylor Huber
Carnegie Fund for Advancement of Teaching
Princeton University, USA

Prof. I.C. Jarvie
Department of Philosophy
York University, Ontario, Canada

Dr M.C. Jedrej
Department of Social Anthropology
University of Edinburgh, UK

Prof. R.S. Khare
Department of Anthropology
University of Virginia, USA

Prof. Victor T. King
Centre for Southeast Asian Studies
University of Hull, UK

Prof. Ann E. Kingsolver
Department of Anthropology
University of California, Santa Cruz, USA

Dr Chris Knight
University of East London, UK

Prof. Henrika Kuklick
Department of History and Sociology of
   Science
University of Pennsylvania, USA

Prof. Michael Lambek
Department of Anthropology, Scarborough
   College
University of Toronto, Canada

Dr Helen Lambert
Department of Public Health and Public Policy
London School of Hygiene and Tropical
   Medicine, UK

Prof. Robert Layton
Department of Anthropology
University of Durham, UK

Prof. John Leavitt
Département d'Anthropologie
University of Montreal, Canada

Dr Pierre Lemonnier
CNRS
Marseilles, France

Prof. I.M. Lewis
Department of Social Anthropology
London School of Economics, UK

Prof. Lamont Lindstrom
Department of Anthropology,
University of Tulsa, USA

Prof. Roland Littlewood
Department of Anthropology
University College London, UK

Prof. Kenneth Maddock
School of Behavioural Sciences
Macquarie University, New South Wales,
   Australia

Dr Marit Melhuus
Department of Social Anthropology
University of Oslo, Norway

Dr Jon P. Mitchell
Department of Social Anthropology
University of Edinburgh, UK

Dr Stephen Nugent
Department of Anthropology
Goldsmiths College, London, UK

Dr Frances Pine
Department of Social Anthropology
University of Cambridge, UK

Dr Johan Pottier
Department of Anthropology and
   Sociology
School of Oriental and African Studies,
   London, UK

Dr Aparna Rao
Institut für Völkerkunde,
University of Cologne, Germany

Dr Nigel Rapport
Department of Social Anthropology
University of St Andrews, UK

Dr Claudia Barcellos Rezende
Institute of Philosophy and Social
   Sciences
University of Rio de Janeiro, Brazil

Dr David Riches
Department of Social Anthropology
University of St Andrews, UK

Prof. Dan Rose
Department of Landscape Architecture and
   Regional Planning
University of Pennsylvania, USA

Prof. Bernard Saladin d'Anglure
Department of Anthropology
Université Laval, Cité Universitaire, Québec,
   Canada

Prof. Philip Carl Salzman
Department of Anthropology
McGill University, Montreal, Canada

Prof. Roger Sanjek
Department of Anthropology
Queens College, City University of New
York, USA

Prof. Gopala Sarana
University of Lucknow, India

Dr Sergey Sokolovskii
Institute of Ethnology and Anthropology
Moscow, Russia

Dr Jonathan Spencer
Department of Social Anthropology
University of Edinburgh, UK

Dr Charles Stafford
Department of Anthropology
London School of Economics, UK

Dr Charles Stewart
Department of Anthropology
University College London, UK

Dr Martin Stokes
Department of Social Anthropology
The Queen's University of Belfast, UK

Dr S.S. Strickland
Department of Anthropology
University College London, UK

Dr Nicholas Tapp
Department of Social Anthropology
University of Edinburgh, UK

Dr Neil Thin
Department of Social Anthropology
University of Edinburgh, UK

Dr Nicholas Thomas
Department of Prehistory and
   Anthropology
Australian National University

Dr Philip Thomas
Department of Social Anthropology
University of Edinburgh, UK

Dr Valery Tishkov
Institute of Ethnology and Anthropology
Moscow, Russia

Dr Christina Toren
Department of Human Sciences
Brunel University, Uxbridge, UK

Dr James Urry
Department of Anthropology
Victoria University of Wellington, New
Zealand

Prof. P.L. van den Berghe
Department of Sociology
University of Washington, USA

Prof. Peter van der Veer
Research Centre Religion and Society
University of Amsterdam, Netherlands

Dr Han Vermeulen
Centre of Non-Western Studies
University of Leiden, Netherlands

Prof. Joan Vincent
Department of Anthropology
Barnard College, Columbia University, NY,
   USA

Prof. Eduardo Viveiros de Castro
Department of Anthropology
National Museum, Rio de Janeiro, Brazil

Dr Francis Watkins
Overseas Development Administration
London, UK

Prof. James Weiner
Department of Anthropology
University of Adelaide, South Australia,
Australia

Prof. Mark P. Whitaker
Department of Sociology
University of South Carolina, Aiken, USA

Dr Roy Willis
Department of Social Anthropology
University of Edinburgh, UK

Prof. Kevin A. Yelvington
Department of Anthropology
University of South Florida, Tampa, USA

Dr Françoise Zonabend
Laboratory of Social Anthropology
CNRS, Paris, France

Analytical table of contents

Ethnographic surveys
Aboriginal Australia
Africa: East
Africa: Nilotic
Africa: Southern
Africa: West
Americas: Central
Americas: Latin America
Americas: Native North
    America
Americas: Native South
    America (Highland)
Americas: Native South
    America (Lowland)
Arctic
Asia: East
Asia: South
Asia: Southeast
Caribbean
Europe: Central and Eastern
Europe: Northern
Europe: Southern
Japan
Middle East and North
    Africa
Pacific: Melanesia
Pacific: Polynesia

History of anthropology
American anthropology
anthropological societies
Boas, Franz
British anthropology
Chinese anthropology
Dutch anthropology
Enlightenment anthropology
French anthropology
German and Austrian
    anthropology
history of anthropology
Indian anthropology
Lévi-Strauss, Claude

Malinowski, Bronislaw
Morgan, Lewis Henry
Radcliffe-Brown, A.R.
Russian and Soviet
    anthropology
scandals, anthropological

**Subdisciplines and
    neighbouring disciplines
    (anthropology and . . .)**
archaeology
biological anthropology
classical studies
cultural studies
ethnopsychiatry
film
history and anthropology
language and linguistics
law
medical anthropology
political anthropology
psychological anthropology
sociobiology
sociology
urban anthropology

**Anthropological concepts
    and methods**
alliance
avunculate
Big Man
cargo cult
cattle complex
cognatic society
compadrazgo
comparative method
complementary filiation
complex society
componential analysis
Crow–Omaha systems
cultural materialism
culture

culture and personality
diffusionism
discourse
divination
dual organization
ecological anthropology
economic anthropology
emic and etic
essentialism
ethnicity
ethnography
ethnoscience
evolution and evolutionism
fieldwork
formalism and substantivism
functionalism
genealogical method
great and little traditions
honour and shame
identity
joking and avoidance
kinship
mana
Marxism and anthropology
methodology
mode of production
nature and culture
network analysis
Occidentalism
Orientalism
patrons and clients
person
postmodernism
potlatch
primitive communism
primitive mentality
rationality
reflexivity
regional analysis and
    regional comparison
relationship terminology
relativism

rite of passage
ritual
sacred and profane
Sapir–Whorf hypothesis
settlement patterns
shamanism
social structure and social
  organization
socialization
society
structuralism
syncretism
taboo
transhumance
world system

**Anthropological objects (the
  anthropology
  of . . .)**
adoption and fostering
aesthetics
age
ancestors
art
belief
body
Buddhism
cannibalism
capitalism
caste
childhood
Christianity
class
classification
cognition
colonialism
community
conception
consumption
cosmology
dance

death
descent
development
dreams
education
environment
exchange
factions
family
feudalism
fishing
folklore
food
friendship
gender
ghost dance
gossip
Gypsies
Hinduism
house
household
hunting and gathering
ideology
incest
individualism
inequality
Islam
kula
land tenure
landscape
literacy
magic
markets
marriage
mass media
memory
menstruation
migration
millennial movements,
  millenarianism
missionaries

money
museums
music
myth and mythology
names and naming
nationalism
nomadism
number
nutrition
oral literature
oratory
pastoralists
pilgrimage
play
plural society
poetics
political economy
pollution and purity
possession
power
preference and prescription
property
race
refugees
religion
reproductive technologies
resistance
sacrifice
science
sharecropping
slavery
state
technology
time and space
totemism
tourism
translation
war, warfare
witchcraft and sorcery
work

Contributions by author

Marc Abélès
state

W. Arens
cannibalism
incest

Lawrence Babb
Hinduism

Marcus Banks
film

Alan Barnard
avunculate
belief
componential analysis
cultural materialism
Dutch anthropology
emic and etic
ethnoscience
joking and avoidance
potlatch
regional analysis and
   regional comparison
relationship terminology
settlement patterns
social structure and social
   organization

**Alan Barnard and
Jonathan Spencer**
adoption and fostering
culture
rite of passage
Sapir–Whorf hypothesis

Gerd Baumann
Islam

Paul Baxter
cattle complex

Barbara Bender
landscape

Bernardo Bernardi
Africa: East
age

André Béteille
caste
Indian anthropology
inequality

Maurice Bloch
alliance
ancestors
cognition
complementary filiation
death
ideology
memory
structuralism

Reginald Byron
Europe: Northern
fishing
identity

Jeanne Cannizzo
museums
art

James G. Carrier
consumption
exchange
Occidentalism
sociology

Michael Carrithers
fieldwork
nature and culture
person

Paul Cartledge
classical studies

H.J.M. Claessen
evolution and evolutionism
feudalism
Pacific: Polynesia

Elisabeth Copet-Rougier
Crow–Omaha systems

Thomas Crump
Americas: Central
Japan
money
number
play

Frederick H. Damon
kula

Michael Dietler
archaeology

Roy Dilley
markets

**Walter Dostal and André
Gingrich**
German and Austrian
anthropology

Dale F. Eickelman
Middle East and North
Africa
pilgrimage

Roy Ellen
classification

Richard Fardon
Africa: West

James Ferguson
development

Ruth Finnegan
literacy
oral literature
poetics
translation

Robin Fox
sociobiology

Sarah Franklin
conception
cultural studies
reproductive technologies
science

C.J. Fuller
Asia: South

John G. Galaty
pastoralists

David N. Gellner
Buddhism

Thomas Gibson
Asia: Southeast
sacrifice

Lisa Gilad
refugees

Anthony Good
kinship
preference and prescription

Ralph Grillo
language and linguistics

Stephen Gudeman
economic anthropology

Ørnulf Gulbrandson
Africa: Southern

C.M. Hann
class
Europe: Central and
   Eastern
land tenure
mode of production
property
sharecropping

Judith Lynne Hanna
dance

Ulf Hannerz
complex society

Simon Harrison
Pacific: Melanesia
war, warfare

Penelope Harvey
Americas: Native South
   America (Highland)

Michael Herzfeld
essentialism
folklore

Signe Howell
cosmology

Mary Tylor Huber
Christianity
missionaries

**I.M. Jarvie and Joseph
Agassi**
rationality

M.C. Jedrej
Africa: Nilotic
primitive mentality
time and space

R.S. Khare
pollution and purity

Victor T. King
cognatic society

Ann E. Kingsolver
power
work

Chris Knight
menstruation
taboo
totemism

Henrika Kuklick
British anthropology
diffusionism
functionalism
Malinowski, Bronislaw

Michael Lambek
possession

Helen Lambert
medical anthropology

Robert Layton
Aboriginal Australia

John Leavitt
French anthropology

Pierre Lemonnier
technology

I.M. Lewis
descent

Lamont Lindstrom
Big Man
cargo cult
discourse
mana
millennial movements,
   millenarianism
oratory
syncretism

Roland Littlewood
ethnopsychiatry

Kenneth Maddock
dual organization
primitive communism
Radcliffe-Brown, A.R.
sacred and profane

Marit Melhuus
Americas: Latin America

Jon P. Mitchell
honour and shame
patrons and clients
ritual

Stephen Nugent
Americas: Native South
   America (Lowland)
postmodernism

Frances Pine
family
gender

Johan Pottier
food

Aparna Rao
Gypsies

Nigel Rapport
community
gossip
individualism

**Claudia Barcellos
Rezende**
friendship

David Riches
Americas: Native North
America
hunting and gathering

Dan Rose
capitalism

**Bernard Saladin
d'Anglure**
Arctic
Lévi-Strauss, Claude
names and naming
shamanism

Philip Carl Salzman
mass media
methodology
nomadism
transhumance

**Philip Carl Salzman and
Donald W. Attwood**
ecological anthropology

Roger Sanjek
Boas, Franz
ethnography
household
network analysis
race
urban anthropology

Gopala Sarana
comparative method

**Sergey Sokolovskii and
Valery Tishkov**
ethnicity

Jonathan Spencer
formalism and
substantivism
kingship

Marxism and anthropology
modernism, modernity and
modernization
nationalism
Orientalism
peasants
psychoanalysis
resistance
scandals, anthropological
symbolic anthropology
violence

Charles Stafford
Asia: East
education

Charles Stewart
dreams
Europe: Southern
great and little traditions

Martin Stokes
music

S.S. Strickland
biological anthropology
nutrition

Nicholas Tapp
Chinese anthropology

Neil Thin
environment

Nicholas Thomas
colonialism
history and anthropology

Philip Thomas

house
slavery
world system

Valery Tishkov
Russian and Soviet
anthropology

Christina Toren
childhood
culture and personality
psychological
anthropology

socialization
James Urry
anthropological societies
history of anthropology
(discipline)

P.L. van den Berghe
compadrazgo
tourism

Peter van der Veer
religion

Han Vermeulen
Enlightenment anthro-
pology

Joan Vincent
American anthropology
factions
genealogical method
ghost dance
law
Morgan, Lewis Henry
plural society
political economy
political anthropology

**Eduardo Viveiros de
Castro**
society

Francis Watkins
migration

James Weiner
aesthetics
myth and mythology

Mark P. Whitaker
reflexivity
relativism

Roy Willis
body
divination
magic
witchcraft

Kevin A. Yelvington
Caribbean

Françoise Zonabend
marriage

Aboriginal Australia

The earliest humans to settle Australia arrived at least 50,000 years ago. At the time of British colonization in 1788 there were two hundred or more Aboriginal language communities within the continent. In areas of intense colonization, the Aboriginal economy was rapidly destroyed and it is only through the reports of explorers that we have records of semi-permanent settlements, the cultivation of edible roots (*Dioscorea sp.*) and the construction of eel dykes. While such practices have recently been confirmed by archaeological research in the southeast and southwest of the continent, much of Australian anthropology has been conducted in areas remote from European settlement and it is from these areas that the image of the 'typical' indigenous cultures of Australia has been derived.

Spencer and Gillen

By far the most influential of the early Australian ethnographers were †Baldwin Spencer and †F.J. Gillen. In late nineteenth-century anthropological theorizing, Aboriginal society occupied the place the Caribs had done in †Rousseau's philosophy; that is, as the living exemplars of humankind's original condition. Spencer and Gillen provided much of the data on which theories about the nature of such societies were constructed. †Frazer asserted in his preface to *The Native Tribes of Central Australia* that Spencer and Gillen had met 'tribes living in the Stone Age', ignorant of metal working, agriculture and even the physiology of reproduction, whose secrets Spencer and Gillen had 'snatched . . . just before the final decadence of the tribes set in' (Frazer, in Spencer and Gillen 1899). Frazer considered that their work pointed to the belief in spiritual conception, in which the unborn baby is animated by the spirit of an ancestral being, as the most probable source of *totemism. He wanted to elucidate the principle of causation that allegedly enabled a *ritual to increase the numbers of a totemic species. †Durkheim, on the other hand, found demonstration of his theory of the sociological origin of religion in the work of Spencer and Gillen and their contemporary, Strehlow. Durkheim emphasized the social character of increase rites rather than their instrumental purpose.

Spencer and Gillen also documented the *kinship terminologies of central Australia. While they committed the error of inferring that classificatory kinship had its origin in 'group marriage', they clarified the relationship of the eight subsection system to rules of *marriage and *descent. In later survey work they demonstrated the existence of similar systems in northern Australia.

Two ideas that pervaded nineteenth-century European thinking about Aboriginal society were: first, that their structure placed them at a given stage in a scheme of unilineal *evolution, rather than displaying an adaptation to the natural *environment; second, that Aboriginal people were about to lose their distinctive culture and either die out or become assimilated to the dominant culture.

Radcliffe-Brown

Although *Radcliffe-Brown carried out fieldwork in western Australia, he worked in an area where Aboriginal life had been far more severely disrupted by colonial settlement than had central Australia in the 1890s. While he had the opportunity to collect detailed genealogies and statements of marriage rules, he did not observe normal, daily interaction and was unaware of how the principles he elucidated translated into social behaviour. Instead, Radcliffe-Brown gained an overview of structural variation in the 130 'tribes' on which he had sufficient information, which was brilliantly conveyed in a four-part analysis published in the first issues of *Oceania* (Radcliffe-Brown 1930–1). A limited range of types of Aboriginal society were identified, each named after a representative tribe: such as the Kariera, Aranda, Mara and Murgin systems. Adopting a (Herbert) †Spencerian perspective, Radcliffe-Brown inferred that the more complex types had developed out of the simpler forms as a consequence of progressive social evolution; indeed, he claimed to have predicted the existence of the simpler Kariera system from his knowledge of the Aranda system described by Spencer and Gillen. Whether he had indeed done so, or learned of systems of the Kariera form from Daisy Bates's field notes, has been hotly debated; there is no doubt that Bates already understood, and had documented, the operation of four-section systems of the Kariera type.

While Radcliffe-Brown and his followers were later ridiculed by †Edmund Leach for indulging in 'anthropological butterfly collecting' when they classified societies according to types and subtypes, his imposition of order upon the accumulating ethnographies of Australia was a substantial achievement. It has nevertheless severe limitations. The method is almost entirely descriptive. There are no hypotheses to explain why the variety of human societies should take particular forms, other than an alleged inherent tendency for systems to develop greater complexity over time.

Unlike Radcliffe-Brown, his student †W.L. Warner conducted extended fieldwork between 1926 and 1929 at Millingimbi, in northeast Arnhem Land, to produce his classic of functionalist ethnography, *A Black Civilisation* (1937). Warner gave the name *Murngin* to the indigenous people of Northeast Arnhem Land; today these people call themselves *Yolngu*. His ethnography provided an integrated account of local organization, kinship, *warfare, *religion and (unusually for the time) the evidence for change and interaction with Indonesian fishermen.

Lévi-Strauss on kinship

Lévi-Strauss's work on †cross-cousin marriage clearly owes a considerable debt to Radcliffe-Brown's work on Australia. He both adopts Radcliffe-Brown's three types of cross-cousin marriage as the three possible †elementary structures of kinship, and re-analyses Australian

material in the first of the ethnographic sections of *The Elementary Structures of Kinship*. While Radcliffe-Brown regarded kinship as an extension of familial relationships to the tribal community in such a way as to achieve progressively higher levels of social integration, Lévi-Strauss regarded kinship as the product of a mode of thought which operated at a global (tribal) level, ordering people into opposed relationship categories such as 'father's father' and 'mother's father'. Lévi-Strauss followed Radcliffe-Brown in hypothesizing that the various types of Australian kinship system offered different scales of social integration, but considered the Murngin system provided the greatest potential for extensive social networks, because the chains of †matrilateral marriage alliance could be indefinitely extended, whereas the †bilateral Kariera and Aranda systems tend toward closure.

Warner had shown that the Murngin had †patrilineal †moieties, but recognized seven patrilines in their kinship terminology. The two 'outer' lines, furthest from *ego*, both belonged to the opposite moiety to *ego's* and therefore could not marry each other. This generated a notorious controversy, as to how many lines of descent actually existed in the Murngin kinship system. Although much of the Murngin debate was arcane, it did highlight an important ambiguity in Radcliffe-Brown's model, where the line of descent in the kinship terminology, the land-owning group and the foraging band appear to be identically-constituted. This ambiguity was resolved, at an academic level, in papers by Hiatt and †Stanner, but resurfaced in anthropological evidence presented on behalf of the first attempt by Aboriginal people to claim legal recognition of their title to land.

The structural study of symbolism

Durkheim argued that the significance of each *totem as a †symbol stemmed, not from any intrinsic attribute, but from its position in the structure of clan totemism. The influence that Durkheim's theory of the social origin of the meaning of totemic emblems had on †Saussure and the formulation of his structural theory of †semiology is well-known. Lévi-Strauss later developed the structural theory of totemism, most notably in Chapter 4 of *The Savage Mind*. He here compares the structural logic of central Australian totemism with that of the Indian caste system. A structural approach is also taken in Stanner's analyses of Murinbata religion, which gains from its basis in Stanner's own fieldwork among the Murinbata. Stanner records, in a footnote, that he only learned of Lévi-Strauss's analysis after he had commenced publication of this series of papers.

The semiological approach to art and ritual was brilliantly taken up by Nancy Munn (1973) in her studies of art among the Warlpiri, and by Morphy (1991) in his work on Yolngu art. Both have taken a more generative approach to art and ritual, made possible by Saussure's development of the Durkheimian theory. In their work the artistic tradition is seen to provide a grammar as well as a vocabulary of visual signs, allowing artists opportunities to create new works rather than simply to reproduce totemic emblems whose form is fixed by tradition. A similar approach has been taken in the study of ceremony. It is questionable how many performances of the major ceremonies which Warner describes in his ethnography he actually observed, but Warner appears to commit the Durkheimian fallacy of assuming that each performance of a ritual is identical and only amenable to one level of interpretation. †Ronald Berndt restudied the two major Arnhem Land cults documented by Warner and, while Warner's 'native' exegesis appeared to support a functionalist interpretation, Berndt's informants opted for a more Freudian reading of the rituals (Berndt 1951). More recently, Morphy has shown how Yolngu ceremonies are to a certain extent constructed to suit the occasion, while Keen (1994) has demonstrated that the Gunabibi and Wawilak cults are merely two among many in the region which interpret common elements in different ways. Special mention should also be made of †Kaberry's pioneering work in the Kimberleys, which showed that Aboriginal women had their own rituals, of which male anthropologists had been unaware (Kaberry 1939).

Marxist and ecological studies

Several *Marxist analyses in anthropology have cited Australian Aboriginal societies as possessing varieties of *'primitive communism', but the power conferred by control of religious cults renders Aboriginal society significantly less egalitarian than the other classic *hunter-gatherers of semi-arid environments, the Kalahari San and the Hadza.

McCarthy and MacArthur's observations of two Aboriginal camps during a three-week period in Arnhem Land provided one of the key pieces of ethnographic evidence in support of †Sahlins's

theory of the 'original affluent society', which argued it was the lack of a political incentive to accumulate resources above subsistence needs that caused the apparent material poverty of hunter-gatherers. McCarthy and McArthur's data showed that the average length of time taken to forage for and prepare food in Arnhem Land was four to five hours per person per day. People stopped foraging as soon as they had enough for their immediate needs, leaving plenty of spare time. From these and similar observations on other hunter-gatherer communities Sahlins derived his concept of the 'domestic mode of production'. Sahlins's domestic mode of production portrays each household as a politically-independent unit of production; a concept which underestimates the importance of reciprocal rights of access between foraging ranges, and meat-sharing between households within camp, as devices for reducing the risks of exploiting scarce and unpredictable resources.

While Sahlins recognized the inadequacy of McCarthy and McArthur's data, it was not until the 1980s that long-term studies of Aboriginal susbsistence practices were published. It is noteworthy that these studies were possible, a century after Frazer had anticipated the imminent extinction of Aboriginal culture, because many communities had, over the previous decade, returned to a more traditional subsistence economy after some years spent on church or government settlements. Both Altman (1987) and Meehan (1982) conclude that women's work has been made easier by the availability of purchased flour and sugar and consequently question Sahlins's picture of leisured affluence in pre-colonial society. Both studies underline the contribution that hunting and gathering can still make to the diet; Altman calculates that it provides 81 per cent of protein and 46 per cent of the calories consumed on the outstation he investigated.

Land claims

Australia was colonized on the basis of the legal fiction that, because they are nomadic and do not 'improve' the soil, hunter-gatherers cannot be said to own land. When, in 1971, three Yolngu clans undertook the first attempt to demonstrate in an Australian court that they held title to their traditional land, the case failed at least in part because an erroneous account of Aboriginal land tenure was put to the court by anthropologists appearing on their behalf.

It was argued that each clan held a territory and its sacred sites through a charter, presented by the totemic *ancestors, which they had never surrendered. The clan was said to have exclusive foraging rights over its territory. Unfortunately, the Yolngu testimony contradicted two elements of this account. Some clans had died out, and others had succeeded to their land. Rather than arguing for a legitimate mode of succession, the anthropologists suggested this was the consequence of *warfare. While clans excluded others from their sacred sites, permission to forage elsewhere on their land was freely given. In his judgement against the Yolngu, Mr Justice Blackburn ruled that they had failed to satisfy two of the three legal criteria for ownership, which he identified as: first, the right to exclude others; and second, the right to alienate (which the Yolngu had disclaimed in arguing for an ancestral charter). He conceded that the third criterion, the right to use and enjoy, had been demonstrated in court.

This case had a considerable impact on anthropology as well as on Aboriginal rights, for shortly afterwards a new Federal Parliament decided to write a definition of Aboriginal *land tenure into the legal system. It commissioned the lawyer who had represented the Yolngu and an anthropologist, Peterson, to research the basis of traditional land ownership and draft an Act of Parliament that would encapsulate it. The consequent Act of Parliament defined traditional Aboriginal landowners as members of a local *descent group who have common spiritual affiliations to the land which place the group in a position of primary spiritual responsibility for sacred sites on that land. Claimants were also required to demonstrate that they foraged as of right over that land, and had retained their attachment to it despite the colonial impact. Given the technical nature of this definition, it was inevitable that anthropologists would be called upon as expert witnesses. Although the Act only applied in the Northern Territory, it provided a novel testing ground for anthropological expertise. Some of the insights into Aboriginal society gained, and aspects of the theoretical debates that ensued, have been published. Perhaps the most important of these has been recognition of temporal process in the constitution of social groups, despite the vicissitudes of colonization, finally breaking with the continuous present/mythic time model of Aboriginal social being perpetuated by Spencer and Gillen. A related issue has been the recognition of Aboriginal traditional law in relation to court sentencing procedures.

Aboriginal empowerment

The growth of Aboriginal self-determination has had a substantial impact on the practice of anthropology in Australia. While *resistance to assimilation has been exercised throughout the present century, it was only in the later 1960s that European Australians began to appreciate the difficulties of enforcing assimilation against sustained indigenous opposition. In 1963, The Australian Social Science Research Council sponsored a project to investigate the policy implications 'arising from contacts between Aborigines and non-Aborigines' which culminated in a three-volume publication by the political scientist C.D. Rowley; the first of which provided a detailed critique of the failure of assimilationist policy. Myers's recent, excellent ethnography of the Pintupi, of central Australia, not only analyses traditional Pintupi social strategies as social adaptations to the harsh, unpredictable environment of the Western Desert, but interprets Pintupi society as the product of intentionally negotiated relationships.

A more fundamental effect on anthropological practice has been felt as Aboriginal people have become aware of what anthropologists had written about them in the past. At least three anthropologists have been criticized for publishing material to which access is restricted by ritual sanctions. In two cases, the offending material has been withdrawn from publication. While *archaeology has been the primary target, anthropology will not be able to escape an indigenous critique. Regrettably, some academics have interpreted these campaigns as a denial of scientific objectivity. Others, who have sustained cooperation with Aboriginal communities, have emphasized that this is not the case. The same issues are being confronted in North America.

A number of Australian Aboriginal authors have recently published studies of the social conditions in which they grew up and of traditional legends from their own communities. Perhaps the most significant influence on the direction anthropological research takes in Australia over the next few years will come from Aboriginal people themselves.

ROBERT LAYTON

See also: totemism, marriage, hunters and gatherers

Further reading

Altman, J.C. (1987) *Hunter-gatherers Today: An Aboriginal Economy in North Australia*, Canberra: Aboriginal Studies Press

Bell, D., and P. Ditton (1980) *Law: The Old and the New; Aboriginal Women Speak Out*, Canberra: Aboriginal History, for the Central Australian Aboriginal Legal Aid Service

Berndt, R.M. (1951) *Kunapipi: A Study of an Australian Aboriginal Religious Cult*, Melbourne: Cheshire

Hiatt, L.R. (ed.) (1984) *Aboriginal Landowners*, Sydney: Oceania Monographs, no. 27

Kaberry, P. (1939) *Aboriginal Woman, Sacred and Profane*, London: Routledge

Keen, I. (1994) *Knowledge and Secrecy in an Aboriginal Religion: Yolngu of North-East Arnhem Land*, Oxford: Clarendon Press

Layton, R. (1985) 'Anthropology and Aboriginal Land Rights in Northern Australia', in R. Grillo and A. Rew (eds) *Social Anthropology and Development Policy*, London: Tavistock, pp. 148–67

Meehan, B. (1982) *Shell Bed to Shell Midden*, Canberra: Australian Institute of Aboriginal Studies

Meggitt, M.J. (1962) *Desert People*, Sydney: Angus and Robertson

Morphy, H. (1991) *Ancestral Connections: Art and the Yolngu System of Knowledge*, Chicago: University of Chicago Press

Munn, N. (1973) *Warlpiri Iconography: Graphic Representation and Cultural Symbolism in a Central Australian Society*, Ithaca: Cornell University Press

Myers, F. (1986) *Pintupi Country, Pintupi Self: Sentiment, Place and Politics Among Western Desert Aborigines*, Washington: Smithsonian; Canberra: Australian Institute of Aboriginal Studies

Peterson, N., and M. Langton (eds) (1983) *Aborigines, Land and Land Rights*, Canberra: Australian Institute of Aboriginal Studies

Radcliffe-Brown, A.R. (1930–1) 'The Social Organisation of Australian Tribes', *Oceania*, 1: 34–63, 206–46, 322–41, 426–56

Spencer, B., and F.J. Gillen (1899) *The Native Tribes of Central Australia*, London: Macmillan

Stanner, W.E.H. (1963) *On Aboriginal Religion*, Sydney: Oceania Monographs, no. 11

—— (1965) 'Aboriginal Territorial Organisation: Estate, Range, Domain and Regime', *Oceania*, 36: 1–26

Utemorrah, D., E. Umbagai, B. Algarra, J. Wungunyet and D. Mowaljarlai (1980) *Visions of Mowanjum*, Adelaide: Rigby

West, I. (1984) *Pride Against Prejudice*, Canberra: Australian Institute of Aboriginal Studies

Williams, N. (1986) *The Yolngu and Their Land*, Canberra: Aboriginal Studies Press

adoption and fostering

Conventionally, fostering involves a parent or set of parents looking after someone else's child, often on a long-term basis, whereas adoption involves in addition the acquisition of a 'kin' relationship between such parents and their (adopted) children. Both practices involve the assumption of parental roles by individuals who are not the child's biological or birthparents, but the addition of *kinship status in adoption makes that concept both more problematic and more interesting.

The original ancient Roman notion of *adoptio* (adoption) was simply one of passing legal authority (*potestas*) over an individual from one person to another, outside his own †lineage, often for the purpose of making alliances and securing the inheritance of *property. In Roman times, the 'adopted' individual was most often an adult male who continued, even after his adoption, to retain the ties of love and duty toward his own, living parents. With *adoptio*, the legal authority of the father over his child was broken and a new relationship established with adoptive parents. In contrast, the Roman notion of *adrogatio* entailed the acquisition of such authority in a case where the adopted person's own father and father's father had died, much as modern adoption usually assumes the death or incapacity of the birthparents.

Thus, modern notions of adoption, including anthropologists' perceptions as to what constitutes the practice cross-culturally, generally combine the legal aspects of the Roman institutions with the nurturing and affective aspects of fostering and 'true' parentage. It also has elements in common with ritual kin relationships, such as *compadrazgo*, though ironically the very fact of acquiring a legal kinship status arguably makes adoption an aspect of 'true' rather than merely figurative kinship. Sometimes adoption is described as a form of fictive kin relation, but the degree of its truth or fiction is a matter of cultural perception (Barnard and Good 1984: 150–4). Ethnographically, adoption in this broadly-defined sense is most commonly found in Europe, North America and West Africa.

Both fostering and adoption reveal important cultural assumptions about processes of relatedness and concepts of *personhood. On the island of Langkawi off the coast of Malaysia (Carsten 1991), for example, people are thought to become kin through sharing common food, and thus common substance, and widespread fostering can be related to other ideas about the fluidity and mutability of kinship (a theme more widely encountered in Austronesian societies). Unlike the Malaysians of Langkawi, for many Americans 'fictive' kinship, in the etymological sense of kinship that is 'made', fits uneasily into Euro-American expectations about the givenness of 'real' kinship (Modell 1994). In America, then, changing adoption practices (and consequent public debate), work as a kind of mirror image of what is considered to be 'real' kinship, and ethnographic research on 'fictive' kinship helps clarify unspoken assumptions about what is 'real'.

ALAN BARNARD
and JONATHAN SPENCER

See also: kinship, *compadrazgo*

Further reading

Barnard, A., and A. Good. (1984) *Research Practices in the Study of Kinship*, London: Academic Press

Carsten, J. (1991) 'Children in Between: Fostering and the Process of Kinship on Pulau Langkawi, Malaysia', *Man* (n.s.) 26 (3): 425–43

Goody, E.N. (1971) 'Forms of Pro-parenthood: The Sharing and Substitution of Parental Roles', in J. Goody (ed.), *Kinship*, Harmondsworth: Penguin Books

—— (1982) *Parenthood and Social Reproduction: Fostering and Occupational Roles in West Africa*, Cambridge: Cambridge University Press

Modell, J. (1994) *Kinship with Strangers: Adoption and Interpretation of Kinship in American Culture*, Berkeley: University of California Press

aesthetics

We can identify two issues which are important with respect to anthropology's approach to aesthetics in non-Western societies: firstly, are we obliged to consider the anthropology of *art and the anthropology of aesthetics as inseparable? We are first confronted by the problem of those societies which either do not produce material objects of art or do not produce many artefacts at all. The Foi of Papua New Guinea and the Dinka of southern Sudan are good examples of societies that have no artefactual or artistic elaboration whatsoever but which have a highly developed form of verbal art in the form of poetic songs (see Coote 1992; Deng 1973; Weiner 1991). There is also the case of the Papua New Guinea

Highlanders, for whom the *body is perhaps the only site of aesthetic elaboration (O'Hanlon 1989; Strathern and Strathern 1983). This throws into relief our Western commitment to the *objet d'art* as the focus of aesthetic elaboration, which has been criticized by anthropologists as †ethnocentric. We can thus picture an aesthetics without art objects; can we similarly picture an artistic world without an aesthetic?

To consider this problem we turn to the second issue: we must separate at least two distinct, though related, senses of the term 'aesthetics'. The first pertains to the judgement of taste, of what is beautiful (identified in Kant's *Critique of Judgement*). The second is more general, and pertains to the form of our sensible intuition (identified in Kant's *Critique of Pure Reason*). Most studies of non-Western artistic practices until recently confined aesthetics to the identification of the beautiful in any society, while more recently, anthropologists of art such as Morphy (1991) have defined aesthetics as the effect of sensory stimuli on human perception. But there is no effect of such stimuli by themselves, that is, apart from some prior cognitive schematism that makes such stimuli recognizable in their particular form, and this is exactly the point of Kant's *Critique of Pure Reason*. While I think a case can be made that we cannot export our notions of the beautiful to other non-Western cultures, as Overing and Gow have recently argued (Weiner 1994), I think no anthropological theory does not contain within its implicit rationale some idea of how form itself is brought forth in different communal usages. It is this general appeal to the transcendental aesthetic of Kant's *Critique of Pure Reason* – without which Kant's notion of schematism (upon which modern anthropology is founded) makes no sense – that anthropologists such as Marilyn Strathern invoke in her concern with seeing Melanesian social process as a matter of making the form of social life appear in a proper manner (1988). The question then becomes why art, whether it be graphic, verbal or whatever, should be the method by which attention is drawn to the form-producing process as such.

The answer may lie in an appeal to transcendance, without which art would scarcely have the special properties we attribute to it. But our Western world of communal life activity, totally mediated as it is by the image industry, has become so thoroughly aestheticized that the ability of art to achieve this stepping-outside has become attenuated (Baudrillard 1983). Our tendency to aestheticize our subjects' social world can perhaps be seen in the increasing attention to the phenomenon of *'poetics', where the expressive and constitutive role of social *discourse is brought into focus (see for example Herzfeld 1985). We thus see our world as well as the world of peoples like the Foi and the Dinka as a total aesthetic fact, because we are both said to inhabit a thoroughly mediated *environment upon which a body image has been projected and expanded. But it is in the very different roles that art plays in these two societies that this similarity is revealed as illusory. Dinka cattle songs focus on men, cattle and their embodied relationship and thus reveal in everyday communal discourse the way human production, reproduction and politics are mediated by bovine fertility. They constitute their economy through the body. But such embodying force has been totally appropriated by the symbolic economy in the West – it is advertising that mediates social body image and conceals the transcendant nature of its own construction; we constitute the body through our economy and leave art to the marginal discourse of the academy.

It could thus be argued that to save the aesthetic from collapsing into a new *functionalism, a new appeal to the transcendance afforded by the work of art might be necessary. The merit of such an approach is that it side-steps the productionist appeals that our ordinary social constructivist view of art contains implicitly within it, and allows us to accept once again the complete interdependence of aesthetics and art, as the form-producing regime in any society, and its mode of revelation respectively. But most anthropologists insist on seeing art and aesthetics as the expressive form of social order or cohesion and attribute to them a function in maintaining such order. It is inevitable that under such conditions, either art or aesthetics is seen to be redundant with respect to that functionality. But the relation between the two demands dialectical thinking, opposed to functionalist thinking. It is reasonable to assume that, just as is the case with our own art, the artistic practices of non-Western people might have nothing to do with making society visible and everything to do with outlining the limits of human action and thought.

JAMES WEINER

See also: art, music, dance, technology, poetics

Further reading

Baudrillard, J. (1983) *Simulations*, New York: Semiotext(e)

Coote, J. (1992) '"Marvels of Everyday Vision": The Anthropology of Aesthetics and the Cattle-keeping Nilotes', in J. Coote and A. Shelton (eds) *Anthropology, Art and Aesthetics*, Oxford: Oxford University Press

Deng, F. (1973) *The Dinka and their Songs*, Oxford: Clarendon Press

Herzfeld, M. (1985) *The Poetics of Manhood*, Princeton, NJ: Princeton University Press

Morphy, H. (1991) *Ancestral Connections*, Chicago: University of Chicago Press

O'Hanlon, M. (1989) *Reading the Skin: Adornment, Display and Society among the Wahgi*, London: British Museum Publications

Strathern, A. and M. Strathern (1983) *Self-Decoration in Mt. Hagen*, Toronto: University of Toronto Press

Strathern, M. (1988) *The Gender of the Gift*, Berkeley: University of California Press

—— (1991) *Partial Connections*, Savage, MD: Rowman and Littlefield

Weiner, J. (ed.) (1995) '"Too Many Meanings": A Critique of the Anthropology of Aesthetics', *Social Analysis* 38 (special issue)

—— (ed.) (1994) '*Aesthetics is a Cross-Cultural Category*', Group for Debate in Anthropological Theory no. 6, Department of Social Anthropology, University of Manchester

Africa: East

In its narrowest sense East Africa includes the three modern republics of Kenya, Tanzania and Uganda. All three of them were heirs to the early British colonies and continue to show a deep British influence. English is one of the official languages of Uganda, together with Swahili and Luganda, while it is of general daily use in Kenya and Tanzania, where Swahili is the official language. Under colonial administration these three states were involved in an agreement for the common promotion of commercial exchange, a connection that has never entirely ceased even after the official termination of the agreement. In a wider and more comprehensive sense East Africa may also include the republics of Burundi, Rwanda, Malawi and Mozambique. However, the influence of the former Belgian administration, and the continuing use of French as an official language, have strengthened the cultural ties between Rwanda and Burundi and francophone Zaïre, rather than with anglophone Uganda and Tanzania, while the recent history of Malawi and Mozambique has favoured continuing cultural and ethnic relations with the neighbouring states of Zambia, Zimbabwe and South Africa rather than with their northern East African partners.

Early ethnography

Our information on the coast of East Africa dates back to classical Greek and Arab sources and, from the sixteenth century, to the reports of Portuguese navigators. Occasional news on the interior of East Africa, merely of a geographical nature, began to reach Europe in the first decades of the nineteenth century; its second half brought in some reliable information of a crude ethnographic type, normally scattered in the daily records of voyagers and explorers, colonial administrators and missionaries. All of these were pioneers in their own ways, but very few had an academic training. When based on firsthand knowledge, their information is still priceless. Normally, however, their reports are uncritical, and even valueless when dependent on hearsay evidence or distorted by stereotyped prejudices. Only a few early twentieth-century sources are distinguished by their accuracy and thoroughness as classics of the anthropological literature, such as the monograph of Gerard Lindblom, a Swedish scholar, on the Kamba of Kenya, and the two volumes on the Thonga of Mozambique by †H.A. Junod, a Swiss evangelist. Both covered the entire spectrum of local culture, aiming at an encyclopedic survey as required by the ethnographic method of the day.

The emphasis on social institutions

The new style of social anthropology, introduced in the 1930s by the teachings of *A.R. Radcliffe-Brown and *B. Malinowski, soon began to affect the type of ethnographic research conducted in East Africa, especially its emphasis on social institutions. This trend was also greatly influenced by the fieldwork of †E.E. Evans-Pritchard in the neighbouring southern Sudan among the Bantu Zande and the *Nilotic Nuer.

It is within this general context that †Jomo Kenyatta's monograph on the Kikuyu, *Facing Mount Kenya* (1938), should be specially mentioned. In his introduction, Malinowski testified to Kenyatta's competence as a trained anthropologist and to the excellence of his work. Malinowski's words were not mere pleasantries, but a clear statement of the need for professional training as a basic requirement for ethnographic research (Malinowski in Kenyatta 1938: viii). Of course

Kenyatta displayed his own bias in writing, as he put it, 'for the benefit both of Europeans and of those Africans who have been detached from their tribal life' (Kenyatta 1938: xvi) and in defence of the land claims of his countrymen. This may at once justify the emotional passages in his writing, and also explain the freshness of his insider's account. Though Kenyatta was involved in the political struggle for independence in Kenya, and went on to become the President of the new republic, his monograph remains the best record of traditional Kikuyu society.

Evans-Pritchard's influence is made evident in his introduction to †Peristiany's monograph on the social institutions of the Kipsigis in which he makes two points: firstly 'that the Kipsigis have a political system', and secondly 'that the †age-set system of the Kipsigis has a very political importance' (Evans-Pritchard 1939: xxiii, xxxi). In the following years these two aspects of East African societies were prominent in anthropological research, especially in Kenya and Tanzania where most societies were based on stateless and decentralized systems. This kind of social organization had been mapped out by †Meyer Fortes and Evans-Pritchard, the editors of *African Political Systems* (1940): out of the eight essays, five were related to African kingdoms, three to stateless and segmentary societies. East Africa was represented by the kingdom of Ankole in Uganda (Oberge in Fortes and Evans-Pritchard 1940) and by the stateless society of the Logoli, one group of the then so-called Bantu Kavirondo, now called Luyia (Wagner in Fortes and Evans-Pritchard 1940). The Ankole were one link in the chain of the Great Lakes kingdoms of Buganda, Rwanda and Burundi. The efficient bureaucracy of these kingdoms, and the majesty of their kings, had provoked such great admiration among early European observers that they became seen in an idealized way – 'fetishized' according to one modern commentator (Chrétien 1985: 1,368) – as heirs of a mythical empire believed by the Europeans to have been founded by the Bacwezi, supposedly a superior race of 'whitish' immigrants. This historical invention was readily endorsed by the standard handbooks of East African history.

Age-systems and stateless societies

The two editors of *African Political Systems* were correct at the time in stressing the need for 'a more detailed investigation of the nature of political values and of the symbols in which they are expressed' (Fortes and Evans-Pritchard 1940: 23). Though they had tried to clarify the political system of stateless and non-centralized societies in their introduction, they failed to explicitly include *age-systems as a discrete kind of political organization (Bernardi 1952). It was only a few years later that †Isaac Schapera drew attention to these systems, recommending them as a special item of enquiry in his survey of anthropological research in Kenya (Schapera 1949). The general category of age-systems included much local variation in sets, classes and generations. These systems had long baffled the early colonial administrators, and only intense research by professional anthropologists was to dispel this puzzling enigma, showing how age-systems formed the political backbone of stateless societies such as, among others, the Maasai (Spencer 1965) and the Borana (Baxter 1954; Bassi 1996). A remarkable contribution by †Monica Wilson brought to the fore a peculiar age-system related to the establishment of new villages by newly initiated age-mates among the Nyakyusa of Tanzania (Wilson 1951, 1959).

Religions and philosophy

African religions were conceived by early European observers in terms of *magic, and as such they were generally condemned by *missionaries as pagan superstition. This attitude changed with time but it was only through professional anthropological research that enquiry on traditional religions became free of conversion bias. John Middleton's monograph on the religion of the Lugbara (1960) may now be reckoned as a classic of the East African literature on religion. A turning point in understanding African religions came when the subject was approached in terms of *cosmological ideas and philosophy. In 1969 a chair of African Religions and Philosophy was instituted at the University of Makerere, Uganda, its first tenant being John S. Mbiti. His work, *African Religions and Philosophy* (1969), provides a general synthesis of African cosmological views. Though not without debatable interpretations, as when he describes the African concept of *time as involving the idea of past and present but no future, Mbiti's book has met with highly popular favour and has been translated into various languages: Japanese, French, Korean and Italian.

The most recent trends in the study of East African religion have focused on cosmological views and their symbolic values, and have especially stressed the ethics of *rituals leading to

reinforced communal relations and traditions (Harris 1978; Parkin 1991). A new interest in traditional medicine and the professionalization of African practitioners, encouraged by the ambitious programmes of the World Health Organization, may also be mentioned as one of the newest fields of anthropological research in Africa as well as in East Africa (Semali and Msonthi, in Last and Chavunduka 1986).

BERNARDO BERNARDI

See also: age, British anthropology, political anthropology

Further reading

Bassi, M. (1996) *I Borana: Una società assembleare dell'Etiopia*, Milan: Franco Angeli

Baxter, P.T.W. (1954) *The Social Organisation of the Galla of Northern Kenya*, unpublished D.Phil. thesis: University of Oxford

Bernardi, B. (1952) 'The Age Systems of the Nilo-Hamitic Peoples', *Africa* 22: 316–32

Chrétien, J-P. (1985) 'L'empire des Bacwezi', *Annales, Économies, Sociétés, Civilisations* 6: 1335–77

Evans-Pritchard, E.E. (1939) 'Introduction', in J.G. Peristiany *The Social Institutions of the Kipsigis*, London: George Routledge & Sons

Fortes, M. and E.E. Evans-Pritchard (eds) (1940) *African Political Systems*, Oxford University Press for the International African Institute

Harris, G.G. (1978) *Casting Out Anger: Religion among the Taita of Kenya*, Cambridge: Cambridge University Press

Kenyatta, J. (1938) *Facing Mount Kenya: The Tribal Life of the Gikuyu*, London: Secker & Warburg

Last, M., and G.L. Chavunduka (eds) (1986) *The Professionalisation of African Medicine*, Manchester: Manchester University Press for the International African Institute

Mbiti, J.S. (1969) *African Religions and Philosophy*, London: Heinemann

Middleton, J. (1960) *Lugbara Religion*, Oxford University Press for the International African Institute

Parkin, D. (1991) *Sacred Void: Spatial Images of Work and Ritual among the Giriama of Kenya*, Cambridge: Cambridge University Press

Schapera, I. (1949) *Some Problems of Anthropological Research in Kenya Colony*, London: International African Institute

Spencer, P. (1965) *The Maasai of Matapato: A Study of Rituals of Rebellion*, Manchester: Manchester University Press for the International African Institute

Wilson, M. (1951) *Good Company: A Study of Nyakyusa Age Villages*, Oxford: Oxford University Press for the International African Institute

—— (1959) *Communal Rituals of the Nyakyusa*, Oxford: Oxford University Press for the International African Institute

Africa: Nilotic

The term 'Nilotic' is used in various senses. First, it describes the geographical region of the upper Nile basin as in *The Pagan Tribes of the Nilotic Sudan*, the title of the †Seligmans' (1932) comprehensive ethnography of the region. Secondly, it refers to a set of cultural traits shared by some, but not all, of the peoples of the upper Nile, with others in an area extending south beyond the Nile basin into Uganda, Kenya, and Tanzania. Finally, Nilotic describes a language family in a classification of languages. Nilotic studies are significant not only in themselves but because they have also produced anthropological works which have had a great influence on the discipline generally.

Historical linguistic research into the Nilotic languages, together with a consideration of the contemporary geographical distribution of languages, suggest that the original proto-Nilotic language community in their homeland to the southwest of the southern Ethiopian highlands probably started to break up into three groups about 4,000 years ago. These groups of proto-Nilotic then began to change independently into the ancestral languages of what are today recognized as the western, eastern, and southern Nilotic groups of languages (Ehret 1971; Greenberg 1955; Kohler 1955).

Those who were to become the speakers of Western Nilotic (e.g. Dinka, Nuer, Luo) seem likely to have moved first and in a westerly direction to occupy the grasslands around the confluence of the Bahr el Ghazal and the Nile. The proto-Southern Nilotes, having been for a long time in contact with neighbouring Cushitic-speaking peoples in their homeland north of Lake Turkana, had acquired from them not only Cushitic vocabularies but also social practices such as circumcision, †clitoridectomy, a prohibition on eating fish, and cyclical *age set naming systems, all of which are not known among the Western Nilotes. By the first century of the present era the Southern Nilotic speakers (e.g. Nandi, Pokot, Marakwet) had moved south, some into what is today Tanzania, and there they encountered agricultural Bantu speaking peoples moving north, and from whom they adopted root crops and banana cultivation to add to their cultivation of grains, sorghum and millet, and their *pastoralism.

Most of the Eastern Nilotic speech communities (e.g. Bari, Lotuko, Turkana) are now found in what is likely to have been their original homeland between Lake Turkana and the Nile, but some of them, the predecessors of the present-day Maasai peoples of Kenya and Tanzania, had followed the Southern Nilotic speakers south. There, during the course of several hundred years up to the end of the first millennium, they absorbed some of the Southern Nilotes and at the same time adopted many of their practices, some of which, such as circumcision, could be traced back to origins among Cushitic peoples. In this way those Eastern Nilotes who followed the Southern Nilotes, adding to whatever Cushitic traits they may already have acquired before migrating south, acquired further Cushitic practices from the Southern Nilotes as intermediaries.

These terms western, eastern and southern Nilotic correspond roughly with the old †ethnological division of the people into Nilotes, Northern and Central Nilo-Hamites, and Southern Nilo-Hamites, terms which will be commonly encountered in literature published before the mid-1960s. This terminology derived from a now discredited speculative theory of racial mixing to account for the distribution of Nilotic social and cultural features. A great deal of scholarship was devoted to adducing evidence that pale-skinned, slim and 'quick witted' mobile pastoral Caucasians of noble disposition, the supposed Hamites, entered northeast Africa and subordinated the sturdy but slow-witted, dark-skinned sedentary agricultural Negroes; and from which process emerged the Nilotes, and those with rather more Hamitic 'blood', the Nilo-Hamites (Seligman and Seligman 1932). The fascination of such a theory for European imperialists in Africa is obvious.

Age and social order

Various forms of institutionalized age organization, †age grades, age sets (linear naming and cyclical naming), generation classes, are especially elaborated in East Africa and particularly among Nilotes (Baxter and Almagor 1978). However, the function and meaning of these often complex cultural constructions have largely eluded social anthropologists. A number of observations can nevertheless be made. First, these institutions primarily concern men rather than women. Among women there may be a parallel organization but it is always a weak reflection of that of the men, and the women themselves are frequently vague and unclear about their own system of age sets.

Secondly, age sets, or generation classes, have no material interests in cattle or other *property rights either in terms of ownership or control. Rights in cattle belong to individuals organized in *households and †lineages. Even the stock acquired through raiding by 'warrior' age sets is distributed to individuals and absorbed into household herds. On the other hand, sets and grades do seem to exercise some sort of sumptuary control among men over the use of titles, insignia, and privileges as regards sexual conduct, meat and drink, especially particular cuts of sacrificial animals, bearing arms, as well as matters of status such as becoming married and establishing a household.

Since Nilotes were generally reported to lack a centralized and hierarchical system of ruling offices, there has always been a strong temptation to see the functions of government being carried out by the ranking involved in age set systems. Among Eastern Nilotes of the southern Sudan, for example, there appears to be evidence of the direct involvement of age classes in indigenous government even into the 1980s. There the replacement of the ruling elders (*monomiji*, 'fathers of the village') is not a continuing process as individuals become too old and die and are replaced by their successors, but is achieved at intervals by what the people themselves compare to a 'revolution', when a junior generation of age sets suddenly takes over responsibility for the village. This transfer of authority is effected by a spectacular ceremony about every twenty years and involves a mock battle for the village between the incumbent generation and the generation about to assume authority. Such inter-generational rivalry also found expression in the wider field of conflict in the Sudan where it seems that in the 1980s support for the rebels and the Khartoum government reflected generational rivalries (Simonse 1992).

Land, lineages and prophets

Among Western Nilotes, such as Nuer, †Evans-Pritchard could attribute no political function to the age sets. Instead he argued, in what was to become one of the outstanding texts of modern social anthropology, that the basis of Nuer social order lies in their †patrilineal *kinship system (Evans-Pritchard 1940). His account was to be generalized into what became known as †'segmentary lineage theory', or *'descent theory', which in the 1950s and 1960s was one of the cornerstones of the discipline of social anthropology.

According to Evans-Pritchard conflict among Nuer is not terminally destructive but mitigated by the lineage system. The segmentary lineage system regulates the number of supporters a man can muster against another individual according to the relative position of the two parties in the lineage system. Since the relationship is symmetrical no one can bring to bear a preponderant force and there is, in effect, a stand off. The dispute is then mediated peacefully by a ritual specialist ('the leopard skin priest') who acts as broker between the two lineages. Where there can be no such mediation, as for instance between Nuer and their neighbours the Dinka, a state of perpetual raiding and counter-raiding prevails.

This theory as it is supposed to apply to the Nuer began to be questioned in the 1970s and 1980s, first by a critical assessment of the evidence presented by Evans-Pritchard in his own publications (Holy 1979), and then by the appearance of new historical evidence (Johnson 1994). A careful re-examination of the case-studies of conflict between lineages cited by Evans-Pritchard seemed to indicate that the local lineages allied with others in the prosecution of hostilities not according to 'the principles of the segmentary lineage system' but according to pragmatic interests and *ad hoc* alliances. These instances of conflict and cooperation were frequently concerned with, as one might expect of pastoralists, access to grazing and here the ecology of the upper Nile basin is crucial.

Historical research into the societies of the upper Nile basin has drawn attention to the consequences of local adaptations to long-term and short-term climatic changes, adaptations which have influenced, and continue to influence, the dispersal of pastoralists throughout the region. Land which has been abandoned because of years of exceptionally high water levels may later be reoccupied and not necessarily by the same people. Changes in drainage patterns can wipe out old grazing lands and produce new ones elsewhere. In addition there are annual movements of people and animals from the limited dry sites above the flood-plain during the wet season to the grasslands of the dry season which are revealed as the flood subsides. This is a fluctuating situation in which access to grazing and settlement sites has therefore to be continually negotiated and contested.

In Evans-Pritchard's view, those spiritual leaders known as †prophets who come to prominence from time to time are the consequence of historical crises between relatively stable conditions of normality. Nuer prophets are represented by him as the effect, and sometimes also the cause, of violent relations between Nuer and other populations, such as the Dinka, or the agents of distant powers such as Arab slavers, the Ottoman Empire, and later the forces of the British Empire. However, historical research has now corrected this vision and removed the prophets from their liminal position and placed them in the centre of Nuer religious and political history.

According to Johnson (1994), Nuer prophets are a continuation by other means of the activities of spiritual leaders whose concern was to define and establish around themselves a 'moral community'. Precisely because they actually experience a life of raiding and counter-raiding, of defending grazing lands from intruders as the erratic movements of the seasonal flooding of the Nile system forces the pastoralists to adapt and change their patterns of herding, so they prize peace and stability. Within the moral community disputes are settled peacefully by mediation. It is this that the prophets attempt to realize and then extend to the widest possible inclusiveness so that all Nuer are under the authority of sovereign, but rival, prophets. When the secessionist Anynya forces entered Nuerland in the 1960s rivalry between prophets became aligned with conflicts between the Anynya and the government.

Divinity and experience

Nilotic religions are characterized by a subtle theism and both †Evans-Pritchard (1957) and then †Godfrey Lienhardt (1961) found it necessary to discuss at length at the beginning of their books on Nuer and Dinka religion the meanings of the words for God, *kwoth* and *nhialic* respectively. God, or Divinity in Lienhardt's more sensitive terminology, does not dwell in some other world, and spiritual beings are only of interest to Nilotes as ultra human agents operating in this world. Many observers have remarked on the religiosity of Nilotes, presumably because they live in and experience a world from which the gods have not departed. There is no ancestor worship but instead shrines, said to have been originally the homesteads of mythical ancestral figures, serve as centres of spiritual power. The best known of these among Western Nilotes are the shrine/homestead of Nyikang (first king of Shilluk) at Fashoda and, east of the Bahr el Jebel, those of the Dinka ancestral figure, Deng, and the first spear master,

Aiwel. The principal religious action is animal *sacrifice and there are also reports of the ritual killing, or interment while alive, of religious figures who have the characteristics of what are sometimes referred to as 'divine kings', as for instance among Shilluk and Dinka.

Lienhardt's study of Dinka religion has endured as one of the most influential and exemplary works in anthropology, and it can now be seen as a precursor of contemporary theory and practice in social anthropology. Lienhardt rejected the crude *functionalism which was predominant in anthropological studies of religion in the late 1950s and early 1960s but successfully avoided reverting to an intellectualist position which supposes that religious ideas are pre-scientific explanatory concepts. It is not a simple matter to divide the Dinka believer from what is believed in. Instead Lienhardt approached Dinka religious utterances as interpretations by Dinka of certain of their experiences. For Lienhardt Dinka religion was not a theology but a †phenomenology. This approach led Lienhardt to question presumptions about mind, self, memory, and experience, in reaching an understanding of Dinka interpretations and imaging of their experiences.

M.C. JEDREJ

See also: age, descent, pastoralists

Further reading

Baxter, P.T.W., and U. Almagor (eds) (1978) *Age, Generation and Time*, London: C. Hurst

Ehret, C. (1971) *Southern Nilotic History*, Evanston, IL: Northwestern University Press

Evans-Pritchard, E.E. (1940) *The Nuer*, Oxford: Clarendon Press

—— (1957) *Nuer Religion*, Oxford: Clarendon Press

Greenberg, J.H. (1955) *Studies in African Linguistic Classification*, New Haven: Compass

Holy, L. (ed.) (1979) *Segmentary Lineage Systems Reconsidered*, Belfast: Queen's University Papers in Social Anthropology (vol. 4)

Johnson, D. (1994) *Nuer Prophets*, Oxford: Clarendon Press

Kohler, O. (1955) *Geschichte der Erforschung der Nilotischen Sprache*, Berlin: Reimer

Lienhardt, G. (1961) *Divinity and Experience: The Religion of the Dinka*, Oxford: Clarendon Press

Seligman, C.G., and B.Z. Seligman (1932) *The Pagan Tribes of the Nilotic Sudan*, London: Routledge and Kegan Paul

Simonse, S. (1992) *Kings of Disaster*, Leiden: E.J. Brill

Africa: Southern

Southern Africa has been the focus of intensive ethnographic research throughout the twentieth century, as well as the source of a disproportionate number of distinguished anthropologists, many specializing in the study of Southern and Central African societies. The region is inhabited by a variety of ethnic groups, including Bantu-speaking populations, San-speaking (Khoisan) populations, and peoples of European and Asian origin. This article will concentrate on the Bantu-speakers and San-speakers – each of these units being divided into a number of smaller ethno-linguistic and political entities – and on the anthropological ideas which emerged through their study.

Studies of Bantu-speaking peoples

Studies concerned with Bantu and San-speaking peoples represent quite different anthropological traditions; the former being central in the development of the British school of *functionalism and †structural functionalism, the latter significantly connected to the materialist-evolutionary tradition in *American anthropology. This difference in theoretical orientation may, at least in part, answer for the fact that there are virtually no studies which systematically address the relationship between them, nor any systematic comparison of them, though one exception is †Schapera's *Government and Politics in Tribal Societies* (1956). The importance of this work is also due to the fact that it went beyond the approach to *'political anthropology', once canonized in *African Political Systems* (Fortes and Evans-Pritchard 1940). Drawing upon a considerable number of solid ethnographic works, especially from the 1930s and 1940s (e.g. Wilson [Hunter 1936;] Krige and Krige 1943; H. Kuper 1947), Schapera gave much more importance to the exercise of leadership. He emphasized the significance of 'the sources and sanctions of political authority' (1956: 1), and he broadened the scope of 'politics' by taking into account all aspects of leadership. This reduced the †ethnocentrism of the concept of political leadership and facilitated his efforts to bring the whole range of Southern African peoples, including hunting-and-gathering bands, into a unified comparative analysis of political organization.

†Gluckman also contributed to expanding the theoretical scope of the study of Southern Bantu polities beyond that of the hitherto Durkheimian tradition, by invoking †Weber in focusing on conflict and tensions surrounding political leaders. In developing what may be labelled 'conflict-functionalism', Gluckman (1954) interpreted a number of political and *ritual processes with particular attention to their display of recurrent conflicts in ways which served to exhaust tensions and thus reproduce 'the system'. These 'rituals of rebellion', as he called them, involved succession disputes and ritualized opposition between senior and junior branches of the respective royal families, a condition which he saw as essential to preserve national unity. Schapera, however, levelled criticism against this notion, emphasizing instead the fission of groups as an effect of succession disputes and civil war (Schapera 1956: 27).

Variations in the character of Southern African societies have been related to an East-West dichotomy, e.g. in terms of such contrasts as clan †exogamy (of the Nguni) versus †endogamy (Sotho-Tswana). Nguni societies include mainly eastern, coastal ones, such as Zulu, Xhosa and Swazi, as well as northern offshoots such as the Ndebele of Zimbabwe. Sotho-Tswana societies include western, inland ones such as the Kgalagadi of Botswana, as well as the Southern Sotho of Lesotho and the Tswana of Botswana and adjacent areas of South Africa. Sansom asserts that 'the contrast between East and West is a contrast in political style that is the result of differential location of power' (1974: 259). Among Sotho-Tswana this was based upon tribal estates managed from central villages and towns, where people are concentrated, whereas amongst Nguni, rulers governed 'checkerboard realms' in which people were more evenly or randomly distributed over the land. While Sansom's essay and earlier ethnographic accounts focused upon the political centre of the major groups, from the 1960s the focus was placed upon societies which had been treated as rudimentary subject communities to the tribal 'super-powers', like the Kalanga and the Tswapong of the present northern and north-eastern Botswana (Werbner 1989). These were now presented as entities in their own right, with cultural and social self-determination. While polity-focusing studies had demonstrated one mode of social integration, Werbner established regional cults as another, representing a variety of activities surrounding a shrine in which a number of groups in a region were linked together.

Recognizing the variations in socio-cultural forms throughout Southern Bantu societies, Adam

Kuper has endeavoured to bring greater order to the diverse and scattered reports on 'traditional' Southern Bantu marriages by means of structural comparison. Dismissing the prominence which previous scholars have often given to the socio-political notions of 'clans' and 'lineages', he gives emphasis to the political significance of marriage, in particular how 'marriages within the ruling line served further to redefine and rearrange status relationships and lines of conflict and support' (Kuper 1982: 58). This function of marriage is widely present, and his comparative exercise demonstrates how a pervasive set of ideas, associated with the exchange of cattle for wives, manifests itself in the varieties of †bridewealth institutions, which, it is argued, represent highly constrained transformations of each other. These variations are especially related to economic adaptation, the different rules governing the marriage of cousins and the varying forms of political stratification.

Earlier monographs which focus upon constitutional aspects have been criticized for reifying Bantu societies and ignoring the extensive inter-action between groups as well as with the expanding European settler communities. It can be argued, however, that the emphasis upon the ethnography of Bantu polities relates to the racism-discourse of the 1930s and 1940s in which liberal anthropologists attempted, in the face of notions of 'barbarism', to bring in substantive knowledge about the rationality and sophistication of these systems. Similarly, there was already from the 1930s keen interest in accounting for the impacts of Western 'civilization', demonstrating both its ill-effects (particularly through labour migration) and the ability of indigenous peoples to adapt Western knowledge and competence. Gluckman, in particular, began to address the complexity of interactions between external forces through his 'extended case method'.

In the 1960s the scope of 'Bantu studies' expanded to urban communities, as pioneered by Mayer's study of Xhosa-speakers in East London, South Africa (Mayer 1961). Mayer identified the contrasting ways in which Africans relate to *'modernity', epitomized in an ideological division of the Xhosa between 'red' (traditionalist adherents to ancestral religion) and 'school' (modernized Christians). Mayer (1980) explains how both ideologies subsequently developed into forms of resistance to White political and economic domination in response to *apartheid* policies. The ability of African cultures to adapt but persist has been most clearly demonstrated in studies of its articulation with Christianity, most apparently with the development of African Independent Churches. While these movements were initially studied as a reaction to racial discrimination, recent studies have emphasized their ability to facilitate African struggles to cope with a demanding urban environment (e.g. Kiernan 1990).

Jean and John Comaroff have approached the issue of domination by focusing upon the agency of cultural imperialism, as exercised by evangelizing missionaries among the Southern Tswana. Rather than the explicit message of the evangelizing voices, they place emphasis upon the establishment of Western cultural hegemony through the long-term and implicit impacts of the 'secular' domain. They argue that 'the seeds of cultural imperialism *were* most effectively sown along the contours of everyday life' (1992: 293). Besides the study of cultural domination, anthropologists have since the 1970s (in part under the influence of the Marxian notion of †'articulation of modes of production') been concerned with the *apartheid*-enforced formation of 'homelands' or labour reservoirs and the socio-economics of labour-migration, with particular attention to its impact upon family and community life (e.g. Murray 1980, Gulbrandsen 1994).

Many of the figures who have worked in Southern Africa have been associated with Manchester University and the so-called †'Manchester School' of anthropology. The Comaroffs' work may well be regarded as a culmination of this tradition, which began with Gluckman, along with Clyde Mitchell, †Victor Turner and others working both at Manchester and at the Rhodes-Livingstone Institute in what was then Northern Rhodesia (now Zambia). Paralleling studies of Southern Bantu-speakers, the studies of South-Central African groups focused on issues of social process and conflict, indigenous law, social networks (especially in the Central African 'Copper Belt') and social change (see Werbner 1990). Even in the post-Gluckman era, studies of South-Central Africa have continued to concentrate on some of these issues, but those focusing on social change came to reject old structural-processual models in favour of a more complex relation between indigenous thought and colonial domination. A good example, which has some parallels with the work of the Comaroffs, is David Lan's (1985) study of spirit mediumship and guerrilla war in Zimbabwe.

Studies of San-speaking peoples

A milestone in the study of San-speakers was Schapera's (1930) comprehensive synthesis of the significant, but scattered, amounts of information available at that time about 'Bushmen' (San *hunter-gatherers) and 'Hottentots' (Khoekhoe cattle and sheep-herders). The latter had been the subject of early studies by †Winifred Hoernlé, who was an early influence on Gluckman. The first major fieldwork on San-speakers in the modern era was conducted by †Lorna Marshall with the !Kung of Namibia in the 1950s (Marshall 1976). The closely-related !Kung on the Botswana side of the border were subsequently the object of a number of studies by anthropologists connected with the Harvard Kalahari Project (see Lee and DeVore 1976). This project was, according to one of its leaders, motivated by the idea that insights from contemporary hunter-gatherer groups could help to develop models of the evolution of human behaviour (Lee 1979: 9). With its strong attachment to *evolutionism, special interest was taken in the cultural ecology of hunter-gatherer adaptation. Lee, for example, asserted that 65 per cent of the people were effective food producers who worked only a few hours a day, and the remaining 35 per cent did no work at all (1969).

A further theme running through this and other projects during the 1960s and 1970s was that of settlement patterns and spatial organization (e.g. Silberbauer 1981). In a major comparative study of the Khoisan peoples which in important respects updated Schapera's work, Barnard (1992) synthesized ethnographic information currently available on various groups of Khoisan peoples. Analysing settlement patterns, for instance, he suggests a correlation between degree of nucleation and availability of water resources and between territoriality and access to resources.

With overtones of romanticism, the notion of 'egalitarianism' has been widely applied to depict the *essential* character of 'San culture'. Thus, Lee portrays the !Kung as 'fiercely egalitarian' with an ideology of equality, allegedly responsible for their current immense problems in coping with the forces of the larger world which, over the past decades, have squeezed them out of their 'aboriginal' hunting-gathering habitat. However true this sad story is, a warning against this kind of essentialism is appropriate in view of recent reports on the establishment of authority figures and the shift to storing economies among sedentary groups

(see Gulbrandsen 1991). By extension, emphasis is increasingly placed upon variation in San culture and adaptation (e.g. Kent 1992).

This issue closely relates to Wilmsen's attack (1989) on the notion of Kalahari San as representatives of the 'primitive' way of life that was a human universal until 10,000 years ago. The alleged 'ahistorical evolutionism' of Lee and his colleagues is confronted with historical and archaeological evidence indicating that Kalahari hunter-gatherers have long vacillated between foraging and food production. Radically breaking with the prevailing closed-system perspective, Wilmsen has combined historical contextualization with a Marxian perspective and identified the San as an 'underclass' within the political-economic context of the larger Kalahari region. He insists that poverty and the appearance of isolation are recent products of a process that has unfolded over the last two centuries. The ensuing controversy was most strongly played out in the pages of the journal *Current Anthropology* (beginning with vol. 31, 1990).

Adding another dimension, Barnard's comprehensive cultural account (1992) qualifies Wilmsen's largely materialist emphasis. Viewing culture as a hierarchical 'structure of structures' Barnard argues that production and exchange relations do not create his postulated deep structure, but more particularly that 'surface structural' elements are influenced by historical changes in modes of production. Accordingly he stresses the distinct and determinative character of Khoisan culture.

Ø. GULBRANDSEN

Further reading

Barnard, A. (1992) *Hunters and Herders of Southern Africa. A Comparative Ethnography of the Khoisan Peoples*, Cambridge: Cambridge University Press

Comaroff, J. and J.L. Comaroff (1992) *Ethnography and the Historical Imagination*, Boulder: Westview Press

Fortes, M. and E.E. Evans-Pritchard (eds) (1940) *African Political Systems*, London: Oxford University Press

Gluckman, M. (1954) *Rituals of Rebellion in South-East Africa* (Frazer Lecture 1952), Manchester: Manchester University Press (reprinted in Gluckman 1963)

—— (1963) *Order and Rebellion in Tribal Africa*, London: Cohen and West

Gulbrandsen, Ø. (1991) 'On the Problem of Egalitarianism: The Kalahari San in Transition', in R. Grønhaug *et al.* (eds), *The Ecology of Choice and Symbol. Essays in Honour of Fredrik Barth*, Bergen: Alma Mater

—— 1994 *Poverty in the Midst of Plenty. Socio-economic Marginalization and Ecological Deterioration in a Southern*

African Labour Reservoir: The Case of the Ngwaketse of Botswana (Bergen Studies in Social Anthropology 45), Bergen: Norse Publications

Hunter [Wilson], M. (1936) *Reaction to Conquest: Effects of Contact with Europeans on the Pondo of South Africa*, London: Oxford University Press

Kiernan, J.P. (1990) *The Production and Management of Therapeutic Power in Zionist Churches within a Zulu City*, Lampeter, Wales: The Edwin Mellen Press

Krige, E.J. and D.J. (1943) *The Realm of a Rain-Queen: A Study of the Pattern of Lovedu Society*, London: Oxford University Press

Kuper, A. (1982) *Wives for Cattle: Bridewealth and Marriage in Southern Africa*, London: Routledge and Kegan Paul

Kuper, H. (1947) *An African Aristocracy: Rank among the Swazi*, London: Routledge and Kegan Paul

Lan, D. (1985) *Guns and Rain: Guerrillas and Spirit Mediums in Zimbabwe*, London: James Currey

Lee, R.B. (1969) '!Kung Bushman Subsistence: An Input-output Analysis', in A.P. Vayda (ed.) *Environment and Cultural Behaviour*, New York: Natural History Press

—— (1979) *The !Kung San: Men, Women, and Work in a Foraging Society*, Cambridge: Cambridge University Press

Lee, R.B. and I. DeVore (eds) (1976) *Kalahari Hunter-Gatherers: Studies of the !Kung San and Their Neighbors*, Cambridge, MA: Harvard University Press

Marshall, L. (1976) *The !Kung of Nyae Nyae*, Cambridge, MA: Harvard University Press

Mayer, P. (1961) *Townsmen or Tribesmen. Conservatism and the Process of Urbanization in a South African City*, London: Oxford University Press

—— (1980) 'The Origin and Decline of Two Rural Resistance Ideologies' in P. Mayer (ed.) *Black Villagers in an Industrial Society. Anthropological Perspectives on Labour Migration in South Africa*, Cape Town: Oxford University Press

Murray, C. (1981) *Families Divided. The Impact of Migrant Labour in Lesotho*, Cambridge: Cambridge University Press

Sansom, B. (1974) 'Traditional Economic Systems', in W.D. Hammond-Tooke (ed.) *The Bantu Speaking Peoples of Southern Africa: An Ethnographic Survey*, London: Routledge

Schapera, I. (1930) *The Khoisan Peoples of South Africa: Bushmen and Hottentots*, London: George Routledge & Sons

—— (1956) *Government and Politics in Tribal Societies*, London: C.W. Watts & Co. Ltd

Silberbauer, G.B. (1981) *Hunter and Habitat in the Central Kalahari Desert*, Cambridge: Cambridge University Press

Werbner, R.P. (1989) *Ritual Passage, Sacred Journey: The Process and Organization of Religious Movements*, Manchester: Manchester University Press

—— (1990) 'South-Central Africa: The Manchester School and After', in R. Fardon (ed.), *Localizing Strategies: Regional Traditions of Ethnographic Writing*, Edinburgh: Scottish Adademic Press

Wilmsen, E.N. (1989). *Land Filled with Flies. A Political Economy of the Kalahari*, Chicago: University of Chicago Press

Africa: West

Generalization about West Africa is made difficult by the size (roughly 3,000 miles west to east, and half that north to south) and diversity of the region, as well as by the problematic character of the terms available to describe it, and the significance that regional scholarship has played in national traditions of anthropology outside Africa.

Region: definition and contemporary states

By convention, West Africa is bounded by the Atlantic Ocean to the south and west and by the world's largest desert, the Sahara, to the north. However these boundaries are most significant for the influences that flowed across them. Via its Atlantic seaboard, West Africa was incorporated into a system of world trade emergent from the late fifteenth century – especially through the *slave trade. Subsequent European colonization and Christian missionization proceeded largely, but not exclusively, from the coast. Trans-Saharan relations, especially trade relations with the Maghreb, have remained crucial in economic, political and religious terms, and established the links by which *Islam became the predominant religion in the north of the region. An eastern boundary between West and Central Africa or the Sudan can be defined only arbitrarily.

Including Chad and Cameroon, West Africa consists of eighteen formally independent states (see map), some of them amongst the poorest in the world. These states were defined in the course of European colonization, which took place largely between 1885 and 1906, and they became independent between 1957 (Ghana) and 1974 (Guinea Bissau). Despite the brevity of the colonial period, and the very uneven effects of colonial rule on different aspects of West African life, among *colonialism's legacies to West Africans were a framework of states varying in size with haphazard relations to existing differences of language and *ethnicity, and three official languages of European origin. The Gambia, Sierra Leone, Ghana and Nigeria were British colonies and are now officially anglophone countries. Liberia, a

West Africa: contemporary states.

fifth anglophone country, was declared a republic in 1847 following the establishment of settlements by freed American slaves. The anglophone states, which predominate in terms of West African population (Nigeria alone accounting for more than half), are surrounded by territorially more extensive francophone states, most of which formed part of *Afrique Occidentale Française*: Mali, Burkina Faso, Niger and Chad are extensive, land-locked states; Mauritania, Senegal, Guinea, Côte d'Ivoire and Bénin have access to the Atlantic Ocean. Togo and Cameroon, initially German colonies of greater extent than today, were mandated to Britain and France after the First World War. As a result, Cameroon is officially bilingual in English and French. Guinea Bissau and the Cape Verde Islands are small Portuguese speaking countries. The coastal states of West Africa are typically marked by pronounced north-south divisions such that southerners are more likely to be Christian and, especially on the coast, may belong to †'creole' cultures. Northerners, in common with citizens of land-locked states, are more likely to be Muslim and relatively less affected by European influences.

Language

West Africa may also be envisaged as a tapestry of language and ethnicity which predates colonialization. Three distinct language families are represented, each found also outside West Africa: in the North, Nilo-Saharan includes both Kanuri and Songhai, while Hausa, spoken by more West Africans than any other indigenous language, belongs to Afro-Asiatic (which also includes Arabic). Languages spoken in the south and west belong to the extensive Niger-Congo family which also included the Bantu languages that predominate in central, eastern and southern sub-Saharan Africa. Among the important members of this group are Wolof and Mande in the west, More (Mossi) in the centre, and Akan-Twi, Fon-Ewe, Yoruba, and Igbo in the south; Fulfulde is the most widely distributed language in this group by virtue of the historically *pastoral mode of life of its speakers, the Fulani (Peul, French). Distinguishable West African languages are extremely numerous – Nigeria alone has in excess of four hundred. Most West Africans are multilingual in African languages, and may additionally speak a language of European origin, Arabic (in the north), or pidgin English (in the south).

Geography

West Africa is characterized by strongly seasonal rainfall which divides the region into ecological bands running from west to east: southwards from the sahel bordering the Sahara, savanna grasslands give way to woodlands, then to rain forests and the coastal regions with local mangrove swamps. Quick ripening grains (millet and guinea corn) are favoured in the north where the rains fall for between three and seven months. In the wetter southern regions, rice predominates in the west where rainfall has a single annual peak, while yam is a staple of the forested east which has a twin-peak rainfall regime. Introduced crops, like maize and cassava, are grown widely. Contrary to some earlier stereotypes, West African farmers respond innovatively to the management of complex local environments using intercropping to achieve reliable yields in the light of labour availability, climatic uncertainties and their requirements for subsistence and cash (Richards 1985). Division of labour varies widely from predominantly male farming, in much of Hausaland, to predominantly female farming, in the Bamenda Grassfields of Cameroon. Most regions fall between these extremes with male farmers carrying out much of the intensive labour of short duration and female farmers taking responsibility for recurrent labour (Oppong 1983).

Ethnic Groups

Ethnic divisions are at least as numerous as languages, to which they are related but not identical. Although †'tribal' names have been used to identify the subjects of ethnographic monographs, the status of these terms is controversial. Contemporary ethnic identities have developed from differences between people that predate colonialization; however, the pertinence of these distinctions, the ethnic names used to label them, and precise criteria of inclusion and exclusion from current ethnic categories have changed demonstrably over the last hundred years. The colonial use of 'tribal' labels for administrative convenience, as well as postcolonial competition between groups defining themselves ethnically for control of resources of the state, mean that the ethnic map of West Africa must be understood as a contemporary phenomenon with historical antecedents, rather than as 'traditional'.

A majority of West African peoples can be classified roughly into peoples of the savannah and peoples of the forest margins and forests. Substantial minorities which do not fit into this binary division include: the peoples of the 'middle belt', especially in Nigeria, the coastal peoples and creolized descendants of African returnees, and the Fulani pastoralists. Developing an argument stated in strong terms by †J. Goody (1971): relative to Europe, West Africa can be characterized as abundant in land and low in population. Precolonially, West African forms of social organization rested on direct control over rights in people defined in terms of *kinship, *descent, *marriage, co-residence, *age, *gender, occupancy of offices, pawnship and *slavery. Political relations were defined by the extent of such relations rather than by strict territoriality. Relations between polities in the savanna depended importantly on their abilities to mobilize cavalry. Centralization of the southern states accelerated with access to the Atlantic trade and to firearms.

History

The documented early states of the western savanna arose at the southern termini of the trans-Saharan trade routes, largely along the River Niger, at 2,600 miles the major river of West Africa. Ghana, in the west, and Kanem near Lake Chad, were known to Arab geographers before AD 1000. The Empire of Mali, dominated by Mande-speakers, reached its apogee in the thirteenth to fourteenth centuries, leaving a profound historical and artistic legacy in the western savanna. Its successor state, Songhai, collapsed in 1591 as a result of Moroccan invasion. The Mossi states (Burkina Faso) rose to power in the fifteenth century, while to their east the Hausa (Nigeria and Niger) lived in numerous city states. Savanna society was marked by distinctions of rank (especially in the west) and ethnicity, under the influence of Islam. From the late eighteenth century, in the course of an Islamic holy war (*jihad*) under the Fulani leadership of Uthman dan Fodio, emirates were created in Hausaland and beyond which together formed the Sokoto Caliphate, the most extensive political formation in West Africa at colonialization. This example was followed by Sheikh Hamadu and al-Hajj Umar who established Islamic states in the western savanna during the nineteenth century.

The forest and forest margins included both relatively uncentralized societies and well-organized states. The kingdoms of Benin and Ife were powerful before European coastal contacts became increasingly important from the mid-fifteenth century. The export of slaves against imports of firearms and other trade goods re-oriented both economics and politics. Kingdoms which became powerful between the seventeenth and eighteenth centuries – including Asante (Ghana), Dahomey (Benin), Oyo (Nigeria) – as well as the city states which arose along the coast, competed with their neighbours to control the wealth to be accrued from the Atlantic trade.

Throughout the savanna and forest regions, and between them, societies of smaller scale than kingdoms were able to resist incorporation by virtue of some combination of their military organization, inaccessibility, and strategic alliances. The internal organization of these societies probably differed even more widely than the centralized societies. Thus, the colonies established when European nations extended their influence beyond the coast during the 'scramble for Africa' in the last quarter of the nineteenth century, consisted of peoples whose diversity posed challenges to colonial and later national governments.

Ethnographic writing: colonial traditions

Historical understanding of West Africa derives from archaeological investigations, oral traditions, the records of Arab travellers and African intellectuals, and, for the last four centuries, the writings of European travellers, explorers, traders and missionaries. From the late nineteenth century, these accounts became more systematic. The establishment of colonial rule in British colonies under the principle of †'indirect rule' – that where possible African political institutions and customs should form the basis of colonial administration – created a requirement for documentation that was met in several ways: from the enquiries of European administrators with varying degrees of anthropological training, by the employment of official government anthropologists (e.g. †R.S. Rattray in Ghana; C.K. Meek, H.F. Matthews and R.C. Abraham in Nigeria), and – probably to a less significant degree – from academic anthropologists. The characteristics of the work of anthropologists derived from the conjunction of colonial, indirect rule, which made research possible and necessary, the ascendancy of structural *functionalism in British anthropology, the foundation of – what is now – the †International African Institute in 1926 under the headship of Lugard, and the ability of this institute to secure funding in significant amounts – especially from such American patrons as the Rockefeller Foundation.

'French' and 'British' traditions of ethnographic writing developed largely with respect to their colonial possessions with theoretical agendas that appear distinctive in retrospect. Africanists predominated among professional anthropologists at the same period with the result that issues of particular concern to the regional study of Africa enjoyed a prominent position within *British and *French anthropology more generally.

The British tradition was especially concerned with the sociological description of tribes and chiefdoms or states. In practice this meant amassing detailed documentation on patterns of residence, kinship, †lineage, membership, †inheritance and marriage that were held to explain the normal functioning of local units. Larger scale political formations were usually investigated in terms of the enduring features of their organization. The landmark collection *African Political Systems* (Fortes and Evans-Pritchard 1940) defined the field of *political anthropology for a generation. It included analyses of the Tallensi of northern Ghana, which became a classic instance of an uncentralized society in West Africa (Fortes 1949; 1983), and of the Nupe kingdom in Nigeria, about which †S.F. Nadel wrote an enduring masterpiece of West Africanist ethnography (Nadel 1942). Under the guidance of †Meyer Fortes and then Jack Goody Cambridge became the major centre for Ghanaian studies in Britain. Like Fortes who also studied the Asante, Goody worked in both centralized and uncentralized societies, producing his most detailed descriptions of the uncentralized LoDagaa. University College London, under the headships of †Daryll Forde, whose ethnography concerned the Yakö of southeastern Nigeria, and then M.G. Smith, who wrote widely on the Emirates of northern Nigeria, became closely associated with studies in history, politics, economics and ecology – initially in Nigeria and later more widely. A nexus of interests in Sierra Leone developed in Edinburgh where Kenneth Little, James Littlejohn and Christopher Fyfe all taught. Not all 'British' West Africanist research emanated from these three centres – the influential work of the Oxford trained Americans Laura and Paul Bohannan on the †acephalous Nigerian Tiv is a clear exception – but these institutional specializations remained powerful beyond the period of African Independence. The literature of this period has attracted criticisms for its aim to reconstruct the lives of West African societies prior to colonialization, its relative neglect of contemporary events, normative bias consistent with the needs of indirect rule, reliance on male informants, and tendency to reify tribal units. This critique forms part of a general reaction to structural-functionalism, but is not equally applicable to all writers on West Africa before the mid-1960s.

The French tradition of the same period – exemplified by the written work of †M. Griaule and †G. Dieterlen (1991) and their collaborators on Dogon and Bambara, and by the *films of J. Rouch – was particularly concerned with the study of *religion and *cosmology among non-Muslim peoples of the western savanna. However, other writers shared the 'British' concern with the documentation of social organization, as for instance M. Dupire's classic studies of Fulani. More recently, the application of Lévi-Straussian *alliance theory has been a relatively distinctive French interest.

An American tradition, cued in part by an interest in African cultures in the New World †diaspora can be identified in †M.J. Herskovits's study of Dahomey, and in the work of his student W.R. Bascom on Yoruba.

Ethnographic writing: contemporary interests

Ethnographic research in West Africa is no less susceptible to simple summary. The French and British schools have lost much of their distinctiveness; considerable American interest has cut across the old association between national and colonial traditions; and, more generally, the disciplinary boundaries between the different social sciences and humanities have become extremely porous in relation to West Africa. Much of this is due to the writings of African scholars critical of anthropology's colonial associations (Ajayi 1965). Two recontextualizations are striking: a turn from ethnographic reconstruction to a historical appreciation of changes in West African societies (evident in M.G. Smith's works on Hausa, J.D.Y. Peel's on Yoruba, or Claude Tardits's on Bamun), and treatment of African peoples in regional and intercontinental perspectives. Researches into some of the larger groups of West African peoples, notably Akan-Twi, Hausa, Mande and Yoruba speakers, have become developed specializations demanding high levels of language proficiency and familiarity with diaspora issues in Africa and beyond.

The person in West Africa: vigorous interest in ideas of the *person in West Africa has been shared by American, British and French ethnographers. In part, this has involved rethinking topics previously dealt with as kinship, marriage, descent, family organization, slavery and pawnship to question ideas of sociality that constitute the person. But the interest also draws upon contemporary debates concerning gender, religion, and the politics of *identity (Fortes and Horton 1983; Oppong 1983; Jackson 1989). Specialists in art, performance studies and literature have contributed significantly to this debate.

Inequality: the problems faced by West African states since independence have prompted contemporary studies of inequality and poverty examining the rapid rate of urbanization in West Africa, development of the †'informal economy' (K. Hart's term), linkages between the state and local communities as well as the dynamics of ethnicity, to which anthropologists have contributed detailed local studies.

West African agriculture: West Africa remains lightly industrialized so that a majority of the population continues to earn a livelihood from agriculture or from trade. French structural *Marxist approaches to the analysis of African *modes of production gave general impetus to re-examination of the nature of African agriculture from the mid-1960s (Meillassoux 1981). Subsequently, problems of food and cash crop production in African countries, the poor performance of *development interventions in improving the agricultural sector, the political sensitivity of food prices in urban areas, and the impact of structural adjustment policies have underlined the significance of agriculture. Ethnographic investigations have emphasized issues of *household composition, gender roles and indigenous agricultural knowledge (Richards 1985).

Religion and conversion: interest in both local and world religions has several strands. These include debates over the nature and explanation of 'conversion' (following Horton's hypotheses), the growth of separatist churches, the expansion of Islam, and concern with local religions especially in the contexts of studies of *art and *performance and the roles of African religions in the diaspora.

Representation of West Africa: vigorous debates have developed around the depiction of West Africa and West African peoples in words and images. Issues of authenticity and authority have been raised in relation to philosophy, African languages, fiction and autobiography, history and ethnography, *oral literature and literature (Appiah 1992).

RICHARD FARDON

Further reading

Ajayi, J.F.A. (1965) *Christian Missions in Nigeria 1841–1891. The Making of a New Elite*, London: Longman, Ibadan History Series

Ajayi, J.F.A. and M. Crowder (eds) *History of West Africa* vol. 1, 3rd edn 1985; vol. 2, 2nd edn 1987, Harlow: Longman

Appiah, K.A. (1992) *In My Father's House: Africa in the Philosophy of Culture*, London: Methuen

Fortes, M. (1949) *The Web of Kinship among the Tallensi: The Second Part of an Analysis of the Social Structure of a Trans-Volta Tribe*, London: Oxford University Press for the International African Institute

Fortes, M. and R. Horton (1983) *Oedipus and Job in West African Religion*, Cambridge: Cambridge University Press

Goody, J. (1971) *Technology, Tradition and the State in Africa*, London: Oxford University Press for the International African Institute

Griaule, M. and G. Dieterlen (1991) *Le renard pâle*, vol. 1: *Le mythe cosmogonique*, 2nd expanded edn Paris: Institut D'Ethnologie

Hart, K. (1985) 'The Social Anthropology of West Africa', *Annual Reviews in Anthropology* 14: 243–72

Jackson, M. (1989) *Paths Towards a Clearing: Radical Empiricism and Ethnographic Enquiry*, Bloomington and Indianapolis: Indiana University Press

Meillassoux, C. (1981) *Maidens, Meal and Money. Capitalism and the Domestic Economy*, Cambridge: Cambridge University Press

Nadel, S.F. (1942) *A Black Byzantium. The Kingdom of Nupe in Nigeria*, London: Oxford University Press for International African Institute

Oppong, C. (ed.) (1983) *Female and Male in West Africa*, London: Allen and Unwin

Richards, P. (1985) *Indigenous Agricultural Revolution. Ecology and Food Production in West Africa*, London: Hutchinson

age

Age, like sex, is basic to the human condition universally, though with different implications in different cultures. Primarily conceived as a chronological measure for reckoning the physical development of human beings, the concept of age has its social significance through the concurrently changing status of a *person. While anthropologists have conducted field research on, for example, old age (Myerhoff 1978; Spencer 1990) or *childhood, or on transitions from one age-related status to another, as in *rites of passage, a specialist literature has developed around the study of polities essentially, if not exclusively, based on †age-class systems. These are overwhelmingly found in Africa, especially among *pastoralists of *East Africa.

This research, however, has long been marked by a *gender bias. In the early phase of scientific anthropology, at the end of the nineteenth century and the beginning of the twentieth, under the influence of *evolutionary theory, male age-classes were thought to have been conceived as a kind of secret association to impose men's supremacy on women's primeval matriarchy. Later on, a similar bias was still apparent because age-class systems are normally found in †patrilineal societies in which women's age-classes, when they exist, play a marginal role and are mostly parallel to men's classes. It is only recently that women's role in age-organizations has become a separate area of analysis (Kertzer 1981; Spencer 1988).

Research and analytical comparison have produced an appropriate terminology which provides a consistent methodological instrument. Thus, 'age-system' indicates the general structure of the whole range of social forms and institutions connected with age. 'Age-group' refers to any collection of people formally or informally based on age. 'Age-class' implies an association of individuals formally initiated into an institutional age-system. 'Age-set' is used either as a synonym of age-class or with reference to one of its minor sections. The collection of individuals forming a set or a class may sometimes be described as a †'cohort', a demographic term referring to all the individuals of a given community born during a definite period who, for that reason, may be considered through their lifetime as a corporate group. 'Age-grade' (or, more rarely, 'age-degree') indicates the position attained by a class (set or cohort) in the scale of promotion of any specific system. Finally, the distinction between 'formal' and 'informal' age-groupings provides a working criterion for distinguishing their character and social significance from any other kind of age qualification. †'Generation', in this context, refers to the *descent aspect of the classes; in fact, it refers not so much to the mass of people born about the same time, but rather to the groups of children who will formally succeed into their parents' social position.

Age-class polities

A new approach to the analysis of age-set systems started with †E.E. Evans-Pritchard's perception of age-sets as a factor in Nuer political organization, in combination (though secondarily) with the †lineage system. Stateless and chiefless societies, like the Nuer, appeared then to be mainly, if not exclusively, based on †segmentary lineage systems (Fortes and Evans-Pritchard 1940). Further research, however, revealed age-class systems to be a discrete type within the category of stateless societies, with their own differences, among which the distinction between †'initiation-' and 'generational-models' is the most significant. Indeed, in these cases the age-classes are so important that the societies might be properly designated as 'age-class polities'. Their social and political structure is, in fact, the outcome of the rhythmic succession of sets and classes which brings about a clear distinction between different grades and an ordered division of powers.

Thus, age-class polities should not be thought of in terms of a concentration of power in the hands of a single class ('the class in power', according to the usage of an earlier ethnographic literature). On the contrary, every class as a corporate body, and all its individual members, are assured of equal opportunities. Equality has deliberately been isolated as a necessary trait of age-class polities, although this needs to be correctly understood as an ideal 'tendency and not an established state of affairs' (Bernardi 1985: 147). Natural differences caused by birth, personal ability and other factors are certainly to be found here as elsewhere, but their effects are in some measure checked.

The distinguishing mark of the initiation model is the performance of post-pubertal initiation for recruiting fresh sets and forming a new class. While normally initiation is aimed at the ritual ratification of the candidates' passage into adulthood, in the age-class context it also effects the entrance of candidates into a set and finally into an age-class, simultaneously causing their movement into the first age-grade and the upward movement of other senior sets and classes. The model is best illustrated by the Maasai of East Africa and their pastoral mode of life. In the past they were consistently moving in search of pastures; this required a constant adjustment to local situations and a protection of cattle from marauding animals and human raiders. Local organization reflected the general social structure with personal duties and prerogatives defined by sets and class membership. Thus, after their initiation Maasai youths were set aside for defence

purposes as warriors – *moran* – for a period of about fifteen years until they were succeeded by a new class. Next, having settled in the upper grade as married men, they attended to their own family affairs, trying to increase their livestock. At the next grade, as family fathers, they were invested with the power of decision in local assemblies which stressed their position of authority. At the next grade they would finally retire as senior elders, highly respected as the holders of tradition and occasionally required for *ritual assistance and performances. This is obviously a standardized scheme but it portrays the ideals to which local organization and personal situations could be adjusted. Tensions and conflicts might always arise between members of two succeeding classes, especially when the time for upgrading was approaching and the holders of a grade tried to postpone the occasion in order to retain their office as long as possible. At present, modern changes have seriously affected the old efficiency of the system and where it still survives it is rarely found in harmony with the ideal standards.

The *gada* system of the Borana Oromo of southern Ethiopia (formerly known as Galla) provides one of the best and perhaps the most complex illustration of the generational model. Based on a chronological cycle of ten grades, each of eight years' duration, it qualifies the whole course of life of a person from infancy (the first grade: *daballe*) to elderhood (*yuba*), through a total of eighty years. The guiding principle for entrance into the system is rigidly dictated by the structural distance of five grades (forty years) between father and sons. So it is only when a class reaches the sixth grade (*gada* – from which the whole system is named) that its members, having spent over forty years in the system, will be invested with the power to conduct the assemblies. It is only through these assemblies that Borana take unanimous decisions under the guidance of the elders: the general assembly – *gumi gayo* – convened every eight years for matters of general interest involving the entire Borana population; †clan assemblies, gathering all the representatives of a clan from wherever they might be scattered for dealing with clan matters; local or family assemblies. Such a system has been described as 'the Boran version of government by committees' (Legesse 1973: 63), and more recently, after prolonged field research, a 'society of assemblies' (Bassi 1996).

†Structural distance between fathers and sons emphasized the distinction between generations,

but its rigidity may sometimes have had serious negative effects, such as the exclusion from the system of a son born at a time when his father had retired. This deprived him of the prerogatives of the age-grades, such as, for instance, performing an official marriage. Another severe effect of the same rule was the norm that male children might only be fathered at the end of the fifth grade – *raba dori* – that is, when the father had reached forty years of age; female children were allowed to be retained at the next grade, *gada*. This has been described as a sort of birth control: †infanticide used to be imposed on breaking the norm. Such terrible consequences have been amended by the general assembly – *gumy gayo* – through the introduction of *adoption instead of infanticide. In the distant past an initiation model, *harriya*, was also devised in order to recruit those youths excluded from the *gada* system in order to let them join the other warriors.

Other models

Other age-related forms of organization are less totalizing than the age-class polities. Thus the 'residential model' refers to some community organizations like the old 'age-villages' of the Nyakyusa of Tanzania, or the villages and wards of the Afikpo of Nigeria. The 'regimental model' was typical of some chieftainships of southern Africa, like the Zulu and the Tswana. Youths were called to join a regiment and had to spend most of their time in barracks under the royal command, a system that was soon broken by colonial administration though some elements may still be recognized in modern Botswana and Zululand.

A high honour for elderhood is certainly a distinguishing mark of the polities discussed so far, although they could hardly be designated as gerontocracies. In fact, *power is not concentrated in the hands of the elders as a general category; instead power is distributed by grades to all sets, and the elders are invested with a power of decision (Maasai) or of direction (Boran), which is only temporary while they hold their position. In other cultures elderhood is frequently experienced as a time of physical decay rather than appreciated as an asset of wisdom and experience. Besides, in modern industrialized societies age is almost exclusively applied as a juridical norm to mark the achievement of maturity and its accompanying rights and duties such as marriage, military conscription or the eligibility to take up (or leave) public office. In these societies elderhood, or

the so-called third (and fourth) age, has recently emerged as a demanding problem of government policy and of serious social responsibility.

BERNARDO BERNARDI

See also: childhood, Africa: East, rite of passage, person

Further reading

Abélès, M. and C. Collard (eds) (1985) *Age, pouvoir et société en Afrique noire*, Paris: L'Harmattan

Bassi, M. (1996) *I Borana: Una societa assembleare dell'Etiopia*, Milan: Franco Angeli

Baxter, P.T. and U. Almagor (eds) (1978) *Age, Generation and Time: Some Features of East-African Age Organisation*, London: C. Hurst

Bernardi, B. (1985) *Age Class Systems: Social Institutions and Polities Based on Age*, Cambridge: Cambridge University Press

Fortes, M. and E.E. Evans-Pritchard (eds) (1940) *African Political Systems*, Oxford: Oxford University Press

Kertzer, D. (1981) 'Women's Age-Set Systems in Africa: The Latuka of Southern Sudan', in C.L. Fry (ed.) *Aging, Culture, and Health*, New York: Praeger

Kertzer, D. and J. Keith (eds) (1984) *Age and Anthropological Theory*, Ithaca: Cornell University Press

Legesse, A. (1973) *Gada: Three Approaches to the Study of African Society*, New York: Free Press

Myerhoff, B. (1978) *Number Our Days*, New York: Simon and Schuster

Spencer, P. (1988) *The Maasai of Matapato: A Study of Rituals and Rebellion*, Manchester: Manchester University Press

—— (ed.) (1990) *Anthropology and the Riddle of the Sphinx: Paradox and Change in the Life Course*, London: Routledge

Stewart, F. (1977) *Fundamentals of Age-Group Systems*, New York: Academic Press

Tornay, S. (1988) 'Vers une théorie des systèmes des classes d'âge', *Cahiers d'Etudes Africaines* 110: 281–91

alliance

The term 'alliance' as it is used in anthropology refers to those social relations created by *marriage. The word derives from the French where it can be used to describe marriage, or the fact of being in an 'in-law' relation.

The reason why a term derived from French is often used in anglophone anthropology, frequently replacing the term 'affinity', is because the importance of this type of relationship came to the fore in a controversy between those anthropologists influenced by the French anthropologist *Lévi-Strauss and those following what has been called *descent theory.

Descent theory was a particular formulation of an old view of the history of human society. It concerned only that part of the latter which referred to what held pre-state societies together and ensured limits on anarchy. According to this theory, what led to stability among primitive people were descent groups, often organized in a †segmentary fashion. Descent theory became elaborated in the work of British anthropologists in a number of studies of non-state societies in Africa and then became extended to many parts of the world where it fitted rather less well. Because of this, when descent theory was at its height, a number of writers challenged it by referring to Lévi-Strauss's book, which was subsequently translated under the title *The Elementary Structures of Kinship* (1969 [1949]).

In this book Lévi-Strauss proposed a quite different view of the history of society to that of the descent theorists. What held primitive societies together was a particular type of relation established through marriage, which Lévi-Strauss called alliance. Societies so organized had an †'elementary structure'. Elementary structures were principally found in places such as *Aboriginal Australia, certain parts of *Southeast Asia, Southern India and Aboriginal South America. These contrasted with †complex structures which were to be found in such places as Europe, Africa or among the Inuit (Eskimos). The marriage rules in societies with complex structures were said by Lévi-Strauss to be negative because they only specified which kin-person one was *not* allowed to marry; for example, in such societies one is usually not allowed to marry a full sibling or a parent. In societies with elementary structures, however, the marriage rule is said to be positive because there the rule says what type of relative one *must* marry.

Lévi-Strauss's book, as its title indicates, only concerns elementary structures and it treats marriage rules as the institution which binds society together. To demonstrate how this occurs, he further distinguishes between two types of elementary structure. In the first type, society is divided into two groups which we can refer to by the letters A and B. In such societies the positive marriage rule states that people of group A must marry people of group B, while people of group B must marry people of group A. Since Lévi-Strauss, following the way of talking of the people studied, sees such marriages as the transfer of women from one group to another, such a system

is said to be one of †*direct* exchange. In the other type of elementary structure, †*indirect* exchange, the rule is different and the society needs to contain more than two groups because, while the women of group A must marry into group B, the women of group B cannot marry back into group A but must marry into another group, group C; and the women of group C may have to marry into yet another group D or, in some cases, into group A. Indirect exchange thus encompasses cases where people marry in a circle and when the chain of groups transferring women is not closed. There is however a great difference between the two cases; when people marry in a circle the relationship between the groups is egalitarian, but if the circle is not closed the relationship between the groups is hierarchical.

Lévi-Strauss's book was not the first to discuss the significance of positive marriage rules. Before him, British and especially Dutch anthropologists working in Southeast Asia, such as van Wouden (1968 [1935]) had also stressed the significance of marriage rules for the linking of groups, but *Elementary Structures of Kinship* was certainly the most wide-ranging of such work.

Since its publication many criticisms have been levelled at it. First of all, the general evolutionary implications of the book have either been criticized or ignored. Second, †Edmund Leach (1954), in a book concerning highland Burma, argued that the social implications of marriage rules always needed to be considered in conjunction with other political and economic factors. Third, the correlation between marriage rules and the linking of groups proposed in the book has been questioned. For example †L. Dumont (1983) has pointed out that although the kind of rule which Lévi-Strauss would have no hesitation as taking to indicate an elementary structure exists in much of South India and parts of Sri Lanka, the social implication of such a rule is quite different from what it would be among, for example, the Australian Aborigines. For him affinity does not necessarily lead to the 'alliance' of social units.

There has also been much discussion about what exactly is meant by a 'positive marriage rule'. †R. Needham (1962), who at first enthusiastically welcomed Lévi-Strauss's book, insisted on drawing a sharp distinction between *'preferential' and 'prescriptive' rules, with only the latter leading to elementary structures. Prescriptive rules were absolute and were normally accompanied with a kinship terminology which equated the term for accompanied spouse with that of the type of kin one had to marry; while systems with preferential rules did not make such an equation and expressed the rule only as a preference. This distinction has proved almost impossible to maintain with clarity and Lévi-Strauss (1965) himself has refused to accept it. This, however, leads to an even greater difficulty for the general theory: *viz.* only if the rule is absolute can the social implications suggested by Lévi-Strauss possibly exist.

MAURICE BLOCH

See also: kinship, marriage, Crow–Omaha systems, and preference and prescription

Further reading

Dumont, L. (1983) *Affinity as a Value*, Chicago: University of Chicago Press

Leach, E.R. (1954) *Political Systems of Highland Burma*, London: Athlone

Lévi-Strauss, C. (1965) 'The Future of Kinship Studies', *Proceedings of the Royal Anthropological Institute for 1965:* 13–22

—— (1969 [1949]) *The Elementary Structures of Kinship*, London: Eyre and Spottiswoode

Needham, R. (1962) *Structure and Sentiment*, Chicago: University of Chicago Press

van Wouden, F.A.E. (1968 [1935]) *Types of Social Structure in Eastern Indonesia*, The Hague: Nijhoff

American anthropology

American (or rather United States) anthropology is a vast professional and disciplinary undertaking. It is taught in many high schools and most colleges and universities. Some ninety universities grant around 400 doctoral degrees in anthropology annually. Applied anthropologists outnumber academic anthropologists and hundreds of persons with doctorates in anthropology practise other professions such as law, medicine, public relations and government service.

Over 370 academic anthropology departments, sixty-four museums, forty-two research institutes and eleven government organizations are affiliated within the American Anthropological Association whose membership of over 11,000 represents only a portion of the profession. Regional, subdisciplinary and area study associations have periodic meetings and produce journals or newsletters. Academic publishers carry extensive lists of anthropological monographs and textbooks. Articles on anthropology appear frequently in newspapers and popular magazines. Fictional anthropologists feature in popular novels, films and cartoons.

American anthropology has a †four-field academic tradition in which *archaeology, *linguistics, *biological and †cultural anthropology maintain debate around certain problems concerning humankind (Silverman 1991). This emphasis developed at the end of the nineteenth century as part of a unifying thrust by university-trained anthropologists to succeed the disparate amateur interests represented in the government's †Bureau of American Ethnology, local ethnological and *folklore societies and *museums.

Trends in American anthropology past and present

American anthropology can be encapsulated thematically in the intellectual history of the discovery and passing of *modernity, not that anthropologists agree on the use of this term (Manganaro 1990). Nevertheless, it is possible to distinguish three phases in modern American anthropology. Voget (1975) characterized them as 'developmentalism', 'structuralism' and 'differentiative specialization'. Since then the onset of *postmodernism in American anthropology must also be acknowledged.

The first phase, from about 1851 to 1889, was a period when †ethnology was practised mainly through the Bureau of American Ethnology. Long periods of *fieldwork were conducted among *Native Americans using the indigenous languages. Artefacts and texts were collected, and photographs were taken. It was believed that deteriorating demographic and material conditions on the reservations necessitated a form of †'salvage anthropology' since the Indian way of life was fast disappearing. Evolutionary theories (specifically those of †Herbert Spencer and *Lewis Henry Morgan) were used to order the field data rapidly accumulating at the Bureau and to explain the nature of Native American society.

The second phase, from 1890 to 1940, was a formative era when academic anthropology was established, and a process of professionalization was undertaken by university departments, many with their own summer training schools, laboratories and funded research programmes. The concept of *'culture', as articulated by *Boas, and subsequently developed by his students (including †Mead, †Benedict, †Lowie, †Kroeber and †Sapir) who dominated professional anthropology, replaced the earlier emphasis on *'society';

and four-field research was advocated to reconstruct the disappearing Native American cultures. The *diffusion of cultural traits was then charted through †material culture and language studies. The influence of *German anthropology (or ethnology) was quite marked throughout this Boasian period.

In the early horse-and-buggy stage of field research, the academic set out from the university to stay on a reservation, interviewing selected, knowledgeable informants. This began to change as the influence of *British †social anthropology encouraged systematic analysis of Native American tribal organization (with particular attention to *kinship and †social organization). Grounded in their continent-wide appreciation of space, place and fast-changing times, American anthropologists were resistant to the natural history methods and the sociological comparisons advanced (at Chicago, for example) by *A.R. Radcliffe-Brown. Instead they advocated methods of †controlled comparison, recognizing that ecological and historical factors might account for structural similarities and differences. American anthropologists were sometimes critical of the narrow sociological focus of British anthropology, deploring its lack of attention to the work of European and American scholars, its ahistorical ethnography and its problematic before-and-after approach to cultural change.

†Alexander Lesser argued for the historicity of †social facts, in the face of the emergent American school of *'culture-and-personality' studies, and challenged the †scientism of both *Malinowski's *functionalism and Radcliffe-Brown's †structural-functionalism. This gave rise to a subterranean stream in cultural anthropology, combining archaeology, †ethnohistory and *history, that only surfaced to any major effect in the discipline with the mainstreaming of anthropological *political economy in the 1970s.

In response to the United States' needs for scientific knowledge about *East Asia and the *Pacific and its newly acquired territories overseas, American anthropology began to expand beyond Native America at this time, but this provided a relatively small proportion of its ethnographic corpus before World War II.

The third phase, from 1940 to 1964, was the period of social-scientific ascendancy when economics, *sociology and political science dominated the academy. Maintaining only a partial allegiance to the social sciences, American anthropology resisted narrower sociological definitions of the field. Nevertheless research *methodology changed. Anthropologists began to study contemporary conditions on reservations, for example, relying on observation as well as elicited information. Anthropologists carrying out observational research in urban and rural American communities began to question the generalizations of sociologists and political scientists about United States society. Overseas fieldwork also expanded significantly, leading to further questioning of, for example, tradition, modernization, continuity and change.

*Lévi-Strauss's *structuralism opened the door again to European ethnology. From the New School of Social Research in New York city, where he spent his wartime exile, Lévi-Strauss launched the structuralist movement that was to sweep the discipline in the 1950s and early 1960s. Francophone scholarship began to replace the German input into American anthropology. Thereafter, in ever quickening succession (marked by the shorter and shorter time it took for Francophone works to achieve English publication), the publications of linguists (†Saussure), Marxist anthropologists (Godelier, Meillassoux), sociologists (†Bourdieu), historians (Braudel), and philosophers (†Althusser, †Foucault) entered American anthropology.

A postwar 'brain drain' from Britain brought several social anthropologists to American shores including †Victor Turner, †Mary Douglas (temporarily), F. G. Bailey, and Aidan Southall. A transatlantic movement in *political anthropology advocating †action theory and a similar Manchester-derived focus on symbols in action and ritual led to further shifts in American field methods. Yet, at the same time and not coincidentally, American anthropology reasserted itself in the neo-evolutionist studies of †White and †Steward, a revival of culture history, and a strong push towards cultural ecology.

The fourth phase started around 1965 and could be said to be still with us. Postmodernism is characterized by crisis and fragmentation. Experience of academic crisis during and after the Vietnam War (1965-73) led to a †paradigm shift in American anthropology towards †hermeneutics (in *symbolic or †interpretive anthropology) and history. Technical advances in the sciences and communications led to increased specialization and a contestation of the interrelationship among the traditional four fields. Further specialization within cultural anthropology increased linkage of its intellectual domains to disciplines other than anthropology, particularly history and literary criticism.

New anthropological interest groups were formed within the profession for humanistic, *medical, *psychological, *urban and visual anthropology, each with its increasingly distinctive discourse. Feminists, homosexuals, black and Hispanic anthropologists became institutionalized in programmes and centres in the universities, their research challenging the anthropological canon. Anthropological postmodernism was itself challenged by those who noted its emergence just at a time when minority and †subaltern voices were beginning to make themselves heard.

American anthropology continued to be remarkably cosmopolitan, this time drawing as much on disenchanted Third-world scholars in history and the humanities, as on European émigré scholarship. The role of the United States as a leading global player and the issues raised by a critical new American anthropology underwritten by public and private funds – especially issues related to localism and globalism, postmodernism, and the literary turn – have had a marked overseas impact on the postmodern global academy.

Continuities in the American tradition

Through all this postmodern flexing of disciplinary and counter-disciplinary muscles, two continuities may be discerned in American anthropology: its four-field practice and its intellectual combativeness towards American social science.

An intriguing collection of essays published in *Current Anthropology* between 1960 and 1990 drew attention to several enduring issues in American anthropology (Silverman 1991). Essays on the emergence of humankind, for example, dealt with connections among tool-making and tool use, forms of *cognition, social organization and language. Several essays on cultural transformation focused on shifts in *food production, trade and the growth of cities. In the first cluster, findings from biological anthropology, archaeology and linguistics were systematically related. In the second cluster, archaeology, ethnohistory and ethnography were intermeshed.

A key text to have emerged out of the continuing four-field approach is Edwin Wilmsen's *Land Filled with Flies* (1989). This revisionist work used archaeological, archival, linguistic, biological and ethnographic evidence to refute the analytically closed-system approaches of structuralists and cultural ecologists. This led to a representation of the !Kung San of the Kalahari as a contemporary instance of the remote way of life of *hunters and gatherers. Wilmsen found the San to have had a long history of regional and transcontinental commerce. Entrenched *ideology in modern society, he argued, perpetuated their dispossession and rural underclass status. Another key text representing this body of distinctively American counter-social science scholarship was Eric Wolf's *Europe and the People without History* (1982), a work first envisaged and outlined in 1969.

Wolf's political economy paradigm and †Clifford Geertz's (1973) literary-interpretivist notion of 'culture as text' were both equally transgressive of the American brand of social science (particularly the burden of the modernization paradigm) that dominated the professionally formative years they shared. Ross (1991) has characterized American social science as exceptional, pragmatic, technocratic and scientistic, centred around liberal individualism and with a shallow historical vision. Hence, working against the grain of American social science, the disciplinary engagement of Wolf and Geertz (political economy and interpretive anthropology) with history and hermeneutics respectively.

Within the discipline itself controversy focused on whether the goal of American anthropology was explanation or interpretation. This epistemological issue – on what basis anthropology contributes to knowledge – quickly becomes enmeshed within the question of how knowledge, *power and authority are produced and reproduced. Michel Foucault's writing (for many American anthropologists mediated through the translations and commentaries of Paul Rabinow) was clearly influential but so too was a strong feminist challenge within anthropology itself. In a *reflexive mood then, both Foucauldian and feminist critiques having entered the mainstream, American anthropology is prepared to face the twenty-first century.

Disciplinary history

A distinctive feature of American anthropology is its research interest in the *history of anthropology. This became virtually a subfield within the discipline after 1962 when the Social Science Research Council sponsored a conference on the subject. Although there had been narrative accounts of American anthropology and its leading practitioners, only Leslie White's research in the Morgan archive provided anything like a corpus of historical inquiry. It also raised the question of historians' and disciplinarians' histories of anthropology.

The research and teaching of A.I. Hallowell at the University of Pennsylvania and later that of Dell Hymes provided a launchpad for the new disciplinary interest. George Stocking's historiographical writing and his teaching encouraged a trend towards specialization by both historians and anthropological practitioners. American anthropology from the 1850s to the 1930s, nineteenth-century German intellectual history, Canadian anthropology, and Victorian anthropology in Britain, as well as the scholarship of Malinowski and Radcliffe-Brown (both of whom taught for short periods in American universities) have been the main areas of concentration.

JOAN VINCENT

See also: archaeology, biological anthropology, culture, folklore, language and linguistics

Further reading

Geertz, C. (1973) *The Interpretation of Cultures*, New York: Basic Books
Manganaro, M. (1990) *Modernist Anthropology. From Fieldwork to Text*, Princeton: Princeton University Press
Mascia-Lees, F., P. Sharpe and C. Cohen (1989) 'The Postmodernist Turn in Anthropology: Cautions from a Feminist Perspective', *Signs: Journal of Women in Culture and Society* 15: 7–33
Morgen, S. (ed.) (1989) *Gender and Anthropology. Critical Reviews for Research and Teaching*, Washington: American Anthropological Association
Murphy, R. (1971) *The Dialectics of Social Life. Alarms and Excursions in Anthropological Theory*, New York: Basic Books
Ross, D. (1991) *The Origins of American Social Science*, Cambridge: Cambridge University Press
Silverman, S. (ed.) (1991) *Inquiry and Debate in the Human Sciences. Contributions from Current Anthropology, 1960–1990*, Chicago: University of Chicago Press
Stocking, Jr. G.W., (1993) *The Ethnographer's Magic and other Essays in the History of Anthropology*, Madison: University of Wisconsin Press
Voget, F. (1975) *A History of Ethnology*, New York: Holt, Rinehart & Winston
Wilmsen, E. (1989) *Land Filled with Flies: A Political Economy of the Kalahari*, Chicago: University of Chicago Press
Wolf, E. (1982) *Europe and the People without History*, Berkeley: University of California Press

Americas: Central

As the table shows, Central America consists of one very large country, Mexico, with some 75 per cent of the total land area and nearly 80 per cent of the total population; and six much smaller countries, Guatemala, Honduras, El Salvador, Nicaragua, Costa Rica and Panama, which form a long and mostly narrow strip of land separating the Caribbean Sea from the Pacific Ocean. (An eighth country, Belize, is treated as part of the *Caribbean region.)

Mexico shares a long northern frontier, approximately 3,000 km in length, with the United States, to which, following the Mexican War of 1847–8, it lost a very considerable amount of territory, consisting of the present American states of Texas, New Mexico, Arizona and California. These all still contain very sizeable and steadily increasing Central American *ethnic minorities.

Following the creation of the North American Free Trade Association (NAFTA) in 1993, the involvement with the United States is only likely to increase. At grass roots this means an increased stream of *migration, legal and illegal, permanent and temporary, across the frontier. This already

Table 1 Central America: basic statistics

Country	Area km² × 1000	Population × 1000	Density /km²	urban per cent	age ≤ 29 per cent	birth rate /1000	literate per cent
Costa Rica	51	2,941	57.8	49.6	66	27.0	93
Guatemala	109	8,935	82.1	36.4	72	36.5	55
Honduras	112	4,377	40.4	40.0	73	39.0	60
Mexico	1,958	84,275	43.0	69.6	68	34.4	92
Nicaragua	131	3,745	31.1	59.2	74	41.8	74
Panama	77	2,370	30.7	51.9	66	27.0	88
El Salvador	21	5,338	244.2	47.7	72	37.0	69
Totals	2,459	111,981	45.5				

reaches the six smaller republics, which since the late 1940s, have been linked to Mexico by the Inter-American Highway.

Historically, the whole of Central America was once part of the Spanish Empire. The result, today, is that Spanish is the official language of the whole region, but this has not prevented the six small republics pursuing quite independent lines of development since freedom from Spanish rule was won at the beginning of the nineteenth century. In all of them economic development has been extremely retarded, with exports being largely confined to the products of tropical plantation agriculture. The plantations themselves were largely developed by foreign capital, mainly German in the case of coffee in El Salvador, Guatemala and the adjacent area of Mexico, and American in the case of bananas in Guatemala and Honduras, or cotton in Nicaragua. Panama is something of a separate case because of the Panama Canal, but even here, in a process whose social and cultural dimensions are described by Gudeman, traditional †subsistence economies are being supplanted by plantation economies focused on export to the United States. This process has led to the slow eclipse of the traditional 'belief in the saints, with the many remifying meanings it carries and functions it performs' (Gudeman 1978: 160).

Mexico is a substantially different case, even though plantations remain important – particularly in the areas furthest from the United States. With an internal market of more than 80 million people, an advanced communications infrastructure, comprehensive education, strong industrial and financial sectors, and the world's largest capital city, many, if not the majority of Mexicans, enjoy the characteristic, mainly urban life of a modern industrial economy. In this sense the country is a sort of poor relation of the United States, the role implicit in the NAFTA agreement of 1993.

Anthropological backwaters

The tens of millions of modern and relatively affluent Mexicans may interest investors, but anthropologists have largely disregarded them. Their focus of interest has been on the 'other' Mexico, which may still constitute more than half the population. Traditionally, the home of the historically dispossessed has been in what Aguirre-Beltran (1967) has designated '*regiones de refugio*', a term equally apt for substantial parts of the smaller republics. Although Aguirre-Beltran's main interest is in rural Indian populations, largely engaged in the subsistence cultivation of maize, with methods going back to before the Spanish conquest in the sixteenth century, his concept can be extended to apply to Spanish-speaking †*mestizo* populations in remote rural areas.

The underlying principle is that, by reason of poor communications, adverse geophysical factors, and, in certain important areas, relatively high concentrations of population, these *regiones de refugio* were left largely undisturbed by the colonial development of Central America. With the help of land reform in the twentieth century, this has made possible the survival, until the present day, of any number of Indian communities, preserving their own language and culture, in which the focus of life is the local centre. Gossen (1974: 16) presents a map drawn by a Chamula informant, in which the outside world (including the rest of Mexico) is consigned to a distant and largely unknown periphery.

Chamula enjoys, in common with the other districts of the highlands of Chiapas in Southern Mexico, a modern Maya culture, but the classic *regio de refugio* is to be found on the other side of the frontier with Guatemala, where the different Indian communities of the western highlands display countless variants of the same basic culture. The whole region is mountainous, with many active volcanoes, and a climate allowing for intensive agriculture, based primarily on maize. Here the new economic opportunities following from the opening of the Inter-American Highway have been offset by the suppression of local attempts at self-development by the Guatemalan Army, whose appalling human rights record has left its mark in Indian communities throughout the area.

Historically the western highland area was always something more than a disjointed collection of isolated subsistence economies, each maintaining its distinctive local culture. Each local economy had its own distinctive contribution to the national *market network, focused on the gigantic market place of the capital city, and market studies are the basis of many familiar ethnographic texts. †Tax introduced the now familiar term, 'Penny Capitalism', to describe 'a society which is "capitalist" on a microscopic scale' (1963: ix).

The society described was that of Panajachel on the shore of Lake Atitlan, where the Indian inhabitants grow onions which they transport far afield for sale on the national market. Tax noted:

a striking peculiarity . . . the combination of a childish, magical or 'primitive' world view with institutions reminiscent of the Great Society. In most 'primitive' societies about which anthropologists write, people behave in our terms irrationally, since they try by devices strange to us to maximize different, hence curious satisfactions. This happens not to be the case in the part of Guatemala about which I write, where the social institutions and cosmology, strange as they may be to us, are as separated from the processes of making a living as are our own . . . the Panajachel economy is like ours.

(Tax 1963: ix)

The dichotomy pointed out by Tax is fundamental to Central American anthropology: the character of any one study is determined by which side the author chooses to describe. Chamula also has an 'economy . . . like ours' in the form of an extremely successful cottage industry devoted to the illegal production of rum (Crump 1987). On the other hand, Gossen's (1974) study of oral tradition and cosmology in the same municipio portrays a world far from mainstream Mexico.

Church and 'fiestas'
Although, from the sparsely populated deserts of northern Mexico to the densely populated highlands of Chiapas and Guatemala, the Indian communities studied by anthropologists vary greatly in climate, topography and demography, certain themes occur almost everywhere. One of the most important is the historical impact of Catholicism on indigenous religious forms. This is summed up by the title of Ricard (1966), *The Spiritual Conquest of Mexico*.

The mission of the Catholic church extended to the remotest areas of Central America, as witness today any number of dilapidated churches and monasteries. The social policy of the church, known as *reducción*, was to concentrate Indian settlement round the parish church. In the less remote areas, with Spanish-speaking *mestizo* populations, this policy led to the foundation of many of the towns which flourish today. In the areas left to the Indians it failed, if only because it conflicted with established *settlement patterns related to traditional subsistence agriculture. The churches were certainly built, but generally the municipal centres attracted no permanent populations, save for a handful of *mestizo* officials and shopkeepers. At the same time, the church as an institution lost most of the wealth accumulated in the first centuries of Spanish colonization, and in Mexico, following the revolutionary years, 1910–20, it was almost completely suppressed.

The result was that local populations were left free to use church buildings for their own religious purposes, with only marginal support from any Catholic clergy (who were never Indians) that survived the revolutionary terror. Today government policy tolerates a revived clergy, throughout Central America consisting largely of expatriate missionaries, but the main religious action is not only controlled by the local population, but also forms the focus of its own political autonomy. The main events in the religious year are the fiestas, each of which is in the charge of an elaborate hierarchy of lay officials, elected anew every year in a process described in detail by Cancian (1965: 126f).

The importance of the system lies in:

the way which fiestas . . . promote order and social control, although they seem to provide a break from ordinary routine and can even appear formless and chaotic. Practically by definition, fiestas provide respites from the constraints and rules of everyday life. Paradoxically, however, they serve to reinforce the power relationships, moral guidelines, and informal sanctioning mechanisms by which people regulate their daily behavior.

(Brandes 1988: 2)

Brandes describes the fiesta system of Tzintzuntzan, not far from Mexico City, but he notes that 'everywhere from the state of Sonora in the northwest . . . to Chiapas in the southeast . . . we find that ethnic identity is affirmed through religious cosmologies and ceremonials' (1988: 3). The same rule applies in the rest of Central America.

The world outside
*Compadrazgo is one particular institution established and maintained by the major sacramental occasions of baptism, confirmation, first communion and marriage, for which the assistance of a priest is required. The key rite is baptism, where the *compadre*, as god-father to the child, is recognized as a key figure in the natural parents' network of fictive or ritual *kinship. The relationship, being essentially hierarchical, can provide the means of access to political support and patronage, but Nash, in her study of Amatenango,

a traditional Mayan community of Chiapas, suggests (1970: 124) that 'its greatest importance is still based on creating or reinforcing group solidarity'.

Medicine is also a field shared between the lore of the outside world and that of the local community. The people of Pichátaro, in the highlands of west-central Mexico, clearly accept the commonly recognized distinction between local *remedios caseros* and trained doctors' *remedios médicos* (Young 1981: 102). The former supports different types of practitioners, or *curanderos*, a term familiar throughout all Central America, who are consulted over particular types of sickness. They can also counteract illnesses recognized as caused by witchcraft (1981: 113).

Finally, the *barrios* of the great cities, with vast populations, often recent migrants from overpopulated rural areas, are also critical in the anthropology of Central America. †Oscar Lewis's (1961) study of one single family is the classic text for establishing a distinctive †culture of poverty, in which every individual must make their own way in life, against a chaotic and unstable background characterized by alcoholism, endless petty crime, prostitution and violence. In a region where birth-rates substantially above the world average (for which see Table 1) lead to a doubling of the population with every generation, the poor *barrios* of the large cities will be the home of a steadily increasing proportion of the total population. At the same time, demographic pressure, exhaustion of land traditionally used for subsistence cultivation and continued extension of the communications infrastructure combine to reduce the capacity of the *regiones de refugio* to support their original populations, and so exacerbate the near insoluble social problems of the large cities.

THOMAS CRUMP

See also: Caribbean, *compadrazgo*

Further reading

Aguirre-Beltran, G. (1967) *Regiones de refugio*, Mexico DF: Instituto Indigenista Interamericano

Brandes, S. (1988) *Power and Persuasion: Fiestas and Social Control in Rural Mexico*, Philadelphia: University of Pennsylvania Press

Cancian, F. (1965) *Economics and Prestige in a Maya Community: The Religious Cargo System in Zinacantan*, Stanford CA: Stanford University Press

Crump, T. (1987) 'The Alternative Economy of Alcohol in the Chiapas Highlands', in M. Douglas (ed.) *Constructive Drinking*, Cambridge: Cambridge University Press

Gossen, G.H. (1974) *Chamulas in the World of the Son*, Cambridge MA: Harvard University Press

Gudeman, S. (1978) *The Demise of a Rural Economy: From Subsistence to Capitalism in a Latin American Village*, London: Routledge & Kegan Paul Ltd

Lewis, O. (1961) *The Children of Sanchez*, New York: Random House

Nash, J. (1970) *In the Eyes of the Ancestors: Belief and Behavior in a Mayan Community*, New Haven CT: Yale University Press

Ricard, R. (1966) *The Spiritual Conquest of Mexico*, Berkeley: University of California Press

Tax, S. (1963) *Penny Capitalism*, Chicago: Chicago University Press

Young, J.C. (1981) *Medical Choice in a Mexican Village*, New Brunswick NJ: Rutgers University Press

Americas: Latin America

The term 'Latin America' is ambiguous, as its connotations are various. As a more encompassing notion, it refers to a territory, and its concomitant nation states, stretching from Mexico in the north, through the *Caribbean and *Central America, to Argentina and Chile in the south. However, as a much looser term, Latin America evokes a series of associated images (not quite mythical nor quite stereotypical): Indian heritage and European dominance; *macho* men and stoic women; violent revolutions and ruthless dictatorships; agrarian reforms and urban congestion; dire poverty and sumptuous luxury; remote hinterlands and advanced industrial enterprises; Liberation Theology and †dependency theory. It evokes the magical realism of their literature; the flair of their *fiestas*; the rhythms of tango and salsa; the flavours of their food; the temperament of their athletes; the *caudillo* of politics; the triumph of *mañana*. In this latter sense, Latin America connotes the culture of the †*mestizo* – in contrast to the *Native American, †indigenous cultures, which have been seen to represent the pre-Columbian heritage.

Most importantly, the term 'Latin America' glosses those aspects of Latin American culture which are perceived to be the products of the particular process of transculturation which ensued as a result of the conquest (initiated in 1492) by the Spanish and Portugese of the indigenous populations, i.e. those historical processes which lend Latin America its singularity. The conquest not only established the invaders as the rulers, but also inculcated a perception of the rulers as radically superior to their subject people. Hence, the *mestizo* – born of Indian mother and Spanish father – was initially seen as a threat to the stability of the social order, and only much later will *mestisaje* come to symbolize a Latin American essence and thereby become the locus of contested national *identity. This attitude of different but *not* equal was nourished initially by the *conquistadores* and the Catholic Church, and subsequently by the various new independent governments to be proclaimed in the first half of the nineteenth century.

In spite of the processes of *mestisaje* and religious and cultural *syncretism, this initial creation of 'the other' has contributed to the construction of a pervasive dichotomy which permeates perceptions of Latin American society (Todorov 1987). Although the roots of this dichotomy can be traced to the original opposition between 'Indian' and 'European', it has over the centuries been transposed and come to encompass a series of oppositions: traditional/modern; backward/civilized; rural/urban; underdeveloped/developed. These oppositions operate both internally in the structuring of relationships between groups and externally, positioning Latin America simultaneously, and hence ambiguously, at the core and periphery of the occidental world.

Since the time of colonization, Latin America was integrated in the *world system, albeit on very unequal terms. Although there are many features which contribute to the shared cultural heritage of Latin Americans, the local conditions at the time of conquest were extremely varied, implying very different forms of articulation and hence different socio-economic and political trajectories (Wolf and Hansen 1972). Any understanding of the complexities and heterogeneity of modern Latin America must take into account these differences.

Anthropological perspectives

The development of anthropology in Latin America has been affected by these perceptions, both with respect to the types of studies carried out and with respect to the theories that have guided the work. At a very general level it is possible to say that anthropological research in Latin America has fallen into two main categories: those dealing with Native American indigenous cultures, and those more concerned with the articulation of social processes that have come in the wake of *modernization and industrialization. Whereas the former studies focus primarily on the internal structurings of indigenous communities and have a specific regional embeddedness (e.g. *Highland and *Lowland South America), the latter, often coined as *'peasant studies', are more concerned with the relations that obtain between local communities and the wider society. These studies are not limited to any particular region, but represent, rather, a perspective which seeks to reflect the complex processes that modernization implies with a specific interest in social change, often with an explicit applied intention. They focus on different forms of socio-cultural integration, exploring forms of social differentiation, *migration and urbanization in order to grasp the transformation of rural societies. Thus, one of the main contributions of anthropology has been to open the space and disclose the tensions that bridge the prevailing dichotomies.

Rural society – folk culture

The particular focus on rural lifeworlds was inspired by *evolutionist theory and the notion that so-called traditional societies represented an impediment to change. The development of anthropology in Mexico is illustrative of this perspective. In the wake of the Mexican Revolution (1910) there was a growing concern for the plight of the indigenous communities and their possible integration into the national society. Under the influence of Manuel Gamio (the founding father of modern Mexican anthropology) the policy of *indigenismo* – based on the notion that indigenous groups were culturally distinct from the wider society – was launched. This policy was to generate a major debate around the question of incorporation: assimilation versus autonomy, integration versus cultural plurality. Later the programme of *indigenismo* was challenged by the concept of †'internal colonialism' and dependency theory and converged in a debate about ethnic identity and inter-ethnic relations (Stavenhagen 1969). At issue was the nature of indigenous communities and, most importantly, their relation to society at large. Being neither †'primitive' nor 'modern', they defied the prevailing categorizations (see Hewitt de Alcantara 1984 for a full discussion on this issue).

The studies of †Robert Redfield, George Foster and †Oscar Lewis, all influenced by the *culture and personality school, insert themselves in this debate. Through his concept of 'folk society' Redfield developed a model of local communities as distinctly integrated and different from urban communities. He considered urban values and lifestyles to be a threat and disintegrating force on local value-systems. He subsequently modified his initial views, developing his folk-urban continuum and the notion of the peasant communities as 'part cultures'. Through his concept of *'great and little traditions' and his focus on the social organization of tradition (1955), he recognized more explicitly the embeddedness of rural communities. With Redfield, peasant studies became an important focus in Latin American anthropology. The criticisms that his work inspired – the romantic view of peasant communities, the *functionalist assumptions, and his emphasis on cognitive categories to the detriment of economic factors in explaining change – led to a continued interest in the forces underpinning the transformation of rural society.

In contrast to Redfield, Foster, in his study on Tzintzuntzan (1967), found a community permeated by mistrust and fear. He introduced the notion of the 'image of †limited good' to explain the prevailing †worldview. Although he related this to the historical and ecological forces that worked to shape the community, he nevertheless stressed psychological factors as the basic impediment to raising standards of living. Oscar Lewis's restudy of the village of Tepoztlán (in the 1940s) challenged Redfield's original findings along similar lines, stressing the prevalence of conflict over harmony. However, Lewis was also interested in the historical processes that linked the community to the nation state, as well as the social processes that linked the rural to the urban. His focus on migration led him to do fieldwork in the urban slums of Mexico City, which resulted not only in innovative ethnographic accounts (e.g. Lewis 1961) but also laid the basis for his controversial theory of the †culture of poverty and many subsequent studies of poor urban communities.

Peasants and relations of power

These studies were not particularly concerned with the issue of *power. Thus, the social organization of peasant communities was largely explained in functionalist terms and with reference to values. This necessarily had implications for the views held with respect to incentives for change. With the work of †Julian Steward (in Mexico, Peru and Puerto Rico) a new approach, cultural ecology, was given to research concerned with rural development. Most importantly this involved a focus on regional developments in a historical perspective and assigning a first priority to material conditions and socio-economic relations.

Eric Wolf and Sydney Mintz developed this perspective within a *Marxist framework. Their work was to have a profound influence on the subsequent development of Latin American anthropology. The shift in the analytic thrust implied a view of the peasant/indigenous community as intrinsically integrated in (as well as a product of) national political and economic relations, but on unequal terms: they were not only dependent but also exploited. The concept of surplus as well as that of domination became central to the analysis of the structural constraints on peasant action. Moreover, particular attention was given to the different social relations that sustain the peasant community, giving weight to both the vertical (*patron-client) and horizontal (*compadrazgo) ties which permeate the community.

The impact of the works of Wolf and Mintz must be seen in the light of both the agrarian unrest which prevailed in Latin America in the 1960s and 1970s, and the prominence of the dependency theories which dominated Latin American social sciences at this time. Countless studies of rural society and processes of rural transformation were informed by these frameworks (e.g. Johnson 1971, Warman 1976), and represent the culmination of the rural-urban problematics. The importance of these studies lies in the consistent effort to relate historical processes, ecological and macro-economic conditions to the everyday organization of social life.

Contemporary perspectives

Whereas earlier studies developed in a context of modernizing projects, with the dual focus of discontinuity and integration, contemporary perspectives, seeking to transcend the former perspectives, recognize Latin America as representing modern, *plural and basically urban societies. Other issues of research are brought to the fore, such as the focus on the various articulations of modernity and identity. One significant development in this direction has been the growing interest in the construction of *gender relations and the meanings attached to gender. As elsewhere, the forerunner to a focus on gender in Latin America was the concern for the position of women, and the central issues were framed in terms of *class and oppression (Nash and Safa 1976), production and reproduction (Deere and León 1987) in line with prevailing Marxist perspectives. However, the narrow †materialist approach has yielded to a more sensitive analysis of the complex meanings of gender in Latin American society, as these are disclosed both in the practice of everyday life, the sexual division of labour and in symbols and values. Thus such themes as football, tango and the notions of *honour and shame are all brought to bear on the construction of masculinity and femininity as expressions of particular moralities (e.g. Archetti 1991; Melhuus and Stølen, forthcoming). A better understanding of the meanings of power, the construction of national identities and ethnic relations seems to rest on a greater appreciation of the significance of gender.

MARIT MELHUUS

See also: Americas: Central, Americas: Native South America (Highland, Lowland), Caribbean, gender, Marxism and anthropology, peasants

Further reading

Archetti, E.P. (1991) 'Argentinian Tango: Male Sexual Ideology and Morality', in R. Grønhaug, G. Haaland and G. Henriksen (eds) *The Ecology of Choice and Symbol: Essays in Honour of Fredrik Barth*, Bergen: Alma Mater

Deere, C.D. and M. León (1987) *Rural Women and State Policy: Feminist Perspectives on Latin American Agricultural Development*, Boulder: Westview Press

Foster, G. (1967) *Tzintzuntzan: Mexican Peasants in a Changing World*, Boston: Little, Brown & Company

Hewitt de Alcántara, C. (1984) *Anthropological Perspectives on Rural Mexico*, London: Routledge & Kegan Paul

Johnson, A.W. (1971) *The Sharecroppers of the Sertaõ*, Stanford: Stanford University Press

Lewis, O. (1961) *The Children of Sanchez: Autobiography of a Mexican Family*, New York: Random House

Melhuus, M. and K.A. Stølen (eds) (forthcoming) *The Power of Latin American Gender Imagery*, London: Verso

Nash, J. and H. Safa (1980) *Sex and Class in Latin America*, Massachusetts: Bergin Publishers

Redfield, R. (1955) 'The Social Organization of Tradition', *The Far Eastern Quarterly* 15 (1): 13–21

Stavenhagen, R. (1969) *Las clases sociales en las sociedades agrarias*, Mexico City: Siglo XXI

Todorov, T. (1987) *The Conquest of America: The Question of the Other*, New York: Harper

Warman, A. (1976) *Y venimos a contradecir . . .*, Mexico City: Ediciónes de la Casa Chata

Wolf, E. and E. Hansen (1972) *The Human Condition in Latin America*, New York: Oxford University Press

Americas: Native North America

The Native people of North America comprise an immense diversity of societies adapted to the full variety of terrestrial environments. From the tundra and coniferous forests of the far north to the swamplands and deserts of the south these societies have in many cases sustained a distinctive lifestyle and identity despite the fact that their lands fall within the boundaries of Canada and the United States, both powerful nation-states with advanced industrial economies. Indeed the deprivation and degradation experienced by most Native American (or Indian) societies during centuries of contact with the larger Euro-American society has in recent years been put into reverse, with greater respect now being afforded both to their political rights and to the value of their particular cultures. For example, in Canada, Indian societies are now termed 'First Nations'. Even so, the loss of population and land will never fully be recovered, and it seems likely that many decades will pass before the North American Indians enjoy the full economic, political and cultural entitlements due them as citizens of the countries into which they have been absorbed.

The first effective European contact with the Native North American societies ranged from the early sixteenth century in the south and east to the early twentieth century in parts of the *Arctic. The records of explorers, missionaries and traders reveal peoples of extraordinary economic and cultural ingenuity. Large political nations and fabulous monumental architecture, both famous from parts of *Central and *South America, are not reported. Yet North American Indians had achieved complex social organizations and sophisticated aesthetic cultures, normally on the basis of relatively simple in technological terms *hunter-gatherer, *fishing, or farming economies. For example, on the basis of hunting, plant collecting and fishing the Calusa of Florida developed a monarchical social structure reminiscent of Ancient Egypt (Marquardt 1988), the Kwakiutl of Vancouver Island evolved spectacular ceremonials of economic distribution (the *potlatch), and in the Arctic the Eskimo (Inuit) accomplished a viable mode of living well beyond the latitude where trees cease to grow (Riches 1982).

The widely varying social organizations and cultures of the North American Indians have stimulated the development of compelling academic studies of inestimable importance to the discipline of anthropology. Thus the work of *Morgan, *Boas, †Benedict, †Eggan and many others reads as a catalogue for the history of anthropological theory over the past century and more.

Morgan and the Iroquois

Lewis Henry Morgan, best known in anthropology for his *evolutionism, is more properly remembered for developing an understanding of human social institutions as components of a broader *social structure. His theoretical insights rest principally on the comparative study of North American Indians, and most especially on his work on the Iroquois, the tribal confederacy in the northeastern United States among whom he conducted both field and archival research. Morgan's studies, principally published between 1851 and 1877, provide landmark accounts of systems of *kinship and *marriage in general, and in particular the shape of †matrilineal *descent structures. Thus the Iroquois matrilineal system, though not †matriarchal, was revealed by Morgan as permitting women to exercise exceptionally high levels of political influence (Morgan 1851). The men who sat on Iroquois tribal and confederacy councils were nominated by the women from their respective †lineages. Correspondingly, women enjoyed enormous influence in the *household, connected with the fact that †uxorilocal postmarital residence meant that the main domestic unit consisted of a stable core of women whose husbands, drawn from different lineages, enjoyed no solidarity. Also to be noted is that the distinctive manner by which Iroquois classify their relatives – for example, using the same terms to label siblings and certain (but not all) cousins – has entered general anthropological parlance as the 'Iroquois' *relationship terminology. This was first reported in 1724 by †Joseph-François Lafitau, the French Jesuit missionary, and was famously developed by Morgan in his discussions of †classificatory kinship (Morgan 1870).

Twentieth-century studies of social organization

The landmark publication, *Social Anthropology of North American Tribes*, edited by Fred Eggan (1937), developed Morgan's approach to the study of North American Indians, though it eliminated its evolutionary dimension. Influenced by the British †structural-functionalist, *A.R. Radcliffe-Brown, the contributors attend mainly to the social and political organization of a large variety of societies, especially the various Plains Indian societies of the north-central United States (e.g. Sioux, Cheyenne, Arapaho). The focus is principally on kinship organization, although other types of relationship, such as the *joking relationship famous among many North American Indian peoples, are considered as well. Another strand in this book, representing an important dimension in the anthropology of Native North America, discusses social change, particularly the religious revivalism which may be associated with the appalling relations with Euro-Americans during the nineteenth and early twentieth centuries. Thus the Plains Indians' *ghost dance, a *millenarian religion foretelling a general catastrophe which only the Indian will survive, may be understood as a reaction to defeat and confinement to reservations experienced by people who until that time had steadily developed a successful buffalo hunting culture based around horses and firearms secured from European immigrants by trade (Mooney 1896). Further south, among the Navajo of Utah and Arizona, the †peyote religion, focused on the ceremonial use of hallucinogens, served similar functions (Aberle 1966).

Inspired by Morgan, Eggan and others, the social organization of the North American Indians has continued to fascinate anthropologists. In particular, the matrilineal societies, though not numerically preponderant, have received considerable attention. As well as the Iroquois, examples range from the Tlingit and Haida, hunters and fishermen of coastal and island southeast Alaska, through to the Hopi, pueblo dwellers of Arizona, and also the Navajo, a people noted for having taken up livestock herding in place of hunting and agriculture. In contemporary times all Native North American Indian societies have diversified their economies because of contact with the wider American society, taking in a range of new livelihoods including lumbering, construction work, fur trading, tourism, and many other types of wage labour. Such involvement with the broader commercial economy has had a fragmenting effect on social structure, and at least the partial demise of all the traditional forms of social organization is widespread.

Boas and the Northwest Coast Indians

The work of Franz Boas and his students provides another major theoretical perspective in anthropology developed through the *ethnographic study of North American Indians. Field research on the Eskimo (Inuit) of Baffin Island in 1883, and, from 1886 onwards, on the Indians of coastal northwest Canada, particularly the Kwakiutl of Vancouver Island, convinced Boas that the hypothetical stages which Morgan and others believed depicted the course of societal evolution everywhere were misguided and unconvincing. In the case of the Baffin Island work Boas's studies put in train discussion of the relation between ecology and social organization which has dominated Inuit studies to the present day (e.g. Riches 1982). It also set the standard for the subsequent field research on the Inuit and other Eskimo-speaking peoples in the Arctic, especially that emanating from the Fifth Thule Expedition of the 1920s which is particularly noted for its classical descriptions of the *shamanistic religion (e.g. Rasmussen 1929). It is only in very recent years that anthropologists have begun systematically to propose that it may be factors other than the natural *environment, such as deep rooted cultural ideas, which shape the form of Inuit social organization and customary practices (e.g. Fienup-Riordan 1990). As to Boas's studies on the 'Northwest Coast Indians', these are a monumental achievement, yet the systematic description of their social organizations, which Morgan's methods would have helped provide, eluded him. Satisfying accounts, using *structuralist methods, were indeed forthcoming only in the 1970s (e.g. Rosman and Rubel 1971).

The category 'Northwest Coast Indians' refers to a remarkable series of 'societies', with broad cultural similarities and coastal adaptations, stretching from southeast Alaska (including the Tlingit and Haida) through to northern California (for example, the Yurok). These societies have in common that their economies are based on hunting, fishing and collecting (for example, of wild plants, nuts, acorns, seeds), and that their social organizations include developed systems of social ranking, the *exchange of food and wealth objects (shells, coppers, bark blankets), and (in the case of most of the societies) the potlatch ceremonial. Yet these features apart, they exhibit enormous diversity, notably in language, *mythology, kinship organization and *art (which in the northern societies includes the totem pole). Boas addressed the complexity of Northwest Coast societies by attending in great detail to historical connections and geographical distributions concerning elements of culture within local

regional areas, a perspective which subsequently came to be labelled †'historical particularism'. Whatever the theoretical shortcomings of this perspective, thanks to Boas the wealth of data now available on the Northwest Coast Indians is unparalleled, and many later theoretical approaches in anthropology have drawn on this material as their testing ground.

As well as his fine-grained approach in tracing particular cultural elements, Boas also developed the concept of a people's *culture as an integrated whole. Among famous developments of this notion, again drawing on North American Indian material, was Ruth Benedict's idea, published in 1934, that cultures thus construed manifest distinct 'patterns' or 'configurations' which could compellingly be described through psychological idioms. Thus Benedict contrasts the Northwest Coast Indians with the various Pueblo Indian societies, peoples whose historical achievements in stone architecture and urban organization (including cliff dwelling) rank them as among the best known Native North Americans. With regard to the characters of the Northwest Coast Indian and the Pueblo Indian cultures, Benedict particularly attended to their developed ceremonial and cultic lives and to their †secret societies and, drawing on Nietzche, labelled them as respectively 'Dionysian' (Northwest Coast Indians) and 'Apollonian' (Pueblo Indians). These labels depict differing orientations of members of society to personal ambition and the constraint of tradition. The Dionysian is individualistic and passionate: thus among the Northwest Coast Indians, ecstasy is the aim in religious ceremonial; and in political life, in the context of social ranking, there is arrogant competition for †status, mainly through accumulation and gifting (in the ceremonial potlatch) of economic wealth such as coppers and blankets. In turn, the Apollonian is committed to tradition and decries individualism: among the Pueblo Indians, for example, there is a cultural emphasis on emotional restraint and the ideal is placidly to submit oneself to the interests of the group. Benedict's writings, though reducing these various societies to crude stereotypes, certainly brought the North American Indians to the attention of a very wide readership.

To the future

In the late twentieth century, as well as enjoying a measure of political redress relating to the original appropriation of their lands by Euro-

American immigrants, North American Indians have won increasing admiration from wider American society for their cultural achievements. In particular, the environmental and 'New Age' movements laud Native Americans for their spiritual and harmonious attunement with the ecological environment, and for the prophecies associated with some Indian societies relating to an impending utopian age. The empirical veracity of New Age representations of the Indian way of life may not be fully accurate; but for the Native Americans themselves, the fact that their cultures command respect can only assist them in their continuing political struggles with the American mainstream.

DAVID RICHES

See also: history and anthropology, Franz Boas, Lewis Henry Morgan, hunters and gatherers, kinship, descent, potlatch, house

Further reading

Aberle, D. (1966) *The Peyote Religion among the Navaho*, Chicago: Aldine

Benedict, R. (1934) *Patterns of Culture*, New York: Mentor Books

Eggan, F. (1937) *Social Anthropology of North American Tribes*, Chicago: University of Chicago Press

Fienup-Riordan, A. (1990) *Eskimo Essays*, London: Rutgers University Press

Marquardt, W. (1988) 'Politics and Production among the Calusa of South Florida', in T. Ingold, D. Riches and J. Woodburn (eds) *Hunters and Gatherers: History, Evolution and Social Change*, Oxford: Berg

Mooney, J. (1896) *The Ghost-Dance Religion and the Sioux Outbreak of 1890*, Washington: Bureau of American Ethnology

Morgan, L.H. (1851) *League of the Ho-de-no-sau-nee, or Iroquois*, Rochester: Sage and Broa

—— (1870) *Systems of Consanguinity and Affinity of the Human Family*, Washington: Smithsonian Institution

Rasmussen, K, (1929) *The Intellectual Culture of the Iglulik Eskimos*, Copenhagen: Glydendalske Borgenhandel

Riches, D. (1982) *Northern Nomadic Hunter-Gatherers*, London: Academic Press

Rosman, A. and P. Rubel (1971) *Feasting with Mine Enemy: Rank and Exchange among Northwest Coast Indians*, New York: Columbia University Press

Sturtevant, W. (1978–) *Handbook of North American Indians*, (20 vols) Washington: Smithsonian Institution

Americas: Native South America (Highland)

Andean anthropology has an enduring fascination with Inka †ethnohistory and the desire to identify the distinctively 'Andean' in a region that has been in constant and intensive contact with the West for over 500 years. Indeed one of the fascinating features of the social and cultural practices of this region is the way in which a sense of 'cultures in contact' has been sustained and reproduced over the centuries in both academic writing and local discourse.

The Inkas operated as the central icon of cultural difference in nineteenth-century Americanist debates on *evolution, †savagery and †civilization, and were the central focus of foundational works of this century on *kinship and *political economy. The richness of the archival and archaeological records has promoted a fruitful collaboration between historians (many of them Latin Americans) and anthropologists of the region. More problematically, the politics of *nationalism has drawn support from academic interest in contemporary manifestations of the pre-Hispanic and what is often an anachronistic search for authenticity that reproduces many of the racist paradigms of nineteenth-century scholarship. Nevertheless, historical understanding is basic to the anthropology of this region.

In the mid-fifteenth century, the Inkas were a small ethnic group of the central-southern Andes. Within 100 years they had come to exercise political and economic control over a territory that stretched from present-day Colombia to central Chile through the use of a large standing army, severe resettlement and colonizing policies and the imposition of labour tribute. Local ethnic groups were obliged to participate in a highly centralized system of hierarchical †reciprocity and redistribution, which drew on local idioms of kinship and affinity for its legitimation. State sponsored ceremonial spectacle, involving both rulers and subjects in the public enactment of the Inkas' sacred genealogy forced subjugated ethnic groups to collaborate in the gendered representation of the 'conquest hierarchy' of empire (Silverblatt 1987).

The Spanish, aided by the epidemics which ravaged the Central and South American populations, ousted the Inka rulers in the 1530s and began to wage their own campaign of cultural and economic domination. The Inka Empire was subsumed by the Viceroyalty of Peru, which in the sixteenth century comprised all the Spanish territories in South America. Unlike the Inkas, who had employed familiar notions of kinship and political organization, the Spaniards used European models of rank and prestige through which to distinguish themselves and to differentiate the indigenous population into local elites and a newly homogenized indigenous mass. In ideological terms their evangelizing mission forced a categorical distinction between the Christian and the pre-Christian and introduced absolute values of good and evil.

The administrative changes brought about by the emergence of the independent republics in the nineteenth century were constructed not just against Spain but also against local indigenous populations. The transfer of power was from one group of white rulers to another. The end of the colonial regime signified changes in national economic policy. Nevertheless until recently the majority of Andean peoples have been *peasant farmers living from the production of potatoes and maize, and the herding of llamas, alpacas and sheep.

Since the middle of this century national governments have orchestrated social change in distinctive ways, but in all Andean nations people have lived through an era of modernization marked particularly by the development of transport infrastructure, the introduction of centralized *education programmes and universal franchise, and an increase in migrant labour and urbanization. Evangelical Protestantism has had a major influence on the religiosity of Andean peoples and the violence associated with warfare and the drugs trade has also dramatically affected many people's lives.

'Scientific' anthropology

In the nineteenth century, Americanists were concerned to trace the similarities and evolutionary connections between the peoples of North, South and Middle America. As a region the Andes became quite central to these debates, particularly in US scholarship. The Inkas, taken as an example of civilized indigenous culture were used as a point of comparison to denigrate both contemporary Andean peoples and, of more significance for US internal politics, the North American indigenous cultures. The supposed gap between past glory and present-day poverty in the Andean region was explained by a theory of degeneration which presumed that the Inkas were a doomed race, with parallel weaknesses to the great oriental civilizations that so preoccupied European writers of the time. Ostentatious displays of wealth, non-Christian religions, †polygamy, etc. were understood as manifestations of decadence and internal weakness (Poole 1995). By the early twentieth century recognizably modern anthropology was emerging. Ethnographers knowledgeable in Andean languages (Germans, French and North Americans and many gifted local students), began to counter the racist depictions of Andean peoples.

The principles and politics of integration

John Murra and Tom Zuidema are the key influences on contemporary Andean anthropology. Both were interested in the principles through which the Inka state cohered as a socio-cultural entity. Murra's analysis of Inka political economy was developed within a broadly *Marxist framework. Employing the notion of 'verticality', he discussed the ways in which the Inkas modified pre-existing systems of *exchange across ecological zones. Under an ideology of reciprocity and redistribution the Inkas controlled both the production and exchange of goods by ensuring that altitude-specific products (particularly potatoes, maize and coca), all technically pertaining to the Inka, passed through the Inka administrative centres and were not exchanged in local markets (Murra 1956).

Zuidema was also interested in political control but he used a *structuralist approach to investigate the underlying symbolic logic of cultural forms and practices such as kinship classification, the spatial organization of irrigation systems, and the agricultural and religious calendars. Principles of †complementary dualism were identified as key features of Inka thought, integrated in a complex system that drew together temporal concerns with spatial organization (Zuidema 1964).

The work of Murra and Zuidema set the agenda for subsequent generations of anthropologists who both continued the work on the Cuzco region of southern Peru and began to contrast these findings with the ethnohistorical records of other Andean regions. An important outcome of the work in contemporary ethnohistory has been the increased awareness of the variable efficacy of Inka control and cultural influence and the reassertion of the cultural differences within the Andean region which had been so comprehensively obscured by both Inka and Hispanic regimes (Salomon 1985).

The ethnohistorical record also serves as a useful source of comparative material through which to discuss various contemporary cultural practices, particularly the widespread importance of principles of asymmetrical dualism and hierarchical complementarity. These principles of *dual organization, recurrent in local understandings of fertility and reproduction, are depicted as a balanced relationship between complementary forces necessary to organic reproduction, a balance that has constantly to be achieved from oppositions that tend to asymmetry (Murra *et al.* 1986).

Defining the Andean

Andean peoples do not think of themselves as culturally equivalent. Nevertheless, the task of defining 'the Andean' set by local intellectuals involved in the politics of modernization, and underwritten by the majority of those working in the region, led to a proliferation of descriptive ethnography on local belief and practice. In the 1950s and 1960s these village studies were concerned to guide planned social change but by the 1970s Andean ethnology was involved in a wide variety of fields, which can be roughly subdivided into four major areas.

First, the anthropological concern with the relationship between *community and economy has generated studies in kinship and productive activity (Bolton & Meyer 1977; Larson & Harris 1995). Relations of reciprocity between bilaterally reckoned kin groups, across ecological zones, between †moieties, among consanguineal, affinal and spiritual kin, and between the human and spirit worlds, are all key features of Andean productive practice. Central to these debates are the varying concepts of community operating in Andean social life, communities that came into existence during the colonial period and whose fiscal status and relationship to the land have varied enormously over time and space. The Andean †*ayllu* is a genealogical and political unit of social action which can be grounded in kinship, territory, and/or labour organization, and operates at the level of the state, the ethnic group, the †kindred, or through relationships of *compadrazgo*. As a principle of differentiation the *ayllu* is relational and operationalized contextually. The ideological force of the concept relates back to the Inka system in which the *ayllu*, as a genealogical unit, was a *descent group centred on the sibling pair and generative of two lineages through

principles of †parallel descent, while the *ayllu* as political unit implied hierarchical subordination and was conceptualized in such a way that the more inclusive group was conceptualized as male.

Secondly, studies of Andean religiosity have discussed the voracious and unpredictable nature of the spirits that animate the local landscape and the centrality of *sacrifice for the regeneration of fertility. The human and the spirit world are frequently found to exist in a relationship of mutual consumption. In return for rain, humans offer their vital substance to the spirits. Scholars of Andean *Christianity have theorized the relationship between *great and little traditions, particularly in relation to *pilgrimage, and described the beliefs and practices of Catholics inextricably involved with the capricious and dangerous authocthonous spirits of the *landscape (Sallnow 1987).

Thirdly, the study of the Quechua and Aymara languages was developed in relation to various national policies for the integration of indigenous communities, educational reforms and the spread of *literacy. Considerable attention has been paid to the history of standardization and codification and to contemporary sociolinguistics, particularly the study of bilingualism.

Finally there is the topic of *ethnicity and *identity which embraces all the above concerns. There has been a continuing fascination with the categorization of the Andean population and constant attempts to define the cultural content of the racial categories of the colonial period. These categories, which both differentiated racial types and homogenized the cultural diversity of Andean peoples, have been sustained in those Andeanist writings which continue to evoke and distinguish Indians from other racial groups (particularly †*mestizos*, Whites, and Blacks). The tendency has been particularly strong in the †acculturation literature which presupposes the gradual elimination of local difference by global concerns.

History and social change in the late twentieth century

As suggested above the salient context for the emergence of these topics of anthropological interest has been the modernizing nation state and the concerns of local intellectuals to influence government policy towards the indigenous populations. This context has affected approaches to Andean ethnicity. Attention is now increasingly paid to the active participation of Andean peoples in identity politics. Instead of treating such practice as the clash of two systems, or the absorption of the local by the global, scholars are looking at the ways in which local practice incorporates the outside as part of itself despite discourses of antagonistic and contending fields. Indeed the constant production and reproduction of an inside/outside distinction can be taken as a central aspect of such practices and attention is now paid to the cultural work required to sustain the living memory of the conquest and the presence of an alien culture 500 years after the arrival of the Europeans. In this respect local understandings of history have been the focus of much attention. Andean accounts of historical process stress the importance of catastrophic events which turn the world upside down and there is much interest in *millenarianism. The ways in which contemporary peoples formulate and reformulate their history involve the creation of moral links (or breaks) with the past through which local people articulate their own distinctive sense of self (Allen 1988). Furthermore historical consciousness is not necessarily a verbal affair but is embedded in public ceremonial and in daily practices such as textile and agricultural production (Howard-Malverde 1996). In some areas history is literally dug into the land as agricultural and ritual activities combine to locate temporal structures in the landscape (Rappaport 1990).

Research into the specificity of Andean modernity has become central to the analysis of contemporary issues such as the war between the state and the Maoist Shining Path movement in Peru, the nationalist Katarista movement in Bolivia, the increasing presence of Evangelical Protestant churches, and the processes of *migration and urbanization which have brought the majority of Andean peoples to the metropolitan centres (Skar 1994). And while it is the case that modernity and the capitalist economy have been and continue to be played out through contemporary understandings of *race, it is imperative to recall that modernity is not a unified coherent project in either practice or ideology, and an understanding of the different procedures of nationalization both within and across the various republics is fundamental to an appreciation of the subjectivities, desires and memories that characterize the contemporary Andean world (Poole 1995).

PENELOPE HARVEY

See also: Christianity, great and little traditions, landscape, peasants, sacrifice.

Further reading

Allen, C. (1988) *The Hold Life Has: Coca and Cultural Identity in an Andean Community*, Washington: Smithsonian Institution Press

Bolton, R. and E. Meyer (1977) (eds) *Kinship and Marriage in the Andes*, Washington: American Anthropological Association

Howard-Malverde, R. (1996) (ed.) *Creating Context in Andean Cultures*, Oxford: Oxford University Press

Larson, B. and O. Harris (eds) with E. Tandeter (1995) *Ethnicity, Markets and Migration: At the Crossroads of History and Anthropology*, Chapel Hill: Duke University Press

Murra, J.V. ([1956] 1980) *The Economic Organization of the Inka State*, Research in Economic Anthropology Supplement no.1, ed. by George Dalton, Greenwich, Conn.: JAI Press

Murra, J.V., N. Wachtel and J. Revel (eds) (1986) *Anthropological History of Andean Polities*, Cambridge: Cambridge University Press

Poole, D.A. (1995) *Vision, Race and Modernity: A Visual Economy of the Andean Image World*, Princeton: Princeton University Press

Rappaport, J. (1990) *The Politics of Memory: Native Historical Interpretation in the Colombian Andes*, Cambridge: Cambridge University Press

Sallnow, M. (1987) *Pilgrims of the Andes: Regional Cults in Cusco*, Washington: Smithsonian Institution Press

Salomon, F. (1985) 'The Historical Development of Andean Ethnology', *Mountain Research and Development* 5 (1): 79–98

Silverblatt, I. (1987) *Moon, Sun, and Witches: Gender Ideologies in Inca and Colonial Peru*, Princeton: Princeton University Press

Skar, S.L. (1994) *Lives Together Worlds Apart: Quechua Colonization in Jungle and City*, Oslo: Scandinavian University Press

Zuidema, R.T. (1964) *The Ceque System of Cusco: The Social Organization of the Capital of the Inca*, Leiden: E.J. Brill

Americas: Native South America (Lowland)

The designation 'lowland peoples' of South America refers, in the main, to indigenous peoples of the Amazon Basin and Circum-Caribbean (Brazil, Peru, Colombia, Bolivia, Venezuela, Ecuador, Guyana, Suriname and French Guiana) and is largely an artefact of †Julian Steward's *Handbook of South American Indians* (1946–50). According to Steward, tropical forest (lowlands) peoples represent societies which, as a consequence of environmental limitations, failed to achieve the levels of political development (chiefdoms, states) characteristic of other pre-conquest South American societies, principally those of the

Andes. Over the past forty years, the 'highlands/lowlands' distinction has emphatically shaped the character of ethnographic research in South America and is represented in distilled form in Meggers *Amazonia: Man and Culture in a Counterfeit Paradise* (1971).

Tribes and culture areas

The focal unit of analysis of lowland peoples has been 'the tribe' (although linguistic and culture area criteria have also been invoked) and the post-World War II era has seen an abundance of detailed monographs. As Jackson has observed, however, despite the richness of the ethnographic record, there has been relatively little synthesis (but see Rivière 1984; Maybury-Lewis 1979; Roosevelt 1994). The absence of a pan-Amazonian framework of analysis (aside from that offered by †environmental determinism) reflects the absolute poverty of the ethnographic record: upwards of 90 per cent of indigenous peoples disappeared within the first 200 years of contact. At present, for example, the Brazilian indigenous population is approximately 250,000, whereas currently cited estimates of pre-conquest population range from 8 to 15 million, and modern anthropological work has been based on peoples whose representativeness of the prior social landscape is questionable.

It is not known how many 'tribes' there were at the time of conquest. In Hemming's survey (1978) there are 240 tribes for which there are some data. In Carneiro da Cunha's *História dos Índios do Brasil* (1992), 126 ethnic groups are referred to (mainly from Brazil). In Ribeiro's oft-cited account, of the 230 Brazilian tribes present in 1900, more than 35 per cent were extinct by 1960. Given the parlous state of indigenous societies at the time serious, systematic anthropological work began, it is not surprising that the focus has been on atomized groups, but as more attention is paid to historical and archaeological data, the gaze may well shift to more general matters concerning the overall configuration of indigenous peoples since the colonial era.

Whether contemporary forest peoples are representative of pre-conquest lowland peoples or not, forest tribes are typically small in population, depend on *fishing, *hunting and gathering, and †swidden horticulture; they are non-sedentary and have a division of labour based only on *age and *gender (religious specialists are a noteworthy exception). Typically characterized as technologically rudimentary (although in recent years close attention to †ethnobiological knowledge and resource management practices has tended to contradict this crude portrayal), lowland societies have long exemplified so-called †'noble savagery', a characterization (or caricature) which owes as much to †Rousseau and *Lévi-Strauss as it does to an environmental determinism. While much anthropological work has detailed aspects of social organization (especially *kinship systems), a major emphasis has been on the complexities of *ritual, *myth, *cosmology and *symbolism of forest peoples. Lévi-Strauss has made a signal contribution in this regard (albeit at some remove from the field), especially in *Tristes Tropiques*, *The Savage Mind*, and the four volumes of *Mythologiques*.

While †Curt Nimuendajú was, from the 1920s, the pioneer of modern ethnography in Amazonia, it is the period since World War II which has seen the consolidation of a distinctive ethnographic literature, and although this literature is diverse in the sense that it reflects the cultural specificities of a wide range of peoples, it is narrow in the sense that it has been projected against a background of theoretical orthodoxy, environmental determinism – Meggers's so-called 'counterfeit paradise' thesis (1971). This is not to say that all authors have subscribed to the thesis, only that the dominance of the thesis has long been institutionalized and has tended to prevent the integration of ethnography and the historical and archaeological records.

In the past twenty years, this situation has begun to change for reasons which bear on scholarly practices as well as geopolitical factors (the 'development' of tropical resources), indigenous rights movements, changed relations between native peoples and the state, increasing recognition of the extent to which the humid tropical forest is an anthropogenic environment, and alliances between anthropologists and the societies they study. While these factors converge and overlap in various ways, two strong tendencies are evident, one toward relating extant indigenous societies to their pre-historical antecedents, the other toward outlining strategies for the survival of indigenous peoples in ever more threatening national and contintental contexts.

Counterfeit paradise and indigenous realities

As noted above, the counterfeit paradise thesis is that rigid environmental constraints precluded the emergence of *complex societies in Amazonia, and corollaries, such as the 'protein shortage' thesis, have long been used to argue that the character of lowland societies is virtually reduceable to an underlying set of natural imperatives. Where there is unimpeachable evidence to the contrary – as on the island of Marajó, for example (and in the area around Santarém and the upriver region of the Omaguas), it has been explained away through recourse to a theory of Andean diffusion (in keeping with the strict 'highlands = complex/ lowland = simple' dichotomy). Although challenged by Lathrap and his co-workers, for example, and more recently and vigorously by Roosevelt, the counterfeit paradise thesis is still the received – although vastly weakened – wisdom. The combination of new archaeological work, a closer reading of historical materials dating from the early years of conquest as well as the continued output of ethnographic work has seriously undermined the thesis, however, and a vastly more complex reconstruction of prehistorical and colonial Amazonia is underway (see Roosevelt 1994 for summary).

Indians and the modern nation-state

Attempts to 'modernize' the lowlands as a great, untapped resource domain have altered the political and social (as well as other) landscapes in the lowlands. Incursions by national governments and their financial allies have given rise to various forms of *resistance and in some cases official recognition of the rights (territorial and otherwise) of indigenous groups as well as modifications of the status of indigenous peoples under various national constitutions.

The foundation in Brazil of the Indian Protection Service (discredited and later transformed into the only marginally less discredited National Indian Foundation – FUNAI), the creation of the first Brazilian Indian reserve (Xingu, 1961), the active role played by indigenous representatives in national and international political arenas, the concessions granted native peoples under various national constitutions, are significant moments in the recent history of lowlands peoples' relations with the state. The role of anthropologists and non-governmental organization colleagues has been important in providing an international platform for the promotion of indigenous rights in the region. The situation of indigenous peoples, however, is still extremely precarious.

Anthropogenecism

One consequence of the increase in research activity following on attempts over the past twenty years to accelerate the 'development' of the lowlands has been the heightened attention granted matters of environmental conservation. In part this simply reflects the abiding view that lowland societies are actually subsumed under nature, that they are contingent and undeveloped, but the privileging of an environmentalist perspective has also drawn attention to the ethnobiological knowledge of native peoples. In studies ranging throughout the Amazon basin, it has been clearly shown that the image of native peoples as dominated by nature is a serious misconstrual. Evidence of significant human modification of the environment over the past 12,000 years has required a re-evaluation of the pristineness of the evironment, and by implication the actual roles of prehistoric and historic indigenous peoples. The persuasive arguments concerning ethnobiological knowledge and the role it has played in indigenous modification of the environment have been a mixed blessing: while on one hand they attest to the malleability of an environment previously widely assumed to be incapable of bearing societies significantly different from those long regarded as typically 'lowland', on the other hand they have led to pressure to promote the 'integration' (a less than benign official euphemism for deculturation/assimilation) of native peoples within national societies through the commodification of their 'native' knowledge.

In the face of a theoretical orthodoxy in which lowland peoples have been regarded as held frozen in check by an array of unbending ecological constraints, modern ethnographic research has revealed a social domain of contrary complexity. With the further integration of archaeological, historical and ethnographic research, coupled with the emergence of new kinds of political movements, the highlands/lowlands distinction may become an archaic boundary in the map of Amerindian research.

STEPHEN NUGENT

Further reading

Carneiro da Cunha, M. (ed.) (1992) *História dos Índios do Brasil*, Sao Paulo: Editora Schwarcz

Gross, D. (ed.) (1973) *Peoples and Cultures of Native South America*, Garden City, NY: Natural History Press

Hemming, J. (1978) *Red Gold: the Conquest of the Brazilian Indians*, London: Macmillan

Hopper, J.H. (ed.) (1967) *Indians of Brazil in the Twentieth Century*, Washington DC: Institute for Cross-Cultural Research

Lyon, P.J. (ed.) (1974) *Native South Americans*, Boston: Little, Brown

Maybury-Lewis, D. (ed.) (1979) *Dialectical Societies: The Ge and Bororo of Central Brazil*, Cambridge MA: Harvard University Press

Meggers, B.J. (1971) *Amazonia: Man and Culture in a Counterfeit Paradise*, Chicago: Aldine Atherton

Rivière, P.G. (1984) *Indian Society in Guiana: A Comparative Study of Amerindian Social Origins*, Cambridge: Cambridge University Press

Roosevelt, A. (ed) (1994) *Amazonian Indians from Prehistory to the Present: Anthropological Perspectives*, London and Tucson: University of Arizona Press

Steward, D.H. (ed.) (1946–50) Handbook of South American Indians, Bulletin of the Bureau of American Ethnology 143

ancestors

The term 'ancestor' is used in anthropology to designate those forebears who are remembered, and to denote specific religious practices as a part of such phrases as 'ancestor cult' or 'ancestor worship'.

Which forebears and in what way they are remembered varies from *kinship system to kinship system. Some Amerindians, for example, seem quite uninterested in ancestors whom they have not known personally, while some Asian and African peoples may remember ancestors up to twenty ascending generations. What may be preserved and cherished may be merely the name of the ancestor, as in Chinese ancestral halls, or the physical remains of the ancestor, as among the Merina of Madagascar, or the memory of their journeys marked in the *landscape, as is the case for many *Aboriginal Australians. Social factors also affect which ancestors are remembered. Men may be remembered to the exclusion of women or men and women may be remembered equally. In †patrilineal systems, ancestors in the male line are remembered much further back than in the female line and the reverse is true in †matrilineal systems. This is because in such systems membership of a socially important group, such as a †clan, may depend on the ability to demonstrate *descent in the appropriate line up to a particular ancestor who may well give his or her name to the group. In hierarchical societies people of higher status usually remember ancestors better than those of lower status.

Ancestor worship is a phrase used to denote religious practices concerned with the belief that dead forebears can in some way influence the living. In his study of ancestor worship among the Tallensi of Ghana, which is very typical of ancestor worship in other parts of Africa, †Fortes stresses how the worship which a patrilineal descendant should carry out reflects, though in a subtly changed way, the relationship of fathers and son when living (Fortes 1959). Similar observations have been made about ancient Rome by Fustel de Coulanges (1864) and for China by †Hsu (1949). In these systems the ancestors are believed to exercise a moral guardianship over their descendants and they are particularly concerned that the group of descendants do not quarrel among themselves. This guardianship, although ultimately thought of as beneficial, is double-edged since the ancestors mainly manifest themselves through the punishment of their descendants; often by sending them diseases. In such a case ancestor worship often involves appeasement in ways such as *sacrifice (Middleton 1960).

The discussion of African ancestor worship has dominated anthropological theorizing on the subject but the phenomenon is very different in different parts of the world. In contrast to Africa, where ancestors are treated with great respect, in Dobu in *Melanesia people used to select specific ancestors whose jawbone they would wear round their neck, only to discard them if they did not bring good luck. In Japan and in China, ancestors are mainly worshipped in the form of ancestral tablets held in temples or ancestral halls (Smith 1974). There the concern seems to be as much a matter of honouring the dead as of separating the ancestors from the world of the living where they might cause trouble.

MAURICE BLOCH

See also: age, descent, kinship, religion, sacrifice

Further reading

Fortes, M. (1959) *Oedipus and Job in West African Religion*, Cambridge: Cambridge University Press

Fustel de Coulanges, N.D. (1956 [1864]) *The Ancient City*, Garden City, NY: Doubleday

Hsu, F.L.K. (1949) *Under the Ancestors' Shadow: Chinese Culture and Personality*, London:

Middleton, J. (1960) *Lugbara Religion*, Oxford: Oxford University Press

Smith, R.J. (1974) *Ancestor Worship in Contemporary Japan*, Stanford: Stanford University Press

anthropological societies

The formation of anthropology as a subject of intellectual study was closely associated with the establishment of distinctive institutions. In the early days these tended to be learned societies which reflected anthropology's amateur origins. As the subject developed academic pretensions, these learned societies were transformed into more professional groupings and new, often more specialized institutions were established to serve the needs of particular sections of the discipline. Special interest groups within and outside academia have also produced separate societies either as sections of existing institutions or as independent entities. The employment of professional anthropologists outside academia has encouraged the establishment of professional societies to represent their interests. Some institutions have remained national in their focus, others have been established to serve regional and even international interests.

Most societies have functioned to provide centres for discussion and debate, to assist in the holding of meetings and conferences, to encourage and occasionally fund research, to publish scholarly work and to disseminate information on the discipline both to members and to outsiders. They have also assisted in promoting employment opportunities for their members, and to establish professional standards including the formulation of ethical rules for members to guide research and scholarly practice. Older societies often have different classes of membership, including honorary fellowships, and present medals and other awards in recognition of an individual's professional and scholarly contributions to the discipline. Some societies provide additional advantages to members including library and bibliographical services, and in recent times certain financial and social services including negotiating commercial advantages to members.

Probably the first anthropological society was the short-lived Société des Observateurs de l'Homme founded in Paris in 1799. But the major European and North American societies were established only after 1840. The most significant British learned society was the Ethnological Society of London (1843) which in 1871 joined with the Anthropological Society of London (1862) to form the (Royal) Anthropological Institute (RAI) which continues to the present. Its original amateur members, later supplemented by colonial officials and missionaries, have been largely replaced by professional anthropologists living in Britain or abroad; its current membership (1992) is 2,408. In 1946 the Association of Social Anthropologists of the Commonwealth (ASA) was founded to represent the interests of professional social anthropologists in Britain and abroad. Its present membership (1993) consists of around 600 people.

Not all the anthropological societies established in Europe have survived as long as the Institute, but notable learned societies, often involved not just with social and cultural anthropology, but also with archaeology and areas of human biology, have included those established in Paris (1858), Berlin (1869), Vienna (1870), Italy (1871), Sweden (1872). Before and after World War II, a number of national societies devoted to ethnology and socio-cultural anthropology were established or re-established in Europe and in recent years these have increased in number. In 1989 the European Association of Social Anthropologists was founded and swiftly overtook the various national organizations, both in membership (which was over 1,100 in 1994) and in the scale of its biennial conferences.

In America the American Ethnological Society was founded in 1842 and in 1879 the Anthropological Association of Washington whose members were associated with the Smithsonian Institution and the National Museum. The incorporation of the American Anthropological Association (AAA) in 1902 reflected the increasing professionalization of the discipline in North America. The Association has grown into a massive organization with a current (1994) membership of 10,810 and 31 sub-sections (units) devoted to a wide range of specialities and interests, regional, topical and professional. Its annual meetings provide an important forum for discussion and debate and the promotion of professional careers. Canada has a number of societies of which the Canadian Ethnology Society founded in 1973 is perhaps the most representative. Other specialized societies in North America include the American Folklore Society (1888) and the Society for Applied Anthropology (1941). A number of societies are also located throughout Latin America.

In Asia an anthropological society was established in Japan in 1884 and another in Bombay in 1887 and a number of more specialized groups have been founded since. These include the Japanese Society for Ethnology (1934) with a current (1993) membership of 1,552. In Australia regional state societies were founded from 1926 (South Australia) and in 1973 the Australian Anthropological Society was established to represent professional anthropologists. Similar moves were made in other ex-colonial societies with for example national Associations of Social Anthropologists being established in New Zealand and in Nigeria.

Regional interests have been represented by the formation of special societies, many of which have included members other than anthropologists. These include the International Société Americanistes (1875), the Polynesian Society (1892), the †International African Institute (1926), the Société Oceanistes (1937) and in the 1960s the Association of Social Anthropologists in Oceania based in North America but including members in Pacific rim countries.

Attempts at international cooperation occurred with the foundation of the International Congress of Anthropological and Ethnological Sciences (IUAES) in Basel in 1933. Meetings have been held since 1934 and in 1948 it established an International Union of Anthropological and Ethnological Sciences to promote research and publication. This Union has a number of specialized interest groupings. In 1941 the Viking Fund was established in New York to fund anthropological research and in 1951 was renamed the Wenner-Gren Foundation which continues to support research, meetings and publications to the present.

JAMES URRY

Further information

American Anthropological Association, 1703 New Hampshire Avenue, N.W., Washington, D.C. 20009, USA

Association of Social Anthropologists of the Commonwealth, 50 Fitzroy Street, London W1P 5HS

European Association of Social Anthropologists, c/o Hon. Secretary Eduardo Archetti, Department and Museum of Anthropology, University of Oslo, P.O. Box 1091 Blinden, N-0317 Oslo 3, Norway

Further reading

Keesing, F.M. (1960) 'The International Organization of Anthropology' *American Anthropologist* 62 (2): 191–201

Thomas Jr., W.L. and A. M. Pikelis (eds) (1953) *International Directory of Anthropological Institutions*, New York: Wenner-Gren Foundation for Anthropological

Research (See also *Current Anthropology* (1961), 2 (3): 286–98 for an update)

archaeology

Archaeology may be broadly defined as the investigation of human cultures and societies of the past through recovery and interpretation of both remnants of ancient †material culture and, most critically, the physical contexts in which they have been preserved. The range of time subject to archaeological investigation runs from the very recent historical past, when interpretation may be aided by written documents, to the earliest evidence of prehistoric hominid cultural activity about 2.5 million years ago. Archaeologists have successfully developed a body of highly specialized excavation and laboratory techniques to extract information from the ground, but they must also grapple with some severe data limitations and epistemological problems peculiar to their field. As Trigger has noted, 'prehistoric archaeology is the only social science that has no direct access to information about human behaviour' (1989: 357). Moreover, in the act of excavating sites to recover information about the past, archaeologists are simultaneously destroying the object of their study. However, despite its limitations and problems, archaeology provides the only means available for exploring the 99 per cent of human 'history' that preceded the very recent invention of writing.

Connections to sociocultural anthropology

Although it is sometimes claimed that archaeology is 'the past tense of cultural anthropology' (Renfrew and Bahn 1991: 9), the relationship between archaeology and sociocultural anthropology is actually rather complex and varies greatly according to regional or national disciplinary traditions. In universities of the United States, archaeology is normally considered one of the †four fields or integrated subdisciplines (along with sociocultural, *biological/physical, and *linguistic anthropology) that combine to form a 'department of anthropology'. On the other hand, in European nations (and their former colonies which have been influenced by European disciplinary concepts), the archaeology of recent prehistoric periods has generally tended to be more closely allied to *history, meaning especially national history, and seen as an extension of that intellectual endeavour. In European universities this kind of archaeology is often housed in separate departments or institutes of archaeology (or prehistory and protohistory) with close ties to history; while archaeologists focused on the deeper periods of prehistory (i.e. the Paleolithic) tend to be more closely linked institutionally to geology and natural history. These kinds of institutional separation from anthropology are rare in the United States. However, in both American and European universities, archaeologists studying the ancient complex societies of certain regions (especially the Mediterranean, Egypt, and the Near East) usually tend to be incorporated with other, text-orientated, humanistic scholars in highly specialized departments or institutes (e.g. Classics, Egyptology, Near Eastern Studies, art history) often having limited contact or intellectual rapport with anthropology.

The contribution of sociocultural anthropology to archaeology is various and important. Anglo-American archaeologists have for many years relied upon analogical models of various kinds drawn from comparative surveys of the ethnographic literature as a basis for making inferences about past societies. They have also generally looked to sociocultural anthropology for appropriate research goals and interpretive theory that can be adapted to their data. This has been less true of a number of Continental European schools of archaeology where comparative ethnographic models and anthropological theory have frequently been eschewed in favour of direct historical analogy and where history has provided a more frequent source of interpretive inspiration.

The contribution, or potential contribution, of archaeology to sociocultural anthropology is perhaps less obvious (and certainly less acknowledged), but no less important. The most subtle and pervasive contributions are an insistent concern with cause and process, a sense of the deep antiquity of human cultural development, and the confrontation of the the very compressed experience of ethnographic *fieldwork with the archaeological perspective of the *longue durée*. Exposure to archaeology should provoke a realization of the dynamic record of continual social and cultural change in prehistory that belies notions of static, pristine, 'traditional' cultures of the kind projected in older *functionalist ethnographies. The archaeological demonstration of the shallow temporal depth of Melanesian *exchange circuits such as the *kula* in their current form (Kirch 1991) is but one striking example of the

need for this kind of long-term historical perspective in ethnographic studies.

As sociocultural anthropologists continue to expand their current rediscovery of the importance of history, archaeology has the potential to play an increasingly integrated and crucial role in studies that link history and anthropology. For people without their own written records, archaeology provides a unique source of access to the long stretch of history beyond the memory of living people which is not dependent solely upon the alien recorded observations of colonial agents. Ironically, the much desired restoration of the history of the 'people without history' by sociocultural anthropologists has to date often turned out to be little more than an account of their encounter with the *capitalist *world system, parting from a static baseline conception of a timeless traditional culture before colonial contact. Archaeology has the potential to redress this problem by demonstrating the equally dynamic history of societies before the colonial encounter, as well as adding important sources of information to an analysis of the process of colonial entanglement and interaction. The rich potential of a closer integration of archaeology and historical anthropology in this vein is well demonstrated by the recent pioneering collaborative study of Kirch and †Sahlins (1992) on Hawaii.

Archaeology also offers the possibility of adding to the theoretical understanding of the expansion of the modern capitalist world system by providing information about the numerous precapitalist colonial encounters that were a common feature of the ancient world. It is important for purposes of comparative understanding to examine the historical dynamics of such processes in as many different contexts as possible, and especially in cases that predate the development of the European capitalist world system. Indeed, archaeological information is critical for resolving debates in this realm between those (e.g. Fernand Braudel, Immanuel Wallerstein) who see the modern world system as a fundamentally new phenomenon which developed in Europe during the sixteenth century and those (e.g. André Gunder Frank) who see it as the inexorable result of a continuous process of expansion of a system which began over four millennia ago.

Another important contribution of archaeology has been the reawakening of an interest in the ethnographic study of material culture, a subject long neglected in mainstream Anglo-American sociocultural anthropology. As Appadurai has noted, material things 'constitute the first principles and the last resort of archaeologists' (1986: 5). In fact, all archaeological inference about past societies hinges critically upon an understanding of the relationship between material and nonmaterial aspects of *culture and *society. Yet, as archaeologists became more sophisticated in their use of ethnographic information for the construction of interpretive models during the 1960s, it became increasingly evident to them that only a rudimentary understanding of this relationship existed. Under the influence of †structural-functionalism and *structuralism, material culture had ceased to be a focus of serious interest for most sociocultural anthropologists; and when information was collected it was generally not recorded in a form that was useful to archaeologists. For example, there was little attention paid to intra-cultural variation, to the spatial distribution of objects and styles, to the process of production and creation, to learning networks and the process of apprenticeship, or to the social roles and *symbolic meaning of material culture.

Beginning in the 1970s, a new research subfield, known as 'ethnoarchaeology', was born in which some archaeologists began to remedy this dearth of information by conducting ethnographic studies themselves. They focused particularly upon understanding material culture in a living social context in ways that were potentially useful for archaeological interpretation. Many of these 'ethnoarchaeologists' found that focusing on material culture provided a remarkably revealing way of penetrating and illuminating social relations and cultural categories and that objects were crucially important elements of symbolic practice (cf. Miller 1985, Kramer 1985). The ethnoarchaeological focus on new ways of understanding material culture has undoubtedly influenced the recent renewal of a more general interest in the subject in sociocultural anthropology, particularly in American cultural anthropology. In any case, it is clear that there is now a good deal more mutual interest and communication between archaeologists and cultural anthropologists studying objects and *consumption (e.g. Appadurai 1986), and ethnoarchaeologists have made important contributions to this discussion.

In France, there is a more long-standing tradition of mutual influence and collaboration between certain archaeologists and sociocultural anthropologists in the study of material culture,

although this work is still little known in Anglo-American circles. The archaeologist †Leroi-Gourhan, who was himself inspired by the work of †Mauss, had a marked influence in the development of a school of the anthropology of *technology, called 'technologie' or 'technologie culturelle' by Haudricourt, one of its most prolific practitioners. This approach, which is today best exemplified in the Parisian journal *Techniques et Culture*, focuses on understanding the social embeddedness of technological choices and technical systems. Its adherents have developed a novel analytical methodology and an impressive body of case studies (e.g. Lemonnier 1993).

History of archaeology as a discipline

Tracing the long historical development of archaeology as a discipline is complicated by the important differences in national and regional traditions noted earlier. Indeed, in many respects it would be more appropriate to eschew the singular altogether and speak instead of the histories of archaeologies. Nevertheless, most of the major works on the subject (cf. Willey and Sabloff 1980, Sklenár 1983, Trigger 1989) are agreed in dividing this complex history into a number of periods broadly characterized by certain shared intellectual perspectives and research orientations, and a highly schematicized rendition is offered here.

An antiquarian fascination with ancient objects and their evocations of prior epochs was already a feature of the societies of antiquity in many parts of the world (Schnapp 1993). However, the origins of archaeology as a systematic discipline are generally traced to the preoccupation with classical antiquity that developed as part of the humanist intellectual movement during the European Renaissance and *Enlightenment. Initially concerned primarily with ancient Roman and Greek texts, the curiosity of humanist scholars was soon directed towards the recovery and description of architecture and material relics dug out of the earth. This passion for ancient objects led to the amassing of large collections, but without the possibility of establishing links to past societies that went beyond romantic speculative fantasy. Texts continued to be the nearly exclusive means of reconstructing the past.

The transition from this 'antiquarian phase' to a new orientation among both European and North American scholars towards systematic description, classification and temporal ordering of objects occurred during the nineteenth century. It was brought about by theoretical and methodological developments that were in large part a response to the challenge of providing more coherence for the growing interest in 'prehistoric' antiquities from areas outside the realm of classical civilizations and their historical texts. Among the most important of these was the development by C.J. Thomsen, in Denmark, between 1816 and 1819, of the 'three age system'. This scheme was based upon both a model of technological evolution from stone to bronze to iron tools and the technique of †seriation; and it was used to provide a rough chronological system for the later prehistory of Europe. Equally important was the adaptation of the newly developed geological principle of stratigraphy as a means of providing relative temporal ordering for objects and fossils recovered from the earth. During the latter half of the nineteenth century, scholars in France and England initiated the field of Paleolithic archaeology and used this new method to dramatically push back the antiquity of human origins. In this act of overturning the biblical compression of the earth's history into a 6,000 year span, and helping to empirically demonstrate the process of *evolution, archaeology was responsible for a conceptual revolution which has had, arguably, a more profound impact on modern Euro-American culture than any of its subsequent contributions.

During the late nineteenth century, archaeologists and early ethnologists (e.g. †Bachofen, †Tylor, *Morgan) were closely united intellectually by their shared orientation toward unilineal cultural evolutionism and their common goal of investigating and classifying examples of evolutionary stages. However, during the early twentieth century, as more refined local chronologies were developed, archaeologists began to turn increasingly towards the identification of geographically defined archaeological 'cultures' (based upon typological analysis of artefacts and their spatial distributions) and the reconstruction of culture history through the study of these reified constructs. Research goals shifted towards a kind of pseudo-historical documentation of the movement of ancient cultural groups and the *diffusion of cultural traits between such groups. The work of Gustav Kossina (particularly his †'Kulturkreis' concept) was extremely influential in the European archaeology of this period, including the ambitious pan-European culture historical syntheses of †Gordon Childe. Much of this work was motivated by a search for the prehistoric origins of historically identified ethnic groups and a desire to push national histories deeper into the past.

The 1950s witnessed a growing dissatisfaction with this kind of research orientation, particularly in American universities; and this turned into a strong polemical attack during the 1960s under the banner of the 'New Archaeology'. Led by such scholars as †Lewis Binford in the United States and David Clarke in Britain, archaeologists operating within this paradigm sought to provide explanations for the social processes that lay behind the largely descriptive accounts of the former culture history approach. They advocated an explicitly anthropological approach to archaeology and reacted strongly against historical interpretation. The version of anthropology adopted, however, was somewhat out of step with contemporary developments in mainstream sociocultural anthropology. It was based heavily upon the neo-evolutionist programmes of †Leslie White and †Julian Steward, and relied upon functionalist ecological models (including especially 'systems theory') to explain social process. Moreover, the misunderstanding of history, and its anachronistic representation as simple narrative in contrast to anthropological 'explanation', was even more out of date with contemporary developments in the field of history.

Despite these problems, this phase in the history of archaeology has resulted in some important contributions, including particularly the opening up of a serious debate about archaeological epistemology and theory, a much greater sophistication in research design, and an ambitious flourishing of new research questions. A critical evaluation of the assumptions underlying explanation, an attempt to improve the rigour of the interpretive process, and an explicit concern to develop anthropological theory were all fundamental goals of the New Archaeology Programme. The pursuit of these goals led to significant improvements in techniques for locating, excavating, and analysing archaeological sites, to experimental and ethnographic research designed to understand the processes by which archaeological sites were formed, and to the ethnoarchaeological study of material culture mentioned above.

Outside North America, Britain and Scandinavia, the influence of the New Archaeology was rather limited. In France and Germany, for example, archaeologists remained firmly committed to developing historical approaches of various kinds and were generally suspicious of anthropological theory. They remained largely insulated from this theoretical ferment (cf. Cleuziou *et al.* 1991, Härke 1991). In the Soviet Union and other East European countries, a rather orthodox, evolutionist *Marxism formed the dominant interpretive framework. Outside Eastern Europe, Marxism had an early influence on a few scholars, such as Gordon Childe; but, with the exception of Italy, explicitly Marxist approaches only became popular with the spread of French structural Marxism in anthropology during the 1970s (ironically because of its isolation from anthropology, this approach had little influence in French archaeology).

Regardless of nationality, temporal focus, or disciplinary traditions, archaeologists today generally share a set of common methods for extracting information from the ground and analysing it in their laboratories (Renfrew and Bahn 1991). To be sure, there are technical differences in, for example, the precision with which an archaeologist excavating a Paleolithic site in Africa and one excavating a Gallo-Roman urban site in France will record the three-dimensional location of all objects found. And the sites and their features will also be dated by quite different means and with very different degrees of precision. But these differences are strategic choices from a range of common options that are determined more by pragmatic considerations than by profoundly divergent conceptualizations of scientific methodology. This common body of excavation and laboratory techniques has been undergoing continual and rapid development since the nineteenth century. Methodological innovations have appeared in various countries with divergent interpretive traditions, and have been quickly adopted in countries that were quite resistant to theoretical developments from those same areas. Progress in the use of physical science techniques for dating artefacts and determining the provenience of their origin have advanced particularly quickly during the past fifty years, and the spread of the use of computers during the past couple of decades has greatly improved abilities to record and manipulate data. Moreover, the recent development of remote sensing techniques has greatly aided in the identification of archaeological sites and the study of regional settlement systems.

In contrast to this methodological homogeneity and the steady improvement of techniques for data recovery, the past few decades have witnessed a remarkable diversification (or what some see more pessimistically as fragmentation) in the realm of interpretive theory. Perhaps the most heated philosophical debate in current Anglo-American archaeology is between advocates of what are called †'processual' archaeology (i.e. an approach which traces its genealogical roots to the New Archaeology of the 1960s) and †'post-processual' archaeology. The latter is a somewhat amorphous perspective which was objectified by being christened with its polemically inspired name during the 1980s. It lays claim to a rather uncomfortable mixture of archaeologists with disparate humanist, *postmodernist, *Marxist, symbolic and structuralist approaches, primarily united by opposition to the scientific-positivist, evolutionist, and functionalist tendencies of the 'processual' school. However, this simplistic dichotomy is irrelevant outside the Anglo-American community (see Cleuziou *et al.* 1991); and within that community this acrimonious debate has tended to reify an unproductive polarization that misconstrues the rich diversity of approaches actually being developed by most archaeologists.

Archaeology and the politics of the past

One important theme that has attracted an increasing amount of attention among archaeologists recently is the use of the past by modern communities and the social situation and responsibilities of archaeologists in this process (cf. Trigger 1989, Gathercole and Lowenthal 1990). A number of scholars from various countries have begun to examine the manipulation of the ancient past in the construction of ethnic, national and regional *identities in modern history. *Ethnicity and *nationalism are clearly powerful forces in the modern world, and archaeology has frequently been conscripted to establish and validate cultural borders and ancestry, sometimes in the service of dangerous racist and nationalist mythologies. It is important for archaeologists to understand the historical processes by which such identities are constructed and transformed by competing groups and factions and how the distant past is marshalled as a symbolic resource to establish an emotionally charged sense of authenticity and continuity. It is equally important for archaeologists, as the principal conduit to that distant past, to develop a critical awareness of their own situation in this process. This is crucial in order to understand how it may subtly inform their practice by conditioning their research goals, their interpretations and their evaluation of knowledge claims, and in order to recognize their responsibilities in presenting the past in the midst of rival appeals to its use in authenticating modern collective identities.

The fact that archaeology acquired its professional disciplinary identity in the context of the development of modern nation states with their demands for the construction of popular traditions of identity has given many scholars cause for serious sceptical examination of the field. Moreover, examples of the unwitting, or occasionally conscious, participation of historians and archaeologists in the manipulation of the past in the cause of ethnic, nationalist, and colonialist mythologies offer clear examples of the risks of unreflective interpretation and the illusion of scientific objectivity. The dangerous abuses and distortions of the archaeological record in the construction of the Aryan myth that served to justify territorial expansion and genocide in Nazi Germany (Härke 1991) are a prominent reminder of the fact that archaeological research may have serious political ramifications. But a host of other, more subtle, examples (from Greek invocations of the legacy of Alexander the Great in efforts to define the territory of modern Macedonia to the attempted use of the archaeology of the ancient Celts as a basis for establishing a sense of cultural unity in the evolving European Union) offer caveats for archaeologists to be vigilantly self-critical in evaluating the social and political context of their interpretive perspectives and their epistemological tools.

A major related controversy has developed over the issue of 'ownership' of the past. This debate centres around questions concerning the authority of competing interpretations of archaeological evidence, the right to control representations of the past, and actual ownership of the physical objects excavated from the ground. Arguments about ownership of archaeological artefacts and sites are not new: archaeologists have been engaged for many years in attempting to secure legislation which would designate these things as public goods under professional supervision and preserve them from becoming private commodities on the thriving international antiquities market. Moreover, many former colonies have also been engaged for some time in attempts to retrieve the archaeological materials which they consider part of their cultural heritage from the museums of foreign colonial powers. What is new

is that indigenous (now minority) populations in some countries, especially in North America and Australia, have begun to demand repatriation of the archaeological materials held in university and state museums and have sought to oppose or control the excavation activities of archaeologists. In many cases, museums are now being forced by legal sanctions to turn over the excavated artefacts and skeletal remains of indigenous peoples for reburial, and excavation projects are required to have indigenous consultants with serious veto powers. Needless to say, a heated debate is being waged over the implementation and justification of these practices.

These developments, as well as a recent relativist critique within archaeology, have also occasioned a greater attention to interpretations of the past which differ from those of professional archaeologists. *Museums, which confer authority in the act of presenting certain interpretations of the past to the public, have been a major battleground for this debate. Not surprisingly, the American celebration of the quincentennial of Columbus in 1992 became a particularly provocative catalyst for discussion. But the same questions have been raised in other contexts around the world.

This new self-consciousness places archaeologists, as the 'producers' of the symbolic resources of the ancient past, in a somewhat delicate position. Wariness of archaeology's manipulation by the state is less morally problematic, although it may require alienating the primary source of funding for research. However, while wishing to be sensitive and open to the interpretations of disenfranchised groups and the needs of local communities to construct popular traditions of identity, the violent effects of ethnic conflict fuelled by emotionally charged appeals to the past show the explosive potential of such apparently more benign manipulations of archaeology in folk traditions. Many archaeologists are seeking ways to be cautiously self-critical about the authority of their own interpretations, while at the same time responsibly engaging in debate about manipulations of the past and exposing ahistorical *essentialist notions to the archaeological record of constant change.

MICHAEL DIETLER

See also: history and anthropology, evolution and evolutionism, museums, technology

Further reading

Appadurai, A. (ed.) (1986) *The Social Life of Things: Commodities in Cultural Perspective*, Cambridge: Cambridge University Press

Cleuziou, S., A. Coudart, J-P. Demoule and A. Schnapp (1991) 'The Use of Theory in French Archaeology' in I. Hodder (ed.), *Archaeological Theory in Europe: The Last Three Decades*, London: Routledge

Gathercole, P. and D. Lowenthal (eds) (1990) *The Politics of the Past*, London: Unwin Hyman

Härke, H. (1991) 'All Quiet on the Western Front? Paradigms, Methods and Approaches in West German Archaeology' in I. Hodder (ed.) *Archaeological Theory in Europe: The Last Three Decades*, London: Routledge

Kirch, P.V. (1991) 'Prehistoric Exchange in Western Melanesia', *Annual Review of Anthropology* 20: 141–165

Kirch, P.V. and M. Sahlins (1992) *Anahulu: The Anthropology of History in the Kingdom of Hawaii*, 2 vols, Chicago: University of Chicago Press

Kramer, C. (1985) 'Ceramic ethnoarchaeology', *Annual Review of Anthropology* 14: 77–102

Lemonnier, P. (ed.) (1993) *Technological Choices: Transformation in Material Culture since the Neolithic*, London: Routledge

Miller, D. (1985) *Artefacts as Categories: A Study of Ceramic Variability in Central India*, Cambridge: Cambridge University Press

Renfrew, C. and P. Bahn (1991) *Archaeology: Theories, Methods and Practice*, London: Thames and Hudson

Schnapp, A. (1993) *La conquête du passé. Aux origines de l'archéologie*, Paris: Editions Carré

Sklenár, K. (1983) *Archaeology in Central Europe: The First 500 Years*, New York: St Martin's Press

Trigger, B.G. (1989) *A History of Archaeological Thought*, Cambridge: Cambridge University Press

Willey, G.R. and J.A. Sabloff (1980 [1974]) *A History of American Archaeology*, San Francisco: W.H. Freeman and Company

Arctic

The term 'Arctic', before it was applied to a geographical region and its inhabitants, first had an astronomical meaning for the ancient Greeks. It signified the apparent trajectory of the Great Bear ('bear' is *arctos* in Greek) around the celestial North Pole. This celestial landmark was then projected onto the terrestrial sphere where it was used to draw what we know as the Arctic Circle (66 degrees N. Latitude).

Arctic peoples have fed the Western imagination for thousands of years, through myths, legends and travellers' tales, before becoming an object of anthropological study at the end of the nineteenth century. It was the ardent quest for a northern short cut to the Indies and China that drew Western sailors to explore the Arctic seas, in the Northwest as well as in the Northeast. The competition between European states which this exploration provoked explains the current political division of the territory occupied by Inuits (Eskimos), which is cross-cut by four state boundaries (Russia, United States, Canada and Denmark). More complex historical reasons produced a similar division of the territory of the Saami (Lapps) between four states (Norway, Sweden, Finland and Russia). Next to these two big regions lies the immense Siberian Arctic, where the following groups of people live, within the present Russian Federation: Nenets (Samoyeds), Mansis (Voguls), Khanti (Ostyaks), Evenks (Tungus), Nganasans, Dolgans, Yakuts, Evens (Lamuts), Yugakirs, Chukchi and Koryaks.

Explorers' and missionaries' accounts

Firsthand accounts based on direct observation of Arctic peoples were published in Europe, thanks to the printing-press, at the beginning of the sixteenth century by explorers, travellers and cartographers. The publication of Heberstein's *Rerum Muscoviticarum commentarii* in 1549 presented more detailed information about the people living at the eastern and northern borders of Moscovia: Tartars and Samoyeds. It is certain that it influenced the creation of the 'Moscow Company' in Great Britain (1555), the aim of which was the discovery and exploration of a northeastern or northwestern passage to Cathay. Yet confusion still reigned for a long time about the configuration of the Arctic lands and their inhabitants.

It was not until the invention of the portable chronometer in the eighteenth century and the ability to evaluate longitude precisely at sea, that the Arctic coasts could be mapped out scientifically. In 1821–23, a British Admiralty expedition searching for a northwest passage spent two winters in close contact with the Fox Bay Inuit, later known as Igloolik. Captains Parry and Lyon, who were responsible for the expedition, later wrote highly succesful accounts of the voyages. Publication, in the mid-eighteenth century, of the ethnographic observations of two missionaries (Hans Egde and David Cranz) concerning western Greenlanders, was the first time Westerners had presented a comprehensive description of the everyday life, beliefs and religious practices of the Inuit.

The pioneers of Arctic ethnography

The books by Parry and Lyon stimulated two great pioneers of Arctic ethnography, *Franz Boas and †Knud Rasmussen to undertake expeditions to the region. Both studied the Igloolik group, although with differing degrees of success. The last quarter of the nineteenth century saw the first scientific research on Arctic peoples. When Russia sold Alaska to the United States in 1870, thus ending the Anglo-Russian political 'Great Game' in the North Pacific, the American Army sent in observers: E. Nelson to the Bering Detroit region (1877-81) and J. Murdock to the Point Barrow region (1881-83). Scientific cooperation in the Arctic also began during this period, with the organization of the first 'International Polar Year' (1882-3). In 1883-4, the American L. Turner was in the Ungava, the German F. Boas was on Baffin Island and the Dane G. Holm was in Ammassalik. All produced the first ethnographic accounts of the groups they visited. It is worth noting that all these ethnographic pioneers came from other disciplines: Nelson, Murdock and Turner were naturalists, Boas a geographer and Holm a marine officer.

Boas later conceived and undertook scientific responsibility for the 'Jesup North Pacific Expedition' (1901–04), the aim of which was to verify the Asian origin of native Americans by comparing the peoples living on each side of the Bering Straits. This expedition was led by two Russians, Bogoraz and Jochelson, who had formerly been exiled in Siberia, and spoke several indigenous languages. They collected an impressive amount of data. From this a series of monographs was produced on the Chukchi, the Koryaks, the Yukagirs, the Chukota Inuit and the Yakuts, which constitutes the best source of ethnographic material on northeastern Siberia, for the period before the Bolshevik Revolution. These ethnographers were also self-taught.

Arctic ethnography and the development of anthropology

The publication in English of all these works introduced Arctic peoples into the nascent field of anthropology. They were to occupy an important place there for several decades. †Marcel Mauss drew material from them for the lectures on which *Seasonal Variations of the Eskimo* ([1906] 1979) was later based. †Robert Lowie also read these early ethnographic accounts very carefully and quoted from them abundantly in several anthropological essays such as *Primitive Society* (1920). He saw such a variety of forms of social organization in Siberia that he held that evidence refuting any doctrine upholding the uniformity of the laws of social progress could be found there. He considered Bogoras's *The Chukchee* an ethnographic masterpiece. He also proposed a typology of Arctic Siberian societies whereby the clanless Chukchis and Koryaks would be at the most elementary level of social organization, the clan-based Samoyeds and Yakuts at the top level and the Yugakirs at an intermediary level.

The communist Bolshevik Revolution, however, was to throw a veil over the Siberian Arctic. Russian ethnographers continued their studies in the region for a while, but strict ideological boundaries were soon to restrict their research and that of the following generation (see *Russian and Soviet anthropology).

On the North American side of the Arctic, two big scientific expeditions had an impact on anthropology. The first, the Canadian Arctic Expedition (1913–18), directed by W. Stefansson, studied the Copper Inuit. The tragic death of Henri Beuchat, a follower of Mauss, who had been in charge of the anthropological aspects of the expedition, forced Stefansson to find a last-minute replacement in the person of the Australian anthropologist †D. Jenness, who oriented the research in a far more descriptive direction. Mauss's thesis that Beuchat wanted to test in the field was, as a result, never verified.

The other major expedition was that of K. Rasmussen. Known as the 'Fifth Thule Expedition', it travelled the length and breadth of the Canadian Arctic and Northern Alaska between 1921 and 1924. Rasmussen spoke the Inuit language fluently. With his companions (the ethnologist †K. Birket-Smith and the archaeologist T. Mathiasen), he gathered data from the central Canadian Arctic unparalleled in quantity and quality. Rasmussen's premature death in 1933 meant that he was unable to analyse his data. During the following fifty years, nobody carried out further fieldwork on his favorite themes: *shamanism, *taboos, rites and myths, except for M. Lantis in Alaska in 1939–40 (*The Social Culture of the Nunivak Eskimos*, 1946). Rasmussen's data were put to productive use in another discipline, the comparative history of religions, especially the Scandinavian school under Ake Hultkrantz. After the end of World War II, the Arctic went through economic development and militarization which brought the inhabitants into the world of urbanization and industrialization. Studies became progressively regionalized, marked by national scientific traditions, and themes were also regionalized: Canadian and American anthropologists focusing on *kinship, social organization or *cultural ecology, Scandinavians on religion and Russians on ethnogenesis.

Arctic peoples in contemporary anthropology

If we examine the impact of Arctic ethnography on anthropology as a whole, several concepts emerge that now seem very far removed from the anthropological mainstream. Examples are the supposed 'sexual communism' and 'economic communism' of the Inuit and Chukchi (Mauss and Lowie). At the beginning of the twentieth century, and especially after World War II, the *'primitive communism' of Arctic peoples seemed like a utopian model of our origins, and for some it was seen as an alternative to Western capitalism and its excesses. It was also believed that the Arctic peoples were the last survivors of the Magdalenians.

Another concept associated with them is shamanism, which has enjoyed a chequered career. The 'Arctic hysteria' often associated with it became fashionable within the *culture and personality movement. As far as the *technology of Arctic peoples is concerned, its importance has always been overestimated compared to social organization and religion. Boas even asserted that the Inuit have no origin myths because they were too busy fighting for survival. Even Lévi-Strauss considered them to be great technologists but poor sociologists.

The concept that has been most resistant to the passage of time has been that of †'Eskimo type' of kinship terminology. L. Morgan stressed the originality of Inuit kinship terminology in his *Systems of Consanguinity and Affinity of the Human Family* (1871), using data collected in dubious conditions. Sixty years later, using D. Jenness's data, †L. Spier defined the 'Eskimo type' terminology as one of the eight main types in his classification of existing systems (*The Distribution of Kinship Systems in North America*, 1925). †G.P. Murdock also adopted this classification, adding an 'Eskimo' type of social organization (*Social Structure*, 1949). His work relaunched interest in Inuit kinship (from 1950 to 1970) and also in descent systems which, in the case of the Inuit,

were described as †bilateral or *cognatic. The attempt to apply this classification to the Inuit was a resounding failure because they could not be said to have a single, homogeneous system, even if one acknowedged the existence among the Inuit of the eastern Arctic of certain features noted by Morgan, Spier and Murdock. Certain groups are even organized patrilineally with patriclans. Research is still being conducted, however, on kinship extensions and alliances.

In the European Arctic, among Saami reindeer herders, R. Pehrson contributed to the development of theoretical reflection on the 'bilateralism' of kinship structures. The subsequent trend in *componential analysis of kinship terminologies dealt a severe blow to studies of kinship. The 1990s have witnessed a revival of Russian anthropology of Arctic peoples, including the defence of indigenous peoples (Vakhtin 1992). There is also a new interest among Western researchers in comparisons with Siberia. Finally, we are witnessing a renewed appreciation of the importance of ethnography involving the holistic approach inspired by symbolic anthropology and the work of Mauss, especially his theory of the gift and of *exchange (Irimoto and Yamada 1994).

BERNARD SALADIN D'ANGLURE

See also: Russian and Soviet anthropology, Native North America

Further reading

Damas, D. (ed.) (1984) *Handbook of North American Indians, vol. 5: Arctic*, Washington, DC: Smithsonian Institution

Garrett, W. (ed.) (1983) *Peoples of the Arctic*, [Map] Washington, DC: National Geographic Magazine

Graburn, N. and B. Strong (1973) *Circumpolar Peoples: An Anthropological Perspective*, Pacific Palisades: Goodyear

Irimoto, T. and Y. Takado (eds) (1994) *Circumpolar Religion and Ecology: An Anthropology of the North*, Tokyo: University of Tokyo Press

Mauss, M. (1979 [1906]) *Seasonal Variations of the Eskimo*, London: Routledge and Kegan Paul

Minority Rights Group (1994) *Polar Peoples: Self-determination and Development*, London: Minority Rights Group

Vakhtin, N. (1992) *Native Peoples of the Russian Far North*, London: Minority Rights Group

Vorren, Ø. and E. Manker (1962) *Lapp Life and Customs*, Oxford: Oxford University Press

art

If little agreement remains on what constitutes the discipline of anthropology, even less exists on what constitutes art, thus posing scholars of the anthropology of art two sets of problematic definitions. Such scholars have sometimes struggled to distinguish themselves from art historians, frequently described as being intent on form while anthropologists pursued function. Nor have anthropological studies of art often been at the centre of theoretical developments, although they frequently illustrated its changing intellectual fashions.

Thus, it is possible to find in *Franz Boas's analysis ([1927] 1955) of non-Western art both a critique of *evolutionary approaches and an example of the †historical particularism which came to characterize much American work at the begining of the twentieth century. Equally, the early *functionalism of *British social anthropology appears in the relatively small number of works about art, such as that by †Raymond Firth (1936) on New Guinea. The increasing interest by the 1960s and 1970s in †symbols and †semiotics is well represented by Nancy Munn's (1973) study of Walbiri graphic signs from Australia. French *structuralism provides the analytical framework for *Lévi-Strauss's (1983) examination of masks and myths on the northwest coast of Canada. By the 1990s, partly inspired by a revival of interest in †material culture as exegesis and evidence, anthropological analyses of art, however defined, became more numerous and informed by theoretical concerns with issues such as *gender and *colonialism (Morphy 1991; Thomas 1991).

Not surprisingly, over the course of these several generations of anthropological studies of art, the questions that have been foremost at any one time have changed, and even when the questions have remained the same, answers are continually reformulated. What was once 'primitive' art has become 'ethnoart'; speculations about origins have been overtaken by those about meaning; description of stylistic elements is joined by a wider concern with *aesthetics. Sometimes these questions have been similar to those asked about European art on the nature of human creativity, the personality of the artist or the role of patronage. Inherent here is an assumption that the anthropology of art is about non-Western forms, although scholars such as Jacques Maquet (1986) have tried to broaden the discussion. Whether such material (most studies of the anthropology of art are of objects rather than performance or the verbal arts) should be displayed in museums or art galleries as 'art' or 'artefact' is an important discussion point in *museum studies.

JEANNE CANNIZZO

See also: aesthetics, museums

Further reading

Boas, F. ([1927] 1955) *Primitive Art*, New York: Dover
Coote, J. and A. Shelton (eds) (1992) *Anthropology, Art and Aesthetics*, Oxford: Clarendon Press
Firth, R. (1936) *Art and Life in New Guinea*, London: Studio
Forge, A. (1973) (ed.) *Primitive Art and Society*, London: Oxford University Press
Layton, R. (1981) *The Anthropology of Art*, London: Granada
Lévi-Strauss, C. (1983) *The Way of the Masks*, London: Cape
Maquet, J. (1986) *The Aesthetic Experience*, New Haven: Yale University Press
Morphy, H. (1991) *Ancestral Connections*, Chicago: University of Chicago Press
Munn, N. (1973) *Walbiri Iconography*, Ithaca: Cornell University Press
Thomas, N. (1991) *Entangled Objects*, Cambridge: Harvard University Press

Asia: East

The Far East, as an expression, suggests a great distance from the West, but it may as well evoke a total disconnection with the familiar. China, Japan, and North and South Korea are the dominant nation-states in what is also called, less ethnocentrically, East Asia. Since the end of World War II, and particularly in response to an expansion of economic activity, Western interest in this seemingly far-away region has increased. Within anthropology, studies of China and Japan (by Western and Eastern scholars) have proliferated, but increasing attention is also being given to many smaller cultural groupings. These studies have at times provided anthropology with challenges, not least because of the special characteristics of some East Asian cultures as ethnographic objects (e.g. because of the vast quantities of written Japanese and Chinese history). But it may also be argued, and perhaps because of these same characteristics, that East Asian ethnography has so far had a surprisingly minor impact on anthropology in general.

Continuity and difference

On one level there are powerful continuities between the dominant cultures of the region, although these manifest themselves in complicated ways. For example, some version of Confucian ideals of social relationships could be said to operate in China, Japan, Korea and beyond. And yet even within China the operation of 'Confucianism' is notoriously difficult to specify, and the history of competing schools of Confucian thought is very complex. There are also linguistic continuities and discontinuities across the region; for example, Chinese characters are used in some forms of Japanese writing, and yet local Chinese dialects, which share a common form of writing, are for the most part mutually unintelligible. Folk religious practice is *syncretic, and in some ways similar, throughout East Asia. Forms of *Buddhism have had a profound and widespread influence. Daoism ('the way') in China and Shintoism ('the way of the gods') in Japan, share common features, as do patterns of *ancestor worship in China, Korea and Japan. And yet even within China there are important regional variations in religious practice, not to even mention the political suppression of 'superstition'.

However, given the background of at least superficial continuity, it is striking that little comparative work has been done in East Asia by anthropologists; on the contrary, it can be argued that ethnography has tended to stress difference. Here the example of China and Japan will be considered. During the postwar era, Japan enjoyed a period of great economic expansion, whereas mainland China entered a period of political isolation and economic hardship (which lasted until the reforms of Deng Xiaoping). During this period both Japan and China have been widely represented in the West as 'traditionalist', but Japan is so in the modern world, whereas the popular image of China has remained, until recently, strangely feudal.

To the extent that Japan could be considered a nation of relatively well-to-do office and factory workers, while China remained a nation of *peasants, it is not surprising that anthropological *fieldwork in these places should address different concerns. But it should also be pointed out that most fieldwork *about* China has been conducted in the very places in and around China which, in a sense, most *resemble* Japan. Until quite recently, it has been virtually impossible to carry out field research in the People's Republic of China, and

even today it remains very problematic (although see Potter and Potter 1990; Davis and Harrell 1993). Most anthropological writing about China has therefore been based on material from Singapore, Hong Kong and Taiwan, all of which have been Japanese or Western colonies, all of which have seen great economic development in the postwar era, and all of which are in many respects resolutely 'modern'.

A great deal of diverse material has been written by anthropologists about China and Japan, and it is difficult to generalize. But the anthropology of China has arguably focused on the most traditionalist aspects of modern Chinese society (e.g. *kinship and *religion) and on questions of *political economy, while de-emphasizing other aspects which might well be seen as equally culturally relevant (e.g. *education or etiquette). Anthropologists of China have conducted historically-based research and collaborated closely with historians (see, for example, Watson and Rawski 1988), which may also have increased the tendency to paint a traditionalist portrait. If a contrast could be made, the anthropology of Japan has arguably been more 'cultural' than 'social', and has often focused on issues such as the construction of self, or on aspects of personality, symbolism, *socialization, sociability and etiquette (see Ohnuki-Tierney 1987, as well as Hendry's 1987 overview and her 1990 essay on 'wrapping'). Does this different emphasis reflect the concerns of our informants, or is it an anthropological projection?

An example: Taiwanese and Korean shamans

If ethnography across East Asia has tended to stress local differences at the expense of regional continuities, it is not surprising. Fieldwork as a methodology directs attention to very profound local differences which can exist in the midst of apparent similarity. In this respect it is interesting to consider two recent books about *shamanism in East Asia, by M. Wolf (1992) and L. Kendall (1988), which share very similar concerns. Each is an account of one woman's life history and of her participation in local religion, but also a consideration of *gender, ethnographic methods, and of the way in which 'tales' of certain incidents are constructed. Kendall relates the story of 'Yongsu's mother', a successful Korean shaman, while Wolf relates the story of Mrs Tan, a Taiwanese woman who seemed on the verge of becoming a shaman.

Many of the folk religious practices in the communities of the two women seem rather similar, including the worship of Buddhist gods, the concerns which are addressed to shamans, the ways in which shamans establish credibility, the significance of gods and ancestors in accounts of misfortune, etc. Several direct Chinese influences are woven into Kendall's account from Korea: the impact of Confucian ideals, the use of classical Chinese in household divination manuals, and the consumption of Chinese herbal tonics against illness.

But for all the similarities between the backgrounds to the accounts, there is one fundamental difference. Most Korean *mansin* (shamans) are women, and even the men who perform this role dress as women to do so. By contrast, although it is possible for Taiwanese women to become *tang-ki* (shamans), it is generally considered inappropriate, and the role is usually reserved for men. This means that while Kendall is writing about Tonga's mother becoming a shaman, and the impact of this upon her life, Wolf is instead writing about Mrs Tan *not* becoming a shaman, and speculating on the reasons for her failure to do so. Although from a regional perspective we might say that the cultural context of these two life-stories is similar, in practice, the impact of local religious beliefs on the fate of the two women could not have been more different. Because anthropologists generally develop their understandings through close interaction with local informants, local understandings are likely to overshadow attempts at regional generalization. It is these local understandings which impinge most directly upon the people with whom anthropologists live and work.

Far from wanting to consider East Asia as an ethnographically continuous entity, anthropologists have increasingly become interested not only in local variations of the dominant cultures, but also in the position of smaller cultural groups within the region. Shepherd is one writer who has found a position somewhat between the regional and the local, in his 'anthropological history' of Taiwan (1993). He relates the history of the interaction between various colonial regimes, the Chinese state, Han Chinese settlers, and the Malayo-Polynesian aborigines of Taiwan. In so doing, he takes account not only of the specific cultural traditions of the island, but also of the political implications, within the Chinese sphere of influence, of cultural difference.

The challenge of the region

As mentioned, East Asia can be seen as providing many challenges for anthropologists. For example, as Kelly (1991) has noted, Japan specialists are studying a *powerful* nation, with great wealth, literacy, and, significantly, with an extensive and independent academic establishment. The implications, for anthropologists, of turning to the study of cultures with ancient literate and scholarly traditions have scarcely begun to be considered. One potential difficulty is that by becoming specialized (or over-specialized) in local concerns (a specialization that is virtually limitless through, for instance, a consideration of Chinese history), it will become difficult for anthropologists of East Asia to relate their findings to anthropologists who rely more fully, in other regions, on the traditional 'long conversation' of participant observation.

Finally, it is clear that some of the power relations implicated in anthropological practice operate differently here, or at least are reflected in different ways. It is significant that much of the best anthropology in East Asia is now conducted by ethnographers from the region. Another indication of the uniqueness of the region is that much of the research being conducted in East Asia is currently funded not from the West, but from local sources, especially from Japan and Taiwan.

CHARLES STAFFORD

See also: Chinese anthropology, Japan

Further reading

Davis, D. and S. Harrell (eds) (1993) *Chinese Families in the Post-Mao Era*, Berkeley: University of California Press

Hendry, J. (1987) *Understanding Japanese Society*, London: Routledge

—— (1990) 'Humidity, Hygiene, or Ritual Care: Some Thoughts on Wrapping as a Social Phenomenon', in E. Ben-Ari, B. Moeran and J. Valentine (eds) (1990) *Unwrapping Japan: Society and Culture in Anthropological Perspectives*, Honolulu: University of Hawaii Press

Kelly, W. (1991) 'Directions in the Anthropology of Contemporary Japan', *Annual Review of Anthropology* 20: 395–431

Kendall, L. (1988) *The Life and Hard Times of a Korean Shaman: Of Tales and the Telling of Tales*, Honolulu: University of Hawaii Press

Ohnuki-Tierney, E. (1987) *The Monkey as Mirror: Symbolic Transformations in Japanese History and Ritual*, Princeton: Princeton University Press

Potter, S. and J. Potter (1990) *China's Peasants: The Anthropology of a Revolution*, Cambridge: Cambridge University Press

Shepherd, J.R. (1993) *Statecraft and Political Economy on the Taiwan Frontier 1600–1800*, Stanford: Stanford University Press

Watson, J.L. and E.S. Rawski (1988) *Death Ritual in Late Imperial and Modern China*, Berkeley: University of California Press

Wolf, M. (1992) *A Thrice-told Tale: Feminism, Post Modernism and Ethnographic Responsibility*, Stanford: Stanford University Press

Asia: South

South Asia includes the modern republics of India, Pakistan, Bangladesh and Sri Lanka – all formerly under British colonial rule – and the kingdom of Nepal. Although the foundations of modern South Asian anthropology lie in the systematic ethnographic reportage begun during the colonial period, the work of post-independence field-workers has had the greatest impact in mainstream anthropology, not least through the reaction to †Louis Dumont's celebrated attempt at theoretical and empirical synthesis, *Homo Hierarchicus* (1980). The first wave of post-independence work was village-based and concentrated on questions of *caste and *kinship. More recent work has focused on *religion, particularly *Hinduism and *Buddhism, *gender, history and the politics of collective (or †'communal') *identities.

Colonial society and ethnography

From the beginning, colonial officials recognized the need to understand the customs and institutions of their subject peoples, and considerable effort was therefore expended on collecting information about *social structure, land systems, political and military organisation, religion and law. On the whole, officials assumed that they were investigating indigenous traditions, but in reality they were participating in an inventive reconfiguration of them that played a formative role in the institutional consolidation of 'traditional' South Asian society under British rule. The consolidating process was complex and should not be caricatured as if the British single-mindedly imagined a 'traditional' India or Ceylon that they then set out to construct. Nevertheless, between the mid-eighteenth and mid-twentieth centuries, the overall direction of change is clear. Partly by design and partly by default, partly with the cooperation of their native subjects and partly in the face of their resistance, British *colonialism – especially in the Indian heartland – brought into

being a social order that was 'traditional' in the sense that it conformed more closely to the *Orientalist image of an unchanging, hierarchical, religiously-minded, mainly village-based society than anything that had actually existed in the pre-colonial era. In the Orientalist vision of 'traditional' society, virtually impotent kings reigned over a mass of ostensibly self-sufficient 'village republics', although the latter were also internally stratified by a hierarchical, hereditary *caste system. This system was regulated by complex rules of ritual *pollution and purity, presided over by the highest caste, the Brahmans, and anciently legitimated by the amorphous religion of *Hinduism. So powerful was caste that in most of South Asia non-Hindus, as well as Hindus themselves, were under its sway.

In establishing caste as the foundation of society in India – and as crucially important even on its periphery – colonial ethnography played a critical role. Systematic ethnography effectively began in 1871, when the first national censuses of India and Ceylon were carried out. The Indian census, like all subsequent ones until 1931, included questions about caste membership. Through the decennial censuses, 'scientific' data about caste were amassed, which would supply the core material for the ethnographic sections of the official gazetteers, the 'Castes and Tribes' compendia, and many influential general treatises on caste written by census commissioners. The same materials were also important for the classic study of Indian religion by †Max Weber (1967). The censuses and the official literature dependent on them are still an invaluable record for modern anthropologists. Yet those works were also a crucial component in the imperial discourse that consolidated 'traditional' Indian society, as well as a principal source of the anthropological image of that society as one founded on a rigid, hierarchical caste system, from which only the marginal tribal populations were seemingly free.

The 'village studies' era and Dumont's theory of caste

Most literature dependent on the censuses was determinedly †empiricist, although the perspective of *evolutionism was generally reproduced. Even publications from the end of the colonial period were largely uninfluenced by the rise of *functionalism during the interwar years. All this changed when a new wave of British, French and American ethnographers arrived in South Asia after 1945 to conduct intensive fieldwork, principally in villages. The first anthropologist to publish a modern, functionalist ethnography, however, was †Srinivas (1952), who completed in Oxford his analysis of the South Indian Coorgs before returning home to carry out a new village study.

From their reading of colonial ethnography, the post-independence ethnographers concluded that caste was the central institution of Indian society, but they also wanted to know how caste actually functioned within a local community. By the mid-1950s, the 'village studies' era had begun (Marriott 1969), and for the next twenty years a stream of publications appeared, mostly about Indian villages, although similar work was also done in villages in Sri Lanka, Pakistan and Nepal. Village studies monographs normally contained either a rounded picture of village society (e.g. Lewis 1958), or a more detailed analysis of the local caste system, often in relation to kinship (e.g. Mayer 1960). In either case, however, the caste system emerged as central to village social structure, so that village studies were simultaneously local caste studies. Even in studies of villages outside India, the influence of Indian ethnography was so strong that caste tended to occupy a disproportionately important place.

Village ethnographies, partly owing to their functionalist orientation, usually depicted 'traditional', caste-based villages as if they were static, bounded communities only very recently affected by significant change. Not until the 1980s was it generally recognized that such villages were themselves the historical product of the consolidation of 'traditional' society during the colonial period. Nevertheless, despite their unhistorical character, village studies formed the bedrock of modern South Asian anthropology and provided the ethnographic basis for significant theoretical progress, especially in relation to caste and †hierarchy.

Indisputably, the most important single theoretical work of the village studies era was Dumont's *Homo Hierarchicus* (1980). In very simple terms, Dumont argued that caste was the unifying institution of Indian society, and that it was founded on a religious principle of hierarchy, defined by both the opposition between the pure and impure, and the absolute separation of religious status from politico-economic power. Hence the caste system, as reported in village ethnographies, was the concrete manifestation of an ancient Hindu system of values. India was an unhistorical, holistic, hier-archical society: the antithesis of historical, individualist, egalitarian society in the modern West. By insisting that India as a whole was the true object of a *structuralist sociology of India, Dumont transcended the empiricist functionalism of the village studies that provided his subject-matter of caste.

The legacy of Dumont's theory

For the anthropology of South Asia during the 1970s and 1980s, Dumont defined the main terms of debate, although his theory was more often criticized than endorsed (Raheja 1988). Post-Dumontian anthropology is very diverse, but five principal bodies of scholarship may be roughly distinguished.

First, there is work (dating back to the 1960s) that focuses on the *political economy of South Asia, notably on the agrarian class structure and rural production systems (Alavi and Harriss 1989). *Class – rather than caste – is treated as primary, particularly by *Marxist anthropologists and sociologists, and neo-Marxist scholarship has increasingly situated itself outside mainstream anthropology. Neo-Weberian analyses focused on the relationship between caste and class, as exemplified by Béteille's work (1991), remain more centrally within anthropology and represent a powerful critique of Dumont's overdrawn contrast between India and the modern West.

Secondly, there is the †'ethnosociological' school developed by Marriott and others at the University of Chicago since the 1970s (Marriott 1990), which explicitly criticizes Dumont's structuralism and draws its inspiration from modern American cultural anthropology. The central axiom of ethnosociology is that in South Asian culture moral 'code' and bodily †'substance' are indivisible, and are constantly subject to transactions in †'coded substance'. Consequently – and contrary to Dumont's theory – South Asian society is not founded on rigid hierarchy, but on an array of †transactions that generates a perpetual fluidity in the constitution of authority, rank and even of *persons themselves.

Thirdly, since the mid-1970s, the anthropology of *religion has expanded greatly. Popular Hinduism and Buddhism have been studied most intensively, and much of this research also draws heavily on textual scholarship. The anthropology of Hinduism in particular (Fuller 1992) has rejected Dumont's very narrow definition of 'religion', which notably excluded any concern with deities, rituals and the *king's religious role. Thus the anthropology of religion in South Asia challenges the sociological reductionism pervading Dumontian theory, and insists that religion must be understood in its own distinctive terms.

Fourthly, especially since the late 1970s, the anthropology of Sri Lanka, and more recently of Nepal, Pakistan and Bangladesh, has progressively escaped from the Indocentric distortions imposed by the Dumontian legacy. Thus, for example, in research among Buddhists and Muslims throughout South Asia, emphasis is increasingly placed on the autonomous – and distinctively non-Hindu or non-Indian – character of their social and cultural systems.

Fifthly, partly owing to the influence of modern historiography, South Asian †ethnohistory has developed since the early 1980s and has convincingly undermined Dumont's premise that 'India has no history' (Cohn 1987). Furthermore, historical writing – together with feminism and other critical scholarship – has encouraged growing interest in women, low-status groups and other subordinate or †subaltern sections of society, whose dissenting voices were marginalized by most earlier anthropologists.

Contemporary change and communal politics

From the mid-1980s onwards, South Asia was subject to unprecedently rapid socio-economic change, although the most dramatic eruptions were in the sphere of communal politics. Hindu-Muslim and Hindu-Sikh violence worsened in India, Sri Lanka was torn by a civil war between Sinhalas and Tamils, and Pakistan witnessed ethnic rioting. These rapid changes, especially the bloody exacerbation of communalism, convinced many anthropologists of South Asia that they had to address these issues directly (Das 1990), and many earlier preoccupations – notably those made central by Dumont – came to look increasingly irrelevant. The anthropology of the region began to free itself from its post-Dumontian legacy, not because Dumont's theoretical achievement was discounted, but because South Asia itself had changed so much.

C.J. FULLER

See also: Buddhism, colonialism, caste, hierarchy, Hinduism, Indian anthropology, Orientalism, pollution and purity

Further reading

Alavi, H. and J. Harriss (eds) (1989) *South Asia*, London: Macmillan

Béteille, A. (1991) *Society and Politics in India: Essays in a Comparative Perspective*, London: Athlone Press

Cohn, B.S. (1987) *An Anthropologist Among the Historians and other Essays*, Delhi: Oxford University Press

Das, V. (ed.) (1990) *Mirrors of Violence: Communities, Riots and Survivors in South Asia*, Delhi: Oxford University Press

Dumont, L. ([1966] 1980) *Homo Hierarchicus: The Caste System and its Implications*, Chicago: University of Chicago Press

Fuller, C.J. (1992) *The Camphor Flame: Popular Hinduism and Society in India*, Princeton: Princeton University Press

Lewis, O. (1958) *Village Life in Northern India: Studies in a Delhi Village*, Urbana: University of Illinois Press

Marriott, M. (ed.) ([1955] 1969) *Village India: Studies in the Little Community*, Chicago: University of Chicago Press

——— (ed.) (1990) *India Through Hindu Categories*, New Delhi: Sage

Mayer, A.C. (1960) *Caste and Kinship in Central India: A Village and its Region*, London: Routledge and Kegan Paul

Raheja, G.G. (1988) 'India: Caste, Kingship, and Dominance Reconsidered', *Annual Review of Anthropology* 17: 497–522

Srinivas, M.N. (1952) *Religion and Society among the Coorgs of South India*, Oxford: Clarendon Press

Weber, M. ([1917] 1967) *The Religion of India: The Sociology of Hinduism and Buddhism*, New York: Free Press

Asia: Southeast

The term 'Southeast Asia' has come to cover all Asian countries south of China and east of India, an area of some 4.5 million sq. km. As of 1985, this region was estimated to have a population of 404 million, of whom 243 million lived in Island Southeast Asia (including peninsular Malaysia) and 160 million in Mainland Southeast Asia.

The region is cross-cut by several significant oppositions. First, the inhabitants of Island Southeast Asia overwhelmingly speak languages belonging to the Austronesian language family, while those of the Mainland speak languages belonging to the Austroasiatic (Mon-Khmer), Tai and Tibeto-Burman families. Second, the region may be divided into four religious zones, with Catholic *Christianity dominant in the Philippines; Sunni *Islam of the Shafiite school of law in Indonesia, Malaysia and Brunei; Theravada *Buddhism in Burma, Thailand, Laos and

Cambodia; and strong Confucian influences in Vietnam and Singapore. All these countries have large religious and cultural minorities, however, Burma being the most diverse. Third, techno-economic differences cross-cut both of the previous two divisions. Everywhere one finds a contrast between 'hill people' practising shifting cultivation, 'valley people' practising irrigated rice cultivation, and 'coastal people' who were historically orientated to fishing and maritime trade. Of these three sets of divisions, the last is most relevant for understanding the theoretical issues that Southeast Asia has raised for anthropology.

Techno-economic adaptations

Rice is the desired staple food throughout Southeast Asia and may well have originated there. Rice can be grown on steep mountain slopes like maize or in deep pools of water (see Geertz 1963). Shifting cultivation in most of Southeast Asia supports a population density of only about 130 per square kilometer (Conklin 1957). This compares with population densities in some wet-rice growing areas of Java of nearly 2,000 per square kilometer. The difference in overall densities is due to the fact that shifting cultivation requires that over 90 per cent of land be held in fallow at any one time. Thus while wet-rice farmers far outnumber shifting cultivators throughout Southeast Asia, they are confined to a relatively small part of each nation's territory. This can give rise to ethnic conflicts when pioneer farmers penetrate the highlands in search of new land.

Hill people

The low population densities characteristic of highland shifting cultivation have made it difficult for élite groups to establish much control over the majority. While highland societies were often stratified as nobles, commoners and slaves, commoners typically outnumbered nobles and slaves combined. Order was maintained chiefly through the institution of the blood feud. One of the issues this raised early in Island Southeast Asia was how feuds were organized in societies lacking unilineal descent groups.

Beginning in 1919, Barton published extensively on the Kalinga and Ifugao of northern Luzon, showing how an elaborate system of peace pacts had developed to regulate tribal warfare between autonomous villages structured only as an interlinking series of bilateral †kindreds

(Barton 1919). Further clarification of the concept of bilateral kindred and of the implications of kindred endogamy were made by †Freeman writing on the Iban of Sarawak, and in a symposium organized by †Murdock.

This discussion provoked a re-evaluation of *descent group theory as it had been developed in the 1930s and 1940s on the basis of Australian and African models by *Radcliffe-Brown, †Fortes, and others. More recently, a number of authors have tried to move the discussion away from a consideration of the idiom of descent and filiation alone, and towards a consideration of the *symbolic structures associated with other types of relationship such as siblingship (McKinley 1981), twinship (Errington 1989), conjugality and companionship (Gibson 1986).

A different sort of criticism of unilineal descent group theory was generated by the work of Southeast Asianists on patterns of *marriage which the Dutch called †'circulating connubium' in eastern Indonesia (van Wouden 1968 [1935]), the British called †'matrilateral cross-cousin marriage' in highland Burma (Leach 1954) and Lévi-Strauss called †'generalized exchange' (see *alliance). Working largely independently of one another at first, these authors showed that rules specifying whom one should marry, and inherited relations between affines, were central to the social, political and ideological structure of certain societies. This appeared to contrast with Africa, where Fortes argued that †affinity merely generated a 'web of kinship' ties for individuals that cross-cut descent group affiliation.

More recently Lévi-Strauss has generated a new debate about kinship systems in the area by postulating that the institution of the noble *house as it developed in medieval France and Japan provides a more general model for societies in transition between kinship-based tribal societies and class-based state societies. His arguments have proven highly stimulating to a number of Southeast Asianists in the last decade (see papers in Carsten and Hugh-Jones 1995).

At the level of *religion, two institutions that are widespread in highland Southeast Asia from Assam to New Guinea have attracted anthropological attention. These are competitive feasting (see Leach 1954) and headhunting. Headhunting has been subject to a variety of 'explanations' over the years. In recent decades, M. Rosaldo provided the most detailed account of the beliefs and practices associated with head-hunting in a specific society, the Ilongot of northern Luzon (Rosaldo 1980, and see references therein to other approaches).

Valley people

There is little evidence that wet rice technology in and of itself requires the large-scale intervention of a central government to organize waterworks or mobilize large workgangs, at least in Southeast Asia (*pace* †Wittfogel's concept of †Oriental despotism). Complex irrigation works can be built and maintained by egalitarian village communities, and have been well described in Bali, Sri Lanka, northern Luzon and elsewhere (see Conklin 1980 for a particularly stunning example). Indeed, the type of local knowledge of the environment that is required for traditional rice-farming means that production tends to decline the more outside bureaucrats get involved. Just as in Europe, the traditional *state in Asia tended to appropriate the agricultural surplus after it had been produced by local *peasants.

Dove argues that the reason wet rice cultivation was so often associated with a 'despotic' state was not a techno-environmental one, but a military one: unlike shifting cultivators, wet rice cultivators were tied to the land by the massive investment they and their ancestors have made in it. It was not population growth which led to the switch from shifting cultivation to wet rice agriculture, which then made possible the development of the state, but the development of the state which led to wet rice agriculture, which made possible the growth of population (Dove 1985).

From the beginning of the Christian era, the Southeast Asian rulers of inland states have looked to neighbouring regions for new political and ideological techniques to consolidate their legitimacy. In the period between AD 200 and 1200 this chiefly took the form of Saivite *Hinduism from South India combined with local forms of Mahayana Buddhism (Coedès 1968 [1944]). In local interpretations, the ruler was conceived as an incarnation of Siva and/or Buddha. The traditional state of both Mainland and Island Southeast Asia was conceived as a mandala focused on the person of the king and surrounded in concentric circles by his palace, capital city, realm and cosmos (Heine-Geldern 1943). Everywhere in Southeast Asia, clearly indigenous forms of spirit cults persisted alongside the world religions emanating from the royal courts. Further complicating the religious picture, from about 1300 on, court élites

in Island Southeast Asia increasingly turned away from the old Hindu-Buddhist models towards Islam, while those on the Mainland turned towards a revitalized form of Theravada Buddhism emanating from Sri Lanka. Both religions had a more egalitarian bias to them and reduced the stature of the king. Only on the island of Bali did something like the old Hindu complex survive. After the Spanish founded a permanent colony in the Philippines, those islands were rapidly converted to Catholicism, putting an end to the Islamic principalities that had taken root as far north as Manila by 1500. It was the *'syncretism' of †animist, Hindu, Buddhist, Islamic and Christian beliefs that posed the primary theoretical problem for early students of lowland culture and religion.

In the 1950s, †Geertz found that the complexity of religion in Java required a more sophisticated approach to religion than the †Durkheimian one then in fashion. He drew heavily on †Weber instead, and mapped out a triadic scheme in which occupation correlated with religious tendency. While 90 per cent of Javanese claimed to be Muslim, peasants tended towards animist forms, merchants towards orthodox Islamic forms, and bureaucrats descended from the old court élites towards Hindu-Buddhist forms (1960). His work has since been criticized for leaning too heavily on what a small group of 'modernist' Muslims belonging to the Muhammadiyah organization considers orthodox, but it remains a pioneering attempt to cover a complex social and religious field.

Tambiah has covered similar material for the Mainland Buddhist states, starting with a monograph on the coexistence of Theravada Buddhism, Brahmanic ritual, and spirit cults in Thailand (1970), and following with a monograph on the historical relations between Buddhist monks and the state (1976). For the Philippines, the best work on the reception of Catholicism by lowland Filipinos continues to be done by historians (Ileto 1979).

Coastal people

During certain periods maritime peoples occupying a narrow coastal zone have dominated long-distance *trade through the region. Such societies were intermediate in scale and complexity between those of the Hill and Valley peoples. Settlements and dynasties were evanescent: the great trading empire of Sri Vijaya that dominated the straits of Malacca from the seventh century until the fourteenth century left so little trace that its very existence was only established in 1918 by Coedès. Great sums of movable wealth, in the form of spices, slaves and bullion passed through the hands of the merchant princes, but there was little fixed capital.

The societies that trace their origin back to these coastal states are more flexible and competitive than the inland societies, and more hierarchical than the highland societies. The peculiar mix of ascription and fierce competition in the ranking system has been most recently described by Errington (1989) for the Bugis of south Sulawesi. She shows how †hypergamous marriage functions as a means of validating the ascriptive rank of women and as an opportunity for men to convert achieved status into socially acknowledged ascribed rank.

It was these societies which first confronted European competition in military technology and in trade. Historians have shown that for a good 200 years after the Portuguese conquered Malacca in 1512 the competition was evenly balanced on land. European naval technology was comparatively more advanced, but was unable to gain a final victory over local 'pirates' until the introduction of the steamboat in the 1840s. During this period, huge numbers of villagers from both the highlands and the lowlands were captured and sold as slaves by predatory raiders drawn from these coastal societies. The structure of these coastal states was described in functionalist terms by Gullick for western Malaya (1958).

*Colonialism and *nationalism

Beginning in the eighteenth century, European powers began investing directly in the production of cash crops, with the Dutch instituting forced coffee cultivation in western Java and the Spanish enacting a tobacco monopoly in the Philippines. Plantation production of sugar, tobacco, rubber and palm oil grew apace in the nineteenth century under conditions described by Stoler in Sumatra (1985) and Geertz in Java (1963). Colonial powers began to train native bureaucrats to staff a more intrusive state, and tax collection was rationalized to the point where peasants were made to bear more of the risk of bad harvests, leading to frequent outbreaks of peasant rebellion. These rebellions were analysed by many American political scientists in the wake of the Vietnam War. Many of them employed anthropological methods,

with the best example being the work by Scott on the effects of the 'green revolution' on a Malaysian village (1985). Ileto takes a more cultural and symbolic approach to revolution, and to nationalism, in the Philippines (1979).

THOMAS GIBSON

Further reading

Barton, R.F. (1919) *Ifugao Law*, Berkeley: University of California Publications in American Anthropology and Ethnology

Carsten, J. and S. Hugh-Jones (eds) (1995) *About the House*, Cambridge: Cambridge University Press

Coedès, G. (1968 [1944]) *The Indianized States of Southeast Asia*, Honolulu: East-West Center

Conklin, H. (1957) *Hanunoo Agriculture*, Rome: F.A.O.

—— (1980) *Ethnographic Atlas of Ifugao*, New Haven: Yale University Press

Dove, M. (1985) 'The Argroecological Mythology of the Javanese', *Indonesia* 39: 1–36

Errington, S. (1989) *Meaning and Power in a Southeast Asian Realm*, Princeton: Princeton University Press

Geertz, C. (1960) *The Religion of Java*, Chicago: Chicago University Press

—— (1963) *Agricultural Involution*, Berkeley: University of California Press

Gibson, T. (1986) *Sacrifice and Sharing in the Philippine Highlands*, London: Athlone Press

Gullick, J. (1958) *Indigenous Political Systems of Western Malaya*, London: Athlone Press

Heine-Geldern, R. (1943) 'Conceptions of State and Kingship in Southeast Asia', *The Far Eastern Quarterly* 2: 15–30

Ileto, R. (1979) *Pasyon and Revolution*, Manila: Ateneo de Manila University Press

Leach, E. (1954) *Political Systems of Highland Burma*, London: Athlone

McKinley, R. (1981) 'Cain and Abel on the Malay Peninsula' in M. Marshall (ed.) *Siblingship in Oceania*, Ann Arbor: University of Michigan Press

Murdock, G. (ed.) (1960) *Social Structure in Southeast Asia*, New York: MacMillan

Rosaldo, M. (1980) *Knowledge and Passion*, Cambridge: Cambridge University Press

Scott, J. (1985) *Weapons of the Weak*, New Haven: Yale University Press

Stoler, A. (1985) *Capitalism and Confrontation in Sumatra's Plantation Belt, 1870–1979*, New Haven: Yale University Press

Tambiah, S.J. (1970) *Buddhism and the Spirit Cults in Northeastern Thailand*, Cambridge: Cambridge University Press

—— (1976) *World Conqueror and World Renouncer*, Cambridge: Cambridge University Press

van Wouden, F.A.E. (1968 [1935]) *Types of Social Structure in Eastern Indonesia*, The Hague: Nijhoff

avunculate

The term 'avunculate' evokes two related images. First, there is the social institution that the term designates. Secondly, there is the complex of theories which have been thought up to explain that insitution where it occurs.

In the first sense, the avunculate is any institutionalized, special relationship between a mother's brother (MB) and a sister's son (ZS). In some societies this relationship is formal or one of authority, as for example, in the well-known Trobriand case. In others, it is an informal indulgent relationship characteristically involving sexual joking, gift-giving on the part of the mother's brother, or permitted 'theft' on the part of the sister's son. This sort of relationship is by far the more common image, thanks to ethnographic examples such as the Tsonga (BaThonga) of Mozambique, the Tongans of the Pacific, and the Nama of Namibia. These three cases are those described in *Radcliffe-Brown's key paper on the subject, 'The Mother's Brother in South Africa' ([1924] 1952: 15–31).

Radcliffe-Brown read this paper before the South African Association for the Advancement of Science in 1924. He intended to draw attention to the fact that the same institution was found in diverse locations across the globe. His purpose was largely to refute the claim made by †Junod that the Tsonga custom of a young man taking his mother's brother's cattle for his own was a survival of a time of †matrilineal *descent. Ironically, the Tsonga probably once had been matrilineal, and the fact that Radcliffe-Brown chose three †patrilineal examples left open the question of the relation of such customs to principles of descent.

This leads us to the second sense of the term 'avunculate'. The debate which ensued from Radcliffe-Brown's paper polarized *kinship studies. *Lévi-Strauss ([1945] 1963: 31–54) postulated an †'atom of kinship' which contraposed structural relations between father/son, and mother's brother/sister's son, and between brother/sister and husband/wife. The saw the avunculate as a cornerstone of marital alliance. Homans and †Schneider (1955) argued against this with a descent-theory approach which took to extreme Radcliffe-Brown's notion that sentiments attached to the mother were extended to the mother's brother, and that the formality observed in the relation to the father was extended to the father's sister. Homans and Schneider said this was the reason why in patrilineal socities matrilineal cross-cousin *marriage seemed to be preferred, while in matrilineal societies patrilineal cross-cousin marriage is said to be more common. However, as †Needham (1962) pointed out, 'cross-cousin marriage' actually involves marriage to people of the cross-cousin category, not necessarily to actual cross-cousins at all. Therefore, Homans and Schneider's argument does not hold water.

Late developments in avunculate studies in both western and southern Africa have stressed relations between descent-group structure, the inheritance of *property, and avuncular indulgence. Radcliffe-Brown's notion of 'extension' had some vogue in *relationship terminology studies in the 1960s, but his concern with 'sentiments' was overshadowed as the field of kinship moved to models more formal than he could ever have dreamed of.

ALAN BARNARD

See also: alliance, descent, kinship, relationship terminology

Further reading

Homans G.C. and D.M. Schneider (1955) *Marriage, Authority and Final Causes: A Study of Unilateral Cross-Cousin Marriage*, Glencoe, IL: Free Press

Lévi-Strauss, C. ([1945] 1963) *Structural Anthropology*, New York: Basic Books

Needham, R. (1962) *Structure and Sentiment: A Test Case in Social Anthropology*, Chicago: University of Chicago Press

Radcliffe-Brown, A.R. ([1924] 1952) *Structure and Function in Primitive Society*, London: Cohen & West

B

belief

Statements like 'The X believe that . . .' or 'The Y believe in . . .' used to abound in *ethnography. Ethnographers regarded belief as an integral part of *culture, with whole peoples being thought uniform and consistent in their sets of beliefs. Such an understanding of belief was characteristic of †Durkheimian and *functionalist writers; e.g. Durkheim ([1912] 1915) and *Radcliffe-Brown ([1945] 1952: 153–77).

However, the study of belief entails a number of interesting problems, if not logical contradictions. How do we know what people really believe? Is it relevant what they believe, or is the statement of belief what ought to really matter to an anthropologist? If belief is an 'internal state' unrelated to language, then it is inaccessible to the ethnographer, even perhaps to the 'external' conscious reflection of the native. If belief can be described, then it is dependent on language, and that language of description may be more formulaic than reflective of the inner state which is supposed to generate belief.

A high point in the study of belief in anthropology was †Needham's *Belief, Language and Experience* (1972), which hints at some of these contradictions. Needham claims he awoke one night with the realization that he did not know how to say 'I believe in God' in Penan, the language of his fieldwork many years before. †Evans-Pritchard had thought of some of these questions earlier too, as he had once remarked: 'The Nuer do not believe in God. He is just there.' Needham explores Evans-Pritchard's claim. The question is, if belief is an 'interior state', as Evans-Pritchard said it was, then can it ever be accessible to ethnographers?

Belief has in the past often been coupled with *ritual, as one of the two pillars of *religion. However, since the late 1970s the theoretical emphasis on †practice has given greater prominence to ritual, with belief now held in the background. The work of Sperber (e.g. [1982] 1985), among others, cast doubt on the notion that *symbols have specific meanings, even in the context of structured sets of symbols. For Sperber, as indeed (though perhaps in different senses), for Evans-Pritchard and Needham, the concept of 'belief' is dependent on the knowledge of the word which describes it. Only those who have a concept of belief themselves have minds which exhibit the properties of belief. Talal Asad (1983) criticized anthropological accounts of belief from a more historical point of view: the emphasis on belief as an interior state was, he suggested, specific to a modern, private Christian religiosity.

As action has come to dominate much of anthropological theory in recent years, with philosophy and language becoming as peripheral as they are problematic, *belief* (as a field of study) has dwindled in importance. Whether it rises will depend on whether anthropology's pendulum will again swing towards its earlier philosophical concerns. The implicit cultural *relativism of those who in the past emphasized the study of belief has thus been overturned in favour of more †behaviourist, †materialist and (in Sperber's case) †rationalist enterprises.

ALAN BARNARD

See also: religion, ritual, language and linguistics

Further reading

Asad, T. (1983) 'Anthropological Conception of Religion: Reflections on Geertz', *Man* (n.s.) 18 (2): 237–59
Durkheim, E. ([1912] 1915) *The Elementary Forms of the Religious Life*, London: Allen & Unwin
Evans-Pritchard, E.E. (1956) *Nuer Religion*, Oxford: The Clarendon Press

Needham, R. (1972) *Belief, Language, and Experience*, Oxford: Basil Blackwell

Radcliffe-Brown, A.R. ([1945] 1952) *Structure and Function in Primitive Society*, London: Cohen & West

Sperber, D. ([1982] 1985) *On Anthropological Knowledge*, Cambridge: Cambridge University Press

Big Man

The Big Man, the prototypical Melanesian leader, is a key figure in the ethnography of *Melanesia. He stands at the centre of a complex of economic and political structures found generally across the region, although the modal Big Man inhabits Papua New Guinea, the Solomon Islands and, to a lesser extent, Vanuatu. He, along with his counterpart the †chief in *Polynesia, together serve to delineate a major ethnographic boundary in the Pacific. Big Man has frequently been defined in counterpoint to chief, each of these twinned Pacific political types shadowing the other. †Marshall Sahlins's influential comparison of the two leadership types, in fact, did much to cement the term 'Big Man' into anthropological parlance (Sahlins 1963). Alternative labels for Melanesian leaders have included 'headman', 'centreman', 'strongman', 'director' and 'manager'. Big Man, however, is apt anthropological terminology because it is a direct translation of indigenous terms for leader in numerous island vernaculars (Lindstrom 1981).

Sahlins, drawing largely on ethnographic accounts of Bougainville Island and Papua New Guinean political systems, characterized the Big Man as 'reminiscent of the free-enterprising rugged individual of our own heritage. He combines with an ostensible interest in the general welfare a more profound measure of self-interested cunning and economic calculation' (1963: 289). This caricature epitomized the archetypal Big Man whose political status flows primarily from economic ability. Whereas a chief succeeds to an †ascribed status, a Big Man achieves his leadership position. A politically ambitious man accumulates both subsistence and prestige goods (e.g. pigs, shell *money, yam, taro and other foodstuffs) in order to give away this wealth. He also plans and takes charge of rituals of economic redistribution. By astute economic generosity and management he secures influence over his kin and neighbours, who become his debtors. People support a Big Man's political endeavours and his

ambitions to build his 'name' because he contributes to their †brideprice funds, bankrolls their ritual obligations and because they also, as a group, profit from investing in his increasing political renown.

The various means and consequences of Big Man status achievement have been important issues within Melanesian ethnography, and the stock Big Man, as quickly sketched by Sahlins, rapidly developed ethnographic complications. Areas of concern have included the sort of person who becomes a Big Man; the various means by which Big Men achieve and maintain their positions; the economic consequences of Big Man politicking; the amount of authority and/or influence that Big Men possess; the structural relations between Big Men and the social groups they lead; the relationship of Big Men to colonial and post-colonial Melanesian states; and whether 'Big Women' might also exist within island societies.

A central question concerns the means by which Big Men acquire and hold *power without the traditional authority that chiefly status accords and without other institutionalized mechanisms of †social control. A Big Man who underperforms or who overdemands may be elbowed aside by his competitors and abandoned by his following. Thus, Big Men typically possess aggrandizing and competitive personalities but they must also be able to accommodate other people's demands for economic equivalence and political cooperation. Big Men must rely on skills of *oratory and persuasion, leading by example or by cajolery in hopes – not always fulfilled – that others will follow.

Many Big Men acquire their influence through economic production and exchange – their political ambitions, as Sahlins noted, fuelling the production of surpluses within Melanesia's †horticultural and cash economies. Big Man competitive politicking encourages people to produce subsistence and prestige goods beyond local needs and to participate in *trade networks that circulate these goods throughout extensive regions. In parts of Melanesia, such politicking has also inflated customary brideprice payments; young women from Paama, Vanuatu, for example, are sometimes called 'Toyotas' after the sort of good their families demand.

Other Big Men are such because of their specialized knowledge of genealogy, *myth and history, curing and *magic; and the influence of some leaders once depended on physical strength and on strategic abilities in war as well. This sort of achieved political influence, too, originates in an unequal exchange although people here transact information and services rather than shell monies, yams, or pigs (see Harrison 1993). Whether transactions involve pigs, money or knowledge, Big Men acquire and maintain their political influence over followers by engaging in ongoing imbalanced reciprocal *exchange.

The Big Man, as a political type, has been generalized and extended outside of Melanesia to label leaders who achieve their positions by engaging in astute exchange. Anthropologists have spotted, for example, Big Men in the halls of the United States Congress as well as within a number of other political organizations worldwide (see, e.g. van Bakel, Hagesteign and van de Velde 1986).

Back in Melanesia, though, the term has lost some of its currency. Leadership patterns are varied and complex in these islands, and the term 'chief' more accurately describes the capacities of leaders in many Melanesian societies (in Fiji, New Caledonia and among Papua New Guinea's Mekeo and Trobriand Islands peoples, for example). Elsewhere, anthropologists, following Maurice Godelier, have bifurcated the Big Man to locate a different sort of Melanesian leader: the 'Great Man'. Great Men exist in societies whose exchange practices are differently constituted to those where Big Men operate. Great Men 'flourish where public life turns on male initiation rather than ceremonial exchange, on the direct exchange of women in marriage and on warfare pursued as homicide for homicide' (Godelier and Strathern 1991: 1). Exchange, in this sort of society, requires a manifest balance – pig for pig, marital partner for partner and homicide for homicide. This equivalence disallows the sort of clever investment and exchange schemes that Big Men elsewhere use to turn economic obligation into political power. Great Men, instead, deal in knowledge and services whose exchange is less constrained by demands for equivalence.

As anthropologists enlarge the company of Melanesian leadership types, many post-colonial local leaders in these islands reclaim for themselves the label 'chief'. There are a variety of local, provincial and national councils of chiefs throughout the region (such as Vanuatu's Malvatumauri and Fiji's Great Council of Chiefs); no one, yet, has organized a National Council of Big Men.

LAMONT LINDSTROM

See also: exchange, patrons and clients, Pacific: Melanesia, political anthropology, power

Further reading
Bakel, M. van, R. Hagesteign and P. van de Velde (1986) *Private Politics: A Multi-Disciplinary Approach to 'Big-Man' Systems*, Leiden: E.J. Brill
Godelier, M. and M. Strathern (eds) (1991) *Big Men and Great Men: Personifications of Power in Melanesia*, Cambridge: Cambridge University Press; Paris: Editions de la Maison des Sciences de l'Homme
Harrison, S. (1993) 'The Commerce of Cultures in Melanesia' *Man* 28 (1): 139–58
Lindstrom, L. (1981) '"Big Man": A Short Terminological History' *American Anthropologist* 83 (4): 900–5
Sahlins, M. (1963) 'Poor Man, Rich Man, Big-Man, Chief: Political Types in Polynesia and Melanesia' *Comparative Studies in Society and History* 5 (3): 285–303

biological anthropology

The closest mammalian relatives of the human species are the apes (chimpanzee, gorilla, orang-utan, and gibbon), monkeys (the catarrhine cercopithecoids in the Old World, and platyrrhines in the Americas), and prosimians. Together these form the Order of Primates. Biological anthropology is the study of the biology of human and other primate species from an evolutionary and comparative perspective. It is concerned with the nature of the *evolutionary process and with modes of †adaptation to the environment. In continental Europe, the field of anthropology has been identified broadly with biological science, as distinct from *ethnography, since the founding of the Société d'Anthropologie in Paris in 1859 by Paul Broca (Barnicot in Harrison 1964) and of the journal *Archiv für Anthropologie* in Göttingen in 1861 by von Baer (Schwidetzky 1992). In the anglophone world, the term '*anthropology*' is sometimes used exclusively to denote social or cultural anthropology, although by etymology it embraces both fields.

Biological anthropology comprises five general sub-disciplines: human evolution, primatology, human genetics, the study of human physical growth, and human ecology. The first two sub-disciplines have sometimes been termed †'physical anthropology' in contrast to the second three as 'human biology'; 'biological anthropology' embraces both. The field has been grounded in the natural sciences and medicine rather than social studies, which on their own have been thought not to provide the requisite biological competence (Harrison 1964). Despite numerous assertions of the need to integrate these various sub-disciplines with *archaeology, social anthropology and associated social science fields, in practice few have succeeded in this aim since *Franz Boas.

Human evolution

Evolutionary studies in biological anthropology have focused on establishing the taxonomic (classificatory) and phylogenetic (evolutionary) relationships between fossil and living primates. In theory, phylogeny provides the necessary basis for taxonomy; but in practice, preliminary phylogenies can permit taxonomy to proceed. The method of cladistic taxonomy, which has become widely used, proceeds by first demonstrating primitive and derived characteristics of the members of a group, and then determining the derived characteristics shared among them (Groves 1989). The term 'hominid' refers to populations and species with which Man shares an evolutionary history excluding any other living primate. The hominid lineage is thought to have evolved between five and ten million years ago. Studies of hominid evolution have attempted to explain where, how and why the human species evolved, hence a longstanding preoccupation with relationships between fossil hominids and their only surviving subspecies Homo sapiens sapiens (Foley 1987). However, the coexistence in the fossil record of species of Australopithecus and Homo indicates that the study of hominid origins is not to be equated with that of human origins (Lewin 1993).

These studies have an historical basis in the comparative anatomy which flourished in the eighteenth century. Their development was greatly influenced by the nineteenth-century works of †Charles Darwin and †T.H. Huxley which sought to take the study of Man away from theology and bring it within the scope of natural history. Their more distant intellectual origins are sometimes sought in the works of Aristotle.

The advent of statistical techniques introduced by Quetelet, Galton and Pearson in the late nineteenth and early twentieth centuries enabled biometric approaches to become sophisticated (Boas [1911] 1938; Barnicot in Harrison 1964; Aiello 1992). A major problem has been separating the anatomical variation characteristic within a species from that expected between species. The use of functional anatomy and environmental physiology, and of comparison between the fossil record and field studies of extant primates in their social and environmental context, has allowed questions such as 'Why are humans bipedal? Why hairless? Why human?' to be asked and in some respects answered. Several competing phylogenies have been proposed and remain controversial (see Figure 1).

In the 1970s, approaches from evolutionary ecology stressed the importance of understanding the ecological context in which evolutionary developments occurred. This has underpinned approaches to quantifying the costs and benefits of alternative evolutionary strategies. These strategies can be framed in terms of 'r' and 'K' selection models. The term 'r' refers to selection for high reproductive turnover associated with small body size and relatively immature (altricial) state at birth. 'K' refers to selection for a low reproductive rate according to the limits of the †'carrying capacity' of the ecological niche; and is associated with relatively advanced (precocial) developmental state at birth (Pianka 1988). Humans show some characteristics of both; and primates in general bear precocial offspring (Foley 1987).

For a large-bodied primate, the human shows a relatively large brain and a long period of childhood dependence. Various theories of nutritional constraints on the origins of these properties have been proposed. Some physical properties may take their form and size purely as a function of body weight. Allometry is a method of comparing animals by scaling features according to body size, and has therefore been an important tool in the analysis of primate relationships. It has been used to argue the central importance of energetic constraints on brain development in determining peculiarly human characteristics (Martin 1983).

The origins of the hominid adaptation of parental provisioning of offspring, extended dependency during childhood and large body size, have been sought in meat-eating, hunting or scavenging, and tool use. Studies of dental development suggest that an extended childhood was not present in the Australopithecines or Paranthropines. However, the nature and extent of meat acquisition and consumption in hominid evolution is a matter of controversy (Ulijaszek and Strickland 1993).

The human species has often been distinguished from others on the grounds of *language, which is itself construed to be essential to *'culture' as a non-biological trait. Theories of the evolution of language are therefore of great importance. It has been argued that language origins lie in cognitive abilities rather than in properties of non-verbal communication (gesture/call) which are shared by all primates (Burling 1993). However, there may also be advantages of social lubrication which are afforded by grooming behaviour in non-human primates. These advantages may be more efficiently achieved by linguistic means in the human, therefore supporting larger social groups (Aiello & Dunbar 1993).

Primatology

Much of Man's evolution has taken place in the Tropics. Most contemporary non-human primates inhabit tropical or sub-tropical climates, although they have not always done so. The skeletal structure, body size, social behaviour and ecology of non-human primates vary considerably across species; and within species there is behavioural variation across ecological zones. Almost all primates are intensely social. Field studies have concerned the social structure and behaviour of primate groups, the biological and social control of reproduction, foraging patterns, and the relationships between these components of primate social systems. These studies comprise primate *sociobiology; and in that one aim is to explain the evolution of such diversity, it contributes to the broader study of human evolution.

Behavioural studies of primates have used methods of animal †ethology. These can give four kinds of explanation for why certain behavioural patterns exist: proximate causes, lying in immediate motivation or physiological processes; ontogenetic causes, which attribute cause to lifetime experiences during development; *functional explanations, which attribute causality to the purpose of the behavioural pattern; and evolutionary explanations, which indicate the sequence of behavioural changes leading to the evolution of the pattern in question. These levels of explanation may interact. Thus all four types of explanation are needed if behavioural patterns are to be explained as part of an integrated biological system (Dunbar 1988). These types of explanation have tended to treat food and its distribution, the avoidance of predators, and the need to locate mates, as primary determinants of species biology including morphology and life-history patterns. Some have preferred to think of primates in terms

of their ecology and behaviour as adaptations which themselves result in morphological characteristics (Harrison *et al.* 1988).

Application of these methods and concepts to human populations comprises human sociobiology, which can be defined as the systematic study of the biological basis of human social behaviour. Early attempts to develop this approach attributed to patterns of human social or cultural diversity a presumptive genetic basis (Durham 1991). This has been controversial among social anthropologists, and in its crudest form this approach is reminiscent of correlations between racial, cultural and mental variation which were postulated in the decades preceding World War II. These were examined critically by Franz Boas (1938). However, the development of theories of the coevolution of biological and cultural characteristics, acknowledging the ways in which they may interact, has been fruitful in the study of diverse *marriage patterns, colour terminology, analysis of *incest prohibitions, patterns of milk use, and *cannibalism (Durham 1991).

Human genetics

The Darwinian theory of evolution by natural selection has been central to the development of biological anthropology. Early workers tended to explain human diversity in terms of migrations and intermixtures. Mendelian (particulate) inheritance of some features was postulated by showing that the variability of quantitative characters in groups of mixed parentage was greater than that of each parental group (Boas [1911] 1938). It was not until immunological and biochemical methods enabled identification of blood groups, abnormal haemoglobin variants, and enzyme polymorphisms that particulate inheritance of such specific traits could be demonstrated (Barnicot, in Harrison 1964). The study of genetic variation within and between human populations, and that of processes of natural selection through effects of isolation, migration and differential reproductive success, have become well established. For example, the changing prevalence of non-insulin dependent diabetes in Polynesians has been attributed to the effects of selection against a genotype which, under less affluent conditions, would have had energy-conserving advantages.

A fundamental question has been the degree of interaction between genetic and environmental sources of human biological variation. This has been investigated for many characters, including stature, obesity, the milk-sugar digesting enzyme lactase, types of muscle fibre, and IQ. However, the method of comparing identical twins reared together with those reared apart does not adequately separate variation due to genetic inheritance from that attributable to non-genetic inheritance, and tends to overestimate the genetic contribution. Other statistical methods attempt to overcome this problem (Shephard 1988). At the sub-cellular level, the conventional distinction between genetic and environmental sources of phenotypic variation is hard to maintain. There is a growing literature on the ways in which nutrients and genes interact to influence gene expression.

The ability to identify individuals by their genetic profiles is useful in forensic investigations. The sub-discipline of forensic anthropology has used a variety of methods of DNA fingerprinting. It has therefore had an important role in public practice, and enabled the determining of relationships between ethnic groups. Mitochondrial DNA is inherited through the maternal line and comparison across populations suggests their degree of genetic relatedness. On this basis, relationships between genetic and linguistic classifications of human groups have been examined. The method has also been used to argue that *Homo sapiens sapiens* originated in Africa rather than in different regions of the world.

In many societies, marriage between close †consanguineous relatives is expected to occur, for example between first cousins or between uncle and niece. This has raised questions about the genetic consequences of such marriage patterns and their implications for health. Some studies have reported a high incidence of congenital malformations and post-natal mortality in the offspring of such unions in South Indian groups. Such marriage patterns may be linked to social controls over property and its inheritance. Studies have also been made of assortative mating for social economic or anthropometric characteristics, and of the relationship between such traits and reproductive success. These illustrate ways in which biological and social anthropological interests can converge: namely in studies of how social stratification may work as a vehicle for processes of natural selection in human groups.

Auxology

Auxology is the study of growth and development. The classical interest of biological anthropologists in the comparative anatomy of human groups is represented in many respects by contemporary anthropometric studies. Growth performance in children is a sensitive index of influences of infectious or congenital disease, nutrition, levels of physical activity, and to some degree mental development. As such, the measurement of growth in height, weight and body composition has been an important means of rating the general physical well-being of populations. Growth performance has been known to mirror social economic inequalities since the mid-nineteenth century (Tanner 1988), and has therefore become a means of identifying vulnerable groups, and of monitoring and evaluating the physical correlates of welfare policies.

The development of growth references as yardsticks for measuring growth performance has relied primarily on longitudinal or semi-longitudinal studies over extended periods. These have been made on ostensibly healthy Caucasian children resident in Europe or North America and have been recommended by the World Health Organization for general use. It has been argued that differences in linear growth performance between reference populations and healthy, well-off study populations tend to be small compared to differences between rich and poor groups within a given study population. If this were true, then there would be a strong case for using a single universal growth reference. However, patterns of growth in height and weight during childhood in healthy study populations do not seem to follow a constant relationship to reference patterns. It has therefore also been argued that there are ethnic differences in genetic growth potential, or in growth pattern appropriate to the local ecology, which may justify the development and use of locally specific references. Universal references may be valuable as a yardstick for the general comparison of groups, locally specific references for the screening of individuals for a particular purpose.

Linear growth is closely associated with rate of maturation, which is in turn related to changes in body composition (relative fatness) and differs according to sex. The nature of this relationship can only be investigated fully in longitudinal studies, such as that conducted at the Fels Institute in America since 1929. Populations in which children show low stature at any given age tend also to be slow to mature and to reach puberty comparatively late. High median ages at menarche of over

18 years have been recorded in Papua New Guinea. However there is no simple relationship between growth performance, reproductive function, and the demographic structure and dynamics of populations. It has been speculated that body fatness itself influences reproductive function, and therefore provides a link between energy balance and reproductive performance. However, this is probably related to one of various stressors of which the effects are mediated by endocrinological mechanisms which are poorly understood (Mascie-Taylor and Lasker 1991).

Human ecology

Ecology is the study of the interaction between organisms and their environment. Human ecology in general studies the adaptations which human groups make to their environment (see also *ecological anthropology). This therefore embraces studies of the epidemiology of infectious disease, patterns of nutrition, reproductive function, demography, human exploitation of and impact on natural resources, and the implications which these various factors may have for each other and for practical policy.

Different diseases affect different human and non-human populations, age groups and the sexes with varying duration, severity and consequences for health and survival. The subject of epidemiology investigates these patterns. Anthropological inquiries of this kind have addressed the historical significance of disease patterns in human populations (Fenner 1980). Some have examined their interaction with *household structure, living density and nutritional status. Assessment of the *nutrition of human groups is an important practical issue. The validity of applying a single universal set of physical measures, for example those derived from healthy Western children, to all populations regardless of ethnic background remains a matter of debate.

Factors influencing human reproductive function include level of physical exercise, dietary pattern, *age, emotional stress, and other factors which act through endocrinological mechanisms. These factors show that human fertility is susceptible to regulation through several biological and social means, and that it is possible to understand some of the observed variation in fertility behaviour in these terms (Mascie-Taylor and Lasker 1991). These investigations therefore contribute to the understanding of demography, the study of population structure and dynamics.

Human interactions with the environment have often been investigated using methods of energy flow analysis. This method became prominent in the early 1970s, after sharp increases in the price of fossil fuels raised public awareness of limits to energy resources. Studies by zoologists, anthropologists, geographers and others attempted to quantify the magnitude of energy inputs to, and outputs from, systems of food acquisition. Quantification of energy flows allows analysis of monetary and non-monetary subsistence patterns, and therefore the comparison of different systems by criteria of energetic efficiency. Ranking societies by these criteria allows analysis of broader relationships between human health and civilization (Boyden 1987). Some such studies have been criticized for methodological deficiencies, reductionism, sociological naivety, lack of attention to the household rather than the whole community, and failure to consider seasonal variation. Nevertheless, quantification of energy flows remains an important tool in the analysis of the biology of human subsistence patterns.

S.S. STRICKLAND

See also: evolution and evolutionism, environment, nutrition, ecological anthropology, kinship, incest

Further reading

Aiello, L.C. (1992) 'Allometry and the Analysis of Size and Shape in Human Evolution', *Journal of Human Evolution* 22:127–47

Aiello, L.C. and R.I.M. Dunbar (1993) 'Neocortex Size, Group Size, and the Evolution of Language', *Current Anthropology* 34 (2): 184–93

Boas, F. ([1911]1938) *The Mind of Primitive Man*, revised, New York: The Macmillan Company

Boyden, S. (1987) *Western Civilization in Biological Perspective*, Oxford: Clarendon Press

Burling, R. (1993) 'Primate Calls, Human Language, and Non-verbal Communication', *Current Anthropology* 34 (1): 25–53

Dunbar, R.I.M. (1988) *Primate Social Systems*, London: Croom Helm

Durham, W.H. (1991) *Coevolution: Genes, Culture, and Human Diversity*, Stanford: Stanford University Press

Fenner, F. (1980) 'Sociocultural Change and Environmental Diseases', in N.F. Stanley and R.A. Joske (eds) *Changing Disease Patterns and Human Behaviour*, London: Academic Press

Foley, R.A. (1987) *Another Unique Species: Patterns in Human Evolutionary Ecology*, Harlow: Longman

Groves, C.P. (1989) *A Theory of Human Evolution*, Oxford: Clarendon Press

Harrison, G.A., J.M. Tanner, D.R. Pilbeam and P.T. Baker (1988) *Human Biology: An Introduction to Human*

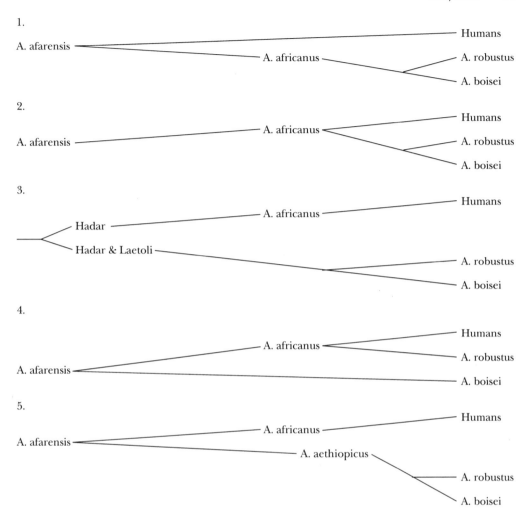

Figure 1 Competing hominid phylogenies (modified from Lewin, 1993, p. 118).

Evolution, Variation, Growth and Adaptability, Oxford: Oxford University Press

Lewin, R. (1993) *Human Evolution: An Illustrated Introduction*, Boston: Blackwell Scientific Publications

Martin, R.D. (1983) *Human Brain Evolution in an Ecological Context*, New York: American Museum of Natural History

Mascie-Taylor, C.G.N. and G.W. Lasker (eds) (1991) *Applications of Biological Anthropology to Human Affairs*, Cambridge: Cambridge University Press

Pianka, E.R. (1988) *Evolutionary Ecology*, 4th edn, New York: Harper and Row

Schwidetzky, I. (1992) *History of Biological Anthropology in Germany*, Newcastle: International Association of Human Biologists

Shephard, R.J. (1988) *Body Composition in Biological Anthropology*, Cambridge: Cambridge University Press

Tanner, J.M. (1988) *A History of the Study of Human Growth*, Cambridge: Cambridge University Press

Ulijaszek, S.J. and S.S. Strickland (1993) *Nutritional Anthropology: Prospects and Perspectives*, London: Smith-Gordon & Co.

Boas, Franz

Born in Germany in 1858, Franz Boas was the dominant figure in *American anthropology from the late 1890s through the 1920s. His major ethnographic research among the Inuit and *Native Americans of the Northwest Coast was complemented by his work in *language and linguistics and *biological anthropology, his influence as teacher, and his professional and social activism (Goldschmidt 1959; Hyatt 1990; Kroeber *et al.* 1943; Stocking 1974). Boas's theoretical contributions are under-appreciated in contemporary anthropology, in part because so much of his legacy is taken for granted. Still, American and world anthropology remain firmly attached to frameworks that Boas established, and many of the ideas he wrestled with continue to haunt the discipline (Wolf 1994), if often in non-Boasian incarnations.

Boas as ethnographer

During 1883–84 Boas undertook his first fieldwork, a study of the Inuit of Baffin Island. His objective was to compare the physical environment, which he mapped and measured objectively, with the knowledge of it held by its inhabitants. Boas discovered that something – *culture – intervened, and that Inuit activities and knowledge were more than a product of environmental conditions. Although he travelled some 3,000 miles during his fieldwork year, Boas approached participant observation as he hunted with his hosts, acquired a deepening knowledge of their language and interpersonal etiquette, interviewed informants and observed performances of folktale-telling (Sanjek 1990: 193–5). His ethnography *The Central Eskimo* (1888) was published by the Bureau of American Ethnology, then the principal organization for anthropological research in the United States. In addition, Boas published popular accounts of his fieldwork in German and English (see Stocking 1974: 44–55).

In Berlin during 1885 Boas was captivated by the museum collections of Northwest Coast art he was assigned to catalogue; he also interviewed some Bella Coola Indians then in Europe with an American Wild West troupe. In 1886 he made his first three-month fieldtrip to Vancouver Island. Typical of much of his subsequent survey work, he travelled from settlement to settlement to transcribe *texts in Indian languages (with interlinear English translation by the informant or an interpreter), collect art and crafts, take †anthropometric measurements of living Indian subjects, and acquire Indian skeletal remains (Sanjek 1990: 195–203).

In all, Boas made twelve fieldtrips to this Alaska-Canada-Washington-Oregon coastal culture area, amounting to a total of twenty-nine months. Most of this work occurred between 1886 and 1900, during summers (when many Indians were working in White-owned salmon canneries). Of his handful of local collaborators, the most important was George Hunt, a man of Scottish and Tlingit parentage who was raised in a Kwakiutl village and was fluent in Kwakwala. Boas met Hunt in 1888 and trained him to record Indian language texts according to Boas's transcription methods when both men were employed at the 1893–94 Chicago World's Fair. Several of the volumes of texts Boas produced were co-authored with Hunt, and their work together continued in person and by correspondence to 1931.

Two dozen books and monographs and many articles resulted from Boas's Northwest Coast work. Half of these 10,000 pages concern the Kwakiutl, and half other groups. Overall, 60 per cent of this corpus consists of texts, most of them in both the Indian language and English translation. But in view of the preceding 100 years of White contact, and the trade, disease, warfare and economic transformation that followed, the texts record primarily cultural reminiscences, and were not transcribed during ritual performances or around ongoing cultural practices. They salvage a culture that flourished around 1850.

Boas had two principal goals in his Northwest Coast work, both of which he regarded as accomplished by 1900. The first was to determine variations and relationships in the languages, physical characteristics and social customs of the Indian groups; the second was 'a presentation of the culture as it appears to the Indian himself', for which the Kwakiutl were his focal group. In mapping out linguistic, physical and cultural divisions, Boas discovered that physical types crosscut language groups, and cultural similarities and differences were distributed without regard to linguistic or biological affinities. Moreover, the cultural traits he studied – folk tales, *myths, ceremonies, *art styles, crafts, *kinship patterns – flowed and ebbed between groups. Overall they demarcated a Northwest Coast culture area of general similarities, but they also revealed past histories of cultural exchange and interpenetration for each of the †culture area's tribal groups.

The paradox was that the trait distributions Boas mapped out, and which supported hypotheses about historical interaction, were independent of the trait integration that was notable among individual groups. Each tribe's mix of separable but intersecting cultural vectors (of folktale types, art motifs, etc.) formed a psychological unity 'to the Indian himself'. It was 'the genius of the people', as Boas put it, that remoulded, shaped and integrated diverse cultural elements into a meaningful whole. For some this might go farther than for others; the Bella Coola, for example, he judged as having 'remodelled and assimilated' borrowed religious elements into the most 'well-defined' and 'co-ordinated' belief system of all the Northwest Coast groups (Stocking 1974: 148–55).

Work on this elusive patterning and integration among the Kwakiutl occupied Boas for much of his career. His first 428-page publication, *The Social Organization and Secret Societies of the Kwakiutl Indians* (1897), included his general description of the tribe, many texts, and nearly 200 pages on the Winter Ceremonial (including fieldnotes from his one sustained period of participant observation during the autumn of 1894). Eight more volumes, mainly unanalysed texts, appeared between 1905 and 1935. (Boas's texts have provided rich material for the *structuralism of *Lévi–Strauss, on whom Boas was an important early influence.) Finally, also in 1935, his capstone study *Kwakiutl Culture as Reflected in Mythology* was published.

This book is organized with a topical outline similar to many conventional ethnographies. Its 'data' however consists solely of things, activities, and beliefs mentioned in Kwakiutl myths. 'In this way a picture of their way of thinking and feeling will appear that renders their ideas as free from the bias of the European observer as is possible' (Boas 1935: v). Here at last the Kwakiutl natural, supernatural and human world was portrayed by Boas 'as it appears to the Indian himself'. This book was neglected in its day, however, as the newer style of *ethnography of *Bronislaw Malinowski and his students, and of Boas's own student †Margaret Mead, had displaced interest in text-based studies. Had *Kwakiutl Culture as Reflected in Mythology* been published when Boas's influence was at its apogee two decades earlier, perhaps this pot at the end of the Boasian rainbow would have received wider professional scrutiny. Since 1935 it has been rarely noted and clearly little-read; two major critics of Boas, †Leslie White and †Marvin Harris, do not even cite it.

Boas as theorist

The lesson that Boas learned on the Northwest Coast – that *race (biological traits), language and culture were not linked to each other – is unobjectionable today, but was hardly so in the late nineteenth and early twentieth-century heydays of *nationalism, racism and White nativism in Europe and the United States. In scientific and popular writings (Boas 1940 and 1945; Stocking 1974) he affirmed his position not only for Native America but for Europe, where Boas argued that maps of language distributions, physical characteristics and cultural groups also cut up the geographical terrain in three different ways. He insisted that each of these aspects of human existence must be studied with different methods – measurements and statistics for biological traits, texts and grammatical analysis for language, and distributional and holistic studies for cultural phenomona. Along with stratigraphic *archaeological methods to study the cultural past (to which Boas devoted concentrated attention at the International School of American Archaeology and Ethnology in Mexico during 1910–12), this defined the †'four field' anthropology Boas taught his Columbia students and which they in turn spread to the departments they and their students founded.

With his understanding of the duality of culture – trait distribution revealing *diffusion and interaction, trait integration indexing patterning and holism – Boas opposed the dominant *evolutionist paradigm of Victorian anthropology. He insisted that positioning individual cultures on the savagery-barbarism-civilization ladder not only discounted their particularity and integrity, but sidestepped the important task of reconstructing unwritten histories for non-Western peoples. Boas launched his attack on anthropological orthodoxy in 1887 by criticizing the organization of the US national museum collections (one room for pottery to illustrate its evolution, others for musical instruments, weaponry, etc.), a gutsy act for a 29-year-old immigrant who as yet had no anthropological employment and few publications (Stocking 1974: 61–7).

Boas reshaped the parameters of anthropological thinking with his concept of 'culture areas': the provinces of general cultural similarity dividing up a continent. In 1910 (Stocking 1974: 257–67) he listed seven areas for North America (Eskimo, North Pacific Coast, Western Plateau-MacKenzie basin, Californian, Great Plains, Eastern woodlands, Southwest), each of which would eventually have its own coterie of Boasian scholars; his student †Melville Herskovits produced a culture area scheme for Africa in 1924. The culture area framework for both museum work and ethnological studies remained dominant until attacked by †Julian Steward and other neo-evolutionists in the 1950s.

Boas as professional

Between 1887 and 1895 Boas held a number of editorial, research and educational positions, but had neither a secure income nor an institutional base. In 1895 he received an appointment at the American Museum of Natural History (which he resigned in 1905) and in 1896 a teaching job at Columbia University (with promotion to professor in 1899). From this joint base he trained his first cohort of PhD students. They worked primarily within Boas's distribution-integration framework, producing general and specific tribal studies in the culture areas of North America. Among the most noteworthy (and their specializations) were †Alfred L. Kroeber (Arapaho, California), †Edward Sapir (North America generally), †Clark Wissler (Plains, Blackfoot), †Robert H. Lowie (Plains, Crow), †Paul Radin (Winnebago) and †Leslie Spier (Havasupai, Plateau-Basin).

Between the end of World War I and his retirement in 1936, Boas trained his second cohort of students. Their interests focused on issues of cultural patterning, and many were women (including Mead), several of whom worked in the Southwest – †Ruth Benedict, Gladys Reichard, Esther Goldfrank, Ruth Bunzel, and the financial sponsor of much of this research, Elsie Clews Parsons.

Boas was an active member and founder of *anthropological societies, and played a key role in reshaping the American Anthropological Association to reflect a more 'professional' stance. As editor of four monograph series between 1900 and 1942 (the year of his death), he provided outlets for the work of his students and colleagues, producing seventy-six titles, including fifteen of his own.

Boas as activist

A victim of anti-Semitic affronts while a student in Germany, Boas abhorred any linkage of group ancestry with feelings of superiority; he actively opposed such popular views on the basis of his understanding of the race-language-culture non-equation. In a commencement address to African-American students at Atlanta University in 1906, Boas stressed the social, not biological, causes of Black subordination in the United States, and urged appreciation of the iron-age civiliza-

tions existing in Africa before European contact 'cut short' their cultural advance. In 1911 he announced that his studies of round-headed and long-headed European immigrants had shown the effect of the American environment on their offspring – this supposedly fixed biological trait in each case had begun to alter towards an intermediate head-form. More generally, he urged opposition to immigration restriction on the basis of any †eugenic devaluing of these 'Alpine' and 'Mediterranean' populations.

Boas also fought the politicization of scholarly work, and tangled with both Columbia University colleagues and Washington establishment anthropologists over his opposition to World War I and his exposure of 'scientists as spies' when he learned that anthropologists were clandestinely gathering information for the US government in Mexico in 1919. In the 1930s, Boas mobilized academics to publicly denounce Nazi racist 'science'; he became an activist during his seventies and early eighties in this cause, speaking and writing in popular venues against the reversal in his homeland of all that his anthropological career stood for (Boas 1945; Hyatt 1990; Stocking 1974: 307–40).

ROGER SANJEK

See also: Americas: Native North America, culture, history of anthropology, race

Further reading

Boas, F. (1888) *The Central Eskimo*, Norman: Bison Books
—— (1897) *The Social Organization and Secret Societies of the Kwakiutl Indians*, Washington: National Museum
—— (1935) *Kwakiutl Culture as Reflected in Mythology*, New York: American Folk-Lore Society
—— (1940) *Race, Language and Culture*, New York: Free Press
—— (1945) *Race and Democratic Society*, New York: Augustin
Goldschmidt, W. (ed.) (1959) *The Anthropology of Franz Boas*, San Francisco: Chandler
Hyatt, M. (1990) *Franz Boas, Social Activist: The Dynamics of Ethnicity*, Westport, CT: Greenwood
Kroeber, A.L., R. Benedict, M.B. Emeneau, M.J. Herskovits, G.A. Reichard and J.A. Mason (1943) *Franz Boas, 1858–1942*, Washington: American Anthropological Association
Sanjek, R. (ed.) (1990) *Fieldnotes: The Makings of Anthropology*, Ithaca: Cornell University Press
Stocking, G.W., Jr (ed.) (1974) *The Shaping of American Anthropology, 1883–1911: A Franz Boas Reader*, New York: Basic Books
Wolf, E. (1994) 'Perilous Ideas: Race, Culture, People', *Current Anthropology* 35: 1–12

body

In anthropology the human body is always recognized as a relative concept, conditioned and conditioning other complex entities that range from society to the cosmos. A key if little read contribution remains †Marcel Mauss's (1935) article 'Les techniques du corps', which draws attention to the universal influence of what today would be called *'culture' on people's use of their bodies and anticipates the later development of kinesics by R. Birdwhistell and others. Mauss instanced the cultural moulding of such activities as walking, running and swimming as well as sexual intercourse and such necessary bodily functions as urination and defecation. It was through what Mauss called 'traditional effective techniques', which were taught by precept and example, that human beings acquired confidence in the control and disposition of their bodies. An example was the distinctive waggle of the hips that Maori women instilled in their daughters.

But the characteristics of the body also serve to structure the world of culture. In his essay on the right hand Mauss's colleague †Robert Hertz surveyed the worldwide existence of dualistic symbolic systems embracing society and the universe, systems which derived from the fact of human physical bilaterality, the complementarity and opposition of right and left sides of the body. It is apparent that the culturally general existence of four cardinal directions originates in the structure of the human body, the east-west axis correlating with the right-left duality and the less emphasized north-south axis with the differentiation of front and back aspects of the body. To these could be added the general equation of the head with the sky and the celestial domain and the lower body and feet with the underworld. In human biology, an influential theory of the role of organic physiology in the perception and construction of cultural worlds has been proposed by Jacob von Uexküll (1982). According to von Uexküll, each natural species constructs a characteristic perceived environment or *Umwelt*. The features of the *Umwelt*, like that of other species, are both realized and constrained by their bodily senses. For example, human beings are naturally unable to discriminate units of astronomical time of less than one-eighteenth of a second in duration.

The work of †Mary Douglas developed the Maussian and †Durkheimian theme of socio-cultural constraints on bodily perception and activity. In *Natural Symbols* (1970) Douglas argues that the 'social body', the organization of society as a system of relations, constrains the way the human body is perceived and thus also constrains social behaviour. In turn perception of the body constrains perception of society. Adapting the sociolinguist Basil Bernstein's distinction of restricted and elaborated codes, Douglas proposes a fourfold categorization of human societies which correlates the type of social organization with culturally prescribed attitudes to the human body, including conventional ideas on trance or *possession states:

> The body itself is a highly restricted medium of expression. The forms it adopts in movement and repose express social pressures in manifold ways ... all the cultural categories in which it is perceived ... must correlate closely with the categories in which society is seen in so far as these also draw upon the same culturally processed idea of the body.
>
> (Douglas 1970: 65)

Within the past two decades comparative research has tended, as against earlier theories of socio-cultural determinism, to highlight the physiological, ultimately genetic, constraints on social behaviour. An interesting example of this trend is Paul Ekman (1974) who reviews evidence that human beings universally possess a repertoire of six elementary facial expressions, each conveying a certain emotion.

Whereas Western biomedicine since Descartes has developed a model of the human body as a complex, self-governing machine, non-Western cultures commonly conceptualize the physical body as the material expression of an invisible causative entity often called a 'soul'. Theories of a subtle body, or bodies, have been developed most elaborately in ancient India and China but the concept is also widespread in tribal cultures around the world. Among the Congo people of Zaire the human being is thought of as endowed with an 'interior' body and soul, the invisible and causative counterpart of the visible 'exterior' body and soul (Jacobson-Widding 1979: 310).

Also widespread is the idea of the human body as a model or microcosm of the universe. This idea is typical of *shamanistic, *hunter-gatherer cultures (Eliade [1936] 1964), but is also found elsewhere. According to the agricultural Hopi

Native Americans, the human body and the 'body' of the planet both reflect the structure of the universe (Waters 1963). The Bambara of West Africa hold that the human body, society and the cosmos conform to a single pattern (Dieterlen and Cissé 1972) and a similar conception pervades the 'Tree of Life' doctrine of the Qaballah in the European *magical tradition.

Humanistic psychologists such as Abraham Maslow and Alexander Lowen and the psycho-analyst Wilhelm Reich have sought to rehabilitate Western perceptions of the body, which they have seen as distorted by culturally transmitted images associating the body with sin and moral pollution (Lowen 1967). Meanwhile, feminist anthropologists have described the ways in which *gendered bodies become the site of powerful discourses (Martin 1987), while recent theoretical work – inspired by †Foucault, †Bourdieu and the French philosopher Merleau-Ponty – has emphasized the †phenomenological priority of the body in our apprehension of the world (Csordas 1993; Jackson 1981).

ROY WILLIS

See also: gender, hunting and gathering, magic, shamanism

Further reading

Benthall, J. and T. Polhemus (eds) (1975) *The Body as a Medium of Expression*, London: Allen Lane

Csordas, T.J. (1993) 'Somatic Modes of Attention', *Cultural Anthropology* 8 (2): 135–56

Dieterlen, G. and Y. Cissé (1972) *Les fondements de la société d'initiation du Komo*, Paris: Presses Universitaires de France

Douglas, M. (1970) *Natural Symbols: Explorations in Cosmology*, London: Cresset Press

Ekman, P. (1974) 'Biological and Cultural Contributions to Body and Facial Movement' in J. Blacking (ed.) *The Anthropology of the Body*, London: Academic Press

Eliade, M. [(1936) 1964] *Shamanism: Archaic Techniques of Ecstasy*, Princeton: Princeton University Press

Jackson, M. (1981) 'Knowledge of the body', *Man* (n.s.) 18: 327–45

Jacobson-Widding, A. (1969) *Red-White-Black as a Mode of Thought*, Uppsala: Almqvist & Wigsell

Lowen, A. (1967) *Betrayal of the Body*, New York: Collier Books

Martin, E. (1987) *The Woman in the Body: A Cultural Analysis of Reproduction*, Boston: Beacon Press

Mauss, M. (1935) 'Les techniques du corps', *Journal de Psychanalyse*, 32 (reprinted in C. Lévi–Strauss (ed.) (1950), *Sociologie et anthropologie*, Paris: Presses Universitaires de France, pp 365–86)

Uexküll, J. von (1982) 'The Theory of Meaning', *Semiotica* 41 (1): 25–82

Waters, F. (1963) *The Book of the Hopi*, New York: Ballantine Books

British anthropology

If anthropology is (somewhat anachronistically) understood to have developed as 'the study of simple and stable societies that are radically different from the complex and changing West' (Carrier 1995: 1), then it has a long prehistory, and dates (at the latest) from the earliest encounters of European imperialists with non-Western peoples. Anthropologists are, however, no different from other scholars: their work is intellectually collaborative – defined by a community determined to reach consensus. Thus, a narrative of the history of British anthropology *per se* commences in the nineteenth century, with the formal organization of a self-referential body of scholars. The enterprise became a coherent pursuit between roughly 1843 and 1871, a period bracketed by the foundation dates of the Ethnological Society of London and of the Anthropological Institute of Great Britain and Ireland (after 1907 the Royal Anthropological Institute).

In the name of science

The Anthropological Institute reunited the Ethnological Society with a group that had seceded from it in 1863, the Anthropological Society of London. The ethnologicals were †monogenists, holding that all human races derived from a single creation, a position initially founded in a religious worldview and associated with anti-slavery agitation. Anthropologicals were †polygenists, maintaining that diverse physical types of humankind were distinct species, a view especially congenial to those who supported *slavery and argued that supposedly congenitally inferior peoples would learn elevated habits only if compelled to do so. The creation of the Anthropological Institute signalled the triumph of monogenism as anthropological orthodoxy, attesting to the power of †Darwinian argument | in the latter part of the century: all humans were members of a single (if differentiated) species. But monogenism had been redefined in quasi-polygenist terms: because Darwinian reasoning (and its antecedents) rested on the presumption that the earth and its lifeforms were of an age far older than that which had once been calculated from biblical chronology, the races of humankind were conceptualized as long-persistent sub-types. In sum, the Institute had succeeded in resolving intellectual conflict, and had in the process moderated the political tone of anthropological debate – conveying, as the society's founders intended, that anthropology was a strictly scientific pursuit (see Stocking 1971). Indeed, the Institute has remained a force in the discipline because it has remained an ecumenical organization, hospitable to persons of diverse theoretical convictions and to every anthropological sub-field.

Thus, anthropology achieved considerable intellectual coherence prior to its recognition by the universities at the end of the nineteenth century, when faculty positions were created and it became a degree subject for undergraduates and postgraduates in turn. Because anthropologists have been wont to represent the campaign for inclusion in university curricula as extraordinarily heroic (see Leach 1984), we should note that the universities were no more reluctant to admit anthropology than such subjects as psychology and English literature, and that in the nineteenth century learned societies rather than universities were the institutional sites of much of British scientific activity (Kuklick 1992: 52–5). But though late nineteenth-century anthropologists were able both to define problems for collective inquiry and to agree on standards for the resolution of disputes – functioning as members of a scientific community that approached †Thomas Kuhn's ideal type – their conception of their enterprise was quite different from that which has prevailed since the second third of the twentieth century (see Stocking 1965).

Explicating human history

Until the 1920s, sociocultural anthropologists, *biological anthropologists, and *archaeologists were joined in a common historical project – one defined by the nineteenth-century assumption that truly scientific explanations (of virtually all phenomena) were historical. And anthropology's purview comprehended Europeans as well as exotic peoples. Late-nineteenth-century anthropologists rejected an old, biblically-derived view of human history – that so-called primitive peoples had degenerated from the original, prelapsarian state of human perfection – judging that primitives were closer than Europeans to primeval humankind. They undertook to chart the course

of human progress, relying on assumptions as much †Spencerian as Darwinian: acquired characteristics were inherited, so progressive improvement was the normal condition of human existence, and racial traits were functions of social behaviour. Evolution involved simultaneous material and moral advance, and followed 'a very similar course even in the most distinct races of man' (Lubbock 1892: 3): progress toward worship of a remote deity associated with an abstract, ethical religious system (implicitly, for many anthropologists, the dissenting Christianity in which they had been reared); the replacement of magical by scientific reasoning; development of formal political offices and impersonal legal systems; and the shift from †matrilineal to †patrilineal kinship structures (supposedly denoting both accurate understanding of the biology of reproduction and elevated moral standards). The *evolutionists' research programme was specification of the characteristics of each developmental stage and of the mechanisms by which transitions from one stage to another were effected (see Kuklick 1992: 78–89).

At the end of the nineteenth century, anthropology's leaders (if not necessarily its rank and file) repudiated the doctrine of the inheritance of acquired characteristics, reconceptualizing the relationship between *race and behaviour. They appropriated Darwin's natural selection model of change among plant and animal species, describing human evolution in a fashion more consistent with it than Darwin's own interpretation of human history: neither biological nor social evolution had an inherent direction, and they were distinct processes. Biological change was so gradual that the human species had barely altered since its formative period, and social change could be so rapid that a people's way of life was transformed in a generation. Human behavioural change was analogous to biological change in plant and animal species, and was explained in the terms of Darwinian biogeography, which stressed the importance of migration and isolation in modification of species' characteristics. A human group changed rapidly by diffusing over extensive, heterogeneous areas, thereby being subjected to rigorous natural selection pressures as it contested with various populations for survival in diverse environments; a large, dispersed group became individually differentiated, developing a broad repertoire of skills, which facilitated adaptation to novel situations. By contrast, a group confined to a small, geographically bounded habitat, often (if not invariably) an island, in which natural selection pressures were relatively light, was a homogeneous population, thoroughly adapted to its particular environment and by this token behaviourally stagnant; should its circumstances change, it would likely suffer cultural if not necessarily physical extinction – as could be witnessed among the exotic peoples newly exposed to European colonial power (Kuklick forthcoming).

The end of synthetic anthropology

The *diffusionist and *functionalist schools which battled for anthropological paramountcy in the World War I era were both engendered by Darwinian biogeography – although they represented themselves as diametrically opposed (and historians have usually taken them on their own valuation). The diffusionists sustained nineteenth-century evolutionists' historical objectives, and resembled their predecessors in their description of the sequence of institutional changes leading to modern civilization. But the diffusionists' explanation of historical change was antithetical to that of evolutionists: human history had no inherent direction; human beings were naturally conservative, rather than innovative, so culture contact effected through migration was the most likely impetus to change; and the distinctive traits of modern civilization were products of historical accident – and did not necessarily constitute a morally superior order. The functionalists, dominant in social anthropology from the late 1920s until the 1960s, focused on the idiosyncratic cultures of isolated peoples. They abandoned the search for laws of world historical change, and, indeed, dismissed historical explanations *qua* explanations. Instead, they sought to define the persistent features of stable social systems: peoples might be distinctive in behavioural particulars, but all societies necessarily exhibited uniform properties of social order; isolated from the historical currents that obscured the stable structural features of Western societies, materially simple societies were ideal anthropological subjects, easily apprehended in their totalities. But the research programmes of diffusionism and functionalism were both conceived in biogeographical terms: the former focused on the consequences of human migration, the latter on those peoples geographically protected from contact with migrant bearers of novel practices. And it is important to note that

the *fieldwork method functionalists embraced was neither original nor peculiar to them. Concern with the phenomenon of diffusion – of interest to many anthropologists at the turn of the century, not just the self-conscious diffusionist school – was arguably a major impetus to the development of fieldwork: when a society was exposed to new influences, some features of its way of life might be unaffected while others were wholly transformed, and only through field research could the anthropologist determine which observed changes were superficial and which fundamental (Kuklick 1992: 121–31; Kuklick forthcoming).

Because diffusionists and functionalists repudiated the link between race and culture, in the twentieth century the research of physical and sociocultural anthropologists became practically distinct. Complete disciplinary differentiation was not immediate, for the (largely medically-trained) diffusionists retained their predecessors' comprehensive conception of anthropology, and undertook to expound a model of universal human psycho-biological nature consistent with their descriptions of cultural change. But the functionalists dispensed with biological inquiries *per se* on the grounds that the same natural imperatives figured in the constitution of all societies, and were therefore irrelevant to explanation of societal variation; the fundamental human drives that were axiomatically antecedent to social institutions were not explicated but posited (if even mentioned). Archaeologists and biological anthropologists, however, remained committed to the objective of nineteenth-century anthropology – documentation of the course of human history. Anthropology's sub-fields became discrete, and interaction among their practitioners minimal – even when they shared concerns.

Toward membership in a global intellectual community

In the post-World War II period, it has become increasingly difficult to identify peculiarly British anthroplogical approaches; while local ties of various sorts must figure in the work of British anthropologists, the reference groups of British scholars are now international. Certainly, the discipline has never been isolated from outside influences. In particular, one should note the importance of the American *Lewis Henry Morgan to the development of *kinship studies – although, at least initially, he served largely as an intellectual antagonist (see Lubbock 1871); the

French †Émile Durkheim, whom anthropologists of virtually every theoretical persuasion have invoked since the early twentieth century; and the German psychophysicists whose work influenced such pioneers as Galton, †Rivers, and *Malinowski. Moreover, since the post-World War I era, British anthropology (particularly †social anthropology) has been an export product; Britain has attracted many foreign students, and anthropologists of British origin have migrated elsewhere. But especially since the 1960s, practitioners in Britain have participated in an international intellectual exchange, finding compelling such theories as the *structuralism of *Claude Lévi–Strauss and varieties of *Marxism (see Ortner 1984). And though British anthropologists may feel that their national variant of the discipline has been especially compromised by its ties to *colonialism (see Asad 1973), they have joined their colleagues elsewhere in redrawing the boundaries of their field's subject matter – perhaps not the least because inquiries conducted under the rubric of anthropology have become highly suspect in former colonial territories – so that social anthropology's purview now resembles that of a century ago.

What have been British anthropology's distinctive features? The most obvious of these are institutional, for different national university systems divide the academic map rather differently. Perhaps because they derived from the intellectual matrix in which (the British) Darwin's comprehensive scheme was embedded, anglophone departments initially joined sociocultural and physical anthropology, unlike their continental counterparts. Notwithstanding their foundational similarities, however, British and American structures have differed: though British functionalists failed in their efforts to excise physical anthropology from the anthropological sphere (see Radcliffe-Brown 1932: 167), they succeeded in effecting complete differentiation among the discipline's sub-fields, whereas, at least on the undergraduate level, American departments retain the aspiration to integrate the field's original components; and British social anthropologists have pursued inquiries that in the United States have often fallen under the rubric of *sociology (albeit based on different subject matter), perhaps thereby contributing to the oft-remarked state of British sociology, underdeveloped relative to its American or continental counterparts. Has British anthropology conveyed distinctive messages? Perhaps its social analyses have often projected

British political values on to exotic cultures, presuming that peoples everywhere are 'imbued with the values of liberty and equality' (Dumont 1975: 338). One must distinguish between problem selection and analysis, however: everyday concerns affect problem selection in every research enterprise, no matter how apparently abstract it is, but these concerns do not preclude conscientious observation and generalization.

HENRIKA KUKLICK

See also: Malinowski, Radcliffe-Brown, functionalism, colonialism

Further reading

Asad, T. (ed.) (1973) *Anthropology and the Colonial Encounter*, London: Ithaca Press

Carrier, J.G. (1995) 'Introduction', in J.G. Carrier (ed.) *Occidentalism*, Oxford: Clarendon Press

Dumont, L. (1975) 'Preface to the French Edition of Evans-Pritchard's *The Nuer*', in J.H.M. Beattie and R.G. Lienhardt (eds) *Studies in Social Anthropology*, Oxford: Clarendon Press

Kuklick, H. (1992) *The Savage Within*, Cambridge: Cambridge University Press

—— (forthcoming) 'Islands in the Pacific: Darwinian Biogeography and British Anthropology', *American Ethnologist*

Leach, E.R. (1984) 'Glimpses of the Unmentionable in the History of British Social Anthropology', *Annual Review of Anthropology* 13: 1–23

Lubbock, J. ([1870] 1892) *The Origin of Civilisation and the Primitive Condition of Man*, Fourth Edition, London: Longmans, Green

—— (1871) 'On the Development of Relationships', *Journal of the Anthropological Institute* 1: 1–26

Ortner, S.B. (1984) 'Theory in Anthropology Since the Sixties', *Comparative Studies in Society and History* 26: 126–66

Radcliffe-Brown, A.R. (1932) 'The Present Position of Anthropological Studies', Presidential Address to Section H – Anthropology of the British Association for the Advancement of Science, in *Report of the Centenary Meeting of the British Association for the Advancement of Science* [1931], London: The British Association

Stocking Jr, G.W. (1965) 'On the Limits of "Presentism" and "Historicism" in the Historiography of the Behavioral Sciences', *Journal of the History of the Behavioral Sciences* 1: 211–8

—— (1971) 'What's in a Name? The Origins of the Royal Anthropological Institute, 1837–1871', *Man* (n.s.) 6: 369–90

Buddhism

Buddhism is a missionary salvation religion, first taught by the Buddha ('the Enlightened One') in the north Indian Gangetic plain in the sixth and early fifth centuries BC. The Buddha came from the edge of the Brahmanic society of his day, and he reacted both against the ritualist exclusivism of Brahman religion and the extreme asceticism practised by renouncers who followed Jainism (Gombrich 1988).

Buddhism began as a form of humanistic, religious *individualism: each person's salvation lay within their own grasp, regardless of background or sex. Salvation in Buddhism means the attainment of nirvana through overcoming desire. Achieving this required long training and meditation and before that the accumulation of spiritual merit (won by moral actions and supporting Buddhist clerics); this accumulation was presumed to take many lives. Buddhism shares with *Hinduism the doctrine of reincarnation according to one's actions, understood in Buddhism to mean in accordance with the moral qualities of one's actions. At any one time there are some practitioners who are more advanced than others, and this is institutionalized in the distinction, found in all traditional forms of Buddhism, between the Sangha (monastic community) and the laity.

Thus traditional Buddhism was egalitarian only in the sense of believing in spiritual equality of opportunity. The closest Buddhism came to propagating the notion of a community of equal believers was the early idea that all monks were equal strivers on the path to salvation; but even this was modified as Buddhist rulers established hierarchies of abbots and other monastic offices. The role of the laity was always the spiritually inferior one of providing material support for the Sangha.

In modern times a new form of Buddhism has arisen which does assert the equality of all believers. Its followers attend meditation centres rather than monasteries, and reject the spiritual leadership of monks. They understand Buddhism to encompass social reform, social work and (sometimes) socialism. Influenced by nineteenth-century European thought, they see Buddhism as a rational 'philosophy'. This kind of modernist Buddhism has been called Protestant Buddhism by Gombrich and Obeyesekere (1988), not just because it was profoundly influenced by Protestantism, but also because, at least in the Sri Lankan case, it arose as part of a Sinhalese protest against Christian missionary activity and British dominance.

Buddhism today can be divided into the Theravada, found in Burma, Thailand, Laos, Cambodia and Sri Lanka, and the Mahayana, found in Nepal, Tibet, China, Korea, Vietnam and Japan. Both have missionary offshoots in many other parts of the world. Theravada is the older and more conservative form. Mahayana Buddhism first arose around the turn of the common era in north India and added many new scriptures and numerous saint-like bodhisattva figures for the laity to worship. Tantric Buddhism is an esoteric current within the Mahayana, based on still later scriptures. It has played a crucial part in the development and legitimation of priestly roles and instrumental rituals within Mahayana Buddhism.

Until the 1980s there was little substantial anthropological work on Mahayana Buddhism, though more has now begun to be published (Gellner 1992, Mumford 1989, Samuel 1993). For various reasons (Gellner 1990) it was Theravada Buddhism which first attracted a very large amount of extremely high quality scholarship (Gombrich 1971, Keyes 1977, Nash 1966, Spiro 1971, Tambiah 1970).

Initial anthropological enquiries on Buddhism attempted to answer a number of interconnected questions, all ultimately focused on the problem of understanding Buddhism as a religious system: What is the relationship between the worship of the Buddha and the cult of spirits or gods whom Theravada Buddhists worship for worldly ends? Do lay Buddhists really accept total responsibility for their actions and future lives? How do they justify performing rituals for the benefit of dead relatives? What do Buddhists believe they are doing when they worship the Buddha? Do they really accept that he is a dead man who cannot help them? Do lay Buddhists want to attain nirvana? Do lay people really understand the simple rituals of Theravada Buddhism as nothing but aids to the generation of good intentions, as the official explanation would have it, or do they also see them as magically effective? What differences are there in the monks' view of Buddhism and the laity's? What motivates people to become monks or nuns? What do the laity receive for their support of the Sangha?

In anthropological terms, these questions boil down to the following issues: (i) How can an individualistic religion provide for collective ends? (ii) How does the austere virtuoso creed of the texts relate to the practice of ordinary lay Buddhists? (iii) What is the relationship of Buddhism to the non-Buddhist practices and traditions with which Buddhism always coexists? Are they complementary opposites within a single system (Tambiah 1970)? Are they dynamically and historically mutually-defining but competing systems (Mumford 1989)? Is Buddhism in a transformation of wider shamanic practices (Samuel 1993)? Buddhism poses in particularly stark form the problem of *great and little traditions. It also raises the question of the universalizability of the concept of *syncretism (Gombrich 1971).

There has also been debate on the extent to which Buddhism can be said to have provided a theory of the *state. Textual scholars assert that the scriptural story of King Mahasammata was originally meant as a skit on Hindu theories of *kingship, not as a serious Buddhist alternative (Gombrich 1988). How far this satirical intent was misunderstood or ignored subsequently, and how sociologically significant the story was in Theravada countries (Tambiah 1976), remain controversial questions. In the 1980s anthropologists increasingly turned their attention to the role of Buddhist institutions, doctrines and personnel in the development of *nationalism and *political violence. In some cases this meant laying aside questions of authenticity; in others a critique of the role of Buddhism in modern politics seemed to be premised on the older concern with identifying what Buddhism is truly about.

DAVID N. GELLNER

See also: religion, syncretism, great and little traditions, Hinduism

Further reading

Gellner, D.N. (1990) 'Introduction: What is the Anthropology of Buddhism about?', *Journal of the Anthropological Society of Oxford* 21 (2): 95–112

—— (1992) *Monk, Householder, and Tantric Priest: Newar Buddhism and its Hierarchy of Ritual*, Cambridge: Cambridge University Press

Gombrich, R.F. (1971) *Precept and Practice: Traditional Buddhism in the Rural Highlands of Ceylon*, Oxford: Oxford University Press

—— (1988) *Theravada Buddhism: A Social History from Ancient Benares to Modern Colombo*, London: Routledge

Gombrich, R.F. and G. Obeyesekere (1988) *Buddhism Transformed: Religious Change in Sri Lanka*, Princeton: Princeton University Press

Keyes, C.F. (1977) *The Golden Peninsula: Culture and Adaptation in Mainland Southeast Asia*, New York: Macmillan

Mumford, S.R. (1989) *Himalayan Dialogue: Tibetan Lamas and Gurung Shamans in Nepal*, Madison: University of Wisconsin Press

Nash, M. (ed.) (1966) *Anthropological Studies in Theravada Buddhism*, Chicago and London: University of Chicago Press

Samuel, G. (1993) *Civilized Shamans: Buddhism in Tibetan Societies*, Washington: Smithsonian

Spiro, M.E. (1971) *Buddhism and Society: A Great Tradition and its Burmese Vicissitudes*, Berkeley: University of California Press

Tambiah, S.J. (1970) *Buddhism and the Spirit Cults in Northeast Thailand*, Cambridge: Cambridge University Press

—— (1976) *World Conqueror and World Renouncer*, Cambridge: Cambridge University Press

C

cannibalism

The assumption that others, representing different times and places, engaged in cannibalism has been a pervasive feature of Western social thought. As such, the cannibal image has made its inevitable way into contemporary anthropology. In the process, every exotic human group from the Highlands of Papua New Guinea to the Lowlands of South America has been obliged to assume the man-eating mantle as a result of western contact. Initiating the trend in the fifth century BC, Herodotus labelled the Scythians anthropophagi (man eaters). Marco Polo also encountered cannibals in the thirteenth century during his travels to the Orient, likewise Christopher Columbus in his voyages to the New World, and eventually anthropologists spreading out through the then colonial world.

In some earlier instances, such as for the Aztecs, the cannibalism has been assumed to be nutritional (Harner 1977) as the participants sought sources of animal protein; in others the deed was only a ritual as, for instance, the natives of New Guinea sought the spiritual sustenance of friends or foes (Koch 1970). Yet, despite the innumerable allusions to such behaviour for other cultures, there is reason to treat any particular report, and eventually the whole genre, with some scepticism.

This preemptory conclusion is warranted for a number of legitimate scholarly reasons, including the absence of eye-witness accounts (Arens 1979). Depending on time or place, the information on the practice entered the historical record after the first contact – in some instances even after the obliteration of the original culture and the decimation of its population. This was the case for the Aztecs, who were reconstructed as cannibals, initially ritual, and then 500 years later nutritional, long after the supposed fact. Moreover, the reporters who documented the now defunct cannibal cultural system were the subsequent agents of the imperial power that had destroyed the society and were now engaged in the secondary process of conversion and exploitation of its sorry remnants. By this time Aztec informants converted to the new faith claimed internal others, such as the nobility or priesthood, had indulged in such practices. Consequently, rather than documenting a custom, reports of alleged cannibalism functioned primarily to legitimize European conquest.

This suspect position could have been rectified later by modern anthropologists living among their subjects. However, second-hand reports on cannibalism in the just recent past continued to accumulate in the twentieth century until the topic became a staple of introductory texts and popular accounts of other cultures (see Harris 1977 and 1987). Thus, the pattern continues to be one of circumstantial rather than direct evidence for the purported custom as 'the other' continues to be exoticized.

This is not to imply that cannibalism has never existed. There obviously have been instances of survival cannibalism under abnormal conditions of stress by individuals and groups. There have also been occasions of deviant cannibalistic episodes in all societies, and in some instances, ritualized or pseudo-scientific practices of this sort. For example, pulverized human body parts were prescribed for medicinal purposes in the West until the early twentieth century (Gordon-Grube 1988); they continue to be used in extract form in contemporary medicine; and there are groups in the United States which consume the placenta of the new-born as a 'natural act' (Janzen 1980).

The problem, then, becomes a matter of cultural translation, in the sense of contextual interpretation, and thus, the meaning of the behaviour. Unfortunately, there has been a simplistic and unwarranted tendency to label non-Western societies in which such instances occur as cannibalistic, while not similarly characterizing our own. Taken together with presumptions of cannibalism with little or no reliable evidence, this proclivity has resulted in a veritable universe of cannibals saying more about the collective mentality of the West than the actual behaviour of others. We are not alone in this tendency, however. In many other parts of the world, Europeans are assumed to be the cannibals (Lewis 1986).

W. ARENS

See also: nutrition, food, pollution and purity

Further reading

Arens, W. (1979) *The Man-Eating Myth: Anthropology and Anthropophagy*, New York: Oxford University Press

Gordon-Grube, K. (1988) 'Anthropophagy in Post-Renaissance Europe: The Tradition of Medical Cannibalism', *American Anthropologist* 90: 405–9

Harner, M. (1977) 'The Ecological Basis for Aztec Sacrifice', *American Ethnologist* 4: 117–35

Harris, M. (1977) *Cannibals and Kings*, New York: Random House

Harris, M. (1987) *Cultural Anthropology*, New York: Harper and Row

Janzen, K. (1980) 'Meat of Life', *Science Digest* (Nov. Dec.): 78–81

Koch, K. (1970) 'Cannibalistic Revenge in Jale Warfare', *Natural History* 79: 41–50

Lewis, I. (1986) *Religion in Context*, Cambridge: Cambridge University Press

capitalism

Capitalism eludes its definitions. It has been called free enterprise and defined as production for a global *market in which goods, services and labour are priced. Ownership is private and alienable and that which is owned can easily change hands in a monetary transaction. Profits are sought in market *exchanges and are made available for further investment. Such definitions tend to create a rupture in history between advanced market economies and earlier periods of time or pre-colonial societies geographically remote from the West. Although *economic anthropologists study capitalist phenomena, other branches of anthropology study them as well by examining such features as the cultural dimensions of the commodity or emergent lifestyles in ↑ popular music in distant areas of the w(

The causes and origins of large-sca¹ formation have been debated by econon. rians; the rise of capitalism has been ↓ in Western Europe and particularly Englan⸤ Fernand Braudel (1977) considered the long-distance, sea-borne trade that opened the Atlantic and Pacific Basins to high-volume markets as a vitally important source of stimulation. Both the London Company of Merchants Trading to the East Indies, chartered by the Crown in 1600, and the Dutch East India Company served to move the state formation of companies to new levels of organization, to pool investment funds, to self-insure against disaster by spreading liability, to create new domestic and international markets, and to sponsor long-distance trade. It has been shown that the national institutions evolving during the early moments of capital development were significant for the rise of *colonialism and also the Industrial Revolution.

The study of capitalism by anthropologists was stimulated after World War II by fieldwork conducted among *peasants who had been radicalized by Marxist ideals and also by the student protests of the late 1960s. In conjunction with *Marxist anthropologists in France, British social anthropologists began to ask if the structure of inequality had preceded capitalist economic development and if capitalist modes of production were substantially different from those that did not make profits. In the US *cultural materialists argued that profit-making constructed anew every aspect of society in all parts of the world. Scholarly meetings, provocative formulations, and the inauguration of studies brought a focus to the workings of capitalism; the neo-Weberians breathed new life into †Weber's definitions and studies of the rise of the market and the Protestant ethic. In addition to Marx and Weber, †Mauss's *The Gift* has been rethought, and changes in exchange as people move from a face-to-face economy to a market system have been explored.

The study of capitalist processes whether foregrounded or backgrounded, has served to shift the field of anthropological inquiry away from predominant concern with non-Western societies and to place the Western and non-Western on a more equal footing. Neither Marx, Weber nor Mauss provide the sole focus for the wide range of study conducted. Issues of *money, the commodity, religious *resistance and *identity formation through the construction of mass markets break out of the easy definitions of capitalism, and anthropologists' case studies reveal the diversity of the phenomena while at the same time pointing to certain regularities that obtain.

Inquiries into contemporary capitalism include a large array of issues and geographical areas. *Gender studies have been prominent due in part to the massive restructuring of the *family induced by the formation of international markets, the introduction of wage-earning and the displacement of local roles. In Africa, substantial research has informed understanding of the course of economic *development through examination of incomes generated outside the official system, prominently a domain of women (MacGaffey *et al.* 1991). Bribery, corruption, smuggling and trade in illegal substances is not only occurring globally, but serves in countries without a highly developed public and legitimized market economy to foster economic growth. Surprisingly, it also fosters an increasing search by the newly affluent for legitimation and the building of legal institutions. In Kathmandu research has shown that new media audiences among the young create new consumer spheres through the introduction of media assemblages; for example, magazine advertisements tied into clothing and musical styles simultaneously. *Possession ceremonies by troupes of Hauka performers among the Songhay in Niger mime the colonial and post-colonial presence while redirecting its power. The effect on local peoples of growth (stimulated by national governments and international lending institutions) in regional economies of third world countries on local peoples has been closely documented. There has been a surge of interest in European ethnography; concern with the entangled growth of *nationalism and the anthropological enterprise; close observation of resistance and rebellion, and inter-ethnic conflicts; studies of commodification and commodities such as coffee and sugar; studies of women's roles in traditional and new markets and the conflicts generated from such transitions. Anthropologists' research interest has expanded into the debates over intellectual property, the legal ownership of such things as brand names, chemical formulae, the 'look and feel' of images produced by software, logos, cartoon figures, songs, poems, and images and texts of all sorts including their electronic storage, retrieval and transmission.

In capitalism, the extended corporate form, traced to its beginnings in the Cluniac order after AD 910, has dominated the recent course of world societies. Contemporary capitalism stimulates three modes of corporate organization: those organized for profit, as in the private firm; those which govern and are public and governmental; and the non-profitmaking, such as the non-governmental organizations (NGOs) that lobby in the halls of the United Nations and represent among other things the interests of native peoples worldwide. Studies of dynastic families (Marcus 1992), non-profitmaking cultural institutions, and old élites who have willingly married family members with industrial fortunes have also been studied in Europe, the US and Asia.

The most neglected area of inquiry has been in the realm of materiality. Whatever else they do, capitalist enterprises produce a plethora of new, often dangerous material substances, many of them rich with their own abilities to act. Few studies focus on the physical agency of materials transformed – in corporate laboratories through science, manufacturing and marketing – into consumer items that form great networks of objects, scientific claims, political responses and consumer anxieties, preferences and identities. Research into the social organization of the material-cultural world is needed. At the same time little critical attention has been paid to the new linguistic formation, both pragmatic and rhetorical, that exemplifies *discourses of the marketplace. It is clearly the case that native languages are being transformed from within, not just new words but by new forms of pragmatic dealings tied to market exchanges.

DAN ROSE

See also: consumption, development, economic anthropology, exchange, markets, Marxism and anthropology

Further reading

Berman, H.J. (1983) *Law and Revolution: The Formation of the Western Legal Tradition*, Cambridge: Harvard University Press

Braudel, F. (1977) *Afterthoughts on Material Civilization and Capitalism*, Baltimore: John Hopkins University Press

Carrier, J. (1990) 'The Symbolism of Possession in Commodity Advertising' *Man* (n.s.) 25: 693–706

Hannerz, U. (1992) *Cultural Complexity: Studies in the Social Organization of Meaning*, New York: Columbia University Press

Marcus, G.E. (1992) *Lives in Trust: The Fortunes of Dynastic Families in Late Twentieth-Century America*, Boulder: Westview Press

MacGaffey, J. *et al.* (1991) *The Real Economy of Zaire: The Contribution of Smuggling and Other Unofficial Activities to National Wealth*, Philadelphia: University of Pennsylvania Press

McDonogh, G.W. (1986) *The Good Families of Barcelona: A Social History of Power in the Industrial Era*, Princeton: Princeton University Press

Rose, D. (1991) 'Wordly Discourses: Reflections on Pragmatic Utterances and on the Culture of Capital' *Public Culture* 4: 109–27

cargo cult

The South Pacific cargo cult was one of the outstanding puzzles of post-World War II anthropology. In the post-war era, the discipline turned its attention away from the colonial management of subject peoples, and the recording of rapidly dying *cultures, to issues of social change, *modernization and *development and its effects. One such reaction to an amplifying global system was the *millennial movement which, in Melanesia, came to be labelled 'cargo cult'. Since 1945, anthropologists and others have located several hundred cargo cults, most of these in Melanesia. Some of these movements continue active, having institutionalized themselves in to local churches and political parties.

The basic lineaments of cargo cults became well known, so much so that a cargo cult provided the climactic scenes of the 1963 cult classic *Mondo Cane*. (The cargo story has also been replotted by novelists, poets and playwrights including Ayi Armah, Maurice Guy, David Lan, Thomas Merton and Randolph Stow.) A cargo †prophet receives a message that *ancestors, or often the Americans or other powerful outsiders, have promised boatloads or planeloads of cargo. This cargo consists of Western manufactured goods, including tinned food, clothing, tools, vehicles and refrigerators, as well as *money. Many Melanesians had enjoyed improved access to such items during the war years, but goods became scarcer when military forces pulled back from the Pacific. A variant of the cargo story is that ancestors are already shipping cargo, but that Europeans have schemed to hijack these shipments so that they fail to arrive.

The typical prophetic message holds that if people establish social harmony and consensus, setting aside disputes and disruptive practices such as sorcery, then cargo will arrive. In some cults, including the John Frumm movement on Tanna, Vanuata, prophets advocated the revitalization of traditional practices of *dance, the use of the drug kava (Piper Methysticum) and restoration of pre-colonial residence patterns. In others, such as Munus Islands Paliau movement, cult leaders recommended wholesale abandonment of tradition and its replacement with European manners. Prophets typically prescribed more specific courses of action to induce cargo's arrival, including mass gatherings on appointed days, the construction of airfields, docks, warehouses and new villages, the raising of flag-poles and short-wave radio masts, burial or washing of money, sexual licence or abstinence, graveyard offerings of money and flowers, military-style marching and drilling and especially dancing.

It was this sort of cultic *ritual, alongside people's increased *resistance to Christian missionaries and to labour and head tax obligations, that excited administrative concern. From the mid-1940s to the mid-1950s, colonial regimes commonly arrested cult leaders, including those of the Solomon Islands' Maasina Rule (organized principally on Malaita Island), the Yali movement of Papua New Guinea's north coast, as well as the Paliau and John Frumm movements. By the late 1950s, government policy towards cults shifted from repression to co-optation. Relations between long-lived movements and the now independent Melanesian states continue to oscillate between suspicion and cooperation.

Beginning also in the 1950s, cargo cults stimulated a rich ethnographic literature of description and comparison; and this literature contributed to important arguments about the nature of anthropological understanding (e.g. Ian Jarvie's *The Revolution in Anthropology* [1964]). Monographs by Jean Guiart (1956) and †Margaret Mead (1956) provided early descriptions of John Frumm and Paliau, respectively. Kenelm Burridge's *Mambu* (1960) and Peter Lawrence's *Road Belong Cargo* (1964) were important cargo monographs; as was Peter Worsley's *The Trumpet Shall Sound* ([1957] 1968), as an influential overview of the cargo literature.

Anthropologists have approached cults from two directions. Some take cargo cults to be a Melanesian version of universal millennial movements that erupt in periods of social crisis and disruption. This sort of explanation seeks the psychological and social functions of cargo cults. Responding to emotions of †relative deprivation and to general confusion precipitated by rapid social change, cults may transform local systems of understanding, work to re-establish people's sense of dignity, provide explanations of/for inequality and so on. Socially, cults may function to create larger unities to resist the colonial or postcolonial oppressor, providing a language of political protest.

Other anthropologists have instead explained cults as emerging from Melanesian culture itself. Rather than a universal form of reaction to social change and oppression, cargo cults are particular Melanesian forms of creativity and cultural imagination. An emphasis on acquiring cargo reflects the cultural importance of *exchange of wealth within Melanesia. Cultic ritual and organization, likewise, reveal island understandings of economic production, of ancestral inspiration, the nature of social change and local *Big Man politicking.

Anthropological explanation of cargo cults, either as reactions to external forces or as internal processes of cultural dynamism, soon raised misgivings about the accuracy of the term. Cargo means much more than simple goods, and cult more than irrational ritual. The label 'cargo cult' first appeared in the November 1945 issue of the colonial news magazine *Pacific Islands Monthly* (Bird 1945). Usage of the term spread rapidly, anthropologists borrowing it to relabel Pacific social movements dating back as far as the 1830s. Previously, many of these had be described as instances of Vailala Madness after F.E. Williams's 1923 analysis of a movement near Kerema, Papua New Guinea.

Although a terminological improvement upon Vailala Madness, use of the label 'cargo cult', within anthropology at least, has declined. While still standard fare in introductory anthropological texts, ethnographers have turned to more politic descriptive alternatives (e.g., nativistic, adjustment, protonationalist, micronationalist, local protest, developmental self-help, regional separatist or Holy Spirit movements).

Journalists and others, however, still apply the term to describe social movements in Melanesia and beyond. Reports of cargo cult, for example, coloured accounts of a secessionist movement on Bougainville Island in the 1990s. Although cargo cults are less commonly discovered in the Pacific, they now erupt globally in a lively politics of labelling. Euro-Disney, the new Australian Parliament House, Japanese enchantment with Hollywood movie studios, Eastern European fascination with capitalism, Third World development

efforts and a panoply of other ventures have all been denounced as cargo cults (Lindstrom 1993). Along with 'culture', †'worldview' and *'ethnicity', the 'cargo cult' is proving one of anthropology's most popular concepts beyond the discipline.

LAMONT LINDSTROM

See also: millennial movements, religion, Pacific: Melanesia

Further reading

Bird, N. M. (1945) 'Is There Danger of a Post-War Flare-up Among New Guinea Natives?' *Pacific Island Monthly* 16 (4, Nov.): 69–70

Burridge, K. (1960) *Mambu: A Study of Melanesian Cargo Movements and their Social and Ideological Background*, London: Methuen

Guiart, J. (1956) *Un Siècle et Demi de Contacts Culturels a Tanna, Nouvelles-Hebrides*, Publications de la Société des Oceanistes no 5, Paris: Musée de l'Homme

Jarvie, I. C. (1964) *The Revolution in Anthropology*, Chicago: Henry Regnery

Lawrence, P. (1964) *Road Belong Cargo: A Study of the Cargo Movement in the Southern Madang District, New Guinea*, Manchester: Manchester University Press

Lindstrom, L. (1993) *Cargo Cult: Strange Stories of Desire from Melanesia and Beyond*, Honolulu: University of Hawaii Press

Mead, M. (1956) *New Lives for Old: Cultural Transformation – Manus, 1928–1953*, New York: William Morrow and Company

Williams, F. E. (1923) *The Vailala Madness and the Destruction of Native Ceremonies in the Gulf Division*, Anthropology Report no 4, Port Moresby: Territory of Papua

Worsley, P. ([1957] 1968) *The Trumpet Shall Sound: A Study of 'Cargo' Cults in Melanesia*, New York: Schoken Books

Caribbean

It can be claimed that the social and cultural anthropology of the Caribbean has been made peripheral to the core of the discipline. This is because of the ways anthropology became professionalized and the concomitant epistemological requirements to look for, and create if necessary, 'pristine' *cultures and *social structures. This situation is *not* a reflection of the Caribbean's intrinsic anthropological value. Centuries of hegemonic *colonialism, *migration, *slavery and forced labour, miscegenation, and 'derivative' cultures broken off from their places of origin, all meant that anthropology defined the Caribbean as 'hybrid' and †'creole'. Thus, anthropology's 'othering' enterprise – simultaneously providing a subject for, and ordering status within, the discipline (the more 'other' the better) – made the Caribbean anthropologically inferior to more 'exotic' ethnographic locales.

Yet, Caribbean anthropology has always involved issues that only became popular in the discipline as a whole in the 1980s and 1990s, including colonialism, *history and anthropology, diaspora processes, plantations, *gender, *ethnicity, the 'crisis of representation' characteristic of *postmodernism, local *world system connections, the links between fiction and anthropology-writing and the connections between ethnology and *nationalism, to name a few.

The notion of 'contact' determines the very anthropological definition of the Caribbean itself. 'The Caribbean' can be defined as the societies of the archipelago located in the Caribbean Sea proper, from Cuba south to Trinidad. In practice, it has also been defined to include the Bahamas islands and Bermuda to the north, Belize in *Central America, and Guyana, Suriname, and French Guiana on the northeast shoulder of South America. A good case is also made to include within this designation the Caribbean diaspora communities created by a history of intra- and inter-regional migration, from Central America to North American and European cities such as Miami, Toronto, New York, Amsterdam, London, and Paris.

Caribbean ontologies

Casting the definitional net wide is justified because of underlying ontological arrangements. Mintz has long argued (e.g. 1974) that despite centuries of colonialism involving at least six imperial powers, certain similarities are visible (but not totally determining) because of the plantation complex, the site of Europe's first industries, and *political economies based on extraction of raw materials, primarily sugar, for the benefit of the metropole, and the resulting ethnic-class division of labour. The Caribbean received up to 40 per cent of the approximately ten million African slaves brought to the Americas from the early sixteenth century to the mid-nineteenth century; as well as indentured labourers from India, China, and Europe's periphery, migrants from as far away as the Middle East, and colonial administrators, plantation owners, merchants and workers from the metropoles. For Mintz, this history was an ever-present reality. Not only did it provide context, but the waves of the *longue durée* continu-

ally affected ethnographic realities. Apparent contradictions and paradoxes were explained by reference to history: the plantation was *capitalist, but depended on forced labour. *Peasantries were, where they existed, 'reconstituted', established, as nowhere else, *after* capitalism and not swept away by it, yet continually affected by movements in the world system. Historical processes informed the region's manifest ethnic and cultural heterogeneity and explained it as a constructed reality for anthropologists, but naturalized this reality for Caribbean peoples. These forces accounted for a historical consciousness among Caribbean peoples, but it was a consciousness which many anthropologists could not (or would not) recognize.

The African diaspora and the cultural politics of ethnology

Twentieth-century Caribbean anthropology began with the collection of *folklore by local ethnologists, even though their contribution was often minimized by professional anthropologists. These included Lydia Cabrera (1900–91) in Cuba, much encouraged by her brother-in-law Fernando Ortiz (1881–1969), Antonio Salvador Pedreira (1899–1939) in Puerto Rico, and Jean Price-Mars (1876–1969) in Haiti – upper and middle-class scholars who dealt with Afro-Caribbean themes. The aims of some were avowedly political. Early North American scholars were the students of *Boas: Martha Beckwith (1871–1959), who collected folklore and data on †ethnobotany in Jamaica; Zora Neale Hurston (1903–60), whose work in Haiti experimented with fiction-writing techniques; and †Melville J. Herskovits, whose *fieldwork was conducted in Suriname, Haiti and Trinidad. The impact of Herskovits's work (often in collaboration with his wife Frances) was substantial. He aimed at exploding racist depictions of New World Blacks by maintaining the conceptual separation of *race and culture and by tracing African cultural survivals in *religion, *language, the *family, etc. from what he called the *West African 'cultural area' with such theoretical tools as †'acculturation', 'cultural focus', and 'reinterpretations' (e.g. Herskovits 1941). In the process, he trained students and inspired others to work in the Caribbean. The opposing theoretical poles of the Afro-American culture question were framed by the debate between Herskovits and the African-American sociologist E. Franklin Frazier. The former stressed the

African origin of (for example) Afro-American family forms, while the latter argued that Africans were stripped of their culture in the enslavement process. This intellectual tension persists. One influential view questions only the levels on which such Africa-New World continuities should be sought: 'less on sociocultural forms' and more on 'values' and 'unconscious "grammatical" principles' (Mintz and Price 1992: 9).

Postwar developments

The debate on the Afro-American family was hardly academic. British colonial administrators, for example, officially decried the high number of what anthropologists came to call 'female-headed' or †matrifocal Afro-Caribbean families (seen in contrast to 'normal' nuclear families). The anthropological response was a plethora of family and *kinship studies. Until the 1970s, Caribbean anthropology was preoccupied with the whys and wherefores of †'matrifocal' families, 'absent fathers', 'female-headed' *households, 'illegitimacy', 'child-shifting', marital 'instability', 'loose' kinship ties, 'outside children', 'visiting' sexual unions, 'extra-residential mating' and a number of other objectifying terms steeped in value judgements. Explicit colonial ideologies became implicit anthropological assumptions as anthropologists often endeavoured to explain these 'pathologies' and 'deviations' from North Atlantic value-norms. This concern was buttressed by imported theoretical orientations, most notably structural *functionalism. Studies focussed on lower-class Black family life in rural areas. Poverty was made to explain the family form and the family form was made to explain poverty. The study of three communities in Jamaica by Clarke, a member of an elite white Jamaican family who studied under *Malinowski at the London School of Economics, is a prime example (1957). And those who lauded the Black family form as a positive 'adaptation' to poverty could not explain why other similarly impoverished groups (e.g. East Indians) did not make the same adaptations.

Later opponents of functionalism emphasized history and *class conflict. Martínez-Alier's (now Stolcke) classic work (1974), based on her Oxford D.Phil. thesis, is an extraordinary anthropological encounter with history. She showed how †hierarchy became 'racially' organized in nineteenth-century Cuba and how this was intimately tied to the *marriage and kinship system and gender ideology. In revising his functionalist stance of three decades earlier, Raymond T. Smith, a Briton based for many years at the University of Chicago and who sent many postgraduate students to the Caribbean, located the family and kinship complex in class relations: 'The family is not the cause of poverty; its particular shape is part of the social practice of class relations' (1988: 182). For Smith, this system was typified by a 'dual marriage' system where status equals marry, but men of higher and women of lower status enter extra-legal unions; a greater emphasis on †consanguineal solidarity than on conjugal ties; a matrifocal (but not matriarchal) family practice (where 'matrifocality' now refers to the 'segregation of sex roles and the salience of mothering within the domestic domain' [1988: 182]); 'domestic' activities not confined to a single 'household'; and sex-role differentiation, all wrapped up in a specific set of local cultural assumptions.

Gender studies tended to arise from family and kinship studies and have thus been underdeveloped as such. Local scholars were at the forefront, questioning why women were only visible within the family, even as some anthropological models depicted an 'independent' Black 'matriarch' as the ideal-type. Others questioned the invisibility of men altogether. Wilson (1973) tied his 'respectability' and 'reputation' dualism to cultural constructions of gender. Respectability is primarily the domain of women and involves the approximation of the value standards of the colonial and local elite. Reputation is primarily, though not exclusively, the domain of men. Reputation is an alternative, egalitarian value system with its roots in local estimations of worth. Descriptively evocative and once theoretically compelling, this schema has been criticized by those who argued that Wilson's overwhelmingly normative focus did not account for power differentials and by those who argued that his depictions of women obscured their activities (see Besson 1993; Yelvington 1995: 163 – 78).

Equally paradigmatic during the postwar decades was the debate surrounding the *plural society thesis. The leading proponent was M.G. Smith, a middle-class Jamaican who studied under †Daryll Forde in London and whose early work was on West Africa. Following British colonial administrator J.S. Furnivall and Dutch pioneering Caribbean scholar Rudolf A.J. van Lier, Smith (1965) posited the existence of separate ethnic/cultural segments in each society that maintained separate and distinct institutions and practices. These segments and corporate groups were held together by the over-arching power of colonial governments. The 1950s and 1960s witnessed a fierce debate between the 'plural society school', the 'stratification school', functionalists like R.T. Smith and Trinidadian sociologist Lloyd Braithwaite who argued for the existence of a common core of values, and the 'plantation society school', who felt that Caribbean culture pertained directly to the exigencies of the plantation. The debate was never resolved. In his later years Smith's thesis was criticized as middle-class ideology parading as theory and Smith himself acknowledged the 'overwhelmingly negative reaction' to his ideas by Caribbean scholars.

In the postwar watershed era, anthropologists from European colonial powers tended to study 'their' colonial societies. As the Caribbean increasingly entered into the US political, military, and economic orbit, and as Caribbean 'social problems' seemed to mirror some at home, American anthropologists increasingly discarded their exclusive focus on Native American groups. Neither North Americans nor Europeans could import their theories or methods wholesale. For example, the 'community studies method' in North America was met with the reality of rural-urban-national-world connections. The *People of Puerto Rico* project (Steward *et al.* 1956) was an ambitious early attempt to specify the workings of these historical links. Yet the Caribbean also came to be seen as a training ground for anthropologists who were to go on to bigger and better things. Even the doyens of postmodernism Michael M.J. Fischer and George E. Marcus did their early fieldwork in Jamaica and Guyana, respectively. Caribbean anthropology has tended to mirror the linguistic and national insularity of the region. Very few scholars did fieldwork in more than one language.

The next generation and beyond

It was natural that later generations of Caribbeanists expressed the contemporary concerns of the discipline at large as well as the themes of their predecessors. For example, in his semiotic analysis of 'race' and 'colour' in pre-independence Trinidad and Tobago, Segal (1993) showed how colonial constructions saw Blacks as culturally naked, who thus could only hope to be infused with European teachings, and East Indians as possessing ancestral culture, albeit an inferior one. Moreover, this theme was utilized by the middle-class Black and 'Brown' Creole inheritors of power as they appropriated lower-class Black popular cultural forms and elevated them to 'national' status.

With a multi-level focus, Williams (1991) demonstrated the articulations of ethnicity and nationalism in Guyana. The construction of ethnic and cultural difference and an ordering of ethnic groups to prove and justify contribution, authenticity, and citizenship was connected to the acts of cultural contestation over which group has historically contributed the most to 'the nation', which therefore gets constructed as 'belonging' to that group. This is achieved through a conceptual move of inversion, where the European-dominated social status hierarchy is turned on its head.

Questions of history and peoplehood have guided the long-term work of Richard and Sally Price among the Saramaka maroons in Suriname. In *First-Time* (1983), Richard Price recorded the Saramaka knowledge of the period 1685 to 1762 when their ancestors escaped slavery, established communities, and resisted European power. Price split the pages of his book to juxtapose these narratives of 'First-time', the 'fountainhead of collective identity', with his own commentaries and citation of Western written sources.

The immediacy of *power and class practice is evident in the urban ethnographies, only prevalent since the mid-1970s. These include Austin's (later Austin-Broos) study of two neighbourhoods in Kingston, Jamaica and the hegemonic 'legitimizing ideology of education' maintained through local class relations and international economic pressure (1984), and a study of women factory workers in Trinidad that traces †hegemony to control over the production process, and the complex ways social identities are dialectically determined and commodified in that same process (Yelvington 1995).

The region Trouillot called 'an open frontier in anthropological theory' (1992) remains relatively understudied. Of the 5,918 anthropologists in academic settings listed by the American Anthropological Association in the 1994–95 *Guide to Departments*, only 180 (3 per cent) list the Caribbean as one of their regional interests. A count of the 584 members of the Association of Social Anthropologists of the Commonwealth in 1994 revealed that only 32 (5.5 per cent) listed the Caribbean as a regional interest. Yet it is interesting to speculate how differently the discipline would have developed if *Radcliffe-Brown had written *The Virgin Islanders* and it featured the stylized grieving of the Afro-Caribbean wake; if *Malinowski had written *Argonauts of the Eastern Caribbean* and it was about reciprocity among fisherfolk in Martinique; if Mead had written *Coming of Age in Jamaica* and it was about female adolescence there; or if †Evans-Pritchard had written *Witchcraft, Oracles and Magic among the Habañeros* and it was about *santería* worshippers in working-class Havana and the *syncretization of Catholic saints and Yoruba *orishas* that characterizes the religion; now that anthropology has begun to recognize that, in terms of 'hybrid' and 'creole' cultures and social structures, and the presence of history, the world has been and is becoming more like the Caribbean.

KEVIN A. YELVINGTON

See also: colonialism, family, household, kinship, peasant, slavery

Further reading

Austin, D.J. (1984) *Urban Life in Kingston, Jamaica: The Culture and Class Ideology of Two Neighborhoods*, New York: Gordon and Breach

Besson, J. (1993) 'Reputation and Respectability Reconsidered: A New Perspective on Afro-Caribbean Peasant Women', in J.H. Momsen (ed.) *Women and Change in the Caribbean*, London: James Currey/Bloomington: Indiana University Press/Kingston: Ian Randle

Clarke, E. (1957) *My Mother who Fathered Me*, London: George Allen and Unwin

Herskovits, M.J. (1941) *The Myth of the Negro Past*, New York: Harper and Brothers

Martínez-Alier, V. (1974) *Marriage, Class and Colour in Nineteenth-Century Cuba*, Cambridge: Cambridge University Press

Mintz, Sidney W. (1974) *Caribbean Transformations*, Chicago: Aldine

Mintz, Sidney W. and R. Price (1992) *The Birth of African-American Culture: An Anthropological Perspective*, Boston: Beacon Press

Price, R. (1983) *First-Time: The Historical Vision of an Afro-American People*, Baltimore: The Johns Hopkins University Press

Segal, D.A. (1993) '"Race" and "Colour" in Pre-Independence Trinidad and Tobago', in K.A. Yelvington (ed.) *Trinidad Ethnicity*, London: Macmillan/Knoxville: University of Tennessee Press

Smith, M.G. (1965) *The Plural Society in the British West Indies*, Berkeley: University of California Press

Smith, R.T. (1988) *Kinship and Class in the West Indies: A Genealogical Study of Jamaica and Guyana*, Cambridge: Cambridge University Press

Steward, J., R. Manners, E. Wolf, E. Padilla, S. Mintz and R. Scheele (1956) *The People of Puerto Rico*, Urbana: University of Illinois Press

Trouillot, M.-R. (1992) 'The Caribbean Region: An Open Frontier in Anthropological Theory', *Annual Review of Anthropology* 21: 19–42

Williams, B.F. (1991) *Stains on My Name, War in My Veins: Guyana and the Politics of Cultural Struggle*, London: Duke University Press

Wilson, P.J. (1973) *Crab Antics: The Social Anthropology of English-speaking Negro Societies of the Caribbean*, New Haven: Yale University Press

Yelvington, K.A. (1995) *Producing Power: Ethnicity, Gender, and Class in a Caribbean Workplace*, Philadelphia: Temple University Press

caste

Caste has been described as the fundamental social institution of India. Sometimes the term is used metaphorically to refer to rigid social distinctions or extreme social exclusiveness wherever found, and some authorities have used the term 'colour-caste system' to describe the stratification based on race in the United States and elsewhere. But it is among the Hindus in India that we find the system in its most fully developed form, although analogous forms exist among Muslims, Christians, Sikhs and other religious groups in *South Asia. It is an ancient institution, having existed for at least 2,000 years among the Hindus who developed not only elaborate caste practices but also a complex theory to explain and justify those practices (Dumont 1970). The theory has now lost much of its force although many of the practices continue.

The English word 'caste' might mean either *varna* or *jati*. *Varna* refers to an ideal model, a plan or design of society whereas *jati* refers to the actual social groups with which people identify themselves and on whose basis they interact with each other. The *varnas* are only four in number – Brahman, Kshatriya, Vaishya and Shudra – and they were the same and were ranked in the same order among Hindus everywhere, from ancient to modern times; this scheme has now lost its legal authority and also much of its social authority. The *jatis* are many in number and often internally segmented; although they vary from one religion to another and have changed their identities over time, they continue to maintain an active existence among most Indians.

Membership in a caste is by birth, and caste is extremely important in *marriage. Most Indians, especially Hindus, marry within their caste. Nowadays individuals might marry in a

different subcaste of their own caste, and sometimes in a different, though cognate, caste; but
marriages without consideration of caste are still
rare. In the past, each caste was associated with
a distinct traditional occupation, and a caste might
be divided into subcastes in keeping with differences in occupational practice. The emergence of
a large number of modern, 'caste-free' occupations has greatly weakened the specific association
between caste and occupation; but there is still a
general association, such that those in superior
non-manual occupations are mostly from the
upper castes, and those in inferior manual occupations mostly from the lower castes. Castes were
elaborately ranked in the past, and the social
ranking of castes is still conspicuous. This ranking
has been characteristically expressed in the ritual
idiom of pollution and purity, although economic
factors were always important and are now
increasingly so.

Caste has been closely associated with a variety
of *ritual practices and with religious beliefs about
a person's station in life. The ritual and religious
basis of caste has weakened greatly, but it has been
given a new lease of life by democratic politics
which encourages the mobilization of electoral
support on the basis of caste. In this respect, caste
loyalties tend to act like ethnic loyalties in many
contemporary societies.

ANDRÉ BÉTEILLE

See also: Hinduism, inequality, pollution and purity,
Asia: South

Further reading

Béteille, A. (1969) *Castes, Old and New: Essays in Social
    Structure and Social Stratification*, Bombay: Asia
    Publishing House
—— (1991) *Society and Politics in India: Essays in a
    Comparative Perspective*, London: Athlone Press
Dumont, L. (1980 [1966]) *Homo Hierarchicus: The Caste
    System and its Implications*, Chicago: University of
    Chicago Press
Srinivas, M.N. (1962) *Caste in Modern India and other Essays*,
    Bombay: Asia Publishing House

cattle complex

The term cattle complex derives from †Melville
Herskovits's PhD thesis, which the *American
Anthropologist* serialized as 'The Cattle Complex in
East Africa'. Herskovits adapted a method, devel-
oped by †Clark Wissler and others, which sought
to classify the different American Indian cultures

according to the complex of traits which each
demonstrated, to understand the diffusions and
mixings of those traits and to map the areas in
which they were found. The method derived from
attempts to bring order into the arrangement of
museum exhibits but attributed equal importance to myths, ceremonies and 'psychological
elements'. A †culture trait, it was argued, is not
static and, as it moves from one region to another,
may so often change both its form and its function as to become almost unrecognizable; so, in
order both to isolate it and classify it, each has to
be examined comparatively and contextually as
part of a culturally integrated cluster or 'complex'.
Herskovits continued to extend the concept.

Cattle-keeping in itself, however economically
important, was not sufficient for inclusion in the
'cattle complex'. Cattle, above all else, had to give
meaning to the life of the people; to be their solace
and passion and the source of the images which
express their social and imaginative lives. Cattle,
the providers of milk, should only be slaughtered
to mark the great transitional events of life, from
birth to final funerary rites. Cattle were known
by their individual attributes. Cattle raiding
according to prescribed conventions was general.
The special honour accorded to cattle often
created both a simple and sparse subsistence
system based on crop cultivation, in which women
did much of the work, and a prestige system
based on cattle ownership restricted to men.
Most enduring social relationships were mediated through the loan, gift or *exchange of cattle.
*Marriage required their transfer in the form of
†bridewealth. A cattleless man could enjoy neither
social position nor respect. In some societies, such
as Rwanda, cattle ownership was the source of
political power and the prerogative of the rulers.
The 'cattle complex' was assumed to overlay agricultural cultures which had preceded it.

Using the 'cattle complex' as his criterion
Herskovits delimited an East African Cattle Area,
extending from the *Nilotic Sudan through the
Great Lakes to the Cape: excluding the pastoral
peoples of the eastern Horn but including, as an
extension, the cattle-keepers of south-western
Angola.

What †Lucy Mair (1985) called this 'moul-
dering cliché' has had little influence on
anthropological thought. Unfortunately it was
misused by some white settlers in Kenya to suggest
that Africans suffered from a complex about
cattle in the way that some people do from an

inferiority complex. This patronizing reversal of meaning has led some Africans and some *development practitioners, who have never read Herskovits, to accuse anthropologists of cultural arrogance and misrepresentation. This is ironic because Herskovits was the only anthropologist invited by Kwame Nkrumah as an honoured guest at the celebrations for Ghana Independence Day.

P.T.W. BAXTER

See also: culture, Africa: East, pastoralists

Further reading

Herskovits, M. (1926) 'The Cattle Complex in East Africa' *American Anthropologist* 28: 230–72, 361–88, 494–528, 633–64
Mair, L. (1985) 'Letter: The cattle complex', *Man* 20 (4): 743

childhood

Studies of children have been central to the development of the social sciences, and especially of psychology, but the social scientists' perspective tended to project onto all children, everywhere, an idea of childhood that was peculiarly Western. Childhood was taken to be a natural state of pre-social *individualism, one which required that children be rendered social by adults. It is perhaps because anthropologists held this idea that the study of childhood in anthropology has been fitful rather than systematic.

The earliest work is Kidd's (1906) *Savage Childhood* – a detailed and, given the prejudices of its time, remarkably sympathetic description of the lives of Bantu children in *South Africa. In Britain, *Malinowksi's followers routinely included children in their accounts and analyses of *kinship but, with the exception of Read (1960), none produced a full-length monograph on children's lives. Read described how, among the Ngoni of *Central Africa, adults transmit certain cultural skills and values to their children. Her account concentrated on how children learned practical skills (e.g. how boys learned cattle herding and hunting), the respect proper to relations between children and their seniors, and respect for the rule of law. But studies of children had little place in the development of theory in British social anthropology.

By contrast, †Margaret Mead, a pupil of the founder of American cultural anthropology *Franz Boas, made children the focus of her ethnographic and theoretical endeavours – working first on adolescent development in Samoa and later with children of all ages in the Manus Islands, Papua New Guinea, and (with †Gregory Bateson) with Balinese children.

Culture, personality and the child

Mead's interest in children was bound up with her concern to demonstrate the 'cultural relativity' of thought, behaviour and personality. Like her teacher Boas and other cultural anthropologists, she argued that culture was the crucial variable in determining differences between human beings. So, for example, while a 'stormy adolescence' might characterize the experience of American young people, and delinquency be common there, this phenomenon was not universal. Comparing the American childhood experience with the Samoan one she argued that:

> Our life histories are filled with the later difficulties which can be traced back to some early, highly charged experience with sex or with birth or death. And yet Samoan children are familiarized at an early age, and without disaster, with all three. It is very possible that there are aspects of the life of the young child in Samoa which equip it particularly well for passing through life without nervous instability
>
> (Mead 1943 [1928]: 167)

Mead's work on Samoa has been criticized for being based on inadequate *fieldwork and infected by ideological considerations, but it remains the case that she was one of the first anthropologists to realize that 'childhood' is culturally variable and that an understanding of *how* exactly a child becomes an adult is important for anthropology as a comparative study of human possibilities.

*Culture and personality theory, of which Mead was a proponent, became a significant subdisciplinary area in cultural anthropology during the 1940s and 1950s. Its attempt to understand first 'personality' and then 'affect' as a function of culture focused attention on the study of children. Thus John W.M. Whiting, whose work was influenced by social learning theory (a reformulation of †behaviourism in the academic psychology of the time), was concerned to show how culture was 'learned'. The first part of his *Becoming a Kwoma* (1941) describes stages of life among this New Guinea people from infancy to adulthood; the second part is devoted to the teaching techniques that 'inculcate' Kwoma children with, for example, a belief in the supernatural. He offered an explanation of this process in terms of drives, cues and rewards.

The culture and personality perspective which, like social learning theory in psychology, was broadly informed by ideas from *psychoanalysis, gave rise to a number of large-scale cross-cultural studies of child-rearing practices. So, for example, Whiting and Child (1953) used data from seventy-five societies (culled from ethnographies and from the †Human Relations Area Files) to examine child training practices concerned with certain behavioural 'systems': oral, anal, sexual, dependence and aggression. They aimed to discover the degree of correlation between cultural 'traits' derived from the child-training practices and beliefs concerning the causes of illness. So, for example, they argued that early or severe weaning practices produced a high degree of 'oral socialization anxiety' and were likely to be associated with adult beliefs that illness was caused by oral behaviour (i.e. by eating something, by something someone said or by magical spells).

The work of Whiting and Child was concerned largely with the differences between 'cultures', so it included few detailed data on actual children's ideas and behaviour. This was partly rectified in the later 'six cultures' studies, which produced a number of publications, culminating in Whiting and Edwards (1988) *Children of Different Worlds*. This includes many sensitive and careful observations of the behaviour of children between the ages of two and ten in communities in Africa, India, the Philippines, Okinawa, Mexico and the United States; and throughout a consistent attempt is made to relate these data on children to 'household structure'. But the reader is still likely to feel the lack of other data concerning, for example, the interrelation between ideas about kinship, *religion and *political economy and how these ideas inform theories of the *person and, more particularly, of 'the child' in each community.

Passive object or active subject?

The studies by culture and personality theorists, like those by social anthropologists of the processes of *socialization, did not lead to children becoming of much greater interest to mainstream anthropology. Indeed, one can argue that the assumption common to both approaches that children 'learned culture' or, more radically, were 'conditioned by culture', made children the more or less passive objects of adult ideas and practices, and thus of marginal interest to anthropologists. Even Erikson's brilliant *Childhood and Society* (1950) – a most careful and detailed attempt to apply psychoanalytic concepts of psychosexual development to the development of identity across cultures – took culture for granted as already 'given', as expressed in the institutions of adult life.

In academic psychology during this same period †Piaget's theory of child development was exerting considerable influence. Piaget used highly detailed observations of children to argue that their ideas were qualitatively different from those of adults. He showed that the process by which children arrived at a mature understanding of adult concepts of, for example, number, volume, time etc. was *constructive*. In other words, children are not passive receivers of adult ideas; rather they have actively to constitute their understandings of the world. But Piaget tended to assume that the conceptual products of cognitive constructive processes were bound to manifest themselves in all people in the same way, and thus that his findings were universally applicable. Piaget was by and large uninterested in the cultural variability of cognitive development and anthropologists found his work uncongenial and paid little attention to it.

By contrast, †Vygotsky (a Russian contemporary of Piaget) was explicitly concerned to integrate history into his theory of cognitive development. He focused on language as the medium of cognitive transformations, but his work remained largely unexamined by anthropologists. And even though both psychoanalytic and Piagetian theories implicitly entailed an idea of ontogeny as a *historical* process, anthropological theorists on both sides of the Atlantic failed to build such an understanding into their studies of children.

During the 1980s, anthropological concern with children in their own right, and especially with child welfare, became more prominent – perhaps in part as a result of a new anthropological awareness of *gender and *power relations (see e.g. Ennew 1986, Scheper-Hughes 1987). Moreover, contemporary anthropology is showing more radical signs of change in that studies of children are beginning to emerge as significant for mainstream analyses of relations between adults (see e.g. Carsten 1990, Gow 1990). This shift towards an interest in children is in large part a function of a more general shift towards a focus on 'meaning'.

94   **childhood**

From the mid-1960s onwards, the massive influence of the great French anthropologist *Claude Lévi-Strauss and his structuralist analyses of, for example, kinship and *myth in a number of different culture areas, had focused anthropological attention on 'systems of meaning'. Many, if not most, anthropologists resisted becoming structuralists in the Lévi-Straussian mould, but both British social anthropology and American cultural anthropology came under his shadow. By and large it came to be taken for granted that the anthropologist's first task was to demonstrate the logic of culture-specific ideas and practices. One might argue that it was inevitable that this focus on meaning would lead eventually to an increasing anthropological interest in precisely how people make meaning over time, and thus to an interest in how children constitute their understandings of adult life. In this perspective, the nature of child cognitive development became more relevant to anthropologists, as did theories of language acquisition in childhood and of the child's earliest competences (see e.g. Ochs and Schieffelin 1984, Trevarthen 1987).

Making meaning
Thus, in marked contrast to earlier conditioning and socialization theories, 'the child' in contemporary anthropology is understood to be an agent, actively engaged in constituting the ideas and practices that will inform its adult life. This is not to say that the child can alone make meaning out of its experience. Rather, because humans are *biologically social* organisms, the process of making meaning is always mediated by relations with others. So the child constitutes its own understandings out of the meanings made by all those others with whom it interacts. Even so, children may produce entirely valid understandings of their own experience that are in direct opposition to those of adults – a finding that demands analysis of how it is that as adults they seem to have discarded their earlier ideas. The process of the cognitive constitution of concepts over time inevitably entails transformation as well as continuity in the meaning of those same concepts; thus child cognitive development has to be understood as a genuinely historical process (see Toren 1993).

It has long been realized that ideas of 'childhood' are historically specific, but this new perspective on children as producers as well as products of history suggests that anthropologists have critically to examine the concepts of 'the child' that inform their own theories (see James and Prout 1992). It suggests too that studies of children are likely to become ever more central to mainstream anthropological analyses of sociocultural phenomena such as kinship, political economy, and *ritual.

CHRISTINA TOREN
See also: cognition, culture and personality, socialization

Further reading

Carsten, Janet (1991) 'Children in Between: Aspects of Sharing and Mediation Between Houses in Pulau Langkawi', Man (n.s.) 26: 425–44
Ennew, J. (1986) The Sexual Exploitation of Children, Oxford: Polity Press
Erikson, Erik (1977 [1950]) Childhood and Society, St Albans: Triad Paladin
Gow, Peter (1989) 'The Perverse Child: Desire in a Native Amazonian Subsistence Economy', Man (n.s.) 24: 567–82
James, A. and A. Prout (eds) (1990) Constructing and Reconstructing Chilhood, London: Falmer
Kidd, D. (1906) Savage Childhood: A Study of Kafir Children, London: Black
Mead, Margaret (1943 [1928]) Coming of Age in Samoa, Harmondsworth: Penguin Books
Ochs, Elinor and Bambi Schieffelin (1984) Language Socialization Across Cultures, Cambridge: Cambridge University Press
Read, Margaret (1960) Children of their Fathers: Growing up among the Ngoni of Nyasaland, New Haven: Yale University Press
Scheper-Hughes, N. (1987) Child Survival: Anthropological Perspectives on the Treatment and Maltreatment of Children, Dordrecht: D. Reidel Publishing
Toren, Christina (1993) 'Making History: The Significance of Childhood Cognition for a Comparative Anthropology of Mind', Man (n.s.) 28: 461–78
Trevarthen, C. (1987) 'Universal Co-operative Motives: How Infants Begin to Know the Language and Culture of their Parents' in G. Jahoda and I.M. Lewis (eds) Acquiring Culture: Cross-Cultural Studies in Child Development, London and New York: Croom Helm
Whiting, B.B. and C.P. Edwards (1988) Children of Different Worlds, Cambridge, MA: Harvard University Press
Whiting, John W.M. (1941) Becoming a Kwoma, New Haven:Yale University Press
Whiting, John W.M. and Irvin L. Child (1953) Child Training and Personality: A Cross-Cultural Study, New Haven: Yale University Press

Chinese anthropology

In 1902 the Japanese Ariga Nagao's *The Evolution of the Family*, based on *Morgan and †Spencer, was translated into Chinese. But there had long been a tradition within China of writings and pictorial representations of minority and neighbouring peoples perceived as exotic or 'barbaric'. Other translations of Morgan and Spencer, †Westermarck and †Durkheim, followed, and a number of ethnographic schools had been established within China before the 1949 Revolution.

From 1928 Cai Yuan-pei (1896–1940), who had studied at Leipzig and Hamburg, directed a number of ethnological studies influenced by *evolutionary theories at the Central Research Institute in Beijing; these included studies of Taiwanese native peoples, the Miao, Yao and She minorities, and the Northern ethnic groups, by ethnographers such as Ling Chun-sheng and Ruey Yih-Fu, Tao Yunkui, Yan Fuli, Shang Chengzu and Lin Huixiang. *Diffusionist influences were dominant at the Catholic Furen University of Beijing, and the works of Durkheim, *Boas and †Kroeber were widely known. A close relationship was established between anthropology and history, with an emphasis on the study of China's minority and border peoples which was ethnological in nature.

The British *functionalist influence of *Malinowski and *Radcliffe-Brown, concentrated in the sociology department of Yanjing University, modified by that of the Chicago school, was to become paramount in China. A number of pioneering studies of minority and Han social organization were directed by Wu Wenzao at the Yanjing-Yunnan Station for Sociological Research set up in 1938. Researchers included *Fei Xiaotong, Lin Yao-hua, Tien Ru-kang, †Francis L.K. Hsu, who had all studied at the London School of Economics, and Martin C.K. Yang.

There were few academic positions in anthropology, however, and the argument put forward by functionalists that Chinese anthropology was a form of *sociology had important repercussions after the Revolution, since sociology was banned from universities after 1952. Many lecturers joined history departments or the Central Minorities Institute, founded in 1951 with Fei Xiao-tong as its Vice-President, or the nine Nationalities Colleges established from 1951. Some ethnographers fled to Taiwan, while others sought refuge in the United States. After 1949 the attempt to apply Stalin's definition of the 'nationality' and five-stage theory of social systems to the Chinese social situation led to a concern with the evolutionary classification of ethnic minorities. Under a twelve-year social history research programme from 1956 Fei Xiao-tong directed extensive studies of the nationalities which have only recently been published.

The anthropology of Chinese society outside China developed from the work of early Sinologists such as †Granet and De Groot. It emphasized the use of historical sources and field research largely based on studies of Chinese communities outside China, particularly in Taiwan, Hong Kong and *Southeast Asia, as a result of restrictions on foreign research within China following the Revolution.

Early monographs included the diffusionist-influenced work of Hans Stubel on the Yao and Li, of †Fortune on the Yao of Guangdong, and Kulp's 1925 study of Phoenix Village. The work of †Maurice Freedman has been particularly influential, from his study of *kinship in Singapore to his work on †lineage organization and *ancestral worship in southeast China (1966). Freedman's work led to what J.L. Watson (1986) termed a 'lineage paradigm' of Chinese kinship which has been criticized as over-reliant on the southeastern coastal region of China. Since then studies based largely on fieldwork in Taiwan have modified and questioned the original thesis. Freedman's interest in Chinese *religion has been followed by a number of recent works concerned with the revival of popular religion and its persistence in Chinese society. Early work by Barbara Ward on the fishing communities and popular culture of Hong Kong was also important in illuminating the extent of regional variation within Chinese society.

Following the creation of the Academy of Social Science in 1978 and the republishing of the journal *Minzu Yanjiu* (Nationality Studies) from 1979, there has been a revival of anthropological interest within China. A national symposium on ethnology was organized in Guiyang in 1980, followed by the re-formation of the Chinese Ethnological Society. In 1979 the Chinese Anthropological Association was established, based at Xiamen University. Socio-cultural anthropology has always been overshadowed by the practical importance of ethnology, taken to refer to the study of non-Han minority peoples. A complex relation has obtained between *folklore studies, somewhat acceptable to the Chinese Communist Party because of its emphasis on popular, non-élite peasant customs, and sociology or anthropology. Debates on the nature of *culture and *feudal tradition, religion and superstition, have taken place. A concern with *modernization and *development is now tending to replace the historical emphasis and *class analysis of earlier studies.

The work of Fei Xiao-tong, who studied under Malinowski, Robert Park, and Shigorokorov, has been crucial in pioneering a vision of a China-specific anthropology as a form of applied sociology, concerned with practical issues of development and modernization, based on field studies of particular communities in combination with the use of sociological methods, and not unallied to political and administrative concerns.

The question of a specifically 'Chinese' anthropology has been an abiding concern since the 1930s. The publication in Taiwan of materials arguing for the Sinification of social science has led to ongoing discussions. Within China debates in anthropology are still often related to political discussions on the preliminary stage of China's socialism, and the identification of the specific characteristics of Chinese socialism.

Currently anthropology within China takes place through a number of institutional media, including the universities and the Academy of Social Science, the Nationality Affairs Commission and Nationalities Colleges, museums under the Ministry of Culture, national and provincial associations (such as the Southwest Nationalities Society) and journals. Academic exchanges with foreign institutes are increasing, and further translations of Western works have been made. A number of joint and individual research projects are in progress by younger scholars which should transform the nature of Chinese anthropology.

NICHOLAS TAPP

See also: Asia: East, Russian and Soviet anthropology, Marxism and anthropology

Further reading

Fei Xiao-tong (1939) *Peasant Life in China: A Field Study in the Yangtze Valley*, London: Kegan Paul

Feuchtwang, S. and Wang Ming-ming (1991) 'The Politics of Culture or a Contest of Histories: Representations of Chinese Popular Religion', *Dialectical Anthropology*, 16: 251–72

Freedman, M. (1966) *Chinese Lineage and Society: Fukien and Kwangtung*, London: Athlone

Harrell, S. (1991) 'Anthropology and Ethnology in the PRC: The Intersection of Discourses', *China Exchange News* 19(2): 3–6

Jordan, D. (1972) *Gods, Ghosts and Ancestors: The Folk Religion of a Taiwanese Village*, Berkeley: University of California Press

Kulp, D. (1925) *Phoenix Village, Kwangtung, China*, New York: Teacher College

Lemoine, J. (1989) 'Ethnologists in China', *Diogenes* 133: Jan-Mar.

Lin Yao-hua (1948) *The Golden Wing : A Sociological Study of Chinese Familism*, London: Kegan Paul

Ma Yin (ed.) (1989) *China's Minority Nationalities*, Beijing: Foreign Languages Press

Pasternak, B. (1972) *Kinship and Community in Two Chinese Villages*, Stanford: Stanford University Press

Watson, J.L. (1986) 'Anthropological Overview of the Development of Chinese Descent Groups', in P. Ebrey and J.L. Watson (eds) *Kinship Organization in Late Imperial China*, Berkeley: University of California Press

Wolf, A., and Huang Chieh-shan (1979) *Marriage and Adoption in China, 1845–1945*, Stanford: Stanford University Press

Yang Kun (1983), *Minzu yu minxuxue* [Nationality and Ethnology], Chengdu: Sichuan renmin chubanshe

Christianity

Christianity, the most intently *missionary of the great world religions, has influenced the social and cultural lives of many of the peoples anthropologists have studied, from its European heartland and the Americas to the mission territories of Asia, Africa, Oceania and mission outposts 'at home'. This evangelical spread has provided the dominant focus for anthropological reflection on Christianity over the years. Often cast in an historical mode, anthropological studies of Christianity have explored the complex ways in which global and local religious institutions and *great and little traditions have been mutually constructed, contested and transformed. In the process they have raised questions about the social bases of religiosity, the dynamics of religious change and the character of transnational institutions and cultural forms.

It must also be said that as a powerful historical force in Europe and the United States, Christianity helped shape the intellectual world that gave birth to anthropology itself. For example, the notion of 'progress' which grounded the evolutionary framework used by nineteenth and early twentieth-century anthropologists resulted from Enlightenment attempts to generalize and universalize the Judeo-Christian conception of time as the medium of sacred history (Fabian 1983: 1–35). Likewise, the meanings of such basic concepts of social and cultural analysis as *person, *religion, *ritual, *sacrifice, *symbol and *belief have been inflected by their specific Christian histories in ways that still are not fully explored (Asad 1993).

Christianity's role in the development of modern society has, of course, provided a fertile ground of analysis and reflection in classic (and contemporary) social theory (Parsons 1968). However, except for †Max Weber's *The Protestant Ethic and the Spirit of Capitalism* ([1904–05] 1958), which has proved a continuing source of inspiration to anthropologists reflecting on the social consequences of religious belief, general or comparative studies of Christianity have had relatively little impact on the development of anthropological thought. Indeed, until the 1970s the anthropological literature on Christianity was quite thin, with a few notable exceptions including community studies that explored the social and cultural significance of Christianity in contemporary Europe, Latin America and the United States, and †ethnohistorical studies of *syncretism in Catholic *Central America. Since then, however, a wider range of anthropological work on Christianity has appeared.

Like other world religions, Christianity proclaims a transcendent truth of universal relevance, which must be communicated in settings that are historically particular, geographically local and culturally diverse. Anthropologists have found this a productive field for social and symbolic analysis, taking into consideration even the ways in which Jesus Christ and his followers transformed local Jewish imagery to convey their message. The eucharist or last supper, a central Christian sacrament representing Christ's crucifixion and resurrection resembles its closest model, the Jewish passover, 'but every critical element in the passover is reversed. . . . The passover is a feast that celebrates kinship and nationhood. Jesus's sacrifice symbolizes the death of family and polity. His new covenant includes all humanity' (Feeley-Harnik 1981: 19).

The social inclusiveness of early Christianity was soon accompanied by the development of Christianity's characteristic concern with doctrinal orthodoxy and the Church, its guarantor across time and space. Historians have explored the social grounding of important elements of ortho-

doxy, such as the rise of the cult of the saints in the turbulent world of late antiquity (Brown 1981) and Saint Anselm's theory of salvation, which reflected medieval notions of compensation and kinship (Bossy 1985). However, ethnographic studies suggest that even in Europe relations between the local and the orthodox have been multiple and complex (Christian 1989). Indeed, as Jane Schneider and Shirley Lindenbaum report in an issue of *American Ethnologist* devoted to Christianity, a central problem for anthropological analysis has been 'how in Christianity as in Islam or Buddhism, the powerful thrust of orthodoxy interacts with, and is changed by, local religious belief and action' (1987: 2).

Tensions between the orthodox and the local have most often been explored by anthropologists in non-Western societies where Christianity has been introduced in *colonial situations. In many of these regions, conversion to Christianity and Christianization – 'the reformulation of social relations, cultural meanings, and personal experience in terms of putatively Christian ideals' – continue to accompany the incorporation of people into the broader social order of the West (Hefner 1993: 3). As Hefner notes, however, anthropological research indicates that Christianity 'has demonstrated a remarkable ability to take on different cultural shadings in local settings' (p. 5). Although missionaries have attempted to keep local expressions within the compass of orthodoxy, Christianity has often been reinterpreted to express local preoccupations and to address political, economic and social concerns (Smith 1994; Comaroff 1985).

Within established Christianity, orthodoxy has historically and often tragically battled its opponents while being subject in turn to moments and movements of revival, renewal and reformation. †Victor Turner and Edith Turner have proposed that Christian *pilgrimage be understood as a 'mode of †liminality for the laity,' which intensifies pilgrims' attachment to their religion by offering temporary liberation from the structural constraints of everyday social life (1978: 4). Elsewhere, the search for religious intensity and purification has led to the formation of denominations and sects which have fashioned identities in opposition to other Christian groups and/or the modernizing, secularizing world. However, the recent return of Christian †fundamentalism to the public arena in the United States underlines the instability of the boundaries between fundamentalist and modern (Harding 1994), and illustrates as well the continuing capacity of people acting in the name of Christianity to challenge powerfully a status quo.

MARY TAYLOR HUBER

See also: religion, missionaries, great and little traditions

Further reading

Asad, T. (1993) *Genealogies of Religion: Discipline and Reasons of Power in Christianity and Islam*, Baltimore: The Johns Hopkins University Press

Bossy, J. (1985) *Christianity in the West: 1400 – 1700*, Oxford: Oxford University Press

Brown, P. (1981) *The Cult of the Saints: Its Rise and Function in Latin Christianity*, London: SCM

Christian, W.A. (1989) *Person and God in a Spanish Valley*, Princeton: Princeton University Press

Comaroff, Jean (1985) *Body of Power, Spirit of Resistance: The Culture and History of a South African People*, Chicago: University of Chicago Press

Fabian, J. (1983) *Time and the Other: How Anthropology Makes Its Object*, New York: Columbia University Press

Feeley-Harnik, G. (1981) *The Lord's Table: Eucharist and Passover in Early Christianity*, Philadelphia: University of Pennsylvania Press

Harding, S. (1994) 'The Born-Again Telescandals,' in N. Dirks, G. Eley and S. Ortner (eds) *Culture/Power/History: A Reader in Contemporary Social Theory*, Princeton, NJ: Princeton University Press

Hefner, R.W. (ed.) (1993) *Conversion to Christianity: Historical and Anthropological Perspectives on a Great Transformation*, Berkeley: University of California Press

Parsons, T. (1968) 'Christianity', in D. Sills (ed.) *International Encyclopedia of the Social Sciences*, New York: The Macmillan Company

Schneider, J. and S. Lindenbaum (eds) (1987) 'Frontiers of Christian Evangelism', *American Ethnologist* (special issue) 14 (1)

Smith, M.F. (1994) *Hard Times on Kairiru Island: Poverty, Development, and Morality in a Papua New Guinea Village*, Honolulu: University of Hawaii Press

Turner, Victor and Edith Turner (1978) *Image and Pilgrimage in Christian Culture: Anthropological Perspectives*, New York: Columbia University Press

Weber, M. ([1904-05] 1958) *The Protestant Ethic and the Spirit of Capitalism*, New York: Charles Scribner's Sons

class

Generations of controversy have done little to alter the centrality of class in the social sciences: it remains an essential theoretical concept, even if its value in operational research has been seriously eroded by changes in the structure of capitalist societies. In anthropology, however, social class understood as a relationship to the means of production has always been less central. Some research traditions have deliberately excluded the study of class differences, preferring to emphasize the unity and homogeneity of bounded cultural units. But even those traditions which have been more open to the study of sociological variation have seldom made much use of class analysis. The concept has been deployed in two principal ways, related through their common debt to the influence of †Marx.

The first is that of nineteenth-century *evolutionist anthropology, in which the emergence of class society is linked to the rise of private property and the state (Engels 1972 [1884]). Such theories have remained influential in accounts of the development of political institutions, for example in distinguishing between hierarchies based on social class and those based on rank, which do not require the presence of the state (Fried 1967). Distinctions between ruling and subordinate classes are upheld by *cultural materialists such as †Marvin Harris, despite their lack of sympathy with other aspects of Marxist analysis.

The second major context in which class analysis has entered anthropology is the neo-Marxist school that began in France in the 1960s, and later converged with a variety of approaches influenced by the rejuvenation of *political economy. Neo-Marxists argued that polarized classes analogous to those detected by Marx and †Engels under early capitalism could also be found across virtually the whole range of pre-capitalist societies. Thus African societies presented in harmonious coherence by earlier *functionalist ethnographers were now shown to be riven by conflict and class struggle. To the extent that male elders appropriated the surplus labour of their juniors and of women, they were to be seen as an exploiting class (or at least they could qualify as a 'class in itself', for even the most enthusiastic neo-Marxists found it hard to detect class consciousness, 'class for itself', among such people). This work added little to earlier ethnographies, but was nonetheless valuable in exposing the implicit bias of functionalist accounts.

The irrelevance of the concept of class as far as self-identifications were concerned was always troublesome to anthropologists working in †'tribal' and *'peasant' societies. Difficulties faced elsewhere in the social sciences, such as the problems posed by the growth of the middle classes in capitalist industrial societies, are posed in accentuated forms in anthropology. The setting and techniques of anthropological research lead the anthropologist away from abstractions that have plausibility at a macro-statistical level. For example, Peter Lloyd (1982) has indicated the difficulties in classifying the occupants of shanty towns around 'Third-world' cities as a proletariat. Others have made similar points concerning rural proletariats, where very often it seems that 'vertical' links across apparent class boundaries impede the formation of horizontal linkages between those sharing the same 'objective' economic situation. Links of *kinship, *religion, *ethnicity and *nation have all tended to seem more powerful than links of class. This has not prevented the more dogmatic neo-Marxists in revisiting earlier studies, from seeing all these as surrogates for the one true ontology of class. Yet it is striking that the original ethnographers seldom found this concept useful, preferring to develop more complex notions such as networks, cross-cutting ties, and *patron-client relations.

China presents a particularly striking case, given the extreme circumstances of the Maoist period when 'class label' had direct and fundamental consequences for the life-chances (or even physical survival) of millions (Watson 1984). Even here anthropologists, when able to carry out fieldwork, have tended to prioritize other forms of grouping, despite the fact that some indigenous pre-socialist concepts of hierarchy can plausibly be glossed in terms of class. Even when the Marxist categories were crudely imposed in the countryside, they were susceptible to local manipulation, and quite different types of class formation in the towns proved even more difficult for the state to control. Some anthropologists, however, argue that the second generation of socialist power is now witnessing the re-emergence of earlier forms of capitalist stratification for which the concept of class remains the appropriate analytic term (Potter and Potter 1990).

On the whole the more successful anthropological accounts of class have been those prepared to shift its definition away from a Marxist rooting in the ownership and control of the means of production. Greater recognition of the importance of status-honour, as emphasized in †Weberian approaches, is one important tendency. The †Durkheimian inspiration that leads †Mary Douglas to adapt the word in its taxonomic sense in her identification of 'consumption classes' is

another. Radical feminists have argued for shifting attention away from relations of production in order to show how the experience of class is structured by *race, *gender and kinship. For example, Sacks rejects a focus on the individual's production activities and instead defines membership of the working class as 'membership in a community that is dependent upon waged labor, but that is unable to subsist or reproduce by such labor alone' (Sacks 1989: 543). From this perspective, 'class emerges as a relation to the means of production that is collective rather than individual, a relation of communities to the capitalist state more than of employees to employers' (Sacks 1989: 547). The drawback, of course, is that in pursuing more culturally sensitive interpretations of stratification and social *inequality and in aspiring to a unified theory of class, race and gender, anthropologists will necessarily have to sacrifice the analytic rigour that made class such a popular term in the Marxist tradition. This is precisely what seems to be happening, for example in burgeoning accounts of *ideology and *resistance.

C.M. HANN

See also: Marxism and anthropology, mode of production, property

Further reading

Bloch, M. (1983) *Marxism and Anthropology: The History of a Relationship*, Oxford: Oxford University Press

Clammer, J. (1978) *The New Economic Anthropology*, London: Macmillan

Engels, F. (1972 [1884]) *The Origin of the Family, Private Property and the State*, New York: Pathfinder Press

Fried, M. (1967) *The Evolution of Political Society*, New York: Random House

Lloyd, P. (1982) *A Third World Proletariat?*, London: Allen and Unwin

Potter, S.H. and J.M. (1990) *China's Peasants: The Anthropology of a Revolution*, Cambridge: Cambridge University Press

Sacks, K.B. (1989) 'Toward a Unified Theory of Class, Race and Gender', *American Ethnologist*, 16(3): 534-50

Terray, E. (1975) 'Classes and Class Consciousness in the Abron Kingdom of Gyaman' in M. Bloch (ed.) *Marxist Analyses in Social Anthropology*, London: Malaby Press

Watson, J.L. (ed.) (1984) *Class and Social Stratification in Post-revolution China*, Cambridge: Cambridge University Press

classical studies

Anthropology and the classics

Anthropology ('the study of humankind'), like so many terms of contemporary social-scientific art, is borrowed appropriately enough from ancient Greek. For although the Greeks themselves did not actually use the term, brilliantly original thinkers like Herodotus and Democritus (fifth century BCE) can be seen as the ultimate progenitors of the field within the Western tradition (Cole 1967). An early landmark of the modern discipline is the classically trained †J.G. Frazer's *The Golden Bough* (original edition 1890), but to conventional late Victorian classicists Frazer remained known, or anyway respected, rather for his six-volume commentary (1898) on Pausanias, the ancient Greek Baedeker who had embarked on a curiously proto-Frazerian pilgrimage of religious antiquarianism around what was to him even then, in the second century of our era, 'ancient' Greece.

By 1898, then, the relationship between anthropology and classics was an established if still a little shaky fact. It had begun as a trial marriage in such foundational works as †H.S. Maine's *Ancient Law* (1861) and †N.D. Fustel de Coulanges's *La cité antique* (1864), when classics was still relatively speaking in its heyday and anthropology its infancy. By 1908, when a group of distinguished scholars was brought together by †R.R. Marett to contribute to a collection entitled *Anthropology and the Classics*, one might have been forgiven for supposing that not only consummation but something like parity of esteem had been achieved. Actually, divorce proceedings were already in the offing.

Traditional classicists repined against what one august American Hellenist colourfully dubbed 'the anthropological Hellenism of Sir James Frazer, the irrational, semi-sentimental, Polynesian, free-verse and sex-freedom Hellenism of all the gushful geysers of "rapturous rubbish" about the Greek spirit' (a loose, not to say crude, reference to the so-called 'Cambridge Ritualist' school of Jane Ellen Harrison, F.M. Cornford and others: Calder 1991). Cutting-edge ethnographic anthropologists, for their part, were on the verge of *Malinowskian participant observation, reporting back to base with mint-fresh data on living societies and often pretty scornful of the irretrievably dead (as they believed) cultures of ancient Greece and Rome, not to mention History more generally.

By 1960, when †Clyde Kluckhohn delivered a lecture-series at Brown University under the same title as the Marett collection, the decree absolute had been granted. In so far as intimate relations still existed, the flow was almost entirely uni-directional, from the erstwhile junior partner, anthropology, to the now seriously moribund elder partner, classics. E.R. Dodds's *The Greeks and the Irrational* (1951) protested eloquently against, but by its very title neatly illustrated, one of the chief reasons for this stand-off. Classicists, many of whom still preferred to bask in the afterglow of Victorian self-identification with the 'Glory that was Greece', were typically not overwhelmingly impressed by Dodds's forays into the shame-culture and *shamanism, let alone the paranormal, that he claimed had flourished even amid the supposed rationalism of classical Greece. When Moses Finley's *The World of Odysseus* was published on this side of the Atlantic in 1956, this unashamed attempt to illuminate the world of Homer from the writings of the French Durkheimian anthropologist †Marcel Mauss (1925) on the northwest American *potlatch and the Melanesian *kula*-ring was thought to need the prefatory imprimatur of a pukka classical humanist, Maurice Bowra (not included in the new, 1978 edition).

In retrospect, Finley's little masterpiece can be seen as the chief seed of the present flowering of anthropologically-related studies of ancient Greek culture and society. The other major tributary of the scholarly flood of anthropologizing Hellenism is French, most famously the so-called 'Paris School' of cultural criticism founded by Jean-Pierre Vernant (originally trained as an ancient philosopher) and the historian Pierre Vidal-Naquet (1986, 1988), who trace their intellectual genealogy back to †Durkheim and Mauss by way of the Hellenist Louis Gernet (1968, 1983; cf. Di Donato 1990). (Anthropological insights have been applied far less frequently, systematically and successfully to Roman society and culture than to ancient Greek. The conspicuous exception is in the field of Roman religion, where the leading inspiration has been the putatively Indo-European trifunctionality of †G. Dumézil: Di Donato 1990.)

Following Finley and the Paris School, many modern scholars of ancient Greece have participated with an unparalleled zest and gusto in the view widespread across all the humanities that anthropology is, if not *the*, at any rate *one* of today's foundational intellectual disciplines. No one has done more to make this appear to be the case than

†Clifford Geertz, patentee of the ethnographic discourse known almost onomatopoeically as †'thick description' (1973) – notwithstanding Geertz's own typically ironic claim (1988) that anthropology, compared with law, physics, music or cost accounting, is a relatively minor cultural institution. Students of the agonistic and masculinist public culture of the ancient Greeks tend to find that Geertz's brilliant interpretation of the Balinese cockfight strikes a particularly resonant chord with them.

It is impossible to mention here more than a sample of recent anthropologically-inspired work in Hellenic classical studies. (For a more complete citation see Cartledge 1994.) But within the last decade alone historians of ancient Greece – both terms are to be interpreted generously – have drawn on comparative anthropological data and/or models to illuminate such institutions, practices and cultural 'imaginaries' as *age-setting and *rites of passage, burial-rituals, the *family, *gender and sexuality, *law, *literacy, *religion and *mythology, ritualized guest-friendship, *science, *slavery, and tragic drama. Selection is invidious, but perhaps worthy of special mention is Thomas (1992), a measured response to the somewhat extravagant claims for the politically determinative function of Greek alphabetic literacy originally made by †Jack Goody (1968).

Continuities or differences

No less important than the sheer range and depth of this anthropologizing research is the sharp – and, almost inevitably, binary – divide that separates its practitioners into opposing camps, partly for theoretical, partly no doubt also for ideological reasons. On the one hand, there are those who believe it is possible and helpful to generalize across all modern Greece (and sometimes more broadly still, to 'the Mediterranean world') and then use such generalized comparative data in the form of a model to supplement as well as interpret the available primary evidence for antiquity – either on the assumption that like conditions produce like effects or, even more robustly, in the belief that there has been substantial continuity of culture and mentality in Greece from antiquity to the present. In anthropology, J.C. Lawson's 'study in survivals', *Ancient Greek Folklore and Modern Greek Religion* (1910) or R. and E. Blum's *The Dangerous Hour* (1970) conspicuously represent this view of Greekness as an essence, a classicizing essence to be sure, impervious to such historic changes as

those from paganism to Orthodox Christianity, or from subsistence peasant agriculture to more or less internationally market-driven *capitalist farming.

For other observers and/or participants, it makes all the difference in the world precisely which historical epoch of Greece is being imagined as constituting the paradigm and standard of Greekness. To many modern Greeks, for example, their supposed classical ancestry is just one more facet of their perceived misfortune to be Greek; this challenged sense of national-ethnic identity has been sensitively analysed by foreign scholars such as Michael Herzfeld (1987), a leading light of the small but vigorous community of anthropologists of modern Greece that acknowledges a debt of inspiration to J.K. Campbell's *Honour, Family and Patronage* (1964). In conscious or unconscious harmony with this stress on difference, many ancient historians either believe on principle, or are simply struck by their supposedly objective observation, that comparison of ancient and modern Hellenism should be used chiefly to highlight fundamental cultural difference rather than conflate heterogeneous cultures or fill gaps in the extant primary sources.

A couple of illustrations, one from each interpretative tradition and both addressing the same area of gender and sexuality, should make this distinction of scholarly approach more concrete and precise. In his *Law, Sexuality and Society: The Enforcement of Morals in Classical Athens* (1991), David Cohen studies the way in which classical Athenian sexuality was policed both formally, by popular adjudication in the democratic lawcourts, and informally, through customary norms. His basic contentions are twofold: that male-generated and male-adjudicated law was just one, and by no means the largest, part of the *honour-and-shame system of values designed to regulate Athenian sexual behaviour, and that in accordance with his 'Mediterranean model' we should postulate quite a radical gap between the officially expressed moral-political norms of Athens and their practical negotiation between the sexes in private.

Cohen (a graduate pupil of Finley) is very widely read both theoretically and empirically – his model draws freely on French and British sociology as well as a vast range of ethnography from all round the eastern Mediterranean, among Muslim and Arab communities in addition to Catholic and Orthodox religious traditions. And his hypothesis of a significant gap between Athenian public cultural ideals and negotiated private practice is important and plausible, especially because it emphasizes the real possibility of a considerable degree of female autonomy. It does not, however, entirely avoid the danger of over-assimilation: crucially, it makes insufficient allowance for the differences between classical Athens, a sovereign democratic political community, and a modern village in Greece (or Lebanon) whose acknowledged norms may well be at odds with those of the officially sovereign national legal culture.

On the other side, the side of local specificity and difference, is the collection of essays by the late J.J. Winkler, *The Constraints of Desire* (1990). This is devoted to understanding what he called gender-protocols in ancient Greece, interpreting the latter far more broadly than Cohen to include texts written in Greek in Egypt or elsewhere in the Greek-speaking half of the Roman Empire as well as in democratic Athens. For Winkler's anthropology of ancient Greek culture the close reading of texts in specific context is of the essence. Thus he, like Cohen, studies the way the Athenians 'laid down the law' on sexual propriety, and agrees that simply knowing the protocols does not tell us how people behaved. But in studying, additionally, the necessarily private textual genre of erotic magical spells, Winkler is able not only to move beyond Cohen's frame of reference but also to provide contemporary evidence that questions the universal validity of the supposed norms themselves (in this case, the official male denial that women did, or rather should, get sexual pleasure). In my view Winkler has the better of this argument. Difference not sameness is the key.

I conclude therefore with the nub of what I no doubt optimistically take to be my own objective observation of fundamental and irreconcilable differences between the mentality and ideology of the classical Greeks and those of any modern Western society, including that of contemporary Greece (Cartledge 1993). Slavery, arguably, was both the principal material basis of society and the governing paradigm of human worth in classical Greek antiquity, affecting not only economics and politics but also, more subtly, the ideological representations of, and interpersonal relations between, the sexes. At the limit of degradation, ancient slavery meant the total deracination and depersonalization, the social death, involved in chattel slavery experienced by the unfree in Athens and elsewhere. At best, it consigned hundreds of thousands of human beings to a vague limbo status

'between slavery and freedom' such as the Helots of Sparta enjoyed (or suffered). There have always been classicists who have objected to the anthropologizing cross-cultural study of the ancient Greeks, on the grounds that it seems to focus on and highlight their least edifying traits. Slavery, however, was an essential and formative part of a culture that was – in many other ways – admirable, and indeed a continuing source of our cultural inspiration today, most obviously in the visual and performing arts. Anthropologizing the ancient Greeks can enable us to come to terms with this rebarbative and seemingly contradictory combination of inhumane servitude and high cultural achievement.

PAUL CARTLEDGE

See also: Europe: Southern, slavery, history and anthropology

Further reading

Calder III., W.M. (1991) (ed.) *The Cambridge Ritualists Reconsidered*, Atlanta, GA: The Scholars Press
Cartledge, P. (1993) *The Greeks: A Portrait of Self and Others*, Oxford: Oxford University.Press
—— (1994). 'The Greeks and Anthropology', *Anthropology Today* 10 (3): 3–6
Cole, T. (1967) *Democritus and the Sources of Greek Anthropology*, Ann Arbor: University of Michigan Press
Di Donato, R. (1990) *Per Una Antropologia Storica del Mondo Antico*, Florence: La Nuova Italia
Geertz, C. (1973) *The Interpretation of Cultures: Selected Essays*, New York: Basic Books
—— (1988) *Works and Lives: The Anthropologist as Author*, Oxford: Polity Press
Gernet, L. (1968) *Anthropologie de la Grèce antique*, ed. by J.-P. Vernant, Paris: Maspéro
—— (1983) *Les Grecs sans Miracle*, ed. by R. Di Donato, Paris: Maspéro
Goody, J. (1968) (ed.) *Literacy in Traditional Societies*, Cambridge: Cambridge University Press
Herzfeld, M. (1987) *Anthropology through the Looking-Glass. Critical Ethnography in the Margins of Europe*, Cambridge: Cambridge University Press
Mauss, M. ([1925] 1954) *The Gift: Forms and Functions of Exchange in Archaic Societies*, trans. by I. Cunnison, London: Routledge & Kegan Paul
Thomas, R. (1992) *Literacy and Orality in Ancient Greece*, Cambridge: Cambridge University Press
Vernant, J.-P. and P. Vidal-Naquet (1988) *Myth and Tragedy in Ancient Greece*, trans. by J. Lloyd, New York: Zone Books
Vidal-Naquet, P. (1986) *The Black Hunter: Forms of Thought and Forms of Society in the Greek World*, trans. by A. Szegedy-Maszak, Baltimore and London: Johns Hopkins University Press

classification

We cannot think about the world unless we assign it to categories. Categories also help us act upon the world, but are probably not essential to all kinds of activity. It is a matter for debate whether categories for thinking and for acting differ. The discussion which follows concerns classifications as objects of intellectual scrutiny (for the most part, *folk* classifications), rather than the classifications which anthropologists use to order their data, though these latter are ultimately subject to the same generalizations.

'Classification' is that activity in which objects, concepts and relations are assigned to categories; 'classifying' refers to the cognitive and cultural mechanisms by which this is achieved; and 'classifications' are the linguistic, mental, and other cultural representations which result. Problems arise when the adjectival and nominal status of the root 'class' are conflated. This reifies schemes as permanent cultural artefacts or mentally-stored old knowledge, when they are more properly understood as the spontaneous and often transient end-product of underlying processes in an individual classifying act. We might call such a misinterpretation 'the classificatory fallacy', and there is every reason to believe that it is potentially evident whenever ethnographers try to make sense of their data, whether these be tables of symbolic oppositions, animal taxonomies or *relationship terminologies.

Ways of classifying the world

Classification as an object of anthropological analysis effectively begins with the publication of *Primitive Classification* by †Durkheim and †Mauss in 1901–02. Their main argument was that social divisions provide the prior model for primitive classifications of the natural world. Durkheim and Mauss, almost as if in passing, establish a distinction between *mundane* (technical, descriptive) and *symbolic* (*ritual, explanatory) schemes which well reflects, and partly determined, the subsequent history of classification studies. Before going any further it will be helpful to unpack this distinction.

Humans classify the world about them by matching perceptual images, words and concepts (Ohnuki-Tierney 1981: 453). The operations work equally in terms of unmodified sense data or their cultural representations. The cognitive and cultural tools available to do this do not distin-guish between the social world and the non-social world, though in the analysis of classification this has become a conventional distinction. Similarly, classification can treat its subject in a pragmatic and mundane way or by using various symbolic allusions. Since so much of what we sense and experience is mediated by social consciousness, and since the boundary between the mundane and symbolic is often unclear, it has sometimes been difficult, in practice, to know where to divide these two axes. It may help to set out the dimensions as a matrix:

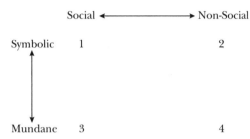

Classifications of type 1 involve the use of symbolic devices to partition and articulate social *time and space: the use of material objects to represent wife-givers and receivers, or the punctuation of time through significant ritual events, are good examples of these. Classifications of type 2 use symbols to make sense of non-social space, as in representations of the cardinal directions in Javanese thought by colours. Classifications of type 3 include descriptive ways of partitioning social space, as with pronouns and relationship terminologies. Classifications of type 4 include much of what passes for biological classification, including †Linnaean scientific schemes. The distinctions cannot always be neatly drawn: symbolic things are in an important sense practical, and practical classifications of the non-social world often rely on metaphors which are ultimately social, as in the use of the terms 'genus' and 'family' to organize plants and animals. Attempts to bring these aspects of classifying behaviour together have met with varying degrees of success. Those who espouse extreme formulations of the universalist (practical)-relativist (symbolic) divide sometimes claim that they are engaged in separate kinds of endeavour, and that one body of work should not invalidate the other. On the other hand, some have stressed the empirical connections between the two, and envisage an ultimate convergence of †cognitive and *symbolic anthropology. The distinctions are entrenched and not wholly avoidable. Here I first discuss some general principles of categorization and then examine mundane and symbolic schemes separately.

Principles of categorization

Categories may be constructed either by reference to their †semantic focus, their boundaries or some combination of the two. In the first case, focus is based on some exemplary instance or cognitive †prototype: thus a sparrow is a focal member of the category 'bird'. Other instances may be non-focal (peripheral) members of their category: as with 'emu', an egg-laying feathered biped which does not fly, and is described in English as a 'bird'. But not all content assigned to categories consists of physical things. Content may include attributes (colour, sound, shape, size and so forth) and abstractions such as time. The visual sense, however, is dominant and there is a tendency to objectivize even the most intangible. The difficulties of assigning things to categories may be made easier by imposing culturally agreed boundaries. Because parts of our experience of the world are complexly continuous, it is occasionally necessary to impose boundaries to produce categories at all.

Many categories are *monothetic*, meaning that the defining set of features is always unique, either coded in some binary way or in terms of the clustering of criteria. Others are *polythetic*: single features being neither essential to group membership nor sufficient to allocate an item to a group. It may seem, therefore, that categories vary according to the complexity of their definition, rather than simply the scope of their content. Many social categories are held to be complex in this sense, though the fact that they are often vague and general (as in Polynesian *tabu* or *taboo) might also suggest that they are semantically primitive.

The relationship between categories and words varies, although the overall developmental primacy of categories over labels is now generally accepted. Language exists within culture and society, but determines the outer parameters of neither. This highlights a major methodological impediment in the study of classification: we rely on language data as the main way of discovering classification, yet words do not always provide an accurate guide. One of the most obvious disjunctions between language and classification is represented by the existence of unlabelled, or *covert categories*. We know that these exist at various degrees of inclusiveness. Thus, many languages

have no words for 'plant', yet there is plenty of evidence to suggest that the category exists. Similarly, many varieties of rice may be recognized by a people who do not consistently label them.

Any consideration of the internal structuring of categories quickly merges into a consideration of how categories relate to one another. In many cases the definition of any one category must be understood in relation to others ('black', 'white'), the part must be related to the whole. What this whole is need not always be clearly distinguished, as in the case where polythetic criteria apply. In some situations the whole may simply be two categories which mutually define each other, in others more inclusive and complex classificatory space which we describe as a *semantic (or cognitive) domain*. Some domains are defined by their physical boundaries, such as a *house or the human *body. Here the internal classificatory architecture is *analytic* in the sense that it decomposes a greater physical whole. The terms which label categories in such classifications are called *partonyms* ('windows', 'doors'; 'arms', 'legs'). Other domains are culturally and cognitively derived from perceived shared resemblances. These we can call *synthetic*, and they are exemplified by domains such as 'animals' and 'plants'. Some are clearly defined *emically, others are vague, and it is here that anthropologists are most tempted to impose etic distinctions, either through ignorance or convenience. Knowing whether or not to treat *kinship categories apart from other social †deictics represents a problem of this kind.

The organization of categories within a domain may vary. Many can be represented in terms of *class inclusion* and contrast, that is as *taxonomies*. In other cases non-hierarchical models are more appropriate. Brent Berlin has consistently argued in favour of the universality of taxonomy for †ethnobiological schemes, but this only works if one also asserts the separation of *general-purpose* from *special-purpose* schemes, that is those that are logical and 'natural', from those that arise to meet the needs of particular cultural requirements. Despite its prevalence, the principle of taxonomy is better represented amongst some populations than others. Its effective demonstration depends on the extent of linkage between categories in (often flexible) ways; ways which undermine implicit taxonomic levels and contrasts and the general-purpose/special-purpose distinction. It also depends upon the ease with which ethnographers can elicit transitivity statements (*a* is a *b* and *b* is a *c*, therefore *a* is a *c*).

Mundane schemes

The systematic analysis of mundane schemes was first initiated during the 1950s, and in its formative phase is associated with *ethnoscience methodologies. It is typified by a rigorous formal analysis of semantic domains. Early work emphasized the role of distinctive features in the allocation of things to categories and class inclusion as the means of ordering segregates. More recent work has shown a preference for core-periphery models and cognitive prototypes.

The kinds of classificatory schemes analysed in this way have been varied (colour, disease types, firewood, soil, and so on), though most work has focused on ethnobiological schemes. The model for work of this kind was established by †Harold Conklin and later Brent Berlin. Their pioneering studies have been swiftly followed by much attention to the evolution of such schemes, the examination of their underlying taxonomic character, regularities in the order of appearance of different degrees of inclusiveness (ranks), and in the order of appearance of life-forms. Much of this work has sought to show the extent to which folk and scientific categories correspond and the relationship between features of a classification and kinds of society. It has also addressed the proposition that plant and animal categories at a particular classificatory level are more salient (basic) than others and have a logical primacy, though there is some dispute as to whether this operates at a consistent level between different natural kinds and across cultures.

Symbolic schemes

Symbolic classification occurs when we use some things as a means of saying something about other things: for example, when *totemic species stand for different social groups. It serves to express formally metaphysical and *cosmological speculation, and may be translated into technical procedures which permit the efficacious manipulation of the world, as in ritual and *divination. Symbols enhance the significance of important categories, such as those involved in social control ('prohibited, non-prohibited'). In this sense, categories imply rules and rules categories.

The study of symbolic classification embarked upon by Durkheim and Mauss was given new impetus in the 1960s by the work of *Lévi-Strauss

and a group of influential British anthropologists, notably †Edmund Leach, †Mary Douglas and †Rodney Needham. This work emphasized the centrality of †*binary opposition* (dualism, polarity) as a principle of social thought. With this basic human organizing idea, best exemplified by the oppositions †'right' and 'left', 'male' and 'female', the elements are usually complementary, but sometimes ambiguously asymmetric. Binary opposition is reflected in symbolic schemes where other even numbers are used as an organising principle. Classifications partitioning semantic space by three may also be important, as in the colour triad (red-white-black) or in dual classifications where a third (mediating) element has been added.

Classification based on the principle of five is exemplified by the Javanese division of the cosmos into four cardinal directions plus a mediating centre. Here, each dimension integrates a large number of different levels of experience (time, colour, state of mind, number, and so on). The case illustrates another pervasive feature of symbolic classification, namely *analogy*, which explicitly occurs in some cultural genres as *semantic parallelism* (Fox 1975). Apart from opposition and analogy, symbolic schemes often display principles of transition (as in marking *rites of passage), exchange and transformation (such as the inversion of left and right in the interpretive logic of the Javanese shadow-play). Transformation is often a way of signifying the ambiguous, which may also be marked by *anomaly*. Anomalies are a means by which significant differences can be highlighted (as in the categories underlying Jewish dietary laws). However, boundaries are not always considered dangerous or polluting, and anomalies are not a necessary result of classificatory process.

Conclusion

While some symbolic classifications strongly reflect social groupings (binary opposition and *dual organization, quaternary schemes and Kariera marriage section systems), the view that all classification (or even symbolic classification) finds its roots in social institutions is now generally considered untenable. Certain features of symbolic classification may evolve autonomously, reflecting underlying general principles of *cognition. What is always striking is the consistent multivocality and economy of symbols, the same oppositions occurring again and again, amongst different peoples.

Classifications of all kinds connect culture, psychology and perceptual discontinuities of the concrete world. Confusion has arisen in the past from failure to distinguish clearly between individual instruments of cognitive process and the collective medium in which these operate, comprising belief, cultural representations and social practice. It is also crucial to distinguish information storage from representation, abstract knowledge of the world and the pragmatic †schemas we use to negotiate our way through it. Our propensity to classify in the ways we do results from the possession of certain innate cognitive skills (some of which we share with non-human primates), plus an ability to organize our perceptions through culture (aided by language) based on models drawn from somatic experience (such as right and left and bodily rhythms), and from social and perceptual experience of the material world. The form a particular classification takes will sometimes be a culturally defined whole, but often as not will be the outcome of interaction in particular circumstances; the interplay of past knowledge, material context and social inputs. Classifications as things, therefore, are not the inventions of individuals, but arise through the historically contingent character of cultural transmission, linguistic constraints, metaphorical extensions, and shared social experience in relation to individual cognitive practice.

ROY ELLEN

See also: ethnoscience, emic and etic, relationship terminology, names and naming, componential analysis, cognition, time and space

Further reading

Atran, S. (1990) *Cognitive Foundations of Natural History: Towards an Anthropology of Science*, Cambridge: Cambridge University Press

Berlin, B. (1992) *Ethnobiological Classification: Principles of Categorization of Plants and Animals in Traditional Societies*, Princeton, NJ: Princeton University Press

Douglas, M. (ed.) 1973) *Rules and Meanings: An Anthropology of Everyday Knowledge*, Harmondsworth: Penguin

Durkheim, É. and M. Mauss (1963 [1901-2]) *Primitive Classification* (trans. R. Needham), Chicago: Chicago University Press

Ellen, R. (1993) *The Cultural Relations of Classification: An Analysis of Nuaulu Animal Categories from Central Seram*, Cambridge: Cambridge University Press

Fox, J.J. (1975) 'On Binary Categories and Primary Symbols: Some Rotinese Perspectives' in R. Willis (ed.) *The Interpretation of Symbolism* (Association of Social Anthropologists, Studies 2), London: Malaby

Harris, P. and P. Heelas (1979) 'Cognitive Processes and Collective Representations', *European Journal of Sociology* 20: 211–41

Leach, E.R. (1964) 'Anthropological Aspects of Language: Animal Categories and Verbal Abuse' in E. Lenneberg (ed.) *New Directions in the Study of Language*, Cambridge, MA: MIT Press

Needham, R. (1979) *Symbolic Classification*, Santa Monica, CA: Goodyear

Ohnuki-Tierney, E. (1981) 'Phases in Human Perception/Cognition/Symbolization Processes: Cognitive Anthropology and Symbolic Classification', *American Ethnologist* 8 (2): 451–67

Rosch, E. (1977) 'Human Categorisation' in N. Warren (ed.) *Studies in Cross-cultural Psychology*, London: Academic Press

Turner, V.W. (1966) 'Colour Classification in Ndembu Ritual' in M. Banton (ed.) *Anthropological Approaches to the Study of Religion* (ASA Monograph in Social Anthropology 3): London: Tavistock Publications

cognatic society

In †Murdock's terms, 'cognatic' refers to a social system in which ideally the ascription of statuses is based on *kinship ties traced equally through both the maternal and paternal lines, or which allows for a choice to be made in affiliation between the mother's and father's kin. Murdock explicitly contrasted cognatic systems with †unilineal ones. The classificatory term 'cognatic' became increasingly popular in anthropology following the publication of Murdock's edited volume (1960). Other terms often used as synonyms are †'bilateral' or, †'non unilineal'. Murdock attempted to classify the main features of cognatic social organization and establish a typology of subcategories of cognatic society.

Major published ethnographies on cognatic societies, mainly from Southeast Asia and Polynesia, did not begin to appear until the 1950s. Among the most important were the Borneo studies by †Freeman (1955) and Geddes (1954). This early work was undertaken in the context of anthropological theories of kinship dominated by ethnographic material from Africa and native North America on †corporate unilineal descent groups. The preoccupation with delineating social groups and mechanisms for the maintenance of social order and continuity explains *Radcliffe-Brown's now famous judgement in 1950:

Cognatic systems are rare, not only in Africa but in the world at large [because] it is difficult to establish and maintain a wide range system on a purely cognatic basis; it is only a unilineal system that will permit the division of society into separate organized kin groups

(1950: 82).

Certainly there was very little information on cognatic societies at that time, but subsequent work on cognation in the 1950s and 1960s was directed, in part, to refuting Radcliffe-Brown's statement. For example, it was established that cognatic systems are found widely, especially in Western industrialized societies and in the Asia Pacific region. Furthermore, Freeman, in particular, showed how the cognatic system of the Iban of Borneo was structured and order maintained; he described and analysed in detail the household as the basic corporate group of Iban society; and he demonstrated how large numbers of people could be mobilized and organized through the mechanism of personal kinship circles or †kindreds (1961). The main purpose of Murdock's volume too was to delimit the structures, systems and order of cognatic societies.

The significant features of these early studies of cognation were the examination of the composition, structure and operation of the *household, or what is sometimes referred to as the small family or domestic unit; the principle of physical propinquity in the organization of neighbourhoods, wards, communities and villages; and the networks of dyadic ties based on kindreds, patronage, shared space or mutual economic and political interest. This literature on cognation, in its concern with personal networks, informal social groupings and †action sets, has also given greater emphasis to mechanisms and processes of individual choice rather than to representative action arising from membership of corporate groups.

The shortcomings of the term 'cognatic society' as a category were emphasized increasingly in debates from the mid 1960s onwards (King 1978; Hüsken and Kemp 1991). First, it has been argued that there is the danger of misplaced emphasis in classifying a society according to its system of reckoning kinship, when this might not be the most important principle of social organization. For example, subsequent studies revealed that such principles as rank, *class or shared residence are sometimes more important than cognation in organizing social relations, and, in consequence, can structure elements of kinship.

Secondly, anthropologists became more aware of the marked variations in societies classified as cognatic in terms of such features as household organization, personal kindreds, and in the degree to which descent plays a role in generating social units. In this regard, peoples such as the Maori of New Zealand recognize cognatic or bilateral descent groups which control or own resources such as land or other valued property (Firth 1963).

Thirdly, the validity of the distinction between cognatic and unilineal societies has been questioned, since, as †Needham has argued, 'The cognatic recognition of relatives is common to all societies and characteristic of none' (1966: 29). In other words, in societies with unilineal descent groups, as in those without them, individuals also recognize kinship ties bilaterally. It is for this reason that some studies of unilineal communities in Indonesia have also explored cognatic linkages between relatives (Hüsken and Kemp 1991).

Finally, the general shift in anthropological perspectives on kinship which gathered pace in the 1970s demonstrated the problems of the static, essentialist view of kinship held by such anthropologists as Murdock. The value of classifying societies into types was called into question and the concept of kinship as a concrete, discrete and irreducible area of social life which could be used to characterize communities was criticized. Instead, anthropologists studying cognatic systems began to examine the complex interrelations between cognatic kinship linkages and other domains of organization and activity, and the strategic and dynamic use of kin ties for economic and political purposes.

The term 'cognatic society' still has some currency in the anthropological literature. However, once the importance of understanding cognatic systems in their own terms was accepted in anthropology, the utility of the category became the subject of intense debate. Some anthropologists specifically abandoned the concept 'cognatic society' because it was used either to lump societies together as a residual or negatively defined class in relation to unilineal societies, or to establish a positively constituted class on the basis of the superficial similarity of bilateral reckoning of kinship. Thus, 'cognatic society' has been deconstructed; but cognation and its interrelations with other modes of organizing social life still remains an important field of anthropological enquiry.

VICTOR T. KING

See also: descent, house, household, kinship, social structure

Further reading

Firth, R. (1963) 'Bilateral Descent Groups: An Operational Viewpoint' in I. Schapera (ed.) *Studies in Kinship and Marriage*, London: Royal Anthropological Institute, Occasional Papers 16

Freeman, J. D. (1955) *Report on the Iban of Sarawak*, London: Her Majesty's Stationery Office

—— (1961) 'On the Concept of the Kindred', *Journal of the Royal Anthropological Institute* 91 (2): 192—220

Geddes, W.R. (1954) *The Land Dayaks of Sarawak*, London: Her Majesty's Stationery Office

Hüsken, F. and J. Kemp (eds) (1991) *Cognation and Social Organization in Southeast Asia* Leiden: KITLV Press, Verhandelingen van het Koninklijk Instituut voor Taal-, Land- en Volkenkunde 145

King, V.T. (ed.) (1978) *Essays on Borneo Societies*, Oxford: Oxford University Press for University of Hull Publications

Murdock, G.P. (ed.) (1960) *Social Structure in Southeast Asia*, Chicago: Quadrangle Books, Viking Publications in Anthropology 29

Needham, R. (1966) 'Age, Category and Descent' *Bijdragen tot de Taal-, Land- en Volkenkunde* 122 (1): 1-35

Radcliffe-Brown, A.R. (1950) 'Introduction' in A.R. Radcliffe-Brown and C.D. Forde (eds) *African Systems of Kinship and Marriage*, London: Oxford University Press

cognition

The word cognition comes from the Latin verb meaning 'to know' and it denotes the knowledge we are able to draw upon to make sense of our environment. Cognition is usually contrasted with perception, which is the way we receive information from the outside world. However, many recent theories in both psychology and anthropology have stressed that there cannot be a hard and fast distinction between the two processes.

The study of cognition is the study of how human knowledge is learnt, stored and retrieved. Clearly what people know includes what they have learnt from others and what they will pass on to the next generation. This is what anthropologists usually call 'culture' and which they consider the subject matter of †cultural anthropology. That part of anthropology which is concerned with culture is therefore concerned with some aspects of cognition but not all. First of all, there is much human knowledge which is not learnt, or not

entirely learnt, from others. For example most psychologists would now agree that although people learn specific languages, the ability to learn language is inherited as part of the general human genetic inheritance and is not learnt from other individuals. Second, although anthropological studies of culture have been concerned with what people know, on the whole, anthropologists have been less concerned with the processes of the acquisition of knowledge and the way knowledge is organized; this has been left to *psychologists.

Psychology and anthropology

Clearly the study of those aspects of cognition of interest to psychologists and those aspects of interest to anthropologists cannot be separated. The history of the two disciplines bears witness to this fact.

Much of the recent history of psychology seemed little concerned with such anthropological issues as how knowledge is passed on among human beings in such natural contexts of learning as family life, play, co-operative work, etc. This was because the discipline was obsessed by the need for careful experimental control which meant that psychologists studied cognition inside the laboratory only. However, even when this point of view was at its height, there were psychologists who were concerned with integrating anthropology and psychology although few talked of the matter in these terms. Thus the Russian psychologist of the first part of this century †Vygotsky stressed that we must understand how the child's individual cognitive growth meshes with the knowledge which is created and transmitted from generation to generation within a social group. This he called the 'zone of proximal development' (Cole and Scribner 1974). In much the same period the Cambridge psychologist Bartlett attempted to deal with the same questions and actively cooperated with anthropologists such as †W.H.R. Rivers and †G. Bateson. As a part of this work he developed the idea of †'schema'. These are simple models of culturally-specific knowledge which inform perception and knowledge. The schema theory thus attempts to explain the way culture affects the psychological (Bartlett 1932).

From the anthropological side, concern with cognition was particularly marked at the turn of the century when anthropologists were arguing among themselves about how far all human beings thought in the same way. The two sides of the argument can be represented by the British anthropologist †E.B. Tylor and the French philosopher †L. Lévy-Bruhl. Tylor was very interested in the evolution of culture and human intellectual progress. For him, however, differences between peoples such as the *Aboriginal Australians and nineteenth-century Britons could be explained by the historical evolution of their culture; they were not due to any fundamental differences in the way they thought. According to him mankind demonstrated a †'psychic unity'. Lévy-Bruhl, on the other hand, argued that primitive peoples (especially South American Indians) had, unlike modern Europeans, a pre-logical form of thought in which basic contradictions would not appear as such. In other words, for Lévy-Bruhl, the principles of *rationality were not the same for all humans. By and large most modern anthropologists would now be on the side of Tylor in this controversy, and even Lévy-Bruhl himself seems to have changed his mind towards the end of his life (Hollis and Lukes 1982).

During most of this century discussions about whether all human beings thought in the same way took on another form. This was due to the influence which *Boas was to have on *American anthropology. Boas's theory of cognition, and that of most of his disciples, was that our culture, i.e. the system of knowledge inherited from other members of our society, determined the way we understood the world; our cognition in other words. This view is perhaps clearest in the work of †Ruth Benedict who argued that anthropology needed psychology, while psychology was merely the study of anthropology at the individual level (Benedict 1935). Such an approach, occurring at the very time when cognitive psychologists were retreating into their laboratories, led to a lack of contact between the two disciplines, at least in the USA.

One aspect of the Boasian cognitive theory did, however, attract the interest of psychologists, first, because it was so provocative and, second, because it appeared less vague than general anthropological pronouncements about culture. This was the theory which merged culture and cognition with *language and which went under the name of its two proponents: the *Sapir–Whorf hypothesis. †Sapir and †Whorf could be understood to say that the grammar and the lexicon of any particular language determined the cognition of its speakers. This proposal was difficult to test but it is clear that the strong claims of the hypothesis are not borne out, and this is most probably true

of the Boasian hypothesis in general (Glucksberg 1988).

Other writers in the middle of the century tried to bridge the gap between cognitive psychology and anthropology. Foremost among these was *Lévi-Strauss who adopted the psychological theories implicit in the work of structural linguists. Others attempted to marry the semantic analysis technique called *componential analysis with psychological findings (Wallace 1965).

Recently there has been a renewal of interest in anthropology in the importance of what psychologists have to say about cognition. This interest has focused on a number of topics, some of the more important of which are listed below.

Concepts

Concepts are small units of cognition through which we make sense of our environment. Thus, we can assume that most humans have a concept 'bird'. Consequently, because we possess the concept, when we see a particular flying animal we *know* it is a bird and instantly and automatically we make a number of assumptions about it: for example, that it lays eggs. The concept of a bird is therefore part of our cognition and if it has been inculcated into us by others who similarly learnt it, in other words it has been created by the history of our people, then it is also part of our culture. However, such a discussion leaves unexamined the question of the relation between the word 'bird' and the concept.

Anthropologists have often thought of less straightforward notions in much the same way. Thus †Evans-Pritchard in his book *Nuer Religion* (1956) discusses the Nuer word *thek*, which partly approximates to the English word 'respect', and assumes that studying how the word is used can lead him straight to Nuer 'concepts'.

Recently, however, cognitive psychology has made clear a number of problems with this common approach. The first is that the assumption that the words used by a person can be a straightforward guide to their concepts is misleading. This is so for a number of reasons (Bloch 1991). Second, the very notion that concepts are phenomena rather like dictionary entries, defined by a checklist of characteristics (a theory which implicitly underlies such writings as those of Evans-Pritchard and most classical anthropologists) is probably very misleading. This has been challenged since it was discovered that many concepts are not organized in terms of abstract characteristics but around prototypical concrete examples with any phenomena being judged as more or less corresponding to the proto-types and not either in or out of the category. This means that concepts are very different to the way anthropologists thought they were and this must lead to considerable rethinking about the nature of culture (Lakoff 1987).

Universals and innate knowledge

As noted above, the Boasian tradition in cultural anthropology stressed how culture directed cogni-tion. One common example was colour terms. The Boasians argued that all humans could see the same spectrum of colour, but since this was a continuum, the way the spectrum was broken up varied from culture to culture. This belief was shown to be quite false in a famous book by Berlin and Kay (1969), and in subsequent studies which showed that there was nothing arbitrary about how the spectrum was divided and that variation between cultures was strictly limited. This study was the first of many which revealed that in many key areas which cultural anthropologists had assumed were variable, all human cultures used the same cognitive principles. These findings were linked by certain anthropologists with advances in linguistics which suggested that the ability to learn human-type languages was the result of genetic programming common to all humans. Some anthropologists suggested that this was true for many areas of culture such as plant and animal *classification, concepts of the *person and of social relationships and face recognition; and even that certain types of narratives were easily learnt because they corresponded to genetic predispo-sitions to remember them while others which did not mesh with the cognitive dispositions would soon be forgotten (Sperber 1985). If proved right, clearly these theories would inevitably lead to fundamental revisions in anthropological notions of culture and *society.

Schemas

Schemas or scripts, two terms used in cognitive psychology to mean very similar things, are really one big concept. An example often given of a schema in an industrialized society is 'going to a restaurant'; or rather, what one can normally expect to happen if one goes to a restaurant. Such a stereotypical sequence is, of course, never exactly what happens in any particular instance, but the knowledge of such a schema enables one to cope efficiently with the various events which occur in any particular instance or to understand stories of what happened when particular people went to a restaurant on a particular occasion. Schemas represent the knowledge which is taken for granted in order that one can pay attention to the less predictable aspects of life. As a number of anthro-pologists have noted, schemas therefore represent the fundamentals of culture, and some writers have attempted to integrate the insights concerning schemas which come from psychology with more traditional anthropological concerns (Holland and Quinn 1987). Some writers (e.g. Strauss and Quinn 1994) have linked schema theory with the theory called connectionism which argues that habitual knowledge is stored and retrieved in ways which make it different in kind from the folk understanding of what knowledge is. As a result, these writers have argued that anthro-pologists have represented cultural knowledge in a way that is fundamentally misleading.

Analogy and thought

The most influential modern anthropologist to have stressed the importance of analogy for culture and thought in general is Lévi-Strauss. In his book *The Savage Mind* (1966), he argues that much inno-vative human thought involves analogy between systems of classification from one domain to another. This insight has received much support from a number of psychological studies which have shown the importance of analogical thinking by means of experiments. The study of analogy, which includes the study of metaphors, is there-fore an obvious area for cooperation between the two disciplines. Also very influential in both anthropology and psychology has been the joint work of a philosopher and a linguist: Lakoff and Johnson (1980; Lakoff 1987). They have argued that nearly all our language, and indeed our culture, is formulated from a very simple basis of bodily states which are used as root metaphors to express almost an infinity of more complex ideas by means of metaphors. This theory has many implications for our understanding of culture and its development, and has had much recent influ-ence in anthropology.

MAURICE BLOCH

See also: childhood, classification, psychological anthropology, socialization

Further reading

Bartlett, F.C. (1932) *Remembering*, Cambridge: Cambridge University Press

Benedict, R. (1935) *Patterns of Culture*, London: Routledge

Berlin, B. and P. Kay (1969) *Basic Color Terms: Their Universality and Evolution*, Berkeley and Los Angeles: University of California Press

Bloch, M. (1991) 'Language, Anthropology and Cognitive Science', *Man* 26: 183–98

Cole, M. and S. Scribner (1974) *Culture and Thought: A Psychological Introduction*, New York: John Wiley

Evans-Pritchard, E.E. (1956) *Nuer Religion*, Oxford: Clarendon Press

Glucksberg, S. (1988) 'Language and Thought' in R.J. Sternberg and E.E. Smith (eds) *The Psychology of Human Thought*, Cambridge: Cambridge University Press

Holland, D and N. Quinn (1987) *Cultural Models in Language and Thought*, Cambridge: Cambridge University Press

Hollis, M. and S. Lukes (eds) (1982) *Rationality and Relativism*, Oxford: Blackwell

Lakoff, G. (1987) *Women, Fire and Dangerous Things*, Chicago: University of Chicago Press

—— and M. Johnson (1980) *Metaphors we Live by*, Chicago: University of Chicago Press

Lévi-Strauss, C. (1966 [1963]) *The Savage Mind*, London: Weidenfeld and Nicolson

Sperber, D. (1985) 'Anthropology and Psychology: Towards an Epidemiology of Representations', *Man* 20: 73–89

Strauss, C. and N. Quinn (1994) 'A Cognitive/Cultural Anthropology' in R. Borofsky (ed.) *Assesssing Cultural Anthropology*, New York: McGraw Hill

Wallace A.F.C. (1965) 'The Problem of the Psychological Validity of Componential Analyses', *American Anthropologist* 67: 229–48

colonialism

Colonialism is significant for anthropology in three senses: (1) anthropology's alleged collaboration with colonial government and broader complicity in the culture of imperialism has been extensively debated; (2) colonial processes have had far-reaching and diverse ramifications for social and cultural phenomena studied by anthropologists; and (3) colonialism and colonial culture have emerged as objects of anthropological analysis in themselves. The order of these points relates roughly to the chronology of debate and analysis around the topic within the discipline and beyond.

Anthropology and colonialism

The key text is understood retrospectively to have been the volume edited by Talal Asad, *Anthropology and the Colonial Encounter* (1974), a book that has often been cited as though it charged the discipline with playing a collaborative role in colonial administration. A polemical stance had in fact been taken in earlier essays by Kathleen Gough (1968) that suggested that anthropologists had colluded in imperialism and neglected to describe the effects of capitalist expansion upon the societies they studied, but contributions to the Asad collection in fact variously exemplified, contested, and moved beyond the critique. James Faris argued persuasively that †Nadel's research in the Sudan was deliberately planned to assist the administration; Wendy James argued carefully if defensively that the liberal political sympathies of individual anthropologists were not accidental but were encouraged by the nature of the discipline itself; conflicts of interest between theoretically-driven research and policy, between ethnographers' and administrators' concerns, among other factors, meant that anthropology rarely served colonial government.

Asad himself moved beyond this literal discussion of collaboration to an analysis of a larger field of representations in a contrast of anthropological and *Orientalist constructions of non-European rule. He suggested that the latter emerged with the process of imperial conquest, and were therefore predisposed to emphasize the essentially despotic and irrational character of Islamic and non-Western polities, while anthropologists worked within a secure colonial order and tended to stress consent and continuity.

Although the caricatured critique was frequently referred to, it was followed up with surprisingly little historical research on the practical colonial involvement of anthropologists, and no further collection on the topic appeared until 1992 (Stocking 1992; for the best review, see Pels and Salemink 1994). As it became represented, the debate was constrained by too narrow a notion of colonialism, and an emphasis on practical collaboration to the detriment of wider discursive and imaginative continuities between anthropology and colonial ideology. †Edward Said's *Orientalism* (1977) charged a range of European disciplines and cultural genres with documenting, reifying, and *essentializing an Orient in a manner that was complicit with, if not always directly in the service of, the effort to dominate. The critique included anthropology more by implication than analysis, but did open up issues concerning the authoritative representation of colonized ethnic groups that had been anticipated by Asad but otherwise passed over.

Although Said concentrated on the nineteenth and twentieth centuries, Orientalism was understood as a discourse that had evolved over a long period, and anthropology could correspondingly also be considered less as a professional discipline and more as a larger body of discourse concerning non-European, or 'less developed' European societies, that was inevitably caught up in projects of dominance and self-definition.

Curiously, figures on both sides of the earlier debate had claimed either that anthropology was the legitimate child of the *Enlightenment *or* the bastard of colonialism (Asad 1974: 16; Firth 1975: 43–4), as though these terms were themselves mutually exclusive. The Enlightenment, however, saw Clive's victory at Plassey and the subsequent expansion of the East India Company in South Asia, the growth of the transatlantic slave trade, and British settlement in Australia, among many other unambiguously colonial initiatives; and the connections between imperial expansion and the growth of knowledge concerning non-European peoples were both evident and disturbing to many eighteenth-century *philosophes* and travellers (cf. Thomas 1994). The debate about the contamination of ethical social knowledge by politics and economics had a much longer history than those writing in the 1960s and 1970s appeared to realize.

So far as the understanding of late nineteenth and twentieth-century developments was concerned, scholarship moved beyond the activities of professional anthropologists and examined representations of others and popular ethnographic knowledge in world's fairs, popular fiction, and postcards. This was also the period for which studies of the relation between ethnography (and related inquiries concerned with population and health, that frequently employed statistical methods), and government really did have something to offer: for colonial administrations in many parts of the world created techniques of observation, statistical classification and discipline that were integral to the culture of government, however unevenly they served its projection. Much recent writing in this area has been informed by †Foucault's arguments about discipline and governmentality, and by the writings of Heidegger and †Derrida on †representation (Cohn 1987; Pinney 1990; Mitchell in Dirks 1992).

Recent critical writing has also raised the issue of whether even liberal or radical texts in fact transcend the distancing and exoticizing textual strategies that characterize earlier, unashamedly authoritative forms of anthropology. It can be argued, in particular, that the emphasis upon the distinctive coherence of other cultural systems, in American cultural anthropology, reproduces the form of Orientalist typification, in the sense that essentialist propositions about Japanese or Balinese culture take the same form as earlier reifications of the Oriental mind, Asiatic society and so on, even if the object is particularized and the analysis more subtle. In riposte, of course, it could be argued that essentialist propositions are pervasive, and that what is problematic is not their presence but their particular character and effect. The earlier critique of anthropological collaboration has thus evolved into two distinct if mutually informed enterprises: one being a more wide-ranging critical history of ethnographic and travel writing, the other being a continuing and unresolved interrogation of contemporary ethnography that draws upon †poststructuralist, feminist, and †postcolonial theory.

Colonial transformations

Anthropological *functionalism tended to ignore the ways in which the societies studied had been altered or influenced by colonial processes, except through inadequate notions of †'acculturation' and 'cultural change'. From the 1960s onward, anthropologists drawing upon Marxist theory, and attempting to historicize the discipline, emphasized the incorporation of apparently traditional societies in wider relations of political and economic dominance, and pointed to various ways in which phenomena that had previously been taken to be integral elements of precontact society were in fact generated, stabilized, or reified because of colonial contact or actual administrative intervention. Peter France's analysis of the Fijian system of land tenure (1969), that was rigidified under the British indirect rule regime, was a path-breaking if not widely recognized exemplar of such analysis, while more recent work in India has suggested that the *caste system was at once rendered more central socially by the British assault upon traditional warrior-kingship and more deeply institutionalized through a range of administrative policies (Dirks 1986).

While postcontact change was certainly earlier underestimated, critique of this kind tended to assume that colonized people passively accepted a variety of administrative impositions. Arguments that societies were remodelled in response or in opposition to European intrusions may overstate the efficacy and importance of colonial processes, and presume that the local social and cultural dynamics ceased to be efficacious from the moment of contact. In most regions, change entailed a more complex pattern of *resistance and accommodation; changes were sometimes accepted not in the terms in which they were projected, but because they articulated with a prior indigenous agenda which was not necessarily understood by colonial agents. Colonialism clearly needs to be understood as an uneven process rather than an all-or-nothing 'impact'. Some scholarship on the invention of indigenous or nationalist traditions has also a debunking character, that assumes a degree of gullibility or bad faith on the part of indigenous peoples and new élites. While this trend is highly problematic, the counter-critique in turn possesses a weakness, in the sense that the resilience of indigenous culture may be romantically overemphasized. If an earlier generation of anthropologists colluded in projects of colonial typification, contemporary ethnographers may collude in traditionalist efforts to validate the present for its elaboration of the past.

These questions need to remain open in part because colonial histories are so diverse. Prolonged settler colonization, entailing dispossession, leads to a different experience and colonial aftermath than the government or exploitation of peasant producers who remain upon their land; further distinctions can be made between mercantilism, informal neocolonialism, socialist colonialism, and so on. While there have been many impressive case-studies, including those concerned with colonialism in the ancient world, the medieval and early modern periods, and non-Western colonialisms (among others, the Japanese in East Asia), the sheer diversity of material has thus far inhibited anthropologically-informed comparative synthesis.

The culture of colonizers

At a surprisingly late stage in the debate, anthropological historians drew attention to the fact that colonialism was not a homogeneous process, and that particular colonizing projects were, moreover, frequently internally divided and contested (Stoler in Dirks 1992). That is, while the emphasis had previously been upon the colonized, anthropologists began to differentiate among agents of colonialism such as *missionaries, traders, and the *state. They drew attention not only to predictable conflicts of interest between such groups (that had long been described if not theorized by historians) but also to deeper contradictions within colonizing efforts, for example around tensions between segregation and assimilation, or between metropolitan imperial and †creole settler interests.

Colonializing societies – that were obviously always divided between metropolitan bases and temporary or long-term settler and trader projections – came to be seen as socially and culturally complex entities, to the same degree as the societies that were experiencing and responding to colonization. A shift of anthropological interest from indigenous peoples to colonizers complemented a move on the part of historians away from archive-based histories of Europeans toward oral histories of the colonized, and in many cases individual scholars worked in both fields. Greater sophistication in historical anthropology thus led to a deeper understanding, not of 'both sides' of colonial processes, but of the fact that there was a plethora of cross-cutting interests and differences among both colonizing and indigenous populations.

Feminist critique further differentiated colonial projects by suggesting the divergent interests of colonizing men and women, by exploring the particular roles of women missionaries and missionary wives, for example, and by examining the differentiated impact of colonial policies on women and men. These were often considerable, given the degree to which, at various times, missions, government policies, and labour recruiting practices explicitly aimed to transform the division of labour and domestic relations (see e.g. Jolly and Macintyre 1989). *Gender has long been significant in colonial and indigenous imaginings of cross-cultural relationships – the feminization of the Oriental other has become a truism of critical discourse – but more can be done on the workings of notions of domesticity, familial forms, and the mutation of indigenous gender identities under colonization.

Parallels have been identified between administrative and evangelical efforts both within metropolitan countries and on the periphery (Comaroff and Comaroff 1991), such as the efforts that were widely projected and implemented from the late nineteenth century onward to sanitize and regulate societies, efforts that entailed much ethnographic, statistical and photographic documentation, and complex interpretive efforts as well as struggles to implement new divisions of space upon recalcitrant English slum-dwellers and African villagers. In this case, 'colonialism' might threaten to evaporate altogether as a category of analysis, to be displaced by modernizing social transformations that were implemented both abroad and at home (and in some cases by national élites in the absence of actual colonial rule; in Thailand and Japan, for example). While these closely-linked projects need to be analysed further, the centrality of *race in colonial imaginings and practices suggests that colonial relationships still need to be considered distinctively, however remarkably diversified they have been and are; and the continuing significance of racism and race makes the study of colonial histories – that are the antecedents to the contemporary global order – a priority for the discipline.

NICHOLAS THOMAS

See also: Orientalism, Enlightenment anthropology, essentialism

Further reading

Asad, T. (ed.) (1974) *Anthropology and the Colonial Encounter*, London: Ithaca

Cohn, B. (1987) *An Anthropologist among the Historians*, Delhi: Oxford University Press

Comaroff, J. and J. Comaroff (1991) *Of Revelation and Revolution*, Chicago: University of Chicago Press

Dirks, N. (1986) *The Hollow Crown: Ethnohistory of an Indian Kingdom*, Cambridge: Cambridge University Press

—— (ed.) (1992) *Colonialism and Culture*, Ann Arbor: University of Michigan Press

Firth, R. (1975) 'The Sceptical Anthropologist? Social Anthropology and Marxist Views on Society', in M. Bloch (ed.) *Marxist Analyses and Social Anthropology*, London: Malaby

France, P. (1969) *The Charter of the Land*, Melbourne: Oxford University Press

Gough, K. (1968) 'New Proposals for Anthropologists', *Current Anthropology* 9: 403–7

Jolly, M. and M. Macintyre (eds) (1989) *Family and Gender in the Pacific*, Cambridge: Cambridge University Press

Pels, P. and O. Salemink (eds) (1994) *Colonial Ethnographies*, special vol., *History and Anthropology* 8: 1–4

Pinney, C. (1990) 'Classification and Fantasy in the Photographic Construction of Caste and Tribe', *Visual Anthropology* 3: 259–88

Said, E. (1977) *Orientalism*, New York: Viking

Stocking, G. (ed.) (1992) *Colonial Situations: Essays on the Contextualization of Anthropological Knowledge* (History of Anthropology 8), Madison: University of Wisconsin Press

Thomas, N. (1994) *Colonialism's Culture: Anthropology, Travel and Government*, Cambridge: Polity/Princeton: Princeton University Press

community

The concept of community has been one of the widest and most frequently used in social science; its examination has been a focus of attention for at least the past 200 years. At the same time a precise definition of the term has proved elusive. Among the more renowned attempts remains that of †Robert Redfield ([1949]1960:4), who identified four key qualities in community: a smallness of social scale; a homogeneity of activities and states of mind of members; a consciousness of distinctiveness; and a self-sufficiency across a broad range of needs and through time. Nevertheless, in 1955, Hillery could compile ninety-four social-scientific attempts at definition whose only substantive overlap was that 'all dealt with people' (1955: 117)! Often, to overcome this problem, community is further specified by a qualifying or amplifying phrase: the 'local community', the 'West Indian community', the 'community of nations' or 'souls'. But this would seem only to beg the question.

Traditional anthropological approaches

In anthropology, one might usefully isolate three broad variants of traditional approach. 'Community' is to be characterized in terms of: (i) common interests between people; or (ii) a common ecology and locality; or (iii) a common social system or structure. Taking these (briefly) in turn, Frankenberg (1966) suggests that it is common interests in achievable things (economic, religious, or whatever) that give members of a community a common interest in one another. Living face-to-face, in a small group of people, with common interests in mind, eventuates in community members sharing many-stranded or multiplex relations with one another; also sharing a sentiment towards the locality and the group itself. Hence, communities come to be marked by a fair degree of social coherence.

For Minar and Greer (1969), physical concentration (living and working) in one geographical territory is the key. For this locale will throw up common problems and give rise to common perspectives, which lead to the development of organizations for joint action and activities, which in turn produce common attachments, feelings of interdependence, common commitment, loyalty and identity within a social group. Hence, communities come to exhibit homogeneity: members behaving similarly and working together, towards common aims, in one environment, whatever their familial or generational differences.

For †Warner (1941), meanwhile, a community is essentially a socially functioning whole: a body of people bound to a common *social structure which functions as a specific organism, and which is distinguishable from other such organisms. Consciousness of this distinction (the fact that they live with the same †norms and within the same social organization) then gives community members a sense of belonging. So long as the parts of the functioning whole (*families, †age sets, †status groups, or whatever) work properly together, the structure of the community can be expected to continue over time.

Whether it be in terms of interests, ecology or social structure, then, anthropologists have conventionally emphasized an essential commonality as the logic underlying a community's origination and continuation. Communities have been regarded as empirical things-in-themselves (social organisms), as functioning wholes, and as things apart from other like things. This was in turn the logical basis of 'the community study': the tradition in anthropology of basing research on what could in some sense be treated as a bounded group of people, culturally homogeneous and resident in one locality, because this 'community' would provide a laboratory for the close observation of the interrelations, the continuing interfunctioning, between interests, sub-groups and institutions; and also serve as a microcosm of a bigger social picture which might prevail as societies grew in size and complexity. Anthropologists conventionally studied communities (villages, tribes, islands) because these were regarded as the key structural units of social life: what the elementary structures of *kinship gave onto; what the complex structures of society were composed of.

Symbolic approaches

However, as varieties of *functionalism and *structuralism have come to share space in the anthropological armoury with approaches which emphasize the extent to which cultural reality is negotiated and contested, its definition a matter of context and interpretation, as anthropologists have come to regard social life as turning on the use of symbolic not structural logics – so notions of 'community' have changed. The idea of something reifiable, essential and singular has been replaced by a focus on how 'community' is elicited as a feature of social life, on how membership of community is marked and attributed, on how notions of community are given cultural meaning, and how such meaning relates to others. In place of the reified notion of community as a thing-in-itself, then, comes the realization that, as †Gregory Bateson put it succinctly: things are epiphenomena of the relations between them; or as †Barth elaborated, social groups achieve an identity by defining themselves as different from other such groups and by erecting boundaries between them (1969). In terms of their field research, anthropologists now admit a distinction between the locus of their study and their object of study: as †Clifford Geertz once put it, they may study in villages (on islands, in cities, in factories) but that does not mean studying villages per se.

Anthony Cohen has applied these ideas perhaps most fruitfully to the concept of community (1985). Community, he argues, must be seen as a symbolic construct and a contrastive one; it derives from the situational perception of a boundary which marks off one social group from another: awareness of community depends on consciousness of boundary. Hence, communities and their boundaries exist essentially not as social-structural systems and institutions but as worlds of meaning in the minds of their members. Relations between members represent not a set of mechanical linkages between working parts so much as 'repositories of meaning', and it is these which come to be expressed as a community's distinctive social *discourse (1985: 98). In short, membership consists not so much of particular behavioural doings as of thinking about and deliberating upon behaviour in common; here is attachment to a common body of †symbols, a shared vocabulary of value. Moreover, it is the ambiguities of symbolic discourse which then allow members to unite behind this vocabulary when facing what they perceive to lie beyond their boundaries but also, when facing inward, to elaborate upon differences in its interpretation and hence affirm a variety of cherished individualities. Community is an aggregating device which both sustains diversity and expresses commonality. Thus it is that community comes to represent the social milieu to which people say they most belong; community, its members often believe, is the best arena for the nourishing of their whole selves.

Furthermore, to say that any understanding of 'community' must be *relativistic, that the concept is a matter of contingent symbolic definition, is also to talk about 'community' in relation to other types or levels of sociation. Here, Cohen continues, community can be understood to represent that social milieu – broader than notions of family and kinship, more inclusive, but narrower, more immediate, than notions of *society and *state – where the taken-for-granted relations of kinship are to be put aside and yet where the non-relations of stranger-ness or the anti-relations of alien-ness need not be assumed; community encompasses something in between the closest and the furthest reaches of sociation in a particular context. Hence, the notion of community encapsulates both closeness and sameness, and distance and difference; and it is here that gradations of sociality, more and less close social associations, have their abiding effects. For members of a community are related by their perception of commonalities (but not tied by them or ineluctably defined by them as are kin), and equally, differentiated from other communities and their members by these relations and the sociation they amount to. In short, 'community' describes the arena in which one learns and largely continues to practise being social. It serves as a symbolic resource, repository and referent for a variety of *identities, and its 'triumph' (Cohen 1985: 20) is to continue to encompass these by a common symbolic boundary.

Evolutionary approaches

Nevertheless, for many social scientists, the problem of defining community is to be explained not by its relativistic qualities but its anachronistic ones. Community is said to characterize a stage in social *evolution which has now been superseded, and the problems of definition arise from the fact that what is seen as 'community' now is a residue and a throwback to a mode of relating and interacting which was once the norm but has now all but been eclipsed by more modern notions of contractual relations in *complex society (cf. Stein 1964). Such ideas are by no means new. They can be seen to imbue the evolutionary schemas of such nineteenth-century visionaries as †Maine, †Durkheim and †Marx. In particular they are associated with the work of German sociologist †Ferdinand Tönnies who, in 1887, posited the transcendence of 'community' (†*Gemeinschaft*) by 'society' (†*Gesellschaft*). What he hypothesized

([1887]1957) was that the traditional, static, 'naturally' developed forms of social organization (such as kinship, friendship, neighbourhood and 'folk') would everywhere be superseded (in zero-sum fashion) by associations expressly invented for the rational achievement of mutual goals (economic corporations, political parties, trades unions). This was not an unmixed blessing, for while community relations may be moral, senti-mental, localized, particular, intimate, ascribed, enduring, conventional, consistent, and based on intrinsic attachments (to blood, soil, heritage and language), societal relations were artificial, contractual, interested, partial, ego-focused, specialized, superficial, inconsistent, fluid, short-term and impersonal. And yet community was inevitably (and absolutely) losing out to the advancing society of *capitalism.

'Community' in current usage

Whatever the evolutionary prognosis, needless to say (whatever 'advances' capitalism may have made over the past century) 'communities' have continued to flourish; as an idea, community has continued to possess both practical and ideological significance for people. Indeed, recent decades have seen an upsurge in 'community consciousness', 'community development and rebuilding' and 'community values and works'. Whether that community is defined in terms of locality, *ethnicity, *religion, occupation, recreation, special interest, even humanity, people maintain the idea that it is this milieu which is most essentially 'theirs', and that they are prepared to assert their ownership and membership, vocally and aggressively, in the face of opposing ideas and groups (cf. Anderson 1983). Thus, anthropologists have continued to be interested in this idea in use; and Robert Redfield's counsel remains pertinent:

> As soon as our attention turns from a community as a body of houses and tools and institutions to the states of mind of particular people, we are turning to the exploration of something immensely complex and difficult to know. But it is humanity, in its inner and more private form; it is, in the most demanding sense, the stuff of community.
>
> (1960: 59)

Anthropologists, in short, continue studying 'community' (cf. Cohen 1987; Meillassoux 1981;

Pitt-Rivers 1954) because this is what their subjects inform them that they live in and cherish.

In sum, perhaps it is sufficient to say that, however diverse its definition, community ubiquitously represents an 'hurray' term (Cranston 1953: 16). Whether 'community' represents a togetherness of the past (Tönnies), contemporary behavioural commonality (Frankenberg, Minar and Greer, Warner), political solidarity (ethnic, local, religious), or a utopian future (a rural idyll, a world order), here, notwithstanding, is a concept of always positive evaluation and evocation, whose usage expresses and elicits a social group and a social environment to which people would expect, advocate or wish to belong.

NIGEL RAPPORT

See also: gossip, symbolic anthropology

Further reading

Anderson, B. (1983) *Imagined Communities*, London: Verso

Barth, F. (1969) *Ethnic Groups and Boundaries*, Boston: Little, Brown

Cohen, A.P. (1985) *The Symbolic Construction of Community*, London: Tavistock

—— (1987) *Whalsay. Symbol, Segment and Boundary in a Shetland Island Community*, Manchester: Manchester University Press

Cranston, M. (1953) *Freedom*, London: Longmans/Green

Frankenberg, R. (1966) *Communities in Britain*, Harmondsworth: Penguin

Gusfield, J. (1975) *Community*, Oxford: Blackwell

Hillery, G. (1955) 'Definitions of Community: Areas of Agreement', *Rural Sociology* 20: 116–31

Meillassoux, C. (1981) *Maidens, Meal and Money. Capitalism and the Domestic Community*, Cambridge: Cambridge University Press

Minar, D. and S. Greer (1969) *The Concept of Community*, Chicago: Aldine

Pitt-Rivers, J. (1954) *The People of the Sierra*, London: Weidenfeld and Nicolson

Redfield, R. (1960) *The Little Community and Peasant Society And Culture*, Chicago: University of Chicago Press

Stein, M. (1964) *The Eclipse of Community*, New York: Harper

Tönnies, F. ([1887]1957) *Community and Society*, New York: Harper

Warner, W.L. (1941) 'Social Anthropology and the Modern Community', *American Journal of Sociology* 46: 785–96

compadrazgo

Compadrazgo (literally co-fatherhood) is the Spanish form of †ritual kinship established through the rites of the Catholic Church (especially at baptism, confirmation and marriage) between a person, his or her biological parents, and his or her godparents. From Spain, *compadrazgo* has spread to *Latin America where it is sometimes even more important than in its place of origin (Mintz and Wolf 1950; van den Berghe and van den Berghe 1966). At baptism, confirmation and marriage, an individual acquires one or more sets of godparents (a *padrino* and a *madrina* who are often a married couple, and who may be biological kin, but most frequently are friends or employers of the biological parents). An individual is known as his or her godparents' *ahijado* or *ahijada*, depending on sex. The relationship between the biological parents and the godparents (who call each other reciprocally *compadre* or *comadre*, according to sex) is at least as important as that between godparents and godchild, and lasts for life. *Compadrazgo* is the generic term to describe the entire complex of these ritual ties. Indeed, the Spanish term is sometimes extended to ritual kinship in non-Spanish speaking countries (Gudeman 1972, 1975).

Normally, the biological parents choose their child's godparents with an eye to both the child's advantage and their own. Godparents (and co-parents from the biological parents' point of view) are chosen to reinforce existing ties with other kin or with friends, or to establish a special relationship to a social superior who can be useful to the child or the parents (e.g. an employer, a politician, a physician, a lawyer, an official). Thus, only individuals of equal or higher status than oneself are normally chosen as co-parents. *Compadrazgo* frequently establishes ties across social *classes or even ethnic groups (e.g. between mestizos and Indians in Mexico, Guatemala, Peru, Bolivia and other Latin American countries with large indigenous populations). This often has the effect of undermining or overshadowing class or ethnic solidarity, and of establishing paternalistic *patron-client ties between persons of quite unequal status who exchange loyalty, favours, gifts, labour, and hospitality over many years.

The terminology of *compadrazgo* is sometimes extended to non-ritual, non-religious events, such as the sponsorship of sport teams, or graduating school classes, but secularized *compadrazgo* is often little more than an attempt to extract a donation from a wealthy sponsor in exchange for social recognition. Being asked to serve as godparent is an honour which cannot be gracefully turned down. The more socially prominent, politically powerful, morally upright, and economically solvent a person is, the more frequently he or she is approached, and number of godparenthoods is one of the best indices of social status in Hispanic societies.

PIERRE L. VAN DEN BERGHE

See also: Europe: South, Americas: Central, Americas: Native South (Highland), kinship

Further reading

Gudeman, S. (1972) 'The *Compadrazgo* as a Reflection of the Natural and Spiritual Person', *Proceedings of the Royal Anthropological Institute for 1971*: 45–71
—— (1975) 'Spiritual Relationships and Selecting a Godparent', *Man* 10: 221–37
Mintz, S. and E. R. Wolf (1950) 'An Analysis of Ritual Co-parenthood (*Compadrazgo*)', *Southwestern Journal of Anthropology* 6: 341–68
van den Berghe, G. and P. L. (1966) '*Compadrazgo* and Class in Southeastern Mexico', *American Anthropologist* 68(5): 1236–44

comparative method

In the nineteenth century the comparative method became the ruler of science. This method was also adopted by the cultural evolutionists. For decades it was assumed that the comparative method was abandoned when *evolutionism was attacked. In truth, not only (†unilinear) evolutionists, but *diffusionists, *functionalists, and *structuralists have all compared. They, however, adopted different strategies for different purposes. †Kroeber stated the position correctly when he contended that the comparative method had never gone out of circulation in anthropology; it had only changed its tactic. Nevertheless, since the heyday of grand comparison in the 1940s and 1950s, †Evans-Pritchard's (1963) scepticism about the possibility of anthropological comparison has become increasingly fashionable (cf. Holy 1987). In the 1980s and 1990s, few anglophone anthropologists were prepared to attempt comparisons above the level of *regional analysis and regional comparison, although more ambitious comparative projects (for example, in the analysis of *kinship structures) remained a feature of *French anthropology.

Units and items of comparison

A *unit* of comparison is the totality which is the point of reference for comparison with another totality of a similar nature. An *item* of comparison is that part of a unit which is actually utilized in comparing. In comparing cultural traits, items and units of comparison may be the same, while whole cultures as units can be compared only through one or more cultural item. *Traits* and *institutions* are the commonest units of comparison. A trait can be defined and isolated with reference to context and is further subdivisible. It may be a biological category (reproduction), a material manifestation (pottery or basketry), a game (patolli or pachisi), or a mere relationship (the mother's brother/sister's son relationship).

Aggregates constitute another class of units of comparison. *Empirical aggregates* like communities, culture areas, cultural wholes, etc., can be located and referred to. A *conceptual aggregate* is constructed through the researcher's conceptualization, rather than from some empirical referent. *Totemism is a notable conceptual aggregate, as are the †*Kulturkreise*, or cultural circles of the German diffusionists.

A cultural whole may be a tribal, folk or civilizational whole. As units of comparison, cultural wholes have to be represented through items like a trait, theme, institution or group. A civilizational whole can be compared through items like speech, *religion, government, *science, *cosmology, etc.

Goals of comparison

Both 'historical' and scientific goals are pursued through anthropological comparison. 'Inferential history', the construction of typologies, generalizations and laws, and generalized processes are the main goals of anthropological comparisons.

History is supposed to tell us what happened. But all history is reconstruction. In *inferential history* the origin or development of a factor (trait, institution, etc.) is hypothesized on the basis of knowledge of its present condition, in the absence of historical evidence, but with free use of the imagination. In inferential history 'theories' (like evolutionism) and facts (like the distribution of cultural elements) may be used to reconstruct cultural sequences. Cultural traits and complexes are the commonest items used for writing inferential history. Studies of the Sun-Dance Complex of the Plains Indians (†Spier), the diffusion of metal forms from the Caucasus to South America (Heine-Geldern) and the distribution of culture elements (Klimeck) are examples of attempts at inferential history.

Typology building is an acknowledged goal of comparison. †Raymond Firth described establishing types and seeking variants from them as the essence of the comparative method in social anthropology. †Edmund Leach denounced comparison because it yields typologies which he famously called 'butterfly collecting'. A *type* consists of a group of manifestations sharing common features which distinguish it from another such unit. It represents a modal tendency of a class of phenomena. A type may refer to empirical reality directly or it may be a reconstruction. †Max Weber's †'ideal type' is a reconstructed type; †Redfield and Leach worked with reconstructed types.

A descriptive-analytic typology deals with †synchronic phenomenal reality and focuses on contextual comparison. It includes morphological (formal) and functional sub-types. A reconstructed type may belong to either category. A historical-developmental typology is concerned with †diachronic factors. Its two main subdivisions are historical-index and whole-culture sub-types.

That the facts of social and cultural anthropology are 'historically-determined' does not mean that regularities cannot be discovered behind them. According to Max Black, a generalization is a principle which asserts some attribute about some or all members of a class of objects. In a uniform generalization *all* the members of the class are represented. A statistical generalization represents *most* of a class of phenomena. When a certain antecedent 'C' is followed by a consequent 'E', under specified conditions, we call it causal. All generalizations need not refer to causes. The correlation (rather than causation) of features is the best we can hope for in the name of generalization in anthropology. A law is a generalization with the universal schema: 'All A is B'; e.g. all crows are black. It is a universal conditional which formulates a constant conjunction of traits, e.g. crow and black.

A process means a movement or transition in time, from one condition to another. To distinguish it from socio-psychological trends or mechanisms – such as cooperation, competition, assimilation, etc. – which are also called processes, we can use the term *generalized process*. Through empirical restudies, like those conducted by Redfield and Firth, a synchronic generalized process is obtainable. From it we may learn how change, generated in a traditional society, may lead to structural readjustments. Using historical material some anthropologists have attempted to formulate diachronic generalized processes. For example, †Julian Steward utilized materials from the Old World and the New World to delineate a pattern of development of social organization of irrigation civilizations, while Kroeber compared whole civilizations as portraying configurations of their growth.

Methods of comparison

†Herskovits once insightfully remarked that the term 'method' should not be confined to the actual processes applied in prosecuting a research investigation. A *method* is not merely an instrumentality; it is a complete set of rules of procedure employed in attaining a given (research) goal. Suitable research techniques are incorporated into the method. A technique is a procedure or a contrivance – verbal or mechanical – for collecting and processing data in the course of an empirical inquiry.

There are four aspects of a comparative method in anthropology: techniques; goals; items and units; and areal coverage of the material which should go together. But only the technique goes with the areal coverage; the picture becomes fuzzy if the other two factors are added to them. The three comparative methods are: the method of illustrative comparison; the method of complete-universe comparison; and the method of hologeistic (sampled) comparison. The three methods, and their particular combination of the aspects are correlated in the table.

The method of *illustrative comparison* lacks a systematic representation of the corpus of ethnographic material. Instead, illustration is the technique. Comparison consists of selecting cases casually or unsystematically to 'prove' one's point. One may claim that through this method empirical support is provided for a formulation which the researcher has already worked out. Illustrations are chosen because the anthropologist is acquainted with them or they ostensively support his or her contention. There is no coverage of all the cultures, either of a defined region or of the whole world, or a representative sample of either of them.

A variety of goals may be pursued through this method – inferential history, validation of concepts and categories, typology construction, supporting general statements, etc. Either a preliminary conceptualization or a preconceived scheme of interpretation guides all such comparisons. Anthropologists of different persuasions – unilinear evolutionists, diffusionists, functionalists, structuralists, etc. – have used this method.

In the method of *complete-universe comparison* a defined and delimited universe of *discourse is

Table 2 A correlation of four aspects of a comparative method

Units and Categories	Areal Coverage	Goals (Purposes)	Technique	Method
Traits, complexes, Institutions, etc.	Unsystematic	Inferential history formulation of types, categories and general laws	Illustration	Illustrative (or causal) comparison
Traits, complexes, institutions, communities and/or whole cultures	Total coverage of a defined universe: regional or global	Inferential history, limited synchronic generalization and diachronic regularity	Delimitation	Complete-universe comparison
Institutions	Global representation through samples	Typology, hypothesis (correlation) and generalization	Sampling and statistics	Hologeistic (sampled) comparison

covered totally. This method utilizes a single empirical order for ethnographic coverage. There are two main sub-varieties of this method with reference to areal coverage: regional, with prominence to geographic ordering; or global, with emphasis on topical and conceptual, rather than geographic ordering.

A region may range from a small geographical area to a whole continent. However delimited, the region must be fully covered or else we shall not be doing complete-universe comparison. This method has been mostly adopted by functionalists. The universe of discourse is clearly defined and delimited. Three main variants are: a comparative description of all the cultures of the region summing up their common features; a single general type pervading the whole region is postulated (other entities are characterized according to the degree of their similarity to or difference from the general type); a general type with two or more varieties forming separate cultural divisions (one of which is chosen for comparative study and its conclusions compared with assumptions about other cultural divisions).

Complete-universe global comparisons have to be selective because not all known cultures can be covered. Julian Steward circumscribed the scope of his study of the development of early forms of agriculture in irrigation civilizations; he hoped to discover the conditions which determined new levels of organization. Kroeber's study of configurations of culture growth is another variant of global comparison. The units of comparison are the great civilizations of the Old and New Worlds. The items of Kroeber's 'inductive comparisons' are categories like philosophy, science, philology, sculpture, etc. Kroeber tried to cover this defined and delimited universe completely in order to find out if there were some regular patterns in the development of civilizational categories, while preserving the phenomena intact as phenomena.

The method of *hologeistic sampled comparison* (from the Greek *holos* = whole; *ge* = 'earth') was called the 'cross-cultural' method by †G.P. Murdock and others. According to John Whiting, this method utilized anthropological data about peoples around the globe in order to test hypotheses concerning human behaviour. The †Human Relations Area Files (HRAF) were devised at Yale, to catalogue a sample representing 10 per cent of all cultures known to date, on which cross-cultural comparisons could be based.

In this method the validity of hypotheses is tested without assuming that the final outcome will be the same as the initial postulate. A defined universe has to be covered through a representative sample; quantitative data and the use of statistics are essential. But only certain social phenomena can be properly isolated from their socio-cultural context for quantitative treatment. This formal approach may, therefore, result in mere enumeration of items. Also all the factors have to be considered identical for statistical treatment, and this may not be true.

Murdock did not find problems in isolating the items of comparison, in order to 'test' social behaviour 'theories', because he remained well within the anthropological tradition. But Whiting and his collaborators in their cross-cultural studies of *childhood also used anthropological source material for testing hypotheses rooted in Freudian and Hullian psychology, although the data were not suitable for their purposes. They imposed their framework on ethnographic data, wrongly assuming that they thus rendered them suitable for testing psychologically-oriented behavioural 'theory'. Actual comparison involved assessing scores on a list of disjointed elements, like the trait list of diffusionists, in order to note the presence or absence of particular data. Realizing the inadequacy of the data, the Whitings launched a programme of collecting proper ethnographic material from six cultures for testing psycho-logically-oriented hypotheses. But, whatever its successes or failures, this effort did not yield sufficient material for hologeistic sampled comparison because this requires sampling, statistical treatment, and the desire to cover the whole globe.

Since the use of sampling and statistics was made the cornerstone of this version of the comparative method its protagonists have to face Galton's problem. Over a century ago, Galton indicated that statistical treatment requires that the researcher ensures that the institutions or traits selected for comparison are unrelated. This cultural and historical requirement is very important. Any historical connection between cultures, peoples or institutions means that for purposes of statistical comparison, related cultures will have to be treated as a single unit.

GOPALA SARANA

See also: methodology, regional analysis

Further reading

Ackerknecht, Edwin H. (1954) 'On the Comparative Method in Cultural Anthropology', in Robert F. Spencer (ed.) *Method and Perspective in Anthropology*, Minneapolis: The University of Minnesota Press

Eggan, Fred (1954) 'Social Anthropology and the Method of Controlled Comparison', *American Anthropologist* 56: 643–763

Evans-Pritchard, E.E. (1963) *The Comparative Method in Social Anthropology*, London: The Athlone Press

Holy, Ladislav (ed.) (1987) *Comparative Anthropology*, Oxford: Basil Blackwell

Kobben, A.J. (1952) 'The New Ways of Presenting an Old Idea: The Statistical Method in Social Anthropology', *Journal of the Royal Anthropological Institute*, 83: 129-46

Kroeber, A.L. (1954) 'Critical Summary and Commentary', in Robert F. Spencer (ed.) *Method and Perspective in Anthropology*, Minneapolis: The University of Minnesota Press

Lewis, O. (1965) 'Comparisons in Cultural Anthropology', in William L. Thomas (ed.) *Current Anthropology: A Supplement to Anthropology Today*, Chicago: University of Chicago Press

Moore, W. F. (ed.) (1961) *Readings in Cross-cultural Methodology*, New Haven: Human Relations Area Files Press

Sarana, G. (1965) 'On Comparative Methods in Social-cultural Anthropology and in Linguistics', *Anthropological Quarterly* 38: 10–40

—— (1975) *The Methodology of Anthropological Comparison*, Tucson: University of Arizona Press

complementary filiation

Complementary filiation was a term introduced by the group of anthropologists of Africa who are often referred to as *'descent theorists', foremost of whom was †M. Fortes. The phrase referred to the fact that in societies with †unilineal descent groups people nonetheless recognize *kinship links with relatives who do not belong to their own descent group. Thus, in societies with †patrilineal descent groups, individuals have important socially-defined links with members of their mother's family, such as, for example, their mother's brother or their maternal grandparents, while in †matrilineal societies individuals have similar ties to their father's family.

Originally the concept was used to describe an important ethnographic characteristic of many African societies, such as the Tallensi of Ghana studied by Fortes, and the anthropologists' theory was little more than a paraphrase of the theory of the people they had studied. Thus Fortes described how Tallensi individuals saw their complementary filiation links as different from their †lineage links, yet essential to their well-being (Fortes 1949). While lineage links always have a political and hierarchical character, complementary filiation is more emotional and more personal. This is because all members of a descent group have different ties of complementary filiation from one another, but are undifferentiated on the basis of descent, so that complementary filiation gives an idiom to feelings of individuality and independence. This sociological perspective is, argued Fortes (1961), also reflected in the religious domain. †J. Goody (1962), following in the same tradition, stressed the importance of †inheritance and showed how, while one inherited a certain type of *property and status inside the descent group, one also inherited different types of property and status along the lines of complementary filiation.

In Fortes's later work the notion of complementary filiation was used to support a much more general claim (Fortes 1953, 1969). Fortes and a number of other anthropologists argued that the existence of groups was, at bottom, always similar and always involved the recognition of the complementary role of the two parents. Thus, in patrilineal societies, while for political, jural and military purposes lineages ignored links through mothers, there nonetheless existed a domestic level where links through women were recognized in the form of complementary filiation.

It is this wider theoretical implication of the theory which came under attack form such writers as †Edmund Leach (1961), who argued that in those patrilineal societies which *Lévi-Strauss would qualify as having an †elementary structure, links through the mother were to be seen, not as manifesting a kind of muted kinship but rather as being part of †affinal links. Thus in such societies one's mother was not seen as a 'mother' in the European sense, nor her brother as a man linked to her, but both would be seen as members of the group who give sexual partners to your own group. Such a distinction might seem of little importance but in fact hides a fundamental theoretical claim, namely that there is nothing universal or 'biological' to human kinship which constrains its representation.

MAURICE BLOCH

See also: alliance, descent, kinship, marriage

Further reading

Fortes, M. (1949) *The Web of Kinship Among the Tallensi*, Oxford: Oxford University Press
—— (1953) 'The Structure of Unilineal Descent Groups', *American Anthropologist* 55: 17–41
—— (1961) 'Pietas in Ancestor Worship', *Journal of the Royal Anthropological Institute* 91: 166–91
—— (1969) *Kinship and the Social Order*, Chicago: Aldine
Goody, J.R. (1962) *Death, Property and the Ancestors*, London: Tavistock
Leach, E.R. (1961) *Rethinking Anthropology*, London: Athlone

complex society

The term 'complex society' came into increasing use in anthropology in the post-World War II period as more scholars turned their attention to *peasant societies, and as *urban anthropology developed. It is used somewhat imprecisely to refer mostly to societies with a developed division of labour and with sizeable populations. State organization, urbanism, organized social *inequality and *literacy tend also to be aspects of the complexity involved. The rather loose usage may be criticized – what society is really not complex? – but anthropologists have obviously found it a convenient alternative to such terms as 'modern society', 'industrial society' or 'civilization', with which it may partly overlap but which entail emphases or connotations one may prefer to avoid.

Varieties of small-scale units

No doubt influenced by the tradition of local ethnographic field study, anthropological research has often focused on smaller-scale units of analysis within complex societies, with varying degrees of attention to the embeddedness of such units in wider structures. The attempt, particularly in the 1940s, by American students of 'national character' to generalize from *culture and personality analyses of interpersonal relations to national cultures is an extreme example; a part of their work was motivated by the desire, during World War II and the period following it, to understand the peculiarities of both adversaries and allies (Mead and Métraux 1953). Another, more durable line of research has been that of *community studies. A great many of these have been done, especially in towns and villages of Europe and North America, by anthropologists or ethnographically oriented sociologists, from the late 1920s onwards. Community studies have often succeeded in offering well-rounded portrayals of places and ways of life, and some even have a certain literary merit. On the other hand, it has been complained that they have contributed little to theory-building or comparative analysis. Frankenberg (1966), however, could draw on a generation of such studies in the British Isles in his comparative exploration of tendencies of social change.

From the 1950s to the 1970s, research on various types of informal organization was prominent in the anthropological study of complex societies. As †Eric Wolf (1966: 2) put it, 'the anthropologist has a professional license to study such interstitial, supplementary, and parallel structures in complex society and to expose their relation to the major strategic, overarching institutions'. The study of *household and *kinship had a part here, but especially characteristic were the increased interest in *friendship, *patrons and clients, social and cultural brokerage, the management of information and reputations (for example through *gossip), and *network analysis. Studies of such topics tended to be strongly micro-sociological, actor-centred, and theoretically oriented towards †transactionalism, and this probably made them less intellectually attractive in the following period with the ascendant interest in *Marxism and anthropology.

A continuous interest in the more recent anthropology of complex societies has been groups whose forms of life for one reason or other diverge from whatever is thought of as the 'mainstream'. Often such groups are defined in terms of *ethnicity. Although the latter term came into more common use only in the 1960s, in North America many ethnographic studies of such groups and their relationships to the surrounding societies had already been carried out under the rubric of 'race relations' or the study of 'minorities'. In Western Europe, similar studies have increased with the growth of immigrant populations.

Clearly, however, these ethnically distinct groups are often at the same time economically and politically disadvantaged, and it has occasionally been a matter of some controversy where the analytical emphasis should be placed: on poverty or ethnicity, on *class or *culture? It may well be that arguments in either/or terms are not always the most helpful here, and that the ambiguity of key concepts is a source of confusion. The debate over the †'culture of poverty' concept in the United States in the late 1960s and the early 1970s offers both an obvious example of how different emphases could be seen to have importantly different policy implications, and of the need for conceptual clarity (Leacock 1971).

Studies of ethnically distinct and disadvantaged groups may well attract anthropologists because they entail both an involvement with a culturally different 'other' and an opportunity to contribute socially relevant understanding; even the possibility of advocacy or †action anthropology. On the other hand, the ethnographic genre has occasionally met with some disapproval; a critical concern with the structure of society, it is argued, would be better served by research on the powerful than on the powerless. Nader (1972) has summarized this view in her plea for 'studying up'. Limited resources and restricted access may well tend to make ethnographic studies of élites rather difficult, yet some such work has also appeared.

Regions, nations and globalization

Anthropologists have given comparatively little attention to developing frameworks of macro-anthropological analysis for complex societies as 'wholes'. There has rather been an inclination to draw, a little too easily, on other disciplines (or on broader intellectual orientations, especially Marxism) for wider frameworks. Yet one may remember here the work of †A.L. Kroeber (more in cultural than social terms) and †Robert Redfield on civilizations (especially the concept of *great and little traditions), †Julian Steward on levels of socio-cultural integration, and M.G. Smith and others on *plural societies.

In later years there has been some interest in developing *regional analysis, drawing inspiration partially from human geography (Smith 1976). The anthropological study of the *state was earlier preoccupied with phases of †state formation, but more recently there has been an increasing concern with contemporary states and state apparatuses, and with the nation-state and *nationalism as cultural constructs. This interest, not confined to anthropology but paralleled in neighbouring disciplines, can perhaps be seen against a background of proliferating transnational linkages and accelerating globalization; in the late twentieth century, it has become ever more problematic to take the state for granted as a universe of analysis, or even as the referent for the term 'society' itself.

Globalization itself is also emerging as one focus of ethnography and conceptual work, in varying degrees tied to *'world systems' formulations elsewhere in the social sciences. Much research has been concerned with earlier periods of Western expansion and *colonialism, and may be seen in part as a critique of classical anthropological conventions of depicting autonomous exotic communities in an 'ethnographic present' (Wolf 1982). The current era of large-scale intercontinental migration, organized institutional diffusion, and spread of *mass media technologies, however, appears to require even more fundamental rethinking of social and cultural thought (Featherstone 1990).

Culture, history and anthropology at home

If much of the anthropology of complex societies has been devoted to the shape of social relationships, there has naturally also been an ethnographic concern with culture. To a considerable extent this has been a matter of detailing the meanings and meaningful forms of neighbourhoods, communities, work settings and other smaller units of face-to-face interaction within which field studies tend to be carried out. In such studies culture has often been understood in the traditional anthropological terms of a 'replication of uniformity'; it is taken to be rather unproblematically shared among the members of the unit. To understand the culture of complex societies in a more macro-anthropological manner, on the other hand, it is obviously necessary to think rather in terms of an 'organization of diversity': there are interrelated subcultures, a more or less overarching cultural apparatus (for example of *educational institutions and mass media), and a division of knowledge in large part matching the division of labour (Hannerz 1992). While the anthropological study of such cultural complexity can be expanded in many directions, the most vigorous development in later years has been in the research area of *ideology, †hegemony and cultural *resistance. Perhaps the long hesitation of anthropologists in engaging with such areas as youth culture, popular culture and the media in complex societies has had some part in the development of the new quasi-discipline of *cultural studies, a discipline also sometimes inclined toward ethnography.

The fact that complex societies are media-using societies (or at least involved with literacy) is surely one reason why anthropological study in these contexts has tended toward an awareness of *history. All human societies have a past, but complex societies have more elaborate records, and with additional media technologies the records become yet more diverse. The possibility of reconstructing past ways of life is there, and a considerable part of the anthropology of complex societies is now historical anthropology in this sense. But there is often an understanding that the anthropology of contemporary life is also the understanding of a moment in history, a portrayal of unfolding processes (Moore 1987).

This sense of the passage through time may also often be intensified by the nature of the anthropologist's personal involvement with the complex society, for relatively frequently this happens to be 'anthropology at home' (Jackson 1987). Although complex society is now everywhere, and it is entirely possible to go far away to study it, the site of research nonetheless often turns out not to be so far away from the anthropologist's home base, and thus its passage through time is more likely to be somehow entangled with the researcher's own biography.

If the study of complex society is conducted 'at home', it may have other intellectual implications as well. Does insider knowledge have a particularly important part in the way anthropology is done there, and is there sometimes a detrimental lack of detachment? Such issues are under continuous debate. It is also true, however, that precisely because complex society is in cultural terms an 'organization of diversity', what is close at hand, in one's own city or country, is not necessarily altogether familiar.

ULF HANNERZ

See also: world system, urban anthropology, great and little tradition, nationalism, state

Further reading

Featherstone, M. (ed.) (1990) *Global Culture: Nationalism, Globalization and Modernity*, London: Sage

Frankenberg, R. (1966) *Communities in Britain*, Harmondsworth: Penguin Books

Hannerz, U. (1992) *Cultural Complexity: Studies in the Social Organization of Meaning*, New York: Columbia University Press

Jackson, A. (ed.) (1987) *Anthropology at Home*, London and New York: Tavistock

Leacock, E.B. (ed.) (1971) *The Culture of Poverty: A Critique*, New York: Simon and Schuster

Mead, M. and R. Métraux (eds) (1953) *The Study of Culture at a Distance*, Chicago: University of Chicago Press

Moore, S.F. (1987) 'Explaining the Present: Theoretical Dilemmas in Processual Ethnography', *American Ethnologist* 14 (4): 727–36

Nader, L. (1972) 'Up the Anthropologist – Perspectives gained from Studying Up', in D. Hymes (ed.) *Reinventing Anthropology*, New York: Pantheon

Smith, C.A. (ed.) (1976) *Regional Analysis I–II*, New York and London: Academic Press

Wolf, E.R. (1966) 'Kinship, Friendship, and Patron-Client Relations in Complex Societies', in M. Banton (ed.) *The Social Anthropology of Complex Societies*, London: Tavistock

—— (1982) *Europe and the People without History*, Berkeley: University of California Press

componential analysis

Componential analysis is a method of †formal analysis or of ethnographic description whose origin is usually traced to †Goodenough's article 'Componential Analysis and the Study of Meaning' (1956). Its essence is the study of 'components', which are the basic building blocks of meaning in a semantic domain. Proponents of componential analysis see such domains as crucial to the understanding, not merely of languages, but also of cultures or significant aspects of *culture.

For example, *kinship terms are not random words for specific relatives, but rather exist in a culture-specific *classification system. Such systems almost always distinguish the sex and generation of relatives, but sets of components such as †direct and †collateral, or †parallel and †cross, will be specific to given cultures or languages. Consider the classification of †consanguines (blood relatives) in English kinship (see table below).

Here the components are sex (or gender), generation (or genealogical level), and lineal versus collateral. *Sex* distinguishes 'father', for example, from 'mother' (both father and mother being first-ascending-generation direct relatives). *Generation* distinguishes 'father' from 'grandfather', 'brother', 'son' and 'grandfather' (all these being male direct relatives). *Directness* distinguishes 'father' from 'uncle' (both father and uncle being male first-ascending-generation relatives). If we were considering †affines as well as consanguines, the 'father' would be distinguished from the 'father-in-law' by the component of *consanguinity* itself.

Proponents of componential analysis, whether in cultural anthropology or in linguistics, often talk about components by the Latin word *significata* (singular: *significatum*). 'Male' would be an example. The terms within the given domain are called *designata* (e.g., 'father'), and the elements which

make up the category are its *denotata* (in this case genealogical position of the father, which kinship specialists call F). There is a logical distinction here between 'father' and F, as the former is a word in English and the latter is a position relevant to any language or kinship system but whose *significance* literally depends on the system. In many languages F is classified with FB (father's brother) as belonging to a different category than MB (mother's brother), and in societies which speak such languages relations between relatives will differ markedly from those in English-speaking societies. A final notion relevant here is that of *connotata*. What 'fatherliness' connotes in English is that which defines 'father' beyond the purely formal componential distinctions drawn above: fatherly attitudes or fatherly behaviour, whatever these might be.

Componential analysis is ideally suited to the study of *relationship terminologies both because of the precision of classification in that domain and because of the sociological importance of such classification. It has been used in other domains too, especially in †ethnobotany and †ethnozoology. Indeed, a loose synonym for 'componential analysis' is *'ethnoscience' (see e.g. Frake 1980). Another is 'cognitive anthropology', reflecting the supposed cognitive reality behind the semantic distinctions which componential analysis reveals. Both these terms were common in the 1960s, when componential analysis was at it height in theoretical interest in *American anthropology (see also *emic and etic).

One semantic domain where things are much more fluid than kinship or ethnoscience is that of colours, and this domain has also attracted much interest especially in cross-cultural comparisons. Here the components are not clearly definable in terms of structural oppositions, but are arranged on sets of continua: the intensity of light (dark to light) and the wavelength of light (red to violet).

Table 3

generation	Direct relatives		Collateral relatives	
	MALE	FEMALE	MALE	FEMALE
+2	grandfather	grandmother		
+1	father	mother	uncle	aunt
0	brother	sister	cousin	
-1	son	daughter	nephew	niece
-2	grandson	granddaughter		

Different languages classify colours very differently, and there may be differences even between languages spoken by people who are bilingual, such as Welsh people who speak both Welsh and English (Ardener 1971). Traditional Standard Welsh (as opposed to Modern Colloquial Welsh) has no equivalent to English *brown*. Some shades of 'brown' are called *llwyd*. Other shades are called *du*. Loosely, *llwyd* means 'grey' and *du* means 'black', but as they encompass 'brown' too their signification is greater than that of the English word. Much the same is true of the Welsh word *glas*, which loosely translates into English as 'blue' but which also includes shades of what English classifies as 'grey' and 'green'. Therefore the Welsh word *gwyrdd*, loosely 'green', is narrower in meaning than its rough English equivalent. Blue-green might be 'green' in English, but it is *glas* (blue) in Standard Welsh. No language classifies everything. With colours, it would indeed be impossible to classify everything, since there is an infinite degree of natural variation. Standard Welsh simply does not need the distinctions which English-speakers take for granted.

ALAN BARNARD

See also: emic and etic, ethnoscience, relationship terminologies

Further reading

Ardener, E. (1971) 'Introduction', in E. Ardener (ed.) *Social Anthropology and Language* (A.S.A. Monographs 10), London: Tavistock Publications

Frake, C.O. (1980) *Language and Cultural Description: Essays by Charles O. Frake* (Selected and Introduced by Anwar S. Dil), Stanford: Stanford University Press

Goodenough, W. (1956) 'Componential Analysis and the Study of Meaning', *Language* 32: 195–216

Tyler, S.A. (ed.) (1969) *Cognitive Anthropology*, New York: Holt, Rinehart and Winston

conception

Theories of conception were of central importance to the nineteenth-century debates about social organization out of which anthropology emerged. Specifically, it was argued by theorists such as †Bachofen that the acquisition of accurate knowledge of physical paternity comprised an elementary transition out of †primitivism, representing a triumph of intellect over nature as a component of human progress towards †civiliza-

tion. Writing at the same time, †McLennan also argued for the central importance of accurate knowledge of physical paternity in the development of *marriage practices foundational to civilized society. *Morgan argued similarly, presuming an instinctive paternal drive to preserve *property through rules designed to consolidate biological and material inheritance. It is Morgan's formulations that are most closely followed by †Engels in the most famous statement of the importance of physical paternity to *evolutionary accounts of social organization, namely *On the Origin of the Family, Private Property and the State* (1884).

Theories of conception, and specifically knowledge of physical paternity, continued to play a central role in debates about social organization occasioning the 'birth' of modern anthropology. As Coward notes in her superb review of this period: 'The role of paternity and the procreative family were obsessive themes in the discussion of familial forms' (1983: 60). Insofar as human history was largely viewed by early anthropologists as the slow but steady advance of human reason and knowledge over ignorance and primitivism, ignorance of physical paternity held a privileged place in their debates. †Frazer (1910), Hartland (1909), †Tylor (1881) and †Westermarck (1891) were all preoccupied with its importance, only the more so as evidence of †matrilineal societies in which no such ignorance could be found were reported.

†Spencer and †Gillen's 1899 report of extensive ignorance among Australian Aborigines of physical paternity set the stage for a more specifically ethnographic rehearsal of earlier debates. Trained by Westermarck, and having completed his doctoral thesis on marriage and the family among the Australian Aborigines, *Malinowski foregrounded the question of ignorance of paternity in his work among the Trobriand Islanders. From early on, Malinowski insisted that the Trobrianders were 'ignorant' only insofar as they adjusted their 'crude' and 'incomplete' theories of conception to fit their overall social pattern of matrilineality. In terms of the basic elements of knowledge (e.g. a virgin cannot conceive), the Trobrianders, Malinowski insisted, were in no way primitive, childlike or ignorant. Developing a model of 'sociological paternity', as had †Durkheim and †van Gennep, Malinowski argued for a separation of †social facts from natural facts in the analysis of conception. His insistence that beliefs about conception cannot be separated from

their specific social context was further bolstered by Montagu's exhaustive compilation of conception beliefs among the Australian Aborigines, confirming their 'ignorance', in which he concludes that: 'Common-sense, in short, like every other aspect of thought, is a cultural trait, and its form is determined in and by the culture in which it must function' (1937: 341).

Malinowski's analysis of Trobriand conception beliefs first became the subject of heated controversy in the 1920s and 1930s when he clashed with Ernest Jones, a champion of Freud's, over the universality of the Oedipus complex, which is premissed on accurate knowledge of physical paternity (see *psychoanalysis). His Trobriand material again became the focus of dispute mid-century, in the exchanges occasioning †Edmund Leach's 1965 Henry Myers lecture entitled 'Virgin Birth'. In these debates, anthropologists wrestled with the broad ramifications of the 'ignorance of paternity' question set against what many (particularly Leach) saw as the racist implications of imputing to any group an ignorance of something so empirically self-evident as the relation between coition and pregnancy.

As Delaney (1986) points out in her excellent review of these debates, the problem can be seen as one of culturally specific theories of knowledge, as well as conception. The paternity question, she points out, has been cast as one of 'possession' versus 'lack' of true knowledge. Such a view obscures the specific conceptual features of paternity itself, which are variable. Insofar as models of paternity are of creation, they are inevitably embedded in *cosmological and *religious systems, as well as models of origins and divinity. As Delaney notes on the basis of her own fieldwork in a Turkish village: 'the symbols and meanings by which procreation is understood and represented provide a means for understanding relationships between such seemingly disparate elements as body, family, house, village, nation, this-world and other-world' (1991: 32).

†David Schneider, in his review of the importance of a presumed set of biological facts at the base of *kinship study, also poses the conception theory question as one of knowledge practices. Insofar as a strict dichotomy between the 'real', 'true' facts of European biology remained the privileged authenticator of beliefs elsewhere, he argued that kinship study remained a product of 'folk European' preoccupations imposed on the ways of life of other peoples.

Theories of conception have again become central to anthropological concerns about kinship, *gender and *personhood in the context of late-twentieth-century Euro-American debates over new reproductive technologies. In this context, renewed uncertainty about parenthood resulting from unprecedented forms of technological assistance to conception has challenged commonsense assumptions about both maternity and paternity. In the context of surrogate arrangements whereby one woman donates her egg and another gestates the fertilized egg to term, it is unclear, for example, who is the 'real' mother. Legislative, judicial and ethical debate on such matters has rekindled anthropological interest in both authoritative knowledge claims about 'the facts of life' and cultural representations of kinship in the age of assisted conception (Edwards *et al.* 1993; Strathern 1992a). In turn, the view of conception as a strictly biological matter has been very broadly challenged by the expanding literature on biology as a cultural system, and on the importance of ideas of the natural in the formation of Euro-American certainties (Yanagisako and Delaney 1994; Strathern 1992b).

Theories of conception thus index to the anthropologist a range of cultural questions. On the one hand, traditional questions about the importance of conception theories to accounts of origins, cosmological systems, social divisions, gender and kinship relations, attitudes to life and death, the structures of marriage, *family and inheritance patterns, concepts of personhood, and so forth have gained new currency in the context of increased technological control over 'the facts of life'. On the other hand, the history of anthropological debate about conception represents an important cultural field in its own right, representing as it does the longstanding 'givenness' of certain assumptions concerning the process of coming into being within Euro-American culture. This dual interest is reflected in the work of a growing number of scholars whose contemporary ethnographic work stands to revive anthropological interest in one of the oldest and most important topics within the discipline.

SARAH FRANKLIN

See also: descent, kinship, person, reproductive technologies

Further reading

Coward, Rosalind (1983) *Patriarchal Precedents: Sexuality and Social Relations*, London: Routledge & Kegan Paul

Delaney, Carol (1986) 'The Meaning of Paternity and the Virgin Birth Debate', *Man* (n.s.) 21(3): 494–513

—— (1991) *The Seed and the Soil: Gender and Cosmology in Turkish Village Society*, Berkeley: University of California Press

Franklin, Sarah (1996) *Embodied Progress: A Cultural Account of Assisted Conception*, London: Routledge

Malinowski, Bronislaw (1929) *The Sexual Life of Savages in North-Western Melanesia*, London: Routledge

Montagu, Ashly (1937) *Coming Into Being Among the Australian Aborigines: A Study of Procreative Beliefs of the Native Tribes of Australia*, London: Routledge

Ragone, Helena (1994) *Surrogate Motherhood: Conception in the Heart*, Boulder: Westview

Strathern, Marilyn (1992) *Reproducing the Future: Anthropology, Kinship and the New Reproductive Technologies*, Manchester: University of Manchester Press

consumption

Consumption is the meaningful use people make of the objects that are associated with them. The use can be mental or material; the objects can be things, ideas or relationships; the association can range from ownership to contemplation. This definition is broad and vague because anthropologists have been less concerned with defining their approach to consumption than with rejecting two previous approaches, those of conventional economics and Marxian *political economy. Researchers criticize these approaches for ignoring the social and cultural processes that underlie needs, generate demand and are satisfied in consumption (Douglas and Isherwood 1978; Sahlins 1976). While anthropologists recognize that some needs have a material basis, they stress the fact that need and demand reflect the ways objects facilitate social relationships and define social identities (e.g. Douglas and Isherwood 1978: ch. 5).

Scholars have long reflected on the meaningful use of objects. †Max Weber and †Thorstein Veblen are two examples from around the beginning of the twentieth century. Despite this history, the systematic social study of consumption is relatively recent, being overshadowed by the study of social organization and production. Social science encyclopedias of the mid-1980s could still discuss consumption solely in economic terms.

One key concern of students of consumption is the way that objects carry significant social meanings. Just about all objects have always carried such meanings to a degree. However, many argue that these meanings became especially pronounced in the West around the time of the rise of *capitalism and mass production; so much so that the West became a consumer society. This period saw a change in the way that Westerners thought about objects, as the symbolic gratifications of consumption loomed larger in people's minds (Campbell 1987). This change was facilitated and exploited by commercial firms, themselves growing larger and more aggressive (McKendrick, Brewer and Plumb 1982). Prominent among these were retail merchants, who were beginning to place their wares in novel and exotic displays in order to generate sales. This was especially true of department stores, the retail merchants who have attracted the greatest scholarly attention (Williams 1982).

For individuals, the first step in consumption is appropriation, establishing a mental association with the objects to be consumed. In capitalist societies this means that *individuals transform objects from being impersonal commodities into things with distinctive meanings for the consumers and distinct places in the consumers' social lives (Carrier 1990; Miller 1987). Once appropriated, people can use the objects to define their place in different social units. For example, the clothes one wears can be important for defining one's gender, social rank, ethnic identity and a host of other social attributes. Less obviously, when and how one eats can be important for defining social cycles of time, whether time of day, season of the year or ritual cycles (Douglas and Isherwood 1978). The cumulative effect of these individual acts of definition is a common structure of consumption at the societal level. This structure of consumption in turn reflects and recreates the identities of social groups that consume in distinctive ways, as well as the differences between those groups (Bourdieu 1984).

Students of Western societies tend to focus on the way that consumption creates the distinction between different entities like *classes or *ethnic groups, probably because mass consumption is so established in the West. On the other hand, mass consumption in the Third World is relatively new, and research there tends to focus on the way that consumption creates novel social identities and entities. Many assert that the spread of Western consumables into Third World countries does not, as some had argued and feared, lead to homo-geneous Westernization. Instead, it leads to the creation of national hybrids (Hannerz 1987; Foster 1991). These hybrids consist of interpretations and adaptations of Western products developed and shared by indigenous people themselves. Such hybrids can generate common national consumption communities that displace pre-existing sub-national or colonial patterns, and so are important in creating the nation itself as a social and cultural entity (Wilk 1995). Equally, those national patterns can become self-sustaining. This can happen when fringe groups within the country adopt national consumption patterns in order to assert their membership in the emerging nation (Hirsch 1990), a process which increases the importance of those national consumption patterns.

As the study of consumption matures it will need to address two issues. One is the denotation of 'consumption' itself, which seems at times to mean little more than 'not production'. This broad, vague, implicit definition is fertile, but is unlikely to help scholars develop a coherent view of the subject. The other issue is more complex. At present researchers tend to investigate the ways that people impose meaning on the objects in their lives. However, many such objects come with complex structures of meaning already in them, such as song and television programmes, or already attached to them through advertising and global cultural imagery, such as soft drinks and sports goods. If they are to develop a rounded account of consumption, scholars will need to address ways that these pre-existing meanings affect those who consume the objects that carry them.

JAMES G. CARRIER

See also: cultural studies, economic anthropology

Further reading

Appadurai, A. (ed.) (1986) *The Social Life of Things: Commodities in Cultural Perspective*, Cambridge: Cambridge University Press

Bourdieu, P. (1984) *Distinction*, London: Routledge & Kegan Paul

Campbell, C. (1987) *The Romantic Ethic and the Spirit of Modern Consumerism*, Oxford: Basil Blackwell

Carrier, J.G. (1990) 'Reconciling Commodities and Personal Relations in Industrial Society', *Theory and Society* 19 (5): 579–98

Douglas, M. and Baron Isherwood (1978) *The World of Goods*, Harmondsworth: Penguin

Foster, R. J. (1991) 'Making National Cultures in the Global Ecumene', *Annual Review of Anthropology* 20: 235–60

Hannerz, U. (1987) 'A World in Creolization,' *Africa* 57 (4): 546–59

Hirsch, E. (1990) 'From Bones to Betelnuts,' *Man* 25 (1): 18–34

McKendrick, N., J. Brewer and J.H. Plumb (1982) *The Birth of a Consumer Society*, Bloomington: Indiana University Press

Miller, D. (1987) *Material Culture and Mass Consumption*, Oxford: Basil Blackwell

Sahlins, M. (1976) *Culture and Practical Reason*, Chicago: University of Chicago Press

Wilk, R. (1995) 'Learning to be Local in Belize' in D. Miller (ed.) *Worlds Apart*, London: Routledge

Williams, R.H. (1982) *Dream Worlds*, Berkeley: University of California Press

cosmology

Cosmology comes from the Greek word *kosmos* which, according to the *Shorter Oxford English Dictionary* means 'the world or universe as an ordered system' or 'order, harmony, a harmonious system'. Cosmology then, means the theory of the universe as an ordered whole, and of the general laws which govern it. In philosophy, it is taken to mean that part of metaphysics which deals with the idea of the world as a totality of all phenomena in space and time. According to Greek thought, cosmos came out of chaos – 'the formless void: a state of utter confusion and disorder' – by differentiating the various elements. The concept is often associated with *cosmogony*, 'a theory, system, or account of the generation of the universe'.

In social anthropology, the meaning of cosmology has broadly followed the dictionary one, and is closely connected to the empirical study of *religions. To a large extent the two words have been used interchangeably, depending upon theoretical fashions and the predilections of the anthropologist. Some have used it to mean no more than religion. †Edmund Leach, for example, defined it as 'the system of beliefs and practices which social anthropologists commonly refer to as "primitive religion"' (1982: 229).

If, however, one tries to abide by the more rigorous definitions, then cosmology in anthropological usage is both more and less than religion. In some way or another the study of cosmology means taking account of the relationship between the whole and the parts: the macrocosm and the microcosm. Because the word *kosmos* can mean 'order' as well as 'world of order', in Greek thought microcosm can signify not only humans in relation to the universe, but also any part of a thing, especially a living thing that reflects or represents the whole it belongs to (Guthrie 1962). In anthropology, †Hocart was an early theorist who sought to elaborate this point. His aim was to establish that the root idea in human existence is the procurement of life. This, he claimed, is done through *ritual which derives its meaning from the 'life-giving myth'. Discussing Vedic religious precepts and practices he states, 'The participants are deliberately seeking to establish an identity between man and the ritual objects, between ritual objects and the world, and so between man and the world, a kind of creative syllogism' (1970: 64).

Cosmology and classification

Anthropologists frequently emphasize *classification and the classificatory principles which link the perceived order of the cosmos directly with the order of social life. We may trace this interest back to an essay by †Durkheim and †Mauss written in 1903, but not translated into English until 1963 under the title *Primitive Classification*. The authors were not interested in cosmology as such, but in the comparative study of the apparent human proclivity to classify. To do so they cast their net wide, both geographically and thematically. They showed, *inter alia*, how spatial categorization often involves religious matters and finds expression in such diverse social facts as house-building, village lay-out, clothing, marriage rules, etc. They conclude that symbolic classifications are of a moral and religious nature and must be distinguished from technological classification. Moreover, the social categorizations determine the religious; the first logical categories were social categories and these determine the cosmologies: 'Nothing shows this more clearly than the way the Sioux retain the whole universe, in a way, within the limits of tribal space . . . universal space is nothing else than the site occupied by the tribe, only indefinitely extended beyond its real limits' (Durkheim and Mauss 1963 [1903]: 87). The essay opened a way for the empirical investigation of cosmological orders, but the reductionist thrust of the argument, together with its *evolutionary ambition, meant that the essay did not inspire such studies among *British or *American anthropologists, although the Dutch found an early use for it.

One may, however, discern a different thread in *French anthropology. From †Granet's studies on Chinese religion (1922) to †Griaule (1965) and his associates' long-term investigations of Dogon cosmology in Mali, as well as to other French studies in *West Africa a series of detailed studies about religion and cosmology were published. However, the Africanists could be accused of turning Durkheim on his head, resulting in what some claimed was a 'cosmological determinism'.

Although a perusal of the British and American anthropological literature from the first half of the twentieth century reveals a spattering of uses of the word 'cosmological' as in 'of cosmological consideration' or 'cosmological beliefs', it is not until the second half that the theme began to be the explicit object of anthropological study. This was partly due to the fact that British social anthropologists had not been interested in the empirical study of religion as a topic of interest above and beyond relating it to social institutions in a *functionalist manner. American cultural anthropologists had not followed the same path as their British colleagues, but their interest in the study of religious matters was too much involved in the *culture and personality approach for them to ask questions about classification. Following the influential work of †C. Geertz (e.g. Geertz 1973), many American anthropologists began to incorporate indigenous cosmological concepts in their ethnographic studies.

Structuralism and after

The new-found interest in cosmology is to a large extent attributable to the influence of the work of *Lévi-Strauss and his notion of the 'order of orders'. Lévi-Strauss makes an analytic contrast between 'lived-in' orders and 'thought-of' orders. The former may be studied as part of the objective reality, he says, but 'no systematic studies of these orders can be undertaken without acknowledging the fact that social groups . . . need to call upon orders of different kinds, corresponding to a field external to objective reality . . . The "thought-of" orders are those of myth and religion' (Lévi-Strauss 1968: 313). In a later essay he seeks to clarify his terms: 'By *order of orders* then, I mean the formal properties of the whole made up of sub-wholes, each of which corresponds to a given structural level' (Lévi-Strauss 1968: 333). Lévi-Strauss made this statement as a response to those who he claimed had misunderstood him and assumed him to be saying that for a given society all orders are homologous. Although in the early days Lévi-Strauss does not use the word cosmology, and hardly does so subsequently, his work inspired a new and different interest in indigenous cosmologies. Data derived from many different cosmologies, together with mythologies, were being used to put forward general theories about the workings of the human mind. But Lévi-Strauss did not appear to be greatly interested in the study of cosmology for its own sake.

Certain parts of the world lent themselves particularly well to *structuralist analysis of *myth and cosmology whereas others did not. *Highland and *lowland South America and parts of *Southeast Asia became regions especially favoured with anthropological studies of this kind. The aim of most of these early structuralist ethnographies was to elicit a form of structural concordance between the cosmological and the social domains (e.g. Hugh-Jones 1979).

In the influential collection of essays entitled *Purity and Danger* (1966), †Mary Douglas alerts us to another aspect of classification as part of cosmology. She suggests that anomalies and ambiguities are necessary as bearers of symbolic meaning in any religious system, and formulates her famous statement that 'dirt is matter out of place.' Anomalies become so, however, precisely because they fail to find a proper place in the overall cosmological order. Thus Jewish food *taboos can be explained in terms of the forbidden animals not being part of the schema of creation; a schema, moreover, which, she argues, necessarily has a moral thrust that informs human social and symbolic orders.

A different tradition developed in Holland where the Leiden structuralist school grew out of the empirical focus on Indonesian societies. Many of these are organized in ways that encouraged the early observers to adopt an untheorized structural model. The Dutch missionary Van Hien wrote an article as early as 1896 in which he discussed the Javanese calendar in direct relationship with the complex Javanese system of organizing the cardinal directions, and showed how these were also embedded within a cosmological order that affected humans and spirits in relation to a whole. The thread of argument was taken up by others who had read Durkheim and Mauss's essay, and were able to bring this theoretical perspective to bear on their own empirical findings (de Josselin de Jong 1983: 10-16). Van Wouden, in his com-

parative study of Eastern Indonesian societies, concludes that not only are these societies distinguished by a clear-cut symbolic dualism, but that *marriage is the pivot to a comprehensive organization of cosmos and society. Although today the pure structuralist approach has been abandoned by most anthropologists, ethnographic accounts from Indonesia cannot ignore this Dutch tradition. Whether the focus of their studies is on *kinship, *ritual, *house construction, or even on social change, most find it impossible to discuss cultural and social practices without relating them in some way to indigenous cosmologies (eg McKinnon 1992, Traube 1986).

With the recent theoretical focus in some academic circles on the individual agent (as opposed to a transcendental cultural order), cosmology has lost some of its interpretative force. In his comparative investigations into the cosmologies of an area in Highland New Guinea, †Barth is critical of the structuralist endeavour and seeks to demonstrate that a better understanding of cosmology comes 'not by construing more order *in* it, but by better accounting for its production' (Barth 1987: 84). However, others would argue that because *ancestors or spirits are integral participants in human social life in many parts of the world, signifying the constituting role of the past in the present and the future, the indigenous values of the individual may often be subsumed by the cosmic. With increased anthropological interest in a globalization of culture, it is becoming clear that this process is far from automatic or easily predictable in particular instances. One reason for the variety of cultural responses to outside influences may be found embedded within cosmological perceptions.

SIGNE HOWELL

See also: classification, myth, religion, society, structuralism

Further reading

Barth, F. (1987) *Cosmologies in the Making: A Generative Approach to Cultural Variation in Inner New Guinea*, Cambridge: Cambridge University Press

Douglas, M. (1966) *Purity and Danger: An Analysis of Concepts in Pollution and Taboo*, London: Routledge & Kegan Paul

Durkheim, E. and M. Mauss (1963) *Primitive Classification* (with an introduction by R. Needham), London: Cohen & West

Geertz, C. (1973) *The Interpetation of Cultures*, New York: Basic Books

Granet, M. (1975 [1922]) *The Religion of the Chinese People*, Oxford: Blackwell

Griaule, M. (1965) *Conversations with Ogotemmeli: An Introduction to Dogon Religion*, Oxford: Oxford University Press

Guthrie, W.K.C. (1962) *A History of Greek Philosophy*, Cambridge: Cambridge University Press

Hocart, A.M. (1970) *Kings and Councillors: An Essay in the Comparative Anatomy of Human Society*, Chicago: The University of Chicago Press

Hugh-Jones, C. (1979) *From the Milk River: Spatial and Temporal Processes in the Northwest Amazon*, Cambridge: Cambridge University Press

Josselin de Jong, P.E. de (ed.) (1983) *Structural Anthropology in the Netherlands*, Leiden: Flores Publications

Leach, E. (1982) *Social Anthropology*, London: Fontana

Lévi-Strauss, C. (1968) *Structural Anthropology*, London: Allen Lane, Penguin

McKinnon, S. (1991) *From a Shattered Sun: Hierarchy, Gender and Alliance in the Tanimbar Islands*, Madison: The University of Wisconsin Press

Traube, E.G. (1986) *Cosmology and Social Life: Ritual Exchange among the Mambai of East Timor*, Chicago: The University of Chicago Press

van Wouden, F.A.E. (1968) *Types of Social Structure in Eastern Indonesia*, The Hague: Martinus Nijhoff

Crow–Omaha systems

From the beginning of the anthropology of *kinship, the systems known as 'Crow–Omaha' have been rich sources of debate. Discovered by *L.H. Morgan (1871), they are characterized by a distinctive type of *relationship terminology with little respect for genealogical levels. Interpretation of these terminologies has varied as different schools of anthropology have come and gone. For *descent theory (principally British and †Durkheimian), they constitute an extreme type of †unilinearity. For *alliance theory (chiefly French and †Maussian), they correspond to *marriage systems founded on numerous marital prohibitions. For American formalism, they obey a classificatory logic which operates through †extension of some kin terms for some authors or through reduction for others. Other interpretations are also advanced now.

Crow and Omaha terminologies correspond to †matrilineal and †patrilineal types respectively. They are named after the North American Indian peoples with whom they were first identified. They are characterized by a principle of †bifurcate merging in the parental level: father and father's brother are designated by the same term, as are mother and mother's sister. In the Omaha type, in †ego's generation †cross-cousins are 'skewed' a generation: the mother's brother's children are raised a generation and classified as 'maternal uncles' and 'mothers', while on the patrilateral side the father's sister's children are classified as 'nephews' and 'nieces'. In the following generations, the same logic is applied, so that the mother's brother's son's children are called 'maternal uncles' and 'mothers', while the children of the mother's brother's daughter (called 'mother') are thus 'siblings' to ego. Thus the set of cross-cousins and their descendants are positioned in an oblique fashion in relation to ego, the †matrilateral ones being 'raised' a generation and the †patrilateral ones 'lowered' a generation. In the Crow version, the positions are reversed: patrilateral cross-cousins are terminologically raised a generation and called 'father' and 'father's sister', while matrilateral cross-cousins are lowered a generation and called 'children'.

The logical consistency of these terminologies, reported from many societies around the world, has sustained a long-standing interest among anthropologists and resulted in diverse explanations. For Morgan they represented evidence of †'group marriage'; for †Kohler, secondary marriage with the widow of the maternal uncle; for Durkheim, simply the primacy of patrilineal descent. †Lowie (1934) regarded Omaha terminology as a product of patrilineality defined by a system of †exogamous †clans, and *Radcliffe-Brown (1952), applying his principle of the solidarity of the sibling group and the unity of the lineage, linked an individual's position to the †lineage he or she represents in relation to ego; in sum, terminology was placed in the service of descent.

This last point was criticized by †Lounsbury (1964) who, through a method of †formal analysis based on rules of equivalence, demonstrated that the logical principle of these systems is founded on a genealogical calculus and is therefore fundamentally bilateral. In the Omaha type, the skewing of cousins is explained by a more fundamental equivalence which claims that, within a chain of consanguinity, a man's sister is regarded conceptually as his daughter. If my father's sister is considered as his daughter, she is then conceptually my sister and her children are my nephews and nieces: they call me 'uncle' because I am their matrilateral cross-cousin. The principle holds throughout the genealogical grid; sometimes, it is yet more explicit and the father's sister is actually called 'sister', or again, the maternal uncle is called 'grandfather' (in this case, the patrilateral cross-cousins are 'grandchildren'). Lounsbury sought the cause of this in the rules of inheritance, a position criticized by Héritier (1981). For her, the terminologies develop out of the central brother–sister relationship, cross-siblingship. In the Omaha case, the primacy of the male sex category combines with the principle of skewing of generations to establish a terminological relationship of 'descent' between a man and his sister. In the matrilineal, Crow type, the logical principle is reversed: the sister takes precedence over the brother, and generations are skewed in an inverse manner.

*Lévi-Strauss (1965) attempted to link Crow–Omaha terminologies to systems of alliance through the extensive marriage prohibitions with which they are frequently associated. More recently, Barnes (1984) has refuted that argument in his distillation of North American Indian ethnography. Nevertheless, one may consider these terminologies as the opposite of †Dravidian systems, mapping out a vast zone of consanguinity within which marriage is forbidden for those linked by descent or alliance.

Héritier (1981) has demonstrated that when these terminological systems are associated with prohibitions, the latter take three forms: prohibition of marriage to a lineal relative, prohibition of marriage to a †cognatic relative, and non-duplication of previous unions. Despite the dispersed alliances apparently implied, several studies in Africa (one of which is based on an informed treatment of genealogies) have demonstrated that such systems do function, despite it all, within an †endogamous framework of non-renewable sister-exchange, with a change in the line of descent at each exchange, and consanguineous marriage to the fifth generation. This has earned them, from this structuralist perspective, the designation 'semi-complex systems' (Héritier 1981, Héritier-Augé and Copet-Rougier 1990).

ELISABETH COPET-ROUGIER

See also: alliance, componential analysis, kinship, marriage, relationship terminology

Further reading

Barnes, R.H. (1984) *Two Crows Denies it: The History of a Controversy in Omaha Sociology*, Lincoln, Nebro: University of Nebraska Press

Dorsey, J.O. (1884) 'Omaha Sociology', *Annual Report of the Bureau of American Ethnology* 3: 205–370

Fletcher, La Flesche (1911) 'The Omaha Tribe', *Annual Report of the Bureau of American Ethnology* 27: 17–654

Héritier, F. (1981) *L'Exercice de la parenté*, Paris: EHESS, Gallimard, Le Seuil

Héritier-Augé, F. and E. Copet-Rougier (eds) (1990) *Les Complexités de l'alliance I: les systèmes semi-complexes*, Paris: Archives Contemporaines

Lévi-Strauss, C. (1965) 'The Future of Kinship Studies', *Proceedings of the Royal Anthropological Institute*, 13–22

Lounsbury, F.G. (1964) 'The Formal Analysis of Crow- and Omaha-type Kinship Terminologies', in W.H. Goodenough (ed.) *Explorations in Cultural Anthropology: Essays in Honor of George Peter Murdock*, New York: McGraw-Hill

Lowie, R. (1934) 'The Omaha and Crow Kinship Terminologies', in *Verhandlungen des XXIV. Internationalen Amerikanisten-Kongresses*, Hamburg: Friederischen-de Gruyter

Morgan, L.H. (1871) *Systems of Consanguinity and Affinity of the Human Family*, Washington: Smithsonian Institution

Radcliffe-Brown, A.R. (1952) *Structure and Function in Primitive Society*, London: Cohen & West

cultural materialism

'Cultural materialism' is a broad heading, but it usually refers to the the specific kind of materialist approach advocated by †Marvin Harris. He developed it in a number of works, the most significantly being *Cannibals and Kings* (1977) and *Cultural Materialism* (1979).

Harris maintains that the material world exhibits deterministic influence over the non-material world. Thus *culture is a product of relations between things. In one of his more famous examples, Harris (1966) argues that the Hindu *taboo on killing cattle stems from Indian society's need to maximize the economic utility of cattle by favouring their use as draft animals rather than as meat. In this example, the implicit *functionalism of the cultural-materialist approach is apparent. Where Harris differs from conventional functionalists is in his emphasis on factors external to society, namely material ones.

Cultural materialism is allied to *ecological anthropology as well, precisely in that material factors are seen as determinant. In the cultural-materialist view, environmental conditions and subsistence techniques together either determine or severely limit the development of many other aspects of culture. Above all, cultural materialism emphasizes etic over *emic categories. Harris and his followers regard observed behaviour as logically and chronologically prior to cultural categories. Thus *cognitive and *ideological aspects of culture must necessarily take second place to *technological ones.

Cultural materialism has been labelled 'vulgar materialism', on the grounds that it is too crude and simplistic to take adequate account of the embeddedness of the material world within the ideological world (Friedman 1974). In contrast, claims Friedman, dialectical materialism (i.e. Marxism) overcomes this vulgarity through a clear distinction between †base and superstructure. Bluntly, to a 'vulgar materialist', there is only base; there is no superstructure. To complicate matters, the phrase 'cultural materialism' has had some currency in Marxist literary circles (e.g., in the work of †Raymond Williams), where it is used in a sense more akin to Friedman's Marxism than to Harris's purer materialist stance.

ALAN BARNARD

See also: ecological anthropology, environment, Marxism and anthropology, emic and etic

Further reading:

Friedman, J. (1974) 'Marxism, Structuralism and Vulgar Materialism', *Man* (n.s.) 9: 444–69
Harris, M. (1966) 'The Cultural Ecology of India's Sacred Cattle', *Current Anthropology* 7: 51–66
—— (1977) *Cannibals and Kings: The Origins of Culture*, New York: Random House
—— (1979) *Cultural Materialism: The Struggle for a Science of Culture*, New York: Random House

cultural studies

Cultural studies was formally introduced into the British university system in 1963, with the establishment of the Centre for Contemporary Cultural Studies (CCCS) at Birmingham, under the direction of Richard Hoggart. Strongly influenced by the work of †Raymond Williams, early work in cultural studies emphasized the need to move beyond the canonical definitions of textuality, in order to locate the culture of literacy in a wider social context. This initiative sought both to counter the elitism of 'high culture' and to widen its definition to be more inclusive. A combination of *sociology and †literary criticism, early cultural studies practitioners often described their work in terms of an 'anthropological turn', referencing the anthropological definition of culture as a way of life in contrast to its more elitist literary rendering as aesthetics or appreciation.

In addition to its anti-canonicalism, the Birmingham Centre also sought to politicize the production of academic knowledge within the university system. In contrast to the emphasis upon competitive individual achievement, the Centre promoted collaborative work, resulting in a series of well-known collections (see further reading). Interdisciplinary, anti-hierarchical and explicitly political in their approach to scholarship, members of CCCS were awkwardly positioned in relation to other departments, faculties and the university system as a whole. Nonetheless, the approaches developed at CCCS held obvious appeal to a wide constituency, and have continued to gain in popularity over time.

A concern with *class inequality was central to the work of both Williams and Hoggart, and much early work in cultural studies drew on Marxist models in which 'culture' was often equivalent to *ideology. In its later ethnographic expansion in the 1970s, work in cultural studies also sought to document culture as ordinary, popular, and ubiquitous, again invoking comparisons to anthropological models in contrast to literary ones. In turn, †Althusserian accounts of culture as part and parcel of the state apparatus, combined with a †Gramscian model of culture as integral to the realization of †hegemony, became central to the cultural studies project at Birmingham and elsewhere. By the early 1980s, these influences began to be both combined with and offset by the growing impact of †poststructuralist, and later †psychoanalytic theory. The work of Stuart Hall, Paul Gilroy, Hazel Carby and others drew attention to the importance of racism and †imperialism to the maintenance of state power, while the anthology *Women Take Issue* foregrounded feminist concerns. By the mid-1980s, CCCS Birmingham had become the site of a large and successful post-graduate research programme supporting a wide range of research and teaching in which concerns related to gender, *race and class remained prominent.

The addition of the polytechnics, where cultural studies was a popular and well-established field, to the British university system in the early 1990s, provided a wider infrastructure for the field. Meanwhile, outside Britain, the subject had also gained influence and grown in recognition, through the establishment of journals, programmes, and associations internationally. Unlike Britain, where the Birmingham initiative had provided a distinctive model, cultural studies in Canada, Australia, Europe and the United States emerged in a more piecemeal fashion. As in Britain, key components of cultural studies elsewhere included interdisciplinarity; a commitment to an explicitly political approach to scholarship; attention to the intersections of gender, race and class; and the use of critical theoretical perspectives drawn from Marxism, poststructuralism, gender theory, critical race theory and, increasingly, *postmodernism. However, cultural studies is best defined internationally in terms of its positionality rather than its content: above all, it has come to denote a space in which critical, theoretical and interdisciplinary research and teaching broadly organized under the rubric of the cultural analysis within developed, industrialized societies is pursued.

In comparison to anthropology, cultural studies has remained more concerned with the analysis of mass, public, dominant, popular or mainstream culture, rather than cross-cultural comparison. Although the analytical status of culture has been extensively debated, critiqued and transformed within anthropology, especially during the latter half of the twentieth century, it remains tied to a model of representing 'other' cultures, different from the anthropologist's own. In contrast, cultural studies has often sought to make visible cultural traditions that are muted, marginal, under-represented or devalued within the society of which the researcher is a part. Alternately, cultural studies has operated as a system of critical perspectives on the production of knowledge itself, indeed at the most local level of disciplinary boundaries and traditions, or the 'way of life' within particular subject fields. As an intervention into scholarly production, cultural studies is above all concerned with the creation of new kinds of spaces for consideration of questions which do not fit neatly within established traditions of intellectual exchange.

Also differentiating cultural studies from anthropology is the range of culture models employed in analysis, teaching and debate. In contrast to the extent to which culture models within anthropology have been explicitly organized in relation to a project of cross-cultural comparison, no such singular aim has united models within cultural studies, save for an overriding concern with issues of *power and *inequality. Hence, within cultural studies may be included a wide range of cultural theory, from the sociology of culture and its concern with *mass media, the culture industries, or culture as a dimension of the social, to the cultural theories derivative of language-based interventions such as †semiotics, poststructuralism, deconstruction or postcolonial theory.

Although in many respects the relationship between anthropology and cultural studies is productive and mutually valued, significant differences divide these two fields. In addition to its commitment to cross-cultural comparison is an empirical tradition within anthropology of detailed ethnographic observation and prolonged submersion in 'the field'. Very much in contrast to cultural studies, anthropology remains strongly connected to the goals of social science, including the rigorous documentation and representation of 'other' cultures. This aim is not shared by cultural studies, which is often explicitly critical of objectivist criteria, in both the humanities and the social sciences. At its worst, cultural studies may be seen by anthropologists as usurping the domain of 'culture' by means of reductionist, elitist, overly-theoretical and speculative or 'journalistic' methods. In particular, the view that texts should be read as part of a wider cultural context can be reversed within cultural studies to argue that culture is readable as a text. For anthropologists, the separation of 'cultural logics' from their lived, embodied social milieu comprises an unacceptable, even capricious, methodology.

At the same time, cultural studies has itself been at the forefront of challenges to the tendency to constitute even 'dominant' culture as monolithic, totalizing or determining. The importance of audience studies, such as Morley's pioneering work on television audiences (1986), or Stacey's thickly-layered account of film consumption (1993), has provided important models for anthropological analyses of the role of media, especially in the context of global, or transnational, cultural phenomena.

As 'culture' continues to demand critical, scholarly and political attention, it is inevitable anthropological and cultural studies approaches will increasingly overlap and inform one another. At the same time, ongoing discordances between the often highly theoretical and critical perspectives generated within cultural studies, and the more conventionally empirical traditions of cultural analysis within anthropology will ensure the two fields remain distinct, if overlapping.

SARAH FRANKLIN

See also: culture, Marxism and anthropology, mass media

Further reading

Brantlinger, Patrick (1990) *Crusoe's Footprints: Cultural Studies in Britain and America*, New York: Routledge

Centre for Contemporary Cultural Studies, University of Birmingham (1978) *Women Take Issue: Aspects of Women's Subordination*, London: Hutchinson

—— (1980) *Culture, Media, Language*, London: Hutchinson

—— (1982) *The Empire Strikes Back: Race and Racism in '70s Britain*, London: Hutchinson

Franklin, Sarah, Celia Lury and Jackie Stacey (eds) (1991) *Off-Centre: Feminism and Cultural Studies*, London: Harper Collins

Johnson, Richard (1987) 'What is Cultural Studies Anyway?', *Social Text* 6 (1):38–80

Morley, David (1986) *Family Television: Cultural Power and Domestic Leisure*, London: Comedia

Stacey, Jackie (1994) *Stargazing: Hollywood Cinema and Female Spectatorship*, London: Routledge

Williams, Raymond (1982) *Problems in Materialism and Culture*, London: Verso

culture

The word 'culture' is probably the single most central concept in twentieth-century anthropology. It has an especially complex history, of which anthropological usage is only one small part. Etymologically it is linked to words like 'cultivate' and 'cultivation', 'agriculture' and 'horticulture'. What these different words have in common is the sense of a medium for growth, a meaning quite transparent in modern biological usage where a mould or bacterium may be grown in a laboratory in an appropriate 'culture'. In English in the seventeenth century it became common to apply this meaning metaphorically to human development, and in the eighteenth century this metaphorical meaning developed into a more general term (Williams 1983). In German (where the word was spelt first *Cultur*, and then *Kultur*), the term was used in works of speculative history from the second half of the eighteenth century and, crucially, started to be used in the plural in the sense of humanity being divided into a number of separate, distinct *cultures*.

What emerged from this history in the nineteenth and early twentieth centuries, was a complex of overlapping, but potentially different meanings. On the one hand, there is what has become known as the 'humanistic' sense of culture, which is singular and evaluative: culture is what a person *ought* to acquire in order to become a fully worthwhile moral agent. Some people have more culture than others – they are more cultured – and some human products are more cultural than others – the visual arts, music, literature. Then there is what has become known as the 'anthropological' sense, which is plural and *relativistic. The world is divided into different cultures, each worthwhile in its way. Any particular person is a product of the particular culture in which he or she has lived, and differences between human beings are to be explained (but not judged) by differences in their culture (rather than their race).

Much ink has been expended – especially in American anthropology in the 1940s and 1950s – on a supposedly 'true' or 'correct' definition of culture, one which would isolate and clarify just what it is we study as anthropologists, while marking off 'our' word and its meaning from other, non-anthropological usage. In this article, we will not attempt any such definition. What makes a word like culture so important for anthropologists is precisely the arguments it generates about disciplinary identity; what makes those arguments important is the way in which the concerns of the non-anthropological world keep leaking into our own private disciplinary disputes, despite all our best attempts to establish boundaries around what we see as our intellectual property. Instead of a definition, we offer an ethnographic history in three phases: the prehistory of the pluralistic concept of culture from its roots in German Romantics like †Herder to its anthropological working out in the writings of *Franz Boas; the competing definitions of mid-century American anthropology, in the context of European suspicion of the term; and the rise and demise of one particular version – culture-as-symbols-and-meanings – in the second half of the twentieth century.

Prehistory: from Herder to Boas

We have already mentioned the proliferation of definitions of culture in mid-century American anthropology. Many of these definitions were collected in an extraordinary survey published by †Kroeber and †Kluckhohn in 1952 (Kroeber and Kluckhohn 1952). This invaluable book collected and analysed dozens of definitions, as well as examining non-anthropological usage in English, German and French. What emerged was a particular story. According to Kroeber and Kluckhohn, the anthropological sense of the word was established by †E.B. Tylor at the very start of his *Primitive Culture* (Tylor 1871), but then languished for another thirty years at least before gaining any wider anthropological currency. This view was resoundingly challenged by George Stocking in two essays from the 1960s (Stocking 1968a, 1968b). In these he argued that not only was Tylor's celebrated definition less 'anthropological' than it looked, but in fact the real roots of the modern anthropological concept lay scattered in somewhat incomplete form through the writings of Boas.

There is a more general point to Stocking's argument (to which we return shortly) which is important here. Words like 'culture' are not invented *ex nihilo* by individual innovators. They are living components of broad languages of description and evaluation, languages which have been used by disparate people in their encounter with the modern world. Moreover, much of what we wish to say when we talk of culture has been said already using one of a range of possible alternatives: custom, climate, civilization, tradition, *society. Nevertheless we can make a start on the anthropological history of culture by insisting on the plural (cultures rather than culture) as the key to the modern anthropological sense.

This would seem to place Herder in the most important position, even though some of what he said about human differences was anticipated by other *Enlightenment writers. Consider the following passage from his *Yet Another Philosophy of History* (1774):

How much depth there is in the character of a single people, which, no matter how often observed (and gazed at with curiosity and wonder), nevertheless escapes the word which attempts to capture it, and, even with the word to catch it, is seldom so recognizable as to be universally understood and felt. If this is so, what happens when one tries to master an entire ocean of peoples, times, cultures, countries, with one glance, one sentiment, by means of one single word! Words, pale shadow-play! An entire living picture of ways of life, or habits, wants, characteristics of land and sky, must be added, or provided in advance; one must start by feeling sympathy with a nation if one is to feel a single one of its inclinations or acts, or all of them together.

(Herder in Berlin 1776: 188)

The spirit of this passage seems strikingly modern. Different peoples are as profoundly different as

different individuals are, and what makes them distinctive cannot be reduced to a simple verbal formula; instead we need a sympathetic grasp of 'an entire living picture of ways of life, or habits, wants' before we can understand any part of it. The use of culture in the plural, and the emphasis on cultures as 'wholes', are both commonplaces of twentieth-century anthropology.

But we also need to note other aspects of Herder's vision. One is the interchangeability of words like 'people', 'culture', and above all 'nation' in his writing. The second is his celebration of the irreducible plurality of human societies: we cannot and should not judge members of one people or culture by the standards of another, nor should we require people of one culture to adapt to the demands of another alien culture. This emphasis on the need for internal cultural purity, or integrity, in any human group provided Herder with the fuel for fierce denunciations of European rule of non-European peoples, even as it also provided a blueprint for later European nationalisms, with their alarming demands for ethnic purity within the nation. Moreover, Herder's usage is as often singular as plural, and his emphasis on the work of artists and intellectuals as the highest point of cultural expression makes him as much a founder of the humanistic sense of culture as of the anthropological.

Despite the large literature on the subject, the history of the word culture in the century after Herder's death in 1803 is confusing and not fully researched. The term culture became an important point of reference in what we would now call cultural criticism in England, through the influence of S.T. Coleridge (who read widely in the German writers of Herder's generation), and later literary figures like Matthew Arnold (Williams [1958] 1963). Stocking has argued that Tylor's famous definition should be seen as part of this tradition, rather than as an anticipation of modern anthropological usage:

Culture or civilization, taken in its wide ethnographic sense, is that complex whole which includes knowledge, belief, art, morals, law, custom, and any other capabilities and habits acquired by man as a member of society.

(Tylor 1871 I: 1)

Although this talk of a 'complex whole' sounds as modern and anthropological as Herder's usage, there are a number of differences. First, when quoting Tylor, later anthropologists have frequently elided the second and third words in the definition ('culture *or civilization*'), thus obscuring the fact that Tylor was writing of a singular phenomenon, which everyone had, but which some people had more or less of. Tylor's purpose was to demonstrate that all societies could be seen as part of one continuous evolutionary process, while his choice of the word 'culture' served as a jolt to those, like Arnold, who would argue that there is an unbridgeable gulf between that which is properly cultured and that which is uncultured or uncivilized (Stocking 1968a).

Stocking has pointed out that Tylor nowhere uses the word culture in the plural. In this respect he was no different from his contemporaries in Britain and America. The link between Herder's early pluralistic vision and modern anthropology is provided by Boas, who was by education steeped in the German tradition of which Herder was a part, and who in his own work accommodated himself to the emerging empirical requirements of Anglo-American anthropology. Boas was alone among American social scientists of his generation in his references to 'cultures' rather than 'culture', even if his usage was neither systematic nor consistent, still less graced by a memorable definition such as Tylor's (Stocking 1968b).

Boas's usage, like other aspects of his anthropology (e.g. the emphasis on *myth and *folklore as the key to any particular culture), grew from the seeds of German romantic nationalism. So, for example, in his 1898 report to the British Association on his fieldwork among Native Americans of the Northwest Coast, Boas refers to 'the three methods of classifying mankind – that according to physical character, according to language, and according to culture', before going on to talk of the 'cultures of the primitive people of British Columbia' (Boas [1898] 1982: 92–3). Then, a few pages later, he discusses the ways in which myths are borrowed or shared between different groups:

It follows that the mythologies of the various tribes as we find them now are not organic growths, but have gradually gained their present form by accretion of foreign material. Much of this material must have been adopted ready made, and has been adapted and changed in form according to the genius of the people who borrowed it.

(Boas [1898] 1982: 96)

These passages illustrate three crucial themes in Boas's work on the idea of culture. First, culture is offered as an explicit alternative to *race ('physical character') in both the classification and explanation of human differences. Secondly, cultures have to be seen as products of highly contingent histories, as fusions of elements which originate in different times and places. This radical historicism is an explicit alternative to the more dogmatic *evolutionists of his time, for whom cultural elements could be effortlessly slotted into place on a single, grand evolutionary scale. Thirdly, despite this emphasis on contingency in the choice of components within a culture, these components are brought together in a specific way according to the 'genius of the people'. In other words cultures need to be seen as wholes, each with its distinctive genius, as well as assemblages of apparently random elements, each with its different history. What Boas left for his students was less a completely coherent theory or definition of culture, but rather a set of tensions or problems which would continue to occupy American anthropologists for much of the twentieth century. On the one hand culture was offered as a pluralistic and relativistic alternative to scientific racism and ethnocentric evolutionism. On the other hand there was an unresolved tension between culture as an assembly of historical fragments and culture as an integrated whole, expressing the 'genius' of a particular people. In this respect, Boas was the true inheritor of Herder's pluralistic vision of human difference, a vision which carried both the possibility of relativistic tolerance, but in the emphasis on internal integrity – the genius or spirit of a people – would also be haunted by the intolerant political possibilities of exclusion and purification.

After Boas

Boas's students, and their students, came to see culture primarily through its diversity. The world was made up of lots of 'cultures' rather than an abstraction called 'Culture'. When they did venture comments on the abstraction, Boasians saw culture as fundamentally human, i.e. not the property of animals, and even declared it the attribute which distinguishes animals from humans, or simply that which has no basis in biology. †Ruth Benedict, for example, in her powerful attack on scientific racism describes culture as follows:

For culture is the sociological term for learned behaviour: behaviour which in man is not given at birth, which is not determined by his germ cells as is the behaviour of wasps or the social ants, but must be learned anew from grown people by each new generation. The degree to which human achievements are dependent on this kind of learned behaviour is man's great claim to superiority over all the rest of creation; he has been properly called 'the culture-bearing animal.'

(Benedict 1943: 9-10)

In these matters the Boasians differed both from the evolutionists who preceded them, in the nineteenth century, and from the modern evolutionists, including the practitioners of *sociobiology and those whose interests lie in topics like tool-use among chimpanzees.

Benedict emphasized both the diversity of culture and the internal integration of specific cultures. Cultures were ways of living, virtually psychological types, which she called 'cultural configurations', which were said to be best perceived as integral and patterned 'wholes': 'Cultures from this point of view are individual psychology thrown large upon the screen, given gigantic proportions and a long time span' (Benedict 1932: 24). This approach drew attention to the †ethos, the characteristic moral, aesthetic and emotional tone of a particular culture. Other anthropologists associated with the emerging *culture and personality school, such as †Edward Sapir put more emphasis on the problem of the individual personality. For Sapir, the 'true locus' of culture lay not in society, which he dismissed as itself a 'cultural construct', but in the 'interactions of specific individuals' and in the 'world of meanings' which guide those interactions: 'Every individual is, then, in a very real sense, a representative of at least one subculture which may be abstracted from the generalized culture of the group of which he is a member' (Sapir [1932] 1949: 151).

There were other challenges to the kind of holism proposed by Benedict. Some, like †Robert Lowie, followed Boas's call for the recognition of cultures as the product of complex, disparate histories. †Clark Wissler (1923), for example, sought culture through its separate †culture traits. While Wissler regarded culture traits as grouped into larger †culture complexes, he nevertheless saw the collectivity of such elements, rather than their interconnection, as the significant feature of

culture. This difference highlights two distinct trends within the Boasian tradition, stemming from the tension in Boas's own work between his interest in the 'genius of a people', and his historicist and diffusionist arguments against the evolutionists. Among the next generation of American anthropologists this tension resurfaced in the division between those interested in psychological aspects of culture, and those committed to the accumulation of ethnographic evidence for its own sake. It is perhaps no accident that Wissler's own specific interest, as a museologist, was in †material culture, and that his anthropology remained closer to the diffusionist origins of Boas's conception of the discipline than did the anthropology practised by most of Wissler's American contemporaries.

Still another dimension of culture prominent in Boasian anthropology was the idea of it as 'superorganic'. This view was first put forward by A.L. Kroeber in a famous 1917 article, and it occupied him through much of his lifetime. Kroeber regarded culture as, above all, *sui generis*: this meant that it could only be explained in terms of itself, and not reduced to racial, psychological or (other) non-cultural factors. It was also 'superorganic' (a term which he borrowed from †Herbert Spencer) in the sense that it had to be explained with reference to a level of understanding above that of the individual organism. Thus Kroeber and his followers came to see culture less as a product of individual human beings, and rather more as that which produced or directed those actions. While his initial formulation of the idea was in part an attack on racism (as stemming from racial determinism), the radical thrust of his more general concern was that culture developed its own logic independently of the thoughts of specific individuals. He cited objects and ideas in the history of science which came to be invented or discovered simultaneously by more than one individual, and later he described cyclical features in culture, most famously women's fashions, which he saw as the product of the laws of culture, and not merely of the whims of individual women or fashion designers.

By 1952 it came time for American anthropologists to take stock of what they meant by 'culture'. In that year Kroeber and Kluckhohn divided 'complete' definitions of culture into six categories: descriptive (e.g. Tylor's), historical (those with an emphasis on tradition), normative (with an emphasis on rules or values), psychological (e.g. with an emphasis on learning or habit), structural (with an emphasis on pattern), and genetic. The last was certainly the most diverse and included definitions with an emphasis on culture as a product or arte-fact, definitions with an emphasis on ideas or on symbols, and residual-category definitions. The last category, including one of Kluckhohn's own definitions, places its emphasis on what culture is not – i.e. on what is left over after biology, or what is human rather than animal – rather than on what distinguishes, in one way or another, one human group from another.

This form of definition was to resurface decades later, when the boundary between human and animal came under greater discussion as a result of intensive studies of non-human primates. When in the early 1960s Jane Goodall first reported on tool-use among the chimpanzees of Gombe, †L.S.B. Leakey is reputed to have remarked: 'Ah, now we must redefine tool, redefine man – or accept chimpanzees as humans!' What really happened, was none of these. Instead, primatol-ogists, and some anthropologists of evolutionist persuasion, called into question the previously-held notion that culture is a phenomenon confined to humans alone (e.g. McGrew 1992). But other evolutionists came to see the advent of *symbolic culture*, rather than either material culture or its transmission, as the significant advance for the human species (e.g. Knight 1991). Although such views are sympathetic to the idea that animals and humans are similar, they have nevertheless come to strengthen the notion that culture is of the utmost importance, especially against those proponents of sociobiology who deny entirely the significance of culture.

Culture versus society

Not all anthropologists of the day were as enthu-siastic about the concept of culture as the Boasians. *Radcliffe-Brown's dismissal of culture as a 'vague abstraction' ([1940] 1952: 190) was echoed else-where in British social anthropology, where 'culturalism' and 'culturalist' were employed as damning epithets for any analysis which sought above all to explicate a culture in its own terms. The usual antonym to 'culturalist' was 'struc-turalist' which, before the 1960s, usually referred to the study of *social structure. The advantage of studying social structure, it was argued, was its tangibility, its unambiguous and bounded properties. This position was, of course, already under threat from the explicitly abstract ideas of structure put forward by †Evans-Pritchard in the 1940s. It was further challenged by †Edmund Leach in the opening pages of *Political Systems of Highland Burma* ([1954] 1964). Leach's 'social structure' is an ideal model constructed by the anthropologist: what makes the world work socially is precisely the fact that it never completely corresponds to anyone's ideal of how it ought to be. Leach's argument about culture derives from the fact that his book concerned an area of extra-ordinary ethnic diversity and mobility, a situation which would challenge any believer in cultures as discrete, bounded systems. In this context, members of different cultures may nevertheless be viewed as components of a single 'social system', and the visible markers of cultural difference (clothing, language, religion) may themselves be political tokens in this wider system. When Leach talks about culture providing 'the "dress" of the social situation' ([1954] 1964: 17), he is very liter-ally illustrating a more pervasive position in British anthropology. As †David Schneider put it just before he died: 'culture for them [British anthro-pologists of the 1950s] was ornaments, different hat styles, things like that' (Schneider 1995: 131).

To some extent this British suspicion of anthro-pological notions of culture might be related to a broader British anxiety about the humanistic sense of culture. This may be even truer in France, where *civilization* predominated over *culture* in general intellectual discourse, and as late as 1980 †Marshall Sahlins's *Culture and Practical Reason* – a book which explicitly argued against the reduction of cultural difference to sociological causes – was retitled for its French translation as *Au coeur des sociétés*.

The exception to this French suspicion was *Lévi-Strauss, whose view of culture was heavily influenced by his close relationship with Boas. Like the evolutionists, Lévi-Strauss saw culture as based on universal principles, but like the Boasians he sought a special recognition for the details which distinguish one culture from another. This problem is what led him to define the *incest taboo as the bridge between *nature and culture: natural because it was inherent in all human society, and cultural since the definition of forbidden sex-partners varied enormously from society to society (Lévi-Strauss [1949] 1969: 3–25). Although Lévi-Strauss has written at length on the issue of cultural differences, his own analyses have rarely been confined to the study of a particular culture. Instead the myths and rituals of neighbouring cultures may be treated as transformations of each other, with the final goal in some sense an elucidation of the human mind as a medium of culture. Cultures-in-particular, for Lévi-Strauss, are illustrations of the logical possibilities of the pan-human capacity for culture-in-general.

Radcliffe-Brown's hostility to the American concern with culture was most forcefully challenged by †Leslie White. As Radcliffe-Brown sought a 'natural science of society', so White envisaged anthropology as a 'science of culture'. For Radcliffe-Brown, this was a contradiction in terms, precisely because culture, for him, was intangible and abstract, whereas social relations were real and observable. White (1949) turned Radcliffe-Brown's argument around, seeing culture as cumulative both for individuals and for humanity as a whole, and as inclusive of social structure. White's position was a curious, and not entirely resolved, combination of radically disparate intellectual elements. Culture, for him, is above all a matter of symbols and meanings, exemplified by the human capacity for language. But this argument, anticipating as it does the claims of the *symbolic anthropologists of the 1960s and 1970s, sat uneasily in an unfashionably materialist and evolutionist intellectual framework.

From meaning to contest

One escape from the apparently fruitless argument between British social anthropology and American cultural anthropology in the 1950s was offered by the theoretical framework of the sociologist †Talcott Parsons. Parsons's theory of social action posited three levels of analysis – that of social structure, culture and personality – none of which could be reduced to any of the others. Culture, in this formulation, was above all the domain of symbols and meanings. †Clifford Geertz and David Schneider, both of whom had been in Parsons' Harvard Department of Socal Relations in the late 1940s and early 1950s, advanced this position in their work of the 1960s, culminating in Geertz's massively influential *Interpretation of Cultures*:

> The concept of culture I espouse . . . is essentially a semiotic one. Believing, with Max Weber, that man is an animal suspended in webs of significance he has himself spun, I take culture to be those webs, and the analysis of it to be therefore not an experimental science in search of law but an interpretive one in search of meaning.
>
> (Geertz 1973: 5)

Geertz, together with Schneider and Sahlins (a late convert to the Boasian tradition), managed something denied to their American predecessors – the partial conversion of non-American anthropology. In Britain, the symbolic or interpretive approach of the 1970s chimed with the vague talk of the 'translation of culture' which had emanated from Oxford under Evans-Pritchard, while the hostility to †positivism, especially in Geertz, was attractive to many of the generation which had been at first seduced, then repelled, by Lévi-Strauss's grand theory. By the 1980s, British anthropologists were convening conferences on 'semantic anthropology', and talking freely about culture, with neither the hostility nor anxiety the word had evoked in the 1950s.

But the 1970s hegemony of culture-as-meaning had an unexpected nemesis. Geertz pointed a new generation of students towards literary criticism, where new theories about language and meaning were emerging in the late 1960s and early 1970s. In particular, French †poststructuralist theorists like †Derrida and †Foucault, provided further ammunition for the assault on positivism, further reasons to privilege language or *discourse in cultural analysis, but also crucially, a radical undermining of any assumption about the stability of particular cultural meanings. What emerged from this – so-called postmodernism in anthropology – was part of a much broader change in the intellectual and political climate of the humanities and social sciences, especially in America. Radical theory became associated with proponents of multiculturalism in American education, while anthropologists had to adjust their arguments to meet the challenge of the new anti-discipline of *cultural studies, not least of which was a much more politicized approach to culture (Turner 1993). In the face of all this, some anthropologists fell back on the new cliché that culture was always a 'site of contestation' (rather as if American higher education in the 1980s could serve as a model for all human societies at all times), while others abandoned the term altogether in favour of apparently less problematic terms like 'hegemony' or 'discourse'.

Two important points need to be emphasized about this crisis of anthropological confidence. One is that the arguments involved were not confined to academic circles, still less to anthropology itself. Culture, like multiculturalism, was a key term in what the philosopher Charles Taylor called the 'politics of recognition', and what others called the 'politics of identity': that kind of politics based on arguments for the recognition of particular categories (African Americans, women, gays and lesbians) in American society. One area of argument concerned who, if anyone, had the 'right' to represent another culture. Anthropologists were especially vulnerable given the discipline's long involvement with *colonialism, and the new arguments which linked academic representation of non-European people to European political domination of those people (Clifford 1988). As Edward Said asked in his *Orientalism*: 'Is the notion of a distinct culture (or race, or religion, or civilization) a useful one, or does it always get involved either in self-congratulation (when one discusses one's own) or hostility and aggression (when one discusses the "other")?' (Said 1978: 325).

In other words, culture, far from isolating anthropological analysis from the world of politics, in fact provided a link between them. This became even clearer as anthropologists turned their attention to the study of *nationalism, only to discover that nationalists were themselves using what looked very like anthropological arguments about culture (Handler 1988). One possible escape from this dilemma might be to abandon talk of different 'cultures' altogether, because of its taint of *essentialism, but to retain some use of the adjectival 'cultural'. But this is to abandon the very important pluralizing element, the element which marked off modern anthropological usage in the first place. Moreover, arguments about the rights and consequences of representations of cultural difference remind us of the evaluative sense of culture in nineteenth-century humanism, a sense few anthropologists have been prepared to acknowledge. Nevertheless, anthropology's recent engagement with the politics of culture brings us back, not merely to Boas's concerns (in his arguments against racist intolerance of human differences), but to the linked meanings, tensions, and problems in early writers like Herder, who was at once the intellectual scourge of the cultural arrogance of European imperialism and one of the unwitting intellectual fathers of the modern politics of ethnic cleansing.

ALAN BARNARD
and JONATHAN SPENCER

See also: Boas, cultural studies, culture and personality, nationalism, nature and culture, relativism, society, symbolic anthropology

Further reading

Benedict, R. (1932) 'Configurations of Culture in North America', *American Anthropologist* 34 (1): 1–27
—— (1943) *Race and Racism*, London: Scientific Book Club
Berlin, I. (1976) *Vico and Herder: Two Studies in the History of Ideas*, London: Hogarth Press.
Boas, F. ([1898] 1982) 'Summary of the Work of the Committee in British Columbia' in G. Stocking (ed.) *A Franz Boas Reader: The Shaping of American Anthropology, 1883–1911*, Chicago: University of Chicago Press
Clifford, J. (1988) *The Predicament of Culture: Twentieth-Century Ethnography, Literature, and Art*, Cambridge, MA: Harvard University Press
Geertz, C. (1973) *The Interpretation of Cultures*, New York: Basic Books
Handler, R. (1988) *Nationalism and the Politics of Culture in Québec*, Madison: University of Wisconsin Press
Knight, C.D. (1991) *Blood Relations: Menstruation and the Origins of Culture*, New Haven: Yale University Press
Kroeber, A.L. (1917) 'The Superorganic', *American Anthropologist* 19: 163–213
—— and C. Kluckhohn (1952) *Culture: A Critical Review of Concepts and Definitions*, Cambridge, MA: Papers of the Peabody Museum, vol. xlvii, no 1
Leach, E. ([1954] 1964) *Political Systems of Highland Burma: A Study of Kachin Social Structure*, London: Athlone
Lévi-Strauss, C. ([1949] 1969) *The Elementary Structures of Kinship*, Boston: Beacon Press
McGrew, W.C. (1992) *Chimpanzee Material Culture: Implications for Human Evolution*, Cambridge: Cambridge University Press
Radcliffe-Brown, A.R. ([1940] 1952) 'On Social Structure', in A.R. Radcliffe-Brown, *Structure and Function in Primitive Society*, London: Cohen and West
Said, E. (1978) *Orientalism*, London: Routledge and Kegan Paul
Sapir, E. ([1932] 1949) 'Cultural Anthropology and Psychiatry', in E. Sapir, *Culture, Language and Personality: Selected Essays*, Berkeley: University of California Press
Schneider, D. (1995) *Schneider on Schneider: The Conversion of the Jews and Other Anthropological Stories*, Durham, NC: Duke University Press
Stocking, G. (1968a) 'Matthew Arnold, E.B. Tylor, and the Uses of Invention', in G. Stocking, *Race, Culture, and Evolution: Essays in the History of Anthropology*, New York: Free Press
—— (1968b) 'Franz Boas and the Culture Concept in Historical Perspective', in G. Stocking, *Race, Culture, and Evolution: Essays in the History of Anthropology*, New York: Free Press
Turner, T. (1993) 'Anthropology and Multiculturalism: What is Anthropology that Multiculturalists Should be Mindful of it?' *Cultural Anthropology* 8 (4): 411–29
Tylor, E. (1871) *Primitive Culture* (2 vols), London: John Murray
White, L.A. (1949) *The Science of Culture*, New York: Grove Press

Williams, R. ([1958] 1963) *Culture and Society 1780-1950*, Harmondsworth: Penguin

—— (1983) *Keywords: A Vocabulary of Culture and Society*, London: Flamingo

Wissler, C. (1923) *Man and Culture*, New York: Thomas Y. Crowell Company

culture and personality

'Culture and personality' is the name given to the earliest school of thought in what came to be the sub-disciplinary field of *psychological anthropology. Its beginnings are associated especially with the great American linguist and anthropologist †Edward Sapir (1884-1939). Sapir was influenced by German †*Gestalt* psychologists, who had argued that perception could be understood only when the thing perceived was viewed not as an assemblage of separate elements, but as an organized pattern (*Gestalt*). So when one looks, for example, at a landscape painting, one sees it not as flat planes of colour laid against one another, but as a whole – 'a landscape'. This example shows us too why a whole may be more than the sum of its parts and have its own essential properties. In this *Gestalt* view, meaning was a function of organized patterns, and Sapir applied this idea to his analyses of language and of culture and personality.

Cultural patterns

Sapir was suspicious of the contemporary concept of *culture, which he described as 'tidy tables of contents' attached to particular groups of people. In an influential 1934 essay he argued that 'the more fully one tries to understand a culture, the more it seems to take on the characteristics of a personality organization' (1985: 594). The study of the development of personality was Sapir's solution to the problems posed by the way that, in anthropological accounts, culture 'can be made to assume the appearance of a closed system of behaviour' (*ibid.*). But in fact, 'vast reaches of culture . . . are discoverable only as the peculiar property of certain individuals' (*ibid.*). He recommended that to understand 'the complicating patterns and symbolisms of culture', anthropologists should study child development.

Sapir's earlier analyses of language, which described the unconscious patterning of sound and grammatical concepts, informed the work of †Ruth Benedict. In her *Patterns of Culture* (1934), she argued that the cultural whole determined the nature of its parts and the relations between them. This work had an enormous impact on anthropologists and lay readers alike.

From ethnographic data concerning *kinship, *religion, economy, political authority, etc., Benedict aimed to derive the 'more or less consistent pattern of thought and action' that informed and integrated all the practices of daily life in four different 'cultures'. The Kwakiutl of America's North West coast, she argued, were characterized by their 'will to superiority'. This found its most intense expression in the *potlatch* – the competitive feast in which a man established, for example, his right to a noble title by giving away, and even destroying, such vast quantitities of valuables that he was able to shame, and thus outdo, his rivals.

Like Benedict, †Margaret Mead analysed culture and personality in terms of dominant cultural 'configurations'. Her best known works are studies of adolescence (in Samoa), *socialization (in the Manus Islands, Papua New Guinea), and the relation between sex roles and temperament (in three contrasting New Guinea groups). Her *Growing Up in New Guinea* (first published in 1930) showed how the children's world may be separate from that of the adults alongside whom they live, how *gender early differentiated the knowledge of boys and girls and how, over time and in the absence of any explicit teaching, the Manus child willy-nilly took on the personality of the Manus adult.

Mead's work was characterized by comparisons between the lives of the peoples she studied and American life. She used her account of the lives of Manus children to draw out lessons for contemporary American educationalists, urging them to recognize how powerful is tradition and how it threatened 'American faith in education as the universal panacea' (1975: 196).

Basic and modal personality

Later research was increasingly influenced by †Freud's *psychoanalysis, certain features of which were taken up by other culture and personality theorists and combined with †behaviourist social learning theory. The psychoanalyst †Abram Kardiner and the anthropologist †Ralph Linton were key figures here. Their *The Individual and His Society* (1939) criticized the configurational approach as being too broad and vague, and put forward the idea of 'basic personality structure'.

Kardiner and Linton argued that, while culture and personality were similarly integrated, there was a specific causal relationship between them. They distinguished between 'primary institutions', which produce the basic personality structure, and 'secondary institutions' which were the product of the basic personality structure itself. The primary institutions were taken as 'given', the product of adaptation to a particular *environment; they included social organization, *technology and child-training practices. In the course of growing up, the child adapted to these institutions, but this process itself produced shared, unconscious conflicts and anxieties which were given form in projective systems – i.e. the secondary institutions such as religion and *ritual.

†Cora Du Bois modified this theory with her concept of 'modal personality', which did not assume that a certain personality structure is common to all members of a society, but that it is the most frequent. Du Bois's data were derived from participant observation, the results of projective tests and detailed biographies of adults (see Du Bois 1961 [1944]). Projective tests – primarily the Rorschach inkblot and the Thematic Apperception Test (TAT) – were also used by other culture and personality theorists in what came to be known as 'national character' studies.

Untenable assumptions

As Bock (1980: 97–101) has pointed out, all the early work on culture and personality rested on five basic assumptions: that childhood experience determined adult personality; that a single personality type characterized each society; that a particular shared basic or modal personality gave rise to a particular cultural institution; that projective tests developed in the West could be used elsewhere; and that anthropologists were 'objective', free of ethnocentric bias.

Each of these assumptions left culture and personality theorists open to criticism, for each assumption itself required empirical investigation. For example, only longitudinal studies of the same persons throughout their lives could actually establish the extent to which very early experience gave rise to adult personality. And what if personality varies as much or more within society as it does across societies? However,

Perhaps the most telling criticism came from within the culture and personality school itself. Melford E. Spiro . . . argued that the school had

failed to clarify its two central concepts, and that most culture and personality work was necessarily circular because 'the development of personality and the acquisition of culture are one and the same process' . . . Instead of seeking causal relationships between personality and culture, we should try to overcome the 'false dichotomy' that separates them into mutually exclusive categories.

(Bock 1990: 101)

Thus the cross-cultural studies of John W.M. Whiting and his colleagues, while they still came within the domain of culture and personality, attempted to test specific hypotheses concerning, for example, the relation between child-rearing practices and puberty rituals for boys. So, for instance, the co-occurrence of long post-partum *taboos on sexual intercourse between parents and exclusive mother-infant sleeping arrangements might produce at once a strong identification between son and mother, and hostility between son and father. Whiting, Kluckhohn and Anthony (1958) argued that their correlational study showed that where these two customs were found together, puberty rituals for boys were likely to be elaborate, and to involve operations such as †circumcision. Their 'psychogenic' explanation was that the rituals helped resolve the profound Oedipus complex induced by the child-rearing practices.

Because of their scope, correlational studies across cultures contained little in the way of detailed material concerning the meanings that different peoples gave for their own practices, nor did they investigate their different concepts of the person, of the child, or of mind. Rather theorists took for granted an idea of the *person as constituted through an interaction between biological and cultural variables – an idea that may have been greatly at odds with the idea of the person held by those who were the objects of their studies.

The notion that anthropologists were justified in assuming that they might use their own culturally constituted concepts to 'explain' other people's behaviour continued to pervade culture and personality studies throughout the 1970s and 1980s. So Robert A. LeVine, introducing an edited collection published in 1974, described culture and personality research as follows: 'Its province, though not sharply bounded, may be defined as the interrelations between the life cycle, psychological functioning and malfunctioning, and social and cultural institutions' (1974: 2).

Nevertheless, LeVine's book included a section entitled 'cultural influence in individual experience: emic views of normal and abnormal behaviour'. Here the papers were concerned not with cross-cultural comparison, but with an attempt to explain the culture-specific logic that integrated categories in particular domains of meaning. So, for example, Hildred Geertz showed how Javanese children learned 'shame' and 'respect' as aspects of a complex of emotional states and the behaviour in which these states were manifested; and Dorothy Eggan analysed Hopi *dream experiences in terms of Hopi ideas of the psyche and how they implicated Hopi cosmology.

This focus on the ideas held by cultural actors, on 'systems of meaning', came to dominate anthropology during the 1970s and 1980s and 'culture and personality' gave way to the larger and more inclusive project of psychological anthropology. In 1951 Melford Spiro had argued that the person is not merely conditioned by culture, rather culture is incorporated into the individual via the psychodynamic processes of identification and internalization. Thus, when contemporary theorists discuss culture and personality, they are likely to attempt to integrate ideas such as Spiro's with a model of cognitive functioning, for example that offered by †schema theory (see D'Andrade 1990).

Cultural schemas

Cultural schemas (or schemata) are mental representations of prototypical events, behaviours and things; these schemas define for the person the nature of any situation in which he or she is involved. Roy D'Andrade has argued that cultural schemas structure how emotion is experienced and what goals are followed. Summarizing his ideas of the 'overlap' between culture and personality he writes:

Some cultural values appear to be incorporated into the individual's superego – to become part of the individual's deepest sense of what is right. Some cultural symbols appear to have unconscious meaning and under certain conditions apparently become an important part of an individual's identity. And some . . . cultural schemata appear to be internalized by most individuals and to function as general goal systems or motives.

This formulation is not perhaps so very different from Sapir's original idea of unconscious 'patterns' in language, but it does not take up his observation that, from the point of view of a child, 'culture is . . . not something given but something to be gradually and gropingly discovered' and that 'the child will unconsciously accept the various elements of culture with entirely different meanings, according to the biographical conditions that attend their introduction to him' (1990: 596).

In other words, 'cultural schemas' have to be *constituted* by children and, in this process, will necessarily be transformed. Thus studies of exactly *how* particular children constitute their ideas of themselves and the world still offer the best means for understanding continuity and change in 'culture' over time, but by and large these studies still remain to be done.

CHRISTINA TOREN

See also: childhood, psychological anthropology, socialization,

Further reading

Benedict, Ruth F. (1934) *Patterns of Culture*, New York: The New American Library

Bock, Philip K. (1988) *Rethinking Psychological Anthropology*, New York: W.H. Freeman & Co

D'Andrade, Roy G. (1990) 'Culture and Personality: A False Dichotomy' in David K. Jordan and Marc J. Swartz (eds) *Personality and the Cultural Construction of Society*, Tuscaloosa and London: University of Alabama Press

Du Bois, Cora ([1944] 1961) *The People of Alor*, New York: Harper and Row

Kardiner, Abram and Ralph Linton (1939) *The Individual and His Society*, New York: Columbia University Press

LeVine, Robert A. (ed.) (1974) *Culture and Personality: Contemporary Readings*, New York: Aldine Publishing Company

Mead, Margaret ([1930] 1975) *Growing Up in New Guinea*, Harmondsworth: Penguin Books

Sapir, Edward ([1949] 1985) *Selected Writings in Language, Culture, and Personality*, Berkeley: University of California Press

Stocking, G.W. (ed.) (1986) *Malinowski, Rivers, Benedict and Others: Essays in Culture and Personality*, History of Anthropology 4, Madison: University of Wisconsin Press

Whiting, John W.M., Richard Kluckhohn and Albert Anthony (1958) 'The Function of Male Initiation Ceremonies at Puberty' in E. Maccoby, T. Newcomb and E. Hartley (eds) *Readings in Social Psychology* 3rd edn, New York: Holt

D

dance

From the dancer's perspective, which is usually shared by audience members of the dancer's *culture, dance is human behaviour comprising purposeful, intentionally rythmical and culturally patterned sequences of non-verbal body movements. Distinct from ordinary motor activities, this motion (in time, space and with effort) has inherent and 'aesthetic' value and symbolic potential.

A subfield of the discipline, the anthropology of dance crosses over the anthropology of *cultural studies, *gender, the *body, *medical anthropology, *music, *politics and *religion. Impediments to Western scholarship on dance were fearful, negative attitudes towards the human body and emotion, the inherent instruments of dance, as well as an exaggerated esteem for verbal language's capacity to describe reality.

When researchers began to study dance, they lacked knowledge of the elements of movement and the training required to associate visual imagery with verbally conceptualized elements. Consequently, descriptions of dance were limited until the mid-twentieth century. Since the 1970s the cognitive and persuasive dimensions of visual imagery, still and kinetic (including dance, especially the original designing of movement), have been recognized.

Most studies emphasized either the text (movement) or context (cultural and social). However, the interrelationship provides a fuller understanding of this human phenomenon of thought, structure and process. An examination of this interrelationship found, for example, that among the Ubakala Igbo of Nigeria, dance movement patterns reflected age and sex-role differentiation patterns. Young people of both sexes have relatively similar dance movements; elderly men and women have similar dance patterns. But when the two sexes are relatively similar in age but markedly different in biological and social role, the dance movement patterns diverge. When the women are life-givers (mothers) and the men life-takers (warriors), women use circles, slow movement and gentle effort, whereas men dance in lines, rapidly, and with intense, percussive energy.

For some researchers a dance study is about the historically unique; for others the study of dance should contribute to a generalizing comparative social science. Anthropologists may focus on dances of a culture, a culture area or on cross-cultural theoretical issues. In *functionalist studies, the meaning of dance lies in its presumed consequences for social and personality systems. Structural studies focus on identifying physical movement patterns of space, time and effort or steps and phrases, the rules for combining these and the resulting regularities in dance form. Communication studies include the interaction between human capacities, sociocultural context, sociological setting, the dynamics of what dance is and what is assigned to dance.

Contemporary anthropologists tend to focus on dance as a medium through which multiple ideologies of *person, gender, generation, social *class and *ethnicity are expressed, negotiated and contested. Dance is an intimate and constitutive aspect of cultural identity, and like language is a window to a person's world view. Aesthetic forms, such as dance, may convey anxieties and aspirations as well as covertly express political feelings that people cannot express directly owing to the perils of challenging the social order.

Studies of dance in *possession, healing and stress reduction have found that the physical activity of dance may cause emotional changes and altered states of consciousness, flow, and secular and religious ecstacy. Dance may increase one's energy and provide a feeling of invigoration. The exercise of dance increases the circulation of blood carrying oxygen to the muscles and brain as well as altering the levels of certain brain chemicals, as in the stress-response pattern. Vigorous dancing induces the release of endorphins thought to produce analgesia and euphoria. Thus dance is a complex physical, emotional and cognitive culturally-patterned social activity.

Meaning

Dance, a symbolic form through which people represent themselves to themselves and to each other, may be a sign of itself, a sign with referents beyond itself and an instrument. Signification is integral to both verbal and non-verbal communication, and dance is a key medium of communication in many cultures. Dance requires the same underlying brain faculty for conceptualization, creative expression and memory as verbal language. In a dance performance, as in spoken and written languages, we may not see the underlying universals and cultural structures and processes, but merely their evidence. Dance usually assembles its linguistic-like elements in a manner that more often resembles poetry, with its suggestive imagery, rhythm, ambiguity, multiple meanings and latitude in form.

Because a symbol condenses a number of affectively linked associations within a meaning system, it may have a powerful charge. Perhaps this is why dance has long held pride of place in religion, ethnic identity, gender, and social stratification. Danced signs may lead to *socialization and †acculturation: reinforcing ongoing patterns of social behaviour, acquiring new responses, weakening or strengthening inhibitions over fully elaborated patterns in a person's repertoire and facilitating performance of previously learned behaviour which was unencumbered by restraints.

Methods to discover meaning

Reliance solely upon an informant's verbal exegesis for indigenous cultural description and analysis may preclude understanding some people's dances. Informants may lie. Performing dances of a native person to elicit the group's aesthetics is problematic. What suffices for an outsider may be an inadequate performance for an insider and criteria for insiders may differ according to age, gender or other category. Many features of dance generally lie beyond the conscious awareness of dancers and viewers. In numerous American and African cultures, most social dancers do not know the names of specific steps in such dances as the waltz, rock and roll, disco and *nkwa di iche*. Just as grammarians and linguists are knowledgeable about vocabulary and syntax, so movement analysts are familiar with the comparable elements in dance. Indigenous views are important in their own right, and discovering them may also modify the anthropologist's comparative categories; but if a people does not analyse the dance it performs, the researcher must then rely upon the disciplinary heritage.

Observing and recording dancing provide data that can be used by itself or in conjunction with dance-participant views (producer, performer, spectator). A problematic consideration is that seeing is creating meaning. Even highly trained movement analysts may variously perceive, interpret and notate a dance. Accurate and speedy notation of dance in its field context is nearly impossible. Some dances may be performed only once during a research visit, and some dancers may be unable or unwilling to replicate a performance. Because of these difficulties, researchers have preserved dance behaviour on *film and video. Notwithstanding the selectivity in what is filmed and how, these recording processes may make the dance more objectively accessible.

Anthropologists draw upon systems for analysing the physical movement of dance such as Labanotation, Benesh and Eskhol. Drawing upon semiotic analyses of visual and verbal texts and the variety of dance worldwide, Hanna (1987) developed a tool to probe for meaning in movement: the *semantic grid*. Its devices and spheres of encoding meaning in movement are intended to evolve with the revelation of new dance knowledge. In probing meaning, the grid can be imposed on the whole dance and used to zoom in on smaller units to bring into focus informant verbalizations, empirical observations and analyses in line with the pattern of associations with some idea, thing or emotion. The researcher can explore whether meaning lies in each cell formed by the intersection of the vertical and horizontal lines separating devices and spheres.

There are at least six symbolic *devices* for conveying meaning that may be utilized in dance. (1) A *concretization* is movement that produces the outward aspect of something. Examples are warrior dances displaying advance and retreat battle tactics. (2) The *icon* represents most properties or formal characteristics of something and is responded to as if it were what it represents. Illustrative is a Haitian possessed by Ghede, god of love and death, who manifests his presence through dance. Haitians treat the dancer with genuine awe and gender-appropriate behaviour as if he were the god. (3) A *stylization* encompasses arbitrary and conventional gestures of movements, e.g. in Western ballet the *danseur* pointing to his heart as a sign of love for his lady. (4) A †*metonym* is a motional conceptualization of one thing representing another of which it is a part, or with which it is associated in the same frame of reference; an example is a romantic duet representing a more encompassing relationship, such as a marriage. (5) The expression of one thought, experience or phenomenon in place of another that it resembles to suggest an analogy is a †*metaphor*, the bringing together of different domains in often unexpected and creative ways. Illustrative is a myth about animals to denote the situation between humans. (6) An *actualization* is a portrayal of one or several of a dancer's usual roles. This device occurs, especially in theatrical settings without a rigid boundary between performer and spectator, when dancers express their own sexual preferences through dance and the audience member accepts or rejects the dancer.

The devices for encapsulating meaning in dance seem to operate within one or more of eight *spheres*: (1) An example of the meaning of dance being in the dance *event* is when people attend a dance to be seen socially or to signal sexual or marital availability and find partners; here, dancing itself is incidental. (2) The meaning of dance may be in the sphere of the total human *body in action*, as in woman or man self-presentation of spectator watching. (3) The *whole pattern* of the *performance* – which may emphasize structure, style, feeling or drama – may be the locus of meaning for participants and observers. (4) Meaning may be centred in the sequence of unfolding movement, including who does what to whom and how in dramatic episodes. (5) Specific *movements* and how they are performed may be meaningfully significant, as when a dancer parodies a leader recognised by certain physical characteristics. (6) The *intermesh of movements* with other communication modes such as speech or costume may be where meaning lies. (7) Meaning may be in the sphere of dance as a *vehicle for another medium*, e.g. dance serving as a backdrop for a performer's poetry or rap recitation. (8) The sphere of meaning may be centred in *presence*,

the emotionality of projected sensuality, raw animality, charisma, or 'the magic of dance'.

It is argued that abstract contemporary Western dance movement has no referent beyond itself. Yet the movement may refer to other genres of dance and the historical development of dance. In addition, dance viewers may read meaning into a performance irrespective of choreographer or dancer intention.

Meaning may be deduced through examining how symbolic elements are developed in other aspects of socioculture (*cosmology, riddles, proverbs, costume, paraphernalia, music, non-dance, *ritual, *myth, polity, economy, social structure and notions of public and private).

Researchers have demonstrated that we must turn to society and not just to the dancer's experience to understand the meaning of dance. It is a reflection of social forces. Society inscribes itself on the body, the body incorporates social meaning, and the individual minds the body. At the same time, however, dance may be more than epiphenomenal and serve as a vehicle through which individuals influence social forces. That is, dance may reflect what is and also *influence what might be*. The persistence of dance in society throughout history, and the religious, civil and political attempts to control it, attest to its potency in human life.

JUDITH LYNNE HANNA

See also: body, music, play, ritual

Further reading

Cowan, J.K. (1990) *Dance and the Body Politic in Northern Greece*, Princeton: Princeton University Press

Fleshman, B. (ed.) (1986) *Theatrical Movement: A Bibliographical Anthology*, Metuchen, NJ: Scarecrow Press

Hanna, J.L. (1987 [1979]) *To Dance Is Human: A Theory of Nonverbal Communication*, Chicago: University of Chicago Press

—— (1983) *The Performer-Audience Connection: Emotion to Metaphor in Dance and Society*, Austin and London: University of Texas Press

—— (1988a) *Dance, Sex, and Gender: Signs of Identity, Dominance, Defiance, and Desire*, Chicago: University of Chicago Press

—— (1988b) *Dance and Stress: Resistance, Reduction, and Euphoria*, New York: AMS Press

—— (1991) *Nigeria's Ubakala Igbo Dance: Life, Death, and the Women's War*, London: Harwood Academic Press

Mitchell, J.C. (1956) *The Kalela Dance*, Rhodes-Livingston Institute Paper 27

Novack, C.J. (1990) *Sharing the Dance: Contact Improvisation and American Culture*, Madison: University of Wisconsin Press

Schieffelin, E.L. (1976) *The Sorrow of the Lonely and the Burning of the Dancers*, New York: St. Martin's Press

Spencer, P. (ed.) (1985) *Society and the Dance: The Social Anthropology of Process and Performance*, Cambridge: Cambridge University Press

death

All human cultures attach a central place to interpreting the processes of human existence. Among these, reproduction and the representation of death, with the associated practices which these representations entail, are always of the greatest importance.

This fact, however, does not mean that death is always visualized in the same way in different cultures. One of the sharpest contrasts was emphasized in a famous study by the French anthropologist †Hertz (1960 [1907]) who stressed the difference between those systems of ideas, like the modern European one, where death is represented as occurring in an instant and as marking a sharp break – the end of life – and those systems of ideas, typical of the traditional societies of *Southeast Asia, where death is mainly thought of as a stage in a longer process which begins before what we call 'death' and goes on long afterwards.

The Merina of Madagascar would be an example of this latter type. There the *person is believed to change gradually throughout life, from being at first wet and soft, like a baby whose bones are still bendable, to an adult who is a mixture of hard dry elements, principally the bones, and soft elements, principally the flesh. At death the corpse should have developed a great deal of the dry hard stuff but will still retain some wet stuff. This, however, will gradually disappear after death through putrefaction, thereby completing the process. For the Merina, therefore, the transformations of the *body throughout life and after death are parts of a single more general process of which death is merely a part.

Dealing with the dead

Such an attitude to death is reflected in the way the funeral ceremonies are carried out. Among the Merina, immediately after death the body is buried in a temporary grave so that the soft parts can finally drain away, then after a period of two years or so, the dry parts of the body are finally buried in the family tomb. The two funerals therefore mark and bring about the completion of the process which occurred in life. Furthermore, the placing of the dry elements in the communal tomb, as is the case in other examples, also marks another change; by then the individuality of the corpse has ceased to matter and he or she becomes merged with the whole family in a monument which should last for ever (Bloch 1971).

The attempt to retain a part of the dead body which is to endure beyond life, often by preserving it in a stone tomb, is very common and is found from China (Watson 1988) to Europe. Often, as in these examples, the tomb is not for an individual, but is a place where the bodies of a family or a †lineage are regrouped. As a result such tombs are likely to become the symbol of family unity. Also, because tombs are permanent, they become the link between the living and a particular area or piece of land, via the presence of the dead in the soil. This explains the crucial role of tombs in *nationalism. For similar reasons *migrants very often attach great importance to their bodies being returned to their place of origin. Thus, Corsican migrants to the Americas spend extraordinary amounts of money on building grandiose family tombs and turning parts of Corsica into a veritable necropolis. By contrast, in hierarchical societies it is often the great and the rich who are most elaborately preserved in monuments such as Lenin's mausoleum or the pyramids, but then they are buried as individuals alone. Inevitably, a result of this is that their subsequent political reputation may affect the way these monuments are treated.

In contrast to these attempts at preservation are practices which seem to be intended to do just the opposite, foremost amongst which is cremation. The reasons for cremation are however varied. In *Hinduism and *Buddhism, cremation is seen as the final stage of that renunciation of attachment to the body and its passions to which the pious dutifully aspire. In Hindu funerals the chief mourner should crack the skull of the deceased in order to liberate the soul from its fleshy entrapment. In the holy city of Banaras in India, thousands of bodies are brought to be cremated on the shores of the river Ganges where the ashes will be dispersed in the hope of attaining final liberation from the cycles of rebirth (Parry 1994). However, cremation may be intended to achieve almost opposite ends. Thus, among the ancient Greeks of Homer's *Iliad* the ideal death was being killed but not disfigured in the prime of youth.

Thus the corpses of heroes killed in battle were burnt so that the memory of their perfect bodies was not contaminated by images of decay and change (Vernant 1982).

In other parts of the world the treatment of the body reflects other concerns. In *Melanesia the creation of the person is above all seen as the result of *exchange – chains of gifts and counter-gifts of which *marriages and marriage payments are a part. Thus among the Gimi of New Guinea (Gillison 1993) each person is thought of as the result of a combination of the bones which come from the natal †clan, and the flesh which is believed to come from the in-marrying women who belong to different clans. It is this combination which makes the person, and death is, therefore, that which unmakes the person. This was traditionally manifested in a dramatic way in that the women had the duty to eat the flesh of the dead so as to liberate the bones of the members of their husband's clan. In doing this they were taking back that which they had brought and ending the *alliance which the living body incarnated. This end of exchange, however, was only the beginning of the possibility for new exchanges; by their *cannibalism Gimi women made it possible for the bones and the flesh to be ultimately symbolically 'reused' in the making of future clan members, something which would be possible through future alliances.

After death

Funerals are not only moments for dealing with the material remains of the dead, but in many cultures there is a belief that an immaterial element remains which is usually labelled by our word 'soul'. In fact in many cases several soul-like elements are thought to survive death. These have several destinations and a part of the funeral may involve guiding them there. In some cases, as among some Melanesian groups (Damon and Wagner 1989), the souls should be reincarnated in future members of the group and funerals attempt to achieve this. In other places, the funeral involves guiding the soul on a long and perilous journey often to some kind of paradise. The famous Tibetan Book of the Dead is precisely such a guide for helping the soul on its journey. In fact, concern with souls at funerals is often not so much a matter of ensuring their safe passage to somewhere else as a matter of ensuring that they do not bother the living. Indeed many of the offerings made at funerals are intended to prevent the soul clinging to the living in the form of a ghost or causing some other sort of unpleasantness (Goody 1962). The condition of the body and the state of the soul are often thought to be closely linked. Thus, in much of Europe, if a body emanated a sweet smell at death this was thought to be a sure sign that the person would go to heaven. The discovery of an incorrupt body was the mark of a saint, though in Portugal it could also be the mark of a great sinner and various practices were needed to sort out which it was (Pina-Cabral 1980).

This distinction between saints and sinners serves to emphasize the fact that within all cultures not all deaths are seen in the same way. Suicide is an example. In some cultures, as in medieval France, death by suicide was thought to be so wicked that no proper church ritual was carried out. In Japan by contrast, suicide was always an honourable thing to do in a number of situations. In other places it is seen as an inevitable part of certain social and physical states (Cátedra 1992). Perhaps the greatest differentiation is sometimes found in the ways the old, the young and the childless are treated in the same culture. In many parts of the world infants are not thought of as fully social beings and so not only is †infanticide accepted but the death of small children is not marked by *rituals; the same is often true of childless individuals. By contrast, the death of the old who have had many children is often the occasion for large rituals which manifest as much joyous celebration as mourning. Indeed it would be wrong to think of funerals as only sad affairs. Funerary rituals are often as much a matter of marking the end of life as organizing and highlighting its continuation and regeneration (Bloch and Parry 1982).

The living and the dead

This leads to a consideration of the emotions aroused by death. In all cultures, death causes sorrow but how far there is a public forum for its manifestation varies. In Madagascar the death of children may cause intense sorrow to the parents but there is no institutionalization of this, though in other places it seems that, in certain situations, the death of children is not necessarily a cause of sorrow (Scheper-Hughes 1992). When it is appropriate to manifest sorrow publicly, this may be organized in quite regimented ways, though what effect such organization has on individual emotions is not known. Certain emotional manifestations which in Europe are thought of as spontaneous and individual, such as weeping, may be orchestrated, as they are in much of the Middle East and many other parts of the world; and may be given to a particular group, often women, to express. The same is true of marking mourning by one's personal appearance. Shaving the head or conversely letting the hair run wild, or wearing specific clothes which mark out mourners for a particular period, are common markers of mourning. In many cases it is as though what is asked of the mourners is not only to show their sorrow outwardly, but to take on some of the *pollution associated with decomposition. Thus in many parts of Melanesia widows are not allowed to wash for a period after their spouse's death.

Death affects the living in yet other ways. The deceased may have had important social statuses and property which must be passed on to others. Because of this, royal funerals may involve long ritual processes which are integral to the coronation of the successor. In certain African cases, these rituals of *kingship involve nationwide ceremonies where it is as if all the subjects, and the natural *environment, die with their ruler and are reborn with the successor. More mundane and much more common are problems caused by *inheritance. The transfer of *property may occur before the death of the property-holder, or after death as is the case with Indian joint families where the division between heirs may be delayed until long after the death. There may be clear rules of inheritance stating whether all, or some, children are to inherit. It is quite possible that some children (e.g. females) will inherit some types of property while males will inherit other types. In many places, however, as in Madagascar, no clear rules exist and the wishes of the dying person expressed either in a will or through 'last words' will be paramount.

In many societies the problems caused by inheritance can become a dominating theme so that all relatives are to a certain extent each other's enemies because of quarrels of this type. At the same time important resources remain unused because they are caught up in disputes. In other cases, certain objects or words associated with the deceased become *taboo, marking the continuing presence of the dead by the stress on their absence.

MAURICE BLOCH

See also: rite of passage, person, body

Further reading

Bloch, M. (1971) *Placing the Dead*, London: Seminar Press

Bloch, M. and J.P. Parry (eds) (1982) *Death and the Regeneration of Life*, Cambridge: Cambridge University Press

Catédra, M. (1992) *This World, Other Worlds*, Chicago: University of Chicago Press

Damon F.H. and R. Wagner (eds) (1989) *Death Rituals and Life in the Societies of the Kula Ring* Northern Illinois University Press

Gillison, G. (1993) *Between Culture and Fantasy*, Chicago: University of Chicago Press

Goody, J. (1962) *Death, Property and the Ancestors*, London: Tavistock

Hertz, R. (1960 [1907]) *Death and the Right Hand*, London: Cohen and West

Parry, J. (1994) *Death in Banaras*, Cambridge: Cambridge University Press

Pina-Cabral, J. de (1980) 'Cults of the Dead in Northern Portugal', *Journal of the Anthropological Society of Oxford* 9: 1–31

Scheper-Hughes, N. (1992) *Death Without Weeping: The Violence of Everyday Life in Brazil*, Berkeley: University of California Press

Vernant, J.-P. (1982) 'La belle Mort et le Cadavre Outragé' in G. Gnoli and J.-P. Vernant (eds) *La Mort, le Mort dans les sociétés Anciennes*, Paris

Watson, J.L. (1988) 'Funeral Specialists in Cantonese Society: Pollution, Performance and Social Hierarchy', in J.L. Watson and E.S. Rawski (eds) *Death Ritual in Late Imperial and Modern China*, Berkeley: University of California Press

descent

Descent refers to relatedness based on common ancestry. Actual biological relationships in a population may well extend well beyond those that are popularly known and socially recognized. Equally, those whose claim to share the same descent is generally accepted may not necessarily all be biologically related. Because of its cultural loading, descent is essentially a social concept, and varies widely in significance in different societies. In Western industrial societies in general, except at the level of *'race' and in other rather specialized circumstances, descent is not a very significant principle of social organization. In traditional societies, however, it is often extremely important. Here, in line with the archaic English aphorism 'blood is thicker than water', social heredity provides a convenient and powerful basis not merely for transmitting *property and office down the generations, but also for social bonding and collective action. Group solidarity, based on descent, is by definition 'natural' and so beyond question since it is, as the saying goes, 'in the blood' – a genetic given. This is reflected in the terms 'nation' and *'nationalism' which makes birth, and therefore ancestry and descent, the basis of individual and collective identity.

Conventionally, anthropologists use the term †'lineage' to refer to a descent-group tracing *kinship from a common (eponymous) *ancestor through named generations, and 'clan' to refer to an often larger descent-group with a vaguer tradition of common ancestry. The clan regularly comprises several component lineages which are often additionally bound together by a rule requiring their members to marry (†exogamously) outside the group. Where family trees are thus not simply objects of curiosity and mild snobbery, but the foundation of collective interests and rights, descent assumes an active and important role in social organization. Here, tracing pedigrees, and re-interpreting (and inventing) genealogies become crucially significant as claims and counter-claims are made to conflicting *identities. Contrary to much that has been written on the subject, *literacy is no guarantee of genealogical accuracy and written genealogies are manipulated as readily as those conserved orally. Where descent is a powerful source of social cohesion and common interest, *adoption is likely to play a prominent role since it enables those who are initially unrelated to assume the same descent as their patrons. Thus, amongst the southern agro-pastoral Somali in contrast to the northern nomads, institutionalized adoption on a vast scale has led to the formation of extremely heterogeneous groups which are formally lineages and trace descent from common 'ancestors' whose genealogies are actually those of only a tiny core population (Helander 1994).

Systems of descent

Descent has been classified according to the way in which relatedness is traced through paternal and maternal ancestors.

Patrilineal descent refers to common kinship traced consistently through male ancestors; the father, father's father, father's father's father, etc. Where male dominance is the norm, as it is traditionally in most societies, and property is mainly controlled by men, patriliny provides an economical arrangement which can be elaborated holistically as a basic organizing principle. The largest human population whose basic social units

are so constituted are the Arabs. The discovery of whole societies which lacked chiefs and whose political organizations, and not merely the primary social units, were based on descent led †Evans-Pritchard (1940) to develop the analytical concept of †segmentary lineage organization. Here essentially descent-based groups mobilize situationally in opposition to other comparable, but genealogically remote, lineages. Ancestors and genealogies are the repositories of political identity which is potentially as wide as a person's ancestry. People interact, in the first place, according to their genealogical closeness or remoteness along the lines of the famous Arab proverb: 'Myself against my brother; my brother and I against my cousins; my cousins and I against the world'.

Although this genealogical ideology provides an actor's model of politics in these societies, the reality is of course more complex since there are a variety of other principles of social cohesion and allegiance. In fact, the purest and most extreme example of this type of society so far described are the several million strong Somali pastoralists of the Horn of Africa (Lewis 1994) who represent themselves in this way and conduct their frequent †blood-feuds accordingly. Everyday political allegiance here is actualized at the level of those patrilineal kin who pay and receive damages for death and other injuries collectively, thus constituting a descent group (a '*dia*-paying group', from Arabic *dia* = blood-money) which has specific insurance functions. In considering its role in such segmentary lineage systems, it has to be remembered that descent is primarily a socio-political (and economic) resource which can be loaded and manipulated in various ways even within one cultural system. It does not in and of itself actually determine action although in these cases it provides an extremely compelling political ideology.

Descent traced patrilineally through the father does not exclude the complementary importance of ties on the mother's side. Indeed, extreme patrilineality tends to be associated with a particularly binding relationship between a man and his maternal uncle and the latter's patrilineage. This is often reinforces by his mother's brother's daughter being regarded as a man's ideal *marriage partner. Where †polygyny is practised, the patrilineal identity of a man's successive wives becomes, for the descendants, the basis of corresponding divisions amongst the ensuing lineages. The existence of such maternally differentiated segments within a patrilineal descent system has often given non-anthropologists (not least historians) the misleading impression that they have found evidence of †matrilineal descent or even of †'matriarchy'. Descent is not without effect on marriage, in that marriage between those who are closely related is generally regarded as *incest. Strongly integrated descent groups often observe a rule of exogamy, forbidding internal marriage and forcing their members to seek partners from other descent groups. This is usually combined with an ideology of marriage as an alliance between antagonistic groups and is represented in popular discourse in aphorisms as: 'We marry our enemies'. In some patrilineal systems marriage incorporates a wife into her husband's lineage: in others a married woman retains her own lineage identity. In the latter case, marriage is frequently more unstable than in the former. The systematic practice of marriage with *prescribed categories of relative (e.g. cross-cousins), widely elaborated particularly in *Southeast Asia, Aboriginal Australia and South America, and frequently associated with status differences between wife-givers and wife-receivers, produces structures where *alliance eclipses descent as a fundamental social principle.

Tracing descent through maternal ancestors is the basis of matriliny, the other form of unilineal descent (see Schneider and Gough 1961). This is a far cry from matriarchy since men are still in control. Here, however, although still under male authority, the hand that rules does not confer citizenship or rights to the inheritance of property and office. Through the rules of matrilineal citizenship, a man is reproduced not through his wife, but through his sister. He inherits from his mother's brother and rears children who will belong to his wife's brother. Matriliny is thus more a matter of 'brother-right' than mother-right (matriarchy). The characteristic domestic tensions entailed here were carefully delineated in *Malinowski's classic study of the Trobriand Islanders referred to, rather colourfully, in W.H. Auden's poem 'Heavy Date': 'Matrilineal races kill their mothers' brothers in their dreams, and turn their sisters into wives'. In matrilineal systems, the sibling and crucial mother's brother-sister's son relationships are constantly threatened by the marriage bond in a kind of institutionalized 'tug-of-love', and marriage is often unstable. In order to exert and maintain authority, a maternal uncle has to be able to control his sister's sons. Hence,

the rules governing where the married couple live in relation to the place of residence of the wife's brother are crucial considerations. The ideal arrangement here would be for brothers and sisters to live together and allow husbands to visit their wives sufficiently frequently to provide for the perpetuation of the descent group. The Nayars of Kerala in India seem to have come closest to exemplifying this model in their traditional practice before it was disrupted by British colonial influence (Fuller 1976). Other societies require both spouses to regularly alternate periods of residence in their own and their partner's matrilineal village. Under a rule of †uxorilocal marriage, the women of the matriline live together in their ancestral settlement and their husbands come to join them there. This, however, has the disadvantage of dispersing the men of the matrilineage who control its affairs and also threatens their control over their sisters' sons who are their heirs. This difficulty can be ameliorated by a rule which requires the sisters' children, especially the males, to live with their maternal uncle once they have achieved puberty. When marriage disperses both the males and females of the matrilineage in separate communities, the matrilineal system loses much of its force as is the situation generally today in the so-called 'matrilineal belt' in Central Africa. Matrilineal ties, may, however, still be important in constituting †cross-cutting ties between local communities.

In the modern setting, where personal wealth becomes available (through commerce or wage earnings), a father tends to try to bypass his traditional obligations to his sisters' sons in favour of his own son. This may be facilitated by encouraging the latter to marry his father's sister's daughter – who has legitimate matrilineal inheritance rights. Under the influence of (patriarchal/patrilineal) colonialism and *Christianity and increasing involvement in money economies, a general drift has occurred from matriliny towards patriliny or †bilateral descent, which is a kind of half-way house. But there are exceptions and examples of traditionally matrilineal societies which have successfully harnessed this form of descent to the market economy.

†Double or dual descent, first analysed among the Yakö of West Africa by †Daryll Forde (in Radcliffe-Brown and Forde 1950), combines both systems of unilineal descent, allocating different social functions to each. Much more common is bilateral or †cognatic descent in which

relationships are traced on both the paternal and maternal sides at each generation. Here genealogies are usually shorter and, in principle, a person belongs to as many cognatic (or †'ambilineal') descent groups as he has known ancestors. Such overlapping identity does not lend itself to the development of a series of clearly defined descent groups in the fashion of segmentary lineage systems, and group cohesion tends to be weak and uncommitting. Where, as among the Amhara of Christian Ethiopia (Hoben 1973), descent from a particular ancestor is made the basis of landholding and regulates marriage (through a rule obliging descendants to marry outside the group), this can give rise to stronger group solidarity. Here again, as with other systems of descent, the official theory of kinship priorities is supplemented and modified in practice by interests based on other principles of association. With bilateral kinship, and indeed under all rules of descent, people also have the opportunity of forming more ephemeral and individually specific groupings, based on common descent, known technically as 'ego-centred †kindreds'. Such kindreds are specific to the individual and only full siblings (having identical ancestry) share the same kindred. Kindreds tend to provide important social networks in most traditional (and some modern) societies even when unilineal descent is strongly developed.

I.M. LEWIS

See also: kinship, property, marriage, Africa: Nilotic, house, alliance, complementary filiation

Further reading

Barth, F. (1973) 'Descent and Marriage Reconsidered' in J. Goody (ed.) *The Character of Kinship*, Cambridge: Cambridge University Press
Evans-Pritchard, E.E. (1940) *The Nuer*, Oxford: Clarendon Press
Forde, D. (1950) 'Double Descent among the Yakö' in A.R. Radcliffe-Brown and D. Forde (eds) *African Systems of Kinship and Marriage*, London: Oxford University Press
Fortes, M. (1953) 'The Structure of Unilineal Descent Groups', *American Anthropologist*, 55: 17–41
Fox, R. (1967) *Kinship and Marriage*, Harmondsworth: Penguin
Freedman, M. (1966) *Chinese Lineage and Society*, London: Athlone Press
Fuller, C. (1976) *The Nayars Today*, Cambridge: Cambridge University Press
Helander, B. (1994) *The Slaughtered Camel: Coping with Fictitious Descent among the Hubeer of Southern Somalia*, Stockholm: Almqvist and Wiksell
Hoben, A. (1973) *Land Tenure among the Amhara of Ethiopia*, Chicago: Chicago University Press
Kuper, A. (1982) 'Lineage Theory: A Critical Retrospect', *Annual Review of Anthropology*, 11: 71–95
Leach, E.R. (1961) *Rethinking Anthropology and Other Essays*, London: Athlone Press
Lewis, I.M. (1969) 'From Nomadism to Cultivation: The Expansion of Political Solidarity in Southern Somalia', in M. Douglas and P. Kaberry (eds) *Man in Africa*, London: Tavistock
—— (1994) *Blood and Bone: The Call of Kinship in Somali Society*, New Jersey: Red Sea Press
Malinowski, B. (1922) *Argonauts of the Western Pacific*, London: Routledge and Kegan Paul
Scheffler, H.W. (1966) 'Ancestor Worship in Anthropology: Observations on Descent and Descent Groups', *Current Anthropology*, 7: 54–98
Schneider, D. and K. Gough (eds) (1962) *Matrilineal Descent*, Berkeley: University of California Press

development

Development is a key concept in Western culture and philosophy (cf. Nisbet 1969; Williams 1985) that figures in anthropology in two different ways. In its broadest sense, the idea of 'development' was central to nineteenth-century social *evolutionism, which pictured human history as a unilinear developmental progression from †'savage' and †'barbarian' levels of social evolution toward the 'civilized' status represented by the modern West. From the mid-twentieth-century, the term has mostly referred to a more specifically economic process, generally understood to involve the expansion of production and *consumption and/or rising standards of living, especially in the poor countries of the 'Third World'. In this second sense, the term is especially associated with the international projects of planned social change set in motion in the years surrounding World War II, which gave birth to 'development agencies', 'development projects', and, ultimately, to 'development studies' and 'development anthropology'. The two usages of the term are normally treated separately, but an understanding of how the concept of development has functioned in anthropology requires that the two be considered together, in their historical relation.

Development and evolution

The origins of anthropology as a discipline are conventionally traced to the late nineteenth century, and to such 'founding father' figures as *Lewis Henry Morgan in the USA, and †E.B.

Tylor in Britain. The dominant conception that such thinkers elaborated, and the key idea that gave to anthropology its early conceptual coherence as a discipline, was the idea of social *evolution. Against the common nineteenth-century assumptions that 'savages' such as the Australian Aborigines or Native Americans were either essentially different kinds of creature than 'civilized' Europeans (the racist supposition), or examples of degeneration, showing just how far from God and original perfection it was possible for miserable sinners to fall (a theological interpretation dating back to the Middle Ages), the social evolutionists insisted that 'savages' and 'civilized men [sic]' were fundamentally the same type of creature, and that if 'higher' forms existed, it was because they had managed to evolve out of the 'lower' ones (rather than vice-versa, as degeneration theory had it). As Morgan put it in the closing lines of *Ancient Society* (1877: 554):

> We owe our present condition, with its multiplied means of safety and of happiness, to the struggles, the sufferings, the heroic exertions and the patient toil of our barbarous, and more remotely, of our savage ancestors. Their labors, their trials and their successes were a part of the plan of the Supreme Intelligence to develop a barbarian out of a savage, and a civilized man out of this barbarian.

The project this implied for the new field of anthropology was to trace the different stages of this development, and to use observations of 'savage' and 'barbarian' peoples as evidence that would fill in what the earlier stages of human history had been. Thus did non-Western peoples end up construed as living fossils, lingering in early developmental stages through which the West had long ago passed. This was a vision of a kind of human unity. But it was also a device of differentiating and ranking different contemporary societies according to their level of evolutionary development, since (in spite of the best laid plans of the Supreme Intelligence) 'other tribes and nations have been left behind in the race of progress' (1877: vi). The metaphor of 'development' invited, too, a fusing of the idea of evolutionary advance with the developmental maturation of an organism or person, thus facilitating the persistent slippage between the contrast 'primitive'/'civilized' and 'child'/'adult' that played a key role in ideologies of *colonialism.

There are three underlying premises embedded in nineteenth-century social evolutionism that are worth emphasizing. First, there is the central idea that different societies are to be understood as discrete individuals, with each society making its way through the evolutionary process at its own pace, independently of the others. Second is the insistence that although each society is in some sense on its own, all societies are ultimately heading toward the same destination; human history is one story, not many. Finally, the social evolutionary schemes posited that differences between human societies were to be interpreted as differences in their level of development. If other peoples differed from the Western standard, it was only because, 'left behind in the race of progress', they remained at one of the prior developmental levels through which the West had already passed. Taken together, these three principles frame a formidable and durable vision of human history and human difference, 'a vast, entrenched political cosmology' (Fabian 1983: 159) that has been of enormous consequence both in anthropology and in the wider world.

Anti-evolutionism and relativism

Within anthropology, the evolutionary schemes of nineteenth-century theorists like Morgan and Tylor are generally taken to have been definitively refuted in the early twentieth century, most of all by the criticisms developed by *Boas and his historically-oriented school in *American anthropology and by the *functionalist school in *British anthropology, led by *Malinowski. In the wake of their devastating criticisms of the empirical adequacy of the nineteenth-century evolutionary schemes, the emphasis on sorting societies according to their level of evolutionary development largely dropped out of anthropology in the first half of the twentieth century. Both in the USA and Britain, though in different ways, a critique of speculative evolutionism was followed by moves toward *relativism in conceptions of progress and development. From whose point of view could one society be seen as 'higher' than another, after all? Evolutionism came to be seen not only as empirically flawed, but as †ethnocentric as well. The task, instead, came to be seen as one of understanding each unique society 'in its own terms', as one of many possible ways of meeting human social and psychological needs (Malinowski), or as one 'pattern of culture' (†Benedict), one 'design for living' (†Kluckhohn) among others.

At one level, such shifts did mark a clear break with evolutionist ideas of 'development': non-Western cultures, in the new view, were no longer to be understood as 'living fossils' trapped in evolutionary stages through which the West itself had already passed. Different societies now really were different, not just the same society at a different stage of development. Yet the break with evolutionism was less complete than it is often made to appear. It is significant, for instance, that mid-twentieth-century relativist approaches (whether Boasian in the USA or functionalist in Britain) preserved the old evolutionist idea (which an earlier emphasis on *diffusion had challenged) that different societies were to be conceived of as so many separate individuals. Even more striking, perhaps, is the way that post-evolutionist approaches preserved the grand binary distinction between primitive and modern societies, and accepted that anthropology's specialization would remain the study of primitive societies. No longer would different primitive societies be placed on a ladder and ranked against each other; all were now equally valid, forming whole culture patterns (USA) or functioning systems (Britain) worth studying in their own right. But they were still seen as a distinctive class set apart from, and in some sense prior to, 'modern', 'Western', 'civilized' society. It is telling that both the label, 'primitive' (or some close synonym), and the underlying category, were accepted by the leading anti-evolutionist anthropological theorists right up until the 1960s and 1970s (and even later, in some cases).

'Practical anthropology' and postwar modernization

A major geo-political restructuring, and with it a new burst of social engineering, reconfigured the political and institutional landscape of the social sciences in the years following World War II. Cooper (forthcoming) has recently begun to excavate the origins of a global project of 'development' from within the postwar planning of the colonial empires. One important early finding of this work is that, in the process of decolonization, a strategically vague story about development came to provide an ambiguous charter both for retreating colonial bureaucrats and for ascendant nationalist rulers. This charter, a broad vision that came to be shared by a wide set of transnational elites, framed the 'problems' of the 'new nations' in the terms of a familiar (at least to those schooled

in nineteenth-century anthropology) developmentalist story about nations (conceived, again, as individuals) moving along a predetermined track, out of 'backwardness' and into 'modernity' (Chatterjee 1986; cf. Ludden 1992).

It was within the terms of this narrative that a host of 'development agencies', programmes of 'development aid', and so forth, were conceived and put into place in the years following World War II (Escobar 1995). One of a number of consequences of this development was that funding and institutional positions became increasingly available for those with the sorts of expertise presumed necessary to bring about the great transformation. It is at this point that 'development' and anthropology began to come together in a new way.

In the years prior to World War II, 'development' had been a central, if often unacknowledged, theoretical concept in anthropology. For Morgan, of course, the question of how societies 'developed' from one evolutionary stage to the next was an explicit theoretical concern. Even for an arch-relativist like Benedict, the distinction between 'primitive' and 'modern' societies was a theoretically motivated one. Yet with the new project of official *modernization, issues of 'development' came increasingly to belong not to the academic world of theory (which remained largely devoted to comparing and generalizing about 'primitive societies') but to a domain of 'applied' work. The explicit coining of the term 'development anthropology' comes only later, in the 1970s. But already in the postwar years, the old domain of applied or policy-relevant work (often focused on such things as †'culture contact', †'acculturation', and 'social change') was beginning to become part of a larger, better funded configuration known as 'development'.

As early as 1929, Malinowski had called for a 'Practical Anthropology', which would be an 'anthropology of the changing Native' and 'would obviously be of the highest importance to the practical man in the colonies' (1929: 36). But though Malinowski readily used his often grandiose claims for anthropology's practical utility for colonialism to beat the drum for more funding, the actual status that such work enjoyed within the discipline is revealed by †Lucy Mair's recollection that 'Malinowski sent me to study social change because, he said, I didn't know enough anthropology for fieldwork of the standard type' (in Grillo 1985: 4). After World War II, the status of applied work on social change (increasingly referred to in terms of 'development' or 'modernization' rather than 'culture contact' or 'social change') would significantly improve (though never fully escaping the stigma of the 'applied'). In British anthropology, for instance, the †Rhodes-Livingstone Institute conducted work that was at least ostensibly applied to practical 'colonial development' policy, while at the same time enjoying a very significant impact on anthropological theory (largely through the leadership of its one time director, †Max Gluckman, and the links between the Institute and a leading academic department at Manchester). In the USA, meanwhile, such a leading figure as †Margaret Mead championed the potential contribution of anthropology to a wide variety of development issues, especially the easing of the transition of 'primitive' peoples into the modern world.

If, as Fabian has argued, anthropology's earlier shift from evolutionism to relativism had resulted in the issue of developmentalist progressions being turned 'from an explicit concern into an implicit theoretical assumption' (1983: 39), the postwar era began to see a shift back to explicit concern. What had been a background theoretical assumption (a fundamental difference between primitive and modern societies) was abruptly shifted from the background to the foreground, and from the passive voice to the active. Increasingly, the question became: How do primitives become modern? And how could they be helped (or made) to make this transition? Significantly, this question was now linked less with theoretical speculation than with explicit programmes of directed social change. The grand project that Morgan had seen as reserved for 'the Supreme Intelligence' – to develop . . . a civilized man out of this barbarian' was now understood to be a job for the merely mortal intelligence of anthropologists.

As the anthropological concern with social and cultural change became increasingly linked (especially in the USA) with 'modernization theory' as formulated in other disciplines (notably political science and *sociology), ideas of linear developmental stages that would have been quite familiar to Morgan began to reappear in surprisingly explicit ways (e.g. Rostow 1960). Theoretically, ideas of social evolution began to become respectable again in American anthropology (starting with †Leslie White in the 1940s, and continuing through the 1950s and 1960s, with figures like †Service, †Sahlins, and †Harris). But

even anthropologists who kept their distance from the neo-evolutionist revival (e.g. Mead, cited above, or †Clifford Geertz, in his early work on Java) began to bend their work in the direction of 'modernization'. A parallel process seems to have allowed British functionalists, also sceptical by training of evolutionary narratives, to endorse and participate in both colonial development schemes, and later projects of state-led 'modernization' (Grillo 1985).

Yet while the nineteenth-century conception of evolutionary 'stages' was nothing if not a theoretical formula, which aimed at the explanation of both human history and human diversity, the mid-twentieth-century revival of a 'stage' theory of development was chiefly linked to applied work, and to the problem of contemporary economic transitions. Studying the development of 'traditional' peoples in modernizing societies was thought to be of mostly 'practical' or 'policy' significance, and the theoretical core of the discipline remained the description and comparison of societies and cultures as little contaminated by 'development' as possible.

Neo-Marxist critique

A major disruption of the received anthropological wisdom regarding 'development' and 'modernization' came with the rise of †dependency theory and a set of neo-Marxist critiques of both modernization theory and traditional anthropology. The contributions of Marxist anthropology are discussed elsewhere (see *Marxism and anthropology, *world systems, *political economy, *mode of production); here it is useful simply to point out that the neo-Marxist critiques of the 1970s fundamentally challenged two key pillars of developmentalist thought in anthropology.

First, and perhaps most profoundly, the new critiques rejected the picture of the world as an array of individual societies, each moving through history independently of the others. This, as I suggested above, was a vision that was largely shared by the nineteenth-century evolutionists and their twentieth-century critics, who disagreed about whether the different tracks all headed in the same direction but accepted the idea of different and separate tracks. In place of this conception, anthropologists influenced by dependency theory, neo-Marxist modes of production theory, and world systems theory, began to insist that differences between societies had to be related to a common history of conquest, imperialism, and economic exploitation that systematically linked them. Supposedly 'traditional' practices and institutions, rather than being relics of a pre-capitalist past, might instead be interpreted as products of, or reactions to, processes of *capitalist penetration, the articulation of modes of production, or world-system incorporation. And poverty, rather than an original condition, might be a result of such processes. Instead of being simply 'undeveloped' (an original state), the Third World now appeared as actively 'underdeveloped' by a first world that had 'underdeveloped' it.

This brings us to the second pillar of developmentalist thought that was brought into question in this period: the assumed identity of development with a process of moral and economic progress. Neo-Marxists insisted that what was called 'development' was really a process of capitalist development: the global expansion of the capitalist mode of production at the expense of existing pre-capitalist ones. And the outcome of such a process might not be 'real development', in the sense of a better life for people in the Third World, at all. 'Development' (really, capitalist development), then, might not be 'progress' in any simple way; indeed, for poor peasants, it was likely to make life much worse. The benign moral teleology of the 'development' story (a central feature of nineteenth-century anthropology and 1960s 'modernization theory' alike) was radically called into question.

These two breaks with anthropology's developmentalist heritage were of fundamental importance. Indeed, it could be suggested that any project for restructuring anthropology's disciplinary relation to 'development' would do well to take them as a promising point of departure. However, it is also evident that for neo-Marxism, world history still had the character of a developmentalist evolution, with the march of the capitalist mode of production leading in a linear, teleological progression toward a future that would culminate (if only after a long process of struggle) in socialism. There remained, too, a tenacious attachment to the idea of 'real development' (in the name of which mal- or 'under-' development could be denounced). And if capitalism could not deliver the 'real development' goods, neo-Marxism was prepared to promise that socialism could and even, all too often, to endorse the exploitation of peasant producers by radical Third World states in the name of 'socialist development' (cf. Phillips 1977; Williams 1978).

'Development anthropology'

It is ironic, but probably true, that the very popularity within anthropology of the radical, neo-Marxist critiques of orthodox development and modernization theory in some ways set the stage for a new era of closer collaboration between anthropologists and the organizations and institutions of capitalist development policy. If nothing else, the radical critiques made it more legitimate, and more intellectually exciting, to study issues of 'development' in the context of an increasingly radicalized and politicized discipline. At a time when university-based scholarship was under pressure to demonstrate its relevance, and when anthropology was particularly challenged to show that it had something to say about change, not just stasis, and about the modern world, not just the 'tribal' one, a politically engaged and theoretically challenging approach to 'development' had considerable appeal.

At the same time, the wider institutional context was changing quite dramatically. Driven by an awareness of the failures of conventional development interventions, and mindful of the apparent successes of communist insurgencies in mobilizing poor *peasants (especially in Asia and Latin America), mainstream development agencies began in the mid-1970s to place a new emphasis on the basic needs of the poor, and on the distinction between mere economic growth and 'real development', understood in terms of such measures of human welfare as infant mortality rates, nutrition, and literacy. The World Bank, under the leadership of Robert MacNamara, and later the US Agency for International Development (USAID), directed by Congressional mandate to focus its aid on the poor, began to pay more attention to the 'soft', 'social' side of development policy, and to turn more readily to social sciences other than economics. This conjunctural moment, fitting nicely with an employment crisis in academic anthropology, gave rise to a burst of anthropological interest in development, and a new, recognized sub-field of anthropology, 'development anthropology'. For reviews of this period see Hoben 1982; Escobar 1991.

The intellectual and political failings of this sub-field have been analysed by Escobar (1991), who shows how anthropological work on 'development' came to be more and more adjusted to the bureaucratic demands of development agencies, at the expense of intellectual rigour and critical self-consciousness. In the process, the ambitious theoretical and political agenda that had characterized anthropological work on 'development' in the days of radical 'underdevelopment theory' largely fell by the wayside, leaving behind a low-prestige, practice-oriented sub-field of 'development anthropology', recognizably anthropological in its 'grassroots' focus and vaguely populist sympathies, but commonly understood to be 'applied', and to have little to do with academic anthropological theory. Academic anthropologists, meanwhile, have mostly kept their distance from 'development', although a few have begun to train an anthropological lens on the 'development apparatus' itself, taking as an ethnographic object the very ideas and institutions on which 'development anthropology' often uncritically relies (e.g. Escobar 1995, Ferguson 1990, Pigg 1992, Robertson 1984).

To make sense of the division between an applied, 'development' anthropology, and an academic, 'theoretical' sort, it is necessary to note that academic anthropology itself continues to be defined in disciplinary terms that are in some ways continuous with its nineteenth-century roots as the science of the less developed. In this sense, 'development' (or its absence), far from defining a mere sub-field within the discipline, continues to be at the heart of the constitution of anthropology itself. In one sense, of course, anthropology's old, developmentalist assumptions have been long overturned; anthropologists today do not seek out untouched primitives, but routinely deal with questions of history and transformation, with the way local communities are linked to a wider world, and with a host of non-traditional substantive questions. The extent to which the field has been able to leave its old developmentalist assumptions behind, however, has been limited by a number of factors.

Perhaps the most important such factor is the way that the anthropological specialization is shaped by the conventional division of academic labour between the social scientific disciplines. What distinguishes anthropology from sociology, political science, and other fields continues, in practice, to be largely a matter of the kinds of societies or settings that they study. Anthropologists, in practice (at least those who are trained and hired by 'leading departments'), continue to work mostly in the 'Third World', and to specialize disproportionately in the study of small, rural, isolated, or marginal communities. Anthropol-

ogists today are expected, it is true, to address questions of the transformation of local communities, and of linkages with wider regional and global processes; but it remains the case that it is a particular kind of people that anthropologists are typically interested in seeing change, and a particular kind of local community that they seek to show is linked to that wider world.

The idea of 'the local', in fact, has come to assume a remarkably prominent place in anthropology's disciplinary self-definitions. Where once anthropology studied 'the savage', 'the primitive', 'the tribal', 'the native', 'the traditional', today we are more likely to be told that anthropologists study 'the local'. More and more, anthropology seems to be defined as a kind of attentiveness to 'local knowledge', or a field that specializes in the study of 'local people' in 'local communities' (thus, not incidentally, a sort of study that must be carried out 'in the field'). Such a definition undoubtedly encompasses a wider range of phenomena than the older conception of 'primitive' or 'traditional' societies. But even if it is true that all social processes are in some sense 'local', it is also clear that, in normal anthropological practice, some problems, some research settings, even some people, seem to be more 'local' than others. Unsurprisingly, it is the least 'developed' who are generally understood to be the most 'local'.

Insofar as a certain opposition of 'us' and 'them', 'the West' and 'the rest', continues to inform the constitution of anthropology as an academic discipline, the concept of 'development' must retain a special salience, sitting as it does astride this venerable binary opposition. For the kind of societies and settings that anthropologists typically study and the kind they do not are separated precisely by 'development' (those that haven't experienced 'development' are most anthropological; those that are 'developed' are least; and those in between, 'developing', are in the middle of the spectrum of anthropological-ness). Indeed, it is clear not only that anthropologists have mostly studied in 'less developed countries', but also that they have tended to study 'less developed' categories of people within those countries (indigenous native peoples in Brazil, 'tribal' or 'hill' people in Southeast Asia, foragers in Southern Africa, and so on). Likewise, when anthropologists work in the 'developed world', they tend to study the poor, the marginal, the 'ethnic', in short, the Third World within.

(Significantly, anthropologists in the West usually work in settings that might also make good sites for 'community development programmes'.) In all these cases, too, those who lack 'development' are those who putatively possess such things as authenticity, tradition, culture: all the things that 'development' (as so many anthropologists have over the years agreed) places in peril.

We are left, then, with a curious dual organization binding anthropology to 'development': the field that fetishizes the local, the autonomous, the traditional, locked in a strange dance with its own negation, its own evil twin that would destroy locality, autonomy, and tradition in the name of progress. Anthropology resents its twin fiercely (hence the oft-noted distaste of mainstream anthropology for 'development' work), even as it must recognize a certain intimacy with it, and a disturbing, inverted resemblance. Like an unwanted ghost, or an uninvited relative, 'development' haunts the house of anthropology. Fundamentally disliked by a discipline that at heart loves all those things that development intends to destroy, anthropology's evil twin remains too close a relative to be simply kicked out. Thus do we end up with an 'applied' sub-field ('development anthropology') that conflicts with its own discipline's most basic theoretical and political commitments (hence its 'evil'); yet which is logically entailed in the very constitution of that field's distinctive specialization (hence its status as 'twin' to a field that is always concerned with the 'less', the 'under', the 'not-yet' . . . developed).

To move beyond this impasse will require a recognition that the extraordinarily tenacious vision of a world divided into the more and less 'developed' has been, and in many ways continues to be, definitive of the anthropological domain of study. It may even be suggested that the idea of 'development' (and its lack) is so intimately inter-twined with the idea of anthropology that to be critical of the concept of 'development' requires, at the same time, a critical re-evaluation of the constitution of the discipline of anthropology itself.

JAMES FERGUSON

See also: evolution and evolutionism, history and anthropology, colonialism, history of anthropology, political economy, world system

Further reading

Chatterjee, P. (1986) *Nationalist Thought and the Colonial World: A Derivative Discourse*, London: Zed Press

Cooper, F. (forthcoming) 'Modernizing Bureaucrats, Backward Africans, and Dualistic Development Theory', in F. Cooper and R. Packard (eds) *Development and the Social Sciences*.

Escobar, A. (1991) 'Anthropology and the Development Encounter: The Making and Marketing of Development Anthropology', *American Ethnologist*, 18 (4): 658–82

—— (1995) *Encountering Development: The Making and Unmaking of the Third World*, Princeton: Princeton University Press

Fabian, J. (1983) *Time and the Other: How Anthropology Makes its Object*, New York: Columbia University Press

Ferguson, J. (1990) *The Anti-politics Machine: 'Development', Depoliticization, and Bureaucratic Power in Lesotho*, New York: Cambridge University Press

Grillo, R. (1985) 'Applied Anthropology in the 1980s: Retrospect and Prospect', in R. Grillo and A. Rew (eds) *Social Anthropology and Development Policy*, New York: Tavistock

Hoben, A. (1982) 'Anthropologists and Development', *Annual Review of Anthropology*, 11: 349–75

Ludden, D. (1992) 'India's Development Regime', in N.B. Dirks (ed.) *Colonialism and Culture*, Ann Arbor: University of Michigan Press

Malinowski, B. (1929) 'Practical Anthropology', *Africa*, 2 (1): 22–38

Morgan, L.H. (1877) *Ancient Society*, New York: Henry Holt and Company

Nisbet, R.A. (1969) *Social Change and History: Aspects of the Western Theory of Development*, New York: Oxford University Press

Phillips, A. (1977) 'The Concept of Development', *Review of African Political Economy*, 8: 7–20

Pigg, S. (1992) 'Inventing Social Categories Through Place: Social Representations and Development in Nepal', *Comparative Studies in Society and History*, 34 (3): 491–513

Robertson, A.F. (1984) *People and the State: An Anthropology of Planned Development*, New York: Cambridge University Press

Rostow, W.W. (1960) *The Stages of Growth: A Non-Communist Manifesto*, Cambridge: Cambridge University Press

Thomas, N. (1989) *Out of Time: History and Evolution in Anthropological Discourse*, Cambridge: Cambridge University Press

Williams, G. (1978) 'Imperialism and Development: A Critique', *World Development* 6 (12): 925–36

Williams, R. (1985) *Keywords*, New York: Oxford University Press

diffusionism

Fundamental to anthropological inquiry in the late nineteenth century was the task of explaining similarities observed in the habits and beliefs of so-called primitives all over the world. Were peoples everywhere essentially identical, joined in the †'psychic unity' postulated by such figures as the German †Adolf Bastian, and therefore capable of independently inventing the basic constituents of social life? Or did common practices denote common origins, indicating that similarities were products of diffusion? At issue was the mechanism of human progress, the process by which humans rose from their primeval condition to superior states. If diffusion rather than independent invention explained resemblances among peoples who were separated by great distances and geographical barriers, then these peoples might once have been joined, or they might each have been affected by contact with migrant bearers of the traits they shared.

Why should accounts of social change not invoke both independent invention and diffusion? The American *Lewis Henry Morgan did so – and infuriated his British contemporaries. Morgan argued that 'the experience of mankind has run in nearly uniform channels', indicating agreement with British sociocultural anthropologists' view of progress as an independently invented passage through an invariant sequence of evolutionary stages; but he also insisted that peoples who shared such traits as †kinship terminology had to be members of the same racial stock – even if they were geographically dispersed. Such prevarication was inadmissible among the founders of British anthropology as a discipline, evoking the †poly-genist argument they successfully suppressed, for equating *culture and *race suggested that the varieties of humankind were separate species. Thus, late nineteenth-century British anthropologists insisted that, at least in the more primitive of societies, independent invention was the primary mechanism of social change; though such figures as †E.B. Tylor allowed that cultural diffusion occurred, they focused on the evolutionary progress which derived from societies' internal dynamics (see Lowie 1937: 59, 60-1; Stocking 1971; Tylor 1888).

By the turn of the twentieth century, the unity of the human species had become incontrovertible. Paleoanthropologists undertook to trace the lines of filiation joining all human varieties to a single (disputed) origin point, and diffusionist interpretations assumed very different significance for sociocultural anthropologists. In Britain, such prominent figures as †A.C. Haddon and †W.H.R. Rivers determined that social change must be explained as a function of *migration and †culture contact, thus embracing the fundamental premises of diffusionist argument. Biologically trained, they reasoned that they were extending Darwinian principles into anthropology: social forms were like lifeforms, migrating over diverse habitats if not presented with geographical obstacles to movement, sustaining adaptive modifications as their circumstances changed. The British extreme diffusionists, led by the paleoanthropologist †G. Elliot Smith, his associate W.J. Perry, and (for a time) Rivers, emboldened by the 1900 re-discovery of Gregor Mendel's genetic findings, declared that human beings were naturally conservative and a new form of social life was analogous to a new species arising from genetic mutation; the basis of Western civilization was a set of practices engendered by historical accident in ancient Egypt. Enjoying considerable prestige within the British scientific community in the years around World War I, the diffusionists were discredited after the war by the emergent *functionalist school of *Bronislaw Malinowski and *A.R. Radcliffe-Brown. Redefining the enterprise of sociocultural anthropology, declaring biological findings irrelevant to sociological inquiries and bracketing consideration of the course of human history, the functionalists rendered the issue of independent invention *versus* diffusion moot: even if some practices in any given society could be identified as imported, their original character was effectively obliterated by incorporation into the ongoing life of the society, in which they might serve functions altogether different from their purposes elsewhere. Formulated in opposition to extreme diffusionism, then, British functionalism was also uncompromisingly schematic (see Kuklick 1992: 119 – 81; Smith *et al.*, 1927).

By contrast, American sociocultural anthropology of the first half of the twentieth century, shaped by *Franz Boas and his students, blended approaches regarded as mutually exclusive in Britain. Trained in Germany as a geographer, Boas attended to factors that figured in the historical school of †Fritz Graebner and †Wilhelm Schmidt, who identified primeval culture complexes, †*Kulturkreise*, which underwent modifications as they diffused throughout the globe; but unlike theirs his approach was historical rather than historicist, postulating neither cultural archetypes nor a pattern in world history. Early twentieth-century American anthropologists might have insisted that the processes of independent invention and diffusion be distinguished, but they considered documentation of the course of diffusion a vehicle for explication of the problematic at the very core of British functionalism. That is, they judged that by identifying the selective principles which determined assimilation of diffused elements, the anthropologist revealed the ethos of the host culture – the coherent interdependence of its habits and beliefs (see Lowie 1937: 142–6, 177–85; Steward 1929; Wissler 1914).

Coda

By the World War II era, the question of independent invention *versus* diffusion had been rendered nonsensical in sociocultural anthropology: either it was irrelevant to explanation of the dynamics of social life or it represented a false dichotomy. It persisted in certain anthropological quarters, however. In particular, *archaeologists remained concerned to specify the nature of innovations, because, unlike sociocultural anthropologists, they had not abandoned the effort to account for world historical change (see Stahl 1994).

HENRIKA KUKLICK

See also: migration, technology, world system

Further reading

Kuklick, H. (1992) *The Savage Within*, Cambridge: Cambridge University Press

Lowie, R.H. (1937) *The History of Ethnological Theory*, New York: Holt, Reinhart and Winston

Smith, G.E., B. Malinowski, H. J. Spindler and A. Goldenweiser (1927) *Culture: The Diffusion Controversy*, New York: W. W. Norton

Stahl, A.B. (1994) 'Innovation, Diffusion, and Culture Contact: The Holocene Archaeology of Ghana', *Journal of World Prehistory*, 8: 51–112

Steward, J. (1929) 'Diffusion and Independent Invention: A Critique of Logic', *American Anthropologist*, (n.s.) 31: 491–5

Stocking, G.W. Jr (1971) 'What's In a Name?', *Man*, 6: 369–90

Tylor, E.B. (1888) 'On a Method of Investigating the Development of Institutions, Applied to Laws of Marriage and Descent', *Journal of the Anthropological Institute*, 18: 245–72

Wissler, C. (1914) 'The Horse in the Development of Plains Culture', *American Anthropologist*, (n.s.) 16 : 1–25

discourse

If the analytical value of some terms derives from their descriptive precision and specificity of meaning, other words – such as discourse – owe their utility to multiple layers of meaning and their ability to stimulate ambiguity. Anthropological discourse about 'discourse' expanded markedly in volume beginning in the 1970s. The term entered the discipline from two directions: it is part of the language of both descriptive *linguistics and *cultural studies. Beyond a common understanding that discourse involves the communication of meaning, the term has divergent uses in these two fields. Moreover, *within* linguistics and cultural studies, as within anthropology, discursive analysis signifies several different sorts of methodological enterprise.

Within linguistics, discourse once labelled utterances longer than the sentence or clause. As linguists move to incorporate contextual factors into their analyses, the term 'discourse' has shifted, slightly, to label the set of utterances that constitutes a †speech event. The tape recorder (and, for ethnographers, notably the cassette recorder) has facilitated the development of discourse analysis. This permits fine-grained transcription of speech events that captures changing rates of conversational speed, notes overlapped talking, measures the length of silences and also remarks prosodic features such as emphasis, intonational flow, loudness and other vocal qualities of utterances.

Linguists study these structural elements of discursive flow, focusing, for example, on how speakers introduce and control topics, on interruption, conversational 'housekeeping' devices that maintain discursive interaction, on markers that define and separate units within discourse, and so forth. Anthropologists, in general, are more concerned with what discourse structuring might reveal about culture at large: 'In every moment of talk, people are experiencing and producing their cultures, their roles, their personalities' (Moerman 1987: xi). The sequential organization of discourse, and conversational features such as overlapping patterns, breaks, silences, repairs and the like, can inform an understanding of both individual intention and cultural order. The genealogy of this technique of paying very close attention to discursive form, often also called 'conversational analysis', also traces back to the †ethnomethodology of the 1960s and 1970s.

A second sort of discourse analysis, associated with cultural studies, takes discourse more globally to refer to particular areas of language use. This approach blurs together three levels of meaning: discourse is the act of talking or writing itself; it is a body of knowledge content; and it is a set of conditions and procedures that regulate how people appropriately may communicate and use that knowledge. Rather than the elemental structures of conversational interaction, this second approach to discourse pursues the connections between orders of communication, knowledge and *power.

†Michel Foucault in large part pioneered discourse analysis of this sort. In *The Archaeology of Knowledge*, he set forth a programme for the 'pure description of discursive events' that sought to answer the question: 'How is it that one particular statement appeared rather than another [in a field of discourse]?' (1972: 270; see also 1981). Foucault's genealogies of European discourses of madness and sexuality have stimulated many other analyses of the ways in which patterned cultural discourses maintain both particular ways of knowing the world and a network of power relations among those who know. (Bauman and Briggs [1990] summarize a selection of this work.) Anthropologists influenced by Foucault have proposed the term 'discourse', with its implicit connotations of power and possible contestation, as an alternative to traditional anthropological notions of *culture (Lutz and Abu-Lughod 1990). The spread of the term reflects anthropology's increasing engagement with oral and written texts as important data for cultural interpretation.

LAMONT LINDSTROM

See also: language and linguistics, postmodernism

Further reading

Bauman, R. and C. Briggs (1990) 'Poetics and Performance as Critical Perspectives on Language and Social Life', *Annual Review of Anthropology* 19: 59–88

Foucault, M. (1972) *The Archaeology of Knowledge*, New York: Harper and Row

—— (1981) 'The Order of Discourse' in R. Young (ed.) *Untying the Text: A Post Structuralist Reader* (48–78), New York: Routledge and Kegan Paul

Lutz, C. and L. Abu-Lughod (1990) 'Introduction' in C. Lutz and L. Abu-Lughod (eds) *Language and the Politics of Emotion*, Cambridge: Cambridge University Press

Moerman, M. (1988) *Talking Culture: Ethnography and Conversational Analysis*, Philadelphia: University of Pennsylvania Press

divination

Divination, or mantic operations, are culturally sanctioned methods of arriving at a judgement of the unknown through a consideration of incomplete evidence. It is likely that divinatory practices have existed since the remote origins of human society. There is documentary evidence on Mesopotamian divination some 4,000 years ago, when priests regularly predicted the outcome of events through the examination of the livers of *sacrificed animals. This practice, called haruspicy, appears to have diffused into Western Asia and to have been adopted by the Etruscan culture of northern Italy. The Etruscans also divined through observation of the effects of lightning and through the examination of the flight of birds, a method still common in insular Southeast Asia. Both customs were incorporated into the culture of the ancient Romans. Scapulimancy, divination from the appearance of cracks in the heated shoulder-blades of sacrificed animals, was general in ancient China, where it replaced an earlier method using tortoise shells, and has been reported elsewhere in Asia and North America. Chinese civilization was also the origin of one of the most sophisticated systems of divination, the book of oracles known as the *I Ching* or Book of Changes which is believed to be at least 3,000 years old. Another mantic procedure of worldwide distribution and immemorial antiquity is divination through spirit *possession, of which a famous classic example was the prophetess called Python at Delphi in Greece. Divination through consideration of the behaviour of celestial bodies, or astrology, was found in ancient Mesopotamia, India and China, in *Central America and Saharan Africa and is still practised in many areas. In Europe the use of Tarot cards, crystal-gazing and a form of automatism called the ouija board enjoy widespread popularity. All these divinatory methods fall into the category of procedures concerned with predicting future events. A second category, typical of small-scale tribal societies, seeks to uncover the hidden causes of present misfortune in the recent or more remote past. Such blame-allocating divinatory methods have been well described by anthropologists in Africa (e.g. Turner 1975; Werbner 1973). In contrast, a predictive African system which rivals the Chinese *I Ching* in formal complexity is the *Ifa* oracle of the Yoruba-speaking peoples of *West Africa (Bascom 1969).

Modern anthropology has generally held divination in low esteem, often regarding it as evidence of primitive irrationality. For all the sensitivity of his celebrated study, †E.E. Evans-

Pritchard's (1937) opinion of the truth value of the Zande poison oracle of Central Africa is essentially similar to †E.B. Tylor's (1871) generalization that divination was 'a sincere but fallacious system of philosophy'. Yet serious consideration of the subject in Western culture goes back at least to the Roman orator and writer Cicero, who in De divinatione (42–44 BCE) usefully distinguished between *deductive* forms, which relied on the un-ambiguous, rule-governed reading of objective phenomena, and *intuitive* methods which called for subjective interpretation. Recent anthropological scholarship, in distancing itself from the implicitly derogatory approach typical of an earlier era, makes similar distinctions between divinatory forms of knowing. However, the latest field studies characteristically discover both logico-deductive and intuitive-interpretive cognitive modes operating within the *same* divinatory system. Further, a recent survey of divination in Africa links this cognitive dualism with the neurophysiologist R.W. Sperry's work on the differential functions in human beings of the left and right cerebral hemispheres (Ornstein 1973). In a typical consultation, it is suggested, the diviner initiates a switch to the holistic, pattern-seeking mode of knowing special to the normally subordinate right brain. Having achieved this altered state of consciousness the diviner then proceeds, with the help of the client, to bring together the information generated in the 'mystical' right-brain state with input from the analytic, linear left-brain (Peek 1991). According to Peek, 'all types of divination aid decision-making by literally re-viewing the problem in light of different knowledge . . . and then the process integrates this perspective with contemporary reality by means of discussion between diviner and client'.

Diviners employ a variety of techniques for achieving the change from ordinary consciousness. In the Americas the use of psychoactive drugs is widespread. In Africa and Asia the same effect is commonly achieved through an auditory stimulus, typically the use of percussive instruments such as drums or rattles. †Victor Turner (1972) describes how the Ndembu diviner of Central Africa is taken out of his 'everyday self' and gains heightened intuitive awareness through drumming and singing, as well as the use of archaic formulae in questions and responses.

This view of divination, so far from seeing it as irrational, credits it with manifesting an unusual, supra-rational form of knowing that provides privileged access to normally hidden information. The view has obvious affinities with the psychoanalyst C.G. Jung's interpretation of the *I Ching*. Jung (1951) saw this ancient oracle, in which the seemingly fortuitous fall of coins or disposition of yarrow stalks directs the client to the appropriate text, as reflecting a principle of 'synchronistic' connection between events which was timeless and entirely distinct from the cause-and-effect connections apparent to ordinary consciousness.

These findings are consistent with earlier anthropological descriptions which have emphasized the abnormal status of the typical diviner. He or she is typically someone who, by reason of ethnic origin, occupation, physical condition or sexual orientation is considered marginal to ordinary society. The transvestite diviners of some Native American societies, the Romany fortune-tellers of Europe, the Untouchable magician-diviners of Hindu India and the blind diviners of the Sudanic Dinka are examples. It seems reasonable to assume that social marginality of some kind helps the diviner to 'see' the situation of the client with the requisite degree of detachment and overall perspective. Frequently also the diviner signals his abnormal status through some standardized but unusual behaviour. Thus the male Nyoro diviner of Uganda symbolically takes on feminine attributes by using his left hand to cast the oracular cowrie shells (Needham 1967).

ROY WILLIS

See also: possession, sacrifice

Further reading

Bascom, W.R. (1969) *Ifa Divination: Communication between Gods and Man in West Africa*, Bloomington: Indiana University Press

Evans-Pritchard, E.E. (1937) *Witchcraft, Oracles and Magic among the Azande*, Oxford: Clarendon Press

Jung, C.G. (1951) 'Foreword', in *The I Ching or Book of Changes* (trans. by R. Wilhelm) London: Routledge & Kegan Paul

Needham, R. (1967) 'Right and Left in Nyoro Symbolic Classification', *Africa*, 37, (4): 425–52

Peek, P.M. (ed.) (1991) *African Divination Systems: Ways of Knowing*, Bloomington: Indiana University Press

Springer, S. P. and G. Deutsch (1981) *Left Brain, Right Brain*, San Francisco: Freeman

Turner, V.W. (1972) *The Drums of Affliction*, Oxford: Clarendon Press

—— (1975) *Revelation and Divination in Ndembu Ritual*, Ithaca: Cornell University Press

Tylor, E. B. (1871) *Primitive Culture*, London: Murray

Werbner, R. (1973) 'The Superabundance of Understanding: Kalanga Rhetoric and Domestic Divination', *American Anthropologist* 75 (5): 1414–40

dreams

Dreaming is a universal human experience which has raised profound questions about human nature, destiny, experience and epistemology since the beginning of history. The earliest preserved dream book is an Egyptian papyrus dated roughly to 2000 BC that presents a catalogue of images seen in dreams alongside their interpretations, divided into good and bad prophecies. If a man saw himself drinking wine or copulating with his mother, for instance, these were auspicious dreams; the first indicated 'living in righteousness' while the second meant that his 'clansmen will cleave fast to him'. Seeing himself drinking warm beer or copulating with a jerboa were bad dreams and meant 'suffering would come upon him' and 'the passing of a judgement against him' respectively (Lewis 1976).

Through Greco-Roman times dreams continued to be considered primarily as a means of prophesying the future. Probably the most complete manual of dream interpretation to survive was written by the second-century AD professional dream interpreter Artemidorus. Artemidorus was very much an empiricist who considered it important to travel and to consider closely the context of a given dreamer's vision. In his opinion traditional dream-interpreting keys often needed to be modified case by case. As an example he presented three different ways of interpreting a man's recurrent dream of not having a nose. The first time it meant that he would lose his perfume business; the second time it predicted that he would be convicted of forgery and exiled (facial disfiguration signifying disgrace); and finally this dream predicted his imminent death since the skull of a dead man has no nose (1975).

Artemidorus was aware that many esteemed thinkers, especially Aristotle and his followers, dismissed the idea that dreams could have prophetic qualities. On this view, dreams were entirely personal thoughts, primarily the residues of waking experiences, anxieties and desires which came to the fore during sleep. Artemidorus acknowledged this tradition of scepticism, but sidestepped it by classifying dreams into different types. Those generated by mundane, personal physiological causes such as inebriation, heat, or indigestion were labelled *enypnia* and were not prophetic and thus not worth interpreting; they referred mainly to the present. Other dreams, called oneiroi, were prophetic and Artemidorus left open the possibility that these could be sent by gods. For the next 1,500 years the Western tradition would fluctuate between viewing dreams as the products of individuals' physical and mental states, or as the results of supernatural visitation.

As Christianity spread during the Middle Ages the Church sought to consolidate its authority by allowing that only the extremely devoted could have prophetic dreams. The dreams of the ordinary laity were approached with suspicion as possible emanations of the devil. The future belonged to God to reveal to those who had achieved spiritual progress and who had, furthermore, developed the faculty of discernment which enabled them to decide the meaning and the divine or demonic provenance of dreams (Le Goff 1988).

At the beginning of the Enlightenment the understanding of dream experiences played an important role in displacing medieval theocentrism and establishing the precepts of natural science. After a dream on 10 November 1619 Descartes began to meditate on the possibility that the physical world was only a dream. The refutation of this idea led to his famous *cogito ergo sum*, the cornerstone of the rationalist movement which posited a clear distinction between mental and physical worlds; between fantasy and reality. The dream could thus be seen as a linchpin of Western epistemology, enabling the distinction between unreal forms of thought and the mechanically governed real world.

As anthropology developed in the nineteenth century under the influence of *evolutionism, the Cartesian view of dreams served as a means of distinguishing 'lower' levels of culture from the civilized culture of Northern Europe. As †Tylor explained in his *Primitive Culture* (1871), 'the savage or barbarian has never learnt to make that rigid distinction between subjective and objective, between imagination and reality, to enforce which is one of the main results of scientific education'. In turn, attempts to explain and understand dreams involving ghosts and nature spirits motivated the elaboration of †animism, the characteristically 'primitive' belief in the manifold operation of souls in both the human and natural worlds. The French philosopher/anthropologist

†Lévy-Bruhl disagreed with Tylor as to whether 'primitives' actually confused subjective with objective phenomena, but nevertheless pointed to their credence in dream visions as exemplifying 'mystical participation', a cornerstone of what he termed 'pre-logical mentality'. As he put it: 'Instead of saying, as people do, that primitives believe in what they perceive in the dream although it is but a dream, I should say that they believe in it because it is a dream' (1910 [1985]).

†Sigmund Freud's monumental *The Interpretation of Dreams* (1900) considered dreams to be the expressions of unconscious desires, distorted and encoded so as to elude the censorship of consciousness. His position continued the Aristotelian tradition of treating dreams as wholly personal matters. In diametrical opposition to Artemidorus and other ancient interpreters, dreams were not about predicting the future, but rather about uncovering an individual's past. The dominance of Freud's psychoanalytic perspective on dreams was such that anthropologists in the first half of the twentieth century largely conceded the topic of dreams to psychology, or else restricted themselves to empirical descriptions of dreaming in particular societies. This in spite of the fact that a psychoanalytic approach says nothing about the meaning which particular cultures attribute to dreams. A Freudian would examine the earlier mentioned Egyptian dream of copulating with one's mother and discern in it an expression of the putatively universal Oedipus complex. Such an interpretation may be correct at one level, but it runs roughshod over the meaning which the ancient Egyptians attributed to this dream, namely that it beneficially signified kin cooperation.

While concerned with the comparative ethnographic probing of Freud's universal theory of the unconscious, J.S. Lincoln (1935) none the less mapped out several useful interrogatives for future socio-cultural anthropological research. It was not until the late 1980s that numerous studies began to appear which, following Lincoln, considered the cultural significance of dreams as well as the practical social and political ends to which they may be applied (Tedlock 1987; Jedrej and Shaw 1992).

CHARLES STEWART

Further reading

Artemidorus (1975) *The Interpretation of Dreams*, (trans. by R.J. White), Park Ridge NJ: Noyes Press
Freud, S. ([1900] 1953) *The Interpretation of Dreams*, George Allen & Unwin Ltd
Jedrej, C. and R. Shaw (eds) (1992) *Dreaming, Religion and Society in Africa*, Leiden: Brill
Le Goff, J. (1988) *The Medieval Imagination*, Chicago: University of Chicago Press
Lévy-Bruhl, L. ([1910] 1985) *How Natives Think*, Princeton: Princeton University Press
Lewis, N. (1976) *The Interpretation of Dreams and Portents*, Toronto: Samuel Stevens
Lincoln, J. S. (1935) *The Dream in Primitive Culture*, London: Cresset Press
Tedlock, B. (ed.) (1987) *Dreaming: Anthropological and Psychological Interpretations*, Santa Fe: SAR
Tylor, E.B. (1871) *Primitive Culture*, 2 vols, London: John Murray

dual organization

A society has a dual organization when it is divided in two, with each of its members belonging to one or to the other †moiety (i.e. half). This widespread type of social organization is an elementary means of obtaining, in †Leslie White's words, 'differentiation of structure, specialisation of function, and co-operation'. The general pattern allows, however, for considerable variation in forms assumed and functions or social role performed by moieties. Among the most elaborate examples of dual organization are those found in *Aboriginal Australia, where it is commonly at work in the regulation of *marriage, allocation of *ritual responsibilities and *classification of nature. As †W. Lloyd Warner said of the Murngin division into the †exogamous †patrilineal moieties Duwa and Yiridja, 'There is nothing in the whole universe – plant, animal, mineral, star, man, or culture – that has not a place in one of the two categories'.

In parts of Arnhem Land there are exogamous †matrilineal moieties named Marawar and Rerwondji and non-exogamous, non-lineal 'ceremonial' moieties named Budal and Gwiyal as well as Duwa and Yiridja. Consequently each person belongs to three moieties, which cut across each other. In this region the most significant dichotomy is into patrilineal moieties. The initiated members of each have distinctive parts to play in such major religious cults as the Gunabibi and the Yabuduruwa. Thus Duwa is said to 'own' the Gunabibi and Yiridja to 'manage' it, these roles being reversed in the Yabuduruwa. The arrangement expresses a division of responsibility: owners do most of the ritual dancing and most of the †totemic images are of their moiety; but managers coordinate the programme and contribute labour, e.g. they make the dancing grounds and most of the objects used in the ritual. Were it not for the cooperation between moieties the cults could not be performed.

Although the dual organization of society is a manifestation of dualism, the latter can exist without it, as has been particularly emphasized by †Rodney Needham in his studies, ultimately inspired by †Robert Hertz, of handedness and symbolic classification. The Chinese philosophy of Yin and Yang is an example of classification without moieties. Husband, summer, etc. are classed as Yang and their 'opposites' – wife, winter, etc. – as Yin. The union of opposites yields wholeness – a conjugal pair, the year, etc. – just as the union of Duwa and Yiridja in Arnhem Land gives us society in its entirety. Needham thinks of a natural proclivity to binary classification (cf. †A.L. Kroeber. who spoke of a psychological trend to dichotomize); such explanations root dualism, including its expression in moieties, in human nature. Hertz himself related it to the antithesis of *sacred and profane, and saw the existence of moieties as 'a reflection and a consequence of religious polarity', but his explanation loses force when it is realized that this antithesis is among the more contestable legacies of the French sociological school.

KENNETH MADDOCK

See also: classification, Aboriginal Australia, totemism

Further reading

Maddock, K. (1979) 'A Structural Analysis of Paired Ceremonies in a Dual Social Organisation', *Bijdragen tot de Taal-, Land- en Volkendunde* 135: 84–117

Maybury-Lewis, D. and U. Almagor (eds) (1989) *The Attraction of Opposites: Thought and Society in the Dualistic Mode*, Ann Arbor: University of Michigan Press

Needham, R. (1973) *Right and Left: Essays on Dual Symbolic Classification*, Chicago: University of Chicago Press

—— (1979) *Symbolic Classification*, Santa Monica: Goodyear

White, L.A. (1959) *The Evolution of Culture*, New York: McGraw-Hill

Dutch anthropology

Dutch anthropology has a distinguished and unique history, and there is no shortage of English-language publications aimed at explaining it to the outside world (e.g., Kloos and Claessen 1975,

1981, 1991). Essentially, there are two main distinctive anthropological traditions in the Netherlands, which in that country are commonly labelled 'cultural anthropology' (including structural anthropology) and 'sociology of non-Western societies'.

Arguably, Dutch cultural anthropology began in colonial Netherlands East Indies, where senior colonial officers of the nineteenth century realized the advantages of recording languages and customs of the indigenous population for their administrative purposes. Chairs were established at Leiden in 1877 and at Amsterdam in 1907, and the incumbents, though at first *evolutionist in persuasion, promoted a long association between colonial administration and ethnographic research. The structuralist tradition, which many outside Holland regard as the essence of Dutch anthropology, took hold in the 1920s and especially the 1930s, and was led by the work of F.A.E. van Wouden, G.W. Locher, and especially †J.P.B. de Josselin de Jong and later his nephew P.E. de Josselin de Jong, among others. Early writings in the tradition were mainly in Dutch, but English translations of the classic texts are included in two important collections (Josselin de Jong 1977, 1984).

Dutch structuralism differs from *structuralism as we usually think of it (i.e., French structuralism) in that the former postulates only structures which are unique to †culture areas or regions, not to all humankind. Such culture areas are known within Dutch anthropology as 'fields of ethnological (or anthropological) study' (*ethnologisch studievelden*). Each is defined by a set of common features known as its 'structural core' (*structurele kern*). These might include, e.g., †patrilineal descent, the †circulating connubium and †hypogamy in the case of the Malay Archipelago, which is the classic example of a field of ethnological study. Each distinct culture within such a 'field' will have differences, but such differences can be accounted for with the larger structural pattern. The motto of Dutch structuralism, like that of the Indonesian nation-state which grew from the same cultural source, might well be taken as 'Unity in Diversity'. This perspective owes much to studies in Indonesian languages, and the idea of culture having structures analogous to language has been much a part of the tradition, which has parallels not only with French structuralism but also with American †cognitive anthropology.

In the last few decades the structuralist tradition in the Netherlands has been in decline, and

†transactionalist, *Marxist, †applied and *development anthropology have all been prominent. In some universities development anthropology is more-or-less equated with the idea of 'sociology of non-Western societies', and includes studies of policy issues, health and nutrition, agricultural systems and even *ethnoscience – the last being an area of overlap between the structuralist and non-Western sociology traditions. Ethnographic interests which are prominent include Africa, Latin America and the Mediterranean, as well as Indonesia. Because of the centralized and bureaucratic nature of the Dutch university system, both regional and theoretical interests are concentrated in different departments according to agreed guidelines drawn up between the departments on a national level. In spite of great differences today in theoretical approach and interest, Dutch anthropology thus retains its unity through these efforts and through its own apparent self-identity as a national institution.

ALAN BARNARD

See also: regional analysis and regional comparison

Further reading

Josselin de Jong, P.E. de (ed.) (1977) *Structural Anthropology in the Netherlands*, The Hague: Martinus Nijhoff
—— (ed.) (1984) *Unity in Diversity: Indonesia as a Field of Anthropological Study*, Dordrecht: Foris Publications
Kloos, P. and H.J.M. Claessen (eds) (1975) *Current Anthropology in the Netherlands*, Rotterdam: Netherlands Sociological and Anthropological Association
—— (eds) (1981) *Current Issues in Anthropology: The Netherlands*, Rotterdam: Netherlands Sociological and Anthropological Association
—— (eds) (1991) *Contemporary Anthropology in the Netherlands: The Use of Anthropological Ideas*, Amsterdam: VU University Press

E

ecological anthropology

Ecological anthropology focuses upon the complex relations between people and their *environments. Human populations, socially organized and oriented by means of particular cultures, have ongoing contact with and impact upon the land, climate, plant and animal species, and other humans in their environments, and these in turn have reciprocal impacts. Ecological anthropology directs our attention to the ways in which a particular population purposely or unintentionally shapes its environment, and the ways in which its relations with the environment shape its culture and its social, economic and political life.

There are several basic points upon which ecological anthropologists agree: any particular population is not engaged with the total environment which surrounds it, but rather with certain selected aspects and elements, which may be called its *habitat*; and the particular place which it occupies in that environment may be labelled its *niche*. Each population has its own particular orientation, or †*adaptation*, to the wider environment, institutionalized in the *culture of the group, particularly in its *technology*, which includes established knowledge of plants and animals, weather and minerals, as well as tools and techniques of extracting food, clothing and shelter. Furthermore, a population's adaptation is often influenced by the *socio-cultural environment* constituted by other human populations, their cultures and adaptations.

The recent history of ecological anthropology

Attention to the impact of environments on human societies is longstanding in philosophy and geography, but in social and cultural anthropology, stress on the ecological dimension is relatively recent. During the first half of the twentieth century, social and cultural anthropology, whether in the British versions of *Malinowski and *Radcliffe-Brown or the American version of *Boas, examined relationships within the social and cultural realm, with little direct attention to relations with the environment. Notwithstanding †Forde's early (1934) contribution and some relevant ethnographic reports, ecological anthropology only became fully established in the 1960s.

By that time, some researchers were drawn to this subject in the hope that the study of adaptations would provide explanations of customs and institutions. A similar development took place in prehistoric *archaeology, reinforcing the interest in ecology among social and cultural anthropologists.

Ecological anthropology in theoretical debate

While increased emphasis upon human-environment relations earned wide acceptance in anthropology, the particular models to be employed fell quickly into dispute, not least in regard to causal explanation. †'Structural Marxist' theorists (Friedman 1974) argued that eco-system analysis was little more than *functionalism, broadened to include environmental factors, and so explained nothing (but see Rappaport's reply [1979]). *Symbolic anthropologists (Geertz 1963) emphasized the position that adaptations were cultural as well as natural, the symbolically-based orientation and social organization of peoples selecting from environmental possibilities and shaping their ecosystems. *'World system' and *'political economy' theorists criticized the local focus of ecosystem analysis, arguing that international political and economic processes are critical determinants of local conditions. Even some of those in sympathy with ecological anthropology, such as the *'cultural materialist'

Marvin Harris (1979), absorbed it into broader frameworks and issues. The effect of these debates was that ecological anthropology was incorporated into more general theoretical discourse.

Ecological ethnography: some illustrations

The *nomadism of many *hunting and gathering and *pastoral peoples is an adaptation to the variable availability of basic resources, such as the animal species hunted, the plant species gathered, and the pasture and water for herded livestock. Technologies of production, such as hunting weapons or selection for livestock breeding, and technologies of *consumption, such as temporary or mobile dwellings, are closely tied to this adaptation. Nomadic pursuit of resources requires flexible composition of local groups, which often fragment into smaller units and then reunite, with individuals and families moving in and out of the group. Because nomadic mobility makes monopoly over resources and coercion difficult, political leadership and decision-making tend to be consensual. Demographic behaviour is also linked to this adaptation: for example, the practice of female †infanticide among some Arctic Inuit groups in response to the high death rate of male hunters, aims to provide a balance of adult females and males in an ecosystem where hunter/non-hunter imbalance means starvation.

The productivity of adaptations varies even within such general categories as 'hunter' or 'pastoralist'. Some hunting groups, such as the Inuit, struggled hard for bare survival; others, such as the Ju/'hoansi of the Kalahari desert in Botswana once supported themselves comfortably by gathering and hunting only 2.4 days each week, on average (Lee 1993: 56); and foragers on the northwest coast of North America were able to draw so much from their rich environment that they lived in large, stable settlements and developed elaborate *ritual systems and chieftainships.

Pastoralists too live in varied environments, from the arid deserts of the Saharan Tuareg and Arabian Bedouin, to the temperate mountains of Atlas Berbers and Zagros Bakhtiari, to the rich plains of the Kenyan Maasai and the Iranian Turkmen. Desert pastoralists are spread thinly across the landscape and follow ever-changing *migration patterns in response to erratic and unpredictable rainfall and pasture. Mountain pastoralists are more densely concentrated, migrating along lineal routes between lowland winter and highland summer pastures in response

to more predictable, seasonal changes. And pastoralists of the rich plains are able remain stable or move only modest distances, although they often maintain their potential mobility for political reasons. External political factors being equal, tribal organization and politics vary in these different environmental settings, with tribal groups being smaller and more dispersed, and with authority more decentralized, in the desert; whereas in the mountains and plains, tribal groups tend to be larger and more concentrated, with more centralized authority. These differences are due not only to production requirements but also to the relative absence of non-pastoral peoples in the deserts and their greater presence in the richer mountain and plains areas.

Adaptations are always specific to particular environments, so general labels such as 'hunter' or 'herder' can be misleading, because hunting or herding is quite different in equatorial deserts and in Arctic tundras. These labels also tend to over-simplify, pointing to one main activity, when the actual adaptation of a particular group involves many diverse activities. As Lee (1993) shows, so-called 'hunters' sometimes live primarily from vegetable matter collected through gathering. Furthermore, different 'hunting' peoples also engage in trading, mining, herding, cultivating and guiding as part of making a living, just as many 'pastoralists' pursue cultivation, hunting and gathering, trading and caravaneering, and extortion and predatory raiding. Most people thus depend upon adaptations involving a variety of activities, each drawing from and contributing to the overall life pattern.

The specificity of adaptations can be seen by examining neighbouring groups in one area of Pakistan. Pathans established themselves in the broad valley of Swat through invasion and conquest, absorbing or displacing the earlier population, the remnants of which are Kohistani. Thereafter, powerful ethnic Pathans controlled the lowland areas of highly productive, irrigated agri-culture, while the politically weaker Kohistanis were allowed to maintain control of the more inhospitable mountain areas, making a living through terrace agriculture and *transhumant herding (Barth 1958). A third group, Gujar nomadic pastoralists, fit in with Kohistanis and Pathans by exploiting areas in periods when they are not used by others. This case illustrates that ecological niches of ethnic groups and the relations between groups are determined by the specific economic and political capacities of the groups rather than by 'natural areas' in the environment.

An ecological enquiry into the dynamics of social evolution, Carneiro's (1961) study of 'slash and burn' or †swidden cultivators in the Amazon Basin addresses the rise of complex *state societies. His data on Amazon cultivators shows that they can and do produce a substantial surplus, thus refuting the argument that *complex societies are not found in the Amazon because the soils are inadequate for producing the necessary surplus. Carneiro suggests that Amazonian cultivators did not come together and form costly complex societies because, having a huge area in which to move around and expand, they were not forced to establish authority hierarchies, social stratification, and other aspects of complex society. Rather, it is populations whose cultivable land was distinctly circumscribed in a geographical sense, such as in narrow valleys or by mountains or deserts, in which population expansion led to the development of complex societies, such as the Circum-Caribbean and the Andean Inka civilizations.

Seemingly arbitrary religious beliefs and customs have been explained in terms of ecological adaptation. According to Harris (1979: 242-53), the granting of sacred status to cattle among Hindus of India and the consequent prohibition on beef consumption was necessary for a high density population of pre-industrial rural cultivators. The high caloric and spatial cost of raising livestock for meat consumption could not be sustained and was rejected in favour of more efficient grain consumption. But in this adaptation of grain production and consumption, cattle play an important part, supplying traction for ploughs, manure for fertilizer, and milk and butter for consumption. Holy status protects cattle from consumption as meat and saves them for supporting grain cultivation. While Harris's argument is controversial, he has shown that the composition of village cattle herds varies predictably in accordance with farmers' pragmatic needs for different ratios of bovine species and sexes in different ecozones, which means that Indian villagers use mainly practical rather than mystical criteria for managing their livestock.

Contributions to the study of global environmental problems

Current awareness of global environmental problems is drawing ecological anthropology into multidisciplinary debates over 'sustainable *development'. The rapid destruction of tropical forests, grazing lands, coastal fisheries, etc., has stimulated interest in the 'tragedy of the commons', a model asserting that resources held in common ownership are inevitably overused and degraded by people pursuing their individual interests. However, ethnographic examples of sustainable common resource management in many regions of the world challenge this model. For example, Swiss alpine villagers have for centuries successfully managed and conserved meadows, forest and irrigation as common resources.

As regards long-term sustainability, small-scale cultivators in many parts of the world have created efficient, flexible and sustainable farming systems. Within a single ethnic group, they may establish different patterns of *household composition and *community organization, depending on their local niches. Contrary to many theories predicting the rapid demise of the world's peasants, smallholders not only endure but may have much to teach concerning flexible and sustainable uses of the land (Netting 1993b). Small farmers are neither simply producers nor victims of environmental crises, for some of them are able to protect both family and community lands.

However, state policies compelling the division of common resources can lead to the 'tragedy of enclosure'. Privatization of grazing lands deprives herds of flexible access to seasonal pastures in climatically variable settings, undermining pastoral adaptations. Forests turned over to commercial loggers leave local farmers deprived of fuel, fodder and other resources, sometimes triggering *resistance movements (Guha 1989).

Irrigated farming entails the dangers of overuse, conflict and depletion of water supplies. Some systems of irrigation management, such as Balinese water temples, have endured for centuries. In the absence of a hydraulic bureaucracy, these temples coordinate entire watersheds; yet they were invisible to *colonial and †postcolonial rulers because they were categorized as 'religious' institutions (Lansing 1991). In South India, farmers organized water-user associations to counter the problems and uncertainties resulting from bureaucratic canal management. In both cases, local systems of knowledge and practice countered the arrogance and ignorance of the technocrats.

Large hydroelectric dams, such as those in northern Canada, central India, and the Amazon Basin, threaten natural environments and human populations alike, provoking resistance. Outsiders seeking to protect natural ecosystems often attempt to do so by excluding indigenous inhabitants. This approach derives partly from ignorance concerning indigenous systems of ecological knowledge and practice. It thus falls to ecological anthropologists to interpret the 'insider's ecology' to outsiders.

PHILIP CARL SALZMAN
and DONALD W. ATTWOOD

See also: environment, technology, cultural materialism, archaeology

Further reading

Barth, F. (1958) 'Ecological Relationships of Ethnic Groups in Swat, North Pakistan', *American Anthropologist* 58: 1079–89

Carneiro, R. L. (1961) 'Slash and Burn Cultivation among the Kiukuru and Its Implications for Cultural Development in the Amazon Basin', *Antropologia*, supplement no 2

Ellen, R. (1982) *Environment, Subsistence and System: The Ecology of Small-Scale Social Formations*, Cambridge: Cambridge University Press

Forde, D. (1934) *Habitat, Economy and Society*, London: Methuen

Friedman, J. (1974) 'Marxism, Structuralism, and Vulgar Materialism', *Man* (n.s.) 9: 444–69

Geertz, C. (1963) *Agricultural Involution: The Processes of Ecological Change in Indonesia*, Berkeley: University of California Press

Guha, Ramchandra (1989) *The Unquiet Woods: Ecological Change and Peasant Resistance in the Himalaya*, Berkeley: University of California Press

Harris, M. (1979) *Cultural Materialism: The Struggle for a Science of Culture*, New York: Random House

Lansing, J.S. (1991) *Priests and Programmers: Technologies of Power in the Engineered Landscape of Bali*, Princeton: Princeton University Press

Lee, R.B. (1993) *The Dobe Ju/'hoansi* (2nd edn), New York: Harcourt Brace

Netting R.M. (1993a) *Smallholders, Householders: Farm Families and the Ecology of Intensive, Sustainable Agriculture*, Stanford: Stanford University Press

—— (1993b) *Cultural Ecology* (2nd edn), Prospect Heights, Illinios: Waveland Press

Rappaport, R. (1979) *Ecology, Meaning and Religion*, Richmond, California: North Atlantic Books

Steward, J. (1963) *Theory of Culture Change*, Urbana: University of Illinois Press

economic anthropology

Economic anthropologists study how humans use the material world to maintain and express themselves in social groups. Researchers examine both the material practices in which humans engage and the ideas they hold about them. As a field, economic anthropology developed in the twentieth century, but it encompasses studies of the past and draws on theories from earlier eras. A single opposition informs much of the subject: either humans live by what they produce or they produce to exchange with others from whom they secure their livelihood. All economies represent combinations of the two practices, but the patterns vary, and their interpretation occasions controversy.

Fieldwork

Humans gain their livelihood in many ways: through †agriculture, *pastoralism, *fishing, *hunting and gathering and industrial production. *Ethnographers gather information about these and other economic features through intensive observation, through lengthy conversations and by using a variety of sampling techniques to secure quantitative data. They have been especially alert to how people are recruited and rewarded for their work, to the *gender division of labour, and to the ways that burdens and rewards for women shift as the market expands into new areas. Since the early studies of †Mauss ([1925]1990) and *Malinowski (1922), *exchange has also been of special interest to anthropologists who have explored how transactions may range from pure gifting to obligated gifting to barter, theft and market trade; this research in turn has stimulated studies on *consumption and display. Economic anthropologists have examined as well the many ways that resources are distributed, goods are allocated, and political regimes are supported. Early on, this led to lengthy discussions concerning the conditions under which a surplus is produced in society, who secures it, and how it may be measured in non-monetary contexts. More broadly, economic anthropologists focus on the ties between material life and *power, ranging from gender control of *food in *households to financial control of monopolies in *capitalist markets. Much ethnographic data defies our common sense categories, however: for example, today farmers on marginal land may work the earth with wooden implements and seed potatoes for home consumption, while listening to tapes on headphones.

Theory

To illuminate their diverse findings, anthropologists draw upon four theories or approaches to economy, three of which were developed outside the field. Most economic anthropologists employ concepts from †neo-classical economics to interpret their data. Material behaviour is seen as an organized way of arranging means to secure valued ends. The human is assumed to be self-interested and *rational; land, labour and capital are said to be the scarce and productive components in the economy. Livelihood practices are presumed to occur as if they were in a *market: they demonstrate ways that humans calculate marginal returns, diversify risk, and measure benefit/cost ratios, often in light of imperfect information. Because social arrangements in other cultures frequently limit the working of markets, neoclassical theorists find their challenge in showing how their model of behaviour can be adapted to diverse ethnographic contexts.

*Political economy constitutes the second model used in the study of other economies. Anthropologists employ concepts from *Marxism but have also developed a broader approach highlighting the connection between power and material activities. In many societies, labour is the motor of material life so research focuses on how labour is expended and connected to value, and on who commands the *work process. By examining the ways that resources are controlled and arranged in economic patterns, anthropologists have also expanded the theory of *modes of production; however, the number of presumed modes has proliferated: anthropologists now claim to have identified kinship, lineage, domestic, tributary, slave and yet other modes. Ethnographers study as well how production modes are connected within larger economic formations and to the world economy. Drawing upon the concept of commodity †fetishism, anthropologists have also explored how *symbolic actions may function as forms of *resistance and express desperation when *peasants or factory workers first sell their labour and experience the power of market forces.

'Institutionalism', and especially the work of †Karl Polanyi (1944), represents the third model of economy. Institutionalists focus on the social framework through which material practices occur. Polanyi argued that land and labour are the universal components of all economies and constitute the basis of society itself. Before the rise of the market, land and labour were controlled and managed through persisting social relationships; consequently, material life was †'embedded' in society. As the market expanded, land and

labour were †'disembedded' from their social moorings and turned into commodities to be transferred through purchase and sale; when this occurred in the West, society experienced a 'great transformation'. Polanyi's concept of embeddedness points to the important fact that in many societies relations of livelihood occur through *kinship, *religious, residential and political ties, and these domains cannot be clearly distinguished one from another. In such cases, the economy does not form a separate or autonomous sphere, governed by an independent set of laws. The Polanyi approach, however, says little about the ways that material livelihood is in fact organized, and it lacks a model of how the social and economic realms are joined. The perspective also fits uneasily with the atomistic, micro-approach of neoclassical economics; and unlike Marxism, it does not emphasize the role of power in material life.

Cultural economics offers the fourth perspective on material life. The most distinctively anthropological approach, this mode of analysis has several variations. Some cultural economists examine how people communicate through the goods and services they produce and use. By looking at how goods are strategically shifted between socially defined exchange circuits and the way these movements connect social positions to prestige, power, gender, competition, and reproduction, these anthropologists have extended Mauss's work on †prestations and †reciprocity. Other cultural economists assert that folk everywhere model their ways of securing livelihood just as modern economists build models of the market economy. But these local models, which are found among agriculturalists, pastoralists, fisherpeople as well as hunters and gatherers, are very different from standard ones. Neither deductive nor written, local models of the economy often have a metaphoric quality: they bring together what the observer may perceive to be distinct domains, and they often employ socially close figures or human images to model material processes. Local economic models may be fashioned after parts and functions of the *body, after *family and *descent relationships, or after images of the stranger and the devil. For example, in some societies, the quality of lineage ties, *ancestral benevolence, and land fertility are conceptually linked so that maintaining proper kin ties helps to secure the goodwill of the ancestors which is made evident in abundant harvests. Local economic models are also found among the marginalized in market society, although their practical emergence and recognition is often suppressed by the dominant, written one. Some cultural economists claim that neoclassical and Marxist models are inappropriately applied to other societies and to parts of market economy as well, because these abstract, written models misconstrue other people's lifeways, do not encode cross-cultural universals, and derive from market experience.

Community and market economies

Cross-cutting the four models and the diverse ethnographic data is the anthropological finding that all economies can be placed along a continuum that ranges from producing for the self to producing for the other. In the first case, productive activities are undertaken for the self or a group; this leads to independence and autarchy with an emphasis on gaining *material sustenance*. In the second case, productive activities are surrounded by exchange; producers transact for their inputs and trade their outputs. This leads to interdependence (or dependence) with an emphasis on *acquisition*. The opposition is between *community economy and market economy. In practice, economies are a combination of the two, but the balance varies and the working out is complex, because cyclical reproduction is an act of mutuality, while exchange breaches social boundaries and leads to competition and rivalry. Most economic theories are focused upon one or the other end of the continuum, but ethnographic studies display the mixed, complementary, and dialectical nature of economic practices; and they suggest some of the ways that a market economy draws upon community.

The dual quality of material practice was clearly seen by Aristotle (1946) and by †Adam Smith (1976: 1) who professed to show how the material 'necessaries and conveniencies of life' were provided through self-interested behaviour in the market. The dialectic of sustenance and acquisition composed part of Ricardian and Marxist theories of the market, and it was developed into a social and evolutionary theory by †Thorstein Veblen. Polanyi's master opposition of the embedded and disembedded economy separated the two dimensions, however, and most contemporary theorists equate economy with market transactions only. Anthropological findings contest this latter representation for many reasons, including its exclusion of household and communal behaviour, its market construction of other economies, and its inability to see the dependence of the economic upon the non-economic.

The market ideal

Consider the ends of the continuum as ideal models. A perfect market is based upon *competition* among anonymous individuals: buyers compete for the goods and services of sellers; sellers compete for buyers. Market participants undertake productive activities in order to exchange and then to resume their productive activity; their goal is *accumulation* of *property or making a profit. Market relationships are ensured only by contract, and market expectations emphasize the need for wariness, caution, and vigilance. As a competitive game, the market should offer a 'level playing field' or free entry to all participants, but in fact some enter with greater resources and secure outcomes based on their financial power.

For participants, the market promises *efficiency* in the use of resources, meaning that in the perfect market no more of one good or service can be produced except by reducing another, or no shift in the allocation of goods would lead to someone being better off with no one else in a worse position. The virtue of efficiency is often used as the reason for ensuring that the rules of community economy do not infringe upon the competitive market, and for seeking market solutions in as many domains of life as possible.

The community ideal

A community economy is made up of a group of people, living in an environment, using their material tools and cultural heritage. In the complete livelihood model, economic processes are cyclical or reproductive, and no exchanges occur outside the community. The aim is not acquisition or the securing of sustenance alone but *maintenance* of a way of living. When rural folk in Thailand resist national forestry planning that would allow for the profitable use of timber by outsiders, they do so not only to hold a needed resource for diversified local use but to preserve and sustain their entire manner of life.

The promise for participation in a community economy is *sufficiency* in access to resources or *adequacy* of material sustenance. This is achieved through social regulation of production, distribution, consumption or exchange; however, few community economies effect or aim to provide complete sustenance for all members.

Locality

A community economy always has a place in space. Its boundaries may be permeable with respect to membership; and a community may be composed of smaller communities, based on households, extended kin groups, local lineages, religious organizations and aggregations around *Big Men. The community economy also may be contained within a larger structure such as a chiefdom, *feudal system or market. Community participation defines as well a local *identity so that being forced to live by a different mode of sustenance, such as fishing on the agricultural island of Dobu in *Melanesia, means leaving aside this identity. Similarly, persons who live in the same space as a community but not by its mode of livelihood, such as Hausa traders in parts of lineage-based Africa, the metics in ancient Greece, or non-Israelites in ancient Israel, are not part of the group. In contrast, the market has no locality. Because the accumulation of gains has no limits and trade respects no social boundaries, market relationships overrun and often break the borders of communities. Participation in the market defines a different sort of identity; since actors strive to accumulate property, their success is often displayed through spectacular consumption and the exercise of power by financial control.

Resources

The market economy consists of many markets in goods and in the *factors of production* which are categorized as land, labour and capital. All are held as private property, traded, and measured against one another by the homogeneous entity, *money. Financial capital, which is an accumulation of past profits, is a principal means for acquiring more, while new successes in achieving profits are gauged by the amount of pecuniary capital used to secure them.

In contrast, a community economy has a single *commons* or base that it shares and on which it relies. The commons is not divided into parts; and its components do not enter distinct markets as separate factors of production, for to divide the base changes the community. Made up of in-commensurate things, the commons is the community's heritage. Often consisting of land, the commons also may include water or fishing rights, crops, tools, ancestors, spirits, ceremonial performances as well as the work habits of the community's members. For example, among subarctic bands of North America, game masters,

animals, hunting leadership, and knowledge of the environment make up the base for securing livelihood. Among groups in Melanesia, magical spells to make crops grow are effective only if they are acquired by †inheritance and used on land in the community whose founders created and bequeathed the incantations. In parts of Africa, local lineage groups plus their ancestors, authority structure, ritual performances and land constitute the commons: to claim lineage land as private property and sell it is the same as selling one's ancestors who are buried in the land and whose spirits reside in the area. Selling lineage land means rejecting membership in the community and the possibility of its continuance. As the people say, land sales yield 'bitter money'. A shared heritage is not static, however, for a community makes its commons by innovating technologies, inventing customs, and accreting land.

Distribution

Based upon †*commensality* and *communion* of its participants, the complete community economy emphasizes qualities such as sharing, care and reliance on others. This is an economy of trust and fostering which extend to all who make up the community, including persons, ancestors, animals and the earth. The household in rural Latin America that shares its food pot, and the urban European family that makes its refrigerator accessible to all members of the house, practise commensality. But group pooling – which makes a commons of the output – does not always imply open access or even equality of shares. Social rules may sustain power differences. For example, in return for his ritual performances that help bring game, a chief may receive the choice parts of quarry caught by hunters who had the benefit of his rituals. Product allocation also may follow rules that encode age or kinship differences: the distribution of household resources is often influenced by gender. In a community economy, principles of the competitive and efficient market – such as allocating shares by *marginal contribution* to the output – do not apply. Some economists may claim that market laws should be applied within households and similar communities; and, to a degree, the ideological dominance of market theory, along with penetration of communities by markets, has wrought these behavioural changes. But the theory still is not fully successful in predicting allocation in real markets, because communal rules and power differentials do leave their mark. Even within the amoral domain of the competitive market, the unrequited gift, corporate charity, and altruism have remained important, because they indicate the negation of self-interest and the public demonstration of commitment to community – after the market has had its effects. More important, markets do not persist without community support systems, such as pension schemes, health plans, welfare programmes, housing projects, entitlements to public education and a material infrastructure. For the neo-classical economist, public subsidies are a category mistake in that private wealth, generated in the market, is being taxed by the community and spent upon projects that are more properly decided upon and financed through market mechanisms. But anthropological evidence suggests that the placing of community limits upon, and exacting redistributions from, the market are just as common as the market itself.

Uncertainty, rationality and pragmatism

In a community economy, expectations of mutuality provide a sense of *certainty* about material life, and this emerges in social and cultural constructions. For example, some studies suggest that hunting and gathering communities have complete *trust* in the environment that game will appear. But such expectations, and the rules that make a community, are *contingent*, for they have no anchorage outside the fact that they are shared by community members. In contrast, competition and the denial of persisting social ties in the market produce *uncertainty* about livelihood. These endemic features of the market, it may be suggested, produce the drive to amass profit as security for the future. But success in accumulating profit is transitory, for the economic game never ends and capital is always at risk. Unlike the community economy, however, the market is said to have an ultimate grounding in human behaviour, because all market participants are presumed to be *rational calculators*. According to the accepted model, market behaviour is anchored in human *rationality. Lying outside the market and cultural formulation, this human attribute is used to explain the presence of markets, deny their historical contingency, and provide market participants with the one certainty that others are reasoning calculators, too.

But the ideology is confusing here, for there is a difference between what really goes on in a market and what the theory urges. Much behaviour in a market economy is not based on the calculated selection of means in order to reach given ends but is *pragmatic*, contingent and rooted in community. Neo-classical theory emphasizes the singular importance of rational behaviour, but ethnographic studies show that material behaviour is often characterized by pragmatic practices, such as adjusting, coping, tempering, and accommodating. Pragmatic action is situated within communal traditions but also reshapes them, for pragmatic practices change in the doing. Industrial relations studies also demonstrate that corporate behaviour in the market is socially embedded, pragmatic, and not necessarily rational. Like community and market, pragmatism and rationality are not exclusive modes of action. But a more important issue lies at stake. The motor of all markets is profit-making, and profits are created by innovations in products or processes. But innovations are unpredictable and occur in conditions of uncertainty; they are fashioned by trial-and-error behaviour or pragmatic practices performed within and shaped by a community and its heritage. In this important way, the central moment of the market or profit-making is dependent on pragmatic action and community, even though this reliance is suppressed in standard models.

Market in community

Ethnographic studies illustrate the ways that markets draw upon and are embedded in community. For example, market economies may swallow community ones through expansion of their frontiers or through the appropriation and use of an unpriced commons. Surpluses also may be extracted from local economies: migratory labourers in cities, at mines, or on plantations may be paid a subminimal wage, forcing them to draw upon their home communities for material support; community economies sometimes produce crops for sale using land that lies outside the profit margin, because they can sell some of their 'costless' subsistence harvests to purchase the inputs and support the labour needed for production of the market ones. In the first case, underpaid labour is subsidized by a community economy; in the second, the use of unprofitable or non-rentable land is subsidized by the community economy. Finally, in market economies themselves, when conditions worsen, participants may withdraw from the sphere of trade by performing services and producing goods for themselves in their households. This process ultimately supports the market's continuance.

If markets depend upon communities, economies of livelihood also leave space for individual acquisition, unobligated manoeuvre, and self-interested transactions. Trade may be undertaken not only to change the composition of the commons and secure sustenance but also out of curiosity or to demonstrate power and prestige through the accumulation of goods. Trade constitutes the Trojan Horse of community persistence, however, because it brings on the contrary practice of acquisition. Adapting Marx's (1967) terminology, one may say that a community economy undertakes trade in two ways: either it swaps part of its commons directly for another, as in 'Commons → Commons', or it trades its commons via a medium of exchange as in 'Commons → Money → Commons'. But the second mode requires that yet another party trade money either via the commodity, as 'Money → Commons → Money', or for itself, Money → Money', which is lending. As observers since Aristotle have remarked, trading money via goods to make a gain is very different from trading goods via money to alter the commons and secure livelihood: practised for its own end and lacking limits, trading for gain is the core of market action. For this reason, a community economy that leaves space for trade outside the bonds of mutuality may threaten its own existence. Within a community, the impulse of human curiosity forges a dialectic with the heritage that sustains it.

In practice, community economies both limit and incorporate trade in diverse ways. In Africa, for example, land may be held and allocated through local lineages, and labour may be performed in the context of household groups; however, agricultural goods may be marketed, and product prices may be determined by the conditions of supply and demand. In the Andes of Latin America, traditional †*ayllus* control water, land rights and marriage; but agricultural goods may be swapped within *ayllus* and sold in markets outside them. Clearly, there has been a long-term trend towards market economies, but even today there is ample evidence of community resilience and opposition; for example, many ecology and resistance movements to the market are inspired by a sense of community.

Models, markets and communities

If the opposition of community and market helps to locate all economies, it also assists in placing the major models used in economic anthropology. neo-classical and Marxist ones are focused on the market; institutionalist models, of the Polanyi type, describe the opposition between the embedded economy of the community and the seemingly disembedded market, but they do not portray this as a continuing dialectic. These three models start with invariants, lay claim to *universality*, and are anthropocentric, for they place human actions and desires at the centre of the material world. In contrast, proponents of cultural analysis assume that folk in communities develop their own models which are local and contextually limited. Often anthropomorphic, *local* models draw upon familiar images to make a world that is neither mechanical nor subject to all human wants. The development of universal models is closely connected to the ascendance of modernity in the West; local models arose before and are located on the periphery of this tradition.

But in a broader respect all models are local. Universal models are limited to the market economy, whose extent is not a function of a human trait but of the political force exercised by communities that constrain and provision it with a heritage. As the market economy encompasses more of the globe, a major task for economic anthropology will be to examine how the two sides of economy conjoin and separate in new ways, and to explore how community economy is freshly formed within and resists the market, even as the market transforms it.

STEPHEN GUDEMAN

See also: environment, formalism and substantivism, house, land tenure, market, Marxism and anthropology, political economy, sharecropping, technology, world systems

Further reading
Aristotle (1946) *The Politics of Aristotle* (trans. E. Barker), Oxford: Oxford University Press

Godelier, M. (1977) *Perspectives in Marxist Anthropology*, Cambridge: Cambridge University Press

Gudeman, S. (1986) *Economics as Culture*, London: Routledge

Malinowski, B. (1922) *Argonauts of the Western Pacific*, London: Routledge

Marx, Karl ([1867]1967) *Capital*, New York: International Publishers

Mauss, M. ([1925]1990) *The Gift* (W.D. Halls trans.), London: Routledge

Plattner, S. (ed.) (1989) *Economic Anthropology*, Stanford: Stanford University Press

Polanyi, K. (1944) *The Great Transformation*, New York: Rinehart

Sahlins, M. (1972) *Stone Age Economics*, Chicago: Aldine

Smith, A. (1976) *The Wealth of Nations*, Chicago: University of Chicago Press

education

The study of formal education has, until recently, been a relatively marginal concern within anthropology. By contrast, a more broadly-defined interest in learning, particularly as it relates to cultural transmission, has been central to the anthropological project. At various times, this broader interest has been reflected in studies of *socialization, *literacy, *cognition, knowledge, *childhood, the *body, apprenticeship and so on. The lack of emphasis on formal education, as such, may in part reflect a tradition of studying communities in which institutionalized education was either non-existent, had little obvious impact on informants, or was effectively beyond local aspirations. The learning processes which existed in such communities seemed to bear little resemblance to Western-style education. More to the point, it seemed a distortion to automatically relate these forms of learning back to Western models.

This was, to cite one example, the position taken by †Audrey Richards in her study of the *chisungu*, an initiation *ritual for Bemba girls (Richards 1988). The ceremonies involved some forms of instruction, and the Bemba themselves stressed that the *chisungu* was partly held in order to teach certain things to young women. But Richards argued against the notion that this process of initiation could be seen as a kind of 'primitive education', not least because the girls were mostly being told things which they already knew. Often during the ceremonies they were told nothing whatever, their heads wrapped in blankets. Richards instead stressed the role of the *chisungu* in enforcing social obligations and promoting traditional Bemba values.

Education as disruption

Formal schooling may indeed not be an integral part of certain cultures, and the impact of education on some communities may be indirect. But this century has seen an enormous expansion of literacy and of educational systems, and anthropologists have increasingly considered this in their analyses (e.g. Spindler 1987). When schools based on Western concepts have been established in 'traditional' communities (often by religious, *colonial and postcolonial authorities) they have been seen to play an important part in cultural transformation.

One anthropological account of this is found in Maurice Godelier's analysis of *gender among the Baruya of New Guinea (Godelier 1986). He describes the role of initiations, particularly the elaborate and prolonged initiations for boys, in transmitting traditional Baruya notions of male superiority and female subordination. But then he goes on to outline the transformations which took place during the colonial and post-colonial eras. Special emphasis is given to the role of *missionary schools which, among other things, taught local children that traditional initiations and *shamanism were evil. In his account, and in many others, the expansion of education is one part of a complex history which has disrupted patterns of social interaction.

Practical mastery and formal learning

In both of the examples cited above education is, in a sense, outside traditional culture and of secondary concern to anthropologists. Education is either a Western *concept*, inappropriate for the analysis of learning in other cultures, or it is an historical *reality* which has been imposed (usually by the West) on traditional communities. To some extent, these two positions, which seem quite justified, still dominate anthropological thinking about formal education. To see why this should be so, it helps to consider the influential work of †Pierre Bourdieu.

Bourdieu's *Outline of a Theory of Practice* (1977) lends itself to different readings, but it can, among other things, be seen as an account of how people learn. In outlining his model of †*habitus*, Bourdieu stresses the development of a 'practical sense' about the world. This learning process, or 'inculcation', is not primarily a matter of formal instruction. Instead it is embedded in a variety of practical contexts: the use of space, the cooking of food, the giving of gifts, etc. The *habitus* disposes people to particular actions, and its power to do so is directly related to embedded and unconscious learning.

Near the end of the book, Bourdieu discusses the profound impact of (among other things) literacy and formal education on such a system. He sets out a contrast between different 'modes of domination', but also between different ways of learning. Indeed, much of Bourdieu's sociology has focused on the role of formal education in France, and in many ways this work contrasts sharply with his anthropology. But continuity is arguably found in the emphasis given to learning, or 'inculcation'. This continuity is shown when, in *Reproduction in Education, Society and Culture* (Bourdieu and Passeron 1990), he analyses the distinction between two different pedagogical forms. The first produces the *habitus* through 'the unconscious inculcation of principles', i.e. the way of learning described in *Outline of a Theory of Practice*. The second pedagogical form produces the *habitus* explicitly through 'articulated and even formalized principles'. Where both forms exist, unconscious and 'practical' learning is crucial because of its influence on the way people later respond to explicit instruction.

Acquiring and constructing knowledge

This broad distinction still characterizes the anthropological analysis of learning. Anthropologists have focused most often on the development of 'practical mastery' outside formal schooling, and in many ways these studies are not about 'education' at all. One example is found in studies of the use of space. Jane Khatib-Chahidi has described sexual segregation and the sharing of space in Iran. She argues that the learning of spatial categories in childhood has a profound impact on notions of gender in adulthood (Khatib-Chahidi 1981). Christina Toren has described how Fijian children develop notions of social †hierarchy (Toren 1990). Toren stresses, however, that children do not simply learn fixed concepts. Indeed, she argues that children's concepts differ in significant ways from those of adults, and that they are actively engaged in the process of producing meanings.

Robert Borofsky's ethnography of learning in Pukapuka (a Polynesian island) also stresses the creative potential of cultural transmission (Borofsky 1987). He argues that when Pukapukans 'acquire' traditional knowledge they are constructing as much as sustaining traditions. This helps to explain why the accounts of anthropologists, who also construct traditions, may differ dramatically from those of informants at different historical moments. Borofsky also seeks to break down the notion that 'traditional' learning is necessarily informal. He describes a broad range of contexts in which Pukapukans teach and learn; many of these contexts are somewhat formal, even

if they do not involve institutionalized education. Borofsky's work complements that of other ethnographers in problematizing the formal: informal opposition which has characterized the anthropology of learning.

Literacy, apprenticeship and cognition

Akinnaso's work, which approaches education from the perspective of *language and literacy, results in a similar problematization (Akinnaso 1992). Here it is argued that formal schooling is *not* necessarily an 'alien practice' in non-literate societies, and furthermore it is ethnocentric to equate schooling with the transmission of literate knowledge. The debate about formal education is thus placed in the wider context of the issues surrounding the social impact of literacy (see also Street 1993). Akinnaso examines as well the distribution of knowledge within societies, and in particular the issue of access to specialized knowledge. Akinnaso's ethnographic material (on Yoruba *divination in *West Africa), like that of Borofsky, suggests considerable cross-cultural variation in experiences of learning.

Apprenticeship is one educational form which has been of particular interest to anthropologists (e.g. Coy 1989). This is partly because it provides a unique perspective on questions of human learning and cognition. Jean Lave argues that learning in apprenticeship is based on co-participation and engagement in a process (through 'legitimate peripheral participation'). This means that the apprentice is not simply acquiring a body of knowledge, but that what is learned is in fact mediated by the perspective of teacher and learner (Lave 1988, Lave and Wenger 1991). Lave suggests that this has implications not only for our understanding of apprenticeship, but also for the process of learning and cognition in general.

Education and power

The anthropological study of institutionalized learning, and of formal education systems, usually focuses on rather different questions, often related to *power. This is true, for instance, of Bourdieu's work on French education; his models emphasize the link between economic and *cultural capital, and the role of the educational system in reproducing *class domination. This work might well be classified as 'sociology of education', but many sociologists have in fact adopted ethnographic approaches in the study of formal schooling. Willis

(1977), for instance, analyses in a very anthropological way the relationship in England between school-based working-class youth culture and shop-floor culture. He attempts to explain the (seemingly wilful) process whereby working-class boys end up in working-class jobs.

Recent anthropological work has examined the role of mass education in the historical development of national (and other) identities, and the implications of this for authority and power. For example, Eickelman has explored the growth of higher education in the Arab world, suggesting that this has a significant impact on religious and national identities (Eickelman 1992). More generally, the development of formal educational systems is seen to have played a key role in the historical expansion of *nationalism (Gellner 1983).

CHARLES STAFFORD

See also: childhood, cognition, literacy, socialization

Further reading

Akinnaso, F. (1992) 'Schooling, Language and Knowledge in Literate and Non Literate Societies', *Comparative Studies in Society and History* 34: 68–109

Borofsky, R. (1987) *Making History: Pukapukan and Anthropological Constructions of Knowledge*, Cambridge: Cambridge University Press

Bourdieu, P. (1977) *Outline of a Theory of Practice*, Cambridge: Cambridge University Press

—— and J. Passeron (1990 [1977]) *Reproduction in Education, Society and Culture*, London: Sage Publications

Coy, M. (1989) *Anthropological Perspectives on Apprenticeship*, New York: SUNY Press

Eickelman, D. (1992) 'Mass Higher Education and the Religious Imagination in Contemporary Arab Societies', *American Ethnologist*, 19 (4): 643–55

Gellner, E. (1983) *Nations and Nationalism*, Oxford: Blackwell

Godelier, M. (1986) *The Making of Great Men: Male Domination and Power among the New Guinea Baruya*, Cambridge: Cambridge University Press

Khatib-Chahidi, J. (1981) 'Sexual Prohibitions, Shared Space and Fictive Marriages in Shi'ite Iran' in S. Ardener (ed.) *Women and Space: Ground Rules and Social Maps*, London: Croom Helm

Lave, J. (1988) *Cognition in Practice: Mind, Mathematics and Culture in Everyday Life*, Cambridge: Cambridge University Press

—— and E. Wenger (1991) *Situated Learning: Legitimate Peripheral Participation*, Cambridge: Cambridge University Press

Richards, A. (1982 [1956]) *Chisungu: A Girl's Initiation Ceremony among the Bemba of Zambia*, London: Routledge

Spindler, G.D. (1987) *Education and Cultural Process* 2nd edn, Prospect Heights: Waveland Press

Street, B. (ed.) (1993) *Cross-Cultural Approaches to Literacy*, Cambridge: Cambridge University Press

Toren, C. (1990) *Making Sense of Hierarchy: Cognition as Social Process in Fiji*, London: The Athlone Press

Willis, P. (1977) *Learning to Labour: How Working Class Kids get Working Class Jobs*, Aldershot: Gower

emic and etic

The terms 'emic' and 'etic' were widely used in the American anthropology of the 1960s and 1970s, and the distinction between 'emic' and 'etic' levels of analysis was a commonplace in the areas of linguistic anthropology known variously as *componential analysis or *ethnoscience. 'Emic' and 'etic' (derived respectively from †'phonemic' and †'phonetic') designate two contrasting levels of data or methods of analysis. An emic model is one which explains the ideology or behaviour of members of a culture according to indigenous definitions. An etic model is one which is based on criteria from outside a particular culture. Etic models are held to be universal; emic models are culture-specific.

Just as phonetic and phonemic levels imply different methods of analysis, so too do etic and emic levels. So-called cognitive anthropologists, especially in the 1960s, were interested mainly in emic analysis (Tyler 1969). They saw culture as possessing structures similar to those of language. In contrast, anthropologists influenced by *cultural materialism, especially in the 1970s, were more interested in etic analysis. They saw culture in terms of minimal units which defined appropriate behaviour, often in direct response to environmental circumstances (see Headland, Pike, and Harris 1990).

The terms 'emic' and 'etic' were first employed by †Kenneth L. Pike in his monumental book, *Language in Relation to a Unified Theory of the Structure of Human Behavior*. As this title suggests, their origin and early use reflect not only the analogy between †phonological (phonemic) and cultural (emic) data, but also Pike's theoretical stance (which sees linguistics as closely related to behavioural psychology) and his search for a grand theory which could encompass both language and culture. The subfields of †'cognitive anthropology', 'the new ethnography' and 'ethnoscience' which emerged in the 1960s all stem ultimately from Pike's original concerns. These approaches emphasized emic over etic approaches through the meticulous analysis of semantic fields and indigenous classifications, and practitioners sought to apply Pike's distinction both as a method of ethnographic research and as an aid to the theoretical understanding of the relation between specific and universal aspects of culture.

Etic and emic in cross-cultural comparison

Etic distinctions are explained in terms of various etic frameworks or classificatory grids. Classic examples of etic frameworks include: †Linnaean taxonomy; disease, in medical science; and the genealogical grid. Linnaean taxonomy is intended as a universal, hierarchical system for the classification of plants and animals on the basis of relative differences and similarities, and it entails an implicit theory of evolutionary relatedness. In contrast, the non-Linnaean classification of plants and animals in different cultures (e.g., the classification of bats as 'birds' rather than as 'mammals') is based on emic criteria, which may be quite different. Medical anthropologists make a similar distinction between 'disease' (a pathological condition, as defined by medical science) and 'illness' (the culturally-specific understanding of disease). Diseases are defined in the same way wherever Western †biomedicine is practised, whereas what counts as a particular illness varies in different cultural contexts.

These distinctions imply a value judgement, that those who have a special knowledge of Linnaean taxonomy or Western medicine understand the true nature of the universe, and that cultures in which ordinary people have access to this specialist knowledge are superior to those in which ordinary people do not have such access. However, not all etic frameworks carry this notion of superiority and inferiority. In the study of *relationship terminology the genealogical grid, which arguably is extrinsic to Western culture, is more neutral. This is a particularly good example for examining the relation between emic and etic distinctions, as well as the problems which can arise in reifying the emic/etic distinction.

The genealogical grid precisely denotes each genealogical position. These positions are presumed to be the same for all languages and cultures. The emic distinctions are those which enable languages to define their kinship categories differently, employing common terms for different combinations of genealogically-defined kin. 'Aunt' and 'uncle', as distinct from 'mother' and 'father',

are not universal notions but rather the specific categories of the English language and of the societies in which this language is used; other languages may classify English-language 'cousins' as 'siblings' or as potential 'spouses', and so on.

Analysts might distinguish the etic notion of the genealogical mother, written 'M', from the emic notion of the biological or social *mother* in British or American culture, written 'mother'. As the italics imply, this 'mother' is a culture-specific one, as foreign to the etic notion as a comparable word in any other language. Yet there are two problems here. First, what 'motherhood' might mean in any specific culture is a question beyond the confines of such simple linguistic distinctions and requires further emic analysis. Etically, it can only be defined very loosely. Secondly, the fact is that anthropologists have cultures and cultural preconceptions like anyone else, and they write in one specific language at a time. Such a language, of course, will have its own emic categories, and the etic grid accordingly remains elusive. In *kinship the etic grid is relatively easy to specify, but in other aspects of thought (say, in the realm of religious belief), etic distinctions are very much more difficult to define and utilize with any precision.

The emic model is not the native's model

A commonplace assumption about emic models is that they are 'discovered' rather than 'invented' by the analyst. However, emic models, like phonemic ones, are ultimately exogenous constructions, formalized by the analyst on the basis of distinctive features present in indigenous usage. They are not in themselves 'the native model', though anthropologists often loosely identify them in this way.

This may be illustrated by †Conklin's (1969) example of the structure of the pronouns in Hanunoo, a language spoken in the Philippines. Conklin argued that the conventional linguistic (etic) distinctions – first, second and third person; singular, dual and plural; and exclusive and inclusive – only describe Hanunoo pronouns in an inelegant and uneconomical way. These distinctions account for all Hanunoo pronouns, but they produce no less than four potential categories which the Hanunoo language does not distinguish. It is better, he suggested, to examine the distinctive contrasts made by the language itself. In doing this, he came up with three sets of emic distinctions for Hanunoo pronouns

– minimal membership, nonminimal membership; inclusion of speaker, exclusion of speaker; and inclusion of hearer, exclusion of hearer. The application of these distinctions generates all and only the eight pronouns found in the language, and the resulting analysis is therefore more elegant and economical than the one employing the etic categories traditionally used by linguists. Yet the emic criteria he identified are distinctions which are not named or even consciously employed by the Hanunoo themselves. They are only implicit in indigenous usage.

As this example shows, an emic model is not necessarily a model held consciously by indigenous thinkers. Here it is clearly an analyst's model, but one which is built up from principles derived from, rather than forced upon, the data. This is equally true of behavioural, semantic or phonological data. Just as no native speaker, simply as a native speaker, can coherently describe the phonological system of his or her language, similarly no indigenous thinker can usually present a complete emic analysis of his actions or of a culturally-significant semantic field of his language. Analysis, even emic analysis, is the job of the observer.

Critiques of emic and etic

Although the emic and etic levels of *culture are intended to correspond analogously to phonemic and phonetic levels in language, there are nevertheless crucial differences between culture and language which make the correspondence problematic. Most obviously, culture is much more variable than language, and cultural behaviour is much more difficult to assign to a single structure than speech is.

†Marvin Harris (1976) has objected to the notion that culture is made of sets of rules or 'grammar', in effect denying the possibility of emic models at all. He argued, especially against †Goodenough (1956), that the methods of linguistics are a poor example for anthropologists to follow, since there is no anthropological equivalent to a native-speaker or one possessing absolute 'cultural competence' in any sense analogous to linguistic competence. Goodenough's view was that the native 'authorities' should be sought and that their ideas should be used in the construction of emic models. In Harris's view, several problematic questions remain. Is there any such thing as a cultural authority? If so, how can such a person be identified? What about the ideas of those who are not considered authorities, but merely average members, of their own culture?

Others have questioned the existential status of etic models. What guarantee is there that the observer's supposedly objective, etic model is not in fact his or her own emic one? Since the 1980s, under the influence of *postmodernism and *reflexivity, critics have challenged the notion of objectivity upon which etic grids depend. These approaches imply instead that an interplay between what might be considered the emic models of the observer and the observed are as close as we can get to an etic level of analysis.

The future of emic and etic

As *Lévi-Strauss (1985: 115–20) has pointed out, the emic level is the level of perception. People do not understand sounds as sounds, but through the phonological structure of their language. Likewise, people understand actions or words only through the culture they possess. Thus, in Lévi-Strauss's view, the materialist objection to the emic as merely culture-specific and not based on objective principles does not hold. The †poststructuralist objection to the etic is more difficult to counter on a philosophical level. However, the simple answer to this apparent dilemma is to seek objectivity, while realizing that it is elusive. Clearly, etic models can exist as heuristic devices, but they are as problematic as emic ones to define precisely.

The concepts 'emic' and 'etic', although less often discussed today than in the past, are implicit in more recent anthropological approaches, even postmodernist and reflexive ones, where they exist as exemplars of the contradictions in anthropology itself. They are also taking on new significance in *regional analysis and regional comparison. A defining feature of the classic emic approach is that ideology or behaviour is studied from 'within' the cultural system. This implies that only one cultural system can be studied at a time, and in the past the cultural system was often taken as equivalent to one culture or society. Yet, for those who define cultural systems more broadly, i.e., who draw their boundaries around a wider geographical area, renewed interest in a more elaborate version of the emic/etic distinction shows promise.

ALAN BARNARD

See also: language and linguistics, psychological anthropology

Further reading

Conklin, H.C. ([1962]1969) 'Lexical Treatment of Folk Taxonomies' in S.A. Tyler (ed.) *Cognitive Anthropology*, New York: Holt, Rinehart and Winston

Frake, C.O. (1980) *Language and Cultural Description: Essays by Charles O. Frake (Selected and Introduced by Anwar S. Dil)*, Stanford: Stanford University Press

Goodenough, W.H. (1956) 'Componential Analysis and the Study of Meaning', *Language* 32 (1): 195–216

Harris, M. (1976) 'History and Significance of the Emic-Etic Distinction', *Annual Review of Anthropology* 5: 329–50

Headland, T., K.L. Pike and M. Harris (eds) (1990) *Emics and Etics: The Insider/Outsider Debate*, Newbury Park: Sage Publications

Jorion, P. (1983) 'Emic and Etic: Two Anthropological Ways of Spilling Ink', *Cambridge Anthropology* 8 (3): 41–68

Lévi-Strauss, C. (1985) *The View from Afar* (trans. J. Neurgroschel and P. Hoss), New York: Basic Books

Pike, K.L. ([1954] 1967) *Language in Relation to a Unified Theory of the Structure of Human Behavior* (2nd edn), The Hague and Paris: Mouton & Co.

Tyler, S.A. (ed.) (1969) *Cognitive Anthropology*, New York: Holt, Rinehart and Winston

Enlightenment anthropology

The period of European intellectual history known as the Enlightenment (roughly corresponding to the eighteenth century) has been frequently acknowledged as central to the emergence of social and cultural anthropology. †Durkheim included †Montesquieu among his scholarly forebears: *Lévi-Strauss adopted †Rousseau (and Chateaubriand); *Radcliffe-Brown and †Evans-Pritchard acknowledged the philosophers of the Scottish Enlightenment as their intellectual ancestors; while *Boas suggested †Herder; and †Edmund Leach, more recently, reclaimed †Vico as the founding father of cultural or social anthropology. More recently still, militant *postmodernists often claim to be attacking a loose entity called 'the Enlightenment project' which has allegedly dominated Western social thought since the eighteenth century. In fact, the anthropology that emerged during the period of the Enlightenment was diverse, with distinct developments occurring in France, in German scholarship, and in Scotland.

What united these distinct developments was the central idea of Enlightenment thought, that humanity as we encounter it is not something simply given by God, but is something unfolding through time, a product, above all, of history. Within this new historical perspective the *development of human *society became a problem worthy of investigation, with particular emphasis on exotic 'others' and their relevance to European identity. In the early eighteenth century it was still considered important to compare indigenous American peoples with the peoples of antiquity (†Lafitau's *Customs of the American Indians Compared with the Customs of Primitive Times* 1724), and similar comparisons were extended to peoples from the East Indies (Krauss 1978; Moravia 1970).

'Savages' (†noble or otherwise) occupied a prominent place in theories on the progression of human society, particularly the four-stage theory of the history of humanity. This theory (often misrepresented as three-stage theory) held that humanity progressed from hunting through animal husbandry and agriculture to commerce. The four-stage theory was first put forward by A.R.J. (Baron) Turgot in 1750 and adopted by J.-J. Rousseau in his *Discourse on the Origins and Foundations of Inequality among Men* (1755). In Scotland †Adam Smith, Dalrymple and Lord Kames presented their own versions in the 1750s (Meek 1976).

French philosophers concentrated on investigating the 'spirit' of laws and nations. Montesquieu set the tone by publishing *The Spirit of the Laws* (1748) which had as its object 'the laws, customs and diverse practices of all the peoples of the world'. Voltaire published his *Essai sur les moeurs et l'esprit des nations* (1756), to which he later added an introduction to philosophy of history. Duchet (1971) has surveyed the anthropology of Voltaire, Buffon, Rousseau, Helvétius and Diderot.

Whereas these French writers connected developments in the mode of subsistence to intellectual developments (in Turgot's case, from the theological through the metaphysical to the empirical stage), the philosophers of the Scottish Enlightenment concentrated on the connection between stages of economic development and socio-political organization. Scottish Enlightenment thought centred on the moral status of 'man'. The concept of morals was important for the transition to 'social principles' and gave the movement its name. The 'moral philosophers' David Hume, Adam Smith, †Adam Ferguson, Lord Kames, William Robertson and †Lord Monboddo concentrated on social and political issues, arguing that man has an innate 'moral sense'. Primitive peoples figured extensively in their theories since, as Ferguson put it in his *Essay on the History of Civil Society* (1767), 'it is in their present condition, that we are to behold, as in a mirror, the features of our own progenitors'. Ferguson's *Essay* contained ethnographic information, particularly in a section entitled 'The History of Rude Nations'; the same holds for Kame's *Sketches of the History of Man* (1774). William Robertson produced two volumes of *The History of America* dealing with the Spanish territories (1777), while two volumes on Native Americans in Virginia and Massachusetts were published posthumously (1793–4). In the historical works of Ferguson, Kames, Robertson and others, ethnographic data on the peoples of the world served to illustrate the presumed development of human society.

The study of universal history was also of great importance in the German Enlightenment. Here a new area of study came to the fore: †*Völkerkunde*, or the science of peoples (in contrast to †*Volkskunde* or the science of the people). In Germany the 'philosophy of history' (developed by Voltaire and others) divided into two branches. One studied the actual history of humankind and its diversity and customs in what could be called a 'culture-conscious' manner; the other branch was more interested in principles of history at the level of humanity, instead of peoples, and worked with the concept of 'spirit' (*Geist*) instead of 'culture' (*Kultur*). †Kroeber and †Kluckhohn claim that the first of these branches resulted in a 'somewhat diffuse enthnographic interest' (1952: 19), but in fact it produced a genuine *Völkerkunde* that was not 'diffuse' but descriptive, historical and universal.

From the 1760s to the 1780s various authors in the German-speaking countries and in Russia formulated, classified and practised a discipline called *ethnographia* (1767) or *Ethnographie* (1771). These terms appeared as neo-Greek synonyms of *Völkerkunde* (1771), in the works of German historians working mainly at the University of Göttingen. The term *ethnologia* came later, in the work of the Austrian scholar A.F. Kollár (1783), followed by *ethnologie* in the work of A.-C. Chavannes (1787). From the 1770s onwards, *Völkerkunde* (ethnography and ethnology) grew into a discipline that developed in relation to history, geography, natural history, anthropology, linguistics and statistics. In 1781 the first issue of the 27-volume journal *Beiträge zur Völker- und Länderkunde* appeared in Leipzig. In 1787 a young scholar-translator, T.F. Ehrmann, published the

first overview of aims and contents of *Völkerkunde* in a popular magazine for women.

The popularity of the subject was greatly enhanced by geographical discoveries in the Pacific, especially reports of Tahiti (1767), which led to a further romanticization of nature and the †'savages' (*les naturels*, as the French called them). Scholars in Germany, Switzerland, Russia, Bohemia, Austro-Hungary, the Netherlands and France rapidly adopted the new disciplinary vocabulary during the last decades of the eighteenth century, and the United States and Britain soon followed. Apparently the concepts met a need, which in the early nineteenth century led to the establishment of 'ethnographical museums' and 'ethnological societies' (Vermeulen 1995). At the same time the physical study of humanity was developed by Buffon, Camper, Monboddo, Hunter, Blumenbach, Soemmerring, White, Cuvier and others (Barnard 1995; Wokler 1988, 1993).

Thus, alongside the comparative study of moral systems. in France, the conjectural study of the development of human society in the Scottish Enlightenment, and the biological study of humanity, we find a strong research tradition in Central and Eastern Europe that focused on the historical relations between people and nations – not only in the non-Western world but also in Europe itself. This tradition was fostered not in centralized states like France and Britain, but in multi-ethnic countries with greater sensitivity to social formations ranging from ethnic groups to national cultures and nation-states.

These diverse approaches were linked by an adherence to the principle of progress by reason, as well as the idea of the 'Great Chain of Being'. This led to a historicization of *science, which was very fruitful for the study of humanity. However, a critique was formulated in the work of early Romantics like Rousseau, and particularly J.G. Herder (*Ideen zur Philosophie der Geschichte der Menschheit*, 1784–91). In their writings, anthropology – especially the emerging tradition of *Völkerkunde* – was criticized for its classificatory method and augmented with a *relativist and pluralist perspective (see Berlin 1976).

The eighteenth century closed with †Wilhelm von Humboldt's *Plan einer vergleichenden Anthropologie* (1795) and Kant's *Anthropologie in pragmatischer Hinsicht* (1798) in Germany; and the short-lived but important *Société des Observateurs de l'Homme* (1799–1804) in Paris. That society adopted ideas developed in Germany, but was inspired by ideas of the *Idéologues* (Cabanis, Volney, Jauffret, Degérando) that already belonged to a later age (Copans and Jamin 1978; Moravia 1970).

Anthropology during the Enlightenment was diverse and diffuse; the early-twentieth-century idea of anthropology as a 'unified science of man' does not apply to the eighteenth century. Nonetheless, steps were taken in a number of fields towards the formation of anthropology as the general study of humankind, its history and diversity, to the extent that the Swiss theologian Alexandre-César Chavannes hailed it in 1787 as *la science nouvelle*. Among these fields were natural philosophy, †comparative religion, historical linguistics, geography, universal history, natural history, †ethnology, and 'proto-sociology'.

HAN F. VERMEULEN

See also: history of anthropology, French anthropology, German and Austrian anthropology, society, culture

Further reading

Barnard, Alan (1995) 'Monboddo's *Orang Outang* and the Definition of Man', in Raymond Corbey and Bert Theunissen (eds) *Ape, Man, Apeman: Changing Views Since 1600*, Leiden: Department of Prehistory

Berlin, Isiah (1976) *Vico and Herder. Two Studies in the History of Ideas*, London: Hogarth

Copans, Jean and Jean Jamin (eds) (1978) *Aux Origines de l'anthropologie française*, Paris: Le Sycomore

Duchet, Michèle (1971) *Anthropologie et Histoire au siècle des Lumières: Buffon, Voltaire, Rousseau, Helvétius, Diderot*, Paris: Maspero

Evans-Pritchard, E.E. (1981) *A History of Anthropological Thought*, (ed. by André Singer), London: Faber and Faber

Krauss, Werner (1978) *Zur Anthropologie des 18. Jahrhunderts*, Berlin: Akademie-Verlag

Kroeber, A.L. and Clyde Kluckhohn (1952) *Culture. A Critical Review of Concepts and Definitions*, Papers of the Peabody Museum of American Archaelogy and Ethnology, Harvard University 47 (1)

Marshall, P.J. and Glyndwr Williams (1982) *The Great Map of Mankind. British Perceptions of the World in the Age of Enlightenment*, London: J.M. Dent

Meek, Ronald L. (1976) *Social Science and the Ignoble Savage*, Cambridge: Cambridge University Press

Moravia, Sergio (1970) *La scienza dell'uomo nel Settecento*, Bari: Laterza

Mühlmann, Wilhelm E. (1948 [2nd edn, 1968]) *Geschichte der Anthrophologie*, Bonn: Universitäts-Verlag

Rousseau, G.S. and Roy Porter (eds) (1990) *Exoticism in the Enlightenment*, Manchester: Manchester University Press

Vermeulen, Han F. (1995) 'Origins and Institutionalization of Ethnography and Ethnology in Europe and the USA, 1771–1845', in Han F. Vermeulen and Arturo Alvarez Roldán (eds) *Fieldwork and Footnotes, Studies in the History of European Anthropology*, London: Routledge

Wokler, Robert (1988) 'Apes and Races in the Scottish Enlightenment: Monboddo and Kames on the Nature of Man', in Peter Jones (ed.) *Philosophy and Science in the Scottish Enlightenment*, Edinburgh: John Donald

—— (1993) 'From *l'homme physique* to *l'homme moral* and Back: Towards a History of Enlightenment Anthropology', *History of the Human Sciences* 6 (1): 121–38

environment

Meanings

In common usage, 'environment' refers to non-human influences on humanity. Like 'nature', it is shorthand for the biophysical context, the 'natural world' in which we live. Less obviously is it linked with *nature/culture dualism, and is intrinsically anthropocentric in its cosmological image of humanity surrounded by relevant biophysical factors. Environment refers not just to biophysical context, but to human interaction with, and interpretation of, that context. When environment is used in its etymological sense of 'surroundings', the term 'environmental anthropology' is tautologous, since all anthropology is worthless if it fails to provide a †holistic analysis of context.

Environment is one of the broadest concepts in the social sciences. Ultimately it is a category residual to the self, and can be extended to include every aspect of context from the body to the limitless cosmos. It has little explanatory use, but may serve as a general rubric for reminders of the different kinds and levels of context which social analysis must heed.

Biophysical factors

Anthropologists have generally followed the common usage of 'environment' to refer to biophysical factors rather than to context in a broader sense. Unmarked, the term refers to nonhuman things so that 'environmental' analysis in anthropology really means biophysical analysis. Marked, as in terms like 'social environment' and 'learning environment' there is usually a strong sense of metaphorical transference from the biophysical to the social domain, as there is in terms like 'economic climate' and 'strained atmosphere'. In other words, even when social aspects of our surroundings are alluded to with the term 'environment', they tend to be understood in ecological metaphors borrowed from the biophysical environment.

Anthropologists must recognize that biophysical factors may not only be shaped by humans in a material sense, but are culturally perceived; the environment, therefore, is not just a set of things to which people adapt, but also a set of ongoing relations of mutual adaptation between culture and material context.

Materialism, idealism, and holism

However it may be used, the term 'environment' refers both to *things* and to *relations* (between humans and biophysical factors). Everything which merits the term 'anthropology' must in some sense also be *environmental* anthropology and avoid the dangers of socio-centrism or the circularity of †cultural determinism. Attempts to interpret culture in purely cultural terms are like attempts to interpret *religion in purely theological terms: they are circular and non-contextual, and therefore don't constitute interpretations at all.

Anthropology which puts more than usual emphasis on the interface between cultural and biophysical factors is variously called *ecological anthropology, *cultural materialism, cultural ecology, or environmentalism. These are all variants of †materialism, differing according to the degree to which they acknowledge *technology (both in the narrow sense of tools and the wider senses of knowledge and productive organization) as a mediator between the biophysical environment and culture.

Among these, †Marvin Harris's cultural materialist approach argues the strongest case for the shaping of culture by material factors. He divides cultural phenomena into *infrastructure*, *structure*, and *superstructure*, and unequivocally attributes causal primacy to infrastructure, the level at which people use technology to interact with their environment. Thus he argues, for example, that the veneration of cattle in India is maintained because of the role of cattle as the key technological adaptation to the environment; religious belief, the superstructural level, is only causative insofar as it facilitates the continuation of the system (see e.g. Harris 1993).

In cultural ecology, inspired primarily by †Julian Steward (1955), there is similar emphasis

on levels of causation but more recognition of mutual causation between culture and environment, and of causation between cultures as recognized in Steward's term 'social environment'. One of the most influential statements of the cultural ecological approach comes from †Sahlins and †Service (1960), who developed †Leslie White's theory of techological, sociological, and ideological 'levels' by insisting that the relationships between cultures should be included in cultural ecology, rather than just people's relationships with natural features of habitat. Their notion of the 'superorganic environment' enormously expanded the scope of what they called 'cultural ecology' to make it include historical, cultural, social, and economic factors – in short, to make it coterminous with 'anthropology' (1960: 49–50).

In the 1960s and 1970s many anthropologists explored the potential of interpreting culture as a †cybernetic system for regulating relations between people and their environments. The most celebrated example of this is Roy Rappaport's interpretation of periodic cycles of ritualized warfare and peace among Maring-speaking Tsembaga people in the New Guinea Central Highlands as a system maintenance strategy for perpetuation of balances between people, pigs, and various resources such as cultivable land and wildlife. Elegant, detailed, and persuasive though his analysis may be, he grossly underestimates the symbolic aspects of the ritual-belief nexus. And by focusing on a community living in exceptional conditions of environmental circumscription, he exaggerates the potential for identifying isolated 'ecosystems' in other parts of the world with which particular cultures might be associated.

In anthropology materialism is contrasted with †idealism, as it is throughout the social sciences and the humanities. As either extreme is approached, so causation is increasingly perceived as unidirectional. Ultimately it is quite true to say that everything we do is determined by our environment, given a sufficiently broad definition of environment. However, environmental determinist arguments overemphasize the influences of specific components in the environment, and exclude or downplay the role of other members of the species (i.e. for us, other people). If our definition is sufficiently broad, our culture is part of our environment.

Most anthropologists lie somewhere between the extremes of materialism and idealism, recognizing that holistic social analysis must analyse the mutual constitution and ultimate inseparability of culture and nature, mind and body. Once this is recognized, then such notions as 'environmental determinism' and 'cultural determinism' are not only untenable but unthinkable. As Croll and Parkin point out, 'human and non-human agency' or 'person and environment' are 'reciprocally inscribed' (1992: 3).

Symbolism and metaphor

The influences of the biophysical environment on human behaviour are never purely material or 'natural', but are always in part cultural since they are mediated by the culturally determined ways in which they are perceived. The influence of seasonal fluctuations in temperature may be perceived as bodily influences restricting our opportunities, but these influences are culturally reconstructed as, for example, the traditional opposition between rugby and cricket, winter and summer, in Britain. Culture is typically perceived as more 'natural' than it actually is; even purely symbolic influences on behaviour such as astrological ones tend to be perceived as influences from our biophysical environment.

Of particular interest to anthropologists has been the exchange of metaphor between culture and its biophysical context. All cultures select features of their environment as a source of terms or images for understanding humanity, and conversely employ the patterning of social relations when coming to terms with the biophysical environment. The term 'mother nature', for example, may be used both to naturalize the socially constructed mother:child relationship, and to humanize aspects of the environment by imputing maternal characteristics to them. Nurit Bird-David, in various articles (see e.g. 1993), has argued that different peoples following similar modes of subsistence 'relate metaphorically to their natural environment' in similar ways: among hunter-gatherers, human relations with the environment are understood in social metaphors such as parent-child, husband-wife, and namesake relationships, which carry expectations of particular kinds of reciprocity.

There is not only an exchange of metaphors between aspects of society and aspects of the environment; human relations with the environment provide metaphors for the construction of relations between humans, and vice versa. Thus relations between husbands and wives, for example, are in many cultures understood in terms of relations between farmers and fields (control, planting, fertility) or hunters and prey (unpredictability, sexual chasing); conversely, people may understand their relations with non-human resources in terms of the husband-wife relationship.

All cultures have a concept of *pollution by which to designate some forms of interaction with the environment as undesirable. These concepts have both biophysical and social referents, and may be used as a way of mapping social space in less abstract, more geographical terms. Among the most dramatic versions of this form of environmental consciousness is the use of pollution concepts by *Hindus as a means of concretizing the asymmetries of inter-*caste relations by insisting that members of more 'polluted' castes keep respectful distance from 'purer' castes.

Dualism and anthropocentrism

The popular association of 'environment' with non-human things derives from the nature/culture dualism whereby humanity is defined in opposition to everything else. The idea of environment as surroundings which are relevant to human existence derives from anthropocentrism, a worldview which places humanity in centre stage. The extent to which dualism and anthropocentrism vary cross-culturally is a matter of considerable debate.

Environmental debates promoted by 'deep ecologists' contrast 'biocentric' (or 'ecocentric') with 'anthropocentric' cosmologies. A biocentric approach denies the distinct and superior moral status of humanity which the anthropocentric philosophy takes for granted. Biocentrists believe in the intrinsic value of nature; but since the notion of value is itself anthropocentric they inevitably end up humanizing the non-human world. The pragmatic element in deep ecology is nonetheless important for anthropology: namely, that the experience of wilderness – of relatively undomesticated nature – is something which all peoples use in various ways, and primarily as a means of coming to terms with their own culture.

Applications

The development of theory and ethnography of human-environment relations can contribute significant opportunities for †applied anthropology. Indigenous environmental knowledge promises to be of great importance in improving environmental management, and by enhancing its status among planners anthropologists can promote participatory *development. Ecological anthropology can inform Environmental Impact Assessments to ensure that these incorporate analysis of socio-economic factors. Understanding of the embeddedness of culture in its biophysical environment helps understand the effect of the displacement of people from one environment to another. Applied anthropologists also frequently have to inform planners of the ways in which traditional common-property resource management systems have been disrupted by †acculturation and externally-planned development programmes.

Environmental anthropology demands good understanding not only of biophysical resources, human needs and uses of those resources, but also of the tenurial and spatial arrangements by which those resources are appropriated, managed, and used. Cross-cultural comparison based on evidence from holistic, long-term, local studies of these arrangements can promote better global understanding of the conditions under which management of resources remains stable and sustainable or else results in deterioration. Such comparison can also remind natural scientists that the concept of 'environmental degradation' is a subjective judgement related to the needs, values, and perceptions of specific interest groups.

Studies of common property regimes and mobility as environmental strategies have been of particular importance since these tend to be more significant among peoples marginal to states. In demonstrating the viability of such systems, anthropologists have played important roles in arguing against those who assume that state control or privatization of resources are the only means of ensuring sound environmental management (see e.g. Berkes 1989).

Most importantly, 'environment' suggests interdisciplinarity. Anthropological concerns, like the livelihoods of most rural people in the Third World, are multidisciplinary and unspecialized. However, the individualism of ethnographic research means that this multidisciplinarity is undisciplined – it generally fails to engage with the various disciplines in whose interests it dabbles.

NEIL THIN

See also: ecological anthropology, economic anthropology, nature and culture, technology, archaeology

Further reading

Berkes, F. (ed.) (1989) *Common Property Resources: Ecology and Community-based Sustainable Development*, London: Belhaven Press

Bird-David, N. (1993) 'Tribal Metaphorization of Human-nature Relatedness: A Comparative Analysis', in K. Milton (ed.) *Environmentalism: The View from Anthropology*, London: Routledge

Croll, E. and D. Parkin (eds) (1992) *Bush Base: Forest Farm. Culture, Environment and Development*, London: Routledge

Ellen, R. (1982) *Environment, Subsistence and System: The Ecology of Small-scale Social Formations*, Cambridge: Cambridge University Press

Harris, M. (1993) *Culture, People, Nature: An Introduction to General Anthropology*, London: Harper Collins

Kroeber, A.L. (1952) *The Nature of Culture*, Chicago: University of Chicago Press

Rappaport, R.A. (1968) *Pigs for the Ancestors: Ritual in the Ecology of a New Guinea People*, New Haven: Yale University Press

Sahlins, M. and E.R. Service (eds) (1960) *Evolution and Culture*, Michigan: University of Michigan Press

Steward, J.H. (1955) *Theory of Culture Change: The Methodology of Multilinear Evolution*, Urbana, Illinois: University of Illinois Press

essentialism

Essentialism commonly appears as both a violation of anthropological *relativism and one of the besetting conceptual sins of anthropology. Exemplified by such totalizing ideologies as *nationalism and biological determinism, it is also frequently conflated with reification, †objectivism, and literalism. All four concepts are forms of reductionism and there is substantive semantic overlap among them. Reification may most usefully be seen as concerned above all with the logical properties of concepts, however, and objectivism primarily entails a priori assumptions about the possibility of definitive description, while literalism may be specifically understood as the uncritical, decontextualized application of a referential and abstract semantics. The distinctive mark of essentialism, by contrast, lies in its suppression of temporality: it assumes or attributes an unchanging, primordial ontology to what are the historically contingent products of human or other forms of agency. It is thus also a denial of the relevance of agency itself.

This is the root cause of its generally bad press in the relativistic anthropological mainstream; it has only rarely been noted as an interesting aspect of ordinary social relations. Attention has been focussed on its centrality to ideologies, such as nationalism, that appear to contradict and supress the local-level and actor-oriented practices that interest ethnographers. In †Geertz's (1973: 234–54) influential study of nationalism, for example, essentialism appears in tandem with 'epochalism' as a defining characteristic of nationalism, and especially as the conflationary notion of 'national character' grounded in such shared symbolic substances as blood. In this sense, epochalism – a modernist Zeitgeist – is temporally the antithesis but also the corollary of essentialism, which requires the construction of a set of age-old national traditions through which national origins are effectively placed beyond real time altogether. One form of essentialism, now much studied by anthropologists, is the search for cultural authenticity as a basis of collective legitimacy. In the study of *religion, this has led to a curious parallel between a lack of anthropological interest in the local uses of orthodox ritual forms and the fundamentalist insistence on a single, all-encompassing hermeneutic. Thus, for example, Bowen (1992) has shown how the uncritical adoption of 'scriptural essentialism' can occlude the local and gendered reconceptualization of central Islamic rituals. Other persistent essentialisms include *Orientalism (Said 1978) and *Occidentalism (Carrier 1995).

In many anthropological treatments of nationalism, essentialism itself has been essentialized as a key, invariant feature. This ironic predicament recalls the historical entailment of anthropology in essentializing classificatory schemes that are closely related to those of nationalism, *colonialism, and other officializing cultural ideologies. Conceptually, however, this fact can be usefully harnessed as a means of maintaining critical awareness of the provisionality of all essentialisms. Both the necessity and the potential benefits of such an epistemological move are apparent in two parallel developments in which concepts of strategy and essentialism, superficially antithetical to each other, emerge in close mutual association: the feminist critique of male power and certain anthropological engagements with the politics of cultural self-ascription.

Strategies – ostensibly actors' creative deployments of the apparent social rules and structures – subvert essentialist claims of immutable authority. But essentialized categories may conversely be viewed as products of the most durable strategies, those which have successfully concealed their own provisionality. This is the practical basis of much bureaucratic classification in the modern nation-state: civil servants deploy an apparently universalist and invariant set of legal precepts, especially those relating to ideas of national character and destiny, in support of what may be sectarian, partisan, or even personal interests.

Such ideas have a long history, and are clearly rooted in debates – central to anthropology and forged in the emergence of *evolutionism – about the relationship between culture and biology. (A particular form of essentialism is sometimes called 'biologism'; it is often ideologically framed – in medicine, for example – as 'naturalism', which is both etymologically and conceptually cognate with 'naturalization' as a bureaucratic procedure conferring citizenship.) In medical philosophy the static character of disease classification is attributable to the pre-Darwinian sense of order that can be found, for example, in humoral theories. Such ideas, as Greenwood (1984) shows, while largely discredited in the biological sciences, formed the basis of †eugenics and other racist ideologies, and also underlie early European attempts to define national identity in terms of biological descent.

Knowing this contested history enables us to focus on the necessarily contingent character of all forms of essentialism. Feminist calls for 'strategic essentialism' as a political response to male-centred definitions and practices (see especially Spivak 1989; see also the special issue of *differences* on essentialism in which this appears), while perhaps liable to relapse into reification in their turn, have offered pragmatic ways of achieving political and epistemological change. A considerable debate about the advantages and drawbacks of thus entering an essentializing contest has emerged, pitting past experience of essentialized (and especially biologized) reductionisms about women against the potential value of harnessing the dangerous powers of essentialism to claim a political space for female subjectivity. In a parallel development anthropologists are now able to acknowledge that charges that particular populations have invented (or 'constructed') histories and identities are politically threatening, especially when such groups are engaged in a political struggle for resources they could not hope to obtain from a more fragmented base. Such charges play into the hands of majority interests and occlude the established essentialisms of the latter. Clearly, this problem is related to the dynamic whereby postcolonial searches for *identity must find themselves engaged in the discursive practices of colonialism in turn, and it also underscores the facility with which self-determination can be transmuted into repression of others. The critical issue here concerns the identification of the social entity *against which* such essentializing strategies are deployed, and requires that these strategies should not be considered independently of this encompassing political context (Lattas 1993). Indeed, it has been pointed out that anthropological relativism may itself be guilty of the kind of selective reading that fosters objectivism about the truth of (majority) history (Gable *et al.* 1992). Essentialism can thus become a decontextualized device for, ironically, essentializing those against whom one claims to defend agency and subjectivity. As a feature of everyday social life, it may encompass both global ideologies and interpersonal relationships. The critical debates that have qualified and modulated its status as an undifferentiated anthropological evil should increasingly illuminate the mutual entailment of local and global strategies of representation.

MICHAEL HERZFELD

See also: colonialism, gender, identity, ideology, nationalism, nature and culture, Orientalism, race

Further reading

Bowen, J. (1992) 'On Scriptural Essentialism and Ritual Variation: Muslim Sacrifice in Sumatra and Morocco', *American Ethnologist* 19 (4): 656–71
Carrier, J. (ed.) (1995) *Occidentalism: Images of the West*, Oxford: Clarendon Press
Gable, E., R. Handler and A. Lawson (1992) 'On the Uses of Relativism: Fact, Conjecture, and Black and White Histories at Colonial Williamsburg', *American Ethnologist* 19 (4): 791–805
Geertz, C. (1973) *The Interpretation of Cultures*, New York: Basic Books
Greenwood, D. (1984) *The Taming of Evolution: The Persistence of Nonevolutionary Views in the Study of Humans*, Ithaca: Cornell University Press
Grosz, E. (1989) 'Sexual Difference and the Problem of Essentialism', in J. Clifford and V. Dhareshwar (eds) *Traveling Theories: Traveling Theorists* (Santa Cruz: Group for the Critical Study of Colonial Discourse & The Center for Cultural Studies, University of California (= *Inscriptions* 5: 86–101)
Herzfeld, M. (1992) *The Social Production of Indifference: Exploring the Symbolic Roots of Western Bureaucracy*, Oxford: Berg
Lattas, A. (1993) 'Essentialism, Memory and Resistance: Aboriginality and the Politics of Authenticity', *Oceania* 63 (3): 240–67
Said, E. (1978) *Orientalism*, New York: Basic Books
Spivak, G. (1989) 'In a Word', interview with Ellen Rooney, *differences* 1 (2): 124–56 (special issue: 'The Essential Difference: Another Look at Essentialism')

ethnicity

The intellectual history of the term 'ethnicity' is relatively short: prior to the 1970s there was little mention of it in anthropological literature and textbooks contained no definitions of the term (Despres 1975: 188; Cohen 1978: 380). Since the mid-1970s the concept has acquired strategic significance within anthropological theory partly as a response to the changing †postcolonial geopolitics and the rise of ethnic minorities activism in many industrial states. The shift has resulted in a proliferation of theories of ethnicity, explaining such diverse phenomena as social and political change, *identity formation, social conflict, *race relations, nation-building, assimilation etc.

There are three competing approaches to the understanding of ethnicity. They could be roughly categorized as primordialist, instrumentalist and constructivist. Roughly speaking, primordialist theories assert that ethnic identification is based on deep, 'primordial' attachments to a group or culture; instrumentalist approaches treat ethnicity as a political instrument exploited by leaders and others in pragmatic pursuit of their own interests; and constructivist approaches emphasize the contingency and fluidity of ethnic identity, treating it as something which is made in specific social and historical contexts, rather than (as in primordialist arguments) treating it as a 'given'.

Primordialist views

The †objectivist theories of ethnicity, which assert that ultimately there is some real, tangible foundation to ethnic identification, can be subdivided into those in which ethnicity is viewed as a predominantly biological phenomenon, and those in which it is construed as a product of culture and history. The conceptual differences are ultimately rooted in different understandings of human nature and *society.

In those theoretical frameworks strongly influenced by *evolutionism, ethnicity is usually conceptualized as based in biology and determined by genetic and geographical factors. Pierre van den Berghe (1981) has explored the contribution of *sociobiology to the explanation of ethnic phenomena and suggests that these are rooted in a genetic predisposition for kin selection, or 'nepotism'. The central concept in a sociobiological approach is 'inclusive fitness', which describes the effect of altruistic behaviour in reducing individual fitness (one's genetic transmission to the next generation) and at the same time increasing one's kin group fitness (by helping more of one's relatives to reproduce, thus transmitting – albeit indirectly – more of one's own genes). This tendency to favour kin over non-kin has been called kin selection, or nepotism. Another concept employed in sociobiological analysis is reciprocity, defined as cooperation among distantly related or unrelated individuals which, in conditions when nepotistic behaviour is impossible, could enhance individual inclusive fitness. In general, ethnicity is defined as a comprehensive form of natural selection and *kinship connections, a primordial instinctive impulse, which 'continues to be present even in the most industrialised mass societies of today' (van den Berghe 1981: 35). Some authors take the view that recognition of the group affiliation is genetically encoded, being a product of early human evolution, when the ability to recognize the members of one's family group was necessary for survival (Shaw and Wong 1989).

Sociobiological interpretations of ethnicity have been severely criticized (Thompson 1989: 21–48) but the main thesis – that human ethnic groups are extended kin groups or collectivities based on *descent – was assimilated by *relativists in talk of 'quasi-kinship' groups (Brown 1989: 6–8).

Explicit primordialism was entertained in *Russian and Soviet anthropology. Taking its origin in †Herder's neo-romantic concept of the *Volk*, as a unity of blood and soil, it was worked out into a †positivist programme for ethnographic research in the work of S.M. Shirokogorov, who has defined the †'ethnos' as 'a group of people, speaking one and the same language and admitting common origin, characterized by a set of customs and a life style, which are preserved and sanctified by tradition, which distinguishes it from others of the same kind' (1923: 122). This approach was later developed in the works of Y.V. Bromley, who has given a very similar definition of ethnos (1981), and L.N. Gumilev (1989). The latter believed in the existence of the ethnos as a 'bio-social organism' and developed a framework

for the study of ethnogenesis as a process which was basically geographically determined: the rise to existence of an ethnos was depicted as a combined effect of cosmic energies and landscape.

Instrumentalist approaches

From the late 1960s, in theories of *modernity and modernization, ethnicity was treated as a remnant of the pre-industrial social order, gradually declining in significance. It was a marginal phenomenon to be overcome by the advance of the modern state and processes of national integration and assimilation ('melting pot', or assimilationist ideology, prevalent in American cultural anthropology from the 1960s to the mid-1970s).

Until the mid-1970s ethnicity was defined structurally i.e. in terms of the cultural morphology of a given society (the linguistic, religious and racial characteristics, treated as 'primordial givens' or 'bases' of ethnicity). It was suggested that objective and perceived differences between the various groups in a society served as a basis for the production of a distinctive group identity, which in its turn created the context for inter-group relations and political mobilization. Cultural affinities might be exploited as a basis for inter-group affiliation in political struggles, but were seen as temporary and minor impediments on the way to the modern nation-state. So, in this cultural approach to the study of ethnicity, it was typically defined in terms of the objective cultural structure of the society (Smith 1969: 104–5). The common observation that not every cultural group develops an ethnic identity or consciousness of group affiliation could be accounted for in the concept of 'latent' or 'silent' ethnicity.

Instrumentalism, with its intelllectual roots in sociological *functionalism, treated claims to ethnicity as a product of political myths, created and manipulated by cultural elites in their pursuit of advantages and power. The cultural forms, values and practices of ethnic groups become resources for elites in competition for political power and economic advantage. They become symbols and referents for the identification of members of a group, which are called up in order to ease the creation of a political identity. Thus, ethnicity is created in the dynamics of elite competition within the boundaries determined by political and economic realities (Brass 1985). Sometimes this functionalism acquired a psychological twist, then ethnicity was explained as an effective means of recovering lost ethnic pride (Horowitz 1985), defeating alienation and alleviating emotional stress as a therapy for suffered trauma. The essential feature of these approaches is their common base in †utilitarian values.

Constructivist theories

†Fredrik Barth, with his colleagues, in a seminal collection *Ethnic Groups and Boundaries*, treated ethnicity as a continuing ascription which classifies a person in terms of their most general and inclusive identity, presumptively determined by origin and background (Barth 1969: 13), as well as a form of social organisation maintained by inter-group boundary mechanisms, based not on possession of a cultural inventory but on manipulation of identities and their situational character. This conceptualization has enabled anthropologists to concentrate upon the situational and contextual character of ethnicity (Okamura 1981; Verdery 1991), to see more clearly its political dimensions, such as the ability to structure inter-group relations and to serve as a basis for political mobilization and social stratification.

With the advent of a new interpretive paradigm based on *postmodernism, attention has shifted to the negotiation of multiple subjects over group boundaries and identity. In this atmosphere of renewed sensitivity to the dialectics of the objective and the subjective in the process of ethnic identity formation and maintenance, even the negotiable character of ethnic boundaries stressed by Barth was too reminiscent of his objectivist predecessors' tendency to reification. It was argued that terms like 'group', 'category' and 'boundary' still connote a fixed identity, and Barth's concern with maintenance tends to reify it still more (Cohen 1978: 386). The mercurial nature of ethnicity was accounted for when it was defined as 'a set of sociocultural diacritics [physical appearance, name, language, history, religion, nationality] which define a shared identity for members and non-members'; 'a series of nesting dichotomizations of inclusiveness and exclusiveness' (Cohen 1978: 386–7).

The future of ethnicity research

All the approaches to understanding ethnicity are not necessarily mutually exclusive, so one possible avenue of research is the integration of the soundest aspects of existing approaches into a coherent theory of ethnicity. There are reasons to believe that a constructivist conceptualization could serve as the nucleus of such a synthesis.

Constructivism has a special significance for these reasons. First, sensitivity to context which could be viewed as the basic feature of relativistic theories of ethnicity. Their stress on its relational character and situational dependence made it possible to study ethnicity in the contexts of different 'levels' and 'contextual horizons': the transnational (as in Wallerstein's theory of the *world-system), and within the nation-state (M. Hechter's theory of †internal colonialism), between groups (F. Barth's theory of ethnic boundary maintenance) and within groups (psychological theories of reactive, symbolic, demonstrative ethnicity, stigmatized identity etc). These approaches are cumulative from the point of view of scale. Second, all of these approaches converge on the problematics of descent and kinship in ethnic identity formation, and these could be viewed as a common conceptual field for testing different hypotheses. Third, the specific experience of the post-communist world, particularly Russia, contains a plethora of examples of constructed and mobilized ethnicity, thus forming a unique field for possible integration of the constructivist and instrumentalist perspectives.

Another direction for ethnicity research is the assimilation of relevant knowledge from other social sciences, such as the integration of research on forms of mass consciousness into the understanding of ethnic group descent mythology, linkage of the psychological theories of attachment with an understanding of ethnic sentiments etc. Our existing understanding of ethnic sentiment as an intellectual construct engendered on the basis of historical differences in culture, as well as myths, conceptions and doctrines that are formed from the deliberate efforts of elite strata to convert myths and mass emotions into programmes for socio-political engineering, is already a synthesis of instrumentalist and constructionist perspectives. The definition of an ethnic community as a group of people whose members share a common name and elements of culture, possess a myth of common origin and common historical memory, who associate themselves with a particular territory and possess a feeling of solidarity, opens further avenues for integration of anthropological, political and psychological knowledge in understanding of ethnic phenomena.

SERGEY SOKOLOVSKII
and VALERY TISHKOV

See also: race, nationalism, culture, essentialism, plural society, urban anthropology

Further reading

Barth, F. (1969) 'Introduction', in F. Barth (ed.) *Ethnic Croups and Boundaries*, Boston: Little, Brown

Brass, P.R. (ed.) (1985) *Ethnic Groups and the State*, London: Croom Helm

Bromley, Y.V. (1981) *Sovremennye Problemy Ethnografii*, Moscow: Nauka

Brown, D. (1989) 'Ethnic Revival: Perspectives on State and Society', *Third World Quarterly* 11 (4): 1–17

Cohen, R. (1978) 'Ethnicity: Problem and Focus in Anthropology', *Annual Review of Anthropology* 7: 379–403

Despres, L.A. (1975) 'Toward a Theory of Ethnic Phenomena', in L. Despres (ed.) *Ethnicity and Resource Competition in Plural Societies*, The Hague: Mouton

Glazer, N. and D. Moynihan (1976) *Ethnicity: Theory and Experience*, Cambridge MA: Harvard University Press

Gumilev, L.N. (1989) *Etnogenez i Biosfera Zemli*, Leningrad: Leningrad State University

Horowitz, D. (1985) *Ethnic Groups in Conflict*, Berkeley: University of California Press

Okamura, J.Y. (1981) 'Situational Ethnicity', *Ethnic and Racial Studies* 4 (4): 452–65

Shaw, P. and Y. Wong (1989) *Genetic Seeds of Warfare: Evolution, Nationalism and Patriotism*, Boston: Unwin Hyman

Shils, E. (1957) 'Primordial, Personal, Sacred, and Civil Ties', *British Journal of Sociology* 8: 130–45

Shirokogoroff, S. (1923) *Etnos, Issledovanie osnovnykh printsipov etnicheskikh i etnograficheskikh yavlenii*, Shanghai.

Smith, A.D. (ed.) (1986) *The Ethnic Origins of Nations*, Oxford: Basil Blackwell

Smith, M.G. (1969) 'Pluralism in Precolonial African Society', in L. Kuper and M.G. Smith (eds.) *Pluralism in Africa*, Berkeley and Los Angeles: University of California Press

Thompson, R. H. (1989) *Theories of Ethnicity*, New York: Greenwood Press

van den Berghe, P.L. (1981) *The Ethnic Phenomenon*, New York: Elsevier

Verdery, K. (1991) *National Ideologies Under Socialism: Identity and Cultural Politics in Ceausescu's Romania*, Berkeley: University of California Press

ethnography

The word 'ethnography' has a double meaning in anthropology: ethnography as *product* (ethnographic writings – the articles and books written by anthropologists), and ethnography as *process* (†participant observation or *fieldwork). The product depends upon the process, but not in any simple A>B relationship. In constructing ethnographies, anthropologists do more than merely 'write up' the fieldnotes they record as part of the process of doing fieldwork. If ethnographies can be seen as the building blocks and testing grounds of anthropological theory, ethnographies and the ethnographic process from which they derive are also shaped and moulded by theory.

Ethnography (in both senses) may profitably be envisioned as one point of an anthropological triangle. The other two points are *comparison* and *contextualization*. Together the three points of this triangle define the operational system by which anthropologists acquire and use ethnographic data in writing ethnographies. Fieldnotes are filtered and interpreted against *comparative theory and against contextual documentary materials. As they are read, ethnographies then stimulate comparative theoretical thinking, which in turn suggests new problems and interpretations to be resolved through further ethnographic fieldwork. Ethnographies, and the comparative theoretical reflection they spur, also regularly lead to new demands and rising standards for documentary contextualization (more history, more ecological or demographic backgrounding, more attention to *state policy, economic trends and the *world system). This anthropological triangle of ethnography, comparison and contextualization is, in essence, the way in which socio-cultural anthropology works as a discipline to explain and interpret human cultures and social life.

Ethnographies as they have evolved over the past century-and-a-half constitute a genre, a form of writing conditioned by the process of knowledge construction epitomized in this anthropological triangle. Ethnographies consequently differ from travel writing, gazetteers, interview-based surveys, or even the personal fieldwork accounts of anthropologists (which form a separate genre). Ethnography, both product and process, has a history and pattern of development of its own.

Ethnography as product: a history of ethnography

As a written account, an ethnography focuses on a particular population, place and time with the deliberate goal of describing it to others. So, often, did the writings of nineteenth-century explorers, *missionaries, military agents, journalists, travellers, and reformers; and these contain much information useful to anthropologists. What distinguishes the first ethnography, *Louis Henry Morgan's *The League of the Ho-de-no-sau-nee or Iroquois* (1851), from these other writings are two qualities: its attempt to depict the structure and operation of Iroquois society from the Iroquois viewpoint (the ethnographic point of the anthropological triangle), and its grounding in the †monogenist anthropological theorizing of its time (the comparative point of the triangle), ideas to which Morgan would make major additions and reformulations. Morgan's book detailed Iroquois †matrilineal *kinship, political and ceremonial life, *material culture, and *religion; the ethnographic basis for this information being Morgan's partnership with the Western-educated Iroquois Ely S. Parker, his translator and cultural interpreter. The book's attention to history, geography, the impact of White settlers and contemporary land-rights issues also established standards for pre-and post-fieldwork contextualization (the third point of the triangle) that anthropologists continue to heed.

Morgan's ethnography, still authoritative and readable, was not joined by comparable works until the 1880s. What ensued instead were increased efforts to provide standardized guides for gathering ethnographic data by local 'men on the spot' (few were women) in accord with the comparative goals of armchair theorists. Although Morgan did himself collect kinship data from American Indian groups on fieldtrips during the 1860s, much of the material he used in later writings arrived from missionary and other amateurs in India, Australia and elsewhere, who filled in and returned his kinship schedules. In England, †E.B. Tylor played a key role in drafting †*Notes and Queries on Anthropology*, first published in 1874 for use around the globe; he and other comparativists like †James Frazer helped shape up the resulting local work for publication, often first as articles in the *Journal of the Anthropological Institute*, which dates to 1872. Through these efforts ethnographic standards slowly improved, and theoretical perspectives became more overt, but contextualization retreated, a victim of anti-historical and †ethnocentric *evolutionism or *diffusionism.

The fieldwork of †Frank Cushing among the Zuni Indians in the early 1880s made a great leap forward in ethnographic method. Cushing learned to speak Zuni, resided at the pueblo over a four-year period, and combined observation of ongoing events with the seated-informant questioning more typical of the anthropological guide-users. Cushing's sensitive *Zuni Fetishes* (1883) revealed the inner world of these people's *cosmology, *mythology and *symbolism, and its connection to practical activities; so did his major work *Zuni*

Breadstuff (1920), but its initial publication during 1884–85 in an obscure journal insulated its impact at the time. Cushing's lack of influence on students and his death in 1899 combined to make his ethnographic advances a false start for anthropology (Sanjek 1990: 189–92).

*Franz Boas's ethnographic research among the Inuit in 1883–84 moved less thoroughly in the participant observation direction than Cushing, and his subsequent fieldwork through the 1890s among the American Indians of the Northwest Coast amounted mainly to the transcription of texts recited by seated informants (Sanjek 1990: 193–203). It was this approach that he taught his cohorts of students during the first three decades of the twentieth century at Columbia University, and they took it with them as anthropology departments sprouted in the United States. Their goal was the †'salvage ethnography' of 'memory cultures' and not the direct †participant observation of human life as it is lived. In view of the devastated circumstances of Native American reservations, the Boasians recognized no other choice before †acculturation and *community studies became acceptable alternatives in the 1930s. Until then, American ethnographies increased in number, and improved in contextualization as historical interests supplanted evolutionary theory. But they stultified in method as participant observation regressed, and in theory as well, with little invigoration from the ethnographic point of the anthropological triangle.

In British anthropology, the division of labour between the armchair theorist and the person on the spot, already dead in the USA, entered obsolescence in the 1890s when Tylor and Frazer's Oxford-trained protégé †Baldwin Spencer collaborated in participant observation with a seasoned local expert on Aboriginal life, †Frank Gillen. Their *Central Tribes of Native Australia* (1899) provided a vivid and detailed view of cosmology, *ritual and social organization that not only revealed unheralded cultural complexity amidst technological simplicity, but also sparked new theoretical currents in the work of †Émile Durkheim and †Sigmund Freud.

Even before Spencer and Gillen's work was published, in 1898 a team of Cambridge scientists arrived on the spot themselves in the †Torres Straits expedition to the islands just north of Australia. Though less theoretically or ethnographically provocative, their results moved fieldwork practice beyond even the Australian ethnographers with crystallization of the *genealogical method of anthropological inquiry by team member †W.H.R. Rivers. Rivers demonstrated that the systematic collection of genealogies could produce far more than kinship terminologies; community history, *migration trajectories, *marriage patterns, demography, †inheritance and succession, and the relation of rules to actual occurrences could all be studied. With his application of this method in *The Todas* (1906), an ethnography of a South Indian group, Rivers also found that prior knowledge of kinship connections enriched an understanding of participation in ongoing ritual events (Sanjek 1990: 203–7).

These British ethnographic innovations were incorporated into a 1912 revision of *Notes and Queries*. Novice ethnographer *Bronislaw Malinowski carried this with him to New Guinea in 1914, but soon became discouraged with the limits of even this more sophisticated use of the seated informant. In his ground-breaking Trobriand Islands fieldwork of 1915–18, Malinowski bettered Cushing. Not only did he learn the language, but he more actively entered the scenes of daily life and made the speech in action he heard and recorded there the basis of his ethnography. Moreover, he maintained detailed fieldnotes that he analysed topically while still in the field, and constantly reread to plan further research activities (Malinowski 1922: 1–25). He found that topics like economics or law or land-use or *magic intruded on each other – the events recorded in his fieldnotes could be analyzed ethnographically from several of these institutional perspectives. Thus was his *functionalism born, 'the mass of gears all turning and grinding on each other' as his American contemporary †Ralph Linton put it (Sanjek 1990: 207–15).

Malinowski's students, a robust and gifted group, produced dozens of classic ethnographies during the 1930s, 1940s and 1950s. Perhaps the most influential has been †E.E. Evans-Pritchard's *The Nuer* (1940). Rich in ethnographic details, it is nonetheless highly selective in their presentation, subordinating them to a powerful theory of how *descent ideology organizes group life and cattle management against the vagaries of annual ecological transformation and population movement. In this work, influenced by the thinking of *A.R. Radcliffe-Brown, a strong relationship was evident between the comparative and ethnographic points of the anthropological triangle, and

its impact was marked over the next quarter century. As critiques of *The Nuer* later mounted, it was the historical-contextual point of the triangle that was seen as most in need of bolstering.

In the US, Malinowskian-style ethnography took hold and Boasian fieldwork methods were largely superceded. †Margaret Mead, one of Boas's later students, appears to have independently invented an ethnographic approach equivalent to Malinowski's, against her mentor's advice (Sanjek 1990: 215–26). From the 1940s, on both sides of the Atlantic and beyond, a combination of strong ethnography but weak contextualization was widely visible in both anthropological theory and in ethnographies themselves. New demands for improved contextualization arose with the impact of *ecology, *regional analysis, *history and anthropology, and *world systems in the 1960s and thereafter. Today, there are hundreds of classic ethnographies, though perhaps none since *The Nuer* would be as readily so designated by a majority of anthropologists, or has been as widely read.

Ethnography as process: doing ethnography

The selection of a particular population or site for ethnographic research is ordinarily related to some unanswered question or outstanding problem in the body of comparative anthropological theory. Personal predilections or connections of researchers also shape this selection, but the fieldworker still must justify his or her choice in terms of some significant theory to which the project is addressed. Usually this justification is made explicit in a written proposal for funds to underwrite the fieldwork.

While ethnographic fieldwork is thus lodged from conception in comparative anthropological theory (in one of the many varieties or schools discussed in this *Encyclopedia*), the comparative point of the anthropological triangle also moulds the ethnographic process in two further ways. First, anthropologists are imbued with a cross-cultural perspective by training and reading. At each step in the ethnographic process they constantly refer to the global range of societies with which they are familiar. When addressing any aspect of social life – marriage, leadership, *ethnicity, etc. – mentally they run through examples of similarities and differences elsewhere. Unlike other social sciences that see Western experience as the centre and as the norm, anthropology fixes each case within the widest co-ordinates – all social formations, globally, through human history.

Second, the comparative perspective focuses ethnographic attention on trends and transitions, not just on similarities and differences at random (which are infinite). Rather than treating each ethnographic instance as unique (which in terms of extreme cultural *relativism it is), ethnographers place the social phenomena they observe within comparative frames (*hunting and gathering, †horticultural, †agricultural, *pastoral, †industrial, *colonial, neo-colonial regimes; co-operative, competitive, individualistic societies; *gender subordination, complementarity or equality; etc.). Ethnographies in turn provoke debate, revision and innovation in theorizing. And behind this, and behind the ethnographic process itself, lies the problem of identifying what is most deserving of close attention within the flux of daily life – the patterns of behaviour and change that effect shifts in the social order at large.

While significant theories bring ethnographers to particular locations, actors and activities, once they arrive they begin to listen as well as watch. Often they must first learn to listen – learn the language, the local vocabulary and the current verbal conventions. Ethnographic fieldwork now turns away from theoretical discourse and to the viewpoints and concepts of the people (informants, subjects, actors, consultants) themselves. Ethnographers aim to document how the people see and talk about their everyday social activities and groupings, and the wider worlds they live in. It is their normal scenes of activity, topics of conversation and standards of evaluation that are the objects of ethnographic fieldwork.

This is not begun by announcing: 'I'm your anthropologist; when can I interview you?' Ethnographers must be honest about their role and sponsorship, but their paramount aim is to listen, and to move as quickly as possible into natural settings of social life, the places people would be, doing what they would be doing, if the ethnographer were not there. Interviews become useful at later stages of fieldwork; participation observation begins by listening to what British anthropologist †Audrey Richards called 'speech in action.' As ethnographers watch and listen in a wide-ranging manner (though within parameters set by the significant theories that bring them there), they learn to understand culturally meaningful conventions, and to formulate culturally appropriate questions.

As this initial stage of the ethnographic process develops, the fieldworker must constantly make decisions about where to be, whom to listen to, what events to follow, and what safely to ignore and leave out. These decisions are guided both by the significant theories prefiguring fieldwork, and by the theories of significance that arise in the field. These latter theories (hunches, hypotheses, ideas about connections and relationships) emerge as participant observation and listening to speech in action proceeds. They suggest what people and activities to focus upon, what places and events to attend, and what objects and their circulation to follow.

As this occurs, the fieldwork 'funnel' narrows, to use Michael Agar's (1980) apt metaphor. The early period is wide, open, and nearly all-encompassing. As theories of significance emerge, pan out, or are discarded, the funnel of informants, events, and activities narrows. Goals sharpen; research design crystallizes as cultural knowledge grows; wide-ranging fieldnotes are reread, and suggest more precise directions to follow; specific bodies of records (of *household composition, *land tenure, ritual performances, life histories, *folklore, etc.) are collected systematically.

One side of ethnography is unmediated by communication with the actors. As observers, ethnographers watch, count, and record things in their fieldnotes – numbers of people in events, their positions, their comings and goings; objects, inventories, exchanges, movements, orderings, sequences, associations, assemblages and arrangements of all sorts. The other side of ethnographic work consists of †speech events, scenes of communication in which the ethnographer is a passive or active participant. And like Agar's funnel, the speech events of fieldwork (here classed in six categories) also move from wide to narrow, from open to more focused.

(1) Ethnography begins with situated listening. Here the actors control topicality (talking to each other about what they usually do), and the anthropologist is admitted to their turf (the locations they usually occupy). Early on, as trust is established, fieldworkers place themselves in a wide sampling of such places; as the research funnel narrows, an ethnographer becomes more selective about where to listen.

(2) Still on the informants' turf, and still in the accustomed activities of daily life, the anthropologist soon starts to enter natural conversations, and begins to shift topicality to his or her own

interests. This process starts gently, by moving appropriately into rounds of chatting, *gossiping, and ordinary comment. As cultural competence increases (and as theories of significance start to emerge), the fieldworker also attempts to direct conversations by introducing questions and suggesting topics for responses from informants.

(3) Though not a major part of ethnographic practice, in some instances, and while still on the informants' turf, the fieldworker may ask direct and pointed questions, and attempt to secure precise pieces of data. Interventions of this sort are dangerous – the inappropriateness of such seizures of topicality in everyday settings may be jarring to the actors. Typically speech events of this sort occur in the final days of fieldwork, when local acceptance is at its peak, research goals are most pressing, and the fieldwork funnel approaches its narrow end.

(4) Usually after some initial period of fieldwork (a few months perhaps), interviews may begin. This class of speech events is disruptive – the informant is removed from her or his turf, either to the ethnographer's household or office, or by transforming an everday location into a scene of ethnographer-informant dialogue (an activity that would otherwise *not* be occurring there). Typically the earliest of these deliberate breaks in time-place flow reserve topicality for the actor. In such open-ended (or discovery) interviews, the informant moves the conversation according to his or her own interests.

(5) In later and more productive interviews, the ethnographer begins to assert control. Topics are introduced, allowing the informant to expand freely upon their own point of view and knowledge. In more structured ethnographic interviews, topicality is more firmly shaped and directed by the fieldworker; informant responses move away from orations and free commentaries, and to more specific responses to questions.

(6) In the most focused form of interview, the ethnographer controls both turf and topicality as fully as possible. Questionnaires and interview schedules may be used, and the objective is to obtain particular types and pieces of data. These typically include household interviews, psychological tests, or reports of disputes, but may also encompass repeated interview sessions to secure lengthy life histories, with the anthropologist guiding the subject according to pre-set standards of scope and comprehensiveness.

The production of notes and records (Sanjek 1990: 92–121) begins to move the ethnographic process towards its ultimate written products. Focused interview sessions with seated informants often permit direct transcription of verbal statements. But in open-ended and ethnographic interviews, brief written notes – what Simon Ottenberg (in Sanjek 1990) terms *scratch notes* – are taken during the session, and these form the basis for the construction later of fuller written fieldnotes. Anthropologists often go through this two-step process even when interviews are tape recorded, both as a backup to and index of the taped session, and because of the analytic gains many ethnographers note in transforming their scratch notes into fuller descriptive fieldnotes.

In participant observation in natural settings, similar brief jottings may be inscribed, but major attention is directed to the event in progress. Often it is not even possible to record scratch notes, and both they and fuller fieldnote description occur later. Margaret Mead wrote about the nagging pressure to type-up fieldnotes from scratch notes, and about the danger of scratch notes growing 'cold' when this is delayed, even by one day. But she also wrote of the satisfaction of being caught up with this work, and of the importance for later ethnographic writing of the insights gained in moving from scratch notes to descriptive fieldnotes. Ottenberg sees this step as the interaction of scratch notes and *headnotes*, the stored memories and interpretations that arise from direct participant observation as filtered by the ethnographer's overall theoretical stance. Headnotes form an essential complement to fieldnotes (and to more formal fieldwork data sets, or records). Headnotes are employed to make sense of one's fieldnotes when they are reread later for ethnographic writing projects. The importance of headnotes is particularly evident when anthropologists attempt to use another ethnographer's fieldnotes, and quickly realize how difficult it is to understand them without any headnotes of their own.

Fieldnotes and records present ethnographers with great masses of information – hundreds, even thousands of pages – that may be arranged minimally in chronological order or by topic. Malinowski urged that fieldworkers constantly read and begin to organize their notes while still in the field, but more focused work on them ordinarily occurs when fieldwork is over. As ethnographers turn to ethnographic writing, they must readdress the theoretical discourse they turn away from in fieldwork. Fieldnotes and headnotes must now be related directly to the comparative and contextual points of the anthropological triangle.

On paper, two types of documents (each with many iterations and subdivisions) link fieldnotes and ethnographic writings. Book or article *outlines* key the writing process to comparative theoretical ideas and contextual data sources against which fieldnote evidence will be weighed and interpreted. *Indexes* of fieldnotes and records are refined to locate relevant data for the topics of concern in the writing outlines. The ethnographer then works back and forth along the fieldnote-index-outline-ethnography continuum. At the same time, considerations are made as to format, style, readership, manner of presentation, and direct use of fieldnotes and informant statements. These issues are considered both through emulation of admired models of ethnographic writing, and through attention to a critical literature on ethnographic writing that arose in the 1980s (Clifford 1983; Geertz 1988; Marcus and Cushman 1982; Sperber 1985). This *postmodernist concern with 'the crisis of representation' adds to earlier forms of ethnographic criticism that focus primarily on faults of contextualization and which have produced ever higher standards in historical, political-economic, ecological, demographic, statistical and legal backgrounding.

Beyond these textual and contextual critiques of ethnography, and those that address an ethnography's acknowledgement of, and relevance to, comparative theoretical work, there are also internal canons of validity by which ethnographic writing may be evaluated (Sanjek 1990: 393–404). The first of these is theoretical candour, the openness with which the ethnographer addresses the significant theories and the local theories of significance that structured the fieldwork process. A second canon calls for explicit depiction of the ethnographer's fieldwork path – the number of informants from whom information was obtained, in what ways, and their relationship both to the wider population the ethnography concerns and to each other. A third canon concerns information about the fieldnote evidence itself: not simply 'how much' and its basis in participant observation or interviews but more significantly the precise relationship of notes and records to the written ethnography. Some ethnographies utilize fieldnotes directly, even masses of them; others, for rhetorical or narrative purposes, do not, and need not. What matters in the end is that readers of an ethnography have a clear picture of what the ethnographer did and why, whom they talked to and learned from, and what they brought back to document it.

ROGER SANJEK

See also: Franz Boas, fieldwork, genealogical method, Bronislaw Malinowski, methodology, Lewis Henry Morgan, postmodernism

Further reading

Agar, M. (1980) *The Professional Stranger: An Informal Introduction to Ethnography*, New York: Academic Press

Clifford, J. (1983) 'On Ethnographic Authority', *Representations* 1(2): 118–46

Cushing, F.H. (1988 [1883]) *Zuni Fetishes*, Las Vegas: KC Publications

—— (1920) *Zuni Breadstuff*, New York: Museum of the American Indian

Evans-Pritchard, E.E. (1940) *The Nuer*, Oxford: Oxford University Press

Geertz, C. (1988) *Works and Lives: The Anthropologist as Author*, Stanford: Stanford University Press

Malinowski, B. (1922) *Argonauts of the Western Pacific*, New York: Dutton

Marcus, G.E. and D. Cushman (1982) 'Ethnographies as Texts', *Annual Review of Anthropology* 11: 25–69

Morgan, L.H. (1962 [1851]) *League of the Iroquois*, New York: Corinth

Rivers, W.H.R. (1906) *The Todas*, Cambridge: Cambridge University Press

Sanjek, R. (ed.) (1990) *Fieldnotes: The Makings of Anthropology*, Ithaca: Cornell University Press

Spencer, B. and F.J. Gillen (1968 [1899]) *The Native Tribes of Central Australia*, New York: Dover

Sperber, D. (1985) 'Interpretive Ethnography and Theoretical Anthropology' in *On Anthropological Knowledge*, Cambridge: Cambridge University Press

ethnopsychiatry

Origins and history

From its origins in the late eighteenth century, clinical psychiatry recognized that mental illness might be influenced, sometimes even caused, by a society's mores, roles and sentiments. Generally, the patterns of severe illness (psychosis) identified in European hospitals were taken as universal, whilst it was accepted that wide variations existed in everyday psychological functioning which could be attributed to *'race', *religion, *gender and *class. In the first explicitly cross-cultural comparison, the German hospital psychiatrist Emile Kraepelin (1904) concluded after a trip to Java that the illnesses which were found universally probably had a biological origin which determined their general form whilst local culture simply provided the variable content through which they manifested. He noted that local understandings could allocate the illness to categories quite different from those of Western medicine such as spirit *possession or a call to a *shamanic role; yet, like the military doctors of the European colonies (Littlewood and Lipsedge 1989), he was confident he could distinguish the universal from the particular when attributing atypical illness to 'a lower stage of evolutionary development'.

Locally recognized patterns which recalled mental illness but could not easily be fitted into Western nosologies were described as †'culture-bound syndromes' which represented a society's character: the *dhat* syndrome being the exaggeration of *Hindu preoccupations with purity; *amok* as a relic of precolonial patterns of redistributive justice; *witiko* as a *cannibalistic impulse consequent on scarcity of food and abrupt weaning of the Ojibwa child; the *kayak angst* of the Arctic solitude; *malignant anxiety* as the individual manifestation of Yoruba sorcery preoccupations; the perennially interesting *voodoo death* ('death by sorcery'); rarely, as with *pibloktoq* ('Arctic hysteria'), as a biological disease such as avitaminosis. Extensive lists of these syndromes were compiled, many now recognized as *folkloric curiosities whose actual behavioural occurrence seems doubtful, but which provided some variety to leaven the mundane tasks of colonial asylum administration. Between World War I and the 1950s, anthropological interest in mental illness was largely restricted to the American *culture and personality school which, following †Freud, emphasized variation in adult character and culture as originating in childrearing practices, and which had little interest in insanity. The standard procedure was to use psychoanalytical measures of personality across societies and relate the findings to levels of anxiety and sorcery accusations. Psychotic individuals occasionally appeared in the classic ethnographies (e.g. *Nuer Religion*) but with little comment, and those European anthropologists trained in clinical psychiatry or psychology (†Rivers, †C.G. Seligman, †Fortes, Carstairs, Field) generally followed psychoanalytical models in examining neurotic illness as an exaggerated form of cultural preoccupations: the cognitive and neurosociological interests of †Mauss excepted. The term 'ethnopsychiatry', coined by the Haitian psychiatrist Louis Mars in 1946 to refer to the local

presentation of psychiatric illness, was popularized in the 1950s by †Georges Devereux in his psychoanalytical study of the Mohave. Devereux, a Hungarian-French anthropologist (1961: 1–2), like Mars uses the term to refer to the medical study of illness in a particular community through looking at its 'social and cultural' setting, but he adds a new emphasis on 'the systematic study of the psychiatric theories and practices [of] an aboriginal group', comparing this to the then established procedures of †ethnobotany (see *ethnoscience). It is in this second sense that the term is now generally recognized. In some hundred papers and books Devereux examined such conventional culture and personality interests as the mental health of the shaman, homosexuality and *millenialism and *dreams, together with studies of suicide and abortion among the Plains Indians and classical Greeks.

In an extended debate with the medical historian Erwin Ackernecht, who objected to the psychoanalytic 'pathologisation of whole cultures' and preferred rather a simple comparison between local and Western ideas of illness, Devereux (1970) firmly privileged an etic (psychoanalytical) analysis, declaring shamans to be 'surrogate schizophrenics' on behalf of their community, insane in what he termed their 'ethnic unconscious' yet able to generate new ideas for their stressed fellows; he warned however that such solutions could only be irrational and lead to further 'catastrophic behaviour'. He later developed his theory of *complementarity*: whereby any cultural pattern could be understood simultaneously from both psychoanalytical and sociological directions, but in practice he reduced sociology to psychology. Devereux's ideas were taken to full development by La Barre who argued that all cultural innovators, successful or otherwise, have been schizophrenic. Psychiatric anthropology now favours Ackernecht's more modest approach: whilst shamans and other inspirational healers and leaders may on occasion be psychotic by Western criteria (at least when they experience their initial 'call'), practising shamans are rarely psychotic. Our etic (psychoanalytic or psychiatric) formulation may fit variously with *emic (local) categorizations of illness.

Devereux focused interest on the problem of etic/emic and normal/abnormal distinctions in psychiatry where, in contrast to *medical anthropology's more evident distinction between disease and illness, its analytical construct – mental illness

– was less evidently an object of observation in nature and indeed on examination appeared closely related to the ideological concerns of Western medicine. His associate Roger Bastide (1965: 9–12) restricted the term 'ethnopsychiatry' to the study of local conceptualizations which recalled those of Western psychiatry, and distinguished it from social psychiatry (the social context of a mentally ill person) and from the sociology of mental illness (its epidemiology and social causes). The latter two are now generally elided. It would be appropriate to see the various overlapping sub-disciplines as ranging from medical to anthropological interests, each marked by fluctuating popularity and influence: starting from the medical end with *epidemiology* and *social psychiatry*, through *comparative psychiatry*, *transcultural* and *cross-cultural psychiatry*, *cultural psychiatry*, and *anthropology and psychiatry*, *ethnopsychiatry* and †*cognitive anthropology*. This closely parallels the spectrum (and recent shift) from empirical cross-cultural psychology to interpretive psychological anthropology, psychoanalytical and evolutionary interest being replaced by ethnoscience with more detailed studies of the context and local meaning of the phenomena. The key issues, though, remain the same.

Are mental illnesses universal?

The epidemiologists of the 1950s to the 1970s, who carried out the first direct questionnaire-based cross-cultural comparisons, had remained influenced by psychoanalysis. They included the McGill group (Wittkower, Murphy, Prince) with its important journal, the *Transcultural Psychiatric Research Review* (Murphy 1980), the North American Society for the Study of Culture and Psychiatry (Lebra, Lin, Westermeyer, Tseng, Jilek, Wintrob), the French-influenced Dakar school (Collomb, Diop) and the Cornell-Aro (Nigeria) study by Leighton and Lambo. The more recent World Health Organization's international studies of schizophrenia and depression similarly use detailed questionnaires, standardized and back-translated, which are derived from Western descriptions. Like Kraepelin, they conclude that formal characteristics of severe psychotic illness can be identified universally and that these are ultimately biologically determined, although the better prognosis identified in non-Western societies may be attributed to local categorization and a less stigmatizing response. These studies do not include small-scale relatively isolated cultures among which psychosis has been argued to be rare

(Fortes, Seligman, Torrey). Recovery may be less likely in capitalist societies due to their delineation of full personhood through the performance of industrial roles (Fortes, †Warner). Arthur Kleinman, the leading American anthropological psychiatrist has argued that cross-cultural comparisons derived from Western criteria are in themselves inadequate, and that the full range of local meanings must always be explored before any comparison (Kleinman and Good 1985). 'Depression' for instance, with its connotation of some downward movement of the self, can be traced as a European idiom for distress only to the eighteenth century, and some alternative idiom of 'soul loss' seems to be more common outside the urban West. Whilst the form/content distinction is widely criticized, it remains debatable as to how in Kleinman's 'new cross-cultural psychiatry' we can derive practical comparative measures from a multiplicity of contexts and at which point local particularity can be ignored (Littlewood 1990). The official diagnostic manual of American psychiatry (DSM IV) now includes a brief cultural section on each category and a glossary of culture-bound syndromes written by ethnopsychiatrists; following recent anthropological and historical interest in Western psychiatry, many Western illnesses such as anorexia nervosa, post-traumatic stress disorder or drug overdoses are now regarded as somehow 'culture-bound'. Are eating disorders to be attributed to a recent 'fear of fatness' or are they rather just a variant of more general gender-based renunciations within the family? If, as Loudon argued, periodical rituals of symbolic inversion in Southern Africa are being 'replaced' by individual neurosis, what sort of social psychological analysis can simultaneously deal with both? Or with the reframing of Western 'hysteria' by the women's movement into a sort of political *resistance?

The mechanism of psychological healing

Psychotherapy has often been said to derive from traditional and religious healing patterns (Janet 1919), contemporary illnesses such as hysteria and multiple personality disorder being closely allied to spirit possession states. The efficacy of both Western ('cosmopolitan' or 'biomedical') medicine and local healing has been argued to be non-specific (empathy and suggestion: Frank) but others have favoured rather a close 'symbolic congruence' between affliction and shared social meanings (Dow, Torrey) or taken the illness as the individual representation of 'social tensions' in a pivotal individual (†Turner, I.M. Lewis, Littlewood). *Lévi-Strauss has proposed that whilst shamanic healing deploys communal myths, Western psychotherapy facilitates the development of private myths: recent interest in the political and gender history of psychoanalysis would argue against the latter assertion. Prince has argued that healing is just the systematization of existing coping styles. Phenomenological and semantic anthropologists (Kleinman, Good, Kapferer, Csordas) criticize the *essentialism implicit in a single notion of 'healing', and look rather at the particular reconstruction of self and agency in a performance of ritual, together with an interest in how both medical and local therapy can be reconfigured in the other context. Whilst Western psychotherapies are rarely available in developing countries, a number of local practices – shamanism, vision quests, fire walking, acupuncture, meditation, sweat lodges – have been assimilated into the 'human potential therapies' of metropolitan North America; whilst 'spirit possession' has emerged again as an acceptable diagnosis among evangelical Christian psychiatrists and social workers.

Somatization and the idioms of distress

That something like 'psychological conflict' may be expressed through bodily preoccupations and physical pain is commonly accepted, and was regarded by psychoanalysts as a primitive psychological defence against anxiety. 'Somatization' is now recognized by ethnopsychiatrists as occurring in all societies; the universal recognition of bodily illness makes pain an available idiom of distress, whether the affliction is to be considered analytically as more truly political or individual (Kleinman and Good 1985). Theoretical approaches to somatization derive from attribution theory and †systems theory, and from ethnoscience particularly its interest in local concepts of self and emotion (Marsella and White 1982), bringing the area close to the psychological anthropology of Shweder and D'Andrade in the United States, and Jahoda, A. Lock and Heelas in Britain. Debate continues in Britain and North America as to whether to take such concepts as actual psychological states, or else as social meanings – and thus, following Wittgenstein, whether we can distinguish the two. The *individual in ethnopsychiatry is now less some unity to which explanations are to be referred that the

embodied locus of contested meanings. A tension remains, as in other areas of contemporary social science, between those naturalistic approaches which emphasise causality and constraints on the individual (whether these are biological or cultural), and those personalistic approaches which emphasize representation, intentionality and instrumentality. In the case of self-starvation, drug overdoses and possession states, should we see these as reflections of male power or some disease process, or rather as active resistances and struggles for identity against the given constraints? Are mental illnesses expressing personal dilemmas or are they standardized strategies to enlist support and influence others (what Devereux called *chantage masochiste* – masochistic blackmail)? Breakdown or restitution? What has been lost from the earlier psychoanalytical approach is its easy conflation of naturalistic and personalistic, with its moralistic equation of health and value, together with the now unfashionable idea that psychopathology may not only be a personal creative act but may at times have a wider importance in social innovation (Littlewood 1990).

Clinically applied ethnopsychiatry

The work of Bateson and Turner has had a direct influence on family therapy and the newer 'expressive' European therapies. Psychiatric anthropologists increasingly work on health and development projects, refining epidemiological measures, evaluating community reception of mental illness, the attribution of responsibility, doctor-patient communications, the pathways into psychiatric care, networks of care and such Western 'cults of affliction' as Alcoholics Anonymous, the consequences of stigma, and the daily life of psychiatric institutions and patients, and have recently turned to record personal narratives of illness and mental handicap (Goffman, Estroff, Skultans, Janzen, Kleinman, Langness and Levine). A particular concern for European anthropologists has been the psychiatric care provided for ethnic minorities and, following the work of Mannoni and Fanon, the psychological consequences of racism, and how Western ideals of health and maturity replicate entrepreneurial values of the self-sufficient individual (Littlewood and Lipsedge 1989).

In the last decade ethnopsychiatry has been profoundly influenced by critical theory, the feminist health movement and by the studies in the epistemology and politics of psychiatry initiated by †Foucault. Against the North American 'critical medical anthropologists' (Singer, Scheper-Hughes, Taussig, M. Lock, Young) who have argued that much of ethnopsychiatry's interest in 'meaning' and 'communication' is intended to accommodate patients to medical treatment through co-opting their own beliefs, Gaines (1992) had objected that these Marxist theorists assert an empirical reality for mental illness more than they admit. He proposes to restrict the term 'ethnopsychiatry' to the study of local meanings alone, arguing that Western science is as much an ethnoscience as any other, and that its various national schools can be examined like other social institutions. How do ethnopsychiatrists deal currently with the naturalistic-personalistic dichotomy? The *Nouvelle Revue d'Ethnopsychiatrie* (France and Quebec) follows Devereux with an eclectic mix of psychoanalysis, biology and romantic ethnography. The interests of the United States and Kleinman's journal *Culture, Medicine and Psychiatry* have remained individualistic and psychological, always more 'cultural' than 'social', and now semantically focused and not easily distinguished from medical anthropology; the Canadians retain an interest in the psychobiology of trance and hypnosis, psychoactive substance use, and other altered states of consciousness; the British and Dutch remain theoretically close to general social anthropology but with a strong emphasis on conflict and on the mental health of minority groups. Increasing numbers of psychiatrists in other countries (Norway, Japan, South Africa, Australia, India, Brazil) and in the World Health Organization now incorporate anthropological critiques into their cultural and epidemiological studies. Psychoanalytical influences on ethnopsychiatry are increasingly marginal but remain significant in Latin American medical ethnography and in the 'cultural and media' studies inspired by Lacan and Kristeva.

ROLAND LITTLEWOOD

See also: culture and personality, emic and etic, medical anthropology, psychoanalysis, psychological anthropology, body, possession

Further reading

Bastide, R. (1965) *Sociologie des Maladies Mentales*, Paris: Flammarion
Devereux, G. (1961) *Mohave Ethnopsychiatry and Suicide: The Psychiatric Knowledge and the Psychic Disturbances of an Indian Tribe*, Washington: Smithsonian Institution
—— (1970) *Essais d'Ethnopsychiatrie Générale*, Paris: Gallimard
Gaines, A.D. (ed.) (1992) *Ethnopsychiatry: The Cultural Construction of Professional and Folk Psychiatries*, New York: State University of New York Press
Janet, P. (1919) *Les Médications Psychologiques*, Paris: Alcan
Kleinman, A. and B. Good (eds) (1985) *Culture and Depression: Studies in the Anthropology and Cross-cultural Psychiatry of Affect and Disorder*, Berkeley: University of California Press
Kraepelin, E. (1904) "Vergleichende Psychiatrie', trans. as 'Comparative Psychiatry' in S.R. Hirsch and M. Shepherd (eds) (1974) *Themes and Variations in European Psychiatry*, Bristol: Wright
Littlewood, R. (1990) 'From Categories to Contexts: A Decade of the New Cross-cultural Psychiatry', *British Journal of Psychiatry*, 156: 308–27
Littlewood, R. and Lipsedge, M. (1989) *Aliens and Alienists: Ethnic Minorities and Psychiatry*, revised edn, London: Routledge
Marsella, A.J. and White, G.M. (eds) (1982) *Cultural Conceptions of Mental Health and Therapy*, Dordrecht: Reidel
Murphy, H.B.M. (1982) *Comparative Psychiatry*, Berlin: Springer

ethnoscience

Ethnoscience, or the 'New Ethnography' as it was often called in the 1960s, consists of a set of methods for analysing indigenous systems of *classification, for example, of diseases, species of plants or types of food. Methods have changed through time. In the 1960s the heyday of ethnoscience, *componential analysis was the primary method through which ethnoscience was practised, and some practitioners regarded a description of the process of eliciting data and constructing the analysis as equally crucial to the exercise (e.g. Black 1969).

The realization that not all hierarchically-ordered classification systems are amenable to componential analysis had already, in the 1960s, led to the notion that some areas of culture and language were practical for ethnoscientific research and others were not. Thus early concerns concentrated on topics like *kinship and on those aspects of botany and zoology in which the components of meaning were quite transparent: e.g. the classification of animals within a species by age and sex, or the classification of species through a complex of differentiating anatomical characteristics.

One important early questioning of the notion of arbitrariness in the cultural classification of observable phenomena occurred in 1969, when Brent Berlin and Paul Kay reported that colours are distinguished in a set order which is universal for all cultures. This helped spur interest in the relation between cognitive categories and cognitive psychology, and even neuropsychology. Also from inside the field of ethnoscience, Roger Keesing (1972) challenged colleagues to rethink the 'new ethnography' they had modelled on the 'old linguistics'. For Keesing, the link between ethnoscience and structural linguistics had to be severed and a new one formed with the linguistic theories of †Noam Chomsky. From outside the field, the main critique of ethnoscience has come from those who favour †interpretive approaches to culture. †Clifford Geertz (1973), in particular, has argued against the formalism and †positivism of ethnoscience.

Over the past twenty years research in ethnoscience has moved closer to cognitive psychology, and in so doing, has jettisoned its former close link with linguistics (see, e.g. Atran 1993). Moreover, the primary focus today among many practitioners is in the way individuals, when as children, learn culture, rather than in the psychological validity of models constructed by anthropologists or linguists (see *emic and etic). Thus the old label 'ethnoscience' has taken on both new meanings and new methodologies. It nevertheless retains its association with methods designed to capture the ways of thought which make up cultural knowledge. It is just that these methods now seem set to find their touchstone less in formal structures of the lexicon *per se*, and more in thought processes which may in fact and indeed ironically, be more universal than culture-specific. If this is the case, then the old label may well have truly changed its meaning well beyond the intentions of its early practitioners.

ALAN BARNARD

See also: classification, componential analysis, emic and etic

Further reading

Atran, S. (1993) 'Whither "Ethnoscience"?', in P. Boyer (ed.), *Cognitive Aspects of Religious Symbolism*, Cambridge: Cambridge University Press
Berlin, B. and P. Kay (1969) *Basic Colour Terms: Their Universality and Evolution*, Berkeley: University of California Press
Black, M.B. (1969) 'Eliciting Folk Taxonomy in Ojibwa', in S.A. Tyler (ed.), *Cognitive Anthropology*, New York: Holt, Rinehart and Winston
Frake, C.O. (1980) *Language and Cultural Description: Essays by Charles O. Frake* (Selected and Introduced by Anwar S. Dil), Stanford: Stanford University Press
Geertz, C. (1973) 'Thick Description: Toward an Interpretive Theory Of Culture', in *The Interpretation of Cultures*, New York: Basic Books
Keesing, R.M. (1972) 'Paradigms Lost: The New Ethnography and the New Linguistics', *Southwestern Journal of Anthropology* 28: 299–331

Europe: Central and Eastern

Definitions and boundaries

Determining the precise boundaries of Central and Eastern Europe has been an awkward task for scholars and politicians alike. For the purposes of this entry the region is taken to comprise the German-speaking countries together with the large swathe of former socialist territory, the extremities of which are formed by Albania, Macedonia and Bulgaria in the south, the Baltic states in the north, and the Ural Mountains in the east.

Many fine lines can be drawn within this large area, e.g. between Germans and Slavs, between Eastern and Western *Christianity, between cultures of wine, of beer and of vodka. Each of these criteria may have significance for anthropology. But of course finer distinctions can always be drawn: within Western Christianity you have Catholics and Protestants, within Protestantism you have Lutherans and Calvinists, and so on. Moreover 'anomalous' groups such as Greek Catholics, found in several countries of the region and still numbering several millions, thoroughly subvert such line-drawing exercises.

It is rather more interesting to enquire into the subjective moral geography and the emotions that lie behind these boundaries. Lines bisecting the European continent longitudinally and latitudinally will cross in an obscure region of the Carpathian Mountains (a monument marks the alleged spot, at Jasinya in the Ukraine) where questions of national belonging remain confused and contested. The inhabitants of this region, often known as 'Sub-Carpathian Rus', are East Slavs. The most important element in their culture is Eastern Christianity, and few would wish to classify them as other than East European. The Hungarians are immediate neighbours of these 'Ruthenians', but Hungarians like to position themselves in 'East-Central Europe', and to imply a particularly sharp boundary between themselves and other neighbours to the southeast ('The Balkans'). East-West stereotypes have figured prominently among the Southern Slavs (especially Serbs against Croats), but they have also emerged with surprising strength within Germany in the years since reunification. Europe itself has become a key symbol, and following the collapse of communism, many countries of this region have seen vigorous debates concerning their proper relation to it.

Ethnicity and nationalism

The political map of this region has been redrawn several times during the last 150 years. After the disappointments of the 'springtime of nations' in 1848, Bismarck's united Germany became the region's first modern state and in spite of all the twentieth-century vicissitudes it has remained the most powerful. Ottoman and Habsburg Empires did not last long into the present century. With the collapse of the socialist supra-national states, the triumph of *nationalist ideology now appears complete: the political boundaries are, more than ever before, congruent with those of the nation.

A good deal of the ethnographic work in this region since the nineteenth century has been undertaken in the service of nationalism, sometimes very explicitly. The task of the scholar was to document an authentic folk culture worthy of veneration by the members of the *'nation-state'. The national museums and folk dance theatres found throughout the region are clear testimony that this political ambition was met. At the same time there is much in the work of native ethnographers that, carefully interpreted, does not support exaggerated focus on the boundedness of the nation. Many ethnographers have emphasized the distinctiveness of small localities; others have pointed to interconnectedness over very large areas, so that 'national ethnography' was never a completely rigid strait-jacket. In many parts of the region these traditions have been explicitly challenged, as ethnographers (increasingly preferring to style themselves anthropologists) have subjected the work of their predecessors and some of the core symbols of the nation to rigorous critique. However, perhaps the most devastating critique remains that of †Ernest Gellner, whose 1983 outline of 'Ruritania' parodies a general type of Eastern European nationalism. For Gellner, whatever the rhetoric of 'awakening' that intellectuals use, the nations are in fact 'invented' to comply with the requirements of industrial social organization. However, this model perhaps needs some modification if it is to account for the spread of nationalism in this region, which contains a good number of 'old' nations and 'high' cultures alongside other countries where the degree of intellectual fabrication was necessarily somewhat greater.

Even after the recent transformations, Central and Eastern Europe – Gellner's ideal type of cultural homogeneity within state boundaries – remains only a distant aspiration. The populations of large border regions such as Silesia and Transylvania remain mixed, and the potential for reviving long-standing antagonisms is everpresent. Other awkward groups are scattered throughout the region. *Gypsies, having resisted socialist attempts at assimilation, have been a renewed target of ethnic or racial abuse in the years after communist collapse. The Jews, their main long-term rivals for the scapegoat role in this region, had been largely eliminated by the middle of the twentieth century. (Some interesting work is continuing, particularly at the Jagiellonian University in Cracow, on the nature of past Jewish relations with other ethnic and national groups.)

At the same time, as elsewhere in Europe, some new minorities have appeared on the scene. In the economically most developed German areas the presence of 'guest workers' and their dependents, particularly Muslim Turks, has already attracted anthropological attention (from Werner Schiffauer, Lale Yalcin-Heckmann and others). In general, anthropological effort, as elsewhere in Europe, has tended to focus on the peripheral and marginal, but some have begun to examine the identities of majorities, including that of contemporary Germans. The region as a whole remains an exciting testing ground for theories of *ethnicity and *identity. In one extraordinary development, the efforts of Paul Robert Magocsi, a Canadian professor, to create a new nation for the Ruthenians suggest that nineteenth-century recipes may still be appropriate in what Gellner terms the 'East European time zone'.

It is not always recognized that tendencies towards a 'Fortress Europe' in the West have themselves been partially responsible for accentuating divisive nationalisms in the former socialist territories. Anthropological investigations of such forces have scarcely begun (but see Goddard et. al. 1993). Nor is there much sign that anthropological expertise has been utilized by political decision-takers in places where ethnic tension has been most extreme, such as Bosnia, Kosova and Transylvania.

Peasantry and underdevelopment

With perhaps a few debatable exceptions, notably the 'tribal' structures described by Hasluck, Whitaker and others for Albania, the inhabitants of most of this region qualify for that loose term: *peasant. Peasantries were usually called upon to provide the *folklore sources for the constructions of new nationalisms, but close attention has also been paid to the more prosaic socio-economic characteristics of peasant farming. This work, although mainly carried out by other specialists, has had some impact on *economic anthropology and *development studies. The contrasting interpretations of the pre-revolutionary Russian peasantry offered by A.V. Chayanov and V.I. Lenin have each inspired anthropological emulation. Chayanov emphasized the fact that inter-household inequality was influenced by demographic composition and by what †Fortes later labelled the †developmental cycle of the domestic group. His arguments were reworked by †Sahlins for a rather different range of societies in the guise of the †domestic mode of production. Meanwhile Lenin sought to explain the same statistical inequalities in terms of *class polarization. Adjudication is difficult in the absence of any satisfying anthropological studies from this period, but Shanin's (1972) careful assessment suggests that Chayanov won the intellectual argument, if not the short-term political one.

As in other parts of the continent, rural family organization in Central and Eastern Europe has continued to attract considerable anthropological attention. Some demographers have proposed a great East-West divide in patterns of *marriage and *household formation, the frontier consisting of a line running approximately from Trieste to Saint Petersburg, but this would appear to be a dangerous oversimplification in the light of the evidence available to date. There are dangers in this field too of exaggerating apparently exotic features of the Eastern region: for example, in the considerable attention that has been bestowed on extended families (the *zadruga*) in a particular period of 'Balkan' history.

Altogether, the historical formation of peasantries in this region is a process of enormous interest, but not yet sufficiently understood. In some cases the patterns are clearly the more or less direct consequences of ecological circumstances: see, for example, the Alpine studies of Cole and Wolf (1974), Netting (1981), and the comparative volume of Viazzo (1989), all of which make effective use of historical data. Peasantries in the region also frequently bear the marks of changing political circumstances: for example, Poland's agrarian structure today still shows the signs of the generations during which the country was partitioned between the very different powers of Russia, Prussia and Austria. But a case can also be made for the proposition that the region as a whole was adversely affected by the onset of commercial expansion, increased urbanization and industrialization in the West. From this perspective, Eastern Europe was a prototype for what later became known as the 'Third World': even earlier than other parts of the European periphery, it was the first region to be systematically *under*developed by *capitalism.

Socialism and the aftermath

It is useful to bear in mind this legacy of underdevelopment when assessing the achievements of the socialist period. We have a number of studies by anthropologists from Western countries, very unevenly spread across the region. The outstanding study of a Soviet-type collective farm was made outside this region; but Caroline Humphrey's Buratian study (1983) still has much to offer East Europeanists. Many of the community studies in Eastern Europe focused on altogether looser forms of collective agriculture (particularly in Hungary), or on the countries which avoided Soviet-style collectivization altogether – Poland and Yugoslavia. Hann developed a comparative approach to the study of rural transformation in Poland and Hungary: in spite of the impact of collectivization on his property rights, the Hungarian farmer in fact benefited substantially from well-integrated processes of rural development in the late socialist period, in contrast to the stagnation and political deadlock experienced in Poland. Hungarian success in combining small-scale farming (organized in Chayanovian manner by the family) with large-scale socialist enterprises was unmatched elsewhere in the region. It proved to be short-lived following the collapse of socialist power, when the pressures for decollectivization accentuated rural instability throughout the region.

Despite the obvious importance of socialism for this region it has only rarely been made the explicit focus of anthropological investigation. Yet it is precisely through the ideologies and practices of socialism that much of this region has obtained a measure of unity in recent generations. We do not really know how deeply this new culture penetrated. It is clear that it did not dissolve a number of older ethno-national conflicts, and it may even have accentuated them in some places. But as to the impact of socialist ideals, symbols and rituals on the generations for whom they were central features of *socialization, anthropological knowledge is thin. Some of the best studies of *ritual, both its manipulation from above and its availability in strategies of *resistance from below) have been made in Romania by Gail Kligman (e.g. 1989). Other American anthropologists have addressed the specifically socialist character of Ceausescu's Romania more directly. Steven Sampson's (1984) investigation of settlement policies and grass roots political mobilization shows how anthropological work can help to demolish some of the familiar 'totalitarian' stereotypes. David Kideckel has contributed a valuable historical community study in the same region (1993). Katherine Verdery (1991) moves beyond the conventional limitations of the community study in her work on the intellectual producers of nationalist ideology in the last years of the dictatorship. She also attempts in this work to elaborate a general model of socialism that draws on the critiques offered by 'dissident' intellectuals themselves (but see also Hann 1994).

Conclusions

It is difficult to speak of any coherent regional tradition in the work that has been done so far on Central and Eastern Europe by anthropologists from outside the region. No doubt problems of access and the general political climate of the Cold War decades play some part in explaining the relatively meagre harvest of this period (though much valuable work has been continued by the local heirs to the traditions of national ethnography). Those who have worked in Eastern Europe reflect the general fashions in the discipline, and it is perhaps ironic that the influence of *Marxism and of *political economy approaches has been particularly strong. Surprisingly, though few of the monographs to date can be regarded as truly outstanding, the position is more favourable if one considers the medium of *film. There have been fine programmes in Granada Television's *Disappearing World* series on Hungarian Rom (Michael Stewart), a Moslem-Croat village in Bosnia (Tone Bringa) and Albanian villagers in the throes of decollectivization (Berit Backer).

Overall, the contribution to international social and cultural anthropology of scholars with roots in Eastern Europe – *Boas, *Malinowski, †Polanyi, †Nadel, Gellner etc. – far exceeds the contribution to date of general anthropology to the study of this region. It is well worth exploring how far the approaches of such scholars derive from their roots in this region: for example, Gellner (1988) has argued that Malinowski's synchronic functionalism is related at least in part by his Polish cultural nationalism in the days when no Polish state existed.

Whether or not this is so, social anthropologists will certainly need to transcend their Malinowskian anti-history heritage as they grapple to understand the region's current problems. The †substantivist approach of Polanyi might serve them rather better as they explore the implementation of a caricatured 'Western free market economy' in the present 'transitional' period. Certainly it is already clear that the enthusiasm that greeted the demise of socialism was far greater outside the region than within it. Some important work in progress is focusing on the cultural misunderstandings which hinder the effective deployment of Western 'aid' to the region; echoing the conclusions of many Third-World studies, Janine R. Wedel has found that some American aid to Poland is totally inappropriate, serving the strategies of donor country rather than the needs of the recipient. Over the longer term, foreign anthropologists in this region, like the aid donors, would be well advised to heed rich traditions of indigenous knowledge, and to work with local researchers whenever possible. They should also be prepared to use the excellent archival and other documentary sources, for which there are good precedents in the literature on this region (e.g. Thomas and Znaniecki 1918–20), in order to address important issues of cultural transmission. High on this agenda must be the dissemination and transmission of the contemporary culture associated with socialism.

C.M. HANN

See also: Russian and Soviet anthropology, history and anthropology, Marxism and anthropology

Further reading

Cole, J.W. and E.R. Wolf (1974) *The Hidden Frontier; Ecology and Ethnicity in an Alpine Valley*, New York: Academic Press

Gellner, E. (1983) *Nations and Nationalism*, Oxford: Blackwell

—— 1988 '"Zeno of Cracow" or "Revolution at Nemi",
or The Polish Revenge: A Drama in Three Acts' in
R. Ellen *et. al.* (eds) *Malinowski between Two Worlds; The
Polish Roots of an Anthropological Tradition*, Cambridge:
Cambridge University Press: 164–94

Goddard, V., J. Llobera and C. Shore (eds) (1993)
Anthropology of Europe: Identity and Boundaries in Conflict,
Oxford: Berg

Hann, C.M. (1985) *A Village Without Solidarity; Polish
Peasants in Years of Crisis*, New Haven: Yale University
Press

—— (ed.) (1993) *Socialism: Ideals, Ideologies and Local
Practice*, London: Routledge

—— (1994) 'After Communism: Reflections on East
European Anthropology and the Transition', *Social
Anthropology*, 2 (3): 229–49

Humphrey, C. (1983) *Karl Marx Collective; Economy, Society
and Religion in a Siberian Collective Farm*, Cambridge:
Cambridge University Press

Kideckel, D.I. (1993) *The Solitude of Collectivism: Romanian
Villagers to the Revolution and Beyond*, Ithaca, NY: Cornell
University Press

Kligman, G. (1988) *The Wedding of the Dead; Ritual, Poetics
and Popular Culture in Transylvania*, Berkeley: University
of California Press

Magocsi, P.R. (1993) *Historical Atlas Of East Central Europe*,
Seattle: University of Washington Press

Netting, R. McC. (1981) *Balancing on an Alp; Ecological
Change and Continuity in a Swiss Mountain Community*,
Cambridge: Cambridge University Press

Sampson, S.L. (1984) *National Integration through Socialist
Planning; An Anthropological Study of a Romanian New
Town*, Boulder, CO: East European Monographs

Shanin, T. (1972) *The Awkward Class: The Political Sociology
of Peasantry in a Developing Society: Russia, 1910–25*,
Oxford: Clarendon Press

Thomas, W.I. and F. Znaniecki (1918–20) *The Polish
Peasant in Europe and America* (2 vols), Boston: Richard
G. Badger

Verdery, K. (1991) *National Ideology under Socialism: Identity
and Cultural Politics in Ceausescu's Romania*, Berkeley:
University of California Press

Viazzo, P.P. (1989) *Upland Communities: Environment,
Population and Social Structure in the Alps since the Sixteenth
Century*, Cambridge: Cambridge University Press

Europe: North

Northern Europe includes Great Britain, Ireland,
Northern France, Belgium, the Netherlands,
Germany, Denmark, Sweden, Norway, Finland
and Iceland. This group of countries is significant
in a number of ways, being mostly characterized
by long histories of maritime trade, upon which
were founded the early development of modern
urban industrial economies associated with the
secularization of society, the rise of scientific
†positivism and *colonial claims upon overseas
territories. Anthropology, as the empirical study
of other peoples, had its origins in the conjuncture
of philosophical liberalism, economic self-interest
and developing forms of political control in
Northern Europe in the eighteenth and nineteenth
centuries. Yet this region, the principal source of
post-Enlightenment Western influence elsewhere
in the world, also contains its own semi-colonized
peripheries: Brittany, Ireland, Wales and Scotland
(the 'Celtic fringe'), and Finland, Northern
Sweden, Norway and Iceland (the 'northern
fringe').

Anthropology, ethnology, folklore and social history

In most of these countries (Britain is the main
exception) †ethnology is the leading discipline
which is concerned with own-society anthropological studies. In general terms, ethnology as a
university subject, *museum profession and
research field arose in the nineteenth century and
is associated with ideologies of nationhood as
embodied in cultural history. The focus is upon
studies of 'the folk'. In practice, this has traditionally meant *peasant cultures and rural history.
In some countries, ethnology also encompasses
*folklore and social history more generally. Each
country has a distinctive national style, more or
less populist in character, informed by its own
charter texts. Rural peasant historical studies
continue to be made, but the field is increasingly
enlivened by infusions of theoretical ideas drawn
from contemporary cultural and social anthropology; and there are new interests in processes
of urbanization and *class formation (e.g. studies
of 'working-class culture'), and contemporary
popular culture and social movements which
borrow from *political economy, historical
demography and *sociology. Ethnological work is
normally published in the national language in
national journals and other local outlets. While
relatively little appears internationally in other
languages, this should not be taken as an absence
of a substantial corpus of knowledge of a broadly
anthropological kind, with which any socio-
cultural anthropologist proposing to initiate
research in a Northern European country will
need to become familiar.

Social and cultural anthropology, whose central
features are *Malinowskian *fieldwork and a set
of (largely Anglo–American) charter texts, is a

somewhat later and unevenly-distributed development. Already well established as a field of academic enquiry in Britain by the 1920s, its growth elsewhere in Northern Europe was slower; the establishment of specialized departments of anthropology in Scandinavia, the Netherlands, Germany, Belgium and France occurred mainly after 1950; they remain, compared with Britain and the United States, relatively few in number. Some departments had their origins in the colonial encounter and postwar traumas of decolonization, and may include *development studies. Others had their origins in purely scholarly interests in foreign cultures, and may include regional studies. Ethnology and anthropology are related in varied ways. In Germany, for example, social and cultural anthropologists are normally located within departments of comparative ethnology; in France, both within ethnology departments and in specialized departments of anthropology. In Scandinavia and the Netherlands, specialized departments were founded; in places, anthropologists conventionally do not infringe upon the academic territory of their colleagues in ethnology departments: anthropologists work overseas, while fieldwork within the country is usually done by ethnologists or visiting foreign anthropologists. See Boissevain and Verrips (1989) for an account of anthropology in the Netherlands. Gullestad (1989) and Gerholm and Gerholm (1990) describe developments in the anthropology and ethnology of Scandinavia.

The anthropology of Northern Europe

†Arensberg and Kimball's study of County Clare in Ireland was, if not the first of its kind in Europe, the most influential in initiating a new genre of *ethnography: the study of the 'traditional' rural *community within a modern European *nation-state, approached through Malinowskian fieldwork. There was more than a hint of †Redfield's *great and little traditions in Arensberg and Kimball's work, which continued to have echoes in subsequent treatments of Irish rural life. Family and Community in Ireland (1940) was the progenitor of more than a dozen monographs on rural Ireland. Yet Ireland remained an exceptional case for a longish period. While a number of similar, local ethnographic studies were being made elsewhere in Europe (principally Spain, southern France, the Alps, Italy and Greece), Northern Europe was largely ignored until the late 1960s. Until then, a sparse anthropological interest was mainly confined to the Celtic and northern

fringes of the region. The region seemed to hold few attractions to visiting anthropologists, perhaps because it was thought to be too familiar, or it was perceived as the already-well-established preserve of sociologists and ethnologists; moreover, the anthropologists then being trained in these countries were being firmly directed towards Africa, Asia, Latin America or Mediterranean Europe. As late as 1950, a certain British university denied a PhD to a candidate at least partly on the grounds that since the fieldwork for the thesis had been carried out in Scotland, it could not be considered as an appropriate work of social anthropology. Anthropology 'at home' had not yet become generally accepted.

There were some exceptions, however. In Britain, there was, notably, James Littlejohn's *Westrigg: The Sociology of a Cheviot Parish* (1963), based on fieldwork between 1949 and 1951; Ronald Frankenberg's *Village on the Border* (1957); and Rosemary Harris's *Prejudice and Tolerance in Ulster* (1972), based mainly upon a study carried out in 1952–53: all three were by 'native' anthropologists working on the geographical fringes of Britain. There were urban studies, also: †Raymond Firth's *Two Studies of Kinship in London* (1956), followed by his pupil Elizabeth Bott's highly influential book *Family and Social Network* (1957). In Norway, Gutorm Gjessing's *Changing Lapps: A Study of Culture Relations in Northernmost Norway* (1954) was another early example of 'at home' anthropology on the northern fringe, as was †Fredrik Barth's *The Role of the Entrepreneur in Social Change in Northern Norway* (1963). Visiting anthropologists making early 'parallel' studies included the Americans John and Dorothy Keur (*The Deeply Rooted: A Study of a Drents Community in the Netherlands*, 1955), Robert and Barbara Anderson (*The Vanishing Village: A Danish Maritime Community*, 1964), and John Messenger (*Inis Beag, Isle of Ireland*, 1969). The British social anthropologist John Barnes based his famous paper, in which *network analysis was first elaborated, on his fieldwork in Bremnes ('Class and Committees in a Norwegian Island Parish', Human Relations 7: 39–58, 1954); and Robert Paine's *Coast Lapp Society II: A Study of Economic Development and Social Values* appeared in 1965.

With the growth of anthropology in the late 1960s, and the questioning of the dominant paradigms, much new work in Northern Europe was stimulated, raising important new issues which fed back into anthropological thinking generally. One of these issues concerned the place of *history in anthropological explanation; another raised the problem of *reflexivity in the practice of ethnography. While previous generations of anthropologists had been enjoined to ignore history and were enabled to do so because anthropology was mainly in the business of studying societies that lacked *literacy, no anthropologist working in Northern Europe from the late 1960s onward was able to behave as if he or she had just discovered a tribe without history, unknown to the Western world. Such communities, even if rural villages, were unquestionably at the centre of the Western world, incorporated within its histories and encompassed within the overlapping orbits of scholarly knowledge by which Europeans knew themselves. Whatever the anthropologist working in Northern Europe wrote would be read and tested not only by a wide range of local experts and scholars in adjacent fields, but also by the informants themselves. Anthropologists of non-literate or semi-literate tribal or peasant societies were unlikely to have as many people looking over their shoulders, questioning and probing their analyses.

Fieldwork in the anthropologist's own *culture, or 'parallel' cultures (Hastrup in Jackson 1987), have thrown up a number of *methodological and ethical problems which are not encountered in anything like the same degree in exotic-society fieldwork. Fluency and literacy in the language are more critical, freedom to impose or negotiate the conventional role of stranger is much more restricted if not entirely absent, †participant observation is highly problematic as in practice subject and object merge, and there are sharp limits upon what can be reported and how it can be said without provoking the antipathy of local people well able to judge for themselves the appropriateness of what is written about them (Strathern in Jackson 1987).

Coverage of the region – in readily-available work published in English – remains, however, surprisingly sparse and extremely uneven. The Celtic and northern fringes continue to be disproportionately represented, while anthropological ethnographies dealing with northern France (apart from Celtic Brittany), Belgium, Germany and Sweden are scarce, and mostly in the form of scattered journal articles or chapters in collections. There are some curious paradoxes. For example, the lively interest in own-society ethnography in the Netherlands, a good deal of which is published in English, contrasts sharply with the situation only a few miles to the east, in Germany, where very few ethnographic accounts have appeared in languages other than German.

Over Europe as a whole, there is a striking imbalance in anthropological interest between the south and the north: of those members of the European Association of Social Anthropologists who stated their ethnographic region in the 1992 EASA Register, more than twice as many were working in Mediterranean Europe as Northern Europe (106:51). Of those with interests in Northern Europe, more than half (28:51) were working in Britain and Ireland. Less than two dozen of EASA's 900 members specifically identified Belgium, Germany, the Netherlands or the Nordic countries as their primary areas of ethnographic interest. The proportions are similar among the nearly 8,000 anthropologists listed in recent editions of the AAA Guide.

Recent trends have been tending towards historically-situated accounts of localities and questions of local and ethnic *identity. In Britain and Ireland, the work of Alan Macfarlane (*The Origins of English Individualism*, 1978), Marilyn Strathern (*Kinship at the Core*, 1981), and Anthony Cohen (*Belonging*, 1982 and *Symbolising Boundaries*, 1986) have informed much subsequent work and are essential reading. Other works in English giving a good general introduction to anthropological studies in Northern Europe include Martine Segalen's historical treatment of French rural life (*Fifteen Generations of Peasants*, 1991); Sandra Wallman's study of modern urban families, *Eight London Households* (1984); Marianne Gullestad's *Kitchen Table Society* (1984), giving an account of ordinary women in Oslo; Ray Abrahams's study of family farming in Finland, *A Place of their Own* (1991); Paul Durrenberger and Gísli Pálsson's collection of papers on modern Icelandic society, *The Anthropology of Iceland* (1989) and Kirsten Hastrup's *Nature and Policy in Iceland 1400–1800* (1990). Anthony Jackson's collection, *Anthropology at Home* (1987) contains useful papers on the methodological and ethical problems of own-society and parallel-society research.

There are as yet no theoretical or ethnographic syntheses of the region as a whole. Volumes of collected papers on the anthropology of Europe, of which there have been several, are heavily biased towards the south. John Davis's *People of the Mediterranean* (1977) has no equivalent in Northern Europe. Such a synthesis is long overdue.

REGINALD BYRON

See also: British anthropology, French anthropology, German and Austrian anthropology, reflexivity, ethnicity, community, history and anthropology, identity, Occidentalism.

Further reading

Boissevain, J. and J. Verrips (1989) *Dutch Dilemmas: Anthropologists Look at the Netherlands*, Assen: Van Gorcum

Cohen, A.P. (1982) *Belonging: Identity and Social Organisation in British Rural Cultures*, Manchester: Manchester University Press

Gerholm, L. and T. Gerholm (1990) 'The Cultural Study of Scandinavia: Where are the Frontiers?', *Anthropological Journal of European Cultures 1* (1): 83–108

Golde, G. (1975) *Catholics and Protestants: Agricultural Modernization in Two German Villages*, New York: Academic Press

Gullestad, M. (1989) 'Small Facts and Large Issues: The Anthropology of Contemporary Scandinavian Society', *Annual Reviews in Anthropology* 18: 71–93

Jackson, A. (ed.) (1987) *Anthropology at Home*, London: Tavistock

McDonald, M. (1989) *'We are not French!' Language, Culture and Identity in Brittany*, London: Routledge

Europe: South

Southern Europe designates those areas bordering on the Mediterranean Sea and their hinterlands – Italy, Greece, Southern France, Southern and Eastern Spain, Albania and the Adriatic coast of former Yugoslavia. Portugal is also usually included even though it does not have a Mediterranean coastline. Anthropologists have in the past grouped Southern Europe together with Western Turkey, the Levant and the north shore of Africa and studied it as part of a broader Mediterranean region. Now that most Southern European countries have become members of the European Union, anthropologists may decide to re-situate them in the context of Western Europe. To focus on Southern Europe apart from the south shore of the Mediterranean is to consider a variety of societies where *Christianity predominates and where there is a common economic and political orientation towards Northern Europe. It is also to study a range of countries that possessed illustrious ancient civilizations, but which have become politically weak states, almost all of which have been governed by military dictatorships at some point in this century.

Oxford beginnings

The anthropological study of Southern European societies got off to a belated start, perhaps because Europe seemed too familiar and its study potentially too much like *sociology. Among the first full-length ethnographies of Mediterranean societies to appear were Julian Pitt-Rivers's *People of the Sierra* (1954) and John Campbell's *Honour, Family and Patronage* (1964), studies of a Spanish village and a Greek shepherding community respectively. Both Pitt-Rivers and Campbell were attached to the Institute of Social Anthropology at Oxford University and were influenced by the †structural-functionalism of the Oxford professor †Evans-Pritchard, as indeed a great many anthropologists were at the time. Many of the early ethnographies of Southern European societies were, in fact, clearly modelled on Evans-Pritchard's *The Nuer*. In exposition they began with considerations of environment and agricultural production, and then proceeded through politics, *kinship and *marriage, moral values and ultimately to *religion. In a memoir of his mid-1950s fieldwork among the Sarakatsani of Northern Greece, Campbell (1992) has acknowledged that *The Nuer* was one of the few books he took with him into the field.

The number of anthropological studies has mushroomed since the 1960s and it now seems that there is hardly a province in Southern Europe which has not been researched. There has, however, been a change in orientation since the first ethnographies. The holistic ideal of the early monographs has been abandoned in favour of studies focusing on particular cultural or political phenomena with ethnographic background material supplied in briefer form and only in so far as it illuminates the central issue. There have been studies of refugees in Cyprus and Athens, local Catholicism in Spain, ritual funeral lamentation in Greece, and migrant labourers and their families in Portugal to name just a few themes.

The Mediterranean as a culture area

As the number of separate village studies mounted in the 1960s anthropologists began to contemplate whether Mediterranean societies could be considered a cultural area. What, if any, were the common features of Southern European societies?

An early contribution to this endeavour was made by the social historian Fernand Braudel ([1949] 1972) who, in the course of a study of sixteenth-century Mediterranean politics and commerce, outlined the geographical and environmental features common to both the north and south shores of the Mediterranean. He pointed to a characteristic climate of hot summers and mild, wet winters that dictated regularities in agriculture, herding and fishing. Furthermore, a common topography of coastal plains closely backed by rugged mountains made for similarities in the structure of habitation and in the interchanges between coastal towns and mountain villages. The ports were wide open to external influences but historically vulnerable to malaria and piracy by contrast with the isolated mountain villages which conserved traditional patterns of agricultural and craft production.

Defining the Mediterranean ecologically as, for instance, all the places where the olive grows, was unlikely to satisfy the social scientific aspirations of anthropologists. They looked instead to social and cultural features common to all Mediterranean societies. For Southern Europe the following catalogue of socio-cultural consistencies has emerged: an unreformed brand of Christianity (Catholicism or Eastern Orthodoxy); a bilateral †kindred often extended by the establishment of ritual kinship conferred on baptismal and wedding sponsors (*compadrazgo); elaborated cults of patron saints; an analogous dependence on the influence of political *patrons; beliefs in the jealous power of the evil eye; and a characteristic gender-based division of labour and morality, labelled the *'honour and shame' complex.

This last complex received extensive comparative treatment (Peristiany 1966) and was held up as evidence for a common set of Mediterranean values. Men displayed and defended honour through swagger, the performance of pride, and sometimes real acts of *violence. Women, by contrast, did not possess honour themselves, but by behaving in a controlled and modest way – staying home as much as possible, if out, avoiding the male gaze by walking with eyes cast downward – they displayed a personal shame, which defended the family against a larger collective shame.

What is perhaps still more suggestive of a Mediterranean cultural unity is the consistency of language, imagery and gesture surrounding honour and shame. Everywhere from Greece to Southern Portugal societies have elaborated a vocabulary predicated on the symbolism of sheep and goats to refer to sexual behaviour (Blok 1981). Sheep are more docile and economically valuable,

while goats are seen to be more difficult, insatiable and have a lower market value. These associations seem to have been recognized already in New Testament times (Matt. 25: 32). In the contemporary Mediterranean it is men, rather than 'saved', who are equated with sheep, or more particularly rams, while women are aligned with goats. A man who has been cuckolded is equated to a goat (e.g. Spanish cabrón), especially if he knowingly tolerates the situation. This association may also be gesturally conveyed by the extension of index and baby finger into the figure of goat horns (in Italian cornuto, in Greek keratás). This gesture is universally taken as an insult or curse in Southern European societies; and it may also be employed to ward off the evil eye, perhaps because it insults and thus pre-empts this humanly sent force.

Compelling as the honour and shame complex appears in the argument for Mediterranean cultural unity, it has not been accepted by all anthropologists (Gilmore 1987). They point out that this pattern of gendered behaviour is not unique to the Mediterranean, and that it may be contradicted within the Mediterranean itself where some communities value modest, lawabiding men most highly. The prominent Mediterraneanist Michael Herzfeld (1984) has objected to the very goal of establishing 'cultural areas' because it produces stereotypes and he has sharply criticized the formation of analytical categories such as honour and shame, and the evil eye. In place of a regional focus. Herzfeld advocates rigorous, particularistic ethnographic research which is then theorized according to central anthropological concerns and global ethnographic data. His objection does not, however, do away with the broad synchronic distribution around the Mediterranean of highly similar ideas, customs and gestures.

History and process in Southern Europe

Undoubtedly the most systematic attempt to compare and contrast Southern European societies is John Davis's *People of the Mediterranean* (1977) which takes into account all the ethnographic data published before 1975. Davis includes Levantine and North African societies in his survey and he is one of the few anthropologists to have fulfilled the early ideal of conducting field research on both shores of the Mediterranean. He views the Mediterranean as primarily a geographical area within which there has been a significant amount of commerce, conquest, conversation and connubium. Over several millennia these interactions have contributed to the formation of overlapping, shared customs and forms of social organization, but not to a pan-Mediterranean core of common cultural features. He stresses that these are matters of historical process and urges anthropologists to increase the historical depth of their studies. Southern European societies have long been literate and there is no sense in treating them as early anthropologists treated pre-literate African and Melanesian communities.

Davis's view may be seen as qualifying our conception of Southern Europe as a cultural area, rather than as a rejection of the idea altogether. Instead of searching for essential cultural traits and timeless beliefs amongst Mediterranean societies, anthropologists have begun to see similarities as common responses to parallel structural situations – constraints such as the Braudelian ecological factors, relative poverty, or modern political and economic dependency on northern Europe. In resisting forces of domination and attempting to ameliorate their conditions, Southern European countries have often responded in similar ways, but these are temporary and contingent similarities in strategy which can and do change; they are not indelible cultural properties. The recognition of factors such as agency, contestation and historical process avoids the pitfall of cultural stereotyping potentially posed by the cultural area concept.

Amoral familism

The example of †amoral familism may be used to illustrate the differences between earlier and recent approaches to Southern European societies. The American sociologist Banfield (1958) coined the term 'amoral familism' on the basis of his research in South Italy to define a characteristic Mediterranean peasant †'ethos', a 'fundamental view of the world', which held that an individual's primary responsibility was towards his or her family. This ethos meant that public projects or initiatives which might benefit the whole community – agricultural co-operatives, the establishment of volunteer ambulance services – were usually scorned and never implemented. Banfield saw amoral familism as impeding *modernization.

A corollary of this idea was the 'image of †limited good' thesis advanced by Foster (1965), who contended that Southern European peasants, like *peasants elsewhere, considered 'goods' – both

moral and material valuables, everything from friendship and honour to property – to exist in a finite quantity within the local community. Individuals or families, therefore, only increased their store of goods at the expense of neighbours and co-villagers. Foster held that this worldview blocked progress because peasants did not hold to a model of hard work and progress, but believed instead that their fortunes were matters of 'fate'. In any case, hard work and manifest ambition were anti-social attributes.

Considering these models today one sees how anthropology has carried forward timeworn prejudices about Southern European 'others'. Already in the nineteenth century †Tylor had considered Mediterraneans as less civilized than Northern Europeans because of their need to gesture while speaking, rather than conveying their message in plain language. In the 1950s and early 1960s models we see Southern Europeans cast as backward, basically because they are unable to adapt to the rational demands of state administration and the ideals of capitalism. If we reconsider the issue, is it amoral to be strongly committed to one's family? And perhaps the image of limited good can better be understood as a mode of *resistance to a capitalist accumulation which threatened communal solidarity with the introduction of economic disparity.

Southern European societies have certainly been structured in similar ways by the features of ecology, history and economy mentioned above. But perhaps, as Herzfeld has argued (1987), they have most significantly been structured, or even invented, by certain pervasive Northern European and North American discourses about the South. In large part these discourses are really concerned with Northern European identity; the South is just a foil, a residual symbolic category expressing what northerners are not.

The Gross National Product of Italy has now surpassed that of Great Britain, but a conviction still persists that Britain is more advanced, if not economically, then at least by virtue of its administrative rationality and fairness. With large numbers of Southern Europeans still migrating in search of wage labour in Northern European countries, while most northerners only visit Southern Europe on holidays devoted to leisurely consumption, a general inequality between North and South remains. Despite the rising number of trained Southern European anthropologists, this economic imbalance continues to make it possible for the north to define the South, both politically and anthropologically.

CHARLES STEWART

See also: Christianity, honour and shame, gender, classical studies, cognatic societies, patrons and clients

Further reading

Banfield, E. (1958) *The Moral Basis of a Backward Society*, New York: Free Press

Blok, A. (1981) 'Rams and Billy-Goats: A Key to the Mediterranean Code of Honour', *Man* 16: 427–40

Braudel, F. ([1949] 1972) *The Mediterranean*, London: Fontana

Campbell, J. (1964) *Honour, Family and Patronage: A Study of Institutions and Moral Values in a Greek Mountain Community*, Oxford: Clarendon Press

—— (1992) 'Fieldwork Among the Sarakatsani, 1954–55', in J. de Pina-Cabral and J. Campbell (eds) *Europe Observed*, London: Macmillan

Davis, J. (1977) *People of the Mediterranean: An Essay in Comparative Social Anthropology*, London: Routledge

Foster, G. (1965) 'Peasant Society and the Image of Limited Good', *American Anthropologist* 67: 293–314

Gilmore, D. (1987) *Honor and Shame and the Unity of the Mediterranean*, Washington DC: American Anthropological Association, (special publication, no 22)

Herzfeld, M. (1984) 'The Horns of the Mediterraneanist Dilemma', *American Ethnologist* 11: 439–54

—— (1987) *Anthropology Through the Looking-Glass: Critical Ethnography in the Margins of Europe*, Cambridge: Cambridge University Press

Peristiany, J. (1966) *Honour and Shame: The Values of Mediterranean Society*, London: Weidenfeld and Nicolson

Pitt-Rivers, J. (1954) *The People of the Sierra*, London: Weidenfeld and Nicholson

evolution and evolutionism

The nineteenth century

The word 'evolution' describes the process of qualitative change. Evolutionism is the scholarly activity of describing, understanding and explaining this process. In cultural and social anthropology the gradual, structural change of human *culture is the subject of study by evolutionists. Interest in evolution goes back to the beginning of the nineteenth century, when scholars of widely divergent backgrounds discovered that the period of time during which humankind had lived on earth was much longer than had been believed till then, and that in the course of time human culture had undergone substantial changes. The interest in the new paradigm ran parallel with the growing accumulation of data on all kinds of peoples, *races, and cultures, prehistoric as well as contemporary. The scholarly world was in urgent need of a method to arrange and classify these data – and evolutionism seemed to offer a workable method for this work.

It soon became clear, however, that the new approach posed many theoretical and methodological problems. And, though much attention and ingenuity was given to the solution of these problems, nineteenth-century scholarship had at its disposal too few reliable data to succeed in this task. Yet, some important works were published before 1900. In England †Sir Henry Maine published his *Ancient Law* (1861), in which he distinguished between human groups composed on the basis of *kinship, and groups defined on the basis of territory. In Switzerland †Johan Jacob Bachofen, basing himself on the analysis of *myths, supplemented with ethnographic data, wrote *Das Mutterecht* (1861), in which he hypothesized that long ago not men, but women had been dominant in human society. The British scholar †Edward B. Tylor wrote *Primitive Culture* (1871), in which an effort was made to describe and analyse the development of *religion. Importantly this work contained the first lengthy consideration of the concept of culture. In the USA, finally, *Lewis Henry Morgan presented a grand overview of the evolution of culture in *Ancient Society* (1877). This was certainly the most elaborate scheme, embracing the widest possible spectrum of institutions within a single framework. It was based on a firsthand knowledge of the Iroquois, and a thorough study of the literature on Aztecs, Greeks, and Romans. Morgan carefully formulated the criteria he employed in ordering his data. His emphasis on orderly arrangements, however, made the book rather more an effort in classification than a study of the evolution of culture.

In evaluating the work of our nineteenth-century predecessors we should be aware of the fact that, even though their answers were sometimes wrong, they posed the right questions. Moreover, several of their views are still considered valuable (Ingold 1986). The central argument was that human culture had developed from very simple beginnings into large, complex systems. In the race to the top, many societies had been left behind, and the task of the scholar was to indicate how this race had been run. Though their works do not figure prominently in the studies mentioned above, there were at least two nineteenth-century scholars who had tried to reach a deeper understanding of the evolutionary process: †Charles Darwin, and †Herbert Spencer. Darwin concentrated his efforts on the evolution of biological forms. In his view the most important principle governing evolution was natural selection: the survival of the better-adapted species. The process of natural selection was accidental: variations were generated at random, and one of them would prove to be most adaptive. In this way new species formed; the process had no specific direction. According to Spencer, however, the evolutionary process had a clear direction: it tended towards growing complexity. He pointed to the great variety in societal forms, and to the substantial differences between, on the one hand, urbanized, industrialized societies, and simple, primitive peoples on the other. Nineteenth-century scholarship was not yet ready to cope with these theoretical considerations, and it remains to be seen whether late twentieth-century anthropologists are in a better position to solve the evolutionary riddle.

Anti-evolutionist interlude

At the end of the nineteenth century the evolutionary paradigm lost its attraction to anthropologists. Even among its adherents criticisms were advanced. Lack of reliable data on the one hand, and rather rigid schemes on the other, produced many errors. Interest shifted to other approaches. Inquisitive scholars went out to visit 'primitive' peoples themselves, and it was felt necessary to develop theoretical and methodological tools for the new technique of *fieldwork. Interest in speculative theories about the past came to a temporary end. In the USA, *Franz Boas called for demonstrability instead of probability; but his neverending search for details prevented him from the construction of more-embracing syntheses. His student, †Robert Lowie, tried to obliterate evolutionism definitively in his *Primitive Society* (1920) but, by following Morgan's argument closely, in fact ended up with a kind of revised evolutionism. For example, his contention that the †clan had been invented four times in North America, was something of an improvement on Morgan's view, rather than its annihilation. In *British anthropology, scholars such as *Malinowski, and *A.R. Radcliffe-Brown called for protracted fieldwork. This interest led to the development of British structural-functionalism. This school, with its emphasis on †holism and *functionalism, and its dislike of 'conjectural history', was not interested in developing evolutionary theories.

The revival of evolutionism

In the 1930s †Leslie A. White and †Julian H. Steward started to revive interest in evolutionism. The central concept in White's approach was culture. Culture is perpetuated by communication, and it develops according to principles and laws of its own. As human culture is dynamic, it consumes energy. This consumption of energy became the core of his evolutionary approach: the greater the amount of energy harnessed per capita per year, the greater the degree of cultural development (White 1949). With enthusiasm and perseverance White defended his views – but did he really explain cultural evolution? A close correlation had been established between the consumption of energy and the development of culture, but establishing a correlation is not enough to provide an explanation. Moreover, White did not explain why complexity emerged in some places and not in others.

In many respects Steward's views were the opposite of White's (Steward 1955). Where White thought in broad, universal schemes, Steward preferred a more limited, multilinear strategy. Characteristic of this line of thought are his efforts to demonstrate that, under specified conditions, cultural phenomena are repeatable. This held for the patrilocal †band, as well as for *state formation in semi-arid regions. In such processes, Steward distinguished basic or constant features, and secondary or variable features.

In *Evolution and Culture* (1960), †Marshall D. Sahlins and †Elman R. Service tried to combine the views of White and Steward. In order to do so, they distinguished between 'general' and 'specific' evolution. General evolution was seen as the evolution of human culture in general. This type of evolution was characterized by growing complexity and unilinearity, with culture apparently leaping from one societal form to another. This approach departs from a classification of societies according to organizational or cultural intricacy. In other words, research starts at the highest level of complexity and then traces back its origins and development. Small wonder then, that such models invariably show ever-growing complexity and unilinearity. If one starts at the other end, however, and asks in what ways the original *hunter and gatherer societies evolved, an entirely different picture emerges, in which multidirectionality looms large. To account for the great variety in historical developments, Sahlins introduced the concept of specific evolution. This borders on the history of the society concerned. It is not so much history, however, which is aimed at, but the explanation of the qualitative reorganizations of that society with the help of general categories.

General evolution can be pictured as either a staircase or a slope. The staircase model, familiar through the writings of Service (*Primitive Social Organization*, 1963), and Morton H. Fried (*The Evolution of Political Society*, 1967), represents social evolution as a series of stages, each higher than the previous one. The less common slope model depicts social evolution as a series of cumulative developments, forming, as it were, a slowly ascending line. Examples of this strategy are Ester Boserup's *The Conditions of Agricultural Growth* (1965), and the seminal essay by Jonathan Friedman and Michael Rowlands, 'Notes towards an Epigenetic Model of the Evolution of Civilisation' (1977).

In an important article, Robert L. Carneiro (1973) demonstrated that there was no contradiction between unilinear and multilinear evolution; a specific institution – say, the state – could be the result of differing developments. Subsequent research into the origin of early states fully proved Carneiro's argument (Claessen and Skalník 1978).

In the same article Carneiro, inspired by Spencer, defined evolution in terms of growing complexity, and though there are many indications that human culture evolved from simple beginnings to complex structures, there are nevertheless reasons not to make growing complexity the cornerstone of social and cultural evolution. The fact that societies with simple cultures exist side by side with complex state societies indicates that stagnation is as real a phenomenon as development. The collapse of (most) civilizations shows that decline and fall are inextricably bound up with growth and florescence. Moreover, the growth of groups and organizations at the same time produces the necessity of efficiency and simplification of rules and regulations (Hallpike 1986). Evolutionary theory thus has to cope with more phenomena than 'growing complexity' alone. Against this background, it seems logical to make qualitative change central to the account of social or cultural evolution. Evolution then can be defined as the process of qualitative reorganization of society (Claessen and Van de Velde 1985).

Since the 1960s the views of †Karl Marx and †Friedrich Engels came to play a considerable role in the discussion of evolutionism. In particular Engels's *Origin of the Family, Private Property and the State* (1884) received a great deal of attention. According to this work the state developed under conditions of population growth and increasing production. A class of managers and rulers was sustained by the appropriation of a surplus produced by others. The institution to keep the haves and the have-nots apart was the state. This scenario differed from an earlier one, presented in *Anti-Dühring* (1878), in which the managerial role of functionaries had been emphasized. Some of Engels's views on management were later repeated, though with a different emphasis, by †Karl A. Wittfogel. In his †*Oriental Despotism* (1957), he defended the view that management of large irrigation works led to the development of the (despotic) state. The book generated heated debate about the Marxist concept of the †Asiatic mode of production, one of the *modes of production originally distinguished by Marx. Though the views of Engels and Marx had the same shortcomings as the works of other nineteenth-century scholars mentioned, they have inspired many later scholars.

Monocausality versus multicausality

Since the 1970s, there has been a growing feeling among scholars that the evolutionary schemes presented thus far were admirable as classifications, but neglected the problem of process. Interest shifted, therefore, towards the question of how social evolution took place. Behind this question loomed the even more difficult one: why?

The problem in explaining how evolution took place is that only the result is known, the outcome of the process. The causes that led to this process are unknown, and one can only speculate about them. For quite some time scholars have tried to find a functional explanation: there must have been a need for which the resulting institution was 'good', or 'productive'. Hallpike (1986: 88), however, has argued cogently that functional explanations are impossible. It is not possible to establish specific connections between the basic forms of relationship in primitive society and the general needs or problems faced by such a society. Moreover, as Van Parijs (1981) argued, the process of selecting solutions to solve problems is a rather vague one; the best that can be said is that there will have been a tendency towards 'local optimization', i.e. people selected from a limited, known range of possible solutions, one that seemed to promise good results. The outcome of such selection was often different from the original expectations. However, once a certain direction had been 'chosen' (deliberately or accidentally), the society in question usually continued in that direction. Investments were made; social relations became oriented towards specific goals, and a return became increasingly difficult. The development of early states was practically always the result of decisions taken in a long forgotten past, with completely different goals in mind. For example the Betsileo of Madagascar, described by Kottak (1980), built hilltop forts to defend themselves against invading raiders, but in doing this they unintentionally also laid the foundations for a state which, after a few hundred years, would emerge out of these hilltop settlements (also cf. Claessen and Skalník 1978).

Several scholars have tried to explain social evolution with the help of one factor only; they look only for monocausal explanations, and try to identify a 'prime mover'. Factors that have been proposed include: population growth and population pressure; war, threat of war, and conquest; economic or material conditions; and ideological influences. Regarding population growth/pressure, it should be pointed out that the first human groups were small, and split easily. This tendency is still observable among hunters and gatherers. Their social organization is not suited to accommodate large numbers of people. Only under exceptional circumstances do *hunters and gatherers become sedentary, and live together in large groups. The Northwest Coast Indians are a case in point. Their rich *environment made it possible for them to produce enough to survive seasonal changes.

For some scholars the production, maintenance and distribution of material resources is the main cause for stratification. In the USA, anthropologists and archaeologists of the ecological school explain all evolutionary changes with the help of demographic factors only. Population growth, in their opinion, is the prime mover. In many cases, however, population growth was a concomitant of †sedentary life and economic prosperity. That population growth has influence on the growth of culture is evident; having to feed more people requires more food, and more organization – provided that they stay together. On this same

basis Carneiro built his circumscription theory, which holds that an increasing number of people in a circumscribed area inevitably produces war and subjugation – and so the state. But it has also been established that too many people in a given area exhaust the environment, which may cause the collapse of socio-political organization (e.g. Easter Island). All this implies that population growth has evolutionary consequences only under specific circumstances (Hallpike 1986).

*War, threat of war or conquest should not be seen as an independent factor: intergroup-fighting occurs because of economic, demographic or ideological reasons. Moreover, it has been argued that war does not occur in 'primitive' society. War is a 'civilized phenomenon'; primitive societies have only raids and fights. Raids or war, however, require organization, leadership, defence works. Because of this they may have evolutionary consequences; by itself war (or raiding) is just a symptom of other underlying developments.

The *economic – or more generally, the material – factor is of great importance. It encompasses production, irrigation works, trade, *technology, and so on. A recognition of the economic factor was found already in Marx and Engels. Recently †Marvin Harris made materialist considerations the cornerstone of development. Yet, many human activities are known which were undertaken on the ground of ideological considerations, or because of managerial problems, in the first place.

*Ideology, in whatever form, is found at the basis of many human activities. Whether we consider the monuments of Stonehenge, the Aztec wars, the building of the Pyramids, the Arab conquests, or the development of Kachin inequality, each time there were ideological convictions that urged people to act. Also there are cases in which development did not take place because of ideological impediments (e.g. levelling mechanisms, rejection of leadership, or religious objections).

Apparently, no single factor can be pointed out as a general prime mover in the evolution of human culture. Rather, a wide variety of factors incites people to act, each of these occasionally playing the role of prime mover. Moreover, the analysis of specific cases of evolution demonstrates that practically always more than one factor is found to play a role in the developments. Only when we are willing to accept that a complex and simultaneous interaction of several factors in a positive †feedback produces evolution will we be able to understand how development took place. As a consequence of these considerations Claessen and Van de Velde (1985: 254–60) proposed the 'complex interaction model'.

Why evolution?

Why did evolution take place? What induced people to give up the 'original affluent society' (Sahlins) and to develop †agriculture, *urban life, or the computer? Put in this way, the question is silly; nobody ever chose deliberately to do so, and nobody envisaged such complex phenomena. They came to happen as unforeseen consequences of earlier decisions and choices, most of which were responses to greater or smaller changes in the way of life of peoples. This illustrates again that most evolutionary changes took place unintended, and without specific planning (Hallpike 1986, Ingold 1986). In this respect social or cultural evolution conforms to Darwin's view that evolution has no direction. Having established this fact, we can try to answer the question of why all kinds of qualitative changes in human cultures occurred; and why – according to Spencer – there is a tendency towards growing complexity.

One point of departure is Malinowski's argument that human beings have basic needs, such as the need for food, shelter and sex. To fulfil these needs people have to undertake activities, and while acting, they usually meet with other people. Action calls for reaction, and human action as well as human reaction will be based on local optimization (see above). Various possibilities present themselves: fear, aggression and defence, or cooperation, *marriage, and *networks. For a very long period of time human groups were but small, and split when their numbers reached a critical point. Relations with other groups were always maintained, however (cf. Tylor 1871; Steward 1955), and in doing so a wide variety of institutions developed, and some of these were better suited to their goals than others. Natural (or rather, social) selection promoted the better, and annihilated the weaker solutions.

Only under certain circumstances will people give up nomadic life, and become sedentary. Once the step was taken, larger settlements emerged, and the need arose for more elaborate leadership, and huts made way for houses. There are, however, people still living today in small villages, where leaders have to keep a low profile. The Amazonian Yanomamö are a case in point. Levelling mechanisms prevent the development of a more elaborate sociopolitical organization, many raids and fights notwithstanding.

The development of more complex social organization is only achieved when a complex interaction of a number of factors is found: population growth, in combination with specific types of resource; an economy which makes it possible that specialists (religious, political, craftsmen) can be maintained; and an ideology which legitimizes the development of *inequality. Some of these more complex societies developed into †chiefdoms, and in the course of time the state emerged. Strong, well-organized societies, which generate more energy than others, dominate the weaker ones (White 1949), and gradually the weaker societies have either been subjugated, or have been dispersed to the more inhospitable quarters of the world. Stagnation or decline, however, occurred perhaps more often because of internal problems than because of external pressure and conquest (cf. Claessen and Van de Velde 1987).

Institutions generally exist longer than the average lifespan of the individuals who form them. This means that there is a continuous influx of new people in the institutions. As no two people are alike, the new ones will be different from their predecessors, and will generate new ideas. Not all of these will be accepted, but in this way a steady flow of smaller or greater changes will be brought about (Cohen 1981).

Human beings have the capacity for learning. They can adapt to better or more efficient ways of living and organization. This means that a tendency in human cultures will be found to reach for higher levels of development. In this way the tendency towards growing complexity, indicated by Spencer (see above), is realized. There is, however, no reason to assume that humans will ever be able to give direction to evolutionary processes, though, paradoxically, they set it in motion themselves.

HENRI J. M. CLAESSEN

See also: archaeology, biological anthropology, development, ecological anthropology, environment, Marxism and anthropology, Lewis Henry Morgan, Russian and Soviet anthropology, sociobiology, state

Further reading

Carneiro, R.L. (1973) 'The Four Faces of Evolution', in J.J. Honigman (ed.) *Handbook of Social and Cultural Anthropology*, Chicago: Rand McNally
Claessen, H.J.M. and P. Skalník (eds) (1978) *The Early State*, The Hague: Mouton

Claessen, H.J.M. and P. van de Velde (1985) 'Social Evolution in General', Chapters 1, 9 and 16 in H.J.M. Claessen, P. van de Velde and M.E. Smith (eds) *Development and Decline; The Evolution of Sociopolitical Organisation*, South Hadley, MA: Bergin and Garvey

Claessen, H.J.M. and P. van de Velde (eds) (1987) *Early State Dynamics*, Leiden: Brill

Cohen, R. (1981) 'Evolutionary Epistemology and Human Values', *Current Anthropology* 22: 201–18

Friedman, J. and M. Rowlands (1977) 'Notes Towards an Epigenetic Model of the Evolution of Civilisation', in J. Friedman and M. Rowlands (eds) *The Evolution of Social Systems*, London: Duckworth

Hallpike, C.R. (1986) *The Principles of Social Evolution*, Oxford: Clarendon

Ingold, T. (1986) *Evolution and Social Life*, Cambridge: Cambridge University Press

Kottak, C.P. (1980) *The Past in the Present; History, Ecology and Cultural Variation in Highland Madagascar*, Ann Arbor: University of Michigan Press

Steward, J.H. (1955) *Theory of Culture Change*, Urbana: University of Illinois Press

Van Parijs, P. (1981) *Evolutionary Explanation in The Social Sciences: An Emerging Paradigm*, Totowa, NJ: Rowman and Littlefield

White, L.A. (1949) *The Science Of Culture. A Study of Man and Civilization*, New York: Grove

exchange

Exchange is the transfer of things between social actors. The things can be human or animal, material or immaterial, words or things. The actors can be individuals, groups, or beings such as gods or spirits. Cast this broadly, exchange pervades social life. Villagers getting foodstuffs at a local market, like city-dwellers at a supermarket, are engaged in exchange. Corporations that contribute to political parties, enemies who hurl insults at each other, hunters who placate the spirit of their prey, and parents who prepare meals for their children, all are engaged in exchange. It should be no surprise that some argue that exchange is a key to social life. For *Lévi-Strauss, true human existence begins when groups begin to exchange women in marriage, while for †Mauss exchange is the earliest solution to the †Hobbesian war of all against all.

Exchange is a central topic in anthropology, but it is more important in the ethnography of some regions than in others. Likewise, exchange is central to all people's lives, but its consequences and cultural elaborations are more marked in some regions than in others. It is in *Melanesia that people and anthropologists have stressed exchange most, and many of the examples used here are drawn from the ethnography of that region.

Structural perspectives

Taken in the aggregate, exchanges can exhibit structure, patterns and regularities. Like †Adam Smith's notion of the invisible hand, these regularities can have consequences whether or not the actors involved intend them or are even aware of them. Perhaps the most famous example is *kula* exchange in Melanesia, described by *Malinowski (1922: ch. 3). The Trobriand Islanders who participate in the *kula* give and receive ornamental armshells and necklaces to and from partners in other villages. However, with their partners in one direction they give only armshells and receive only necklaces, while the situation is reversed for their partners in the other direction. Seen as a whole, the kula trade exhibits a clear structure that is unintended by participants, a giant circle covering hundreds of miles, with armshells travelling in one direction around it and necklaces travelling in the other.

Another sort of structure is defined by the things that can be exchanged against each other. Even in societies permeated by *money, there are things that should be, and typically are, transacted only for certain other things. In the West, for example, this includes promotions, academic degrees and honours of all sorts, which are given in return for merit and should not, and typically cannot, be given in return for money. When exchange is restricted in this way, there is a structure of †spheres of exchange. A classic example of such spheres is the Tiv, a society in Nigeria. Bohannan (1955) describes three Tiv spheres of exchange. One concerns everyday foodstuffs and petty consumables, traded freely against each other. Another and more restricted sphere includes *slaves, cattle, metal bars and a type of cloth – items of prestige rather than subsistence. The most restricted consists of rights in people (other than slaves, who are part of the middle sphere), such as dependent women and children. Typically one cannot exchange across spheres; exchange, for example, cattle for a daughter in marriage, or petty consumables for metal bars. However, these spheres have decayed somewhat. The colonial imposition of a money economy has meant that items from different spheres can be traded against each other, using cash as an intermediate step. However, in many societies money does not dissolve spheres altogether, but becomes incorporated into one sphere or another.

Probably the most renowned structural analysis of exchange is Lévi-Strauss's (1969 [1949]) work on patterns of *marriage, which he casts as the exchange of women between descent groups that are dominated by men. Lévi-Strauss argues that rules about whom a woman should marry produce structures of relationships between groups and so produce a larger social order. One set of rules, those of restricted exchange, produces pairs of groups linked to each other through the exchange of women and so produces a social order that incorporates only a small number of groups. The other sort is generalized exchange, where groups are linked more widely through the irregular giving of women in marriage. This can order a large number of descent groups in an extensive social system.

Relational perspectives

Complementing the structural approach is the relational. This approach is concerned with how exchanges reflect and shape the identity of the social actors involved, as well as the relationship those actors have with each other, with the thing exchanged, and even with the act of exchange itself. Two themes in work on the relational aspects of exchange are the way that exchange can create groups within a society, and the way that exchange links people and objects.

One example of the way exchange creates groups is the *Big Man system found in Melanesia, described by †Sahlins. In this system, aspiring leaders use generosity to attract a body of supporters, and so create a social group. In the relationship between leader and group, supporters give material objects and allegiance to their leaders. In return they get the prestige of being in the Big Man's faction. They also get a share of what is given to their leader by competing Big Men, for Big Men and their factions are in competition with other leaders and their associated factions. Consequently, these groups do not only emerge through exchange, their survival and renown depends upon their success in exchange with other such factions. This example points out how, as exchange creates groups, so it creates boundaries between groups. When these sorts of socio-political structures become stable, exchange can be a way of marking allegiance and obligation between leader and group, as with the *jajmani* system in *South Asia.

Exchange can also create relationships of *kinship, for in many societies membership in a kin group is not, and even cannot be, defined solely by birth. In defining these kin relationships, exchange thereby creates kinship groups. Among the Daribi, in Melanesia, people do not become members of a kin group because they are descended in the appropriate way from group members. Instead, they become members, and hence the group is constituted, because other people make the appropriate exchanges on the behalf of those individuals and because those individuals exchange in the appropriate ways with the appropriate people in the appropriate circumstances (Wagner 1967).

Types of exchange and types of relationship between actors reinforce each other, with the result that types of exchange are a part of the creation of groups and the boundaries between them. Sahlins (1974: ch. 5) makes this point when he notes that, generally, exchange within the group is tinged with generosity and without stipulation of when and how a return is to be made; exchange at the boundaries of the group is balanced, with a concern for adequate and timely reciprocation; exchange with strangers tends toward 'negative reciprocity', the desire to get something for nothing, and it ranges from sharp bargaining to theft (see †reciprocity). However, it is important to remember that negative reciprocity is itself a social relationship, distinct from sheer indifference. Moreover, the exchange of blows by raiding and warfare can be a basis of social groups and relationships, for defining adversaries can be as important for the group as defining members.

Other work describes how exchange links actors to each other and to objects. In his discussion of the †fetishism of commodities, †Marx addressed this issue, observing that commodity exchange masks the real relation between actors and the objects they exchange. For many anthropologists, however, the formative statement is Mauss's (1990 [1924]) analysis of exchange in societies in Melanesia and elsewhere. Mauss's classic formulation states that parties to a relationship of gift exchange are obligated to give gifts, to receive them and repay them in the appropriate ways. In such relationships, the object given bears the identity of the giver, which the recipient acquires along with the object itself. Mauss made this point particularly with regard to the Maori *hau*, the 'spirit of the gift' that demands the return of the gift to its owner. Mauss's interpretation is important in work on exchange, and has been subject to extensive debate (e.g. Sahlins 1974: ch. 4; Parry 1986; Weiner 1980).

The relational approach has been taken to its extreme in Melanesia, pre-eminently by Marilyn Strathern (1988). Melanesians do not, it is argued, conceive of objects and *persons as independent entities that are involved in exchange. Rather, persons and objects acquire their identities from the relationships in which they are transacted. The person who gives does not exist prior to the giving and the relationship in which it occurs, but has an identity only as part of and as a result of that relationship. Consequently, people bear the identities of the people and things that were involved in the relationships that created and maintained them, and the same is true of objects.

Work on the relational aspects of exchange, particularly in Melanesia, is bedevilled by a number of problems. Foremost among these is a tendency to focus on cultural principles at the expense of attention to social practice. Too often, the result is sweeping generalizations about how people think, in the absence of detailed and qualified analyses of the various ways that people actually act (see Bourdieu 1977: ch. 1; Davis 1992). Without such analyses, assertions about the spirit of the gift or the link between people and exchange relationships must be treated with extreme caution. It is not possible to know the degree to which these generalizations are more than ideal types constructed by anthropologists (though often they are presented as valid generalizations), types that are subverted frequently in people's daily lives. More scholarly attention to social practices of exchange would allow a consideration of when such abstract statements apply and when they do not. This in turn would open a range of questions about how circumstance affects people's thinking about exchange, identity and relationship, and what are the practical consequences of these effects.

Exchange and economy

The relational approach is involved in what is perhaps the most popular recent topic in the analysis of exchange, the relationship between exchange and economy. This topic springs from an old question: why do people spend so much time and energy to exchange items that seem worth so little? This question reveals an implicit assumption that exchange ought to be about individuals transacting objects of utility and value.

This topic appears as a debate about how we should approach exchange, a debate that exhibits two general orientations (Parry 1986). One is more social and is associated with Mauss, who stressed the way that actors are linked and obligated to each other and who saw the things exchanged as bearers of social identities and relationships. Much of the relational work on exchange reflects the more social thread, and there is no need to describe it again here.

The other is more individualistic and is associated with Malinowski, who saw actors as relatively self-interested and autonomous, and concerned with equivalence, with getting as good as they give. Much of the classic sociological work on exchange falls into the Malinowski stream (see Emerson 1976). Writers such as Blau, Gouldner and Homans describe exchange in terms of the costs and benefits that accrue to actors. Thus, they root exchange in an individual, utilitarian calculus, even if that utility can be esteem or self-satisfaction rather than just money or material utilities. While this approach has an individualist foundation, some writers who use it base social relationships and social order on these exchanges.

Although it has produced interesting arguments, the conflict between the Maussian and Malinowskian perspectives is probably pointless. For one thing, the more individualistic approach frequently becomes a philosophical position rather than a falsifiable hypothesis: it is always possible for the determined analyst to discover some reward or satisfaction that the giver gets in return, even if the giver neither anticipated nor was aware of it (Davis 1992). Equally, though a view of individuals concerned with equivalence may accord with Western utilitarianism, it tends to ignore the fact, documented in studies of *consumption, that value and utility themselves are not naturally given, but are products of social and cultural identities and relationships. Finally, the varieties of exchange that anthropologists have described cannot be understood adequately from either viewpoint alone.

However, the differences among writers who make this last point are interesting. Some seem to argue that, in different sorts of societies, exchange is routinely of the more social or utilitarian sort. Consequently, for them 'exchange' is broad, but only because it varies across types of societies – typically Western capitalist societies and non-Western, often village-based, societies (e.g. Strathern 1988; Gregory 1982). Others challenge the idea that exchange within any given society is in fact relatively uniform. One challenge asserts that in most societies some exchange is more individualistic and concerned with short-term gain, while other exchange is more social and concerned with long-term cultural values and goals (Bloch and Parry 1989). Another challenge asserts that it can be misleading to classify exchanges, as there may well be disagreement among people in a society over whether a particular transaction is more relational or utilitarian. Most telling is the objection, echoing Mauss, that the very notion that material gain and social identity and obligation are or can be distinct is peculiar to Western capitalist society.

Conclusion

Two general trends in anthropology are likely to influence the study of exchange in the near future. One is a growing concern with complex societies, especially the West. This is leading to a more critical investigation of the *Occidentalist assumption that exchange in the West is overwhelmingly of the Malinowskian sort , as well as attacks on the economists' notion of the *market itself. Another general trend in anthropology is the growing interest in the symbolic aspects of consumption. This increasing interest in objects as bearers and creators of cultural meanings may lead scholars to approach exchange in terms of the symbolism of the things that people transact.

JAMES G. CARRIER

See also: economic anthropology, kula, markets, money, potlatch

Further reading

Bloch, M. and J. Parry (eds) (1989) *Money and the Morality of Exchange*, Cambridge: Cambridge University Press

Bohannan, P. (1955) 'Some Principles of Exchange and Investment among the Tiv', *American Anthropologist* 57 (1): 60–70

Bourdieu, P. (1977) *Outline of a Theory of Practice*, Cambridge: Cambridge University Press

Davis, J. (1992) *Exchange*, Buckingham: Open University Press

Emerson, R.M. (1976) 'Social Exchange Theory' *Annual Review of Sociology* 2: 335–62

Gregory, C.A. (1982) *Gifts and Commodities*, London: Academic Press

Lévi-Strauss, C. (1969 [1949]) *The Elementary Structures of Kinship*, rev. edn, Boston: Beacon Press

Malinowski, B. (1922) *Argonauts of the Western Pacific*, London: Routledge & Kegan Paul

Mauss, M. (1990 [1924]) *The Gift* (trans. W.D. Halls), London: Routledge

Parry, J. (1986) 'The Gift, The Indian Gift and the "Indian Gift"' *Man* 21 (3): 453–73

Sahlins, M. (1974) *Stone Age Economics*, London: Tavistock

Strathern, M. (1988) *The Gender of the Gift*, Berkeley: University of California Press

Wagner, R. (1967) *The Curse of Souw*, Chicago: University of Chicago Press

Weiner, A. (1980) 'Reproduction: A Replacement for Reciprocity', *American Ethnologist* 7 (1): 71–85

F

factions

In *Enlightenment political thought, factions were viewed disapprovingly as small dissenting groups formed to advance particular persons or policies within formal political structures. *Political anthropology has contributed to a broadening use of the concept as well as to its specific use as a technical term for a particular type of political organization within a cluster of similar, informal, political alignments.

Factions are fluid groups recruited opportunistically and 'vertically' by leaders to contest specific issues. They may cut across other forms of 'horizontal' cleavage within a society, such as those of *class, *religion or *gender. Usually only two factions come into being around any one issue, breaking up when that issue is resolved. Anthropologists tend to view such cross-cutting formations favourably since cross-cutting ties encourage reconciliation. Yet the possibility exists that factional hostility might become permanently institutionalized and prolonged violence ensue.

Anthropologists conceptualize factionalism as simply one form of political organization on a continuum of †action groups ranging through informal †action sets, cliques, gangs, coalitions and interest groups to formal political parties. During the Cold War this perception contributed to the work of historians and political scientists charting leadership struggles within the communist parties of China and the Soviet Union.

Studies of factionalism have a long history in anthropology. In the nineteenth century, for example, fieldworkers from the †Bureau of American Ethnology reported the emergence of factionalism among *Native North Americans being settled on reservations. This revolved around whether they should retain their own traditions or accept modern ways. Jeremy

Boissevain's research in Malta provided a classic account of factionalism. In a detailed analysis (1974) of the beginning of factional rivalry over the introduction of a new cult in the village of Harrug he established several factors which relate to the structure, evolution, number and strategy of factions under conditions of political competition. Many excellent studies have been carried on the Indian subcontinent where factionalism appears to be commonplace. Adopting a processual approach, observing individuals and groups in action over time, Indianist ethnographers found that factions were most prevalent in villages where there were many castes but with no one being dominant. Factionalism was thus a form of struggle among equals. Recently, though, radical historians have argued that the importance of factionalism has been exaggerated at the expense of ties of class, *caste and *community in writings on Indian political culture (Hardiman 1982).

Ethnography from many countries supports a contention that factions are contingent groupings based on competition over new resources. *Development projects introduced new spoils into local political and economic arenas and peasants adopted development *discourse to establish and maintain factional divisions within their villages. Factionalism is, apparently, less likely to be an urban phenomenon. It has been suggested that factionalism became more common in some Third World societies when parliamentary electoral systems were introduced on the eve of independence.

JOAN VINCENT

See also: political anthropology, patrons and clients

Further reading

Boissevain, J. (1974) *Friends of Friends. Networks, Manipulators and Coalitions*, Oxford: Blackwell

Bujra, J. (1973) 'The Dynamics of Political Action: A

New Look at Factionalism', *American Anthropologist* 75
(1): 132–53

Hardiman, D. (1982) 'The Indian "Faction": A Political
Theory Examined' in R. Guha (ed.) *Subaltern Studies
I*, Delhi: Oxford University Press

Schmidt, S., J. Scott, C. Lande and L. Guasti (eds)
(1977) *Friends, Followers, and Factions. A Reader in Political
Clientelism*, Berkeley: University of California Press

family

'Family' is one of the words most commonly used
in anthropological writings and discussion, and yet
its meaning is neither always clear nor a matter of
consensus. This is partly because in everyday use
in Euro-American culture, the word covers a
multitude of senses of relatedness and connection.
It may for instance refer to the domestic group or
*household, to close kin who are not co-resident,
such as parents and adult offspring, or to a much
wider network or deeper genealogy of *kinship, as
in 'the entire family attended the funeral', or 'the
house has been in the family for seven generations'. People know what they mean when they use
the word family, and the meaning is usually made
clear to others by the context in which it is used,
but most would find it difficult to define precisely
what sorts and range of relationships the word
covers. The same complexity of meaning often
exists within anthropological writing and, furthermore, the way in which the concept is used, and
the sets of assumptions it embraces, have changed
radically as new theories of kinship, *gender, and
*social structure have been developed.

A related point is the fact that in Euro-
American discourse the concept of the family is
politically and ideologically 'loaded', or imbued
with sets of politically and culturally contested
ideas about the correct or moral ways in which
people should conduct their lives, and the people
with whom they should conduct them. In the postmodern intellectual climate of the 1980s and
1990s, the term has been increasingly subjected
to re-analysis, deconstruction, and radical redefinition: as is the case with many other cultural and
social categories, emphasis has shifted from one
meaning to a plurality of meanings. 'Families' have
increasingly replaced 'the family' as an analytic
concept, and the family itself, singular or plural,
has come to be seen less and less as a 'natural'
form of human social organization, and more and
more as a culturally and historically specific
symbolic system, or *ideology.

Types of family

In anthropological writings, different congregations of kin and †affines have been labelled as
specific types of family. The †conjugal family refers
to a heterosexual pair and their offspring, while
the †extended family refers to at least two related
conjugal families, and for instance may consist of
a woman and man, their children, and the spouse
and children of at least one of these, or two or
more siblings, their spouses and children. The
†stem family includes a couple, their unmarried
children and one married child with spouse and
offspring. Other labels have also been devised to
refer to specific types of situation. In most of these
definitions the family overlaps with the household
or domestic group: that is to say, the family is
identified as those kin and affines who live together
in the same dwelling, share a common hearth, and
jointly participate in production and consumption.
As will become clear, this identification of the
family with the domestic group has given rise to
various analytic problems.

Theoretical origins

Late nineteenth and early twentieth-century
writers, influenced by ideas of social *evolution,
saw the conjugal family as growing out of more
complex systems of kinship, cohabitation or
*marriage, and divisions of labour. †Engels for
example explicitly linked the rise of the monogamous nuclear family to sedentary agriculture,
the development of private *property, and the
elaboration of *exchange relations between men.
In his evolutionary scheme of things, a gendered
division of labour which associated women with
the domestic sphere and childcare, and men
with the outside domain, was both natural and
egalitarian; initially neither the domestic nor the
external domain was valued over the other. The
transformation of this balanced division into a
hierarchical order in which women's labour was
undervalued and women's persons and sexuality
controlled by men was effected through the rise
of the patriarchical nuclear family and property
relations between men.

The three ideas, of first a 'natural' gendered
division of labour, secondly a linked association of
women with the domestic and men with the jural
sphere, and thirdly a narrowing of wider kinship
relations to those of the patriarchal nuclear family
concurrent with increased economic specialization, were to remain essential premises in theories
of the family for a long time to come. Goode (in

Goody 1971) for instance drew on *Marxist theory to argue that with the growth of urbanization and industrialization there was a world change in family patterns, as the *state increasingly took over kinship functions such as *socialization, health and welfare, and the organization of labour and the extended family came to be replaced by the nuclear family. †Talcott Parsons, following a †positivist, *functionalist line of thought, maintained that the nuclear family provided the basis for socialization of children and for the personal development and stability of the adult couple, and identified the 'isolated nuclear family' as the ideal family form for the mobile workforce of industrial society.

The conjugal family as building block

Early social theorists defined the family in terms of its functions, and implicitly saw it as a natural form based on a heterosexual conjugal pair and their offspring. Anthropologists developing kinship theories based on cross-cultural analysis, however, were more interested in identifying universals than in developing theories of social evolution and change. For †G.P. Murdock, the nuclear family was a universal feature of society, through which the needs of *consumption, socialization, sexuality and labour were met and regulated. *Malinowski, writing in rather a different vein about what he termed the 'principle of legitimacy' argued that universally 'the father is indispensable for the full sociological status of the child as well as of its mother, that the group consisting of a woman and her offspring is sociologically incomplete and illegitimate . . . [and that] . . . the father, in other words, is necessary for the full legal status of the family' (in Goody 1971: 39). Malinowski had done his own research among the †matrilineal Trobriand Islanders, and he had argued that in this cultural context motherhood was perceived as a biological relationship, while fatherhood was seen as a purely social one. Thus, his insistence that both parents are necessary for the social legitimacy of the child must be seen in the context of his other claims, quite revolutionary for their time, about the ways in which biological and social kinship may be differentially perceived. Throughout such works, the nuclear or conjugal family, so ideologically central to the Euro-American social order of the time, was taken to be the basic 'building block' of kinship organization which, even when elaborated upon in such residential patterns as the extended family or the stem family household, still provided the basis for the regulation of consumption, production, socialization and sexuality.

The conjugal family and the developmental cycle

†Meyer Fortes's work on the †developmental cycle of the domestic group shifted the discussion of the family away from function and towards comparison of structures. For Fortes, the minimal unit of kinship was the mother-child dyad, which he saw as 'demonstrable' and hence natural. Fatherhood and other kinship relations, it followed, were socially rather than obviously biologically based, and could be organized in a variety of different ways in different cultures. Fortes's great achievement, however, was to distinguish between the domestic group and the family, and following this to recognize that any static picture of the domestic group was misleading. Following *L.H. Morgan and other earlier thinkers, Fortes made a distinction between the domestic and the juro-political domain. The domestic domain was associated with the mother-child dyad, or the 'matricentral cell', and the juro-political domain with wider, more instrumental social and economic relations:

> Where the conjugal relationship and patrifiliation are jurally or ritually effective in establishing a child's jural status, the husband-father becomes a critical link between the matricentral cell and the domestic domain as a whole. In this case the nuclear family may be regarded as the . . . reproductive nucleus of the domestic domain. It consists of two, and only two, successive generations bound together by the primary dependence of the child on its parents for nurture and love and of the parents on the child as the link between them and their reproductive fulfilment.
>
> (Fortes in Goody 1971: 91)

The domestic group, on the other hand, is a 'householding and housekeeping unit organized to provide the material and cultural resources needed to maintain and bring up its members' (ibid.: 92).

Thus, the family consisted of a heterosexual conjugal pair and their offspring, which formed the core but did not limit the parameters of the domestic group. Further, the domestic group went through phases, which involved different residential patterns and different personnel, beginning with the marriage of a woman and man, changing with the birth of their first child, and changing again when that child entered adulthood and set up her or his own household. The juro-political domain was implicitly organized around male relations of exchange, power and authority; the family around the mother and child and affective relations of love and nurture; while the domestic group, a residential unit based on production, reproduction and consumption, mediated the two domains through the husband-father.

While Fortes's picture added flexibility and structural variation to the notion of the universal family, it still rested on an assumption of a conjugal family based on a heterosexual conjugal unit and, further, it promoted a gendered dichotomy between the natural matricentral family at the core of the domestic domain and the social male domain of jural polity. Variation and difference were added to the model, but the variation was cyclical and to a great extent uniform, as the term 'developmental cycle' itself implies. Fortes, like Malinowski, had done path-breaking research in a matrilineal society; Ashanti children received their social *identity from their mother and belonged to their mother's lineage, but their spiritual core, their *ntoro*, came from their father. For Fortes, as for Malinowski, two parents were therefore necessary for complete social identity. Both Fortes and Malinowski extended the idea of a socially complete *person to their definitions of the family: if a person could only be complete with two legitimate parents, then the family should consist of two parents and their children, regardless of the lineage affiliation. Ironically, Fortes's own work on Ashanti family structure and the developmental cycle of the domestic group showed how transitory and fragile the conjugal family could be, particularly in relation to the more enduring matrilocal extended family. In his later writings, however, he stressed the universality of †bilateral affiliation, and by extension the conjugal family. As Raymond Smith commented, this insistence upon the importance of bilateral affiliation as a moral principle of universal significance serves to re-establish the nuclear family (or something very like it) as the universally necessary matrix for the reproduction of social beings. It also forges a strong link in the theoretical chain between domesticity and kinship, and comes dangerously close to reintroducing the confusion between biology and kinship (Smith 1973: 122).

Even some quite early ethnographic accounts, however, attested to the fact that the conjugal family was not as ubiquitous as the dominant theories maintained. †Evans–Pritchard had recorded the existence of 'woman to woman' marriages among the †patrilineal Nuer, in which a woman could pay †bridewealth for another woman, and by so doing attain rights over that woman's labour and the right to claim any children she bore for her own †lineage, just as a man would have the right to claim for his lineage any children born to a woman for whom he had paid bridewealth. While it could be argued that in such a case the woman paying bridewealth was acting as a 'sociological male', or that the rights to which she was entitled were closer to those over a servant or *slave than a marital partner, the existence of the institution cast doubt on the universal and exclusive nature of the heterosexual conjugal union as the basis of the family. Other examples were even more problematic to the universal model because they represented not a sociological anomaly but the norm. †Kathleen Gough's account of the Nayar, a South Indian matrilineal group in which women underwent a ritual like marriage at puberty and afterwards took a number of lovers who fathered their children, while continuing to live with their brothers, cast doubt on the universality of the 'fit' between conjugal family and domestic group. These examples, and others like them, suggested that there was no universal natural family, nor any automatic correlation between family form and domestic group which could be taken as universal. While the assertion that two social parents give the child a complete social identity is probably correct in many if not most cultures, an automatic link between this bilateral affiliation and the practical, lived-in form of the conjugal family is less clear.

A further problematic dimension to the family in anthropological studies was its connection with an evolutionary bias in theory, and an unstated but omnipresent connection with *modernity. Thus, non-industrial societies were depicted as having kinship systems, in which, à la Fortes, the family played the part of the basic building block, while Europe and middle-class North America, and at a broader level industrialized societies generally, were seen to have families rather than complex kinship systems. This harks back to the social evolutionists' idea that, with increasingly complex divisions of labour and the development of formal political institutions, the importance of wider kinship structures such as the lineage diminishes and that of the nuclear family increases. One result of this perspective was that analyses of non-industrial societies concentrated on kinship, while those of industrial societies tended almost to ignore it, and to emphasize instead the conjugal or nuclear family.

The family and the household

This model of the evolution from kinship to nuclear family has been criticized from two quite different perspectives. Those associated with the Cambridge Group for Population Studies, most notably Peter Laslett, questioned the widespread existence of the pre-industrial extended family, and used census materials and other historical data to show that even in 'past times' *households based on the small conjugal family were often the norm (Laslett and Wall 1972). MacFarlane (1978) specifically linked the conjugal family household, strong notions of private rather than corporate property, and an ideology of *individualism to pre-industrial England. Other studies, however, such as Anderson (1971) on nineteenth-century family structure in Lancashire, showed that the family structure and household membership were far more flexible than a static census-based picture would imply. At times of crisis or hardship families pooled resources among households, and kin moved between households, extending the nuclear family to the more complex forms. This was neither a regional nor a nineteenth-century phenomenon; the work of Wilmott and Young (1962) in East London in the 1950s revealed very similar patterns of resource-sharing beyond the boundaries of the household, and of very strong, regular ties between extended families, particularly between mothers and married daughters, and sisters. Grieco's (1987) research in Scotland and northern England in the 1980s also suggested that the extended family was as important as the conjugal family in patterns of residence, household composition and access to resources during periods of unemployment. This research specifically refuted the Parsonian theory of the isolated nuclear family as the ideal, moveable unit for employment in the modern, industrial state: Grieco's data show not only that local management recruit through extended kin networks – a syndrome also discussed by Wilmott and Young as the 'lads of dads' employment pattern – but that ties of kinship are used to find employment over long distances, to recruit labour from other regions, and to provide housing and other support when labour migration takes place.

An important implication of these studies is that family and household are not the same thing. While they often overlap, it is also frequently the case that households consist of members who are not family, such as servants or lodgers, while family membership, in terms of shared consumption, production and ties of intimacy, often extends over several households. An interesting similarity between the findings of Wilmott and Young and of Grieco is the significance of links between female kin and of matrilateral links generally in the workings of the extended family. In this they resemble what has been labelled the matrifocal family.

The matrifocal family

The matrifocal family occupies a curious position in anthropological writings, sometimes seen as a definite family structure based on a cultural valuing and centrality of the mother, and sometimes as a temporary or *ad hoc* response to poverty and exclusion. Raymond Smith's study of family and kinship in Guyana showed that a high proportion of villagers lived in female-headed households, and that often the core of the domestic unit consisted of a woman, her children and her daughters' children. Arguing that the 'family is not based on marriage or the nuclear family' (1973: 137), Smith describes a developmental cycle in which households are established when a man and woman, who may or may not be married and may or may not already have children either with other partners or together, set up house together. While the children of the household are young the woman is most dependent on the man economically, 'but while men contribute to the support of the household they do not participate very much in child-rearing or spend much time at home' (ibid.: 124). As the children get older, leave school and begin to earn money or to work on the farm, they contribute more economically to the household. The woman has always been the centre of affective ties in the family; at this point she also becomes 'the centre of an economic and decision-making coalition with her children . . . *whether the husband-father is present or not*' (ibid.: 125, emphasis added). Sons and daughters begin to engage in sexual relations while still living at home; if these result in children, they are incorporated into the maternal grandmother's household, resulting in the three generation 'matrifocal' family.

Smith suggests that in this family form the mother-child bond forms the affective and economic core, and the conjugal relationship is neither central nor necessary either to childrearing or to the family itself. He stresses that the term 'matrifocal' applies both to households where the husband-father is present, and where he is absent, and links matrifocality to three factors: a separation between the domestic and the politico-jural spheres, and an exclusion of men from domestic tasks and responsibilities; an emphasis on the mother-child and sibling relationship, and an expectation that the conjugal relationship will be 'less solidary, and less affectively intense (ibid.: 141); and stratification and economic factors, notably the absence of property.

Female-centred families attracted the attention not only of anthropologists but also of policy-makers and politicians. In the United States in the 1960s, as racial tension was growing and the civil rights movement was increasingly drawing attention to the poverty in which many Black Americans lived, the 'dysfunctional' family was increasingly singled out as the cause of poverty. In the early 1960s Daniel Moynihan's now famous report blamed the 'pathology of the Negro family' on the absence of men in the family, the high numbers of single-mother families, and the failure of unemployed men to take responsibility for their families and to provide role models for their children. A study by Stack (1974) of kinship and survival strategies among Afro-American families on a housing estate in Detroit showed that rather than being 'dysfunctional', female-centred house-holds and kin networks provided reasonable and rational responses to poverty and racial exclusion. Stack argued that the combination of high rates of male unemployment and a national welfare system which denied benefit to women who were cohab-iting with male partners favoured the develop-ment of female-centred households. In The Flats, the housing estate studied by Stack, high empha-sis was placed upon the sharing of both scarce resources and childcare and domestic responsibil-ities among female kin and friends. Long-term affective relationships between men and children were encouraged and maintained, but the female-based extended family formed the core of eco-nomic activity, resource-sharing and consumption. While this type of kin and household interdepen-dence was in many ways contrary to the dominant American ideology of the conjugal nuclear family, Stack showed that rather than being 'dysfunc-tional' it was a highly effective, strategic response to a situation of poverty and exclusion.

Families and ideologies

In studies of kinship and the family, anthropolo-gists are increasingly looking at discrepancies between ideology and lived practice, at differences based on *class, region, or *race and ethnicity, and at the relationship between the state and the family. Goody's (1983) historical work on the family in Europe specifically linked changes in marriage rules and in inheritance patterns and dowry payments within families to developments within the church and the state, thereby empha-sizing the changing nature of family and property relations in the context of external power struc-tures. Feminist social scientists have examined the relationship between gender and family, arguing that the ideology which represents the conjugal family and the household as 'natural' units serves to mask inequalities arising from an association of women with reproduction and men with produc-tion, a division which renders a great deal of women's labour invisible. Similarly, social histo-rians have shown that this association of women with the domestic sphere and men with the politico-jural or productive domain was histori-cally specific, arising in Britain in the nineteenth century with the growing influence of a middle-class morality which promoted government legislation removing children from the labour force, relegating their care to women, and repre-senting women as the core of the household, the 'haven in a heartless world' to which men could return after their long day in the brutal world of commerce and waged labour. These theories stress the links between capitalism, state legislation and changes in family ideologies, and emphasize the different ideologies of gender and family which obtained at various specific periods among different classes.

Increasingly, as single-parents families, same-sex unions, cohabitation without marriage, serial monogamy, and households based on friendship rather than sexual partnerships are becoming both more numerous and more visible to the public eye in Euro-American societies, established ideas about the 'natural' family are being challenged. Simultaneously, cross-cultural data which stress different types of family and house-hold structure place claims about the universality of the conjugal family in question. While the family will doubtlessly continue to be a major focus of analysis in social science in the foreseeable future, the parameters of the subject are currently being redefined, and the emphasis of enquiry is increasingly on plurality and difference rather than universality.

FRANCES PINE

See also: gender, house, household, kinship, marriage

Further reading

Anderson, M. (1971) *Family Structure in Nineteenth Century Lancashire*, Cambridge: Cambridge University Press

Gittins, D. (1985) *The Family in Question: Changing Households and Familiar Ideologies*, London: Macmillan

Goody, J. (ed.) (1971) *Kinship*, Harmondsworth: Penguin

—— (1983) *The Development of the Family and Marriage in Europe*, Cambridge: Cambridge University Press

Grieco, M. (1987) *Keeping it in the Family: Social Networks and Employment Chance*, London: Tavistock

Laslett, P. and R. Wall, (1972) *Household and Family in Past Time*, Cambridge: Cambridge University Press

MacFarlane, A. (1978) *The Origins of English Individualism: The Family, Property and Social Transition*, Oxford: Basil Blackwell

Smith, R. (1973) 'The Matrifocal Family', in J. Goody (ed.) *The Character of Kinship*, Cambridge: Cambridge University Press

Stack, C. (1974) *All Our Kin: Strategies for Survival in a Black Community*, New York: Harper and Row

Wilmott, P. and M. Young (1962) *Family and Kinship in East London*, Harmondsworth: Penguin

feudalism

Feudalism is a specific type of patronage-based political structure. Generally speaking, feudalism means that in exchange for support a lord makes land available to a vassal. Specifically, feudalism refers to a very particular kind of political structure found in medieval Europe, although the term may be applied in a much looser way to a variety of pre-modern *states outside Europe.

The 'invention' of feudalism is attributed to Charles Martel (689–741), mayor-domo of the Frankish kingdom of Austrasia, who needed mounted soldiers to combat the invading Saracens. Though the actual situation was more complicated, in essence this view still holds true (McKitterick 1983, Reuter 1991). To reward his cavalry Charles handed out land, which he extracted partly from the royal domains, but mainly from the extended landed property of the Church. In doing this he combined three long-established institutions: (1) the retinue, the group of warriors around a leader, who pledged oaths of fidelity, and who lived and died with their leader; (2) the vassalage, the custom, that

a free man placed himself under the protection of some lord, and in return had to give military service and counsel; and (3) the *beneficium*, the custom that a lord gave a piece of land to a man to earn a living, or in order to help him cover certain expenses (Bloch [1940] 1965, Ganshof 1957). To indemnify the Church it was decided that, though the land remained de facto in the hands of the warriors, when the holder of the land died it would return to the Church, unless the military situation did not allow it. The king would then endow another vassal with the land and the Church would receive a tithe. In this way the original gift of the land became a fief.

In the course of time the feudal system underwent considerable changes. The landed aristocracy gained more power and the position of the king eroded. When after the death of Louis the Pious (840) his sons battled each other fiercely for succession, each of them tried to contract as many vassals as possible, and in doing so spread their power thinly over more and more lower-ranked lords. Soon the territorial princes in their turn lost their influence to the local seigneurs. In the end these castellans possessed the military, judicial, and economic powers that once were the prerogatives of king and counts (Bloch [1940] 1965). It would take till the twelfth century until under the Capetians royal power and the *state in France were restored. Under the influence of Abbot Suger new concepts of *kinship and feudalism developed. The king became the highest feudal lord; he owed homage to no one but God; all other lords had to pay homage to the king. In this way feudal kingship was given its own place, with a religious legitimation that none of the territorial princes could ever hope to claim.

Ideally, the fully developed feudalism of the thirteenth and fourteenth centuries had the following characteristics:

1 A pyramidal, hierarchical power structure headed by a king, whose power was believed to be god-given; his position thus was legitimized sacrally. Under the king came the feudal lords. Their power was derived from, and legitimized by the king. Higher-placed feudal lords could have their own vassals who, indirectly, were also legitimized by the king. In the service of a feudal lord were keepers of manors, sheriffs, soldiers and servants, some of whom were authorized by their lord to exercize power in his name. Finally there were the humble subjects, who tilled the land and

owed the lord food, goods and service. In return the lord was supposed to protect them.

2 The relations between the members of the feudal hierarchy were asymmetrical, vertical, formal, dyadic, personal and reciprocal (Bloch [1940] 1965, Wolf 1966). A man commending himself to another paid homage by ceremonially placing his hands between those of his lord and taking an oath of fidelity to him. From that moment on there existed feudal relations between the two. Taking the act of homage as defining the feudal relation, it will be clear that the subjects of a lord fell outside the feudal system. It is also doubtful whether many members of the servant category had feudal relations with their lord. Yet, the servants, as well as the subjects, were inextricably bound up with the feudal system.

3 Positions in the feudal system were gained in principle by achievement, though in the course of time heredity played an increasing role. As the feudal lord received land in recompensation for his services, he was economically independent of the king. This made it difficult for the ruler to keep his lords under control; this was the main weakness of the feudal system.

'The feudal system meant the rigorous economic subjection of a host of humble folk to a few powerful men' (Bloch [1940] 1965: 443, Wolf 1966). In fact, the exploitation of *peasantry made the whole system possible. *Marxist scholars paid much attention to the exploitative aspects of the system, and the concept of the feudal *mode of production was developed (see below). Though feudalism dominated the social, political and economic relations during the Middle Ages, people such as clergy, monks, free cultivators, townsfolk and traders did not belong to the system. Bishops or abbots often played a role as feudal lords, however, but they did this in their capacity as worldly administrators, not as clergymen.

In the fifteenth century the feudal system gradually lost its dominating position. Heavy losses of the aristocracy on the battlefields, a growing influence of the money economy, an increasing role of towns and townspeople, and a new balance of power, were among the factors causing the emergence of new social and political conditions in Europe.

Feudalism poses a particular problem for *political anthropology. On the one hand, it bears sufficient superficial resemblance to pre-modern state forms in Asia and Africa – in the dependence on dyadic ties between lord and follower, or the use of overlapping tenurial rights in land – to suggest all may be usefully compared as variations on a single type. On the other hand, though, some of the features of the European case are more distinctively European – the emphasis on bearing arms and military service for the higher lord, for example. The situation is rendered even more unclear by feudalism's historical position as the political-economic predecessor to the emergence of *capitalism in Europe. In the doctrinaire Marxism that prevailed for many years in *Russian and Soviet anthropology, all pre-capitalist state forms had to be defined as 'feudal', however awkward that might be empirically.

HENRI J. M. CLAESSEN

See also: caste, Marxism and anthropology, peasant, political economy, power, state

Further reading

Bloch, M. ([1940] 1965) *Feudal Society*, 2 vols. London: Routledge and Kegan Paul

Ganshof, F.L. (1957) *Qu'est-ce que la féodalité*, Brussels: Office de Publicité

McKitterick, R. (1983) *The Frankish Kingdoms under the Carolingians, 751–987*, London and New York: Longman

Reuter, T. (1991) *Germany in the Early Middle Ages 800–1056*, London and New York: Longman

Wolf, E. (1966) *Peasants*, Englewood Cliffs, NJ: Prentice Hall

fieldwork

There is a troubled relationship between the representation of anthropological fieldwork and the actuality of any particular fieldwork. In sober fact, fieldwork can take as many forms as there are anthropologists, projects, and circumstances. Jean Briggs (1970) spent 17 months with a family group of Inuit in the Canadian *Arctic, 150 miles from anyone else. It is difficult to conceive of a more intense, total, and perhaps ill-advised abandonment to the ethnographic project. No-one spoke English. She was dependent on her hosts for shelter, for much of her food and clothing, and in an immediate and frightening sense for her very survival. Only once did she briefly leave the field, for a tiny and hardly less austere outpost of civilization. Malcolm Young (1991), on the other hand, did his fieldwork on the police of Newcastle while being a Newcastle policeman, and so never left home – or perhaps never left the field. My own fieldwork with Sri Lankan forest monks was different again (Carrithers 1983). I lived in Sri Lanka for nearly three years, but only occasionally among the monks: after all, they live in the woods to get away from people.

The representation of fieldwork is another matter. In the 1920s *Malinowski published a series of works representing the Trobrianders and – even more momentous for subsequent anthropologists – the character of his fieldwork in the Trobriands. George Stocking called these works 'mythopoeic' (Stocking 1983: 110) because they set out a grandly heroic and vivid image of fieldwork against which later anthropologists measured themselves. To immerse himself in local life, the intrepid fieldworker isolates himself completely from the consolation of his fellows: 'imagine yourself set down surrounded by all your gear, alone on a tropical beach close to a native village while the launch ... which has brought you sails away' (Malinowski 1922: 4). He spends months or years in his task, learns the language and thoroughly documents every aspect of local society. It is hard to imagine a more thorough devotion to science, and indeed the Malinowskian ethnographer is a paid-up member of the scientific guild, possessing special methods of collecting, manipulating, and fixing evidence (1922: 6), thus making an experimental contribution (1922: 2) on the analogy of chemistry or physics. Malinowski captured this composite picture brilliantly in the phrase †participant observation, which evokes what was then considered the scientific method *par excellence*, observation, and adds a twist of first-hand knowledge from the man on the spot.

It is now easy to find this image quaint, and certainly Malinowski's practice was not so monumental as his precept, but it is important to retrieve the tremendous impact the ideal of the heroic ethnographer has had on the practice of anthropology. It set out an aspiration which enabled later anthropologists, not only in Britain but elsewhere, to work in extraordinarily difficult circumstances under the fortifying assumption that if it had been done once it could be done again. Moreover the quality and quantity of Malinowski's information seemed fully to justify the role he claimed for himself as founder of modern anthropological fieldwork. On the other hand, there were significant silences in his work, and in that of those who followed him. Methods were frequently invoked, but in print little of use was said. The actual process of fieldwork, the sense of it being a day-

to-day experience and a deeply problematical one at that, was largely missing. And participation was understood largely to be a superior form of observation, for anything more might seem unscientific.

The Malinowskian image held unchallenged for more than forty years (for discussions of fieldwork in that period see the bibliography to Powdermaker 1966). But in 1960 Joseph Casagrande edited *In the Company of Man*, a collection in which a long list of anthropologists, including several elder statesmen, each discussed a key informant met during fieldwork. This book signalled a more human-sized and less scientistic view of the research enterprise. Casagrande wrote that 'we wish to share with the reader the personal experience of field work, and to communicate the essentially humane quality of our discipline in a way that is at once aesthetically, emotionally, and scientifically satisfying'. He stressed that the capacity for imaginatively entering into the life of another people becomes a primary qualification for the ethnographer (Casagrande 1960: xii). This is no doubt true of most fieldwork, indeed of Malinowski's, but it had not so far figured as a part of anthropology's official self-image. In 1965 Kenneth Read's *The High Valley* was the first serious ethnography to use a largely autobiographical style, revealing his own feelings and failings in the service of scholarship. And in 1966 Hortense Powdermaker, a one-time student of Malinowski, wrote quite explicitly of anthropology as a humanistic discipline in a monograph-length personal-cum-scholarly retrospective over her professional life (Powdermaker 1966). To bolster her rejection of a purely scientistic anthropology, she chose an image that was intentionally subversive, that of the anthropologist as a 'human instrument' studying other human beings (1966: 19). She probably meant scientific instrument, but the direction of her argument suggests that she could as well have meant sensitive musical instrument.

There followed an explosion of writing about fieldwork, ranging from handbooks for gathering information, through personal reminiscences, to new styles of *ethnography using personal experience and feelings, and this broadening stream carries on right to the present. Some of the Malinowskian mystique still hovers over fieldwork, and some of the fieldwork manuals make it out to be at least as orderly and scientific as Malinowski ever did: but for the most part we now understand the ethnographer as a more complex, flawed, human-sized figure whose efforts and exposure to the unfamiliar bring forth a less absolutely certain, but also a richer and more nuanced account. Jean Briggs's *Never in Anger* (1970) became one of the most widely quoted ethnographies. She showed how an outburst of anger, unremarkable among Yankees but unacceptable among Inuit, led to their ostracizing her, but also to a more profound understanding on her part, and so ours, of Inuit social relations. The use of personal experience in this way is now an acceptable scholarly and writerly device for anthropologists, and can sometimes be extremely revealing (see, for example, Favret-Saada 1980).

This shift in the representation of fieldwork is tied to a larger change in the character of anthropology in general (see Carrithers 1992 for a fuller treatment). The natural scientific image of anthropological research regarded *culture and *society chiefly as collectible or countable, whereas now we regard culture and society as matters to be learned. On this view, there are two kinds of knowledge involved in fieldwork. One kind is the practical, everyday knowledge that the people studied use to get around in their lives. The anthropologist must engage with this, both to survive and work in local circumstances and to discover local reasons, motives and standards. The anthropologist may never totally command the local language or local styles of relating, but she does achieve a good passive knowledge of them. She then rehearses and reflects upon what she has learned – and also upon what she has counted and collected – and transforms this first knowledge into a second knowledge, no longer a personal knowledge of how to handle persons, but a critical knowledge of how to compare one society and culture with others, particularly her own. It would be more faithful to the anthropological enterprise if we called this process engaged learning.

In this light, the present understanding of fieldwork might be something like this. Fieldwork encompasses much more than the time you spend in the field. You must prepare by reading and talk, and by cultivating knowledge of your own ignorance and an attitude of intense and pure curiosity, rather like the feeling you have just before you utter a question to which you deeply want to know the answer. Then, in the field, you must be able to tap this sense and turn it upon anything you meet. For you will find that your experience there

is mostly a brash, awkward, hit-and-run encounter of one sensibility with others, as Kumar (1992: 1) so aptly remarked, and only curiosity and hope – with a measure of self-organization – will get you through. Whatever preparations you made, you will still have to make it up as you go along. You will struggle to produce that second knowledge, the knowledge re-worked for scholarly purposes, even while you are struggling to achieve the first knowledge, how to live with people. You will gain a measure of peace from successfully counting and collecting things, but only towards the end of your stay might you expect the reward Kumar discovered toward the end of her fieldwork in Banaras:

> I felt part of my surroundings; I was like a finely tuned instrument from which a complex sound could emerge and all the resonant strings vibrate in analogy with the sitar when the correct note was plucked. Reports confirmed one another, facts were buttressed by more facts, interpretations rallied to one another's defense ... I was interacting with only a few informants on one level but on many other levels I was interacting with other components of the city. I felt beyond the shadow of a doubt that I was interacting with the city itself.
>
> (Kumar 1992: 230)

But it doesn't end there. Back home at your desk you will continue to be engaged laboriously with the people you study, through imagination, recollection and reconstruction. It is easy to forget that writing is as much a part of fieldwork as any choice passage of travel or startling encounter.

MICHAEL CARRITHERS

See also: ethnography, methodology, Malinowski

Further reading

Briggs, J. (1970) *Never in Anger: Portrait of an Eskimo Family*, Cambridge, MA: Harvard University Press

Carrithers, M. (1983) *The Forest Monks of Sri Lanka*, Delhi: Oxford University Press

—— (1992) *Why Humans Have Cultures: Explaining Anthropology and Social Diversity*, Oxford: Oxford University Press

Casagrande, J. (ed.) (1959) *In the Company of Man*, New York: Harper

Ellen, R. (ed.) (1984) *Ethnographic Research: A Guide to General Conduct*, London: Academic Press

Favret-Saada, J. (1980) *Deadly Words: Witchcraft in the Bocage*, Cambridge: Cambridge University Press

Kumar, N. (1992) *Friends, Brothers and Informants: Fieldwork Memoirs of Banaras*, Berkeley: University of California Press

Malinowski, B. (1922) *Argonauts of the Western Pacific*, London: Routledge

Powdermaker, H. (1966) *Stranger and Friend: The Way of an Anthropologist*, New York: W.W. Norton and Company

Rabinow, P. (1977) *Reflections on Fieldwork in Morocco*, Berkeley: University of California Press

Stocking, G.W. (ed.) (1983) *Observers Observed: Essays on Ethnographic Fieldwork*, Madison: University of Wisconsin Press

Young, M. (1991) *An Inside Job: Policing and Police Culture in Britain*, Oxford: Clarendon Press

film

Any consideration of the place of film within anthropological theory and practice must take into account two contextual factors: first, its place within the wider subdiscipline of visual anthropology, where it should be seen as a medium of visual representation that shares much in common with other forms of visual representation employed by the anthropologist (photography, diagrams) and forms employed by the anthropological subject (photography, video, *art and decoration); and second, its place within many cultures as an art form which shares much in common with drama and literature.

So-called ethnographic films thus have two aspects, the documentary or *ethnographic and the artistic or cinematographic. Of course, film shares this duality with other modes of representation such as writing and *oratory; however, while most written or oral texts employed in anthropological teaching or research – such as published monographs, seminar papers and lectures – are produced by anthropologists who give little prominence to their 'artistic' qualities, many ethnographic films are produced by professional film makers who attach at least as much value to the cinematographic qualities of their films as to the ethnographic. In his pioneering work *Ethnographic Film* (1976), Karl Heider argues that the documentary or ethnographic component of an ethnographic film should always take precedence over the cinematographic so that, for example, a shot which is slightly out of focus should be included in a film if it is essential to an holistic ethnographic understanding. However, it is clear that many of the best known and best distributed ethnographic films, such as those of

the American film maker Robert Gardner (who collaborated with Heider in the making of *Dead Birds* [1963], a film about local warfare amongst the Dani people of Irian Jaya) are appreciated as much for their cinematographic qualities as their ethnographic ones. The possible conflict between these two interests has led to much debate, and some confusion.

Brief history

As with photography, anthropologists have used moving film as a medium of record (the documentary aspect) from the beginning of the modern anthropological project. Only three years after Louis Lumière launched the first portable moving film camera in 1895, the British anthropologist †A. C. Haddon took one to the †Torres Straits Islands off the northern coast of Australia as a tool for his influential expedition. By 1901, †Baldwin Spencer was filming *Aboriginal dances in Australia, and over the next twenty-one years a number of anthropological expeditions were equipped with a film camera for documenting the customs and habits of the natives. A new direction was taken in 1922 when the American explorer and film maker Robert Flaherty publicly released his influential *Nanook of the North*. Ironically, 1922 is seen by many as the year in which British *functionalist anthropology was born, with the death of the *evolutionist and *diffusionist †Rivers and the publication of *Malinowski's and *Radcliffe-Brown's major monographs. Functionalism is the anthropological paradigm perhaps most closely associated with the documentary aspect of ethnographic film, yet above all else *Nanook* is clearly a film remarkable for its cinematographic qualities. While it does certainly document aspects of the lives of the Eskimo (as they were known) of Hudson Bay, Canada, it does so in a way that is driven by narrative, suspense, tension and resolution – qualities of the cinema or of theatre, not of anthropology or science.

However, the natural-science paradigm of most functionalist anthropology had little use for film, claiming (quite rightly) that the highly particularistic nature of filmic data was of little use in documenting or analysing society-wide †social facts, such as *kinship or *social structure. There was a brief surge of interest in the United States in the years leading up to World War II when †Margaret Mead and †Gregory Bateson, following a paradigm later known as the *'culture and personality' school, made extensive use of still photography and film in their investigations into Balinese character. Similar work was carried out after the war by Alan Lomax, particularly in his †choreometric studies of *dance. But as the theoretical influence of this type of analysis waned, so too did this very specialized use of film.

However, in some parts of the world (particularly in *German and Central European anthropology) anthropology – while still heavily functionalist and positivistic – retained an †ethnological and *folkloristic component in the postwar years that had withered in North America and especially in Britain. The ethnologists' interests in †material culture fitted well with the representational properties of film. In particular, from the 1950s onwards, the Institut für den Wissenschaftlichen Film (IWF – Institute for Scientific Film) at Göttingen in Germany produced a number of 'scientific' films which paid close attention to material culture and productive processes in European and non-European societies. In marked contrast, the renowned French film maker and anthropologist Jean Rouch began in the mid-1940s to produce a remarkable corpus of films, some of which freely mixed fictional narration and documentation (such as *Moi, Un Noir* [1957] in which three young men from Niger act out their experiences and fantasies as migrants in the Ivory Coast). In almost all of Rouch's many films the cinematographic quality has dominated. There are several other important historical trends that should be noted, but space does not permit an adequate discussion (see instead the contributions to Hockings 1995). The 1970s and 1980s have seen an extraordinary explosion in the production of ethnographic film, through much of which the tension between ethnographic and cinematographic qualities has remained. The two are well reconciled in the films produced by the British television company, Granada, in their 'Disappearing World' series. Many of these films incorporate some kind of narrative device (for example, the preparations leading up to some large-scale event or ritual) to drive the film forward and to carry ethnographic detail. Of course, these films, while made with an anthropological consultant, are produced by professional television film makers and intended for a mass audience, and this has led to some criticism of them by professional anthropologists. Elsewhere similar television projects have been seen, with the PBS 'Odyssey' series in the USA, and the Japanese NTV 'Man' series (see Ginsburg 1988).

The uses of film

The single most important use of ethnographic film today is in teaching, although in the case of televised films the didactic purpose cannot be separated from their entertainment value. In many cases teachers (of anthropology, but also of dance, art, behavioural science and so forth) show the films for their ethnographic content, and play down or ignore the cinematographic qualities. It is partly for this reason that some of Robert Gardner's films – especially his *Forest of Bliss* (1985) shot at the Banaras cremation grounds in India, and containing no commentary or subtitled speech – have been rejected by several anthropologists. In the United States Tim Asch pioneered the production of films especially for use in teaching, most notably the Yanomami series produced with the anthropologist Napoleon Chagnon. Some corpuses of film however – particularly those of Jean Rouch, Robert Gardner and the Australian-resident David and Judith MacDougall – have attracted the attention of film theorists, who see in them innovatory cinematographic practices (see Loizos 1993 for an anthropologist's account of such innovation). Several anthropologists have used film – and more specifically video – as an aid to *fieldwork. Videotape permits an anthropologist to record long and sociologically complex sequences of action (such as *rituals or political oratory) far more efficiently than would be possible with a stills camera and a notebook. Very often these tapes are never intended for public screening (except perhaps to those who participated in the event), but they can be viewed again and again by the anthropologist in the course of research. The use of video in this way also permits anthropologists to 'return' some of their work to the people they have lived among in a form that is perhaps more accessible than a printed book or article.

Some anthropologists have also noticed that video (and to a lesser extent experiments in 'neighbourhood television') has been taken up as a means of communication within certain societies, effectively bypassing the state control of media and even the need for literacy. The American anthropologist Terence Turner has both documented and facilitated this process amongst the Kayapó Indians of Brazil (see Turner 1992).

Theorizing film

It is only in recent years that anthropologists have begun to make anything other than a purely historical or chronological assessment of the place of film within the discipline. Some earlier uses of film attempted to expand or verify certain theoretical positions. For example, Sol Worth and John Adair's 1966 Navajo filmmakers project was an attempt to transplant the *Sapir–Whorf hypothesis from language to vision (Heider 1976: 43). Theoretical questions since then have, however, shifted away from functionalist anthropology and communication science, towards literary theory, film theory, and *cultural studies. The position advocated by Heider which calls for ethnographic integrity and veracity, while influential in its day, rests on a rather naive understanding of visual representation, the so-called 'window on the world' approach to cinema, that has now largely been rejected for its inherently functionalist view of social reality. On the other hand, some of the more experimental films shown at ethnographic film festivals, which employ mixed filmic genres, appear to display a poor understanding of the cultures they are supposed to represent, particularly when the filmmaker is a student who does not speak the local language and has not spent very long in the field.

The issue of ethnographic 'truth' preoccupied much American writing during the 1970s and 1980s. Anthropologists such as Jay Ruby praised the *reflexive quality of film which provides the chance for anthropologists to be far more explicit about their field methodology and thus allows the viewer greater insight into the circumstances that produced the data (Ruby 1980). Similarly, writers influenced by literary theory have suggested that the cinematographic features of film can be used to emphasize the constructed nature of texts about other societies, leading to a more critical anthropology. The nature of the film-watching event has also attracted attention, drawing on work in both literary theory, particularly 'reception theory' or 'reader-centred criticism', and media studies. Several writers on ethnographic film have been disturbed by Wilton Martinez's findings that North American student audiences appear to 'read' ethnographic films in a way that confirms rather than corrects the prejudices they hold about non-European societies (see Martinez in Crawford and Turton 1992).

Just as there are a number of possible interpretations of what might constitute an ethnographic film in the first place (hence my initial use of the phrase 'so-called ethnographic film' – see also Banks in Crawford and Turton 1992), so there are many interpretations of the place of such films within anthropological investigation, teaching and research (including some that reject it completely). The tensions of the cinematographic and documentary qualities of film, however, together with the particularizing tendency of film when contrasted with the generalizing project of anthropology, would seem to lie at the heart of most of these interpretations.

MARCUS BANKS

See also: aesthetics

Further reading

Crawford, P. and D. Turton (eds) (1992) *Film as Ethnography*, Manchester: Manchester University Press in association with the Granada Centre for Visual Anthropology

Ginsburg, F. (1988) 'Ethnographies on the Airwaves: The Presentation of Anthropology on American, British and Japanese Television' in P. Hockings and Y. Omori (eds) *Senri Ethnological Studies No. 24: Cinematographic Theory and New Dimensions in Ethnographic Film*, Osaka: National Museum of Ethnology

Heider, K. (1976) *Ethnographic Film*, Austin: University of Texas Press

Hockings, P. (ed.) (1995) *Principles of Visual Anthropology* (second edition), The Hague: Mouton

Loizos, P. (1993) *Innovation in Ethnographic Film: From Innocence to Self-consciousness, 1955–1985*, Manchester: Manchester University Press

Ruby, J. (1980) 'Exposing Yourself: Reflexivity, Film and Anthropology', *Semiotica* 3: 153–79

Turner, T. (1992) 'Defiant Images: The Kayapo Appropriation of Video', *Anthropology Today* 8 (6): 5–16

Films

The following films are a small number of those that have been considered influential in the development of an anthropological cinema.

Asch, T. and N. Chagnon (1975) *The Ax Fight*, USA: Pennsylvania State: University [colour, 30 mins]

Dunlop, I. and R. Tonkinson (1967) *Desert People*, Australia: Film Australia [black and white, 51 mins]

Flaherty, R. (1922) *Nanook of the North*, USA: Revillon Frères [black and white, 55 mins]

Gardner, R. (1963) *Dead Birds*, Boston, USA: Film Study Center, Harvard University [colour, 83 mins]

Kildea, G. and J. Leach (1975) *Trobriand Cricket: An Indigenous Response to Colonialism*, Papua New Guinea: Office of Information [colour, 53 mins]

MacDougall, D. and J. MacDougall (1971) *To Live With Herds: A Dry Season Among the Jie*, USA: University of California Ethnographic Film Program [black and white, 90 mins]

Moser, B. (1971) *The Last of the Cuiva*, Manchester, UK: Granada Television [colour, 50 mins]

Rouch, J. and E. Morin (1960) *Chronique d'un été*, Paris: Argos Films [black and white, 90 mins]

fishing

There is evidence of specialized fishing adaptations in the archaeological record dating from Paleolithic times, which parallel technological developments in the exploitation of terrestrial resources. Fishery resources are in places abundant and reliable. Year-round livelihoods are possible with minimum technical elaboration. Shellfish may be picked off the rocks at low tide, artificial pools built of rocks to trap fish as the tide flows out; streams and rivers may be dammed with sticks and stones. Middens at coastal, riverine and lacustrine sites demonstrate long, continuous occupation with strata of shells and fish bones several metres deep.

A fishing economy may be supported either by simple gathering, active hunting, or both. Fishing may be a full-time specialization, or it may be a seasonal, part-time or occasional pursuit. It may rely upon sedentary or slow-moving animals which are easily gathered; it may exploit locally-resident populations of fish and sea mammals which require more active techniques of trapping or hunting; or it may pursue seasonal migrations of these animals with a variety of technical means, including boats operating offshore, out of sight of land. Depending upon the nature of the resources exploited, and the technical basis of the economy, relatively dense populations of people can be supported, since the †carrying capacity of the immediate environment is not limited by the natural distribution of terrestrial plants and animals, as in a *hunting and gathering economy.

The Kwakiutl, Nootka, Tsimshian and other peoples of the west coast of Canada give examples of pre-industrial maritime economies founded upon sea-mammal hunting and the seasonal capture of salmon and candlefish. Much of their food supply was garnered during a relatively short season; preserved fish was the staple foodstuff for the rest of the year, which left ample time for other activities. These peoples were largely sedentary, living in large, permanent, year-round village communities. Elsewhere, there are †Mesolithic and †Neolithic sites which suggest similar features, and have given rise to speculation that maritime peoples, having stable food supplies, adequate leisure and sedentary settlement patterns, were more favourably placed to experiment with domestication and cultivation at lower risk and opportunity costs than nomadic or *transhumant populations reliant upon terrestrial resources only.

There is uncertainty, therefore, whether fishing should be classified as a sub-type of hunting and gathering, or as a distinct mode of livelihood, intermediate between hunting and gathering and horticulture. While fishing economies rely upon wild resources which are hunted or collected, social complexity of a kind normally associated with domesticated resources is demonstrated in the archaeological and ethnographic records. The classical theorists, upon whom contemporary anthropologists rely for authority, evidently knew little about fishing, or found the anomalies methodologically too troublesome to be fitted into their schemes. For example, *Morgan treated fishing as identical with hunting and gathering; and †Marx did not mention fishing at all, a circumstance which has given rise to difficulties in anthropologists' attempts to devise analyses of fishing economies using Marxist principles.

Attempts to theorize fishing have had mixed success. One concept that has proved useful in explaining certain kinds of fishing that involve active hunting is the 'tragedy of the commons'. If the fish in the sea are a common resource, over which no one is able to assert a proprietorial claim, then the tendency will be for the numbers of fishers to expand and for all to take as much as they can until the catches available to each decline below the point of economic viability. At this point, some or all of the fishers drop out. Gradually numbers build up again and the cycle repeats itself. In practice, however, fishers may seek to counter declining catches with improved forms of organization and technical equipment. Ultimately, the fish may be caught faster than they can reproduce themselves, leading to the complete collapse of the fish populations upon which the fishers depend. There have been several such collapses in recent years. Anthropologists have played a significant role in identifying the social and economic variables leading to instances of over-exploitation in modern commercial fisheries, and their advice has been sought by national and international agencies seeking to create new regulatory frameworks.

In other respects, a 'theory of fishing' remains elusive. People like the Nuer of the Southern Sudan, who spear fish during a brief season in years when the Nile floods, are fishers only as occasional opportunists; they have little in common with the Nootka, still less with contemporary Norwegian trawler operators and crews. Nevertheless, maritime anthropologists have attempted to apply the label †'petty commodity producers' or 'artisanal fishers' to a wide variety of modern fishing peoples with little apparent regard for the local origins of fishing or its relationship to *capitalism. In some places, it may indeed be a semi-subsistence *peasant activity; in other places fishing can be adequately understood only in relation to the rise of mercantilism and industrial capitalism, and where the fishers themselves are no less capitalists and industrial workers than city dwellers. Comparative research on the differential penetration of *markets in fish, capital and labour at various periods and in various places still requires to be done if an adequate 'theory of fishing' is to be advanced.

REGINALD BYRON

See also: economic anthropology, hunting and gathering

Further reading

Acheson, J. (1981) 'The Anthropology of Fishing', *Annual Review of Anthropology* 10: 275–316

Cole, S. (1991) *Women of the Praia: Work and Lives in a Portuguese Coastal Community*, Princeton: Princeton University Press

Faris, J. (1972) *Cat Harbour: A Newfoundland Fishing Settlement*, St John's: Institute of Social and Economic Research

Firth, R. (1966) *Malay Fishermen: Their Peasant Economy*, London: Routledge and Kegan Paul

Hardin, G. (1968) 'The Tragedy of the Commons', *Science* 162: 1243–8

McCay, B. and J. Acheson (eds) (1987) *The Question of the Commons: The Culture and Ecology of Communal Resources*, Tucson: University of Arizona Press

Orbach, M. (1977) *Hunters, Seamen and Entrepreneurs: The Tuna Seinermen of San Diego*, Berkeley: University of California Press

Robbens, A. (1991) *Sons of the Sea Goddess: Economic Practice and Discursive Conflict in Brazil*, New York: Columbia University Press

Tunstall, J. (1962) *The Fishermen: The Sociology of an Extreme Occupation*, London: Macgibbon and Kee

folklore

The term 'folklore' means both a body of material and the academic discipline devoted to its study.

Although the description of customs, verbal lore and, more rarely, material culture was not unknown even in medieval Europe, the idea of the systematic collection and analysis of such data emerged most strongly with the dramatic rise of European romantic *nationalism in the first half of the nineteenth century.

Inspired by philosophies such as those of †G.B. Vico (1668–1744) and †J.G. Herder (1744–1803), nationalist scholars sought in folkloric materials the empirical basis for their claims about essentialized national character. In many cases they also sought demonstrable connections with the cultural glories of supposed collective ancestors. Nationalism gave folklore its greatest impetus, charging it with preserving the evanescent treasures of the oral archive for a literate posterity. It even legitimated textual 'emendation', which sometimes amounted to outright forgery, on the combined grounds of scholarly sophistication and insiders' instinctive knowledge, and for the practical reason that the defence of national interests demanded cultural cleansing (analogous in some countries to concurrent linguistic 'purification'). In Finland Elias Lönnrot (1802–1884) 'reconstructed' the *Kalevala* from texts collected at geographically dispersed sites; in Greece N.G. Politis (1852–1921), while a philological comparativist of extraordinary erudition and scope, reconstructed 'original texts' from similarly dispersed oral variants, treating them as if they were chronologically fixed manuscript versions. In a very real sense, the attempts to reconstitute *Urtexte* expressed metonymically the programmes of national regeneration they were intended to serve.

Just as anthropology reached maturity as the study of colonized others, academic folklore first appeared to reach coherence as the study of the domestic exotics to be found in the rural hinterland of nation-states (initially in Europe, then in many Asian countries – notably India, Japan, and Korea – as well as virtually the rest of the world). As a discipline, indeed, folklore partially shares the institutionalized genealogy of anthropology, notably in its early adherence to forms of survivalism and *evolutionism – epistemologies, however, that folklore was far slower to reject. Although they did not long retain the original survivalist tenet – namely, that the folklore of countryside and colony was the residue of an earlier, childhood phase of human history – they easily inverted it to argue that this lore instead represented in degenerate form the lost glories of newly reconstructed pasts (see Hodgen 1936). In totalitarian ideologies such as Nazism, folklore was used to invest notions of national and racial purity with scientific authority. In almost all cases, a romantic form of censorship suppressed the lore of sexuality, subjecting the peasantry to a bourgeois moral code. The city – again Nazism provides an extreme example – represented the 'corruption' of the pure national virtues. It was not until the post-World War II era, and especially with the influential work of the psychoanalytic folklorist Alan Dundes in the United States, that the categories of urban and industrial folklore began to gain currency, and that obscene or politically subversive folklore gained academic respectability.

The philological origins and direction of much academic folklore prompted a strongly taxonomic emphasis. In the early nationalistic studies, this often served the purpose of drawing a clear line between allegedly historical and *mythological texts. As folklorists began to engage in more global and comparative research, however, it produced less parochial and politically motivated work. Already in the nineteenth century Child's (1857) study of balladry allowed subsequent scholars to trace the migration of specific themes and motifs to the New World. Such philological approaches remained tied to genealogical models of textual interrelationships (stemmatics). Notable among the later products of the classificatory tradition was Stith Thompson's monumental Index of Tale-Types (1932–36), a work of such comprehensive scope that later scholars continue to find it a sure guide requiring modification only in matters of detail. Another tradition, powerfully influenced by French *structuralism and its Russian antecedent, †Vladimir Propp's (1968) taxonomic and formal study of Russian folktales, attempted to organize oral traditions according to structural and semantic properties; developments in literary theory have also promoted a focus on such themes as genre theory – permitting greater attention to the conceptual and social contexts of performance – as well as on audience reception and performance. These moves have permitted a more perceptive view of humour, irony and insult as culturally negotiated assessments rather than as intrinsic properties of inert texts.

In the United States, where folklore played an important role in establishing both the European origins and the New World distinctiveness of the earlier settlers, a more theoretical approach has been energized by the study of indigenous *aesthetics and by what has become known as 'the ethnography of communication' as well as the active development there of †semiotics. Especially prominent in this arena has been the work of R. Bauman; working in a Jakobsonian linguistic idiom and with a strong interest in †speech act theory, he and others (including a number of prominent †ethnomusicologists) have developed a performative perspective on folklore that frees it from the rigidity of older taxonomic approaches. Framing, play, ambiguity, and the contested evaluation of competence emerge as no less important than formal textual features.

Material culture is an increasingly studied dimension of folklore, and is especially relevant to the discipline's role in museums. While museum displays often serve ideological ends such as promoting a sense of national unity by highlighting commonalities in artefact form and use, they may also focus on use, aesthetic principles, and processes of the transmission of technical knowledge. Studies of material objects may also situate them in wider matrices of use and meaning – for example, the utensils used to prepare ritual and ordinary foods and the relationship of this entire culinary complex to cosmology, ritual and social practices. Here, in fact, the most careful folkloric research is indistinguishable from *ethnography. More generally, it can be said that, as folklore moves from philological classification to social and performative contextualization, its relationship to aspects of social structure and practice ceases to warrant a distinct epistemology, but that, concomitantly, it demands that anthropologists pay serious attention to the constitutive (or performative) properties of expressive forms.

MICHAEL HERZFELD

See also: ethnography, history of anthropology, language and linguistics, music, oral literature

Further reading

Bauman, R. (1977) *Verbal Art as Performance*, Newbury, MA: Rowley House
—— (ed.) (1992) *Folklore, Cultural Performances, and Popular Entertainments*, New York: Oxford University Press
Child, F. (1857) *English and Scottish Ballads*, Boston: Little, Brown
Cocchiara, G. (1981) *The History of Folklore in Europe*, Philadelphia: Institute for the Study of Human Issues
Dorson, R. (1972) *Folklore and Folklife: An Introduction*, Chicago: University of Chicago Press

Dundes, A. (1980) *Interpreting Folklore*, Bloomington: Indiana University Press

Herzfeld, M. (1982) *Ours Once More: Folklore, Ideology, and the Making of Modern Greece*, Austin: University of Texas Press

Hodgen, M. (1936) *The Doctrine of Survivals: A Chapter in the History of Scientific Method in the Study of Man*, London: Allenson

Janelli, R. (1986) 'The Origins of Korean Folklore Scholarship', *Journal of American Folklore*, 99 (391): 24–49

Propp, V. (1968) *Morphology of the Folktale*, 2nd edn Austin: University of Texas Press

Thompson, S. (1932–6) *Motif-Index of Folk-Literature: A Classification of Narrative Elements in Folk-Tales, Ballads, Myths, Fables, Mediaeval Romances, Exempla, Fabliaux, Jest-Books, and Local Legends*, Bloomington: Indiana University/Helsinki: Suomalainen Tiedeakatemia

Wilson, W. (1976) *Folklore and Nationalism in Modern Finland*, Bloomington: Indiana University Press

food

As the most powerful instrument for expressing and shaping interactions between humans, food is the primary gift and a repository of condensed social meanings. Any food system has multiple dimensions (material, sociocultural, nutritional-medical), all of which interrelate. Food derives its 'power' from the web of the interrelations it evokes. Besides being of academic interest, the interconnectedness of production, distribution and *consumption has been acknowledged as central to the formulation of effective food policies.

Fieldworking anthropologists are well placed to research the levels and intersecting nodes at which food must be understood. They have long been interested in human diets, specifically in the socio-cultural determinants of diet; changing patterns of food production and *markets; and food security at community and *household levels. Increasingly, anthropologists are turning their attention to the socioeconomics of hunger, famine and food aid; and †agricultural development and food policy.

Anthropological studies of food draw inspiration from the pioneering research of †Audrey Richards (Richards 1939), in which the social dimensions of production, preparation, distribution and consumption were outlined, along with the dynamics of commensality. Food-focused ethnographies remain a model for those studying the social and nutritional impact of economic development. D'Souza (1988) has called for similar studies – famine ethnographies – to help prevent famine and improve relief efforts. Such studies require emphasis on the interrelationships between local, national, regional and international variables.

Anthropologists take a flexible approach to food and culture, because individuals at times have to choose between contradictory norms. The semiotic approach to food, championed by Appadurai (1981), highlights how the intellectual properties of food may be manipulated to solve this problem of choice.

Food as cultural construction

Studies of the sociocultural dimensions of food take either a cultural/structural or semiotic approach. The former treats food as 'good to think' within a fairly static cultural environment, as illustrated in numerous studies of binary classifications (hot-cold, wet-dry, male-female, etc.), and introduces the idea that diets can be analysed as parts of a food code. In contrast, semiotic studies show that people manipulate food to make statements about and challenge social relations. While all cultures use food to mark or build relative prestige and social status, the ways in which Hindu castes manipulate food transactions to improve relative status, and the emotions with which food preparations are charged, set Hindus apart (Messer 1984). Using food to protect or protest social positions, Hindus are experts in *gastropolitics* (Appadurai 1981). The semiotic approach is indebted to *Lévi-Strauss, who first developed the theory that food was of the order of language.

Changing patterns of production and the role of markets

The inquiry into food as idiom can be extended to the study of agriculture and agrarian change, because fields and field crops carry social meanings. For instance, the transition from upland/male farming to swampland/female farming in Gola, Sierra Leone, has been facilitated conceptually by the 'power' of associated images. The shift in terrain reflects engendered concepts about danger and safety (Leach 1994).

While the literature on changing food production patterns has many references to environmental symbolism, the dominant focus is on labour relations and *land tenure. Changes are set against the backdrop of global transformations. In Africa earlier this century, no one who needed land went landless. Inequalities existed, but communal groups and individuals had †usufruct rights to land. The *class and *gender inequalities of today result from the recent introduction of cash and cash crops, through which new production relations emerged between and within *households. As commodity relations destroyed bonds that secured non-free labour (e.g. that of sons), men increasingly took the major production decisions, while married women became involved as unfree labourers (Whitehead 1990).

Agrarian societies in transition are marked by widening separations in the division of labour by gender. Gender separation also pertains to new responsibilities for meeting consumption needs. Whereas men and women used to share responsibilities through sharing complementary production tasks, gender separation leaves women more and more solely responsible for household food provisioning. In addition, women must regularly supplement their agricultural activities to keep their families' food secure. This has been noted for both Africa and Asia, especially in areas where the adoption of †high-yielding crop varieties has left smallholders in heavy financial debt.

Empirical studies of agrarian change in Asia (as in Africa) highlight how macro and micro variables fuse, and reveal shared experiences as well as regionally specific ones. Javanese women, for example, share with African women exceptionally heavy labour burdens, yet, with regard to land rights, they have maintained their rights to private ownership (Stoler 1977). The literature on Asia centres on the accentuation of social distinctions under Green Revolution regimes. For India, studies of agrarian change outline a polarization between permanent (high-tech) agricultural labourers and casual labourers, the latter being mainly women employed during peak labour times. The narrowing of the range of female tasks causes 'crowding' and devalues women's work. Women take part in waged labour mostly as unfree members of households with restricted access to land and credit (Harriss 1977). Research in Southeast Asia confirms the rise of gender separation, crowding and the devaluation of women's work (Stoler 1977). Here too, women take on additional paid work to achieve basic food security.

Against over-optimism about the technological benefits of modern agriculture, anthropologists argue that gains have been offset by increased social differentiation and equity losses. Gender and class intersect here. Although women bear the brunt of modern hardships, real costs fall disproportionately on women from poorer households.

In keeping with the holistic approach to food, anthropologists regularly link the concept of a dynamic, gendered agriculture with the domain of food marketing. In Bwisha, Zaire, for instance, where commercialization began around independence, land scarcity and cash scarcity combine to give rise to a non-seasonal, individuated approach to farming, with household food security now being dependent on markets that prove difficult to control. This dependence stimulated gender negotiations regarding roles, rewards and duties. Since the 1985 famine, Bwisha women have regained some control over marketing and food security through a strategy whereby they introduced crops they control unambiguously (Pottier and Fairhead 1991).

Field studies of actual market performances usefully complement market analyses by economists, because the broad systemic approach by anthropologists integrates many domains of social life. Market studies often focus on how farmers and marketeers cope with the volatile nature of markets. In some cases, protection is offered by traders who enter into equilibrating relationships with farmers; in others the state attempts to increase household security through better producer prices or by opening up markets for staples not normally bought by national marketing boards. State interventions, however, regularly fail, because planners divorce market performance from conceptual and production aspects of food. Market performance must be seen in conjunction with other domains of the food system. On this basis Russell attacks the concept of equilibrating relationships, pointing out that peasant farmers in the Philippines must borrow from commercial middlemen in order to obtain credit; a practice leading to an indebtedness that obliterates the voluntary nature of personalized exchanges (Russell 1987). The need for linking markets and production relations has been heightened by the imposition of †structural adjustment programmes.

Food security at community and household levels

The debate on food security generates awkward *methodological questions regarding observation and measurement. The key problem is that measuring food intake is virtually impossible as it involves a specific set-up that distorts behaviour. The advice by anthropologists is to develop a resource control perspective which considers intra-household food allocations in relation to who controls which resources.

Some nutritionists, however, are less than enthusiastic about the theory that the cause of much malnutrition in women and small children is unfair distribution within households. The objection is that it is extremely difficult to establish whether such discrimination occurs. Rather than adopt the maldistribution theory, nutritionists may accept the *functionalist perspective that households and individuals modify their patterns of food use and adjust to seasonal or occupational changes in food entitlement (Wheeler and Abdullah 1988). While anthropologists do not dispute that households and individuals adapt to predictable fluctuations in food supply, they note that deepening poverty makes sharing much harder than when periodic, predictable hunger occurs (Schoepf and Walu 1991).

Given the paucity of empirical studies that have explored and backed the functionalist perspective, it is suggested that both the 'resource control' and the 'functionalist' approach deserve further investigation. The value of the resource control approach, however, is being enhanced because of the damaging impact of structural adjustment measures on the poor.

Hunger, famine and food aid

The anthropological concern with combining global and local variables is reflected in studies of hunger and famine. Thus, while most food crises share key features (e.g. upheaval, social differentiation, climatic disturbance) and develop along predictable lines, each crisis must also be regarded as unique. It is for this reason that detailed famine ethnographies are encouraged (D'Souza 1988).

D'Souza argues that social scientists should go over, in some detail, the harrowing events which precede mass starvation and make the world better prepared in future (D'Souza 1988). Famine ethnographies should also look at the immediate post-famine recovery period, since the details there can be just as harrowing as the story of the famine itself (Pottier and Fairhead 1991).

Famine ethnographies focus on detailing famine coping strategies and fine-tuning Sen's †entitlement theory (Sen 1981). This theory shows that hunger and starvation result from the loss of entitlement to food, rather than from a decline in food availability. Famines therefore run through predictable stages and give rise to predictable responses. Coping mechanisms, however, may change over time, which requires continuous monitoring. Besides documenting patterns and changes, famine ethnographies must reveal the heterogeneity of responses at the community level; showing, for instance, how gender and class and agricultural cycles combine to determine which responses are open to which groups or individuals. This heterogeneity partly explains why all famines are different.

Aware of the significance of entitlement, relief organizations focus on how and when to intervene. Discussion here is marked by contradictory views on the timing of emergency aid. The first view is that farmers adjust to weather fluctuations by accumulating assets during good times and drawing down stocks in lean years. Proponents of this view believe that officials habitually misread farmers' 'adjustments' as distress signals and dispatch aid when it is not needed. The counter-view contends that mortgaging land or liquidating productive capital to meet current needs are signals of acute distress and detrimental to recovery, so aid must arrive well before such desperate measures are taken.

To maximize the potential of food aid, anthropologists argue that donors should do more than simply throw grain at famine victims. Instead, emergency supplies must be utilized in ways that strengthen existing food channels and bolster the mechanisms for post-famine recovery. This could mean regulating livestock prices during and after famine through purchase-and-resale policies by government or outside agencies. Such policies can be effective in mitigating distress sales and enabling herds to be rebuilt, as Sperling reveals in her Samburu study of the 1984 famine and its aftermath (Sperling 1987). Cases of positive intervention through learning suggest that improved flows of detailed information create the potential for improved targeting and long-term recovery.

In addition to micro-level studies of hunger, famine and famine relief, anthropologists have developed an interest in the impact of broad food aid programmes. An excellent example is Doughty's study of how the 'Food for Peace' programme in Peru affected the lives of its beneficiaries (Doughty 1986).

Agricultural development and food policy

Agricultural policy interventions can have devastating consequences. This is attributed, within anthropology and increasingly beyond, to the fact that food policy design and implementation remain in the hands of agricultural advisers who fail to anticipate how their interventions will affect people's ability to access food. Local people have virtually no say in the process that determines market prices and produce availability.

The pitfalls of policy approaches that ignore the interconnectedness of the major food domains are well illustrated in the regular observation that higher incomes as a result of cash cropping do not necessarily lead to nutritional benefits. The obstacle is a set of mitigating factors, e.g. the need or tendency to spend lumpy payments on consumer goods other than food.

The absence of an integrated approach is also characteristic of feeding programmes that assume that if women only knew what to do, they would deploy existing resources to feed their families better (Wheeler 1986). By isolating mothers and their children as a target-group, programme implementors avoid confrontation with the full range of structural factors that impede food supply at the household level. The importance of the critique is reinforced by contributors to McMillan's *Anthropology and Food Policy* (1991).

The structural constraints on food security warn against taking an overly functionalist approach to food and resource sharing. The need for caution is well illustrated by Walu Engugu who studied the activities of women traders in Kinshasa (Schoepf and Walu 1991). These women traders, who *must* trade in order to earn substantial additional incomes to secure for their households even modest living standards, all gave evidence of gender struggles over income and assets.

Being ideally placed to comment on household activities and organization, which is the level at which much of the food policy debate is pitched, anthropologists are stepping up their participation in the search for more effective food policies. The key to policy success, they argue, is that policy thinking must address the three main food domains (production, distribution, consumption) within a single framework of theory and action. Dealing analytically with food allocations at household level also requires dealing with aspects of authority and *power, while setting the discussion in a wider economic context.

JOHAN POTTIER

See also: development, economic anthropology, land tenure, household, markets, nutrition

Further reading

Appadurai, A. (1981) 'Gastro-politics in Hindu South Asia', *American Ethnologist* 8 (3): 494–511

Doughty, P.L. (1986) 'Peace, Food and Equity in Peru', *Urban Anthropology* 15 (1/2): 45–59

D'Souza, F. (1988) 'Famine: Social Security and an Analysis of Vulnerability', in G.A. Harrison (ed.) *Famine* Oxford: Clarendon Press

Harriss, J. (1977) 'Implications of Changes in Agriculture for Social Relations at the Village Level: The Case of Randam', in B.H. Farmer (ed.) *Green Revolution? Technology and Change in Rice-growing Areas of Tamil Nadu and Sri Lanka*, London: Macmillan

Leach, M. (1994) *Rainforest Relations: Gender and Resource Use among the Mende of Gola, Sierra Leone*, London: International African Institute

McMillan, D. (1991) (ed.) *Anthropology and Food Policy: Human Dimensions of Food Policy in Africa and Latin America*, Athens and London: The University of Georgia Press

Messer, E. (1984) 'Anthropological Perspectives on Diet', *Annual Review of Anthropology* 13: 205–49

Pottier, J. and J. Fairhead (1991) 'Post-Famine Recovery in Highland Bwisha, Zaïre: 1984 in its Context', *Africa* 61 (4): 537–70

Richards, A.I. (1939) *Land, Labour and Diet in Northern Rhodesia*, Oxford: Oxford University Press

Russell, S.D. (1987) 'Middlemen and Moneylending: Relations of Exchange in Highland Philippine Economy', *Journal of Anthropological Research* 43 (1): 139–61

Schoepf, B.G. and W. Engundu (1991) 'Women's Trade and Contributions to Household Budgets in Kinshasa', in Janet MacGaffey (ed.) *The Real Economy of Zaïre: The Contribution of Smuggling and other Unofficial Activities to National Wealth*, London: James Currey; Philadelphia: University of Pennsylvania Press

Sen, A. (1981) *Poverty and Famines: An Essay on Entitlement and Deprivation*, Oxford: Clarendon Press

Sperling, L. (1987) 'Food Acquisition during the African Drought of 1983–84: A Study of Kenyan Herders', *Disasters* 11 (4): 263–72

Stoler, A. (1977) 'Rice Harvesting in Kali Loro: A Study of Class and Labor Relations in Rural Java', *American Ethnologist* 4 (4): 678–98

Wheeler, E. (1986) 'To Feed or to Educate: Labelling in Targeted Nutrition Interventions', in G. Wood (ed.) *Labelling in Development Policy: Essays in Honour of Bernard Schaffer*, London: Sage

Wheeler, E. and M. Abdullah (1988) 'Food Allocations within the Family: Response to Fluctuating Food Supply and Food Needs', in I. de Garine and G.A. Harrison (eds) *Coping with Uncertainty in Food Supply*, Oxford: Clarendon Press

Whitehead, A. (1990) 'Food Crisis and Gender Conflict in the African Countryside', in H. Bernstein *et al.* (eds) *The Food Question*, London: Earthscan

formalism and substantivism

The terms 'formalism' and 'substantivism' were used to mark the antagonistic positions in a controversy that dogged *economic anthropology in the 1960s. The distinction between 'formal' and 'substantive' approaches to economic phenomena was made by the influential economic historian †Karl Polanyi (Polanyi 1958), echoing †Max Weber's distinction between formal and substantive rationality. The 'economic', according to Polanyi can be defined in formal terms – as a kind of rationality which assesses choices between scarce resources by calculating in terms of means and ends, costs and benefits. Or it can be defined substantively – as whatever processes people employ in their relationship with the material world. The formal definition is that employed by modern economics and is a product of a society in which the economy has been isolated from other areas of social life. The substantive definition is potentially much broader in its application, and is explicitly intended to deal with societies and historical epochs in which the economy has not been †disembedded from other areas of social life like religion or kinship.

In brief, what was at stake in this controversy was the status of modern Western economics in cross-cultural and historical research. Did economics provide a viable and reasonably culture-free way to approach other people's economic life? Or was it hopelessly attached to assumptions about choice, maximization and scarcity which were only to be found in modern *market economies? Interestingly, this debate in 1960s economic anthropology was paralleled by contemporary arguments in the anthropology of *kinship and *law. In each case anthropologists were divided by their use of Western models: did these provide more rigorous and scientific tools for the study of other societies, or were they hopelessly inappropriate because of their culturally and historically specific origins?

Polanyi's argument was enthusiastically adopted by anthropologists like G. Dalton and †Marshall Sahlins, and as enthusiastically opposed by more mainstream economic anthropologists (e.g. Burling 1962; Cook 1966; the most important arguments are collected in Leclair and Schneider 1968). Sahlins's *Stone Age Economics* (1972) was explicitly presented as one more contribution to the argument. In the introduction,

though, Sahlins made an important historical shift, claiming as antecedents for the two positions †Adam Smith and †Karl Marx. Whatever its qualities as intellectual history, this ancestral gesture marked the beginning of the end of the controversy. The Marxist anthropology of the 1970s was, like the work of the substantivists, critical of the supposed value-free neutrality of Western economics, but it was also (as Sahlins subsequently conceded) indifferent to the cultural peculiarities of other people's material life; as such it could not be easily fitted on either side of the 1960s divide. By the end of the 1970s the issues which had seemed so divisive a decade earlier had been almost forgotten. Ten years later, at the end of the 1980s, the starting point of the controversy – the distinction between embedded and disembedded, primitive and modern economies – was itself challenged by the growing ethnography of *capitalism and the *market as cultural phenomena.

JONATHAN SPENCER

See also: capitalism, economic anthropology, markets

Further reading

Burling, R. (1962) 'Maximization Theories and the Study of Economic Anthropology', *American Anthropologist* 64: 802–21

Cook, S. (1966) 'The Obsolete "Anti-market" Mentality: A Critique of the Substantive Approach to Economic Anthropology', *American Anthropologist* 68: 323–45

Leclair, E. and H. Schneider (eds) (1968) *Economic Anthropology: Readings in Theory and Analysis*, New York: Holt, Rinehart and Winston

Polanyi, K. (1958) 'The Economy as Instituted Process', in K. Polanyi, C. Arensberg and H. Pearson (eds), *Trade and Markets in the Early Empires*, New York: Free Press

Sahlins, M. (1972) *Stone Age Economics*, Chicago: University of Chicago Press

French anthropology

The modern tradition of French anthropology, which dates from the beginning of this century, has always been stretched between the two poles of grand theory, on the one hand, and the minute and exacting study of data on the other. In the history of the discipline, these have sometimes been integrated into single bodies of work and have sometimes represented complementary or rival approaches (Jamin 1991). At the pole of specific data, French anthropology has been characterized by penetrating thoroughness of description, exhaustiveness, and craftsmanly care. At the theoretical pole, it has been centrally concerned with human societies as wholes, with a particular leaning towards the analysis of systems of social †representations. A characterization of the 'French school' before 1935 may be taken for the tradition as a whole: 'The French school maintained the primacy of the whole over the parts, the functional interdependence of the elements of a system, and the importance of establishing correlations among these elements' (Menget 1991: 332). The central thrust of French anthropology has thus been quite distinct from that of both British and North American anthropology.

A few characteristics of French anthropology deserve particular mention. Firstly France possesses a general intellectual culture which involves the educated public in a way unknown in Britain or North America: *Lévi-Strauss, for instance, is a recognized public figure, respected, in particular, as a writer of fine prose. Through its participation in this broader culture, French anthropology has always been connected to other human sciences, to philosophy, and to literature, so that each major development in anthropology has had repercussions outside the field.

Secondly, much of French anthropology, particularly that which has been most influential outside France, has been theory-driven. In France, †Lowie wrote, 'it was not *ethnography that stimulated the theory of culture, and through it other disciplines. On the contrary, the impulse to field research finally emanated from philosophy' (Lowie 1937: 196). The internationally recognized French masters – Lowie cites †Durkheim, †Mauss, and †Lévy-Bruhl, and Lévi-Strauss fits the pattern almost uncannily – have been philosophers by training and temperament, who promulgated their theories on the basis of what field ethnographers, often of other nationalities, were bringing in. The burgeoning of French field research has provided a counterpoint to this style of armchair construction; but at its best, French ethnography either teases out indigenous philosophies (†Leenhardt, †Griaule) or seeks in ethnography answers to fundamental questions in the human sciences (e.g. †Dumont).

Thirdly French scholarship takes place in a web of institutions, each with its own character, history, responsibilities, and centres of power, that is unique in the world. This includes, in no particular order: university departments; a chair in anthropology at the Collège de France; the École

Pratique des Hautes Études and the École des Hautes Études en Sciences Sociales, which are devoted to research and graduate training; the Institut National des Langues et Civilisations Orientales, which trains field linguists and does research in linguistic anthropology; and the vast structure of the Conseil National de Recherche Scientifique, with its cadre of researchers. Also important are the institutional bases of French-language anthropology outside France, in academic departments and research centres in Europe, Canada, Africa, and other parts of *la Francophonie*.

Origins

From the sixteenth century, with Rabelais's 'ethnography' of the late medieval imagination and †Montaigne's ruminations on cannibals, French thinking on cultural differences has had a distinctive contour: a cool eye for one's own society and a sympathetic curiosity about the other, often using the exotic to criticize the familiar. This tradition involves most of the great names of the *Enlightenment. Through these centuries, reports were coming in from missionaries, explorers, and colonists about the wonders of the newly discovered world. Specific reportage and broad theory came together in the Jesuit †J.-F. Lafitau's 1724 comparison of the peoples of North America with those of *les premiers temps*.

The nineteenth century

The nineteenth century was one of institutional foundation and consolidation. Until mid-century, new efforts were made to carry out an essentially philosophical agenda, incorporating the information coming in from around the globe. In 1799 a group of philosophers who came to be known as the Idéologues founded the Société des Observateurs de l'Homme, whose manual 'on the observation of savage peoples' urged observers to live with the people studied and learn their language (see Stocking 1968). The Académie Celtique, founded in 1807, promoted the collection of folk practices and beliefs, understood as survivals of a pagan past (Belmont 1986). The Société Ethnologique de Paris, founded in 1839, produced its own manual for the collection of representative ethnographic data.

By mid-century, the philosophical agenda was being incorporated into a colonial one, requiring information that would be of use to administrators of empire. This shift is marked by that from the term *ethnologie*, the study of specific languages and cultures for the purpose of understanding humanity, to an *anthropologie générale*, an overall science that would include physical anthropology and human geography along with culture and language. The second half of the century saw the founding of a chair in *anthropologie* at the Natural History Museum, of the École d'Anthropologie de Paris, and of the Musée d'Ethnographie, which would later become the Musée de l'Homme.

The sociological synthesis

The development of French anthropology has gone through periods of consolidation and of relative drift. The former have gelled around groups of scholars working in Paris and have always centrally involved links to other disciplines.

At the turn of the twentieth century, Émile Durkheim and his collaborators created a comparative sociology that was to become the basis of modern French anthropology. The Durkheimians understood social life as an autonomous level of analysis constituted centrally of collective representations. The school published major comparative analyses of social, symbolic, and religious institutions, many in their journal the †*Année Sociologique*. Associated with this group was the philosopher Lucien Lévy-Bruhl, who assumed fundamental differences between civilized and *primitive mentalities, but sought to explain these through differences in social life rather than through innate capacities.

The Durkheimian school was decimated by World War I. Marcel Mauss, the most important survivor, continued to promote sociology and particularly ethnology, playing a role comparable to that of *Boas in North America. Mauss's book *The Gift* (1925) proposed that the social whole could be conceived as a system of *exchange, an idea that would have a profound effect on later anthropology; his 1934 essay on 'Body Techniques' prefigures many of today's concerns.

The Durkheimian approach directly influenced †Saussure and the development of a systemic *linguistics; the school of social and cultural *history that formed around the journal *Annales*; and *folklore, in the person of †Arnold van Gennep, whose book on *rites of passage is a comparative study of Durkheimian scope.

The development of field research

The institutionalization of French ethnology continued between the wars with the 1925 founding of the Institut d'Ethnologie by a philosopher (Lévy-Bruhl), a sociologist (Mauss), and an ethnographer/physical anthropologist (Paul Rivet). The Institut itself, and French anthropology of the period, juxtaposed the two poles of grand theory and the meticulous concern for particular data in the form of Mauss's vision of a theory-driven and autonomous ethnology versus Rivet's ideal of anthropology as the meeting-place of descriptively exact disciplines in the social and natural sciences.

This was the classical period of French ethnography, and most of the major practitioners of the craft combined these two poles. The French-speaking world has produced a series of great field scholars, some devoting much of a lifetime to the explication of a single social and intellectual universe, most often through the analysis of its *language and symbolism. One exemplar of this tradition was Maurice Leenhardt, a missionary, then an ethnographer on New Caledonia, whose book *Do Kamo* is a landmark in the comparative study of the *person (Clifford 1982). But the great bulk of French ethnography has focused on Africa. The Dakar-Djibouti Expedition of 1931, the ostensible purpose of which was to collect museum artifacts, was at the beginning of (at least) three major contributions: the work of †Michel Leiris, ethnographer, critic of colonialism, and a celebrated poet; the pioneering *films of Jean Rouch; and the many years of analysis of the *ritual, language, and philosophy of the Dogon of *West Africa associated particularly with the names of Marcel Griaule, †Germaine Dieterlen, and Geneviève Calame-Griaule. The work with the Dogon remains the world model for long-term elucidation of levels of *cosmology (cf. Clifford 1988, ch. 2).

The period between the wars was also marked by the overlapping between ethnology and literature (Clifford 1988, ch. 4). The journal *Minotaure* published Griaule alongside Picasso and Eluard, and just before World War II, the Collège de Sociologie brought together social science, in which ethnology held pride of place, and avant-garde literature.

The structuralist synthesis

During the occupation, while anthropology in France virtually froze, European anti-fascist scholars were meeting in New York under the auspices of the École Libre des Hautes Études. Here the exiled Claude Lévi-Strauss came into contact with the linguist †Roman Jakobson and with North American anthropology, notably in the person of Franz Boas. Lévi-Strauss welded these influences into the new synthesis of *structuralism, seeking to define the mechanism of culture as parallel to that of language, which is systemic (Saussure) and based on binary oppositions (Jakobson); like language, other aspects of culture can be understood as systems of exchange (Mauss). The structuralist paradigm took shape in the 1950s, after Lévi-Strauss's return to France, linking his work in anthropology with that of †Lacan in *psychoanalysis and †Barthes in literary studies.

Within anthropology the decade saw an expansion of French interest in new regions of the world (notably *Asia and *Latin America), in linguistic anthropology, studies of the *environment, and prehistory. A new theoretical thrust came with the politically committed, sociologically oriented anthropology of †Georges Balandier. But it was structuralism that emerged as a great consolidating force in the 1960s, both within anthropology and between it and other fields, with anthropology playing a privileged role in general intellectual life, as illustrated by the famous cartoon showing Lévi-Strauss, Lacan, Barthes, and †Foucault sitting around talking in the jungle in grass skirts. Lévi-Strauss's own work set the anthropological agenda, reorienting research in several key domains. In *kinship, French anthropology came to stress *alliance, that is, exchange, over *descent (Dumont, Héritier); *myth and ritual were seen primarily as forms of language and *cognition, rather than as social charter or expression of psychological drives (Izard and Smith 1979); the *economy, in structural *Marxism, came to be seen as one aspect of a systemic whole (Godelier), rather than as either a simple quest for maximization or a simple determinant of everything else. This structural Marxism developed autonomously into an influential school insisting on the multiplicity of *modes of production in particular cases and the complexity of relations among levels of analysis (Meillassoux, Rey, Terray). Structuralism also reinvigorated regional anthropologies (Dumont on *South Asia, Condominas on *Southeast Asia, de Heusch on *Africa, Lévi-Strauss on *North and *South America) and such 'anthropologies' of the past as Indology, Sinology, *classics, folklore, and Indo-European studies (†Dumézil).

After the millennium

Even during the heyday of structuralism, dissenters were objecting to its attack on personal †agency, its often scientistic tone, and its apparent lack of interest in contemporary problems. After the student uprising of May 1968, intellectual trends in France became more free-flowing and pessimistic, and structuralism came in for severe criticism from Marxists and anti-authoritarians. On the whole, however, French anthropology has remained more committed to learning things about others in a structural and/or a detailed ethnographic mode than to worrying about whether such knowledge is possible or permissible.

The field is curently suffering or enjoying a period of relative dispersion. Thematic interests stand out more than grand-theoretical monoliths. Major work is being done again, (listed here in no particular order) in field linguistics and the collection and analysis of *oral texts; in *medical anthropology; in a continuing tradition of *ethnopsychiatry; in the study of cognition and ritual; in the study of the past and present, particularly that of *Northern and Southern Europe; in a new anthropology of the *modern. These last two themes draw on an increasing integration of history and anthropology. At the same time, structuralist projects continue on kinship and exchange, on religious symbolism, and on *classification and cognition. Most of these thematic tendencies are institutionally based, and some have their own journals. Particularly striking is the renewal of passion for the 'Griaule option' of long-term, detailed ethnography. Much of French anthropology is being carried out in regionally-defined research teams, which now exist for most parts of the world. The field is also undergoing a process of Europeanization and internationalization, with increasing collaboration in the context of multilingual conferences and publications.

JOHN LEAVITT

See also: Lévi-Strauss, structuralism

Further reading

Belmont, N. (1986) *Paroles païennes*, Paris: Imago

Bonte, P. and M. Izard (eds) (1991) *Dictionnaire de l'ethnologie et de l'anthropologie*, Paris: Presses Universitaires de France

Clifford, J. (1982) *Person and Myth: Maurice Leenhardt in the Melanesian World*, Berkeley: University of California Press

—— (1988) *The Predicament of Culture*, Cambridge, MA: Harvard University Press

Copans, J. and J. Jamin (1978) *Aux origines de l'anthropologie française*, Paris: Le Sycomore

Izard, M. and P. Smith (eds) (1979) *Between Belief and Transgression* (trans. J. Leavitt), Chicago: University of Chicago Press, 1982.

Jamin, J. (1991) 'L'anthropologie française', in P. Bonte and M. Izard (eds) *Dictionnaire de l'ethnologie et de l'anthropologie*, Paris: Presses Universitaires de France

Lowie, R. (1937) *The History of Ethnological Theory*, New York: Holt, Rinehart and Winston

Menget, P. (1991) 'Histoire de l'anthropologie', in P. Bonte and M. Izard (eds) *Dictionnaire de l'ethnologie et de l'anthropologie*, Paris: Presses Universitaires de France

Stocking, G. (1968) 'French Anthropology in 1800' in G. Stocking, *Race, Culture, and Evolution*, New York: Free Press

The journal *Gradiva* specializes in the history of French anthropology.

friendship

Friendship until recently has been a subject of only secondary importance in anthropology. Anthropologists have always tended to view friendship in relation to *kinship, generally comparing friends to kin. In non-Western societies, kinship was often considered as the chief set of relations upon which communities were structured. Friendship was mainly regarded as a residual category for people who were neither kin nor enemies. In studies of Western societies, kinship was no longer thought to have a central role in organizing social life. But precisely because of the greater instability and diminished functions of the family, anthropological interest was directed at revealing how significant it still was as a set of social relations. Friendship, in turn, was taken to be basically affective in character and too informal to be treated as the main focus of research.

The few studies of friendship conducted between the 1950s and 1970s (Paine 1974, Gilmore 1975, Reina 1959) emphasized the instrumental functions of friends and their structural significance. Analyses of social *networks (e.g. friends, *patrons and clients) in urban centres (cf. Boissevain 1974, Whyte 1955) also attempted to uncover a structured form for urban relationships.

Instrumentality, or the exchange of practical and emotional support between friends, was the chief aspect of friendship emphasized by *functionalism. But this is only one of the possible characteristics of friends. Above all, friendship is often perceived and valued as an affective and voluntary relationship, in which sociability and equality between friends are stressed. Although these elements tend to be cross-culturally present in friendship relations, distinct discourses emphasize different values. For instance, among English middle-class people, friendship privileges personal disclosure as a way of counteracting the impersonality of the work sphere (Rezende 1993). For the Arawete of lowland Amazonia, friendships between married couples stress not only economic cooperation but also sexual mutuality (Viveiros de Castro 1992). Among women in Andalusia, friendship values the possibility of sharing secrets without the fear of *gossip (Uhl 1991). Discourses and practices of friendship also vary within cultures. Factors such as *gender, *age and *class affect how friendship is perceived and experienced. Thus, the study of friendship in itself, rather than as a comparative instance for the analysis of kinship, can become one possible means for the investigation of central cultural values and notions.

CLAUDIA BARCELLOS REZENDE

See also: kinship, network analysis, complex society

Further reading

Boissevain, J. (1974) *Friends of Friends: Networks, Manipulators and Coalitions*, Oxford: Blackwell

Gilmore, D. (1975) 'Friendship in Fuenmayor: Patterns of Integration in an Atomistic Society', *Ethnology* 14 (4): 311- 24

Paine, R. (1974) 'An Exploratory Analysis of "Middle-class" Culture' in E. Leyton (ed.) *The Compact: Selected Dimensions of Friendship*, Newfoundland: Memorial University of Newfoundland

Reina, R. (1959) 'Two Patterns of Friendship in a Guatemalan Community', *American Anthropologist* 61 (1): 44–50

Rezende, C.B. (1993) *Friendship among some Young Men and Women Residents in London, 1991–1992*, PhD Thesis, London School of Economics

Uhl, S. (1991) 'Forbidden Friends: Cultural Veils of Female Friendship in Andalusia', *American Ethnologist* 18 (1): 90–105

Viveiros de Castro, E. (1992) *From the Enemy's Point of View: Humanity and Divinity in an Amazonian Society*, Chicago: University of Chicago Press

Whyte, W.F. (1955) *Street Corner Society: The Social Structure of an Italian Slum*, 2nd ed., Chicago: University of Chicago Press

functionalism

Broadly speaking, 'functionalism' refers to a range of theories in the human sciences, all of which provide explanations of phenomena in terms of the function, or purpose, they purportedly serve. In the period spanning the last decades of the nineteenth century and the first half of the twentieth, virtually every human science generated a school that identified itself as functionalist, and in nearly every instance that school dominated its discipline for a time. Darwinian evolutionary theory provided the initial impetus to functionalist reasoning. But †Darwin's multifarious argument admits of variable interpretation, so different constructions of his model yielded varieties of functionalism. The earliest schemes, those of psychology and economics, were promulgated at the turn of the century. These were not equally important, however; functionalist psychology was extremely influential, while functionalist economics was nearly inconsequential. But in both, the *individual was the basic unit of analysis, and individual action was conceptualized in terms of recursive processes of evolutionary adaptation. That is, both functionalist psychology and economics relied on an interpretation of the inherent nature of the human organism, and constituted fundamentally historical approaches to explanation.

In the late 1920s, a rather different type of functionalism became the dominant paradigm among British social anthropologists, thereafter diffusing to anthropologists elsewhere, as well as to sociologists – who judged that observation of non-Western societies had revealed the fundamental constituents of human sociability, unconfounded by the workings of 'organized state machinery' (Parsons 1934: 230). (After World War II, this type was embraced by practitioners of other disciplines, perhaps most notably political scientists studying colonial societies then making the transition to independence, but these contributed little to its elaboration.) In its original formulation if not necessarily its subsequent permutations, this scheme was informed by Darwinian reasoning, but differed from its precursors in psychology and economics in its basic unit of analysis: functionalist anthropology and *sociology considered the group, not the individual, judging that it was in groups that humans withstood processes of natural selection. And the group had to be analysed as a social, not a biological, entity. Because all groups possessed roughly equivalent human resources – individuals differing in talent and temperament – variable natural endowments did not explain given groups' survival. Human adaptation was effected through

social organization. Thus, notwithstanding some functionalists' professed concern with individual personality structure and volitional action, in analysis of this type individuals were judged derivative creatures of their social orders – practically epiphenomenal as individuals (see Radcliffe-Brown 1949; Wrong 1961).

For anthropologists and sociologists, the point of functionalist investigation was to identify the standardized habits that maintained the social organism in a condition of dynamic equilibrium – the 'more or less stable social structures' regulating individuals' relations 'to one another, and providing such external adaptation to the physical environment, and such internal adaptation between the component individuals or groups, as to make possible an ordered social life' (Radcliffe-Brown 1932: 152). The historical antecedents of any given social order were of no interest: they did not explain either the meaning of its practices for those who sustained them in the present or the roles these practices played in maintaining the social organization as a whole – roles which exhibited the general properties of social life the functionalist sought. Moreover, scientific inquiry by definition entailed direct observation. Thus, the very designation †'ethnology', which denoted efforts to reconstruct the histories of peoples who left no written records, became a term of opprobrium for functionalists: ethnological findings were at best descriptions of probable pasts (and more likely conjectural ones), yielding accounts of idiosyncratic experiences rather than identification of scientific regularities (see Radcliffe-Brown 1932: 144–8).

The politics of knowledge

Functionalism became the predominant analytic mode in anthropology and sociology following fierce disputes during the 1920s and 1930s; and when functionalism came under concerted attack in the late 1950s, it ceased to be the discipline's reigning theory only after extraordinarily acrimonious debate. Indeed, the issues raised in the latter controversy have yet to be thoroughly resolved. The social sciences' current theoretical irresolution may be variously construed. Perhaps it indicates that the disciplines have abandoned naive scientism, achieving intellectual maturity; if, as †E.E. Evans-Pritchard argued as early as 1950 (1951), the study of social behaviour has closer affinities with the humanities than with the natural sciences, then the human sciences should share with the humanities a tolerance for interpretative pluralism. Or perhaps the lack of †paradigmatic unity is lamentable, the product of the crisis of identity the disciplines have been suffering since roughly 1960; if the mission of the human sciences is to replicate the pattern of inquiry characteristic of the natural sciences (as authoritatively defined by Kuhn 1962), then their research must be guided by some (almost any) dominant paradigm so that their findings may be cumulative. Thus, recent theoretical controversy has embroiled practitioners in consideration of the fundamental constitution of the human sciences.

Moreover, debates over the merits of functionalist analysis have been significant because they have constituted sites for convergence of the disciplines' academic politics and intellectual conflicts. Both the functionalists of the 1920s and 1930s and the anti-functionalists of the 1950s and 1960s were younger practitioners determined to discredit their elders' theoretical commitments. And at stake in both controversies were also the disciplines' material resources – positions in university departments, as well as the funds for research dispensed by government agencies and private philanthropies (see Kuklick 1992: 208–16). We cannot overestimate the importance of academic political considerations in prolonging theoretical dispute, for in the 1950s and 1960s members of the social scientific establishment were able to frame the debate over functionalism in terms that still persist. Their position, perhaps most clearly articulated by the American sociologist Kingsley Davis, was that non-functionalist scholars were not really social scientists of any sort, for the functionalist creed entailed only the explanatory habit of recognizing interdependence among any given social order's constituent parts (1959). That Davis's formulation was widely acknowledged as authoritative may be judged from its reverential treatment in such definitive texts as the *International Encyclopedia of the Social Sciences*, which reported that functionalism as he defined it was 'the most widely used type' of functionalist analysis, and was so pervasive in anthropology and sociology that 'it is misleading to distinguish it by a special name' (Cancian 1968: 29–30).

Davis's definition of functionalism was an invitation to ignore differences of social scientific opinion far more significant than those of the 1950s and 1960s. If concern to establish patterns of correlation among elements of a social order

denotes functionalist analysis, then such figures as the British evolutionist anthropologist †E.B. Tylor should be counted among its proponents – since he developed a method for identifying such patterns – although his was one of the very approaches functionalism was intended to supplant. Moreover, Davis's own analyses provided compelling illustrations of the very interpretative defects functionalism's critics identified: the tendency to confound the actual and the optimal, as well as to presume consensus and stability in the absence of incontrovertible evidence of societal breakdown. Unless we disaggregate his (re)interpretation of the model from its characteristics during its era of paramountcy, we will be unable to appreciate the distinctive properties of functionalist theory. And from the points raised in the theoretical debate of the 1960s, we may deduce that any useful definition of functionalism has to specify at least two properties. One, it is one example of a theoretical type often termed 'grand theory' – a category that admits of Tylor's *evolutionism among other theories – a scheme that is intended to comprehend the behaviour of peoples at all times and places. Two, it is holistic analysis of a sort that Tylor's most certainly was not. That is, it asks a specific question about every habitual practice: How does this contribute to the maintenance of the whole?

Since the 1960s, no grand theory has compelled collective effort among either anthropologists or sociologists. Indeed, it has become a commonplace that their fields no longer exist as such, having dissolved into specialized sects devoted to specific subject areas and/or documentation of particular perspectives. But many still insist that the social sciences ought to be guided by some dominant paradigm – which must represent a comprehensive scheme; their view accounts for the disciplines' reluctance to repudiate functionalism definitively, and, indeed, for some significant recent efforts to rehabilitate it. It is important to stress, however, that many disciplines were seized by paradigmatic crisis at the same time as anthropology and sociology were – indicating that irresolution within the social sciences does not necessarily derive from distinctive problems raised by the study of human behaviour; perhaps in consequence of the embattled state of the university in the 1980s and 1990s, and particularly of the politics of research funding, practitioners of such fields as biology and chemistry also see their enterprises as fragmented. Furthermore, the social scientific consensus of the era of functionalist dominance may have been more apparent than real, an artefact of prosperous conditions. Until 1960, British social anthropologists were beneficiaries of relatively generous funds from the Colonial Social Science Research Council, and researchers of somewhat disparate views were able to coexist peaceably; and the incompatibility of functionalist principles with the sociological nominalism of survey research went unremarked among their sociologist contemporaries (see Platt 1986) because these were able to appeal to financial patrons with the claim that sociology was truly rigorous science, its surveys providing empirical documentation for its theory.

An origin story

Virtually all functionalists have invoked †Émile Durkheim's *The Rules of Sociological Method* ([1895] 1938) as their first programmatic manifesto, placing its author at the head of their intellectual lineage, if not necessarily identifying him as their sole progenitor. In no small degree, functionalists' equation of Durkheimian sociology with their scheme constitutes historical revisionism. That is, as his contemporaries knew, although we have been wont to forget, Durkheim enjoyed an extraordinarily diverse readership during his lifetime, and the proto-functionalists of the turn of the century represented only a fraction of his audience. Moreover, in its mature form functionalism represented the confluence of various theoretical and methodological trends: anthropologists and sociologists differed from one another in the routes they took to reach the functionalist position they eventually came to share; and the intellectual trajectories that led to functionalism differed from country to country as well as from discipline to discipline. Nevertheless, at last, if not at first, a stylized version of Durkheim's scheme provided many functionalists a covering rationale for their enterprise. And once social scientists had devised their revisionist origin myth, Durkheim's ideas became in fact central to self-conscious articulation and dissemination of functionalist argument. Indeed, the importance of these ideas as a legitimating creed for the functionalist school in *British anthropology, at least, may be judged from the self-conscious identification of its creators and followers as 'sociologists'.

Durkheim provided nothing less than a justification for the existence of sociology as a separate discipline, arguing that it addresses a 'new variety of phenomena', qualitatively different from those of other disciplines. These are †'social facts', the only data to which 'the term 'social' ought to be applied' – 'ways of acting, thinking, and feeling, external to the individual, and endowed with a power of coercion, by reason of which they control him' ([1895] 1938: 3). Thus, Durkheim dismissed the so-called reductionist research programme, which was widely endorsed by scientists in his day (and many find compelling in ours), premised on the assumption that scientific inquiries become more rigorous in direct proportion to the degree to which the phenomena they treat are understood in terms of their presumed underlying causes – sociology translated into psychology, psychology into biology, biology into chemistry, chemistry into physics, and so on. Indeed, he questioned the value of reductionism for any sort of scientific inquiry: because the whole is invariably greater than the sum of its parts, even the chemist considering the inorganic molecular constituents of organic matter should perceive that 'these molecules are in contact with one another, and this association is the new phenomena which characterize life, the very germ of which cannot possibly be found in any of the separate elements' ([1895] 1938: 102). The apparently counter-intuitive, sociological interpretation of such data as suicide rates exemplified the explanatory power of the Durkheimian paradigm: a reductionist, psychological account of suicide seems mandated because it seems a quintessentially individual act, the product of an individual's 'temperament, character, antecedents, and private history' ([1897] 1951: 46); yet, in both their frequency and motivational type, suicides are consequences of broad social trends. Certainly, Durkheim was not entirely consistent. He allowed that fundamental 'sociological laws can only be a corollary of the *more general laws of psychology*', because 'the ultimate explanation of collective life will consist in showing how it emanates from human nature in general' ([1895] 1938: 98, emphasis mine). And Durkheim also made assumptions about the relationship between the sociological phenomena he observed and human biological nature, tacitly resting his generalizations on Lamarckian biology.

Durkheim's anti-reductionist pronouncements served as rallying cries for anthropologists and sociologists, and had perhaps particularly strong force for the British social anthropologists who developed functionalism. We should note that their two founding figures, *Bronislaw Malinowski and *A.R. Radcliffe-Brown, were joined in accepting Durkheim's fundamental premises, notwithstanding their critiques of each other's work (and the very real differences between them). Malinowski taught his students to repudiate Radcliffe-Brown's 'dangerous and one-sided . . . sociological determinism of culture' (quoted in Kuklick 1992: 120), and Radcliffe-Brown charged that Malinowski was not a genuine functionalist because he invoked the biological needs of individual human beings (1949). Yet, in his *Argonauts of the Western Pacific* (1922), which together with Radcliffe-Brown's *The Andaman Islanders* (1922) heralded the emergence of the functionalist school, Malinowski proclaimed that 'as sociologists, we are not interested in what A or B may feel *qua* individuals . . . only in what they feel *qua* members of a given community' (1922: 23).

Installing Durkheim at the head of functionalism's lineage required a somewhat revisionist construction of his research programme, however, for he was an evolutionist, concerned to identify the developmental trajectory that led to the emergence of modern society. He explicitly decried sociologists' assumption that 'they have accounted for phenomena once they have shown . . . what social needs they satisfy . . . To show how a fact is useful is not to explain how it originated or why it is what it is' ([1895] 1938: 89, 90). Observing that a given practice could assume variable significance for social actors over time, he concluded that attention to the processes of historical transformation is essential ([1895] 1938: 91). But his functionalist followers judged that anthropology could not become 'the science it should be' if it persisted in the search for origins – and that Durkheim himself was 'misled', rendering his theory in a form 'which has caused it to be misunderstood by many of his readers', and clinging to 'some of the ideas and some of the terminology of the older social anthropology' (Radcliffe-Brown 1932: 153).

Functionalism embattled

By the late 1940s, a standard litany of objections to functionalism was developing. The functional unity of society should not be assumed (and, indeed, could not be assumed when the society in question was a Western one); in the study of any given society, integration was a variable to be measured by empirical test. Routinized practices were likely to be functional for some members of a society and dysfunctional for others – and some

practices might have no meaningful consequences for a society whatsoever. That a given practice could have variable significance for social actors indicated that patterns of conflict might be inherent in a social order, and that significant social change might derive from endogenous as well as exogenous factors. When such criticisms were made in the period immediately following World War II, however, they usually represented efforts to render functionalism more rigorous. The habit of explaining all observed practices as indispensable for the maintenance of the whole, for example, could be identified as merely the product of conceptual confusion, rather than a telling illustration of the defects of the functionalist mode of analysis *per se* (see Merton [1949] 1968: 76–93).

Perhaps more important to the future debates over functionalism was the charge levelled in the 1940s that it conveyed an inherently conservative political message, that its analyses of thoroughly integrated communities suggested that any sort of change in them was inadvisable. There was an irony in this accusation, for as political argument functionalism arguably began as social criticism – as an elaboration of a vision of optimal social order shared by many European and American intellectuals in the era of World War I, described in such tracts as R.H. Tawney's *The Acquisitive Society* (1921), a meritocratic polity in which individuals and groups would be rewarded in direct proportion to their contributions to the collective good. Post-World War II critics could, however, point to presumptive evidence that functionalism was the ideology of the status quo: the rhetoric of its chief spokesmen. In no small part, functionalism prevailed in the disciplines because its entrepreneurs made calculated appeals to powerful patrons. By arguing that only the functionalist brand of anthropology could serve the practical needs of colonial administrators, Malinowski became the broker of much of the research support available to anthropologists during the interwar period, eliminating his rivals from the field. Nevertheless, his consummate grantsmanship must be recognized as just that. Malinowski and his students were highly critical of all manner of colonial practices. Furthermore, colonial administrators made little use of functionalist anthropology – and frequently suspected that the functionalists who came to do fieldwork in their jurisdictions were fomenting discontent among colonial subjects (Kuklick 1992: 182–241).

A similar story can be told for sociology. In the United States, such figures as †Talcott Parsons persuaded Congress that the national interest required inclusion of the social sciences in the National Science Foundation established after World War II, arguing that the sociologist's role was analogous to that of a physician – that of an objective professional dedicated to curing social pathology. And in the postwar decades, those universities which were centres of functionalist argument consumed a disproportionate share of the funds available from both government sources and private philanthropies (see Buxton 1985: 117–25; Geiger 1988). Privileged access to funding did not enable functionalist sociologists to police their field as ruthlessly as social anthropologists: because few aspirant anthropologists can finance their own fieldwork – which functionalists made a necessary prelude to an anthropological career – the discipline's gatekeepers have been those who hold the purse strings; by contrast, sociological research has taken many forms (particularly in the large and diversified American university system), a number of which can be pursued without lavish funding. But sociologists' position in the disciplinary prestige hierarchy has tended to be a straightforward function of their ability to attract research support. It should not be presumed, however, that 1950s functionalist sociology invariably assumed the Panglossian posture exemplified by American interpretations of social stratification; by contrast, at this time British sociologists undertook to expose the routinized practices that perpetuated inequities in the British *class system – and they counted among their most important mentors Edward Shils, an American Parsonian who maintained a recurrent presence in British academe (Halsey 1982).

During the 1960s and 1970s, the chorus of functionalism's critics swelled, reiterating earlier arguments – in louder tones. The usual interpretation of their motivation has become a cliché, but is a reasonable explanation nonetheless: in every country in which functionalism had dominated social scientific inquiry, ideological differences grounded in cleavages of class, *ethnicity, and generation belied the consensual model of society embodied in functionalist analysis. And the crisis of authority in Western democracies, coupled with the politics of decolonization in erstwhile subject territories, facilitated recognition of routinized conflicts in even the most apparently stable of societies – the non-literate, technologically underdeveloped polities on which the functionalist model had been based.

Functionalism's critics in the 1990s

Functionalism could withstand the critiques of the post-World War II generation, with relatively minor modifications. The accusation that functionalism had constructed an 'oversocialized conception of man' (Wrong 1961) by confounding 'what A or B may feel *qua* individuals' with 'what they feel *qua* members of a given community' (Malinowski) could be countered with the observation that many functionalists – such as Malinowski – had never made this equation. The charge that functionalism exaggerated social integration could be met with attention to structured patterns of conflict within a social order. In the 1980s and 1990s, however, the very idea of a coherent social order – one which may be understood 'as a whole composed of parts' – became suspect; instead, social scientists posited 'lasting incongruities between actors, others, and third parties in their construction of the meaning of events' rather than 'norms and shared ideas [that serve] as blueprints for acts', so that what order obtains is an 'emergent property' of individuals' interactions – and 'differently positioned persons . . . live together in differently constructed worlds' (Barth 1992: 19, 23, 24 and passim). Indeed, even 'unitary accounts of 'the person' have . . . become deeply problematic' (Lave *et al.* 1992: 257). When social scientists emphasize historical contingency, situational particularity, and conceptual disjunction, *no* sort of grand theory can seem plausible.

HENRIKA KUKLICK

See also: British anthropology, Malinowski, Radcliffe-Brown, society

Further reading

Barth, F. (1992) 'Towards Greater Naturalism in Conceptualizing Societies', in Adam Kuper (ed.) *Conceptualizing Society*, London: Routledge

Buxton, W. (1985) *Talcott Parsons and the Capitalist Nation-State*, Toronto: University of Toronto Press

Cancian, F.M. (1968) 'Varieties of Functionalist Analysis', in D.L. Sills (ed.) *International Encyclopedia of the Social Sciences*, New York: Macmillan

Davis, K. (1959) 'The Myth of Functional Analysis as a Special Method in Sociology and Anthropology', *American Sociological Review* 10: 757–72

Durkheim, É. ([1895] 1938) *The Rules of Sociological Method* (trans. by S.A. Solovay and J.H. Mueller), Glencoe: Free Press

—— ([1897] 1951) *Suicide*, (trans. by J.W. Swain), Glencoe: Free Press

Evans-Pritchard, E.E. (1951) *Social Anthropology*, London: Cohen and West

Geiger, R.L. (1988) 'American Foundations and Academic Social Science, 1945–1960', *Minerva* 26: 315–41

Halsey, A.H. (1982) 'Provincials and Professionals: The Post-War Sociologists', *European Journal of Sociology* 23: 150–75

Kuhn, T.S. (1962) *The Structure of Scientific Revolutions*, Chicago: University of Chicago Press

Kuklick, H. (1992) *The Savage Within. The Social History of British Anthropology, 1885–1945*, Cambridge: Cambridge University Press

Lave, J., P. Duguid, and N. Fernandez (1992) 'Coming of Age in Birmingham: Cultural Studies and Conceptions of Subjectivity', *Annual Review of Anthropology* 21: 257–82

Malinowski, B. (1922) *Argonauts of the Western Pacific*, London: Routledge

Merton, R.K. ([1949] 1968) 'Manifest and Latent Functions', in his *Social Theory and Social Structure*, New York: Free Press

Parsons, T. (1934) 'Society', in E.R.A. Seligman (ed.) *Encyclopaedia of the Social Sciences*, New York: Macmillan

Platt, J. (1986) 'Functionalism and the Survey: The Relation of Theory and Method', *The Sociological Review* 34: 501–36

Radcliffe-Brown, A.R. (1922) *The Andaman Islanders*, Cambridge: Cambridge University Press

—— (1932) 'The Present Position of Anthropological Studies', Presidential Address to Section H – Anthropology, of the British Association for the Advancement of Science, in *Report of the Centenary Meeting of the British Association for the Advancement of Science* [1931], London: BAAS

—— (1949) 'Functionalism: A Protest', *American Anthropologist* 51: 320–3

Wrong, D. (1961) 'The Oversocialized Conception of Man in Modern Sociology', *American Sociological Review* 26: 84–93

G

gender

Models of subordination

Although the distinction between female and male is one common to all known human *cultures, the ways in which male and female *bodies are distinguished, the role each is seen as playing in reproduction, local understandings of the biological basis of difference, cultural attributes assigned to the masculine and the feminine, and the importance attached to these differences, all vary enormously from culture to culture. In recent anthropological work, 'sex' is generally taken to refer to the anatomical, biological and physiological characteristics of female and male bodies, and 'gender' to the culturally specific †symbolic articulation and elaboration of these differences. The concept of gender came into popular use in the theoretical and ethnographic writings of social and cultural anthropologists in the early 1980s. As a term which addressed both the female and the male, the cultural construction of these categories, and the relationship between them, it offered an alternative to the emphasis on 'the problem of women' which had dominated feminist anthropology for the previous decade and had itself become increasingly problematic.

The feminist anthropology of the 1970s grew out of a general theoretical reappraisal in the social sciences, itself an aftermath of the widespread political unrest of the late 1960s. Social scientists went back to *Marxist theory in their search for tools to understand political and economic *inequality, and to reassess issues of *development and underdevelopment. A similar search for the roots of women's position as 'the second sex' (in Simone de Beauvoir's term) led Western feminists to look to anthropology for ways of understanding women's situation in different social, political and economic orders, and simultaneously fed into anthropology a variety of questions concerned with the possibility of egalitarian social order, the roots of female subordination, and the general roles of women in different cultures and economies.

A major aim of the feminist project of the 1970s was to establish 'an anthropology of women' (Reiter 1975), which would fill the gaps in the anthropological literature resulting from male bias. Traditional anthropology was seen as suffering from a double male bias: first, it was argued that professional anthropologists tended to be male or, whether male or female, to accept and work within male-centred models of social organization and culture and, second, that anthropologists tended to rely on male informants during *fieldwork, and therefore replicate the indigenous male view. The 'anthropology of women' focused on what women said and did, and gave equal or greater weight to female domains and spheres of activity and to the symbolic representation of the categories female and male. Two quite different lines of argument were developed during this period. One maintained that neither female oppression nor exclusive male power was universal, while the other grew out of an assumption of universal male dominance and female subordination.

Authors such as K. Sacks and E. Leacock, who followed a Marxist line and drew on †Engels's theories, maintained that female oppression was an historically specific phenomenon, linked to relations of production, private *property and either *colonialism or *capitalist economic relations. Thus, they assumed the existence of a prior egalitarian social order, in which men and women did different tasks but were equally valued. Other anthropologists also rejected a straightforward model of female subordination, but stressed individual transactions and interpersonal relations

rather than wider economic and political determinants. Such anthropologists as Friedl ([1967]
1987) and Lamphere (1974), for instance, argued
that although women appeared to be denied
formal *power and authority in the public or political sphere, they were not without individual
power. Foreshadowing to some extent the problematic relationship between individual action or
†agency and encompassing *social structure which
was to become a major concern in the late 1980s,
they emphasized the domestic power of women,
manifested in individually negotiated relations
based in the domestic sphere but influencing and
even determining male activity in the public
sphere. In terms of these arguments, gender difference was assumed, as was an apparently natural
division between domestic/female and public/
male domains, but these differences did not
automatically result in female subordination.
Subordination and inequality rather arose as a
result of specific economic and political conditions.

Other feminist anthropologists of this period,
however, did assume a universal subordination of
women, and sought to explain its origins and
perpetuation in sociological, cultural or symbolic,
or material terms. Each of these explanations
rested upon a major dichotomy which was taken
to be universal: public/domestic (Rosaldo 1974),
*nature/culture (Ortner 1974), and production/
reproduction (Edholm *et al.* 1977).

Rosaldo, in her seminal article in *Women, Culture
and Society*, argued that the roots of female oppression cross-culturally lay in the division between
the public and the domestic spheres, and the
systematic undervaluing of the domestic, which
was defined as those roles and activities revolving
around women and children. The extent to which
women were subordinate in a given society
depended on the degree of division between the
public and the domestic spheres. In *hunting and
gathering societies, for instance, where the two
domains were least likely to be highly differentiated, relations between women and men were
likely to be most egalitarian. In *peasant and
industrial societies, where a far greater division
between the two spheres in ideological, political
and economic terms was likely to be found, women
were associated primarily with the domestic sphere
and men with the public. The domestic sphere
was subordinate to the public, and women, by
their association with the domestic and their
exclusion from the public, were subordinate to
men. For Rosaldo, therefore, some degree of

female subordination was universal, but the extent
of male dominance depended upon the degree of
separation between the domestic and the public
sphere.

Ortner (1974), writing in the same volume as
Rosaldo, pursued a different line of theoretical
enquiry, but one which was to be equally
influential. She re-examined the binary opposition
between nature and culture which the French
structural anthropologist *Lévi-Strauss had
posited as a universal dichotomy, and argued that
cross-culturally women were represented as closer
to nature because of their role in childbearing,
lactation and *socialization of children. She was
careful to stress that this identification of women
with nature and men with culture was not 'natural'
but was culturally constructed; in other words
women were not in fact any closer to nature than
men, but were universally perceived as being
so. She argued further that women to some
extent mediated between nature and culture, by
transforming the 'raw' child (natural) into the
'cooked' social person (cultural). In this structural/
symbolic analysis, the roots of female subordination were to be found in the cultural explications
of biological difference.

For Marxists, the subordination of women
resulted from their association with reproduction
within the household, and their exclusion from
relations of production and exchange in the public
sphere. These ideas were first developed by Engels
and Marx, most specifically in Engels's classic
volume *The Origin of the Family, Private Property and
the State*. Engels, writing within the framework of
social *evolutionism, suggested that the association
of women with the household and reproduction
and men with the wider *political economy and
production was a 'natural' division because of
childbearing and childrearing; the oppression
of women, however, only arose with the development of sedentary agriculture, monogamous
*marriage and private property relations; at which
point, as male productive labour and property
became the source of value, the 'natural' division
of labour ceased being egalitarian. Some of these
ideas were removed from their rather problematic
evolutionist context and elaborated upon in
comparisons of contemporary societies. Edholm *et
al.* (1977), for example, questioned the idea that
an association between women and reproduction
and men and production was 'natural', but looked
at the ways in which production and reproduction were related in different types of economies.

They suggested that in hunting and gathering societies, where concepts of private property were not highly developed, there was little distinction between women's productive and reproductive activities, and hence little undervaluing of women. The socio-economic centrality of the male-headed household as the unit of production, *consumption, property and exchange (the †'domestic mode of production') in 'peasant' societies, on the other hand, led to an undervaluing of women's role in production and an overemphasis on their role in reproduction. In this Marxist feminist analysis, the position of women was inextricably linked to economic relations of production and reproduction.

Each of these three theoretical approaches located the source of women's oppression in culture and social structure, rather than in biology, and stressed that the idea that women's biology placed them closer to nature, outside production, or within the domestic sphere, was not a natural fact, but a cultural elaboration on biological difference. And yet each ended up caught in a conundrum of exactly the type it was trying to avoid: regardless of sociological, cultural or material explanation, the origin of women's universal subordination seemed to lie in the biological 'facts' of reproduction (Collier and Yanagisako 1987).

The work of sociobiologists, and of some anthropologists influenced by *sociobiology, explicitly applied models drawn from animal behaviour to human society, and developed arguments around a biological basis for sex role differentiation. While most feminist anthropologists rejected these models as inapplicable to human social life, or at least as not neatly transferable to human social organization and behaviour, the role of biology and by extension *essentialism, remained unresolved problems in the feminist writings of the 1970s. The way out of this seemed to lie on the one hand in the separation of gender from biological sex, and on the other in a wider understanding of the diversity of local concepts of gender themselves.

Theorizing beyond dichotomies

By the late 1970s emphasis on the universal nature of women's subordination was being challenged by Third World academics and political activists, by women of colour in Europe and North America, and generally by theorists influenced by *postmodernism. Increasingly throughout the 1980s 'gender' replaced 'women' as a focus of academic enquiry and as the subject of courses, workshops and conferences. Gender appeared to provide the key for talking about difference without assuming universal male dominance and female subordination, and without relying upon linked dichotomies based on Western philosophy and Western ideas about the biological basis for sexual difference. The 'universal' dichotomies were rejected as reflections of dominant Western discourse, historically situated and socially and culturally specific.

The use of the concept of gender to some extent freed the discussion of difference and inequality from biological referents. It was argued that it cannot be assumed that all cultures represent difference in the same ways, or give sexual difference the same emphasis. In many ways †Margaret Mead had anticipated these arguments in her much earlier works on *Male and Female* and *Sex and Temperament*, in which she used a range of ethnographic material to show not only that the tasks and economic activities assigned to each sex varied enormously from culture to culture, but so too did the emotional and temperamental characteristics associated with females and males. The 1980s discussions of gender, however, also raised new and more complex issues of cross-cultural *translation, universality, and the relationship between thought systems or systems of *classification and individual action, and *ideology and material conditions.

The contributors to MacCormack and Strathern's edited volume, *Nature, Culture and Gender* (1980), were among the first to point out the ways in which Western political philosophy, located in specific historical periods, had taken a dominant position of assumed and unquestioned universality. The articles by Bloch and Bloch and by Jordanova particularly demonstrated that the nature/culture dichotomy was a creation of European philosophical discourse. Nature and culture, and the associated linking between nature and female and culture and male, were shown not to be universal dichotomies at all, but rather culturally and historically specific ones which were developed and elaborated in Europe by philosophers such as Rousseau during the *Enlightenment. The location of these dichotomies in their proper historical and cultural context undermined assumptions about the universal subordination of women and dominance of men, and called for recognition of gender as a component of far more complex systems of thought. In Jordanova's words:

> [The belief in the universal secondary status of women] assumes a model of society where there are unambiguous, rigid hierarchies, and so clear criteria for assigning their rank to any individual. Even if we clearly separate issues of value (bad/good) from those of control (sub/superordinate), there are no simple scales on which men and women can be ranged. Women are deemed both good *and* bad, and both evaluations may be represented as stemming from their naturalness. Similarly, they may be subordinate in some areas of life (e.g. legal rights) and superordinate in others (e.g. control of the house), and both descriptions could be based on their putative natural qualities.
>
> (Jordanova 1980: 65–66)

The importance of shifting the analytic focus from simple dichotomies and apparent universals to far more complex systems of thought pertaining to gender was also emphasized by other authors in this volume. Olivia Harris, for instance, questioned not only the association between female and nature and male and culture, but also implicitly the dichotomy of domestic/female and public/male in terms of the cultural constructs of the Laymi, rural cultivators in the Bolivian Andes. The Laymi distinguished between the wild and the domesticated or fully cultural, but both male and female were symbolically represented in each category. Both men and women were involved in cultivation, care of livestock, and weaving, and the married couple was represented as the core of the household and of production and consumption. Unmarried men and women were seen as undomesticated, and their courtship and sexual encounters took place outside the house, in the wild. In this case, a distinction between wild and domesticated did not coincide with one between female and male; rather, gender, *age and *kinship status together served as concepts for classifying both females and males in relation to the domestic and the wild. Laymi children were viewed as undomesticated until they had language; their hair was left matted and uncut, like that of a wild mythical creature, until they could speak. Women were vulnerable to the evil spirits who occupied the wild at night, because these spirits would try to impregnate them. It was therefore men who had command of the ritual language through which to speak to the evil spirits, and men rather

than women who could walk about alone at night. The circumscription of women's movements was given as a reason for their exclusion from full political participation in the community. However, Harris was careful to stress that this was not an essentialist representation:

> There are women who do travel alone at night. In the case of ritual specialists who talk to the devils, Laymis were most insistent that it was possible for women too to hold this position . . . and of course men are afraid of the devil as well . . . Men and women are not pre-given, eternal categories but change their relationship to the symbolic in the course of their lives
>
> (Harris 1980: 92)

Gender, age and generation, and marital status were interwoven in the Laymi symbolic order in ways far too complex to be elucidated by a straightforward female/nature – male/culture dichotomy.

In her article 'No nature, no culture', Strathern (1980) made explicit the important point that gender is a symbolic system. The people of Mount Hagen in Papua New Guinea had words for the wild and the domestic, but both men and women could be represented in either category, and neither category was 'naturally' dominant over the other. Strathern argued that the identification of such binary categories, and the assumption that one is dominant over and one subordinate to the other, were Western concepts inappropriate in a non-Western context. In Hagen thought two distinct categories, *mbo* and *romi*, were recognized but either could be associated with male or female according to context, and neither dominated the other. Further, while 'male' activities in exchange and reciprocity were valued and 'female' activities generating domestic consumption were 'rubbish', men who failed to perform adequately in these highly valued activities were seen as 'rubbish', while women who actively support the exchange networks of men were likened to *Big Men. Gender was thus a symbolic system through which certain attributes were assigned to males and females: particular women and men could, through their actions, transcend these boundaries. Gender, rather than being fixed in a simple dichotomy between female and male and nature and culture, was a symbolic system referring to ideal behaviour. In her complex analysis, Strathern argued that the ideas of dominance and subordination which apply in Western thought to both nature and culture (the domination of nature by culture), and to female and male (the subordination of women by men), cannot be transposed onto Hagen cultural constructs. In Mount Hagen the wild and the domestic do not exist in a hierarchical order; neither is considered to be prior, nor are male and female attributes or relationships perceived in straightforward terms of dominance and subordination. Women may be culturally associated with the selfish interests of the individual household, and men with the greater social good of exchange relations, but this does not imply hierarchy or domination.

J.A. Barnes (1973) had demonstrated a decade earlier that Western beliefs concerning biology, although represented as natural 'facts', were culturally determined. What the articles in *Nature, Culture, Gender* and similar works established was that neither Western ideas about sexual difference itself, nor the gender symbolism and relations written onto this difference, could automatically be assumed to be adequate or even relevant theoretical tools for understanding meanings in other cultures.

If the application of simple domestic/public or nature/culture dichotomies to gender analysis is clearly of limited value in non-European cultures, the ideas are problematic even within Europe. In Portugal, as in other parts of Europe, particularly *Southern Europe, women are associated with the Devil and uncontrolled female sexuality is regarded as dangerous to men, who are associated with God and Jesus. *Marriage brings the male and female together, and unites them in the *house, which stands as a metaphor for gender complementarity, correct reproduction, and social good (Piña-Cabral 1986). In rural Poland young men to some extent are expected to be wild and violent until they marry, when their energies should turn to production and reproduction based in the house and farm, and centred on the adult married couple. Men who fail to make this transition, and who continue to drink excessively and behave violently within marriage, are judged negatively by their peers, and are likely to be excluded from the circles of reciprocity which are central to farming and community life. In these examples, it is not only gender but also age and marital status which provide the basis for symbolic distinctions between categories of persons and normative behaviour. Gender combines with age and kinship in the depiction of different ideal

types, and individual social actors move from one type to another at different stages of their lives. The domestic and the public may be recognized as separate domains, but neither is exclusively linked to either the male or the female; rather, both women and men have a culturally appropriate part or parts to play in each domain.

Sex, gender and inequality

When gender is seen as a symbolic construction, or as a metaphor for types of action, it is possible to unpick the relationship (assumed as unproblematic and hence little analysed in early feminist work) between 'natural' sexed bodies, symbolic representations of female and male, and the actual behaviour of individual women and men. In their introduction to *Sexual Meanings*, Ortner and Whitehead argued that:

> [When] gender, sexuality and reproduction are treated as symbols ... the approach to the problem of sex and gender is ... a matter of symbolic analysis and interpretation, a matter of relating such symbols to other cultural symbols and meanings on the one hand, and to the forms of social life and social experience on the other.
> (Ortner and Whitehead 1981: 2)

To facilitate the understanding of these relationships, they proposed a model of prestige structures, which they defined as 'the sets of prestige positions or levels that result from a particular line of social evaluation, the mechanisms by which individuals arrive at given levels or positions, and the overall conditions of reproduction of the systems of statuses' (ibid.: 13). Gender, they argued, is one such prestige structure, and 'in every known society, men and women compose two differentially valued terms of a value set, men being as *men*, higher' (ibid.: 16). They suggested that male prestige is linked to 'public' roles, such as chief or Brahman, while female prestige is defined in relation to men, in such roles as wife, sister and mother; in other words, the female prestige structure is encompassed by the male structure.

While this idea of an encompassing male system is similar to that of a dominant public or politico-jural domain, treating gender as one of several prestige structures which together reproduce social relations pushed gender analysis in new directions. Thus Ortner (1981) looked at sexual hierarchy in *Polynesia and explored the complex interplay between gender, kinship and social status. She argued that within the kinship system hierarchy was based on gender and age, placing males above females and senior brothers over junior brothers. Within marriage, the husband occupied a chief-like status in relation to his wife and children. The kinship and gender structures, however, were encompassed by the structure of social stratification: 'At any given level in the system, men's and women's statuses are more similar to one another's than to persons of either sex at other levels'. Ortner linked this to women's access to property, through dowry or inheritance: 'they are, in varying degrees in various hierarchical societies, full-fledged members of their "classes", and their rights to a share of their natal units appear, at one level, as "natural"' as the men's' (Ortner 1981: 397). Within each stratum, however, gender and kinship provided the basis for inequality.

In her article on the Maasai, *East African *pastoralists, Llewelyn-Davies elaborated on this idea of female and male prestige structures, arguing that 'age/gender organization' defined not only the relations which obtain among members of the same sex, but also those between the sexes. Circumcision symbolically marked the transition from girl to woman. Warriors, who were in a liminal state between boyhood and manhood, had rights of sexual access to uncircumcized girls, and it was through these sexual relations that the girls' breasts began to grow and they could undergo circumcision. After the circumcision ritual, they were considered socially mature, and ready for marriage and childbirth. Thus, female maturity and fertility were 'asserted to be the artificial creation of men and of ceremonial' (Llewelyn-Davies 1981: 353). Male circumcision was also a crucial symbol of adult manhood, but was only one part of a much longer three-stage transition from boy, to *moran* (warrior), to elder. Each *moran* †age-set spanned about fourteen years; during this period, the young men lived outside the village, raiding, hunting and fighting. They paid great attention to body care, and with their magnificent feathers, beads and plaited hair, represented the public face of the Maasai. In the third male stage, Maasai men became elders, and gradually obtained property rights over cattle and non-property owning persons – that is, women and children. The labour of women and children was essential in tending the herds, and women had rights of distribution over milk, but only men had property rights over cattle. With the payment

of †bridewealth cattle, the husband acquired rights over his wife's person, labour and fertility. Female fertility and male bravery were both valued by the Maasai, but Llewelyn-Davies argued that they were not balanced: 'Females never become *moran* and they are seen as lacking in the desirable qualities of masculinity. Indeed, to some extent femininity is thought of as an absence of masculinity' (ibid.: 352). The rituals of the *moran* age-set transformed boys into elders, who controlled property and reproduction. Circumcision and marriage transformed non-reproductive girls into reproductive women, but that very fertility was itself transactable by men, through marriage alliances and bridewealth payments. In the case of the Maasai, age and gender worked together as symbolic systems through which production and reproduction were generated, and hierarchy reproduced and maintained.

While Ortner focused on kinship, status and gender as complex interrelated systems of classification and Llewelyn-Davies analysed the mutual construction of gender, generation and kinship, Whitehead considered the cultural basis for gender ascription itself. Drawing on historical accounts and early anthropological descriptions of the North American Native Indian berdache, a socially recognized transsexual category, she questioned the existence of a universal primal link between anatomically sexed bodies and gender. Berdache were anatomical males who dressed, spoke, and participated in the division of labour as females. They were often identified in childhood, by their preference for female clothing, and by their choice of female tasks and female implements such as spade or spindle (rather than male ones such as bow and arrow). Sometimes identification came through a vision:

> It is said that the moon would appear to a man having in one hand a burden strap, in the other bow and arrows, and the man would be bidden to make a choice. When he reached for the bow, the moon would cross its hands and try to force the strap on the man.
>
> (Fletcher and LaFlesche, quoted in Whitehead 1981: 87)

The berdache were not classified in terms of their sexuality; the homosexual was generally a separately recognized category of person defined by sexual activity rather than gender transformation. Neither were the berdache apparently regarded as gendered females; rather, they were part-men/part-women. In fact, their sexuality and sexual preferences seem to have been of little importance. What was significant was their performance of work classified as female in the sexual division of labour and, slightly less importantly, their adoption of characteristically female dress, movement and speech. The berdache were apparently socially accepted as part-men/part-women, rather than being viewed as transgressive. The key to this acceptance seems to lie partly in the relatively autonomous status accorded to female production within the sexual division of labour. In most *Native North American cultures, women were producers of durable goods, such as textiles, basketry and pottery, which were included in intratribal exchange and trade, and women as well as men were curing specialists. Whitehead suggested that although men were granted greater esteem than women because of their activities in warfare, hunting, and decision-making, they were not entitled to appropriate the products of female labour, and women were not excluded from distribution. Hence, the berdache could cross the male/female boundary and still, through perfecting 'female' skills, gain wealth and prestige. In these North American cultures, gender distinctions were based both upon anatomical and social difference, and in the case of the berdache it was not the anatomical but the social which was most salient in personal identity.

Gender distinctions can be inextricably linked, as in the Maasai example, to the cultural construction of the body – through circumcision, through the male 'opening the (female) path' for reproduction, or through decoration which embodies for public appraisal and appreciation 'masculinity' or 'femininity'. In the case of the Native North American berdache, body anatomy played a less important part in gender classification than did performance through the body – clothing, speech and gestures, demeanour and above all labour.

What emerges from the articles in *Sexual Meanings* and other works from the early 1980s is a conception of gender as one symbolic system which, in combination with others, 'talks about' or provides metaphors for the ordering of social persons in relation to each other and to the social system as a whole. As such, it should be seen as a differentiating system, ascribing ideal attributes rather than determining or speaking to individual behaviour. As the case of the berdache performing like a woman, or the Mount Hagen woman

behaving like a Big Man make clear, however, it is also important to distinguish symbolic systems and cultural meanings from the range and diversity of things which individual people actually do. As La Fontaine points out:

> It is increasingly obvious that to link the categories of gender, especially as they are symbolically displayed in myth and ritual, directly with the social behaviour of living individuals *creates* problems of interpretation rather than solving them.
>
> (La Fontaine 1992: 91)

She suggests that both personhood and kinship are 'critically implicated' in the understanding of gender. Symbolic systems provide cultural metaphors for roles, statuses and behaviour; they do not dictate what individual men and women actually do. Strathern, for example, showed that in Mount Hagen individual self-interest was associated with the female and social good with the male, but these gender concepts were metaphors for social value, not prescriptions for – or reflections of – individual men's and women's behaviour.

Deconstructing difference

Postmodern theory and deconstruction have had a profound influence on the study of gender since the late 1980s, bringing into even finer focus the problems of translation and of the dominance of Western models, and above all stressing difference and diversity. Strathern (1988), for example, argued that the application of Western analytical concepts such as 'exploitation' and 'oppression' to gender relations is inappropriate in the Hagen case. In her discussion of female labour, male pig exchanges and the circulation of women and wealth in marriage payments, she maintained that even though it may appear that men are alienating and appropriating the products of women's labour, in Mount Hagen concepts of the person did not encompass such distinctions. Although women provided the labour for rearing the pigs which men exchanged, and thereby enhanced men's reputation and political power, and although women are exchanged by men, along with wealth, in marriage transactions, the Hagen people themselves did not make the Western distinction between production and property, or subject and object of production, and women therefore did not experience the situation as one of exploitation or oppression. Rather, women and the pigs and other wealth which were the material of male exchange were not 'alienated' in the Western sense of the word, as labour was not the basis of profit in Mount Hagen. Strathern argued that neither the products of labour, nor persons themselves, could be seen to be appropriated and exploited if the Western distinction between subject and object, and the connection between labour and ownership, were inappropriate. Here again we come back to the relationship between women and men as ideal categories, and individual action or agency. Strathern did not deny female agency, but showed how individual women could and did act both in their own interests and in the interest of 'social good'; what she stressed was the relationship between individual agency and social structure, and the inappropriateness of applying Western concepts of the individual, the person, or the collective to Mount Hagen cultural constructs.

This insistence on using indigenous categories as the basis of interpretation has been criticized for failing to take into account power or recognize ways in which ideology masks exploitation and inequality. The argument is one which pertains not only to the study of gender, but to the interpretation of social acts and structure generally; should priority be given to indigenous categories and concepts, or to materialist or other external explanations which can themselves be seen either as objectively revealing truths 'masked' by indigenous ideologies or, conversely, as imposing Western categories in a way which is in itself mystifying? Can we dismiss exploitation as a Western concept when it is women's labour which provides the basis for men's prestige, or power when it is male violence to women which is a common and culturally condoned occurrence? Part of the problem implicitly addressed in these questions is the relationship between local meanings, individual action, and theoretical models of social structure.

In *Kinship and Gender: Essays Towards a Unified Analysis*, Collier and Yanagisako (1987) attempted to develop a 'systematic model' of inequality which took into account structural models, local cultural meaning, and historical context. They argued that gender and kinship are mutually constituted symbolic systems containing specific cultural meanings which are not static but can only be understood through consideration of historical process. Suggesting that all social systems are systems of inequality, they proposed a three-tiered approach which comprises cultural analysis of meaning, construction of models of inequality, and historical analysis.

Yanagisako's article on first and second-generation Japanese American marriages is an example of this approach. She showed that what appeared to be parallel gender patterns in the marriages of Issei (first generation) and Nisei (second generation) were in fact reflections of quite different ideologies of gender, the family, *work and the *state. Issei divided their socio-spatial world into 'inside', which related to the family, and 'outside', which related to the public domain. Women were associated with 'inside' and men with 'outside', and although women often worked in the family business, this was considered to be 'inside' because it took place within the context of the family. Marriage was a hierarchical relationship in which authority rested with the husband, who was the mediator between the world of the family and the wider society or state. Nisei on the other hand made a division between 'work' and 'family', the latter being the domain of the husband, and the former that of the wife. Nisei represented care of the family, childcare and domestic labour as the woman's job, balanced by, and equivalent to the men's job of waged work to support the family. Rather than seeing the inside/outside and family/work oppositions as variations of the domestic/public or encompassing/encompassed dichotomies, Yanagisako presented them as 'core metaphors' which referred to different sets of gender/kinship relations, and arose from different historical circumstances. The Issei core metaphors reflected the 'blend of Western European and elite (*samuri*) Japanese ideologies of gender, kinship and polity' which was promoted by the leaders of the Meiji Restoration and which the Issei brought with them to America; the Nisei core metaphors reflected the ideology of industrial capitalism, particularly the separation of the family from the workplace, which was part of the socialization of the second-generation American-Japanese. The former was a hierarchical ordering of social relations within gendered space, reflecting a division between kinship and polity, the latter a separation of reproductive work from productive work, 'which in turn is symbolically associated with an opposition between love and money, cooperation and competition, expressive and instrumental activity' (Yanagisako 1987: 111). In this discussion, local meanings were related to wider structural models of gender, kinship, family and state and further, were shown not to be fixed or static but to transform in response to the process of historical change.

In the feminist anthropology of the 1970s and early 1980s, the subject of enquiry was above all 'woman'. This emphasis continued after the shift in analytic emphasis to 'gender', to the extent that gender itself could almost be seen as a gloss for 'women'. Gradually, however, 'men' and 'masculinity' also came to be the focus of study in their own right. Loizos and Papataxiarchis's *Contested Identities* (1991) was one of the earliest collections in which the contributors paid equal attention to the cultural construction of masculinity. The editors themselves saw gender and kinship not as mutually constituted categories, as Collier and Yanagisako had argued, but as symbolic systems which were at times in conflict; thus, they argued that the kinship roles of the Greek male, which located him in the context of household and family, were often in conflict with other roles such as 'friend', which prescribed quite another set of behaviours in the external domain of the street and the coffee house. Cornwall and Lindisfarne in *Dislocating Masculinity* (1994) also shifted the focus from women to men, and the articles in this volume subjected male sexualities, bodies, and social interactions to the type of scrutiny usually reserved for females. These works represent an important change in emphasis, with male and female both being considered as complex and changing symbolic categories, and masculinity itself viewed as just as problematic as femininity.

There are now few if any areas of social enquiry which have not been subjected to a 'gendered' enquiry. Gender is an element in the most abstract theories of anthropological discourse, such as notions of personhood, *identity and morality, and in the most material or practical, such as *development, *migration or, on a different level, biology (Di Leonardo 1991). The range covered by gender questions has come to parallel that of anthropology itself. With the deconstructionism of the 1990s, the distinction between sex and gender has itself become murky, as anthropological studies of sex and sexuality, drawing on the theories of †Foucault, have increasingly presented not only sexual practice but also the sexed body itself as historically and culturally constructed. Martin's *The Woman in the Body* (1987), for example, demonstrated that North American women of diverse classes and backgrounds experience, speak about and explain bodily functions such as *menstruation and childbirth in profoundly different ways. On a rather different level, Boddy (1989) argued that in the Sudan, infibulation 'creates' virginity, and reinfibulation may restore a sexually experienced woman to the status of virgin; virginity is therefore in this context a social elaboration on the female body rather than a natural condition (Boddy 1989). As Collier and Yanagisako maintain

> It is impossible ... to know what gender or kinship mean if they are to be entirely disconnected from sex and biological reproduction. We have no choice but to begin our investigations of others with our own concepts. But, we can unpack the cultural assumptions embodied in them, which limit our capacity to understand social systems informed by other cultural assumptions.
>
> (Collier and Yanagisako 1987: 34)

FRANCES PINE

See also: body, family, house, household, kinship, nature and culture

Further reading

Barnes, J. (1973) 'Genetrix: Genetor:Nature:Culture?', in J. Goody (ed.) *The Character of Kinship*, Cambridge: Cambridge University Press

Bloch, M. and J.H. Bloch (1980) 'Women and the Dialectics of Nature in Eighteenth-century French Thought', in C. MacCormack and M. Strathern (eds), *Nature, Culture and Gender*, Cambridge: Cambridge University Press

Boddy, J. (1989) *Wombs and Alien Spirits: Women, Men and the Zar Cult in Northern Sudan*, Madison: University of Wisconsin Press

Collier, J. and S.J. Yanagisako (eds) (1987) *Gender and Kinship: Essays Towards a Unified Analysis*, Stanford: Stanford University Press

Cornwall, A. and N. Lindisfarne (eds) (1994) *Dislocating Masculinity: Comparative Ethnographies*, London: Routledge

Di Leonardo, M. (ed.) (1991) *Gender at the Crossroads of Knowledge: Feminist Anthropology in the Post-modern Era*, Berkeley: University of California Press

Edholm, F., O. Harris and K. Young (1977) 'Conceptualizing Women', *Critique of Anthropology*, vol. 3, 9 and 10: 101–130

Friedl, E. (1987) 'The Position of Women: Appearance and Reality', in J. Dubisch (ed.) *Gender and Power in Rural Greece*, Princeton: Princeton University Press

Harris, O. (1980) 'The Power of Signs: Gender, Culture and the Wild in the Bolivian Andes', in C.P. MacCormack and M. Strathern (eds) *Nature, Culture and Gender*, Cambridge: Cambridge University Press

Jordanova, L.J. (1980) 'Natural Facts: A Historical Perspective on Science and Sexuality', in C.P. MacCormack and M. Strathern (eds) *Nature, Culture and Gender*, Cambridge: Cambridge University Press

La Fontaine, J.S. (1992) 'The Persons of Women', in S. Ardener (ed.) *Persons and Powers of Women in Diverse Cultures*, New York and Oxford: Berg

Lamphere, L. (1974) 'Strategies, Cooperation, and Conflict among Women in Domestic Groups', in M. Rosaldo and L. Lamphere (eds) *Woman Culture and Society*, Stanford: Stanford University Press,

Leacock, E. (1981) *Myths of Male Dominance*, New York: Monthly Review Press

Llewelyn-Davies, M. (1981) 'Women, Warriors, and Patriarchs', in S. B. Ortner and H. Whitehead (eds) *Sexual Meanings: The Cultural Construction of Gender and Sexuality*, Cambridge: Cambridge University Press

Loizos, P. and E. Papataxiarchis (eds) (1991) *Contested Identities: Gender and Kinship in Modern Greece*, Princeton: Princeton University Press

Martin, E. (1987) *The Woman in the Body*, Milton Keynes: Open University Press,

Ortner, S.B. (1974) 'Is Female to Male as Nature is to Culture?', in M. Rosaldo and L. Lamphere (eds) *Woman, Culture and Society*, Stanford: Stanford University Press

—— (1981) 'Gender and Sexuality in Hierarchical Societies: The Case of Polynesia and Some Comparative Implications', in S.B. Ortner and H. Whitehead (eds) *Sexual Meanings: The Cultural Construction of Gender and Sexuality*, Cambridge: Cambridge University Press

Ortner, S.B. and H. Whitehead (eds) (1981) *Sexual Meanings: the Cultural Construction of Gender and Sexuality*, Cambridge: Cambridge University Press

Piña-Cabral, J. de (1986) *Sons of Adam, Daughters of Eve*, Oxford: Clarendon Press

Reiter, R. (1975) *Toward an Anthropology of Women*, London: Monthly Review Press

Rosaldo, M. (1974) 'Woman, Culture and Society: A Theoretical Overview', in M. Rosaldo and L. Lamphere (eds) *Woman, Culture and Society*, Stanford: Stanford University Press

Strathern, M. (1980) 'No Nature, No Culture: The Hagen Case', in C.P. MacCormack and M. Strathern (eds) *Nature, Culture and Gender*, Cambridge: Cambridge University Press

—— (1981) 'Self-interest and Social Good: Some Implications of Hagen Gender Imagery', in S.B. Ortner and H. Whitehead (eds) *Sexual Meanings: The Cultural Construction of Gender and Sexuality*, Cambridge: Cambridge University Press

—— (1988) *The Gender of the Gift: Problems with Women and Problems with Society in Melanesia*, Berkeley: University of California Press

Whitehead, H. (1981) 'The Bow and the Burden Strap: A New Look at Instutionalized Homosexuality in Native North America', in S.B. Ortner and H. Whitehead (eds) *Sexual Meanings: The Cultural Construction of Gender and Sexuality*, Cambridge: Cambridge University Press

Yanagisako, S.J. (1987) 'Mixed Metaphors: Native and Anthropological Models of Gender and Kinship Domains', in J.F. Collier and S.J. Yanagisako (eds) *Gender and Kinship: Essays Towards a Unified Analysis*, Stanford: Stanford University Press

genealogical method

The genealogical method was invented by †W.H.R. Rivers (1864–1922) during the †Torres Straits Expedition of 1898–99. He described it most fully in †*Notes and Queries on Anthropology* (1912), after which it became standard procedure in †social anthropology. Its primary purpose, as Rivers saw it, was to improve the analysis of social organization, i.e. the concrete actuality of inter-personal relations and living arrangements. The method required extensive interviewing of named individuals in order to: (1) collect vital statistics among a non-literate population, and (2) record their pedigrees, which reflected rights and respon-sibilities relating primarily to *descent, succession, and †inheritance.

The method was used, along with censuses and settlement plans, in field research for classical monographs on the Todas (Rivers), Tallensi (†Meyer Fortes), Tikopia (†Raymond Firth), Ndembu (†Victor Turner) and Sinhalas (†Edmund Leach) among others. Robin Fox added a further dimension to the method by showing that, because a genealogy is a cultural form, care has to be taken that names are elicited in accordance with local practice. Fox's Irish islanders began not with a named individual (an †ego) but with ancestors. Alan Barnard and Anthony Good (1984) added further procedural refinements to ensure that no †patrilineal bias affects the use of the genealogical method.

The value of the genealogical method extends beyond the specialized realm of *kinship studies yet it has been neglected by anthropologists who do not work in kin-structured societies. Thus it provided the foundation of a kind of struc-tural demography in anthropology as advocated by *Lévi-Strauss. This aims at a mathematical expression of the relationship between the functioning and durability of *social structure and the actual size of population. It is based on accumulation of individualized demographic and social data and the charting of pedigrees, mapping residences and household surveys.

The genealogical method has been used in modern *urban anthropology where it is often combined with ego-centred *network analysis. It has also been foundational in studies of the *migration of ethnic groups to the United States. Most striking has been its application in *medical anthropology. Thus, for example, among certain groups of New Guinea highlanders the disease *kuru* was proved not to be hereditary, as first thought, but associated with the spread of *cannibalism throughout their territory. Anthropologists have also used the genealogical method in AIDS research in Africa. Indeed, the nature and problems encountered in these two cases eerily echo Rivers's concerns when he first confronted Melanesian depopulation and inexplicable illnesses at the turn of the twentieth century, the setting in which he first began to develop the genealogical method.

JOAN VINCENT

See also: kinship, fieldwork, comparative method, methodology

Further reading

Barnard, A. and A. Good (1984) *Research Practices in the Study of Kinship*, London: Academic Press

Fox, R. (1978) *The Tory Islanders*, Cambridge: Cambridge University Press

Hackenberg, R. (1973) 'Genealogical Method in Social Anthropology: The Foundations of Structural Demography', in J. Honigmann (ed.) *Handbook of Social and Cultural Anthropology*, Chicago: Rand McNally

German and Austrian anthropology

It is almost impossible to treat the anthropological traditions of Germany, Austria, and the German-speaking parts of Switzerland independently before the 1960s. To take a few examples, key figures in post-World War II Swiss anthropology were German or Austrian citizens; most leading members of the former 'Vienna school' (1924–57) were German priests, and †R. Thurnwald, perhaps the most prominent 'German' anthropologist, was an Austrian by birth and academic education.

From their intellectual and organizational beginnings in the nineteenth century until today, the closest equivalents to social and cultural anthropology in the German-speaking countries were the two separate fields of †'*Volkskunde*' and †'*Völkerkunde*'. Although other names have recently been substituted (mostly *Ethnologie* for *Völkerkunde*), the institutional separation continues. *Volkskunde* (science of *the* people) was dedicated to the study of local cultures within Switzerland, the German and Habsburg empires and their successor states. *Völkerkunde* (science of peoples) was primarily concerned with the study of non-European societies and has had closer relations with academic social and cultural anthropology in Western Europe and North America. This entry primarily considers *Völkerkunde*.

Amidst elements of *Enlightenment thought and early Romanticism, the classical period in German philosophy, literature and science of the late eighteenth and early nineteenth centuries prepared the ground for anthropology's later development. A few great travellers and authors combined their humanistic ideals with detailed description. The father and son, J.R. and G. Forster (1727–98, 1754–94) accompanied Captain Cook on his second expedition, resulting in G. Forster's famous account of the voyage. †Alexander von Humboldt, brother of the linguist and political reformer †Wilhelm von Humboldt, was the influential author of 30 volumes on the regions and peoples of South America. But, apart from these early exceptions, the intellectual mainstream in the first decades of the nineteenth century was less inspired by enlightened ethnographic reports from outside Europe, but became preoccupied with local folk cultures. The fragmented political and territorial status of civil society in the German-speaking areas of Europe, and the absence of serious colonial expansion outside Europe were decisive reasons for this. †J.G. Herder had already introduced the distinction between '*Naturvölker*' (natural peoples) and the German people. Herder's influence favoured emotional empathy, rather than reason, in constructing the collective essence of a people's soul and spirit. The beginnings of pan-Germanic *nationalism, and the accompanying interest in *folklore, promoted the formation of *Volkskunde* in the first half of the nineteenth century, while *Völkerkunde* became institutionalized from the second half onward. Its institutional beginnings were related to the establishment of a large number of *museums and collections, which promoted a rising interest in questions of †material culture, its distribution, *diffusion and history.

*Evolutionism did not play any significant role in late nineteenth-century German-speaking anthropology. Evolutionist works were rejected by most scholars, not so much because of any scientific disagreement with *Morgan's *Ancient Society*, but rather for political reasons. Morgan's favourable reception by †Marx and †Engels, at a time of political emancipation for the labour movement, led to a strongly negative reaction from mainstream anthropology, which mostly favoured bourgeois and related political options.

In the period from the late nineteenth century to the immediate post-World War II years, German-speaking anthropology was predominantly concerned with the development of four areas. †A. Bastian's theory of '*Elementargedanken*', i.e. of the †psychic unity of *homo sapiens*, treated parallel cultural developments as the result of independent convergence. Bastian was the founder of *Völkerkunde* as an academic discipline. †L. Frobenius's cultural †phenomenology basically postulated that each socio-cultural phenomenon is built upon an inner experience in soul and mind; i.e. in †Husserl's language, upon an intentional experience. Although its primary meaning may then be modified through forms of application and regional distribution, it is possible to reconstruct it by phenomenological *reductio* (compare L. Volhard's work on cannibalism, 1939). Frobenius's successor A.E. Jensen (1899–1965) developed this method through a shift of focus towards the study of *cosmology (*Das religiöse Weltbild einer frühen Kultur*, 1940). R. Thurnwald's sociological and psychological orientation is often regarded as a variant of 'comparative sociology' or *functionalism. He did emphasize the interrelations among various elements of a social system, but differed from British functionalists in his emphasis on historical aspects. In this theoretical context one also has to place W.E. Mühlmann, who tried to combine philosophical phenomenology with comparative sociology and after 1945 broadened his interest towards cultural anthropology.

Apart from these three theoretical programmes (and †culture history), there were a remarkable number of individual scholars who, having received their first training in German-speaking countries, did not follow its main directions in anthropology, but emigrated for academic or non-academic reasons. The long list of researchers covers several generations and includes such prominent names as *Boas, †Kirchhof, and †Nadel.

The ideas described so far were at least partly developed on the basis of extensive ethnographic experience, but nevertheless they did not altogether succeed with most German-speaking anthropologists. This was largely due to the strong position of *Kulturhistorie* or 'culture history'. The beginnings of this tradition can be traced back to early authors like J.R. Forster and C. Meiners (1747–1810), especially their interest in a general history of cultures, including 'primitive' societies. But the methodological basis was established by the anthropo-geographer †F. Ratzel and the historian †F. Graebner. Ratzel explained the spatial distribution of similar material elements of culture in terms of previous *migration from a few centres. In support of his diffusionism he introduced an axiom that contradicted Bastian, namely the alleged 'narrowness and poverty of human consciousness' in †primitive societies. According to Ratzel, low population density limited the creativity of non-literate human beings; if inventions occurred at all, their diffusion seemed more plausible. On this basis, Ratzel also defined the '*Formkriterium*' (criterion of form for comparing material culture) and postulated the identification of temporal sequences out of the spatial distribution of cultural elements. His ideas were taken up by Graebner, who elaborated them in his more systematic method of cultural-historical ethnology (*Methode der Ethnologie*, 1911). This was conceived as a historical discipline that would explore cultural relationships by means of '*Beziehungskriterien*' (criteria for identifying affinities and chronologies). In addition to this methodological inventory, Graebner defined the term †'*Kulturkreis*' (culture-circle), which was to become central to the so-called Vienna school of cultural-historical ethnology. The 'culture-circle' was understood as a complex of central cultural elements in a specific area. Graebner's version was accepted and modified by several other German-speaking anthropologists, such as B. Ankermann, H. Baumann, and R. Heine-Geldern.

Within this larger framework, the Vienna school of cultural-historical ethnology had a special status. Its founder, †Pater Wilhelm Schmidt adopted Graebner's method, but altered it considerably for his own purposes (*Handbuch* der Methode der kulturhistorischen Ethnologie, 1937). Together with P.W. Koppers (1886–1961) he developed the 'Kulturkreislehre' (culture-circles concept), which attempted a cultural history of non-literate humanity on the basis of culture-circles, existing above any regional level, and placed in a relative chronological sequence ('primitive', primary, secondary and tertiary). This was aimed against Morgan, and contrasted his model with cultural history. The chronological vagueness implied in the notion of 'primitive' cultures (which were seen as being closest to creation in the Biblical sense) enabled Schmidt to engage in other ideological arguments of his times through his anti-evolutionist and anti-Marxist work; for example, in his attempt to demonstrate the primary importance of private *property in 'primitive' cultures (Das Eigentum der Urkulturen, 1937). These concepts were supported by a research programme carried out among societies of the 'primitive culture-circle' (†Gusinde, Schebesta, Koppers).

A considerable number of well-known scholars were more or less active in integrating Völkerkunde into the Nazi regime, which nevertheless favoured Volkskunde and *biological anthropology more directly for its own racist and totalitarian purposes. Those who rejected Nazism or were persecuted – apart from those of 'non-Aryan descent' (Heine-Geldern, 1885–1968) and explicit supporters of the left (Cunow, 1862–1936) – include Jensen and several representatives of the Vienna school (Dostal 1994).

The period after World War II was marked by the dissolution of the schools that had dominated the previous decades. J. Haekel (1907–73) put the Kulturkreislehre to a definite end in 1957 and renounced it once and for all. Because of the experience of subordination to Nazi ideology, and with the disintegration of the schools, Völkerkunde in the German-speaking West was characterized by a certain reluctance towards ambitious theories of any kind, preferring instead historical and empirical research strictu sensu. In the GDR of course, Soviet Marxism dominated an East German ethnography that was nevertheless to some extent able to achieve remarkable empirical results, and sometimes developed more sophisticated theoretical approaches than in comparable *Russian and Soviet anthropology

In Switzerland, West Germany and Austria a generation of social anthropologists trained immediately after the war now structures the present institutional landscape of Völkerkunde. Broadly speaking, one tendency in today's social anthropology of the German-speaking countries is towards close cooperation with *archaeology, historiography and history in the form of regional ethnohistorical and cultural-historical research. Another group of scholars has emphasized the involvement of anthropological research in *development and applied studies of an empirical and sociological orientation. Thirdly, a steady and continuous evaluation of Western theories and methods has established the closest forms of interaction with the main existing tendencies in international anthropological research.

WALTER DOSTAL
and ANDRE GINGRICH

See also: Enlightenment anthropology, culture, diffusion, Europe: Central and East

Further reading

Conte, E. (1987) 'Wilhelm Schmidt: Des letzten Kaisers Beichtvater und das neudeutsche Heidentum', in H. Gerndt (ed.) Volkskunde und Nationalsozialismus, Münchner Beiträge zur Volkskunde 7: 261–78

Dostal, W. (1994) 'Silence in the Darkness: German Ethnology in the National Socialist Period', Social Anthropology 2 (3): 251–62

Hildebrandt, H.-J. (1989) 'Einleitung', in H-J. Hildebrandt (ed.) Albert Hermann Post, Einleitung in das Studium der ethnologischen Jurisprudenz, Göttingen: Ed. Re

Hirschberg, W. (ed.) (1988) Neues Wörterbuch der Völkerkunde, Berlin: Reimer

Steiner, G. (1977) Georg Forster, Stuttgart: Metzler

ghost dance

The ghost dance remains an important part of *Native North American cultural history in part because of the savage butchery of the United States Army on the battlefield at Wounded Knee in 1890. This was the subject of a classic monograph by James Mooney (1861–1921). Mooney's first-hand inquiry dealt with the spread of the ghost dance movement in Western North America in the early reservation period and the actions taken by the military to suppress it. His own sympathy for the Irish nationalist struggle for independence from Britain led Mooney to see the ghost dance as a product of Euro-American contact history and the powerlessness of the Native Americans. The dances promoted solidarity and *resistance to domination or assimilation. Mooney also compared the ghost dance with *millenarian religions in Europe, Asia, and elsewhere and his monograph remains a model for the study of such movements, both theoretically and methodologically.

Ethnohistorians have reported considerable local and regional variation in ghost dance performances. Some dances stressed militancy and included a belief in bulletproof ghost shirts. Many involved feasting to encourage the return of ancestral warrior heroes, and *ritual to bring the dead back to life. Others were more concerned with warding off disease and promoting fertility. Scholars have argued that calls for cultural and demographic revitalization enhance the likelihood of cultural survival and the building-up of new forms of moral community. Thus it is not surprising to find that the dances continue on many tribal reservations to this day.

Academically, the ghost dance lies at the heart of discussions of the boundaries of †ethnohistory, *history and anthropology. Ethnohistorians consider it a reaction to Euro-American settler incursion onto reservations and hunting grounds. They shun global generalizations, preferring to emphasize circumstances within each tribe, arguing the historical occurrence of the dance mainly among those smaller groups that suffered most disease and loss of refuge areas. Historians trace the dance to social and cultural deprivations following the colonization and dispossession of native peoples. Government policies brought increased disease, poverty, and diaspora. Some historians see the ghost dance as part of a global process of European expansion and the marginalization of *indigenous peoples dating from the the fifteenth century.

Anthropologists have found cultural forms comparable with the ghost dance in many parts of the world and have employed a plethora of terms to characterize them: religions of the oppressed; nativistic movements; messianic movements; transformative movements. Recent North American ghost dance ethnography has begun to examine the dancers' own categories of meaning and *agency, in the context of novelty and cultural continuity. This has established a new precedent for the anthropological study of similar movements elsewhere in the world.

JOAN VINCENT

See also: millennial movements, Americas: Native North America, political anthropology, resistance

Further reading

Kehoe, A. (1989) *The Ghost Dance: Ethnohistory and Revitalization*, New York: Holt, Rinehart and Winston
Lesser, A. ([1933] 1978) *The Pawnee Ghost Dance Hand Game*, Madison: University of Wisconsin Press
Mooney, J. ([1896] 1965) *The Ghost Dance Religion and the Sioux Outbreak of 1890*, edited by A.F.C.Wallace, Chicago: University of Chicago Press

gossip

In any social milieu, people may be occupied in gossip for a substantial part of their every day lives. Recognizing, since *Malinowski, that studying the world of the everyday is the key to an understanding of how people behave, anthropologists have long appreciated gossip to be a key sociocultural phenomenon.

Nevertheless, sustained analysis of gossip *per se* remained intermittent (†P. Radin, †M. Herskovits, †E. Colson) until the 1960s, when three broadly distinct approaches emerged: the *functionalist, the †transactionalist, and the †symbolic-interactionist.

The functionalist approach is exemplified by †Max Gluckman (1963). Gossip, Gluckman begins, is a culturally determined and sanctioned process, a social fact, with customary rules, and with important functions. Notably, gossip helps maintain group unity, morality and history; for the essence of gossip is a constant (if informal and indirect) communal evaluation and reaffirmation of behaviour by assessment against common, traditional expectations. Furthermore, gossip enables groups to control the competing cliques and aspiring individuals of which they are composed; for through gossip, differences of opinion are fought out behind the scenes (through customary innuendo, ambiguity and conceit) so that outwardly a show of harmony and friendship can be maintained. Finally, gossip is a hallmark and a privilege, even a duty, of group membership. A group gossips, gossip is group property, and to be a member is to gossip – about other members.

The transactionalist approach, spearheaded by Robert Paine (1967), eschews the presumptions of seeing groups as united and equilibrated, and social-structural convention as being always geared towards this end. Paine argues that it is more apposite to see gossip as a means by which individuals manipulate cultural rules, and to see individual gossipers as having rival interests (in *power, *friendships, *networks, material) which they seek to forward and protect. Individuals not groups gossip, and they gossip primarily not about group values but individual aspirations, others' and their own. Indeed, any appeal to group unity should rather be seen as a managing of self-interest: an attempt to have a particular definition of a social situation prevail. In short, gossip allows the moral order to be bent to individual purpose. It is instrumental behaviour which uses a genre of informal communication for the partial effecting of competition between individuals through the selective imparting and withholding, the manipulating, of information.

To an extent, the above dichotomy between group- and individual-oriented analyses is collapsed in the symbolic-interactionist approach. Here (John Haviland 1977; Stanley Heilman 1978) the emphasis is on how, through everyday talk, cultural reality and social relations are continually being represented and debated; in gossip, individuals can be seen actively speculating together on the nature of their lives and world. Hence, gossip provides individuals with a map of their social environment and with current information about happenings, inhabitants and their dispositions. This then provides the resource by which they can devise a programme of action. Also, gossip is the means by which individuals align their actions: negotiate between themselves the scope and import of cultural rules and the social behaviours to which they apply. Gossip is essentially a meta-cultural process: an activity through which individuals examine and discuss together the rules and conventions by which they commonly live. Moreover, since rules are relative and ambiguous in their application, such interpretation is never final or consensual. Hence, gossip continually disassembles, evaluates and reconstitutes the everyday world.

In anthropological analysis – and contrary to common designation – gossip is never idle.

NIGEL RAPPORT

See also: community, language and linguistics, friendship

Further reading

Du Boulay, J. (1974) *Portrait of a Greek Mountain Village*, Oxford: Clarendon Press

Gluckman, M. (1963) 'Gossip and Scandal', *Current Anthropology* 4 (3): 307–15

Haviland, J. (1977) *Gossip, Reputation and Knowledge in Zinacantan*, Chicago: University of Chicago Press

Heilman, S. (1978) *Synagogue Life*, Chicago: University of Chicago Press

Paine, R. (1967) 'What is Gossip About? An Alternative Hypothesis', *Man* 2 (2): 272–85

great and little traditions

The issue of great and little traditions did not arise for the first generation of anthropologists who, following the example of *Malinowski, mainly studied remote, self-contained, small-scale societies. It was only after World War II, when anthropologists began to study communities integrated within larger states and participating in centuries-old religious traditions such as *Buddhism or *Christianity, that the problem arose. The terms 'great' and 'little' traditions were actually introduced and elaborated in the 1950s by the University of Chicago anthropologist †Robert Redfield. In Redfield's vision: 'The studies of the anthropologist are contextual; they relate some element of the great tradition - sacred book, story-element, teacher, ceremony, or supernatural being - to the life of the ordinary people, in the context of daily life as the anthropologist sees it happen' (1956).

An important early contribution to the study of great and little traditions came from Redfield's protégé McKim Marriott (1955) who contrasted Indian village religion with the Sanskritic textual tradition of *Hinduism. Marriott observed that fifteen of the nineteen village festivals celebrated in the village were sanctioned by at least one Sanskrit text. To explain the interaction between little and great traditions he theorized a two-way influence: local practices had been historically promoted into the Sanskrit canon in a process he labelled 'universalization', and ideas and practices already contained in this canon were locally adapted in a process of 'parochialization'. Of course some rites may have been parochialized and then re-universalized in a circular fashion.

Additionally, Marriott stressed that in the North Indian context, the great Sanskritic tradition could be viewed as an 'indigenous civilization'; a body of cultural forms elaborated in an orthogenetic fashion from a regional pool of ideas. Great tradition Hinduism thus constituted a primary civilization by contrast with other great traditions such as Spanish Catholicism in Latin

America which were foreign impositions rather than the orthogenetic outgrowth of indigenous culture. Such heterogenetic great traditions did nonetheless amalgamate, or syncretize, with indigenous traditions to form 'secondary civilizations'.

Marriott's views on great and little traditions were disputed by †Dumont and Pocock (1957) in the very first issue of their journal *Contributions to Indian Sociology*. They pointed out that the villagers themselves were unconcerned with distinguishing between the presence of separate traditions – 'For them there are not two traditions but simply the one which is their life'. In their view local religious practices required consideration as a whole, understandable as the realization of general principles such as the opposition between *pollution and purity or the recourse to the sacred through either priests or *possession. A common ideology of Hinduism could be discerned at all levels and in all localities. The recognition of different 'levels' in Hinduism (1959), however, came close to reproducing the great and little tradition distinction against which they were protesting. The difference was that for Dumont and Pocock the little tradition was not a residual category of rituals not found elsewhere, but the whole cycle of festivals found in their local context.

Tambiah (1970) objected that a distinction between two traditions was an ahistorical artefact of anthropological enquiry because the great tradition for religions like Hinduism and Buddhism consists of a variable selection of texts written in widely different historical periods yet often presented as if they were a synchronic totality. This objection may apply in Asia, but not in the study of European Christianity where the principal sacred texts and ritual liturgies are very much agreed upon within each denomination (Stewart 1991). One cannot so easily accuse anthropologists of European Christianity of running amok in the library and inventing their own great tradition. In place of a distinction between great and little traditions, Tambiah proposed substituting a distinction between historical and contemporary religion with the primary task being to look for continuities and transformations between them.

Another promising line of approach may be borrowed from studies of *orality and *literacy. A focus on the differences between the written and the spoken word enables us to qualify and better specify the transformations which knowledge and practices undergo when they are translated into texts, or from texts back into oral and practical repertoires. Writing fixes a given text and facilitates the elaboration of consistent, often highly abstract, philosophical principles. It converts practical local religion into universal theology while also permitting the dissemination of these complicated ideas over broad areas. Literacy is one of the keys in creating a system of rules which can be used to keep a tradition orthodox partly through its power to define local traditions as heterodox or 'superstitious' (Goody 1986).

Mastery of great tradition texts usually brings prestige, but it is not the exclusive prerogative of the urban or the wealthy. Poor villagers may also gain access to great tradition knowledge either through their own learning or through the mediation of local priests or monks. These villagers are often capable of discerning the hegemonic authority and status value of great tradition knowledge. If visited by a bishop, or a government minister, they might try to conceal those aspects of local practice which they know to be part of a divergent little tradition. This situation weakens Dumont and Pocock's assertion that there is only one tradition. Analytically it may be useful to consider village practices as an integral whole, but the villagers themselves recognize the existence of another, more prestigious tradition.

The distinction between great and little traditions thus remains valid and vital although relatively few anthropologists have, over the years, been able to achieve the balance of philological, historical and anthropological talents required for their ideal study. As Redfield (1956) understatedly acknowledged when he outlined his vision, 'It makes anthropology much more difficult and very much more interesting'.

CHARLES STEWART

See also: syncretism, complex society, literacy

Further reading
Dumont, L., and D. Pocock (1957) 'Village Studies', *Contributions to Indian Sociology*, 1 :23–41
—— (1959) 'On the Different Aspects or Levels in Hinduism', *Contributions to Indian Sociology*, 3:40–54
Goody, J. (1986) *The Logic of Writing and the Organization of Society*, Cambridge: Cambridge University Press
Marriott, M. (1955) 'Little Communities in an Indigenous Civilization', in M. Marriott (ed.) *Village India: Studies in the Little Community*, Chicago: University of Chicago Press
Redfield, R. (1956) *Peasant Society and Culture*, Chicago: University of Chicago Press

Stewart, C. (1991) *Demons and the Devil: Moral Imagination in Modern Greek Culture*, Princeton: Princeton University Press

Tambiah, S. (1970) *Buddhism and the Spirit Cults in North-East Thailand*, Cambridge: Cambridge University Press

Gypsies

The term 'Gypsy' is used in Anglo-American anthropology for †endogamous communities who refer to themselves variously as Rom, Sinti, Manush, Kale, etc. and live scattered throughout Europe and North America (Salo 1990), in parts of Southern and Central America, Northern Africa and Southern Africa (*Encyclopedia of World Cultures* 1992). 'Gypsy' derives from the misnomer 'Egyptian', which resulted from the erroneous notion that 'Gypsies' originally came from Egypt. Philologists examining the dialects of the Romanes language spoken among these communities in the eighteenth century discovered their Indic structure. Lexically the six to seven major contemporary dialects of Romanes have been largely influenced by diverse European languages, in addition to Persian, Greek, Armenian and probably Arabic. This points to a westward migration from South Asia at an as yet unknown period. Although some Gypsies such as the Kale of Spain (the 'Gitanos') no longer speak Romanes, for most groups some Romanes dialect is mother tongue.

There has been much speculation about the early history of Gypsies. From the fifteenth century onwards their presence in Western Europe is attested in documents, and they probably entered the Balkans around the thirteenth century. It is difficult to affirm their presence here earlier, since they were often confused with local peripatetic communities (Rao 1987). Individuals from the so-called 'dangerous classes' in Europe probably joined Gypsy bands time and again, yet the latter have by and large valued and defended their separate *identity. *Pollution taboos whose violation implies expulsion from the group still help preserve this identity. These relate as much to activities like eating and washing as to behaviour towards the dead, and are essential to Gypsy religious belief and practice (Okely 1983; Piasere 1985). Yet everywhere Gypsies also share the religious denomination of their non-Gypsy neighbours, and in Christian areas they are Christian, in Muslim areas Muslim.

The Gypsy economy traditionally corresponded with their peripatetic niche, and seasonal *nomadism has been used to engage in petty trade and provide various services and crafts to a wide range of clients. In Western Europe many are no longer nomadic, or only sporadically so, and in countries such as Spain they have been sedentary for generations. While in socialist East Europe many were forced into wage labour in generally low-status, unskilled jobs (Kaminski 1980; Mirga 1992), some from Southern Europe are employed as migrant labour in the more industrialized countries of Western Europe. The hallmark of Gypsy economy is extreme flexibility, and both within the socialist and capitalist systems many communities have managed to retain some degree of independence (Stewart 1993).

The social and political organization of Gypsies is community-specific. *Kinship systems range from bilaterally reckoned †kindred to an absence of formalized kin groups; kinship terminology also varies between groups, and examples of both †Eskimo type (e.g. 'Vlach Gypsies') as also of the †Sudanese type (e.g. 'Slovensko Roma') may be found. Most communities are characterized by the †acephalous nature of small, local groups, accompanied by a strong *gender hierarchy.

Most Gypsies now live in caravans or houses in underprivileged areas. This is symptomatic of their low social status and of the discrimination and harassment they have been subjected to, and still are especially in Europe, where most of them live. Over the centuries they have been banished, imprisoned, tortured, hanged, enslaved or deported to European colonies overseas. This persecution culminated in the Holocaust in which more than half a million were exterminated. Estimates of the contemporary Gypsy population in Europe range between 2 and 5.5 million (Vossen 1983).

APARNA RAO

See also: ethnicity, identity, nomadism

Further reading
Kaminski, I.-M. (1980) *The State of Ambiguity*, Gothenburg: The University Press

Mirga, A. (1992) 'Roma Territorial Behaviour and State Policy', in M.J. Casimir and A. Rao (eds) *Mobility and Territoriality*, Oxford: Berg

Okely, J. (1983) *The Traveller-Gypsies*, Cambridge: Cambridge University Press

Piasere, L. (1985) *Mare Roma: Catégories humaines et structure sociale*, Paris: Études et Documents Balkaniques et Méditerranéens

Rao, A. (ed) (1987) *The Other Nomads: Peripatetic Minorities in Cross-cultural Perspective*, Cologne: Bohlau

Salo, M.T. (ed.) (1990) *100 Years of Gypsy Studies*, Cheverly, MD: Gypsy Lore Society

Stewart, M. (1993) 'Gypsies, the Work Ethic and Hungarian Socialism', in C. Hann (ed.) *Socialism: Ideals, Ideologies, and Local Practices*, London: Routledge

Sutherland, A. (1975) *Gypsies: The Hidden Americans*, London: Tavistock

Vossen, R (1983) *Zigeuner*, Frankfurt: Ullstein

Hinduism

'Hinduism' is an English term coined in the nineteenth century to designate the religious traditions of the non-Muslim majority of *South Asia. The term has no exact and well-established equivalent in Indian languages. The word 'Hindu' was originally used by Muslims as an ethnographic term to describe the non-Muslim inhabitants of the lands beyond the Indus river; its marriage to the English suffix '-ism' was a joint product of *Orientalist scholarship, British administrative convenience, and the responses of some Indian intellectuals to the challenges of *colonial rule. About 83 per cent of the population of the Republic of India and a majority of the population of Nepal may be said to be Hindu as the term is normally used; significant numbers of Hindus have also migrated from South Asia to other regions of the world.

The traditions falling under this general label are derived historically from Indo-Europeans who first arrived in the subcontinent in the second millennium BCE and from the peoples already present at the time they came. The result of the mixture and interaction over subsequent centuries is a multi-levelled and highly diverse patchwork of sects and traditions. At the subcontinental level we find a textualized religious culture, itself immensely variegated, carried in Sanskrit texts and propagated mainly by Brāhman priests and other religious specialists. Here are to be found the abstruse philosophies and great sectarian theologies for which India is justly famed. While no single philosophy or belief system predominates at this 'Sanskritic' level, the soteriologies, deities, values, and ritual styles associated with the texts enjoy great prestige and constitute a pan-Indian framework for more parochial traditions. The several major linguistic regions of India (roughly comparable to European nations in size) have produced their own distinctive high religious cultures expressed in regional literatures. Coexisting with these textual traditions, and always interacting with them, are the largely unsystematized local traditions of India's mostly rural masses.

Underlying the diversity of these traditions are certain widely shared concepts and themes that impart some unity to an otherwise fragmented picture. One such concept is that of the soul's rebirth after death. Associated with rebirth is the concept of *karma*, the idea that one's destiny in this and future lives is influenced by one's actions. The idea of the liberation (*mokṣa*) of the soul from the cycle of transmigration, the cycle seen as a concatenation of karmic effects, is the common goal of all Hindu soteriologies. Asceticism is not a universal value among these traditions, but the world-renouncer – the spiritually disciplined ascetic who achieves liberation by inwardly attaining what is regarded as the changeless, and thus deathless, true self – commands nearly universal respect.

The worship of deities, seen as powerful beings who can respond to supplications with both worldly boons and help in achieving salvation, is central to most Hindu traditions. Deities in great profusion populate the Hindu world; some are figures of subcontinental renown whose attributes and deeds are celebrated in well known texts; others are regional or local figures. At the apex of a subcontinental pantheon are the male deities Brahmā, Viṣṇu and Śiva together with their goddess-consorts. Brahmā, the creator of the world, is rarely worshipped, but Viṣṇu and Śiva, presiding over the preservation and destruction of the world respectively, are the foci of two predominant sectarian traditions: the *vaiṣṇava*s (worshippers of Viṣṇu) and *śaiva*s (worshippers of Śiva). Viṣṇu periodically appears in the world in the form of *avatāra*s (descents), of which the best known are Rāma and Kṛṣṇa. Śiva, usually worshipped in the form of the phallic *linga*, is a paradoxical figure whose character combines asceticism and eroticism, and who is associated with creative energy as well as destruction. Hindu goddesses, whose worshippers are often called *śakta*s, are viewed as embodiments of *Śakti*, divine energy, which underlies fertility and abundance but is also manifested as disease, destruction and death.

Religious symbols express and support crucial features of social rank in Hindu society. The *varṇa* system, the ancient idealized scheme of four ranked classes – Brāhmans (priests), Kṣatriyas (warriors and rulers), Vaiśyas (husbandmen and traders) and Śūdras (servants) – is sanctioned in religious texts and focuses on the relationship between Brāhmans and Kṣatriyas as performers and sponsors, respectively, of sacrificial rites. Contrasting with the all-India *varṇa* system are regional and local hierarchies of *castes (known as *jāti*s in Indic languages); these local ranking systems are at least partly ordered on a continuum of ritual *pollution and purity, with the Brāhman, seen as a mediator between the human and divine worlds, at the system's top, and the polluted 'untouchable' at its nadir. The concepts of transmigration and *karma* are sometimes treated as a †theodicy of rank, with one's position in the hierarchy of beings in the world (of which the human social hierarchy is only a part) interpreted as an outcome of one's actions in previous existences.

The degree to which Hinduism corresponds to any social or political reality is a hotly contested matter. Common themes and a web of historical connections are sufficient to justify the idea that Hinduism is a cultural entity of some sort. The idea of Hindus constituting an actual confessional community is a purely modern concept and meshes poorly with the highly fissured traditional religious landscape of South Asia. Hindu nationalists, however, vigorously promote the notion that Hindus constitute the 'majority community' of the Republic of India.

L.A. BABB

See also: Asia: South, caste, Indian anthropology, Orientalism, pollution and purity

Further reading

Babb, L.A. (1986) *Redemptive Encounters: Three Modern Styles in the Hindu Tradition*, Berkeley: University of California Press

Brockington, J.L. (1981) *The Sacred Thread: Hinduism in Its Continuity and Diversity*, Edinburgh: Edinburgh University Press

Fuller, C.J. (1992) *The Camphor Flame: Popular Hinduism and Society in India*, Princeton: Princeton University Press

Thapar, R. (1985) 'Syndicated Moksha', *Seminar* no. 313 (September): 14–22

history and anthropology

Since the 1980s, anthropology and history have converged, through mutual interests, overlapping methods, and reciprocal borrowing of methods and concepts. There are now significant areas of overlap between the two disciplines, even if certain basic orientations toward chronological narrative and contemporary fieldwork make them fundamentally distinct. While these recent developments suggest growing areas of mutual interest, a longer view of anthropology's development would muddy a story of increasing mutual engagement on the part of the two disciplines. Anthropology has in fact had a succession of historical moments and unhistorical ones; while for Scottish Enlightenment writers among others, 'history' could refer to the comparative analysis of political institutions as well as to annalistic narrative.

Anthropology was a historical inquiry up to the early twentieth century, in the sense that the *comparative method for the study of institutions entailed developmental narrative and drew upon a range of classical, biblical, and ethnological sources. In some forms anthropology's history was frankly teleological and *evolutionist, and in others it was *diffusionist. By modern standards, its use of sources was opportunistic and uncritical. Diffusionist arguments, in particular, tended to be highly speculative and tendentious. What was indeed 'conjectural history' was dismissed by *Radcliffe-Brown and others as the professional discipline of social anthropology was established over the first decades of the twentieth century. Although scope for the study of cultural affinities and migrations persisted in *Boasian anthropology in the United States, such 'history' became increasingly marginal in synchronic studies of cultural and symbolic systems; longer-term †diachronic processes came to be studied by archaeologists employing a whole battery of sophisticated techniques that had been unavailable earlier.

Converging disciplines

As †Evans-Pritchard noted (1981: 200), Radcliffe-Brown's exclusion of 'guesswork history' in fact entailed the exclusion of all history. He was concerned to establish a sociologically rigorous inquiry, that had a definite identity as a separate discipline, and could not tolerate the messy complexities of historical contingency (Thomas 1989). He and most other British social anthropologists consequently disembedded intensive ethnographic studies from their historical contexts, not only from a prehistory of hazy migrations, but also from colonial interactions and other developments over the decades immediately preceding the time of fieldwork. Just as some ethnographic photographers such as E. S. Curtis notoriously persuaded subjects to resume traditional dress, and airbrushed-out signs of †acculturation, anthropologists elided foreign contacts that detracted from the authenticity of the cultures studied. Interactions between traditional societies and *colonial powers were reduced to 'social change' that might be dealt with in a brief introduction or in a concluding chapter to the classic *functionalist monograph.

From the 1960s on, anthropologists became increasingly concerned to situate small-scale societies in wider economic and political processes. This interest, more evolutionist than historical, was at first closely linked with the development of *Marxist anthropology and with theories of imperialism. The prevailing view was that fine-grained historical research was 'empiricist'. Any close integration of anthropological and historical knowledge was therefore retarded, as theories of the *world system, dependence, *modes of production, and articulation were elaborated, notably in journals such as *Critique of Anthropology* and *Economy and Society*.

The failure to historicize culture during the 1960s and 1970s is only surprising in retrospect. Materialist and culturalist perspectives were more sharply polarized than has subsequently been the case; and history was generally a conservative discipline more remote from anthropology than it has since become. Histories of the non-European world, in particular, were often limited to narratives of the development of colonial policy, and moreover frequently focussed less on administrative problems in colonized regions than on metropolitan decision-making – which, it must be said, made for some pretty dull monographs. History generally remained strongly biased towards documentary as opposed to oral records, and perforce therefore toward the perspectives of those who produced documents rather than those whose lives might be marginally noticed in them. This bias was exacerbated by the fact that not only documents, but official documents, were privileged as sources for colonial histories: the more revealing private correspondence and memoirs of officials, *missionaries, and traders 'on the ground', who frequently conveyed more ironic and revealing accounts of the disordered and partial implementation of colonial policies, were not extensively drawn upon until historians moved toward a more 'social' orientation in the 1960s. The essentially 'democratic' orientation of anthropological work, the tendency to deal with values and perceptions at the level of local communities, was plainly not compatible with histories in which white officials remained central.

The discipline of history was itself to change both in its approaches to European and non-European societies. Interests in oral history and ethnohistory emerged earlier in Africa than in other regions, but significant studies were being done in the Pacific, Asia and elsewhere by the late 1960s. In European studies, histories of working-class movements, *peasants, and women emerged; E.P. Thompson's classic, *The Making of the English Working Class* (1963), was especially important. Broader interests in 'history from below' and social history generally – drawing in part from the several generations of the French †*Annales* school – led to a dramatic broadening of historians' vision. The issue of what was studied was intimately connected with the question of how it was studied; unconventional sources, oral history, and critical and imaginative readings of canonical documents were required, if the lives and perceptions of those beneath or at the margins of the historical record were to be even partially recovered.

From then on, shifts within both disciplines produced common ground. Historians inspired by †Victor Turner and †Clifford Geertz, among other anthropologists, became increasingly interested in culture, drama, and ritual. Although their insights were often only loosely applied, †'thick descriptions', *reflexivity, and sensitivity toward questions of performance, were enlivening in a discipline still generally characterized by precise primary research and objectivistic narrative, particularly in the hands of such eloquent writers as Greg Dening, Natalie Zemon Davis, Rhys Isaac, Inga Clendinnen, Robert Darnton, and Simon Schama.

Studies of colonial processes compelled them to consider how 'both sides' of the relationship might be recovered, which was to raise methodological and epistemological questions concerning the form of historical knowledge. As it became increasingly clear that Marxist anthropology needed to move away from the sterile formalism of †Althusserian structuralism to more particular accounts of 'social formations', anthropologists were prompted to examine colonial histories and relationships more specifically. The kind of historical anthropology that emerged had nothing in common with the earlier conjectural history, but at its best instead aimed to integrate extensive archival research with anthropological sensitivity to the complexities of cross-cultural relationships. This trend had been anticipated, in South Asian studies, in a fine series of essays produced from the 1960s on by Bernard S. Cohn; it is symptomatic of wider intellectual shifts in the discipline that these were not published together and widely appreciated until the late 1980s (Cohn 1987). Among other pioneering works might be mentioned James Fox's remarkable political and ecological history of eastern Indonesia (1977) and Renato Rosaldo's *Ilongot Headhunting* (1980).

Over the same period, a new rigour emerged in *histories of anthropology as a discipline. Earlier these had often been no more than exercises in collective self-congratulation, highly directed toward the validation of current theoretical concerns, and often based more on anecdote than extensive research. The more deeply researched studies were marginal to the discipline, and regarded as being of little more than antiquarian interest. Together with Fabian's critique of the denial of coevalness in anthropological writing (1983), the publications of Stocking (1983–1991; 1987), Urry (1993), and others did much to bring this area of inquiry back into the centre of the discipline. The formation of anthropological knowledge became an issue increasingly linked with colonial practice, and with the 'invention of tradition' (Pels and Salemink 1994).

Structural history

Historical anthropology has at no point been a unified approach. However, the broader level of interest in the field intensified in the mid-1980s in response to †Marshall Sahlins's stimulating interpretations of the death of Cook in Hawaii and contact histories in Fiji and New Zealand (1981, 1985). His culturalist arguments emphasized that history was ordered differently in different societies, that it was not necessarily antithetical to a structuralist frame of analysis but could be integrated with it, since events, at least in Pacific societies, were understood to recapitulate in the short term the mythic structures that they transformed in the longer term. Sahlins's essays revitalized studies in a number of fields – on divine *kingship, that was now correlated with the 'heroic history' that assimilated accomplishments to the agency of the king – and on *myth, that was drawn out of a dehistoricized *Lévi-Straussian domain and into a processual account.

But at the same time Sahlins's work failed to speak to those exploring labour history, peasant *resistance, *migration, and colonial histories that entailed deep social and cultural disruption. Just as its key case-studies were derived from the 'heroic societies' of early Polynesia, its salience as a model seemed restricted to those societies, at the moments in their histories when interaction with outsiders was limited and occasional. Under such circumstances intrusions could indeed be assimilated to prior categories; although the argument did address the transformation of structure in the longer run, in so far as it dealt with the very Hawaiian way in which the Hawaiians 'abandoned' their religion for Christianity, it was hard to see how the arguments could be extended to the second half of the nineteenth century in Hawaii, when plantation economies dispossessed and proletarianized many Hawaiians. A number of critics suggested that Sahlins's arguments could only account for externally stimulated change and introduced no dynamism into local cultures themselves. Sahlins implicitly responded to the point in a subsequent essay (1991) concerning cultural reformulation within the Fijian chiefdoms; but the equally significant line of criticism, that the more radical restructuring of indigenous societies attendant upon later phases of colonization requires some different set of arguments, seemed to require a fundamentally different approach.

Debunking the exotic

While Sahlins's studies have inspired scholars working in many regions to pursue the dynamic interplay of myth, ritual and history further, historical anthropology elsewhere – in Melanesia and South Asia for example – has emphasized the transformative power of colonial processes, generally from a critical perspective.

A range of phenomena that anthropologists had previously interpreted for their social and cultural logic were shown to arise from a wider historical dynamic, from the interaction between local societies and colonial powers. In many cases precisely the features taken by anthropologists to be hallmarks of cultural difference, such as the Indian *caste system and the Balinese 'theatre state', arguably emerged in the specific forms that had intrigued anthropologists as a result of colonial interventions.

†Louis Dumont's celebrated study of caste, *Homo Hierarchicus* (1980) rigorously segregated religious and secular status, and associated kingship with a symbolically-impoverished political domain, while affirming the centrality of caste and hierarchy in Indian society. While Dumont's elaborate theory had been questioned from many perspectives, a particularly decisive critique emerged from Nicholas Dirks's detailed ethnohistoric study of the 'little kingdom' of Pudukkottai (1986). Because Dumont neglected colonial history, he failed to consider the degree to which the very separation of religion and politics was a product of colonial intervention. On the basis of a mass of ethnohistorical information Dirks argues convincingly that hierarchy, kingship and status had previously been intimately connected. The British truncated the power of warrior kings, and created a bureaucracy in which literate Brāhmans assumed privileged positions, not least in the codification of the social order in terms that emphasized their own high status.

In debate that is in many ways parallel, Clifford Geertz's characterization of the Balinese states as preoccupied with theatre rather than politics (1980), has been challenged by scholars including Tambiah (1985), Schulte Nordholt (1986, 1994), and most recently and comprehensively, Margaret Weiner (1994). They have reconstructed the political dynamism that Geertz elided, and argued that the specific conditions described by Geertz could only be associated with the attentuated states subordinated to Dutch rule. Tambiah mischievously suggested that Geertz's *Negara* might more aptly have been titled *The Twilight of the Balinese State* (1985: 336). In both the Indian and Balinese cases, an ambitious anthropological argument, that drew attention to stark contrasts between the

West and Asia, would seem flawed by exoticism. In this context, the deeper and more critical approach to the history of anthropological thought, alluded to above, gave a new and powerful edge to the critique. As critics like Inden and Appadurai had argued, Dumont's argument was less a distinctive sociological or anthropological analysis than the culmination of a tradition of colonial discourse, that fashioned India as a mystical and archaic domain, and in general as the antithesis of the West. The mutual influences between colonial and professional anthropology, between anthropology and a wider field of discourse, and between anthropology and indigenous representation, were attested to further by Bernard Cohn (1987: 58–64) who argued, on the basis of Peter France's work, that Fijian origin myths, still widely current in Fiji in official versions that have entered school textbooks, possessed no authenticity, but were adapted versions of migration histories postulated by colonial ethnologists.

The 'debunking' style of this criticism was initially refreshing, as was the wider project engaged in by Hobsbawm and Ranger (1983), that drew attention to inventions of tradition, in many contexts. It became clearer, however, with the controversy surrounding similar claims that Allan Hanson made with respect to Maori histories (1989), that such arguments relied in some cases upon the same notions of 'authenticity' that they might overtly disavow, and presumed the unique validity of Western ways of knowing the past, effectively discounting local historical understandings. A conflict between foreign scholars and indigenous people with particular investments in the traditions being deconstructed also emerged, that might prove peculiarly difficult to negotiate or overcome. While the immediate repercussions of the controversy were for debates about tradition and identity, there are broader implications for historical anthropology in general: how can a multiplicity of constructions of the past and modes of constructing the past be acknowledged, without lapsing into an uncritical *relativism?

One history or many

Oral history projects often had two motivations, one being the recovery of particular groups' perceptions of the past, the other being more simply the collection of information concerning events that were undocumented in other ways. There is clearly a tension between these projects: the scholar may be prompted to use vernacular accounts as a kind of quarry for shreds of evidence concerning happenings that preceded European contact, or were unnoticed by Europeans, without necessarily acknowledging underlying differences between different expressions and genres of historical knowledge. Data concerning political expansion, migrations, or genealogy, may be extracted from oral narratives without reference to the structure of a narrative or the intentions of narrators.

This positivistic approach to oral history has been displaced by an anthropological relativism that is concerned to do justice to the particular styles and genres of indigenous historicities. Again, Sahlins's discussion (1985) of Polynesian 'heroic history', provides a relevant model. This history is not annalistic or event-structured but tends rather to condense genealogies, to identify deeds in the present with those of ancestors, and to assimilate consequential acts and states to the person of the ruler. The king may encompass the deeds of his subjects and provide a plethora of precedents that may be alluded to in the ongoing rationalization of present strategies. This is, then, an indigenous 'great man' theory of history that may be more thoroughgoing than the European variant: the point is not merely that prominent individuals are privileged, but that their practices encompass the historical space.

Many modes of understanding events, agency, continuity, and change in other cultures might similarly be acknowledged. It is indeed important that they be recognized. Yet it is problematic if the result of such interpretive efforts is simply a sense that the world consists of cultural islands, each with its singular culture and history. This was never the case, and is still less so now: cultures are structured as much by interaction as by internal logic, as are histories and historical consciousness. As Dirks and others have shown, phenomena that once seemed to belong to 'other cultures' were shaped by the West's interactions with those cultures, or rather by the intrusive efforts of particular European political and cultural agencies. The futures of historical anthropology and the anthropology of history must lie in inquiries that avoid imposing Western notions of historical action and causation and seek out distinctive indigenous historical narratives and understandings – yet strive also to ground those narratives in the intersocial colonial histories that we share.

NICHOLAS THOMAS

See also: history of anthropology, classical studies, colonialism

Further reading

Cohn, B. (1987) *An Anthropologist Among the Historians and Other Essays*, Delhi: Oxford University Press
Dirks, N. (1986) *The Hollow Crown: Ethnohistory of an Indian Kingdom*, Cambridge: Cambridge University Press
Dumont, L. (1980) *Homo Hierarchicus*, Chicago: University of Chicago Press
Evans-Pritchard, E.E. (1981) *A History of Anthropological Thought*, London: Faber & Faber
Fabian, J. (1983). *Time and the Other: How Anthropology Makes Its Object*, New York: Columbia University Press
Fox, J. (1977) *The Harvest of the Palm*, Cambridge, MA: Harvard University Press
Geertz, C. (1980) *Negara: The Theatre-State in Nineteenth-Century Bali*, Princeton: Princeton University Press
Hanson, A. (1989) 'The Making of the Maori: Cultural Invention and Its Logic', *American Anthropologist* 91 (4): 890–902
Hobsbawm, E. and T. Ranger (eds) (1983) *The Invention of Tradition*, Cambridge: Cambridge University Press
Pels, P. and O. Salemink (1994) *Colonial Ethnographies* special vol., *History and Anthropology* 8, 1–4
Rosaldo, R. (1980) *Ilongot Headhunting, 1883–1974*, Stanford: Stanford University Press
Sahlins, M. (1981) *Historical Metaphors and Mythical Realities: Structure in the Early History of the Sandwich Islands Kingdom*, Ann Arbor: University of Michigan Press
—— (1985) *Islands of History*, Chicago: University of Chicago Press
—— (1991) 'The Return of the Event, Again', in A. Biersack (ed.) *Clio in Oceania*, Washington: Smithsonian Institution Press
Schulte Nordholt, H. (1986) *Bali: Colonial Conceptions and Political Change: From Shifting Hierarchies to 'Fixed Order'*, Rotterdam: Comparative Asian Studies Program, Erasmus University
—— (1994) 'The Making of Traditional Bali', in P. Pels and O. Salemink (eds) *Colonial Ethnographies*, special vol., *History and Anthropology* 8 (1–4): 89–127
Stocking, G. (1987) *Victorian Anthropology*, New York: Free Press
—— (ed.) (1983–91) *History of Anthropology* (series), Madison: University of Wisconsin Press
Tambiah, S.J. (1985) 'A Reformulation of Geertz's Conception of the Theatre State', *Culture, Thought and Social Action*, Cambridge, MA: Harvard University Press
Thomas, N. (1989) *Out of Time: History and Evolution in Anthropological Discourse*, Cambridge: Cambridge University Press
Thompson, E.P. (1963) *The Making of the English Working Class*, Harmondsworth: Penguin
Urry, J. (1993) *Before Social Anthropology*, Chur: Harwood Academic Publishers

Weiner, M. (1994) *Visible and Invisible Realms: Power, Magic and Colonial Conquest in Bali*, Chicago: University of Chicago Press

history of anthropology

History has its uses and no more so than in defining a discipline like anthropology. Stressing continuity in discontinuity can legitimate current practice; emphasizing discontinuity can assist in making current unorthodoxy orthodox; resurrecting neglected ancestors can establish fresh genealogical links and diminish the status of ancestor figures. In accounts of the discipline's history such approaches which interpret the relevance of the past only in terms of present-day concerns are referred to as †'presentist'. They are often employed by anthropologists when they write or teach on the history of their discipline. Approaches which attempt to apply historical methods and to place anthropology's past in its wider contingent context are called †'historicist' (Stocking 1968).

Insider presentist histories

Although anthropology was established as a subject only in the nineteenth century, the study of humankind has a greater antiquity. However, reflection on anthropology's past really only began in the early years of the twentieth century as the subject began to acquire academic status. In Britain †Haddon's brief survey (1910) stressed the continuity and unity of anthropology, detailing its steady development from the writers of classical antiquity through to the present. The academic development of the discipline also encouraged individuals to reflect upon the discontinuities inherent in their past. This assisted them to differentiate their ideas and methods from those of earlier writers and to legitimate their current position in relation to competing academic approaches. Thus accounts of the history of the discipline were made to serve presentist aims. This approach can be clearly seen in the writings of *Boas and his followers in *American anthropology who attempted to distance themselves from the evolutionary ideas and methods of earlier American anthropologists. Internal differences among the Boasians and differences between American and European traditions were also discussed in historical terms. This approach is most clearly articulated by †Lowie, but is also apparent in the writings of †Radin and †Kroeber.

The first generation of *British social anthropologists who emerged in the 1920s and 1930s were less concerned than American anthropologists with establishing a legitimate ancestry. Unlike the Boasians, the founders of British social anthropology rejected historical approaches, including reflections on their own past. The view that real anthropology only began with the founding figures of *Malinowski and *Radcliffe-Brown required more time before a history of the discipline's development could be written, an event which occurred with the appearance of Kuper's study of British social anthropology (1973). Kuper later revised this account and has gone on to make significant contributions to the history of anthropology viewed from an insider's perspective, mixing presentism with a degree of historicism (1988).

After 1960, as the unity of British social anthropology declined, some second-generation anthropologists wrote accounts of anthropology's past to assert their own ideas and identities. †Evans-Pritchard, for example, charted a personal intellectual biography, relegating the founding fathers to footnotes and locating the origins of the discipline not in the nineteenth century but in the writings of eighteenth-century *Enlightenment Scots and English moral philosophers. Others resurrected past anthropologists to strengthen their own position, hoping to legitimate their current views by rediscovering and reasserting what they claimed were lost traditions. The postcolonial situation generated an initial flurry of critiques of social anthropology's links with imperialism and *colonialism and invoking defensive responses by anthropologists who had worked in colonial societies for colonial governments.

The emergence since 1945 of a number of distinctive and often competing approaches to anthropology in North America has generated a number of histories also aimed at legitimating particular approaches. Most notable among these is that by †Marvin Harris, the most sustained attempt to date at a presentist history of anthropology. Harris attacked a wide range of ideas and approaches often with polemical insight, but his ultimate aim was to enhance his own *cultural materialist approach to anthropology by dismissing most others.

Insider/outsider historicist approaches

Directly and indirectly presentist approaches have been challenged from both within and outside anthropology by more historicist approaches, often utilizing a wide range of published and archival sources. Some early historicist accounts (Hodgen 1936) were written from outside the discipline but were neglected by most anthropologists. Hallowell, writing from within the discipline, made an initial plea for an historicist approach. In Britain one intellectual historian placed nineteenth-century anthropological interest in the origin and evolution of *society in the development of philosophical reflection on human society (Burrows 1967). More recently Bowler (1989) has situated nineteenth-century anthropological ideas in the context of the development of evolutionary ideas in Victorian science. Urry (1993) has applied an historicist approach to the formation of British institutional and academic anthropology in the late nineteenth and early twentieth century.

But it has been the American historian George Stocking, trained in the history of science and using an historicist approach, who has had the major impact on the study of the history of both British and American anthropology. Stocking's original research was on the issue of *race in American social science, but his major early publications deal with Franz Boas and the development of American cultural anthropology. Later research, tracing the development of British anthropology – from its ethnological foundations before 1840, through evolutionism to the emergence of social anthropology in the twentieth century – has resulted in numerous articles and a major study of nineteenth-century anthropology (1987). Closely connected with anthropology and anthropologists, Stocking writes with the privileged eye of an insider/outsider. While maintaining an emphasis on historicism, he has increasingly come to see the value in certain contexts of presentist approaches. He has also applied new approaches to the interpretation of anthropology's past (1992).

As well as publishing widely on the subject, Stocking has also acted as a major promoter of research on the history of anthropology, most notably through his *History of Anthropology Newsletter* (*HAN*) and by editing essays on specific topics in the series 'History of Anthropology' published by the University of Wisconsin Press. In this work Stocking has encouraged both anthropologists and non-anthropologist historians to research and write on the history of the discipline, opening a new field of enquiry and setting new standards of scholarship.

Recent research and writing

Recent research and writing on the history of the discipline, apart from leaning towards either presentism or historicism, has concentrated on three areas: intellectual history (ideas and methods), the history of institutions (*museums, learned *societies, research institutes, universities) and the careers of particular individuals, their schools and followers often through the use of biography and autobiography. These areas are far from exclusive, but reflect major emphases in research and writing.

Insider anthropologists, often lacking historical training and with a natural tendency towards presentism, have favoured the explication of ideas and methods (see Kuper's writing) and the biographical/autobiographical approach. The rise of feminist anthropology has encouraged a number of anthropologists to write accounts of the life and work of women anthropologists. An extensive memoir literature of second and third-generation anthropologists, either autobiographical or obtained through interviews with younger anthropologists (published mainly in *Current Anthropology*), now exists. The publication of *fieldwork diaries (Malinowski's diary set the trend), the notes and correspondence of early anthropologists and autobiographical accounts of fieldwork experience have also become popular. Often these are published without much scholarly commentary and the same is true of the new editions of the published and unpublished collected writings of past anthropologists which have appeared.

Historicists, including professional historians, have made major contributions to biographical studies and published collections of texts. But most have concentrated more on accounts of anthropological institutions and relate these to the persons and ideas involved as well as to the broader social and intellectual contexts in which the discipline has developed (see Hinsley 1981 on the Smithsonian Institution and many of Stocking's essays on British and American anthropology). While outsiders often possess superior historical research skills to anthropologists, some reveal an inadequate understanding of anthropological ideas and their context as some recent accounts of British anthropology clearly illustrate.

In the 1980s, the influence of †Michel Foucault, mediated through †Said's polemic on *Orientalism, shifted some historical concerns into the fashionable mainstream of anthropology. Intellectual historians of a broadly *postmodern persuasion like James Clifford and Donna Haraway (whose writings on the history of *biological anthropology are probably more widely read by social and cultural anthropologists) reworked anthropology's past, either in search of unacknowledged intellectual precursors or in order to argue the case that disciplinary concerns are inextricably linked to the issues of *gender, colonialism and *power.

Currently a number of anthropologists and historians have written or are writing research theses in the field and there are regular conferences and sessions at anthropological meetings devoted to the history of the discipline (see regular reports in *HAN*). The history of local traditions in research, ethnographic writing and institutional developments are also being rediscovered in many countries. In *Central and Eastern Europe, Asia and Latin America these often involve the linking of older ethnological, †material culture and *folklore studies to current research in social and cultural anthropology.

Resources for further study

Kemper and Phinney (1977) provide a good review of the published literature to the mid-1970s and this can be supplemented by *HAN* which publishes bibliographies of current published literature. The *Newsletter* also has regular accounts of archival collections, work in progress and other news relevant to those studying the history of the discipline. In France the journal *Gradhiva* is devoted to the history of (mostly francophone) anthropology.

Some established learned societies, such as the Royal Anthropological Institute, maintain archives and like collections in universities, scholarly libraries and museums. These often contain not only institutional material, but also the private papers and correspondence of significant figures in the development of the discipline. Important collections include the Haddon Papers at Cambridge University, the Malinowski papers at the London School of Economics and Yale University, the Boas papers at the American Philosophical Society and the †Margaret Mead papers at the Library of Congress and the Institute for Intercultural Studies in New York. The Melanesian Archive at the University of California, San Diego, provides a basis for a regional collection helpful in research and writing

on the discipline and in ethnographic studies. At present there is no overall listing of archives on the history of the discipline, but details on many individual collections can be found in *HAN*.

The following serial publications give the best overview of current work on the history of the discipline: *Gradhiva: revue d'histoire et d'archives de l'anthropologie* 1981 – Section Histoire de l'Ethnologie du Musée de l'Homme and École des Hautes Études en Sciences Sociales; *History of Anthropology Newsletter* (*HAN*) 1972 – Department of Anthropology, University of Chicago; *History of Anthropology* (G.W. Stocking, Jr. (ed.) 1983–1995; Richard Handler (ed.), 1995–), Madison: University of Wisconsin Press.

JAMES URRY

See also: American anthropology, British anthropology, Chinese anthropology, French anthropology, German and Austrian anthropology, Indian anthropology, Russian and Soviet anthropology

Further reading

Bowler, P.J. (1989) *The Invention of Progress: The Victorians and the Past*, Oxford: Blackwell

Burrow, J.W. (1966) *Evolution and Society: A Study in Victorian Social Theory*, Cambridge: Cambridge University Press

Haddon, A.C. (with A.H. Quiggin) (1910) *History of Anthropology*, London: Watts

Hinsley, C. (1981) *Savages and Scientists: The Smithsonian Institution and the Development of American Anthropology, 1846–1910*, Washington: Smithsonian Institution Press

Hodgen, M.T. (1936) *The Doctrine of Survivals: A Chapter in the History of Scientific Method in the Study of Man*, London: Allenson

Kemper, R.V. and J.F.S. Phinney (1977) *The History of Anthropology: A Research Bibliography*, New York: Garland

Kuper, A. (1973) *Anthropologists and Anthropology: The British School 1922–1972*, London: Allen Lane

—— (1988) *The Invention of Primitive Society: Transformations of an Illusion*, London: Routledge

Stocking, G.W.,Jr (1968) *Race, Culture and Evolution: Essays in the History of Anthropology*, New York: Free Press

—— (1987) *Victorian Anthropology*, New York: The Free Press

—— (1992) *The Ethnographer's Magic and Other Essays in the History of Anthropology*, Madison: University of Wisconsin Press

Urry, J. (1993) *Before Social Anthropology: Essays on the History of British Anthropology*, Reading: Harwood

honour and shame

The *gender-based system of honour and shame has been seen as the quintessential moral code of the Mediterranean. Indeed, it has been seen as a defining feature of the region (Gilmore 1987). Honour defines prestige or reputation, and so the honour and shame system is linked to the political system of *patrons and clients. It defines people's – usually men's – trustworthiness, and therefore their status as good and reliable patrons or clients. Honour is not simply related to the social standing of individual men, however, but also to the standing of the social groups in which they live (Pitt-Rivers 1965: 35). It is in some degree hereditary, and is therefore centred around the Mediterranean's predominantly †patrilineal *kinship unit, the *household.

The honour of a household is inextricably linked to the reputation of the women who live there. Their reputation in turn is sealed by the public display of shame. Shame is an index of female reputation, just as honour is an index of male. It is related to the notion of female chastity, and the dual importance of ensuring that men marry virgins, and preventing them from being cuckolded once they do. Having shame involves having, or displaying the requisite reticence in public places, and particularly avoiding situations where it could be considered that women are engaging in extra-marital sex. Shame is therefore connected to women's association with the domestic domain of the *house itself, and sometimes involves almost complete female seclusion.

Individual women's reputation for shame is managed through the collective sanction of local *gossip. This means that the honour and shame complex links the individual to wider society. Shame is directly related to honour, in that a reduction of the shame of a household's women becomes a direct reflection on the honour of its men. The man whose wife is adulterous, or who fails to demonstrate the virginity of his new bride, is dishonoured.

For example, in †Julian Pitt-Rivers's (1961) study of the Spanish village of Alcalá, he observed the phenomenon of *vergüenza*, which he glossed as shame. The mechanism by which it operated amounted to maintaining a moral reputation in the face of the community. It was therefore related not necessarily to female activity *per se*, but to it being publicly exposed through gossip (1961: 113).

To maintain *vergüenza*, women had to avoid the suggestion of sexual impropriety. Men were considered inherently shameless, but to possess a form of honour through their inherent manliness, and the *vergüenza* of their female kin, particularly their wife. Thus, whereas a man's sexual adventures were largely ignored, his wife's were censured, because they disrupted the moral unity of the family (1961: 115). They made the man a cuckold, a *cabrón* or billy-goat, whose 'lack of manliness has allowed . . . [an]other to replace him'. (1961: 116). In short, they dishonoured him.

Anton Blok (1981) has related the †symbolism of the billy-goat to a general theory of the honour and shame system. This in turn relates it to the broader issue of masculinity in the Mediterranean. He argued that the use of the billy-goat as a symbol for a cuckold contrasts with the use of the ram as a symbol for an honourable man. The persuasiveness of these symbols lies in the actual reproductive practices of rams and billy-goats. For where the ram has only one sexual partner throughout his life, and jealously guards her, the billy-goat has many. Thus the Mediterranean cuckold is habitually associated with the goat. However, Blok's argument goes further than defining a Mediterranean moral system. This symbolic structure used to be common to the whole of Europe, he suggested, but now only survives in the relatively marginal Mediterranean.

This picture of a pan-Mediterranean honour and shame system, that is a survival of some more pervasive moral code, has been criticized. Michael Herzfeld (1987) saw the image of the honour and shame system as one of a number of mechanisms whereby anthropologists from Northern Europe and the United States have marginalized and stereotyped the Mediterranean. He argued that although these scholars acknowledged their roots in the Mediterranean – and particularly Greece – there was still an enduring assumption that the region was somehow backward. The honour and shame system, therefore, was part of a hegemonic discipline of 'Mediterraneanism', akin to †Edward Said's *Orientalism, which marginalized and exoticised the Mediterranean.

The stereotype of Mediterranean morality has also been criticized from a feminist perspective, for portraying only an official version of *gender ideology, and thereby supporting the patriarchal status quo (Lindisfarne, 1994: 83). The version of honour and shame outlined above implies a passivity of women not born out in ethnographic evidence. In the real Mediterranean, women have a much more active role in the creation of society and morality, it is argued (Dubisch 1991). Similarly, in the real Mediterranean, men do not simply re-enact the timeless moral structure. Just as women subvert the ideology of a chaste woman who possesses shame, by concealing sexual activity (Lindisfarne, 1994: 89–90), so men can be seen manipulating the notion of a good, honourable man (1994: 85).

In the real Mediterranean, particularly the urban Mediterranean (Goddard, 1987), a variety of different gender identities and roles coexist. One of these, perhaps the official one, relates to honour and shame. However, to state that this is the single and defining moral code amounts to the reification of a stereotype to the level of an analytic tool. Rather than defining gender roles, and the behaviour of men and women, honour and shame should be seen as a dominant version of gender roles, or an ideological gloss on the multiplicity of gender identities.

JON P. MITCHELL

See also: patrons and clients, gossip, Orientalism, Europe: South

Further Reading

Blok, A. (1981) 'Rams and Billy-goats: A Key to the Mediterranean Code of Honour', *Man* (n.s.) 16 (3): 427–40

Dubisch, J. (1991) 'Gender, Kinship and Religion: 'Reconstructing' the Anthropology of Greece', in P. Loizos and A. Papataxiarchis (eds) *Contested Identities: Gender and Sexuality in Modern Greece*, Princeton: Princeton University Press

Gilmore, D. (ed.) (1987) *Honor and Shame and the Unity of the Mediterranean*, Washington DC: American Anthropological Association

Goddard, V. (1987) 'Honour and Shame: The Control of Women's Sexuality and Group Identity in Naples', in P. Caplan (ed.) *The Cultural Construction of Sexuality*, London: Routledge

Herzfeld, M. (1987) *Anthropology Through the Looking Glass: Critical Ethnography in the Margins of Europe*, Cambridge: Cambridge University Press

Lindisfarne, N. (1994) 'Variant Masculinities, Variant Virginities: Rethinking "honour and shame"', in A. Cornwall and N. Lindisfarne (eds) *Dislocating Masculinity: Comparative Ethnographies*, London: Routledge

Pitt-Rivers, J. (1961) *The People of the Sierra*, Chicago: Phoenix Books, University of Chicago Press

—— (1965) 'Honour and Social Status', in J.G. Peristiany (ed.) *Honour and Shame: The Values of Mediterranean Society*, London: Weidenfeld and Nicolson

house

In the past the house has often figured in ethnographies as an item of †material culture, as an object replete in symbolic meanings, or as the locus of the domestic domain and systems of *household production. Various studies have revealed ways in which aspects of architecture are used to symbolize social relations and categories, whilst others have shown how *gender representations involve the house, through the division of domestic space and the role of women in the domestic economy, itself frequently modelled on the house. More recently however an anthropology of the 'house' has emerged which aims to unite these diverse elements, combining an analysis of the house as built environment with the 'house' as a category and idea central to the conceptualization and practice of social relations.

Much of this work forms part of current attempts to rethink the anthropological study of *kinship, adopting a cultural approach which focuses on native categories as a better basis for analysing indigenous understandings of relationships (Schneider 1984), and in the process criticizing various elements of established kinship theory. Studies from Africa, for example, have used the concept of the 'house' to question the usefulness of *descent theory (Kuper 1993; cf. Saul 1991), whilst the concept has been fruitfully employed by others working in *Southeast Asia and *lowland South America (Macdonald 1987; Carsten and Hugh-Jones 1995). Although many draw inspiration from the writings of *Claude Lévi-Strauss, some see a need to move beyond his model of 'house societies', which is arguably mired in the sort of problems more recent work has attempted to overcome.

Lévi-Strauss and 'house societies'

Whilst Lévi-Strauss's thinking on 'house societies' (*sociétés 'à maison*) represents his most recent engagement with the study of kinship, he has written no extended account of the subject in the manner of his earlier work on elementary structures, nor does he fully contextualize what he does say in terms of that earlier work. Despite this however, Lévi-Strauss's writings on the house can be seen as an attempt to deal with an institution which lies somewhere between †elementary and †complex systems, combining elements of descent and *alliance, and found in widely separated societies.

The initial discussion of the 'house' comes in Lévi-Strauss's re-analysis of Kwakiutl social organization (Lévi-Strauss 1982: 163–187), where he attempts to overcome some of the complex problems encountered by *Boas in trying to describe the kinship system of a society that exhibited both †patrilineal and †matrilineal elements, and for which all available analytic terms proved misleading. Using both comparative ethnography and history, Lévi-Strauss comes to the conclusion that the basic unit of Kwakiutl society was similar to that of the Yurok of California (studied by †Kroeber) who had similar institutions named 'houses', which in turn closely resembled the 'houses' of medieval Europe and feudal Japan. Here Lévi-Strauss defines the 'house' as a 'moral person' (sometimes taken to mean †corporate group) which perpetuates itself through time, this continuity expressed in the 'language of kinship or affinity', and quite often both (1982: 174). These 'houses' exhibit organizing principles that are usually seen as mutually exclusive in kinship analysis: patriliny and matriliny, †filiation and residence, †hypergamy and †hypogamy, †exogamy and †endogamy. However, it is the peculiarity of the 'house' as an institution that it in fact transcends these theoretically irreconcilable traits, rather than being undone by them.

In a subsequent work, Lévi-Strauss (1987: 149–94) extends the discussion of the 'house' to various societies of the Pacific, Melanesia, Indonesia and Africa, seeking 'common social-structural characteristics that might explain [the] appearance of the same institutions among peoples far distant in both time and space' (1987: 152). Having previously stressed the continuity of the 'house' in a 'real or imaginary line' (1982: 174), Lévi-Strauss here suggests that the 'house' acts to 'solidify' the 'unstable relation of alliance', a form of 'objectification' born of the oppositions characteristic of 'house societies', in particular the competing principles of descent and alliance (1987: 155–9). This instability coincides with a situation where political and economic interests have begun to invade the social field without entirely undermining the importance of kinship. Indeed, Lévi-Strauss suggests that the 'language of kinship' is borrowed to talk of political and economic interests, there being none other available to 'house societies' (1982: 186–7). This tension between kinship and political and economic interests is referred to in terms of the 'duality of 'blood' and 'land'', and is seen as typical of 'house societies' (1987: 181–2).

Although Lévi-Strauss's writings on the 'house' have provided inspiration for some, his theory arguably 'raises as many problems as it solves' (Carsten and Hugh-Jones 1995: 19). Whilst some have tried to refine Lévi-Strauss's theory (see e.g. some of the contributors to Macdonald 1987), most have used it as the starting point for a more holistic analysis of social relations, criticizing Lévi-Strauss's view of 'house societies' as a strict category. There are problems for example with the applicability of the model, for whilst Lévi-Strauss ranges with breathtaking ease across vast tracts of cultural and historical time and space in the defining of a social type, some question the usefulness of a model which encompasses such diversity. In addition, some criticize the rigidity of the definition of the 'house', finding it a useful model outside the contexts in which Lévi-Strauss has used it. Furthermore, although Lévi-Strauss talks of the house as the 'objectification' of the relation of alliance, there are cases where the 'house' is associated with the conjugal couple rather than alliance *per se*, whilst elsewhere the 'house' is associated with siblingship, or a form of generational continuity akin to the notion of descent.

For most who have attempted to use Lévi-Strauss's ideas there is agreement that some of the limiting aspects of his definition of 'house societies' must be abandoned, a move which particularly leads to a questioning of the notion of kinship underlying Lévi-Strauss's discussion of the 'house'. Besides a latent *functionalism in Lévi-Strauss's writings, such that the role of the 'house' is to overcome the problems of opposing principles, there is also a quasi-evolutionism, whereby 'house societies' exist somewhere between elementary and complex structures, as well as between pre-literate and modern societies. Nowhere is this clearer than in his discussion of Africa, where Lévi-Strauss links an account of the 'house' in the Niger delta region to the emergence of 'kings' who 'based their power, not on ties of descent, but on military and economic success' (1987: 186). When political and economic forces come into play, Lévi-Strauss suggests that the institution of the 'house' overcomes the duality of 'blood' and the 'genealogical chain' on the one hand, and 'land' and 'ancestral soil' on the other (1987: 181–2). As with his earlier work on elementary structures, here Lévi-Strauss assumes that kinship is principally about 'blood' and genealogy. But there is a missed opportunity in his discussion when he notes that the 'representation of social relations in material form' (1987: 160) may appear in shapes other than the 'house', a point he fails to develop by taking it to its logical conclusion: that whilst the 'house' is one form of the representation of social relations, so too is 'blood' or 'land', none logically prior to the other (cf. Carsten and Hugh-Jones 1995: 19). In his work on *myth Lévi-Strauss has brilliantly revealed the complexity and subtlety of the ways in which the human mind classifies and categorizes the world; however he fails to bring this understanding to the 'house', where instead of seeing in the 'house' the basis of a radical critique of the theory it fails to be classified by, he instead creates a model of an institution which, whilst transcending previous categories of kinship analysis, remains premised upon them. The fundamental problem with the model is thus that whereas Lévi-Strauss claims that it is 'house societies' which employ the 'language of kinship' to talk about political and economic interests, it is in fact Lévi-Strauss who employs the 'language of kinship' to talk about relations which a variety of societies phrase in the 'language of the house'.

Although Lévi-Strauss may have 'reminded us of a sound anthropological principle: the priority of native categories' (Carsten and Hugh-Jones 1995: 20), it is not a principle that Lévi-Strauss himself fully adopts. However, those who have sought to go beyond Lévi-Strauss's theory have usually found his discussion useful in situations where the 'house' is a salient native category of social relations. But, as one frequently finds the word for 'house' employed as a term for a social grouping in a wide range of societies, the problem becomes 'not one of discovering which are 'house societies' but of discovering which ones are not' (Carsten and Hugh-Jones 1995: 18). Such classic examples in the field of kinship studies as the Lovedu, Nuer, Tallensi and Tikopia all use 'house' terms for groups related by descent and/or alliance. These and other examples therefore suggest that Lévi-Strauss's model of 'house societies' needs to be reformulated in the process of creating a 'holistic anthropology of the house' (Carsten and Hugh-Jones 1995: 4) which combines the analysis of native kinship categories with the study of architecture, symbolism, and indigenous models of political and economic organization.

Recent work in this vein aims to move beyond the outmoded categories and formalist typologies of kinship theory, taking a processual view of social relations. The study of the 'house' is thus not simply an attempt to explain the social organization of those societies which previously resisted typologies, for it can also be used to shed light on societies previously classified as descent-based or alliance-based, such as the Kachin. A brief look at Kachin ethnography reveals the house to be central to Kachin thinking about kinship, politics, economics and religion, and an account which focuses on Kachin categories and metaphors arguably gives us a better understanding of the Kachin sociological imagination than does an account framed in terms of descent and alliance.

'Houses' and the Kachin

Among other things, the Kachin (Leach 1954) are famous in anthropology as an example of a society that practises †matrilateral cross-cousin marriage, an exchange relationship of alliance that takes place between two or more lineages related as wife-givers (*mayu*) and wife-takers (*dama*). †Leach tells us that among the Kachin there exists a system of patrilineal clanship, with †clans made up of a number of localized †lineages (1954: 55), although he adds that within villages, people of one lineage are usually related to everyone else by affinal ties rather than common clanship, that is by alliance rather than descent (1954: 68).

When one looks at the Kachin terms for these groups and relations (see 1954: 108–36), some rather interesting things emerge. Those of one lineage are said be of 'one household' (*htinggaw*), and share a 'household name' (*htinggaw amying*) which they inherit from their father. Glossed by Leach as 'lineage', the term *htinggaw* literally means 'people under one roof', and in addition Kachin refer to 'lineage' members as 'brothers' (*kahpu-kanau*), those who are of the same 'branch' (*lakung*), or the same 'hearth' (*dap*), and those who are of the same 'sort' (*amyu*), a term which Leach glosses as 'clan'. Although members of a *htinggaw* do not necessarily live together in a single dwelling, the social group is still referred to as 'people under one roof', whilst Kachin refer to a 'family' as 'people of the house' (*nta masha*). Finally, the individual household is the basic unit of economic organization, working its own swiddens and gardens, a unit which comes into being through marriage, when a man is said to 'extend the roof' (*htinggaw rawn*), and the husband and wife become 'owners' or 'lords' (*madu ni*) of their house.

The architecture of the Kachin house is also important, particularly as it relates to the differences between chiefs' houses (*htingnu*) and those of commoners (*nta*). As well as being larger than other houses, their grandeur a marker of status and prestige, chiefs' houses have oversized hardwood house posts (*nhpu daw*), a sign of chiefly rank, and some chiefs are reported to have surrounded their houses with elaborate stone walls. Within the house another feature differentiates chiefs' houses from other dwellings, the possession of the *Madai dap*, a shrine to the chief Sky Spirit, Madai (*dap*, 'hearth'). Members of a *htinggaw* are said to be 'people who worship the same set of household spirits', and all houses contain a shrine to the *masha nat*, spirits of the ancestors of the husband of the house. However, the right to sacrifice to the chief Sky Spirit is the perquisite of chiefs, and it is only in their houses that one finds the *Madai dap* shrine.

As for the term for chief's house itself, *htingnu* literally means 'house of the mother' or 'the mother house' (*nu*, 'mother'), for which Leach offers two interpretations: first, 'that the chief's house is the parent house from which other houses of the village have segmented off; the other that the house of the chief is *mayu* [wife-giver] to the houses of his followers' (1954: 112). The gendered nature of the term however appears confusing, particularly given that Madai 'represents the male principle' (1954: 112) and that the wife-giver/wife-taker relationship appears to be gendered male. It is therefore surely significant that although Madai is wife-giver to all the chiefly 'lineages', their common ancestor is Madai's daughter, 'mother' to all those of chiefly ancestry.

A chief's house, Leach suggests, 'is more than a dwelling-house, more than a palace, it is also a kind of temple to the *Madai* [spirit]' (1954: 113). But the Kachin 'house' is also more than a religious building and a place to perform rituals. It figures as the basic unit of economic organization, and is associated with the continuity of a group of 'brothers', men of the same 'hearth' who worship in their house their own 'ancestor spirits' and who pass on to their children their 'household name'. The 'house' is similarly central to marriage, for besides the fact that alliance relations exist between groups known as 'people under one roof', the conjugal union itself is said to 'extend the roof' when a man sets himself up with his wife as 'owner' of a house. Finally, the difference between chiefs and commoners is marked through differences in domestic architecture. Kachin categories therefore reveal a conceptualization of social relations premised on metaphors about the 'house', which rather than simply being

an 'objectification' of the relation of alliance, emerges as an object significant in various domains. It is by trying to combine elements such as those used in the foregoing analysis that the anthropology of the 'house' has begun to rethink the study of kinship, focusing on connections between houses as items of vernacular architecture and the people who build and live in them.

Rethinking kinship

As well as attempting to bring together various domains of anthropological enquiry which often remain separate, recent work on the 'house' has joined a more widespread critique of anthropology's own metaphors. In some of this work there has been a move away from seeing kinship in terms of a set of structured relationships lying at the heart of systems of descent and alliance, and an emphasis on the need to analyse native categories as a basis for understanding the practice and conceptualization of relationships as an ongoing process. In many cases the 'house' emerges as a category better suited to such analysis than our own metaphors of 'lineage' and 'clan'. That the 'house' crops up so often as a metaphor of social relationships is perhaps not surprising, given that the house is the place where much that is usually taken to constitute kinship is practised. As Carsten and Hugh-Jones point out, kinship is about 'sleeping together . . . living together, eating together and dying together, not just about bed but also about house, hearth and tomb' (1995: 19). Nowhere are these relations more vividly realized than in some parts of the Austronesian world, where the house is a salient category and metaphor of social relations as well as being the dwelling place of the living built over the burial place of the dead.

PHILIP THOMAS

See also: kinship, household, Japan, Asia: Southeast

Further reading

Blier, S.P. (1987) *The Anatomy of Architecture: Ontology and Metaphor in Batammaliba Architectural Expression*, Cambridge: Cambridge University Press

Carsten, J. and S. Hugh-Jones (eds) (1995) *About the House: Lévi-Strauss and Beyond*, Cambridge: Cambridge University Press

Fox, J. (ed.) (1993) *Inside Austronesian Houses: Perspectives on Domestic Designs for Living*, Canberra: Research School of Pacific and Asian Studies, Australian National University

Gudeman, S. and A. Rivera (1990) *Conversations in Colombia: The Domestic Economy in Life and Text*, Cambridge: Cambridge University Press

Kuper, A. (1993) 'The "House" and Zulu Political Structure in the Nineteenth Century', *Journal of African History*, 34: 469–87

Leach, E. (1954) *Political Systems of Highland Burma*, London: Athlone Press

Lévi-Strauss, C. (1982) *The Way of the Masks*, trans. by S. Modelski, Seattle: University of Washington Press

—— (1987) *Anthropology and Myth: Lectures 1951–1982*, trans. by R. Willis, Oxford: Blackwell

Macdonald, C. (ed.) (1987) *De la Hutte au Palais: Sociétés 'à Maison' en Asie du Sud-Est Insulaire*, Paris: Editions du CNRS

Saul, M. (1991) 'The Bobo "House" and the Uses of Categories of Descent' *Africa*, 61 (1): 71–97

Schneider, D. (1984) *A Critique of the Study of Kinship*, Ann Arbor: University of Michigan Press

Waterson, R. (1990) *The Living House: An Anthropology of Architecture in Southeast Asia*, Singapore: Oxford University Press

household

Many keystrokes have been registered, and much ink spilt, in attempts to produce a universal, *etic, one-size-fits-all definition of household. None exists. More realistically, anthropologists have recognized the particularities of the situations they study, and directed their efforts to analysing them. Most agree with Hammel (in Netting *et al.* 1984: 40–1) that households simply are 'the next bigger thing on the social map after an individual', and proceed then to answer the 'who', 'what' and 'where' questions that concern householdly things.

Household ideology and composition

Aside from single-person domestic units, households consist of groups of persons. What ties these groups together? Often, but not always, it is *kinship and *marriage, and household members can trace such links among themselves. Some households consist of *families – groups constructed of spousal, parent-child, and sibling bonds – but families may also be distributed in two or more households, or one household may contain relatives beyond these primary kin (as well as non-kin members). Families are *emic and ideological groupings that knit persons together on grids of marital, parental and filial relations. Households have their own cultural dimensions, and these need to be examined separately from those of families, even when household and family

personnel largely overlap (Gray and Mearns 1989; Netting *et al.* 1984; Yanagisako 1979).

In *Japan they do not, and a series of cultural concepts exists that sorts people into groupings different from the Western folk notions of family and household. *Shotai* is the set of persons who share a common budget, regardless of kinship connections; *kazoku* is a group that has a sense of belonging together, whether or not they co-reside (and might include an adult child not living with a parent); *ie* means both the *house itself and its transgenerational line of occupants (ancestral and living), of which there can be only one married pair per generation; *dozoku* is a larger group that includes an *ie* and branch houses founded by sons other than the one in any generation who continues the *ie* line (but by no means all sons form such branch households); *shinseki* includes houses linked to an *ie* through out-marriage of its daughters (Kitaoji 1971; Yanagisako in Netting *et al.* 1984).

Which is family, which is household? Or is it better to approach Japanese social organization through Japanese categories? If we focus on *ie*, the salient unit in rural Japan, we learn that its table of organization and terms of address have their own logic, which does not coincide with that of biological families and kinship. Males (in English translation) may be 'old man, retired', 'househead', 'successor', 'younger son' (who must leave to marry), or 'grandchild'; women may be, 'old woman, retired', 'housewife', 'bride/young wife', 'daughter' (who also must leave to marry), or 'grandchild'. Men may be recruited as 'successor' by either birth to their 'househead' father, marriage to his daughter, or *adoption; a family bloodline may die out, and the *ie* continue.

Such positional household systems may be culturally elaborated as in Japan, or less so, but still behaviourally significant (Carter in Netting *et al.* 1984). In Accra in *West Africa, adult household residents may occupy the mutually exclusive roles of child in their household of rearing, employee, independent co-member, solitary adult, conjugal partner, single parent, or grandparent; *gender-patterned, life-cycle household role sequences may also be identified. For many Ghanaian adults their household of rearing may not be a parent's household; a large proportion are fostered in other households as children, just as many of the children resident at any point in time live with adults other than their own parents (Sanjek 1982, 1983). More broadly, adoption and fosterage occur widely beyond Japan and Ghana, and are important in understanding both the ideology and composition of households where these practices are of organizational significance.

One cross-cultural scheme that is sensitive and adaptable to such ethnographic variation categorizes five major household types (Hammel and Laslett 1974; Sanjek 1982). *Solitaries* are single-person households; subtypes consist of single, divorced, widowed or duolocally-married persons. *No family* households have no spousal pair or parent-child members, but may be comprised of other relatives (siblings, cousins, grandparents and grandchildren), or only of non-related room-mates. *Simple family households* include both spousal couples with or without children, and male and female single-parent households; an important subtype in many societies are mother-child households in which the father resides elsewhere, sometimes with another adult woman. *Extended family households* are simple family cores that add other kin, but not other spousal couples or parent-child units; they may be extended laterally (with siblings of simple family core adults), or lineally, both up (to include perhaps a parent of a married pair) and down (adding a co-resident grandchild). *Multiple family households* contain two or more discrete simple families (e.g. a couple and two married sons, two divorced sisters or widowed co-wives and their children, or a four-generation Japanese *ie*), and may be extended with other kin as well. All five types may also include live-in household workers, less satisfactorily labelled 'servants', a term with unneeded connotations; boarders, who pay to eat and often to sleep in a household, and lodgers, who pay only to sleep, may also be counted as members.

This framework permits an overview by ethnographic region of ideologically dominant, and often numerically prominent, household forms, without resorting to such local usages as 'the Hindu joint family' or 'the *zadruga*'. In composition, these Indian and Balkan lineal-lateral multiple family households, each with much symbolic elaboration, resemble Chinese and patrilineal African counterparts. Lineal multiple family households include the Japanese *ie* and Western European and Irish †stem families (Goody 1972; Gray and Mearns 1989; Netting *et al.* 1984). Simple family households, with the husband-wife or 'nuclear family' subtype normative, are characteristic of England, the USA, *Latin America, the *Caribbean and many *hunter-gathering

societies. In these cases, extended families often form to meet physical or economic distress; and among elites (which excludes the hunter-gatherers), multiple family households are not uncommon, especially at family seats and retreats.

In all household regimes, the phenomenon of †developmental cycles occurs, meaning that a household may assume different forms through time as members arrive and depart, and new households begin (Goody 1972); the normative form may occur only rarely, although strategies to achieve it or adjust to its passing may preoccupy many members of the society otherwise. Berreman (1975), for instance, shows neatly how the North Indian Pahari †polyandrous household ideal (one wife, multiple husbands) actually produces other classifiable forms as members age and die. Too many developmental cycle analyses, however, take only the household as the focal unit; more careful study exposes how domestic cycles may differ by gender (especially where conjugal separation is frequent), and that household management and socialization strategies probably anticipate this (Sanjek 1983).

Household activities

For some anthropologists, to consider household ideology and composition before 'domestic functions' is to put the normative cart before the behavioural horse. They ask first what a person must *do* to be considered a member of a household. Ethnographers generally answer this question in three different ways: a person must sleep there, or eat there, or make some economic contribution, whether or not they sleep or eat there.

As to other activities there is less contention. Households are agreed to be crucibles of *identity (Gray and Mearns 1989), primary locations in which life cycle phases are enacted (*childhood, family establishment, elderhood), *rites of passage celebrated or planned, †inheritance decided, and *ancestors (who may symbolically and even physically underlie the household) be venerated. But must the persons who perform these and other activities in householdly places also be householdly groups?

No. Goody (1972) distinguishes dwelling (sleeping) units, reproductive (eating) units, and economic units, pointing out that each may be organized independently, with personnel of one including individuals from two or more of the others. Sanjek (1982) documents how, in an Accra neighborhood, the universal activities of production (gainful work), social reproduction (the day-to-day reprovisioning of labour power emphasized in *feminist anthropology), *consumption, sexual union, and *socialization of children are organized within, across, and outside of household units (compare Vatuk in Gray and Mearns 1989; Netting *et al.* 1984). Social relations among local residents and †consociates elsewhere involved in these activities constitute a platform on which *class alignments and political ideologies are constructed. Households in urban Ghana are not the building blocks of larger social forms (if they may be elsewhere; see Gray and Mearns 1989); social practice is.

Sanjek defines these Accra households, which social practice variously joins and cuts against, on the basis of where persons sleep and store possessions, a decision following a West African cultural logic also identified by other regional ethnographers. Vatuk (in Gray and Mearns 1989) presents similar data concerning social practice for a South Indian Muslim group, but defines households according to where people eat, a decision in accord with South Asian cultural logic. There are also anthropologists who define households neither by sleeping nor eating groups but by pooled economic contributions – remittances sent one way by urban *migrants for instance, or foodstuffs sent the other way by rural members. Again, this decision follows local cultural logic ('two locations, one household'). Thus, Goody's three units may each appropriately be used for answering the 'what' question about households.

Structures, locations, and activities again

Hunter-gatherers, †shifting cultivators and tent-dwelling *pastoralists may move their household groups as their economies require and their impermanent or portable dwellings permit. In more permanent built environments, like West African savannah settlements or Southwestern American pueblos, house owners may reassign, divide or add new rooms as household composition changes. But when space is a commodity that households rent, or laws regulate building use or redesign, household groups (that may not wish to) must sometimes divide into separate locations, even though they may continue to organize themselves as one economic unit or cooking group.

Other people's households are also workplaces for millions of persons worldwide (in contrast to artisans, business proprietors, professionals or job contractors whose own home is also their workplace). Women and men who are hired by households to cook, clean, care for children or elders, and other tasks are found throughout the world (Sanjek and Colen 1990). Some live-in, frequently with an ambiguous relationship to household members ('She's just one of the family'; 'I hate not living in my own home'). Others live elsewhere in their own households, and see the household of their employment simply as a workplace.

Trajectories of change

Although some anthropologists argue convincingly that enlarging households is adaptive in circumstances of extreme poverty, the global trend is to smaller household size. Often this is accompanied by ideological strictures concerning household composition (nuclear 'family values') and canons of domesticity (Lofgren in Netting *et al.* 1984; Williams 1994). Beyond this, with increasing world population the result is *more* households – more consumption units, more renters and mortgage payers, more telephone and cable subscribers, more furniture buyers and credit-card holders. Moreover, the fastest growing household type in the USA and elsewhere is solitaries.

Anthropological research on household ideology, composition, activities and location also confronts new territory. The study of lesbian and gay households raises easily-settled typological questions, but also more challenging organizational ones (Lewin 1993). Major social policy debates centre on households, including issues regarding growing numbers of elderly persons and criminalized young males who reside in institutional and congregate settings. The number of teenage mothers in the USA is actually declining, but the 'problem' is magnified both by their greater current likelihood of independent household formation, and by later and fewer births among the female majority (Williams 1994). Finally, anthropologists who document the lives of homeless persons confront dilemmas of how households survive without homes.

ROGER SANJEK

See also: adoption and fostering, age, childhood, consumption, family, gender, house, kinship, marriage, migration, rite of passage, socialization

Further reading

Berreman, G. (1975) 'Himalayan Polyandry and the Domestic Cycle', *American Ethnologist* 2: 127–38

Goody, J. (1972) *Domestic Groups*, Reading MA: Addison-Wesley

Gray, J.N. and D.J. Mearns (eds) (1989) *Society from the Inside Out: Anthropological Perspectives on the South Asian Household*, New Delhi: Sage

Hammel, E.A. and P. Laslett (1974) 'Comparing Household Structure Over Time and Between Cultures', *Comparative Studies in Society and History* 16: 73–109.

Kitaoji, H. (1971) 'The Structure of the Japanese Family', *American Anthropologist* 73: 1036–57

Lewin, E. (1993) *Lesbian Mothers: Accounts of Gender in American Culture*, Ithaca: Cornell University Press

Netting, R.McC., R. Wilk and E.J. Arnold, (eds) (1984) *Households: Comparative and Historical Studies of the Domestic Group*, Berkeley: University of California Press

Sanjek, R. (1982) 'The Organization of Households in Adabraka: Toward a Wider Comparative Perspective', *Comparative Studies in Society and History* 23: 57–103

—— (1983) 'Female and Male Domestic Cycles in Urban Africa: The Adabraka Case', in C. Oppong (ed.) *Female and Male in West Africa*, London: Allen and Unwin

Sajek, R. and S. Colen (eds) (1990) *At Work in Homes: Household Workers in World Perspective*, Washington: American Anthropological Association

Williams, B. (1994) 'Babies and Banks: The "Reproductive Underclass" and the Raced, Gendered Masking of Debt', in S. Gregory and R. Sanjek (eds) *Race*, New Brunswick NJ: Rutgers University Press

Yanagisako, S. (1979) 'Family and Household: The Analysis of Domestic Groups', *Annual Review of Anthropology* 8: 161–205

hunting and gathering societies

Hunter-gatherers as a social category

Hunting and gathering societies in the contemporary world are relatively few in number, yet they have commanded an intense interest through the history of anthropology, and in recent years have become the centre of a major controversy. Peoples like the San (Bushman) of *Southern Africa and the Pygmies of the Central African forests, their *technologies small-scale and their social organizations strikingly †egalitarian, were long held to exemplify a pristine form of human society – the way of life of humans everywhere until the dawn of *pastoralism and agriculture around 12,000 years ago. But since the 1980s the validity of this *evolutionary picture has been called into question. Much may be learned by reviewing the issues that touch on this debate.

First the label 'hunter-gatherer society' implies that we are dealing with a correspondence between a type of social organization and a type of economy: that people who rely for subsistence on undomesticated plants and animals inevitably organize themselves in a distinctive fashion. However it is now clear that, perhaps for millenia, most hunter-gatherers have been engaged in activities other than hunting and gathering, such as trading with agricultural and pastoral neighbours or even practising a small amount of cultivation or animal rearing themselves. Hunters and gatherers in India and *Southeast Asia, their populations small and their forest locations often remote, are classic examples, but the Pygmies, San and the pockets of hunter-gatherers in the tropical and temperate regions of the Americas would fall under this stricture as well. Only the Australian *Aborigines, the Inuit (Eskimo) and some Native groups in northern North America were traditionally independent from other types of economy; but even here this has changed dramatically in recent decades because of these peoples' heavy involvement in a Westernized monetary economy. These varying circumstances have led some anthropologists to argue that it is the total regional system, of which the hunting and gathering economy may be only a part, which should be the focus of study (Barnard 1992; Myers 1988). And, more radically, other anthropologists surmise that the egalitarian social organizations of such peoples as the San may be the result of their dealings – normally politically disadvantaged dealings – with their agricultural and pastoral neighbours (Wilmsen 1989).

A second major concern attends to the fact that some contemporary hunter-gatherers have quite complex social organizations. For example the Northwest Coast Indians of the coastal and island areas of western Canada and southern Alaska display social stratification (nobles, commoners and slaves), competition for rank among both individuals and local groups, and *descent groups which exercise corporate control over delimited tracts of resources such as fishing stations, hunting grounds, and berrying areas. Such social features are conspicuously absent among egalitarian peoples like the San, Inuit and Pygmies, among whom interpersonal competition and hierarchy are strongly muted, and whose social groups, often rather amorphous collections of kin, merely associate themselves with areas of territory and may not claim rights of ownership. A further complication is the case of the Australian Aborigines. Many Australians live in semi-desert environments similar to the San, yet unlike the San they display marked hierarchies in relations between men and women and between elders and youth; they also manifest quite complex social subdivisions which are articulated by marriage *alliances requiring one's spouse to be selected from a particular category of kin. *Archaeological studies on hunter-gatherers concentrating on the †Palaeolithic period strongly suggest that when the entire human population lived by hunting and gathering relatively complex social organizations would have been prevalent. Thus the contemporary Northwest Coast Indians, pursuing a semi-sedentary lifestyle in a relatively temperate environment, may better exemplify the form of early hunter-gatherers than the San, Pygmies or Inuit, who are confined to nomadic hunting and gathering in more extreme environments.

This, in turn, is not an entirely satisfactory position. In the first place, the complex hunter-gatherers are themselves not likely to exemplify the 'original' human society about which anthropologists keenly speculate when considering the emergence of a distinctively human social organization from a (non-human) primate past; they will have evolved from a simpler social organization. Secondly, there is the example of the Inuit and of such peoples as the Hadza of northern Tanzania where, before the colonial period, outsiders appear to have had minimal impact on the hunting and gathering way of life. These societies have egalitarian social organizations comparable with the San. This suggests that egalitarian arrangements among hunter-gatherers are highly versatile: they are adaptive in the context of pressure from outsiders and they are also viable in circumstances when hunter-gatherers stand alone (Kent 1992). In sum, it may be argued that the first human societies, from which all others evolved, were indeed 'simple', egalitarian ones.

The culture of hunter-gatherers

Nurit Bird-David, in a series of stimulating articles (e.g. 1992a, 1992b), has argued that hunter-gatherers have a highly distinctive †ethos, which influences their social pose even when they are involved in non-hunting activities. She bases her argument on the Nayaka, a South Indian hunting

and gathering people, but maintains that the fundamental principles of Nayaka culture are shared among such varied hunter-gatherers as the Inuit, San, Pygmies, Australian Aborigines and the Indian groups of the North American coniferous forests (for example, the Cree of Ontario and Quebec). Bird-David demonstrates that in all these hunter-gatherer societies people conceive of the relation between humans and the *environment as one of very close kinship. The environment is imbued with spirits (which exercise control over animals, the weather, health, good fortune, and so on) and these relate to humans as parents to children or husbands to wives. The result is that hunter-gatherers view their relationship with the environment as one of trust, confident that the environment will provide for their material needs. An exemplification of this is the Inuit belief that the spirit world is inherently benevolent, dispatching animals to the waiting hunter from the sky or from underwater lairs. The hunter's important duty is to take the animals when they appear and to offer them respect, by the performance of small rituals acknowledging their generosity; these ensure the release of the animals' souls and their return to the spiritual domain whence they came. Here the important supplementary belief is that when hunting brings no success it is because the spirits, angered by human misdemeanour (such as failure to observe religious edicts), have withheld the animals from human view.

In the contemporary world, hunter-gatherers engage not just with a natural environment but also with governments and entrepreneurs, and they participate in commercial enterprises, such as trapping, craft work and wage labour; government transfer payments may also importantly contribute to their cash wealth. However Bird-David argues that hunter-gatherers strike up a distinctive attitude to these opportunities, not differentiating them from the natural environment. Such opportunities offer resources that may be 'procured', and the hunter-gatherers, confident that these resources will be made available, do not endeavour to seize control of them, or invest in them, as agriculturalists or pastoralists might do. In short, in relation to the present-day situation of employment and welfare state, their culture constrains hunter-gatherers to behave in a highly flexible and partial way, moving from wage work to hunting to securing welfare benefits, in much the same strategic fashion as traditional hunter-gatherers would seasonally move from hunting locale to hunting locale taking advantage of different plants and animals as and when they became available.

Bird-David's interpretation is useful and original and offers an important insight into the way family-type metaphors are at the root of hunter-gatherer culture. But it is doubtful that it fully explicates hunter-gatherer behaviour in the contemporary world. This is especially so with regard to northern North America and Australia where Indians, Inuit and Aborigines are engaged in vigorous political disputes with governments, multinationals and the wider, mainstream society, about 'native rights' and 'land claims'. Here with partial success hunter-gatherers have upheld the entitlement of 'original peoples' to benefit from economic exploitation originating from the outside, including mining and hydroelectric production, and to exercise managerial responsibility over their lands. An intrinsic dimension of such aggressive political activity is the hunter-gatherers' insistence that their way of life – their hunting and gathering way of life – be defended, and that 'Native' control over their homelands should be discharged in a distinctively 'Native' fashion. The complexion this puts on the position of hunter-gatherers relative to their culture is not the somewhat passive one that Bird-David evokes, but one where people are actively manipulating, controlling and even inventing their culture on behalf of down-to-earth political and economic ends. In this way hunter-gatherers are seen not as prisoners of their past but active agents for whom, in present times, culture may be mobilized as a symbol of solidarity.

Social structure and ideology

The range of social structures exhibited by hunter-gatherers, from the past through to the present-day, may be best addressed by analysis which examines the structures' essential features, the corresponding ideologies, and the factors which precipitate change from one structure to another. A good example is Wodburn's distinction (1982) between †'immediate-return' and 'delayed return' hunter-gatherer societies which grasps the difference between egalitarian and more complex hunter-gatherer social structures in terms of different types of social bonding implicated by differing technological and economic constraints. From another perspective, discussion of egalitarian hunter-gatherers often makes much of the unrestricted access to territory

and ungarnered resources which uniquely seems central to their cultures. Thus Ingold (1986) notes that in these societies the prevalent food sharing among members of the community replays the fact that the means of subsistence are held in common, and that this differs from more complex societies where sharing amounts to the giving up of that which is first personally owned. Other writers have attended to the essential instability of egalitarianism and how 'immediate-return' hunter-gatherers must work to sustain it, for example by employing joking, teasing, put-downs and other 'levelling mechanisms' against those who might seek to translate superior ability (e.g. in hunting) into higher †status. Meanwhile, the attempt to grasp what precipitates the emergence of the more complex social structures has resulted in a variety of proposals ranging from the development of systems of food storage, the intensification of control over women, and the emergence of notions of ownership associated with the conservation of resources. Among the Australian Aborigines, more complex social structures may be connected with large-scale †initiation ceremonies such as do not generally occur among egalitarian hunter-gatherers.

Peoples with flexible, egalitarian social structures commonly subscribe to religions which embrace shamanistic principles, and hunter-gatherers are no exception. In *shamanism direct contact by humans with the spirit domain, usually in order to relieve misfortune, is achieved through soul loss, and this is normally discharged by a specialist – the shaman – whose techniques of ecstasy and trance have been refined through a long period of apprenticeship. Shamanism, a religion marked by social unpredictability, seems less compatible with complex social structures with their more rigidly organized social groupings. Thus Australian Aboriginal religion, once thought to exemplify *the* elementary religion, revolves around *totemic beliefs which are connected with the existence of discrete social subdivisions, including descent groups. Among the Northwest Coast Indians there are closed religious 'societies' into which young men are initiated, and inter-group ranking celebrated by ceremonial *potlatch feasting.

In more recent times many hunter-gatherer peoples have come to subscribe to world religions such as *Christianity, melding indigenous beliefs with new, and radically different, concepts and notions. Underpinning such religious change may be the heterogeneous economic values to which many contemporary hunter-gatherers now subscribe and the serious disruptions in the indigenous economy wrought by colonial contact. Thus Tanner (1979) shows, in the case of the Cree Indians, that merging both subsistence and commercial economic concerns can pose enormous ideological dilemmas, which may be rationalized through selectively, and situationally, upholding beliefs from more than one religious tradition. This sort of analysis will increasingly be required to grasp the changing circumstances of hunter-gatherers throughout the world.

DAVID RICHES

See also: environment, Aboriginal Australia, shamanism, potlatch

Further reading

Barnard, A. (1992) *Hunters and Herders of Southern Africa: A Comparative Ethnography of the Khoisan Peoples*, Cambridge: Cambridge University Press

Bird-David, N. (1992a) 'Beyond the 'Original Affluent Society': A Culturalist Formulation', *Current Anthropology* 31 (1): 25–48
—— (1992b) 'Beyond the 'Hunting and Gathering Mode of Subsistence': Observations on the Nayakas and Other Hunter-Gatherers', *Man* 27 (1): 19–44
Ingold, T. (1986) *The Appropriation of Nature*, Manchester: Manchester University Press
Ingold, T., D. Riches and J. Woodburn (eds) (1988) *Hunters and Gatherers* (2 vols), Oxford: Berg
Kent, S. (1992) 'The Current Forager Controversy: Real versus Ideal Views of Hunter-Gatherers', *Man* 27 (1): 45–70
Myers, F. (1988) 'Critical Trends in the Study of Hunter-Gatherers', *Annual Review of Anthropology* 17: 261–82
Tanner, A. (1979) *Bringing Home Animals: Religious Ideology and Mode of Production of the Mistassini Cree Hunters*, London: Hurst
Wilmsen, E. (1989) *Land Filled with Flies: A Political Economy of the Kalahari*, Chicago: Chicago University Press
Woodburn, J. (1982) 'Egalitarian Societies', *Man* 17 (3): 431–51

I

identity

Anthropological uses of 'identity' are ambiguous. In one sense, the term refers to properties of uniqueness and individuality, the essential differences making a *person distinct from all others, as in 'self-identity'. In another sense, it refers to qualities of sameness, in that persons may associate themselves, or be associated by others, with groups or categories on the basis of some salient common feature, e.g. 'ethnic identity'. The term may also be applied to groups, categories, segments and institutions of all kinds, as well as to individual persons; thus families, communities, classes and nations are frequently said to have identities.

The term 'identity' was brought into general use by the *psychoanalytic theorist Erik H. Erikson (1959). Personal identity, for Erikson, was located deep in the unconscious as a durable and persistent sense of sameness of the self; whatever happens, however traumatic the experience or dramatic the passage from one phase of life to another, the non-pathological individual does not normally consider himself or herself to have become someone else. Individuals conceive of the self in terms of the *cognitive models or paradigm types of personality or moral character available in their historical time and within spatial range of their experience. While the term 'identity' is frequently employed by anthropologists to refer to selfhood in a loosely Eriksonian way, the concept is usually treated more sociologically, emphasizing the individual's social and *cultural surroundings, and the mechanisms of *socialization and cultural acquisition. The anthropological concern with selfhood considerably antedates the recent adoption of the term 'identity', in the United States exemplified by the works of †Margaret Mead, †Ruth Benedict and the *culture and personality school, from the late 1930s. Anthropologists have also found inspiration in the works of pioneering social theorists such as †Georg Simmel, †Émile Durkheim, †George Herbert Mead, Alfred Schutz, and others.

In its sense of sameness, 'identity' refers to commonalities associated with groups or categories. The starting point is classificatory: the social and cultural world is held to be composed of segments, membership in terms of which individuals must define themselves, or be defined by others. While sharing some features of the well-established concept of 'status and role', the usage is less prescriptive and mechanical, giving greater attention to individuals' conscious self-typifications. The groups and categories are accorded significant cognitive content 'of a type'. These include evaluative or emotional characteristics from which the individual derives self-esteem, or a sense of knowing or belonging. These features are highly variable in intensity and salience, as are any associated normative expectations which may furnish individuals with guides to their social behaviour. Individuals' identities are, then, emergent properties of their categorical memberships.

REGINALD BYRON

See also: person, socialization, culture and personality, ethnicity, psychological anthropology, classification, cognition

Further reading

Erikson, E.H. (1980 [1959]) *Identity and the Life-Cycle*, New York: W.W. Norton
Giddens, A. (1991) *Modernity and Self-Identity: Self and Society in the Late Modern Age*, Cambridge: Polity Press
Jacobson-Widding, A. (ed.) (1983) *Identity: Personal and Socio-Cultural*, Stockholm: Almqvist and Wiksell

ideology

The term 'ideology' has a history going back to the late eighteenth century. In politics and *sociology it has been used in a great variety of meanings, but as far as anthropology is concerned only two senses of the term are important.

The first use of the term refers to the system of social and moral ideas of a group of people; in this sense ideology is contrasted with †practice. In this usage, ideology is close to *'culture', except that it suggests a necessary coherence which means that an ideology, in this sense, can be formulated as a set of interlinked propositions. The best example of such a use in anthropology is to be found in the work of †Louis Dumont. In his book on caste, *Homo Hierarchicus* (1970 [1966]) he talks of the governing ideology of Indian social systems as focused on the concepts of *pollution and purity. In a later book, *Homo Aequalis*, which bears the subtitle 'Genesis and development of the economic ideology' he contrasts Hindu ideology to modern Western ideology, centred as it is on the irreducibility of the individual.

†C. Geertz, in an article entitled 'Ideology as a Cultural System', defines ideology as 'maps of problematic social realities and matrices for the creation of social conscience' (1973: 220). For him ideology is a part of culture concerned with a representation of the social and a commitment to central values. He is particularly interested in those social conditions under which coherent ideologies are formulated.

The other use of the term 'ideology' in anthropology is inspired by *Marxism, although Marx's own use of the word was somewhat inconsistent (Bloch 1983). The best example of the concept in this tradition can be drawn from *Capital*. The aim of the book is to show how the capitalist system is exploitative in that it transfers the fruit of the work of the majority, the workers, to a minority, the capitalists. If this is so the question of why the workers put up with this state of affairs then arises. One answer could be physical coercion, but although that is certainly present, it is not a sufficient explanation since the workers are not menaced by soldiers at all times. Marx's answer to this puzzle is ideology. A representation of the economy is present, no doubt favoured by those who benefit from it but partly accepted by all, which makes the whole system appear fair. It works in the following way. The basis of the system is the fact that the means of production are unequally divided so that some people, the capitalists, control them and others, the workers, do not. This unequal distribution is seen as beyond question, natural, the God-given right to private property (as it says in the American Constitution). This unequal distribution having been taken for granted, attention, by contrast, is focused on the *market, especially the market for wages, where workers can exchange their labour 'freely' for the right to receive a part of the product which is obtained through the coming together of capital and labour. The rate of exchange is the wage which is determined, apparently, by the quasi-mechanical, therefore natural, operation of supply and demand. Rather as a conjuror is able to perform tricks by making the audience pay attention to the non-essential, the image of a relation of capitalists and workers as non-exploitative and simply inevitable is created by diverting attention away from the allocation of the means of production to the market. Such a representation is ideological.

A number of anthropologists have attempted to carry over this type of analysis onto more familiar anthropological terrain. Thus Terray (1975) explains how a small group of people, the Abron, who ruled over a much larger subject population in nineteenth and twentieth-century *West Africa, maintained their power without disposing of overwhelming physical force. Terray shows how the Abron, at the time of their initial conquest, systematically destroyed all the traditional legal and peacemaking institutions of the conquered people and then established a system of courts manned only by Abrons which settled disputes among their subjects. The Abron were therefore able to appear as ideologically necessary and indeed beneficial by shifting attention from their destructive activities to their peacemaking. Consequently it could seem only right that they should receive tribute in labour and produce. In this analysis we have all the traditional elements of a Marxist analysis of ideology. The ideological representation serves to legitimate the exploitative position of a ruling class. It does that by hiding, but not falsifying, the real situation by an ideology which is powerful because it appears natural and inevitable.

There are a number of objections to such a theory. The first is that it makes ideology a kind of plot thought up by the ruling class to mystify the subjects – but this is unlikely. First of all, in these examples, the rulers seem just as taken in by ideology as their subjects, so they can hardly be consciously misleading others. Second, it is not clear how such ideas are propagated so that they become generally accepted. An attempt to answer these questions was made by the philosopher †L. Althusser (1977) who argued that ideology is created as part of the historical process in a way which makes its construction, at least in part, beyond anybody's intentionality. He also argued that it is propagated by what he called 'ideological state apparatuses' such as the *family, the church, the school and various forms of *ritual. In modern societies, the school and the family are most important, in others it is *religion. An attempt to translate some of Althusser's ideas into anthropology is found in Bloch's *From Blessing to Violence* (1986).

The other problem with the Marxist notion of ideology is that ideology's place in relation to other forms of knowledge is unclear; indeed, what would be the source of alternative theories of society? A number of anthropologists and historians have stressed that studies should pay attention to understanding the situation from the point of view of the oppressed, emphasizing †subaltern perspectives rather than merely examining ideology (Guha 1982). Others have looked more theoretically at the issue, and have discussed the sources of non-ideological consciousness which would make it possible for ideology to be resisted in the right circumstances (Godelier 1984).

MAURICE BLOCH

See also: Marxism and anthropology, capitalism, resistance, political economy

Further reading

Althusser, L. (1977) *Lenin and Philosophy*, London: New Left Books
Bloch, M. (1986) *From Blessing to Violence*, Cambridge: Cambridge University Press
—— (1983) *Marxism and Anthropology*, Oxford: Oxford University Press
Dumont, L. (1970 [1966]) *Homo Hierarchicus*, London: Weidenfeld and Nicolson
Geertz, C. (1973) 'Ideology as a Cultural System', in *The Interpretation of Culture*, New York: Basic Books
Godelier, M. (1984) *The Mental and the Material*, London: Verso
Guha, R. (ed.) (1982) *Subaltern Studies 1*, Delhi: Oxford University Press
Terray, E. (1975) 'Classes and Class Consciousness in the Abron Kingdom of Gyaman', in M. Bloch (ed.) *Marxist Analyses and Social Anthropology*, London: Malaby Press

incest

Incest and its prohibition or avoidance are closely related social phenomena. However, the two topics have very distinct if not contrary intellectual histories in the social sciences. Incest, usually defined as sexual relations between close kin such as members of the same nuclear family, has merely been assumed to be a natural inclination of humanity to be guarded against by explicit social rules. This essentially psycho-biological explanation for the deed, and its implicit assumptions about human nature, was exemplified by †Freud's *Totem and Taboo* (1950). In this influential essay, set against the imagery of primate society and human origins as then conceived, Freud drew a stark contrast between *nature and culture: as the chaotic impulses of the former are denied and controlled by the latter. Indeed, as *Lévi-Strauss later argued in similar fashion, the establishment of a rule prohibiting incest creates the conditions for human culture as 'nature transcends itself' (1969: 25).

But the evidence for such a proposition about human sexual impulses was merely assumed, reflecting a deep-seated aspect of Western cosmology rather than detailed knowledge of the evolutionary differences between human and non-human primate societies. Eventual studies of these social systems demonstrated the very opposite pattern, since inbreeding is strictly avoided by other primates. Thus, if incest is not a feature of our animal nature as previously supposed, its existence has gone unaccounted for in any theoretical sense.

The incest prohibition

In contrast to a mere set of assumptions, some explanation for the existence of the incest prohibition in human societies has been offered by almost every major figure in the history of Western social science. The early American anthropologist *Lewis Henry Morgan proposed, in sound Darwinian fashion, that the recognition of the reproductive advantages of outbreeding eventually became apparent to primitive societies and as such, it was a 'good illustration of natural selection at work' (1877: 425). Taking a more sociological approach to the problem, †Edward Tylor argued that 'savage tribes had the alternative between 'marrying out or being killed out' (1889: 267). In this instance, the social advantages of creating alliances was recognized and institutionalized by early humans. (It should be noted here that Tylor unwittingly changed the topic from sex to *marriage rules. While related, these are distinct phenomena since incestuous sexual behaviour and †exogamy – marrying outside a particular social group – can coexist.)

In some form or another, these arguments continue to hold sway in mainstream contemporary social science. As a result, it is a commonplace in *sociology to note that the incest prohibition effectively excludes potentially disruptive sexual competition among nuclear family members. In addition, it had been argued as a corollary that the prohibition eliminates the role confusion that would result from reproduction by members of the same nuclear family, such as father/daughter or mother/son mating. The result is that children are reared in a relatively harmonious and orderly social setting. In time each family member will seek reproductive partners outside the family, and in the process forge a series of linked and presumably co-operative social units. Thus, as Tylor implied, this process set in motion by the incest prohibition ensures that society itself will come into existence and be continually reproduced with every new generation.

There is no denying that the incest prohibition has the eventual positive outcomes suggested by these arguments. Contemporary genetics indicates that nuclear family inbreeding has deleterious effects on offspring as a group, expressed in the form of higher morbidity, i.e. congenital illnesses and higher mortality rates. As a consequence, an inbreeding group would have difficulty in maintaining a viable population over time. (It is important to note that such conclusions do not hold for reproduction by first cousins.) The sociological commentaries are equally perceptive in pointing to the positive results of exogamy, since nuclear family sexual competition and role confusion would be dysfunctional, while larger related social units are socially beneficial for all concerned. Yet, their *functional arguments have serious flaws in attempting to account for the origin of the incest prohibition and rules of exogamy.

First and foremost is their teleological nature. In effect these lines of reasoning assume that the *functions* of the incest taboo are the original *cause* of this prohibition. Even though these functions may emerge, there are no logical reasons to assume, for example, that the prevention of inbreeding or the creation of alliances are actually the *reason* for the creation of the incest prohibition. These responses may merely be the unintended consequences of the custom. Furthermore, these functional arguments all implicitly assume that the incest prohibition was at some point in time created by human beings in recognition of its benefits. Again, there is no evidence from the anthropological or historical record to assume that this is the case. Finally, with regard to the deed itself, the incidence of human incestuous behaviour is no reason to conclude that our species is naturally inclined to engage in it. The existence of what we would characterize as an incest taboo for other primate species – they all outbreed – suggests that human beings have not in fact created this arrangement, and therefore, no consequences – biological, psychological, or sociological – were intended. Indeed, as this outbreeding arrangement is characteristic of all primate societies, it is assumed to have been a feature of our last common ancestor extant at least 400,000 years ago (Maryanski and Turner 1992). In effect, humans must have evolved with the outbreeding pattern and then created the rule against incest as social reinforcement for the behaviour somewhere along their more recent historical path. However, the sporadic occurrence of incest indicates the human ability to engage in such behaviour but not as the result of natural forces, for these apparently encourage the very opposite.

Incest avoidance

This avoidance argument was originally proposed in the late nineteenth century by the Finnish moral philosopher and early anthropologist †Edward Westermarck ([1926] 1968). He argued that human beings were naturally attracted to unfamiliar potential sexual objects, normally those outside the nuclear family. In other words, Westermarck suggested that, like other species, we avoid incest. This 'familiarity breeds contempt' argument was derided by Westermarck's contemporaries with the eminently sensible rejoinder: If this were the case, why do all societies have an explicit rule against incest? Westermarck himself was unable to provide a satisfactory response to this objection at the time. However, we are now aware that some societies lack the proscription, indicating that incest can indeed be avoided as he suggested. Moreover, subsequent ethnographic studies from China (Wolf and Huang 1980), the Middle East (McCabe 1983), and Israeli kibbutzim (Sherper 1983) suggest that children raised together from early infancy, even if they are not siblings (as in these instances), make for unappealing sexual and, if eventuated by social pressure, unsatisfactory marriage partners. Although not uncontested (see Spiro 1982; Roscoe 1994), these data have provided renewed interest in and support for Westermarck's initial avoidance hypothesis.

Finally, as mentioned, inbreeding is also unintentionally avoided among other primates and mammals in general, usually by transfer out of the natal group by either males or females in search of more exotic sexual partners. Controlled laboratory experiments also demonstrate captive animals' preference for mates other than those with whom they were raised. Significantly, those given no option but to mate with both familiar and close genetic sexual partners fail to reproduce at a rate necessary for the continued survival of the group (McGuire and Getz 1982). Thus, it appears from the relevant evidence that, for a variety of biological and psychosocial reasons, incest is not an attractive sexual alternative for any species, including our own. However, the question remains: if incest is not a natural human inclination, why does it exist? For an answer to this query, we must look to the realm of human culture rather than nature.

Explaining incest

Initially it should be noted that incest exists in a variety of forms. There is the uncondoned variety which occurs in societies such as our own in violation of explicit rules against it. There are also numerous examples from other times and places such as Pharaonic Egypt and the pre-contact Hawaiian and Incan states, to name only a few. In these instances incestuous marriages were a characteristic prerogative of royalty despite the societal rules against such unions for others. (As marriage arrangements, sex and reproduction were not necessarily at issue in these cases, especially for the male, who typically had numerous other sexual partners. Thus, it is best to view these unions as pseudo-incestuous symbolic representations of the divine right to rule.) In addition, there is the telling and well-documented instance of the Greek minority in Roman Egypt (300 BC to AD 300) which, as a group, regularly engaged in sibling marriage to avoid reproduction with surrounding ethnic groups held in low esteem (Shaw 1992).

This latter example is particularly important, for it demonstrates that for culturally-defined reasons human beings are quite capable of overcoming their natural inclination to avoid inbreeding. In attempting to account for this, and all other, exceptions to the overall pattern, it must be recognized that the source of the impetus to engage in incest is a human cultural capacity not a feature of our animal nature. (Animals kept in 'cultured' situations such as laboratories, zoos and households will also engage in such behaviour.) In response to this possibility (and indeed likely eventuation), most societies, though not all, have generated rules against such sexual, and therefore potentially negative, reproductive behaviour. In effect, humans have the ability to create social rules and, at the same time, the individual ability to reflect on them and to choose alternatives, for a variety of anti-social and even social reasons.

It is interesting that the most popular 'scientific' explanations attempting to account for the existence of the incest prohibition have failed to grasp this possibility. As indicated above, these arguments simply assume at the outset that: (1) human beings consciously create their behavioural rules; and (2) their cultural inclinations are morally superior to their natural ones. This is not always the case. The presumption that culture is superior to nature is just that; it is not a sound basis for the theoretical interpretation of profound cross-cultural human social patterns.

W. ARENS

See also: family, kinship, nature and culture, biological anthropology

Further reading

Arens, W. (1986) *The Original Sin: Incest and Its Meaning*, New York: Oxford University Press

Freud, S. (1950) *Totem and Taboo*, New York: W.W. Norton

Lévi-Strauss, C. (1969) *The Elementary Structures of Kinship*, London: Eyre and Spottiswoode

McCabe, J. (1983) 'FBD Marriage:Further Support for the Westermarck Hypothesis of the Incest Taboo', *American Anthropologist* 85: 50–69

McGuire, M. and L. Getz (1981) 'Incest Taboo between Sibling Microtus Ochrogaster', *Journal of Mammalogy* 213–215

Maryanski, A. and J. Turner (1992) *The Social Cage: Human Nature and the Evolution of Society*, Stanford CA: Stanford University Press

Morgan, L.H. (1877) *Ancient Society*, New York: Holt

Roscoe, P.B. (1994) 'Amity and Aggression: A Symbolic Theory of Incest', *Man* 29 (1): 49–76

Shaw, B. (1992) 'Explaining Incest: Brother–Sister Marriage in Graeco-Roman Egypt', *Man* 27: 267–99

Sherper, J. (1983) *Incest: A Biosocial View*, New York: Academic Press

Spiro, M. (1982) *Oedipus in the Trobriands*, Chicago: Chicago University Press

Tylor, E.B. (1889) 'On the Method of Investigating the Development of Institutions: Applied to the Laws of Descent and Marriage', *Journal of the Royal Anthropological Institute* 18: 245–69

Westermarck, E. ([1926] 1968) *A Short History of Human Marriage*, New York: Humanities Press

Wolf, A. and C.S. Huang (1980) *Marriage and Adoption in China, 1845–1945*, Stanford, CA: Stanford University Press

Indian anthropology

The term 'Indian anthropology' may be used to refer either to the study of society and culture in India by anthropologists irrespective of their nationality, or to the study by Indian anthropologists of society and culture in and outside India. The focus of this article will be on the study by Indian anthropologists of their own society and culture, although their studies have been and continue to be significantly influenced by the work of anthropologists the world over. With a few significant exceptions, they have mostly studied society and culture in South Asia. They have from time to time addressed themselves to general problems of theory and method, but the main emphasis, particularly in the early work has been on the description and analysis of specific aspects of Indian society and culture.

Adopted initially as an amateur pursuit by a few, the subject soon became established as a profession with its own centres of study and research and its own journals. The first postgraduate department of anthropology was established in the University of Calcutta in 1920; several new departments were started after independence in 1947, and the subject is now taught at both undergraduate and postgraduate levels in many universities. The first professional journal in the subject, *Man in India*, was founded in 1921, and it was followed in 1947 by *Eastern Anthropologist*. Departments of anthropology in most Indian universities have a composite character, combining social and cultural anthropology with physical anthropology and prehistoric archaeology, and this composite character is also maintained by the two journals mentioned above.

There are centres of anthropological research outside the universities as well, and the Anthropological Survey of India, one of the largest organizations of its kind in the world, has conducted research on a variety of topics throughout the country in the last fifty years. One of its major recent undertakings is a study of the people of India, and the first few volumes of a projected series of forty-three volumes have already been published.

Anthropological studies began in India at the turn of the century with the ethnographical mapping of the country led by British civil servants. Indians soon entered the field, and the first two prominent anthropologists were L. K. A. Iyer (1861–1937) and S. C. Roy (1871–1942). Iyer published extensively on the ethnography of Travancore and Cochin (Kerala), and became the first head of the department of anthropology in the University of Calcutta. Roy published a number of outstanding monographs on the tribes of Chotanagpur (Bihar) such as the Munda, the Oraon and Birhor; he became the founder-editor of *Man in India*.

By the 1920s, there were professional anthropologists who had received academic training in the discipline either abroad, mainly in Britain, or at home in Calcutta. G. S. Ghurye (1893–1983), the first professor of sociology at Bombay and K. P. Chattopadhyay (1897–1963), the first professor of anthropology at Calcutta, had both been trained at Cambridge by †W. H. R. Rivers and †A. C. Haddon, and they both published in professional journals in India and abroad. Prominent among those who came immediately after them were N. K. Bose (1901–72), D. N. Majumdar (1903–60) and Irawati Karve (1905–70). Majumdar built a strong department of anthropology at Lucknow, and published extensively in both social and physical anthropology. Bose and Karve had very broad intellectual interests, not confined only to ethnography, and they wrote on society, culture and politics in both English and Indian languages, Bengali in the case of Bose and Marathi in the case of Karve. Their writings brought anthropology to the attention of a public extending well beyond the circle of professional anthropology. We see in the works of these anthropologists a concern for the subjects they studied that is different in some respects from that generally encountered in anthropological writings in Britain and the United States in the corresponding period.

In India, there has been almost from the very beginning a closer relationship between social anthropology and *sociology than in most Western countries. The distinction between the study of other cultures and the study of one's own society, so conspicuous in Europe and North America, has never been sharply maintained. Because of the great size and diversity of the Indian population, sociologists as well as social anthropologists continue to investigate tribal, agrarian and industrial social and cultural systems. Again, because of the continuing importance of a long historical tradition, anthropology has always had close links with historical and classical studies. Although intensive fieldwork has been part of the regular training of the professional anthropologist, literary material is also extensively used, particularly in the study of cultures associated with written languages.

In the beginning, Indian anthropologists concentrated a great deal on the study of 'primitive' or 'tribal' communities, but they soon extended their range of observation and enquiry. The 1950s and late 1960s witnessed the publication of a large number of village studies by Indian and other anthropologists; more village studies have been made by anthropologists in India than probably anywhere else in the world. These studies have investigated practically every aspect of society and culture, from *family and *kinship to social stratification, and they have raised significant questions about the relationship between the local community and the larger society of which it is a part. More recently, anthropologists and sociologists have entered fields of investigation such as schools, hospitals, factories, trade unions, and so on.

Indian anthropology in the 1990s is much concerned with the problems, both empirical and normative, involved in the study of one's own society. There is a growing engagement not only with new types of data but also with new ways of looking at those data. Now, as before, anthropological research is influenced substantially by the concepts, methods and theories being continually shaped and reshaped by anthropologists all over the world; but it is influenced no less by the cultural and political concerns that animate the intellectual environment within which Indian anthropologists work in their own country. It is this tension between the general and the specific that gives to anthropology in India many of its distinctive features.

ANDRÉ BÉTEILLE

See also: Asia: South, Hinduism, caste

Further reading

Bose, N.K. (1963) *Forty Years of Science in India: Progress of Anthropology and Archaeology*, Calcutta: Indian Science Congress Association

Indian Council of Social Science Research (1985–6) *Survey of Research in Sociology and Social Anthropology 1969–1979*, 3 vols, Delhi: Satvahan

Ray, S.K. (1974) *Bibliographies of Eminent Indian Anthropologists*, Calcutta: Anthropological Survey of India

individualism

Individualism should not be confused with individuality, difficult though it has been to separate their definition and implication in anthropologists' work. To attempt this as a starting-point here, individualism pertains to a particular historico-cultural conceptualization of the *person or self, and might include: notions of the ultimate value and dignity of the human individual, his or her moral and intellectual autonomy, *rationality and self-knowledge, spirituality, voluntary contracting into a *society, market and polity, the right to privacy and self-development (cf. Lukes 1990). Individuality, by contrast, refers to the universal nature of human existence whereby it is individuals who possess †agency. Moreover, since individuals engage with others by virtue of discrete sense-making apparatuses (nervous systems and brains) – discrete centres of consciousness in discrete bodies – their agency necessarily accords with distinct perspectives on the world. Not only is an individual's being-in-the-world universally mediated by very particular interpretive prisms which distance the individual from the world, but while intrinsically 'of the world', the individual also inexorably comes to know the world as 'other'. Finally, this individuality of consciousness and agency is extant whatever the currency of individualism as a cultural norm.

In much anthropological writing on individualism, however, a conflation is apparent. The study of the conceptualization of the person in a particular socio-cultural milieu spills over into a positing of the nature of the individual actor. The society or culture to which the individual belongs is looked to for the ultimate origination of action and its interpretation, the source of agency. Hence, individuality comes to be depicted as as much prone to the niceties of socio-cultural fashion as individualism.

The root of the confusion lies in the nineteenth-century tradition of social thought from which twentieth-century anthropology derives. In attempting social-scientifically to come to terms with what were felt to be grand societal changes (the French Revolution, the American Revolution, the Industrial Revolution), to discover causatives and predict evolutions in mimicry of the sciences of natural organisms, *sociology began predicating grand historical patterns and forces. Explanatory narratives were fashioned which turned on the origins and development of such collective organisms as society (generally in Europe) and *culture (generally in North America).

While *Boas and American anthropology owed debts to the writings of †Herbert Spencer and *L.H. Morgan (and later, †Weber), perhaps the key nineteenth-century influence on the twentieth-century development of anthropological explanation – the key exponent of a collectivist narrative which subsumed individual agency within grand societal workings – was †Emile Durkheim. It was from him that *Radcliffe-Brown and *Malinowski, †Lowie and †Kroeber adopted much of their theoretical programme and problematic, and it is from Durkheim's French followers, especially †Marcel Mauss and †Louis Dumont, that a theorizing which conflates individualism with individuality has been propagated and elaborated. Let me outline this thinking.

The Durkheimian individual

Durkheim conceived of human beings as *homo duplex*, as leading essentially double existences, one rooted in the biological organism and one (morally, intellectually, spiritually superior) in a social. And while the former was naturally egoistic and selfish (the individual body with its material senses and appetites), the latter, accruing from society, effected by †socialization, was able to be 'conscientious': altruistic and moral. Between the two there was constant tension, but through inculcation into a public language and culture, humans became capable of rising above mean (animal) individuality and becoming part of a †collective consciousness in which the (sacred) traditions of a society were maintained. If people were yet conscious of themselves as individuals, then this too derived from their socialization and served a social function. The Western 'cult of the individual' related to the complexities of the collective division of labour in European societies, and could be traced back to the Christianity of the

Enlightenment and to the rise of Protestantism. Individualism was a †social fact like all moralities and all religions.

Mauss (in Carrithers *et al.* 1985) takes it upon himself to show in more detail how society exerted its force upon the physiological individual: how †collective representations and collectively determined habitual behaviours submerged the individual within 'a collective rhythm'. In different ages and societies, Mauss begins, people have been differently aware of themselves as social beings, differences which can be related to different forms of social structure and an evolution between these. First, then, comes the tribal stage of *personnage*. Here individuals are conceived of as ephemeral bearers of a fixed stock of names, roles and souls in †clan possession. These individual name-holders have no recognized existence independently of the clan (each merely reincarnating an original mythical *ancestor), and they possess no inner conscience. Next comes the Classical stage of *persona*. Here individuals are conceived of as free and responsible citizens of a state; they are legal persons with civic identities. But still they are social-structural facts, possessing no individual inner life. Then, with the rise of Christianity, comes the stage of *personne*. Here the individual is conceived of as indivisible and rational, with a conscience, indeed, with a unique sacred soul, who serves as the foundation of all political, economic and legal institutions. And finally, accompanied by modern schools of psychology, there is the peculiar Western stage of *moi*: the individual as a 'self' with increasing self-interestedness and self-knowledge.

Agreeing with Mauss that the Western notion of the individual is an exceptional stage in the evolution of civilizations, Dumont attempts more precisely to plot its origination and progress through a comparison with an archetypal civilization: India. Looking (as a Durkheimian would) to *religion as the cardinal element, Dumont finds *Hinduism providing the first clue. For despite the constraining interdependence ubiquitously imposed by Indian society on its members, in the Hindu figure of the 'world-renouncer' – one who seeks ultimate truth by forgoing the world in favour of an independent spiritual progress and destiny – he finds a Western-like individualist. For the renouncer, society is recognized as having lost its absolute reality and value. The crucial difference between the Hindu world-renouncer and the modern individualist is that the former can continue to exist only outside the everyday social world.

Dumont's second clue is that this same 'other-worldly individual' can be seen to be present at the birth and ensuing development of *Christianity. For Christ's teaching – that humans possess souls of infinite worth and eternal value which absolutely transcend the world of social institutions and powers, which are absolutely individual in relation to God – engenders a community of other-worldly individuals who meet on earth but have their hearts in heaven. The history of Christianity over the ensuing centuries (the conversion of Emperor Constantine and thereafter the Roman Empire; the Protestant Reformation) then represents a triumphant overcoming of the dualism between the Christian and the societal, a Christian repossessing of the world, so that life-in-society becomes synonymous with that of the other-worldly individual.

Nevertheless, Dumont concludes, the evolution need not end here. The individualistic West and holistic India represent two diametrically different conceptualizations of society, and although the former Western 'liberal' model is enshrined in the United Nations' Universal Declaration of Human Rights (recognizing the inherent dignity and equality and the inalienable rights of all individuals), it is the latter conceptualization which still represents the common type. Indeed, through movements as diverse as multiculturalism, *nationalism, fascism and Islamic †fundamentalism, the cultural future of individualism is, to say the least, unpredictable.

Anthropological applications

Characterizing the above line of thought, then, is the idea that the individual †actor of Western society is the result of a recent, particular and exceptional historico-cultural development. Moreover, it is not surprising that, learned in this (or commensurate) thinking, anthropologists have been prone to find a lack of individualism (and hence an absence of individuality) in their ethnographies of traditional societies (cf. Carrithers *et al.* 1985).

'The African', for example, is someone who is only conscious of himself or herself as a member of some general category: a *race, people, *family or corporation. The New Guinean 'Gahuku-Gama tribesman' lacks a concept of the individual person, recognizing only relationships between socially defined positions; if personalities are

recognized as distinct, then this is simply the issue of unique combinations of social relationships. There is no *a priori* differentiation made here between individual and role, self and society. In short, it might be concluded, the ethnographic record demonstrates the specificity of the individual to Western thought; the concept and its moral and social significance is otherwise absent.

The non-Durkheimian individual

Nevertheless, there have been exceptions to Durkheimian expectations and conclusions: ethnographies and analyses which distinguish between individualism and individuality, deny the priority (ontological, developmental, historical) of the societal, and ground themselves in individual agency.

Notably, Alan Macfarlane, tracing the 'origins of English individualism', disagrees spectacularly with those theorists (Marx, Weber, Durkheim, Dumont specifically) who would see individualism as a recent socio-cultural development, within previously holistic, collectivist, close-structured milieux. For in England at least, historical records evidence an individualistic, open, egalitarian society – with political and intellectual liberty, with private property rights, with legal rights of the person against the group – in existence since the 1200s if not before. He claims: 'the majority of ordinary people in England from at least the thirteenth century were rampant individualists, highly mobile both geographically and socially, economically 'rational', market-oriented and acquisitive, ego-centred in kinship and social life' (1978: 163). Here at least, the traditional anthropological evolution towards individualism must be abandoned and the conventional anthropological eschewing of conscious individuality obviated, for one does not find a time when 'an Englishman did not stand alone . . . in the centre of his world' (1978: 196). Contrariwise, it is the individual and his †nuclear family which may be looked to for originating those socio-cultural changes which elsewhere have been taken to be causative.

Moreover, even focusing on non-Western milieux, †Godfrey Lienhardt observes how talk in Africa celebrates individual eccentricities and inner consciousnesses which defy and subvert collective judgement and behaviour (in Carrithers *et al.* 1985). Meanwhile, drawing on his fieldwork in New Guinea, Kenelm Burridge describes how people are 'individuals' and 'persons' in different respects and at different times – where 'persons' may be understood as those who realize a given social order and embody categories which are prescribed by tradition, while 'individuals' are those who use their intuition and perception to create anew. As persons are products of socio-cultural environments, so individuals exist in spite of them; if persons are created by current moralities, then individuals are creative of new intellectualizations – including new persons. Moreover, each 'spatially bounded organism' is able to switch between the two: leave personhood behind and realize their individuality. This realizing may take a variety of ethnographic forms (besides its Western recognition as 'individualism'), but realization is everywhere possible. Certainly, in New Guinea there are individuals who seek a truth which goes beyond convention and transcends materialism. Indeed, Burridge concludes, such individuality would seem constitutive of our very human being, deriving from an agency which pre-exists culture.

Burridge's ethnographic summation is also commensurate with †Edmund Leach's theoretic stance that it is the individual actor and not the social system which should be looked to as source and guarantor of cultural vitality and social process. Indeed, the essence of humanity is an ubiquitous individual proclivity to break with normative social structures, reinterpret cultural conventions and create afresh (Leach 1977: 19–21).

Leach's concerns have been perhaps most famously extended in the work of †Fredrik Barth and the †transactionalist school (F. Bailey, R. Paine et al.). However, an emphasis on the individual actor – an interest in individualism; an appreciation of individuality – also finds expression in the theorists of *culture and personality (†G. Bateson, A.F.C. Wallace, †W. Goodenough), of *network analysis (J. Barnes, C. Mitchell, J. Boissevain) and more recently in a flowering of studies within *symbolic anthropology which focus on the interactive constructions and individual interpretations of symbolic realities (E. Bruner, M. Jackson, V. Crapanzano). Imbuing all of these approaches, perhaps, is an insistence that, in Macfarlane's formulation, 'individuals and their attitudes, their assumptions and mental life' should not lose out to macro-social (statistical, material, collectivist) 'facts' (1970: 3).

Current approaches

Despite periodic attempts to theorize in terms both of individual and society (†T. Parsons, H. Blumer, P. Berger, A. Giddens), in current anthropological analyses the dichotomy would seem set to continue.

In much mainstream debate, sensitivity to the individualistic is yet denigrated as †methodological individualism, the axiom that the individual is the fundamental unit of analysis and explanation, a term which is often used perjoratively by anthropologists, as erroneously couching explanation in terms of characteristics of individuals, their behaviours and interests, and hence gaining insufficient purchase on the broader and deeper conditions of socio-cultural 'realities'. Meanwhile, the centre-ground of anthropology continues to be a preserve of 'methodological collectivism': positing social phenomena as determined by factors which bypass individual rationality, and envisaging cultural development quite independently of individual consciousness. Here is an insistence (now blessed by the thinking of †Foucault, †Derrida, †Bourdieu) that the distinction between the individual and the societal is specific to the West and must be collapsed in favour of the latter – or at least of 'social relations' – for anthropology persuasively to encounter cultural others.

On the other hand, there is the continuing belief that it is a peculiar †ethnocentrism for anthropologists to fail to 'extend to the 'others' we study a recognition of the personal complexity which we perceive in ourselves' (Cohen 1989: 12). We are persons and individuals, role-players and rebels, conventional and creative; we may be self-contradictory, paradoxical, situated actors, but we are always (helplessly, proudly) interpretively autonomous and agential, inevitably and inexorably ourselves (cf. Rapport 1993). Hence, it is not good enough simply to say that since only Western culture valorizes the concept of the individual ('individualism'), only in Western society do individuals act distinctively ('individuality'). Whether it is socio-culturally confirmed or not, discrete individual consciousness is the crucial factor in the ongoing effecting and interpreting of socio-cultural reality.

NIGEL RAPPORT

See also: psychological anthropology, culture and personality, person

Further reading

Burridge, K. (1979) *Someone, No One. An Essay on Individuality*, Princeton: Princeton University Press

Carrithers, M., S. Collins and S. Lukes (eds) (1985) *The Category of the Person*, Cambridge: Cambridge University Press

Cohen, A.P. (1989) 'Against the Motion', in T. Ingold (ed.) *Anthropology is a Generalising Science or it is Nothing*, Manchester: Group for Debates in Anthropological Theory

Dumont, L. (1986) *Essays on Individualism*, Chicago: University of Chicago Press

Leach, E.R. (1977) *Custom, Law and Terrorist Violence*, Edinburgh: Edinburgh University Press

Lukes, S. (1990) *Individualism*, Oxford: Blackwell

Macfarlane, A. (1970) *The Family Life of Ralph Josselin, a Seventeenth-Century Clergyman*, Cambridge: Cambridge University Press

—— (1978) *The Origins of English Individualism*, Oxford: Blackwell

Morris, B. (1991) *Western Conceptions of the Individual*, Oxford: Berg

Rapport, N.J. (1993) *Diverse World-Views in an English Village*, Edinburgh: Edinburgh University Press

inequality

In the last hundred years, empirical studies of inequality have been significantly influenced by normative theories of equality. Social theorists have recognized the presence of inequalities of many kinds in the societies of which they have direct knowledge and experience, but they have also speculated about the existence and prospects of equality in past and future societies. Here there has been a major division: some have argued that inequality is an inherent feature of all societies, whereas others have maintained that egalitarian societies have existed in the past and can be brought into existence in the future.

Anthropological studies have made a significant contribution to these discussions since they have given special attention to †'primitive' or 'pre-literate' or 'simple' societies which, according to some, provide the best approximations to societies based on equality. The work of †Marx and †Engels, and particularly the latter (Engels 1948 [1884]), did much to give currency to the theory of *'primitive communism'. Engels and others argued that the real basis of social and political inequality was *property, and that, since there was no private property in primitive societies, there was no *state and no *class or inequality. They used many examples selected from ethnography and ancient history to illustrate their argument.

The subject of primitive communism was re-examined as better ethnographic evidence from contemporary primitive societies became available in the twentieth century. In a major study, first published in 1921, †R.H. Lowie (1960) contested the theory on the basis of a careful and systematic scrutiny of the evidence. He showed that property existed in many forms in most if not all primitive societies. Others have shown that inequalities of rank and status are also commonly found independently of the ownership of property. The theory of primitive communism as a demonstrable, universal stage of human evolution is now no longer widely accepted among anthropologists. It was for a long time part of the orthodoxy of *Russian and Soviet anthropology, but with the demise of the Soviet Union, it now has few defenders left.

Egalitarian societies

In recent years, a number of anthropologists have drawn attention to what they call 'egalitarian societies', some of which they have investigated directly through the method of participant-observation. These societies are found in different parts of the world, usually in isolated ecological niches, and they include the Hadza of Tanzania, the Mbuti of Zaire, the !Kung Bushmen of Botswana and Namibia, and the Batek Negritos of Malaysia. There are no clear inequalities of wealth, power or status among them; moreover, they are not 'egalitarian' merely by default, but consciously stress the value of equality and actively practise it (Woodburn 1982: 931–2). However, the special nature of these egalitarian societies must be noted. They all have a very simple †material culture based on *hunting and gathering. Again, not all hunter-gatherer groups meet the conditions of egalitarian societies, but only those based on †immediate-return (as against †delayed-return) economies. They consist of small, scattered bands of individuals, often of no more than ten to twelve households, and are without any clear structure or organisation; so much so that one student of the subject (Ingold 1986) has questioned the appropriateness of the term *'society' in their case.

Apart from 'immediate-return' hunter-gatherer bands, many forms of inequality of status, power and wealth have been observed and described among simple and tribal societies all over the world. One particular form of inequality among them has recently become a subject of controversy among scholars. Earlier anthropologists had often noted the presence of sharp, and sometimes harsh, inequalities between men and women even among hunter-gatherers such as the *Australian Aborigines; and, after the waning of the initial enthusiasm for the theory of primitive communism, it came to be generally accepted that the subordination of women to men is a universal feature of all human societies, including primitive ones (Evans-Pritchard 1965: 37–58). This is now seriously questioned. A number of contemporary anthropologists, mainly women, have argued forcefully that *gender relations were often misrepresented by earlier anthropologists who were predominantly male, and that equality between men and women was much more common in simpler societies than was generally acknowledged (Leacock 1978). This debate clearly shows the difficulty of separating judgements of reality from value judgements in the understanding of equality and inequality.

Unequal societies

Modern anthropologists no longer confine their attention to the study of simple, small-scale, preliterate societies, whether bands or tribes. During the last fifty years, they have contributed significantly to the study of large and complex societies with long historical traditions, often described as civilizations. Here they have investigated the problems of inequality or hierarchy directly through *fieldwork in small face-to-face communities as well as through textual and other forms of historical analysis dealing with whole traditions.

South Asia has received considerable attention from anthropologists, and as far as equality and inequality are concerned, the traditional civilization of India stands at the opposite extreme from the hunter-gatherer bands mentioned earlier. Indian civilization has been represented in the literature of anthropology as the epitome of rigid social stratification, and, indeed, a major anthropological study of India has been entitled *Homo Hierarchicus* (Dumont 1980a). A large number of detailed case studies of Indian communities have described and analysed the division of the population into numerous groups that are ranked in an elaborate and complex hierarchy (Béteille 1965; Berreman 1963; Bailey 1957). These studies have shown, while dealing with *caste, the salience of the *ritual opposition of *pollution and purity; but they have also drawn attention to the importance of the unequal distribution of land and other material resources.

The French anthropologist †Louis Dumont has drawn a sharp contrast between India and the West in which the former represents *Homo Hierarchicus* and the latter *Homo Equalis*. It should be made clear that Dumont's contrast is on the plane of values, and not of facts about the distribution of resources or even interactions among persons (Dumont 1980b). There are no doubt all kinds of inequalities of wealth, power and status in every modern society, but these exist in a moral and cultural environment whose basic premise is equality, whereas in India the basic premise of that environment is hierarchy. There is, therefore, a fundamental difference between equality in modern Western societies and in hunter-gatherer bands characterized by immediate-return transactions.

Kinds of inequality

In Western, and indeed in all modern societies, social practice is marked by different expressions of inequality, and these have been investigated in detail at the level of the local community as well as the wider society, but more by those who are called *sociologists rather than social or cultural anthropologists. Of all these many inequalities, the ones that are most distinctive of modern societies are those relating to the social grading of occupations (Blau and Duncan 1968). In these societies, one's social identity is defined to a considerable extent by one's occupation: a great deal of one's adult life is devoted to it, and one's early life is largely a preparation for it. Occupations are differentiated and ranked in very elaborate ways (Goldthorpe and Hope 1974), and one may detect broadly similar patterns of occupational ranking across a very wide range of societies, such as the United States, Poland and India (Treiman 1977).

One striking feature of many modern societies is the simultaneous presence of inequalities of many kinds. In the United States, for example, inequalities of *race and of gender co-exist with, and to some extent cut across, those due to occupation. It is true that a very high value is placed on equality in what has been called the 'American creed'. When, on the other hand, one looks at all the multifarious inequalities there – of wealth, income and occupation; of power and prestige; between blacks and whites; and between men and women – one cannot but ask what it might mean to say that equality, and not hierarchy, is the basic premise of American culture. The contrast between *Homo Hierarchicus* and *Homo Equalis* may illuminate the past to some extent, but so far as the present is concerned, it would appear more reasonable to say that modern societies 'are both egalitarian in aspiration and hierarchical in organisation' (Aron 1968: xv).

Much of the research actually conducted by anthropologists consists of detailed investigations of specific communities or societies, but the aims of anthropology are in addition both comparative and general. The *comparative method has been a central part of anthropology from the very beginning, although there have been some distinguished critics of it (Béteille 1991). At first it was used to discover the origin and evolution of every kind of social arrangement, including inequality; later it was used to discover the general laws of the structure and functioning of societies; and today it is still widely used, more or less systematically, to throw light on similarities and differences in the forms of social and cultural life, including the nature and types of inequality.

In examining inequality comparatively, the sociologist or social anthropologist is less concerned with inequalities of ability, aptitude or talent among individuals than with inequalities that are an inherent part of collective existence and that arise from the evaluation of qualities and performances and the organization of persons into more or less stable arrangements (Béteille 1977). These studies aim at investigating not only the existing patterns of inequality but also the mechanisms of their reproduction over time (Bourdieu and Passeron 1972). A major change between the past and the present has been the shift of attention from the origin to the reproduction of inequality. The reproduction of inequality can be investigated empirically, whereas it is hard to see how this can be done for its origin.

Human beings differ from animals, it is said, because they have *culture, and every human culture, irrespective of scale or complexity, *classifies and evaluates all manner of objects, beings, positions, arrangements and so on. Some qualities are highly esteemed while others are not; some types of performance rate higher than others; and persons and positions associated with qualities and performances considered superior are themselves considered in some sense superior. What is at issue here is not just individual (or idiosyncratic) tastes and preferences, but standards of evaluation that are widely shared or at least acknowledged by the bearers of a particular culture. Persons with sophisticated tastes and preferences may find it strange, but it is true never

the less that a sense of distinction is a part of every human culture, no matter how impoverished it may appear from outside.

If the argument above is correct, then scales of evaluation are used for discriminating among persons and positions, and ranking them as superior and inferior in all human societies. In simple societies, the scales may be largely implicit and the ranking rudimentary. In complex civilizations, they tend to be articulated, elaborated, systematized, justified, contested and also overthrown and replaced by other scales and other standards. While no society can accommodate an infinity of scales of evaluation, it may be a mistake to believe that any society is likely to maintain only one single scale that encompasses all the evaluations made by its members.

The fact that in a given society some evaluations predominate and prevail over others indicates that there are inequalities of power among individuals and groups. Inequalities of power are a general if not universal feature of human societies, and they have many different sources. Some have taken the view that they are all ultimately rooted in inequalities of wealth and property; these may be called 'class theorists'. As against these, there are the 'élite theorists' whose position, broadly speaking, is that *power is the source of riches. Those who stress the importance of power as a source of inequality point out that every society has some division of labour, no matter how rudimentary, and some organization involving more or less regular chains of command and obedience. This involves a differentiation of social positions, some of which carry more authority or power than others. In this view, the hunter-gatherer bands, referred to earlier, are at best limiting cases and not typical ones.

ANDRÉ BÉTEILLE

See also: caste, class, power, property, work

Further reading

Aron, R. (1968) *Progress and Disillusion*, London: Pall Mall Press

Bailey, F.G. (1957) *Caste and the Economic Frontier: A Village in Highland Orissa*, Manchester: Manchester University Press

Berreman, G.D. (1963) *Hindus of the Himalayas*, Berkeley: University of Californian Press

Béteille, A. (1965) *Caste, Class and Power: Changing Patterns of Stratification on a Tanjore Village*, Berkeley: University of California Press

—— (1977) *Inequality Among Men*, Oxford: Basil Blackwell

—— (1991) *Some Observations on the Comparative Method*, Amsterdam: CASA

Blau, P.M. and O.D. Duncan (1968) *The American Occupational Structure*, New York: Free Press

Bourdieu, P. and J.C. Passeron (1972) *Reproduction in Education, Society and Culture*, Beverley Hills: Sage

Dumont, L. (1980a [1966]) *Homo Hierarchicus: The Caste System and its Implications*, Chicago: University of Chicago Press

—— (1980b) *On Value*, London: The British Academy

Engels, F. (1948 [1884]) *The Origin of the Family, Private Property and the State*, Moscow: Progress Publishers

Evans-Pritchard, E.E. (1965) *The Position of Women in Primitive Societies, and Other Essays*, London: Faber & Faber

Goldthorpe, J.H. and K. Hope (1974) *The Social Grading of Occupations*, Oxford: Clarendon Press

Ingold, T. (1986) *Evolution and Social Life*, Cambridge: Cambridge University Press

Leacock, E. (1978) 'Women's Status in Egalitarian Society', *Current Anthropology* 19: 247–75

Lowie, R.H. (1960 [1921]) *Primitive Society*, London: Routledge and Kegan Paul

Treiman, D.J. (1977) *Occupational Prestige in Comparative Perspective*, New York: Academic Press

Woodburn, J. (1982) 'Egalitarian Societies', *Man* (n.s.) 17: 431–51

Islam

This entry should perhaps be titled 'Islams' (el-Zein 1977) since anthropologists have for long stressed the plurality of social forms and conceptions within the religion of some 15 to 20 per cent of humankind. This emphasis on internal plurality is not surprising, given such factors as geographical spread, doctrinal distinctions, authority structures, and academic imperatives. Geographically, Islam is the dominant religion in not only all Arabic-speaking countries, but also in most of the northern half of Africa, about half of Central Asia, and influential parts of Southeast Asia. Doctrinal differences can be located between the major branches of Sunni and Shi'a, between either of these and their so-called 'sects', and in the long-standing divisions among four major schools of Islamic law (*shari'a*). Contending authority structures are most clearly seen in the frictions and conflicts between authorized religious authorities ('*ulama*) and the more believer-centred ('mystical') teachings of Sufi 'saints' whose shrines can spawn highly distinctive regional cults. Finally, anthropologists' stress on variety followed the academic imperative of substituting their tradition of

historial particularism for the *Orientalism and *essentialism of textual scholars who helped to create 'the Islamic' as the prototypical 'Other' of the Christian West.

Among anti-essentialist work that precedes the critique of Orientalism and continues to be influential, one may stress two approaches. One, usually cast in the language of *political economy, uses local histories and sometimes revised macro-level periodizations in order to counteract stereotypical ideas of Muslim 'essences'. The other, cast in the language of religion as a 'cultural system' and championed by †Clifford Geertz, relates local, regional or even national characteristics of Islam to the ethos of the civilization within which they make sense. In Geertz's *Islam Observed* (1968), it is the underlying 'Fabianism' of Moroccan civilization and the 'Utopianism' of Indonesia that appear to shape both the external distinctiveness and the internal unity of Islamic ideas there. The argument develops against the backdrop of a dualist modern tendency which favours a progressive 'secularization of thought . . . and the major response to it – the ideologization of religion' (Geertz 1968: 103). It may be doubted, however, whether such a separation of 'religion' from 'politics', as well as the secularism ascribed to the latter, are not themselves the outcome of *modernist ideologies.

This question has been foregrounded by the growing power and appeal of so-called 'fundamentalist' movements (that challenge state policies aimed at *modernization) and state structures (geared toward the secularist division of political from religious moralities). The term 'fundamentalist' is widely conceded to be historically misleading and analytically toothless, but it has helped to pull together the work of political scientists, historians and anthropologists (Marty and Appleby 1994). There are, as yet, no detailed micro-level ethnographies of Islamist initiatives placed in their local political, economic and cultural contexts, perhaps because of the difficulties of †participant observation and the endlessly-celebrated 'crisis' of *ethnography. They would have much to offer, however, especially since they could build upon the heightened anthropological awareness with which we now perceive the social ambivalences, seeming cognitive dissonances, and subtly articulated antinomies of 'Islamic' ideas cast and recast in contests for power (Gilsenan 1982). In placing activist Muslim ideas within their 'political economy of meaning',

Roff (1987) has revived the use of the *comparative method, one of anthropology's greatest ambitions, but also one of its most neglected projects. It may require intra-regional or local-level comparisons between 'different' Muslim activisms in order to re-imagine Islam as a discursive universe that allows for, and indeed encourages, different interpretations of a few basic axioms about the link between private and public moralities. This link flies in the face of the key idea of Western secular modernity, as exported through *colonialism, and it throws into question the most tangible inheritance of decolonization: the idea of the *nation-state (Piscatori 1986). This has consequences both for the formerly colonized and for their erstwhile colonizers.

On the Indian subcontinent one can see how nation-state ideologies are challenged, as well as used, by the protagonists of a 'religious nationalism' (van der Veer 1994), be they Muslim or Hindu. Anthropologists have begun to leave behind the methodologically indefensible myopia of studying Muslims regardless of the surrounding 'others' that they construct and are constructed by. Such an emphasis on the interactive dynamics between co-existing religious constituencies has become increasingly important also in the anthropology of Muslims living in the United States and Europe. Given that millions of Muslims took part in the great labour migrations from the 1950s to the 1970s, ideas of 'assimilation' came to be replaced by a state-sanctioned ideology of 'multiculturalism'. Yet the so-called Rushdie Affair ended the civic dream that Islam, or for that matter any other religion, could be confined to the 'private', as opposed to the public and political 'sphere' of social life. Most Islams are known to query this dichotomy which is so fundamental to the secular nation-state, and anthropologists have been alerted by what might be called the 'New Orientalism': a populist construction of Islam as a threat to Western civic values and of Muslims as the post-migration 'enemy within'. The crisis of nation-state ideologies which serve an economic system dependent on a global labour market and normative pluralism has also sparked the beginnings of interest in the study of Islam, and of Muslim movements and initiatives, from a transnational perspective.

GERD BAUMANN

See also: Middle East and North Africa, Orientalism, religion, state

Further reading

Geertz, C. (1968) *Islam Observed. Religious Development in Morocco and Indonesia*, New Haven: Yale University Press

Gilsenan, M. (1982) *Recognizing Islam. An Anthropologist's Introduction*, London: Croom Helm

Marty, M.E. and R. Scott Appleby (eds) (1994) *The Fundamentalism Project*, vol. 4: *Accounting for Fundamentalisms*, Chicago: University of Chicago Press

Piscatori, J.P. (1986) *Islam in a World of Nation-States*, Cambridge: Cambridge University Press

Roff, W.R. (ed.) (1987) *Islam and the Political Economy of Meaning. Comparative Studies of Muslim Discourse*, Berkeley: University of California Press

van der Veer, P. (1994) *Religious Nationalism. Hindus and Muslims in India*, Berkeley: University of California Press

el-Zein, Abdul Hamid (1977) 'Beyond Ideology and Theology: The Search for the Anthropology of Islam', *Annual Review of Anthropology*, 6: 227–54

J

Japan

The empire of Japan, located in the Northern Pacific Ocean off the coast of China, consists of four large islands – Hokkaido, Honshu, Kyushu and Shikoku – and innumerable smaller islands, many of which are inhabited. The total area is 377,835 square kilometres; the present population is more than 120 million. The majority lives on the largest island, Honshu, which also provides the location of such important and well-known cities as Tokyo, Osaka, Yokohama, Nagoya, Kyoto, Sendai, Niigata and Hiroshima. With more than 80 per cent of Japanese territory consisting of uninhabitable, mostly forest-covered mountains, the inhabited area – with ten cities of more than a million inhabitants – is among the most densely populated in the world. Land is either used very intensively, for terrace agriculture, infrastructure, industry or residential building, or left in its primary vegetative state, with, generally, very clearly defined local boundaries between the two categories.

The Japanese speak just one, very distinctive language, and enjoy a remarkably uniform culture. For such a large population, ethnic minorities are few in number, and are denied any chance of real integration. Members of the quite sizeable Korean minority (mainly concentrated in Osaka) are still not allowed to adopt Japanese names. Such marginalization is shared with an important autochthonous group, that of the two million odd '*eta*', or 'special status people', historically consigned to 'defiling' occupations, associated with culturally defined dirt (Ohnuki-Tierney 1987: 91). A much smaller number of Ainu, representing an earlier population once spread over the whole of Japan, still survive in Hokkaido maintaining something of their original culture.

Extreme attitudes of national self-consciousness, known as 'nihonjinron' ('discussions of the Japanese'), are the subject of many recent publications, such as Yoshino (1992). With a national holiday, 'bunka no hi' ('day of culture') to commemorate their own traditions, Japanese are positively encouraged to esteem their own culture. Carried to excess, this esteem characterizes countless small *nationalist groups whose political influence is quite disproportionate to the number of members. In fact many so-called traditions hardly reach back to the restoration of the power of the Emperor in 1868 which, with the opening of Japan to the outside world, marks the beginning of modern Japanese history. This event, in the first year of the Emperor Meiji (whose great grandson now sits on the Chrysanthemum throne) encouraged a parallel discourse, about the so-called 'tennôsei', relating to both the political, and the religious status of the Emperor (Crump 1991: 94). Furthermore, the trauma of the Pacific War (1941–5), followed by six years of Allied occupation, required the reformulation of many basic traditions – an historical process now underplayed by many influential Japanese.

One problem facing contemporary Japanese, in relation to their own culture, and the social organization which it supports, is that their roots are to be found in a rural society with an economy based on intensive wet-rice cultivation. Although government policy still pays excessive regard to the cultivation of rice, the traditional village *household, or *ie*, which was always its focus, now defines the lifestyle of only a small minority. The *ie* is, however, still central in any anthropology of Japan. It is an enduring corporate unit, centred on the household, seen both as an economic and a social unit, with a prescribed rule of succession to headship. Because of the dominant principle of †patrilineal descent, the *ie* essentially provides the topos of the Japanese family from one generation to another.

The essential continuity of the *ie* is enhanced by the worship of former members, as *ancestors, at the household altar. Although this commonly takes the form of a *butsudan* ('Buddha shelf'), reflecting the fact that mortuary rites in Japan are the primary responsibility of *Buddhism (Reader 1991: 77); a Shinto alternative, the *kamidana*, is not unusual. The problem with religion, in this form, is that it is difficult to place in the context of a young family, living in a modern city apartment and separated from its historic rural background. The result is that while a colourful ritual cycle appears to flourish at countless local temples and shrines, there is little religious observance in the modern Japanese home. Some new sects, such as the rapidly expanding Agonshû, described by Reader (1991: 219) as 'user-friendly', use the media to reach within the modern home, deprived of spirituality, but for the most part Japanese are content to visit religious centres, to pray for *riyaku*. These 'blessings' may be anything from peace of mind to examination success (Reader 1991: 33).

Japan pays inordinate attention at every level to *literacy and *education. The idiosyncratic form of written Japanese, with its thousands of characters borrowed from Chinese, defines the main focus of primary education. In science and mathematics, little concession is made to oriental tradition, so that the notation used, together with the specific subjects taught, is truly international; and so that, for instance, modern computer science relies on standard computer languages originating in the West. None the less, traditional crafts, in fields such as pottery and wood-carving, are still widely taught and practised, providing employment for countless Japanese.

In modern Japan, any international orientation conflicts with the sharp distinction made between 'inside' (*uchi*) and 'outside' (*soto*). For the individual the contrast is expressed in terms of *tatemae*, behaviour expected by the outside world, and *honne*, true feelings, suppressed in actual behaviour. A well-known proverb condemns those who draw too much attention to themselves. Not surprisingly, then, *soto* connotes not only foreigners (*gaijin*), but also deviance within Japanese society, as already illustrated by the cases of ethnic Koreans and the *eta*. None the less, other deviant characters as wandering players, acrobats and jugglers, and even the criminal fraternity of the *yakuza*, do have

a place in Japanese culture, as if their presence were needed to counteract the dominance of *uchi* in the life of the average citizen.

THOMAS CRUMP

See also: Asia: East, household, ancestors

Further reading

Benedict, R. (1946) *The Crysanthemum and the Sword*, Boston: Houghton Miflin

Crump, T. (1991) *The Death of an Emperor*, Oxford: Oxford University Press

Embree, J. (1939) *Suye Mura: A Japanese Village*, Chicago: University of Chicago Press

Ohnuki-Tierney, E. (1987) *The Monkey as Mirror*, Princeton: Princeton University Press

Reader, I. (1991) *Religion in Contemporary Japan*, London: Macmillan

Yoshino, K. (1992) *Cultural Nationalism in Contemporary Japan*, London: Routledge

joking and avoidance

The concepts of 'joking' and 'avoidance' emerged in *kinship studies between the 1920s and the 1940s, when publications by Marcel †Mauss, Henri Labouret, Denise Paulme, R.E. Moreau, F.J. Pedler, †Fred Eggan, †Meyer Fortes, and especially *A.R. Radcliffe-Brown, hinted at the ethnographic importance, particularly of joking relationships. While some, such as †Marcel Griaule, denied the significance of these relationships, the growing body of ethnographic evidence suggested enough cross-cultural uniformity for the concepts to become a standard part of the descriptive mechanism of the emerging subdiscipline of kinship studies.

Essentially, joking relationships are defined as those which necessarily involve free, familiar discourse between individuals occupying specific kin categories in relation to one another, while avoidance relationships are defined as those which similarly involve great formality by virtue of the respective kin categories to which those in the relationship belong. The notion of compulsion is important. One must 'joke' with those in one's genealogy classified as 'joking relatives', typically one's grandparents, mother's brothers, or cross-cousins. This may involve real jokes, but much more commonly the English term 'joking relationships' is a misnomer; the French term *parentés à plaisanterie* is more accurate.

Radcliffe-Brown's two articles on joking relationships, published in the journal *Africa* in 1940 and 1949, are usually taken as the definitive statement on the subject. These were later reprinted in his *Structure and Function in Primitive Society* (Radcliffe-Brown [1924] 1952: 90–116). Radcliffe-Brown saw joking relationships as involving essentially 'permitted disrespect', of a sort that would arouse hostility in any other context. Avoidance relationships, in contrast, involve extreme respect, such that avoiding the relative in question is the most satisfactory way of ensuring that the implicit tensions of the relationship do not result in conflict. Radcliffe-Brown argued that joking and avoidance relations limit conflict and increase social solidarity by directing sentiments in such a way as to control potentially threatening social interaction. He expressed the processes relevant as ones of 'social disjunction' (involving the potential for strife) and 'social conjunction' (involving the avoidance of strife), but these terms otherwise never caught on.

The classic case of joking is that found in many societies, especially †patrilineal ones, between a mother's brother and his sister's son. Radcliffe-Brown himself described this in his essay on 'The Mother's Brother in South Africa' ([1924]1952: 15–31), and the resulting notion of the *avunculate became a much-debated problem in kinship studies. In many societies, the mother's brother is treated with great licence. His sister's son may tease him, insult him, and steal his possessions. This 'joking' behaviour is one-way, in that the mother's brother has no recourse against his sister's son, but has to accept his behaviour as a willing spirit. However, in contrast to this one-way, non-reciprocal relationship, other joking relationships may involve fully reciprocal joking. For example, †cross-cousins who are marriageable may be expected to 'joke' with one another, in the sense that they treat each other with great sexual licence and indulge in conversation which would be regarded as rude or indecent if directed towards anyone else.

The classic example of an avoidance is that found, some would say universally, between a man and his mother-in-law. In extreme cases, notably in many parts of *Aboriginal Australia, special 'mother-in-law languages' have been devised, used only to express this extreme avoidance relationship. Although 'joking' and 'avoidance' are rarely to be taken literally, mothers-in-law may be the exception. They are avoided lest intense conflict ensue from the virtually unthinkable: close contact between them and their children's spouses.

Some kinship specialists prefer to think of joking and avoidance relations as those which operate between consanguines, while similar relations between affines are best termed relations of 'familiarity' and 'respect'. However, this usage has not met with much support, especially in that, in very many relevant societies, no semantic or behavioural distinction is made between relations with affines and relations with consanguines.

ALAN BARNARD

See also: avunculate, kinship, Radcliffe-Brown

Further reading

Griaule, M. (1948) 'L'alliance cathartique', *Africa*, 18: 242–58

Radcliffe-Brown, A.R. ([1924] 1952) *Structure and Function in Primitive Society*, London: Cohen and West

K

kingship

Ever since †James Frazer's *Golden Bough*, in which
the ritual slaying of the divine king provides a
central motif, as well as a conscious echo of the
Christian account of Christ's death and resurrection, kingship has been most convincingly treated
by anthropologists as a problem of *ritual and
symbol, rather than an issue for what became
*political anthropology. Despite Frazer's precipi-
tous fall from anthropological fashion in the 1920s
and 1930s, discussions of kingship continued, not
least because of the sheer amount of fascinating
evidence amassed from Africa and Polynesia,
where the rites of kingship were performed in front
of fieldworkers, and Asia and South America,
where kingship was a central theme in both historical records and local social idioms (there are
excellent bibliographies in Feeley-Harnik 1985
and Galey 1990).

Frazer's two greatest successors as comparative
theorists of kingship were the French scholar
†Georges Dumézil, for whom the king fulfilled one
of the three functions in his comparative account
of Indo-European mythology, and †A.M. Hocart,
whose work almost dropped from sight during his
lifetime but was enthusiastically revived in the
1950s and 1960s. In *Kings and Councillors* ([1936]
1970) Hocart employed a Frazerian melange of
evidence – contemporary ethnographic reports,
extracts from literary sources in the Indic and
Classical traditions – to put forward the case that
kingship, and with it government, was originally
a ritual activity directed to the collective regeneration of 'life', and only subsequently acquired the
executive and governmental functions we now
take for granted. In other words, ritual is not some
secondary feature of politics; politics is, as it was,
primarily a matter of ritual onto which secondary

features to do with ordering and running mundane
life may be attached.

Hocart's apparently extravagant argument,
which was quite at odds with the stern pragmatism
of British political anthropology of the time, in
fact finds plentiful support from historical and
ethnographic accounts of South, and especially
*Southeast Asian kingship. (In *South Asia, the
situation was complicated by †Louis Dumont's
influential mischaracterization of Hindu kingship
as secular, and encompassed by the ritual role of
the Brahmin: see Raheja 1988.) In those regions
strongly influenced by Hindu and Buddhist
theories of kingship, premodern *states were
focused on ritual centres (rather than ritual boundaries, as in modern nation-states), and built on
pyramidal ties of lordship and fealty, in which
*peasants recognized the ritual centrality of their
local lord, and local lords in turn paid ritual
homage to the greater lord at the ritual centre.
The king, as the focus of all this attention, held
power, but power of a quite different sort from
that invoked in modern Western theory. Benedict
Anderson, in a classic account of Javanese ideas
of power, has argued that the ruler's task was to
demonstrate the concentration of 'power' at the
centre – paradoxically often through inactivity
– rather than to transform the world though its
exercise (Anderson [1972] 1990).

In these regions, although kings themselves only
barely survive (in Nepal and Thailand, for example)
representations of kingship are pervasive, and the
idiom of lordship structures all manner of everyday
activities, from inter-caste relations within a village,
to ties of patronage with local politicians, to grand
attempts to project the modern nation-state as the
legitimate successor to the precolonial kings. In so
far as this idiom is rooted in the kind of idea of
*power explored by Anderson, then modern mass
politics are likely to be subtly different from politics

in the West. With a few exceptions (e.g. Burghart 1996) this possibility has barely been explored in anthropology since Anderson's important essay, partly because of the obvious dangers of essentializing other people's politics as trapped in frozen tradition, but mostly because of the lingering attachment to a curiously acultural, or anti-cultural, vision of political anthropology.

The second regional strand in the study of kingship has been in Africa, where anthropologists like the Belgian Luc de Heusch, have systematically explored the rituals and myths of kingship. What emerges from this literature is another important facet of kingship. Rituals of kingship, often involving the reversal of everyday values and norms, are as much as anything about making ordinary *persons into extraordinary kings (Feeley-Harnik 1985). †Sahlins (1985), in an analysis of Polynesian kingship which draws upon Dumézil, Hocart and de Heusch, suggests that the representation of kings as strangers or outsiders, and their ritual transgressions of the world of culture, are again part of a radically different view of power and the political. Power, in this kingly idiom, is not something inherent in society, and thus inherent in every individual; rather it is something which can only be dealt with by representing it as coming from outside the world of normal persons and normal sociability.

Recent work on kingship has quite profound, and mostly unexplored, implications for the anthropological study of politics in contemporary societies. Unfortunately, while the study of kingship and its implications has been focused on 'traditional' (i.e. pre-modern, precolonial) kingship, political anthropology has shown relatively little interest in different cultural understandings of power and its implications. Bringing the two together is both necessary and, historically and analytically, extremely difficult.

JONATHAN SPENCER

See also: ritual, power, state

Further reading

Anderson, B. ([1972] 1990) 'The Idea of Power in Javanese Culture', in B. Anderson, *Language and Power*, Ithaca: Cornell University Press

Burghart, R. (1996) *The Conditions of Listening: Essays on Religion, History and Politics in South Asia*, Delhi: Oxford University Press

Cannadine, D. and S. Price (eds) (1987) *Rituals of Royalty: Power and Ceremonial in Traditional Societies*, Cambridge: Cambridge University Press

Feeley-Harnik, G. (1985) 'Issues in Divine Kingship', *Annual Review of Anthropology* 14: 273–313

Galey, J.C. (ed.) (1990) *Kingship and the Kings*, London: Harwood

Hocart, A.M. ([1936] 1970) *Kings and Councillors: An Essay in the Comparative Anatomy of Human Society*, Chicago: University of Chicago Press

Raheja, G. (1988) 'India: Caste, Kingship and Domination Reconsidered', *Annual Review of Anthropology* 17: 497–523

Sahlins, M. (1985) 'The Stranger-King, or Dumézil among the Fijians', in M. Sahlins *Islands of History*, Chicago: University of Chicago Press

kinship

The study of kinship is so central to anthropology that Robin Fox has likened it to logic in philosophy, as 'the basic discipline of the subject' (1967: 10). This is hardly surprising, since it deals quite literally with matters of life and *death, not to mention *identity and *personhood, *honour and shame, control of *property, and †succession to positions of authority.

Despite the importance of these themes, anthropologists have never agreed on what kinship is, let alone how to deal with it. Their views on these matters are as varied, contested and multidimensional as human life itself, and †Needham's iconoclastic statement that there is 'no such thing as kinship' (1971: 5) was not meant to deny the significance of the topic, but rather to emphasize that like all such notions in comparative anthropology, kinship is not a clearly delimited 'thing' but an amorphous, polythetic concept (Barnard and Good 1984: 188–9). This lack of precise definition may even be liberating rather than restrictive, since it helps undermine the persistent delusion that the task of kinship studies is to isolate and analyse semi-algebraic kinship 'systems'. For any individual, kinship does not constitute a closed system, but an open-ended set of opportunities and constraints.

Kinship and biology

It is crucial to understand that kinship relationships are quite distinct from biological relationships. Kinship systems vary greatly, but as physiological processes are the same everywhere, these variations are clearly social rather than biological. There is more to it than this, however. It had long been conventional to distinguish social parents (†pater and †mater) from physiological ones (†genitor and †genetrix), but John Barnes (1961) introduced a further distinction between genitor and genetrix, the supposed biological parents of the child, and the genetic father and mother from whose sperm and ovum the child was actually produced. Like mater and pater, genetrix and genitor are socially-ascribed roles, assigned according to prevailing ideas about the biology of *conception, combined with assumptions about the sexual activities of possible parents. Of these three levels – social kinship, *emic views about physical kinship, and genetic relationship – social anthropology is concerned only with the first two. It deals not with biology itself, but with biological kinship as culturally defined by the society concerned.

Trobriand Islanders' views on paternity illustrate the need for Barnes's distinctions. *Malinowski (1932) reported their belief that a child's spirit entered its mother's body through her head and was nourished in her womb. Sexual intercourse was seen as a necessary preliminary to conception, but its sole function was the mechanical one of opening the vagina and providing space for the child to grow, so although Trobriand children presumably do have genetic parents, they have no genitors according to local dogma. Yet the role of pater is crucial, and for a woman to bear a child having no social father is highly dishonourable. Interestingly, Trobrianders were perfectly familiar with notions of biological paternity but denied their validity; in other words, this denial was ideological rather than an indication of their state of empirical knowledge. The same probably applies to many emic statements about biological kinship, even those purporting to be 'scientific' or factual.

Analytical levels

For heuristic purposes, kinship can be seen as having three coexisting aspects. (1) At the categorical level it comprises forms of nomenclature and *classification. These provide the conceptual framework whereby people experience and understand their environment. The *relationship terminology is the most obvious example in kinship, but *Aboriginal Australian section systems also qualify. (2) At the jural level, it includes the rules which affect people's kinship behaviour, covering everything from criminal laws to ideas about good manners. Jural rules are phrased in terms of the categories just mentioned, but whereas these categories are normally taken for granted, rules are explicit, subject to disagreement, and can be broken. (3) The behavioural level consists of what people actually do. It can be subdivided into collective behaviour, expressible statistically through such notions as *marriage or divorce rates; and individual practice, which depends upon the circumstances at the time. Practice is influenced by jural rules of course, but in a more complex way than is often assumed.

The three levels are far from congruent, and none fully determines the forms taken by the others. Consider choosing a spouse, for instance. In a few societies one finds *prescription, whereby the relationship terminology positively defines marriageable categories of relative. In these and many more societies, there are also jural preferences for people to marry particular relatives such as first cousins. This obligation is never absolute, however, and whether individuals actually make such marriages depends on the political, economic and emotional advantages of choosing an alternative spouse rather than the 'preferred' partner. Marriage choice is therefore not a matter of blindly obeying a rule: obedience is only one possible strategy, and although conformity often has advantages, these may be outweighed by other considerations.

This example shows that in order to comprehend kinship fully, all three levels must be taken into account. Many anthropological arguments about kinship arose because the protagonists failed to do this; having defined the problem at different levels, they proceeded to talk past each other. Nineteenth-century scholars emphasized jural aspects, partly because many – like *Morgan and †J.F. McLennan – were lawyers, but also because reports of local customs were the most accessible data for armchair theorists. Among later writers, *Radcliffe-Brown also saw kinship primarily in jural terms, as a means of allocating rights and responsibilities and regulating their transmission from one generation to the next, while *Lévi-Strauss dealt with it mainly as a means of classifying persons. This was not always clear in their writings however, because Radcliffe-Brown often discussed rules in language more appropriate to statistical behaviour, while Lévi-Strauss conflated the classification of relatives with rules of marriageability.

Approaches to kinship: (1) descent theory

Historically, there was a clear division between those who saw kinship as based upon *descent links between parents and children, and those who concentrated on *alliance relationships created by marriage. Radcliffe-Brown was foremost among those who saw kinship primarily in terms of descent (1950: 4). Along with other descent theorists like †Fortes and †Jack Goody, he drew a clear distinction between kin, relatives by descent, and †affines, relatives through marriage; hence his frequent use of the phrase 'kinship and marriage', implying that the latter was somehow external to the former. He further distinguished †agnates, persons descended from a common *ancestor through males only, from *cognates, descendants of a common ancestor or ancestress counting descent through both males and females.

Unilineal descent

Radcliffe-Brown classified kinship systems according to how descent was recognized. Two particularly distinctive forms are †patrilineal descent, reckoned through males only, and †matrilineal descent, reckoned only through females. These should not be confused with †patriarchy and †matriarchy, for in both cases official power resides primarily with men; under patriliny a child acquires social status primarily from its father, whereas under matriliny its mother's brother is the key figure (the *avunculate). Patrilineal descent is more common worldwide, perhaps because of the added complexities involved when men transmit rights to other men in the female line.

However, this kind of typology was criticized by †Edmund Leach (1961: 4) as 'butterfly-collecting'. The mere fact that two societies are labelled 'matrilineal' does not mean they have anything predictable in common. As no societies are wholly regulated by a single descent principle, they cannot be termed 'matrilineal' without specifying which social contexts are involved. †Rivers (1924: 85–8) long ago stressed the distinction between: descent proper, i.e. membership by birth of a particular group such as a lineage; †inheritance of property; and succession to a title or office. The latter processes are not necessarily governed by descent-based principles, and even when they are these do not always operate in a simple way. Succession to the British throne is basically patrilineal, for example, but a directly-descended female takes precedence over a collateral male; by contrast, succession to noble titles is purely patrilineal, so women cannot inherit under any circumstances. The possible permutations are almost endless.

Turning to descent in Rivers's strict sense, Fortes portrayed Tallensi society in Northern Ghana as entirely built around the †lineage system (1970: 34). Whether he is worshipping ancestors, arranging marriages, allocating work, or exerting judicial authority, a Tallensi man's rights and responsibilities are determined by his position in his patrilineage. So although lineage membership is determined by kinship criteria, its functions are economic and political. For this reason Fortes drew a distinction between †filiation and descent. Filiation stemmed from being the legitimate child of one's parents and was normally †bilateral, i.e. children were filiated to both parents. By contrast, jural status was determined by pedigree – descent from a particular ancestor. In patrilineal cases, a man had descent and filiation links on his father's side, but only filiation on his mother's side. Filiation was relevant only in domestic contexts, whereas descent was a politico-jural matter, though the fact that it was expressed in the vocabulary of kinship provided an ideological bridge between the two domains.

Unlike Radcliffe-Brown, then, Fortes saw descent as external to kinship proper, which he limited to the domestic domain. As for marriage, it was an ephemeral matter concerning only those directly involved, quite different from the enduring lineages on which Tallensi *social structure was based. Yet marriages did form a 'web of kinship', which held society together by transcending the social barriers between lineages (1970: 82). It was in this context, too, that Fortes employed his controversial notion of *complementary filiation.

Groups and categories

Is 'descent' best seen as an empirically-observable characteristic of real groups out there in society, or an emic ideology for making sense of social life? Barnes (1962) argues that despite their superficial similarities to Tallensi-style †segmentary lineages, local groupings in the New Guinea Highlands cannot be understood using theoretical models developed in Africa. Whereas lineage membership is irrevocably determined by birth for a Tallensi man, New Guinea communities are *ad hoc* groupings round charismatic *Big Men, based on individual choice. Many men do join their fathers' groups, but the all-embracing descent ideology so prevalent in Africa is absent.

Harold Scheffler (1966) draws an important distinction between descent groups composed of people related by †unilineal descent, and descent constructs, which are classificatory concepts used to help visualize one's society. It is quite common to find one in the absence of the other. Wherever sons inherit land from their fathers local males are likely to be related by patrilineal descent, yet as in New Guinea people may not think of their society in that way. Conversely, communities may be spoken of in lineage terms even when most people are not actually members (or spouses of members) of that lineage. This happens among the Nuer of the Sudan, whose villages contain many persons linked to the local lineage in other ways (†Evans-Pritchard 1951: 28). Local group composition may be very similar in societies with strong descent ideologies like the Nuer, and societies lacking such ideologies, as in New Guinea. The difference lies not in the residential pattern itself, but in how people think about it.

Approaches to kinship: (2) alliance theory

Descent theory made sense in some lineage-based African societies, but proved inappropriate for much of Australasia and the Americas, either for the reasons just discussed or because marriage alliance, far from being ephemeral, forms enduring patterns which persist over time. For example, marriage among the Kachin of Burma is †hypogamous, i.e. the bride's family is higher status than the groom's family (Leach 1961). It follows that marriage can only occur in one direction, and that any two lineages are in a wife-giver/wife-taker relationship which is just as persistent over time as the lineages themselves.

Alliance theory, which stresses marriage as a structural principle, is especially associated with †Dumont, Leach and Needham, but its pioneer was Lévi-Strauss (1969). He saw marriage as the other side of the coin from *incest prohibitions: both helped prevent local groups from becoming sexually self-sufficient, and so encouraged wider social cohesion. Although this conflation of incest rules and †exogamy is open to criticism, it is certainly true that marriage in some societies follows regular, enduring patterns. These 'elementary structures of kinship' therefore involve both positive and negative marriage rules, whereas complex structures only have negative rules. He identified three elementary structures, though others have argued that these can be reduced to two, symmetric and asymmetric *exchange.

Symmetric exchange

In the symmetric case, women from group A marry men from B, and conversely B's women marry A's

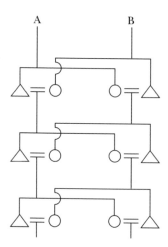

Figure 2 Bilateral cross-cousin marriage

men. Similar reciprocal marriages occur between C and D. Lévi-Strauss views this as a fairly rudimentary form of social cohesion, and terms it †restricted exchange because it seems to link only a few people. This need not actually be so, however, as B and C could also be linked symmetrically.

In the simplest case (Figure 2), where A and B are nuclear families, all marriages involve first cross-cousins. †Cross-cousins are the children of a brother and sister, whereas †parallel cousins are the children of two brothers or two sisters. This particular form is called bilateral cross-cousin marriage, because the spouses are related on both their fathers' sides (patrilaterally) and mothers' sides (matrilaterally).

Do not take such diagrams too literally, however! It is more realistic to envisage A and B as two large descent groups, containing hundreds or even thousands of people. First cousin marriage may be rare, and most marriages will involve second, third, or Nth cross-cousins. In the extreme case, that of *dual organization, A and B together make up the entire society. Finally, these units need not even be descent groups at all, and could just as easily be local groups such as villages.

Asymmetric exchange

Suppose A's women marry B's men, but B's women cannot marry A's men and must marry men from C instead. Similarly, C's women marry D's men, and so on. This entails a clear distinction between wife-givers and wife-takers, as with the Kachin.

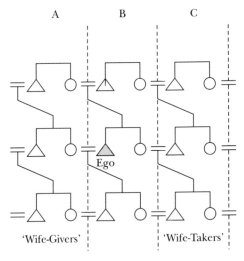

Figure 3 Matrilateral cross-cousin marriage

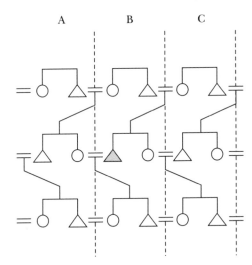

Figure 4 Patrilateral cross-cousin marriage

Lévi-Strauss calls this †generalized exchange, arguing (controversially) that it provides greater social cohesion than restricted exchange, and so permits more complex social systems to develop. If the exchange units are single families, as in Figure 3, every man marries his †matrilateral cross-cousin (MBD). The same caveat applies as before, however; in practice they are much larger groups, so most people do not marry actual first cousins.

Patrilateral cross-cousin marriage
Lévi-Strauss regards the converse case, where men marry their patrilateral cross-cousins (FZD), as a third distinct type in which exchanges reverse in each generation. But is this just an illusion fostered by Figure 4? As the real exchange units are much larger than single families, there can be no sharp distinction between generations. Even as the youngest people in one generation are marrying, so are the oldest of the next; at any given moment exchange is occurring in both directions, making the situation indistinguishable from symmetric exchange. Figure 4 cannot therefore be taken literally, though it is always possible that people may visualize their society in this way – as with descent, we should perhaps distinguish exchange groups from exchange constructs.

Approaches to kinship: (3) the cultural approach
Although some kin relationships, like those between 'in-laws', are seen as purely social, most

are felt to have a biological basis. †David Schneider found that Euro-Americans define relatives both in terms of common 'blood', and by the fact that they behave like relatives. In his memorable phrase, kinship involves both natural substance and code for conduct (1968: 29) – though *'natural' is itself a cultural notion, of course.

Fieldworkers adopting this approach are often led to examine emic ideas about the person. As Schneider found, personhood is commonly seen as constituted partly by kinship practices, and partly by genetics as locally understood. For example, Marriott and Inden (1977) argue that *South Asia is characterized by monistic thinking quite different from the mind-body dualisms of much Western thought. Every kin group, from caste to family, has its own specific 'code for conduct', yet this moral code is thought to take physical form, such as shared blood or substance. Group members must adhere to the codes regarding marriage and sexual intercourse, so that their personal identity will remain secure and their distinctive substance will be passed on to their offspring.

All group members broadly share this common substance, but there are also individual differences and fluctuations. Daniel (1984) shows that Tamils see the timing, location, and style of sexual intercourse as having auspicious or inauspicious implications for the well-being of a couple, and the gender, health, and fortune of their offspring.

Moreover, mere mixing of sexual fluids is not enough. To mix properly they must be compatible, and this is investigated by studying horoscopes before marriage. As social and physiological factors are dialectically related, a horoscope is simultaneously an account of one's social destiny, and a biopsy revealing the character of one's bodily substance. Incompatible sexual fluids produce unhealthy children, or none at all in extreme cases.

Such accounts are vital because they indicate the means whereby people represent their own actions to themselves and others, but they also have potential pitfalls. First, ethnographic evidence is rarely clearcut: some South Asians say that substance derives from semen and 'spirit' from uterine blood, but others say substance comes from both parents and spirit derives from the ether. Moreover, the sociology of such theories is complex; rival views are often current, and many people have no coherent theory at all. Second, somewhat ironically given the insistence on working through indigenous rather than Western concepts, there is a tendency to write individuals out of the script in favour of abstractions like 'Indian thought'. Third, it is often implicitly assumed that indigenous explanations have the same purpose as anthropological theories, namely, to provide abstract explanations of social phenomena. As the next section shows, this is far from the case.

Approaches to kinship: (4) kinship practice

Classic kinship writing emphasized jural rules, but conformity to such rules was usually seen as unproblematic and explanations were sought only when they were 'broken'. Yet obedience and disobedience are both matters of choice, so it is necessary to explain why some people adhere to the rules as well as why others ignore them. Even this takes too naive a view of the connection between rules and behaviour, however. In brief, rules do not direct (or fail to direct) behaviour; rather, they are used to interpret, explain or justify it.

The atemporal character of earlier approaches led to a downplaying of the strategic aspects of kinship behaviour. By contrast, †Bourdieu (1977) sees kinship as an open-ended set of †practices employed by individuals seeking to satisfy their material and symbolic interests. Thus, marriage choice is made in the light of one's social situation at the time, including the options available in the form of marriageable persons and the material and

symbolic capital to be gained by choosing each of them. One factor in this complex calculation is that by 'obeying the rules' one gains respect. However, such rules refer to official, publicly-acknowledged kinship entities – lineages and the like – rather than the practical kinship units called into existence for specific purposes. Whereas official kin generally come to the fore in celebrating marriages, many other kinds of practical, *ad hoc* kinship links may be involved in setting them up.

The major determinants of kinship behaviour, therefore, are not the explicit rules themselves but people's largely implicit knowledge about 'how things are done', i.e. about social practice. Explicit ideologies are manifestations rather than explanations of this practical knowledge, which Bourdieu terms †*habitus*. For these reasons, the study of rules alone yields a picture of kinship which is not only incomplete but also seriously misleading. For example, because anthropologists use *genealogies to depict 'real' relationships, they tend to forget that informants often use genealogical discourse in other ways, to support or justify particular activities and concerns.

Analyses of this kind can be criticized for reducing human motives to cynical attempts at maximizing personal, material advantage. But just as it is necessary to steer a middle course between descent theory and alliance theory, using insights from either as the situation demands it, so too this approach based on †praxis provides a necessary dynamic and inherently sociological counterweight to the somewhat asocial, atemporal insights provided by the study of emic theories of personhood.

Kinship and gender

The central place occupied by kinship in anthropological history has gone hand-in-hand with an emphasis on its socio-structural rather than domestic aspects. The *locus classicus* for the kinship ethnographer has been the public arena of lineage politics and ostentatious weddings, rather than the private one of the cooking hearth or vacuum cleaner. In small-scale societies, kinship – or at least the kinship metaphor – often encompasses politics, economics and religion too, making the resulting theoretical debates central to the discipline as a whole. This is in marked contrast to the status of the sociology of the *family as an empirical backwater. Yet the downplaying of *household and family relationships has undesirable consequences too; for example, kinship theorists are ill-equipped to say much of value about those intimate contexts to which kinship in urban, large-scale societies is increasingly confined. Above all, it leads to the major paradox that kinship studies have paid almost no attention to issues of *gender.

Most kinship writing has been thoroughly chauvinistic – a feature not wholly eradicated above because the terminology itself usually presumes the male viewpoint. To some degree this can be empirically justified by the fact that in many societies groups of men exchange women in marriage rather than the other way round, but this argument again privileges the public domain over the private. In any case, there is a world of difference between consciously assuming the male perspective in order to depict events as male participants see them, and doing so unthinkingly, which was what normally happened in the past. The problem was not that ethnographers mis-represented indigenous views, but that they represented only one such viewpoint, that of men.

Howell and Melhuus (1993) argue that such distortions were inevitably exposed once the focus of interest shifted from the first two approaches outlined above to the second two. There are self-evidently at least two kinds of person in every society, male persons and female persons. Similarly, when ethnographers look at kinship practices rather than social structure, they frequently discover that whereas 'official kin' are indeed predominantly male, 'practical kin' are far more likely to be female. It may seem bizarre that it has taken so long for kinship studies to take gender relations fully into account, but at least there is no longer any excuse for not doing so.

Reproductive technology and future kinship

This article began with the premise that biolog-ical facts are universal and unchangeable, yet the *reproductive technologies now available have the potential to bring about previously unimaginable changes in kinship. Two particular areas of interest are the changing patterns of rights and obligations involved; and the possible redefinition of kinship relations themselves. Even that (as culturally defined) most natural of all notions, motherhood, is called into question by the emergence of previously unknown statuses like 'egg-donor' or 'surrogate mother', while genetic fingerprinting, which allows paternity to be unambiguously established, may lead to conflation of the roles of

'genitor' and 'genetic father'. A new kinship entity has also made its appearance, with distinctive rights and a legal personality – the embryo. Even more basically, ideas about 'nature' itself, which have always been fundamental to cultural notions of kinship, seem bound to change (Strathern 1992).

ANTHONY GOOD

See also: age, alliance, ancestors, avunculate, *compadrazgo*, complementary filiation, componential analysis, conception, Crow–Omaha systems, descent, dual organization, family, genealogical method, gender, house, household, incest, joking and avoidance, marriage, preference and prescription, relationship terminology, reproductive technologies, socialization, sociobiology

Further reading

Barnard, A.J. and A. Good (1984) *Research Practices in the Study of Kinship*, London: Academic Press

Barnes, J.A. (1961) 'Physical and Social Kinship', *Philosophy of Sciences* 28: 296

—— (1962) 'African Models in the New Guinea Highlands', *Man* 1962: 5–9

Bourdieu, P. (1977) *Outline of a Theory of Practice*, Cambridge: Cambridge University Press

Daniel, E.V. (1984) *Fluid Signs: Being a Person the Tamil Way*, Berkeley: University of California Press

Dumont, L. (1971) *Introduction à Deux Theories d'Anthropologie sociale*, Paris/The Hague: Mouton

Evans-Pritchard, E.E. (1951) *Kinship and Marriage Among the Nuer*, Oxford: Clarendon Press

Fortes, M. (1970) *Time and Social Structure, and Other Essays*, London: Athlone Press

Fox, R. (1967) *Kinship and Marriage*, Harmondsworth: Penguin Books

Howell, S. and M. Melhuus (1993) 'The Study of Kinship; The Study of Person; A Study of Gender?', in T. del Valle (ed.) *Gendered Anthropology*, London: Routledge

Leach, E.R. (1961) *Rethinking Anthropology*, London: Athlone Press

Lévi-Strauss, C. (1969 [1949]) *The Elementary Structures of Kinship*, (2nd edn) London: Eyre & Spottiswoode

Malinowski, B. (1932) *The Sexual Life of Savages in North-Western Melanesia*, London: Routledge & Sons

Marriott, McK. and R.B. Inden (1977) 'Towards an Ethnosociology of South Asian Caste Systems', in K. David (ed.) *The New Wind: Changing Identities in South Asia*, Paris/The Hague: Mouton

Needham, R. (1971) 'Remarks on the Analysis of Kinship and Marriage', in R. Needham (ed.) *Rethinking Kinship and Marriage*, London: Tavistock Press

Radcliffe-Brown, A.R. (1950) 'Introduction', in A.R. Radcliffe-Brown and D. Forde (eds) *African Systems of Kinship and Marriage*, Oxford: Oxford University Press

The Kula Ring
Standard English names in parentheses

Rivers, W.H.R. (1924) *Social Organization*, London: Kegan Paul, Trench, and Trubner

Scheffler, H.W. (1966) 'Ancestor Worship in Anthropology: or, Observations on Descent and Descent Groups', *Current Anthropology* 7: 541–51

Schneider, D.M. (1968) *American Kinship: A Cultural Account*, Englewood Cliffs, NJ: Prentice-Hall

—— (1984) *A Critique of the Study of Kinship*, Ann Arbor: University of Michigan Press

Strathern, M. (1992) *Reproducing the Future: Essays on Anthropology, Kinship and the New Reproductive Technologies*, Manchester: Manchester University Press

kula

The *kula* system is an exchange system in †Melanesia. In *kula* people rank themselves by exchanging two sets of shell valuables, counter-clockwise circulating *mwal* and clockwise circulating *bagi*, through a circle of island cultures in Southeastern Papua New Guinea. The institution has been central to twentieth-century anthropological theories about *society, 'primitive' and 'modern,' 'non-Western' and 'Western,' 'reciprocity-based' versus 'market-based' and †'gift' versus †'commodity'.

Although partially described by late nineteenth and early twentieth-century observers, *Bronislaw Malinowski carved it into the anthropological imagination with *Argonauts of the Western Pacific* (1922), a monograph written to shatter existing theories and stereotypes and reformulate what then existed of anthropological *methodology. †Marcel Mauss immediately reinterpreted Malinowski's data in *The Gift* (1990; *Essai sur le don* [1924]). Both works appeared as anthropology was becoming professionalized and at a time when Western intellectuals were forced to re-examine certainties eclipsed by the horrors of World War I. The *kula*'s eminence derives partly from the role it played in both processes. Although Malinowski thought he was describing something unique, Mauss discussed similar institutions through time and space. Together these two fashioned *kula*, along side the *potlatch, as the ethnographic prototype for theories about †reciprocity. Malinowski inspired much of *British anthropology's *functionalism. Mauss's reinterpretation launched *Lévi-Strauss's *structuralism and *exchange theory. Although the *ethnography was reworked (e.g. Uberoi 1962), theoretical constructs built from Malinowski, Mauss and Lévi-Strauss lasted into the 1970s (Ekeh 1974) when new *kula* data played a role in redefining these theories.

The Trobriand Islands provided the setting for Malinowski's description. 'Kula' is a Trobriand word. In nearby islands cognates are *kun, kune*, and related practices called *niune* (Young 1985). These words may be used as nouns, noun classifiers for counting *kula* valuables, and as verbs encompassing activities epitomized by the shell exchanges.

Many consequences follow from *kula* activity. These run from distributing different products among ecologically and socially diverse islands to warfare, witchcraft, and murder. Yet, the institution's expressed purpose is to create a person's 'name' or 'fame,' this being realized by the exchange of the two sets of ranked objects along a 'road' or line of people.

A thousand or more of each valuable move in two waves. It may take four or five years for a crest to circle the course, but every year smaller numbers of valuables precede and follow each crest. Although actors describe *kula* as circular, some valuables continue to leak out of the system and others are traded into neighbouring cultures. Hence the fashioning of new ones.

Although exchange rules vary among the islands, the basics are simple. When one person gives a *mwal* to another, the recipient must return a commensurately sized *bagi*. The return ends the relationship created by the initial object. Since the desired name or fame derives from relationships, actors struggle to transcend basic exchange rules. They do this by returning valuables of different sizes, returning more than they owe, or delaying returns for as long as possible. These strategies become very complex. The simple going and coming of a few valuables defines younger participants' ties. Experienced actors, however, embed themselves in networks as tangled by new links as they are by redefined older ones.

To create a successful *kula* relationship people build other productive and exchange relationships, ultimately tying together an area's ecological and social diversity. Eventually a whole community flows into a successful *person. Consequently, all exchanges are public. As the most important form of wealth in these societies, *kula* valuables and their paths are visible signs of persons understood in relation to multiple others.

The exchange items have distinctive appearances and meanings. *Mwal* are cut from the broad end of a conus shell (*Conus leopardus*). Natural spots are polished off new ones until they are white. *Bagi* are made from small red pieces of shells (*Chama (pacifica) imbricata*) strung through locally produced string and ground to a round glassy texture. New necklaces approach a metre in length, individual shell pieces several centimetres in diameter. People rank the valuables, the highest being more decorated and carefully handled than the lowest. Makers or first owners name all but the lowest ranked. Successful traders name children with the highest. *Kula* articles are personified. The smallest are likened to irresponsible youths whose ties rarely endure, the largest to mature, wise elders who move only in well defined paths. Most islanders assert that *mwal* are male, *bagi* female. The completed exchange of one for the other is likened to marriage. Marriage varies among the islands, but everywhere it organizes male and female labours. Personified *kula* valuables and relationships draw from ideas about marriage, for *kula* too is a (if not the) major productive activity.

Why and how one valuable has to be returned for its complement is the *kula*'s major analytical problem. Theories of reciprocity provided one answer. New research contributed others through the discovery of the *kitoum* concept, another way of classing the objects (see essays in Leach and Leach 1983, and Weiner 1992). *Kitoum*, or close cognates, mediate the *mwal/bagi* distinction since both can be equated to it, though not to each other. Further, they facilitate reciprocal conversions among products, persons and *kula* articles.

Excepting Rossel Islanders, the traditional *bagi* makers, all *kula* people speak Austronesian languages. These language speakers arrived in the region two to three thousand years ago coincident with the expansion of Austronesian populations into *Polynesia. Long-distance trade was a characteristic of such peoples, but when *kula* started is not known. European expansion simplified indigenous cultures. Although late twentieth-century *kula* remains a leading passion, its underlying conditions have changed significantly since 1900 and earlier.

FREDERICK H. DAMON

See **also:** economic anthropology, exchange, Malinowski, Pacific: Melanesia

Further reading

Ekeh, Peter (1974) *Social Exchange Theory: The Two Traditions*, Cambridge, MA: Harvard University Press

Gregory, Christopher (1982) *Gifts and Commodities*, London: Academic Press

Leach, J.W. and E.R. Leach (1983) *The Kula: New Perspectives on Massim Exchange*, Cambridge: Cambridge University Press

Macintyre, Martha (1983) *The Kula: A Bibliography*, Cambridge: Cambridge University Press.

—— (1989) 'Better Homes and Gardens', in Martha Macintyre and Margaret Jolly, *Family and Gender in the Pacific*, Cambridge: Cambridge University Press: 156–69

Malinowski, Bronislaw (1922) *Argonauts of the Western Pacific*, London: Routledge and Kegan Paul

Mauss, Marcel (1924) 'Essai sur le don', *L'Année Sociologique* (n.s.) (1): 30–186

Munn, Nancy (1986) *The Fame of Gawa*, Cambridge: Cambridge University Press

Uberoi, J.P.S. (1962) *The Politics of the Kula Ring*, Manchester: Manchester University Press

Weiner, Annette (1992) *Inalienable Possessions*, Berkeley: University of California Press

Young, Michael (1985) 'Abutu in Kalauna: A Retrospect', *Mankind* 15 (2): 184–97

L

land tenure

Because of the importance of land for the liveli-hood of the peoples among whom anthropologists have traditionally worked, the ways in which it is held, by persons and by groups, have long been an important subject of enquiry. Well before the end of the *colonial period the study of non-Western forms of land tenure had begun to escape the confines of Western ideological debate that emphasized a stark contrast between 'individualist' and 'communal' systems. Besides being an area of considerable theoretical interest, for a long time this was one of the most important areas of work in †applied anthropology. It has been less promi-nent in the postcolonial period, but remains a topic of great importance for *economic anthro-pology and *development.

Nineteenth-century attempts to understand non-Western land tenure, notably those of British administrators in *South Asia, typically proceeded either in terms of familiar European ideas of ownership (such as the pattern of private owner-ship established by English landlords in Ireland), or their presumed antithesis, communal owner-ship. This dichotomy remains powerful in Western thought, and receives one of its strongest formu-lations in the *Marxist account of the evolution from *primitive communism to progressively more exclusive forms of private property.

Twentieth-century anthropologists who base their accounts on prolonged *fieldwork have painted a more complex picture. Much of this work was carried out for practical purposes, in the spirit of †'indirect rule', but it was also designed to faciliate a transition to cash-cropping and the commercialization of land (Meek 1946). Colonial peoples (or at least some of them) were to be allowed to 'hold' their land in 'traditional' ways. In practice this required all kinds of intervention that altered previous practice, sometimes dramat-ically. For disputes to be settled, the authorities needed to work out a full legalistic understanding of 'traditional land tenure', and anthropologists helped to construct this hypostatized tradition. The importance of land tenure for anthropology was clearly recognized by *Malinowski, who insisted on the need to transcend the legal stand-point. He defined land tenure as 'a relation of human beings, individuals and groups, to the soil they cultivate and use' (1936: 376). Distinguishing between narrower and broader senses of the term, he advocated a broad approach in which investi-gation of how people related to the soil would reveal all the 'invisible facts' on which tribal society was founded. Numerous later students of agrarian societies attempted to follow this advice: for example, John Davis argued in the very different context of a small town in southern Italy that 'Rules about land, how it is allocated to different purposes, how it is distributed within the popula-tion, and how it is then transmitted reveal the basic structure of Pisticci society' (1973: 162).

This stance is best demonstrated in a large number of tribal ethnographies, particularly in Africa, where rights to use land were shown to form part of a series of reciprocal duties and obligations between subjects and their political superiors. The most elegant theoretical formula-tion was that of †Gluckman (e.g. 1965), who explained land tenure among peoples such as the Lozi in terms of 'hierarchies of estates of admin-istration'. The number of such estates would depend on the complexity of the group, but typically a *king or paramount †chief would be the 'ultimate owner' of all the land; he would delegate to village headmen the responsibility for allocating sufficient land to *household heads, who might in turn allocate plots to individual wives. What Gluckman termed the 'estate of production' was generally farmed in an individualized way (though for many purposes individuals combined to form co-operating groups). Individuals could not alienate the land: any land not required for cultivation would revert up to the next level of the hierarchy for potential reallocation. Such a system of 'serial' rights was neither communal nor individualist as these terms are normally used in Western ideologies.

Gluckman developed this schema as a general model, but it clearly works better in some cases than others. Lozi cultivators may have depended on their headman for plot allocation, but in other groups where land was more plentiful it may be misleading to imply any process of allocation: people such as the Bemba, studied by †Audrey Richards, seem to have had considerable freedom in the selection of their sites. Yet it can still be argued that Bemba subjects held land in virtue of their general social and political status, and again there was no freedom to alienate. The usefulness of Gluckman's schema extends similarly to †acephalous societies where, in the absence of a central ruler, rights over land revert up to the groups as a whole. This model is confirmed in †J. Goody's analysis (1980) of conflicts over land in Northern Ghana, when members of an acephalous society reacted strongly to attempts to convert collectively – held land to a modern form of private ownership. But it is equally confirmed in the well documented attempts to promote the communal use of land in the name of 'African socialism'. The 'collectivist' element in traditional land tenure systems did not mean communal use of the land; when the policies of post-colonial governments, such as *ujamaa* in Tanzania, failed to recognize this, they encountered *resistance among farmers and most such schemes were costly failures.

Rights over land are not equally important in all societies. Some *hunting and *pastoralist peoples attach greater importance to rights over animals than to rights over specific territories. But even groups that are otherwise disengaged from property frequently acknowledge not only general territorial rights but also more specific rights, such as access to scarce water-holes. However, to the extent that such rights are shared by all members of the group, land tenure practices among some hunting and gathering peoples lend support to the theory of primitive communism.

Land is often considered, for example, by substantivist economic anthropologists, as one of the last resources to be transformed in the course of *capitalist commoditization processes. However, even the market in land is apparently active and commoditization complete, it generally remains the focus of strong loyalties and sentiment among family farmers. And of course, ownership rights are never in fact absolute: they remain subject to social and political constraint in all societies, as is regularly demonstrated in controversies concerning road-building schemes, or the rights of *Gypsy travellers to occupy 'private property'. It is interesting in this context to examine the ex-socialist countries as they abandon their collectivized systems of land tenure. Caroline Humphrey (1983) has provided an ingenious application of Gluckman's model to the hierarchy of a Soviet collective farm. Just as this differed in its working from the ideal type of communal farming, so the new systems of land tenure, whatever the rhetoric used to promote them, will not in fact be based on individuals and absolute private ownership. Rather, it is likely that families will be reaffirmed as the main unit of production, but many kinds of cooperative links will remain important, and the operation of farms and the use and transmission of the land will be closely regulated by various levels of political authority.

This remains a field of importance for applied anthropology at various levels. It is insufficient to rely upon the technical data provided by other disciplines in seeking the optimum forms of land tenure for particular crops in particular environments: anthropological exploration of past local practices and †indigenous knowledge can ensure smoother adjustments when changes are introduced. The establishment of the main features of a 'traditional' land tenure system has been a vital part of political strategy in the defence of †indigenous peoples: for example in Australia, where *Aboriginal groups have been threatened by the exploitation of mineral wealth on their territories, anthropological expertise has sometimes assisted groups to work out more satisfactory compromises in such situations. Land reform projects have attracted anthropological attention in many parts of the world, and it is at least arguable that many projects might have had greater success in achieving the aims of greater equity and greater efficiency in land use patterns had more anthropologists been involved in the actual implementation of reform packages. Gradually this point has been recognized by agencies such as the World Bank, and anthropologists are now regularly involved in rural resettlement schemes. However, involvement in land disputes can also raise serious ethical and political dilemmas for the discipline (see e.g. Whiteley and Aberle 1989). In contexts of increasing threats to natural and human environments, anthropological interest in the management of common-property resources seems sure to increase (see McCay and Acheson 1987). The question of how land tenure principles relate to general development aspirations as well as to conservation is a vital one almost everywhere. In promoting a better understanding of these relationships, anthropologists may be able to contribute to informed decision – taking, not just by bureaucrats and politicians but also by the ordinary people most directly concerned.

C.M. HANN

See also: property, development, primitive communism

Further reading

Davis, J. (1973) *Land and Family in Pisticci*, London: Athlone
Gluckman, M. (1965) *The Ideas in Barotse Jurisprudence*, New Haven: Yale University Press
Goody, J.R. (1980) 'Rice-burning and the Green Revolution in Northern Ghana', *Journal of Development Studies* 16 (2): 136–55
Humphrey, C. (1983) *Karl Marx Collective: Economy, Society and Religion on a Siberian Collective Farm*, Cambridge: Cambridge University Press
McCay, B.M. and J.M. Acheson (eds) (1987) *The Question of the Commons: The Culture and Ecology of Communal Resources*, Tucson: University of Arizona Press
Malinowski, B. (1936) *Coral Gardens and Their Magic (Vol. 1)*, London: Allen and Unwin
Meek, C.K. (1946) *Land Law and Custom in the Colonies*, London: Geoffrey Cumberlege, Oxford University Press
Whiteley, P.M. and D.F. Aberle (1989) 'Can Anthropologists be Neutral in Land Disputes? The Hopi-Navajo Case', *Man* 24 (2) :340–4 (Correspondence)

landscape

Anthropologists have been slow to appreciate the potential of landscape studies. They have tended to think of landscape either in terms of 'landform' – something already in place – or 'land-use', whereby something is done to the land. Either way, the land is thought of as neutral and passive. It is only since the 1980s that anthropologists have begun to recognize the way in which people's perceptions of their world and their material engagement with it are intimately bound together and are creative of, as well as created by, the landscape. Such an approach makes it clear that the separation of *'nature' from 'culture' and the passive role given to 'nature' form part of a quite specific Western 'viewpoint'. This alternative way of thinking about landscape owes much to the work of literary critics, cultural geographers, historians, sociologists, philosophers, and novelists.

There is, however, one area of the world where there has been a longer anthropological commitment to landscape, and this is Australia. It could be argued that the total intermeshing of Aboriginal †sociality and landscape more or less forced anthropologists to think more creatively about the meaning of landscape. Thus, for example, Aboriginal birch-bark and sand paintings provide important insights into the †polysemic nature of landscape – the way in which it works simultaneously at a number of levels. The representation of landscape is at one and the same time a topographic map, a cosmological exegesis, a 'clanscape', and a ritual and political landscape. Moreover, people differentiated by *age and *gender will have different understandings of the land, and some will be empowered by their knowledge of sacred sites and associated rituals. These landscapes, which appear timeless and unchanging, are, in fact, constantly renegotiated, as government agencies have found to their cost in land-claim battles.

Outside of anthropology, landscape studies have moved in several different directions. Already in the 1950s Hoskins explored landscapes as palimpsests, and showed how, in a British context, a history of occupation and land-use materializes in the shape of a hedge or the angle of a road. 'One could write a book about every few square inches [of the ordnance survey map]. It is like a painting by Brueghel or a major symphony' (Hoskins 1985: 3). Alternatively, †Raymond Williams's seminal *The Country and the City* explored 'structures of feeling' in the context of English literature and analysed the way in which people's engagements with the landscape were, and are, rooted in historically constituted social relations. Again, at any given time and place, people's attitudes will vary according to who they are and how they are placed. Williams noted that while Jane Austen, William Cobbett and Gilbert White all lived in the same area at the same time, they percieved the land in very different ways. †Edward

Said (1993) took the analysis of *Mansfield Park* a stage further and explored the wider context of *colonial exploitation. Not only are people differently placed, but, as Naipaul showed brilliantly in his novel *The Enigma of Arrival*, the same person may hold many and often contradictory and changing notions of the world.

Geographers and sociologists have also worked on the †hermeneutics of landscape: the way in which people's understanding of who they are is created – and negotiated and subverted – by spatial constraints. †Bourdieu's classic study of the Berber *house created a gendered world of social relations; while Giddens has explored movement – the intersection of time and place – at the level of the locale and the larger region, and also worked with †Goffman's notion of backstage and frontstage, private space and public space (Bourdieu 1990; Giddens 1985). Recently, *archaeologists have mapped the increasing constraint on movement and vision within the Neolithic and later Bronze Age landscapes and monuments of southern Britain (Barrett 1994).

Many of these studies have focused on the engagement with landscape in the Western world. Thus, for example, Cosgrove and Daniels (1988) concentrate on a Western iconography of landscape that, from the sixteenth through to the nineteenth century, moved from landscape as a particular form of painting, to landscape as a class-defined way of seeing – an ego-centred, perspectival, patrician gaze – and then to the active creation of landscaped parks and gardens. The Western 'gaze' also formed part of the colonial enterprise, and both the iconography of maps and the variable guises of Orientalism have recently been deconstructed.

In recent years anthropologists have not only extended discussions of the 'imperial eye', including the accounts by explorers of what they 'saw' in Africa or South America, but have also used landscape studies to map the politics of unequal encounter. Moreover, in many contemporary contexts, both Western and non-Western, the 'imperial eye' transmutes into the 'tourist gaze' and the politics of 'heritage'.

Anthropologists have also begun to explore in greater depth non-Western ways of seeing and being in the landscape (Bender 1993; Hirsch and O'Hanlon 1995). Landscape, too, has finally begun to be gendered.

Landscape is never passive. People engage with it, rework it, appropriate and contest it. It is part of the way in which identities are created and disputed, whether as individual, group or nation-state. Operating at the juncture of history and politics, social relations and cultural perceptions, landscape is a concept of high tension. It is also an area of study that forces the abandonment of conventional disciplinary boundaries and creates the potential for innovative cross-fertilization.

BARBARA BENDER

See also: archeology, house, time and space

Further reading

Barrett, J. (1994) *Fragments from Antiquity*, Oxford: Blackwell

Bender, B. (ed.) (1993) *Landscape: Politics and Perspectives*, Oxford: Berg

Bourdieu, P. ([1971] 1990) The Berber House or the World Reversed, in *The Logic of Practice*, Oxford: Polity

Cosgrove, D. and S. Daniels (eds) (1988) *The Iconography of Landscape*, Cambridge: Cambridge University Press

Giddens, A. (1985) 'Time, Space and Regionalisation', in D. Gregory and J. Urry (eds) *Social Relations and Spatial Structures*, London: Macmillan

Hirsch, E. and M. O'Hanlon (eds) (1995) *The Anthropology of Landscape*, Oxford: Oxford University Press

Hoskins, W.G. (1985) *The Making of the English Landscape*, Harmondsworth: Penguin

Naipaul, V.S. (1987) *The Enigma of Arrival*, Harmondsworth: Penguin

Pratt, M.L. (1992) *Imperial Eyes*, London: Routledge

Said, E. (1993) *Culture and Imperialism*, London: Vintage

Tilley, C. (1994) *A Phenomenology of Landscape*, Oxford: Berg

Williams, R. (1973) *The Country and the City*, London: Chatto & Windus

Wood, D. (1993) *The Power of Maps*, London: Routledge

language and linguistics

What is language?

Language usually refers to the human system of units of sound (†phonemes) compounded into words, in turn combined through grammatical rules (syntactically) to form a mode of communication that may be realized in both speech and writing. †Saussure suggested that linguistics, the study of language in this narrow sense, was part of a wider field of investigation of signs and signification in general which he called †'semiology'. A notable instance of the application of a semiological perspective is *Lévi-Strauss's analysis of *mythology, though terms such as 'grammar' of myth, or of clothing, should be understood as analogies with language in the narrow sense, and do not mean that all human sign systems necessarily share common principles of organization.

Many anthropologists have adopted this broad view, studying all the channels and modes of communication that humans use to organize and convey meaning, including paralinguistic features such as gesture, facial expression, tone of voice and so on. It has the advantage of revealing the controversy over whether other animals have language as, in many respects, misplaced. Detailed studies of bees, birds, apes and dolphins, among many others, have conclusively demonstrated that they have very complex systems of intra-species communication which, with considerable difficulty, can be decoded by human observers. That cross-species communication, not least between humans and other animals, also occurs will be confirmed by anyone familiar with domesticated beasts. Apes, certainly, dogs and horses, up to a point, cats and sheep, barely, can all be trained to interact quite meaningfully with human beings, and to an extent vice versa (i.e. with convergence on a mutually satisfactory channel and style of communication). Nonetheless, experiments with primates reveal that the faculty for language narrowly defined seems to be confined to humans: it is a species-specific characteristic.

All human groups have a language in the narrow sense, and each of the many thousands of languages can, eventually, be learned and understood by speakers of other languages. Although, therefore, anthropologists take a broad view of communication, they share with linguists the perception that human language is sufficiently distinct, complex and wide-ranging to require understanding in its own right. This does not mean that anthropologists and linguists agree on what constitutes the nature of language and how it should be studied.

Anthropologists versus linguists

Linguists sometimes complain that other academics treat their subject as if it were a social rather than a cognitive science. Like most disciplines linguistics is very diverse, but the transformational revolution associated with †Chomsky led to acceptance of a view of language as an abstract system, which for theoretical and practical reasons may be studied in isolation from its social and cultural context. For Chomsky, the core subject matter is grammar, and the universal human ability to generate and understand grammatical utterances: linguistic competence. Chomsky has remarked

that other disciplines are 'presumably concerned not with grammars ... but rather with concepts of a different sort, among them, perhaps, 'language', if such a notion can become an object of serious study' (1979: 190).

This conception of an 'autonomous linguistics', as it is sometimes called, poses fundamental problems for anthropologists, and indeed some linguists, who believe that the cognitivist emphasis marginalizes language's role in human communication. A similar point had been made much earlier against Saussure, when, in the 1930s, *Malinowski, like the Soviet linguist Voloshinov, expressed serious reservations about the distinction between †langue (the abstract linguistic system) and †parole (actual speech). Since the 1960s, one of Chomsky's most vociferous opponents has been the linguistic anthropologist Hymes (e.g. 1977). In the USA, there was a long and fruitful association between pre-Chomskyan linguists and anthropologists working in the tradition of *Boas, †Kluckhohn, †Kroeber and †Sapir, who attached considerable importance to the study of language. Hymes sought to reaffirm that tradition, and rescue the study of language from the transformationalists.

There are four main points on which Hymes diverges from Chomsky: speech (or *parole*) is accorded priority over grammar (or *langue*); competence is redefined to mean communicative competence in general, and treated as a behavioural rather than a cognitive phenomenon; universal forms of speech and language must be discovered by research in specific cultures and in cross-cultural comparison, not assumed in advance; and, crucially, language must be investigated in its social and cultural context. There is a very substantial body of work in anthropology and other disciplines which explicitly or implicitly shares these and similar assumptions. It includes, for example, research on *class, both historically and in contemporary, especially urban, society; on *education, *ethnicity, *gender relations, *law, *literacy, *politics; and on the language of and in literature, both written literature and *oral literature.

Language in context

Social linguistics, as it may be called, is by no means a uniform field, theoretically or methodologically: *functionalism, *structuralism, *Marxism (structural and other), feminism and not least *postmodernism have all shaped how social scientists and others have conceptualized the relationship between *culture, *society and language. American linguistic anthropology illustrates one influential approach.

In the 1940s, the dominant issue was the relationship between language and world view. The abandonment of the so-called *Sapir-Whorf hypothesis, that the structure of a language determined our conceptualization of the world, led to a period in which folk categories and taxonomies and their organization became a distinct specialism. How different cultures classify flora and fauna (ethnobotany, ethnozoology, *ethnoscience generally) yields rich data with practical implications for rural *development programmes needing to take into account †indigenous technical and environmental knowledge (Posey 1984). Folk linguistics (how people talk about their own language and speech) has also attracted attention. Stross (1974), discussing what he calls the 'metalinguistics' of speakers of the Tzeltal language of Chiapas Province, Mexico, identifies a key term, *k'op*, which may roughly be glossed as 'speech'. He lists 416 phrases in which *k'op* is modified to refer to various kinds of speech, speaker, or styles of speaking: *bolobem k'op*, 'drunken talk'; *pawor k'op*, 'asking a favour'; *niwak k'op*, 'speech of adults', and so on. This extensive lexicon reflects the propensity to evaluate people by reference to their speech styles. Tzeltzal themselves divide *k'op* into two main categories: 'recent speech' and 'traditional speech', which also includes prayers, flute music and drum sounds. Both have their own highly valued style: *rason k'op*, eloquent, sensible, slow and deliberate, associated with old men; and *ʔista k'op*, humorous speech used by 'clever and witty younger men'.

In the early 1960s, seeking to go beyond uncovering indigenous systems of classification and develop a more dynamic approach to language as social process, Hymes suggested that attention should be focused on 'ways of speaking'. This idea generated a great deal of research (of which Stross's work may be considered part) under the broad heading of the 'ethnography of speaking' or 'communication'. In this approach, speech is treated as the property of persons and social groups. People who share ways of speaking (i.e. who have a common set of linguistic practices) are said to be members of the same †speech community. This is not the same as a society within which there are likely to be numerous speech communities. The totality of languages or linguistic varieties in a society, or those available to an individual speaker, constitute the verbal or linguistic repertoire. At the micro-level are †speech events, activities involving verbal exchanges which participants may well recognize as distinct, and duly label: a funeral oration, a diagnosis by a physician. Speech events are in turn composed of †speech acts: greeting, explaining, apologizing, commiserating etc. This definition is similar to that found in a separate field of 'speech act theory', associated with linguistic philosophers such as Austin, Grice and Searle.

The *ethnography of speaking is important because it emphasizes language in use, and locates that use within a social and cultural context. Its approach also forces attention on higher order linguistic practices (i.e. above the level of the phrase). In linguistics, these are what constitute *discourse though that term has a number of other meanings. Discourse includes conversation, and for anthropologists, it is axiomatic that all conversation is culturally embedded, and only understandable through what Moerman (1988) calls 'culturally contexted' investigation. Many linguists say they accept this, but in practice ignore its implications. What those implications are becomes apparent if we consider what participants in a verbal exchange require to know in order to understand the meaning of references to persons. The answer is cultural knowledge, and the anthropological understanding of such exchanges demands ethnography. This is illustrated in Moerman's analysis of conversation in Thai, showing just how much background information may be crammed into a single utterance whose significance can only be revealed by a complex process of cultural unpacking. Moerman demonstrates this in a chapter entitled 'Society in a Grain of Rice' where he discusses a conversation with a Thai District Officer on a village visit. Overtly it is about arrangements for supplies, hence the rice; more subtly it is about ethnicity and bureaucracy. Moerman claims that conversation analysis is doubly important for anthropology: *methodologically because most *fieldwork is talk, and theoretically since culture 'gets done' in and through conversation. He therefore criticizes anthropologists such as †Geertz whose interpretation of cultural symbols, he says, deals with concepts as category labels, omitting the practices through which symbols are given meaning. †'Thick description' must, so to speak, be grounded in thick, interactive, data.

Language and social differentiation

Contextualization, then, is crucial. So is linguistic heterogeneity. In most societies there co-exist different languages and †dialects, and different modes of speaking which linguists call 'registers', 'styles', or 'codes'. These languages and modes of speaking are often hierarchically ordered and their speakers of unequal status, power and authority. This is common in modern nation-states with their 'standard' languages, but also occurs in traditional societies. Contextualizing language means understanding heterogeneity in terms of social differentiation at large.

The 'sociology of language', pioneered by Fishman, Haugen and Ferguson, has specialized in analysing linguistic differentiation within the nation-state. Ferguson (1959) devised the term †'diglossia' for situations where two varieties of a language (e.g. a standard language and a dialect) are spoken by members of the same community, with each variety having its own function and situationally defined range of usage. One variety he termed 'H(igh)', the other 'L(ow)' by reference to the generally perceived status of the variety's functions. For example the H language might be used for education, the L for family conversation. Diglossia is therefore associated with a division of social life into sets of institutions or activities (domains) in which, generally, one language (say the H variety) is expected or appropriate or obligatory.

Mapping the domains of language use is, of course, important, but analysis must do more than summarize the results of statistical investigations showing that the H language tends to be spoken in this context, the L language in another. There are invariably social and political reasons for the restriction of the L language to a limited range of domains, and there is need for a 'political economy' of language to understand how and why such restriction occurs. One approach is to see it as an effect of processes of nation-state formation which create powerful centres or 'cores', with subordinate, dependent, peripheral regions. This has the danger that language may be construed only as an epiphenomenon of economic processes of marginalization, whereas culture may be crucial in the creation and experience of dependency. Writers on 'Occitanie', the region of southern France in which the Langue d'Oc was historically spoken, see the way in which that region came under the economic and political hegemony of a French-speaking centre as fundamentally entailing a cultural, and hence linguistic, imperialism. This perspective is widely shared by proponents of minority or subordinate languages, not least in the Third World. The novels and critical essays of the Kenyan writer, Ngugi wa Thiongo, for example, respond extensively to the cultural and linguistic effects of *colonialism and neo-colonialism.

Macroscopic perspectives of this kind, however, need to be complemented by micro-level studies which show how people handle diglossia in their daily lives. By contrast with sociolinguists such as Labov and Trudgill, who seek statistical correlations between linguistic features (often phonological) and their use by specific social groups, the work of Gumperz provides just such a dynamic, interactional view. An account of a small commercial and industrial town in northern Norway, where a dialect of Norwegian (Ranamal) is spoken alongside one of the Norwegian standard languages (Bokmal), examines the social meanings attached to the use of these varieties in particular contexts (Blom and Gumperz 1972). Ranamal, learned at home, is the language of the family, of friendship, of local loyalty, and of equality. Bokmal, learned at school and in church, was historically associated with non-local landowners, business people, and administrators. It is thus the language of outsiders and of inequality, and its use by locals is interpreted as 'putting on airs'. Language use is not solely determined by social position, however. Setting, too, is important, and even within the same setting participants may change their definition of the event in which they are engaged, and indicate this by changing the language they use. This is called 'situational switching'. There is also 'metaphorical switching', for example when two people conduct business in an office in Bokmal, and then move to dialect when the topic of conversation turns to personal matters, or when one or other manages to define the encounter in a different way. The participants are engaged in what †Gluckman called 'multi-plex', or many-stranded, relationships, different aspects of which may be emphasized at various points in an interaction.

In modern nation-states it is usually assumed that the standard language is a superior mode of communication, a view completely at odds with that of both linguists and anthropologists who hold that no language is inherently inferior to any other. Hierarchies of language are social phenomena; they have nothing to do with intrinsic linguistic features. The pre-eminence of the standard often means that speakers of non-standard varieties and dialects are put at a serious disadvantage when obliged to interact in the dominant code. Other work by Gumperz has shown how the different cultural conventions that structure conversational exchanges in multilingual societies may give rise to the drawing of incorrect inferences, misunderstandings, and communicative breakdown. For example non-native English speakers even those with a high level of formal competence in the language, may be thus affected, when under stress in a job interview or in a courtroom. In contemporary society, access to jobs, housing, social services etc. often depends on the communicative resources that can be brought to bear, and lack of competence in the appropriate language or code has serious consequences, especially for those who already occupy a subordinate social, cultural, economic and often political status.

Many studies of ethnicity and class concern the disadvantages experienced by speakers of non-standard varieties, such as †creoles, notably in education. Anthropologists and linguists have frequently been caught up in the political debates surrounding the value of such languages and dialects. In the USA, for example, researchers into what is called the Black English Vernacular (BEV), have argued strenuously, and with considerable success, against the idea that such varieties are in some sense 'deficient' (Labov 1982). In western Europe, the USA and Canada, bilingualism and multicultural education have, relatedly, raised major questions of policy. Since World War II, many European countries have seen the growth of immigrant populations, with origins in Asia, Africa, the Middle East, and the Caribbean, whose different cultural traditions and languages often put them at variance with the receiving societies. The Linguistic Minorities Project (1985) provided extensive documentation of what this change meant for linguistic diversity in British cities. Holding that Britain had become an inescapably multilingual society, they urged (vainly) that bilingualism be considered a valuable resource, and promoted within mainstream education. The USA, whose cities have, in general, a population which is more varied ethnically, and often more influential, than those of European cities, has probably gone further in accepting this than most other countries, and many communities in the USA are effectively bilingual.

Subordination through language?

The study of linguistic heterogeneity therefore rapidly leads to questions of disadvantage, and thus to politics. There is, however, another, some would argue more profound, way in which language and *power are related. Drawing on theories of *ideology and discourse, it is suggested that language, rather than simply reflecting or reinforcing non-linguistic structures of domination, itself fashions subordination. Bloch, for example, found that among the Merina of Madagascar speeches in village councils are highly formalized, using a restricted syntax and vocabulary. One formalized speech must be followed by another whose content is shaped by the first. Thus, 'communication becomes like a tunnel which once entered leaves no option of turning either to left or right' (1975: 24). For the Merina, the only acceptable reply is one which acknowledges the previous speech and its premises.

Something comparable may characterize the situation of women in many societies. The ways in which women are excluded from linguistic exchanges, or allowed to intervene in a restricted way, are well documented. An interesting experiment is to watch a video of a mixed class of students, or perhaps a social science conference, and observe how and in what way women speak, and the extent to which their contributions are overridden, or cut off by men. There is more to it than this, however, †Ardener (1975) proposed the concept of 'muteness' (not to be confused with silence) to refer to situations in which a group (in this case women, though the concept may also be applied to subordinate ethnic groups or classes) can only articulate what it wishes to say through the dominant (male) voice. There are problems with this view (Cameron 1985) but Ardener, like Bloch, points to an important area in which language and power combine in a form of repressive control. This is not to concur with any simplistic notion of 'man made language'. Mutedness is an instrument of exclusion from power and authority, and, as with the Merina, 'It is not formalism in language which represses people and their thoughts, but the degree to which speakers impose such discourse on others' (Parkin 1984: 362).

Nor should those constrained by mutedness or formalism be seen as passive victims of language, as 'subjects' constructed in and through discourse. Like anything else, language, and linguistic practice is a site of contestation, and of creativity, in which a multiplicity of 'voices' struggles for attention. This is illustrated in Hill and Hill's account (1986) of the experience of diglossia by peasant farmers in the Malinche area of Mexico. Mexicano refers to Nahuatl, an Indian language which coexists with Spanish. In the colonial period bilinguals were rare, but nowadays most people 'speak two', as they say. Historically, Mexicano was the code of the 'inside', Spanish of the 'outside', and in contemporary society Spanish still represents external power: it is dominant in religion, law, work (though not agriculture), commerce and the media, and exerts a strong influence on the way Mexicano itself is spoken. Using data mainly from interviews designed originally to collect examples of linguistic usage to be later counted and correlated with social factors, the Hills demonstrate what these codes signify, who uses them, and how they are realized in daily speech. But they discovered that the interviews were themselves significant speech events. Interviewers and interviewees engaged in verbal duels embodying the 'symbolic strategies' through which individually and collectively the peasants manage their changing relationship with national society.

The Linguistic Minorities Project, too, found that surveys were not inert fact-finding devices. They could and did change or create linguistic consciousness, as when pupils were asked to set down their own language practices, or simply to state the languages they spoke. There is a bewildering variety of labels which parents, children, teachers, administrators and linguists attach, for example, to a single South Asian language, and negotiating those labels is a fundamental part of the experience of speaking 'other' languages in predominantly monolingual England.

The need for a dynamic perspective, giving prominence to creativity and contestation, is further illustrated by work dealing with the †'performative force' of language. This concept, which influenced Bloch and Parkin, refers to the idea that the social significance of a word or phrase is to be found less in its propositional content (what it says) than in its effect (what it does). An early attempt to show this was Malinowski's notion of †'phatic communion', a way of speaking which serves a social function; that of establishing human solidarity, Malinowski thought. Greetings in most cultures have this form: elaborate enquiries into an interlocutor's health should not be taken literally. Developed by the linguistic philosopher, Austin, the concept of the performative force of language has been highly influential in studies of *oratory, especially of political and religious rhetoric, and of the persuasive nature of devices such as metaphor. Expressive language generally has proved a very fertile field of inquiry, and much of what is written about language and *identity, especially ethnic identity, explores the creative use of language. Such use need not, however, be solidaristic. †Evans-Pritchard once demonstrated how a veiled and ambiguous style of speaking known as *sanza* enables Azande to indulge, relatively safely, in personal and social criticism.

Conclusion

There is an enormous range of data, oral and written, available to the social linguist, and this review has not attempted comprehensive coverage of the whole field. What has been emphasized is the way that anthropologists depart from linguists, first by emphasizing speech, rather than the language system, and then by studying speech in its social context. The Azande example offers a good illustration of this. With *sanza*, where the surface meaning of what is said may be exactly the opposite of what is intended (something not entirely unknown to speakers of English), an account which confined itself to specifically linguistic features such as phonology and syntax would be pointless, though linguistic data in the narrow sense may well, of course, give crucial clues for a social interpretation.

The anthropologist, therefore, studies linguistic, or more broadly, communicative, practice, the social activities through which and within which language or communication is produced, as well as the form that they take. This entails working in and through detailed ethnography, balancing structure and construction, actors' interpretations and observers, judgements, micro and macro levels of analysis. Above all, it means locating speech within the prevailing system of social differentiation and of power relations which both shape language and are shaped by it.

RALPH GRILLO

See also: componential analysis, discourse, emic and etic, ethnoscience, literacy, oral literature, oratory, poetics, Sapir–Whorf hypothesis, translation

Further reading

Ardener, E. (1975) 'Belief and the Problem of Women', in S. Ardener *Perceiving Women*, London: Dent

Bloch, M. (ed.) (1975) *Political Language and Oratory in Traditional Society*, London: Academic Press

Blom, J.P. and J.J. Gumperz, (1972) 'Social Meaning in Linguistic Structures: Code-Switching in Norway', in J.J. Gumperz and D. Hymes (eds.) *Directions in Sociolinguistics: The Ethnography of Communication*, New York: Holt, Rinehart and Winston

Cameron, D. (1985) *Feminism and Linguistic Theory*, London: Macmillan

Chomsky, N. (1979) *Language and Responsibility*, Brighton: Harvester Press

Ferguson, C.A. (1959) 'Diglossia', *Word* 15: 325–40

Hill, J.H. and K.C. Hill (1986) *Speaking Mexicano: Dynamics of Syncretic Language in Central Mexico*, Tucson: University of Arizona Press

Hymes, D. (1977) *Foundations in Sociolinguistics: An Ethnographic Approach*, London: Tavistock Publication

Labov, W. (1982) 'Objectivity and Commitment in Linguistic Science: The Case of the Black English Trial in Ann Arbor', *Language in Society* 22: 165–201

Linguistic Minorities Project (1985) *The Other Languages of England*, London: Routledge and Kegan Paul

Moerman, M. (1988) *Talking Culture: Ethnography and Conversation Analysis*, Philadelphia: University of Pennsylvania Press

Parkin, D.J. (1984) 'Political Language', *Annual Review of Anthropology* 13: 345–65

Posey, D.A. *et al.* (1984) 'Ethnoecology as Applied Anthropology in Amazonian Development', *Human Organization* 43 (2): 95–107

Stross, B. (1974) 'Speaking of Speaking: Tenejapa Tzeltzal Metalinguistics', in R. Bauman and J. Sherzer (eds) *Explorations in the Ethnography of Speaking*, Cambridge: Cambridge University Press

law

†Clifford Geertz (1983) has labelled the anthropology of law, or legal anthropology as lawyers call it, a centaur discipline. It was first given clear recognition as a subfield in 1941 when law professor Karl Llewellyn constructed a genealogy for it and argued its relevance for the study and teaching of jurisprudence. Fifty years later, lawyers view legal anthropology as one of the booming fields of jurisprudential study. They view one of their own, †Sir Henry Maine, as directly responsible for its beginnings. Almost with one voice they single out for attention *Malinowski's (1926) study of why the Trobrianders followed assessable rules in the absence of visible enforcement, †Gluckman's legal ethnographies of the Barotse in central Africa (1955, 1965), and Llewellyn and †Hoebel's work on dispute settlement among the Cheyenne (1941). Frequently in their textbooks,

†Margaret Mead appears in discussions of Natural Law theories; occasionally Clifford Geertz appears in a review of 'critical legal studies'.

The law professors' view both legitimates and confines the anthropology of law. It is a product of an era (1850–1907) when a so-called black-letter tradition, that law is an internally coherent and unified body of rules, predominated in legal education and scholarship. The anthropology of law is much broader than this, embracing many aspects of law excluded by Western normative legal philosophy. Anthropologists scrutinize Chinese, Indian, Japanese, Islamic and African legal philosophies, for example. At the same time, categories of law derived from the Roman civil law tradition and the British common law tradition receive uneven attention from anthropologists. The common law tradition with its ideological emphasis on courts and the judiciary has received most attention, largely because most anthropologists have worked in colonial and postcolonial states in which this tradition was implanted.

Anthropological jurisprudence

Anthropology is among the disciplines credited with the final dismantling of the doctrinal tradition of law – the long-standing *Enlightenment discourse that defined law as the unfolding of reason. Thereafter it passed through three phases. By the mid-nineteenth century, the jurisprudential paradigm was one of the legal order as a system of rules. Social order rested on *property relations and relations of †consanguinity and †affinity. Change in the laws came about through the expression of public opinion and education – the growth of knowledge.

Attention then turned to recognition of law's unity or homogeneity expressing certain structural features of society. This first involved 'early' or ancient societies, including both ancient Rome (Maine) and modern Morocco (†Westermarck), and later twentieth-century 'primitive' societies. Field research provided two distinctive contributions to jurisprudence. First, working largely in *kinship polities, anthropologists documented the embeddedness of law within the social and cultural milieu. Secondly, they reported law observed as much as law breached.

At this point a divide opened up between scholars drawing on Western jurisprudence for their inspiration, distinguishing judicial institutions and codified rules (†Schapera, Fallers, Pospisil among them) and those who studied ongoing interaction to arrive at broader notions of order and dispute settlement (Malinowski and Gulliver among them). Gluckman's ethnography encompassed both: having trained as a lawyer and at home with jurisprudential discourse, he deliberately sought operational field procedures that straddled the two domains.

The development of an action-oriented, processual anthropology of law in the 1950s led to a focus on courtroom procedure and dispute settlement that had much in common with the American legal realists (among them Llewellyn), whose work was highly compatible with the work of the anthropologists. Both operated, at that time, within the narrowly defined paradigms of social science but more recent work within this paradigm has begun to shift towards historical analysis (Starr and Collier 1989) while retaining a view of law as politics. For this reason †Foucault's *Discipline and Punish* (1975), with its conceptualization of law as part of a larger set of institutions of surveillance, †normalization and control, has been used selectively by legal anthropologists since he rules out of consideration †agency, tension, contest and change – the defining features, in short, of processual legal anthropology.

The regionalization of legal anthropology

Anthropologists working in different regions of the world represent different law-centred concerns. These are a blend of the legal traditions of the societies in which fieldwork is conducted and the ideological orientation towards 'law' of the ethnographer. Three examples may be given.

Many ethnographies from *South Asia describe attempts to transform aspects of society by legal means. These include affirmative action at the national level for so-called untouchables and tribals. National law also serves local ends and a multitude of forums for dispute-processing exist in every village. Here the ideological interests of religious groups, dominant *castes, and the state are all represented, each with its different history, different philosophy of justice, different procedural and substantive law. Villagers have recourse to more than one 'law'. It would appear that the only common feature is law's †patriarchy, and women frequently seek alternatives to courts of any kind. To seek justice they turn to spirit healing, witchcraft, or cultural ways of 'being sick' instead. Whether this diffuse, relativistic view of law has gone too far may be debated; anthropological views of law as culture are diametrically opposed

to perceptions of law as force, domination, and control.

Law has always formed the core of *Islamic civilization. Anthropological studies of Islamic courts in the interpretive vein have suggested that law is about causality and responsibility, and that moral order and judicial discretion is a variable cultural phenomenon. How 'law' travels from the particular courtroom of a Moroccan qadi to become Islamic justice tends to be unexamined. Starr's *Law as Metaphor: From Islamic Courts to the Palace of Justice* (1992) is a study in historical ethnography. Fieldwork was conducted in Turkey, the only Islamic state to have become secular. Starr views law as a contested domain, as events in a process happening through time. Law as *discourse is fought over by very real agents with disparate political agendas. Thus 'the growth of Turkish law and legal structures comes . . . as metaphor, [in] that it represents the embodiment of struggles between groups that were worked out in compromises within the legal system' (1992: xxiii) – a far cry indeed from the disembodied jurisprudence of rules and obligations.

Africanist studies of †customary law have brought about a metamorphosis in jurisprudence. Customary law is now perceived as a refraction of legal centralism or state law, as belonging to history rather than culture (Starr and Collier 1989). The historical moment at which it was constructed within the colonial state and the manner in which it entrenched the interest of dominant elders, and men in general, is becoming clearer. First used for personal aggrandizement or as 'folk law' to defend local autonomy against the colonial state, it then became a means of legitimation in the postcolonial nation state. Customary law has thus become a problematic issue for the legal profession in African nations, particularly those which seek to eliminate injustices inherited from colonial law. Chanock's (1985) study of law in colonial Zambia and Malawi shows how customary law developed in conjunction with criminal law in colonial African societies, drawing attention to the criminalization of women's activities and the way in which patriarchal tendencies in law bred new conflict between men and women.

Legal pluralism

A recognition that several categories of law exist in most post-colonial societies has led to a focus on what anthropologists call, controversially,

†legal pluralism. Since this is based on the proposition that the state does not have a monopoly on law, lawyers find the concept problematic. In postcolonial societies a recognition of pluralism may be viewed as a roadblock to nation-building and development.

Analytically, legal centralism and legal pluralism are contending processes. Legal centralism impinges on local knowledges and peripheral situations of *resistance, contingencies or simply pure contradictions. Anthropologists analyse competing legal registers, each with its own historical trajectory and historical consequences. They view legal pluralism in the light of historical struggles over sovereignty, nationhood and legitimacy.

The ethnography of United States law

Significant changes in the domains and procedural forms of legal regulation in the West have made the unitary paradigm of legal order more problematic for lawyers too. Bureaucratic and regulatory law has increased and public law has begun to make social provision for welfare, accident compensation and the like. With increased use of the courts for the settlement of disputes in contested areas of social relations, arguments from anthropology are entering into legal discourse. In the courtrooms of the United States, the so-called cultural defence pleads religious or ethnic pluralism without challenging centralized law; persons found guilty are given milder sentences.

In the wake of substantive ethnographic studies, it is clear that not only the state shapes legal conformity. In a case study of the garment industry in New York City, Moore distinguishes between law and *reglementation*, thus defining that vast activity of everyday rule-minding and regulation which affects most people – and, particularly, women and the poor (Smart 1991) – far more than does statutory legislation. *Reglementation* includes statutory provisions, forms of delegated legislation, administrative regulations, directives, codes of practice and other features of law which both lawyers and anthropologists have tended to neglect.

Ethnographers working at the grassroots have found an unwillingness to embark on litigation, even a culture of avoidance. A paralegal mediation industry has grown up around interpersonal disputes. The tendency of officialdom to direct poor litigants to mediation rather than law is the subject of Sally Merry's *Getting Justice and Getting Even* (1990). As legal institutions have been subjected to closer scrutiny, the procedures by which some persons may be disempowered on the basis of age, gender, ethnic origin, race and class have begun to emerge. Anthropologists thus go beyond lawyers' views of their own society as they expose the extent to which forms of disempowerment lie behind the ostensible rule of law (Comaroff 1990).

Conclusion

Satisfying continuities and disconcerting discontinuities coexist within the anthropology of law. New world-historical issues challenge the established competence of jurisprudence: law as †hegemony; law as war by other means; the jurisprudence of terror and legal restraint; civil and human rights; sovereign entitlements and oppositional legal practice. In a world of †genocide and forensic anthropology, the ethnography of law embarks on new comparative world-historical issues (Comaroff 1990). At home, substantively it carries critical legal studies forward. Legal ethnography worldwide now focuses on how difficult it is to 'get justice'. Working within the context of the legal profession's own heightened consciousness of the apparent powerlessness of representative government – national and international – to ensure peace and security this would appear to augur well for the future of the centaur discipline.

JOAN VINCENT

See also: colonialism, plural society, political anthropology, violence

Further reading

Chanock, M. (1985) *Law, Custom, and Social Order: The Colonial Experience in Malawi and Zambia*, Cambridge: Cambridge University Press

Comaroff, J. (1990) 'Re-Marx on Repression and the Rule of Law', *Law and Social Inquiry* 15: 671–8

Fuller, C.J. (1994) 'Legal Anthropology, Legal Pluralism and Legal Thought', *Anthropology Today* 10 (3): 9–12

Geertz, C. (1983) *Local Knowledge: Further Essays in Interpretive Anthropology*, New York: Basic Books

Merry, S. (1990) *Getting Justice and Getting Even: Legal Consciousness among Working-class Americans*, Chicago: University of Chicago Press

Moore, S. (1978) *Law as Process: An Anthropological Approach*, London: Routledge and Kegan Paul

—— (1986) *Social Facts and Fabrications: 'Customary law' on Kilimanjaro, 1880–1980*, Cambridge: Cambridge University Press

Smart, C. (1991) 'Feminist Jurisprudence', in P. Fitzpatrick (ed.) *Dangerous Supplements. Resistance and Renewal in Jurisprudence*, Durham, NC: Duke University Press

Starr, J. (1992) *Law as Metaphor: From Islamic Courts to the Palace of Justice*, Albany: S.U.N.Y. Press

—— and J. Collier (eds) *History and Power in the Study of Law*, Ithaca: Cornell University Press

Lévi-Strauss, Claude

Few anthropologists have acquired in their lifetime the international fame and audience of Claude Lévi-Strauss. Since the end of World War II his ideas have taken hold throughout the human sciences. Although his work is not easily accessible to the uninitiated (Leach 1970), nor have all been convinced by his propositions – far from it – he has radically transformed the way anthropologists pose questions and define their object in central areas like *kinship, *classification and *mythology. In advocating an approach inspired by structural linguistics, his work has brought about an epistemological break with previous methods of analysis. We can thus refer to a period 'before Lévi-Strauss' and one 'after Lévi-Strauss'.

This is all the more remarkable since, like most of his French contemporaries, he was self-taught as an anthropologist, having received his academic training in philosophy and law (at a time when only a few of the major British and American universities were offering programmes in anthropology). Nevertheless, we must not overlook the fact that he has always paid homage to his predecessors (†Mauss, *Boas, †Lowie, and *Radcliffe-Brown, among others) whether or not he agreed with them. On the other hand, he has not hesitated to engage in controversy with philosophers, who have taken him to task on a number of occasions. No one who reads his work is left indifferent and he has contributed much to anthropology's reputation in the human sciences.

From the aesthetic to the sensual

Lévi-Strauss has been described as sensitive, dignified and reserved, someone who has always privileged rigorousness in his professional life, and no doubt striven, as a result, to maintain a certain distance from events, people and facts. In order to know more about him we can turn to his own testimony (Charbonnier [1961] 1969; Lévi-Strauss [1975, 1979] 1983; Lévi-Strauss and Eribon

[1981] 1991), concerning his roots and intellectual development, and relate certain aspects of his work to his life and personality.

Those close to him all agree on his distinctive sensibility, which leads him sometimes to prefer the company of nature, rocks, plants and animals, to that of people. Undoubtedly this is the key to his aesthetic sensitivity, whether in relation to painting, music, poetry or simply a beautiful ethnographic object (Lévi-Strauss 1993). Is this aesthetic refinement part of his family heritage? This is quite plausible when one takes into consideration that his great grandfather was both a composer and a conductor, that two of his uncles were painters, as was his father who was also passionately interested in both music and literature. This aesthetic sense can be found in most of Lévi-Strauss's books; it is expressed in the choice of titles, in the choice of images (on the covers of the French editions of *Mythologiques*, or *The Savage Mind*, even in the colours of the characters of the titles (e.g. *the raw*, green and red; *the cooked*, brown), and the organization of the contents (e.g. the musical arrangement of *Mythologiques* beginning with *The Raw and the Cooked*, which is devoted to music, and concluding with the 'finale' of *The Naked Man*).

In his remarkable autobiographical volume, *Tristes Tropiques* (Lévi-Strauss [1955] 1976) he wrote about his early interest in nature and a taste for geology which led him to scour the French countryside in search of the hidden meaning of *landscapes. We can add to this youthful fascination a close reading of Freud and a discovery of *Marxism. Although each operates on a different level, he tells us that these three approaches (geology, Marxism and *psychoanalysis), show that true reality is never that which is the most manifest, and that the process of understanding involves reducing one type of reality to another. For each, he adds, the same problem arises, that of the relationship between the sensory and the *rational; and the objective of each is a kind of super-rationalism which can integrate the sensory and the rational without sacrificing any of the properties of either. Although he has distanced himself gradually from Marxism and pschoanalysis, this is nevertheless the programme that Lévi-Strauss has striven to realize throughout his work.

From the view from afar to the discovery of the other

Lévi-Strauss has the qualities required to carry out this programme, particularly a distinct taste for formal logic and an exceptional memory, both reinforced by a solid academic training. Yet it is his two long periods of residence outside France in the New World – more than ten years altogether – which have most determined the orientation of his scientific life and work. The first period began in 1934 when, as a young twenty-six year-old teacher of philosophy, he received an offer from one of his former teachers to go and teach sociology at the University of São Paulo. His reading of Robert Lowie's *Primitive Society* had already filled him with a desire to exchange the closed, bookish world of philosophical reflection for that of ethnographic work and the immense field of anthropology. He stayed in Brazil until 1939, gaining the opportunity to make contact with the Amerindian cultures which occupy such an important place in his work. At the end of his first academic year at São Paolo he spent several months in the Matto Grosso among the Caduveo and the Bororo – his baptism into the world of *ethnography – and published his first article on Bororo social organization. In 1938 he carried out a new expedition, this time among the Nambikwara, a relatively unknown group, whose social and family life he subsequently described in a monograph.

After returning to France in 1939, he was compelled by the war to leave once again. This time he went to the United States where in 1941 he was offered a new teaching post at the New School for Social Research, moving in 1942 to New York's École Libre des Hautes Etudes. His stay in New York lasted until 1947, including three years as cultural adviser to the French Embassy. This was an opportunity for him to familiarize himself with American anthropology and to have access to a wide range of anglophone ethnography which he used for his doctoral thesis *The Elementary Structures of Kinship* (Lévi-Strauss [1949] 1969). During this period he met many eminent European intellectuals who like himself had come to North America as refugees, amongst them the linguist †Roman Jakobson, who introduced him to structural linguistics and exerted a decisive influence on his thinking.

His final return to France marked the beginning of a brilliant and prolific academic career which took him to the Collège de France (1958, Chair in Social Anthropology), after the Centre National de Recherche Scientifique, the Musée de l'Homme (1948) and the École Pratique des Hautes Etudes (1950, Department of Religious Studies), where he was elected to the chair of Comparative Religions of Pre-Literate Peoples, a post once held by Marcel Mauss. He has received the highest national and international honours, including election in 1973 to the Académie Française. He has produced more than twenty books (translated into most of the major languages of the world) in this forty-five year period, continuing well after his retirement from the Collège de France in 1982. Under his impetus, and that of the Laboratoire d'Anthropologie Sociale which he created in 1960, *French anthropology has gone through a period of great development and its influence has spread throughout Europe and the rest of the world.

A theory of kinship based on alliance

Far from confining himself to the data he had gathered in South America or to the problems that were preoccupying his North American colleagues, Lévi-Strauss tackled, in his first major theoretical work (Lévi-Strauss [1949] 1969), one of the most ambitious anthropological projects of the period, the unification of the theoretical field of kinship; a field dominated for half a century by *British anthropology. Reversing the prevalent perspective of the time which considered relations of *descent as the key to kinship systems, Lévi-Strauss based his theory of kinship on relationships of marital *alliance, showing that the *exchange of people as spouses is the positive counterpart to the *incest prohibition. This is founded on reciprocity, in Mauss's sense of the term (in his essay on *The Gift*), and the relationships associated with it are the binding force of the social fabric. Lévi-Strauss showed that the rules that regulate these relations and the structures that express them can be reduced to a small number. He even suggested an analogy between the exchange of goods (after Mauss), the exchange of messages (after structural linguistics) and the exchange of women between groups. The question remained, however, of whether these 'structures' were a reflection of social reality, or were instead to be traced back to the properties of human thought. He returned to settle this question in his other major work, the four volumes of *Mythologiques*. He had intended to follow *The Elementary Structures of Kinship*, which dealt with societies in which the choice of spouse is prescribed and restricted to one particular category of kin (so-called †elementary structures), with another work devoted to †complex structures of kinship. But, except for several courses and lectures in the years immediately prior to his retirement, and his development of the idea of *sociétés-à-maison* (*house-based societies), this project has never been realized.

From primitive thought to mythical thought

In 1950 Lévi-Strauss was elected to a chair of Comparative Religions which led him to put kinship temporarily to one side in order to devote himself, and his structural method, to mythology and indigenous classifications. First of all, he deconstructed the concept of *totemism (Lévi-Strauss [1962] 1963). In the *evolutionary perspective that prevailed at the end of the nineteenth century and the beginning of the twentieth, totemism had been considered as one of the first forms of primitive *religion, in which human groups identified themselves with animal or plant species. Several British anthropologists (†Fortes, †R. Firth, *Radcliffe-Brown and †Evans-Pritchard) had tried to reinterpret totemism in the light of their own ethnographic data, but had failed to reach the level of logical abstraction to which Lévi-Strauss raised the debate. For Lévi-Strauss, totemism is a system of classification of social groups based on the analogy with distinctions between species in the natural world. The relationship between the individual animal and the species as a whole provides a natural intellectual model for the relationship between a person and a broader social category; animals were not made totems because, as *Malinowski had claimed, they were 'good to eat', but because, in Lévi-Strauss's phrase, they were 'good to think'.

Lévi-Strauss went further in *The Savage Mind*, originally published in the same year (1962), in which he demolished the evolutionist idea of a pre-logical stage of primitive thought. The French title, *La pensée sauvage*, involves an untranslatable pun – it means both 'wild pansies' and 'savage thought'. This type of thought is, according to Lévi-Strauss, logical, but non-domesticated, natural, and wild. Close to sensory intuition, it operates by working directly through perception and imagination. It is universal and manifests itself both in art and popular beliefs and traditions.

The *Mythologiques* (four volumes published between 1964 and 1971) developed the line of enquiry initiated in these two books since 'mythical thought' is a product of 'primitive thought'. These volumes constitute Lévi-Strauss's most important work, not only because of their innova-

tive approach to the field, but also because of their immense scope (close to a thousand myths taken from 200 Amerindian groups), their size, and the duration and intensity of their author's intellectual investment. To these we can add three later works which also deal with mythology: *The Way of the Masks* ([1975, 1979] 1983), *The Jealous Potter* ([1985] 1988) and *The Story of Lynx* ([1991] 1995).

In focusing on material from the two Americas where he spent ten years of his life, Lévi-Strauss not only returned to the site of his first anthropological studies but also drew on his first-hand knowledge of the natural environment of several of the groups studied, as well as the rich ethnographic literature housed in the great libraries of New York. With these he refined his structural method and showed that the structures of myths could be traced back to the structures of human thought. No longer was there any uncertainty about the possible effect of social constraints on structure: he stressed that mythology does not have an obvious practical function, and that myths function as systems of transformations. Through analysis he was able to describe their workings in terms of relations of opposition, inversion, symmetry, substitution and permutation.

He broke new ground by superimposing on the †diachronic order of the narrative, which expresses itself in †syntagmatic relations between elements, a †synchronic and †paradigmatic order between groups of relations. He also innovated by defining myth as the summation of its variations, no one being more true than the others. By a series of analogical substitutions, the variations provide a logical mediation which resolves the contradictions found in the myth. In other words, within a given myth we can compare elements and recurring relationships which might be obscured by concentrating on the narrative thread alone; and we can elucidate these relationships by looking at other related myths, from the same culture or from neighbouring peoples, in which variations on these relationships recur. These variations and their mediating function constitute a group of transformations, the logic of which has been represented by what Lévi-Strauss refers to as the canonical formula:

$$Fx \, (a) : Fx \, (b) : : Fx \, (b) : Fa\text{-}l(y)$$

in which a and b are terms, and x and y functions of these terms. In *The Jealous Potter*, he clearly demonstrates the scope of this formula. If one replaces a by n (nightjar), b by w (woman), x by j (jealousy) and y by p (potter), this gives:

$$Fj\ (n) : Fp\ (w) : Fj\ (w) : Fn\text{-}1(p)$$

The function 'jealousy' of the nightjar is to the function 'potter' of the woman, what the function 'jealousy' of the woman is to the inverted function 'nightjar' of the potter. From the two known relationships nightjar/jealousy and jealousy/potter one can infer the relationship potter/nightjar (confirmed by other myths) the inversion of which allows the logical circle to be closed. Mythical thought, Lévi-Strauss tells us, viewed from the perspective of logical operations, cannot be differentiated from practical thought; it differs only with respect to the nature of the things to which its operations apply.

For Lévi-Strauss, then, anthropology must investigate the structures underlying the diversity of human *cultures, structures which refer to the properties of the human mind and the *symbolic functions which characterize it. This intellectualist approach to humans and human culture, which raises the logic of sensory qualities to the rank of scientific thought, has been acclaimed by some and denounced by others. Yet it constitutes one of the most stimulating and powerful theories in twentieth-century anthropology.

BERNARD SALADIN D'ANGLURE

See also: alliance, classification, French anthropology, house, kinship, marriage, mythology, structuralism, totemism

Further reading

Boon, J. (1973) *From Symbolism to Structuralism: Lévi-Strauss in a Literary Tradition*, Oxford: Blackwell
Charbonnier, G. ([1961] 1969) *Conversations with Claude Lévi-Strauss*, London: Cape
Hayes, E.N. and T. Hayes (eds) (1970) *Claude Lévi-Strauss: The Anthropologist as Hero*, Cambridge, MA: MIT Press
Hénaff, M. (1991) *Claude Lévi-Strauss*, Paris: Pierre Belfond
Leach, E. (1970) *Lévi-Strauss*, London: Fontana
Lévi-Strauss, C. ([1949] 1969) *The Elementary Structures of Kinship*, Boston: Beacon Press
—— ([1955] 1976) *Tristes Tropiques*, Harmondsworth: Penguin
—— ([1958] 1963) *Structural Anthropology*, New York: Basic Books
—— ([1962] 1963) *Totemism*, Harmondsworth: Penguin
—— ([1962] 1966) *The Savage Mind*, Chicago: University of Chicago Press
—— ([1964] 1969) *The Raw and the Cooked* (Mythologiques I), London: Cape
—— ([1967] 1973) *From Honey to Ashes* (Mythologiques II), London: Cape
—— ([1968] 1978) *The Origin of Table Manners* (Mythologiques III), London: Cape
—— ([1971] 1981) *The Naked Man* (Mythologiques IV), London: Cape
—— ([1973] 1977) *Structural Anthropology II*, London: Allen Lane
—— ([1975, 1979] 1983) *The Way of the Masks*, London: Cape
—— ([1985] 1988) *The Jealous Potter*, Chicago: University of Chicago Press
—— ([1991] 1995) *The Story of Lynx*, Chicago: University of Chicago Press
—— (1993) *Regarder, Ecouter, Lire*, Paris: Plon
Lévi-Strauss, C. and D. Eribon ([1988] 1991) *Conversations with Claude Lévi-Strauss*, Chicago: University of Chicago Press
Sperber, D. (1985) 'Claude Lévi-Strauss Today', in D. Sperber, *On Anthropological Knowledge*, Cambridge: Cambridge University Press

literacy

Literacy is on the face of it something simple and straightforward, familiar in both everyday life and academic discourse, and the natural subject of study by a range of different disciplines. But like many such concepts, it is both more complex and less value-free than it seems at first. It is mainly over the last generation that anthropologists, together with social historians, have pointed to its complexity, ethnographic interest, and *socially-shaped* attributes.

What is literacy?

Human beings have over the ages developed a series of media to express or represent features of the social and natural world or to translate one medium into another through culturally-acceptable analogues: drum beats experienced as if spoken words, Asian contour graphics or Western notations representing musical performance, hand gestures carrying cognitive meaning, cartography representing spatial relationships. Writing is just one of these culturally-developed forms. It is true that it is currently an extremely widespread and highly-valued medium, but seen in comparative perspective it is no more transparent or 'obvious' than any other communication *technology. Nor can we assume that the elusive relationships between writing and what it 'represents' – is it really 'visible speech' for example? – are necessarily the same in all cultures.

One common model of 'literacy' is the type well-known in recent centuries of Western history:

phonetically-based alphabetic writing, tied to the concept of a linear text, often with the (unspoken) connotations of something validated through high *culture and, at the same time, rightfully open to mass use. But there are other writing systems too. These include – to follow one standard typology – pictographic, ideographic and †phonetic (syllabic *or* alphabetic) forms; manuscript as well as print; and a number of different materials: stone, clay, papyrus, parchment, paper, computer screen. These varied forms are not just of anti-quarian interest – merely precursors of the alphabetic achievements of Western civilization – but represent differing ways in which human beings have developed technologies which expand human control over time and space, and built these into their cultural institutions.

Literacy in this wider sense is not confined to Western societies or the recent past. Writing has been around a long time, whether in Chinese, Arabic, the alphabetic scripts of Western European languages, or Maya hieroglyphs (Boone and Larson 1994). As †J.Goody put it:

> At least during the past 2000 years, the vast majority of the peoples of the world (most of Eurasia and much of Africa) have lived ... in cultures which were influenced in some degree by the circulation of the written word, by the presence of groups or individuals who could read and write.
>
> (Goody 1968: 4–5)

As Goody also points out, we cannot assume *mass* literacy either, for 'restricted literacy' is a common pattern too. Furthermore, the *presence* of literacy in a society does not mean that everyone partici-pates in literate practices in the same way or to the same extent – these may (or may not) be quite marginal to people's everyday lives. Similarly there is little evidence that literacy automatically 'drives out' oral forms: on the contrary, there is plenty of evidence that the two interpenetrate (Finnegan 1988).

The recent Western paradigm of literacy is of a symmetric process, with reading and writing 'naturally' going together. But they can also be split or, at the least, differentially developed. Historians have, for example, analysed 'signature literacy' – people sometimes signed their names on, say, marriage registers, but did not necessarily read or write otherwise. Indeed it is sometimes to the advantage of rulers to encourage their subjects to *read* but not to master more active *writing*, skills. Literacy turns out to be not so much one undif-ferentiated thing as a cluster of skills which people deploy differentially, more, or less, fully, and in a series of different ways, depending both on their own individual situations and the culture within which they live.

Approaches to the study of literacy

Literacy has long been a topic of interest, and more interdisciplinary than most. Thus there has been a series of both specific and wide-ranging studies by, for example, psychologists, socio-linguists, development experts, educationalists and, especially, social and economic historians. However, although anthropological voices are now increasingly heard, anthropologists actually got into the subject rather late – not surprisingly, perhaps, given their earlier focus on primitive or non-industrial society (for which read 'non-literate society'), with written forms disregarded as intrusive and 'non-traditional'. It was not really until 1968 that Jack Goody's edited collection *Literacy in Traditional Societies* (1968) raised anthro-pologists' interest in both general theories and ethnographic questions. Together with Goody's later writings, this set the agenda for many sub-sequent studies of literacy.

There have been many approaches, by both anthropologists and others. The view of unidirec-tional progress upwards to the predestined Western pinnacle of alphabetic writing and, finally, print has been enormously powerful (even among anthropologists) and still appears in author-itative publications. Quantitative studies are also influential, particularly in educational and govern-mental contexts: counting how many people 'are literate' (sometimes in terms of UNESCO's 'functional literacy') or linking it to other social or demographic characteristics like *age, *gender, wealth or status. In addition general questions about the effects of literacy have been pursued by historians, classical scholars, psychologists and, from 1968, anthropologists: while more historic or culture-specific studies have also been carried out by specialist historians and (particularly from the 1970s) by anthropologists.

Among these various approaches, some issues have been of particular interest to anthropologists.

(1) The *consequences* of literacy have drawn much discussion: its 'impact' either at a local level or in more general, even universal, terms. Its suggested effects (some more convincingly argued than

others) have included: the requirements for empire; political and religious control; political and religious freedom; 'modernization'; *rationality; secularism; religious obscurantism; history; *science; linearity of thought and expression; the 'take-off' for economic *development; innovation; a transition from auditory to visual perception; bureaucracy; *individualism.

The arguments around these possible effects have partly drawn on specific ethnographic and historical evidence (Heath 1983 and Graff 1979 being particularly influential). They have also brought in the familiar theoretical issues of the distinctions between sufficient and necessary conditions, or between possibilism and determinism, and the anthropological interests in *both* comparative *and* culture-specific studies (Finnegan 1988, Street 1993). Obviously not all the suggested consequences could be true in a generalized automatic way, not only because they comprise just about every social and cognitive characteristic that could be associated with Western civilization, but because several are mutually contradictory. Many would thus now regard the compendium of possible effects more as a useful checklist of the roles literacy sometimes fulfils – since, like any other set of practices, it is used in different ways in different situations – rather than as a set of predetermined consequences. They also prefer to speak less of 'effects' than of 'implications', some of which may perhaps be of particular significance (for example the role of literacy in extending face-to-face communication and transcending time and space). Single-factor 'impact' studies have anyway become less fashionable, especially those associated with the now-challenged earlier certainties about the mission of the West. In the 1990s the emerging anthropological consensus thus seems to be to emphasize the cultural context and, as with any other technology or form of communication, to see the manifestation and meaning of 'literacy' not as an autonomous *cause* but as intertwined with the constitution of the society or societies in which it is set: the cultural, economic, political, religious and symbolic features which both influence and are influenced by the accepted practices of reading and writing and other forms of communication. What it *is* to be 'literate' thus depends on local symbols and practices: on how it is distributed; on who is literate and for what purposes; on ideas about history or about the self; on educational and economic arrangements; on the sexual or social divisions of labour; and on local power relations

and their interaction with literacy – all questions to which anthropologists are increasingly turning their attention in culture-specific ethnographies.

(2) Partly covering the same ground, but involving more extreme positions, is the cluster of arguments dubbed '*the orality-literacy debate*'. On the one side were writers like McLuhan and Ong (1982) (partially associated with Jack Goody's early writings) who not only sharply contrasted 'literacy' and †'orality', but also envisaged the development of human civilization as a series of revolutionary leaps from orality, to writing, to print and finally to the electronic age. Each medium had its own consequences, leading to the 'Great Divide' between 'primitive' and civilized marked by literacy. Their opponents pointed to the ethnographic and theoretical difficulties of such uni-causal and sweeping explanations, their evocations of the older *primitive mentality arguments, and their underlying †technological determinism (Finnegan 1988, Schousboe and Larsen 1989, Street 1993). This debate may now have run its course within anthropology (it continues to be rehearsed elsewhere) as few anthropologists would by now see either literacy or orality in unitary or universal terms. But it was useful in drawing attention to the comparative study of literacy, in bringing influential anthropological insights to the (interdisciplinary) debate, and, ultimately, in stimulating detailed ethnographic investigations in both urban and rural settings.

(3) There has also been an increasing appreciation of the †*ethnocentric* basis of many approaches to literacy. Our concept of literacy is linked to cultural assumptions about language, education, and power: in many ways a folk rather than (as we too easily presume) a universal notion. It carries deeply-felt images about individual and Western identities and historical experiences, sanctioned by our Greek roots, the scholarly élite, Whig view of progress, expansion of Europe (bringing book-based culture and religion to 'traditional primitive' peoples), and the vision and industries associated with education and with 'development' both at home and overseas. For these reasons literacy can be analysed as a powerful folk symbol, as a 'mythical charter' or, as in Street's 'ideological approach', as a reflection and mask of the current power relations.

(4) Consonant with other trends in anthropology, the 1980s and 1990s have also seen increasing emphasis on studying not the general ideals or formal structures of literacy but its

detailed *processes* as actually practised on the ground, and the *multiple* ways in which these are manifested. Such aspects come out partly in cross-cultural ethnographies, partly in detailed analyses of how different forms of communication – such as writing, reading, or speaking (and non-verbal media too) – are used and interact in actual situations (Basso 1974, Boyarin 1993, Keller-Cohen 1994, Kulick and Stroud 1990, Street 1993).

A sceptical approach to the older view of literacy as one unitary thing opposed to 'orality' or as having universal culture-free 'consequences' had thus by the early 1990s become the prevailing consensus among anthropologists (also many historians), with an interest in the social and cultural – rather than purely technological – nature of literacy. Ethnographic studies are increasingly unravelling the complex processes of local communication and the local understandings of these. Perhaps the next steps will be further work setting these ethnographies into a wider (most likely an interdisciplinary) framework: whether relating them to the expressive and communicative features of other human senses and media (rather than privileging the Western status of word/text/writing), or linking the implications of the permanent and distance-communication qualities of literacy with recent interests in †globalization and the study of *complex societies (Hannerz 1992).

RUTH FINNEGAN

See also: education, great and little traditions, language and linguistics, oral literature

Further reading

Basso, K.H. (1974) 'The Ethnography of Writing', in R.Bauman and J.Sherzer (eds) *Explorations in the Ethnography of Speaking*, Cambridge: Cambridge University Press (2nd ed, 1989)

Boone, E.H. and W.D. Larson (eds) (1994) *Writing without Words: Alternative Literacies in Mesoamerica and the Andes*, Durham: Duke University Press

Boyarin, J. (ed.) (1993) *The Ethnography of Reading*, Berkeley, Los Angeles: University of California Press

Finnegan, R. (1988) *Literacy and Orality: Studies in the Technology of Communication*, Oxford: Blackwell

Goody, J. (ed.) (1968) *Literacy in Traditional Societies*, London: Cambridge University Press

—— (1986) *The Logic of Writing and the Organization of Society*, Cambridge: Cambridge University Press

Graff, H.J. (1979) *The Literacy Myth. Literacy and Social Structure in the Nineteenth Century City*, New York: Academic Press

Hannerz, U. (1992) *Cultural Complexity. Studies in the Social Organization of Meaning*, New York: Columbia University Press

Heath, H.B. (1983) *Ways with Words. Language, Life, and Work in Communities and Classroms*, Cambridge: Cambridge University Press

Keller-Cohen, D. (ed.) (1994) *Literacy: Interdisciplinary Conversations*, New York: Hampton Press

Kulick, D. and C. Stroud (1990) 'Christianity and Ideas of Self: Patterns of Literacy in a Papua New Guinea Village', *Man* 25: 286–304

Ong, W. (1982) *Orality and Literacy. The Technologizing of the Word*, London and New York: Methuen

Schousboe, K. and M.T. Larsen (eds) (1989) *Literacy and Society*, Copenhagen: Akademisk Forlag

Street, B. (ed.) (1993) *Cross-Cultural Approaches to Literacy*, Cambridge: Cambridge University Press

magic

Magic, the purported art of influencing the course of events through occult means, has generally had a dubious reputation in Western civilizations. Its doubtful status seems implicit in the origin of the term itself in the name of the priestly clan of the Persians: for classical Greek writers, the word *Magi* suggested both alienness and charlatanry. However, the return to ancient wisdom that characterized the fifteenth- century Italian Renaissance included a new scholarly interest in magical ideas. A major contribution in this context was Marsilio Ficino's Latin translation in c. 1480 of the *Corpus Hermeticum*, a mysterious Greek manuscript supposedly written by a certain Hermes Trimestigus about the fifth century BC and collating the main themes in the magical traditions of the ancient Middle East. The best known statement in the *Corpus* is the aphorism 'As Above, so Below', an assertion of the essential unity of the spiritual and material domains.

Ficino, like most of his contemporaries and followers in Renaissance magical scholarship, was careful to frame his arguments so as to avoid charges by the Christian Church of heresy and encouraging resort to diabolical agencies. Ficino's appeal to the authority of Thomas Aquinas, the celebrated Christian theologian, apparently satisfied the ecclesiastical authorities. Ficino's younger contemporary Pico della Mirandola was less fortunate: his presentation of a body of magical doctrines based on the Qabalah – the so-called Tree of Life of esoteric Judaism – earned the condemnation of the Pope and the ruling of a Church commission that any kind of magic was evil and Satanic. However, a later pope, Alexander Borgia, took a more liberal view of Pico's work, stating that magic and the Qabalah were valuable aids to Christian practice.

But the perils associated with magical thought in Christian Europe were plain to see in the fate of Giordano Bruno, a one-time Dominican monk who openly espoused the obviously pagan elements in the Hermetic tradition and was burned at the stake by the Inquisition in 1600. Other Renaissance theorists of what was then called Natural Magic achieved social acceptance by their proficiency in other branches of learning. The noted Swiss magician Paracelsus (1493–1541) made important contributions to medical knowledge while John Dee (1527–1608) advanced the science of geography in Elizabethan England along with his learned contributions to magic and alchemy.

The eighteenth-century Enlightenment saw the triumph of scientific rationalism in Western Europe as scholars generally became persuaded that only the material world apparent to the senses was ontologically real. In such an intellectual climate the medieval and Renaissance debates on magical causation appeared absurd. 'Magic' was driven underground, to re-emerge later as part of the Romantic counter-movement to the nineteenth-century progress of scientific †materialism. Such figures as Eliphas Levi (A.L. Constant) in France and the groups of artists, writers and mystics associated with the Order of the Golden Dawn in England embodied this largely clandestine magical resurgence. But mainstream scholarly theorizing on magic during this period was represented by the work of the English anthropologist †Edward Tylor who in *Primitive Culture* (1871) described magic as 'the most pernicious delusion that ever vexed mankind'. That raised the question of why, in the primitive societies that were just becoming known to anthropological scholarship, belief in this 'delusion' was so general. Tylor discerned several reasons for the persistence of magical beliefs, including their association with practical behaviour, the ascription of magical failure to breach of *taboos or the machinations of rival magicians, and the cultural authority of magical thought.

Tylor's theories were further developed by †J.G. Frazer. In *The Golden Bough* (1890) Frazer endorsed Tylor's description of magic as a 'pseudo-science', seeing it as the first stage in the *evolution of human thought; next came *religion, the ascription of superhuman powers to non-existent deities; and the final phase was true, experimental *science. Frazer also noted that magical ideas of causation universally fell into two categories. One was the notion that like produced like, which he called the Law of Similarity or homeopathic magic: an example was the then current belief among peasants in the Balkans that swallowing gold could relieve the symptoms of jaundice. The other causal idea was that things which had once been in contact continued to act on each other at a distance, the Law of Contact or contagious magic: an example was the common practice of magically operating on clippings from a person's hair or nails in order to change the condition of that person.

In France †Émile Durkheim and his disciples in the †*Année Sociologique* school of sociology and anthropology pointed to the private and often secretive nature of magical operations, which contrasted with the public form of religious congregations. †Marcel Mauss in *A General Theory of Magic* ([1902] 1972) seemed to echo ancient distrust of magic arts which he saw as always tending towards evil-doing (*maléfice*). Mauss further developed the Tylorian and Frazerian perceptions of the essentially systematic character of magical thought, which he saw as having properties similar to language. It was not mere association of ideas that determined the action of like on like, as Frazer had implied: there was always a selection of one particular quality of an object as the vehicle of magical action, and the choice reflected social convention. The repertoire of sympathetic and antipathetic items in a given system amounted to a classification of collective representations.

In the United States †Robert H. Lowie argued against both Frazer's evolutionary theory of magic and his (and Tylor's) distinction between 'natural' and 'supernatural', a distinction he saw as foreign to primitive thought. But †A.L. Kroeber placed himself firmly in the evolutionist camp, asserting that magic was a characteristic of 'retarded' cultures. Where magical beliefs occurred in 'advanced' cultures they were to be found among the socially disadvantaged and the 'psychotic, mentally deteriorated, or otherwise subnormal'.

A similar view of magic was propounded by †Sigmund Freud, the founder of *psychoanalysis. In *Totem and Taboo* ([1918]1950) Freud drew a parallel between 'primitive' magical beliefs and neurotic and infantile delusions that attributed causal efficacy to thought alone.

Magic in the field

This apparently plausible but essentially †ethnocentric theory did not long survive the rise of modern anthropology with its emphasis on prolonged field studies which produced the first detailed accounts of magical ideas and practices among tribal peoples. The classical work in the Melanesian Trobriand Islands by Bronislaw Malinowski included copious descriptions of Trobriand magic, notably of spells directed towards the success of horticulture and *kula* expeditions, which involved the inter-island exchange of prized *ritual objects. Malinowski observed that magical operations were undertaken when the outcome of empirical actions was uncertain: thus a fishing trip into the perilous ocean called for magic whereas fishing in the calm waters of an inland lagoon did not. Every magical act comprised three elements: the spell or actual words used (in Melanesia and Oceania generally spells were characteristically private properties, inherited within families); the rite, a stereotyped sequence of symbolic acts; and the moral or ritual condition of the performer (frequently involving sexual and dietary taboos). Malinowski (1935, 1948) also saw magical rituals as having a functional utility in the case of communal activities such as canoe-building, where the mandatory character of associated magical operations ensured the mobilization of the necessary labour force.

Malinowski's student †Edward Evans-Pritchard showed in another classical study, *Witchcraft, Oracles and Magic among the Azande* (1937) how the magical ideas and practices of this African people of the southern Sudan formed a total system with their notions of *witchcraft and the institution of oracular *divination. This complex of ideas and institutionalized behaviour patterns provided Azande with ways of making sense of, and dealing with, the misfortunes of sickness and death. Evans-Pritchard's detailed analysis demonstrated the logicality of Zande thought within the constraints of the system. However, as

Evans-Pritchard saw it the system finally reposed on 'mystical' notions about non-existent occult forces.

Beyond explanation

Subsequent studies of magic in non-Western, tribal cultures, while sharing Evans-Pritchard's presumption of the empirical non-efficacy of magic and related practices such as witchcraft and sorcery, have tended, probably from a laudable concern to protect 'primitive' peoples from accusations of irrationality, to emphasize the 'symbolic' and 'metaphorical' elements in these practices. In the words of †John Beattie (1964), in magic 'we are dealing with the imagined potency of symbols and symbolism'. The whole basis of this approach, which rested on a †worldview inherited from the Enlightenment, has been brought into question since the so-called *postmodern critique of anthropology of the late 1970s and 1980s. Inspired in some case by the controversial works of Carlos Castaneda, which introduced readers to the 'separate reality' supposedly known to the Yaqui Native Americans of the Mexican Highlands, certain anthropologists have written of magical phenomena as objectively real, even if inexplicable in terms of Western scientific knowledge. An early example is Michael Harner's account of the magical world of Conibo and Jivaro *shamans of South America. Other recent examples of this school are the works of Stoller and Olkes, de Surgy and Edith Turner, all based in African field experience. Michael Jackson, another anthropologist of Africa who also adheres to this approach, has dubbed it 'radical empiricism'.

A further notable contribution to this postmodern rehabilitation of magic is Jeanne Favret-Saada's ([1977] 1980) study of 'magic force' in a community in rural France. Taking issue with Evans-Pritchard (1937), Favret-Saada states her aim of taking magical forces seriously, and not being content to describe it as 'a logical error, or someone else's belief'. A more recent study (Luhrmann 1989) describes the apparent 'conversion' to belief in Renaissance-style ritual magic of a group of prosperous middle-class English people in the town of Cambridge. Luhrmann identified four ways in which these converts rationalized to themselves, and to outsiders, the validity of their practices. One category she calls 'realists', those who argue that there are precepts and assumptions that differ from those recognized by orthodox science, but

which can be empirically proven to be valid. Others argue for the existence of 'separate realities', physical and spiritual, which are governed by different laws. Another category are the 'relativists', who argue that there are different ways of knowing the same underlying reality, with no one way having absolute worth. Yet others, who espouse 'metaphorical' explanation of their magical practices, emphasize the subjective value of their experiences rather than their objective validity.

The recent shift in anthropological approaches to magic has been summarized by Winkelman (1982). The 'traditional' assumption has been that magical beliefs are empirically untenable and that there can be no such cause-and-effect relations as these beliefs imply. An impetus to the reformulation of theories of magic that takes account of their possible empirical validity has come from laboratory research in parapsychology. This research, Winkelman says, has produced support for some of the phenomena claimed by magical traditions. Thus, it has been shown that human beings can exercise psychokinetic influence on radioactive decay, on computerized random-number generators, on the growth rate of plants, fungi and bacteria, and on healing in animals. Other commentators draw attention to the apparent congruence between traditional magical philosophy which posits an organic universe in which human beings play an actively creative role and theories of the New Physics on the unity of mind and nature (Roney-Dougal 1991).

ROY WILLIS

See also: divination, *kula*, ritual, shamanism, witchcraft, science

Further reading

Beattie, J.H.M. (1964) *Other Cultures*, London: Cohen & West

Evans-Pritchard, E.E. (1937) *Witchcraft, Oracles and Magic among the Azande*, Oxford: Clarendon Press

Favret-Saada, J. ([1977] 1980) *Deadly Words: Witchcraft in the Bocage*, Cambridge: Cambridge University Press

Frazer, J.G. (1890) *The Golden Bough*, London: Macmillan

Freud, S. ([1918]1950) *Totem and Taboo*, London: Routledge & Kegan Paul

Luhrmann, T. (1989) *Persuasions of the Witch's Craft: Ritual Magic in Contemporary England*, Cambridge, MA: Harvard University Press

Malinowski, B. (1935) *Coral Gardens and their Magic*, London: Allen & Unwin

—— (1948) *Magic, Science and Religion*, Glencoe: Free Press

Mauss, M. ([1902] 1972) *A General Theory of Magic* (trans. by R. Brain), London: Routledge

Roney-Dougal, S. (1991) *Where Science and Magic Meet*, Longmead: Element

Tylor, E.B. (1871) *Primitive Culture*, London: Murray

Winkelman, M. (1982) 'Magic: A Theoretical Reassessment', *Current Anthropology* 23 (1): 37–66

Malinowski, Bronislaw

A formidable personality in life, Bronislaw Malinowski (1884–1942) is still a somewhat controversial figure, long after his death. Born in Poland, he was educated there through the PhD level, receiving his degree in 1908. Subsequently, he travelled to Leipzig to study with †Wilhelm Wundt, notable both as a pioneering experimental psychologist and as a student of *Völkerpsychologie*, and Karl Bücher, an economist with special interest in primitive societies, and then won a Polish fellowship for prospective university teachers which took him to Britain in 1910 to study anthropology with †Edward Westermarck and †C.G. Seligman at the London School of Economics. He received his DSc in 1916 on the basis of a library study published in 1913, *The Family Among the Australian Aborigines*, as well a report on his first fieldwork published in 1915, *The Natives of Mailu*. He spent most of his career at the LSE, where he first lectured in 1913, became reader in social anthropology in 1923 and professor in 1927 – the only one in the subject at a major British university at the time. He was a founder of the *functionalist school of social anthropology, and its undisputed leader in Britain until 1937, when *A.R. Radcliffe-Brown became professor at Oxford after years in academic exile. His training programme revolved around his famously lively seminars, which attracted many who were not formally his students. Most of the leaders of British social anthropology in the post-World War II era were his disciplinary progeny (a number were to adopt Radcliffe-Brown as their intellectual mentor, however); and these were the first generation of anthropologists able to be professionals – who enjoyed careers in academe and wrote largely for other social scientists rather than amateur enthusiasts – in no small part because Malinowski's promotional efforts encouraged proliferation of academic positions. And Malinowski's influence was global, for he attracted many foreign students, and many recipients of PhD degrees from the LSE found employment outside Britain. In 1939 he secured an appointment at Yale University, determined to remain outside Europe for the duration of World War II; he died in New Haven (see Firth 1957, Thornton and Skalník 1993).

Bulletins from the field

There has never been any doubt about Malinowski's role as a pioneer of *fieldwork. He came to the LSE just as British anthropology was in the process of repudiating so-called †armchair research, the scholarly synthesis of data gathered in the field by disparate amateurs. Anthropology's methodological revolution had been heralded by the 1898 Cambridge Anthropological Expedition to †Torres Straits, of which Malinowski's teacher Seligman was a member. Represented as natural science, joining direct observation and theoretical generalization, the Expedition did not do fieldwork as it came to be understood, however; its seven members were in the field a scant seven months, and they acted as a survey team, each performing a portion of the collective project. But from the Expedition's experience derived a new field method, defined by another of its members, †W.H.R. Rivers: a lone anthropologist should live for 'a year or more' in a 'community of perhaps four or five hundred people', mastering the vernacular and developing a personal relationship with every inhabitant, gaining access to 'every feature of life and custom in concrete detail' (Rivers in Freire-Marreco and Myres 1912: 143).

Malinowski was not the first of the Expedition's progeny dispatched to work in the new mode: Rivers's student Radcliffe-Brown went to the Andamans in 1906. But Malinowski was the first to realize Rivers's injunctions, and, indeed, corresponded with Rivers while he was in the field. As has been common among anthropologists (as well as practitioners of other field sciences), his long-sustained fieldwork was undertaken at the beginning of his career: his research in an area of Papua of special interest to Seligman, among the Mailu of Toulon Island from September of 1914 to March of 1915; and his two stints in the Trobriand Islands, a site Seligman did not approve, between June of 1915 and May of 1916, and between October of 1917 and October of 1918 – on which his major monographs were based. Perhaps he would not have remained in the field so long, with intermittent breaks in Australia, had he not been a virtual prisoner in the region; World War I had broken out while he was *en route* to the field, rendering him an enemy alien unable to move freely for the duration. Later, he would visit briefly among peoples in Africa and in the American Southwest, and at the end of his life he was preparing to undertake research in Mexico; but he did no more prolonged fieldwork.

Certainly, Malinowski's actual field experience differed from the heroic ideal in a number of respects. He began his research among the Mailu living as a paying guest in the home of a missionary, W.J. Saville, daily venturing from it into the village (guarded in at least one instance by a native policeman). In the Trobriands he was never very far from European pearl traders, with whom he consorted when he found unbearable the company of the islanders – frequently described in his diary as 'niggers', as his professional descendants were horrified to learn when it was published in 1967. And he occasionally behaved imperiously, availing himself of colonialists' prerogatives. Nevertheless, during his first bout of fieldwork he removed himself from Saville's home to live 'quite alone among the natives', determining that he was thereby able to do 'incomparably more intensive' work. And though while working in the Trobriands he confided to his diary his 'feeling of ownership' as 'master of this village with my boys', he demonstrably succeeded in fulfilling his declared intention to take the 'native's point of view'. He identified sufficiently with his subjects to assume a protective attitude toward them, in opposition to the colonial officials, missionaries, and commercial agents who were determined to eradicate their way of life, and frequently bent on ruthless exploitation – an attitude he would sustain throughout his career (see Stocking 1991: 37–47).

Malinowski produced ethnographic accounts populated by sympathetic figures, described in a deliberately vivid literary style (see Stocking 1983). And he was contemptuous of those who would eliminate from anthropology descriptions of recognizable human beings. Against those who would represent *kinship in 'formulae, symbols, perhaps equations', for example, he observed that 'kinship is a matter of flesh and blood, the result of sexual passion and maternal affection, of long intimate daily life, and of a host of personal intimate interests' (1930b: 19). Functionalist man in his Malinowskian guise was not the automaton who has been so often identified in critical analyses of functionalist writing, a person incapable of imagining – let alone pursuing – action contrary to his normative socialization; rather, Malinowskian man's conformity to societal expectations was 'partial, conditional, and subject to evasions', tempered by his individual purposes (Malinowski 1926: 15).

Financing functionalism

Among Malinowski's talents was self-promotion of a high order. He was wont to speak of his aristocratic ancestry, even including in his *Who's Who* entry the boast that his 'parentage on both sides' was of the 'landed gentry and nobility' – although his paternal grandfather had lost the family lands, and his childhood was spent in impoverished circumstances. By fawning shamelessly upon that archetypal armchair anthropologist †J.G. Frazer, he gained a powerful champion – whose work he had criticized severely in essays written prior to his emigration. He claimed a scientific background which enabled him to cast his anthropological generalizations in a form more rigorous than his predecessors'; but though his studies prior to his emigration included mathematics and physics, his Polish PhD dissertation was in truth an exercise in the philosophy of science with special reference to psychology ([1906] 1993). His propensities served him well, however, advancing functionalist anthropology.

Because functionalists made fieldwork indispensable for every professional, their research programme was expensive. At the very beginning of his career, Malinowski received an object lesson in scientific finance: Seligman would have preferred to send him to the Sudan to do his first fieldwork, but only appealed successfully to patrons prepared to support research in the Antipodes. And when Malinowski was stranded there during World War I, he himself had to find the funds to carry on, provided by Australia's Department of External Affairs. He learned from this experience that anthropologists could appeal to potential patrons by advertising the utility of their knowledge, which almost invariably meant claiming that their work would serve the practical needs of colonialists.

He acted on this knowledge after the war. Describing functionalist anthropology as the study of 'the actual way in which primitive politics are worked' – and thus the only sort of anthropology that could serve as the theoretical basis of colonial management – he commended himself to the alliance of colonial officials, missionaries, and philanthropists who founded the †International African Institute (IAI) in 1926. The American Rockefeller Foundation, by far the most generous patron of the IAI (and accustomed to supporting scholars associated with the LSE because it was an institution in which 'the academic and the actual come together'), changed its policies so that Malinowski's students would be eligible for IAI fellowships, responding to Malinowski's claim that the application of anthropology as 'social engineering' in areas 'into which Western capitalism is pressing' could 'prevent untold waste and suffering'. Because the Institute provided the bulk of research funds available for fieldwork in the interwar period, most of Malinowski's students became Africanists. And, not the least because they enjoyed the status that inheres in prosperity, they became the leaders of British social anthropology. Malinowski was hardly an apologist for colonial rule, however. Echoing statements he had made while in the Trobriands, he proclaimed that the colonial situation was founded on antagonism: all parties to the colonial situation had 'deeply rooted personal interests at stake' that created 'irreconcilable differences' among them. And, in fact, his students' work proved unappealing to British colonial administrators, whose notion of useful anthropology was a highly stylized evolutionist scheme contrived by generations of officials themselves which rationalized modification of indigenous polities to suit the system of Indirect Rule – which ostensibly (but hardly actually) preserved traditional order so that it might serve as the willing instrument of colonial power (see Kuklick 1992: 182–241).

Of theories and legacies

After Malinowski's death, Radcliffe-Brown established his theoretical distance from Malinowski: unable to articulate theory that might be tested by a community of researchers, Malinowski acted as an individualist rather than a scientist; and his theory was not functionalism but 'Malinowskianism' because he derived social processes from 'biological needs of individual human beings', rather than recognizing that social life was constituted of 'interactions and joint actions of persons who are brought into relation by the [social] structure' (Radcliffe-Brown 1949: 49, 51). These accusations were not unfounded. Malinowski did judge that all societies had to develop institutions that served the basic biological needs of self-preservation (Malinowski 1930a); and he did find

'innate emotional attitudes' grounded in physiology antecedent to social forms (Malinowski 1930b: 28).

Taken up initially by those whose resentment of Malinowski's professional power derived from personal contact with him, Radcliffe-Brown's accusations became received opinion among many sociocultural anthropologists in the post-World War II decades. Granting that Radcliffe-Brown was 'incomparably the poorer fieldworker', they judged him 'the more powerful theorist'; his model represented 'a comparative anatomy of societies', lending itself to 'systematic comparison' of populations, in contradistinction to Malinowski's scheme – which admitted only of universal generalization (see Wolf 1964: 5). As functionalism came under attack in the 1960s, however, the differences between the two men began to seem relatively unimportant; perhaps they emphasized different social institutions, but both fostered analysis that documented the fundamental functionalist problem – the coherence of any given society's parts into a whole. And Malinowski's evocative ethnographies, inviting the reader to contemplate the satisfactions of exotic ways of life, may prove more enduring than Radcliffe-Brown's schematic formulations.

HENRIKA KUKLICK

See also: fieldwork, ethnography, *kula*, British anthropology

Further reading

Firth, R. (1957) 'Introduction: Malinowski as Scientist and Man', in R. Firth (ed.) *Man and Culture*, London: Routledge and Kegan Paul

Freire-Marreco, B. and J.L. Myres (eds) (1912) *Notes and Queries on Anthropology*, London: The Royal Anthropological Institute

Kuklick, H. (1992) *The Savage Within*, Cambridge: Cambridge University Press

Malinowski, B. ([1906] 1993) 'On the Principle of the Economy of Thought' trans.by L. Krzyzanowski, (PhD dissertation, Jagiellonian University), in R. Thornton and P. Skalník (eds) *The Early Writings of Bronislaw Malinowski*, Cambridge: Cambridge University Press

—— (1926) *Crime and Custom in Savage Society*, London: Kegan Paul

—— (1930a) 'Parenthood: The Basis of Social Structure', in V.F. Calverton and S.D. Schmalhausen (eds) *The New Generation*, New York: Macaulay

—— (1930b) 'Must Kinship Studies Be Dehumanised by Mock Algebra?', *Man* 30: 19–29

Radcliffe-Brown, A.R. (1949) 'Functionalism: A Protest', *American Anthropologist* 51: 320–23

Stocking Jr, G.W. (1983) 'The Ethnographer's Magic', in G.W. Stocking Jr (ed) *Observers Observed*, Madison: University of Wisconsin Press

—— (1991) 'Maclay, Kubary, Malinowski', in G.W. Stocking (ed.) *Colonial Situations*, Madison: University of Wisconsin Press

Thornton, R. and P. Skalník (1993) 'Introduction: Malinowski's Reading, Writing, 1904–1914', in Thornton and Skalník (eds) *The Early Writings of Bronislaw Malinowski*, Cambridge: Cambridge University Press

Wolf, E.R. (1964) *Anthropology*, Englewood Cliffs: Prentice-Hall

mana

The word *mana* and its cognates exist in a number of languages within the Oceanic branch of the Austronesian language family, most of these within the Eastern Oceanic subgroup that includes languages of Northern Vanuatu, Fiji, Rotuma, Polynesia and Central Micronesia. Social evolutionary theorists of the nineteenth and early twentieth centuries worried over the defining characteristics of the various evolutionary stages, and vigorously debated the exact sequencing of those putative stages of human progress. Argument about the evolution of religion fixated partly upon the Austronesian word *mana*, and this term has since been a staple of anthropological and comparative religious analytics.

†Robert Marett, drawing on the work of missionary ethnographer Robert Codrington (1891) who had lived in Vanuatu and the Solomon Islands, borrowed '*mana*' to describe the 'supernatural in its positive capacity' (1909: 128). He paired *mana* with a second Austronesian word, *tabu* (*taboo), which would label the supernatural's negative mode. Marett disputed †Edward Tylor's claim that the simplest form of human religion was †animism, or the belief in spiritual beings. Marett, rather, advocated an even more primitive stage – belief in an *impersonal* supernatural force that he split into positive *mana* and negative *tabu*. †Émile Durkheim also borrowed *mana* to describe his 'totemic principle' – an indefinite sacred power, an anonymous force which is 'the source of all religiosity' (1915: 229).

This *mana* is an incorporeal supernatural force that energizes people and things, conferring efficacy upon them. Codrington's original examples of people and things with *mana* included magical stones that govern the fertility of fruit trees; effective spells and charms; influential chiefs; skilful warriors; and celebrated gardeners (1891: 118–20). *Mana*, as a powerful substance that people can acquire and that serves to explain their abilities and accomplishments, thus has much in common with another comparative religious term, †charisma.

The concept of *mana* has facilitated comparative religious analysis but it mistranslates Pacific religious sensibilities. Roger Keesing (1984) assayed Eastern Oceanic linguistic data and established that *mana* is almost always a stative verb (which expresses a state or condition), not a noun. People and things, accordingly, *are mana*; they do not have *mana*. Keesing suggests that *mana* might be translated as 'be efficacious, be successful, be realized, 'work'' (1984: 137). *Mana* is not a universal supernatural force that animates a miscellany of people and things, but rather the quality of efficacy. This explains odd, secular usages in which Islanders may characterize ancient but still functional outboard canoe motors as *mana*.

Notions of *power as a substance or thing reflect European, rather than Pacific, *cosmology. They similarly underlie European metaphors of electrical energy as a sort of tangible 'power', metaphors whose development paralleled that of the comparative religious discourse of *mana* in the nineteenth century. It is not surprising, for example, that Marett wrote of *mana*'s relative 'voltage' (1909: 138).

Anthropological interest in *mana*, however, has boosted that term's modest popularity beyond the discipline, particularly in the urbanized Pacific where Western understandings of *mana* as a substance may now have overwritten more traditional Pacific notions of *mana* as a quality. The Polynesian Cultural Centre in Hawaii billed one of its flamboyant stage shows as 'Mana'; and a glance through the Honolulu telephone directory discovers Mana Productions, Mana Publishing and Mana Trucking.

LAMONT LINDSTROM

See also: evolution and evolutionism, Pacific: Melanesia, Pacific: Polynesia, power, religion

Further reading

Codrington, R. (1891) *The Melanesians: Studies in Their Anthropology and Folklore*, Oxford: Clarendon Press

Durkheim, É. (1915) *The Elementary Forms of the Religious Life*, London: George Allen and Unwin

Keesing, R. (1984) 'Rethinking *Mana*', *Journal of Anthropological Research* 40 (1): 137–56

Marett, R. (1909) *The Threshold of Religion*, London: Methuen & Co.

markets

The analysis of markets and marketing has been one of the central issues in *economic anthropology, and of course it is a subject much theorized in economics. The relationship between anthropology and economics is often uneasy, and this tension is apparent in the attempts to reconcile exotic ethnographic material with the theoretical interests of economics. Of major theoretical significance is the simple grammatical step of contracting the plural form 'markets' to its singular 'market' to suggest a formal, ideal model which some commentators take to explain culturally diverse types of markets and trade practices.

A market, in its rudimentary sense, entails the buying and selling of things by persons, as distinct from †barter or other forms of social *exchange that do not use an intermediary token of common exchange value – namely, *money of some sort. Characteristically, exchange of this former type is immediate and not delayed over time, and is conventionally contrasted with †gift exchange. A market-place denotes an arena in time and space to which these interactions are confined, and marketing generally denotes the process of buying and selling not necessarily confined to one place. The fact that people may or may not buy and sell things within or outwith a market-place is not simply at issue; but whether what they do can be described in terms of Western market theory, and whether such description sheds light or obscures the nature of people's practices, have been points of contention.

Formal models

Market models developed by economists have supplied many of the theoretical underpinnings for those anthropologists attempting to find continuities between diverse forms of trading practice in different cultures. For economists, a market is an arena of 'perfectly competitive transactions' between many buyers and sellers sharing complete market information (about price, quality of goods and so on); thereby an efficiency in production and distribution is achieved. Real markets only ever approximate to this ideal; nonetheless, it is a model against which actually-existing markets and practices are compared and explained.

Much of the *formalist-substantivist debate focused on the two referents of the term 'market': market-places as physical locations and market-principles as abstract factors determining wider economic processes. The substantivists' own position, however, was perceived as increasingly untenable – as they themselves recognised – due to the spread of market-principles over the global system. As Plattner (1985) argues, 'the pretense that theories of markets and marketing were irrelevant became less viable' in a world that increasingly resembled a market system.

Developments in theory in the 1970s were twofold: formal models grounded in a broad anthropological knowledge of local contexts gained increasing sophistication; *Marxist-inspired theory displaced an interest in systems of exchange alone to a concern with local *modes of production and distribution and *world systems. Whilst these latter trends deflected attention away from the issues of liberal economics and towards questions of *political economy, the extent to which these approaches took market theory for granted is, however, open to question.

Central-place analysis of *peasant markets was also developed (see *settlement patterns), and G.W. Skinner's work in 1964 on market-place systems in rural China was particularly influential. The formal model was further elaborated by Carol Smith from the early 1970s onwards in various publications, and she argues that central-place theory helps reduce the confusion of market activity to economic patterns through which a complex commodity economy is integrated. As a formal model, the predictions of central-place theory are reconciled to the 'real-world deviations', which are explained with reference to social, political or geographical factors. The universality of central-place theory provides a model against which actually-existing markets are compared. Moreover, it concentrates primarily on the material flows of traded items, types of trader, and the social integrative effects of these flows. Markets thus form part of a social system and structure.

The micro-level behaviour of individuals in market contexts is also subject to formal methods that attempt to make sense of market behaviour as rational, and of individuals as decision-makers (see *individualism). Over-simplistic notions of †economic man as individual maximizer of economic value have now receded in the face of theoretical criticism that such assumptions provide few convincing explanations of socio-economic action. The *rationality of economic action as a relationship of means-to-ends has been increasingly contextualized, and these issues have been challenged by ideas about intentionality of exchange and differing styles of reasoning. That it has to be shown that rationality, however defined, is not confined to Western industrial society should be seen in some measure as part of a political debate in social anthropology that defends exotic others from the charge of irrationality. Whether such a specific focus on forms of individual behaviour leads to further insights into the differences in trading practice in various cultures is moot. Indeed, questions about our own 'rationality' in economic matters have also been raised.

The treatment of markets as systems of information is a further aspect of the analysis of market behaviour. Evidence suggests that, contrary to market models, information is not evenly shared, but it is differently allocated and is difficult to acquire not only for local traders but also for ethnographers. These 'inefficiencies' in the flow of information arise from particular kinds of social and cultural organization, such as traders dealing in small quantities of unstandardized †commodities that are subject to variations in supply. Various institutional practices are recognized as ways of dealing with such 'inefficiencies' and 'uncertainties' in markets.

That issues such as information and uncertainty are defined as problematic arises from assumptions deriving from our own market models, which are predicated on the perfect distribution of information. A series of important publications from the mid-1980s by Jennifer and Paul Alexander (e.g. Alexander and Alexander 1991), which focus on bargaining, price-setting, market information and trading partnerships in Java, shows that the control of the flow of information is strategically important for traders to make profits. Market buyers and sellers are not autonomous individual agents, but are linked by power relationships in which knowledge and †agency are intimately connected in trading practice.

A formal definition of a market such as 'any domain of economic interactions where prices exist which are responsive to the supply and demand of items exchanged' bears perhaps little resemblance to *any* real market. Indeed, bar-

gaining over prices in Javanese markets may appear economically more efficient as a method of price-setting than Western posted-prices (Alexander in Dilley 1992). What needs explanation, in Alexander's view, is the simultaneous presence in industrial economies of a dominant ideology of market efficiency through the price mechanism, and a method of price-setting that inhibits the efficient operation of the market. Prices in Western markets, he points out, are less responsive to changes in demand than to changes in cost, and cultural notions of 'fairness' are important in price-setting.

Cultural economics

Stephen Gudeman's work represents a different approach, termed 'cultural economics', to questions of economic theory and modelling. Formal analyses drawing on Western economic models, he suggests, 'continually reproduce and discover their own assumptions in the exotic materials' (1986: 34). The centrality of culture must be recognized in the analysis of economics. Culture does not stand opposed to economics such that, say, cultural explanations are given to account for why *their* market practice does not coincide with *our* market theory. Rather, culture and economics are mutually constitutive. A more comprehensive and dialectical process of comparison between actual market *practices* in both Western and non-Western markets is needed, and, as Alexander argues, *all* markets are cultural constructs (see his chapter in Dilley 1992).

Gudeman focuses on the cultural models and metaphors produced by ourselves and others to account for the economic practices we all engage in. By treating our own economic theories as cultural models that are produced in specific socio-historical contexts (see his *Conversations in Colombia*, 1990), we see how models are generated and how they form parts of longer conversations amongst ourselves, between ourselves and others, and amongst others. Investigations of market models and practice from a similar perspective include Dilley 1992 (see also Friedland and Robertson's 1990 volume which adopts a critical interest in the market). The inspection of market models, rhetoric, and *discourse, as well as their deployment in specific social contexts, links with concerns expressed by some economists about the metaphors and meanings within economic discourse (see, for example, McCloskey 1986). One aim is to situate the conversations we conduct about economics as well as those that other people conduct about the systems they inhabit. Native accounts (including our own) of how people conceive their engagement with a global system of trade and power relationships (conventionally glossed as the 'world market') require further study. Knowledge of 'local models' (Gudeman) not only adds to an understanding of how peoples may act in relation to this global network, but the method contextualizes the processes of cultural-economic modelling and reveals the ways these models are invoked in political activity.

This project moves beyond the early substantivist perspective, which accepted the ideological separation of economy and society in Western *capitalism (a distinction that may not hold at the level of practice); and which failed to seriously challenge the cultural construction of market theory. The inspection of how we construct our notions of markets is as important as the analysis of how other cultures construct theirs. A parallel development is Appadurai's work on the social life of things (1986), which traces the social biographies of items as they move through different networks of exchange. The conventional dichotomies labelling systems – for example gift versus commodity; non-market versus market and so on – appear less relevant once it is seen that the processes of social exchange within any one culture (or even between cultures) can transform the status of an item.

Morality and the market

The great transformation in European society, for †Karl Polanyi, was the replacement of morality by the market; similarly, for Bohannan and Dalton the †moral economies of tribal or peasant peoples were being overrun by an amoral market system. But market theory embodies its own special morality: economic action is seen as oriented towards the common good; exchange is advantageous to all parties (cf. a gain for one is a loss to another). The market as a self-regulating system of apparent discord produces a harmony of interests and social co-ordination, through what economists take to be †Adam Smith's notion of the 'invisible hand' of the market. These are two contrasting moral positions relating to the market: on the one hand, market negates traditional moral systems; on the other, it is a 'civilizational process' through which humans and societies reach their full potential (see Blanton in Ortiz 1983).

The connection between the market and morality is also made by social agents involved in exchange. Moral evaluations of trade and commerce – negative or positive – must be viewed empirically as arising from the context of changing politico-economic relationships (see also Appadurai's notions of pathways and diversions, 1986). The establishment of market systems is as much a political struggle as an economic matter, and negative moral representations of trade practices arise from a loss of control over previously known and indigenously transparent relationships. Moral outcries at the introduction of market relationships are a response to a sense of uncertainty and opaqueness often triggered by the activites of high-profile middlemen or women who redefine the politics of exchange. The analytical positions of theorists over morality and markets reflect native perceptions on the morality of exchange generated from experiences in trading.

Power, agency and the market

The term 'market' carries a significant political weight in a post Cold War world represented as the triumph of Western liberal market economics over state-planned, communist economic systems. This marriage of market theory and political *ideology is a potent union, and its forms of discourse dominate many local, national, as well as global, debates about how we should conduct our lives. The apparent triumph of market ideology in the 1980s has paradoxically spawned an increasing sense of unease about the status of the market concept. Whilst the concept has become hegemonic, it is also in crisis; and this crisis concerns one of the master concepts of social and economic science.

The †fetishization of the market as a powerful transformative social agent is an issue which reveals the nature of our own cultural constructions of market phenomena. The ideological strength and attractiveness of market rhetoric and its construction as an agent of change connect with Western political agendas that dominate contemporary social debate. To disentangle these complex matters has become an urgent issue for the analysis of actual market practice, for the anthropology of *development, and for social theory itself.

The market and the domain of market relations is a contested field of *power played out through the medium of economic and cultural value. The market as an ideological representation of capitalism fails to portray power in terms of either the imbalances within individual exchange relations, or the connections between market structures and political institutions. But the problem goes beyond conventional issues in political economy.

The hegemony of market discourse reveals itself in the 'power to name' other people's trading activities in Western market terms; in its ability to intervene in other discourses and to impose its own metaphors. The voices of non-Western cultures, speaking of their participation in global relationships, has hitherto remained muted. The attention given to alternative ways of making sense of, and making a living within, the global system not only redresses the balance between our models and theirs, but also suggests the idea of multiple discourses about 'the market'. How these discourses are employed and invoked in relation to social and political practices on local as well as global stages has, and no doubt will have, continued relevance for all our lives.

ROY DILLEY

See also: capitalism, consumption, economic anthropology, money.

Further reading

Alexander, J. and P. Alexander (1991) 'What's a Fair Price? Price-setting and Trading Partnerships in Javanese Markets', *Man* 26 (3): 493–512

Appadurai, A. (ed.) (1986) *The Social Life of Things: Commodities in Cultural Perspective*, Cambridge: Cambridge University Press

Dilley, R. (ed.) (1992) *Contesting Markets: Analyses of Ideology, Discourse and Practice*, Edinburgh: Edinburgh University Press

Friedland, R. and A.F. Robertson (ed.) (1990) *Beyond the Marketplace: Rethinking Economy and Society*, New York: Aldine de Gruyter

Gudeman, S. (1986) *Economics as Culture: Models and Metaphors of Livelihood*, London: Routledge and Kegan Paul

Gudeman, S. and A. Rivera (1990) *Conversations in Colombia: The Domestic Economy in Life and Text*, Cambridge: Cambridge University Press

McCloskey, D.N. (1986) *The Rhetoric of Economics*, Brighton: Wheatsheaf Books

Ortiz, S. (ed.) (1983) *Economic Anthropology: Topics and Theories*, New York and London: University Press of America

Plattner, S. (ed.) (1985) *Markets and Marketing* (Monographs in Economic Anthropology, no 4), New York and London: University Press of America

Smith, C. (ed.) (1976) *Regional Analysis* (vol. I: Economic Systems; vol. II: Social Systems), New York and London: Academic Press

marriage.

The institution of marriage, which has been defined as 'the union of man and woman such that the children born from the woman are recognised as legitimate by the parents' (*Notes and Queries on Anthropology* 1951:) has constituted a central area of anthropological research, usually in the context of studies of the *family (Morgan 1871, Westermarck 1921). *Claude Lévi-Strauss has made the most spectacular contribution to the development of this field; by placing marriage *alliance at the very heart of *kinship, he has shown how marriage is a structure of *exchange resulting from the *incest prohibition. The prohibition of incest, which is universal and requires the avoidance of union between close relations, has as its positive counterpart the institution of †exogamy, the obligation to choose a marriage partner *outside* the close family group. Alliances are, nevertheless, not made randomly: exogamy has its own counterpart in †endogamy, which demands or recommends marriage *within* a prescribed group or locale. Modern societies, for example, combine strict prohibitions on marriage between close or distant kin and affines, with what might be termed a less restrictive class and ethnic 'homogamy' (marriage with the 'same kind'). Most so-called primitive societies have both strict exogamy between certain close relations and an equally strict endogamy between other relations or prescribed groups.

Thus it can be seen that this 'universe of rules' (Lévi-Strauss [1949] 1969) governing the organization of all human groups, has many implications. The prohibition of incest leads to exogamy, which implies marriage with others, and this in turn produces exchange and reciprocity. These marriage exchanges, in which women are exchanged by men for other women, do not take place between individuals but between groups of 'givers' and 'takers' who thus circulate women between them. In certain societies, these groups are always the same, with the result that they find themselves linked to each other by an endless series of matrimonial exchanges, each of which reinstates the first alliance and in so doing reaffirms their solidarity. As it is women who are at the heart of this exchange and as they are 'a priceless good', they transform it, adding a sort of extra value. It is this which justifies the giving of a woman as a wife to seal political alliances and to cancel debts of blood, honour or money.

But marriage is not only an opportunity to create new social bonds, it is often accompanied by †prestations, of greater or lesser importance, and as much symbolic as material, which firmly establish the marriage and set up long-lasting bonds between the two groups party to the exchange. Within the broad category of marriage payments, one can distinguish societies that practise †bridewealth, involving prestations, in nature or kind, which the family of the groom must give to the family of the bride, from those which practise †dowry, whereby a collection of goods and services are offered by the bride's family to that of her future husband, either with or without the dower (the part of the goods to be returned to the wife if her husband dies before her). The structure of marriage prestations can have important political, economic and ritual consequences for the society as a whole (Comaroff 1980), and there have been a number of attempts to construct grand comparisons. For †Jack Goody (1973), the choice between bridewealth and dowry derives from a more general opposition between societies that have †unilineal kinship systems, emphasizing *descent, and societies that have †bilateral systems, valuing alliance. For Collier and Rosaldo (1981), important symbolic and political consequences of *gender relations can be correlated with a slightly different distinction: between bridewealth societies, in which *objects* are transferred from the groom's side to the wife's side, and †bride-service societies (often, but not always, relatively egalitarian *hunting and gathering societies) in which the groom's *labour* is given to the wife's side.

Although emphasis is often put on the economic aspects of marriage or on marriage as a form of exchange, it should not be reduced to these functions alone, nor can we justify its neccessity in terms of these functions. The variation in forms of conjugal union between different societies clearly indicates its relative nature. Everyone knows that there are societies in which men or women have more than one marriage partner at the same time. These societies are referred to as †polygamous. The term †'polygyny' is used when a man can have more than one wife at the same time, and †'polyandry' when a woman can have

more than one husband. However, there are also societies where marriage may occur between people of the same sex: among the Nuer for instance, studied by †Evans-Pritchard (1951), there is the institution of †woman-marriage. In this case a woman can give bridewealth to the relatives of another women and marry her. She then has absolute control over this woman and her children, delegating to a male †genitor the duties of procreation. In addition, the death of the spouse does not bring to an end the rights and obligations brought about by marriage. The Nuer also practise †ghost-marriage, contracted by a widow on behalf of her dead husband if he has no heirs, or by a sister on behalf of her deceased brother if he has no progeny. We should also mention the †levirate, which is the institution obliging a brother to marry his widowed sister-in-law; and the †sororate which obliges a widower to marry his deceased wife's sister. In the 1950s, †Edmund Leach used examples like these, especially the marriage practices of the †matrilineal Nayar of South India (see *family), to query the universality of the *Notes and Queries* definition with which we started (Leach 1955).

These varied forms of conjugal union pose several questions. They may appear to us as aberrant, even absurd, but they cannot be dismissed as archaic or primitive elements of societies yet to reach civilization. On the contrary, such institutions occur in demographically important populations which have highly developed cultures and can in no way be regarded as at the dawn of humanity. Besides, do not our own changing practices, for example as a consequence of new *reproductive technologies – allowing a mother to be impregnated by her dead husband, or a woman to rent her womb to beget children for another mother – suggest that we might be discovering equally unexpected arrangements ourselves?

It is also clear that all of these marriage institutions cannot be reduced to rational causes. In each case the particular form of the institution is an essential element of the social system to which it belongs. And, taken in their entirety, they are 'the illustration of a series of logical possibilities derived from the application of very simple conceptual principles that appear to us as strange because we have not been able to imagine them for ourselves' (Muller 1976). Finally these polygamous marriages between women, between the living and the dead, provide little evidence of the stability of the marriage institution. The divorces and remarriages, the common law marriages and free unions which are on the increase in Western societies, also point to the fragility of the institution and show above all that the functions that have been ascribed to marriage – the transfer of goods, the solidarity between the relations, the sexual division of labour, reering of children – cannot be the consequence of any natural imperative. Therefore we can only call for a rethinking of the universality and durability of marriage.

FRANÇOISE ZONABEND

See also: alliance, Crow-Omaha systems, family, gender, incest, kinship, preference and prescription

Further reading

Collier, J.F. and M. Rosaldo (1981) 'Politics and Gender in Simple Societies', in S. Ortner and H. Whitehead (eds) *Sexual Meanings: The Cultural Construction of Gender and Sexuality*, Cambridge: Cambridge University Press

Comaroff, J.L. (ed.) (1980) *The Meaning of Marriage Payments*, London: Academic Press

Dumont, L. (1971) *Introduction à Deux Théories d'Anthropologie Sociale: Groupes de Filiation et Alliance de Mariage*, Paris: Mouton

Evans-Pritchard, E.E. (1951) *Kinship and Marriage among the Nuer*, Oxford: Oxford University Press

Goody, J. (1973) 'Bridewealth and Dowry in Africa and Eurasia', in J. Goody and S.J. Tambiah (eds) *Bridewealth and Dowry*, Cambridge: Cambridge University Press

Héritier, F. (1981) *L'Exercice de la Parenté*, Paris: Gallimard

Leach, E.R. (1955) 'Polyandry, Inheritance and the Definition of Marriage', *Man* 55: 182–6

Lévi-Strauss, C. ([1949] 1969) *The Elementary Structures of Kinship*, Boston: Beacon Press

Morgan, L.H. (1871) *Systems of Consanguinity and Affinity of the Human Family*, Washington: Smithsonian Institution

Muller, J.-C. (1976) *Parenté et Mariage chez les Rukuba (Bénoué, Nigéria)*, Paris: Mouton

Westermarck, E. (1921) *The History of Human Marriage*, London: Macmillan

Marxism and anthropology

The relationship between marxism and anthropology has been both fruitful and often antagonistic. There are several distinct phases which can be described. First of all, there are Marx and Engels's own writings on anthropological topics which formed the basis for much self-consciously orthodox research in official *Russian and *Chinese anthropology. Secondly, there is anthropological work inspired by later marxist theorists: most of this has been carried out since the early 1970s and can be divided into two broad streams, structural Marxism and what I shall call cultural Marxism. Finally, we can also point to important areas of work which could be characterized as 'post-Marxist', in the sense that they have been deeply influenced by the authors' encounter with Marxist ideas, but with little or no trace of dogmatic attachment to Marxist principles.

Marx, Engels and the official line

Marx himself was a revolutionary whose theoretical efforts were above all directed to the understanding, and eventual overthrow, of industrial *capitalism. A strong case can be made for starting any appreciation of Marx with his most complete and mature statement of his position in the first volume of *Capital*. This is above all a work of *political economy, and its empirical content is derived from the secondary literature on British industrial capitalism in the mid-nineteenth century. As such it seems to have relatively little to say about classic anthropological problems and anthropological topics. The more theologically inclined Marxists have managed to glean a more complete anthropological programme from Marx's notebooks and early writings, but the key source for official Marxist anthropology has been Engels's *The Origin of the Family, Private Property and the State* ([1884] 1972).

Marx and Engels's writings on anthropological topics, heavily influenced by the work of *L.H. Morgan, provide one possible research agenda for a Marxist anthropology. In particular, they provide a typically nineteenth-century model of social *evolution in which contemporary ethnographic evidence could be fitted into appropriate positions in the movement from the primitive, through the ancient and feudal, to the capitalist and eventually the communist *mode of production. The argument for the primacy of the economic base, or †infrastructure (forces and relations of production), over the †superstructure (religion, law, *ideology) provides a wonderfully clear heuristic, even as it opens up an empirical nightmare (for superstructures vary with scant regard for infrastructural similarities). And the central role accorded to *class antagonisms in the movement from one stage to another provides further opportunity for empirical research, either by locating 'classes' in widely different socio-historical contexts, or – as in the lengthy arguments about the †Asiatic mode of production – analysing the implications of a political order based on class but apparently lacking class conflict.

This, broadly, was the research agenda pursued – often with great ingenuity and considerable scholarship – by the official anthropology of the Soviet Union and the People's Republic of China for much of the twentieth century (see Gellner 1980 for a survey of this work). Not surprisingly, though, it had much less impact in Europe and North America (except in *archaeology, where all kinds of materialism have their obvious attractions). The combined influence of *Malinowski and *Boas rendered schematic views of social evolution deeply unfashionable, while the cruder versions of the base/superstructure distinction seemed inadequate to cope with the empirical richness produced by the fieldwork boom of the 1930s, 1940s and 1950s. Individual anthropologists, such as †Leslie White in the USA and †Max Gluckman in Britain, shared certain political and intellectual affiliations with Marxism, but these appeared in oddly muted form in their own anthropological work. The political climate of the 1950s was hardly conducive to Marxist scholarship in Britain and the US – known Marxists were barred from access to British colonial research sites as well as university employment in the USA. Individual scholars like Peter Worsley and Ronald Frankenberg in Britain, Eric Wolf and Stanley Diamond in the US, did begin to use Marxist theory in their work from the late 1950s onward, but there is little sense in which we can talk of a distinctive Marxist anthropology outside the former communist states before the late 1960s.

Structural Marxism

What has come to be called, in retrospect, structural Marxism was a product of a very specific historical and intellectual conjuncture. Intellectually, structural Marxism was based on two major French influences: the revisionist interpretations of Marx provided by the philosopher, †Louis Althusser, and applied to ethnographic problems by Claude Meillassoux and Emmanuel Terray; and the more pervasive linguistic turn occasioned by *Lévi-Strauss's *structuralism, and rendered into appropriate Marxist form by his protégé Maurice Godelier. Historically, structural Marxism was taken up by graduate students and young university teachers, especially in Britain, the Netherlands and Scandinavia in the 1970s (Melhuus 1993), but also in many post-colonial contexts – the 1970s debates on the articulation of modes of production, for example, were probably most vigorously pursued in India (Guha 1994).

Structural Marxism was characterized by a number of concerns. The issue of infrastructural determinism was a source of recurring anxiety – often resolved by recourse to the phrase 'determination *in the last instance*', but also met by fairly radical revision of the very idea of the infrastructure itself. Godelier, for example, argued that in non-capitalist societies (or 'social formations') *religion or *kinship could 'function' as the infrastructure, a point which owed much to †Karl Polanyi's earlier arguments about the †embeddedness of the economy in pre-capitalist societies. Althusser's writings on *ideology encouraged the study of language, symbols and ritual as sources of both domination and integration. Subsidiary debates emerged about the relationship between kinship, other sources of social classification (*age, *gender), and socio-economic class.

Most energy, however, was expended on the question of modes of production. On the one hand, this raised issues of *classification: is Indian agriculture usefully characterizable as *'feudal'; are *peasants components of a specific mode of production, or are they more usefully viewed as †petty-commodity producers? It also raised important issues of scale and integration, not least as †dependency theory and *world-systems theory both seemed to suggest that the politically and economically crucial relations in the modern world were not between classes *within* a society, but between societies of the core and societies of the periphery. These were important issues for any understanding of the modern world (Wolf [1982] provides a skilful and judicious synthesis of this work), yet the results were oddly unimpressive. Too often, empirical analysis was subsumed under the typological demands of the theory, while there was little evidence of what made particular places particular in the modern world order. In short, structural Marxism was threatened by two opposing possibilities: as Marxism it was relatively indifferent to issues of ethnography and culture, and thus was not particularly anthropological; or, in the hands of ethnographers like Godelier and Maurice Bloch, it did become more obviously cultural, but looked less and less convincingly Marxist.

Cultural Marxism

In his *Culture and Practical Reason* (1976), one of the most influential theoretical books of the 1970s, †Marshall Sahlins renounced his own earlier 'Marxish' tendencies, arguing that while Marxism was revealing as a portrait of industrial, capitalist society it was ultimately restricted by its inability to deal with culture as a distinct and irreducible order of signs and meanings. Sahlins's argument was directed against the francophone theories which dominated structural Marxism, but was oddly silent on the impressive theoretical work done by other Western Marxists on issues of culture and consciousness throughout the twentieth century. The key figures before World War II were the Italian communist †Antonio Gramsci, and the German cultural critics of the Frankfurt School, especially Adorno and Walter Benjamin. After World War II, literary critics and historians in Britain, like †Raymond Williams and E.P. Thompson, developed their own analyses of the relationship between culture and Marxist theory, and their work was especially important in the emergence of that mélange of Marxism, sociology, ethnography and †poststructural theory which came to be known as *cultural studies.

Interestingly, 1970s structural Marxists showed remarkably little interest in this work. Instead it was taken up by younger, historically-inclined anthropologists like Michael Taussig and Jean Comaroff in the US. Taussig's *Devil and Commodity Fetishism in South America* (1980) and Comaroff's *Body of Power, Spirit of Resistance* (1985) both drew on work by Marxist historians and social theorists in a much more open and creative way than the Althusserians of the 1970s. Both examined the ways in which local cultural resources might be deployed in acts of *resistance to the spread of capitalist work practices. Marxism here was used in an interpretive spirit, as the writers sought to explicate the hidden moments of resistance in people's religious and symbolic life (a theme anticipated thirty years earlier in Peter Worsley's writing on *cargo cults). At the same time, †Pierre Bourdieu's immensely influential *Outline of a Theory of Practice* (1977) mixed influences from Marx, †Weber, Lévi-Strauss and †Wittgenstein in the creation of a practice-based theory of social life, with particular emphasis on the reproduction of structures of domination.

All of these writers, and the many that followed them in work on *power and resistance, were strongly influenced by earlier Marxist writers (few of them anthropologists). Yet none could be straightforwardly classified as 'Marxist' themselves. This has now become the pattern as young radical anthropologists, especially in North America, often build their work on unacknowledged Marxist assumptions about the importance of class and inequality in social life, without properly confronting either the strengths or the weaknesses of Marxist theory proper. That is only one legacy of the impact of Marxism on anthropology. Another, possibly more profound one, comes from the experience of reading Marx himself. Marx's own writing – for example, on the commodity-form in *Capital* I – introduced a whole generation of anglophone anthropologists to the subtleties of German dialectical argument. Althusser's influence in the 1970s may seem difficult to explain from the perspective of the 1990s, yet his work inspired an important reaction against the empiricism of so much British and American anthropology. In the 1970s it was possible for young anthropologists to claim that a correct reading of Marx would provide the answer to the discipline's many problems. If we can now speak of a 'post-Marxist' anthropology, it is because so many anthropologists have now undertaken that reading, to the extent that they have learned that the greatest value of Marx's work is in the problems it raises and the questions it fails to answer, rather more than in the ready-made analytic solutions it provides.

JONATHAN SPENCER

See also: capitalism, Chinese anthropology, class, development, evolution and evolutionism, mode of production, political economy, power, resistance, Russian and Soviet anthropology

Further reading

Bloch, M. (ed.) (1975) *Marxist Analyses and Social Anthropology*, London: Malaby
—— (1983) *Marxism and Anthropology*, Oxford: Oxford University Press
Bourdieu, P. (1977) *Outline of a Theory of Practice*, Cambridge: Cambridge University Press
Comaroff, J. (1985) *Body of Power, Spirit of Resistance: The Culture and History of a South African People*, Chicago: University of Chicago Press
Engels, F. ([1884] 1972) *The Origin of the Family, Private Property and the State*, New York: Pathfinder
Gellner, E. (ed.) (1980) *Soviet and Western Anthropology*, London: Duckworth
Godelier, M. (1977) *Perspectives in Marxist Anthropology*, Cambridge: Cambridge University Press

Guha, R. (1994) 'An Anthropologist Among the Marxists', *Civil Lines* 1: 73–94

Melhuus, M. (1993) 'Pursuit of Knowledge – Pursuit of Justice: A Marxist Dilemma', *Social Anthropology* 1 (3): 265–75

Sahlins, M. (1976) *Culture and Practical Reason*, Chicago: University of Chicago Press

Taussig, M. (1980) *The Devil and Commodity Fetishism in South America*, Chapel Hill: University of North Carolina Press

Wolf, E. (1982) *Europe and the People Without History*, Berkeley: University of California Press

mass media

The mass media is one form of communication found in many societies throughout the world, and has become increasingly important in recent centuries. Communication is a prerequisite for human society. Humans are not genetically programmed for one pattern of behaviour, but rather have the capacity to learn many different patterns. Any particular society institutionalizes a specific set of behaviours selected from the wide range of possible ones. Basic to this institutionalization is communication with the young, in order to *socialize them to the †norms of the society, to pass on the cultural †symbol system that carries the norms of the society, and to teach them the language that serves as the major means of communication. Furthermore, people must communicate to coordinate their actions in accomplishing the tasks necessary to maintaining their lives and their society.

Traditional forms of mass media
The most general and common forms of communication are face-to-face verbal communication using language and face-to-face non-verbal communication using body language. Mass communication, in which messages are passed to large groups or collections of individuals, can be seen in traditional forms widespread for millennia, such as sermons, plays, town criers, musical concerts, and the more long-distance medium of loud instruments such as drums or horns. Traditional forms of mass communication have required the co-presence of the individuals communicating, and beyond the moment of communication, rely upon *memory for conservation.

The use of traditional mass media can be seen in Indian villages (Hartman *et al.* 1989). In the Southeast province of Andra Pradesh, tom-toms,

locally called *dandora*, were used to attract attention for public announcements. Drama, locally *natakam*, was well established, as was a concert of sung narration, *katha*, in which several people or a group presented epic themes from regional history and religion. In West Bengal:

> Indigenous mass media . . . disseminates ideas and information. Folk drama, folk songs, folk tales, the repertoire of itinerant minstrels and musicians at festivals – all serve as media of mass communication . . .
> Here *jatra* (a folk drama performed in the open) is still prevalent and very popular . . . it runs on non-commercial lines, and is open to everyone without any barriers of class, caste, religion, age or sex. A jatra . . . serves as a reflector of traditional or existing social norms.
> There are three drama clubs in Ranabanda [village]. . . .
> There are a number of professional drama companies in Calcutta who perform their shows in the countryside towns for about six months in the year. . . .
> Another type of traditional folk drama is the *Bhanumatir Gan.* . . . It is a song-based drama, with a group of singers playing the harmonium and singing with the actors forming the backbone of the play. . . .
> Folk songs and lyrics are powerful means of propagating the ideas and experiences of the wise and learned to village people who cannot read and write.
>
> (Hartman *et al.* 1989: 190–2)

Plays, concerts, recitations and sermons continue to be important means of communication in contemporary societies. From the influential after-prayer sermons in Muslim mosques and Christian churches, to punk and rap music concerts, to plays in Africa and Asia (Peacock 1968), traditional forms of media are used to express established norms and ideals and to challenge the established.

The written word was a great breakthrough, for it allowed communication across space and time. Traditional use in mass communication was however limited to the reading of proclamations and the limited engraving of public monuments. Texts central to particular cultures, such as the Old Testament to the Jews, the New and Old Testaments to the Christians, and the Koran to the Muslims, were arduously reproduced, sometimes memorized, and then passed on to the general populace through sermons, which became an established and regular part of religious *ritual, and through religious schools.

The printed media

The development of printing made the written word into a medium of mass communication. For the first time, copies of messages could be economically produced and distributed widely, bridging great gaps of space and time. It became possible to communicate with large numbers of people, as opposed to the minuscule few of the elite who had access to the manuscripts. The availability of technology for disseminating written texts did not, however, automatically provide everyone, or even most, with the ability to read and understand; it could not eradicate the widespread barrier of illiteracy resulting from lack of *education. The slow increase in education, albeit uneven geographically and across economic classes, in the nineteenth and early twentieth centuries, and the corresponding spread of newspaper, pamphlet, and inexpensive book production and dissemination, resulted in the growing impact of the printed word as a medium for mass communication. In spite of the large and increasing number of literate people and the proliferation of printed material, large portions of the population in even the most technologically developed societies could not or did not read, and in the great rural populations of the agrarian societies of Africa, Asia and South America, reading remained a rare skill of the elites.

At the end of the twentieth century, in the large rural districts and in the poorer classes everywhere, the reading of newspapers and books is limited at best. Even in successfully developing countries such as India, with large indigenous publishing industries, major impediments remain in the diffusion of information via the printed word. One major problem is that the level of literacy is not high enough for many people to read with comprehension, ease and pleasure, and so they do not read. The other main difficulty is that newspapers and books are comparatively expensive, and the costs can be sustained only by members of the richer classes (Hartman *et al.* 1989). Some indirect diffusion does take place, as in those who read printed information verbally to others. But the limitations of the written mass media as a cultural influence remain, with a consequent ineffectiveness as a spur to change.

The electronic media

The development of the electronic media – film, telephone, radio, television, video – provided the means for communication over space and time as well as inexpensive and efficient diffusion, coded through the same human skills of speech and body movement that are characteristic of face-to-face communication. The electronic media bypass the need for special communication skills, such as *literacy, thus opening communication to those who, for lack of literacy skills, are excluded from communication via printed media. Even the cost of the electronic media is less than that of the printed media, for portable radios and audio tape players cost little more than one or two books, and the price of a year of newspapers or a dozen books will in most places buy an inexpensive television set.

Ordinary people everywhere are capable of receiving communication through the electronic media, and increasingly people throughout the world, even in the remotest forest, desert, and mountain settlements, are regularly receiving radio and television broadcasts from multiple sources. These sources are at the same time highly diverse and notably similar. They are diverse because media broadcasts – including series such as soap operas and comedies, films, musical performances, and news and documentaries – travel and are transmitted across cultural boundaries, from one country to another and from one ethnic group to another. These sources are similar because, for economic and technological reasons, they tend to come from industrial countries and regions to non-industrial countries and regions, from large countries to small, and from urban to rural areas. Consequently, the material heard or viewed is often diverse from the conditions and norms of the viewer's local life, while there is a consistency or similarity in the broadcast material because of the commonalities of the urban, industrial sources of production.

Mass media and culture

The production of messages for mass communication is rooted in the *culture of the producers and that of the supposed audience. Messages are sets of cultural meanings and are effective as communication only if they fit with the structure of cultural meanings held by the audience. For example, the Brazilian prime time, evening television *telenovelas*, social dramas or soap operas, that have become a national obsession in Brazil, incorporate and reflect basic cultural assumptions, such as the dominance of the †extended family in social life and the emphasis on †status rather than work in values and *identity (Kottak 1990).

The producers of Brazilian *telenovelas*, which run for many episodes, keep a close watch on audience reaction, and shift story lines and juggle characters to hold audience interest and enthusiasm. In this case as in most others, ongoing production is maintained and producers prosper by drawing audiences and thus making profits, either directly from audiences or from commercial advertisers. Directors of Tamil films in South India, as with producers everywhere, must therefore cater to the tastes of the audiences, such as for escape fantasies or heroic violence, even if they do not directly approve of those tastes (Dickey 1993). These directors, like others, sometimes insert morals to instruct and 'improve' the audiences.

In addition to commercial factors, producers must deal with the power and governmental structures in the societies in which they work. Media regulation and censorship boards are used, to one degree or another, by powerful societal elites to control and limit messages disseminated in the media. Producers and their programmes vary in degree of conformity and subversion. Producers do have at their disposal many symbolic ways of expressing views and representing problems which may not be expressed explicitly and represented directly.

Symbolic codes that make up the content of programmes speak to issues in the lives of the audience. The long-running, popular space programme 'Star Trek', which has spawned several 'spin-off' programmes, expresses basic themes in American life, such as space travel representing the quest for adventure and exploration and the interaction, collaboration, and co-membership of beings from different planets representing 'the incorporation of strangers and diversity within an expansive American culture' (Kottak 1990: 101)

To be successful, films or programmes must be 'culturally appropriate, understandable, familiar and conducive to mass participation' (Kottak 1990: 43). At the same time, success requires satisfying the culturally-conditioned psychological needs and desires of the audience. In the case of Tamil films, 'viewers . . . seek out movies as entertainment and as an escape from the difficulties of their lives' (Dickey 1993: 141). But they also look for relevance to their lives.

[Viewers] see very personal connections between themselves and their relationships, on the one hand, and the characters and relationships shown on the screen on the other, and occasionally see more general class level connections as well . . . They focus on themes . . . central to [their] lives: . . . among other things the effects of marriage on individuals and families, possibilities for romantic love, the responsibilities of children or siblings, and the disregarded inner virtues of the poor. Films create utopian resolutions of these issues. Escape and reality are intimately connected.

(Dickey 1993: 141)

Viewers are active in responding to the messages sent through the mass media; they do not passively absorb what the mass media brings them. There is an ongoing interplay and feedback between producers and audiences of the mass media.

The active nature of audience response does not mean that the audience is unaffected or uninfluenced by messages sent through the mass media. Some messages may be rejected or ignored, as in the case of *development information in Indian villages (Hartman *et al.* 1989). But other messages, intended or inadvertent will be consciously or unconsciously accepted and assimilated. At the very least, the mass media has an 'agenda setting' function; it cannot successfully tell people what to think, but it can effectively tell them what to think about by including some issues and ideas in messages and excluding others.

The interplay between mass media and culture becomes even more complicated when, as often is the case, messages are transmitted across cultural boundaries. Much of the world's film and television production takes place in a small number of urban centres: San Paulo, Delhi, Rome, New York, Paris, Tokyo, Hollywood, London and Bombay. The economics of production and the technology of transmission favour wide distribution, and so audiences in small countries, in less developed countries, in rural remote regions, see films and programmes that have grown out of quite different cultures, in codes based upon those cultures, and which tend to advance values from those cultures, such as individualism, commercialism, consumerism, and romanticism, which sometimes clash with the established norms, values, and beliefs of local society. Such influence can be seen, depending upon one's point of view, as liberation or as cultural imperialism.

PHILIP CARL SALZMAN

See also: culture, complex society, cultural studies, film, literacy, world-system

Further reading
Abu-Lughod, L. (ed.) (1993) 'Screening Politics in a World of Nations', *Public Culture* II: 463–604
Cruz, J. and J. Lewis (1994) *Viewing, Reading, Listening: Audiences and Cultural Reception*, Oxford: Westview Press
Dickey, S. (1993) *Cinema and the Urban Poor in South India*, Cambridge: Cambridge University Press
Hartman, P., B. Patil and A. Dighe (1989) *The Mass Media and Village Life*, London: Sage Publications
Heider, K. (1991) *Indonesian Cinema: National Culture on Screen*, Honolulu: University of Hawaii Press
Kottak, C.P. (1990) *Prime Time Society: An Anthropological Analysis of Television and Culture*, Belmont, California: Wadsworth Publishing Company
Lull, J. (ed.) (1988) *World Families Watch Television*, London: Sage Publications
McLuhan, M. (1964) *Understanding Media*, London: McGraw-Hill
Martín-Barbero, J. (1993) *Communication, Culture and Hegemony: From the Media to Mediations*, London: Sage Publications
Newcomb, H. (1994) *Television: The Critical View* 5th edn, Oxford: Oxford University Press
Peacock, J.L. (1968) *Rites of Modernization: Symbolic and Social Aspects of Indonesian Proletarian Drama*, London: University of Chicago Press

medical anthropology

'Medical anthropology' is generally understood to refer to the study of social and cultural dimensions of health, ill health and medicine. A founding ancestor was the anthropologist and doctor †W.H.R. Rivers, although his work on medicine (posthumously published) did not prompt the establishment of an identifiable subfield in anthropology. Rivers argued that 'primitive medicine' could be studied as a social institution employing the same principles and methods that are used to study other social and cultural phenomena. 'Primitive medicine' was seen as a coherent body of practices underpinned by particular ideas about the causation of disease that are, in turn, shaped by the general worldview of the members of that society. Clements's attempt in the 1930s to identify universals in etiological categories of disease, and Ackerknecht's series of *functionalist publications on comparative aspects of 'primitive' medicine and surgery in the 1940s, proved more influential in giving rise to a subdiscipline that in the 1960s came to be known as 'medical anthropology'. Until that decade anthropologists assumed non-comparability between 'primitive' and 'modern' medicine on the grounds that the former was magico-religious and the latter scientific in nature.

Medical anthropology is, as the phrase implies, unavoidably concerned with the paradigm of modern Western medicine, whether implicitly or explicitly. Struggles to produce objective accounts of non-Western medical concepts and traditions among peoples who often lacked a medical domain of thought and practice that was indigenously distinguished from that of *religion or *ritual, characterized debates in the field during the 1960s and 1970s. One approach – to study only those forms of sickness and modes of treatment that were considered symbolically significant by the people under study – rendered the problem of equivalence explicit, but was simply a rationalization for anthropologists' continuing focus on the more exotic phenomena, such as spirit *possession and ritual healing, in which they had traditionally been interested. Studies of this type (see 'Ethnomedicine' below) have indeed tended to be more properly ethnographic than those in the applied domain. However, the demise of both functionalism and the treatment of societies as homogeneous cultural isolates, together with increasing interest in the practice of anthropology both 'at home' and as applied to *development issues, has led Western medicine itself to become an object of study for anthropologists working in a variety of geographical contexts. With the realization that the modern Western tradition of medicine is itself socially constructed and historically situated as well as globally practised, implicitly evaluative terms such as 'Western', 'modern' and 'scientific' have gradually given way to the use of the more neutral term 'biomedicine' to describe this tradition.

Ethnomedicine, medical pluralism and medical systems
The term †'ethnomedicine' is frequently used to characterize the object of study in ethnographic research on indigenous, usually non-Western, forms of healing and *classifications of disease. Such research is often, though erroneously, itself designated as 'ethnomedical' since the focus of enquiry is the elucidation of *emic or indigenous concepts of sickness and its treatment. Many prominent anthropologists from †Victor Turner to †Evans-Pritchard have discussed aspects of

illness and healing in the course of describing mechanisms of social regulation, religious systems or aspects of *cosmology in particular cultures, but these ethnographic works were not regarded as studies in 'medical anthropology' by their authors, nor did they take illness and healing to be their central concern. In such research the investigation and analysis of indigenous understandings of sickness and modes of treatment were undertaken as means through which to elucidate broader cultural themes.

The ethnographic investigation of indigenous modes of healing and their relationship to underlying conceptualizations of sickness and health as part of a particular world view has continued to be one of the three major orientations historically identifiable in medical anthropology. Many of these studies have focused on single medically-related traditions such as indigenous midwifery and childbirth practices within specific Latin American Indian cultures, *shamanism in Nepal, †ethnobotanical knowledge among Amazonian peoples or classical Ayurveda in the Indian subcontinent. Another favoured research domain is the study of traditional healers; investigation of the comparative efficacy of 'traditional' and 'biomedical' approaches to the treatment of mental illness, or *ethnopsychiatry, has been a popular topic among both 'transcultural' psychiatrists and medical anthropologists.

Increasingly, however, research in non-Western settings has turned to the study of †medical pluralism, the coexistence of a variety of different medical traditions within a chosen context. Much attention has been paid to the description and comparative analysis of national 'medical systems' comprising a variety of forms of healthcare and on the degree to which these configurations can be considered 'systems' at all. An initial focus among applied anthropologists was local responses to biomedicine in non-Western settings (see 'Applied anthropology in public health' below) and the putative conflicts between different conceptual systems produced by this encounter. More recent work, however, places the changing relations between biomedicine and indigenous medical traditions (and, especially, processes of professionalization among indigenous healers) within a broader social and historical context that gives proper weight to the influences of *colonialism and state legislation. The character of medical pluralism and the place of alternative (non-biomedical) forms of therapy within Western

industrial societies is another topic of growing interest among medical anthropologists.

Applied anthropology in public health and clinical medicine

The main focus of †applied anthropology here is the elucidation of practical problems in the fields of public health, clinical medicine and psychiatry. This approach has become increasingly influential as anthropologists and others practice anthropology beyond academia. Repeated failures of context-insensitive health programmes in the developing world, and difficulties in providing effective medical care within Western multi-ethnic societies, have prompted a growing awareness in the health professions of the need to attend to social and cultural dimensions of health. American anthropologists began to be employed in institutions of international public health from the 1950s and 1960s. The task assigned to the anthropologist was to identify 'cultural barriers' to modern healthcare and the means for overcoming resistance to change in non-Western settings; an example of this kind of work is *Health, Culture and Community* (1955) edited by Paul, one of the first anthropologists to be employed in this field. Applied studies of this type argued for a greater degree of cultural sensitivity in the formulation and implementation of health education and disease prevention programmes imported from Western settings.

Contemporary anthropologists in the field of public health often work within multidisciplinary research teams and focus on the adaptation and refinement of anthropological methods for application to specific health problems (such as diarrheal disease and acute respiratory infections). 'Community based' research tends to concentrate on conceptual discrepancies and conflicts within these *communities between local beliefs about the causation of illness and biomedical approaches to disease prevention. Meanwhile, ethnographic studies of organizational culture in health care settings and sociocultural analyses of risk, for example, seek more explicitly to employ and develop theoretical insights through ostensibly 'applied' research.

Ecological studies

*'Ecological' or 'biocultural' anthropology focuses on the ecology of disease in human groups and takes an evolutionary approach to human adaptation. This orientation is frequently invoked to

support the claim that medical anthropology exemplifies the holistic ideal of the parent discipline (anthropology as a whole), since it entails studies of the relationships between social practices, such as †agriculture and *food or *marriage patterns; *environmental stressors, such as high altitude or urban *migration; and biological conditions, such as the incidence of genetic disorders or of malaria. Due to these emphases, however, cultural practices become dependent variables for the explanation of certain *etic observations deriving from biomedical models of disease, while the elucidation of their meaning to those who engage in them and the role of human agency in changing cultural practices takes second place. This orientation is more prominent in the work of *biological anthropologists and has increasingly been subsumed within epidemiology, medical sociology and population genetics. Indeed the concurrent development of the nascent fields of modern epidemiology and medical anthropology from the 1950s onwards ensured that a significant proportion of the health-related studies that were reviewed under the aegis of 'medical anthropology' in the 1950s and 1960s could as easily be classified as social epidemiology.

Disease, illness and clinical applications

Efforts to characterize non-biomedical views of ill health and approaches to its treatment in relation to the biomedical paradigm led to the development of the single most utilized analytic dichotomy in medical anthropology as a whole; that of the disease/illness distinction (Eisenberg 1977). 'Disease' is taken to be the biomedical, measurable identification of bodily disorder central to the process of biomedical diagnosis and is contrasted with patients' experiential awareness and understanding of their 'illness'. The disease/illness distinction has been regarded as valuable for its benefits in enhancing communication, compliance and patient satisfaction in clinical practice and it is significant that it was first proposed and explored by practising psychiatrists, some of whom had training in anthropology, rather than by academic anthropologists. A tradition of *psychoanalytic and psychological approaches to cultural variations in manifestations of mental illness already had roots in the *culture and personality school of anthropology within the US from the 1940s.

Since the 1970s, increasing levels of dissatisfaction with Western medicine among patients, and communication difficulties between doctors

and patients of culturally diverse backgrounds within North American society, has led medical professionals to take a more direct interest in the possible contributions of anthropology to clinical practice. This includes the recognition of cultural variability in the expression of signs and symptoms of distress and disorder through a focus on meaning and symbolization. Kleinman's (1980) delineation of 'Explanatory Models' – conceptual templates variously constructed by individual patients and practitioners to explain episodes of illness – has been widely utilized in clinical settings and in academic medical anthropology.

The emphasis in such approaches is on cultural influences in the manifestation of ill health and the effectiveness of treatment, while relatively little account is taken of social determinants. This interpretative approach has come to be known, at least in the US, as 'clinically applied anthropology' and is contrasted with a materialist 'critical medical anthropology' that considers the *political economy of health and the macro level determinants that influence understandings of and responses to ill health ('sickness') at the micro level. It tends to regard biomedicine as an instrument of social control that is only aided in its effectiveness by the contributions of 'clinical applied anthropology', since the latter accords little recognition to the structural determinants of ill health such as poverty, *class, racism and the influence of global *capitalism. Most work in this genre comes from the USA and mainly derives from research within this national economic context.

The anthropology of medicine

Applied approaches take lay perceptions of ill health and modes of dealing with it ('health behaviour') as central to medical anthropology. The application of anthropology to clinical medicine and public health is ultimately a means for increasing the appropriateness, and thus effectiveness, of biomedicine in a variety of settings from the clinic to the community. In contrast, more academically-oriented medical anthropology critically examines biomedicine itself as a form of ethnomedicine. Research in this vein ranges from the study of international health institutions and bureaucracies (Justice 1986) to the cultural construction of biomedical concepts and epidemiological categories. The latest and single most influential impetus in the anthropological study of health issues, however, has been the AIDS pandemic. Research on this topic includes the study of indigenous theories of etiology and their application to the design of culturally appropriate HIV prevention programmes, ethnographies of commercial sex work, critiques of epidemiological assumptions and explorations of the dialectic between medical and social representations of the deviant 'other'. This range illustrates the inappropriateness of assuming any strict division between 'applied' and 'academic' approaches.

Medical anthropology began to gain general respectability among academic anthropologists only in the early 1980s. While much ethnographic research in medical anthropology focuses on symbolic aspects of healing and the meaning of sickness within particular cultural contexts, the work of some academic anthropologists integrates an interpretative approach to ethnographic material with analysis of the structural forces and relations of power that shape cultural constructions of ill health and healthcare. Some of the more successful attempts to combine interpretative and materialist approaches in the analysis of medical phenomena lie within the field of feminist anthropology and the *gender-related studies which comprise an important influence on the field of medical anthropology (for instance Martin 1987 on reproduction in the USA). Associated with these is a growing interest among academic anthropologists in health-related issues such as the new *reproductive technologies and studies of the *body and emotions that hold potential for the theoretical development of anthropology as a whole. In its broadest sense, 'medical anthropology' ranges from strictly applied work to topics of study that have long been integral to mainstream anthropology (from *pollution and purity ideas to food, *nature/culture and concepts of *person), but this diversity means that, overall, the subdiscipline lacks the character of a truly coherent field.

HELEN LAMBERT

See also: biological anthropology, body, ecological anthropology, ethnopsychiatry, nutrition, psychoanalysis

Further reading

Bolton, R. and M. Singer (eds) (1992) *Rethinking AIDS Prevention: Cultural Approaches*, New York: Gordon and Breach
Eisenberg, L. (1977) 'Disease and Illness: Distinctions between Professional and Popular Ideas of Sickness', *Culture, Medicine and Psychiatry* 1: 9–23

Farmer, P. (1992) *AIDS and Accusation: Haiti and the Geography of Blame*, Berkeley: University of California Press
Johnson, T.M. and C.F. Sargent (eds) (1991) *Medical Anthropology: Contemporary Theory and Method*, Westport: Greenwood Press
Justice, J. (1986) *Policies, Plans, and People: Foreign Aid and Health Development*, Berkeley: University of California Press
Kleinman, A. (1980) *Patients and Healers in the Context of Culture*, Berkeley: University of California Press
Lindenbaum, S., and M. Lock (eds) (1993) *Knowledge, Power, and Practice: The Anthropology of Medicine and Everyday Life*, Berkeley etc.: University of California Press
Martin, E. (1987) *The Woman in the Body: A Cultural Analysis of Reproduction*, Boston: Beacon Press
Nichter, M. (1989) *Anthropology and International Health: South Asian Case Studies*
Paul, B. (ed.) (1955) *Health, Culture and Community: Case Studies of Public Reactions to Health Programs*, New York: Russell Sage Foundation
Scheper-Hughes, N. (1992) *Death without Weeping: The Violence of Everyday Life in Brazil*, Berkeley: University of California Press

memory

Memory is a topic which closely links the interests of psychologists, anthropologists and historians. Psychologists have traditionally studied how individuals remember but have paid little attention to what they remember. Anthropologists have studied what individuals remember and how this is affected by what it is acceptable to recall. They have focused on the relation of individual and social memory. Historians too have studied what people remember of past events since many of their sources take this form, but more recently they have begun to see their work as one kind of remembering, in the end, not fundamentally different to other kinds of recall. This view is elaborated in an extreme form in the work of the American cultural historian Hayden White (1973).

Psychologists distinguish between short-term, or working memory, and long-term memory and it is psychologists' views of long-term memory which are most important to anthropologists. Long-term memory is itself further divided into episodic memory which relates to individuals' experiences during their lifetimes, and semantic memory which relates to individuals' decontextualized knowledge. For example, those people who know that the capital of Greece is Athens are people who have stored this information in their long-term semantic memory. It is therefore possible to equate what anthropologists have called *culture with the shared knowledge which different members of a society have stored in their long-term memory.

Although many anthropologists ignore the fact that the concept of culture inevitably raises issues about memory, a number of writers have argued that the psychological and anthropological side of things cannot be separated. One of the most influential was the Cambridge psychologists Bartlett, who was much influenced by anthropologists such as †W.H.R. Rivers, and who was subsequently to have a direct influence upon †Gregory Bateson. In a particularly influential book, *Remembering* (1932), he demonstrated that what people remembered of a story was influenced by their way of seeing things, a way which had been created by their culture. Thus when Cambridge undergraduates were asked to remember a North American Indian myth they could only do this on a long-term basis when they had transferred this myth into a story which accorded to the principles of their culture. The implication of this is that culture filters what is remembered, and that new information is unlikely to challenge people's ingrained preconceptions, since this new information will only be retained in a form which accords with these preconceptions.

Anthropologists and *sociologists have reached similar conclusions from their side. †Durkheim saw knowledge as closely linked to the organization of society, and Halbwachs, a French student of his, wrote a book, *La Memoire Collective* (1950), which stressed that the act of remembering was always social, because what was recalled had to be socially approved and constructed through a process of interaction and accommodation of which the individual participants were not fully aware. Similarly a number of writers have developed the idea of 'distributed memory'. What is meant by this is that the social memory of a group may be distributed unequally in the minds of its members but that this distributed memory can be brought together at moments such as *rituals. A similar point has been made by †Frederick Barth (1987) who has also argued that in certain societies rituals can first serve to organize distributed memory, then fix certain representations and meanings which subsequently inform perception and future performances.

British anthropologists such as *Malinowski, *Radcliffe-Brown and, later, †Edmund Leach tended to stress the pragmatic side of things, arguing that what people recalled in social contexts was used to legitimate institutions or to back a claim to †status or rights. These writers paid attention especially to the kind of selective forgetting which they called 'structural amnesia'. Thus Laura Bohannan (1952) demonstrated how, among the Tiv, only *ancestors relevant to the present situation were evoked from the past, while others were forgotten. Subsequent writers working in this tradition have stressed how all narratives of the past have to be understood in terms of the nature of the society in which they are told and how such factors as the construction of the *person and the nature of the *kinship system affect such stories (Bloch 1992; Dakhlia 1990; Kilani 1992).

A more radical and highly controversial theory of the relation of memory and culture has been recently proposed by Dan Sperber (1985). Sperber draws his inspiration from the theories of †Chomsky in linguistics. Chomsky had argued that humans learn language extraordinarily fast and efficiently because they are genetically predisposed to be on the lookout for the specific forms which all human languages share. When the infant identifies these forms it can remember them with amazing ease. Sperber argues that this might also be the case for certain cultural forms, and certain types of narrative in particular. Thus humans would be genetically predisposed to remember only certain types of information while other types would not be retained or transmitted. This psychological disposition would therefore, in the long run, be a strong determinant and limitation on what kind of human culture is possible.

Anthropologists have also been concerned with memory in a way which is less directly linked to individual mental processes. Many writers have pointed to the importance of †material culture as a way by which societies deliberately choose to encode memory (Connerton 1989). Often, monuments are made precisely in order that an event or a person will not be forgotten. This is the case with statues and war memorials, but such phenomena are common in the non-industrial world too; thus the standing stones found in Madagascar which are intended to mark a whole variety of events are called memory stones. Elaborate tombs and funerary buildings such as the pyramids of Egypt or the Taj Mahal in India serve similar purposes. In New Guinea elaborate carvings of spatial configurations often represent complex stories and their making and destruction are seen as devices for the evocation, transformation and even abolition of certain forms of memory of alliances and events (Küchler 1987; Munn 1986).

MAURICE BLOCH

See also: cognition, psychological anthropology, history and anthropology.

Further reading

Barth, F. (1987) Cosmologies in the Making: A Generative Approach to Cultural Variation in New Guinea, Cambridge: Cambridge University Press

Bartlett, F.C. (1932) Remembering: A Study of Experimental and Social Psychology, Cambridge: Cambridge University Press

Bloch, M. (1992) 'Internal and External Memory: Different Ways of Being in History', Suomen Anthropologi 1: 3–15

Bohannan, L. (1952) 'A Genealogical Charter', Africa 22: 301–15

Connerton, P. (1989) How Societies Remember, Cambridge: Cambridge University Press

Dakhlia, J. (1990) L'oubli de la Cité: La Mémoire Collective à l'épreuve dans le Jerid Tunisien, Paris: Editions La Découverte

Halbwachs, M. (1950) La Mémoire Collective, Paris: Presses Universitaire de France

Kilani, M. (1992) La Construction de la Mémoire, Geneva: Labor and Fides

Küchler, S. (1987) 'Malangan: Art and Memory in a Melanesian Society', Man (n.s.) 22: 238–55

—— and W. Melion (eds) (1991) Images of Memory: On Representing and Remembering, Washington: Smithsonian Institution Press

Munn, N. (1986) The Fame of Gawa, Cambridge: Cambridge University Press

Sperber, D. (1985) 'Anthropology and Psychology: Towards an Epidemiology of Representations', Man 20: 73–89

White, H. (1973) Metahistory: The Historical Imagination in Nineteenth Century Europe, Baltimore: Johns Hopkins University Press

menstruation

The human female menstruates considerably more copiously than any other primate. Since ovulation in the human case has become concealed, this bleeding is one of the few indicators of fertility to have remained externally detectable. This may help explain the extraordinary attention focused upon it in virtually all *hunter-gatherer and other traditional cultures.

Biologically, sex around the menstrual period is both possible and enjoyable. Yet most cultures treat marital relations at such times as highly risk-laden. Recurrently, menstruants are also prohibited from cooking meat, touching men's hunting weapons or allowing the sun to shine on them. *Lévi-Strauss's Mythologiques (see especially 1978) is largely taken up with such themes. European fairy tales such as The Sleeping Beauty centre on the spell-casting potency of a girl's flow. When women are out of circulation, *mythology places the moon, too, in its dark, secluded phase. Among the Amazonian Barasana, 'mythology says the moon copulates with menstruating women and that during an eclipse of the moon, called the 'dying moon', the moon becomes a small red ball of menstrual blood which comes to earth and fills the house and its objects' (Hugh-Jones 1979).

Such is the ritual potency of menstruation that over much of Australia, men underwent a genital operation (†'subincision') enabling them to bleed on ritual occasions. Counterparts in other parts of the world abound. Wherever 'male menstruation' is central to initiation ritual, myths attribute it to a culture-hero who violently stole such secrets from women (Knight 1983, 1991).

Kalahari San women are ritually most powerful when menstruating, and use this power to obtain much-desired meat. A girl in seclusion is metaphorically a bleeding, wounded game animal; in her special hut, she is sexually inviolable – having only to snap her fingers to bring down lightning. Whilst secluded, other women dance around her, pantomiming the mating behaviour of antelope. This 'Eland Bull Dance' spurs men to success in the hunt (Lewis-Williams 1981).

This illustrates that menstrual *taboos are not necessarily rooted in †patriarchy. Indeed, there is evidence that joyful dances like those of the San once empowered women by structuring the first sexual division of labour. Instead of gaining meat by chasing after male hunters, in this view, earliest culturally organized women made the meat move. They did this by refusing sex until men brought their kills home, using their blood to signal their solidarity and defiance (Knight 1991).

CHRIS KNIGHT

See also: taboo, ritual, pollution and purity

Further reading

Buckley, T., and A. Gottlieb (eds) (1988) Blood Magic: The Anthropology of Menstruation, Berkeley: University of California Press

Hugh-Jones, C. (1979) *From the Milk River: Spatial and Temporal Processes in Northwest Amazonia*, Cambridge: Cambridge University Press

Knight, C.D. (1983) 'Lévi-Strauss and the Dragon: *Mythologiques* Reconsidered in the Light of an Australian Aboriginal Myth', *Man* (n.s.) 18: 21–50

—— (1991) *Blood Relations: Menstruation and the Origins of Culture*, New Haven and London: Yale University Press

Lévi-Strauss, C. (1978) *The Origin of Table Manners (Introduction to a Science of Mythology)* 3, London: Cape

Lewis-Williams, J.D. (1981) *Believing and Seeing: Symbolic Meanings in Southern San Rock Art*, London: Academic Press

methodology

How does one actually carry out *ethnographic research? There is one well established, basic strategy that is common ground among anthropologists since *Malinowski set the standard early in the twentieth century. That strategy is †'participant observation', long-term residence among the population being studied. It is generally agreed that ethnographic *fieldwork should be carried out for a year or more, that the researcher should be able to converse effectively, preferably in the local language, with the people being studied, and that some kind of engagement with the flow of ordinary life and ongoing activities of local people in the research setting is desirable.

Beyond this strategy, there is a large range of methodological techniques for collecting different kinds of information. Which techniques a researcher chooses depends upon the appropriateness of any particular technique for any specific topic being studied, the logistical difficulties of applying the methods under consideration, and the researcher's theoretical views about the validity of various techniques. Of equal importance, but beyond the scope of this discussion, are modes and techniques of information or data analysis.

Some exemplary methods

A variety of techniques (Johnson 1978; Pelto and Pelto 1978; Poggie *et al.* 1992) can be directed to the collection of the specific topical information desired by the researcher, whether it focuses upon decisions and choices, concepts and precepts, status and power, etiquette and morality, or resources and their use. There follow some examples of information collection techniques, presented in alphabetical order to avoid suggestion of priority or relative value:

Archival documents which are the records of various aspects of people's lives, and are found in local, regional, national institutions, both public and private. Everything from parish records of births, marriages, and deaths, to those of court cases, taxes, employment and unemployment, school attendance, job competitions, and medical cases, can be rich sources of historical and contemporary information. Gaining access to such records, and finding a way to copy them, are serious logistical difficulties. Learning the limitations and biases of such material is also important.

Collection of information from two or more distinct cases, usually communities or research sites, allows the juxtaposition of different social and cultural patterns in *comparative analysis. That specific differences between cases are not random, but related to other observable differences, indicates that some factors vary together. These concomitant variations, suggest that certain factors influence others in these settings and perhaps more widely (Nadel 1953).

In *extended †case-study analysis*, the researcher focuses upon the evolution of a particular series of events in the population being studied, following the involved parties, their interventions and reactions, and the consequences of the events upon people and their activities (Van Velsen 1967).

Interviews, whether formal or informal, unstructured or highly structured, with individuals or with groups, are widely used and versatile means of eliciting responses from informants. Such responses provide valuable information, usually culturally significant, but require careful analysis, for the content cannot always be taken literally. Furthermore, the relationship between a response on a particular occasion and how people might respond in a different setting is rather unclear, as is the relationship between a particular verbal response and some other (non-verbal) behaviour. A major logistical problem is how to conserve the responses, for memory is weak, notes are selective and transcription of verbatim recordings is usually unmanageably arduous or expensive.

The collection of *life-histories* provides full, first person accounts of a wide range of experiences over time. These reports, based upon recollection, have the same limitations as interviews, but benefit from being on one of most subjects' favourite topics.

For some kinds of information, direct *measurement* is required. This may be the only way to gain information important to a particular account, such as the size of fields under cultivation, the amount produced in a period, the margin between calories used and calories produced, the time necessary to accomplish certain tasks, the number of animals in flocks, weight gain and loss in different periods and classes, the number of people visiting holy sites, doing two jobs, or marrying within or outside the group or up or down the social ladder. Any one of these measurements may necessitate complex techniques and protracted procedures.

*Social *network analysis* is directed toward the ties between individuals, with the combination of individual reports providing a map of relationships within and between social settings (Boissevain 1974).

Observation of life in natural settings, whether in homes, bars, offices, fields, or churches, whether at work, sport, politics, or religion, is a mainstay of 'participant observation', and a good way to test, through anticipation, what one thinks one understands about the way things work. Formal recording of frequency of behaviour is difficult but possible, although rarely used, the more informal 'taking in what one can' the common strategy.

Quantitative case-study analysis subjects a series of separate cases, such as of disputes, marriage negotiations, or witchcraft accusations, to numerical or statistical examination in order to elicit patterns (Marwick 1967; Poggie *et al.* 1992).

Sampling is a way of deciding from whom, within a larger population, one wishes to collect information. This allows the researcher, depending upon her or his purpose, to deal with information from a set of people representative of the population, or a set of people which represents various specified kinds of diversity, whether economic, religious, linguistic, generational, or gender.

Surveys are used to collect specific information from a wide range of individual cases, as in demographic surveys of households to ascertain who, of what ages, sexes, and relationships, live together, or occupational surveys to determine how everyone makes a living, or activity surveys to see who plays what sports, attends church, or goes to movies, or attitude surveys to establish people's views. Surveys provide a broad but thin base of information which may be useful for providing a contextual framework. Surveys depending upon

informants as opposed to direct observation have similar limitations to interviews, namely that responses may have an uncertain relationship to what people surveyed would say in other contexts and how they would act.

Tests, presumably designed or adapted for use in the specific research setting, provide a uniform stimulus for the elicitation of a set of complex responses, not always conscious, from a number of informants. Tests differ from surveys in lengthy application and the greater depth of results, which allows various internal tests of validity. Tests of cognitive ability, personality structure, and social attitudes, usually adapted from psychology or sociology, have been used by anthropologists. The validity of such tests cross-culturally has been questioned.

Common problems in applying methods

Methodology is not a popular concern in anthropology, and students, even at the PhD level, receive little instruction in it, and even less in quantitative analysis. Even for those who are enthused, opportunities for learning methods, and particularly for practical training, are rare, excepting a few scattered departments and summer field schools. So few researchers actually know any methods for collecting information, beyond hanging around with the folks and trying to figure out what is going on. Some researchers develop or reinvent methods as they go along.

Another impediment is the customarily individualistic nature of ethnographic research, with the individual researcher going to the field and trying to do everything on his or her own. That research is usually limited to a year or so, and is poorly funded, not allowing for much in the way of equipment or assistance, compounds the problem. The result is that ethnographers do not have the time or energy to apply, in any extended or systematic fashion, more than one or at best two methods of collecting information (Salzman 1993). Perhaps this is why 'methodology' is so unpopular in anthropology.

On the other hand, the freedom to use a wide range of methods and the benefit of being able to cross-check results is a great strength of anthropological research. Increased collaboration with other anthropologists and social scientists, with researchers from the country of fieldwork, and with local assistants, can provide some opportunity to overcome the logsitical difficulties of applying many methodological techniques.

Theoretical foundations of methodologies

A researcher's methodological approach is influenced by her or his vision of the goals of social or cultural anthropology and by heuristic theoretical position.

Two visions of objectives and goals are well established in contemporary social and cultural anthropology. These visions might be labelled 'humanistic' and 'scientific', and are perhaps better seen as poles around which researchers situate themselves, and between which they shift in one direction or another from time to time, thus shifting somewhat the tendency of the entire discipline.

In the humanistic vision, the goal of anthropology is the understanding of people's lives, their social life, and their culture, an understanding which requires an empathetic grasp of the point of view of the people studied. Thus the anthropologist provides a qualitative account of the cultural 'web of meaning' shaping the society and the lives of its members. Such an account is thought to reflect the researcher as well as those studied, the description being one of many possible interpretations. The work of anthropology is likened, in this vision, to history and to literature, emphasizing the particular and the idiographic.

In the scientific vision, the goal of anthropology is the discovery of descriptive generalizations and explanatory laws about the way society and culture work which can account for the commonalities and variations among societies and their trajectories over time. To accomplish this, attention must be given to behaviour as well as ideas, and precise information is required, quantitative as well as qualitative. To maximize the value of the information, and to limit errors resulting from human subjectivity and bias, systematic forms of data collection are needed, and checks, as in repeat studies, are required. Comparative studies juxtaposing different societies and cultures allow the formulation of general explanations.

The works of founding authors such as †Weber, *Boas and †Evans-Pritchard have inspired many anthropologists with a humanistic bent, while those of †Marx, †Durkheim, and *Radcliffe-Brown have inspired many with a scientific bent. Contemporary authors who have influenced this debate include †Clifford Geertz (1983) on the humanistic side and †Marvin Harris (1979) on the scientific side. The current intellectual shift toward the humanistic pole called *postmodernism has challenged intellectual authority in general, and that of science in particular, the postmodern position being that no particular viewpoint can be justifiably privileged, each being one of many possible interpretations, and that all opinions, perspectives, and viewpoints are equally legitimate.

The methodologies favoured by humanistic anthropologists would include the use of empathy, as in participation in local activities to gain a feeling for local life, the collection through casual conversation, interviews and life-histories of expressions by local people of their perspectives, understandings, and experiences, and the recording of collective expressions of local culture such as *myths, proverbs, songs, stories, *rituals, and ceremonies. (See below for more detail.) Humanistic anthropology in its more extreme postmodern form has no place for information collection that smacks of †'objectivism' and †'positivism', such as distanced observation, surveys, testing, quantitative data, or any method which makes the people being studied into research objects. In fact, from this perspective, the very idea of 'methodology' is unacceptable because of its disreputable objectivist connotations.

The methodologies favoured by anthropologists of a scientific leaning would include general surveys, observations of behaviour patterns, tests and other formal exercises of information collection, structured interviews, sampling of the population studied, and comparison of different neighbourhoods, communities or cultural groups. (See below for more detail.) Often these methods are marshalled to test a specific hypothesis about the relationship between certain variables, such as the argument that control of wealth determines the relative power of the sexes, or that in †patrilineal societies, kin group †endogamy provides higher status and security for young wives than does kin group †exogamy. The intention is to use methodological techniques to collect systematic and precise information on the relevant variables so as to test decisively the hypothesis, thus adding to firmly established knowledge about social and cultural patterns and the nature of human life.

Theoretical differences other than that of humanities versus science similarly influence research agendas and methodological application. For example, those committed to proactive, advocacy anthropology, such as some Marxist and feminist anthropologists, take the position that all anthropological accounts are political, implicitly or explicitly supporting either the status quo or some kind of change. In their view, one must pick a conceptual framework and methodology to advance the interests of those identified as oppressed. *Class analysis or *gender analysis based upon the analyst's criteria allow the researcher to disregard the 'false consciousness' of the people studied and pinpoint their 'real interests' as members of economic classes or gendered subjects. Methodologically, emphasis would be upon the researchers' observations of economic exploitation or gender oppression, rather than upon the perspectives and opinions of the people being studied, whose awareness has been clouded by mystifying ideologies promulgated by the oppressors.

One further example is the differing theoretical emphasis upon the collectivity versus the individual. Some researchers follow Durkheim and Geertz in emphasizing the determining collective nature of consciousness and culture, while others follow Weber and †Barth in emphasizing individual consciousness and †agency in shaping society and societal change. Methodologically, the collectivist orientation leads to the study of collective phenomena, such as society-wide institutions, belief systems and rituals. In contrast, the individualist orientation leads to focus upon individual interests, actions and decision-making, and upon the goal-oriented activity manifested in transactions, innovations, and manipulations.

PHILIP CARL SALZMAN

See also: comparative method, fieldwork, emic and etic, history of anthropology, reflexivity, poetics, componential analysis, network analysis

Further reading

Boissevain, J. (1974) *Friends of Friends: Networks, Manipulators and Coalitions*, Oxford: Blackwell
Geertz, C. (1983) *Local Knowledge: Further Essays in Interpretive Anthropology*, New York: Basic Books
Harris, M. (1979) *Cultural Materialism: The Struggle for a Science of Culture*, New York: Random House
Johnson, A.W. (1978) *Quantification in Cultural Anthropology*, Stanford: Stanford University Press
Marwick, M.G. (1967) 'The Study of Witchcraft', in A.L. Epstein (ed.) *The Craft of Social Anthropology*, London: Tavistock
Nadel, S.F. (1953) *The Foundation of Social Anthropology*, Glencoe: The Free Press
Pelto, P.J. and G.H. (1978) *Anthropological Research*, Cambridge: Cambridge University Press
Poggie, Jr, J.J., B.R. DeWalt and W.W. Dressler (eds) (1992) *Anthropological Research*, Albany: State University of New York Press
Salzman, P.C. (1993) 'The Lone Stranger in the Heart of Darkness', in R. Borofsky (ed.) *Assessing Cultural Anthropology*, New York: McGraw-Hill
van Velsen, J. (1967) 'The Extended-case Method and Situational Analysis', in A.L. Epstein (ed.) *The Craft of Social Anthropology*, London: Tavistock

Middle East and North Africa

In historical terms, today's Middle East coincides roughly with the three largest Muslim empires at their greatest extent (except for Spain) – the Umayyad (661–750), the early 'Abbasid (750–c. 800), and the Ottoman from the sixteenth through the eighteenth centuries. In current usage, the Middle East encompasses the region stretching from Morocco to Turkey and Iran – many include Pakistan and Afghanistan – and it is used in this sense by the people of the region itself.

As a whole, the region is semi-arid, so that irrigation agriculture is more characteristic of many areas, including oases (such as Marrakesh in Morocco and Nizwa in Oman) and a narrow belt of cultivated land on either side of the region's major rivers, such as the Nile, the Tigris, and the Euphrates. Elsewhere, annual rainfall varies so much in timing and quantity that even where agriculture is possible, the yields from wheat and barley, the most common rainfall-fed crops, are highly irregular. As a result, seasonal farming is often combined with *transhumant pastoralism.

Most Middle Eastern countries also possess mountainous regions which have served as zones of refuge from state control. Thus the Kurds of Iraq, Iran, and Turkey, the Berber-speaking tribal groups in the mountainous regions of Morocco and Algeria, and some of the tribal groups of southern Iran remained relatively autonomous until the early twentieth century.

Traditionally, the Middle East has been a region of irrigation, †agriculture, *pastoralism, and long-distance trade, making important the shifting interrelations between *nomads, farmers, and city-dwellers. Despite the prevailing image of the region as populated by nomadic and semi-nomadic peoples – until the 1960s most anthropological studies of the region focused on pastoralists – nomads today constitute less than one per cent of the population and never constituted a majority of the non-urban population in the past. Most non-urban Middle Easterners are *peasants, even if some are tribally organized. Only in recent years, however, have studies of the region's peasants encompassed changing international and regional economic conditions, which have often led to the substitution of cash crops for subsistence ones, and changes in gender roles as women perform agricultural tasks formerly assumed by men who have sought work elsewhere.

The popular image of the region also belies its rapidly emerging urban profile. If roughly ten per cent of the Middle East's population was urban in 1900, today it is nearly half. The rate of urbanization continues to increase as a result both of rapid population growth – the Middle East birth rate is one of the highest in the world – and economic transformations which make agriculture less economically viable than labour emigration. Even for countries lacking mineral wealth, oil revenues in neighbouring states have significantly altered social and material life, facilitating transnational and transregional patterns of labour *migration. The effects are not just economic – the high density of first and second generation North African immigrants in France and Turks in Germany have profound religious and political implications both for countries of origin and for host countries.

*Islam is the region's predominant religion – the obvious exception is Israel – but even in other countries there are important non-Muslim minorities. Christians form significant minorities in Egypt, Lebanon, Iraq, Syria, and Turkey, and European settlers gave the Maghrib states sizeable Christian populations until the end of the colonial era. Today small but often influential Jewish communities remain in Morocco, Turkey, Tunisia, and Iran. Prior to the founding of Israel in 1948, only Saudi Arabia and the Persian Gulf states lacked Jewish communities. Popular religious practices often coincide between the major religious traditions. Thus in North Africa, Muslim maraboutic, or saint, festivals (*musims*) and pilgrimages (*ziyaras*) have their Jewish equivalents (*hillulas*) (Deshen and Shokeid 1974), and some Moroccan shrines are equally venerated by both Muslims and Jews. These practices also distinguish communities from one another, including between Sunni and Shi'i Muslims (who comprise about ten per cent of Muslims worldwide, with most located in Iran, Southern Iraq and Lebanon), and Christians from Muslims.

The region's history is dominated by its Arabic, Turkic, and Persian-speaking peoples, but these are heavily influenced by the significant linguistic minorities throughout the region. Many Moroccans and Algerians speak one of North Africa's several Berber languages, although as national education spreads, most adult males have become bilingual in Arabic. In Iran, many people speak Azeri Turkish, Kurdish, Arabic, and Baluch as their first language; and Kurdish is the first language of many Turks. Nor are the region's major languages necessarily uniform. Colloquial Moroccan and Algerian Arabic, for example, are difficult for Arabs from other regions to understand, although educated speakers of Arabic readily communicate through the more standardized language of classrooms and the media. Former colonial languages continue to be widely used, especially French in North Africa, notwithstanding official Arabization policies.

Anthropologists in the Middle East

In the latter part of the nineteenth century, the Middle East inspired major anthropological thought. A prominent example is the polymath Biblical scholar, †William Robertson Smith (1846–1894), who used ethnographic and historical texts and ideas to formulate explicit assumptions about the interrelated evolutionary stages of *kinship, *religion, and political organization (Smith 1889). His work had a major impact on subsequent anthropological thinking, notably inspiring †Evans-Pritchard's analysis of the *social structure of the feud and of †segmentary lineage systems and the French sociologist, †Émile Durkheim. However, because of the region's complexities, the Middle East receded to the periphery of the specifically anthropological imagination for the first half of the twentieth century, when the central concern of social anthropology was so-called 'elementary' or 'primitive' societies (Vatin 1984).

The first major synthesis of the region's ethnography appeared with Carleton Coon's *Caravan*, first published in 1951 and revised several times over the next decade. The book's unity is sustained by a 'mosaic' metaphor, a device useful for portraying the region's complex and varied modes of livelihood, peoples, religions, and linguistic groupings, but this metaphor had built-in limitations. Coon writes that the region's 'mosaic' pattern becomes clear only if the 'little pieces of plastic and broken glass are removed'. By plastic and broken glass he meant everything which was modern or in transition: 'a culture in transition is hard to describe and harder to understand; we must find some period in history when the culture was, relatively speaking, at rest' (Coon 1951: 8). The result was to juxtapose and inventory cultural and social forms, rather than unravel their shifting dynamics, a concern of later interpretive essays on the region's ethnography (Eickelman 1989, with extensive bibliography; also Abu-Lughod 1989).

Until the 1960s, Middle Eastern ethnography concentrated on anthropological puzzles, such as †patrilateral parallel cousin *marriage. By the 1970s this 'problem' gave way to recognition of the multiple marriage strategies by which both peasants and elite in the Middle East, as elsewhere, seek to control property and persons. Likewise, if earlier studies of tribal and pastoral groups stressed segmentation theory, or how groups supposedly without formal political structures could maintain social order, later studies, including those by Emrys Peters (1990) on the Cyrenaican bedouin, †Fredrik Barth (1965) on the Basseri nomads of Southern Iran, Talal Asad (1970) on the Sudan, and Richard Tapper (1990) on pastoralists in Iran and Afghanistan, focused on the complex relationships between access to resources and the subtle relationships between tribal leadership and 'external' authority. Recent studies such as Paul Dresch (1989) on tribes, government, and history in Yemen, Steven Caton (1990) on the cultural rhetoric of tribal poetry and its relation to politics and moral authority, and John Davis (1987) on contemporary Libya, have de-exoticized studies of tribes and placed them in the mainstream of anthropological studies.

The Middle East has also been a locus for innovative studies of *gender and *person. Boddy (1989), for example, shows how Sudan's spirit (*zar*) cults, far from being confined to women's religious imagination and practice, provide a conceptual matrix for both men and women to imagine alternate social and moral realities, much as did saint cults in early Latin Christianity. Far from treating the spirit (*zar*) cults of the Sudan as specific to women, she indicates how they complement male-dominated 'orthodox' religious practices and are inseparable from wider discussions of gender as it relates to ideas of person, community, and religion.

The multiple loyalties, pervasive multilingualism, and complex, often transnational, ties characteristic of the Middle East could rarely be encompassed in the earlier framework of locality-specific anthropological studies. Since the 1970s,

however, studies of transregional religious orders and *pilgrimage centres in the Middle East have contributed significantly to the study of complex societies, as have efforts to explore the permutations of cultural order in economics, kinship, and regional ties, and the pivotal role of *literacy and religious *education in creating new forms of communication, community, and authority. Such studies have also collapsed the prior conventional assumption of a †'great divide' separating the region's 'tribal' and urban, non-literate and literate populations. This trend has been further accelerated as scholars from the Middle East increasingly join anthropological discussions of its societies – and representations of their pasts (e.g. Elboudrari 1985; Hammoudi 1993).

DALE F. EICKELMAN

See also: Islam, Orientalism, pilgrimage

Further reading

Abu-Lughod, L. (1989) 'Zones of Theory in the Anthropology of the Arab World', *Annual Review of Anthropology* 16: 267–306

Asad, T. (1970) *The Kababish Arabs: Power, Authority and Consent in a Nomadic Tribe*, London: C. Hurst

Barth, F. ([1965] 1986) *Nomads of South Persia*, Prospect Heights, Il.: Waveland Press

Boddy, J. (1989) *Wombs and Alien Spirits: Women, Men, and the Zar Cult in Northern Sudan*, Madison: University of Wisconsin Press

Caton, S.C. (1990) *'Peaks of Yemen I Summon': Poetry as Cultural Practice in a North Yemeni Village*, Berkeley: University of California Press

Coon, C.S. (1951) *Caravan: The Story of the Middle East*, New York: Holt, Rinehart and Winston

Davis, J. (1987) *Libyan Politics: Tribe and Revolution*, London: I.B. Tauris

Deshen, S. and M. Shokeid (1974) *The Predicament of Homecoming: Cultural and Social Life of North African Immigrants in Israel*, Ithaca: Cornell University Press

Dresch, P. (1989) *Tribes, Government, and History in Yemen*, Oxford: Clarendon Press

Eickelman, D.F. ([1981] 1989) *The Middle East: An Anthropological Approach*, Englewood Cliffs, NJ: Prentice Hall

Elboudrari, H. (1985) 'Quand les saints font les villes: Lecture anthropologique de la pratique sociale d'un saint marocain du XVIIe siècle', *Annales E.S.C.* 40 (3): 489–508

Gilsenan, M. (1982) *Recognizing Islam: Religion and Society in the Modern Arab World*, New York: Pantheon

Hammoudi, A. (1993) *The Victim and Its Masks: An Essay on Sacrifice and Masquerade in the Maghreb*, Chicago: University of Chicago Press

Peters, E. L. (1990) *The Bedouin of Cyrenaica: Studies in*

Personal and Corporate Power, ed. by J. Goody and E. Marx, Cambridge: Cambridge University Press

Smith, W.R. ([1889] 1972) *Lectures on the Religion of the Semites*, New York: Schocken Books

Tapper, R. (1990) 'Anthropologists, historians, and tribespeople on tribe and state formation in the Middle East', in P.S. Khoury and J. Kostiner (eds) *Tribes and State Formation in the Middle East*, Berkeley: University of California Press

Vatin, J.-C. (ed.) (1984) *Connaissances du Maghreb: sciènces sociales et colonisation*, Paris: Editions du Centre National de la Recherche Scièntifique

migration

The study of migration has been and continues to be an important area of innovation in anthropological theory. It is an area of research which by its nature focuses on change and which has frequently challenged preconceived notions of *society and *culture. Some have argued that the study of migration was well established by the end of the nineteenth century in the works of †Marx, †Engels and †Weber (Eades 1987). Yet, for much of its history, migration has remained at the periphery of theoretical developments in the subject.

Early studies of migration to urban areas in North America by Wirth and the Chicago sociologists reflected a certain ambivalence about the results of these movements. The American anthropologist, †Robert Redfield, developed the ideas of Wirth and suggested the notion of a †folk-urban continuum. He argued that the distinction between the city and the countryside corresponded to distinctions between developed and underdeveloped, modern and traditional. The migrants who move from the countryside to the city were, according to his analysis, progressive types, who through their move contributed to development and the breakdown of tradition. †Oscar Lewis, in research which followed the informants of his early fieldwork in rural areas of Mexico to the cities and shantytowns, began to find inconsistencies in the Wirth-Redfield model of urbanization. Lewis suggested that urbanization could take place without development necessarily following and talked in terms of *'peasants in the city'.

British anthropologists working in Southern and Central Africa, such as †Audrey Richards and †Isaac Schapera, were similarly critical of the results of migration, describing a situation of a failure of social ties and a decline of tradition. As the economic climate improved after 1945, others began to make more positive evaluations. Members of the †Manchester school like J. Barnes and J.C. Mitchell, working out of the †Rhodes-Livingstone Institute in the Central African copperbelt, pointed to the importance of *networks of family and friends in these newly emerging settlements. Their studies described the processes by which existing networks of social ties were maintained and utilized in urban situations – an on-running theme in the anthropology of migration which continues today (see for example articles in Eades 1987 and the work of Gardner 1995). According to Eades (1987) this work by British and American anthropologists marked a shift from the use of a simplistic notion of *modernization to a more realistic analysis of the social and economic contexts within which migration took place.

Political and economic events of the 1960s and 1970s forced further re-evaluations in the anthropology of migration and also prompted a renewed interest in the work of Marx. French theorists such as †Althusser and Meillassoux inspired new Marxist approaches to the study of small-scale societies. Meillassoux's classic study of migration in colonial *West Africa, *Maidens, Meal and Money* (1981), sought to identify and characterize the different modes of production that existed in pre-colonial times and to analyse their reaction to each other and to the colonial impact. He describes the way in which the indigenous domestic economy was maintained within the sphere of circulation of the capitalist *mode of production in order to be exploited for commodities and particularly labour power. Other writers, such as Wallerstein and Frank, developed macro-models of the *world system. Their theories of underdevelopment described the ways in which underdeveloped countries operated within capitalist economies. Such analyses brought about a critical evaluation of the neo-colonial processes of modern *capitalism and of anthropology's role in these processes.

At the same time anthropologists turned their attention to the communities of migrants who had come to the industrialized West in the 1950s and 1960s to work. Fieldwork was carried out throughout Europe, examining for instance, communities of Turkish migrants in Germany and Scandinavia. In Britain work such as Watson's collection *Between Two Cultures* (1977), looked at the differences between groups of migrants in terms of *social structure and culture. Research on minority communities in Britain continues today and can in some senses be said to have marked the starting point of anthropology at home, the process of bringing anthropological fieldwork closer to the study of the anthropologist's own society.

The 1980s and 1990s saw renewed interest among anthropologists in global migration, looking, for example, at the huge movements of workers from Asia to the Arab Gulf states. Much of this work was based on detailed analyses of the social and economic contexts that migrants, their families and communities operated in (see for example Ballard, Marx and Mascarenhas-Keyes in Eades 1987). This work challenged the economically determined and macro-models of migration in which individuals are 'pushed' and 'pulled' by the forces of capitalism. More recently there has been a greater interest in the cultural contexts of migration, examining the ideas and values around which migration is organized and the changes in these ideas and values that migration brings. Katy Gardner's book *Global Migrants, Local Lives*, which examines the long history of migration from a rural area in Bangladesh to the UK and latterly to the Arab Gulf is particularly interesting. She comments directly on recent theories of globalization, challenging notions of homogenization, which she argues are a trendy substitute for modernization. Gardner analyses the very local responses to global processes and thus seeks to draw together macro and micro approaches to the study of migration. Similarly, the Comaroffs, working in those areas of Southern Africa where migration has become an inescapable feature of everyday life, have drawn out the complex historical and cultural mediations involved in people's understandings of the meaning of migration (Comaroff and Comaroff 1987).

When anthropologists habitually thought of the world as divided into neat, discrete 'cultures', 'societies' or 'tribes', migration presented, if nothing else, something of an embarrassment. As such, it became a marginal topic, often confined to the theoretical dustbin of 'social change' or 'applied anthropology'. When, in the relentlessly postmodern 1980s, it became *de rigueur* to challenge earlier assumptions about a world of bounded, internally homogeneous cultures, migration suddenly emerged into the limelight of full theoretical fashion. Now spoken of in terms of 'transnational' processes and †'diaspora'

communities, migration became crucial to arguments about *identity and hybridity (see, for example, Clifford 1994; Rouse 1995). Such work is in fact merely the continuation of the trend of the anthropology of migration challenging accepted notions of society and even of change. Though often viewed as peripheral in the past, the anthropological study of migration has now finally been acknowledged as a valuable source of innovation.

FRANCIS WATKINS

See also: capitalism, complex society, network analysis, urban anthropology, world system, work

Further reading

Clifford, J. (1994) 'Diasporas', *Cultural Anthropology* 9 (3): 302–38
Comaroff, J. and J. Comaroff (1987) 'The Madman and the Migrant: Work and Labor in the Historical Consciousness of a South African People', *American Ethnologist* 14: 191–209
Eades, J. (ed.) (1987) *Migrants, Workers and the Social Order*, ASA Monographs, London: Tavistock Publications
Gardner, K. (1995) *Global Migrants, Local Lives: Travels and Transformation in Rural Bangladesh*, Oxford: Clarendon Press
Kearney, M (1986) 'From the Invisible Hand to Visible Feet: Anthropological Studies of Migration and Development', *Annual Review of Anthropology* 15: 331–61
Meillassoux, C. (1981) *Maidens, Meal and Money. Capitalism and the Domestic Economy*, Cambridge: Cambridge University Press
Mitchell, J.C. (ed.) (1969) *Social Networks in Urban Situations*, Manchester: Manchester University Press
Rouse, R. (1995) 'Thinking through Transnationalism: Notes on the Cultural Politics of Class Relations in the Contemporary United States', *Public Culture* 7(2): 353–402
Watson, J. (ed.) (1977) *Between Two Cultures: Migrants and Minorities in Britain*, Oxford: Blackwell

millennial movements, millenarianism

Anthropologists, sociologists and historians have extended the term 'millenarianism' from the Christian tradition to categorize religious movements worldwide that predict an impending, supernatural transformation and perfection of human society. Jesus Christ's Kingdom on Earth will last 1,000 years – a round and solid number – or so foretold the prophet John in the Book of Revelation:

I also saw the souls of those who had been slain
for their testimony to Jesus and for God's message,
and of those who had not worshipped either the
beast or his statue, nor had received his mark on
their foreheads or on their hands. They came to
life and reigned with Christ a thousand years

(Revelation 20:4)

Theologians and †eschatologists have much
debated this revealed 'millennium' and its sched-
uling. The prediction also inspired numerous
revolutionary agitations throughout the history of
Christian Europe. These were campaigns and
movements of disaffected people seeking a
miraculous and imminent act of salvation that
would completely 'transform life on earth' (Cohn
1957: 15).

Generalized from its Christian origins, the label
'millennial' describes a broad variety of social
movements that have in common an aspiration to
reform or to overturn the social order with supernatural assistance. Daniels (1992) included more
than 5,900 different millennial movements in an
international bibliographic compendium. Among
these are the *ghost dance and †Peyote (Native
American) Church of North America, the New
Zealand Maori Hau Hau, South African Zulu
zionism, Brazilian Umbanda, and Melanesian
*cargo cults (see also Wilson 1973).

The term 'millenarianism' encompasses, or
overlaps, other labels that anthropologists have
used to classify movements, including messianic,
†acculturation, nativistic, revitalization and cargo
cult. (A conference in 1960, 'Millennial Dreams
in Action', helped consolidate anthropological
approaches to various forms of religious protest
under the rubric of millenarianism – see Thrupp
1962). Many have proposed to regularize anthropology's terminology in this neighbourhood of
religious protest, but no standard typology exists.
Generally, however, the label 'messianic' describes
movements that focus on the advent or the return
of a saviour; acculturation movements respond to
the disruptions of colonial domination; nativistic
movements seek to revive or perpetuate endan-
gered aspects of culture and so re-establish a
golden age (Linton 1943); the label 'revitalization'
highlights the reconstructive and socially therapeutic functions of movement belief and ritual
(Wallace 1956); and cargo cults are a specific,
Melanesian case in which the anticipated
millennium will be a supermarket of Western
commodities.

Millennial movements emerged as a significant
anthropological problem principally after World
War II in conjunction with pressing issues of social
change, and of economic and political *development in the postwar era. The term proved useful for
anthropology's attempts to theorize people's reactions to colonial political orders (that had been
shaken by the war) and to an expanding global
economic system that promised development and
*'modernization'. The Cold War and the rise of
communist states in Eastern Europe, China, Korea,
Vietnam and Cuba also made revolution a conspicuous problem; anthropologists along with other
scholars inspected millenarian and other sorts of
social movements with the potential to unsettle the
social order, seeking general theories that might
explain political revolution or, if necessary, forestall
this. The civil rights and youth movements of the
1960s in North American and Western Europe also
gave issues of millenarianism a new urgency. Of
note, here, were arguments between Marxists,
who typically took millennial movements to be a
primitive form of class struggle (e.g. Hobsbawm
1959; Lanternari 1963), and those who suggested
that *Marxism itself was millenarian.

Explanation of millenarianism begins with
locating tension and disruption within a society.
Famine, plague, price inflation, political oppression, colonial disruption of traditional lifeways or
some other source of stress unsettles people's lives.
Increasingly desperate, they collectively pursue
supernatural salvation from their problems in
promises of a New Age. †Prophets surface with
messages that reveal an impending millennium
of transformed or revitalized human sociability
on earth, and they prescribe what people must do
in order to sweep away the present, debased
political and economic orders.

Theorists have approached movements from
both psychological and sociological directions.
Psychologically, the problem is to explain why
people lose confidence in the present order,
trusting instead in promises of glorious social transformation. Drawing on Aberle (1962), some have
used the notion of †relative deprivation to account
for millenarian motivations. People who are *used*
to being politically and economically deprived
typically are not driven to escape their dismal,
although familiar circumstances. It is only when
everyday deprivation becomes conspicuous and
measurable, relative to some other imagined or
experienced state, that it can impel people to act
in order to change their lives.

Others have approached movements sociologically, seeking commonalities in their organization and in their life-cycles, and in the broader social contexts that influence their emergence and relative success at obtaining their goals (Wallace 1956; Smelser 1963). A key element, here, is the failure of mechanisms of social control that ordinarily defuse or derail political action that challenges ruling social orders. These controls range from gross physical repression (such as the 1993 attack by US government forces on the Branch Davidian movement compound in Waco, Texas) to the more subtle operation of everyday *discourses that maintain cultural boundaries between the normal and abnormal, ordinary religion and *outré* cult, sensible aspiration and crazed desire. Millenarian movements have their best chance of organizing, expanding and eventually unsettling ruling orders when ordinary policing mechanisms fail.

LAMONT LINDSTROM

See also: cargo cult, colonialism, religion

Further reading

Aberle, D. (1962) 'A Note on Relative Deprivation Theory as Applied to Millenarian and Other Cult Movements' in S. Thrupp (ed.) *Millennial Dreams in Action*, The Hague: Mouton

Cohn, N. (1957) *The Pursuit of the Millennium: Revolutionary Millenarians and Mystical Anarchists of the Middle Ages*, Oxford: Oxford University Press

Daniels, T. (1992) *Millennialism: An International Bibiliography*, Hamden, CT: Garland Publishing

Hobsbawm, E. (1959) *Primitive Rebels: Studies in Archaic Forms of Social Movements in the 19th and 20th Centuries*, New York: W.W. Norton & Company

Lanternari, V. (1963) *The Religions of the Oppressed: A Study of Modern Messianic Cults*, London: MacGibbon and Kee

Linton, R. (1943) 'Nativistic Movements', *American Anthropologist* 45: 230–40

Smelser, N. (1963) *Theory of Collective Behavior*, New York: The Free Press

Thrupp, S. (1962) *Millennial Dreams in Action: Essays in Comparative Study*, The Hague: Mouton

Wallace, A. (1956) 'Revitalization Movements: Some Theoretical Considerations for their Comparative Study', *American Anthropologist* 58: 264–81

Wilson, B. (1973) *Magic and the Millennium: A Sociological Study of Religious Movements of Protest among Tribal and Third-World Peoples*, New York: Harper & Row

missionaries

Strictly speaking, missionaries are people sent to other countries to extend religious teaching and institutions, although the term can also refer to proselytizers at home, and to those who work on behalf of humanitarian as well as religious causes. *Christianity, *Buddhism, and *Islam have all been missionary religions, but in social and cultural anthropology, the term 'missionary' is most closely associated with Christianity. This is because Christian missionaries and anthropologists have long crossed the same borders to work side by side in what both groups call 'the field'.

Since the age of Western expansion, Christian missionaries have been important parties in the encounter between the West and people throughout the rest of the world. Through missionary efforts Christianity has become a global religion, and mission schools, clinics, transportation, and economic development projects have helped transform life in places far away. Missionaries typically engage the people to whom they minister in a moral critique of local culture and society, encouraging far-reaching change in belief and practice, and they have sometimes played consequential roles in the politics of empires, colonies, and postcolonial states. Historically, many of the world's people have learned about Western culture through encounters with missionaries, while many Westerners at home have learned about these same people through missionaries' eyes.

At times collaborative and at times competitive, anthropologists' relations with missionaries have been deeply ambivalent. Early ethnologists depended on missionaries for information about indigenous people. Missionaries also contributed to linguistic surveys and museum collections, sponsored and published ethnographic research, and a few, like †Maurice Leenhardt, were noted ethnologists themselves (Clifford 1982). Still, the professional identity of academic anthropology was negotiated in part against missionaries, who were generally considered by many anthropologists to be biased and amateur observers, and in some cases irresponsible meddlers in native life.

Although Christian missionaries have long appeared in the anthropological record as agents of social and cultural change, it has only been since the 1970s, when anthropology took a more reflexive and historical turn, that missionaries have become subject to sustained ethnographic attention. Perhaps reflecting the critical stance anthropologists have adopted towards missionaries historically, many studies of missionaries are cast in an ironic mode. The distinguishing features of this literature are a focus on the contradictions and ambiguities that have so often attended missionary work in colonial and postcolonial societies, and attention to the unintended consequences of missionary practice (Beidelman 1982; Huber 1988: Comaroff and Comaroff 1991). The significance of missionary studies, for many anthropologists, is the light they shed on some of the historical processes *colonialism entails.

Missionaries have been a highly varied lot. They have been men and women from different social classes and different countries, working in quite distinct historical circumstances in disparate parts of the world. They have been Protestants from a dizzying array of denominations, and Catholics from a wide variety of religious orders and societies. Although social anthropologists like K.O.L. Burridge (1991) argue that Christianity has provided a common logic to missionary work, others like T.O. Beidelman (1974) suggest that some of the more interesting sociological questions concern the ways in which ideologies like Christianity, which are framed in universal terms, have taken on particular historical forms. Indeed, mission projects have varied considerably depending not only on ecclesiastical and theological differences among denominations, but also on the social and cultural backgrounds from which particular groups of missionaries have come (Langmore 1989).

Mission projects do, however, share distinctive social and temporal horizons which give the cultural life of missionaries a common cast. Missionaries of most denominations stand somewhat outside ordinary church authorities, and the mission churches they first establish also stand apart from the 'mature' form of the church as it is found at home. Missionaries usually draw a close connection between time and the organization of a church, so that movements in time are marked by changes in the position of the missionaries and by change in ecclesiastical form. The story missionary historians usually tell is one of progress, in which the temporal flow is inflected, if not precisely defined, by the promotion of a mission through varying stages of maturity until it achieves the status of a church. The hope expressed is that eventually missionaries from other countries will

no longer be necessary, that personnel will be locally recruited, and that the new church will be able to support missions of its own.

Missionaries' experience can be profoundly shaped both by the ideals of the church that they are trying to reproduce, and by the detours they often must take for their work to be effective in local conditions. For example, nineteenth-century missionaries who embraced 'anti-materialism' faced special problems when organizing hundreds of carriers for a caravan across East Africa (Beidelman 1982), while in nineteenth-century South Africa missionaries who believed in separating religion from politics were nonetheless drawn into the contentious secular sphere (Comaroff and Comaroff 1991). Familiar categories can be displaced in unfamiliar circumstances, and missionaries in their practical activities have frequently exposed to relatively severe risk such basic cultural categories as spiritual and material labour, hierarchy and community, ministry and authority, family and gender.

The consequences of mission work can be disruptive for the local people, as well, making familiar ways of life untenable, and putting into question the certainties by which they live. But that is not the whole story, for the encounter can also be creative. One theme, for example, concerns the ways in which people come to objectify and critique their own societies, and the cultural resources that enable individuals to transcend their social milieux. From this perspective, Christian missionaries may play a privileged role in the origination and dissemination of a culture of reform. But missionaries have also helped create conditions which have encouraged the growth of *millenarianism and other experiments in community sometimes at odds with the missionaries' own project (Burridge 1978; 1991). And, although the work of missionaries has often supported other colonial efforts, Christianity has also provided local people with tools for *resistance to oppression of many kinds (Comaroff and Comaroff 1991).

MARY TAYLOR HUBER

See also: Christianity, colonialism

Further reading

Beidelman, T.O. (1974) 'Social Theory and the Study of Christian Missions in Africa', *Africa* 44 (3): 235–249
—— (1982) *Colonial Evangelism: A Socio-Historical Study of*

an *East African Mission at the Grassroots*, Bloomington: Indiana University Press

Burridge, Kenelm (1978) 'Missionary Occasions', in J.A. Boutilier *et. al.* (eds) *Mission, Church, and Sect in Oceania*, Ann Arbor: University of Michigan Press

—— (1991) *In the Way: A Study of Christian Missionary Endeavours*, Vancouver: UBC Press

Clifford, James (1982) *Person and Myth: Maurice Leenhardt in the Melanesian World*, Berkeley: University of California Press

Comaroff, J. and J. Comaroff (1991) *Of Revelation and Revolution: Christianity, Colonialism, and Consciousness in South Africa*, vol. 1, Chicago: University of Chicago Press

Huber, M. (1988) *The Bishops' Progress: A Historical Ethnography of Catholic Missionary Experience on the Sepik Frontier*, Washington DC: Smithsonian Institution Press

Langmore, D. (1989) *Missionary Lives: Papua, 1874–1914*, Honolulu: University of Hawaii Press

mode of production

Although there were interesting attempts in the eighteenth century to periodize human history according to modes of production (notably †Adam Smith's fourfold scheme: hunting and fishing, pastoral, agricultural and commercial), it is only with the development of *Marxism in the later nineteenth century that we find a more rigorous formulation of this concept and its deployment in a philosophy of history. Both the concept itself and the various uses made of it have had considerable appeal among some anthropologists, while attracting the opprobium of others.

In a famous passage †Marx summed up his general position as follows:

> In the social production of their life, men enter into definite relations that are indispensable and independent of their will, relations of production which correspond to a definite stage of development of their material productive forces. The sum total of these relations of production constitutes the economic structure of society, the real foundation, on which rises a legal and political superstructure, and to which correspond definite forms of social consciousness. The mode of production of material life conditions the social, political and intellectual life process in general.
>
> (1970: 181)

Later in this same passage Marx explains how a dialectic between the material forces and the social

†relations of production establishes the motor of history: revolutions occur when the latter have come to be 'fetters' on the development of the former and 'With the change of the economic foundation the entire immense superstructure is more or less rapidly transformed' (ibid.: 182).

It is not difficult to detect inconsistencies in Marx's discussion of modes of production, and he sometimes uses the phrase in a less exalted sense, to indicate a specific technology. Because Marx was above all concerned with *capitalism, he pays relatively little attention to pre-capitalist modes of production; and even his relatively detailed accounts of the transition from *feudalism to capitalism have been much criticized by later historians. Both Marx and †Engels paid close attention to anthropological writings in their later years, especially those of *L.H. Morgan. The results of this interest were presented by Engels in 1884 (1972) in a work which became the basis of orthodox Marxist research in *Russian and Soviet anthropology and *Chinese anthropology (its rigid unilinealism later undergoing ingenious modifications). According to this theory, humankind had progressed from *primitive communism through *slavery and feudalism to capitalism, all three of which featured antagonistic social *classes. The communist society of the future would transcend such antagonisms.

The difficulties with this theory are legion. It is at least arguable that twentieth-century anthropological research provides some support for the notion of primitive communism. However, given the information available to him, it is scarcely surprising that Engels's attempts to generalize from European historical evidence have been shown to be highly unsatisfactory as far as slavery and feudalism are concerned. Attempts to insert an †'Asiatic mode of production' into the general schema have been similarly flawed. For example, the work of †J. Goody and others has shown that none of these terms is very helpful in understanding pre-colonial African societies. There is moreover a general danger of ahistoricism in the application of these labels to non-Western societies.

It is sometimes argued that production was relatively neglected in the early decades of modern *economic anthropology (though valuable descriptive accounts were provided by †Firth and also by *Malinowski himself). Attempts to remedy matters through an explicit theorization of the concept of mode of production, far more explicit indeed than anything written by Marx and Engels themselves, began during the efflorescence of neo-Marxism in the 1960s. Most of this work took place in France, and the major source of theoretical inspiration was the distinctive *structuralism of †Louis Althusser. This work provoked a radical critique of earlier controversies in economic anthropology. Althusser's invitation to diagnose a plurality of modes of production within the same †'social formation' led to some creative and subtle analyses, e.g. of the co-existence of individualized and communitarian production systems, and the transformation of traditional systems by a new, dominant capitalist mode of production.

In less able hands the apparent rigour of these approaches could easily become a strait-jacket, as in numerous sterile attempts to rework classic *functionalist ethnographies in the newly fashionable jargon. It was not always clear that the neo-Marxist formulations enabled an escape from the woolliness of functionalism, for example, if kinship or religious factors were allowed to enter the material base and 'function as' the social relations of production in pre-capitalist societies. Those who developed the concept under the influence of *political economy and *world-systems theory were still too often inclined to overlook the historicity of non-Western peoples. Within a comparatively short period of time a phrase that initially seemed to promise conceptual breakthrough was generating disputes that seemed increasingly arid. For example, there was controversy over whether there existed a general 'peasant mode of production', or only many distinct *forms* of peasant production (usually relabelled †petty commodity production), each compatible with a variety of encompassing modes of production.

With the decline of Marxist anthropology in the 1980s, controversies concerning modes of production have also waned. It is clear that a powerful legacy remains, stronger perhaps in America than in Europe; but it is by no means a straightforward task to disentangle its contradictory elements. At one extreme stands the *'cultural materialism' of †Marvin Harris, which emphasizes material causation but without the dialectical sophistication central to the Marxist tradition. At the other we might locate the culturalism of †Sahlins, whose elaboration of a †'domestic mode of production' has even less in common with Marxism. But the work of Eric Wolf (1982) is a noteworthy attempt to overcome the Eurocentrism of the original Marxist categories, while

remaining faithful to their radical spirit. Others, such as Scott Cook, have shown how the Marxist framework can help in the analysis of development at various levels, from the global to the petty commodity producing household. Finally, the work of Donham (1985, 1990) shows how the concept of mode of production can be brilliantly deployed in a particular case, with appropriate ethnographic and historical sensitivity.

C.M. HANN

See also: Marxism and anthropology, class, economic anthropology

Further reading
Bloch, M. (1983) *Marxism and Anthropology: The History of a Relationship*, Oxford: Oxford University Press

Donham, D.L. (1985) *Work and Power in Maale, Ethiopia*, Studies in Cultural Anthropology 8, Ann Arbor, MI: University Research Press

—— (1990) *History, Power, Ideology; Central Issues in Marxism and Anthropology*, Cambridge: Cambridge University Press

Engels, F. (1972 [1884]) *The Origin of the Family, Private Property and the State*, New York: Pathfinder Press

Kahn, J.S. and J.R. Llobera (eds) (1981) *The Anthropology of Pre-Capitalist Societies*, London: Macmillan

Marx, K. (1970 [1859]) 'Preface to a Contribution to the Critique of Political Economy', in K. Marx and F. Engels, *Selected Works in One Volume*, London: Lawrence and Wishart, pp. 180–4

Seddon, D. (ed.) (1978) *Relations of Production: Marxist Approaches to Economic Anthropology*, London: Frank Cass

Wolf, E.R. (1982) *Europe and the People Without History*, Berkeley: University of California Press

modernism, modernity and modernization

The word 'modern' has served as an important, if shifting, point of reference in anthropology's developing sense of disciplinary identity and purpose. So, for example, anthropology may be thought of as the work of 'modern' people studying other 'traditional' (or 'premodern', or †'primitive') people. The people it studies may be thought of as undergoing a process of 'modernization' in the course of economic *development. Anthropology itself may be treated as part of a broader intellectual and cultural movement in the West known as 'modernism'. And, in recent years at least, those social, cultural and intellectual features which mark out the West as distinctive may be collectively referred to as 'modernity', a condition which could be investigated ethnographically like any other.

These different projects and terms overlap in meaning, and have been deployed differently at different points in anthropological history. Nevertheless we can discern a broad historical movement from the first example (modern anthropologists studying traditional societies), which covers the greater part of the work done in the first half of the twentieth century, through the second (modernization as a process and an intellectual problem), which most obviously covers work done in postcolonial societies in the 1950s and 1960s, on to the third (anthropology as one kind of modernism), which is a view propagated by self-consciously *postmodern anthropologists in the 1980s, culminating for now in the fourth position (modernity as an ethnographic object), which is only beginning to take shape in areas such as the anthropology of *science, *capitalism, *consumption and the *mass media. There is some continuity linking these different usages: even when we study the most apparently different and non-modern society, we seem to be implicitly asking what it is about 'us' that marks us off as 'modern'? In other words, understanding our condition as modern people is – usually implicitly but occasionally explicitly – one part of the anthropological problem. Nevertheless there has been an important change in recent years as 'our' sense of 'ourselves' as modern has become increasingly problematic and open to empirical critique. One possible consequence of the ethnographic study of modernity is a quite radical undermining of fundamental, mostly unarticulated, assumptions about anthropology, anthropologists and their place in the world.

The modern and the modernizing

It is impossible not to discuss these words in anything other than sweeping terms. The self-conscious use of the word 'modern' has its roots in European intellectual life in the second half of the nineteenth century. Not coincidentally, the concern with 'modern life' as a cultural and intellectual problem, coincides with the florescence of classic social theory in the works of †Marx, †Durkheim, †Simmel and †Weber. Classic social theory is predicated on the assumption that there is something radically new about the modern world and its social and intellectual arrangements. Our era has no precedent, so the models of the past can only serve as contrasts to what we now

have, and all we know for sure about the future is that it too promises to be different in equally unprecedented ways. The use of contrast as a means to come to terms with the present is the source of many of our most pervasive theoretical structures – tradition and modernity, †status and †contract, †mechanical and organic solidarity, †*Gemeinschaft* and *Gesellschaft*, †hot and cold societies. But in applying such contrasts to empirical situations in the present we displace our subjects to another time – the primitive, savage, premodern – somewhere in our past.

In this respect, *evolutionary assumptions have lingered on in anthropology long after the demise of grand nineteenth-century theories of social evolution. This is most obvious in the anthropology of development, a term which itself implies a process of regular qualitative change through time. In the first phase of the Cold War, so-called modernization theory dominated social scientific understandings of development. In its crudest version, modernization theory treated development as a unilinear process toward the 'modern' (an imaginary *telos* apparently located in the suburban United States, but with its intellectual roots in Weber's account of the growing rationalization of capitalist societies) and away from the traditional. This process involved both social and cultural change, particularly the shedding of those aspects of traditional culture which served as a hindrance in progress to the modern.

For some anthropologists (for example those, like †Clifford Geertz and Lloyd Fallers, involved with the University of Chicago's Committee for the Study of the New Nations in the 1960s), modernization theory took them into close interdisciplinary collaboration with economists and political scientists, and opened up areas such as the study of *education and intellectuals, popular culture, mass politics and postcolonial *nationalism (Geertz 1963). But the cruder versions of modernization theory received their richly deserved comeuppance from radical critics in the 1960s and 1970s who pointed out that there were structural features in the world economy which might provide better explanations for 'backwardness', in which case attributing poverty to some irrational attachment to traditional culture was rather missing the point. Unfortunately, modernization theory's empirical concerns went down along with its theoretical pretensions, not least because its intellectual successors such as structural *Marxism and *world-systems theory showed little interest in the study of such quintessentially modern topics as mass education or urban popular culture outside the West.

Modernism

The term 'modernism' has its intellectual foundations in the study of literature and the visual arts. There it usually refers to a broad cultural movement characterized by a spirit of constant challenge to received forms – modernism opposes itself to the figurative tradition in the visual arts and to realism and naturalism in literature. It is the source of the 'modern' in 'modern art', and its exemplars are Picasso and T.S. Eliot, Schoenberg and Le Corbusier, Ezra Pound and Gertrude Stein, Charlie Parker and Ornette Coleman. As some of these names suggest, modernism in this sense is a movement of a relatively small avant-garde, usually working in the rarified atmosphere of elite *culture. Moreover, its proponents were far from unanimous in their celebrations of the modern: many were politically conservative, nostalgic for a lost world of tradition, although some (like Le Corbusier) saw their own work as a positive force for social change.

It is fair to say that no adequate account exists of anthropology's relationship with modernism in this sense (although Manganaro 1990 provides the beginnings of such an account). On the one hand, the empirical concerns of the founding giants (*Malinowski, *Boas and his circle) overlap with a wider interest in 'primitivism' among modernist writers and artists of the time: Picasso's use of African masks, D.H. Lawrence's interest in the Native American rituals of the American Southwest, Max Ernst's collection of Hopi dolls (Torgovnick 1990). On the other hand, anthropology's own cultural productions – *ethnographies – were characterized by stylistic conventions such as naturalism and realism, modes usually associated with modernism's nineteenth-century predecessors. Formal experimentation in modes of representation, the defining feature of literary modernism, is usually taken to be the defining feature of anthropological *post*modernism. (As all this probably indicates, this is not the most coherent field in the history of ideas.)

Without postmodernism, it is quite likely that these problems of definition and periodization would never have arisen. But from the point of view of the most grandiose accounts of postmodernism, modernism has a much broader meaning than that discussed so far. It is no longer

merely a particular phase in Western high culture, but can be taken to denote the whole era of *grandes histoires* (or †metanarratives in the clumsy translator's rendition of †Lyotard's 'big stories'), what has come to be known as the 'Enlightenment project'. This version of modernism would collect together all attempts at the application of universal reason to the understanding of human affairs, along with all attempts at planned intervention in the cause of human emancipation. It may be difficult to think of modernism in this sense as an ethnographic problem, but there are signs of a new anthropology *of* modernism (as apart from a modernist anthropology) in recent studies of architecture and urban space in colonial Morocco (Rabinow 1989) and contemporary Brazil (Holston 1989).

Modernity

So far I have discussed a point of reference (the modern, the moment without precedent), a process (modernization as the shedding of tradition), and a cultural movement characterized by certain kinds of cultural product (modernism). Finally we arrive at a condition of the world – modernity. At its most general, modernity may serve as a broad synonym for capitalism, or industrialization, or whatever institutional and ideological features are held to mark off the modern West from other, traditional societies. With the political demise of Marxism in Eastern Europe in the late 1980s, and the academic ascendancy of postmodernism, 'modernity' has become an increasingly fashionable term in revisionist social theory.

Paradoxically, because most theorizing about modernity and the modern has been conducted at a lofty level of generalization, the possibilities for an anthropological approach to modernity are extremely rich. Since the late 1970s there has been a growing number of ethnographic studies of quintessentially modern institutions and practices – scientific laboratories, capitalist corporations, consumer cultures, as well as the studies of architecture and planning already mentioned – both within and outside the 'West'. Needless to say, empirical scrutiny reveals that supposedly modern institutions fail to live up to Weberian expectations of impersonality and rationality, and the anthropology of modernity might go no further than repetitive, if amusing, empirical challenge to Western self-images of modern life. As such it would remain parasitic on those self-images, rather as much other anthropology has remained dependent on *Occidentalist stereotypes of 'the West', 'Western thought' and 'Western institutions'.

There is, however, another more radical possibility. Developing his own empirical research in the history and ethnography of science, Bruno Latour ([1991] 1993) has argued that the very idea of the modern world is based on a set of impossible intellectual distinctions – between the objective knowledge of nature and the subjective world of culture, between science and politics, between the modern and the traditional. Empirical research swiftly shows these distinctions to be untenable: science and politics are connected in complex social networks, while our public life is increasingly concerned with hybrids, objects and problems which are at once social and natural. An anthropology of modernity would employ ethnographic holism to dissolve the illusions that convince us that 'we' are modern, unprecedented but objective observers of other people's cultural worlds. As yet such an anthropology hardly exists, and it is difficult to imagine quite what an 'amodern' (rather than postmodern) intellectual landscape would look like, except to say that it would be far more empirically challenging and far more genuinely 'decentred' than any of the oddly Eurocentric products of scholastic postmodernism.

JONATHAN SPENCER

See also: capitalism, consumption, development, evolution and evolutionism, occidentalism, science, society

Further reading

Geertz, C. (ed.) (1963) *Old Societies and New States: The Quest for Modernity in Asia and Africa*, New York: Free Press

Holston, J. (1989) *The Modernist City: An Anthropological Critique of Brasilia*, Chicago: University of Chicago Press

Latour, B. ([1991] 1993) *We Have Never Been Modern*, Cambridge, MA: Harvard University Press

Manganaro, M. (ed.) (1990) *Modernist Anthropology: From Fieldwork to Text*, Princeton: Princeton University Press

Miller, D. (1994) *Modernity: An Ethnographic Approach*, Oxford: Berg

Rabinow, P. (1989) *French Modern: Norms and Forms of the Social Environment*, Cambridge, MA: MIT Press

—— (1992) 'Studies in the Anthropology of Reason', *Anthropology Today* 8 (5): 7–10

Torgovnick, M. (1990) *Gone Primitive: Savage Intellects, Modern Lives*, Chicago: University of Chicago Press

money

To the anthropologist money is the means for effecting one particular ritual, *payment*.

> Payment is the transfer, from one person (the 'payer') to another person (the 'payee') of an interest which is always expressed as a multiple of a recognized unit with its own name, or 'denomination'. Money is the means which represents this interest and enables payments to be made. The ostensible result of a payment, so far as the money used to make it is concerned, is to put the payee in what, before the payment, was the position of the payer.
>
> (Crump 1981: 3)

This definition makes it clear that money, to fulfil its function, must circulate indefinitely, which requires an extremely durable 'money stuff'. In principle, though not so often in practice, the actual quantity circulating at any one time is fixed, and given the demand for money by those wishing to perform the ritual – whatever its purposes may be – it should be in short supply. It is therefore a pre-eminent instance of *Lévi-Strauss's (1969 [1949]: 32) 'system of the scarce product' which is described as 'a model of extreme generality'. Suitable scarce products hardly occur in nature: cowrie shells, used as money in many different parts of the world, are about the only important case. Otherwise money, in the form of coins, tends to be made out of metal.

The ritual of payment is pervasive in almost any monetized society, but its meaning depends on the circumstances of every single performance. Western economics is founded on the assumption that the main monetary ritual is a particular form of *exchange, known as 'sale', in which a sum of money, known as the 'price' is paid for some commodity. This particular use of money (as any other) gives rise to its own distinctive institutions, such as *markets and long-distance trade, which have provided the material for many detailed studies such as Beals (1975). This book describes a local autonomous market system of very long standing, which, while using ordinary Mexican money, is still largely independent of the national economy.

> Long-standing market systems are but one example of a quite general phenomenon, to be

found with almost every form of monetary exchange, which is the relationship between a cycle of short term exchange, which is the legitimate domain of individual – often acquisitive – activity, and a cycle of long term exchanges concerned with the reproduction of the social and cosmic order.

(Parry and Bloch 1989: 2)

Furthermore, the two cycles are

organically essential to each other. This is because their relationship forms the basis for a symbolic resolution of the problem posed by the fact that transcendental social and symbolic structures must both depend on, and negate, the transient individual.

(Parry and Bloch 1989: 25)

Many illustrations of the interaction between short and long-term exchange are provided by *ceremonial* exchange, 'a technical term for a type of reciprocity ... in which every payment may be seen as a gift importing the obligation to make a return gift – often in the same 'coin' – at some future time' (Crump 1981: 42).

Among the 'Aré 'Aré of Malaita in the Solomon Islands, the nodal points of the primary system of distribution of money are to be found in the rites which consummate the funeral cycle of any individual and which establish, in numerical terms, rank among the ancestors. Individuals, while still alive, do their best to ensure the future 'success' of their funerals by participating, on the basis of an increasing scale of money gifts, in other funerals. The money so given is returned to the realm of short-term exchange by using it to pay for 'the products of horticulture and husbandry which the gravediggers bring to the feast' (de Coppet 1970: 780), but the unceasing long-term exchange, focused on the funerals, is seen by the 'Aré 'Aré as much more important. The fact that between funerals the money is returned to individual holders is quite secondary, for the dead are represented exclusively in terms of money, and this is its main purpose.

The 'Aré 'Aré funeral cycle and the Oaxaca market system illustrate the point that no general rule defines the sphere of payment. Although there is little systemic overlap between the 'Aré 'Aré and Oaxaca, the Kapauku of West New Guinea appear to have monetized almost every conceivable exchange transaction, not only in the field of economic but also in that of social relations (Pospisil 1963: 402), creating a sphere of payment of far wider range than that of a modern industrialized economy.

In the modern world banking provides the link between short and long-term exchange. Specie, in the form of coin, is the traditional medium of short-term exchange: when deposited with a bank it is then converted into a negotiable credit, known as 'scriptural' money. Traditional societies are also able to transfer and give credit where circumstances require it: this is one way in which the considerable expenses of local religious offices are funded among the Indian tribes of the Chiapas highlands in Southern Mexico (Cancian 1967: 101).

In whatever form, for whatever purposes and in whatever circumstances it is used, the use of money gives rise to a particular world view, which in turn defines the ways in which money itself is represented. But 'what money means is not only situationally defined but also constantly renegotiated' (Parry and Bloch 1989: 22). At the same time, the essential simplicity of the phenomenon of money means that 'it will always tend to symbolise much the same sort of things' (Parry and Bloch 1989: 19) regardless of any local cultural attributes.

THOMAS CRUMP

See also: exchange, economic anthropology, markets, capitalism

Further reading

Beals, R.L. (1975) *The Peasant Marketing System of Oaxaca, Mexico*, Berkeley: University of California Press

Cancian, F. (1965) *Economics and Prestige in a Maya Community: The Religious Cargo Cult System in Zinacantan*, Stanford, CA: Stanford University Press

Crump, T. (1981) *The Phenomenon of Money*, London: Routledge & Kegan Paul

Coppet, D. de (1970) 'Cycles de meurtes et cycles funéraires. Esquisse de deux structures d'échange', in *Mélanges offerts à Claude Lévi-Strauss*, vol. II, Paris: Mouton, pp. 759–81

Lévi-Strauss, C. (1969) *The Elementary Structures of Kinship*, London: Eyre and Spottiswood

Parry J. and M. Bloch (eds) (1989) *Money and the Morality of Exchange*, Cambridge: Cambridge University Press

Pospisil, L. (1963) *Kapauku Papuan Economy*, Yale University Publications in Anthropology, no 67

Morgan, Lewis Henry

Lewis Henry Morgan (1818–1881) was a founding father of professional anthropology in the United States and his notebooks, letters and manuscripts provide a mine of information for the historian of the discipline. He was the first ethnographer of an Indian tribe and the first ethnologist of repute to write on *Aboriginal Australian social organization. For more than half a century, Morgan's work lay at the heart of epistemological debates on *evolutionism, idealism, *Marxism, and *structuralism.

Born in Aurora, New York, Morgan's ethnological investigations grew out of his membership of a secret literary society, The Grand Order of the Iroquois, which engaged in scientific study of Native Americans and in offering humanitarian and political aid to them. Morgan's work lay particularly with the Seneca. Ely S. Parker, a Seneca and a member of the Order, was his critical ally and resource.

As a lawyer, Morgan combined his work for railroad investors with visits to Indian reservations further west. His main objective was to collect *kinship terminologies but his journals also indicate his keen interest in Indian †acculturation. Although he deplored intermarriage between Indians and Euro-Americans, he nevertheless argued that Indians had the potential to be American citizens. Morgan twice ran for the New York State legislature and hoped (but failed) to become US Commissioner for Indian Affairs. His work was influential in shaping the †Bureau of American Ethnology, and his intellectual stature was recognized by his elevation to the American Association for the Advancement of Science, the most prestigious scientific organization in the country.

Between 1851 and 1877 Morgan published five books. Today only one remains uncontestedly in the anthropological canon. This is *League of the Ho-de-no-sau-nee, or Iroquois*, published in 1851. Based on direct inquiry and observation, it owed much to Morgan's training as a lawyer. He was intrigued by the Iroquois †matrilineal kinship system as comparative jurisprudence. Because of its format, *League* has been called the first modern ethnography of a native people and a pioneer study in *political anthropology. Adopting a natural history approach, Morgan described systematically the *environment, †subsistence, kinship, ceremonial, *religion and politics of the Iroquois people.

Long a classic among evolutionary and structural studies of kinship, Morgan's *Systems of Consanguinity and Affinity of the Human Family* (1871) is now seen to be sadly misguided. Over a third of the book consists of tables of kinship terms Morgan collected on his fieldtrips and by correspondence. Changes between earlier and later drafts of the book show how Morgan was led to transform a systematic, structural classification into an evolutionary thesis by incorporating a friend's fallacious idea that *relationship terminologies provided evidence for growth in the idea of the family.

Morgan may be said to have invented kinship studies by realizing that the semantic patterning underlying kinship terminologies, the internal logic of kinship systems, could be studied comparatively. He was the first to make a distinction between †descriptive and †classificatory kinship terminologies and to use the †ethnographic present tense, 'time being immaterial' (1877: 13) in the collecting mode of structural kinship studies. Morgan's structural paradigm was later replaced by *Lévi-Strauss's linguistic model, by cultural accounts of kinship, and by the study of kinship in processual and historical context.

In *Ancient Society* (1877) Morgan developed more fully an evolutionary schema for mankind's intellectual and material progress. For him, the growth of ideas, changes in the family, and, especially, property, shaped the unrecognized social processes of human history. His emphasis on 'the arts of subsistence' provided a mechanism for progressing from †savagery, through †barbarism, to †civilization. This became foundational in modern *archaeology and in ethnological distinctions between *hunters and gatherers, sedentary †agriculturalists, and *urban dwellers.

Morgan's work, along with that of other evolutionists, was read critically by Karl Marx between 1879 and 1882. Morgan deplored what he called the 'property career' of Euro-American society and predicted a return to democratic, communal principles which he believed were once universal. In changing Morgan's narrative sequence, Marx brought *property into conjunction with the *state rather than with the *family. †Engels restored Morgan's original emphasis in *The Origin of the Family, Private Property and the State* (1884). As a result, Morgan's work remained important in *Marxist anthropology, and especially in *Russian and Soviet anthropology. Engels's interpretation of Morgan took on a new lease of life among feminists in the 1970s.

Morgan wrote two less well known books, *The American Beaver and his Works* (1868) and *Houses and House-life of the American Aborigines* (1881). The first reflects his views on man's relationship to the animal kingdom, progress, intellect, and race. Part of an American debate on †monogenism and †polygenism, it was read in the context of slavery and civil war. The second is of interest today for its exploration of spatial design in relation to family structures, laws of hospitality, communal living, and the holding of lands in common by Indian groups.

JOAN VINCENT

See also: American anthropology, evolution and evolutionism, kinship, primitive communism

Further reading

Bieder, R.E. (1986) *Science Encounters the Indian: The Early Years of American Ethnology*, Norman: University of Oklahoma Press

Morgan, L.H. ([1871] 1985) *Ancient Society*. Foreword by Elizabeth Tooker, Tucson: University of Arizona Press

Resek, C. (1960) *Lewis Henry Morgan, American Scholar*, Chicago: University of Chicago Press

Trautmann, T.R. (1987) *Lewis Henry Morgan and the Invention of Kinship*, Berkeley: University of California Press

museums

The popular image of the museum, a neoclassical temple acting as national treasure chest or tomb for the relics of past civilizations, visited by families on rainy afternoons, was well established by the end of the nineteenth century in much of Europe and North America. However the origins of the museum, as idea and institution, remain obscure, although its later development in European society has been well described (Impey and Macgregor l985). Since their invention over 100 years ago in Sweden, open air or 'living history' museums, which usually feature costumed artisans at work in period homes or studios, have attracted large numbers of visitors worldwide.

Most contemporary definitions revolve around the collecting, conserving, researching and displaying of objects or specimens. It is probable that some, if not all, of these functions can be found in other contexts, such as the care a ritual specialist might extend to the objects associated with an ancestral altar. There is no agreement if such activity should be described as museological.

Museums dedicated to *ethnography have often been based on collections stimulated by cross-cultural encounters, sometimes within a *colonial framework. While this may have seemed unremarkable to collectors and keepers at the time, the exploration of the history of particular collections as an exhibition theme has been a noticeable, if sometimes controversial, development in 'decolonizing' anthropological practice.

Indeed the anthropology of museums, that is, the treatment of the museum itself as a social artefact, has increasingly attracted scholarly attention. From this grows the examination of a collection to reveal the underlying cultural or ideological assumptions which have informed its creation, selection, and interpretation while on display. Within such a collection, objects act as an expression not only of the †worldview of those who choose to make and use them, but also of those who chose to collect and exhibit them.

As both anthropologists and art historians use galleries and museums to exhibit and analyse objects, it is perhaps not surprising that disciplinary approaches have sometimes overlapped and at others collided in the exhibition hall. The issue is occasionally oversimplified and presented as a dilemma over whether to present, and hence guide the viewer's response to, an object as an artefact or as an *art form. Should it be interpreted within an ethnographic context or be described in such a way as to bring to the fore its aesthetic attributes? To make explicit the undoubted artistic equality between, for example, African and Pacific objects with those from European traditions, it has been argued, it is necessary to jettison labels on the function and meaning of an object in its originating culture. Counter-charges that this is a distortion and merely imposes a European sensibility and set of categories are sometimes heard. There is, of course, no need for the anthropological and art historical approaches to be seen as antithetical and the debate itself has been on display as an exhibition.

Demands for the repatriation of cultural material and human remains (primarily skeletal) from museum storerooms to their owners or descendants have occasionally soured diplomatic relations between states (for example between Greece and the United Kingdom over the so called Elgin marbles), but more often raised legal and moral issues between states and indigenous or

†aboriginal populations. The museological response has ranged from a non-negotiable refusal to return any material, to innovative reformulations of the relationship itself. There are a growing number of museums, run by and for indigenous communities, based on repatriated collections which had been housed in national or regional institutions.

This is part of a wider concern with 'appropriation', what has been called 'the politics of representation', which deals most broadly with the ability to exercise control over the content and context of images and interpretations (Karp and Lavine l992). As such, this debate affects not only museum and gallery exhibitions, but literary works, films and television series, and advertising campaigns in reference to many things including *gender, *ethnicity and *class.

It has been suggested that the golden age of the great museums in the nineteenth century was the product of historical processes which met specific social and political needs through the display of material culture (Horne 1984). Inevitably, as new modes of communication have been invented and ideas of educational instruction changed, the success of museums in fulfilling their original missions has been questioned within and without the museological profession. Fears that the museum is being eclipsed by a wide variety of leisure activities have generated efforts to increase accessibility, reduce the primacy of the object for carrying the curatorial message, and provide a high level of visitor services. The introduction of admission fees for institutions which receive public money remains a contentious issue as does the balance between, to simplify, education and entertainment.

JEANNE CANNIZZO

See also: art, aesthetics, technology

Further reading

Hinsley, Jr, C.M. (1981) *Scientists and Savages: The Smithsonian Institution and the Development of American Anthropology 1846–1910*, Washington, DC: Smithsonian Institution Press

Horne, D. (1984) *The Great Museum: The Re-presentation of History*, London: Pluto Press

Hudson, K. (1987) *Museums of Influence*, Cambridge: Cambridge University Press

Impey, O. and Arthur Macgregor (eds) (1985) *The Origins of Museums*, Oxford: Clarendon Press

Karp, I. and Steven Lavine (eds) (1991) *Exhibiting Cultures: The Politics and Poetics of Museum Display*, Washington, DC: Smithsonian Institution Press

Pearce, S. (1992) *Museums, Objects and Collections*, Leicester: Leicester University Press

Stocking, G. (ed.) (1985) *Objects and Others: Essays on Museums and Material Culture*, Madison: University of Wisconsin Press

music

Music can be situated in anthropological analysis in two distinct ways. First, music can be defined as any communicational practice which organizes sound in terms of pitch, duration, timbre and loudness. A wide range of practices can be included in this definition, extending from the human to the natural world (for example, birdsong, the 'languages' of dolphins and whales). This approach permits analysis of the social uses of sound in highly structured communicational and expressive systems in ways that are often ignored by anthropologists, but has the disadvantages of foisting a culture-bound definition of music on areas of activity in which it is not necessarily appropriate, and of concealing indigenous definitions and explanations which might be of more analytical use. In this sense, the problems faced by an anthropology of music are similar to those faced by an anthropology of *art or *aesthetics. Whilst a category such as 'music' is a useful way of focusing on aspects of performance and ideas which are of great cultural significance, it encourages the application of musicological concepts whose scope is limited outside of the practice of Western European art music, and also divides experiences (through defining 'music' in opposition to 'speech' or *'dance') which other people might not consider divisible.

A second approach, therefore, is to look for indigenous terms that cover roughly the same areas of experience as those covered by the term 'music'. This approach roots any analysis firmly in the social and cultural worlds being discussed, and reveals the connections that are made by the people involved between performance and the socio-cultural domain. It also allows one to see the ways in which 'musical' practice is involved in the reproduction or transformation of other social and cultural practices without imposing an alien and inappropriate analytic framework. The problems inherent in this approach are, typically, that terms corresponding to 'music' do not exist, and that performances that we might readily consider to be 'musical', on account of qualities that we might translate as 'melody' and 'rhythm', are not classified as such in indigenous discourse. In many Middle Eastern contexts the chanting of the Koran and certain kinds of poetic declamation are classified as 'recitation', since the terms for 'music' or 'song' connote immorality. Therefore, if the contours of indigenous discourse are respected, it might be inappropriate to think of the object of analysis as 'music' at all. Any anthropological approach to music has to confront this dilemma at some point.

Brief history of ethnomusicology

The question of how music should be understood in the context of anthropological analysis has been addressed systematically in the discipline of †ethnomusicology, although intellectual traditions of interest in musical 'others' go back at least to classical antiquity. Speculation about the origins and development of music with reference to what was known of other musics was a consistent feature of philosophical and moral commentary from the Renaissance to the Enlightenment period. Histories of ethnomusicology tend to begin in 1885 with the Viennese musicologist Guido Adler's 'Umfang, Methode und Ziel der Musikwissenschaft', which set out to explore the theoretical, aesthetic, pedagogical and comparative aspects of music in the context of a 'systematic musicology'. The academic legitimacy thereby accorded to the study of non-Western European musics, the movement of musicians from the colonial domains to world fairs in major European cities, and later the invention of the phonograph and establishment of sound archives ignited a storm of 'scientific' fascination with other musics. This fascination was largely directed toward the psychology of perception; music provided conveniently measurable data. Primarily on the basis of Javanese gamelan tunings, Alexander John Ellis established in 1885 that musical consonance could not be understood, as had hitherto been assumed, in terms of the physiological effects of whole number ratios. His establishment of the 'cent' as a unit of pitch measurement enabled the tonal properties of all musics to be understood on an equal footing, without recourse to Eurocentric evaluations of consonance or dissonace. The Berlin psychologist, Carl Stumpf, and the director of the Berlin Phonogram archive, Erich von Hornbostel, followed the same trajectory over the next twenty years with their investigations into perceptions of consonance and dissonance in non-European

tonal systems, organizing these systems into an *evolutionary and *diffusionist framework. Many of those associated with the 'Berlin school' left Germany when the Nazis came to power and found academic jobs in the United States.

After the term 'ethnomusicology' was coined in 1950 by the Dutch scholar of Javanese gamelan, Jaap Kunst, Berlin-trained 'systematic musicologists' and their students rapidly provided the backbone for ethnomusicology teaching in the United States. Anthropological models entered ethnomusicology decisively with the publication of Alan Merriam's *Anthropology of Music* in 1964. Drawing heavily on his field research among the Basongye and the Flathead Indians, this was conceived broadly in terms of American cultural anthropology; music was seen as an integral and inseperable aspect of cultural life which could be conveniently understood in terms of a three part model, in which concepts relating to music, behaviour in relation to music and the structural aspects of musical sound all impinged upon one another. Merriam's project opened up a dispute which still lingers today. For those who continued to identify with the Berlin comparativist project, such as Kolinski (1967), Merriam's approach was so involved in culture-specific qualifications and connections that the possibility of asking comparative musicological questions had become remote, if not impossible. The one exercise in comparative musicological thinking which appeared to unite the two camps was the debate over musical universals which ran through the pages of *Ethnomusicology* in the early 1960s. The last major comparative venture in ethnomusicology was Alan Lomax's 'Cantometrics' project, which succeeded in alienating both. Lomax classified songs' styles according to a 'profile' of acoustic and social features, and proposed systematic and global relationships between song style and cultural traits (1968). Lomax's tendency to characterize on the basis of a small number of songs, the lack of †participant-observer fieldwork, and the †positivist orientations of the project have been much criticized; the comparative project can be considered to have reached its logical conclusion at this point, leaving 'musicologists' and 'anthropologists' without obvious areas of cooperation. Merriam later spoke of his regret that ethnomusicologists 'do not seem to have been able to create a true discipline of ethnomusicology, as opposed to a musicology of music and an anthropology of music living rather uneasily together under an artificial rubric' (1975: 59).

Since the mid-1970s, ethnomusicology has been predominantly driven by anthropological methods and fashions. The *functionalist implications of Merriam's three part model have been thoroughly criticized; others have argued for a more dynamic model (see Rice 1987). Merriam himself accurately forecast the *Boasian trajectory of ethnomusicology in the United States in the 1970s and 1980s as a progression 'from a focus on music sound structure, through a concern with music as a socio-cultural phenomenon, and now to a preoccupation with musical emotion, feeling and meaning' (1975: 64). Outside this trajectory, †Chomskian linguistics provided a number of models in ethnomusicology as in anthropology (see for example Boiles 1967). Anthropological analyses of *urbanism, *gender and *class that emerged from the collapse of †structural-functionalist paradigms and village/tribe based ethnography have shaped a number of significant ethnomusicological studies (see respectively Nettl 1978; Koskoff 1989; Pena 1985). On the other hand, the ethnomusicological concern with performance perhaps predates its rise to prominence in anthropology. The disciplinary proximity of *folklore has perhaps helped ethnomusicologists in this respect. Seeger's study of the Suya of Northern Brazil (1987) outlined the significance of understanding music in the context of an anthropology of performance. Reversing a conventional and somewhat reductive understanding shaped by Merriam's definition of ethnomusicology as 'the study of music in culture' within an 'anthropology of music', Seeger speaks of social life as something taking place in musical performance, and describes his approach as a 'musical anthropology'. The prevailing movement amongst ethnomusicologists in the United States appears to be towards the ethnography of performance, and away from the interpretative paradigms of the 1980s.

In Europe, ethnomusicology has not attained the disciplinary critical mass that it has in the United States, and as a consequence ethnomusicologists have been drawn more decisively towards either anthropology or musicology. In the United Kingdom, John Blacking's ethnomusicology was conceived as part of an ongoing anthropology of the *body. His overriding interest lay in the attempt to understand music in relation to bodily movement, neurology and biology. Understood as a species-specific biological proclivity, 'musical' processes (which were often taken to include other

movement systems) could be seen to provide primary patterning devices either underpinning, or contradicting and transforming, other social domains. On the continent, ethnomusicological thinking tends to be divided between those with anthropological training and inclinations, such as Hugo Zemp and Gilbert Rouget, and folklorists. Rouget's *Music and Trance* (1985) drew on a vast range of ethnographic material to construct a *Lévi-Straussian theory of trance states and the symbolic relationships of various kinds of music and dance to these states. Folklore, heavily influenced by Bela Bartok and Constantin Brailoiu, dominates much of the study of non-Western art music in Southern and Eastern Europe: much is explicitly concerned with preserving what is seen as a disappearing traditional world, and contributing to 'modernized' national musical forms.

New directions

Those interested in understanding music today find themselves faced with the task of understanding social worlds thoroughly penetrated by new media systems, the apparatus of transnational industrial, political and military structures, and the collapse of scientific certainties in the study of society and culture. These problems are keenly felt in disciplines with a tradition of commitment to the local and small-scale such as ethnomusicology and anthropology. Recent ethnomusicology has been absorbed by issues of *reflexivity. The second edition of Steven Feld's Kaluli study (1990) concluded with a lengthy analysis of the reception of the book by his Kaluli informants. Feld brings the varied voices of the participants in his field research into the picture, and discusses fieldwork as a kind of collaborative dialogue. The role of observers is particularly marked in musical contexts, especially where music is involved with forms of exploration and play, and 'informants' are keen to benefit from the expertise of those who study them. One also cannot ignore the ways in which the music industry has promoted certain forms on a global basis, and has drawn non-European music (including that of the Kaluli) into its commercial ambit.

The role of the music industry in a variety of contexts has consequently been the subject of a number of studies, notably Wallis and Malm's *Music In Small Countries* project (1984). Peter Manuel's investigation of North Indian popular genres (1992) is explicitly situated in *Marxist cultural theoretical debates concerning the political effects of *technology in cultural production, in particular the extent to which patterns of domination are reproduced or challenged. His conclusion is based on a careful ethnography of North Indian media systems: the effects of cassette culture are complex and cannot be reduced to this kind of either/or dichotomy. Manuel's approach is particularly useful in outlining the possibilities and problems of a contemporary anthropological approach to music. Anthropologists continue to investigate the role of music in shaping *identity and experience in a rapidly changing world, in confronting or assisting established or newly emerging patterns of *power and domination. However, the issues of power, †hegemony, domination and reflexivity are shared in a number of disciplines, *cultural studies in particular, committed to a critical and democratic understanding of society and culture. An anthropological approach will certainly continue to stress that the answers to questions of interpretation cannot be answered by reference to texts in a social and cultural void; a picture of which interpretations and representations are used, appropriated and mobilized by musicians and their audiences can only be built up from ethnography, and a conception of music as a form of creative social practice.

MARTIN STOKES

See also: aesthetics, art, dance, folklore, poetics

Recordings

The following series of ethnographic recordings are accompanied by extensive and reliable notes: Smithsonian/Folkways, Ocora, UNESCO Collection/Auvidis, Museum Collection Berlin, Archives Internationales de Musique Populaire, and Le Chant du Monde (CNRS/Musée de l'Homme). A large number of good 'world music' recordings, usually made in studios, can be found on labels such as Real World, Earthworks, EUCD, World Circuit, Hemisphere, and Nimbus. These tend to provide very little information about the music beyond the translation of texts, and brief biographical notes. For regional discographies see Post (1992). The journal *Ethnomusicology* also provides detailed regional discographies in each edition.

Further reading

Adler, G. (1885) 'Umfang, Methode und Ziel der Musikwissenschaft' in *Zeitschrift für Musikwissenschaft* 1: 5–20

Blacking J. (1973) *How Musical Is Man?*, London: Faber

Boiles, C. (1967) 'Tepehua Thought-Song', *Ethnomusicology* 11 (3): 267–92

Ellis, A.J. (1885) 'On The Musical Scales of Various Nations', *Journal of The Society of Arts* 33: 485–527

Feld, S. (1990) *Sound and Sentiment: Birds, Weeping, Poetics, and Song in Kaluli Expression* (2nd edn), Philadelphia: University of Pennsylvania Press

Kolinski, M. (1967) 'Recent Trends in Ethnomusicology', *Ethnomusicology* 11 (1): 1–24

Koskoff, E. (ed.) (1989) *Women and Music in Cross-Cultural Perspective*, Urbana: University of Illinois Press

Lomax, A. (1968) *Folk Song Style and Culture*, Washington, DC: American Association for the Advancement of Science

Manuel, P. (1992) *Cassette Culture: Popular Music and Technology in North India*, Chicago: University of Chicago Press

Merriam, A. (1964) *The Anthropology of Music*, Evanston, IL: Northwestern University Press

—— (1975) 'Ethnomusicology Today', *Current Musicology* 20: 50–67

Nettl, B. (ed.) (1978) *Eight Urban Musical Cultures: Tradition and Change*, Urbana: University of Illinois Press

Pena, M. (1985) *The Texas-Mexican Conjunto: History of a Working-Class Music*, Austin: University of Texas Press

Post, J. (1992) 'Research Resources in Ethnomusicology', in H. Myers (ed.) *Ethnomusicology: An Introduction*, London: Macmillan

Rice, T. (1987) 'Toward a Remodeling of Ethnomusicology', *Ethnomusicology* 31 (3): 469–488

Rouget, G. (1985) *Music and Trance: A Theory of the Relations Between Music and Possession*, Chicago: University of Chicago Press

Seeger, A. (1987) *Why Suya Sing: A Musical Anthropology of an Amazonian People*, Cambridge: Cambridge University Press

Wallis R. and K. Malm (1984) *Big Sounds From Small Peoples: The Music Industry in Small Countries*, New York: Pendragon

myth and mythology

Since †Frazer's *The Golden Bough* (1890), mythology has been viewed as the repository of central *cosmological formulae and explanations of origin. Writers such as *Malinowski (1954) felt that myth and social reality were functionally interrelated. Myth confirmed, supported and maintained the social state of affairs. It provided an account of origins – of the world, of people and of their conventions. The *structuralists, who succeeded Malinowski, while discarding such overt *functionalism, nevertheless retained a somewhat more abstract version of it: they maintained that myth provided the conceptual rather than normative supports for a social world. If the members of a society were seen to be in possession of something as coherent as a cosmology, this was largely an effect of the anthropologist's search for a stable or ordered cultural world in which to place them. Accordingly, myth and ritual came to stand to semantic structures much as *joking and avoidance relations and †'rituals of rebellion' (for the last three generations of British social anthropologists) stood to social convention, and both were said to function in the same paradoxical manner: to preserve the integrity of society by subverting its conventional premises in other worldly, supernatural terms, and thereby focusing people's attention on them.

But there is an alternative way in which we can view myth that avoids this paradox, or, at the very least, allows the articulation of the paradox to be part of its methodology. We can assume that nothing so substantial as *culture or *language or convention exists except as it is tacitly revealed by the continuously innovative, extemporized, and experimental behaviour of people in interaction with each other (see Weiner 1992). We can view culture, convention, the utterances that defer to it and invoke it, and the body of rules by which we codify it, as things that emerge *post facto*, varieties of retrospective judgement on the part of actors, singly and collectively, as to the appropriateness, creativeness, felicity, infelicity, etc. of particular actions (including speech actions, that is, the utterances themselves).

This view would not encourage us to draw a sharp divide between language and the world, or between myth and language. It would see all actions and utterances as potentially subversive, introducing distinctions (temporarily, for the most part) in an otherwise undifferentiated world, drawing boundaries between words, people, and objects so as to release a flow of meaningful relations between them. Myth in such a world does not concern itself with origins as such. An origin story asks the listener to consider the kinds of things that cannot possibly have origins – language, *gender, †clan organization, humanity – and the myths that tell these stories produce an allegorical effect on language itself, a recognition of its contingency and the contingency of the conventional representations established through it. Each story provides an insight, an oblique and novel perspective that disabuses us from the normal, everyday habit of taking our world, our descriptions of it, our way of acting in it, and our beliefs as true, natural and self- evident.

The possibility of such an anti-charterist view of myth was first recognized by *Lévi-Strauss in his classic article, 'The Story of Asdiwal' (1976) where he began by commenting on the mythographic work of *Franz Boas. In the early years of this century, Boas, together with his Native American assistant George Hunt, undertook to record, as fully as possible, the myths of the Tshimshian, a people of the Pacific coast of Northwest America. His goal, in analysing this corpus of material, was to arrive at 'a description of the life, social organisation and religious ideas and practices of a people . . . as it appears in their mythology' (Boas and Hunt 1916: 320). Yet Lévi-Strauss, in his reinterpretation of one of the myths that Boas collected – the story of Asdiwal – argues that in the formulation of his programme, Boas failed to stipulate a relationship between myth and other social phenomena:

> The myth is certainly related to given facts, but not as a representation of them. The relationship is of a dialectic kind, and the institutions described in the myths can be the very opposite of the real institutions. This conception of the relation of the myth to reality no doubt limits the use of the former as a documentary source. But it opens the way for other possibilities; for in abandoning the search for a constantly accurate picture of ethnographic reality in the myth, we gain, on occasions, a means of reaching unconscious categories.
>
> (Lévi-Strauss 1976: 172–3)

With this aim in mind, Lévi-Strauss goes on to analyse myths only in relation to other myths – his intent in the four volumes of *Mythologiques*, his comprehensive survey of Native American mythology. Since their relationship to social organization is at best problematic, myths afford no more than a partial window on ethnographic reality. Myths provide a guide or template, sure enough, but only to other myths, only to other forms of *classification.

Lévi-Strauss approached the question about the relationship between language and world correctly: by rephrasing it as a problem of the relationship between one kind of language and another. He therefore forced us to consider the broader analytic problem of representation itself, and of how anthropologists construe the relationship between myth and the rest of social *discourse, and more generally, between vehicles of representation and that which is represented. Lévi-Strauss sees myth as similar to *music: it shares superficial syntactic and contrapuntal similarities with language but is essentially non-linguistic in form and effect. It could then be said that a myth must stand outside language if it is to represent something other than itself. We would then have to agree, as did Lévi-Strauss, with Richard Wagner, who thought that music and myth have the power to convey messages that ordinary language cannot. But both Richard Wagner and Lévi-Strauss felt that these extra-linguistic forms ultimately functioned to unify and coordinate the †worldview and morality of a community. In other words, though the forms of myth and music are not conventional, their effects are. And this is just another version of the functionalist paradox.

We could say, on the other hand, that myth must stand outside convention by proposing meanings that are interstitial or tangential to it. We would then be taking the position of Roy Wagner who holds that myth does not express conventional significances, it only makes the latter visible by way of its innovative impingements upon them. Thus he says, 'A myth, a metaphor, or any sort of tropic usage is ... an event – a dislocation, if you will – within a realm of conventional orientations' (1978: 255), a formulation that shares much in common with †Clifford Geertz's notion of the dialectical relationship between the 'is' and the 'ought', and with †Gregory Bateson's theories of rules and communication. A similar view has been propounded by Burridge in his landmark study of the narrative of the Tangu people of Papua New Guinea (1959). Myth 'juxtaposes [images], it does not classify' according to †Maurice Leenhardt (Clifford 1982: 181); it interprets rather than squarely represents, and from this point of view, its role in maintaining some represented social order is more ambiguous and complex than a functionalist or charterist theory would have us believe. Lévi-Strauss himself says, at the end of the last volume of *Mythologiques* that *contre* (to tell a story) is always *conte redire* (to retell a story) which can also be written *contredire* (to contradict) (1981: 644).

Myth and structural analysis

Lévi-Strauss was careful to point out that a myth could only be compared with another myth. Between myth and other forms of language and activity there is only a relationship of aesthetic impingement or impressionistic rendering. Some practitioners of structural analysis, however, sought to establish this relationship in more

normative, †Durkheimian terms. Of the myths of the Kwakiutl, for example, Walens says that the story of the creator being Q!aneqelaku, the Transformer, 'expresses the charter of Kwakiutl society' (1981: 137). This charter enjoins the control of hunger in the interests of maintaining an orderly sociality. 'Kwakiutl rituals enact the ideas embodied in this myth' (ibid.). Walens sees language in semantic terms, that is, in terms of sign relations. And in the same manner that a sign can only signify in one direction – the signifier can only represent the signified and not the other way around – so, for many anthropologists, myth and *ritual represent a more significant social reality. From this initial assumption of the gap between language and everything it describes, the assumption of discrete levels of all social discourse necessarily follows. What Lévi-Strauss (1976) once described as a multiplicity of explanatory levels came to be seen as reflecting a multiplicity of institutional perspectives. That is, where myth, ritual and politics are assumed to be separate phenomena, the relationship between them always appears to be problematic. And in the elucidation of this relationship is seen to lie the 'function' of structural analysis. Stephen Hugh-Jones elaborates upon this function in his study of the myth and ritual of the Barasana Indians of Northwest Amazonia (1979). Ritual for Hugh-Jones mediates between myth and social praxis, but in contrast to the assumed discontinuities between these modes of social discourse lies the Barasana's encompassing notion of He:

> The word He is ... used in a more general sense as a concept which covers such things as the sacred, the other world, the spirit world, and the world of myth. Used in this latter sense, the word is often added as a prefix to other words ... He pertains to the world of myths ...
>
> Barasana myths describe the establishment of a differentiated cosmos from an undifferentiated life-principle, and describe the establishment of order from chaos. This ordered cosmos, implied by the concept of He, and established as changeless in the mythic past, is seen by the Barasana as being the 'really real' (Geertz 1966) of which the human social order is but a part.
>
> (Hugh-Jones 1979: 139, 248)

It seems that the Barasana, like the Foi, accord to humans the task of differentiating themselves and their society from a more encompassing and immanent cosmos. As is the case with *Aboriginal Australians, their myth and ritual is the ongoing attempt to reconcile these social differentiations with what they perceive to be a natural continuity between humans and their surrounding world. A Barasana myth may not be a repository of semantic equations so much as a form through which to elicit an insight into the nature of man's He.

Wagner (1978) identifies myth among the Daribi of Papua New Guinea as an instance of symbolic obviation, which can be described as forcing a social image to collapse into its means of elicitation, thus revealing social protocol as contingent upon the language we bring to bear to describe it. In this view, myth dissolves the boundary between the conventional and the contingent that social life, at some level, always depends on.

JAMES WEINER

See also: Lévi-Strauss, structuralism, poetics, oral literature

Further reading

Boas, F. and G. Hunt (1916) *Tshimishian Mythology*, Bureau of American Ethnology, 31st Annual Report, 1909–10, Washington, DC: Smithsonian Institution

Burridge, K. (1959) *Tangu Traditions*, Oxford: Clarendon Press

Clifford, J. (1982) *Person and Myth: Maurice Leenhardt in the Melanesian World*, Berkeley: University of California Press

Hugh-Jones, S. (1979) *The Palm and the Pleiades*, Cambridge: Cambridge University Press

Lévi-Strauss, C. (1976) 'The Story of Asdiwal', in *Structural Anthropology*, vol. 2, New York: Basic Books

—— (1981) *The Naked Man (Mythologiques* vol. 4), New York: Harper and Row

Malinowski, B. (1954) *Magic, Science and Religion*, Garden City, NY: Doubleday Anchor Books

Wagner, R. (1978) *Lethal Speech: Daribi Myth as Symbolic Obviation*, Ithaca, NY: Cornell University Press

Walens, S. (1981) *Feasting with Cannibals*, Princeton, NJ: Princeton University Press

Weiner, J. (1992) 'Against the Motion (II)' in *Language is the Essence of Culture*, Group for Debate in Anthropological Theory, 4, Department of Social Anthropology, University of Manchester

N

names and naming

The anthropological study of personal names (or anthroponyms), ethnonyms and toponyms aroused little interest before the 1960s. This field seemed of secondary importance when compared with themes such as *kinship, social organization and *religion. Several pioneers of anthropology had indeed studied certain aspects of it. *L.H. Morgan, for example had investigated the use of personal names among Native Americans, *B. Malinowski had examined *cosmology and reincarnation among the Trobrianders, and †M. Mauss had compared the notion of *person and 'self' amongst various indigenous peoples (in Carrithers *et al.* 1985), and there were many others. It was not until the publication of *Lévi-Strauss's *Savage Mind* ([1962] 1966), however, that the importance of a comparative theoretical study of the classificatory functions of personal names, as a point of intersection between the social and the religious, became apparent.

Research and reflection on this subject has increased since then, as is evidenced by the number of seminars, symposia and publications which have been devoted to it. Nevertheless the subject is no easier to study in the field, because it requires a good knowledge of the language and the local culture studied, and also because it is often the case that personal names are not used outside specific social contexts. Although there is no standard *methodology for this kind of enquiry, a good inventory of personal names and of naming processes should be made in the initial stages of all social anthropological *fieldwork, because it enables one to perceive a group's social and symbolic relationships with others in *time and space. Combined with the study of *genealogies and systems of naming/reference, such an inventory permits a more general investigation of all aspects of social and religious life.

The success of studies carried out using this perspective, in non-Western as well as Western societies, allows us to predict interesting future developments in this field. For instance, C.J. Crocker and several other specialists on Amazonia have been able to show that †clan membership among certain groups was based on a stock of shared names rather than on †unilineal descent groups, and that the system of names and the system of descent reinforced one another (Tooker and Conklin 1984). Among Inuit, Guemple and Saladin d'Anglure have demonstrated how names noticeably affect the use of kinship terms and the conduct associated with them due to the identical nature of homonyms (Mills and Slobodin 1994). In *Southeast Asia, a substantial secondary literature has developed on the implications of †teknonyms (e.g. '*father of* Clifford', '*mother of* Hildred') and birth-order names, both for systems of kinship and concepts of personhood (Geertz and Geertz 1964). Names of persons, like names of groups and places, are used in all known societies to define a group's *identity, while also demarcating its otherness, i.e. the boundary separating it from other groups.

All these systems also bear the mark of †diachrony. In the absence of descendants personal names can be lost, while others are introduced, often the nicknames of deceased ancestors. Clans can merge, clan names become tribal names, whereas others may disappear for demographic reasons. Toponymy also bears the mark of history, event and individuals.

If the attribution of personal names has been recorded in all known human societies, and thus considered as a universal by †G.P. Murdock, the nature and forms of naming processes are extremely varied across the world, as shown by

Alford's (1988) comparative study in the †Human Relations Area Files. Alford distinguished four aspects of 'naming', the first of which is the initial naming process, usually taking place at birth, and sometimes having a provisional or private character (the 'umbilical name' described by Lévi-Strauss would fall into this category, as would the provisional name given by the midwife in some Amazonian groups). The second aspect is the way in which personal names individualize and classify people. Names can be chosen to match the child's sex, birth rank or clan. They can create a bond of homonymy or have a sacred character. Thirdly, there are changes of name – nicknames as well as new names given after birth, during the main transitions in the life cycle, during an illness, or after an exploit. The final aspect mentioned by Alford is the use or non-use of names and role terms: avoidance of a name, symmetrical or asymmetrical usage for certain relations, and a distinction between usage in address and usage in reference. This work far from exhausts the subtlety of the classificatory or religious functions of personal names; its objective – the quantification of selected traits present in diverse monographs and articles, restricts its field, mainly due to the absence of a standard methodology of data collection.

On the other hand, to approach naming systems using the concept of 'reincarnation' (Mills and Slobodin 1994) as happens customarily in religious studies, is to run another risk, namely that of attaching greater importance to the content of the belief than to its social construction. In fact, conceptions of the person, of identity and of the psychic principle associated with the name, in societies such as those of the Amerindians and the Inuit, are so polymorphous and different from what we usually understand by the term 'reincarnation', that there is a danger of a certain reductionism. Fruitful debates are still possible, however, on this central theme of social life, its practices and its representations.

BERNARD SALADIN D'ANGLURE

See also: individualism, person, relationship terminology

Further reading

Alford, R. (1988) *Naming and Identity: A Cross-Cultural Study of Personal Naming Practices*, New Haven: Human Relations Area Files

Carrithers, M., S. Collins and S. Lukes (eds) (1985) *The Category of the Person*, Cambridge: Cambridge University Press

Geertz, H. and C. Geertz (1964) 'Teknonymy in Bali: Parenthood, Age Grading and Genealogical Amnesia', *Journal of the Royal Anthropological Institute* 94: 94–108

Lévi-Strauss, C. ([1962] 1966) *The Savage Mind*, London: Weidenfeld and Nicolson

Mills, A. and R. Slobodin (eds) (1994) *Amerindian Rebirth*, Toronto: University of Toronto Press

Tooker, E. and H. Conklin (eds) (1984) *Naming Systems*, Washington, DC: American Ethnological Society

nationalism

Nationalism is the political doctrine which holds that humanity can be divided into separate, discrete units – nations – and that each nation should constitute a separate political unit – a *state. The claim to nationhood usually invokes the idea of a group of people with a shared *culture, often a shared *language, sometimes a shared *religion, and usually but not always a shared history; to this it adds the political claim that this group of people should, by rights, rule themselves or be ruled by people of the same kind (nation, ethnicity, language, religion, etc.). Understood like this, the idea of nationalism as a political doctrine can be traced back to German Romantic philosophers like †Herder and Fichte, whose ideas were also crucial in the development of the anthropological concept of culture. Anthropology, then, shares an intellectual history with nationalism, and nationalism serves as a reminder of the political implications of common anthropological assumptions about the world – for example, the idea that people can be naturally classified as belonging to discrete, bounded cultures or societies. *Boas (who explicitly acknowledged the influence of Herder) and his students, for example, fought a long battle against the idea of *'race' in the inter-war years, but in substituting instead the idea of culture they failed to question the assumption that people naturally belonged to one culture and one culture only.

In fact this assumption is so widespread in the modern world that it has rarely been subjected to sustained intellectual scrutiny. The great social theorists like †Weber and †Marx often treated nationalism, and the vision of human cultural difference on which it is based, as a self-evident feature of the world, whereas other kinds of collective category, like *class, received endless theoretical scrutiny. Their followers in *sociology, history and political science usually followed suit so that nationalism, despite its pervasive effects on twentieth-century world history, was the great forgotten topic of the human sciences. Similarly, anthropologists rarely questioned the idea of nationhood, preferring the less politicized topic of *ethnicity in some cases, or even contributing to the construction of nationalist stereotypes of national culture in other cases.

Although anthropological writers like †Mauss, †Dumont, †W.L. Warner, and †Clifford Geertz had all written important essays on nationalism and the rituals of the nation, nationalism only really emerged as an anthropological problem in the 1980s. There were several reasons for this, none of them inherent to anthropology. In Europe, the growth of separatist nationalisms in the 1960s and 1970s was strongest in those periph-eral areas – Brittany, the Basque country, Scotland – most attractive to anthropologists; ethnogra-phers in those areas, therefore, had to come to terms with nationalist representations of local cultural differences. Elsewhere, the optimistic project of 'nation-building' in former European colonies was sometimes replaced by civil war and violent movements towards separatism – in India and Sri Lanka, as well as parts of Southeast Asia, East and West Africa. Ethnographers in these areas had to deal with the political and human cost of †postcolonial nationalisms. Finally, the collapse of communist rule in Eastern Europe in 1989 was followed by an apparent explosion of nationalist and separatist conflict, most spectacu-larly in former Yugoslavia. Anthropologists who had worked in these areas often found themselves unexpectedly sought out for comment and analysis, as relatively few political scientists had either the sensitivity or knowledge to offer plau-sible interpretations of what was happening.

The 1980s also saw the publication of a number of important theoretical books on nation-alism. †Ernest Gellner's *Nations and Nationalism* (1983), offers a general sociological model of links between nationalism and *modernity. He argues that industrial society is based on a necessary cultural homogeneity which allows for continuous cognitive and economic growth. In order to ensure that homogeneity, the state takes control over the process of cultural reproduction, through the institution of mass schooling. Nationalism, an argument for the political pre-eminence of cultur-ally homogeneous units, is the political correlate

of this process. As such, far from the 'primitive', 'atavistic' or 'tribal' phenomenon of journalistic cliché, nationalism is unquestionably modern. Benedict Anderson's *Imagined Communities* (1983) shared Gellner's conception of nationalism as a modern phenomenon, but, influenced in part by the work of †Victor Turner, focused more on nationalism as a mode of political imagination, to be analysed more like religion or kinship, for instance, than like other political ideologies such as Marxism or liberalism. Chatterjee's *Nationalist Thought and the Colonial World* (1986) examined the paradoxes and contradictions of anti-colonial and postcolonial nationalisms, drawing on the history of Indian nationalism.

Anderson's work has had the most obvious impact on anthropology so far, not least because his emphasis on the imaginary work of nation-alism opens up potentially fascinating areas for new research on nationalist cultural production: for example, in the *mass media, *consumption, *art and *folklore (Foster 1991). Gellner's argu-ments, in fact, often offer somewhat tougher theoretical propositions which could be usefully tested by historical and ethnographic research; but these are in anthropologically unfashionable areas like *education, while Gellner's unapologetic †positivism is out of kilter with the *postmodern *zeitgeist* (in British and American anthropology, that is, not Central and Eastern Europe, or soci-ology, where his work commands wider respect).

In general, anthropologists have been slower to respond to nationalism as a specifically political phenomenon, and slower still to deal with its undoubted power to mobilize people politically in modern societies. Much ethnographic research has instead concentrated on the rituals and symbols of nationalism, pursuing a line of enquiry opened up by Hobsbawm and Ranger's *Invention of Tradition* (1983). In this research, intellectuals and cultural producers become an unexpected object for anthropological enquiry, as in Verdery's important study of Romanian nationalism under Ceaucescu (1991) and McDonald's work on Breton nationalism (1990). Handler's research on Québécois nationalism 'as a cultural system', turned into an important examination of the intellectual genealogy of anthropological and nationalist ideas, not least the very idea of a 'cultural system' which Handler had taken from the *symbolic anthropology of his teacher †David Schneider (Handler 1988: 26–7). The result, though, is disturbing because Handler's argument is as much a critique of Québécois nationalism as it is a critique of the anthropological ideas he brought to its study (cf. Handler 1985).

This element of critique – which occurs again and again in recent ethnography, as nationalist claims to authenticity and historical rootedness are challenged and exposed – suggests that nationalism occupies a sensitive place in the anthropological collective consciousness. After all, most anthropologists are expected to take a charitable line on the deeply-held convictions of the people they write about, and it is unusual to find a political and social phenomenon subject to such unremitting criticism. Politically this is not a mystery, as nationalism can be held accountable for many of the gravest crimes in the bloody twentieth century. Intellectually, it should be more problematic, though. If nothing else, it serves as a salutary reminder that anthropologists cannot, and should not, employ assertions of *relativism as a smokescreen to conceal their own inevitable political engagement with the subjects of their study.

JONATHAN SPENCER

See also: colonialism, culture, education, essentialism, ethnicity, folklore, identity, state

Further reading

Anderson, B. (1983) *Imagined Communities: Reflections on the Origins and Spread of Nationalism*, London: Verso
Chatterjee, P. (1986) *Nationalist Thought and the Colonial World: A Derivative Discourse?*, London: Zed
Foster, R. (1991) 'Making National Cultures in the Global Ecumene', *Annual Review of Anthropology* 20: 235–60
Gellner, E. (1983) *Nations and Nationalism*, Oxford: Blackwell
Handler, R. (1985) 'On Dialogue and Destructive Analysis: Problems in Narrating Nationalism and Ethnicity', *Journal of Anthropological Research* 41: 171–82
—— (1988) *Nationalism and the Politics of Culture in Quebec*, Madison: University of Wisconsin Press
Hobsbawm, E. (1991) 'Ethnicity and Nationalism in Europe Today' (with responses by K. Verdery and R. Fox) *Anthropology Today* 8 (1): 3–13
Hobsbawm, E. and T. Ranger (eds) (1983) *The Invention of Tradition*, Cambridge: Cambridge University Press
McDonald, M. (1990) *We are not French! Language, Culture and Identity in Britanny*, London: Routledge
Verdery, K. (1991) *National Ideology under Socialism: Identity and Cultural Politics in Ceausescu's Romania*, Berkeley: University of California Press

nature and culture

At the foundation of †cultural anthropology lies the notion of a great fault line sundering the world of human culture from the rest of the living world. On this view, part of our human constitution falls on one side of the line, the side explicable by biological and allied sciences. On that side we resemble other animals. But on the other side, dominated by our capacity for learning, language and the use of symbols, we reach beyond the ken of biology and attain our essential, unique and, so to speak, super-animal character. In his presidential address to the American Association for the Advancement of Science in 1958, †Leslie White captured this doctrine in a memorable myth.

> [Using symbols] man built a new world in which to live . . . He still trod the earth, felt the wind against his cheek, or heard it sigh among the pines; he . . . slept beneath the stars, and awoke to greet the sun. But it was not the same sun! . . . Everything was 'bathed in celestial light'; and there were 'intimations of immortality on every hand'. Between man and nature hung the veil of culture, and he could see nothing save through this medium . . . Permeating everything was the essence of words: the meanings and values that lay beyond the senses.
>
> (quoted in Sahlins 1976: 105)

The imagery of this just-so story dividing humans from animals is fanciful, but the message is sincerely intended: human *cognition and action are mediated by learned and therefore cultural, rather than by instinctive or inborn, responses. Since this is so, culture is a separate object of study, cultural variation is different in kind from biological variation, and cultural anthropology is an autonomous discipline, separate from the biological sciences.

Culture

Nevertheless the development of a notion of culture has from the beginning been driven hard from behind by the intellectual struggle against attempts to explain human behaviour and human variety using purely natural scientific means. It is therefore impossible to understand the concept 'culture' clearly without reference to its opposing concept, 'nature'. In a wider perspective this struggle is but a fragment of the greater conflict over human nature which has been so pervasive a feature of intellectual life in the North Atlantic societies of the nineteenth and twentieth centuries. For as the assurance of the natural sciences grew, and as more of the living world fell under their confident surveillance, so a conception of nature began to grow that was to be subject to an increasingly authoritative style of enquiry, which we know today as biology. The burning question then became: to what extent do humans fall into nature and therefore under the sovereignty of biological explanation? For some – and this is as true today as it was in the last century – the sway of such explanation was to be total. For others in *sociology and related disciplines, however, humans and human society participate in a different order of existence altogether.

In the province of intellectual endeavour that became anthropology, the province concerned with human diversity, the struggle for a distinct science of humanity was led by *Franz Boas (1858 – 1942) in the United States. To Boas we owe the creation of both the cultural anthropological attitude and the very profession of cultural anthropology itself. When he began work in the 1880s, Boas found in place a theory hardly fifty years old, but already very elaborate, which purported to explain the different varieties of people, their customs, and their apparently different mental capacities by reference to *race. The race theory was firmly anchored in the new science of biology by evolutionary ideas which suggested that some races were more primitive than others, and therefore more animal-like, or 'theromorphic', in bodily form, mental ability, and moral development. The theory measured each race against the supposedly most advanced, the Northern Europeans.

Boas broke the evidently seamless simplicity of this theory. He showed that bodily form is not linked to language or to any of the matters we associate with culture: attitudes and values, customs, modes of livelihood and forms of social organization. He argued that there is no reason to think that other 'races' (or, more accurately, other ways of life) are less moral or less intelligent than Northern Europeans, and so there is no single standard for evaluation. Moreover by his own strenuous example he showed that different cultures could, and should, be the object of intensive field research which would reveal forms and patterns in human life that were hitherto unsuspected. These patterns are so various, he argued, that they could not have arisen from a uniform

process of social or cultural evolution but must rather be the fruit of complex local historical causes.

These ideas were set out in Boas's *The Mind of Primitive Man* in 1911, but they were elaborated in the next generation by Boas's large and brilliant group of students, which included †Edward Sapir, †Alfred Kroeber, †Margaret Mead, and †Ruth Benedict, and by their students in turn. On this view, human culture is marked by its extreme plasticity, such that human beings, possessing everywhere much the same biological heritage, are nevertheless able to sustain kaleidoscopically differing sets of values, institutions and behaviours in different cultures. Yet if culture seems to this extent arbitrary in its variety, its possession is central to the human constitution, for without culture – without some learned collection of language and habits of thought and action – human beings could most literally not live. These ideas were well in place by the publication of Benedict's *Patterns of Culture* in 1934. To achieve Leslie White's just-so story of 1958 only a slight extra stress was needed, to the effect that humans are 'symboling' and classifying creatures, creatures who possess meaning. These ideas were hugely successful. They became the *pons asinorum*, the bridge separating those who understand anthropology from those who do not, and they serve even today as the entry to what grew into a vast professional academic discipline in the United States.

Culture and nature

The Boasian doctrine expanded and changed as well. Along one line of development nature/culture became, for anthropologists who now studied culture alone, an unexamined or even dogmatic presupposition, an unquestioned feature of reality. Hence the distinction came to be applied just like any such general and governing idea, as a conceptual Swiss Army knife, useful for many purposes beyond its designers' plans. The French anthropologist *Lévi-Strauss is perhaps the most influential representative of this turn. He argued that the nature/culture divide is not just an anthropologist's concept, but is to be found among all societies in some form as a cognitive device for understanding the world. Indeed he went further, suggesting that it is the very making of a distinction between nature and culture that distinguishes humans from animals. Few have been willing to follow him around so many corners (and he later scaled down his claims about the universality of the distinction), but his example has given warrant to the use of nature versus culture as an interpretive device throughout anthropology. Some writers, for example, have suggested that the divide falls between men and women, such that women, or perhaps the processes of childbirth, are natural, whereas men, or the ritual and political processes they control, are cultural (for a critical review see MacCormack and Strathern 1980). The nature/culture divide is often used to great and illuminating effect, but it is worth remembering that the very concept is a product of, and is used by, only a small segment of the societies of the North Atlantic Rim in the twentieth century, and so may not enjoy the universal explanatory penetration that is sometimes claimed for it.

One of the other alternatives was to accept a notion of culture, but to turn back to scientific styles of explanation to give an account of it. The rise to prominence of the biological field of ecology after World War II stimulated some anthropologists to look for a new material logic underpinning cultural forms. The most famous, and least persuasive, example is †Marvin Harris's attempt to explain the worship of cattle in India by reference to the usefulness of cowdung to Indian farmers. A more plausible example is Roy Rappaport's painstaking attempt to explain the religion of a Papua New Guinea people by their ecology and mode of livelihood. The force of such arguments often lies not so much in themselves as in their demonstration of weaknesses in the Boasian inheritance, which often glosses over complexities in social and material life that are not amenable to traditional cultural explanation.

In any case the vigour and anger of the replies to such arguments reveal how fervently many anthropologists cling to the autonomy of culture. Indeed the temperature of the continuing conflict between the parties of biological and cultural determinism remains high. This conflict has ranged in the twentieth century across race, sexuality, *gender, aggression, intelligence, *nutrition and many more issues besides. It may seem merely antiquarian to stress the importance of Boas . . . until we realize that the research project on adolescent sexuality in Samoa proposed by him for Margaret Mead, a project which then seemed to demonstrate decisively the force of cultural over biological explanation, was challenged fiercely in the 1980s in the name of new forms of biological explanation. On the one hand, the notion of nature/culture has worked its way into conceptual vocabularies across the learned disciplines of the North Atlantic societies, and into the thought of psychologists, †ethologists, and even evolutionary biologists. Even British social anthropology, which for so long resisted the concept of culture, has silently accepted its importance. Yet on the other hand the disciplinary disputes continue because the biological sciences have very different schemes of training, and very different aspirations, than the cultural disciplines. And if anthropologists have grown in number and confidence, so have biologists: the biologists' nineteenth-century claim for decisive authority has only been magnified by a growth in the professionalization and the accomplishments, and a fabulous growth in the authority and the funding, of biological sciences in the twentieth. In the mutual misunderstanding of the two parties it is often difficult to judge who are the more ignorant of the other and the more arrogant.

Synthesis

Yet the late twentieth century has seen the beginning of an extraordinary cooperative effort, by behavioural biologists, psychologists and anthropologists, not so much to reconcile the disciplines as to channel their conflicting energies into a greater project. Suppose, for a moment, that we took the two parties each to have revealed a broken fragment of the truth. Humans do vary greatly in their cultural endowments and those endowments bear heavily on their behaviour; yet humans, like other animals, came into being through forces best described as Darwinian. It follows then that humans evolved to have culture, so to speak: our big brains with their ability to manipulate symbols, along with our abilities to use our respiratory tracts for speech, comprise the Darwinian heritage that makes us the culture-bearing animal *par excellence*. This much might be admitted by even a very reductionist biologist or a very doctrinaire cultural anthropologist. What is only now coming to light, however, is a subtler picture, which shows that we have evolved not in the first instance as culture-bearing animals, but as social animals. Studies of *childhood cognitive and emotional development, and comparative studies of other primates, show that beneath and around the stuff of culture there stands a scaffolding of social abilities and distinctly social intelligence. We can learn culture because we come richly equipped, even as the smallest infant, to enter into conscious and responsive social relations with our fellows. We become culturally knowledgeable because we first become socially knowledgeable, able to grasp and react to the moods and intentions of those around us in a way recognizably akin to, but a good deal more powerful than, that of our primate cousins. And because this scaffolding intelligence is both relatively powerful and flexible – because, in other words, it is a creative and imaginative intelligence – we can begin to see how humans have, quite naturally, been so productive of a rich panoply of differing cultures across the world.

MICHAEL CARRITHERS

See also: biological anthropology, environment, ecological anthropology, Lévi-Strauss

Further reading

Benedict, R. (1934) *Patterns of Culture*, London: Routledge and Kegan Paul

Boas, F. ([1911] 1938) *The Mind of Primitive Man*, New York: Macmillan

Carrithers, M. (1992) *Why Humans Have Cultures: Explaining Anthropology and Social Diversity*, Oxford: Oxford University Press

Caton, H. (1990) *The Samoa Reader: Anthropologists Take Stock*, Lanham, MD: University Press of America

Freeman, D. (1984) *Margaret Mead: The Making and Unmaking of an Anthropological Myth*, Harmondsworth: Penguin Books

Harris, M. (1966) 'The Cultural Ecology of India's Sacred Cattle', *Current Anthropology* 7: 51–62

Horigan, S. (1988) *Nature and Culture in Western Discourses*, London: Routledge

Ingold, T. (1986) *Evolution and Social Life*, Cambridge: Cambridge University Press

Lévi-Strauss, C. (1969) *The Elementary Structures of Kinship*, Boston: Beacon Press

MacCormack, C. and M. Strathern (eds) *Nature, Culture and Gender*, Cambridge: Cambridge University Press

Mead, M. ([1928] 1943) *Coming of Age in Samoa*, Harmondsworth: Penguin Books

Rappaport, R. (1984) *Pigs for the Ancestors: Ritual in the Ecology of a New Guinea People* (enlarged edn), New Haven: Yale University Press

Sahlins, M. (1976) *Culture and Practical Reason*, Chicago: University of Chicago Press

Stocking, G.W. (1968) *Race, Culture and Evolution: Essays in the History of Anthropology*, Chicago: University of Chicago Press

network analysis

Network analysis in anthropology is more than the study of 'networking' – expanding and making strategic use of the stock of contacts a person has. Minimally, a network consists of points and lines. Points can be persons, marketplaces, or organizations, and lines can be social relationships, †commodity or information flows, or shared board members.

*Sociologists have been more interested in organizational networks and interlocking directorates, and often study them with existing documents. No particular centre to the network need exist, and the strength or weakness of connections among the organizations is the object of 'block analysis' (Scott 1991). Similarly, in anthropological studies of *market networks, no individual marketplace is given centrality; the place of each market in a hierarchical network is determined through fieldwork and quantitative analysis (Skinner 1964–5).

Networks that have a person at their centre are termed 'egocentric' networks, and this was the focus of network analysis as developed by social anthropologists in the 1950s and 1960s (Sanjek 1974; Scott 1991). In exploratory studies and conceptual papers, hope was expressed that charting and analysing egocentric networks would be as valuable in urban settings (where alters include many non-kin) as the *genealogical method was in kin-based societies.

The problem is how to determine that an alter is 'in' an ego's network (Sanjek 1974). Some anthropologists see this as a cognitive question, and ask an ego to list their alters. One exhaustive study of two Maltese networks found 638 alters in one and 1,751 in the other; the first Maltese, however, exchanged conversation or visits with only 128 alters, and the second with 700. With no clear theoretical goal set for this data-gathering, however, the investment in research time was enormous, and few more such studies were undertaken.

Another methodogical tack is to observe (or recover through interviews) the alters actually encountered by an ego. The study of action-sets – the alters whom candidates interact with during an Indian electoral campaign, for example, or who appear at English christenings, Navajo ceremonies or Zambian funerals – is one way to isolate a discrete portion of a behavioural network, and to make comparisons among a set of egos. A second behavioural network method uses data on alters encountered by an ego over a delimited time period. Thus Sanjek (1978) compared networks of forty Ghanaians, each studied over four days, in terms of theoretical issues regarding the extent of 'tribalism' in urban life. He found that more than half the interaction scenes in the networks were polyethnic, and that in many others the co-ethnic alters were kin of the egos.

Since the 1970s, few network studies have been published by anthropologists. Network analysis requires diligent fieldwork, and even then needs to be contextualized and interpreted with other sorts of information. In sociology, a vast technical vocabulary related to formal measures now marks network analysis (Scott 1991); in anthropological discourse, network appears today more often as metaphor (when speaking about 'networking') than as method. But when theoretical questions that can be answered with network data are posed, network analysis remains a valuable if under-used research tool (Boissevain 1979; Sanjek 1978).

ROGER SANJEK

See also: markets, complex society, urban anthropology

Further reading

Boissevain, J. (1979) 'Network Analysis: A Reappraisal', *Current Anthropology* 20: 392–94
Sanjek, R. (1974) 'What is Network Analysis, and What is it Good For?', *Reviews in Anthropology* 1: 588–97
—— (1978) 'A Network Method and its Uses in Urban Ethnography', *Human Organization* 37: 257–68
Scott, J. (1991) *Social Network Analysis: A Handbook*, London: Sage
Skinner, G.W. (1964–5) 'Marketing and Social Structure in Rural China', *Journal of Asian Studies* 24: 3–43, 195–228, 363–99

nomadism

Nomadism is movement of the residential social group in the course of regular social, economic, and political activities. Nomads move, from one place to another, taking their families and homes, neighbours and kin with them, as they go about joining with or separating from other people, engaging in the activities of making a living, and avoiding the threats of enemies and supporting their allies. Whether there is a permanent 'home' site or not, mobility of the *household requires a

*technology of travel and transport, including baggage and in some cases burden animals, and of shelter, either mobile dwellings, such as tents or yurts, or the ability to construct dwellings from local materials, as with igloos.

Nomadism is common among peoples living in difficult environments, such as rain forests, deserts, and arctic lands, because the useful resources are thinly and irregularly distributed across space, and nomadism is the most efficient way of harvesting those resources. The demographic correlates of this low †carrying capacity are usually a small population and low population density, that is, few people spread thinly across the land.

From an economic point of view, nomadism is important in traditional forms of *hunting and gathering and *pastoralism. People engaged in hunting and gathering, such as the Inuit of the Arctic (Balikci 1970), the San of the Kalahari desert (Lee 1979), and the Mbuti of the Ituri forest (Turnbull 1965), migrate from exploited to fresh territory, to follow the movement of target species, and to shift from one species to another. People engaged in pastoralism, raising livestock on natural pasture, such as the Somali of the deserts in the Horn of Africa (Lewis 1961), the Bedouin of Arabia (Lancaster 1981), and the Zagros mountain tribes of the Western Iran (Barth 1964; Beck 1991), migrate seasonally to take their livestock to better climates and pastures, but also to take them away from disease and predators. There are also nomads who live in small groups scattered amongst sedentary peoples, providing services such as blacksmithing or engaging in trade (Rao 1987).

Most peoples who engage in hunting and gathering and in pastoralism do so as part of broader multi-resource or mixed economies (Salzman 1971). This is particularly true of people who are oriented toward producing for their own subsistence, rather than toward sale in the *market, because they must produce a wide variety of foods and raw materials to satisfy their needs. While the Bedouin of Arabia could specialize in camel production for the caravan market, in turn receiving a variety of goods from the market, the subsistence oriented Baluch of Southeastern Iran (Salzman 1971) engaged in small stock pastoralism, runoff cultivation of grain, date palm arboriculture, hunting and gathering, and predatory raiding. Nomadism provides the spatial flexibility necessary for carrying out, contemporaneously or sequentially, the myriad tasks of these diverse activities.

In addition to these economic dimensions of nomadism, there is an important political dimension, which in some cases may dominate. Mobility of residences and of capital resources, such as domesticated livestock, allows people to move away from threatening enemies. Hostile relations with neighbours can lead groups which have little pressing need for economic nomadism, such as the yurt-dwelling Yomut Turkmen (Irons 1975) in the rich Gorgon plain of Northeast Iran, to live in mobile dwellings and maintain transport animals, so that they could escape from attacks, in this case Persian Government military reprisals in response to Turkmen raiding of Persian villages. Groups using nomadism for economic reasons will also use it in this political fashion, to avoid political pressure or military threat by escaping through spatial mobility.

It is clear that nomads do not 'wander', but rather strategically select migratory routes and new residential locations after carefully sifting information – gathered by scouts from the group or visitors – about many environmental, economic, and political factors. This selection comes after the weighing of alternative trajectories and sites and their benefits and shortcomings, often through debating among themselves for weeks, while trying to balance their multiple common interests with the different interests of the constituent individuals and *families arising from their different economic preferences, repertoires, and commitments. Furthermore, people are usually nomadic within a customary range or territory which they know well and to which they have some political claim. One of the main functions of the tribal organization common among pastoralists is the control of territory within which constituent groups may engage in nomadic exploitation. Commonly any natural resource – uncultivated pasture, natural water sources, wild fruits and vegetables, game – is regarded as common property, available to any member of the larger political entity, while constructed resources – domesticated livestock, wells, cultivation, dwelling or storage structures – are regarded as the property of those who made them. Outside individuals or groups often customarily ask permission to enter and make use of the natural resources.

Because household mobility makes leaving and joining others relatively easy, local groups among nomads tend over time to be somewhat fluid, with a regular flow of households coming and going.

This allows relatively easy adjustment to a variety of pressures, such as changing environmental conditions, as in a drought which requires a lower population density, or changing economic circumstances, as when new opportunities lead some members to choose different activities than others, or interpersonal and political pressures, as when conflict develops among group members. Seasonal changes in the local group, aptly called 'structural poses' by Gearing (1958), are found among some nomadic peoples, such as the Inuit (Balikci 1970) and the Plains Indians (Oliver 1962), from large groups of many score or hundreds in summer, to small groups of a few families in winter. This fluidity not only allows precise adaptation to environmental conditions, but social adjustments which minimize conflict within the residence group. If people cannot get along or are in conflict, they can easily separate from one another and resolve the difficulty through avoidance. As a consequence, the personality structure of nomads (Edgerton 1971), in contrast with non-nomadic, spatially stable peoples who must live together decade after decade however they feel about one another, tends to be more emotionally open and expressive, quick to fight and quick to forgive, whereas †sedentary villagers tend to hide anger, carry grudges, and engage in indirect aggression such as *gossip and vandalism.

PHILIP CARL SALZMAN

See also: transhumance, ecological anthropology

Further reading

Balikci, A. (1970) *The Netsilik Eskimo*, Garden City, NY: Natural History Press

Barth, F. (1964) *Nomads of South Persia*, New York: Humanities Press

Beck, L. (1991) *Nomad: A Year in the Life of a Qashqa'i Tribesman in Iran*, Berkeley: University of California Press

Edgerton, R.B. (1971) *The Individual in Cultural Adaptation*, Berkeley: University of California Press

Gearing, F.O. (1958) 'The Structural Poses of 18th Century Cherokee Villages', *American Anthropologist* 60: 1148–56

Irons, W. (1975) *The Yomut Turkmen*, Ann Arbor: Anthropological Papers 58, Museum of Anthropology, University of Michigan

Lancaster, W. (1981) *The Rwala Bedouin Today*, Cambridge: Cambridge University Press

Lee, R.B. (1979) *The Kung San*, Cambridge: Cambridge University Press

Lewis, I.M. (1961) *A Pastoral Democracy*, London: Oxford University Press.

Oliver, S.C. (1962) 'Ecology and Cultural Continuity as Contributing Factors in the Social Organization of the Plains Indians', *University of California Publications in American Archaeology and Ethnology* 48 (1): 13–18, 46–9, 52–68

Rao, A. (ed.) (1987) *The Other Nomads*, Cologne: Böhlau Verlag

Salzman, P.C. (1971) 'Movement and Resource Extraction among Pastoral Nomads', *Anthropological Quarterly* 44 (3): 185–97

Turnbull, C.M. (1965) *Wayward Servants*, London: Eyre and Spottiswoode

number

Numbers are a problem for anthropologists because they defy the assumptions implicit in the idea of cultural *relativism. Davis and Hersh, following Kant, suggest that

> The truths of geometry and arithmetic are forced on us by the way our minds work; this explains why they are supposedly true for everyone, independent of experience. The intuitions of time and space, on which arithmetic and geometry are based, are objective in the sense that they are universally valid for all human minds.
>
> (1981: 329)

This proposition does not close the subject to anthropologists, but rather requires them to ask two questions. First, how are the truths of arithmetic accessed within any given culture; and second, how are they then applied?

To conceptualize number requires the insight that two collections of objects can share the property that if their members are placed side by side, there is a perfect isomorphism between them (Crump 1990: 8). Since this property is independent of the character of the objects themselves, the principle can be extended indefinitely. At the same time, other collections, will prove, as a result of the matching procedure, to contain either fewer, or more, members. This insight is the crucial step along the path to numeracy. The Indians of Zinacantan in Southern Mexico – who, far from being primitive are fully equal to the numerical demands of the modern world – still maintain a ritual based on counting the value of a sacred hoard of coins against a fixed number of maize kernels kept in a sack (Vogt 1976: 128).

If the property common to 'matching' collections is then defined as the 'number' of these collections, one then has an adjectival property that can be expressed in language. This is essential for advancing numeracy beyond the level of this matching procedure. Once this step is taken, then a whole series of words are required, which can then be ordered according to the principle that the place of any word in the series is such that the words preceding it define collections with fewer members, while those following it define those with more members. There will then be a single word, in English 'one', with no predecessors, followed by an ordered series of number words, such as the English 'two, three, four . . .' and so on indefinitely. The process of uttering these words, in the order established in this way, is then known as 'counting'.

Where then do these words come from in the first place? There is no general answer to this question, but a process known as 'body-counting' has been recorded from many different parts of the world. The term 'designates the number sequence arrived at by some primitive peoples, in which the parts of the human body – the head, the eyes, the arms, and so forth – are arranged in a certain order' (Menninger 1969: 34). The fact that five, ten or twenty, are key words in almost all languages containing number words, confirms that the human *body provides the basic model for number words. This is true even for languages in which the present form of these words cannot be related to those for any part of the human anatomy.

There are, however, cultures, such as that of the Iqwaye of New Guinea, in which

> the twenty fingers and toes on the body . . . function as the irreducible units of reference and together with the whole body provide the basis of the counting system and the numerical series by means of which the Iqwaye count other things in their world
>
> (Mimica 1988: 13)

In this case, according to Mimica (1988: 6), mathematics as a 'specific form of Occidental cultural knowledge' has no part to play. In practice this excludes every form of calculation, a restriction acceptable to the Iqwaye and other similar cultures.

Mimica's view may be tendentious, but certainly the use of numbers in calculation does require a systematic linguistic means for representing the series of numbers to an extremely high level. The simplest possible system, in its purest form, is to be found in Chinese, which combines the number words from one to nine with other special words for ten, hundred, thousand, and so on. The principle that large numbers must be conceived of, implicitly, in terms of arithmetical formulae based on a limited number of standard signs is almost universal, and even extends to the Iqwaye.

Spoken language has severe limitations in working with numbers, so it is not surprising that numbers are fundamental to visible language, even in the first stages of development. The case is significant for the fact that numbers can be represented by visible signs much more transparently than is possible in spoken language. The most perfect system, developed independently in both the old world and the new, is that of place value. The so-called Arabic numerals exemplify this, so that the numbers appearing in say, 5,387, indicate, by their position, the relevant power of ten, as becomes immediately apparent when such a number is read out aloud. This property is shared also by the most elementary and widespread calculator, the abacus.

Finally, once numbers, in popular *cognition, are detached from any collection of things being counted, and combine efficiently in calculation, an essential numerical dimension is common to *time and space, *music and poetry, every form of *exchange, *sport and games, in ways varying from one culture to another, but as the same time capable of wide diffusion.

THOMAS CRUMP

See also: rationality, relativism, cognition

Further Reading

Crump, T. (1990) *The Anthropology of Numbers*, Cambridge: Cambridge University Press
Davis, P.J. and R. Hersh (1981) *The Mathematical Experience*, London: Penguin
Menninger, K. (1969) *Number Words and Number Symbols*, Cambridge, MA: MIT Press
Mimica, J. (1988) *Intimations of Infinity*, Oxford: Berg
Vogt, E.Z. (1976) *Tortillas for the Gods*, Cambridge, MA: Harvard University Press

nutrition

Adequate nutrition is required for survival and successful reproduction. However, there is great variety in human dietary patterns. The saying

'Man ist was man ißt' (man is what one eats) can be construed both to refer to the chemical composition of the body as the product of flows of nutrients and energy, and to the sociological sense in which dietary choice reflects the social persona of the individual. The science of nutrition has developed from chemistry and physiology and remains an essentially biological discipline. Social economic factors play an important role in influencing access to nutritional resources, but have tended to be seen as peripheral to the discipline.

The emergence of nutritional anthropology in the 1970s has tended to replicate the 'two cultures' of an anthropology divided methodologically and by theories into social and biological sciences. The former have been concerned with the social role of foodstuffs, the determinants of their production and distribution, and the management of shortages. This has historically been a concern of social anthropology at least since the early work of †Audrey Richards (1939). For example, Freedman has defined nutritional anthropology as 'the study of the interrelationship between diet and culture and their mutual influence upon one another' (1976). In a practical context, this becomes the application of social anthropological data and methods to solving 'the cultural aspects of human nutritional problems', for instance where health programmes need to overcome what are seen as cultural barriers to improved nutrition (Freedman 1976). Jerome *et al.* (1980) adopt a similar approach which delineates the significance of four areas: dietary pattern; non-nutritional aspects of food related to ethnic identity, culinary tradition, social structure, social status and cultural change; cognitive aspects of food understood as part of ideological systems; and food as a vehicle of energy in studies of the human ecosystem.

By contrast, *biological anthropologists and nutritionists have treated food mainly as a vehicle of energy and nutrients. Nutritionists have focused on determinants of variation in nutritional status and its measurement, the nature of energy and nutrient requirements, ethnic differences in nutrient utilization, and the possibility of nutritional adaptation by biological and social means (Blaxter and Waterlow 1985; Ulijaszek and Strickland 1993). Biological anthropologists have tended to see nutrition as a dimension of the complex human-environment relationship. Thus, Haas and Pelletier (1989) and Haas and Harrison (1977) postulate several ways of approaching nutrition in human population biology: as a constraint or stressor; as a modifier of other environmental stresses; and as contributing to limits to human biological adaptation.

Nutrition as a constraint or stressor has been investigated in various ways. The focus can be on behavioural responses to the nutritional limitations set by staple foodstuffs. For example, an association between sago consumption and infanticide has been argued where this staple is a poor weaning food and long inter-birth intervals are desirable for successful child rearing. Seasonal nutritional stress can be managed by varying body weight and growth performance within limits, as well as by behavioural and social mechanisms, although the biological limits to this are unknown. The need to develop systems for predicting famines has given rise to models of household strategies for coping with shortages of varying severity and duration.

Nutrition as a modifier of other environmental stresses concerns its role in adaptation to climatic variation (Haas and Harrison 1977). Some protection against cold stress is afforded by insulative adipose tissue or muscle, and by an efficient, active thermogenic response. It is sometimes argued that this can also occur by the growth and development of a physique which reduces the ratio of surface area (potential heat loss) to body mass (heat source); and conversely, heat stress would favour a greater surface area to weight ratio. Some differences in physique between populations inhabiting cooler and warmer climates, or different climatic zones of the same region, have been attributed to this but the issue remains contentious. Climate can also influence nutrition through its effects on synthesis of vitamin D by the action of ultra-violet radiation on the skin. Where climate also promotes high-altitude living conditions, low oxygen tension (hypoxia) will interact with blood haemoglobin and iron nutriture to influence health.

The role of nutrition in defining limits to biological adaptation is significant in several ways (Haas and Harrison 1977). There is known to be variation across populations in the frequency of genetically determined enzyme and other polymorphisms. For example, this results in differences in the capacity to digest lactose (milk sugar), sucrose, and alcohol; and in the variable distribution of conditions such as coeliac disease, which depends on sensitivity to the wheat protein gluten. However, there is much that remains unknown about variants in nutrient utilization in different groups, and about the interactions between genes and nutrients which influence gene expression (Walcher and Kretchmer 1981). Relationships between nutritional deficiencies and behavioural disorders have been shown for iodine in regions of endemic cretinism in Asia, Melanesia, Europe and South America. However, protein-energy malnutrition during early childhood can also significantly influence later mental and motor development.

The concept of malnutrition rests on demonstrable impairment in physical, behavioural or psychological *function*. Without this criterion, the interpretation of nutritional data must remain unclear. The degree to which social values influence judgement of malnutrition is debatable. The lines of debate resemble those of arguments over the concept of health. A strictly biological definition would seem to allow the social context of malnutrition to be delineated separately, as for any disease; but the social and biological properties of disease may often seem to be confused (Lewis 1993).

The extent of human biological plasticity in nutritional requirements remains unknown. Studies of semi-starvation and individuals undergoing prolonged total fasts suggest that absolute adaptive limits will vary with initial body size. However, the timescale over which adverse effects occur is likely to vary. Through their consequences for reproductive function, intra-uterine nutrition and post-natal growth performance, nutritional insults exert influences which often become apparent only across generations.

Population biology is not the only type of approach used in nutrition, a subject of which the interests range from the molecular to the international, and which uses a diversity of methods from atomic mass spectrometry to macro-economics. Closer to anthropology, factors influencing the distribution of food within *households will determine access to nutrients and energy for many dependants. Studies of those factors which govern patterns of food distribution have helped in the understanding of sex-related patterns of undernutrition and early mortality in the Asian subcontinent (Wheeler 1988; Harriss 1990). The relationship of these patterns to systems of *kinship and †inheritance, and to social ideas of responsibility, right and obligation is an area which would repay future careful inter-disciplinary investigation.

S.S. STRICKLAND

See also: food, medical anthropology, biological anthropology, environment

Further reading

Blaxter, K.L. and J.C. Waterlow (eds) (1985) *Nutritional Adaptation in Man*, London: John Libbey

Freedman, R.L. (1976) 'Nutritional Anthropology in Action: An Overview', in T.K. Fitzgerald (ed.) *Nutrition and Anthropology in Action*, Amsterdam: Van Gorcum

Haas, J.D., and G.G. Harrison (1977) 'Nutritional Anthropology and Biological Adaptation', *Annual Reviews in Anthropology* 6: 69–101

Haas, J.D. and D.L. Pelletier (1989) 'Nutrition and Human Population Biology', in M.A. Little and J.D. Haas (eds) *Human Population Biology: A Transdisciplinary Science*, Oxford: Oxford University Press

Harriss, B. (1990) 'Food Distribution, Death and Disease in South Asia', in G.A. Harrison and J.C. Waterlow (eds) *Diet and Disease*, Cambridge: Cambridge University Press

Jerome, N.W., R.F. Kandel and G.H. Pelto (eds) (1980) *Nutritional Anthropology: Contemporary Approaches to Diet and Culture*, New York: Redgrave Publishing Co.

Lewis, G.A. (1993) 'Some Studies of Social Causes of and Cultural Responses to Disease', in C.G.N. Mascie-Taylor (ed.) *The Anthropology of Disease*, Oxford: Oxford University Press

Richards, A.I. (1939) *Land, Labour and Diet in Northern Rhodesia*, Oxford: Oxford University Press

Rivers, J.P.W. (1988) 'The Nutritional Biology of Famine', in G.A. Harrison (ed.) *Famine*, Oxford: Oxford University Press

Ulijaszek, S.J. and S.S. Strickland (1993) *Nutritional Anthropology: Prospects and Perspectives*, London: Smith-Gordon & Co.

Walcher, D.N. and N. Kretchmer (eds) (1981) *Food, Nutrition and Evolution*, New York: Masson

Wheeler, E.F. (1988) *Intra-household Food Allocation: A Review of Evidence*, London: Department of Human Nutrition, London School of Hygiene and Tropical Medicine, Occasional Paper 12

Occidentalism

An Occidentalism is a distorted and stereotyped image of Western society, which can be held by people inside and outside the West and which can be articulated or implicit. The term emerged as the reciprocal of the notion of Orientalism, itself a generalization by anthropologists of †Said's (1978) *Orientalism*, his name for a particular distorted rendering of the Middle East by Western academics.

Behind both Orientalism and Occidentalism is an assumption about how people define themselves and others. One's own social unit and the alien unit are compared, and certain features of each are identified as contrasting elements that are taken to express the essences or crucial distinguishing features of the two units. The resulting characterizations are dialectical, because they emerge only as the negation of each other. Said (1978) describes at length the emergence of an *essentialist rendering of the Orient, but pays less attention to the paired rendering of the West to which it is opposed.

These renderings are shaped by political relationships within the societies in which they exist. Thus, in one of the earliest uses of 'Occidentalism', Nader (1989) describes Orientalist and Occidentalist renderings of the place of women in Middle Eastern and Western societies by Middle Eastern and Western commentators. She suggests that in each case, the pairs of depictions served the political purpose of protecting existing *gender relations by describing the place of women in the opposed society as being much worse. Likewise, Carrier (1995) describes essentialist renderings by Western scholars in which the West is occidentalized as the land of autonomous, calculating individuals. He suggests that such renderings reflect the self-conception of powerful groups in the West, and that they serve to legitimate that power by defining as deficient those in the West who do not conform to the stereotype.

Some studies of self-conceptions among Pacific societies anticipate the idea of Occidentalism even though they do not use the term. For instance, Thomas (1992) describes how some Pacific people generate an essential, Orientalist definition of themselves in opposition to a West that they Occidentalize as a land of mercenary individuals. Thomas makes the point that these opposed Occidentalisms and Orientalisms are conspicuous in *colonial settings.

Finally, Carrier (1992) has argued that anthropologists themselves are prone to Occidentalize the West, which facilitates anthropologists' Orientalist renderings of non-Western societies and so helps exaggerate the difference between Western and non-Western societies. He argues that critics of anthropological Orientalism have erred in failing to consider how these Orientalisms are shaped and sustained by anthropological Occidentalisms.

Because the politics of self-representation is an important issue in the discipline and in Western societies, it seems likely that interest in Occidentalism will increase in anthropology.

JAMES G. CARRIER

See also: ethnocentrism, identity, Orientalism

Further reading

Carrier, J.G. (1992) 'Occidentalism', *American Ethnologist* 19 (2): 195–212
—— (1995) 'Maussian Occidentalism', in J.G. Carrier (ed.) *Occidentalism* Oxford: Oxford University Press
Nader, L. (1989) 'Orientalism, Occidentalism and the Control of Women', *Cultural Dynamics* 2 (3): 323–55
Said, E. (1978) *Orientalism*, Harmondsworth: Penguin
Thomas, N. (1992) 'Substantivization and Anthropological Discourse', in J.G. Carrier (ed.) *History and Tradition in Melanesian Anthropology*, Berkeley: University of California Press

oral literature

'Oral literature' is used by anthropologists and others to refer to unwritten forms which can be regarded as in some way possessing literary qualities. It thus broadly covers such oral forms as *myths, narratives, epics, lyrics, praise poetry, laments, and the verbal texts of songs; also sometimes riddles, proverbs and perhaps *oratory and drama. The study of such forms is an area in which both literary or linguistic scholars and *folklorists have for long interacted with anthropologists.

The concept of oral literature, already found among some nineteenth-century collectors, was brought into wider currency by H.M. and N.K. Chadwick's comparative work (1932–40) on the 'growth of literature', and, later, by Albert Lord's influential *The Singer of Tales* (1960) which treated the fluidity of texts and 'oral-formulaic' principles of composition-in-performance. Since then the term has been used extensively both by literary scholars and by anthropologists (e.g. Bauman 1986, Finnegan 1970, 1977, Görög-Karady 1982, and the journal *Cahiers de Littérature Orale*). It is sometimes confined to oral-formulaic works composed in performance, sometimes used more widely of genres transmitted, composed or performed orally, in literate as well as non-literate contexts.

The term is controversial however. Some literary scholars consider it self-contradictory ('literature' – from Latin *litterae* – could not be *un*written), while others hold that the anthropologists' *comparative method has always relied on extending terms from their 'original' Western referents and that we regularly use words in senses far from their root etymologies. Some writers regard 'oral literature' as having potentially negative connotations and prefer the more positive neologism 'orature' (further references and discussion can be found in Finnegan 1992; Tonkin 1992).

More constructive controversies revolve round the argument that the term 'oral literature' risks imposing an †ethnocentric model on activities which may have other elements than the verbal or aesthetic. Calling something 'oral literature' is helpful in allowing for an analysis of literary or artistic aspects, of individual creativity and of new as well as old forms – aspects missing in earlier *functionalist or folkorist approaches. It also points to the possibility of studying a range of genres rather than undifferentiated 'oral tradition' and can draw on comparative insights from the analysis of written forms. But since this entails highlighting verbal and textual rather than performative aspects, there are the corresponding dangers of overemphasizing apparent parallels to the Western written canon which may misrepresent local meanings or interactions. Work by linguistic anthropologists, furthermore, has elucidated the performance qualities which are of the essence in any *oral* form but arguably obscured by the model of 'literature'. Some analysts thus prefer 'verbal art', 'performance', or simply the specific genre term. But whatever the term used, many anthropologically-inclined scholars would now regard the study of oral literature as going beyond just the *words*, to include also performance features like *music, *dance, the qualities of the speaking and singing voice, kinetic features, visual aspects, multivocality, the role of audiences and the communicative context.

As often in anthropology, some research issues relate to boundaries and the processes which intersect or challenge these apparent divisions: for example between *art/non-art; prose/poetry (problematic in *oral* literature); literature/history; speech/music; oral/written. The long-standing questions about distinguishing 'literature' from other verbal formulations also arise for oral literature, particularly intriguing for *oral* forms. There is also the position that, rather than trying to delimit the 'literary', there are merits in considering *all* forms of heightened verbalization together (Howell 1986).

The study of oral literature is more interdisciplinary than most, and the many differing approaches to its analysis depend on mutual interchange between anthropology and – in particular – literary and sociolinguistic theory and folklore. Among the most influential approaches have been the so-called 'Finnish' historical-geographical method; comparative philology and mythology; functionalist, *structuralist and †poststructuralist approaches; and a series of approaches inspired by *Marxist perspectives. Developing anthropological interests in *psychological aspects, in the emotions, in feminist critiques and in the *poetics and politics of texts have all had their impact on the study of oral literature. So too have the analyses of narratologists, and of performance-oriented anthropologists such as Dell Hymes or Richard Bauman, combining insights from sociolinguistics, performance theory and the *ethnography of speaking (for fuller discussion see Finnegan 1992: esp. 29–52, 183ff.)

Amidst these various methodologies the familiar anthropological puzzles remain: In what ways are works of art constructed and interpreted in their social contexts? Are they 'emergent' processes and practices rather than 'products'? Who controls them? How do they interact with power relations and whose voices are heard? Do people use them to represent society, validate their lives, narrate the past, or somehow 'create reality' – and if so how? Far from treating a marginal activity of interest only to specialists, the study of oral literature brings us to the heart of how we and others represent the human condition and its dilemmas.

RUTH FINNEGAN

See also: language and linguistics, literacy, play

Further reading

Barber, K. and P.F. de M. Farias (eds) (1989) *Discourse and its Disguises: The Interpretation of African Oral Texts*, Birmingham: Centre of West African Studies, Birmingham University African Studies Series 1

Bauman, R. (1986) *Story, Performance, and Event: Contextual Studies of Oral Narrative*, Cambridge: Cambridge University Press

Chadwick, H.M. and N.K. (1932–40) *The Growth of Literature* 3 vols, Cambridge: Cambridge University Press

Finnegan, R. (1970) *Oral Literature in Africa*, Oxford: Clarendon Press

—— (1977) *Oral Poetry: Its Nature, Significance and Social Context* Cambridge: Cambridge University Press (2nd edn, Bloomington: Indiana University Press, 1991)

—— (1992) *Oral Traditions and the Verbal Arts. A Guide to Research Practices*, ASA Research Methods Series, London: Routledge

Görög-Karady, V. (ed.) (1982) *Genres, Forms, Meanings: Essays in African Oral Literature*, Oxford: JASO

Howell, S. (1986) 'Formal Speech Acts as One Discourse', *Man* 21: 79–101

Lord, A.B. (1960) *The Singer of Tales*, Cambridge, MA: Harvard University Press

Tonkin, E. (1992) *Narrating our Pasts: The Social Construction of Oral History*, Cambridge: Cambridge University Press

oratory

Anthropologists, drawing on Western traditions of rhetoric and homiletics, have restricted the term 'oratory' to refer to public *discourse whose style is remarked as somehow dramatic, persuasive or both. These styles are part of the verbal repertoire – the linguistic capital – of †speech communities; oratory is thus rule-governed and it must be learned by those who wish appropriately to declaim. People everywhere practise public speaking of one sort or another; and oratory is particularly important in communities where orality, rather than literacy or an electronic transmission of words and images, is the principal medium of politicking and, more generally, of the circulation and transmission of culture at large. Declamation at political meetings, judicial moots, religious rituals, curing ceremonies and the like have all attracted a receptive anthropological audience. These discourses are both public (and thus recordable for later analysis by attentive anthropologists) and dramatic in the sense that oratory is a performance. Such oratorical performance typically relies upon special and formalized genres of speaking that can both seduce and demand an audience's attention and participation.

Anthropologists have inspected the linguistic features of oratorical speaking styles, and the underlying structures that shape oratorical discourses and the †speech events in which people orate. They have also debated the social and political functions of oratorical performance. Oratory may serve to remark and thereby help reproduce social relations (particularly power relations) that antedate the speech event; conversely, oratory may excite new or transformed relations between orators and their audiences that emerge within a speech event itself. Oratory displays but also persuades. It can sustain existing social orders, and it may sometimes engender new political formations.

Public discourse must somehow be marked stylistically for audiences (including anthropologists) to recognize this as oratorical performance. Other sorts of public speaking besides oratory may take place within political debates, marital and funerary rituals, courts, curing events and the like. Oratory is more than just speaking in a public place (although the logistics of talking to more than one person no doubt influence certain widespread aspects of oratorical style including loudness, intonation, speed, etc.).

Formal oratorical style differs from one speech community to another. Relatively common linguistic features, however, include distinctive loudness and intonation patterns; a formalized syntax; and a special, sometimes arcane or archaic lexicon. Oratory often also conspicuously deploys a variety of figures of speech (including metaphor, proverbs, songs), and favours repetition and an indirect rather than direct mode of expression (see, for example, Yankah 1991).

Orators typically work with standard scripts. Their forensic renown depends on their discursive skills at following, but sometimes strategically violating, expected frameworks of oratorical speech. Orations (*kabary*) of Madagascan Merina elders, for example, include four stock components: initial excuses, followed by thanksgiving, the speech's core, and then finally more thanksgiving and blessings (Bloch 1975: 7–8; Keenan 1974). Speech events as wholes, beyond single orations, may be similarly scripted by discursive expectations about who may speak, about what, and in what order (see for example, Salmond 1975 on the scripting of Maori *whaikoorero*, 'exchange of speeches'; and Duranti 1994 on Samoan *fono*, 'chiefly assemblies').

Bloch (1975: 13) characterized rigidly formulaic oratorical styles as 'restricted' and even 'arthritic' speech codes that are unable to shoulder much meaning beyond rehearsing already agreed upon understandings, expectations and social hierarchies. He argued that since formulaic oratorical speech is often predictable, indirect and ambiguous, this restricts 'what can be said so that the [oratorical] speech acts are either all alike or all of a kind, and thus, if this mode of communication is adopted, there is hardly any *choice* of what can be said' (1975: 17).

Others, however, have protested that oratorical codes, although stylized, do permit speakers creatively to define events, shape public opinion and inform subsequent political action (Paine 1981; Myers and Brenneis 1984). For example, genre demands for oratorical 'indirectness' can be a tactical resource rather than a linguistic fetter that merely constrains what speakers can say. Indirectness may permit orators to suggest and strategically insinuate rather than rashly declare, just as oratorical ambiguity permits clever speakers to encourage usefully multiple understandings among their audience.

These two contrary evaluations of the political functions and capacities of formal oratory depend, in part, on philosophies of language as well as on the broader political context of oratorical events. Does language just reflect reality so that rhetorical flourish must always distort the truth, or does language frame our perceptions of the world? Those who accept that discourse may create social order, and not just reflect this, more readily seek the constituting capacities of oratory and other forms of discourse to construct or transform human relations. Here, speech is 'constitutive of the system' – a form of action (Myers and Brenneis 1984: 8). Oratory's politically constructive functions, however, are generally greater in egalitarian societies: 'Public political discourse has a different flavor in those communities where the maintenance of individual autonomy is a concern from that which it has in those where relations of dominance/subordination are crucial' (Myers and Brenneis 1984: 28). Thus, it is no surprise that the leaders of many egalitarian communities are well-spoken.

In contexts of political hierarchy, oratorical performance comes closer to Bloch's arthritic speech code that allows speakers only hollow phrases that remark, and perhaps mystify, those inequalities that already exist. Beyond this sort of decorous political display, however, oratory's capacities to constitute and persuade also operate in the midst of the most stubbornly hierarchical systems. Here one may often locate circumscribed speech arenas (such as courts, some electoral campaigns and backstage conferences) where people orate persuasively in ways that do not imperil or transform ruling political orders (Bloch 1975: 26; O'Barr 1982; Atkinson 1984).

The Polynesian 'talking chief', or chiefly spokesman, similarly serves to circumscribe some of the dangers of oratory within hierarchical political systems. He talks so that his silent chief may occupy a secure position above and beyond the political dangers of oratorical fray (Duranti 1994). Academic anthropologists, who themselves are sometime public speakers, may also appreciate the capacity of oratory to create the atmosphere in which the discipline's various social theories and concepts have come to sound useful and true.

LAMONT LINDSTROM

See also: discourse, language and linguistics, oral literature, political anthropology

Further reading

Atkinson, M. (1984) *Our Masters' Voices: The Language and Body Language of Politics*, London: Methuen

Bloch, M. (1975) 'Introduction', in M. Bloch (ed.) *Political Language and Oratory in Traditional Society*, London: Academic Press

Duranti, A. (1994) *From Grammar to Politics: Linguistic Anthropology in a Western Samoan Village*, Berkeley: University of California Press

Keenan, E. (1974) 'Norm-Makers, Norm-Breakers: Uses of Speech by Men and Women in a Malagasy Community', in R. Bauman and J. Sherzer (eds) *Explorations in the Ethnography of Speaking*, Cambridge: Cambridge University Press

Myers, F. and D. Brenneis (1984) 'Introduction: Language and Politics in the Pacific', in D. Brenneis and F. Myers (eds) *Dangerous Words: Language and Politics in the Pacific*, New York: New York University Press

O'Barr, W. (1982) *Linguistic Evidence: Language, Power, and Strategy in the Courtroom*, New York: Academic Press

Paine, R. (1981) *Politically Speaking: Cross-Cultural Studies of Rhetoric*, Philadelphia: Institute for the Study of Human Issues

Salmond, A. (1975) 'Mana Makes the Man: A Look at Maori Oratory and Politics', in M. Bloch (ed.) *Political Language and Oratory in Traditional Society*, London: Academic Press

Yankah, Kwesi (1991) 'Oratory in Akan Society', *Discourse and Society* 2 (1): 47–64

Orientalism

Orientalism conventionally describes those academic disciplines, like history and comparative philology, which specialize in the study of 'the Orient', usually taken to mean Asia and the *Middle East. Specialists in the anthropology of *Islam, *Buddhism and *Hinduism have all had to work out a *modus vivendi* with Orientalist scholars, textual experts and historians of religion, in this sense (for example, through distinctions such as that between *great and little traditions). But as a consequence of †Edward Said's powerful polemic of the same name (Said 1978), Orientalism has come to refer to a distinctive body of academic work, built up in the shadow of nineteenth-century colonial domination and continuing long after the demise of the formal structures of European empire, in which the 'Orient' and 'Orientals' are stereotyped, denied history and †agency, and represented in ways that reflect the continuing interests of the West in the East. Since the publication of Said's *Orientalism*, virtually all anthropologists have had to come to terms with an argument that links stereotyped academic representations of non-European peoples to structures of *colonial and neo-colonial political and economic domination.

In fact, anthropology came off relatively well in Said's original argument (although he has subsequently taken a more critical tack [Said 1989]). His argument concentrated on scholarly work on Islam and the *Middle East, explicitly targeting the pro-Israel, anti-Arab bias of 'area studies' work from the 1950s, 1960s and 1970s. In the conclusion of the book, †Clifford Geertz is – somewhat surprisingly – one of a number of scholars whose work is singled out for post-Orientalist approval. Yet that same conclusion contains the argument which, more than any other, would disturb anthropological complacency:

> How does one *represent* other cultures? What is *another* culture? Is the notion of a distinct culture (or race, or religion, or civilization) a useful one, or does it always get involved either in self-congratulation (when one discusses one's own) or hostility and aggression (when one discusses the 'other')?
>
> (Said 1978: 325)

On the one hand, this links with the *postmodern concern with the issue of representation in ethnographic writing, but it also seriously undermines the assumption that liberal talk of cultural difference is inherently benign and tolerant: the idea of *'culture', as critics of *essentialism have pointed out again and again, can also be employed as a source of stereotyping and denigration, as well as providing a liberal counter to arguments based on *race.

Said's argument chimed with other critiques of academic representation of non-Western people, such as Fabian's suggestion that the anthropological other is placed in a different temporal frame in anthropological writing, rendered different through the denial of a shared history (Fabian 1983). It was also extended beyond the Middle East to writing about *South Asia (Inden 1985), for example, as part of a valuable re-examination of the ways in which colonial knowledge and colonial assumptions have structured both anthropological research and the self-knowledge of people living in †postcolonial societies. It was even extended beyond the East, and applied to the examination of *Occidentalist stereotypes about 'the West' (Carrier 1995).

Nevertheless, Said's critique of Orientalism was not without its own problems. As a polemic, it contains its fair measure of simplification and overstatement, and outraged Middle East specialists subjected him to often vicious attacks. But even sympathetic readers had their problems. His argument, as James Clifford pointed out in an incisive critique (Clifford 1988), moves inconsistently between a fairly traditional liberal humanism and a more unsettling stance borrowed from the work of †Michel Foucault. Clifford clearly feels Said has been too timid in his commitment to Foucault's approach, yet it could as well be argued that it is Foucault who provides the legitimation for some of Said's weaker arguments. Certainly Said's use of *discourse in Foucault's sense allows him to build up a portrait of a totalizing and undifferentiated Orientalism, with (despite his protestations to the contrary) little or no room for the idiosyncracies of different Orientalists working in different historical moments and in different political contexts. Moreover, his Orientals become oddly mute and passive in the face of the Western knowledge-power axis: there is little sense that the inhabitants of 'the East' have themselves contributed to Orientalist discourse, still less that Orientalist stereotypes are as likely to be encountered in, say, communal politics within India as in Western foreign policy in the 1990s.

JONATHAN SPENCER

See also: colonialism, culture, essentialism, Occidentalism, postmodernism

Further reading

Carrier, J. (ed.) (1995) *Occidentalism: Images of the West*, Oxford: Oxford University Press

Clifford, J. ([1980] 1988) 'On Orientalism', in J. Clifford *The Predicament of Culture: Twentieth-Century Ethnography, Literature, and Art*, Cambridge, MA: Harvard University Press

Fabian, J. (1983) *Time and the Other: How Anthropology Makes its Object*, New York: Columbia University Press

Inden, R. (1985) 'Orientalist Constructions of India', *Modern Asian Studies* 20: 401–46

Said, E. (1978) *Orientalism*, London: Routledge and Kegan Paul

—— (1989) 'Representing the Colonized: Anthropology's Interlocutors', *Critical Enquiry* 15: 205–25

P

Pacific: Melanesia

Melanesia is a group of islands in the Southwest Pacific. Although its boundaries are not entirely agreed, it corresponds approximately to the territories of Papua New Guinea, the Solomon Islands, Vanuatu, New Caledonia and Fiji. It also includes the Torres Straits Islands, which are part of the Australian state of Queensland, and the Indonesian province of Irian Jaya (the western part of the island of New Guinea). During the second half of the nineteenth century, the different parts of Melanesia were claimed by Britain, Germany, France, Holland and Australia, and this situation changed little in its essentials until post-colonial states began emerging in the 1970s. The interior of the island of New Guinea, with the largest population in Melanesia, was not brought under external control until after World War II. A few, small 'uncontacted' groups probably still remain in the remoter parts of the New Guinea Highlands.

Throughout most of the history of ethnography in Melanesia, the two dominant themes of research in this region have been *exchange and *gender. These have provided the encompassing rubrics under which other important aspects of Melanesian society have tended to be studied, and have been the two fields in which research in Melanesia has made its greatest contributions to anthropology. Signs of a new formulation of the central issues in Melanesian studies have begun to appear only recently, with the emergence of an interest in the politics of tradition and the construction of *ethnicity.

Ethnography and society before World War II

Melanesia is a region of very great ethnic and linguistic diversity. Most estimates place the number of indigenous languages, for instance, at 700 or 800 at least, spoken by some 3.5 million people. Yet it is possible, at the risk of some simplifications, to sketch certain broad character-istics of pre-colonial Melanesian societies. Their economies were typically based on root-crop horti-culture supplemented by pig husbandry, and many Melanesian peoples also traded extensively in both subsistence and luxury goods, often over long distances. They often had elaborate prestige economies and gift-exchange systems, in which special high-status valuables made from precious materials such as shell, feathers or boars' tusks were employed in †bridewealth payments, peace-making and other ceremonial transactions.

†Secret societies and male initiatory cults were prominent features of many societies, and were the focus of much of the region's artistic creativity, involving as they often did the produc-tion and display of masks, statuary and elaborate body decorations. The political units of most Melanesian societies were small, usually no more than a few hundred people. *Feuding and *warfare between these communities were common, though temporary alliances were made, and truces called, as enemies came together for initiation ceremonies, feasts or gift-exchanges. Few societies recognized inequalities of birth or had political offices; the powers of leaders were usually imper-manent and derived from personal renown gained in activities such as warfare, ceremonial exchange and *ritual.

The first significant academic study of a Melanesian people was carried out by the Cambridge †Torres Straits Expedition of 1898–9, the ethnologists associated with which (†A. Haddon, †W.H.R. Rivers and †C.G. Seligman) published extensively in a *diffusionist vein on var-ious aspects of Melanesian societies. It was also in the course of this fieldwork that Rivers established the *genealogical method in anthropology. But the figure who looms largest in the early history of Melanesian anthropology is *Bronislaw Malinowski, whose studies of the Trobriand Islands (off the southeastern tip of New Guinea) during World War I established in anthropology the theory of *functionalism and its accompanying method of intensive ethnographic *fieldwork. Although the Trobriands are in certain respects atypical of Melanesia, many of the topics on which Malinowski focused – *magic, sexuality, †social control and the economics of the *kula gift-exchange system, for example – anticipated what later came to be seen as some of the central features of Melanesian societies.

The other major figure in the pre-war period was †Margaret Mead, who carried out studies of *childhood and *gender roles in a number of Melanesian societies, envisioning the rich diversity of these cultures as a laboratory for testing theories in the field of *culture and personality.

African models of social structure

The New Guinea Highlands, which had the last substantial unstudied populations in the world, were opened up after the war, and the 1950s and 1960s saw a huge growth of anthropological research in this part of Melanesia. The preoccupation of anthropology at the time with the study of *kinship and *social organization was reflected in this early postwar research, much of which was concerned with understanding Highland *social structure. Some studies (e.g. Meggitt 1965) sought to apply to the Highlands models of African †segmentary lineage systems, and to correlate variations in the apparent 'strength' of †patriliny in different Highland societies with factors such as land shortage. A number of important later analyses of kinship and social structure, drawing on *Lévi-Strauss and *alliance theory, constructed models in which †reciprocity figured as the central principle, positing exchange as the distinctively Melanesian equivalent of the principle of *descent in Africa (e.g. Forge 1972).

Ceremonial exchange and Big Men

The spectacular ceremonial economies of the Highlands and elsewhere in Melanesia attracted considerable attention, and were often interpreted as promoting social integration by creating alliances and providing a non-violent outlet for inter-clan rivalries (e.g. A.J. Strathern 1971). With the suppression of warfare and the growing availability of wealth, many of these systems had hypertrophied and became major arenas for the activities of politically ambitious men. At the time, it appeared that these self-made entrepreneurs, or *Big Men, were the quintessentially Melanesian type of leader, distinguishing this region of the Pacific from the stratified, chiefly polities of *Polynesia (Sahlins 1963). Studies of economic development in the 1950s and 1960s often suggested that this Big Man pattern of individualistic and †transactional politics had a special compatibility with Western capitalism. The centrality of the Big Man to Melanesian politics and economic life has in recent years been reconsidered. Godelier (1986), for instance, argues that the classic entrepreneurial figure of the Big Man arose only in societies where wealth was essential to processes of †social reproduction in transactions such as bridewealth payments; otherwise, Melanesian societies had what he calls Great Men, leaders of various sorts whose power ultimately derived from the domain of ritual.

Religion

Melanesian *religion, ritual and *cosmology have been approached from a variety of perspectives, though three have tended to predominate. The role of initiation ceremonies in male psychosexual development has attracted the attention of a number of studies inspired by *psychoanalysis (e.g. Herdt 1981); scholars influenced by *Marxism have examined the role of religion in maintaining the control of senior men over women and juniors (e.g. Keesing 1982); while the symbolism of ritual has been analysed from various *structuralist, †semiotic and other †interpretive perspectives (e.g. Gell 1975).

Some Melanesian societies seem to have highly elaborated cosmologies and systems of religious belief, while others appear to have decidedly secular and pragmatic cultural orientations. An early comparative study of Melanesian religions suggested a 'secular' emphasis in the New Guinea Highland societies, and a 'religious' emphasis in seaboard and insular Melanesia (Lawrence and Meggitt 1965). More recently, there was controversy over whether the apparent variations in the elaboration of religion in Melanesia are real or merely artefacts of analysis, a controversy which debated among other issues the nature of the 'order' apparent in some Melanesian religions, the political and other factors that may serve to promote or subvert this order, and the role that indigenous exegesis should be allowed to play in the interpretation of ritual (Brunton 1980).

From the very beginning, Western observers in Melanesia had been intrigued by *cargo cults, *millenial movements in which believers await the arrival of large quantities of 'cargo' (Western manufactured goods) sent by their *ancestors. Cargo cults continue to flourish in many parts of Melanesia, sometimes in close integration with national party politics, and they remain an important focus of anthropological interest.

Gender and personhood

Early researchers were often struck by what they variously described as a marked sexual inequality, a male-female polarization, or antagonism between the sexes, evident in a number of Melanesian societies, especially in the New Guinea Highlands. Often, women seemed excluded from religious and political affairs. For instance, while Highland women raise pigs and carry out much of the agricultural work, the wealth they create is converted by means of feasts, rituals and †prestations into prestige for their husbands; in this respect, men seem to appropriate and exploit women's labour for their own political ends (e.g. Josephides 1985). At the same time, many of these societies have ideologies, such as beliefs in *menstrual *pollution, that appear to demean women and legitimize their oppression. Since the 1970s in particular, there has been a burgeoning of interest in Melanesian gender constructs, a field which developed further during the 1980s into a preoccupation with Melanesian concepts of the *person, culminating in Strathern's (1988) synthesis of the extensive literature on Melanesian political economy and gender relations. Drawing on Gregory's (1982) characterization of Melanesian economies as 'gift' economies oriented to the creation and maintenance of social relationships, Strathern's work is essentially an attempt to deconstruct Western notions of the 'individual' and *'individualism'. In Melanesian cultures, she argues, social relations exist before persons, so that persons are produced by these relations and composed of them. These Melanesian constructs thus contrast fundamentally with the Western ideas (associated with the profit-maximizing 'commodity' economies of market capitalism) of the 'individual' as an entity ontologically prior to any relationships.

Contemporary trends in Melanesian ethnography

Current research in Melanesia continues to have as its central focus the symbolic dimensions of exchange, and in particular the role of exchange in the constitution of power relations, gender and personhood. But a trend apparent recently is an interest in history, including the constructions that Melanesians themselves now make of their own past. The experiences which (now, of course, elderly) Melanesians had of 'first contact' with Europeans have attracted interest (e.g. Schieffelin and Crittenden 1991). Some scholars have begun to examine the processes by which tradition is being 'invented' in the post-colonial era as new Melanesian states seek to establish their national cultures and identities, while others are questioning the assumption, which they regard some earlier research as having made, of a 'timeless' Melanesia before European contact (e.g. Jolly and Thomas 1992; Keesing and Tonkinson 1982; Thomas 1991).

SIMON HARRISON

See also: Big Man, cargo cult, exchange, gender, *kula*, person

Further reading

Brunton, R. (1980) 'Misconstrued Order in Melanesian Religion', *Man* (n.s.) 15: 112–28

Forge, A. (1972) 'The Golden Fleece', *Man* (n.s.) 7: 527–40

Gell, A.F. (1975) *Metamorphosis of the Cassowaries: Umeda Society, Language and Ritual*, London: Athlone Press

Godelier, M. (1986) *The Making of Great Men: Male Domination and Power among the New Guinea Baruya*, Cambridge: Cambridge University Press

Gregory, C. (1982) *Gifts and Commodities*, London: Academic Press

Herdt, G.H. (1981) *Guardians of the Flutes: Idioms of Masculinity*, New York: McGraw-Hill

Jolly, M. and N. Thomas (eds) (1992) *The Politics of Tradition in the Pacific*, Special Issue of *Oceania* 62 (4)

Josephides, L. (1985) *The Production of Inequality: Gender and Exchange among the Kewa*, London: Tavistock

Keesing, R.M. (1982) *Kwaio Religion: The Living and the Dead in a Solomon Island Society*, New York: Columbia University Press.

—— and R.Tonkinson (eds) (1982) *Reinventing Traditional Culture: The Politics of Kastom in Island Melanesia*, Special Issue of *Mankind* 13 (4)

Lawrence, P. and M.J. Meggitt (eds) (1965) *Gods, Ghosts and Men in Melanesia: Some Religions of Australian New Guinea and the New Hebrides*, Oxford: Oxford University Press

Meggitt, M.J. (1965) *The Lineage System of the Mae-Enga of New Guinea*, New York: Barnes and Noble

Sahlins, M.D. (1963) 'Poor Man, Rich Man, Big Man, Chief', *Comparative Studies in Society and History* 5: 285–303.

Schieffelin, E.L. and R. Crittenden with contributions by B. Allen and S. Frankel, P. Sillitoe, L. Josephides and M. Schiltz (1991) *Like People You See in a Dream: First Contact in Six Papuan Societies*, Stanford: Stanford University Press

Strathern, A.J. (1971) *The Rope of Moka: Big Men and Ceremonial Exchange in Mount Hagen*, Cambridge: Cambridge University Press

Strathern, M. (1988) *The Gender of the Gift: Problems with Women and Problems with Society in Melanesia*, Berkeley: University of California Press

Thomas, N. (1991) *Entangled Objects: Exchange, Material Culture, and Colonialism in the Pacific*, Cambridge, MA: Harvard University Press

Pacific: Polynesia

The Polynesian islands are scattered over the Pacific Ocean, forming roughly a triangle with the Hawaii Islands, Easter Island, and New Zealand as its angular points. A number of small islands west of Fiji are considered as Polynesian outliers (including Tikopia, Kapingamarangi). Most Polynesian islands are high, with volcanic mountains, abundant rain and a tropical climate. Others are atolls, small circles of coral reefs and sand in the ocean, only a few meters above sea-level, crowned by coconut palms. Though European voyagers passed through the region of the 'many islands' several times after 1519, it was not until the second half of the eighteenth century that 'discoveries' of importance were made here. The three voyages (1768–80) of James Cook were especially successful; after him there was little left to discover. His journals are still counted among the most important sources on traditional Polynesia. Soon other Europeans (and Americans) followed these first 'discoverers' to Polynesia: missionaries of the Protestant London Missionary Society and the Roman Catholic Marists, traders, whalers, and colonizers (British, French, German, American and Japanese). In the course of the nineteenth century most of the Polynesian islands were colonized by the European powers. Exceptions were the Tonga Islands which became a 'protectorate' of England, and the Hawaii Islands which finally became the fiftieth state of the USA in 1959 (Campbell 1989).

Colonial interests in Polynesia were mainly strategic. The islands became first naval bases, and later air bases. Economically they had little to offer. Most islands were small, and there was a shortage of labourers. Fruit, coconuts, palm oil, sugar, and coffee were grown, but the large distances and the high costs of transport made the Polynesian producers poor competitors on the world market. Since World War II *tourism has been a growing influence, but its profits are relatively low because of the high investments in the necessary infrastructure. After the 1960s most of the colonies gained independence and have struggled to survive economically since. Thousands of Polynesians migrated to Australia, New Zealand and the USA. In 1991 about 1.7 million people lived in Polynesia, of whom 1.1 million were in the Hawaii islands. The most important region still colonized is French Polynesia (Robillard 1992).

Prehistoric explorers and colonizers

There is a growing conviction among scholars that the forebears of the Polynesians came by way of *Melanesia. They are associated with the makers of the so-called Lapita pottery, which is found scattered on the coasts of the Melanesian islands. Some bearers of the Lapita culture reached the Tonga/Samoa region about 2000 BC, where in relative isolation the 'Ancestral Polynesian Culture' (APC) emerged (Kirch 1984). The construction of this culture is based on archaeological, linguistic and ethnohistorical research. It is assumed that the characteristics of the Polynesian cultures described by the eighteenth-century discoverers were found in their basic forms in the APC. From this region the other Polynesian islands have been colonized. There are indications that settlers reached the Marquesas Islands as early as the second century BC; the Hawaii Islands were settled between AD 300 and 400. For other islands, such as the Society Islands, data are scarce or insufficient because of geomorphological disruptions. New Zealand, which was relatively near to the Tonga/Samoa region, was not colonized before AD 1000, most probably because of difficult sailing conditions. The question of whether the Polynesians discovered the island deliberately or by accident has caused heated debates. It is believed now that the ancient Polynesians quite often went out to sea to search deliberately for unknown islands. Their capacity for making voyages of discovery and returning safely was remarkable (Irwin, 1992).

When sailing for colonization the settlers took with them their families, animals (pigs, dogs, rats), food (coconut, bananas, tubers), utensils and weapons – and also their technical knowledge, and ideas on social organization, religion and magic. In short, they took as much of their home culture – the APC – with them in their canoes as was possible. Once settled they adapted this culture to the new surroundings.

Aspects of traditional Polynesian culture

The Polynesians travelled with large seagoing vessels, suitable to transport dozens of people with goods and livestock over large distances. The master navigated during the day with the help of wind and waves, and during the night with the help of the stars. There were two types of vessels: the large 'double-canoes', consisting of two hulls connected by a platform, and the canoes with outriggers. The vessels had heavy plaited sails, but could also be rowed. These canoes were mostly seaworthy. In 1976 a copy of a Polynesian double-canoe sailed from Hawaii to Tahiti and back, using traditional navigation methods.

Though the Polynesians were descendants of the people which once made the Lapita pottery, ceramics hardly played a role in Polynesia. Polynesians were, however, able woodcutters and accomplished stone workers. In many islands megalithic monuments can be found, varying from the Tongan trilithon to the large statues of Easter Island. There were constructed tombs, temples, platforms, and waterworks on Tahiti, Hawaii, and the Marquesas Islands, too (Jennings 1979). Food was occasionally prepared in earth ovens, pits in the sand lined with hot stones, in which meat and vegetables packed in palm leaves were cooked. The high, volcanic islands were rich in food: yams, taro, coconuts, vegetables, and fruits were harvested in great quantities. The sea and the lagoon were rich sources of fish, and shell fish; pigs and fowl were raised. In some of the high islands the food situation eventually worsened, mainly because of too large a population for the resources available. In some cases there were even serious shortages (Easter Island, Mangareva, Marquesas). The atolls had but limited resources: coconuts and fish being the staple diet here. Atolls measured only a few square kilometres, and the population counted a few hundred people (Alkire 1978).

Though the socio-political structure of the various islands differed, the same basic principles were found everywhere. Polynesian society was organized along the lines of the †ramage,

defined as a non-exogamous, internally stratified, †unilineal – here †patrilineal – *descent group (Sahlins 1958). Distance from the senior line of descent from the common ancestor was the criterion for stratification. The 'common ancestor' was usually a mythical figure, a descendant of the gods. This descent invested the senior line of the ramage with sacred powers or *mana. To protect people against the dangers of mana, the sacred leaders were surrounded by tabus (*taboo). Though chiefs had some religious obligations, most religious activities were carried out by priests. There were found also people who, like *shamans, were temporarily possessed by the gods or spirits. In the temples (marae) *sacrifices (sometimes human) were made (Siikala 1982).

Every brother in the family was ranked according to the principle of seniority, and sisters might also be integrated into this hierarchy. This system of ranking was extended outwards to embrace the whole society. In theory each individual occupied a different †status position, in accordance with his or her distance from the senior line of descent in the group. In the large islands (Hawaii, Tahiti, Tonga) the direct descendant in the senior line of the reputed founder of the society was the sacred ruler (alii nui, arii rahi, tui tonga). Usually the all-embracing ramage was split into a number of sub-ramages – each with a sacred ruler at its head. In smaller islands the ramage was less complex, and counted fewer members. Here the senior leader occupied a chiefly rank rather than a royal (Cook Islands, Marquesas, Mangareva). The socio-political system of atolls was even simpler, though also here the principles of the ramage were found. Interestingly in the Samoan Islands a complex socio-political structure never became realized. Though in theory all-embracing titles did exist, they were hardly ever realized in terms of power; there are reasons to suspect that the relatively small population here made further developments unnecessary as well as impossible (Goldman 1970; Sahlins 1958; Van Bakel 1989).

In the course of time the traditional ramage structure became modified by other forms of social stratification. The social and economic distances between the senior and junior branches of the same (sub) ramage grew so great that marriages between members of these groups were no longer considered attractive, and the ramages fell apart into †endogamous groups (the nobles, a middle group and a large category of smallholders, tenants and landless people or servants). Only among the nobles did descent and rank continue to play a role. Here the custom developed that not only the rank of the father counted, but also the rank of the mother; later even the ranks of the grandparents were brought into play (Goldman 1970). Tensions arose between those who claimed positions on the basis of †ascription, and those who claimed positions on the basis of †achievement – a phenomenon called status rivalry by Goldman. Because of this, many islands became ravaged by war and strife. The arrival of European visitors made the existing situation even more complicated, and after some years of contact the traditional structures collapsed under the pressure of *Christianity, trade and colonization (Campbell 1989).

Anthropology in Polynesia

Polynesia has been traditionally a region of anthropological interest, stimulated perhaps on the one hand by the *Romantic, *Rousseau-coloured journals of Bougainville and his shipmates, and on the other hand by the availability of detailed descriptions of Polynesian islands by explorers such as Cook, Foster, or Dumont d'Urville, and missionaries like Ellis, Bingham, Laval and Turner. But Polynesia, from the writings of the early explorers, through the self-mythologization of European visitors like Paul Gauguin, through to early ethnographies like †Margaret Mead's *Coming of Age in Samoa* (1928), has been the site of European fantasy as well as European fascination. Mead's romanticized account of Samoa was, nevertheless, balanced by the more prosaic (and careful) work of †Raymond Firth in Tikopia, or †A.M. Hocart in Fiji, not to mention the researches of her own nemesis, †Derek Freeman, in Samoa itself.

Since World War II, and the era of decolonization, the ethnography of Polynesia has become far more self-conscious about its origins in European domination. Sahlins's historical reconstruction of the events surrounding Cook's death in Hawaii (1985) has become the focus of an extraordinary controversy as a result of Obeyesekere's polemical postcolonial challenge (1992). Hanson's (1989) investigation of the politics of Maori tradition in New Zealand has provoked controversy and challenge from Maori activists. To some extent, these controversies, like the Mead-Freeman *scandal, all involve the growing recognition of the political complexity of romanticized versions of the region, whether these are presented in the name of indigenous activism or American cultural criticism. As anthropology has outgrown its own roots in romantic primitivism, younger anthropologists (like N. Thomas, A. Biersack, R. Borofsky, J. Kelly, M. Kaplan and J. Siikala) have started to construct much more historically sophisticated accounts of the region, both in the colonial and the postcolonial context (Borofsky and Howard 1989; Thomas 1990).

HENRI J.M. CLAESSEN

See also: missionaries, Pacific: Melanesia, scandals, taboo

Further Reading

Alkire, W.H. (1978) *Coral Islanders*, Arlington Heights, IL: AHM Publishing Corp.

Borofsky, R. and A. Howard (eds) (1989) *Developments in Polynesian Ethnology*, Honolulu: University of Hawaii Press

Campbell, I.C. (1989) *A History of the Pacific Islands*, Berkeley: University of California Press

Firth, R. (1936) *We the Tikopia*, London: George Allen and Unwin

Goldman, I. (1970) *Ancient Polynesian Society*, Chicago: University of Chicago Press

Hanson, A. (1989) 'The Making of the Maori: Cultural Invention and its Logic', *American Anthropologist* 91: 809–902

Irwin, G. (1992) *The Prehistoric Exploration and Colonialisation of the Pacific*, Cambridge: Cambridge University Press

Jennings, J.D. (ed.) (1979) *The Prehistory of Polynesia*, Cambridge, MA: Harvard University Press

Kirch, P.V. (1984) *The Evolution of the Polynesian Chiefdoms*, Cambridge: Cambridge University Press

Mead, M. (1928) *Coming of Age in Samoa*, New York: William Morrow

Obeyesekere, G. (1992) *The Apotheosis of Captain Cook: European Mythmaking in the Pacific*, Princeton: Princeton University Press

Robillard, A.B. (ed.) (1992) *Social Change in the Pacific Islands*, London: Kegan Paul International

Sahlins, M. (1958) *Social Stratification in Polynesia*, Seattle: University of Washington Press

—— (1985) *Islands of History*, Chicago: University of Chicago Press

Siikala, J. (1982) *Cult and Conflict in Tropical Polynesia. A Study of Traditional Religion, Christianity and Nativist Movements*, Helsinki: Academia Scientiarum Fenica

Thomas, N. (1990) *Marquesan Societies: Inequality and Political Transformation in Eastern Polynesia*, Oxford: Clarendon

Van Bakel, M.A. (1989) *Samenleven in gebondenheid en vrijheid: Evolutie en ontwikkeling in Polynesië* (Living Together in Restraint and Freedom: Evolution and Development in Polynesia), PhD Thesis, Leiden

pastoralists

Societies dependent on domestic animals for subsistence and predominantly occupied with herding on natural pasture are characterized as pastoral, after the Latinic term *pastor* for 'pasture'. The early domestication of herd animals – first goats and sheep, later cattle – was coterminous with plant domestication and early agriculture (Digard 1990). Specialized pastoralism was first practised by mountain herders who hived off from lowland sedentary communities. Subsequently, other marginal areas unoccupied by settled villagers were utilized by extensive herders, who often derived agricultural produce through trade (Clutton-Brock 1989; Smith 1992).

Pastoralists often give cultural emphasis to a 'dominant' species. Dominant animals are important for subsistence, and serve as measures of value, objects of investment, metaphors for conceptualizing the social world and tropes for expressing group *identity: cattle for the Maasai, Fulani and Nuer; camels for the Tuareg, Somali, Kababish and Bedouin; yaks for Tibetans and Mongols; sheep for the Basseri, Pashtun and numerous Southwest Asian and Mediterranean communities; llama and alpaca in the Andes; and reindeer for the Saami and the Chukchi of the Sub-Arctic. But pastoralists invariably maintain a complex mix of species, reducing risks by diversifying their resources and dispersing their assets (Dahl and Hjort 1976). However, this strategy often requires mobility, complex labour sharing, and differentiated *households, so that separate species can be managed in diverse environments in different seasons.

Given dispersed vegetation, pastoral households move opportunistically whenever and wherever grasses or shrubs grow. In turn, rights in pasture resources are usually held by pastoral communities rather than local groups, while the *family serves as the stock-owning group, responsible for herd management, routines of production and food preparation (Galaty and Johnson 1990). Perhaps due to combining *community and individual *property across levels of political organization, pastoralists are both highly individualistic and solidary in character (Edgerton 1971). This may also account for the capacity of pastoralists to aggregate for collective action, yet retain local autonomy and flexibility.

Most pastoralists are characterized by similar patterns of husbandry, division of labour, rights in pastures and animals, forms of political organization and cultural character. Yet they often share forms of social organization, religion, language and culture with settled communities to whom they are tied through *descent, *marriage, trade and *exchange (Barth 1961). Even where status hierarchies are found, diffuse egalitarianism often characterizes the attitudes of pastoralists towards one another.

Intensive animal husbandry is practised under widely varying environmental, economic and social conditions: in drier regions, where animal densities are low, herd mobility is necessary, while in wetter regions, where densities are high, sedentary husbandry is practised. Among agro-pastoralists, such as the Nuer, cultivation supplements the pastoral diet (Evans-Pritchard 1940), and in densely populated agricultural areas, such as *South Asia, animals are valued for milk, manure and traction, and as objects of strong cultural and religious emphasis. But in drier regions, which sustain fewer animals per land area, pastoralists paradoxically possess greater *per capita* animal wealth, so depend more on livestock for subsistence (Galaty and Johnson 1990).

Pastoralists are essentially milk rather than meat producers; by primarily living off renewable products of the herd, namely milk and blood, and only eating meat from animals that die naturally, from disease or through sacrifice, they strive to increase their herds. In this regard, pastoralists' strategies fall midway between those pursued by agro-pastoralists and ranchers. In agro-pastoralism, since holdings are low and labour inputs high, animals have great social value, so slaughter is rare. In ranching, technology reduces labour requirements and animal holdings are high, so animals – as †commodities – return value only when sold for slaughter. In contrast, pastoralists follow an 'optimal' strategy: a medium-sized community invests a medium amount of labour in a medium-sized herd, sustaining itself on a mix of renewable and non-renewable products in areas of marginal habitation, limiting its involvement in either cultivation or the *market.

Many attempts have been made to forcibly settle pastoralists during the twentieth century; continued *nomadism is often a political strategy for resisting state encapsulation. But pressure of population growth and the spread of market relations have affected pastoralists everywhere (Salzman, Galaty *et al.* 1981; Salzman and Galaty 1990). Resources have been taken out of pastoral control, producing greater pressure on remaining lands. And growing demand for meat has raised the commercial value of domestic animals and natural pastureland alike. Most pastoralists – some pressured or wooed by *development projects – increasingly pursue a dual strategy: fattening some animals for market while preserving others for domestic use (Sandford 1983). Similarly, pastoral lands are increasingly subdivided and privatized, enclosure undermining integrated systems of coordinated or common resource management (Behnke 1994).

Pastoralism represents one of the world's great cultural achievements, one that has made possible the flourishing of human societies across vast areas of grassland, in steppes, deserts, mountains and tundra that would otherwise have been virtually uninhabitable. Today, pastoralism is increasingly constrained by sedentarization and diversified use of rangelands, decreasing the land base of herding. Yet, for many regions, no other effective means of sustaining human populations has been developed. Thus the continuing use of natural pastures for extensive husbandry of domestic animals potentially remains a viable and desirable strategy for the future.

JOHN G. GALATY

See also: nomadism, environment

Further reading

Barth, F. (1961) *Nomads of South Persia*, Boston: Little, Brown
Behnke, R. (1994) *Natural Resource Management in Pastoral Africa*, London: Commonwealth Secretariat
Clutton-Brock, J. (1989) *The Walking Larder: Patterns of Domestication, Pastoralism and Predation*, London: Unwin Hyman
Dahl, G. and A. Hjort (1976) *Having Herds: Pastoral Herd Growth and Household Economy*, Stockholm: Department of Anthropology, University of Stockholm
Digard, J.-P. (1990) *L'homme et les animaux domestiques: Anthropologie d'une passion*, Paris: Fayard
Edgerton, R. (1971) *The Individual in Cultural Adaptation*, Berkeley: University of California Press
Evans-Pritchard, E.E. (1940) *The Nuer: A Description of the Modes of Livelihood and the Political Institutions of a Nilotic People*, Oxford: Clarendon Press
Galaty, J., D. Aronson and P. Salzman (eds) (1981) *The Future of Pastoral Peoples*, Ottawa: International Development Research Centre
Galaty, J. and D. Johnson (eds) (1990) *The World of Pastoralism: Herding Systems in Comparative Perspective*, NY: The Guilford Press; London: Belhaven Press
Salzman, P.C. and J. Galaty (eds) (1990) *Nomads in a Changing World*, Naples: Istituto Universitario Orientale
Sandford, S. (1983) *Management of Pastoral Development in the Third World*, Chichester: John Wiley and Sons
Smith, A. (1992) *Pastoralism in Africa: Origins and Development Ecology*, London: Christopher Hurst

patrons and clients

The categories 'patron' and 'client' describe the two participants in a particular type of political relationship. Generally speaking, patrons are considered politically superior and clients inferior, but accounts vary as to the precise nature of the relationship. The basis of the patron-client relationship is the assumption that the patron has, and controls, access to political, economic or cultural resources that the client wants or needs. The means by which the client gains access to them is not through appeals to formal bureaucracy, but by the manipulation of personal relationships of reciprocity. The patron-client relationship is therefore considered to lie on the margins of the *state.

Writing on patron-client relations in the Mediterranean, John Davis argued that the relationship occurred 'whenever men [sic] adopt a posture of deference to those more powerful than they and gain access to resources as a result' (Davis 1977: 132). The relationship is based on the personal reputation of the patron, and in the Mediterranean this links patron-client politics with the moral system of *honour and shame. The relationship involves the client honouring the patron by gift-giving or political support, in return for access to resources. It is therefore a personal relationship of *exchange that although asymmetrical, is assumed to be mutually beneficial.

For example the Sarakatsani, a group of *transhumant herders in Northern Greece who were dependent, as clients, on the local village patrons, strategically deployed deference to gain access to resources (Campbell 1964). They were dependent on the village presidents for access to grazing land and for signing documentation, and on local shopkeepers and cheese-merchants for credit.

They created with these local patrons relationships of *'friendship' based on reciprocity. Friendship, for the Sarakatsani, was impossible to develop with non-kin, and so was always based on complementary favours. With the cheese-merchants and shopkeepers the return for credit was a steady supply of Sarakatsani sheep's milk. Friendship with the presidents was achieved by offering them votes in return for access to land. It was consolidated by the giving of unsolicited gifts, particularly during times of trouble, and sealed by establishing ties of spiritual kinship (Campbell 1964: 217 – 24). Established through marriage sponsorship and godparenthood, the spiritual kinship between Sarakatsani and their village patrons was similar to the *compadrazgo observed in Spain and Latin America. Creating a link that supplemented and subsumed natural kinship, it added a spiritual dimension to the relationship between patron and client.

In the 1970s, a *Marxist critique of patron-client relations emerged, which argued that rather than being purely personal relations, they were actually structural, and related to *class. The patron-client relationship was an *ideology, it was argued, both from the point of view of the relationship itself, and in its elaboration by anthropologists (LiCausi 1975). Michael Gilsenan (1977) argued that, rather than being a personalized relationship between individuals, patronage was a class relationship. Seeing it as personal merely served to conceal the wider structural relations of class domination behind an ideology of mutual benefit. It also served to contrast the types of political organization found in 'other' societies from those found in the 'West'.

The study of patron-client relations was initially most common in Southern *Europe and *Latin America, but has increasingly emerged in other parts of the world, where the rise of patron-client relations was seen as part of the faltering development of democracy. This in turn was based on the assumption that patron-client relations developed as the result of a dysfunctional state. Where the state fails to provide universal access to resources, patrons emerged to control what access there is. For example, Anton Blok (1974) has linked the rise of the Sicilian mafia to its marginality from the state. They emerged in the late nineteenth century as mediators between landowners and peasants.

Debate also emerged in the 1970s concerning the difference between patrons, clients and 'brokers'. Robert Paine argued that the mediating role, such as that of the Sicilian mafia, was that of a broker, rather than of a patron. Whereas patrons adopt a superior position to further their own interests and values, brokers do so to maintain the interests of a third party (Paine 1971).

The linkage of patron-client or broker-client relations to a dysfunctional state assumed that the development of the state, †civil society and democracy would necessarily lead to their disappearance. As †Ernest Gellner put it, 'where power is effectively centralized, or on the other hand, well-diffused, patronage is correspondingly less common' (Gellner 1977: 4).

However, a new wave of studies on patron-client relations, that emerged in the wake of the international political developments of the late 1980s, suggested the opposite. They saw the insistence on the importance of the functional state as an element in the †hegemony of Western ideas of democracy and civil society. They therefore form a reaction to evolutionary models of state development (Roniger 1994: 3). Patron-client relations, it was argued, not only persisted in so-called well-developed democracies, but also emerged alongside, and in some degree complementary to, other political forms in the new democracies of the former Soviet world (Vorozheikina 1994). The disappearance of patron-client politics was therefore no longer seen as an inevitable consequence of democratization. Rather, it was increasingly seen as another mode of political activity, which was not necessarily dysfunctional.

Changes in *political anthropology began to see different types of political organization as legitimate political cultures. The implications of this can be extended from Gupta's (1995) analysis of corruption in India. Corruption is often linked with patron-client relations, as the personalization of what should be an anonymous relationship. Gupta demonstrates how corruption, rather than being anti-political, can be seen as simply a different, and no less functional, mode of political action. The same can be said of patron-client relations.

JON P. MITCHELL

See also: honour and shame, state, political anthropology, factions

Further reading

Blok, A. ([1974] 1988) *The Mafia of a Sicilian Village 1860–1960: A Study of Violent Peasant Entrepreneurs*, Oxford: Polity Press

Campbell, J.K. (1964) *Honour, Family and Patronage: A Study of Institutions and Moral Values in a Greek Mountain Community*, Oxford: Clarendon Press

Davis, J. (1977) *People of the Mediterranean: An Essay in Comparative Social Anthropology*, London: Routledge and Kegan Paul

Gellner, E. (1977) 'Patrons and Clients', in E. Gellner and J. Waterbury (eds) *Patrons and Clients in Mediterranean Societies*, London: Duckworth

Gilsenan, M. (1977) 'Against Patron-Client Relations', in E. Gellner and J. Waterbury (eds) *Patrons and Clients in Mediterranean Societies*, London: Duckworth

Gupta, A. (1995) 'Blurred Boundaries: The Discourse of Corruption, the Culture of Politics, and the Imagined State', *American Ethnologist* 22 (2): 375–402

LiCausi, L. (1975) 'Anthropology and Ideology: The Case of "Patronage" in Mediterranean Societies', *Critique of Anthropology* 4 (5): 90–107

Paine, R. (1971) 'A Theory of Patronage and Brokerage', in R. Paine (ed.) *Patrons and Brokers in the East Arctic*, Newfoundland: University of Toronto Press

Roniger, L. (1994) 'The Comparative Study of Clientelism and the Changing Nature of Civil Society in the Contemporary World', in L. Roniger and A. Günes-Ayata (eds) *Democracy, Clientelism, and Civil Society*, London: Lynne Rienner Publishers

Vorozheikina, T. (1994) 'Clientelism and the Process of Political Democratization in Russia', in L. Roniger and A. Günes-Ayata (eds) *Democracy, Clientelism, and Civil Society*, London: Lynne Rienner Publishers

peasants

A broad definition of the term peasant would invoke three important characteristics (Shanin 1987): peasants are agriculturalists (or possibly engaged in *fishing), for whom both production and *consumption are oriented to the *household, and who are also under some economic and political obligations to outside power-holders. A definition of this sort brings into one comparative frame, pre- and post-revolutionary Chinese peasants, Indian farmers, African smallholders, Southeast Asian rice farmers, as well as modern and pre-modern agriculturalists in many areas of Europe and Central and South America. Although peasants have formed the greater part of the world's population for most of anthropology's existence as an empirical discipline, they only began to be treated as a distinctive object of scrutiny from the 1950s, with an explosion of cross-disciplinary interest in the late 1960s and early 1970s.

Analytically such a broad category teeters on the verge of incoherence. Nevertheless, it has been extremely useful in reminding anthropologists that potentially fruitful comparisons can be made across the world (for example, in the analysis of production and consumption within the peasant household); that in †Clifford Geertz's famous dictum anthropologists study *in* villages, but that doesn't mean that they study villages (for peasant lives are shaped by far broader economic, political and cultural forces than can be contained within a closed local *community); and that anthropologists cannot and should not close their ears to colleagues in other disciplines (*sociology, history, political science). In other words, studying peasants has forced anthropologists to acknowledge that their particular ethnographic knowledge is only a small part of some greater whole. †Robert Redfield made this explicit in his theoretical delineation of peasantries as 'part-societies', positioned on a 'folk-urban continuum', and culturally aligned to both a *great and a little tradition; while all of these concepts have since been found wanting in one way or another, the general orientation remains valuable.

Theoretically, the peasantry have had a precarious existence. Their rise to prominence in the late 1960s was a direct consequence of the success of twentieth-century revolutionary movements not, as †Marx might have predicted, among industrial workers but in predominantly rural, peasant populations. The Vietnam War was just the latest in a line of peasant-based radical movements which had changed the political shape of the world – most obviously in China and Russia. In other words, peasants held a special fascination for the academic left even as they seemed to challenge the certainties of classical Marxist-Leninism. Politically and culturally, then, what often needed to be explained about peasants was either their capacity for rebellion or, just as often, their tendency to conservatism and acquiescence in structures of *inequality.

Economically, studies of peasant life have concentrated on the questions raised by the Russian scholar A.V. Chayanov ([1925] 1966). He argued that peasants constituted a distinctive *mode of production, characterized by the domestic unit of production and consumption, in which production is oriented first and foremost towards household reproduction rather than individual profit. Chayanov died in Stalin's purges, and his arguments have been attacked by later adherents to Marxist orthodoxy (who emphasized instead peasants either as †petty commodity producers, or as rural proletarians). In anthropology they were taken up by †Sahlins in his concept of the †domestic mode of production (a concept which Sahlins did not apply to peasant economies, but rather to *kinship-based societies without adequate hierarchical structures to increase the extraction of economic surplus). The key dynamic in the peasant economy, in this view, was household structure and Chayanov's explanatory frame could be mapped onto earlier anthropological work, such as †Fortes's idea of the †developmental cycle of the domestic group (discussed in the article on *family). And, while feminist scholars were able to deconstruct Sahlins's gendered assumption about what constituted a 'natural' household, their critiques emphasized again the value of detailed empirical study of the link between kinship, gender relations, economy and polity.

Politically, the anthropological focus has shifted from peasant quiescence to radicalism and then back to a modified understanding of the hidden *resistance which may be uncovered beneath the surface of apparent conservatism. Writers of the 1950s and 1960s, heavily influenced by the assumptions of *modernization theory, emphasized peasant attachment to collective norms and values, such as *honour and shame in *Southern Europe, E. Banfield's †amoral familism, or C. Geertz's †ethos of 'shared poverty' in Indonesia, and particularistic political styles, such as a dependence on *patron-client ties and the development of *factions. Writing at the height of anti-Vietnam radicalism in the late 1960s, and partly in reaction to the complacencies of modernization theory, Eric Wolf (1969) identified a key group – the so-called middle peasantry – as potential agents of social transformation. A decade later, Michael Adas (1981) pointed out the extent to which peasants in the past had dealt with exploitation by simply walking away from it; premodern *states in Africa and Asia were based on control over people rather than bureaucratic control over territory, and people who sensed their overlord was requiring too much could, and frequently did, respond by moving elsewhere and shifting allegiance to another authority. In this interpretation, overt rebellion was a distinctively modern response to the increased bureaucratic penetration and control of colonial and postcolonial states. James Scott (1985), whose earlier work had emphasized the collectivist and risk-reducing ethos of the peasant †moral economy, argued against the privileging of moments of outright rebellion; his own ethnography of 'everyday forms of peasant resistance' in rural Malaysia drew attention to the ways in which peasants employed covert tactics of resistance like foot-dragging and gossip rather than overt and dangerous confrontation (albeit in a context of rural proletarianization and dramatic change in the technology of rice production).

What is interesting about this broad theoretical trend is the extent to which individual writers have moved from the privileging of either *social structure, or political relations, or cultural values as explanations of peasant political action, to much more sophisticated combinations of cultural exegesis, historical research and political economic theorizing. Although the drift to the cities in many parts of the world, and the increasing penetration of the *world-system, may seem to herald the demise of peasant life, it remains the case that many, if not most, anthropologists continue to study what can broadly be characterized as peasant societies.

JONATHAN SPENCER

See also: family, household, Europe: Central and Eastern, Europe: Southern, Marxism and anthropology, mode of production, great and little traditions

Further reading
Adas, M. (1981) 'From Avoidance to Confrontation: Peasant Protest in Precolonial and Colonial Southeast Asia', *Comparative Studies in Society and History* 23: 217–47
Chayanov, A. ([1925] 1966) *The Theory of Peasant Economy*, Homewood, Il: Irwin
Redfield, R. (1956) *Peasant Society and Culture: An Anthropological Approach to Civilization*, Chicago: University of Chicago Press
Scott, J. (1985) *Weapons of the Weak: Everyday Forms of Peasant Resistance*, New Haven: Yale University Press
Shanin, T. (ed.) (1987) *Peasants and Peasant Societies* (2nd edn), Oxford: Blackwell
Wolf, E. (1966) *Peasants*, Englewood Cliffs, NJ: Prentice-Hall
—— (1969) *Peasant Wars of the Twentieth Century*, New York: Harper and Row

person

The concept of the person, like other comparative concepts such as kinship or the state, designates a zone of enquiry within which there is enough commonality across societies to ensure that comparison is reasonable, yet enough variation between them to make enquiry fruitful. Enquiries in this zone concern conceptions of the human psychophysical *individual. This is territory for the psychologist and the philosopher as well, of course, but anthropologists are guided by two special considerations. First, we expect that a society's conceptions of people as individuals, of how people work, can be related compellingly to its forms of social institution, of how society works. Second, we have come to learn that other societies' ways of anatomizing individuals' thought and form may be profoundly, and startlingly, different from those we take for granted.

Indeed the differences between versions of the person are a matter not only of thought but of feeling and experience as well. Consider, for example, †Godfrey Lienhardt's (1961) ethnographic account of the Dinka, in which he shows that Dinka regard themselves, indeed experience themselves, very differently to the way people of the North Atlantic do. In the matter of a bad debt, for example, North Atlantic peoples assume that the power to recollect a bad debt – the faculty of the conscience, in other words—is wholly internal to the thinking subject, the person. But among the Dinka such recollection is not a property of the debtor's own mind or conscience. Rather, the debtor who owns up to his debt does so because the spirit *Mathiang Gok* has laid hold of her and forced her to recollect the debt and respond to it. Rather than an internal conscience directing her, in other words, the debtor experiences an external power. Similarly, members of certain clans among the Dinka have as a special divinity, the spirit which Lienhardt translates as Flesh. The divinity Flesh appears within them as their own flesh when their muscles begin to quiver and they become *possessed during ritual *sacrifices. In other words, their own body becomes at once spiritual and subject to another power, neither of which properties are familiar in a North Atlantic perspective. To this extent, the person is very differently conceived and experienced in the two societies.

Persons and individuals

Lienhardt's writing is extraordinary in its sensitivity and stands as a monument to the achievements of anthropology as an exploration of the human condition. It is the more notable, therefore, that the early development of the notion of the person for anthropology was concerned, not with experience, but with an abstracted and generalized view of the topic. Thus †Durkheim and †Mauss, writing at the beginning of the twentieth century, described 'person' as a *category* of thought, by which they meant that it is a fundamental and inescapable component of human *cognition, like the categories of *time and space, without which

thought itself would be impossible. Such cognition is governed by the force that *society exerts upon individuals, but, beyond that, the categories of society actually constitute the person, such that there could be no human †agent in any intelligible sense without such categories. Mauss, in the seminal 1938 article which summarizes and expands the Durkheimian position, makes clear that he is writing of the person as a matter of 'law and morality', and not of the internal or psychic sense that anyone might have of themselves: his interest is 'not the sense of 'self' (*moi*) – but the [collective] notion or concept that men in different ages have formed of it' (Mauss [1938] in Carrithers *et al.* 1985). On this view the concept of the person held by a society differs sharply from a psychologist's concept of individual human beings in their biological, experiential or idiosyncratic nature, and the psychologist's concept is of no relevance.

In the 1938 article Mauss lays out a grand historical and comparative sketch of the person so understood, a sketch drawn from a mass of evidence on past and present societies. The greatest contrast lies between concepts of the person belonging to the earliest human communities – or at least to early communities as Mauss attempted painstakingly to reconstruct them from widely scattered signs found among contemporary societies – and concepts of person eventually achieved in contemporary North Atlantic societies. These are the beginning and end of a great species-wide development. Archaic society was comprised of 'roles' (*personnages*): the stock of roles was fixed and each role was inherited by a successor or perhaps filled by the reincarnation of an *ancestor. There was correspondingly a fixed stock of names to go with each role and some form of mask or body painting associated with each role in collective ritual. Each role had a clear set of rights and duties attached to it, so that the role or *personnage*, which might be called the 'proto-person', was wholly defined by its social ties and socially bestowed names and forms.

Nothing could contrast more markedly with the practices and attitudes of the contemporaneous North Atlantic, the end of Mauss's historical narrative. In these societies we regard each individual person as unique and not as the incarnation of one among a fixed stock of roles. Similarly, we now regard the possession of an inner self or consciousness as the qualification for personhood, in contrast to the putative early societies, which placed emphasis on one's place and name in a †clan or †kin group. And whereas contemporary North Atlantic societies consider each living human being to achieve consciousness and therefore personhood at birth or even, as anti-abortionists argue, well before birth, other societies have considered that full personhood can only be achieved by certain categories of people and perhaps only with time. The only full persons may in such cases be mature men, while others are excluded, such as women, children or slaves. (For full commentary and case studies see Carrithers *et al.* 1985.)

No writer today could expound Mauss's ideas without remarking the opprobrium which has fallen, and had begun to fall even when Mauss published his essay, on the project of a grand sociocultural history of the whole human species. A large part of such history must always be irre-deemably speculative, nor is there reason to suppose that history culminates among North Atlantic peoples. But even leaving Mauss's universal history aside we can still salvage a very important double insight. On the one hand, North Atlantic societies do, *as a matter of law and public ideology*, place value upon each unique individual, such that the individual person is regarded as sacred, as both Mauss and Durkheim observed. Thus, for example, the American Constitution enshrines rights pertaining to persons without specifying their age, sex, or relationship to others: it is sheer personhood that matters. Indeed Mauss's perspective can help us to understand the very development of individual psychology and of an interest in 'selves' in North Atlantic societies (and in *psychological anthropology): it is a conse-quence of our collective preoccupation with the individual human being, the individual person, quite apart from any social setting.

On the other hand, there are societies which *as a matter of law and public ideology* place emphasis elsewhere, such as on the value of social relations and the fulfilment of social obligations specific to each role, e.g. mother and wife, father and husband, dutiful son or daughter. Chinese society does so, at least as far as it has been governed by Confucian ideas, and so do many African societies, so far as they are governed by local ideas and practices. †Louis Dumont, standing in the direct line of pupillary succession to Mauss, has devoted his life's work to exploring a related idea, namely that Indian society, in its organization and atti-tudes, places value upon society as a whole rather

than on the 'individual' (as he terms the North Atlantic version of the person). Correspondingly he explored how the contrasting ideology of the sacred individual arose in the West, largely through the agency of Christians and Christian thought. And these ideas of Dumont have helped to inspire work by Marilyn Strathern (1988) and McKim Marriott (1989) suggesting that, in India and *Melanesia respectively, it would be more faithful to the character of those societies to regard people within them not as individuals – that is, as indivisible and autonomous wholes – but as being constituted by properties, goods and substances *exchanged or shared with others.

Persons and selves

This broad stream of Durkheimian thought treats the person in a distinctly †social anthropological style, in that the overt topic of the investigation is a social system and that system is treated as a system of ideas collectively and uniformly held among the participants in that social system. Apart from some ethnographic work (e.g. Harris 1978 and writers in Östör *et al.* 1982), this tradition has tended to produce writing which, in its scope and abstraction, lies rather closer to the social theory of sociologists than is usually the case among anthropologists, and has remained separate and autonomous within anthropology. This autonomy is the more remarkable in that another tradition of work on the psychophysical individual devel-oped and flourished alongside work on the person, namely American psychological anthropology.

On the face of it, the lack of mutual inspira-tion between these two schools is puzzling, since psychological anthropology – and more broadly, †cultural anthropology with its psychological lean-ings – has been concerned with individuals, with the description of individuals and their experience, and with the relation of individuals to the larger social setting. Yet in fact there are strong ideo-logical reasons for the lack of mutual attention. For the Durkheimians, the psychophysical indi-vidual is of interest, indeed exists for enquiry, only insofar as it is recognized in collective ideas and attitudes. But for the psychological anthropolo-gists, who write of 'selves' rather than 'persons', the individual embodied self is of importance, and bears its own character, quite apart from a cultural setting. The self so considered can be at odds with its society or marginalized by it, and even well-adjusted selves may depart from cultural norms from time to time. So the difference between self and society can be diagnostic of both. And indeed this divergence of norm from reality – surely a human universal if ever there was one – is a strong argument against the Durkheimian assumption of massive conformity to collective values. Durkheimians, on the other hand, could reply that psychological anthropologists have drawn their portrait of such selves-beyond-society from American academic psychology, which is just American folk psychology in polysyllabic words. Such psychology is therefore merely an †ethnocentric form of evaluation, the product of the North Atlantic's particular stress on individuals in themselves. Indeed this accusation of ethno-centricity has often been made against psychological anthropology within American cultural anthropology itself (see Rosaldo 1984 for sources).

Yet despite their deep differences, these traditions can be reconciled. In a collection of articles on Oceania with the revealing title *Person, Self and Experience* (White and Kirkpatrick 1985), American anthropologists demonstrated a systematically subtler anthropology of the self/person. Some writers in the volume began to recognize the constitutive character of ideas of the person, following Mauss, and most rejected to very great effect the simplifications of older psychological views. But at the same time most preserved experience as a valid topic of study, *contra* Mauss. In the same year British scholars published a collection, *The Category of the Person* (Carrithers *et al.* 1985), directed entirely to Mauss's seminal 1938 article. Several writers in this volume argued that scholarship must recognize notions of self and personal experience, in addition to the matters of 'law and morality' that Mauss prescribed. And some suggested that notions of the person are more embroiled in social controversy and historical change, and more subject to individuals' agency, than Mauss's theory comprehended.

At present, writing on these issues is being carried forward mostly by ethnography, sometimes under the rubric of experience, a notion which stresses a meticulous concentration on the illuminating details of interaction in everyday life. Two recent examples will suffice. Myers (1986), in his ethnography of the Pintupi of Australia, shows how emotions are not to be regarded as events in the depth of the psyche, as our North Atlantic folk psychology would have it, but are instead the necessary and compelling evaluations of people and circumstance people must make in

order to live successfully in the rapid flow of social life. The point is one Mauss might have appreciated, though it is arrived at from a tradition, psychological anthropology, and a language of the 'self' quite alien to Mauss's own. Myers stresses the interactive character, the swiftly flowing give and take, of social life much more than did the Durkheimians.

Wikan (1990), in her splendid ethnography of Bali, *Managing Turbulent Hearts*, shows how anthropologists' notions of both the person and the self have failed through assuming that people simply follow a cultural program in constructing their *personae*. On the older assumption, Balinese culture ordains – out of its ineluctable power, so to speak – that Balinese become graceful, composed, and theatrically imperturbable persons through and through (see for example Geertz [1966] 1973). Yet, as Wikan observes, for Balinese

> face, expression, and action are perceived *as* appearances that may require a great deal of emotional work to bring about and sustain. Balinese have a concept – *ngabe keneh* – to connote the effort frequently entailed. Literally, it means to 'bring or guide the. . .heart.' Actually it refers to a process of shaping and mustering one's feelings by deliberate, willful effort.
>
> (Wikan 1990: 29)

Wikan illustrates this with the example of a young woman who maintained a smiling facade though her fiancé had died tragically: 'on the basis of the facts of the case that were generally known, people inferred what went on behind bright faces and closed doors. And they reacted accordingly – with compassion *(kelangen/inda)*' (1990: 29). So as anthropologists we can learn how persons *should* be in Bali (they should have bright faces), but beyond that we need also to learn something else as well, namely that Balinese are fully aware that actual persons may diverge painfully from that ideal. This subtler awareness is not so readily useful for comparative purposes as the earlier simplifications. Yet if anthropology remains committed to firsthand knowledge and to the sovereignty of *fieldwork, then we will have no choice but to take our comparativism in that more challenging direction.

MICHAEL CARRITHERS

See also: individual, body, gender, slavery, symbolic anthropology

Further reading

Carrithers, M., S. Collins and S. Lukes (eds) (1985) *The Category of the Person: Anthropology, Philosophy, History*, Oxford: Oxford University Press

Geertz, C. ([1966] 1973) 'Person, Time and Conduct in Bali', in C. Geertz *The Interpretation of Cultures*, London: Hutchinson

Harris, G. (1978) *Casting Out Anger: Religion among the Taita of Kenya*, Cambridge: Cambridge University Press

Lienhardt, G. (1961) *Divinity and Experience: The Religion of the Dinka*, Oxford: Clarendon Press

Marriott, M. (1989) 'Constructing an Indian Ethnosociology', *Contributions to Indian Sociology* (n.s.) 23 (1): 1–40. (See also (1990) *Contributions to Indian Sociology* (n.s.) 24, (2) for full and excellent comments by a number of writers on this article.)

Myers, F. (1986) *Pintupi Country, Pintupi Self: Sentiment, Place, and Politics among Western Desert Aboriginals*, Washington: Smithsonian Institution Press

Östör, Á., L. Fruzzetti and S. Barnett (eds) (1982) *Concepts of Person: Kinship, caste, and Marriage in India*, Cambridge MA: Harvard University Press

Rosaldo, M. (1984) 'Toward an Anthropology of Self and Feeling', in R. Shweder and R. Levine (eds) *Culture Theory: Essays on Mind, Self and Emotion*, Cambridge: Cambridge University Press

Strathern, M. (1988) *The Gender of the Gift*, Berkeley: University of California Press

White, G. and J. Kirkpatrick (1985) *Person, Self, and Experience: Exploring Pacific Ethnopsychologies*, Berkeley: University of California Press

Wikan, U. (1990) *Managing Turbulent Hearts: A Balinese Formula for Living*, Chicago: University of Chicago Press

pilgrimage

Pilgrimage in all religions is pre-eminently a journey of the religious imagination. It obviously constitutes physical movement from one place to another, but at the same time involves spiritual or temporal movement. Pilgrimage may project the believer across lines of *gender, *ethnicity, *language, *class, and locality. Yet even as pilgrims believe that they are transcending the 'imagined community' of their immediate locality or group, pilgrimage creates new boundaries and distinctions. In the hope of creating new horizons or reaffirming contact with a spiritual centre, pilgrims set off from home, encounter 'others' and return with a sharpened awareness of difference and similarity. In sacred centres shared by pilgrims from different faiths, such as Jerusalem or the Tomb of Abraham in Hebron/al-Khalil, the heightened sense of distinction can be particularly intense

(Webber 1985). Pilgrimage may also create a different sense of 'home', so that some pilgrims come to identify it with some place other than their place of origin or departure.

The study of pilgrimage has challenged anthropology. Anthropologists have generally explored its impact in small-scale, face-to-face communities, but since the 1970s, like scholars in neighbouring disciplines such as the history of religion, they have increasingly taken its historical, doctrinal, political, and transnational dimensions into account (Eickelman and Piscatori 1990).

†Victor Turner (1973, 1974; Turner and Turner 1978) was one of the first modern anthropologists to explore systematically the translocal implications of pilgrimage, adapting the sociological concepts of 'centre' and 'periphery' and †Van Gennep's notions of *rites of passage to conceive of pilgrimage as a process involving three stages: separation (from one's 'home' or conventional surroundings); the 'liminal' stage of the journey itself, including an intensified sense of the sacred, a strong sense of †*communitas* ('community') and temporary release from ordinary social bonds; and the reaggregation of 'homecoming'.

Turner's generalizations on the similarities of all pilgrimage movements did not go unchallenged. Thus Sallnow (1981) argues that pilgrimages to Andean shrines indeed temporarily abrogate existing patterns of social relations and create a supralocal arena in which novel social alignments may arise, but that these directly engender endemic competition and conflict. He argues that assuming *communitas* as the pilgrims' goal is spurious, leading to a deterministic view of what is essentially a polymorphic phenomenon. Likewise Nissan (1988) argues that the major Buddhist pilgrimage centres in Sri Lanka reflect multiple collective historical representations rather than a unified tradition. Finally, the claim that pilgrimage is 'initially unstructured and outside the bounds of religious orthodoxy' (E. Turner 1987: 330) is belied by *Islam, in which the pilgrimage to Mecca (*hajj*) is a highly structured and 'orthodox' event, the rules for which are set out in the Qur'an.

It would be tempting to assume a fixed hierarchy of sacred space and sacred journeys in world religious traditions, but the sense of 'centre' and 'periphery' is in constant flux. What is 'central' to some believers in a given space and time may be peripheral to others. Thus the multiple belief systems within *Hinduism preclude identifying any formal hierarchy among the hundreds of holy places which over twenty million pilgrims visit annually; in Islam, Shi'i Muslims – roughly 10 per cent of Muslims worldwide – consider Mecca only as one spiritual centre among others (such as Karbala and Najaf in Iraq and Qum in Iran); and for the Alevi Muslims of Turkey, the genuine pilgrimage is one of the heart and not one of physical movement.

In all religious traditions, pilgrimage is complex and multilayered. It can subvert local orthodoxy, but it can also link local and regional pilgrimage traditions – called 'visits' (*ziyarat*) in many parts of the Muslim *Middle East – to more universal ones, embed universal religious practices in the local religious imagination, and sustain complementary gender roles. The creative tension between pilgrimage as envisioned by priests and the religious elite and popular practices can even contribute to a major reorientation in thought and practice – in late medieval Europe, the rise of long-distance pilgrimages facilitated shifting popular religious sensibility to assuming that God acted for saints rather than through them (Kieckhefer 1984: 10, 25). In Judaism, visitational dreams have encouraged Tunisian and Moroccan Jewish immigrants to Israel to 'transplant' shrines of saints and sages to their new home (Deshen and Shokeid 1974). Finally, in modern times, the lines between religious pilgrimage and reunions reaffirming 'family values' or other non-religious ones have increasingly blurred, as among American southerners of Scottish origin (Neville 1987).

DALE F. EICKELMAN

See also: Islam, religion, rite of passsage

Further reading

Deshen, S. and M. Shokeid (1974) *The Predicament of Homecoming: Cultural and Social Life of North African Immigrants in Israel*, Ithaca and London: Cornell University Press
Eickelman, D.F. and J. Piscatori (eds) (1990) *Muslim Travellers: Pilgrimage, Migration, and the Religious Imagination*, London: Routledge
Kieckhefer, R. (1984) *Unquiet Souls: Fourteenth-Century Saints and their Religious Milieu*, Chicago and London: University of Chicago Press
Neville, G.K. (1987) *Kinship and Pilgrimage: Rituals of Reunion in American Protestant Culture*, New York: Oxford University Press
Nissan, E. (1988) 'Polity and Pilgrimage Centres in Sri Lanka', *Man* (n.s.) 23 (2): 253–74
Sallnow, M.J. (1981) 'Communitas Reconsidered: The Sociology of Andean Pilgrimage', *Man* (n.s.) 16 (2): 163–82
Sumption, J. (1975) *Pilgrimage: An Image of Mediaeval Religion*, London: Faber and Faber
Turner, E. (1987) 'Pilgrimage: An Overview', in M. Eliade (ed.) *Encyclopedia of Religion*, vol. 11, New York: Macmillan
Turner, V. (1973) 'The Center Out There: Pilgrim's Goal', *History of Religions* 12 (3): 191–230
—— (1974) 'Pilgrimage as Social Process', in *Dramas, Fields, and Metaphors*, Ithaca: Cornell University Press
—— and E. Turner (1978) *Image and Pilgrimage in Christian Culture*, New York: Oxford University Press
Webber, J. (1985) 'Religions in the Holy Land: Conflicts of Interpretation', *Anthropology Today* 1 (2):3–9

play

Play is a type of 'free' activity, familiar in the lives not only of humans, but also of certain animal species, that takes place 'within its own proper boundaries of time and space' (Huizinga 1950: 13). This activity is particularly characteristic of the young of any relevant species, who use special playful, and immediately recognizable expressions to indicate that they are engaged in it. This signal shows that the ostensible character of the activity, for instance, combat, does not reveal its true nature as understood by its participants. In other words, play has something of the character of acting, or make-believe.

In human society, the growing child soon discovers that play has its own characteristic instrumentality. Sometimes this is provided by improving upon nature, as when trees are used for playing hide and seek, but more often, balls, tops, boards, dice, cards and any number of different kinds of sticks, darts and bats, often carrying special symbols, together with lines and other markings drawn on the ground or on walls, clearly and unequivocally define the context of a game.

Games also have a pronounced social dimension. Lacrosse, a game first played by the Plains Indians, is defined not only by the stick and ball with which (and the field on which) it is played, but by the division of the players into two sides. Furthermore, within each side the prevailing ethic is cooperation, whereas between them it is competition. What goes for lacrosse goes for any number of other games, belonging to countless different cultures.

The result is that play, as an adult activity, is no longer recognizable by the facial expressions of the participants (which can reflect a wide range of emotions), but, instead, by the imposition of elaborate rules establishing in detail not only the number of players, the size of the arena, the duration of the contest, but also such apparently extraneous matters as the clothes to be worn and the appropriate season of the year. In many familiar cases, the rules are necessary to constitute the game, which could not exist in any form without them: this is particularly true of such intellectual pursuits as chess, backgammon, or card-games, including solitaire.

This latter case is also exemplified by a game known in different parts of Africa as *oware* (Ghana), *omweso* (Uganda), *soro* (Tanzania) (Zaslavsky 1979: 116f), but also played as far afield as the Phillipines and Suriname. This is a board game for two opposing players, who score by moving counters around two rows of holes, one for each side. Although there are local variants in the number of holes, and of the counters to fill them, there is only one underlying principle. At the same time there is considerable local variation in the game's cultural attributes: in the old kingdom of Baganda, a new king, or *Kabaka*, picked brown seeds from a local tree, for use on the *omweso* board kept in the royal hall. In Suriname the game is played at funerals. This illustrates a point, characteristic of play, that each separate type, whether it is *oware* or lacrosse, can be diffused over a very wide area, but in such a way that every local instance has its own distinctive social and cultural niche. Just consider the difference between lacrosse, as it was played by Lakota warriors in the mid-nineteenth century, and its present day manifestation in English girls' schools.

The human player, in the process of growing up in society, moves from a type of innocent, solitary play, characteristic of the very young child, and defined by Caillois (1979: 27) as *'paidia'* to serious adult games, with intricate rules creating obstacles to be overcome, which are defined as *'ludus'*. At an early stage, according to †Victor Turner, 'the rules of a game provide a framework of action within which anything that does not properly belong . . . is screened out as irrelevant. This enables the players to enter into an altered state of consciousness called 'flow', in which their action and their awareness become one and their skills and the tasks confronting them are precisely matched' (Turner 1982: 98).

In this process play becomes increasingly a matter of competition, in principle between equal sides, generally two in number. This symmetrical case, although extremely common, and exemplified by such diverse games as *oware* and lacrosse (to take examples already given), is by no means inherent in the rules of all competitive games. In some special cases, such as casino gambling, there is no question of equal chances, if only because the rules are designed to ensure that one side, in this case the 'bank', has a privileged status.

This is just one type of case in which winning or losing are matters of pure chance: any such case is defined by Caillois (1979: 17f) as *'alea'*, but nothing in this definition requires unequal chances. The alternative case, where the players' skill counts in determining their chance of winning, is *'agon'* (1979: 14f). The two can combine, in games such as poker, where the hands dealt and the cards drawn, are determined by *alea*, but the choice of any card actually played, by *agon*. In all such cases, the more skilful players, in the long run, always win, however great the element of chance.

Finally, the cultural domain of play can extend far outside 'the framework of action', to involve non-players such as spectators, betters, trainers and promoters, each with their own distinctive role. †Geertz's study (1973: 412–53) of the Balinese cockfight shows how this can happen, at different levels of society, in a contest in which the ostensible protagonists, the fighting cocks, are not even human. But then, 'it is only apparently cocks that are fighting . . . Actually, it is men' (1973: 417).

THOMAS CRUMP

See also: childhood, ritual

Further reading

Caillois, R. (1979) *Man, Play and Games*, New York: Schocken Books
Geertz, C. (1973) *The Interpretation of Cultures*, New York: Basic Books
Huizinga, J. (1950) *Homo Ludens: A Study of the Play Element in Culture*, Boston: Beacon Press
Turner, V. (1982) *Celebration: A World of Art and Ritual*, Washington, DC: Smithsonian Institution Press
Zaslavsky, C. (1979) *Africa Counts*, Westport: Lawrence Hill

plural society

The paradox of the plural society entered anthropology with J.S. Furnivall's discussion of colonial policy and practice in Burma and Indonesia. He described a plural society as one in which racially distinct peoples met only in the market place, a feature of colonial *political economy. Critiques of the concept followed in rapid succession. It was suggested by Maurice Freedman, writing about Malaya, that although *ethnicity might be recognized as a preliminary to the useful fiction of a plural society, and although members of each ethnic *community recognized commonality, these were cultural categories (mental constructs) and not organized entities (groups). None of the ethnic divisions distinguished was politically autonomous; none constituted a unit; none was a valid group. How such categorical labels became instituted in colonial societies, often in the face of local opposition, later became the subject of anthropological inquiry.

Furnivall's term was taken up by M.G. Smith, the most prolific exponent of plural society theorizing in anthropology. Smith found the concept useful first in order to delineate the structural forms to be found in *Caribbean societies and then to compare them. In Smith's formal analysis, the plural society model based on *race ignored all other cleavages between individuals and groups, such as those of *class or *religion.

Smith argued polemically for an umbrella concept of pluralism to be used comparatively in social anthropology; Caribbean ethnographers suggested that he failed to recognize the historical context of the so-called plural societies there. They suggested that societal pluralism was more usefully viewed not as a structural form but as a phase in a historical process. In the ethnographic cases they presented, the plural society was a colonial construct. This led to discriminations based on racial – and sometimes ethnic – categorization and legal codification. In its most extreme form, racial pluralism was used to segregate, enclave and exclude, as in apartheid South Africa where there was at one time a Ministry of Pluralism.

Plural society theory underscored the polyethnic character of most Third World societies but it did not significantly influence the trend in either post-colonial or ethnic studies. Adjusting constantly to his critics, Smith's own theorizing eventually became so conceptually involuted that it was superseded by theories of cultural pluralism.

Cultural pluralism embraces the idea that historic cultural differences among peoples should be both admitted and respected by a legal order which assures them equal rights within the national society. This has proved a concept of more universal application than the plural society model. It took hold first with concern over the cultural survival of indigenous peoples such as Amazonian Indian groups, and today anthropologists have organized to ensure international protection against †genocide in such societies. Among them are David Maybury-Lewis who founded the organization *Cultural Survival* and Leo Kuper who campaigned for the protection of *indigenous peoples at the United Nations.

JOAN VINCENT

See also: ethnicity, complex society, colonialism

Further reading

Furnivall, J.S. (1948) *Colonial Policy and Practice: A Comparative Study of Burma and Netherlands India*, Cambridge: Cambridge University Press
Maybury-Lewis, D. (1984) *The Prospects for Plural Societies*, Washington: American Ethnological Society
Smith, M.G. (1965) *The Plural Society in the British West Indies*, Berkeley: University of California Press

poetics

'Poetics' has two different – if related – meanings for anthropologists: first the long-established meaning of the study of patterns in literary texts, traditionally carried out in the context of literary analysis; and second the approach to analysing the genres of anthropological writing itself which became popular in the 1980s.

Poetics in the first sense broadly covers both general issues such as the study of genres or the principles underlying literary formulation, and specific analyses of the stylistic and structuring properties in particular works or genres. Such questions are relevant in a general way to any anthropologist encountering examples of verbal or literary art as part of the *culture being studied, whether under the label of 'myth', 'tale', 'life history', 'lament', 'song' or whatever. They are also central for anthropologists with a specialist interest in, for example, *aesthetics, literary forms, verbal art, or the 'ethnography of speaking'. In this context anthropologists often focus on performed genres (under headings like *oral literature, verbal art, *myth or *folklore); detailed analyses have been undertaken particularly by the 'performance oriented' American anthropologists and folklorists such as Dell Hymes, Joel Sherzer, Steven Feld and Dennis Tedlock. There is also work in narratology, a development from the structuralist analyses pioneered by †Propp and other *formalist writers. Topics include the differentiation of genres (more multi-faceted than once supposed); the analysis of stylistic and structural features such as rhythm, rhyme, parallelism and other prosodic properties; narrative themes; the interplay of different voices; figurative language, allegory and allusion; openings and closings; the structuring of episodes and themes.

For anthropologists the scope of such poetics has moved beyond merely the *verbal* elements of 'texts', to encompass paralinguistic features and wider patterns of communication and action: the 'communicative event', the role of audience and context, multiple voices, †dialogic meanings, the political setting, and the deeper emotive implications. The concept of 'text' as a bounded verbal unit for analysis is under challenge by anthropologists (and others) partly for being culture-bound, partly because even in print-based cultures it may be too simple to regard 'the text' as an autonomous and context-free entity. Such challenges have been reinforced by interdisciplinary †poststructuralist approaches and analyses of †intertextuality. Anthropologists now regard the *performance* features as part of poetics, for instance in Sherzer's analysis of the poetics of Kuna verbal art which 'requires attention to the interplay of linguistic and sociolinguistic structures and processes along with such aspects of the dramatization of the voice as pause, intonation, volume, and musicality' (Sherzer 1990: 16). Such poetics necessarily include consideration of *music, *dance and visual communication. The approach known as 'ethnopoetics' (Hymes 1981, Tedlock 1983) parallels and overlaps these developments, emphasizing particularly the poetic voices of non-Western peoples and the creative aspects of performance.

The second sense of poetics draws, similarly, on the interaction between literary and anthropological theory, analysing the conventions through which texts are constructed and interpreted. But, following Clifford and Marcus's influential *Writing Culture: the Poetics and Politics of Ethnography* (1986), it was the writings of anthropologists themselves that became the subject for analysis. Far from being objective and scientifically-neutral reports, *ethnographies are – like any poetic or narrative texts – shaped by rhetorical conventions. So it was appropriate to engage in narratological analysis of the varied 'voices' in such texts, and in critical assessment of the implicit claims to authority or the politi-

cal contexts in which they were formulated as 'persuasive fictions'. Similarly the sub-genres of ethnographic writing were scrutinized, as for example in Van Maanen's account (1988) of the types of 'tales of the field': 'realist'; 'confessional'; and 'impressionist'. This approach also often carried political and ethical overtones: anthropological writing should not only be self-critical but also convey a plurality of viewpoints rather than the single would-be authoritative voice of the researcher.

The early 1990s have seen a reaction against the extreme versions of this approach as – arguably – concerned more with navel-gazing than with attempting to communicate a responsible and valid account of the conditions and findings of anthropological research. A common middle position is to insist on the importance of being explicitly aware of the politics and poetics of one's writing and certainly no longer to take the author's authority for granted as the only objective word on the topic – but all the same not to give up writing monographs.

Despite the different slants on 'poetics', there has been some convergence. In the 1980s and 1990s anthropologists have more generally recognized that the conventions of communication – whether in oral performances encountered in the field, acclaimed art-texts of their own culture, or anthropologists' own academic writings – are, indeed, *conventions* rather than 'natural', and thus worth ethnographic and critical analysis in the context of the cultural and political settings in which they are produced and interpreted. Similarly anthropologists are increasingly aware of the poetic and plural qualities of communication: that ambiguity, figurative language, poetry, communicative context, contested meanings, the exercise of power or a multiplicity of voices may be as significant as 'straightforward' information-transfer – and that, furthermore, this kind of 'poetics' may apply to their own varied performances (written or other) as well as to those of the cultures they study.

RUTH FINNEGAN

See also: discourse, language and linguistics, aesthetics, art, folklore, oral literature, ethnography, postmodernism, reflexivity

Further reading

Atkinson, P. (1990) *The Ethnographic Imagination: Textual Constructions of Reality*, London: Routledge

Brady, I. (ed.) (1991) *Anthropological Poetics*, Savage MD: Rowman and Littlefield

Clifford, J. and G.E. Marcus (eds) (1986) *Writing Culture: The Poetics and Politics of Ethnography*, Berkeley: University of California Press

Feld, S. (1982) *Sound and Sentiment: Birds, Weeping, Poetics, and Song in Kaluli Expression*, Philadelphia: University of Pennsylvania Press (new edn 1990)

Finnegan, R. (1992) *Oral Traditions and the Verbal Arts. A Guide to Research Practices*, ASA Research Methods Series, London: Routledge

Hymes, D.H. (1981) *'In Vain I Tried to Tell You': Essays in Native American Ethnopoetics*, Philadelphia: University of Pennsylvania Press

Sanjek, R.(1991) 'The Ethnographic Present', *Man* 26: 609-28

Sherzer, J. (1990) *Verbal Art in San Blas*, Cambridge: Cambridge University Press

Spencer, J. (1989) 'Anthropology as a Kind of Writing', *Man* 24: 145-64

Tedlock, D. (1983) *The Spoken Word and the Work of Interpretation*, Philadelphia: University of Pennsylvania Press

Van Maanen, J. (1988) *Tales of the Field: On Writing Ethnography*, Chicago and London: University of Chicago Press

political anthropology

Political anthropology has proved to be a late and comparatively short-lived subfield specialization within social and cultural anthropology. Between 1940 and the mid-1960s a generation of political anthropologists was exceptionally cohesive, establishing a canon and setting out a programme for the subfield. But, apart from that short period, anthropology's definition of politics and its political content has invariably been so broadly defined that politics may be found everywhere, underlying almost all the discipline's concerns during its nearly one-hundred-year professional history. In 1950, political scientist David Easton criticized political anthropologists for viewing politics simply as a matter of power relationships and inequality; today anthropology's sensitivity to the pervasiveness of *power and the political is considered one of its strengths.

The objective world fashions political anthropology as much as anthropology constructs and reconstructs the world in which its practitioners find themselves (Vincent 1990). The anthropology of politics can be narrated in terms of an intellectual history framed first by British cultural †hegemony over an anglophone imperial world

and then by United States cultural hegemony over a *world-system dominated by Cold War concerns. A critical turning point in the subdiscipline came with the decline of empire and American defeat in the war in Vietnam. These two events marked, for many scholars, a shift from *modernity to *postmodernity.

Three phases may be recognized in anthropology's relationship with politics. In the first formative era (1879–1939) anthropologists studied politics almost incidentally to their other interests, and we can speak only of 'the anthropology of politics'. In the second phase (1940–66) political anthropology developed a body of systematically-structured knowledge and a self-conscious discourse. The third phase began in the mid-1960s when all such disciplinary specialization came under severe challenge.

As new paradigms challenged the earlier dominating, coercive systems of knowledge, political anthropology was first decentred and then deconstructed. The political turn taken by geography, social history, literary criticism and, above all, feminism, revitalized anthropology's concern with power and powerlessness. The writing of non-Western scholars in these fields was particularly influential. Anthropologists concerned with things political began to read †Edward Said as keenly as they read †Evans-Pritchard and found the work of Homi Bhabha as challenging as that of †Victor Turner.

A recognition that anthropologists must review critically their own intellectual equipment and the politics of its production led to a renewed interest in the material and intellectual history of the texts that constituted political anthropology as a subfield.

The evolution of political society

The first professional studies of political organization were carried out among Native American peoples by the Smithsonian Institution's †Bureau of American Ethnology, established in 1879. By this time the reservation system was in place and questions of law and order, as well as problems of Indian development, were high on the agenda of the US government. Bureau publications provided three kinds of political ethnography: (1) somewhat idealized reconstructions of pre-reservation political society; (2) reports of observed tribal organization and legal practice; and (3) documentary accounts of government-Indian treaty relations. †Herbert Spencer and *Lewis Henry Morgan provided the conceptual underpinning for many Bureau studies; long periods of field research provided the ethnographic substance. Exceptional for its narrative method was James Mooney's account of the *ghost dance movement and its suppression by the United States military in 1890.

Morgan's *The League of the Ho-de-ne-sau-nee, or Iroquois* (1851) has been pronounced the first political ethnography. In delineating the political organization of the Iroquois confederacy in relation to its social, ritual and economic aspects this work established a form that later became standard. It was, however, Morgan's later volume *Ancient Society* (1877) that established *evolutionary theory as the bedrock of political studies. His title reflected Morgan's affinity for the work of †Sir Henry Maine, whose *Ancient Law* was published in 1861. Yet their approaches to political evolution differed quite markedly. Maine was concerned with the evolution of law and his studies of classical Roman law and village communities East and West were designed in accordance with philological rather than sociological methods. His research was imbued with a concern for †controlled comparison and transformations rather than with organic societal evolution. Morgan, on the other hand, followed †Montesquieu in projecting the evolution of societies through the three stages of †savagery, †barbarism and †civilization. He envisaged progress from †clan organization to the establishment of political society on the basis of territory and *property.

An interest in the evolution of civilization and the *state continues within European and American anthropology to this day, often closely linked with *archaeology and *museum research. The terminology of savagery, barbarism, and civilization has given way to that of egalitarian tribes, ranked and stratified societies, providing a neo-evolutionist taxonomy which is pervasive in American college textbooks. Among British and French scholars evolutionary terminology was replaced by a binary recognition of primitive (or simple, small-scale) and advanced (or *complex) societies.

In the early twentieth century, evolutionary schemata were used to order the ·mass of ethnographic data that was being 'collected' among so-called simpler peoples around the globe. Ethnologists, *missionaries, travellers and administrators had responded avidly ever since the first issue of †*Notes and Queries on Anthropology* was published in 1874.

The most ambitious use of evolutionary schemata was made by L.T. Hobhouse, G.C. Wheeler and M. Ginsberg in their *The Material Culture and Social Institutions of the Simpler Peoples* (1915). Here the four-stage theory of the eighteenth-century Scottish political economists provided for a more detailed classification than the three-stage projection of Morgan. The authors (two sociologists and an anthropologist) attempted to correlate statistically government, economics, justice, *war and *social structure among some 600 of the world's peoples. Several features of this work became standard in political anthropology as it developed: (1) the sociological *comparative method; which required (2) closed units of analysis (in the form of *'societies' or 'tribes'); and encouraged (3) tendencies towards †primitivism (and less attention being paid to 'ancient' societies or civilizations such as that of *Islam); (4) Material cultural differences between *hunters and gatherers, *pastoralists and †agriculturalists (subdivided into higher and lower where necessary) provided the economic base on which other social, political and religious domains rested. *Functionalist holism (i.e. a conceptualization of homogeneous, integrated societies) thus embedded political institutions within closed analytical units.

The anthropology of politics in colonial settings

At the end of the nineteenth century most anthropologists carried out field research in imperial and quasi-imperial settings. Europeans consolidated their colonial territories throughout Africa, the Middle East and Oceania. The United States acquired territory from a defeated imperial Spain in the Caribbean, Hawaii and the Philippines and also began to evince interest in China, West Africa and Latin America. Their national and transnational connections provided anthropology with its *fieldwork settings as the twentieth century progressed, yet few ethnographies explicitly took *colonialism into account. Later the construction of the colonial 'other' entered political anthropology, first in the work of North African writers on the colonial experience and then more generally in critiques of anthropology and imperialism.

Roy Franklin Barton's multifaceted monographs on Ifugao *law, society, economy and religion, published between 1919 and 1930, reflect the modern ethnographer's goal of providing a rounded description of the way of life of a 'native' people at a particular moment in time. For many, a distinction between society and politics was meaningless. Barton's work was distinctive in that he saw the Ifugao, a mountain people among whom he worked in the northern Philippines, as interacting *individuals. Barton wrote *Ifugao Law* (1919) at the request of the American government. Its categorization of law was orthodox (looking like something out of a law school textbook) but his long residence in the village of Kiangan and his familiarity with his Ifugao neighbours render his case materials a rich source of political ethnography. Barton's classic monograph was a pioneer study in the anthropology of law, but a shift within functional anthropology towards the study of †social control rather than law led to it being unjustly neglected. Yet, for those who consider *Malinowski's landmark *Crime and Custom in Savage Society* (1926) 'one of the reddest herrings ever dragged into the working of orderly jurisprudence', as Paul Bohannan put it, or for those who like a little sex and a lot of economics in their ethnographies, Barton is one of the most grounded practitioners in the business of political anthropology.

He was also a somewhat atypical American. At this time most work in the anthropology of politics was being done by the students of *Franz Boas among *Native North Americans either on reservations or, in the western states, in small clusters of habitation scattered among Euro-American settlers. Political reconstructions of tribal organization continued to be the order of the day along with studies of *diffusion and *classification. By the 1920s a peculiarly American social science had emerged within the academy which divided those who traced continuities with European history from those who argued that it was unlikely that American society would develop along European lines. The presence of Native Americans and the role of the frontier supported notions of what came to be called 'American exceptionalism'. The divide was reflected within anthropology between those who specialized in describing particular tribal polities (such as the Crow, Hidatsa, Zuni and so on, each with its own university-based anthropologist) and those who retained a larger vision of Native Americans as conquered peoples, examining their place within a larger historical scheme of things.

The work of William Christie MacLeod falls into the latter category. His book *The American Indian Frontier* (1928) was not well received by the social science-oriented anthropologists of the time

in either Britain or the United States. A study of encounters between Native Americans and Europeans and their respective political and economic interests, it was subsequently taken up in the 1950s when political anthropology in the United States again took on a historical stance.

In general, throughout the colonial and quasi-colonial period, practical differences in surveillance, control and the administration of 'native' peoples, as well as their very different histories encouraged marked regionalization in anthropology and the adoption of particularistic frameworks for political analysis. Thus one found a selective focus on *Big Men in New Guinea, lineages and *descent in Africa and war in North America, for example, in spite of the fact that Big Men, lineages and war could be said to be found in all three places.

The 'clash of cultures'

The interests of capital were not invariably aligned alongside those of empire. Political change and potential trouble spots were matters of concern to business interests overseas. On both sides of the Atlantic, the anthropology of politics followed the money trail. The Social Science Research Council funded †Robert Redfield's fieldwork in Tepoztlan in Mexico, for example, and the Rockefeller Foundation sponsored the study of †culture-contact by Malinowski's students in Africa.

Funding agencies and scholars alike must have been somewhat disappointed with the results. Although Mexico had been colonized by Spain, and although Bolsheviks fought in the streets of Tepoztlan while Redfield was there, he returned with a paradigm for the study of timeless folk societies. His critics introduced *feudalism, *peasantry and rural proletarians into anthropology. The culture-contact studies proved almost equally fruitless for the development of political anthropology. An exception was †Monica Hunter's fine *Reaction to Conquest: Effects of Contact with Europeans on the Pondo of South Africa* (1936) but, like MacLeod's earlier historical narrative of contact situations in North America, this too was not well received within the academy.

No paradigm held more potential for the study of political change than that of culture-contact, but so engrained were the †synchronic and holistic principles of functional analysis that *methodology dominated the discourse rather than political relations and political change. Its timing was unfortunate, too. After the war (1939–46) a rather different, more orthodox, political anthropology emerged to capture the field. This focused not on political contact and change but on the structure of government and the systemic nature of political organization.

Systems theory in political anthropology (1940–53)

The real impetus to political anthropology came when British †structural-functionalism confronted large African centralized states, functioning as units of †indirect rule. These were more akin to the monarchies and republics of Europe than the small-scale communities or †aboriginal societies to which political anthropologists had become accustomed. Structural-functionalists operated with a classically simple dichotomy between states and stateless (or †acephalous) societies, with an absent-minded nod towards †bands.

The major work of this era, *African Political Systems* (1940), was a collection of eight essays edited by †Meyer Fortes and †E.E. Evans-Pritchard whose own structural analyses of the Tallensi and Nuer became classics in the field. The book was sharply criticized by a few Africanists and many American anthropologists for being unnecessarily limited in scope, obsessed with lineage systems and kinship polities, neglecting history, stressing the primitive at the expense of the complex, serving colonial administration, neglecting forebears, neglecting other social sciences and being gratuitously critical of political science. Structural-functionalism provided anthropology with a model for the comparative study of political systems, some of its concepts even being applied, albeit critically, to newly pacified highland New Guinea peoples in *Melanesia. Momentarily it provided an alternative to the historically-oriented *political economy approach to the analysis of Native American political organization. For the next two decades in African political ethnography, the taxonomy of *African Political Systems* was elaborated to include village councils, †age grades, †secret societies and the like.

Structural-functionalism's constitutional approach focused on political institutions, offices, rights, duties and rules. Little or no attention was paid to individual initiatives, strategies, processes, struggles for power or political change. †Edmund Leach's *Political Systems of Highland Burma* (1954) provided an internal critique of the systems paradigm, offering in its place the existence of political alternatives with change coming about through individual and group decision-making. Crucially, Leach suggested that individuals' choices are the result of conscious or unconscious power-seeking. Leach took this to be a universal human trait.

Process and action theory (1954–66)

Largely in response to other social sciences as they began to undertake field research in newly independent Third World nations, political anthropology set out to establish a distinctive agenda for itself. Rejecting constitutional reconstruction and the earlier typological trend, as well as political scientists' characterization of their role as being restricted to delineating the traditional and the local, anthropologists began to study interstitial, supplementary and parallel political structures and their relation to formal power. The politics of *ethnicity and of elites in new nations encouraged a focus on social movements, leadership and competition. Historically immersed in field situations of rapid institutional change, anthropologists constructed their political analyses around contradictions, competition and conflict.

†Action theory (later called †agency or †practice theory) provided the subfield's dominant paradigm. Political ethnographers, such as Bailey and Boissevain, studied individual actors, strategies and decision-making in political arenas. Related paradigms such as †transactionalism, †game theory, and †symbolic interactionism also embraced politics. A new spatial and processual vocabulary began to replace the systems vocabulary: field, context, arena, threshold, phase and movement emerged as keywords. Critical to this paradigmatic shift was Victor Turner's richly detailed ethnography of schism among the Ndembu of Northern Rhodesia (now Zambia) and his hand in writing a long expository introduction to a challenging new set of essays, *Political Anthropology* (1966). In this volume, politics was defined as 'the processes involved in determining and implementing public goals and in the differential achievement and use of power by the members of the group concerned with these goals' (Swartz, Turner and Tuden 1966: 7).

Much of the impetus for the new political analysis drew on the work of †Max Gluckman and his colleagues and students, first at the †Rhodes-Livingstone Institute in Central Africa and later at Manchester University. Among them were Africanists Barnes, Mitchell, and Epstein, Bailey (India) and Frankenberg (Britain). Bailey's trilogy on Indian politics, published between 1957 and 1963 was a *tour de force* within the genre. His political ethnography followed the action from the village (*Caste and the Economic Frontier*, 1957) through the district level to national electoral politics.

Postmodernity, anthropology and politics

The modern social science era of political anthropology came to an end in the late 1960s when new concerns and new voices entered the discipline. By this time six paradigms had emerged and co-existed successfully within the subfield: neo-evolutionism, cultural historical theory, political economy, *structuralism, action theory and processual theory.

In the context of Third World political struggles, decolonization and the recognition of new nations, a mounting critique of new forms of imperialism and neo-imperialism (sometimes called economic imperialism) confronted the sub field. The Vietnam War (1965–73) was the catalyst for Kathleen Gough who spoke out (literally, in a radio broadcast from California) calling for the anthropological study of imperialism, revolutions and counter-revolutions. Talal Asad's *Anthropology and the Colonial Encounter* (1973) launched critical analysis of the problematic relationship of anthropology to British colonialism. †Pierre Bourdieu used the vast legacy of French colonial scholarship to examine descriptive accounts for systematic relations, seeing what was left out, reading the silences in more orthodox Algerian ethnography.

Political economy again came to the fore with one of its more radical forms, *Marxism, gaining ground in the analysis of Third World politics. A new revisionist †structural Marxism directed attention to political forms ranging from the *household and lineage to the colonial and postcolonial worlds of uneven exchange, dependency and underdevelopment. Much of this analysis was contributed by scholars working in francophone North and West Africa but, given the range of its subject matter, the paradigm quickly spread.

It was not uncontested. Reaction stimulated another of anthropology's recurrent moves towards history. Intellectual rapprochement with historiographic British Marxism, and particularly the work of E. P. Thompson, reinforced political anthropology's engagement with agency and process. A parallel concern centred around peasant *resistance, labour movements and crises in *capitalism in Africa and Latin America (Cooper, Isaacman, Mallon, Roseberry and Stern

1993). Neglect of historical conditions, *class and competing interests in what was called in this paradigm (following Wallerstein) the periphery of the modern world system drew some criticism. One of the most exciting trends was developed by historians of *South Asia under the rubric †'Subaltern Studies'. Historians along with anthropologists and literary critics began to dismantle the sub continent's imperial historiography in an attempt to recover the political activities of subordinated groups. The leading anthropological voice was that of Bernard Cohn, whose studies of power relations in colonial India stimulated the anthropology of politics into further rethinking imperialism, *nationalism, peasant insurgency, class and *gender. The invention of tradition became a resonant theme as did the imposition of colonial rule and the transformation of the political economy. Historical explanations began to replace those of the sociologist and economist in the new anthropology of politics.

The relative salience of global and local politics divided political economy from interpretive theory. The former was characterized as Eurocentric, the latter as apolitical; practitioners of both denied these charges. Eric Wolf's *Europe and the People without History* (1982) became the key text of global, historical political economy; †Geertz's *Local Knowledge* (1983) asserted the interpretive paradigm with a particularly strong (and long) chapter on fact and law in comparative perspective. An attempt was made to reintroduce practice theory but a trend towards history in both camps rendered this reversion to social science methodology a non-starter.

State politics, hegemony and resistance

Political anthropology inclined more towards the study of past colonialisms the more it became difficult or unpleasant to do field research in states where political insecurity, civil war, *violence and terror had become commonplace. Studies of such situations did indeed appear along with specific critiques of state power and its abuse, but political anthropologists more generally contributed localized and particularistic tales of resistance and accommodation, challenge and riposte. Micropolitical resistance to the state has been discerned in †counter-hegemonic oral histories, folk tales, *cargo cults, drum festivals, and women's illnesses to name just a few ethnographic case studies.

Resistance became a key concept, even to the extent of being romanticized and overused, a reflection, perhaps, of an uncritical adoption of notions of hegemony from †Gramsci and †Raymond Williams. Hegemony has been ethnographically located in exhibitions, commemorations and monumentalism, felicitously bringing *property notions and †material culture back into political anthropology. Anthropological play with the notion of hegemony succeeded its longstanding concern with order (derived from †Durkheim and *Radcliffe-Brown) since it captures what is, in effect, the *struggle* for order.

Critique

A distinguishing hallmark of postmodernity is critique and a major critical thrust in postmodern anthropology was directed towards re-examining its intellectual equipment. Political anthropology was not slow to point out the effects of its virtual obliteration of *imperialism* and *colonialism* as critical sites of ethnographic investigation. *Time and space, which once provided introductory settings and closing frames in political ethnographies, were 're-viewed' by postmodernists as constructed, controlled, and transformed features of political design. Edward Said's discussion of *Orientalism heightened anthropology's established concern with the politics and ethics of representation, particularly the representation of subordinated peoples. Anthropologists received his work critically, making the point that neither the discourses of Western imperialism nor the voices of subject peoples were as monolithic, localized, and unchanging as he suggested.

The literary turn in anthropology that attention to Said's thesis reflected had several positive repercussions. It introduced into the sub field a *'poetics and politics trope' that succeeded in combining interpretive anthropology and political economy. Controlled comparative studies of Fiji-Samoa-Hawaii, for example, inspired by †Marshall Sahlins's work but moving critically beyond it, showed how 'symbolic capital', for example, might be a mechanism of state power and authority or a mechanism of insubordination and irredentism. †Praxis, history and political economy were interpellated to determine whether at any one time in any one place the political agenda of the nation was being enriched or undermined. The poetics and politics trope thus opened up a new analytic space for a political anthropology of symbolic action (Comaroff and Comaroff 1993).

Conclusion

A concern with the mechanics of power and the relation of power to knowledge (derived primarily from the writings of †Michel Foucault) halted the involution of disciplinary and subfield specialization in its tracks. Within the anthropology of politics, a new post-Foucaultian micro-political paradigm emerged (Ferguson 1990) at the same time as global transdisciplinary movements – subaltern studies, black studies, and feminist studies – made familiar concepts such as power, history, culture and class problematic.

The political context in which fieldwork is done, the politics involved in constructing and reproducing political anthropology's canon, and critical assessments of the political agendas of the discipline all feature on the postmodern agenda. Foucault's connections between disciplines, knowledge and relations of authority, along with counter-Foucauldian treatises, mark the return of politics to the heartland of intellectual debate. After a century in which the concepts of society and *culture have predominated even within the subfield of political anthropology, this is a change indeed.

JOAN VINCENT

See also: colonialism, factions, kingship, law, Marxism and anthropology, political economy, power, resistance, state, violence, war

Further reading

Asad, T. (ed.) (1973) *Anthropology and the Colonial Encounter*, London: Ithaca Press

Bailey, F. (1980) *Stratagems and Spoils: A Social Anthropology of Politics*, Oxford: Basil Blackwell

Comaroff, Jean and John Comaroff (eds) (1993) *Modernity and its Malcontents: Ritual and Power in Postcolonial Africa*, Chicago: University of Chicago Press

Cooper, F., A. Isaacman, F. Mallon, W. Roseberry and S. Stern (1993) *Confronting Historical Paradigms: Peasants, Labor, and the Capitalist World System in Africa and Latin America*, Madison: University of Wisconsin Press

Dirks, N., G. Eley and S. Ortner (eds) (1993) *Culture/Power/History*, Princeton: Princeton University Press

Ferguson, J. (1990) *The Anti-politics Machine: 'Development', Depoliticization, and Bureaucratic Power in Lesotho*, Cambridge: Cambridge University Press

Fortes, M. and E.E. Evans-Pritchard (eds) (1940) *African Political Systems*, Oxford: Oxford University Press

Foucault, M. (1980) *Power/Knowledge: Selected Interviews and Other Writings 1972–1977*, Colin Gordon (ed.), Brighton: The Harvester Press

Leach, E. (1954) *Political Systems of Highland Burma: A Study of Kachin Social Structure*, London: Bell & Sons

Swartz, M., V. Turner and A. Tuden (eds) (1966) *Political Anthropology*, Chicago: Aldine

Vincent, J. (1990) *Anthropology and Politics: Visions, Traditions and Trends*, Tucson: University of Arizona Press

political economy

Discourse on anthropological political economy provides several overlapping genealogies (Roseberry 1988; Vincent 1990; Moore 1993). All agree, however, that the juxtaposition of 'political' with 'economy' came with the invention of the concept of *capitalism by eighteenth-century ideologues such as James Steuart: what 'economy' was in a family, political economy was in a *state. Nation-states became actors in a worldwide drama. Thus political economists considered as a single project, for example, the colonization of India, the rise of the textile industry in Britain, and the status of Egypt within what they called the cosmopolitical economy.

Bifurcation set in early in the development of political economy as scholars began to question whether the state *ought* to act as paterfamilias. Increasingly the moral and governmental aspects of political economy were set aside and a separate discipline, economics, came into existence. In opposition to the classical focus on the *market and *consumption, popular political economists developed theories of *property and labour. Based on experience with expanding industrial capitalism, they argued that capitalism did not simply adjust to, but positively required, crisis. The term political economy was thus revitalized and transformed into a rallying point for those critical of rampant capitalism.

Several features of classical and popular political economy have been assimilated into anthropology. When, in *Ancient Society* (1877), *Lewis Henry Morgan deplored what he called the property career of mankind, †Engels suggested that Morgan's ethnology validated †Karl Marx's critique of capitalism. The idea that what was thought of as 'natural' – the family, the difference between men and women, women's work, for example – was interlinked and connected with the political economy of the society and the existence of the state, did not gain wide circulation until the 1970s when feminism began to contribute critically to anthropological political economy.

Nineteenth-century German economists and historians developed a substantive critique of British political economy, questioning its focus on *homo oeconomicus*. Arguing the inapplicability of the British model of capitalism to agrarian Germany, they focused instead on cultural otherness. This, too, entered anthropology when political economists within the discipline began to question even more broadly whether neoclassical economics could be applied to non-Western, non-capitalist societies. This was taken up initially as a *formalist-substantivist debate between economic historians and anthropologists and was later revived in connection with *modernization theory and the analysis of capitalism's impact on the non-Western world.

Anthropological political economy enters the mainstream

Anthropological political economy entered the academic mainstream in the 1970s. At that time two paradigms prevailed in the social sciences: the *development and †underdevelopment paradigm that emerged to challenge modernization theory, particularly in its focus on newly independent Third World nations; and the modern *world-system model of sociologist Immanuel Wallerstein. Anthropological political economy defined itself in contradistinction to both.

It would be unrealistic not to relate the emergence of these paradigms to the historical events of these years. Politically, in the Third World, this was an age of advocacy of armed revolution: Mao Tse-tung, Ho Chi Minh, Castro, Regis Debray, Che Guevara, Fanon. *Peasant revolutions were clearly the order of the day rather than social science analyses of nation states. The work that most influenced anthropology was that of Samir Amin, Arrighi and Rodney in Africa; and Andre Gunder Frank and Cardoso in Latin America. Eric Wolf's *Peasant Wars* appeared in 1969.

The term 'political economy' became widely used in anthropology during the Vietnam War (1965–73). Teach-in movements in the universities, radical political economic and history journals and a campus movement, Students for a Democratic Society, spearheaded the emergence in the United States of a New Left. The critical thrust of these radical movements was applied to society at home, to the university system, and to anthropology itself in the United States, Britain and France. Critiques of structural anthropology's representation of African societies, with its emphasis on *kinship and its neglect of political economy, appeared in re-evaluations by Kathleen Gough, Peter Worsley and Talal Asad of classic ethnographies. These seminal studies stimulated more explicit discussion of the theories of political economy and their application in Third World countries, by Joel Migdon in Indonesia, for example, and Keith Hart in Africa. An entire cadre of French Marxist anthropologists and Africanists – among them Godelier, Meillassoux, Terray and Coquery-Vidrovitch – became prominent exponents of economic anthropology worldwide. With the emergence of a new group of radical Left scholars within the American academy, *Marxism became academically respectable. Propagation by American publishers of the work of European Marxists led to the sequential introduction to anthropology of Lenin, †Gramsci, and †Althusser. Africanists, for example, drew on Lenin's thesis of the uneven development of the capitalist economy in agrarian societies and emergent rural differentiation, documenting the increasing pauperization of the mass of the people in Africa's so-called 'development decade'. Marxist theories of †petty commodity production were criticized by anthropologists, stimulating valuable historical ethnographies of petty commodity production in, for example, Minangkabau in *Southeast Asia (Kahn 1980) and the Peruvian Andes in *Highland South America (Smith 1989).

An intellectual connection with Marxism has, at different times and in different places, both strengthened and undermined anthropological political economy. Yet, when political economy came of age in academic anthropology in 1978 in a special issue of *American Ethnologist*, it was apparent that there was no one unifying vision or discourse among its self-proclaimed practitioners. Thus when Wolf published a †subaltern alternative to prevailing paradigms of expanding western capitalism, *Europe and the People without History* (1982), his book was subjected to keen debate among anthropological political economists, historians and social scientists. Criticisms of the paradigm it offered both consolidated anthropological political economy and moved it forward.

Anthropological political economy and its critics

In the tradition of both classical and popular political economy (of which Marxism is a variant) internal critiques have shaped and reshaped the

†metanarratives of anthropological political economy. By the end of the 1980s, it could no longer be said that anthropological political economy was no more than a simple-minded representation of *Enlightenment thinking and that it was not political enough. Always attentive to history, anthropological political economy had achieved much of its coherence through analyses of colonial capitalism and economic imperialism, initially in a critique of ethnographic representation of non-Western societies and cultures, but subsequently as a genre in its own right. It is currently taking up the challenge of feminist and post-colonial theory with a somewhat belated recognition that historically specific determinations of *gender, *race, and *class come into conflict with one another. Anthropological political economists studying colonial and post-colonial capitalism in Africa, Latin America and Oceania have thus begun to delineate numerous capitalisms.

That political economy did not analyse the structures and history of non-Western communities penetrated by capitalism and that it appeared unwilling to incorporate *culture into its analyses were more problematic matters. At issue is the historical tension between ethnographic particularism (local knowledge) and universalizing social theory. Jane Schneider's many essays on complex European 'cultural codes' exemplify political economy's resolution at its best. With their enigmatic titles – 'Peacocks and Penguins', 'Trousseau as Treasure', 'Rumpelstiltskin's Bargain' – they consistently blend culture, *ideology, symbolism and *folklore with historical materialism. They interpret and explain at the same time: why peasant women wore black clothes; why embroidery was valued in peasant Europe and what has taken its place today; why weaving cloth was viewed with suspicion. Status emulation, class formation, demographic change, female *purity, the seclusion of women and †dowry systems as liquid wealth in regional spheres of exchange are all linked in her analysis of the changing social topography of *Central and *Southern Europe.

The peripheral situation

The end of modernism in anthropology brought no resolution to the problem of employing universalistic analytic categories. What it did bring was a more explicit application of Marxism. The question in anthropological political economy remained one of the relationship between capitalism and those societies conceptually located on its periphery. Was capitalism to be understood as a single world-system or as a heterogeneous assemblage of subsystems which Western capitalism had penetrated to varying degrees?

For such peripheral situations, Michael Taussig's *The Devil and Commodity Fetishism* (1980) and Jacques Chevalier's *Civilization and the Stolen Gift* (1982) provided key texts for a clear formulation of the issues involved. Both provided ethnographies of communities in highland South America. Chevalier found non-capitalist modes of production to be subsumed within the dominant framework of capitalism. Taussig described a cultural system that had internalized the contradictions of capitalism in several different ways but most notably through beliefs in 'the devil' as an indigenous critique of commodity forms of exchange and wage relations.

In a critical review of the two books Terence Turner urged appreciation not simply of the possible integration of two systems of economic production but of the qualitative differences that might be attached to defining and articulating production itself. With absorption into capitalism, †indigenous peoples lost the ability to define themselves in their own way. Turner thus argued for moving beyond the analysis of economic production to †social reproduction. This raised the question of whether on the periphery subsistence might *not* simply be an alternative *mode of production to capitalism but a form of *resistance to it.

Analyses of such relations in the historically earlier peripheries of Northeast Scotland and colonial Africa had suggested that developing industrial capitalism required a peasant subsistence sector so that the costs of reproduction might be borne by the agrarian sector as both food resources and labour power. The South American peripheral situations suggested the very real need in anthropology to distinguish more precisely between †mercantile, industrial and finance capitalism.

Discussion of the peripheral situation opened up space beyond the debate between those who saw capitalism as largely determinate of local social systems and those asserting the relative autonomy of local peoples and their cultures. Appreciating that the periphery of capitalism is but the furthest extension of the core (Nugent 1988) is not unrelated to the growing corpus of political economic research carried out in modern

Western cities and within the apparatus of the modern state. Thus anthropological political economy provides ethnographies of race in the inner cities, educational discrimination, poverty and the underclass. It has sometimes questioned the validity of sociological paradigms and, indeed, the very way in which phenomena have been defined as problems within *complex societies. The current challenge of anthropological political economy is to interrogate its own intellectual equipment.

Conclusion

Anthropology's engagement with political economy reflects its somewhat ambivalent role within the social sciences. Anthropologists tend to put forward alternative and even oppositional analyses to those offered by the other social science disciplines. The endurance of political economy owes much to its emergence within capitalism as a discourse on crisis. New theoretical movements in anthropology tend to define themselves in contradistinction to political economy's long intellectual career. Thus †interpretive anthropology attempts to set the logic of political economy against the autonomy of culture just as *postmodernism attempts to decentre political economy by labelling it modern (in its attention to capitalism and class) and canonical (by virtue of its historically-situated intellectual origins). Ironically, that which appears most characteristic of postmodernism – fragmentation and the diffusion of *power – is to the political economist a further indication of capitalism's success in masking its hegemonic powers.

JOAN VINCENT

See also: economic anthropology, Marxism and anthropology, political anthropology

Further reading

Chevalier, J. (1982) *Civilization and the Stolen Gift: Capital, Kin and Cult in Eastern Peru*, Toronto: University of Toronto Press

Kahn, J. (1980) *Minangkabau Social Formations: Indonesian Peasants and the World-economy*, Cambridge: Cambridge University Press

Moore, J. (1993) *The Political Economy of North American Indians*, Norman and London: University of Oklahoma Press

Nugent, S. (1988) 'The "Peripheral Situation"', *Annual Review of Anthropology* 17: 79–98.

Roseberry, W. (1988) 'Political Economy', *Annual Review of Anthropology* 17: 161–85

Smith, G. (1989) *Livelihood and Resistance. Peasants and the Politics of Land in Peru*, Berkeley: University of California Press

Taussig, M. (1980) *The Devil and Commodity Fetishism in Latin America*, Chapel Hill, NC: University of North Carolina Press

Turner, T. (1986) 'Production, Exploitation and Social Consciousness in the "Peripheral Situation"', *Social Analysis* 19: 91–115

Vincent, J. (1990) *Anthropology and Politics: Visions, Traditions and Trends*, Tucson: University of Arizona Press

Wolf, E. (1969) *Peasant Wars of the Twentieth Century*, New York: Harper and Row

—— (1982) *Europe and the People without History*, Berkeley: University of California Press

pollution and purity

Every human society subscribes to ideas of human purity and pollution in some form. Certain agents, activities, contracts, periods and substances are known to pollute, while others purify. Pollution, as opposed to purity, disturbs equilibrium, destroys or confuses desirable boundaries and states, and engenders destructive natural forces or conditions. Though also of much significance to modern temper (e.g. as in *food, medicine and *environment), purity, pollution and *taboo are anthropologically well documented for widely different societies (e.g. the Dogon, the Western Pueblo Hopi, the Samoan, and the Bedouin). All major religions (e.g. *Hinduism, Judaism, *Buddhism, *Christianity and *Islam) also variously elaborate on matters of sin, taboo, pollution and purity.

The sacred and 'magical uncleanness'

The early sociological studies of †William Robertson Smith ([1889] 1927) distinguished states and rules of holiness (purity) from those of 'magical' uncleanness, pollution or taboo. With the social reflecting the desirable *sacred, societies continually tried to separate and protect themselves from the dangerous profane by suitable rituals. †James Frazer ([1890] 1955), who compiled wide-ranging supportive evidence on the magical powers of contagion in 'primitive thinking' observed that confusion between holiness and pollution often led to dangerous or anomalous consequences.

Next came the important work of †Durkheim ([1912] 1954), the founder of modern *sociology, who showed how the sacred reflected the *sui generis* social. His study examined diverse religious belief and ritual systems in 'primitive societies'. Echoing Robertson Smith, Durkheim also saw a distinct social need in different societies to protect their fragile religious sacred from the surrounding (and threatening) profane, often by elaborate *magical injunctions (the precursors of modern medicine). With tendencies in each to invade the other, the sacred and profane for Durkheim had to be carefully demarcated, separated and contained by suitable interdictions.

Pollution as danger to social order

But these early studies retained a significant 'us' versus 'them' cultural polarity. They evaluated other human cultures largely by applying European standards of cultural *evolution and progress. Besides, there still was no scheme for clearly organising and explaining the baffling diversity in rules and practices on purity, pollution and taboo in different cultures (Steiner 1956). The definition, organization and meanings of the religious pure and impure (*vis-à-vis* the sacred and profane) remained unclear under certain situations, particularly in conditions which fell outside the religious domains and were called either 'non-sacred', 'non-profane', or 'secular'.

A distinct breakthrough on such issues came with †Mary Douglas's works (particularly 1966). Relying on the Durkheimian conceptions of social order and social cohesion, she examined the underlying structures and meanings guiding diverse cultural beliefs, rules and practices of purity and pollution. With examples from both simple and complex societies, she showed how purity stands for (and stresses a recognition of) clear boundaries and orders, while pollution invites unwanted ambiguity, confusion, and disorder. Societies related pollution to their moral values, with rites and practices aimed at reducing risk and danger to their people. And they devised ways of clearly demarcating, ordering and controlling sources of pollution, with the overall goal to protect their social and cosmological orders.

In this way, as she argued in *Purity and Danger*, pollution helped explain rules and practices found in 'primitive worlds' as well as complex civilisations. Her explanations concerned the sacred and the secular, the inner and the outer, and the physical and the symbolic. Also, notions of 'dirt', hygiene, uncleanness, and symbolic representations of the human *body occupied the centre stage to explain how – and why – different peoples treat contaminated foods, bodily fluids, secretions, excretions, remainders, and refuse. Similarly, Douglas explicated how societies handle what the human in nature finds impure, abnormal, anomalous and frightening (e.g. earthquakes, floods, eclipses and disasters).

Ritual purity and pollution in *South Asia

Several anthropological studies of Indian *castes and religions contribute to our subject at this point. For, as †Dumont remarked, 'what can India teach us chiefly, if not precisely the meaning of pure and impure?' (1980: xxxix). Since India ranks its thousands of castes by placing the ritually purest Brahman at the top and the Untouchable at the bottom, its contributions are in some ways distinct and instructive. After World War II, especially with the advent of intensive *fieldwork, a host of modern systematic accounts of castes and villages appeared from different parts of India, elaborating 'lived rules' and practices on purity and pollution.

However, Louis Dumont (1980) soon succeeded with his striking 'structural explanation' of the Indian caste system, arguing that ritual purity/pollution is *the* fundamental †binary opposition organising the traditional Indian (mainly Hindu) †hierarchy, society and power structure. Here the ritual status of the Brahman encompasses the 'temporal authority' of Kshatriya rulers. This unique value configuration made, he insisted, India's ideology traditional, holistic, and ahistorical, while the modern West emphasized history, *individualism and secular power.

Dumont's studies prompted a wave of close examinations of Indian ideals, texts, terminologies, rules, and practices surrounding purity and pollution. Some yielded 'taxonomies' and 'grammars' of Hindu pollution, distinguishing, for instance, 'timed pollution' (e.g. at birth and *death) from those 'internal' and 'external', which came from either a polluting action (e.g. killing) or an object (bodily secretions, excretions, refuse). But the focus of these studies slowly moved from functions of purity and impurity to those of wider social order and meanings. Not unlike Douglas, India also recognised connections between ritual purity and matters of hygiene and sanitation (Khare 1962).

The next development crystallised when McKim Marriott criticized Dumont's dualist approach to caste ranking and developed his distinct †'ethnosociology' of India (1989). In a series of exercises, he controverted Dumont's

dualist view of India, showing that the Hindu world is constructed by multiple transactions of †substances and their 'markings' rather than by the ideological opposition between purity and impurity. Marriott's 'transactional' markers are 'fluid' rather than binary, stressing the 'joining' and 'flow' of constituent substances like blood, foods, humours, interactions, residues and dispositions along with the Hindu alchemy of intrinsic 'heating' and 'cooling' in persons, groups and physical surroundings.

The auspicious and the inauspicious

At the same time there appeared a number of studies critically examining the comparative ritual status (and changing positions) of renouncers, kings, and women within both classical and popular Hinduism. These considerably widened the cultural ground in which to place the issue of purity and pollution in Hindu India, and showed some clear limitations in Dumont's binary approach to pure and impure. For example, there appeared the need to understand the crucial role of concurrently occurring notions of auspiciousness (*subha* or *mangala*) and inauspiciousness (*asubha* or *amangla*) in foods, gifts, events, rites, and gods (Carman and Marglin 1985; Khare 1976). Auspiciousness here was not just a synonym for purity, and inauspiciousness for impurity. Instead, the auspicious and the inauspicious signified meanings, ambiance, and goals which purity and impurity did not represent. Besides, they also criticised the caste hierarchical order. Unlike Dumont's dependence on the binary pure/impure opposition, later investigators found the four categories working in tandem, by context and cultural purpose. The meanings and messages thus reached explained more and better across the flow of time, events, persons, and contexts.

During the 1970s and 1980s anthropologists investigated more puzzles which purity, auspiciousness and defilement (under different combinations, and in different strengths) produced within Indian society. For instance, if there is an anomalous god Shiva (sometimes pure but inauspicious, and sometimes impure and auspicious), we also encounter degraded and inauspicious Brahmans, impure but auspicious low servicing castes (e.g. washerwomen or *dhobin* in the north), and the polluting and inauspicious (eclipse-causing) planets Rahu and Ketu. Similarly, those practices which produce anomalous relations across purity, rank, power, and inauspiciousness have long remained a puzzle. For example, consider the issue of meat-eating Brahmans *vis-à-vis* 'purer' vegetarianism; the nature of divine 'left overs' or 'blessed foods' (*prasad*); and the impurity or inauspiciousness removing persons and gifts (Babb 1975; Parry 1980; Raheja 1988).

New directions

Further work on pollution and purity might concern the issues of modern society and its conflicts and antagonistic politics. For instance, in many colonial and †postcolonial societies, a study of the politics of '†subalterns' increasingly opens the rules of purity and pollution to political interpretations of domination and control. Some subaltern historiographers and anthropologists have detected sacred and non-sacred power conflicts hidden behind the 'traditional rules' of caste and purity and pollution. Thus both the 'elitist historiography' as well as the 'anthropology of order' must be criticised for their blind spots. Others detect a distinct trace of the 'colonial knowledge' in 'documenting' and 'representing' many of those castes, rules and rituals with which anthropologists start their inquiry.

Mary Douglas and Wildavsky (1982), to date, however, show best how the politics of pollution, social risk and national borders interrelate in a modern society. They find 'abuse of technology' as a potent source of environmental 'pollution' in modern America, risking economic prosperity, stable political and power boundaries, and a rise in crime. But the risk perception in all forms of pollution, the authors argue, still remains culturally conceived and socially ordered, a vindication of anthropological insights. America thus tends to skew its risks from environmental pollution according to the way it conceives of its own cultural centre, borders and frontiers.

R.S. KHARE

See also: taboo, food, ritual, caste, Hinduism, Asia: South, classification, menstruation

Further reading

Babb, L. (1975) *The Divine Hierarchy*, New York: Columbia University Press

Carman, J.B. and F.A. Marglin (eds) (1985) *Purity and Auspiciousness in Indian Society*, Leiden: Brill

Douglas, M. (1966) *Purity and Danger*, London: Routledge

Douglas, M. and A. Wildavsky (1982) *Risk and Culture*, Berkeley: University of Califronia Press

Dumont, L. ([1966] 1980) *Homo Hierarchicus*, Chicago: University of Chicago Press

Durkheim, E. ([1912] 1954) *Elementary Forms of the Religious Life*, New York: Macmillan

Frazer, J. ([1890] 1955) *The Golden Bough* (abridged edn), New York: St Martins

Khare, R.S. (1962) 'Ritual Rules of Purity and Pollution in Relation to Domestic Sanitation', *Eastern Anthropologist* 15: 125–39

—— (1976) *The Hindu Hearth and Home*, Delhi: Vikas

Marriott, M. (1989) 'Constructing an Indian Sociology', *Contributions to Indian Sociology* (n.s.) 23: 1–39

Parry, J. (1980) 'Ghosts, Greed and Sin: The Occupational Identity of the Benares Funeral Priests', *Man* (n.s.), 15: 88–111

Raheja, G.G. (1988) *The Poison in the Gift*, Chicago: University of Chicago Press

Smith, W.R. ([1927] 1889) *Lectures on the Religion of the Semites* (3rd edn), New York: Macmillan

Steiner, F. (1956) *Taboo*, New York: Philosophical Library

possession

The term 'possession' has been applied to Africa, the African diaspora (especially Brazil and the Caribbean), the Middle East, the Pacific, and sometimes South and Southeast Asia in contexts in which humans are said to be temporarily displaced, inhabited, or ridden by particular spirits. During these often highly framed episodes, voice and †agency are attributed to the spirit rather than the host; the host is not held accountable for what occurs and indeed may claim subsequently to have no knowledge of it, or at least no ability to have influenced its direction. The spirits are generally conceptualized and experienced as discrete persons, whether *ancestors, foreigners, historical figures, gods or members of an alternate species. These persons may be viewed as more or less distinct from their hosts according to the particular performance tradition at issue as well as the stage the relationship between an individual host and spirit has reached.

Some commonly recognized cultural forms (which may cover a range of local variations) include *Zar* (Northeast Africa), *Bori* (Hausa), *Vodou* (Haiti), and *Umbanda* and *Candomblé* (Brazil). While some writers have sought to clarify differences between possession and *shamanism (a term generally applied in Asia and indigenous America), a categorical distinction does not appear to be useful and much of the South and East Asian material can be framed in the same general terms as the African. Nor does it make sense to firmly distinguish possession as a sociological type from other instances in which people find themselves subject, in varying degrees, to the influence of disembodied external powers. The choice of whether to exorcize a demon or assimilate a spirit generally represents less a distinction of kind than a local politics of religion as well as an informed reading of the immediate social context and personal circumstances of the particular host.

Spirit possession has long exercised the anthropological imagination. This may be, in part, because it is itself an imaginative construction. Indeed in many instances possession forms a sort of unrationalized counterpart to anthropology itself, whereby what is foreign or distant is appropriated, framed, inspected and used for local reflection. The main difference is that while anthropological knowledge is objectified, rationalized and reproduced in textual form (such as this encyclopedia), spirit possession is embodied, reproduced in the bodies of human hosts. The presence of spirits is made manifest in episodes of illness, dissociation, *dreams and *taboos, as well as in performances in which the spirits may dress in their own clothing, eat their own foods, speak in their own voices and generally display behaviour which contrasts with that of their human hosts. Spirit possession thus occurs in the real time of human life and is experienced as an impingement upon it.

Spirit possession forms a complex and exciting subject for anthropological analysis for two main reasons. First, it combines both an order of collective thought in the distinctions among the spirits as a semiotic system (*myth, *totemism) and an order of collective practice (*ritual, therapy, oracles) whereby hosts are initiated, particular voices are legitimated, and spirits are provided with the spaces in which to perform. Possession thus provides a context in which contemporary experience can be actively mediated by past myth models and vice versa. Second, it provides an instance in which the collective and personal clearly interpenetrate. Collective forms are internalized by individuals and become self-transforming. Likewise, individual intentions are externalized and given form through the voices and acts of the spirits and the careers of their hosts (Obeyesekere 1981). Performances of possession therefore have a degree of unpredictability that many other kinds of rituals lack. Possession raises fascinating questions of agency and accountability for participants and anthropologists alike.

Performance and the play of agency

If we take seriously the idea of spirits and possession as imaginative phenomena, it follows there is no single essence that underlies them. Hence reductive attempts to explain particular local practices as simple expressions of illness, hysteria, or relative deprivation (Lewis 1971) have been replaced by more nuanced forms of understanding. To the degree that possession is embodied, it constitutes a specific performance. Performances may be comic or dramatic, suspenseful or gay, establish hierarchies or invert them. They make use of music, dance, distinct clothing, and unusual speech patterns and body movements. Different features may be highlighted in different performance traditions but one of the most striking will be the evident discrepancy between the features of the host as a recognized member of the community and the transformation that overlays them as she is possessed by the spirit. Possession may be linked to broader ritual cycles or political processes. It may be displayed before a crowd, restricted to privileged audiences, or embedded in *kinship relations. Some of the most significant episodes of possession may take place in private settings among intimates (Lambek 1981).

As mimetic forms and practices that are always also skewed, altered, distorted versions of their original objects (Taussig 1993), spirits are often taken to represent 'Difference' itself, an 'other' world against which the quotidian is set off and from which it can be reflected upon. In precolonial times the salient difference often depended heavily upon imagery drawn from nature. The critical gap that spirit possession established and mediated may have been, as *Lévi-Strauss had it, that between *nature and culture. At the same time, the spirits also drew upon signs of social otherness or cultural distance. Since the colonial period, the salient opposition has often shifted to what might be called culture : superculture (local: global). Possession attempts to think through or capture the relationship between indigenous forms of authority, *power and practice and those manifestly stronger, external ones, often exemplified by the seductiveness of foreign commodities. Since the object of †mimesis is almost always conceived of as very powerful, an interpretation of possession must address questions of †hegemony and *resistance (Comaroff 1985). Moreover, since power is not merely represented but addressed, possession is almost certain to be at least implicitly a discourse on morality (Boddy 1989, Lambek 1981). As a mimesis of power and a discourse on morality, possession is attuned to contemporary circumstances. Frequently bringing the authority of the past to bear on the present, it is also highly flexible and ready to change.

If spirits are imagined, they may become like works of art that, in turn, seize our imaginations, overwhelm, and captivate us with their power, interest, beauty or sublimity. They may, indeed, 'possess' us. Drawing on the classic analysis of †Godfrey Lienhardt (1961), Kramer (1993) makes a strong case for treating possession as *passiones*, a term that has dropped out of ordinary usage but means something like the opposite of action. Kramer delineates African 'spirits' as the images of *passiones* embodied in people and shrines. To be possessed is to be 'carried away'. Kramer argues, however, that modernity ultimately locates agency within the self, replacing cosmology with psychology, passion with action. Devotion to the other has been lost and our links to the external, but intrinsically interconnected world have been reconstituted as internal qualities of mind. This broad discursive transformation may be partially responsible for the spirits' withdrawal to the shadows, in some parts of the world, although it cannot explain their persistence and even expansion in others.

There is a significant difference between possession and such captivating aesthetic forms as poetry or film that enfold us in their worlds. Possession demands to be taken literally; the displacement is marked. Possession is an embodied phenomenon, manifesting itself in physical pain, spiritual trauma, anxiety, hyperconvulsive behaviour, temporary and partial amnesia. It invites a therapeutic response, one that usually requires addressing the spirit as a distinct entity from the sufferer, from the one impassioned. Social recognition is granted to the displacement of agency. But this means that out of passion stems a course of action.

Any viable institution of possession must retain the social means to render its spirits 'real'. Naturalization (*vraisemblablisation*) develops from the fact that negotiation between the host and spirit is a public, social event. Possession takes place in the presence of at least a third party, a therapist, mediator, spectator or, if the spirit's appearance in the host is already well authorized, a client. The existence of the spirit is corroborated through public witnessing of the embodied

transformation of the host, legitimated through collaboration in dialogue with the spirit, and, subsequent to the possession episode, by the actions and statements of the host who must exhibit competence at shifting frames. The performative constitution of the spirits as distinct persons is mystified to the participants so that they come to understand themselves as simply 'meeting' entities whose existence is independent of such acknowledgement (Lambek 1981).

The difference between disembodied and embodied spirits is one of focus. *Bodies provide the vehicle by means of which spirits can be held in focus, as it were; through which they can be sustained in steady communication and from which they can be expected to respond. These are not necessarily the effects of radically different belief systems, but of weaker and stronger forms of collective authorizing. The more the *passio* is understood as an external, even autonomous entity, the less need there will be for recourse to a psychological discourse. But this in turn is enabling of greater agency.

The nature and transformations of agency are apparent when possession is understood as a system of communication, providing alternative, authoritative voices and critical distance, but also anti-language and ambiguity (Boddy 1989), and the possibility for the simultaneous transmission of opposed messages (Lambek 1981). As Besnier (1996) demonstrates, possession is truly †heteroglossic.

Selfhood and therapy

To the degree that spirits are embodied, they are lived through and with, and to this extent also they impinge on the selfhood of their hosts. Boddy (1989) describes how possession expands culturally overdetermined selfhood for Northern Sudanese women. Kapferer (1991) examines the unmaking and remaking of the self during the conduct of specific rituals in Sri Lanka, while authors in Crapanzano and Garrison (1977), and Obeyesekere (1981) drawing on *psychoanalysis, view possession from biographical perspectives. However this need not be understood pathologically; possession implies weakly bounded egos, but not necessarily weak egos *per se*. Moreover possession can be a vehicle for the growth of psychological insight or maturity. Once again, the emphasis on passion needs to be complemented by noting the agency, especially moral agency, and †dialogical qualities of spirits and hosts (Lambek 1993).

Spirits are often associated with trauma and healing. As such, possession is full of moral references and contextualized by accountability narratives. A diagnosis of possession may provide an entrée into therapy or a rationalization for its inadequacy. But at times illness is simply an idiom of possession, one of its embodied, †indexical qualities that contributes to the legitimation of spirits as autonomous entities and marks their arrival in human bodies as independent of the wills of their hosts. Some of the possessed may become therapists or oracular voices in their turn. To perform as a medium requires psychological insight and social savvy as well as the capacities for empathy, context shifting and making full use of the communicative properties of possession.

There is a great deal of excellent work on possession from many parts of the world. Boddy (1994) provides an extensive bibliography.

MICHAEL LAMBEK

See also: body, cosmology, divination, person, religion, shamanism

Further reading

Besnier, N. (1996) 'Heteroglossic Discourses on Nukulaelae Spirits', in J. Mageo and A. Howard (eds) *Spirits in Culture, History and Mind*, London: Routledge

Boddy, J. (1989) *Wombs and Alien Spirits: Women, Men and the Zar Cult in Northern Sudan*, Madison: University of Wisconsin Press

—— (1994) 'Spirit Possession Revisited: Beyond Instrumentality', *Annual Review of Anthropology* 21: 407–34

Comaroff, J. (1985) *Body of Power, Spirit of Resistance*, Chicago: University of Chicago Press

Crapanzano, V. and V. Garrison (eds) (1977) *Case Studies in Spirit Possession*, New York: Wiley

Kapferer, B. (1991) *A Celebration of Demons: Exorcism and Healing in Sri Lanka*, Washington: Smithsonian Press

Kramer, F. (1993) *The Red Fez: Art and Spirit Possession in Africa*, London: Verso

Lambek, M. (1981) *Human Spirits: A Cultural Account of Trance in Mayotte*, New York: Cambridge University Press

—— (1993) *Knowledge and Practice in Mayotte*, Toronto: University of Toronto Press

Lewis, I.M. (1971) *Ecstatic Religion: A Study of Shamanism and Spirit Possession*, Harmondsworth: Penguin

Lienhardt, G. (1961) *Divinity and Experience: The Religion of the Dinka*, Oxford: Clarendon Press

Obeyesekere, G. (1981) *Medusa's Hair: An Essay on Personal Symbols and Religious Experience*, Chicago: University of Chicago Press

Taussig, M. (1993) *Mimesis and Alterity: A Particular History of the Senses*, New York: Routledge

postmodernism

The development of postmodernism in anthropology since the early 1980s has provided a major focus of debate and commentary. While few anthropologists as such have been regarded as seminal in the larger postmodernist field, anthropology in general has been viewed as a particularly sympathetic arena of the human sciences within which to pursue the postmodernist agenda, especially with regard to issues of 'otherness', critiques of the programmes of the *Enlightenment and elaborations of the notion of *culture. Postmodernism has been incorporated in anthropological discourse, yet a 'postmodern anthropology' is still inchoate, represented more by critiques of traditional disciplinary shortcomings (and critiques of such critiques) than by a new kind of anthropological praxis (although there is a growing corpus of 'postmodernist ethnography'; see Marcus 1992).

By some accounts, postmodern anthropology is the culmination of a series of internal critiques (e.g. feminist anthropology, †structural-Marxism, *ethnoscience) which – however germane – failed to confront with sufficient *reflexivity the dilemmas of a field torn between affiliation to the Enlightenment project (science, *rationalism, universalism) and affiliation to the diverse constituencies represented in the ethnographic record (Clifford in Clifford and Marcus 1986; di Leonardo 1991). According to this view, a postmodernist critique represents an overdue – and swingeing – reassessment of anthropology *tout court*, one in which the filtering of exotic otherness through the constructions of social theory is exposed as a literary excursion disguised as scientific reportage. By this reading, anthropology is a representational genre rather than a clearly bounded scientific domain and the rise of postmodernism in general has made possible a more critical self-awareness in the field without necessarily effecting more wide-reaching transformations.

While the postmodern shift in anthropology is part of a larger tendency in cultural criticism, a number of specifically anthropological antecedents are widely cited – the interpretive (†Clifford Geertz) and symbolic (†David Schneider) approaches, for example – approaches whose continuity from pre-postmodern to postmodern phases both validates a traditional anti-scientific strain within anthropology and also – uncomfortably – subverts the idea of 'postparadigm' break. Similarly, issues of *reflexivity and political positioning raised in critiques of *colonialism and *Orientalism are no less compelling for having laid down markers before postmodernism came to be viewed as a decisive break.

While there is acknowledgement of some precursors, citation is selective: the contribution of *Lévi-Strauss (especially with regard to *The Savage Mind*) is slighted, and the so-called 'rationality' debate – which could lay strong claim to having mapped the philosophical parameters of postmodernism within anthropology – is rarely invoked. Significantly, the most unapologetically postmodernist anthropological position is occupied by a major contributor to the now largely discarded ethnoscience approach of the late 1960s, Stephen Tyler.

Part of the reason for the differential visibility of anthropological postmodernist antecedents is – paradoxically, given the frequent claims for a postmodernist *Zeitgeist* – that within the national traditions mainly represented in the debates – French, British, US – the relationship between anthropology and cultural criticism in general varies significantly. In the US, anthropological postmodernism has been directly implicated in national debates about multiculturalism and the 'Western civilization' canon; in France, the anthropological contribution – filtered through *structuralism and poststructuralism – has been largely overshadowed by explicitly literary and philosophical debates (although anthropology does not go unmentioned; cf. Lyotard 1984); in Britain, postmodernist debate has fallen within the fiefdoms of social theory and *cultural studies. As a result, postmodernism as a pan-anthropological phenomenon is internally differentiated, the different terms of reference being shaped not by anthropology itself, but by its varying roles in national cultural traditions.

The literature

Writing Culture (Clifford and Marcus 1986) was a benchmark publication indicating several possible trajectories for a postmodernist (or critical) anthropology. A major theme in the collection is that anthropology has moved (or should move) from the espousal of scientific ethnography to the study of ethnographic texts themselves. According to Marcus and Fischer (1986) this shift is not only in accord with general tendencies toward a 'reassess-

ment of dominant ideas across the human sciences' (1986: 7) (the so-called 'postparadigm'), but in the specific case of anthropology, the shift marks an increasing preoccupation with issues of contextualization and reflexivity in the face of the declining coherence of †metanarrative and grand theory. Where anthropological approaches significantly part company with the general tendencies of 'postparadigm' cultural criticism is in the continued affiliation with peoples and traditions outside the 'Western' nexus. The tension generated by anthropology's dual allegiance has thwarted a hegemonic postmodern outlook: if the field were to relinquish 'the other' in the name of a Baudrillardian 'implosion of the the hyperreal' it would have little role to play, except as provider of ethnographic detail.

Marcus and Fischer (1986) and Clifford (1988) also outline the possibilities of a postmodern anthropology and confirm not only the view of the maturing of the expressive qualities of anthropological writing, but also that postmodernism is a synthesis of previous critical postures constrained by their misguided adherence to the certainty of the notion of explanation. Significantly, in a recent collection Marcus (1992) explicitly situates these new tendencies within anthropology as openings into the field of cultural studies.

Postmodernist ethnography

A relatively small number of ethnographies are frequently cited as informed by a postmodernist sensibility (Taussig, Crapanzano, Shostak, Rabinow etc.), yet as Pool has observed (1991), the claims made for an experimental, postmodernist ethnography are often so broad as to include many 'traditional' ethnographies (from *The Nuer* to *Naven*). Pratt (in Clifford and Marcus 1986) has drawn attention to the traditional use of literary devices in ethnographic writing drawing particular attention to the restricted use of narrative, a failing which is directly addressed in the 'experimental' emphasis on polyvocality. Taussig's *Shamanism, Colonialism and the Wild Man* (1987) is among the most celebrated efforts so far, but while invoking the anti-aesthetic markers of a literary postmodernism, he also displays a strong interest in questions of history which are quite in keeping with pre-postmodernist, critical traditions (see Fabian 1983).

Critiques of postmodernist ethnography have largely focused on the way in which attention has shifted from examination of the power relations according to which 'the other' has been constructed, to examination of the rhetorical devices and preoccupations of ethnographers themselves (Polier and Roseberry 1989; Sangren 1988; Spencer 1989). In keeping with this shift toward the examination of anthropological discourse itself, ethnographic attention has also shifted to a new arena, namely cultural domains in the centre (cf. Marcus 1992). The work of members of the Birmingham Centre for Cultural Studies has been particularly influential in this regard, especially that of Paul Willis and Dick Hebdige.

The future of postmodernism in anthropology

Given the strong continuities between pre-postmodern critical anthropology and postmodern anthropology, it could be argued that the 'post-paradigm' shift is more imagined than real. The most intense arena of debate, for example, concerning the central (or perhaps only heightened) role of postmodernism in anthropology, is a traditional one: the status of economic and political determinants of anthropological discourse. The critiques of ultra-relativism within postmodern tendencies are similar to those levelled against 'value-free' social science decades ago (cf. Hymes 1969) and underscore the political agnosticism which has characterized debates about texts wrenched free from their socio-historical determinants.

In other ways, however, postmodernism in anthropology has established an institutional base which ensures the durability of debates about postmodernism for some time to come. The journal *Cultural Anthropology* is both 'the property of a long-established "professional society" (the AAA)' (Marcus 1992: ix), and also part of a new constituency represented by such like-minded (if not necessarily anthropological) journals as *Representations*, *Semiotext(e)* and *Cultural Critique*. At the macro-level, the programmatic claims for a new kind of anthropology are emboldened by the nascent field of cultural studies, one which in many ways represents a shift away from the ethnography of exotic others (the historical role of anthropology) to the ethnography of adjacent others (the lumpen and marginal in the core). In this light, postmodernism in anthropology does not merely provide a new theoretical focus in the linear development of the field, but may also be perceived as a threat of larger dimensions, with both traditional and critical concerns of the field gradually dismantled in the name of finding a position in the intellectual division of labour of the 'postmodern cultural condition'.

Unlike other fields in which postmodernist discussions have set the pace in recent years, anthropological postmodernism has laboured under a distinctive tension, namely that between the ethnographic texts and the *fieldwork experiences upon which those texts are based. The strategies according to which the truth of texts is endlessly negotiable – in certain literary versions of poststructuralism and postmodernism, for example – are to some degree blocked by an anthropological praxis in which the (most often disguised) naivety of fieldwork has entailed at least a nod toward a 'truthful' rendition in the resulting ethnographic texts.

STEPHEN NUGENT

See also: ethnography, reflexivity, symbolic anthropology

Further reading

Clifford, J. (1988) *The Predicament of Culture: Twentieth-Century Ethnography, Literature and Art*, Cambridge, MA: Harvard University Press
Clifford, J. and G. Marcus (eds) (1986) *Writing Culture: The Poetics and Politics of Culture*, Berkeley: University of California Press
Derrida, J. (1974) *Of Grammatology*, Baltimore: Johns Hopkins University Press
di Leonardo, M. (ed) (1991) *Gender at the Crossroads of Knowledge: Feminist Anthropology in the Postmodern Era*, Berkeley, Los Angeles and London: University of California Press
Fabian, J. (1983) *Time and the Other: How Anthropology Makes Its Object*, New York: Columbia University Press
Hymes, D. (ed) (1969) *Reinventing Anthropology*, New York: Vintage
Jameson, F. (1990) *Postmodernism or the Cultural Logic of Late Capitalism*, Durham, NC: Duke University Press
Lyotard, J.-F. (1984) *The Postmodern Condition: A Report on Knowledge*, Minneapolis: University of Minnesota Press
Marcus, G. (ed.) (1992) *Rereading Cultural Anthropology*, Durham, NC: Duke University Press
Marcus, G. and M. Fischer (eds) (1986) *Anthropology as Cultural Critique: An Experimental Moment in the Human Sciences*, Chicago: University of Chicago Press
Polier, N. and W. Roseberry (1989) 'Tristes Tropes: Postmodern Anthropologists Encounter the Other and Discover Themselves', *Economy and Society* 18: 245–64
Sangren, S. (1988) 'Rhetoric and the Authority of Ethography: 'Postmodernism' and the Social Reproduction of Texts', *Current Anthropology* 29, 3: 405–35

Spencer, J. (1989) 'Anthropology as a Kind of Writing', *Man* 24: 145–64

Taussig, M. (1987) *Shamanism, Colonialism and the Wild Man: A Study in Terror and Healing*, Chicago: University of Chicago Press

potlatch

A potlatch is a gift-giving ceremony as practised on the Northwest Coast of North America, in societies such as Kwakiutl, Tlingit, Haida and Chinook. It was recorded by numerous ethnographers, including *Franz Boas, and has been re-analysed by others in more recent times. The term is also employed in a looser sense for ceremonies in other parts of the world, such as *Melanesia, where feasting and gift-giving practices are similar to those of the Northwest Coast Indians.

From an ecological-functional perspective, the instability of resources in the Northwest Coast (including salmon and wild plants) made redistribution desirable – from those with resources in any given season to those who lacked them. People who accumulated sufficient resources to hold a feast could do so, and even barter away food beforehand in order to acquire other goods to give. Kin would assist their kin, and commoners their chiefs, in building up the necessary stockpile of goods to give away. The gift-giving was ostentatious. By giving, the donor showed off his wealth and reaffirmed his social position. Accepting †gifts was a mark of recognizing the superior status of the donor.

Typical occasions when potlatches were held included births and deaths, initiations into secret societies, and weddings. They were also held at the death of a chief (when his successor would hold one in order to assert his authority and influence), after a public embarrassment (as a face-saving device) and simply when one kin group acquired enough wealth to give it away. The potlatch system was highly competitive; it depended on rivalry between powerful individuals as well as on the principle that the donor is morally superior to the recipient.

The institution reached its most elaborate form among the Kwakiutl from 1849 to 1925. What had been gift-giving evolved into the wilful destruction of wealth. Those who could afford to burn blankets in front of their rivals, for example, not only showed off their higher status; they denied their rivals the potential for acquiring the goods for themselves. Government authorities eventually banned the practice, but potlatches of a more benign nature continue today: Northwest Coast Indians still use this Chinook word to describe feasts held, for example, at weddings, where cash give-aways keep alive the spirit of the potlatch system.

The potlatch is a classic example of an economic institution embedded in a wider social structure. For this reason, it is often used by †substantivist economic anthropologists to show the impossibility of analysing *exchange divorced from its social context. It was important for †Marcel Mauss ([1925]1990) for much the same reason: it illustrates well his notions that society functions to redistribute material resources, that there is in cases like potlatch societies a 'totality' made up of gift-exchange and its wider context, and consequently that 'gifts' are never really free.

ALAN BARNARD

See also: Americas: Native North, economic anthropology, exchange, formalism and substantivism

Further reading

Drucker, P. and R. Heizer (1967) *To Make My Name Good: A Re-examination of the Southern Kwakiutl Potlatch*, Berkeley: University of California Press

Mauss, M. ([1925]1990) *The Gift: The Form and Reason for Exchange in Archaic Societies* (trans. by W.D. Halls), London: Routledge

Rosman, A. and P. Rubel (1971) *Feasting With Mine Enemy: Rank and Exchange among Northwest Coast Societies*, New York: Columbia University Press

power

Power has been defined in a great variety of ways by anthropologists, ranging from physical domination to symbolic empowerment. Of course, for there to be talk of power at all, anthropologists must be speaking of distinctions: either between an *individual and a group, as in the power legitimized through acknowledged, often redistributive, leadership; or one group and another group, as in *colonial domination; or between humans and their *environmental energy sources, as in the power of a collectivity to organize and maintain itself. Social and *political anthropologists have theorized about forms of social organization in non-state and *state societies which legitimize the power of specific †lineages, *classes, or individuals to make decisions pertaining to others' lives and the organization of social and material resources. Conflict theorists have studied *factionalism and how claims to power are asserted and contested. *Resistance theorists have studied more closely the ways in which those who seek to dominate others through the use of language, *ritual, and force, are resisted by those seeking self-determination or, in turn, domination also. A study of power implies not only a study of social distinctions but also of the *inequalities implied in those distinctions – whether one is following †Marx in thinking about the extraction of surplus labour or more recent theorists of the inequalities embedded in *racial and *gender distinctions. Power has been thought of by anthropologists as human influence and †agency, and even as – reflecting various world views – situated outside humanity (see, for example, the cross-cultural notions of power described in Fogelson and Adams 1977). Attention to power goes in tandem with attention to power-lessness, although not all theories of power are binary.

While most anthropological analyses of power have investigated social stratification and †hierarchy, some have looked at forms of social organization which assure that power is not individually concentrated, as in the industrial collectives or collectives not organized within state societies. Just as Marx was preoccupied with the question of how labourers came to give up their labour power, anthropologists have studied historically, and prehistorically, the question of how individuals might have come to dominate groups and how one group might have come to dominate another. *Archaeological theorizing of inequality has been accompanied with method-ological innovations in studying relational power over time (McGuire and Paynter 1991). Social theorists †Max Weber and †Émile Durkheim influenced anthropological conceptualization of bureaucratic power in state societies and the perpetuation of institutional authority. Anthro-pological studies of social movements and state-making, and of national policy, have furthered conceptualization of institutional power and the rituals of its replication. *Legal anthro-pologists, too, have studied cross-culturally the different systems through which power is legit-imized, enforced, and contested.

Anthropologists undertaking studies of institu-tional power must engage the debates formulated

within *sociology about structure and agency. C. Wright Mills (1956) argued influentially that social stratification and hierarchy are forcefully maintained by the 'power elite', those who, between themselves, mobilize the power to tran-scend 'ordinary' social environments and make decisions that pertain to the lives of people they will never meet, in nations they might never visit. This kind of structural analysis can be seen, for example, in anthropological studies of the itinerant power of transnational corporations. Class analysis has been used by anthropologists to study in-equality in many social contexts, not all of them industrialized (see, again, McGuire and Paynter 1991). Anthropologists have also argued that class analysis has its limits, especially in contexts where exploitation is multidirectional, and have been drawn to reformulations of historical materialism, as in Giddens's theory of structuration – in which 'power is regarded as generated in and through the reproduction of structures of domination' (Giddens 1981: 4), across *time and space, whether those structures of domination rely on the alloca-tion of material resources (as emphasized by Marx) or on, for example, information and surveillance.

The power relations, between nations and between individuals, organized through colonial-ism have been the most important influence, in several ways, on conceptualizing power within anthropology. While colonial political structures gave rise to early anthropological studies of the distribution of power through political systems, they also stimulated a variety of intriguing critiques, led most notably in anthropology by Asad (1973) and those in his collection, *Anthropology and the Colonial Encounter*. Writers outside anthro-pology greatly influenced the way many anthropologists have conceptualized power and powerlessness, whether between colonizers and colonized or within societies as similar power relations, racialized, have been enacted. Colonial and neo-colonial relations between nations became a useful trope for anthropologists seeking to critique institutional power and the discipline of anthropology's epistemological role in perpet-uating institutionalized power relations. Colonial critiques made more obvious, for example, the ways in which 'observers' assigned themselves the power to summarize others' experience (and that power was reinforced through institutional resources and legitimacy), and the 'observed,' as encapsulated in those analyses anyway, were without the power to define themselves or assert autonomy in many other ways. A 'reinvented' or 'decolonized' anthropology was envisioned as work done by anthropologists with diverse ethnic, class, and political *identities on not only traditional topics, but also, as Nader put it (in Hymes 1969), 'studying up': to really learn how those who held institutional power did so, and to use that knowledge to address – rather than simply document – social inequalities.

†Hegemony, the concept of totalizing power (in which the state and/or a popular majority dominate, through every means, 'civil society') articulated by †Gramsci (1971), provided anthropologists with a way to think about pervasive institutionalized power. The *Subaltern Studies* group (Guha and Spivak 1988), worked through a critical deconstruction of colonial historiography to recognize the powerful ways in which colonial subjects had been left without a voice in strategic discussions of their identity, resources, and future. Earlier, as anthropologists in the US and in France rethought the political role of intellectuals in reaction to their nations' protracted war in Vietnam, the concept of hegemony became a way to think about how the state did indeed have agency, through a militarized institutional apparatus, to repress – ideologically, socially, and physically – those citizens who held contradictory views about state actions. That was also a time when, in anthropology, theories of resistance took their cue from political movements.

The social theorist who has most shaped anthropologists' recent discussions of power is †Michel Foucault (1980), although not all those writings influenced by him reproduce Foucault's views of power. In contrast to the binary views of power articulated by so many, whether cast in terms of gendered power relations focusing on patriarchy and those oppressed by it, or domination and resistance, Foucault saw power as being produced and reproduced through constant social interaction, from many different directions. He countered arguments about power as constituted through structural positions between individuals or social classes with arguments about power as being problematic, contested, and requiring constant, disciplined persuasion to convince those construed as powerless of their powerlessness and those construed as powerful of their powerfulness. Although he wrote about institutional sites as important for reproducing power relations, Foucault (1981: 93) described power as 'not an institution, and not a structure; neither is it a

certain strength we are endowed with; it is the name that one attributes to a complex strategical situation in a particular society'. Influenced by Foucault's analysis, Kondo (1990: 307) stated in her ethnography of the crafting of identity in Japan that power is 'creative, coercive, and coextensive with meaning'. A view of power as not simply embedded in structural relations – maintained by force of one kind or another – but also as constituted through language and everyday practice (Bourdieu 1991) engendered many ethnographies exploring the specific, historicized ways in which power has been constructed and challenged in different social contexts (cf. Comaroff 1985). Foucault's work has drawn anthropological attention to the relational aspects of power, with a concentration on the contexts of actions and interpretations, and away from structural control of resources by individuals with fairly static institutional authority. Some critics of Foucault think that attention has strayed, in the late 1980s and 1990s, too far from structural power; some feminist theorists, for example, have argued that Foucault and other writers of *postmodern social criticism have – while meaning to eliminate 'big stories' – replaced binary structural models of power which have been useful for theorizing oppression (especially by those working to understand the social mechanism of their own disempowerment) with a less useful totalizing model of overdetermination (e.g. power is everywhere, thus what social site does one go about working to transform?). They also argue that, once again, the 'powerless' have not been left space, or agency, in the discussion to articulate their own theories of power. (This, of course, has continued to happen despite the actions of any social theorist.)

The historical focus that Foucault brought to his discussion of the disciplining of bodies and minds through hospitals, prisons, courts, and schools, has had its effect in *medical, legal, and *educational anthropology, or at least coincided with trends in these and other areas of anthropological study, as more anthropologists have turned from synchronic ethnographic studies to diachronic discussions of social institutions. For example, Emily Martin's comparative study of birthing practices (1987) demonstrates the institutional ways in which women are empowered or disempowered in relation to control of their own bodies and actions. Anthropologists have been informed, also, by researchers working in sociology and other disciplines on collective – or participatory – research strategies that challenge the epistemological leverage of an 'expert,' whether the researcher or some other person asserting 'legitimate authority' in a social setting, and recentre the 'subjects' of study as those with the power to legitimize research design and documentation.

In addition to studies of power as evidenced in times and sites of *war, where claims to power are forcefully clear, if contradictory, anthropological analyses have increasingly also been focused on the elusive power of transnational capital in determining social relations in various localities and on manifestations of *symbolic power. †Bourdieu (1991: 164) described symbolic power as 'that invisible power which can be exercised only with the complicity of those who do not want to know that they are subject to it or even that they themselves exercise it.' Such a form of power can be studied in such diverse social arenas as the very public scripts of television advertising and the very private rituals of the Ku Klux Klan (Kertzer 1988). Thus, power and its social legitimacy and contestation continue to be puzzled through creatively in anthropological analyses.

ANN E. KINGSOLVER

See also: kingship, political anthropology, violence

Further reading

Asad, T. (ed.) (1973) *Anthropology and the Colonial Encounter*, Atlantic Highlands, NJ: Humanities Press

Bourdieu, P. (1991) *Language and Symbolic Power*, ed. by John B. Thompson, Cambridge: Harvard University Press

Comaroff, J. (1985) *Body of Power, Spirit of Resistance: The Culture and History of a South African People*, Chicago: University of Chicago Press

Fogelson, R.D. and R.N. Adams (eds) (1977) *The Anthropology of Power: Ethnographic Studies from Asia, Oceania, and the New World*, New York: Academic Press

Foucault, M. (1980) *Power/Knowledge: Selected Interviews and Other Writings*, ed. by Colin Gordon, New York: Pantheon Books

—— (1981) *The History of Sexuality, Vol. 1: An Introduction* trans. by R. Hurley, London: Pelican

Giddens, A. (1981) *A Contemporary Critique of Historical Materialism Vol. 1 Power, Property, and the State*, Berkeley: University of California Press

Gramsci, A. (1971) *Selections from the Prison Notebooks of Antonio Gramsci*, (ed.) Quintin Hoare and Geoffrey Nowell Smith, London: Lawrence and Wishart

Guha, R. and G.Ch. Spivak (eds) (1988) *Selected Subaltern Studies*, New York: Oxford University Press

Hymes, D. (ed.) (1969) *Reinventing Anthropology*, New York: Vintage Books

Kertzer, D.I. (1988) *Ritual, Politics, and Power*, New Haven: Yale University Press

Kondo, D. (1990) *Crafting Selves: Power, Gender and Discourses of Identity in a Japanese Workplace*, Chicago: University of chicago Press

Martin, E. (1987) *The Woman in the Body: A Cultural Analysis of Reproduction*, Boston: Beacon Press

McGuire, R.H. and R. Paynter (eds) (1991) *The Archaeology of Inequality*, Oxford: Basil Blackwell

Mills, C. Wright (1956) *The Power Elite*, New York: Oxford University Press

Vincent, J. (1990) *Anthropology and Politics: Visions, Traditions, and Trends*, Tucson: University of Arizona Press

preference and prescription

When individuals or families select spouses, some types of person are ruled out or disapproved of, while others are thought particularly appropriate, either because a preference exists in favour of such *marriages, or because the persons concerned are already related in a particular, prescribed way. Marriage preferences are found in all societies, but prescriptions are confined to those exhibiting what *Lévi-Strauss called †elementary structures of kinship (Lévi-Strauss 1969).

Because many elementary structures involve †cross-cousin marriage, Homans and †Schneider (1955) assumed that Lévi-Strauss was trying to explain the widespread *preference* for marriage among *first* cross-cousins, but †Needham (1962) argued that this was a misunderstanding. Elementary structures are not just unusually strong preferences for marrying specific close relatives, but global systems of classification, whereby prescriptive *relationship terminologies divide up a person's entire *kinship universe into marriageable and non-marriageable categories. The marriageable category may include cross-cousins, but is not limited to them.

In this technical context, therefore, both terms have meanings differing significantly from their dictionary definitions (Needham 1973: 177). With regard to the three aspects of kinship – classification, rules, and behaviour – 'preference' seems to imply the exercise of choice at the level of individual behaviour, while 'prescriptions' ought to be requirements or rules. In fact, however, ethnographers normally take marriage preferences to be customs with some degree of †jural force, whereas prescriptions are now usually seen as classificatory phenomena.

Generation	Parallel		Cross		Age
	Male	Female	Female	Male	
+2					
+1					Senior
+0				attan	
−0			kolundiyal		
−1					Junior
−2					

Figure 5 The structure of the Maravar relationship terminology

South Indian Maravars, for example, are able to classify all their caste fellows – potentially hundreds of thousands of people – according to gender, relative age, generation, and whether their relationship with ego is parallel or cross, as shown in Figure 5 (Good 1981). Only one such category of relative is marriageable. Men marry women classed as *kolundiyal*, junior cross-relatives of their own generation, while women marry *attans*, senior cross-relatives of their own generation. The prescribed categories include relatives on both the †patrilateral and †matrilateral sides, but Maravars also state a preference for men to marry their father's sister's daughter (FZD); i.e. for patrilateral first cross-cousin marriage. This asymmetric preference for one particular close relative therefore distinguishes more precisely among the broad categories of relatives classed as marriageable. However, whereas all Maravar marriages accord with the prescription, for reasons explained below, their stated asymmetric preference is scarcely reflected in their behaviour, since mother's brother's daughter (MBD) marriage is just as common as FZD marriage. This illustrates the important general point that categories, rules and behaviour are – within limits – independent variables (Needham 1973: 174).

In the second edition of his book Lévi-Strauss tried to downplay the distinction between prescription and preference, which he first equated to that between model and reality (1969: xxxiii), then to the difference between †mechanical and statistical models (1969: xxxv). In these mutually inconsistent statements, categories, rules, and behaviour are thoroughly muddled up. Even Needham partly conflated categorical and jural phenomena in his notion of prescriptive *alliance (1973: 176), since alliance is a jural phenomenon rather than a matter of classification. However, the two basic types of alliance structure, symmetric and asymmetric exchange, are indeed often associated with prescriptive terminologies

(Maybury-Lewis 1965: 224). The terminologies are usually differently structured in the two cases (though not necessarily, since categories and rules vary independently), because the former implies direct reciprocity and the latter a distinction between spouse-givers and spouse-takers.

The diagnostic test for distinguishing between preferences and prescriptions is to look at what happens when behaviour does not conform to them (Good 1981). When people marry, their choice of partner conforms to or conflicts with a set of preferential rules having customary or judicial force. (It is better not to speak of 'obeying' or 'disobeying', since rules serve more to criticize or justify behaviour after the event than to coerce people to behave in certain ways; cf. Bourdieu 1977). Violating such rules generates social disapproval or even formal punishment, whose severity depends on how seriously the rule concerned is taken; certain marriages may simply be thought inappropriate to one's status, while others may even be criminal offences. In either case there is no undoing what has taken place; as with any other 'crime', the breach of rules may be forgiven, but cannot be wished away. Prescription, by contrast, is characterized by the existence of an entire category of 'marriageable relatives', so if you marry a previously unrelated person, then of course – since s/he is, *ipso facto*, marriageable – your spouse and in-laws are thenceforth categorized as if s/he had belonged to the marriageable category all along. Crucially, the same thing happens when people marry relatives from a non-marriageable category; that is, their spouses – whom they have married and who are therefore again *ipso facto* marriageable – are reclassified, and so are all their immediate relatives. Every marriage in a prescriptive system thus conforms to that prescription *by definition*, at least in retrospect. The fact that such redefinitions are infrequent in practice does not mean that a prescription is merely an extremely strong rule. Rather, to violate a prescription is to violate a system of classificatory meaning; it is 'hard to think', and for many people actually unthinkable.

In short, then, marriage preferences are jural rules or customs saying that certain types of relative must, should, or could marry, though the sanctions backing them up vary greatly in strength, and the punishments for ignoring them may be correspondingly strong or weak. Marriage prescriptions, on the other hand, arise where the entire kinship universe is divided up into marriageable and non-marriageable categories; and where the terminological relationships between all actual couples and their respective families are defined on the premise that – by definition – people who marry must stand in marriageable categories with respect to one another.

ANTHONY GOOD

See also: alliance, complementary filiation, Crow-Omaha systems, descent, dual organization, kinship, marriage, relationship terminology

Further reading

Barnard, A.J. and A. Good (1984) *Research Practices in the Study of Kinship*, London: Academic Press

Bourdieu, P. (1977) *Outline of a Theory of Practice*, Cambridge: Cambridge University Press

Good, A. (1981) 'Prescription, Preference and Practice: Marriage Patterns among the Kondaiyankottai Maravar of South India', *Man* (n.s.), 16: 108–29

Homans, G.C. and D.M. Schneider (1955) *Marriage, Authority and Final Causes: A Study of Unilateral Cross-cousin Marriage*, Glencoe: Free Press

Lévi-Strauss, C. (1969) *The Elementary Structures of Kinship* (2nd edn), London: Eyre & Spottiswoode

Maybury-Lewis, D.H.P. (1965) 'Prescriptive Marriage Systems', *Southwestern Journal of Anthropology* 21: 207–30

Needham, R. (1962) *Structure and Sentiment*, Chicago: University of Chicago Press

—— (1973) 'Prescription', *Oceania* 42: 166–81

primitive communism

The doctrine of primitive communism represents a fusion of speculative social theory with anthropological understanding. In its classic form it imputes to early, and also some contemporary, primitive societies the complete sharing of economic goods, including food, and a concomitant absence of any private *property. In such a life the distinction between mine and thine has no significance. Sometimes the doctrine is extended beyond economics to sex, it being postulated that a state of †primitive promiscuity used to exist. Under this regime, vestiges of which have survived into modern times, a man mates indiscriminately with the women of his group and a woman with the men; consequently children belong to the mature adults of the group rather than to individual parents. The emergence of separate *families within an original larger and undifferentiated group causes the system to collapse by giving rise to economic and sexual exclusiveness, i.e. to an emphasis on what is mine, not yours.

Associated especially with such names as *Lewis Henry Morgan and †W.H.R. Rivers, the doctrine of primitive communism is a part of their legacy which most modern anthropologists have preferred to forget. It is interesting, however, that *A.R. Radcliffe-Brown (1922) felt its appeal when describing the Andaman Islanders. While land is the only thing they hold in common, all portable property being owned by individuals, a variety of their customs 'result in an approach to communism'. Presents are constantly exchanged; it would be bad manners to refuse a request for an article; practically all food obtained is evenly distributed within the camp; and generosity is not only highly esteemed but 'unremittingly practised by the majority'.

Radcliffe-Brown's guarded acceptance of the ethnographic utility of the concept invites comparison with the more generalizing approach of his contemporary, G. H. L-F. Pitt Rivers (1927). Pitt Rivers admitted the prevalence of 'preconceptions, false analogies, and widely speculative ideas' on the subject of communism, but he wanted to keep the word to denominate a tendency which everywhere exists in inverse proportion to the *individualist tendency. In effect, there is a continuum on which all societies must be placed. At one pole resources are deployed to further the corporate purposes of a *community and to satisfy 'instincts and impulses with which each member of the community is endowed'. At the other pole resources are appropriated by enterprising individuals for 'personal use and gratification'.

Communism, on such a view, is not a state of affairs which has ever existed in its entirety, but nor is it a utopian dream projected on to the past (as by †Friedrich Engels and †Peter Kropotkin) or hoped for in the present or future (as by Kropotkin and some Israeli kibbutzniks). It belongs to a pair of terms which enable us to conceptualize permanent tension within human society. It is therefore as much a tool of moral criticism and political speculation as of social analysis. In the latter capacity its most sustained recent employment has been in debates over Kalahari Bushmen and other hunter-gatherers (Barnard 1993).

KENNETH MADDOCK

See also: evolution and evolutionism

Further reading

Barnard, A. (1993) 'Primitive Communism and Mutual Aid: Kropotkin Visits the Bushmen', in C.M. Hann

(ed.) *Socialism: Ideals, Ideologies and Local Practice*, London: Routledge

Piddington, R. (1950) *An Introduction to Social Anthropology*, vol. 1, Edinburgh: Oliver and Boyd

Pitt Rivers, G.H.L.-F. (1927) *The Clash of Culture and the Contact of Races*, London: George Routledge and Sons

Radcliffe-Brown, A.R. (1922) *The Andaman Islanders*, Cambridge: Cambridge University Press

primitive mentality

The idea of a primitive mentality is closely associated with the French philosopher †Lucien Lévy-Bruhl (1857–1939) who attempted to delineate its attributes (1910, 1922, 1927). Lévy-Bruhl remarked that he became interested in the possibility that modes of thought are not everywhere the same when a colleague at the École Normal Supérieure sent him a translation of the works of ancient Chinese philosophers, a text which he found quite incomprehensible. At the same time Lévy-Bruhl was not convinced by the English anthropologists †Frazer and †Tylor who assumed that the intellect of people everywhere was the same except that some people, 'primitives', were in varying degrees ignorant, and that this accounted for any apparent differences.

A primitive mentality is one side of a simple dualism of which the other side is European ('civilized') mentality. To this extent Lévy-Bruhl was working in a manner common enough at the time, when short cuts were being taken through history by attempting to characterize the development of human society in terms of a movement between dualities such as †mechanical and †organic social solidarity (†Durkheim), †status-based and †contract-based societies (†Maine), †*Gemeinschaft* and *Gesellschaft* (†Tönnies). However, Lévy-Bruhl was less successful in describing his duality of mentalities in positive terms. Primitive mentality was defined negatively, in terms of an absence (rather than the presence) of attributes. Thus, Lévy-Bruhl describes the first characteristic of primitive mentality as 'mystical', but this simply means that primitive people do not make the distinction between the natural and supernatural which is typical of modern thought. The second distingishing feature is that it is pre-logical. But, again, Lévy-Bruhl can only explain this quality by saying that the primitive mentality 'does not tie itself down as our thought does, to the avoidance of contradiction'. Instead a primitive mentality obeys something he called 'the law of participation', which means that thoughts can be joined by connections which having nothing in common with those of our logic. These qualities were inferred by Lévy-Bruhl from ethnographic reports such as, for example, that the Bororo of the Amazon claim to be red parrots, or that among the Asante of Ghana if a husband learns that another man has dreamed of sexual intercourse with his wife then he will sue the dreamer for adultery.

Although Lévy-Bruhl consistently viewed the analysis of primitive mentality as a sociological rather than a psychological task, and emphasized the collective nature of the mentality, deploying such Durkheimian notions as †'collective representations', he did not, unlike Durkheim, relate cognitive structures to social structures. Mentalities, whether primitive or civilized, were autonomous. Moreover, in Lévy-Bruhl's sense of collective, there can be no room for deviants. The idea of a mentality identifies a mode of thought which is absolutely pervasive: that a Bororo might not be a red parrot is therefore inconceivable to the Bororo mind.

The word 'mentality' is also used in a rather weaker sense. Just as a society may have a characteristic style of architecture, of music, of cuisine, and the like, so it is supposed to have a style of thought, a usage which is close to a word such as 'culture'. It is this sense of mentality which French social historians such as Lucien Febvre, Marc Bloch and members of the †*Annales* school intend. It refers to the taken for granted in a particular society, the practical knowledge of its members, rather than to explicit systems of belief and doctrine. But what is being documented, and sometimes invoked to explain a course of events, may merely reflect the different interests of the people of the societies being investigated, and it is not at all obvious that the introduction of a word such as 'mentality' does more than contribute to a distancing of the people from ourselves by importing a suggestion of an alternative mode of thought.

Attempts since Lévy-Bruhl to identify the attributes of a primitive mentality have proved to be equally unsuccessful. For example, Hallpike (1979), like Lévy-Bruhl, took as his point of departure ethnographic reports of concepts of cause, space, *time, *number, self, and then related these to †Piaget's theories of developmental psychology; theories which, as Hallpike notes, were not available to Lévy-Bruhl. Hallpike concluded that the cognitive abilities of six-year-old children, as described by Piaget, are sufficient to understand what people in a primitive society know about, for example, shadows, and therefore probably also describe the attributes of a primitive mentality. However, the validity of Piaget's theories have been questioned within psychology, and research by comparative psychologists among the people whose cultures provide the evidence for Hallpike's account of primitive mentality indicate that this approach is mistaken (Shweder 1982).

As against the notion of a distinct primitive mentality some anthropologists have taken the view that when presenting accounts of the beliefs and experiences of the people of another culture we are not exploring some mysterious primitive mentality but the further potentialities of our own thought and language. This is sometimes taken to mean that attention has to be given to feelings and to imaginative thought as well as to the reflections of the reasoning mind. Anthropologists such as James Fernandez (1986) appeal to an anti-Cartesian tradition in philosophy associated with the work of †Vico, and emphasize the importance of the figurative and the play of †tropes in human understanding, in the way people come to terms with and define their ultimate circumstances. The difficulty here is the danger of deploying Western distinctions between the metaphorical and the literal to describe situations where the same distinctions are not recognized by the people involved. Tylor's enquiring intellectual, but ignorant, primitive is replaced by an anxious symbolist poet.

M.C. JEDREJ

See also: rationality, relativism, cognition

Further reading

Fernandez, J. (1986) *Persuasions and Performances*, Bloomington: Indiana University Press

Hallpike, C. (1979) *The Foundations of Primitive Thought*, Clarendon Press: Oxford

Lévy-Bruhl, L. (1910) *Les fonctions mentales dans les sociétés inférieures*, Paris: Alcan (English translation, 1926, *How Natives Think*)

—— (1922) *La mentalité primitive*, Paris: Alcan (English translation, 1923, *Primitive Mentality*)

—— (1927) *L'âme primitive*, Paris: Alcan (English translation, 1928, *The Soul of the Primitive*)

Lloyd, G.E.R. (1990) *Demystifying Mentalities*, Cambridge: Cambridge University Press

Shweder, R. (1982) 'On Savages and Other Children', *American Anthropologist* 84 (2): 354–66

property

Property was a key subject in the *evolutionist arguments of several of the greatest pioneers of anthropology. For *L.H. Morgan (1877: 6), 'A critical knowledge of the evolution of the idea of property would embody, in some respects, the most remarkable portion of the mental history of mankind'. However, property has been a casualty of increasing specialization in intellectual practice in modern anthropology. It tends to fall between the sub-disciplines of *economic anthropology and the anthropology of *law, and much of the work on property has been polemical: e.g. †Leach's (1961) investigation of whether property relations should take priority over *kinship relations. The true significance of property is precisely that it supplies the necessary link between material economic factors on the one hand and ideal or ideological factors on the other. Understood in this way it could again become a central integrating concept for anthropology.

Following †Morgan (1877), †Engels ([1884] 1972) provided a cogent outline of the role of property in an evolutionist perspective. The decline of communal property and the rise of its antithesis, bourgeois private property, are here associated with the origins of the *state and of *class society. The clarity and radicalism of this vision have been largely lost in the twentieth century, as most anthropologists have worked with shorter time frames or †synchronically. *Malinowski, the main instigator of such approaches, attacked the crude dichotomy between individualist and communal that animated so many studies of colonial *land tenure. His lack of sympathy with communist agendas led him to exaggerate the individualist aspects of Trobriand property rights, and to argue that collective use of tribal land was no different in essence from rival businessmen making common use of the streets of New York. Other *functionalists, notably †Max Gluckman, argued from a rather different perspective that all property relations were ultimately social and political relations. Gluckman revived †Sir Henry Maine's insistence that property be understood as a 'bundle of rights'. He rejected the standard †Notes and Queries definition, which viewed property in terms of the relations of persons to things. Whatever the language in which we convey our sense of ownership, most anthropologists would now agree that rights over things are better understood as rights between people. In Gluckman's terms, 'ownership cannot be absolute, for the critical thing about property is the role that it plays in a nexus of specific relationships' (1965: 45). There is a clear continuity here with the Morgan–Engels critique of bourgeois property relations, though Gluckman was cautious in developing such links (perhaps understandably, given the conservative climate in the subject as it was by now consolidated in universities).

Thus an anthropological analysis must go beyond the formal, legalistic definitions of property rights to penetrate 'real' distributions of rights. Concepts of ownership must be related to ideologies of distribution and sharing, and supplemented by analyses not just of position in the status hierarchy, as emphasized by Gluckman, but of control and *power. Although the subversive potential of this anthropological tradition has been made explicit in some recent Marxist work (Bloch 1975), this potential has not been fully realized. †Jack Goody, paying particularly close attention to the rights of women, is perhaps the only modern researcher to investigate the mechanisms for the 'devolution' of property on a broad comparative basis (1962, 1977). The importance of inheritance practices is now widely recognized for the understanding of agrarian societies, but there has been little anthropological treatment of property in industrial societies. This is regrettable, for the subject has considerable practical as well as theoretical importance. For example, it is argued by some economists that a failure to specify private property relations rigorously lies at the heart of the failure of socialist attempts to organize industrial economies. The current reconstruction of such economies throughout Europe and Asia along capitalist lines provides a unique research opportunity for anthropologists interested in studying the relationships between changes in property relations and changes in productive systems and in *social structure.

Property rights need not, however, be exclusively understood in terms of social relationships concerning material objects. For example, the recent work of Harrison (1990) on prestige economies in Melanesia marks an exciting revival of interest in what †Lowie called 'incorporeal property'. There has been a radical questioning of the concept of property in other recent work, including feminist studies. The Marxist critique of bourgeois property theory does not challenge the basic Western assumption that an individual has property rights in his or her own *person; indeed this is the basis of the labour theory of value. If it is established that persons are quite differently constituted in many non-Western cultures, the comparative value of the property concept may be seriously undermined. But if property is broadly understood to refer to the social organization of rights and entitlements over resources, both physical and intellectual, there is no reason why it cannot regain the central place it used to occupy in anthropological enquiry.

C .M. HANN

See also: law, economic anthropology, land tenure, class, person

Further reading

Bloch, M. (1975) 'Property and the End of Affinity', in M. Bloch (ed.) *Marxist Analyses in Social Anthropology*, London: Malaby Press: 203–28

Engels, F ([1884] 1972) *The Origin of the Family, Private Property and the State*, New York: Pathfinder Press

Gluckman, M. (1965) *Politics, Law and Ritual in Tribal Society*, Oxford: Basil Blackwell

Goody, J.R. (1962) *Death, Property and the Ancestors; A Study of the Mortuary Customs of the LoDagaa of West Africa*, Stanford, CA: Stanford University Press

—— (1977) *Production and Reproduction; A Comparative Study of the Domestic Domain*, Cambridge: Cambridge University Press

Hann, C.M. (1993) 'From Production to Property; Decollectivization and the Family-Land Relationship in Contemporary Hungary', *Man* 28 (2): 299–320

Harrison, S. (1990) *Stealing People's Names: History and Politics in a Sepik River Cosmology*, Cambridge: Cambridge University Press

Hirschon, R. (ed.) (1984) *Women and Property: Women as Property*, London: Croom Helm

Leach, E.R. (1961) *Pul Eliya: A Village in Ceylon*, Cambridge: Cambridge University Press

Morgan, L.H. (1877) *Ancient Society*, New York: Henry Holt

psychoanalysis

Psychoanalysis is at once a distinct intellectual discipline, a theory of the human mind and human body, and a kind of therapeutic practice. It was founded by †Sigmund Freud in turn-of-the-century Vienna, where he swiftly gathered a group of like-minded practitioners around him. By the second decade of the twentieth century Freud's arguments were spreading beyond his Viennese circle, especially in North America. Freud himself published at least one contribution to

contemporary anthropological debates – his theory of the origins of *incest in *Totem and Taboo* ([1913] 1950) – while his heterodox former protégé C.G. Jung made promiscuous use of ethnographic data in his theory of †archetypes. Freud's own anthropological writings are so mired in the speculative *evolutionism of their time that a sympathetic reading requires great interpretive charity, even from anthropologists with a strong psychoanalytic commitment (e.g. Paul 1991). Since the early years of psychoanalysis, there has been a small but distinguished group of psychoanalytic anthropologists, including †Georges Dévereux, †Géza Roheim and †Abram Kardiner, all of whom were trained analysts with anthropological field experience, and in more recent years, Melford Spiro and Gananath Obeyesekere.

The tense history of anthropology and psychoanalysis has been well described by George Stocking as the 'sometimes fruitful and often contentious relationship of two twentieth-century discourses that seek, in somewhat different ways, rational explanations of the apparently irrational' (Stocking 1986: 13). The similarities go further than this: both disciplines have roots in the turn-of-the century discovery of new empirical procedures which could help make sense of the alien and disturbing: the long hours of shared conversation between analyst and analysand for psychoanalysis; the long months of intensive *fieldwork for anthropology. In the 1920s anthropology and psychoanalysis both contributed to a general movement concerned to open up discussions of sexuality to rational argument. From the earliest years, though, a main source of tension has been psychoanalysis's recourse to apparently universal explanatory models, rooted in unconscious desires, which many anthropologists have felt to be culturally insensitive, and often reductionist, when applied outside Western Europe and North America.

A good example of this would be Malinowski's attempt at Freudian revisionism in the 1920s (an episode illuminatingly described by Stocking). In a series of papers *Malinowski developed the argument that, in the †matrilineal Trobriand Islands, physiological paternity was denied and the familial distribution of sentiment and authority was so radically different as to call into question Freud's so-called Oedipus Complex: the child's desire for the mother and hostility to the father. Malinowski's attempt to revise the psychoanalytic argument in the light of ethnographic data was brusquely dismissed, not by Freud himself, but by his principal British follower, Ernest Jones, who argued that matrilineality itself was better seen as a 'defence' against the more fundamental reality of Oedipal desires (Stocking 1986: 33–8). The product of Malinowski's intervention was less a debate than an early agreement on the sheer impossibility of debate.

There followed a long period of hostility to Freudian ideas in British anthropology (even though prominent anthropologists, like †Meyer Fortes and A.L. Epstein, were personally sympathetic to psychoanalytic arguments). This hostility was fuelled by almost ritualistic critiques of crude attempts by non-anthropologists to impose psychoanalytic arguments onto ethnographic data, for example by †Edmund Leach in the 1950s and †Mary Douglas in the 1960s. More broadly, psychoanalysis was identified with American *culture-and-personality studies (although key figures in this movement, like †Ruth Benedict, avoided Freudian explanations), and hostility to psychoanalysis became part of a more general hostility to all kinds of 'psychological' explanations, and even to those areas of life apparently privileged in those explanations – *childhood, sexuality and emotion.

Fieldwork and the work of culture

Anthropological hostility to psychoanalysis, more pronounced in Britain but also discernible in the USA, has tended to concentrate on a vision of psychoanalysis as providing a set of ready-made, usually sexual, explanations for all social and cultural phenomena. We can certainly find enough in Freud's own writing, not least his †positivist desire to establish psychoanalysis as a science of the unconscious, to justify such anthropological suspicions. But this is to ignore an equally important aspect of Freudian theory and practice: its grounding in the constant and unending work of interpretation. In the late 1960s, the social philosophers Paul Ricoeur and †Jurgen Habermas provided influential reinterpretations of psychoanalysis as a form of †hermeneutic practice. As such it could provide one model for the new interpretive, or *symbolic, anthropology that was emerging in the US.

In particular, psychoanalytic reflection on the ambiguities and dramas in the relationship between analyst and analysand, the phenomena known as 'transference' and 'countertransference', could be profitably applied to the anthropological fieldworker's relationship with his or her informants. This argument was first developed by the analyst and fieldworker Georges Devereux in his *From Anxiety to Method in the Behavioral Sciences* (1968), a book which anticipated many of the themes of 1980s *reflexive anthropology. The same concerns were turned to brilliant ethnographic effect by the Sri Lankan anthropologist Gananath Obeyesekere in his *Medusa's Hair* (1981). This study of female religious innovators in Sri Lanka hinged on the author's own moment of anxiety when confronted with a disturbing new symbol – the matted hair of a female ecstatic at the jungle shrine of Kataragama. Through a series of sensitive case-studies, Obeyesekere endeavoured to trace the path from individual trauma to symbolic innovation and thence to new cultural forms. Although Obeyesekere's Freudian interpretations remained too Freudian for some of his own anxious critics, they were far looser and more open, less dogmatic and reductionist, than the usual anthropological caricatures of psychoanalytic interpretation. In his subsequent *The Work of Culture* (1990), Obeyesekere drew on Ricoeur and Habermas in an attempt to provide a fuller theoretical framework for his attempts to reconcile social, cultural and psychoanalytic levels of explanation, while also reflecting on the well-worn theme of the alleged nonuniversality of the Oedipus complex.

If anthropologists like Obeyesekere have profitably drawn on psychoanalysis as a kind of hermeneutic practice, they have also been oddly attached to the work of Freud himself and relatively uninterested in revisionist, or postFreudian, psychoanalytic theorists. The main exception has come from feminist anthropologists who have drawn heavily on the work of †Jacques Lacan and his followers in problematizing the supposed universality of the human subject; although Lacan's work has been increasingly influential in feminist theory, it is only just beginning to be brought into fruitful dialogue with ethnographic problems (Heald and Deluz 1994). Other postFreudian theorists, such as the British 'objectrelations' analysts Ronald Fairbairn and Donald Winnicott, in focusing on the child's relationship with the external social world, may in fact provide an even more fruitful point of contact with anthropological concerns, although this is an area which has been even less developed to date (Mahoney and Yngvesson 1992). The most promising development in recent years, though, has been the emergence of a new generation of psycho-analytic fieldworkers (e.g. G. Gillison, R. Dévisch, S. Heald) who combine a particularly strong commitment to ethnographic particularity with a non-dogmatic approach to psychoanalytic theory.

JONATHAN SPENCER

See also: childhood, culture and personality, ethnopsychiatry, psychological anthropology, socialization

Further reading

Dévereux, G. (1968) *From Anxiety to Method in the Behavioral Sciences*, The Hague: Mouton

Freud, S. ([1913] 1950) *Totem and Taboo*, London: Routledge and Kegan Paul

Heald, S. and A. Deluz (eds) (1994) *Anthropology and Psychoanalysis: An Encounter through Culture*, London: Routledge

Mahoney, M. and B. Yngvesson (1992) 'The Construction of Subjectivity and the Paradox of Resistance: Reintegrating Feminist Anthropology and Psychoanalysis', *Signs* 18 (1): 44–73

Obeyesekere, G. (1981) *Medusa's Hair: An Essay on Personal Symbols and Religious Experience*, Chicago: University of Chicago Press

—— (1990) *The Work of Culture: Symbolic Transformation in Psychoanalysis and Anthropology*, Chicago: University of Chicago Press

Paul, R. (1991) 'Freud's Anthropology: A Reading of the "Cultural Books"', in J. Neu (ed.) *The Cambridge Companion to Freud*, Cambridge: Cambridge University Press

Stocking, G. (1986) 'Anthropology and the Science of the Irrational: Malinowski's Encounter with Freudian Psychoanalysis', in G. Stocking (ed.) *Malinowski, Rivers, Benedict and Others: Essays on Culture and Personality* (History of Anthropology IV), Madison: University of Wisconsin Press

psychological anthropology

Mind is the condition of human being in the world; it follows that mind, and the processes that constitute mind, should be of central interest to any human scientist, including any anthropologist. Certainly the French sociologist †Émile Durkheim thought so, as did *Franz Boas, the founding father of cultural anthropology. Durkheim's *The Elementary Forms of the Religious Life* (1915) enquired at once into the origins of *religion and the sources of the logical categories of mind; Boas, in *The Mind of Primitive Man* (1911), argued for the †psychic unity of humankind even while he celebrated the different cultural forms to which mind gives rise. Both men had been (like *Malinowski) pupils of

the great German psychologist †Wilhelm Wundt, one of whose later works (the ten-volume *Volkerpsychologie* [*Ethnic Psychology*], published between 1900 and 1920) was devoted to an attempt to derive psychological explanations of 'folk mentalities' from ethnological data. Nevertheless, mind as an object of anthropological theorizing came to be relegated to the sub-disciplinary area of psychological anthropology. How this came about is by and large the consequence of our Western intellectual inheritance of Descartes's distinction between mind and matter and the subsequent gradual institutionalizing of scholarly investigation into discrete human sciences: biology, psychology, anthropology, sociology, economics, law.

Descartes's distinction between mind and matter still informs theory in each of these disciplines. In anthropology, we find a prevailing acceptance of a distinction between *culture and biology which is mapped onto other binary distinctions such as *society and *individual, mind and *body, structure and process, *rationality and emotion and so on. What distinguishes psychological anthropology as a sub-disciplinary domain is an explicit concern to reconcile psychology's focus on the individual with anthropology's focus on culture and society; but how, precisely, this objective is to be achieved is the subject of continuing debate. At the same time, it is becoming increasingly apparent that the terms of this debate are themselves problematic and so, in contemporary anthropology, there is a shift away from psychological anthropology to a more general concern with how to derive an anthropological theory of mind that is able to realize its own historical specificity, even while it attempts to analyse mind as the fundamental condition of human existence.

Defining psychological anthropology

The definition of psychological anthropology and its proper concerns have been more closely associated with *American anthropology than with anthropologists elsewhere in the world, who appear to be less inclined to define their interests in sub-disciplinary terms. Indeed, it can be argued that the carving out of such a domain led mainstream anthropologists to consider psychological anthropology a parochial concern, of only marginal interest to themselves.

Psychological anthropology was initially an outgrowth of *culture and personality studies – the new title for the sub-discipline having been proposed by †Francis L.K. Hsu in his 1972 introduction to his edited collection, *Psychological Anthropology*. There Hsu argued that:

> [a] sound theory which aims at explaining the relationship between man and culture must not only account for the origin of psychological characteristics as they are molded [sic] by the patterns of child rearing, social institutions, and ideologies, but must also account for the maintenance, development, and change in the child-rearing practices, institutions and ideologies.
>
> (1972: 13)

Nevertheless, even while he argued that cultural, social and psychological anthropology were all concerned ultimately to study the same phenomenon – human behaviour – he also maintained that:

> [it] is probably desirable, however, for the student from one viewpoint to hold on to his particular viewpoint as he probes deeper and deeper into his data . . . the field worker who shifts from one viewpoint to another . . . is likely to bring back little that is of coherent signficance.
>
> (ibid.: 14)

So those who continued to define themselves as cultural anthropologists tended to take the view that, in so far as psychology was an attribute of 'the individual' and culture an attribute of 'society', they were, by definition, covering more ground than any psychological anthropologist possibly could – a view that appears to be endorsed by psychological anthropologists themselves. In general they accept the characterization of psychology and culture as phenomena that occur at different 'levels' – a position that has militated against any attempt to forge a psychological anthropology that denotes a coherent theoretical perspective. So 'psychological anthropology' is most often used as a catchall which, in broad historical terms, takes in culture and personality studies, *socialization theories, *psychoanalytic approaches, ethnosemantics, *ethnopsychiatry and cognitive anthropology.

Bock's survey of the development of psychological anthropology makes the problems inherent to the sub-discipline clearly apparent. He begins his book with the statement that 'all anthropology is psychological' and ends with a discussion of the limitations of a psychological perspective: 'Failure

to recognize the origins of Western psychology in our own cultural tradition, with its unconscious values, biases and habits of thought, is the crudest kind of ethnocentrism' (1988: 212). In other words, as Bock points out, 'all psychology is cultural'.

One of psychological anthropology's most influential theorists, Melford E. Spiro, has struggled throughout his career to overcome the problems posed by the Cartesian separation of matter and mind. In 1978 he argued that:

> the nature/history dichotomy is a false dichotomy . . . even a radical cultural determinism does not imply a radical cultural relativism; however much societies may differ, they must all cope with man's common biological features.
>
> ([1978] 1987: 27)

Despite this eminently useful insight, however, Spiro continued to hold to 'culture' as an analytical category, a position that inevitably rendered 'biology' and 'the individual' as analytical categories in their own right. So, some years later, we find him asserting that:

> 'culture' designates a cognitive system, [but] it is not the only . . . source of the cognitions and schemata held by social actors. The other source, of course, consists of their own experience.
>
> (1984: 324)

This distinction between 'culture' and 'experience' implies that a set of historically specific concepts exists independently of the people whose behaviour at once constitutes and expresses them. So, in so far as it refers to a system of meanings, 'culture' can only be an abstraction. But this is problematic, because meaning does not reside anywhere 'out there'. Rather, meaning is manifest in behaviour – in what people do and in what they say (and write) – only in so far as living persons make it so.

That psychological anthropologists still hold their domain of investigation to be distinctive is clear in White and Lutz's assertion in their introduction to *New Directions in Psychological Anthropology* that 'psychological anthropology . . . remains the field most centrally concerned with putting people and experience into theories of culture and society' (Schwartz *et al.* 1992: 1). But this is a tall order, because 'people' and 'experience' refer us not only to actual persons' actual lives and to their ideas about themselves and the world, but to their engagement in the world as visceral, passionate, lived. And because living seems to us to be more about process and transformation than it is about static structures, we are thrown back on the problem of how, exactly, we can deal with the messy complexity of living in terms of theoretical abstractions like 'culture' and 'society'.

It is thus unsurprising that the papers in the *New Directions* collection (referred to above) are characterized by pleas for the necessity of addressing problems arising from a continuing inability to deal effectively with Cartesian distinctions. So, for example, we find discussions of the theoretical schism between biological and psychological anthropology (James S. Chisholm), the relationship between 'knowledge structures and their conceptual and situational contexts' (Janet Dixon Keller), the question of how 'cultural models get elaborated during the course of human development' (Sara Harkness), and 'the divide between views of human behaviour as determined or emergent' (Carol M. Worthman).

Cultural psychology and social construction theory

Neither have the problems inherent to psychological anthropology been solved by the creation of the new sub-disciplinary domain of 'cultural psychology'. Here the intention is to acknowledge the validity of other people's understandings of the world and themselves and to use these understandings as the basis for analysis. Even so, and despite a good deal of fascinating ethnography that suggests otherwize, Descartes's emphasis on conscious thought as the existential ground of knowledge by and large continues to be taken for granted by cultural psychologists. In Stigler, Shweder and Herdt's (1990) edited collection, this emphasis is evinced in the very titles of the papers, for example, 'culture and moral development' (Shweder, Mahapatra and Miller), 'the socialization of cognition' (Goodnow), and 'the relations between culture and human cognition' (D'Andrade). And this despite the fact that, in an introductory essay, Shweder claims 'cultural psychology' to be distinct from 'psychological anthropology':

> Cultural psychology is the study of intentional worlds. It is the study of personal functioning in particular intentional worlds. It is the study of the interpersonal maintenance of any intentional world. It is the investigation of those psycho-

somatic, sociocultural and, inevitably, divergent realities in which subject and object cannot possibly be separated and kept apart because they are so interdependent as to need each other to be.

> (ibid.: 3)

But if realities are 'inevitably divergent', then where exactly can the analyst locate any 'particular intentional world'? Yet again, as the titles of the papers indicate, we find outselves willy nilly caught in the distinction between the 'personal functioning' of the consciousness of particular actors and an abstraction – that is, the 'intentional world' that is the artefact of the anthropologist's analysis.

Any analysis of *what* is known inevitably requires an analysis of *how* it comes to be known and this implicates concepts of the *person. Shweder, elaborating his arguments for cultural psychology, suggests that we should view concepts of the person as 'social constructions':

> The 'constructive' parts of a social construction theory are the idea that equally rational, competent, and informed observers are, in some sense, free . . . to constitute for themselves different realities; and . . . that there are as many realities as the way 'it' can be constituted or described. . . . The 'social' parts of a social construction theory are the idea that categories are vicariously received, not individually invented; and . . . that the way people divide the world into categories is, in some sense, tradition bound, and thus transmitted, communicated and 'passed on' through symbolic action.

> (Shweder 1991: 156)

But if, as studies of child language demonstrate, we do not passively *acquire* our native language, but have rather (each one of us) to *constitute* its very categories, then language as 'structure' cannot be separated from construction as 'process'; rather structure and process have to be conceived of as aspects of one another – a point that is taken further below. In locating the constructive process in the person and what is social in an abstract space *between* persons (i.e. in language categories), social construction theory reproduces the very theoretical impasse it pretends to dismantle.

Even so, there have been attempts to arrive at genuinely synthetic theories able to grapple at once with the subjective experience and understandings of actors and the analytical description of the anthropologist observer as itself a form of subjectivity. But while the authors of such works may justly be said to be concerned with mind, they are unlikely to characterize themselves as psychological anthropologists or even as cultural psychologists. Rather, they are concerned to understand 'embodied mind' as an emergent, historically constituted and, at the same time, universal condition of human existence through an examination of its inevitable particularity.

Mind and habitus

One of the key texts to prompt a re-examination of anthropological theories of mind, at least among European anthropologists, has been †Bourdieu's *Outline of a Theory of Practice* (1977). He argued that the anthropologist observer was bound to produce a distorted account because, in making the lives of others an object of analysis, the anthropologist re-ordered the dynamic flow of people's day-to-day practice into a set of explicit 'representations' or worse, 'rules' for behaviour. But in going about our own everyday lives, in doing the things we do and saying what we say, our behaviour is so highly nuanced, so subtly accommodating to novel situations, that we cannot be following 'rules' or acting in terms of 'representations'; it follows that there is no reason to suppose that others are doing so. Bourdieu proposed the idea of the †'*habitus*', a set of predispositions to certain behaviours inculcated in the course of socialization, to account for the way that people everywhere come to have a 'sense' of how to behave, and thus to take for granted their own ideas and practices as right, as the only proper way of being in the world. But Bourdieu's habitus, while it almost managed to collapse the mind-body distinction, was not sufficiently well theorized to bring about a paradigm shift in respect of theories of mind.

Nevertheless, Bourdieu's theory of the *habitus* as embodied practice has been fruitful in forcing anthropologists to recognize that mind is constituted *in practice* by persons relating to one another as subjects. In other words, I do not relate to others as if they were simply objects in my world, but as persons who, like me, are the active subjects of their own actions. Moreover, I do not have to reflect continually upon what I do because my habitual mode of being in the world – for example, the way I walk, eat, talk, feel and in general relate to others is constituted by me over time and embodied in me as taken for granted, as 'the way

I am', and as such may never be made the object of conscious scrutiny.

But how, exactly, is 'the taken for granted' (or what Bourdieu calls *doxa*) constituted in active, intersubjective relations between particular persons? Lave (1988) on arithmetic as social practice and Toren (1990) on cognitive development as a microhistorical process offer ethnographic attempts at an answer.

Embodied mind

The focus on practice has developed alongside attempts to use the insights of †phenomenology to analyse 'embodied mind'. Here the theoretical emphasis is on the body as 'the existential ground of culture' and thus as at once manifesting and constituting mind (see, for example, Csordas 1990). A phenomenological perspective is becoming increasingly important for theory in contemporary anthropology and biology, and is beginning to penetrate academic psychology (see, for example, Varela *et al.*, 1991).

As a school of philosophy, phenomenology strives at once to render transparent the validity of the *variety* of human experience of the world *and* to show how this variety is referrable to the processes through which mind is constituted. Anthropological studies that take a phenomenological perspective tend to focus on how human beings 'live their world', on how they come to embody their consciousness of that world as a function of experience that is always mediated by meaning, even while it is always concrete and material – that is to say, real and lived. By the same token the reality of lived experience crucially informs the processes by which we make meaning.

So, for example, Bruce Kapferer (1986) shows how, in Sinhala (Sri Lankan) exorcism, the elaborate performance of the rite is crucial not merely for the patient but also for all the other participants, including the exorcist. The *performance* frees all the participants from 'the solitude of subjective experience', but at the same time it 'demands that they take a variety of standpoints on the world as experienced and as it achieves its diverse meanings'. In other words, it is through performance as embodied experience that any given participant renders the rite personally meaningful and comes to understand what it might mean for any other participant.

A remarkable ethnographic example of the relevance to anthropology of a radical phenomenological approach is provided by Jadran

Mimica's work on the counting system and conception of *number of the Iqwaye of Papua New Guinea. Mimica shows how the binary mathematic of the Iqwaye 'is generated on human fingers and toes ... [and] although this systematic expression has a very concrete, indeed substantial, form, the number is simultaneously constituted in it as an abstraction' (1988: 7). Moreover he is able to show how the cognitive structures that are constitutive of the Iqwaye system of counting 'became entangled and developed as a unified mathematical form in relation to the Iqwaye view of the cosmos, their system of kinship and marriage' (ibid.: 140).

By virtue of his analysis of the specific characteristics of Iqwaye rationality, Mimica's anthropological theorizing is also a systematic critique of Western mathematics as a form of cultural knowlege. By demonstrating the validity of the Iqwaye conception of number, Mimica throws into question the taken-for-granted Western assumption that our vaunted 'scientific objectivity' is the only valid form of knowing the world.

This critical perspective is intrinsic to an understanding of mind as embodied for, as the phenomenological psychology of Merleau-Ponty makes plain, perception is immanent in consciousness (see Merleau-Ponty [1945] 1962). In other words, if perception is not, as most cognitivists assume it to be, an autonomous process that precedes and is theoretically separable from conscious experience, then we can no longer hold to the idea that the facts and, more particularly, the scientific facts are 'out there' waiting to be discovered. In Merleau-Ponty's view, intentionality as a function of embodied mind has to be considered as historically constituted.

History and embodied mind

An understanding of historical continuity and transformation is central to the anthropological endeavour; it requires an investigation of how the history of our social relations enters into the constitution of meaning over time by each and every one of us. This brings us to the problem of how we conceptualize 'history' and its significance for the study of embodied mind.

The prevailing tendency in the social sciences makes history inhere in 'social structures', in 'institutions', in 'ideologies', in 'collective representations' – which are represented as independent of the living persons whose actions make these abstractions material (see e.g. Spiro 1978). Here

history is conceived of as what is past but persistent, as inhering in the *products* of human action as divorced from their producers: in the *environment as modified by human practice, in *technologies, in *ritual, in oral traditions, in what has been written down, in the very categories of language. And because these alienated products of the past are understood to pre-exist any given human being, they are taken for granted as 'ready-made' – the implicit assumption being that in so far as they carry meaning, that meaning declares itself. Thus †Sahlins, in his influential attempt to synthesize structure and process, refers to a 'cultural totality' which he conceives of as 'the system of relations between categories without a given subject' (1985: xvi–xvii); here cultural categories are received ready-made, open to being transformed only when they are 'risked in action' (cf. Shweder 1991). But this cannot be so for people have actively to *constitute* the categories in whose terms they understand and act in the world, and each one of us does this rather differently as a function of a unique set of relations with others (see e.g. Bowerman 1982). It follows that even while the past inheres materially in the present, it can manifest in the present only as the constituted, but never finished, always emergent product of particular human minds.

Re-defining mind

Thus one can argue that mind is the fundamental historical phenomenon because each one of us, over time, constitutes mind anew *and* manifests it in intersubjective relations with particular others. In this view, mind cannot be an isolated function of the nervous system or, more narrowly, of the brain; neither can it be located in 'culture' or 'collective representations' or 'social constructions' or 'cultural models'. Rather, mind is manifested in the whole person, considered as a particular person with a particular history in relation to other persons who are similarly constituting themselves over time – from birth to death – as unique manifestations of mind.

In this perspective, each one of us is the locus of manifold relations with others that inform the endogenous constitution of embodied cognitive schemes; so each one of us constitutes cognitively the social relations of which we are the transforming product. Humans have a common biology, are subject to the same general physical conditions and the same physiological processes, and all of us are compelled to make meaning of the world by virtue of engaging with the meanings others have made and are making (for language is a condition for what we call mind). And it is because we have, all of us, to live in and through the world that we constitute our categories as guarantors of the world in which we live – that is, as valid. So while we all live the same world, we have no choice but to live it autonomously as a function of our own, always unique, histories as particular persons. It is common to us all, therefore, to be different from one another.

This assumption of the commonality that resides in our difference informs †participant observation as the fundamental research method of anthropology. Moreover, it brings us to the heart of the human existential dilemma: that we assume and act on the assumption that meanings made by others (and especially by intimate others) can be rendered as ours; but it is in the nature of mind that this can never entirely be achieved. Nevertheless, because sociality is the very condition of our human autonomy, we *can* come to understand others, even radically different others, to the extent that we allow their meanings to inform, and thus transform, our own.

Thus any given person is at all times at once a manifestation of his or her history and an historical agent. He or she at once maintains the continuity of meanings and transforms them by virtue of actively constituting an understanding of the world in and through relations with others (see e.g. Toren 1993).

So, in contemporary anthropology, distinctions between body and mind, individual and society, biology and culture are beginning, at last, to be discarded as inadequate to encompass the complex data with which anthropologists have to deal; and a new analytical vocabulary is being forged to address new formulations of the anthropological endeavour. A growing awareness of the central importance of ideas of the person for ethnographic analyses have made anthropologists more generally aware that their own analyses are bound to implicate a particular, Western, theory of person and mind. Thus our attempts to explain ideas of the person and of mind held by others have thrown into relief the necessity for a re-examination of our own taken-for-granted anthropological concepts.

CHRISTINA TOREN

See also: childhood, classification, cognition, culture and personality, ethnopsychiatry, person, socialization

Further reading

Bock, P.K. (1988) *Rethinking Psychological Anthropology*, New York: W.H. Freeman & Co.

Bourdieu, P. (1977) *Outline of a Theory of Practice*, Cambridge: Cambridge University Press

Bowerman, M. (1982) 'Reorganizational Processes in Lexical and Syntactic Development', in E. Wanner and L.R. Gleitman (eds) *Language Acquisition: The State of the Art*, Cambridge: Cambridge University Press

Csordas, T.J. (1990) 'Embodiment as a Paradigm for Anthropology' *Ethos* 18: 5–47

Hsu, F.L.K. (1972) 'Psychological Anthropology in the Behavioural Sciences', in F.L.K. Hsu (ed.) *Psychological Anthropology*, Cambridge, MA: Schenkman Publishing Co.

Kapferer, B. (1986) 'Performance and the Structuring of Meaning and Experience', in V.W. Turner and E.M. Bruner (eds) *The Anthropology of Experience*, Urbana: University of Illinois Press

Lave, J. (1988) *Cognition in Practice*, Cambridge: Cambridge University Press

Merleau-Ponty, M. ([1945] 1962) *Phenomenology of Perception*, London: Routledge and Kegan Paul

Mimica, J. (1988) *Intimations of Infinity. The Mythopoeia of the Iqwaye Counting System and Number*, Oxford and New York: Berg

Sahlins, M. (1985) *Islands of History*, London: Tavistock Publications

Schwartz, T., G.M. White and C.A. Lutz (1992) *New Directions in Psychological Anthropology*, Cambridge: Cambridge University Press

Shweder, R.A. (1990) 'Cultural Psychology – What is it?', in J.W. Stigler, R.A. Shweder and G. Herdt (eds) (1990) *Cultural Psychology: Essays on Comparative Human Development*, Cambridge: Cambridge University Press

—— (1991) *Thinking Through Cultures. Expeditions in Cultural Psychology*, Cambridge, MA: Harvard University Press

Spiro, M.E. (1984) 'Some Reflections on Cultural Determinism and Relativism with Special Reference to Emotion and Reason', in R.A. Shweder and R.A. LeVine (eds) *Culture Theory. Essays on Mind, Self and Emotion*, Cambridge: Cambridge University Press

—— ([1978] 1987) 'Culture and Human Nature', in B. Kilborne and L.L. Langness (eds) *Culture and Human Nature. Theoretical Papers of Melford E. Spiro*, Chicago: University of Chicago Press

Stigler, J.W., R.A. Shweder and G. Herdt (1990) (eds) *Cultural Psychology: Essays on Comparative Human Development*, Cambridge: Cambridge University Press

Toren, C. (1990) *Making Sense of Hierarchy. Cognition as Social Process in Fiji*, London School of Economics Monographs on Social Anthropology No 61, London: Athlone Press

—— (1993) 'Making History: The Significance of Childhood Cognition for a Comparative Anthropology of Mind', *Man* (n.s.), 28: 461–78

Varela, F.J., E. Thompson and Eleanor R. Thompson (1991) *The Embodied Mind. Cognitive Science and Human Experience*, Cambridge, MA: The MIT Press

R

race

Race is a framework of ranked categories dividing up the human population. It was developed by Western Europeans following their global expansion which began in the 1400s. Several key elements of this racialization of the world made race vastly different from earlier localized †ethnocentric or *caste ideologies which stressed differences between 'them' and 'us'. Race was *global*, applied to the entire human species. Race consisted of a *small number of categories*, most frequently just five, although sometimes with sub-races and mixed-race types added to them. Race *ranked* these categories in terms of assumed and imputed fixed quanta of cultural worth, intelligence, attractiveness and other qualities. Race reinforced *pervasive *inequality* in terms of the political, economic, social, and frequently legal, conditions of everyday existence accorded to persons judged to be of different races. Race was *essentialized* – it came to seem real, natural and unquestionable to millions of human beings, including both victims and beneficiaries of racialized social ordering.

Race resulted in *racism*, the cultural and ideological formation that shapes perception and evaluation of self and others according to racial identity, which is institutionalized in both interpersonal and larger-scale behavioural social orders. Racism has met *resistance and contestation at many levels, from community-based political struggle to academic scholarship. Racism in its regional, national and local forms is seen by some analysts as many different racisms, each culturally interpretable in its own terms. Others, like Michel-Rolph Trouillot (in Gregory and Sanjek 1994), prefer to see these local manifestations (in South Africa, the United States, Haiti, etc.) as refractions of 'the international hierarchy of races, colours, religions, and cultures' that has pervaded one increasingly racialized *world system since the 1400s. In either view, racial ranking has consistently assigned White persons to the top and Black persons to the bottom. Other racial identities have occupied either bottom or intermediate locations according to varying impositions and refractions of, and resistances to, racist identification and institutionalization.

Before race

Race arose with the perception of global variation in human physiognomic and bodily appearances, variation which is certainly real but vastly more complex than can be contained within a small number of racial types. The entire spectrum of human packaging was not apprehended anywhere on the globe until regular European sea travel linked the Old and New Worlds after 1492, and completed the planetary picture with Pacific Island reconnaissance in the 1700s. Before then, what was more apparent everywhere was the gradual transition in physical types found in all continuous geographic areas. It was the ocean-borne *migration and enforced transportation of Europeans and sub-Saharan Africans into the Americas that first brought large blocks of non-contiguous peoples into intimate contact, and fertilized the ground for the emergence of race and racism.

Race built upon the ethnocentrism of the various European *colonialist peoples. Ethnocentric feelings of superiority to nearby groups ('we're better than them') are as widely encountered in human societies as are more tolerant views ('their customs are different'). The ethnocentric ancient Greeks, for example, saw themselves as first among the civilized and barbarian peoples around the Mediterranean. Yet physical appearance and cultural attainment were not linked by the Greeks. They granted civilized status to the

Nile Valley Nubians, who were among the darkest people they knew, but not to the light-skinned European barbarian peoples to the north.

Regimes of caste, like racial formations, arrange their members hierarchically, with comparable material and political deprivation for those at the bottom. In *South Asian caste societies individuals vary widely in skin colour, but intra-caste (*jati*) variation overlaps with that of other local castes; dark colour and high status is no rarity, nor is its reverse. *Hindu †*karma* ideology posits higher or lower caste status as a distinct possibility for all persons, either in previous lives or future rebirths. The disabilities of *harijan* ('untouchable') status are something a soul is born into, and not the unquestioned consequence of one's visible physical appearance. Other caste-situations, such as those in Africa and Japan, have their own cultural and geographically-limited circumstances, and also do not institutionalize physical appearance into caste (except perhaps in Rwanda where the rulers were darker than their subjects).

*Slavery, which both long preceded and continued after the emergence of race, assumed a new dimension with global racialization. Before the 1400s, slavery was widespread in *state societies, but its victims, either recruited internally or from neighbouring groups, were largely physically indistinguishable from slave-holders; slavery was a status that, as fortunes changed, might be held by anyone. In pre-1400 Europe and in indigenous non-Western societies, slave descendants (even those few of more distant origins) gradually disappeared, blending into the dominant cultural group. Since systemic racial ordering did not distinguish free and enslaved populations, slave descendants could †acculturate and usually had no other choice. They did not remain perpetually demarcated by race as happened following the emergence of the racialized enslavement of Africans by Europeans between the 1400s and 1800s (see Drake 1987, 1990; Sanjek in Gregory and Sanjek 1994).

The rise of race

As the post-1400s racial order solidified from its ethnocentric beginnings, the devaluation of Africans, Native Americans and colonized Asians, and reluctance to sanction intermarriage or to admit persons of mixed background to the full entitlements of solely European ancestry, were evident in all the European colonial societies by the late 1600s. In the 1700s, efforts mounted within the citadels of science in Western Europe to place the exploited peoples into natural schemes, culminating in the division of humankind into Caucasian, Mongolian, Ethiopian, American and Malayan races by Johann Friedrich Blumenbach in 1795. Ranking of these races followed, with early nineteenth-century anthropology (as the science of races was called) divided between †polygenists who believed in separate divine creation of each race, and †monogenists who accepted one creation for all humankind, with different races the divergent products of natural history.

Chief among the polygenists was Samuel Morton whose long-accepted cranial studies during the 1830s and 1840s 'proved' the larger brain size, and therefore superiority, of Whites over other races. Only in 1977 did biologist Stephen Jay Gould (1981) reanalyse the data and discover that Morton's overt racist bias had prevented identification of what clearly were fully overlapping measurements among the 'racial' skull samples he used. A radical break with the assumptions of continuing racist †anthropometry and psychological testing (see Gould 1981) came with the famous separation of race, *language and *culture (and methods to study each) by *Franz Boas. After proclaiming during the 1890s his inductive discovery that mappings of Northwest Coast Native American biological traits, cultural similarities and linguistic affinities each yielded different results, Boas delighted in criticizing European *nationalism, pointing out that a similar historical flow of traits and peoples had occurred on that continent and from beyond.

Boas also applied his anthropology to combat racism. He used his study of changes in head form among descendants of Southern and Eastern European immigrants to counter nativist and †eugenic antagonism to what were seen as sub-races inferior to Northern Europeans. In his 1906 address at Atlanta University, he urged pride among African-Americans in the accomplishments of African civilizations, and appreciation that the condition of Black people was of historic making, and could change in the future. During the 1930s he mobilized scientists against Nazi racialism, and his writings and those of his students moulded the liberal view opposing racial discrimination that became widely acceptable in the United States in the 1950s.

By the 1960s anthropology moved beyond the Boasian critique of racial ranking and the target became the very idea of race itself (Montagu 1964). The new anti-racists attacked the notion that the human species was divisible into five, or any other, small number of races. They pointed out that racial appearance is determined by very few of the many genetic loci, and like the far greater number of invisible biological traits, the few visible 'racial' features vary in expression continuously across continents. Hair form types and skin colour shades grade into each other; there is no line in nature between a 'white' and a 'black' race, or a 'Caucasoid' and a 'Mongoloid' race. Historical movement of peoples and intermingling of populations complicate but do not disguise the fundamentals of continuous, clinal distribution. Even more destructive of categorical race thinking was the point that the many more numerous invisible traits – for example blood factors and enzymes – also vary continuously across populations, and each varies independently, not in parallel with visible racial markers or in concordance with each other. Simplistic racial categories based merely upon a few 'package' traits hardly constitute a scientific approach to human biovariability.

Racism

As global consciousness over racial inequality sharpened during the 1960s, a liberal anthropology affirmed that race does not exist. But racism, the socially-organized result of race ranking, clearly did. During the 1930s and 1940s in the USA, several social anthropologists had studied racism in southern bi-racial communities and in northern black ghettos, and their work highlighted contradictions between the US creed of equality and the practice of racial segregation and oppression (Bond 1988; Davis *et al.* 1941; Drake 1987: 44–6, 341). Anthropologists also began to explore the historical formation of racialized societies, comparing local regimes (in *Latin America, the *Caribbean, the USA, South Africa, Britain) in terms of racial categorization and political economy (Banton 1983; Drake 1987, 1990; Harris 1964). But with few exceptions – Eleanor Leacock's study (1969) of institutionalized racism in New York City public schools was one – by the 1970s anthropologists focused more on *ethnicity (expressive processes of cultural identification) than race (repressive processes of social exclusion). While some went as far as to subsume race within ethnicity, or to euphemize race with 'colour caste', *'plural society' or 'duality', others joined

Banton (1983) in stating the need to study ethnicity *and* race, particularly in societies marked by both White/Black racialization and by White (and Black) ethnic heterogeneity (Drake 1987: 58–60).

Still, ethnicity has captured more of the anthropological imagination in recent decades than has race. Ethnographic studies of race in community politics, in schools and housing estates, and in household worker-employer relations (see Cock 1980 on South Africa) are few; Benson's (1981) careful study of the social networks and acceptance of inter-racial couples in South London is virtually alone. This situation is likely to change in the 1990s. Global South-North and East-West movements of people are making European and North American societies increasingly more multiracial. As 'the empire strikes back', *refugees flee repressive societies, and the world's poor see the future as much in transnational terms as do the rich, so do racial heterogeneity, *identity politics and resistance to inequality more and more mark the major institutional landscapes of neighbourhood, workplace, university and political arena, and even *kinship and *marriage (Gregory and Sanjek 1994).

In these circumstances anthropologists ponder not only new research topics, but also the effects of racism and its institutionalization (which no longer requires overt racist attitudes) within their own discipline. The African-American social anthropologist St Clair Drake began his career in the 1930s but despite professional achievements could not do fieldwork in Africa during the 1940s because †Melville Herskovits, who chaired the principal funding committee, believed that Whites could do objective research in that continent but Blacks could not (Bond 1988). Closer to the present, while anthropologists work and the discipline is widely established in a people-of-all-colours world, by 1989 some 93 per cent of US anthropologists in full-time academic positions were White, even higher than the 89 per cent White figure for all full-time US academics (Alvarez in Gregory and Sanjek 1994), or the 76 per cent White population (which includes persons of North African and Middle East origin) counted in the 1990 US census.

ROGER SANJEK

See also: biological anthropology, Franz Boas, caste, colonialism, essentialism, ethnicity, nationalism, slavery

Further reading

Banton, M. (1983) *Racial and Ethnic Competition*, Cambridge: Cambridge University Press

Benson, S. (1981) *Ambiguous Ethnicity: Interracial Families in London*, Cambridge: Cambridge University Press

Bond, G.C. (1988) 'A Social Portrait of John Gibbs St. Clair Drake: An American Anthropologist', *American Ethnologist* 15: 762–81

Cock, J. (1980) *Maids and Madams: A Study in the Politics of Exploitation*, Johannesburg: Ravan Press

Davis, A., B.B. Gardner and M. Gardner (1941) *Deep South: A Social Anthropological Study of Caste and Class*, Chicago: University of Chicago Press

Drake, St C. (1987, 1990) *Black Folk Here and There: An Essay in History and Anthropology*, 2 vols, Los Angeles: Center for Afro-American Studies, University of California

Gould, S.J. (1981) *The Mismeasure of Man*, New York: Norton

Gregory, S. and R. Sanjek (eds) (1994) *Race*, New Brunswick: Rutgers University Press

Harris, M. (1964) *Patterns of Race in the Americas*, New York: Walker

Leacock, E. (1969) *Teaching and Learning in City Schools: A Comparative Study*, New York: Basic Books

Montagu, A. (ed.) (1964) *The Concept of Race*, New York: Free Press

Radcliffe-Brown, A.R.

Born in the industrial Midlands of England in 1881, the last of three children of a family fallen on hard times, Alfred Reginald Brown was to enjoy a brilliant career which took him from King Edward VI School, Birmingham and Trinity College, Cambridge to chairs at Cape Town, Sydney, Chicago and Oxford and visiting professorships in China, Brazil, Egypt and other countries. In 1926 he added his mother's maiden name to his own by deed poll, thus putting the seal on a form he began adopting during World War I.

Radcliffe-Brown spent most of his adult life outside England, with particularly formative periods in Australia and South Africa, where his brother and sister were settled. Whether because of a restless temperament, the precarious state of anthropology or his hope, invariably disappointed, that the discipline might somewhere become solidly enough established to allow research to flourish, he never stayed more than a few years in one place. Through his peregrinations, which evoke the wanderings of a culture hero, he spread the message of social anthropology widely, both

in and beyond academe. The process was aided by the charm and theatrical flamboyance Radcliffe-Brown often displayed, qualities which co-existed with a deep inner reserve. In 1931, shortly before he left for Chicago, a woman journalist gave an impression of the figure he cut:

> Sydney is to lose her Radcliffe-Brown, the tall, slender professor of anthropology, who has graced her ballrooms and, in the De Chair reign, so many Government House parties. In spite of his violent prejudices in favour of modern art, Radcliffe is a gentle soul, very popular with the undergraduates.

Natural science fascinated Radcliffe-Brown from boyhood. His interest in it can only have been strengthened by admiration for Bertrand Russell, whom he had taken as his philosophical guide. However his vision of a natural science of society, propounded in the posthumously published but unrevised Chicago lectures of 1937, was never fully developed and was to be dismissed out of hand by his successor at Oxford, the Catholic convert †E.E. Evans-Pritchard, who maintained that anthropology is akin to history and that the search for laws is vain.

*Art, especially painting, was another early interest of Radcliffe-Brown's. Known among artists and bohemians in Sydney and Cape Town, his aesthetic leanings found further expression in a passion for classical Chinese culture and in drama and music. Not one to wear heart on sleeve, Radcliffe-Brown had an attitude to life which can be gauged from his lecture at the Society of Artists' Exhibition in Sydney in 1929: the modern painter hates vagueness and sentimentality, seeks clear-cut and definite results and, in keeping with the scientific spirit, appeals to intellect rather than emotions. The words could be used to describe his own outlook on anthropology and life, provided allowance is made for a romantic streak, the manifestation of which included attachment to the name Radcliffe and championship of the theory that Shakespeare's plays were written by the Earl of Oxford.

Radcliffe-Brown trained in anthropology under †A.C. Haddon and †W.H.R. Rivers at Cambridge. *The Andaman Islanders*, his first book, carried a warm dedication to them; in 1922 he described Haddon to a correspondent as 'my own master, to whom I am gratefully indebted for what success I have had'. But although he and Rivers had in common a deep interest in problems of *kinship and social organization, his conception of them and of the methods by which they might be solved had come by 1912–14 to diverge sharply from his mentor's. It seems, too, that by the same period his growing enthusiasm for a 'sociological' approach had gained the upper hand over the 'ethnological' which retained Haddon's primary allegiance and on which he himself had relied when planning his Andamanese fieldwork of 1906–8. The definitive pronouncement of a characteristically Radcliffe-Brownian position, in which †ethnology and social anthropology are clearly distinguished and historical surmise and conjecture called into question, had to wait until 1923, however, when 'The Methods of Ethnology and Social Anthropology' appeared.

Even before going to university Radcliffe-Brown had turned in the direction of anthropology through the influence of †Peter Kropotkin and Havelock Ellis. His early anarchism would have made him receptive to Kropotkin who, around the turn of the century, was prepared to recommend that the study of society should precede attempts at reforming it and that the path to understanding a complex civilization lay through simpler societies. Of the Siberian tribal life he experienced in the 1860s, Kropotkin had written 'to live with natives, to see at work all the complex forms of social organisation they have elaborated far away from the influence of any civilisation, was, as it were, to store up floods of light'. The words are virtually prophetic. Taken together with Rivers's passion for kinship, they define the direction in which Radcliffe-Brown would make his major contribution.

Nevertheless, it would be wrong to stereotype him as a Kropotkinian. He rejected such labels (*functionalist was another) as unscientific, though his description of Andamanese social life carries a distinct flavour of Kropotkin. The islanders are described as living in local groups, each of them 'independent and autonomous, leading its own life and regulating its own affairs'. They knew 'no organised government' and 'no such thing as the punishment of crime'. Community affairs were 'regulated entirely by the older men and women', but of authority they had 'little or none'. Despite the existence of private *property in portable things, 'the Andamanese have customs which result in an approach to communism'.

It was to Ellis, who began reading †Émile Durkheim in the 1890s, that Radcliffe-Brown owed his introduction to the ideas of the French sociological school. The influence is apparent in lectures he gave in Cambridge and Birmingham in 1910 and 1913–14. In 1923 he was recommending, to second-year students at Cape Town, *The Elementary Forms of the Religious Life* and *De la division du travail social* (not then available in English) and also the *Mélanges d'histoire des religions* of Henri Hubert and †Marcel Mauss.

Radcliffe-Brown considered that the best chapters of *The Andaman Islanders* were those in which he interpreted *myth and ceremony through the concepts of meaning and function formulated by Hubert. But far from being an unquestioning disciple of this school, Radcliffe-Brown criticized much in Durkheim's treatment of the social organization and the religion of *Aboriginal Australia. He had the advantage of first hand knowledge through fieldwork, principally in 1910–12 but also for shorter periods in later years.

Australia is the part of the world with which he is perhaps most closely associated. His work on kinship, *cosmology and local organization, conceptualized in terms of structure and function and aiming at comparative generalization, remains of interest, notwithstanding criticism. It is both curious and instructive that the models of local organization Radcliffe-Brown constructed as early as 1913 have been almost universally rejected since the 1960s (and indeed were criticized before then), yet they are often referred to in the burgeoning literature on land rights. The paradox is explicable if one assumes that he alone has been able to introduce order, even if erroneously, into multifarious Australia-wide data.

Radcliffe-Brown was not a prolific writer. To understand his style of anthropology it is helpful to read work inspired or influenced by him, as presented in such collections as *Social Anthropology of North American Tribes* (Eggan 1937), *African Political Systems* (Fortes and Evans-Pritchard 1940) and *African Systems of Kinship and Marriage* (Radcliffe-Brown and Forde 1950). Together with his papers on 'The Social Organisation of Australian Tribes' (1930–1) they illustrate the application of *comparative method to restricted regions. He did not, however, regard this as the only way in which generalisation might be pursued. In 'The Comparative Method in Social Anthropology' (1951) he used the Heraclitean notion of a union of opposites, governed by tension and complementarity, to elucidate Australian and other cosmology. Contrary to the opinion of *Claude

Lévi-Strauss, it was not a late development in his thought but had, as †Raymond Firth has pointed out, been expounded more than two decades earlier in his lectures at Sydney.

Little interested in bourgeois accumulation, Radcliffe-Brown died in relative poverty in London in 1955. A surviving sister-in-law remembers him as a man who had loved the life he led.

KENNETH MADDOCK

See also: British anthropology, functionalism, Aboriginal Australia

Further reading

Eggan, F. (ed.) (1955 [1937]) *Social Anthropology of North American Tribes*, Chicago: University of Chicago Press

Firth, R. (1956) 'Alfred Reginald Radcliffe-Brown 1881–1955', *Proceedings of the British Academy* 62: 287–302

Fortes, M. and E.E. Evans-Pritchard (eds) *African Political Systems*, Oxford: Oxford University Press

Gordon, R. (1990) 'Early Social Anthropology in South Africa', *African Studies* 49: 15–48

Maddock, K. (1992) 'Affinities and Missed Opportunities: John Anderson and A.R. Radcliffe-Brown in Sydney', *The Australian Journal of Anthropology* 3: 3–18

Radcliffe-Brown, A.R. (1922) *The Andaman Islanders*, Cambridge: Cambridge University Press

—— (1952) *Structure and Function in Primitive Society* , London: Cohen & West

—— (1958) *Method in Social Anthropology*, Chicago: University of Chicago Press

Radcliffe-Brown, A.R. and D. Forde (eds) (1950) *African Systems of Kinship and Marriage*, Oxford: Oxford University Press

Stanner, W.E.H. (1985) 'Radcliffe-Brown's Ideas on "Social Value"', *Social Analysis* 17: 113–25

rationality

Rationality and its cognates (rational, reason, reasonableness), are, in anthropology, usually ascribed to ideas or thought ('magic is irrational, science is rational'), to action ('cloud-seeding is rational, rain dance is irrational'), or to social arrangements ('feud is an irrational feature of social organization, bureaucracy a rational feature'). Some history will help explain this proliferation, while more recent debates show how to make some simplification.

To begin with ideas or thought, how can we recognize rational ideas? Intuitively, only true ideas are rational, erroneous ideas are not. The ancient Greeks were well aware that diverse societies had diverse ideas. They also made the shattering proto-anthropological discovery that all societies are symmetrical in taking it for granted that only their ideas are true, throwing into question the truth and rationality of the ideas of all societies, including the anthropologist's own (and hence anthropological ideas). Most important, it vacates the intuitive standard, only true ideas are rational.

As a solution, Greek thinkers distinguished between two kinds of truth, truths by nature and truths by convention. The former are true, regardless of the history of local convention, because they accurately capture the world and hold for all times and places; they transcend history, geography and convention. Truths by convention are true by virtue of the historical fact that they enjoy local endorsement; elsewhere, they may not be endorsed. Truths by nature are always rational, truths by convention are at best locally rational.

A marked preference for universal truths of nature over limited truths by convention is the root of all versions of the problem of rationality: everyone thinks it is most rational to prefer universal truth. The Greek distinction raises the question: which view is true? Or, which views should I endorse as true? Even the relativists, who say universal truth is inaccessible to mortals, and the sceptics, who deny its very possibility, were compelled by the very distinction between two kinds of truth to face this problem of choice. Both sceptics and relativists insist that rationality is local, so they commend some limited local orthodoxy, usually a truth by convention if not always current convention. By contrast, Western natural science and technology assume that truths by nature are accessible, that only they can be rationally endorsed, and with the aid of logic and method. What logic and method? Variously: the logic of proof, of probability, of plausibility, of justification, of giving good reasons. A large and inconclusive literature discusses the precise meanings of these competing suggestions and their combinations. Anthropologists need a theory of rationality that escapes this quagmire.

It seems easy: descriptive reports on truths by convention can be true by nature, so *ethnography is rational even if its subjects are not. Instead, anthropology is wracked by disputes over the rationality of other societies (and over its own practice). How are such disputes to be adjudicated? The simplest answer is, some anthropologists say one thing and other anthropologists say another. †Thomas S. Kuhn (1962) gained great influence by labelling competing views †'paradigms' and legitimizing them all as truths by convention; especially those from different historical periods. He accepted the philosopher †Michael Polanyi's (1958) picture of scientists as tribes centred around workshops. There is something to this but, as intellectual tribes trade in ideas, it gives no solution to the problem: which idea is it rational to endorse?

Primitivity as lack of rationality

Anthropology traditionally specialized in displaying the rationality of societies supposedly innocent, even in their technology, of the distinction between nature and convention. Yet anthropological discussions of the theory of rationality get lost in the conceptual mazes left by generations of debate over †primitive society and thought. Each refuted theory left behind conceptual dead-ends.

All anthropology, Greek, Renaissance and modern, begins with the wish to understand differences between societies. Each period considered itself better than its ancestors and neighbours. Greek thinkers wondered about barbarians; Renaissance thinkers wondered about the newly encountered North American Indians; modern anthropology wondered about 'our contemporary ancestors'. Why did none of these anthropological 'others' possess universal truths as we do? Perhaps, one theory went, they were not properly human; alternatively, perhaps they were deficient in the power to reason their way to universal truths. The influence of Plato and Aristotle on posterity ensured this latter theory a hearing, and left definite traces on current concepts of rationality. The theory that primitivity is a deficiency in the rational faculty is refuted by many kinds of evidence: such as the anthropological others' ability to assimilate quickly and quite successfully into any society, and to excel at any endeavour; such as the successful transplantation of universalist *science to other societies and cultures; such as the offspring of mixed couples, predicted by this theory to be feeble in body and mind (even †Darwin endorsed this view), shown to be nothing of the sort (enriching gene pools being deemed advantageous nowadays).

A more recent theory had it that the limited, conventional ideas of anthropological others reveal a subtle difference of rationality, perhaps a more practical and less theoretical orientation, or

a greater proneness to emotion, or a less-than logical or *primitive mentality (Lévy-Bruhl 1923). This theory is refuted by the same evidence. †Michel Foucault (1972) revived it under the name *epistemes*, which is no more testable, or plausible, than other theories of collective †mentality such as the discredited 'spirit of the nation', '*Zeitgeist*', etc. (Lloyd 1990). The Piagetian Hallpike attempted another revival (1979).

A variant of the false theory that other societies harbour rationally inferior mentalities is still surprisingly popular: anthropological others are guided by types of thinking that have atrophied among us, such as magical or allegorical or metaphorical or poetic or symbolic thinking. *Myths, *Malinowski held, are a way of thinking, a kind of knowledge of the world. Myths think for us, added *Claude Lévi-Strauss. Refusing to assess myths as universal scientific theories, because their holders make no universal claim, symbolist anthropologists still view them as compelling because they charter the society in which they thrive; myths maintain social cohesion and the collective economic pulse. This theory is *functionalist; it confuses effect with cause, error with fault, and alternative with contradiction; it is anti-historical in accord with Malinowski's dictum that there are no survivals: institutions are explained by their function, not their past. Yet myths both explain and charter, exist as poetry and transform into scientific theory. Survivals do exist (men's evening dress tails, English spelling, the monarchy).

Another variant, †worldview or framework theory, allows that anthropological others possess both the faculty and the mentality for rationality, yet pictures them as trapped within worldviews flexible enough to explain and assimilate any information save their own limitations. Thus the universal assimilates the conventional (Evans-Pritchard 1937); in particular, social regularities are treated as laws of nature. This is natural monism. Though refuted by the ability to shed myths that is regularly observed in *modernizing and secularizing societies, and by some of the cross-cultural evidence mentioned above, it retains some explanatory power.

This is captured in †Popper's social theory of rationality, according to which sophisticated techniques distinguish the pursuit of truth by nature: logic and methodology, and social institutions to incorporate and mandate them (Popper 1945). The result is to foster cooperative self-checking. Thus, the difference between us and the anthropological others is social: it is certain kinds of action in search of truth that are rational, neither mental capacities nor types of thought.

This final theory can help simplify the opening triad of rational ideas, rational action and rational social arrangements. We present this against the background of twentieth century debates over rationality.

A single conception of rationality for anthropology

The rationalist theory that some ideas are more rational than others was advanced in order to explain the scientific and technological superiority (what Gellner [1964] calls the 'cognitive power') of European societies over the societies they subjected to anthropological research. The difference seems to be qualitative. The various attempts to pin down that quality can be expressed in a series of contrasts:

THEIR IDEAS ARE	OUR IDEAS ARE
historical	universal
anthropomorphic	mechanistic
speculative	calculated
imaginative	empirical
emotional	intellectual
intuitive	cerebral
personal	impersonal

Admittedly, modern science and technology eschew all equivalents to the notion of the ritual states of actors affecting the technology they employ; the cloud-seeding pilot neglects the rain dance with impunity. Yet it is difficult to explain how humanity got from there to here – an inescapable problem in the Darwinian intellectual atmosphere within which modern anthropology emerged. The story of the unity of the human race demands a coherent account of intellectual progress. The notoriously Darwinian functionalist anthropologists tried to evade this problem by the observation that any social form that has survived to the present has thereby demonstrated its functionality. This exciting move bridged the gulf between the universalism of the rationalist tradition and the historical approach that seemed equally desirable. The same move also bridges between the universalism demanded by the unity of humanity and the diversity disclosed by social and cultural anthropology.

Between the wars, influential rationalists, the logical †positivists, claimed to have found a clear,

purely natural demarcation between scientific ideas and all other ideas, especially those counterfeits in which anthropologists specialized such as pseudo-science, primitive science, folk science, old wives tales and such. This claim was doomed by the obvious fact that scientific method could hardly have come fully-fledged from nowhere, and could not, therefore, put stamps of approval on particular ideas without begging the question of the approval of its own stamp. Logical positivism dismissed most of past science, particularly the speculations which populate ethnography and the history of science alike. To dismiss the speculative atomism of Democritus is awkward, as it was an ancestor of modern scientific notions.

The collapse of logical positivism spread a sense of calamity: if scientific method did not demarcate scientific ideas, what would? Popper developed his answer: shift the focus to stance or attitude towards ideas – any ideas, including myths, pseudo-science, etc.

This is a forceful proposal, and it suggests a general strategy: characterizing scientific method, as a rational treatment of ideas, makes science a special case of rational action (Agassi and Jarvie 1987). If rational action is assessed as a matter of degree, rationality is thereby relativized and non-invidiously graded. Now earlier anthropological theories make sense as they pass through the mangle to have incoherencies and condescension squeezed out, the disingenuous pretence rejected that recognizing moral equality compels one to admit the equality of the cognitive powers of all societies. Not magic, but the uncritical attitude to ideas embedded in the social institutions of magic-oriented groups is what inhibits the jump to universalist science: members are doing their top rational best as long as they have no science.

Rational thinking becomes a version of internalized rational action. As an interesting consequence, rational thought, namely, orderly, systematic, mental concentration is a clearly universal human disposition, manifest in the ability to plan a hunt, lay up stores for winter, compute, and design a scientific experiment. Construed as a form of rational action, rational thought is a universal competence. If rationality is identified with rational action in the prosaic sense of goal-directed, and rational thinking is taken as a type of rational action, especially planning, then it is ultra-rational to create institutions that promote and improve efficiency, including intellectual efficiency. The social arrangements that produce science are more rational in this sense than those which produce magic: they foster correction and improvement of ideas, improvement charted in the history of ideas.

The error of traditional rationalism goes deeper: dividing all endorsed ideas into truths either by nature or by convention makes thought ahistorical. Not only are truths by nature abstracted from history; all falsehoods can be summarily dismissed. The only intellectual progress allowed then is from truth by convention to truth by nature in one rationally inexplicable step. To disallow this step on grounds that truth by nature is inaccessible deprives the history of ideas of its rationality. In a desperate effort to retrieve the lost rationality, the traditional equation (rationality = truth-by-nature) has been replaced by the equation, rationality = truth-by-convention. This reverts to a pre-philosophical view, under the label *'relativism'. Relativism of truth recently decayed into the textualist view that anthropology and all science simply tell stories, and all intellectual activity is reduced to a generalized anthropology of story-telling. Stories can be assessed by aesthetic or psychological criteria, but these are local and conventional.

An extreme form of relativism inspired by †Kuhn (1962) and the 'Strong Programme in the Sociology of Knowledge' (Bloor 1976) emerged in the 1970s. It views anthropological story-telling as a Western ritual activity. If anthropology is to be declared rational, then, on the principle of 'study the ritual not the belief' (Jarvie 1964), it requires functional rather than historical or intellectual explanation. Anthropological ritual consists in the production of texts that construct the societies and cultures of 'others' in service to the powers that be (Clifford and Marcus 1986). This relativism of truth makes all doctrine true by convention, promotes conservatism and stagnation, and gladly denies the rational superiority of science over magic. (It also evades the awkward question of whether the relativism is true by nature or by convention.)

These recent moves are excessive. It suffices to relativize rationality: denying its traditional identification with truth permits the recognition of truth by nature as superior – even though seldom accessible: it suffices to maintain the concept of truth by nature as the ideal, and for the refusal to bow to local teachings as superior just because they are ours.

I.C. JARVIE and JOSEPH AGASSI

See also: relativism, science, cognition

Further reading

Agassi, J. (1977) *Towards a Rational Philosophical Anthropology*, Dordrecht: Kluwer

Agassi, J. and I.C. Jarvie (eds) (1987) *Rationality: The Critical View*, The Hague: Martinus Nijhoff

Bloor, D. (1976) *Knowledge and Social Imagery*, London: Routledge

Clifford, J. and G.E. Marcus (1986) *Writing Culture: The Politics and Poetics of Ethnography*, Berkeley and Los Angeles: University of California Press

Evans-Pritchard, E.E. (1937) *Witchcraft, Oracles and Magic Among the Azande*, Oxford: Clarendon Press

Foucault, M. (1972) *The Archaeology of Knowledge*, London: Tavistock

Gellner, E. (1964) *Thought and Change*, London: Weidenfeld and Nicolson

Hallpike, C.R. (1979) *The Foundations of Primitive Thought*, Oxford: Clarendon Press

Hollis, M. and S. Lukes (eds) (1982) *Rationality and Relativism*, Oxford: Blackwell

Jarvie, I.C. (1964) *The Revolution in Anthropology*, London: Routledge

Kuhn, Thomas, S. (1962) *The Structure of Scientific Revolutions*, Chicago: University of Chicago Press

Lévy-Bruhl, L. ([1922]1923) *Primitive Mentality*, London:

Lloyd, G.E.R. (1990) *Demystifying Mentalities*, Cambridge: Cambridge University Press

Polanyi, M. (1958) *Personal Knowledge*, London: Routledge

Popper, K.R. (1945) *The Open Society and Its Enemies*, London: Routledge

Wilson, B. (ed.) (1970) *Rationality*, Oxford: Blackwell

reflexivity

The concept of reflexivity, after some hectic years as the pennant of a seminar revolution, has at last settled into a kind of comfortable convention. Perhaps too comfortable. Reflexivity, in practice, has become the recognition by most ethnographers of the symbolic wing of American cultural anthropology that adequate anthropological accounts cannot be crafted without acknowledging the forces – epistemological and political – that condition their writing. At its most useful and bland, this has developed into a form of *ethnographic writing with distinct features. A typically reflexive effort, hence, will contain a discussion of its writer's biographical ties (or lack thereof) to the events or peoples being discussed; an admission that the anthropological project of describing human diversity was created as part of the larger Western colonial project of *divide et impera (divide and rule)*; all leading to a reanalysis of the concepts and analytic techniques that biography and the discipline's dubious history may have brought to the ethnographic process as unspoken givens. The result is supposed to be, and often is, an account that illuminates both what the ethnographer set out to discuss as well as the always contingent grounds of such a discussion.

At its most interesting and disruptive, however, reflexivity has sometimes manifested itself as the epistemological claim that any ethnographic investigation of some 'other' is really, inevitably, only a process of self-definition played out within the disciplinary, individuating, Western, 'self'; and an associated political claim that this revelation, masquerading as observation, is part of a process of writing the 'other' back into a kind of textual colonialism (Abu-Lughod 1991). This more radical kind of reflexivity, of course, hints that anthropology, or at least its associated concepts of *'culture' and *'society', should end with the colonial arrogance that gave it birth. This terminal negativity, along with the tendency of some avowedly reflexive ethnography to ooze autobiographical treacle, has led a few dismissive critics to write off reflexivity as both self-serving and self-indulgent. The epistemological and political charges it raises, however, remain all too painfully undeniable.

Reflexivity first became an issue to American cultural anthropologists in the late 1960s because of the Vietnam war. (The term already had some usage in radical *sociology; see Bourdieu and Wacquant 1992.) Anthropologists doing *fieldwork in an antagonistic 'Third World' could not help but feel the falseness of their position when challenged by locals outraged by the United States of America's international power playing. The collection, *Reinventing Anthropology*, edited by Dell Hymes, which appeared in 1969, crystallized this sense of political unease in a series of essays which confronted American anthropology's till then largely unexamined colonial past, and contemplated the international and national power dynamic within which its contemporary professional activities continued to be carried out. Bob Scholte's article in that volume, 'Toward a Reflexive and Critical Anthropology', was probably the first to use the term 'reflexive' in the sense it now carries today; i.e. by suggesting that anthropologists must always note 'reflexively' how the political assymetries their activities presupposed were connected, in the process of ethnography, to the epistemological privileges of 'objectivity' and

'neutrality' they also claimed. Talal Asad's 1973 collection, *Anthropology and the Colonial Encounter*, levelled a similar critique at *British social anthropology. In the late 1970s, a trio of semi-autobiographical 'ethnographies', Paul Rabinow's *Reflections on Fieldwork in Morocco* (1977), Kevin Dwywer's *Moroccan Dialogues: Anthropology in Question* (1982), and Vincent Crapanzano's *Tuhami* (1980), carried things a step further, challenging the normal distinction between 'subjective' field memoir and 'objective' ethnographic monograph by melding the two together in their various accounts of fieldwork in Morocco. Their works, like Barbara Myerhoff's more subtle *Number Our Days* (1978), tended to concretize the charge that the ethnographer's own racial, national, political, financial, and professional position was inextricably at play in the processes of recording and interpreting the field. Rabinow, in particular, isolated a concept central to such accounts by hauling forth, as an accurate characterization of the fieldwork encounter, Paul Ricoeur's definition of hermeneutics as 'the comprehension of the self by the detour of the comprehension of the other'; and then pointing out, acutely, that this is the very process reflexivity critiques when it highlights the political preconditions of such 'detours' (Rabinow 1977: 5, 161–2). Their often tragi-comic accounts of conceptual disillusionment and confused, cross-cultural betrayal also left traces of elegiac bemusement and wounded revelation that continue to mark much reflexive ethnographic writing.

In the mid 1980s, reflexivity was turned in a direction at once more textual and philosophically sophisticated with the publication, in the same year, of two books: George E. Marcus and Michael M.J. Fisher's overview of anthropology, *Anthropology as Cultural Critique* (1986); and the collection, edited by James Clifford and George E. Marcus, *Writing Culture: The Poetics and Politics of Ethnography* (1986). These works, together, raised a selfconscious call for the doing of more experimentally reflexive ethnographic writing, and, to simplify them mercilessly, derived their feeling of critical urgency as to why this was suddenly so necessary from three interrelated factors. First, a sense, variously articulated, that anthropology's foundationalist epistemology and scientism – that is, its unspoken presumption that, in the end, anthropology is somehow about discovering the perfect language for articulating either a 'really real' universal human essence, or a set of equally 'real' if various cultural essences – had been fatally called into question by a growing recognition of that epistemology's Western provincialism, historical specificity, and unsavoury political implications. Second, a *'postmodern' distrust and, sometimes, outright rejection of the standard Western †'meta-narratives', or big stories, of how history tendeth as it listeth (as implied by terms like 'modern' and 'traditional') occasioned by the inevitable unifica-tions and violent juxtapositions that occur when things like, say, Hausa drumming and Charlie's Angels, formerly separated by these same histor-ical narratives, are forced together into the single space, time, and value of the inexorable, world market. Finally, third, the fatal observation (first made by †Clifford Geertz) that since ethnography was, above all else, a form of writing, much of its self-proclaimed objectivity and empirically-grounded authority would be better seen as rhetorical effects of the way the ethnographic genre was constructed rather than as either defen-sible claims or incontestable givens – with the corollary implication that, if constructed, such texts could be, should be, opened up for inspec-tion, and strategically de- and reconstructed. The shorthand way to refer to this kind of text-focused reflexivity is as 'a politics of writing'; an investi-gation, that is, of the implications of that hidden struggle in the ethnographer's office, where larger, generally unacknowledged political and profes-sional hegemonies quietly slouch toward anthropological pronouncement. The appearance of this politics in American anthropology was of a piece with 'reflexive' reconsiderations of *Orientalism (Said 1978) by literary critics, critiques of the historiography of *colonialism by postcolonial scholars, and of the popular media by *cultural studies.

All this, of course, has given rise to some passionate objections. Leaving aside, as a momen-tary dyspepsia, the grumpy disdain of those discomforted by a few too many intimate revela-tions, these criticisms tend to be of two sorts. On the one hand, there are claims by the epistemo-logically conservative that reflexivity implies a form of radical *relativism that would make ethnographic comparison and anthropological generalization impossible. This critique, which at times seems to be taken seriously as a positive claim even by some rather unreflective reflexive anthropologists, is undercut by the difficulty attending any attempt to imagine what 'relativism' might mean in the absence of the kinds of claims about cultural essences that most reflexive

anthropologists have refused to make. Rather more serious are the charges, levelled by some feminists, postcolonial scholars, and students of science studies, that the reflexive 'politics of writing' were often more about the struggle for academic prestige than for social justice – because, that is, the theorists of 'reflexivity' merely took old insights into the production of anthropological knowledge offered years before by feminists and Marxists, and redrafted them into an elite post-structuralist language of calculated uniqueness. Some feminists and activists have also argued, in a more interesting, partial application of the conservative epistemological critique, that reflexive anthropology's non-foundationalism – its forswearing, that is, of the possibility of a 'really real' ground underlying its accounts – also desta-bilizes the political positions activists, such as feminists and some postcolonial critics, require for political engagement. Other critics of anthro-pology, like Donna Haraway, unwilling to reapply foundationalism in this way, have proposed instead a notion of 'situated knowledge', of knowing constructed according to an objectivity locally but nonetheless firmly constrained (Haraway 1991: 188-96), that would also allow critique to continue without disabling the critic. This position also causes Haraway to reject, as epistemologically naive, the very idea that one can 'fix' ethnographic representation by being more self-conscious about how one does it.

However these controversies pan out, it remains that reflexivity has proven itself a fertile concept. Most anglophone ethnography now written, whether in Britain or the United States, pays at least routine heed to the whys and where-fores of its own production. And although this very routinization has resulted in a certain staleness in application, it has also allowed entirely new kinds of questions to be asked; a questioning originally initiated, it is to be remembered, by the very people anthropology had so often silenced in the past.

MARK P. WHITAKER

See also: colonialism, ethnography, relativism, cultural studies, Orientalism

Further reading

Abu-Lughod, L. (1991) 'Writing against Culture' in Richard G. Fox (ed.) *Recapturing Anthropology: Working in the Present*, Santa Fe School of American Research Press

Asad, T. (ed.) (1973) *Anthropology and the Colonial Encounter*, Atlantic Highlands, NJ: Humanities Press

Bourdieu, P. and L. Wacquant (1992) *An Invitation to Reflexive Sociology*, Oxford: Polity

Clifford, J. and G.E. Marcus (eds) (1986) *Writing Culture: The Poetics and Politics of Ethnography*, Berkeley: University of California Press

Crapanzano, V. (1980) *Tuhami: Portrait of a Moroccan*, Chicago: University of Chicago Press

Dwyer, K. (1982) *Moroccan Dialogues: Anthropology in Question*, Baltimore: Johns Hopkins University Press

Haraway, D.J. (1991) *Simians, Cyborgs, and Women: The Reinvention of Nature*, London: Routledge

Hymes, D. (ed.) (1969) *Reinventing Anthropology*, New York: Pantheon

Marcus, G.E. and M.M.J. Fisher (1986) *Anthropology as Cultural Critique: An Experimental Moment in the Human Sciences*, Chicago: University of Chicago Press

Myerhoff, B. (1978) *Number Our Days*, New York: Simon and Schuster

Rabinow, P. (1977) *Reflections on Fieldwork in Morocco*, Berkeley: University of California Press

Said, E.W. (1978) *Orientalism*, New York: Vintage

Scholte, B. (1969) 'Toward a Reflexive and Critical Anthropology', in Dell Hymes (ed.) *Reinventing Anthropology*, New York: Pantheon

refugees

The 1951 United Nations (UN) Convention on the Status of Refugees defines a refugee as a person who has a well founded fear of persecution by reason of one of five grounds (race, religion, nationality, political opinion, or membership in a particular social group) and whose country of nationality or former habitual residence is unable or unwilling to provide protection. Some 23 million refugees are distinguished from other kinds of *migrants – even those fleeing natural disasters or environmental destruction – by their right to claim international protection. The elements of international protection are 'admission to safety, exemption from forcible return, non-discrimination, and assistance for survival' (UNHCR 1993: 5). Refugees are often the kin of persons who are internally displaced (of whom there are now 24 million), but they have fled to other parts of their countries rather than cross borders.

The right to seek and enjoy asylum from persecution is recognised in article 14 (1) of the Universal Declaration of Human Rights. Yet states have no obligation to grant asylum, particularly when they are not party to at least one of the international instruments for setting out the rights and obligations of states to refugees. Persons who have committed serious non-political crimes, war crimes, or engaged in acts contrary to the purposes and principles of the UN are excluded from benefiting from the Convention.

In 1969, the Organisation of African Unity (OAU) adopted a broader definition to encompass massive refugee flows in Africa where the harm feared also resulted from external aggression, occupation, foreign domination or events seriously disturbing public order. In 1984, the ten Latin American states enacted the Cartagena Declaration, adopting a similar definition to that set out by OAU and including fear of generalised violence and massive violations of human rights as enumerated grounds for regional protection (Hathaway 1991: 16–21). Enlightened interpretation of the UN definition, even in the age of increasingly restrictive access to asylum procedures, can go some way towards protecting persons fleeing civil war, provided it can be demonstrated that a person faced heightened risk of serious harm because of civil or political status. However, refugee status is often not given to victims of civil war, but some states provide for interim status to remain until it is safe to return.

There are disruptions to virtually every phase of a refugee's life. Marginality characterises the phases of the refugee experience: anticipated harm, flight, search for asylum, resettlement or repatriation. Few who become refugees can anticipate the experience that envelops them. There is an oppressive time component: generations can be born into refugeehood. There is also a gender component: women and children comprise 80 per cent of the world's refugees and often experience persecution differently from men. The irony is that while international protection is meant to protect persons who have become disenfranchised from their own states, these same persons may remain marginalised throughout refugeehood.

The anthropological study of refugees is noted for *in situ* fieldwork: in camps, in cities, in asylum seeking-procedures, or in repatriation movements back home. It is concerned with questions of meaning, perception, and *survival* as viewed by the refugees themselves and by the assisting agencies (Gilad 1990; Maalki 1995). The anthropologist may be led to criticism of the agencies and hence to applied research for the improvement of the lot of refugees (Harrell-Bond 1986). Finally, the anthropological study of refugees requires more than lip service to interdisciplinary understanding of law, international relations, psychology and *sociology.

LISA GILAD

Lisa Gilad is a Member of the Immigration and Refugee Board of Canada (IRB). The views in this entry are those of the author and do not necessarily reflect the views of the IRB.

See also: migration, state

Further reading

Forbes, S. (1991) *Refugee Women*, London: Zed Press
Gilad, L. (1990) *The Northern Route: An Ethnography of Refugee Experiences*, St John's: ISER Books
Hansen, A. and A. Oliver Smith (eds) (1982) *Involuntary Migration: The Problems and Responses of the Displaced*, Boulder: Westview Press
Harrell-Bond, B.E. (1986) *Imposing Aid: Emergency Assistance to Refugees*, Oxford: Oxford University Press
Hathaway, J. (1991) *The Law of Refugee Status*, Toronto: Butterworths
Hirschon, R. (1989) *Heirs of the Greek Catastrophe: The Social Life of Asia Minor Refugees in Piraeus*, Oxford: Clarendon Press
Kay, D. (1987) *Chileans in Exile: Private Struggles, Public Lives*, London: Macmillan
Knudsen, J. (1992) *Chicken Wings: Refugee Stories from a Concrete Hell*, Bergen: Magnet Forlagin
Loescher, G. (1993) *Beyond Charity: International Cooperation and the Global Refugee Problems*, New York: Oxford University Press
Maalki, L. (1995) *Purity and Exile: Violence, Memory and National Cosmology among Hutu Refugees in Tanzania*, Chicago: University of Chicago Press
Morgan, S. and E. Colson (eds) (1987) *People in Upheaval*, New York: Centre for Migration Studies
Tollefson, J. (1989) *Alien Winds: The Reeducation of America's Indochinese Refugees*, New York: Praeger
United Nations High Commissioner for Refugees (UNHCR) (1993) *The State of the World's Refugees; The Challenge of Protection*, London: Penguin

regional analysis and regional comparison

Three kinds of regional analysis

The term 'regional analysis' has at least two, and possibly three, completely different senses. In the first instance, the term has come to be linked closely with the idea of regional comparison, which entails comparing different societies or cultures, or elements of them, within a region. Regional analysis, in this sense, further involves the search for explanations as to why such cultural

phenomena are constant across a region, or why differences occur within a region. It is this first sense that will be of primary concern in this article.

In a second sense, the term can refer to the study of a region as a structural or dynamic system, with different social and cultural units interacting. It has been used in this way, or more often simply implied, by social scientists of all kinds who are interested in *colonialism and †pluralism, and especially by Marxist and other materialist thinkers whose emphasis is on units larger than single small-scale societies (see *Marxism and anthropology). The idea is that such 'societies' are not really independent, but themselves part of larger politico-economic entities, namely regions. In their different ways, Kahn's (1993) analysis of social change in colonial Indonesia and Wilmsen's (1989) study of the political economy of the Kalahari are examples.

Finally, there is a third sense in which the word 'regional' has been used in anthropology, if not quite a third meaning of 'regional analysis'. This is in the sense of regional traditions. As Fardon (1990), and contributors to his volume have shown, anthropologists themselves create regional traditions of ethnography through their engagement in dialogues within their respective regions – dialogues from which the *images* of ethnographic regions emerge. The relation between this concept of region – Melanesia, Middle East, West Africa, etc. – and the *ethnography which is produced in its name does bear relation to the first sense of regional analysis. The difference is that in this third sense it is the anthropologist as creator of regional texts who is emphasized, rather than the social facts he or she encounters within the region in question.

Early regional studies

Early attempts at understanding regions were made in order to compare those regions to others, rather than to understand the internal aspects of a region for its own sake. In the early twentieth century, in German and Austrian anthropology, the †*Kulturkreis* school sought to map out the history of the world according to their postulated expanding and overlapping 'culture circles', which were supposedly spread by both *diffusion and *migration.

About the same time, American anthropologists were developing models which drew on the notion of the †culture area. †Clark Wissler (e.g. 1923), especially, consolidated efforts made by other American anthropologists to understand the regions of *Native North America and devised theories to explain relations between cultures within a region and between regions. Culture areas were often equated with environmental zones, each of which would have a centre from which †culture traits diffused. Marginal areas might have elements in common with more than one culture area. Sets of functionally related traits, called trait complexes, were supposed to diffuse together. Their presence would mark the bounds of various regional levels of analysis – e.g. 'sub areas', 'culture areas' and 'grand areas'.

Theoretical advances

Comparison is both a method and a theoretical concept. Its theoretical importance is enhanced when we compare not just two or three societies, but a range of similar societies, such as those which define a region or culture area. This kind of comparison has been labelled, with increasing degrees of theoretical refinement, 'controlled', 'intensive regional', and 'regional structural' comparison. The idea is that an element of control is introduced when we compare societies which are similar. This does not always suggest comparing within regions: controlled comparisons beyond regional boundaries might be within a range of similar economic systems, e.g. desert-dwelling hunter-gatherers of different parts of the world. However, the regional dimension tends to add an additional element of control, as well as to highlight historical relations which connect cultures of the same area.

Regional studies differ logically from large-scale, cross-cultural, 'global sample' studies (e.g. Murdock 1949). Equally, they differ from studies in which comparison is merely illustrative, whether the illustration involves a culture trait found only in two or three societies or in many societies across the globe. A good examples of a study which both goes beyond mere illustration and narrows the focus by concentrating on closely-related cultures or societies is †Jack Goody's (1959) essay on the mother's brother among the LoDaggaa and LoWiili of Northern Ghana. In these cultures, or arguably different social groups within the same culture, opposite forms of behaviour between a mother's brother and his sister's son can be ascribed to differences in the rules of †inheritance. Goody sacrifices broader ethnographic coverage in order to maintain a tighter control over his comparisons, and thus is able to claim strong grounds for his supposition that *property rela-

tions affect the way kinsmen treat each other (see also *avunculate). As in a chemical experiment, here he narrows the range of variables in order to find the single determinant one.

An interesting contrast is †Nadel's (1952) essay on *witchcraft in four African societies. Two of his examples are Sudanese and the other two are Nigerian. Each regional pair shows both similarities of historical relationship and divergences, but cross-regional comparisons also reveal features which seem to be associated with variations in *kinship, *age, and *gender relations, among other things. Nadel's study is loosely concerned with regional structures, but it is also partly illustrative rather than controlled. Unlike Goody, he sacrifices control in order to illustrate structural contrasts which would otherwise not be apparent.

Regional structural comparison

Early developments of regional structural comparison include elements within the traditions of both Dutch and French *structuralism. The Dutch structuralists of the 1920s and 1930s engaged, probably unwittingly, in controlled regional analysis in their work on kinship, marital *alliance, social hierarchy, *ritual and *belief among the inhabitants of the Malay Archipelago. The most explicit statement on the subject was †J.P.B. de Josselin de Jong's inaugural lecture at Leiden University (Josselin de Jong [1935] 1977), which commented on a number of common features of the diverse indigenous societies of the Dutch East Indies, such as the form of marriage known as †circulating connubium, and suggested that scholars search further for the reasons for the apparent diversity within this unity. Among the French, much of *Lévi-Strauss's work, and †Dumont's, is also regional, and certainly structural, though it is doubtful that either of them developed their approaches to South American or South Asian ethnography as part of a conscious effort to maintain control in their work.

More formal understandings of the notion of regional structural comparison have been developed by Kuper (e.g. 1982). His studies of patterns of marriage and the spatial symbolism of the homestead emphasizes the fact that differences between divergent southern Bantu cultures are not random or merely historical, but related to complex economic and political relations. In traditional *Southern Africa, higher-status individuals can often maintain power and wealth by making appropriate †bridewealth transactions. Predictable patterns emerge. The Tswana, who tend to marry †hypergamously, have relatively low bridewealth. The southern Sotho, who tend to marry †hypogamously, have relatively high bridewealth. The Swazi marry either way, and those Swazi men who marry high-status women tend to pay higher bridewealth. Similarly, close kin †endogamy among the Lovedu and †exogamy among the Tsonga can be explained according to contrasting features of their economic circumstances. Different strategies are appropriate within different southern Bantu cultures, because different conditions apply. Yet, what all these groups have in common is a set of fundamentally similar structures of kinship. The differences are but permutations of that underlying structural similarity.

More recently, Kuper's methods have been applied to the study of the *relationship terminologies, *settlement patterns and religious beliefs of the Khoisan peoples of Southern Africa (Barnard 1992). These peoples, more distantly related than southern Bantu-speakers are to each other, have provided a test case for the notion of culture as a regional structure larger than an individual society. Specific societies, it is argued, are analogous to dialects within a language, and diversity can be explained through an interplay between underlying constraints and environmental, technological and historical factors. For example, the transition from hunting to herding has effects on group structure and the classification of relatives. Similarly, settlement patterns are related both to (a) common structural features of *environment or *society, such as seasonality or egalitarian group structure among *hunter-gatherers, and (b) divergent ones, such as the availability of specific resources in certain areas. The comparison of micro-environmental differences among hunting-and-gathering societies of this region should enable the building of models which can both explain and predict the way in which land is or can be used within the constraints of cultural practice. With Khoisan religious beliefs, regional analysis is more complicated but equally intriguing, due in this case to the very fact that a central, common element of Khoisan religion is its great fluidity. Individuals can manipulate symbols according to *other* underlying principles of Khoisan thought, within structures of relations between their deities and other elements of their common cultural universe.

ALAN BARNARD

See also: comparative method, culture, Dutch anthropology.

Further reading

Barnard, A. (1992) *Hunters and Herders of Southern Africa: A Comparative Ethnography of the Khoisan Peoples*, Cambridge: Cambridge University Press

Fardon, R. (1990) 'General Introduction', in R. Fardon (ed.), *Localizing Strategies: Regional Traditions of Ethnographic Writing*, Edinburgh: Scottish Academic Press

Goody, J.R. (1959) 'The Mother's Brother and the Sister's Son in West Africa', *Journal of the Royal Anthropological Institute* 89: 59–88.

Josselin de Jong, J.P.B. de ([1935] 1977) 'The Malay Archipelago as a Field of Ethnological Study', in P.E. de Josselin de Jong (ed.) *Structural Anthropology in the Netherlands*, The Hague: Martinus Nijhoff

Kahn, J.S. (1993) *Constituting the Minangkabau: Peasants, Culture, and Modernity in Colonial Indonesia*, Oxford: Berg

Kuper, A. (1982) *Wives for Cattle: Bridewealth and Marriage in Southern Africa*, London: Routledge & Kegan Paul

Murdock, G.P. (1949) *Social Structure*, New York: Macmillan

Nadel, S.F. (1952) 'Witchcraft in four African societies: An Essay in Comparison', *American Anthropologist* 54: 18–29

Wilmsen, E.N. (1989) *Land Filled with Flies: A Political Economy of the Kalahari*, Chicago: University of Chicago Press

Wissler, C. (1923) *Man and Culture*, New York: Thomas Y. Crowell Company

relationship terminology

A relationship terminology is, in any given language, the set of words used to classify a person's relatives. The phrase *'kinship terminology' is a near-synonym, but many anthropologists prefer the former term because it does not imply that the society in question makes a precise distinction between kin and †affines, or even between 'real' and 'metaphorical' kin (e.g. 'sisters' in the women's liberation movement).

The idea that different societies classified relatives differently was noted in the early eighteenth century by the missionary-ethnographer †Joseph-Francois Lafitau who lived and worked among the Iroquois Nations of North America. However, the true founder of the study of relationship terminologies is generally agreed to be *Lewis Henry Morgan who, coincidentally, repeated Lafitau's discovery among the same linguistic group more than a hundred years later.

Morgan's theory

Morgan posited historical and sociological reasons for differences in kinship classification, as well as noting the structural features of the specific terminologies found among Native North Americans. His theory was influential because he suggested that relationship terminologies change because of transformations in *property relations. Thus relationship terminologies could be a clue to working out a materialist history of preliterate societies, such as that of his followers †Marx and †Engels.

More specifically, in the final chapter of *Systems of Consanguinity and Affinity of the Human Family* (1871), Morgan advanced a theory of the evolution of the *family based on the notion that relationship terminologies change only slowly, and thus retain clues to customs which are no longer practised. For example, if the same term is used for father and father's brother, this might imply a former practice of *marriage of a group of brothers all to the same woman. If mother and mother's sister are also called by a single term, this might further suggest an ancient system of †group marriage, where a group of brothers would collectively be married to a group of sisters. Morgan was attacked by †McLennan for overrating the significance of relationship terminologies. Yet, when anthropology moved on from *evolutionism, Morgan's interest was nevertheless retained as a keystone to later *functionalist and *structuralist theories of kinship. In both these cases, relationship terminologies were seen as important elements of *social structure because they frequently reflect aspects of *descent group structure or rules of marriage.

Three typologies

Morgan's classification of relationship terminologies included only two types: †'descriptive' and †'classificatory'. 'Descriptive' terminologies were defined as those which distinguish direct relatives (direct ancestors and descendants of †ego, plus ego's siblings) from †collaterals (all other †consanguineal relatives). 'Classificatory' terminologies were defined as those which fail to make such a distinction. By these means, Morgan classified all the Amerindian terminologies he came into contact with. He also sent questionnaires to *missionaries and American consuls throughout the world, in order to compare terminologies with each other and decipher through them what he could of world history.

However, as Morgan's own work suggests, the division of all the world's terminologies into only two types proved to be inadequate. It is not merely the presence or absence of one distinction (direct/collateral) which is important. Other distinctions are equally interesting. †Kroeber (1909) found eight distinctions altogether. Of these one emerged as being of special importance: the distinction between †parallel relatives and †cross relatives. On the basis of these two distinctions – Morgan's direct/collateral and Kroeber's parallel/cross applied in the generation of ego's parents – †Lowie (1928) recognized four ideal types. Consider females of the mother's generation, for example. One might (1) call mother, mother's sister, and father's sister all by a single term (as in the Hawaiian language). Alternatively, (2) one might classify mother and mother's sister by one term and father's sister by a different one (as in Iroquois). Another possibility (3) is to classify mother by one term and mother's sister and father's sister by another (as in English). Finally, (4) one might classify each genealogical position by a distinct term (as in Gaelic). Lowie called these four ideal types †'generational', †'bifurcate merging', †'lineal', and †'bifurcate collateral', respectively. 'Generational' terminologies make neither direct/collateral nor parallel/cross distinctions. 'Bifurcate merging' terminologies make parallel/cross distinctions. 'Lineal' terminologies make direct/collateral distinctions. 'Bifurcate collateral' terminologies make both sets of distinction.

While Lowie emphasized the classification of relatives in the first ascending generation, †Murdock (1949) emphasized the classification of relatives in ego's own generation. His typology consists of six classes. †'Hawaiian' terminologies make no distinction between siblings and cousins. †'Iroquois' terminologies distinguish cross-cousins from parallel cousins and often classify siblings by the same term as that for parallel cousins. †'Eskimo' terminologies do not make parallel/cross distinctions, but rather, distinguish cousins (collaterals) from siblings (direct relatives). †'Sudanese' terminologies, like Lowie's 'bifurcate collateral' ones, make both kinds of distinction. In other words, they lack any general word for 'cousin' and call all cousins by strings of possessives.

Murdock's other two types, *'Crow' and 'Omaha', like 'Iroquois', distinguish parallel from cross-relatives. The difference is that they treat generational differences in a peculiar way. The defining feature of Murdock's 'Crow' (or 'Choctaw') type is that it classifies father's sister and father's sister's daughter by the same term. The defining feature for 'Omaha' is that it classifies mother's brother and mother's brother's son by the same term. Such terminologies often make further equations across the generation lines. For example, 'Crow' terminologies may classify father and father's sister's son by the same term, and 'Omaha' terminologies, mother and mother's brother's daughter. These classifications reflect descent group structure. In societies which possess 'Crow' terminologies, †matrilineal groups are usually present, and ego simply assimilates all members of his or her father's matrilineal group and calls them by two terms (one for males and one for females). 'Omaha' terminologies tend to be found in strongly †patrilineal societies, where similar equations are made in reference to ego's mother's patrilineal group. Where such terminology structures generate (or reflect) *alliance, they are known as *Crow-Omaha systems.

The formal analysis of relationship terminologies has been used to provide a key to understanding different systems of marriage and descent. Much depends, though, on what connection is thought to hold between the classification of relationships and kinship practice: the confusions and arguments about the terms *prescription and preference, for example, stand or fall on this connection. In general, anthropologists have grown increasingly sceptical of claims that there is any necessary connection between systems of classification and kinship practice. Similarly, grand typologies, of the sort advanced by Murdock, have fallen almost entirely out of fashion.

ALAN BARNARD

See also: alliance, descent, emic and etic, kinship, Crow–Omaha systems, preference and prescription

Further reading

Barnard, A. and A. Good (1984) *Research Practices in the Study of Kinship*, London: Academic Press

Fox, R. (1967) *Kinship and Marriage: An Anthropological Perspective*, Harmondsworth: Penguin Books

Héritier, F. (1981) *L'exercice de la parenté*, Paris: Gallimard

Kroeber, A.L. (1909) 'Classificatory Systems of Relationship', *Journal of the Royal Anthropological Institute* 39: 77–84

Lowie, R.H. (1928) 'A Note on Relationship Terminologies', *American Anthropologist* 30: 263–8

Morgan, L.H. (1871) *Systems of Consanguinity and Affinity of the Human Family*, Washington: Smithsonian Institution

Murdock, G.P. (1949) *Social Structure*, New York: Macmillan

Radcliffe-Brown, A.R. (1941) 'The Study of Kinship Systems', *Journal of the Royal Anthropological Institute* 71: 49–89

relativism

To define relativism is, of necessity, to take a position in the controversy surrounding it. This is because, as †Geertz (1984) has suggested, relativism, especially in its oft-derided 'epistemological' form, has become one of those peculiar by-products of anthropological spleen more deplored, and therefore more fully developed, by its opponents than held by those accused of being its adherents. For this very reason, it is helpful to begin by distinguishing three different kinds of relativism: conventional cultural relativism, ethical relativism, and epistemological or 'cognitive' relativism. These three notions, defined below, sometimes overlap, as nothing precludes someone from holding two or more of these positions at once; nonetheless, they constitute quite different concerns, and, more importantly, are subject to quite different degrees of controversy.

Many anthropologists since World War II would probably find themselves agreeing with a conventional cultural relativism – and disagreeing with its being called a form of relativism. Less a philosophical position than a vague methodological attitude, the conventional cultural relativism that most anthropologists, British or American, take to work with them is a combination of two notions: first, that insofar as there are behavioural differences between various populations of people, these differences are the result of cultural (sometimes societal) variation rather than anything else; and, second, that such differences as do exist are deserving of respect and understanding in their own terms. In its weakest, most popular version, conventional cultural relativism is agnostic about whether or not some universals, like death, eating, reproduction, or even class conflict and pan-psychological desires, might exist to define the limits of human diversity. Some anthropologists would make this list of universals large, many more would keep it small, and a few would argue against any; but any anthropologist not supposing all human action (or any human behavioural variation) the result of in-built universal forces would still qualify, in this sense, as a relativist. As applied in practice, this kind of relativism has also generally held most Western epistemological presumptions constant, and has often avoided troubling ethical issues altogether by reducing them to matters of local causation or design. This is, perhaps, because not questioning the first allows one to avoid debating epistemological relativism; and keeping the second issue from ever surfacing neatly side-steps the conundrums of ethical relativism. Still, this sort of conventional cultural relativism remains a kind of relativism, since, as per disciplinary convention, it assumes that the behavioural variations which interest anthropologists must be understood within the cultural or social frameworks which contain them.

This conventional cultural relativism is not a very thorough-going kind of relativism, for the strength of its claims tend to fade at the edges of its ethnographic interests; but it is a very safe view to propound. Hence, conventional cultural relativism is what students often take home with them from introductory anthropology classes. Moreover, it has proven a good club with which to batter arguments about *race and †ethnocentrism, and a practical attitude with which to approach ethnographic research. Still, this form of relativism is obviously not a proper philosophical position – nor, practically speaking, could it be. Rather it is a conveniently sloppy framework – a kind of 'work-ethic', or disciplinary 'common sense' – within which many anthropologists are comfortable discussing human variation, and which is the residual end-result of the more properly philosophical debates about ethical and epistemological relativism that have swirled around ethnographically-based anthropological research since its inception. The arguments about these forms of relativism, thus, are really struggles over what will ultimately constitute the conventional cultural relativism, which is, really, anthropology's practical core. And so we must turn to these more blatant controversies.

Ethical relativism

Ethical relativism is the notion that the business of making universal, cross-cultural, ethical judgements is both incoherent and unfair because moral values are a product of each culture's unique developmental history, and can, thus, only be judged in relation to that history. Versions of this form of ethical relativism, varying in strength from a weak call for mutual intercultural tolerance to the (rare) strong demand for ethical compartmentalization, have been part of anthropology and the traditions of thought that gave rise to it since,

at least, †Montesquieu's De l'esprit des lois (1948). This kind of relativism was most popular, however, in the 1930s in both British social anthropology and American cultural anthropology. *British anthropology's various forms of *functionalism, for example, seemed to suggest that any given society's ethical practices were the result of long-standing structural or practical developments, served complex and subtle purposes, and thus were not to be tampered with. Similarly, in the United States, *Boas (1911) and his students †Benedict (1934), and †Herskovits (1972), held to a *diffusionist view of cultural development which tended to undercut universalist claims, and made ethical relativism seem empirically obvious, methodologically necessary (to avoid ethocentrism), and obviously just. They also found it a useful jumping-off place for launching attacks on American provincialism, racism, and anti-Semitism.

These notions were, perhaps, best laid out by Melville Herskovits. In the late 1940s and early 1950s, Herskovits, inspired by his repugnance for racism and cultural imperialism, claimed that 'cultural relativism', as he termed it, was not merely pragmatically useful but empirically proven by the ethnographic record; and then went on to flirt with a form of epistemological relativism (Herskovits 1972), suggesting that perhaps not only mores but perceptions as well were products of enculturation. However, Herskovits, for whom relativism was really more a way of criticizing colonial imperialism than a proposal for a thorough-going philosophical doctrine, was soon brought to the dock by philosophers, and some anthropologists, on a charge of paradox: i.e. for asserting, as an absolute truth, the claim that all truths are culturally relative, and was thus, perhaps, unfairly, hoisted by his own petard. In any case support for ethical relativism began to erode during and after World War II, for various, sometimes ironic, reasons: the inadequacy of applying relativist tolerance to that period's sanguinary ideologies; the postwar demand for, and expectation of, development by the 'New States'; and the devastating postcolonial critique that ethical relativism, and the 'don't touch' approach to intercultural contact it seemed to approve, was merely a Western ideology that played into the hands of colonial masters by justifying their repressive status quo.

Still, this controversy has by no means died out. In the 1980s and early 1990s, for example, a claim by the cognitive psychologist Lawrence Kohlberg to have substantiated the existence of a universal developmental sequence of moral reasoning (one culminating, rather suspiciously, in something like Western liberalism) was met by equally passionate counter-claims by Shweder, Mahapatra and Miller (1990) that this 'confirmation' was merely an effect of the Western presuppositions built into his data-gathering technique. More painfully, current arguments among anthropologists about *power, human rights, and ritual genital mutilation reveal an old tension between the cosmopolitan tolerance of ethical relativism, with its corollary suspicion of the motives of those wishing to find or impose 'universal values', and an activist intolerance of repressive or violent conditions, with its equally apposite distrust of those who would allow such conditions to continue in the name of cultural autonomy. Nor has the routinization of some *reflexivity in much American ethnographic writing effaced this issue. Indeed, by questioning the authorial motives of both those who would remain relativistically neutral and those who would sometimes hazard judgement, reflexivity actually serves to heighten this dilemma. So the debate goes on, revealing an inevitable tension within the field, and discomforting, by extension, the sometimes complacent political/ethical neutralism of anthropology's conventional cultural relativism.

Epistemological relativism

This stands in contrast, however, to the debate about epistemological relativism which shows some signs, lately, of breaking down. Epistemological relativism, sometimes called 'cognitive' relativism, is often defined, by its critics, as the assertion that systems of knowledge possessed by different cultures are 'incommensurable' (i.e. not comparable, not translatable, utterly alien, etc.), and that people in different cultures, therefore, are believed by epistemological relativists to live in different, equally 'true', cognitive 'worlds'. Of course, defined this way, epistemological relativism is a straw man, and one embraced by very few of those accused of being its adherents (Rosaldo 1989: 218–24). This is partly because, so posited, it is obviously self-refuting. That is, the thesis that, as different cultures are incommensurable, therefore comparison and universal assertions are impossible, is, as Herskovits found out, one of the very class of statements that it has

just declared impossible. Moreover, this definition of epistemological relativism also misses its mark. For its self- refuting character has not in practice entailed (nor, by its own logic, need it only imply) the epistemologically conservative alternatives its critics favour; the epistemological agnosticism of many *symbolic anthropologists, for example, neatly sidesteps this critique.

Nevertheless, this kind of epistemological relativism could be said, with varying degrees of justice, to have arisen in connection with, or even out of, three major anthropological debates. The first such debates were among linguists in the 1950s about the, misnamed, *Sapir–Whorf hypothesis. These concerned whether, or if, one could say that the language one spoke, and its capacity for expressing certain kinds of concepts, determined, fully or partly, the kind of experience (or 'reality') one could have. These discussions were flawed, however, by ambiguity over whether this was a debate about first principles in epistemology or about an observational finding in linguistics, and were not helped by being concerned with a 'hypothesis' that was never actually formalized as such by either †Sapir or †Whorf. The second round of debates, in the late 1950s and 1960s, were about the extent to which *rationality, or the way humans think, is or is not universal. This was sparked by the use made by some philosophers, such as Peter Winch and Willard Van Orman Quine, of the discussions of proof and 'primitive' thought in †Evans-Pritchard's ethnographic work (Evans-Pritchard 1956) – work which was, itself (as can be seen in Evans-Pritchard's discussion of Nuer religious symbols) a refutation of †Lévy-Bruhl's earlier theories that posited a radical difference between 'modern' and 'prelogical primitive' thinking (Evans-Pritchard 1956: 123–43). Unfortunately, Quine's (1960) carefully illustrated doubts about the possibility of literal *translation – and, therefore, of comparison – from one language to another have received fairly little discussion among anthropologists. More attention has been paid to Winch's (1958) argument that if rules of thinking are socially constructed; and if, therefore, rationality could be said to differ validly from culture to culture; then the social sciences must be seen as simply obscuring what they hope to understand whenever they try to 'explain', in Western scientific terms, the apparently irrational statements and behaviours of, say, Western religious believers, or almost all non-Western peoples.

However, the ensuing discussion of whether, or to what extent, rationality was indeed culturally constructed (with most of Winch's critics answering 'no' and 'only in part', respectively) was flawed by far too little ethnographic consideration of whether the Western scientific rationality almost all (including Winch) used as a backdrop to this discussion was itself, in daily scientific practice, quite so 'rational'.

Finally, more recently, some epistemologically conservative critics have assumed, inaccurately, that epistemological relativism constitutes the core of many approaches with which they disagree: symbolic anthropology, †hermeneutics, *reflexivity, sometimes feminism, *cultural studies, and the denial of universal epistemological foundations by *postmodernists and poststructuralists. This is a rather odd list, however, since it is very difficult to find an anthropologist from this extremely heterodox collection of approaches who also claims, or recommends, epistemological relativism. Moreover, the term 'relativism' is more often thrown about among this group, especially by some feminist scholars, as an accusation than as an accolade. What all these groups do have in common, however, is having argued (in various ways) for a critique of conventional Western scientific rationality. And this is the real nub. For it is, indeed, the very idea that Western rationality as such is vulnerable to political or epistemological critique that is seen, by epistemological conservatives, as implying an underlying relativism, and by many of those so accused as implying nothing of the sort.

The resulting disagreement about who is or who is not a relativist reveals, perhaps, that the debate about epistemological relativism has an underlying instability, and, at long last, may be falling apart. Or, at least, a number of reasons have been offered as to why it may eventually do so. Clifford Geertz, for example, has suggested that anti-relativism is really just a symptom of pre-ethnographic nostalgia, an attempt to put the apple of human diversity back into the tree of Enlightenment rationality. But the option of staying home for home truths, despite odd arguments by the philosopher Richard Rorty in favour of a kind of educated ethnocentrism (1991: 203–11), seems to be fading even for the most determinedly provincial. Moreover, although arguing about epistemological relativism by arguing about the presence, character, or number of human universals – the form taken by all the arguments above – made some sense in regard to the Sapir–Whorf hypothesis or the rationality issue, where both the concept of culture and of Western scientific rationality were held fairly constant by both sides, in more recent debates, where this is often not the case, such an approach to 'refuting relativism' (along with the concept of epistemological relativism itself) hovers on the edge of incoherence. After all, it is hard to accuse those who question the concept of *culture of believing in a culturally-based epistemological relativism. It is no surprise, then, that recent postcultural attempts by theorists in feminism, *science studies, and symbolic anthropology to construct alternative 'objectivities' (Haraway 1991: 183–202), truly 'relative relativisms' (Latour 1993: 91–129), or stances of epistemological agnosticism, though shot through with their own problems, are not affected by the traditional critiques of epistemological relativism. They simply are not good examples of what they are accused of being. Yet, precisely because of this, their approaches to the relativism debate also threaten, for good and ill, the political complacency and comfortable epistemological sloppiness of anthropology's old conventional cultural relativism, and thus leave the discipline again uncertain at its very heart. But, perhaps, for anthropology, that is only to be expected.

MARK P. WHITAKER

See also: reflexivity, rationality, Sapir-Whorf hypothesis, science, cultural studies, symbolic anthropology

Further reading

Benedict, R. (1934) *Patterns of Culture*, Boston: Houghton Mifflin

Boas, F. (1911) *The Mind of Primitive Man*, New York: Macmillan

Evans-Pritchard, E.E. (1956) *Nuer Religion*, Oxford: Oxford University Press

Geertz, C. (1984) 'Anti Anti-Relativism', *American Anthropologist* 86: 263–78

Haraway, D.J. (1991) *Simians, Cyborgs and Women: The Reinvention of Nature*, New York: Routledge

Herskovits, M.J. (1972) *Cultural Relativism: Perspectives in Cultural Pluralism*, ed. Francis Herskovits, New York: Random House

Latour, B. (1993) *We Have Never Been Modern*, Cambridge, MA: Harvard University Press

Montesquieu, Charles-Louis de Secondat, Baron de ([1748]1979) *De l'esprit des lois*, Montreal: Garnier-Flammarion

Quine, W. van Orman (1960) *Word and Object*, Cambridge, MA: MIT Press

Rorty, R. (1991) *Objectivity, Relativism, and Truth*, Cambridge: Cambridge University Press

Rosaldo, R. (1989) *Culture and Truth: The Remaking of Social Analysis*, Boston: Beacon Press

Shweder, R.A., M. Mahapatra and J.G. Miller (1990) 'Culture and Moral Development', in J.W. Stigler, R.A. Shweder and G. Herdt (eds) *Cultural Psychology: Essays on Comparative Human Development*, Cambridge: Cambridge University Press

Winch, P. (1958) *The Idea of a Social Science and its Relation to Philosophy*, New York: Humanities Press

religion

Anthropological interest in religion extends as far back as the nineteenth-century emergence of anthropology as an academic discipline. In nineteenth-century anthropology, religion was often opposed to *science, and placed in an earlier position on a universal model of human *evolution. Religion could, therefore, be used to mark out the non-rational, or non-modern elements in any society. In the twentieth century, as social and cultural anthropologists freed themselves from the evolutionist assumptions of their predecessors, most field studies were of so-called 'primitive religions'. The most important theoretical influence was †Durkheim, especially his emphasis on *ritual as a kind of collective action in which society celebrates its own transcendent power over its individual members (Evans-Pritchard 1965). But, from the 1950s in particular, ethnographic attention shifted to local forms of world religions such as *Islam, *Buddhism and *Christianity, and theoretical attention shifted from Durkheim's *functionalism to †Max Weber's comparative sociology of religion. More recently still, Weber's theoretical assumptions about the place of religion in the modern world have been subject to historical criticism. Ironically, the anthropology of religion has now come full circle to return to the Western arguments about science and religion from which it first emerged in the nineteenth century.

Definitions and history

Probably the most influential definition of religion in anthropology today is that of †Clifford Geertz:

> A religion is a system of symbols which act to establish powerful, pervasive and long-lasting moods and motivations in men by formulating conceptions of a general order of existence and

clothing these conceptions with such an aura of factuality that the moods and motivations seem uniquely realistic.

(1973: 90)

Geertz's definition hinges on a conception of religion as symbolic communication, in which a *'symbol' is simply seen as a vehicle for its meaning. These symbols synthesise the †ethos of a society and its †'worldview'. In Geertz's interpretation ritual plays the important role of making the worldview seem real. One of the ways ritual may do this is by resisting historical change. While the way people live, and the way in which their society is organized, changes considerably over time, ritual action tends to be highly conservative.

In a study of the circumcision ritual of the Merina in Madagascar, Maurice Bloch (1985) explains this by arguing that the ritual refers to the other-worldly, which is removed from historical events, and that its form of *discourse (singing, dancing, the use of material objects – activities that have no ordinary referential meaning) also distances it from the everyday. The ritual provides an *ideology in which this world is denied, or hidden, while the other higher world (of the *ancestors) is shown to be more real. While this argument might be accommodated in Geertz's perspective, a related point, made by Bloch, complicates it considerably. In Bloch's view ritual legitimates several types of domination in its authoritative discourse: *gender †hierarchy as well as *state domination. Ritual often contains an antagonistic discourse, which works by violently conquering and subjugating death and, by extension, whatever is 'demonic', 'other', 'weak', and so on. This perspective allows for attention to antagonism and violent conflict between groups in society which almost disappear from view in Geertz's analysis. What these two anthropologists seem to agree upon, however, is that there is a field of religious ritual to be distinguished from other social practices and that this field can be read, interpreted and translated by the anthropologists as if it were a text. Ritual thus becomes a universal category of symbolic behaviour and part of that larger universal category, called religion.

A fundamental problem for a universalist, ahistorical definition of religion, such as Geertz's, is that it ignores the genealogy of the modern Western understanding of religion. The universalization of a concept of 'religion' is closely related to the emergence of *modernity in Europe and the spread of this modernity over the world. One issue here is the distinction between the religious and the secular. Talal Asad (1993) has argued that, while the boundary between religious and secular has been constantly redrawn in Christianity, a major shift occurred in the seventeenth century when the Roman Catholic Church lost its ultimate authority to draw this line. What came to be called 'religion' now became both universal in the widest sense, as exemplified in the seventeenth-century notion of 'natural religion' existing in every society, but also individual in the deepest sense, that is to be found in the inner beliefs of individuals. Geertz's understanding of 'religion' belongs firmly to this modern period and, Asad argues, would not be understood in medieval Christianity nor, for that matter, in a number of non-Western societies.

Asad's genealogy of universal definitions of religion is important. It calls for a social history of religion with an emphasis on the social conditions of particular discourses and practices. This demand is also of great importance for the anthropology of religion, since it is only through historical analysis that one can deconstruct the commonplace dichotomy of a supposedly secular and modern West and a supposedly religious and backward rest. Non-modern forms of religion – especially when they are not forms of Christianity – gradually come to stand for irrationality. A standard formula in nineteenth-century anthropological thought was to assume an evolution from *magic to religion. Non-Christian religion is perhaps more than anything else the sign of difference in the Western representation of the non-Western world. As †Edward Said (1978) and others have pointed out, this representation is at once instrumental in the making of the world in which non-Western subjects have to live, and also crucial in the production of the self-image of the West. The enlightened secularism of modern Western society is one of the most entrenched aspects of this self-image. It is therefore important to note not only the importance of religious dissent in the spread of the Enlightenment, but also the enduring importance of religious organization in the modern Western nation-state.

Religion and European expansion

It is a fundamental assumption of the discourse of modernity that in modern societies religion loses its social creativity and is forced to choose between either sterile conservatism or self-effacing assimilation to the secular world. In fact, new and highly original religious organizations proliferated in modern nation-states like Britain and the Netherlands in the nineteenth century, resulting in unprecedented levels of lay involvement. Ideological pluralization, resulting in ecclesiastical and theological strife, only served to reinforce these mobilizations. Given the importance of theological and ecclesiastical strife and conflict in sixteenth and seventeenth-century Western Europe, it is interesting to note that nationalism in Britain and the Netherlands in the eighteenth century was imbued with a 'generalized' Protestantism, which transcended the differences between the various Protestant Churches.

The 'secularism' of modern European society, assumed for instance by †Ernest Gellner (1983), only makes sense as a *colonial theory. In India, for example, colonial rule was justified by the argument that the British were an enlightened and rational 'race' of rulers who had to lead and develop the Indian people, steeped as they were in ancient prejudices. An important element in this argument was the view of the British as a secular but Christian nation who could thus take a rational interest in establishing a †utilitarian morality. Hindu society, in contrast, was depicted as completely under the sway of priests and given to endless, absurd ritual. The Muslims of India at this period were portrayed as 'backward' and 'bigoted', prone to zealous revolutionary activism. This *Orientalist view of Muslim 'fanaticism' was also a crucial element of Dutch rule in Indonesia.

It was not universal secularism, but Christianity, which spread along with European expansion. The missionization of non-European peoples was an important feature of European expansion. In the early modern period the Spanish and Portuguese brought the Roman Catholic Church to *Central and *South America and the Philippines. These early *missionaries were highly successful, to the extent that the majority of the population became Catholic. In these cases the expansion of the religious regime was intimately tied up with the expansion of colonial states. It strongly resembles Islamic expansion, from the twelfth century onwards, over large parts of *South and *Southeast Asia. An important element in both the expansion of Islam and of Catholic Christianity has been the establishment of regional cults round sacred centres in the colonized regions. While the principal centres might continue to be far outside these regions (Mecca, Jerusalem, Rome), regional *pilgrimages, supported by a local infrastructure of clergy and monks, became the central conduit for combining local traditions and global religions. It may be noted here that pilgrimage routes and networks of shrines are also important in many cultures for long-distance trading, combining, as usual, the religious and the economic. It should also be noted that it is not only 'world religions' which connect the local with the regional, as regional cults can also be found in, for example, African religions and in highland South America.

Spain and Portugal were followed by Protestant nations, such as Britain and Holland, in the European expansion and they continued the Christianization of the world in the eighteenth and nineteenth centuries. In early modern times, Protestant Churches had always been closely tied to a particular political regime. They had had neither the opportunity nor the will to organize missions. But the great Protestant missionary societies, founded at the end of the eighteenth century, were not controlled or run by Churches. Their nineteenth-century history can serve as an important indication of the fundamental changes which took place in the ways the Churches conceived of themselves. The sheer scale of the advertising undertaken by the missionary societies to raise funds served to introduce new notions of religion and conversion in the West.

John and Jean Comaroff (1991) rightly insist on the dialectical nature of the missionary encounter, which has to be studied both in the West and in the mission areas. They examine at length the social conditions in Britain from which the London Missionary Society (founded in 1795) and the Wesleyan Methodist Missionary Society (established in 1813), both active in the South African field, emerged. In their analysis the great eighteenth- century evangelical movements out of which the missionaries came were both causes and consequences of the rise of European modernity, a process that turned upon newly salient differences between †civilization and †savagery. The heathen 'other' of the dark continent provided a language for talking about the rising working classes, employed in the 'dark, satanic mills' at home. This suggests that we should compare the rhetoric of upliftment and improvement of the working class and the urban poor as a parallel to the civilizing mission in the areas of colonization.

Tswana Christianity, with which the work of the Comaroffs is concerned, is shown to be the product of the dialectic between particularly British missionary projects and Tswana cultural and political projects.

Translation

Because of this particular history, in which European modernizing power met non-European societies, the subject of conversion has to be regarded as one of the most important in the anthropology of religion. †Rodney Needham (1972) has drawn attention to the great conceptual difficulties involved in dealing with conversion. He begins his discussion with †Evans-Pritchard's statement that the Nuer language does not have a word which could stand for 'I believe'. This leads him to an argument about the particular intellectual baggage of the term 'belief' in English, which tends to refer to an 'inner experience'. Missionaries soon discovered how misleading it can be to translate ideas and practices in terms of 'belief', and of William James's individualized, inner experience. It is not surprising that missionaries were so strongly involved in philology and linguistics, since the practice of conversion is very much a matter of translation. One of the early activities of missionaries in a new target area was to make dictionaries and grammars of the language in order to produce translations of the Bible. The particular understandings and misunderstandings in this area were themselves productive in transforming colonized cultures, but not always in the ways intended by colonizers and missionaries.

The project of translation in the colonial encounter also involves the description of the 'heathen' practices of the people who had to be converted. Some of the terms used to describe these practices found their way into the scholarly discourse of the nineteenth century. An example is the term †'fetishism' which derives from the pidgin *fetisso*, a term used by Portuguese and Dutch slave traders on the Gold Coast of Africa in the sixteenth and seventeenth centuries. The fetish was a hybrid object pieced together from bits of bone, beads, feathers. It came to stand for the irrational religion of the enslaved African peoples, but, interestingly, it was taken up by †Marx to point out the irrationality of Western modernity. Marx developed a theory of †'commodity fetishism' as the heart of *capitalism's mystification.

While this example shows the extent to which, to use *Lévi-Strauss's expression, the non-religions of others are 'good to think with' in the critique of Western practices, it also allows us to compare precapitalist economic formations with capitalist ones. In a study of belief in the devil in Colombia and Bolivia, Michael Taussig argues that:

> The fetishism that is found in the economics of precapitalist societies arises from the sense of organic unity between persons and their products, and this stands in stark contrast to the fetishism of commodities in capitalist societies, which results from the split between persons and the things that they produce and exchange. The result of this split is the subordination of men to the things they produce, which appear to be independent and self-empowered.
>
> (Taussig 1980: 37)

In Taussig's analysis of the beliefs of *Latin American plantation workers and tin miners who are half peasants, half proletarians, the devil is the hybrid object that bridges precapitalist and capitalist *cosmologies. This transformation was not only examined by Marx, but also by †Marcel Mauss (1990 [1925]), who compared gift *exchange in a large number of societies. In Mauss's most famous example, from the Maori, it is the life-force, or *hau*, of the thing given which forces the recipient to make a return. Mauss's investigations have spawned a large amount of anthropological research on gifts and *sacrifice. Mauss's student †Louis Dumont (1980), for instance, makes the argument that the precapitalist economy of India's *caste system is based on fundamentally religious conceptions of hierarchy and interdependence and is modelled on the Vedic sacrifice.

One term which received a new lease of life in the colonial encounter is †'syncretism'. While Erasmus of Rotterdam used the term in 1519 in the sense of reconciliation and tolerance among Christians, it acquired a negative meaning in Protestant theological disputes where it came to stand for the betrayal of principles at the expense of truth. This negative sense continues to adhere to the term when, like fetishism, it is used to point to the hybridity inherent in the Christianization of the world. Sincerity and insincerity of conversion are therefore perennial themes of missionary discourse. While missionaries are aware of the fact that Christianization entails the articulation of the local and the global, syncretism as an illicit contamination of the Eternal Truth is the enemy

to be fought tooth and nail. This view is not only found among Christians, but also among, for instance, Muslim theologians who condemn any form of syncretism as 'innovation'. On the other hand, the Erasmian positive sense of tolerance also continues to adhere to the term, as in attempts to resolve often antagonistic relations between religious communities in multicultural societies. This is especially true in the †postcolonial world in which the civilizing mission of the West seems to have been replaced by a celebration of hybridity, †creolization and syncretism.

Conversion to a world religion is not conversion to transcendent religious essences, but to new self-understandings which only become possible as part of particular historical formations. It is therefore interesting to note that Christian missionary activities have been conspicuous in their lack of success in areas which were already Islamicized, such as the *Middle East, or Hinduized such as South Asia, or resisted colonization, such as *East Asia and *Japan. African, Latin American and Pacific religions seem to have been much more amenable to syncretic combinations with Christianity. In an influential contribution, Robin Horton (1971) argued that the religions of sub-Saharan Africa often had two tiers, a lower level of local spirits and a higher one of a (largely inactive) supreme god. The local spirits were concerned with the daily affairs of the local community, the microcosm, while the supreme god was concerned with the macrocosm. Similar arguments have been made for other religious systems, such as Theravada Buddhism where anthropologists make a distinction between spirit cults which deal with daily concerns and Buddhism as a salvational religion. However, when sub-Saharan Africa was drawn into the *world system, Christianity, with its elaborate macrocosmic cult, replaced the African supreme god.

Reform, 'fundamentalism' and transnationalism

Horton's understanding of religion and religious change, despite his emphasis on cognitive aspects, neglects the Christian missionaries' monopoly over formal education in Africa. While this was also attempted in other parts of the world, it failed in the face of strong resistance from competing religions. In the colonized parts of the Middle East and Asia, Muslim, Hindu and Buddhist reformist movements which originated in the nineteenth century often got a strong impetus from the

Christian educational challenge. While formal religious *education had existed in the pre-colonial period in all these societies, modern schools were founded to combine Western education with indigenous religious training. Indigenous religion in these regions became more the site of anti-colonial *resistance. Religious nationalism brings together discourse on the religious community and discourse on the nation in the argument that colonial (Christian) domination is an attack on one's religious life (van der Veer 1994). Modern reformist movements, confronted by Western modernization, have redefined the boundaries of religious beliefs and practices in the name of tradition. These movements are often called 'fundamentalist', since they share certain characteristics with Fundamentalism, an early twentieth-century movement in American Protestantism. They are simultaneously truly modern and implacably opposed to certain aspects of Western modernity.

In Islam, reformist movements also agitate against the widespread Sufi practice of saint worship, because they object to the idea that there is an intermediary between god and the worshipper. Because these Sufi practices were traditional links between the global and the local, and thus the site of syncretism, reformist changes have caused the redrawing of boundaries with other religious communities in multicultural societies, with inevitable political consequences. In other religions, such as Hinduism and Buddhism, reformist movements sometimes incorporate other communities' practices into their own, but deny these origins in efforts to suggest doctrinal purity.

There is a complex relationship between religious *community and nation because of the inherent transnationalism of 'world religions'. Some Islamic thinkers, for example, have pointed out that there is a contradiction between *nationalism and the transnational universalism of Islam. But, rather than a contradiction, there seems to be a fertile dialectic between nationalism and transnationalism in many of these movements. Transnational *migration brings people into nation-states in which religion is often the crucial badge of *identity and the place of worship the prime site of communal solidarity. Migrants are therefore especially under the influence of radical religious movements which promise to sustain their identity in an often hostile cultural environment and to bring about changes in their countries of origin. These migration-fuelled movements

often succeed for reasons outside their own control; secular nation-states, for example, often unwittingly encourage them by their own inability to accommodate religious difference in the institutions of the state, and especially in education. A good example of this difficulty is the refusal of the French government to allow Muslim girls to wear veils in the school. The French Minister of Education argued in 1994 that a secular ideal is the very substance of civic education in the French Republic. It is small wonder that in such a situation the veil becomes a clear symbol of resistance to an assimilationist state which wants to make immigrants into Frenchmen, without offering sufficient employment or protection against discrimination.

Students of the nation-state have pointed out that official secularism does not prevent the staging of a more or less elaborate 'civil religion' which includes the worship of the Tomb of the Unknown Soldier, the Pantheon of the 'great souls' of the nation, national holidays and a political rhetoric of the 'civilizing mission' of the nation. Moreover, Robert Bellah (1970) has demonstrated that American civil religion at least, though distinct from particular Churches, was clearly built on Christian symbolism. Obviously, large groups in American society cannot be entirely incorporated in this religious self-definition of the nation.

The definition of religion is to a considerable extent a product of the interaction between the global and the local. Nineteenth-century anthropological understandings had an evolutionist character and, despite their secular character, accepted that Christian monotheism was the apogee of religious evolution. Although this evolutionist optimism is gone, anthropologists still need a critical understanding of the historical fact that missionaries often preceded them in the field, while the fact that many theoretical assumptions derive from Christianity, and from the recent religious history of the West, remains of crucial importance.

PETER VAN DER VEER

See also: magic, ritual, Buddhism, Christianity, Hinduism, Islam, great and little traditions, syncretism, sacred and profane

Further reading

Asad, T. (1993) *Genealogies of Religion: Discipline and Reasons of Power in Christianity and Islam*, Baltimore: Johns Hopkins University Press

Bellah, R. (1970) *Beyond Belief: Essays on Religion in a Post Traditional World*, New York: Harper and Row

Bloch, M. (1985) *From Blessing to Violence: History and Ideology in the Circumcision Ritual of the Merina of Madagascar*, Cambridge: Cambridge University Press

Comaroff, J. and J. Comaroff (1991) *Of Revelation and Revolution: Christianity, Colonialism and Consciousness in South Africa*, Chicago: University of Chicago Press

Dumont, L. (1980) *Homo Hierarchicus: The Caste System and Its Implications*, Chicago: University of Chicago Press

Evans-Pritchard, E.E. (1965) *Theories of Primitive Religion*, Oxford: Clarendon Press

Geertz, C. (1973) *The Interpretation of Cultures*, New York: Basic Books

Gellner, E. (1983) *Nations and Nationalism*, Oxford: Basil Blackwell

Horton, R. (1971) 'African Conversion', *Africa* 41: 85–108

Mauss, M. (1990 [1925]) *The Gift: Forms and Functions of Exchange in Archaic Societies*, London: Routledge & Kegan Paul

Needham, R. (1972) *Belief, Language and Experience*, Oxford: Basil Blackwell

Said, E. (1978) *Orientalism*, New York: Vintage Books

Taussig, M. (1980) *The Devil and Commodity Fetishism in South America*, Chapell Hill: University of North Carolina Press

van der Veer, P. (1994) *Religious Nationalism: Hindus and Muslims in India*, Berkeley: University of California Press

reproductive technologies

Anthropological interest in new reproductive technologies (NRTs) combines long-standing debates about *conception, *kinship and *personhood with more recent interests in *science, *technology and *gender. International debate on new forms of technological assistance to conception and heredity in the 1980s catalysed the emergence of a rapidly expanding social scientific literature addressing their ethical, legal and social implications. In concert with legislative, parliamentary and policy-related committees in various parts of the world, anthropologists began in the mid-1980s to address the specifically cultural dimensions of rapid advances in reproductive and genetic science. Topics such as prenatal screening, genetic counselling, *in vitro* fertilization, surrogacy, embryo research and artificial insemination have emerged as significant areas of both ethnographic and theoretical analysis. By the early 1990s, this field gained increasing importance, not only as an exemplary and expanding topic within the anthropology of science, but as a notable context of kinship study.

'New reproductive technologies' does not accurately describe all of the techniques often discussed under this rubric, such as artificial insemination or surrogacy, which are neither new nor necessarily 'technological'. However, the advent of an increasing array of technological capacities to alter, modify and control the reproductive process has precipitated the sense of an urgent need for some ability to limit, or contain, what is often described as the 'impact' or 'implications' of such techniques. While some anthropologists, such as Peter Riviére, have argued that the dilemmas in relation to parenthood posed by new forms of assisted reproduction are familiar to anthropologists by comparison to traditions such as the †levirate, or *adoption, other researchers have emphasized the distinct set of cultural changes accompanying the advent of new kinds of choices and decisions derivative of rapid technological change.

Kinship has emerged as a central theme in relation to the new reproductive technologies, both because traditional anthropological expertise in this area is seen to offer an appropriate and useful terminology for the analysis of the social and cultural dimensions of the NRTs, and the reverse; that is, that the dilemmas produced by NRTs shed new light on some of the presumptions of traditional kinship theory. Hence Strathern (1992a, 1992b), for example, extends and also critiques †David Schneider's account of kinship by arguing that in the level of explicit public and parliamentary debate about NRTs are revealed the workings of ideas of the natural, which are altered by being 'assisted' by technology. Whereas Schneider theorized American kinship systems in terms of a symbolic distinction between the order of nature (blood ties) and the order of law (marriage), Strathern uses the context of assisted conception to destabilize this opposition, and reveal kinship as the hybrid organization of seemingly distinct domains, such as the individual and society, or *nature and culture. In turn, she argues, such hybrid effects illustrate the cultural specificity of Euro-American knowledge practices, or ways of making sense.

Methodologically, the question of the 'implications' of new reproductive (and new genetic) technologies poses significant challenges. Edwards *et al.* (1993) explore kinship in the age of assisted conception by using various social arenas of their contestation (clinical, parliamentary, familial, conjugal) as contexts for one another. By so doing, and in tandem with the approach outlined by Strathern, the NRTs are understood as a site of cultural production in which established ways of understanding are recombined to new effect. They note that the NRTs not only create new persons, but new forms of knowledge and connection.

Rayna Rapp's research on genetic counselling has also emphasized the multiple contexts of interpretation invoked in the encounter between patients and clinicians, in what are often difficult and ambiguous contexts of decisionmaking. The process of translation involved in communicating technical scientific information to women and couples for whom it may not be meaningful knowledge traces both the operations of authoritative knowledge, and its resistance or accommodation. In addition, such encounters yield valuable insights into the processes by which scientific knowledge is both produced and consumed.

At the other end of the spectrum, ethnographic research on surrogacy (Ragone 1994) has illustrated the remobilization of traditionally gendered activities, such as maternal gestation and nurture, to new effect in the pursuit of the 'gift of life'. Under-recognized dimensions of social *class have been demonstrated to be operative in the negotiations surrounding the gift no amount of money can buy from largely working-class surrogates to their largely middle- to upper-class commissioning couples.

Cross-cultural studies of assisted conception have drawn on established anthropological debates about conception to situate the confrontation with infertility in relation to established gender codes and cultural traditions. In comparison to American studies of IVF, such studies reveal important points of both continuity and difference (see also Franklin 1996, for the UK). As accounts of new reproductive technology increasingly overlap with those of the new genetics, the meaning of reproduction is expanded to encompass not only human, but also plant, animal and unicellular reproduction, raising questions both about the emergent cultural value of biodiversity and of genetic property .

This expansion of the meaning of reproduction parallels increasing recognition of its neglected importance within anthropological theory (Ginsburg and Rapp 1995). Likewise, the increasing interest in the anthropology of Euro-American culture, kinship theory, science studies and technological change contribute to the importance of NRTs as an emergent field in anthropology. Both new methodological approaches and the refiguration of traditional anthropological problems feature centrally in this important area of late-twentieth century anthropological scholarship.

SARAH FRANKLIN

See also: conception, gender, kinship, science

Further reading

Edwards, Jeanette, Sarah Franklin, Eric Hirsch, Frances Price and Marilyn Strathern (1993) *Technologies of Procreation: Kinship in the Age of Assisted Conception*, Manchester: Manchester University Press

Franklin, Sarah (1996) *Embodied Progress: A Cultural Account of Assisted Conception*, London: Routledge

Ginsburg, Faye and Rayna Rapp (eds) (1995) *Conceiving the New World Order: The Global Politics of Reproduction*, Berkeley: University of California Press

Ragone, Helena (1994) *Surrogate Motherhood: Conceived in the Heart*, Boulder, CO: Westview

Sandelowski, Margarette (1993) *With Child In Mind*, Philadelphia: University of Pennsylvania Press

Strathern, Marilyn (1992a) *Reproducing the Future: Anthropology, Kinship and the New Reproductive Technologies*, Manchester: University of Manchester Press

—— (1992b) *After Nature: English Kinship in the Late Twentieth Century*, Cambridge: Cambridge University Press

resistance

Some of the most influential new ethnography of the 1980s was concerned with resistance to structures of inequality or oppression, whether these were based on differences of *class, *gender or *ethnicity. As a topic, resistance was especially attractive to those anthropologists concerned to reconcile the 1970s influence of *Marxism in anthropology, with the more culturally sensitive approaches of *symbolic anthropology; it also appealed to feminist anthropologists.

Whereas most Marxist anthropology of the 1970s was influenced either by French structural Marxism, with its somewhat formal language of *mode of production and †social formation, or by *world-systems theory, which left little apparent space for the culturally or ethnographically particular, ethnographies of resistance in the 1980s drew on different theoretical inspirations. Particularly important were the British cultural Marxists like †Raymond Williams and E.P. Thompson, the Italian Marxist †Antonio Gramsci (whose idea of †hegemony and counter-hegemony itself achieved a kind of theoretical hegemony), the Indian historians of the †Subaltern Studies group, and the

French social theorists †Michel Foucault and †Pierre Bourdieu.

The combination of †interpretive approaches, derived from symbolic anthropology, with historical and material concerns was a heady one. The work of the cultural Marxists opened up new areas for enquiry: inequality was not just a matter of economic relations and was not just to be found in the workplace. It was inscribed in all social relations and took culturally-specific forms, and so resistance might also be found, often in elusive or disguised form, in unexpected areas of life. Important ethnographic analyses covered areas as different as women factory workers and labourers in rice fields, members of native churches in South Africa, Bedouin women and tin-miners in Bolivia. Ethnographers were able to connect 'classic' anthropological concerns like *shamanism, *ritual, and spirit *possession to issues of power and resistance and thence to broader structures of inequality.

'Resistance' provided a broad rubric for innovative work which, above all, showed how local cultural resources could empower people confronted by global structures of inequality. Its chief drawbacks were the vagueness of what was taken to be 'resistance' – i.e. action which *impeded* or subverted unequal power relations, as apart from moments of relative autonomy when the apparently powerless could step aside from the realities of oppression – and consequently the considerable interpretive licence used by some ethnographers in reading resistance into acts and symbols which people themselves might describe in quite different terms. At its most extreme, this could lead into a kind of neo-functionalism in which all social and cultural phenomena might be reduced to the role they play in maintaining or subverting power relations.

JONATHAN SPENCER

See also: colonialism, cultural studies, political economy

Further reading

Comaroff, J. (1985) *Body of Power, Spirit of Resistance*, Chicago: University of Chicago Press

Ong, A. (1987) *Spirits of Resistance and Capitalist Discipline: Factory Women in Malaysia*, Albany: SUNY Press

Scott, J. (1985) *Weapons of the Weak: Everyday Forms of Peasant Resistance*, New Haven: Yale University Press

rite of passage

Rites of passage are *rituals which mark the passing of one stage of life and entry into another, e.g. birth, puberty, *marriage, initiation to the priesthood, or *death. They are also known in English by the French equivalent, *rites de passage*, and by the term 'life-crisis rituals'. The concept was first brought to attention by the Belgian scholar †Arnold van Gennep and became an important part of the analytical framework of many in British anthropology of different theoretical persuasions, including †Audrey Richards, †Max Gluckman, †Edmund Leach, †Mary Douglas, and especially †Victor Turner.

Van Gennep ([1909] 1960: 1-13) distinguished three kinds of rites of passage: rites of separation, transition rites, and rites of incorporation or aggregation. He noted that rites of separation often take prominence in funeral ceremonies, that transition rites may be important in pregnancy, betrothal or initiation, and that rites of incorporation are often highly developed in marriage ceremonies. However, it is more usual to think of these three as elements in a single rite which includes each form – separation, transition, incorporation – as a separate phase.

A key concept here is that of †'liminality' (from Latin *limen*, 'threshold'). Van Gennep saw transition rites as 'liminal', while rites of separation are 'preliminal', and rites of incorporation are 'postliminal'. The liminal phase is when things are not as they are in the ordinary world: roles may be reversed (men acting as women, the elderly as if they were young, etc.). The best examples to illustrate van Gennep's classification are initiation ceremonies. Commonly these involve an individual leaving his or her group and even experiencing a symbolic 'death' (the separation), then proceeding through a phase in which he or she is secluded, perhaps taking on roles otherwise inappropriate for the individual's *age or *gender (the transitional or liminal phase), and finally rejoining the group but with a new, adult status (the incorporation). Initiation rituals the world over take this form, and indeed van Gennep himself compared examples from Africa, Australia, North America, Europe, and Asia.

Turner's contribution was to emphasize the implications of these rites for our conceptions of *society itself. Like many who have found the concept 'rites of passage' useful, he conducted fieldwork in *Central Africa, where at puberty both men and women undergo extensive ritual activities in order to mark initiation into adulthood. Turner remarked (e.g. 1969) that these rites of passage negate normal rules and the social hierarchy of society, and emphasize instead the bonds between people which enable society to exist. He called the latter †*communitas* – the very negation of *social structure which the liminal phase of initiation (and other) rituals draws on for its symbolic power.

As the title of one of Turner's best-known books indicates, he used van Gennep's schema as a way of emphasizing the processual nature of ritual. This also enabled him to expand his concern with the liminal moment from life-crisis rituals to other moments of social transition, such as *pilgrimages. Leach (1961) had already emphasized the importance of symbolic reversals in marking the passage of time. The classic example in European history was the moment of carnival, when the lower orders were able to enjoy a brief, but bounded, moment of licence – *communitas*, or anti-structure, in Turner's terms – and the poor could mock and laugh at the rich. While *functionalists like Gluckman had stressed the conservative results of such rites of reversal, recent inter-disciplinary research in history, anthropology and literary studies, influenced by †Bakhtin's work on the carnivalesque, has reopened the question of possible links between symbolic reversals and political *resistance (Bakhtin 1984; Ladurie 1979).

ALAN BARNARD and JONATHAN
SPENCER

See also: age, death, pilgrimage, ritual, time and space

Further reading

Bakhtin, M. ([1968] 1984) *Rabelais and his World*, Bloomington: University of Indiana Press
Ladurie, E. Le Roy (1979) *Carnival in Romans*, Harmondsworth: Penguin
Leach, E. (1961) 'Time and False Noses' in E. Leach, *Rethinking Anthropology*, London: Athlone
Turner, V. (1969) *The Ritual Process: Structure and Anti-structure*, Chicago: Aldine
van Gennep, A. ([1909] 1960) *The Rites of Passage*, London: Routledge and Kegan Paul

ritual

According to most theories, ritual either involves different forms of action from everyday life, or at least different purposes. For example, in Christian ritual, the act of ingesting bread during holy communion is different from eating bread at any other time. The difference relates to the meaning attached to the ritual act, which is suggested by the use of †symbols. Paraphrasing †Clifford Geertz's definition of *culture, David Kertzer defines ritual as 'action wrapped in a web of symbolism' (1988: 9). This assumes that ritual has a communicative role. Thus, despite the idea that ritual denies the everyday relationship between an action and its purpose, it is assumed that this denial is not gratuitous. There is assumed to be a purpose, a function and a meaning behind ritual action. This has implications for the relationships between ritual, politics and *social structure.

Accounts vary as to the purpose, function and meaning of ritual. As Kelly and Kaplan have pointed out, unlike a riot for example, ritual is habitually connected to 'tradition', the sacred, to structures that have been imagined in stasis' (1990: 120). This has led to the †synchronic pursuit of an inevitable and generalized ritual form. Appeals to a universal ritual form imply a generalized ritual function; the assumption being that what looks the same is the same. Attempts to define this function have generally seen ritual as either supporting social structure by directly representing it, or legitimizing social authority by concealing it. Thus ritual's social role is either to bolster, or conceal, the prevailing political order.

The turn towards an anthropology of † practice has drawn attention to the †diachronic study of particular rituals as they are performed and experienced by their participants. Rather than playing out of eternal pattern, the actors in ritual are seen as conscious agents in the reproduction of that pattern. This means that rather than directly representing, or even concealing, social structure, ritual itself becomes part of the political process.

Ritual and social integration

Taking their lead from †Émile Durkheim, the British *functionalist anthropologists of the 1950s and 60s concentrated on the integrative function of ritual. Durkheim had argued that because the apparent function of ritual is to strengthen the bonds attaching the believer to god, and god is no more than a figurative expression of *society itself, so ritual in fact serves to attach the individual to society (Durkheim 1915: 226). Because ritual is a direct representation of society to itself, studying ritual tells us important things about society.

In many societies, god comes in the form of a king or chief. The strengthening of bonds between king and subjects is a most clear demonstration of the strengthening of social bonds, or the legitimation of authority. A celebrated example of this process at work is provided by †Max Gluckman, who examined the *incwala* ritual performed by the Southern African Swazi people. This was an annual ritual which reaffirmed the relationship between the king and the nation by deliberately drawing attention to the potential conflict his authority could cause. Gluckman called such rituals 'rituals of rebellion', the power of which lay in 'exaggerating real conflicts of social rules and affirming that there was unity despite these conflicts' (Gluckman 1963: 18).

A similar conclusion was drawn by †Victor Turner, although with rather different implications. In his seminal account of *The Ritual Process* (1969), Turner examined the installation ritual of an Ndembu senior chief, in Northwest Zambia. The ritual involved the building of a small shelter a mile from the chief's capital village. The chief was taken there and systematically jostled and insulted by ritual functionaries, before his installation was finally celebrated with great revelry. The central part of the ritual, which Gluckman would have seen as a structured rebellion, was for Turner a ritual phase of 'anti-structure', that lay outside social structure altogether. He argued, after †van Gennep (1960), that such installation rituals, as *rites of passage, involve three phases; separation, †liminality and reaggregation.

Separation involves the physical detachment of the participant from normal life, and entry into a liminal, transcendent phase. Liminality, which Turner sees as by far the most important phase, involves a prolonged period in which the participant is both literally and symbolically marginalized. Reaggregation is when the participant returns to society.

During liminality, the status of the participant is deliberately made ambiguous, so as to separate the ritual process from normal social life. The symbolism of the installation ritual suggested that the Ndembu chief was dead, and his identity was negated. For Turner, this period of liminality was critical in the ritual process. He argued that long periods of liminality lead to the development of a transcendent feeling of social togetherness, which he called †*communitas*.

This is a generalized and eternal social bond, which transcends social structure, and brings the ritual participant under the authority of the community. It is represented by symbolic inversion during the liminal phase. During this phase of the installation, the Ndembu chief becomes like a slave, and is therefore forced to confront the mutual dependence of different strata of society. Because he becomes literally nobody, he can be abused and insulted by anybody. He therefore submits to the authority of nothing less than the total community. With all structural relations abandoned, he becomes a *tabula rasa* for the group knowledge that reconstructs him as chief.

Thus, where Durkheim saw ritual as a representation of social structure, Turner saw it as a process that transcends it. Turner's model of ritual has been used in a variety of contexts, particularly by anthropologists who see ritual as performance or *play. Liminality is seen as a creative phase of anti-structure, to which activities such as riots do conform, despite not explicitly appealing to tradition. Thus Richard Schechner (1993) argues that the pro-democracy demonstrations in Beijing in 1989 can be seen as a type of political theatre, or ritual performance, because they involved *communitas*.

Despite appeals to the creativity of liminality, the centrality of *communitas* still sees ritual participants submitting to the communal will, and a universal ritual form. This means that the Turnerian scheme is still essentially conservative. No matter how revolutionary the intention of the ritual performance at Tiananmen Square, it is still seen as a representation of political will which conformed to a determinate ritual form.

Ritual as mystification

In his broadly *Marxist critique of theories of ritual, Maurice Bloch (1989) sees it as a form of *ideology, which provides an alternative to, or gloss on, everyday life. Because it is highly formalized, ritual restricts debate or contestation, and there is a certain predictability to the ways in which people construct ritual across different social and cultural contexts. In *Prey into Hunter* (1992), Bloch argues that the archetypal form of ritual is to demonstrate the power of the transcendental over the everyday. The transcendental may take the form of a sacred king or an eternal community, but it need not necessarily. Thus Bloch's irresistible ritual form is more ambiguous than those of Durkheim or Turner, though no less determinate. For Bloch, ritual is a dramatic process through which the vitality of everyday life is conquered by the transcendence of *death and the eternal. This is played out in a process he calls 'rebounding violence'. He maintains the same three-phase model as Turner and van Gennep, but argues that the phases are inseparable. Where Turner privileges the liminal phase, Bloch merely sees this as part of an overall process that involves people entering the transcendental only to return to and conquer the vital, through the use of literal or symbolic violence.

Bloch uses many examples to furnish his theory. One of these is of a Ladakhi *marriage ritual, which involves the symbolic capture of a bride in one *household by the groom of another. The event is surrounded by the symbolism of sexual, military and *cosmological conquest; a violence that only becomes recognizable as rebounding violence when seen in the context of the enduring household group. For whilst the symbolism of a single marriage sees the vital, reproductive bride and her household conquered by the transcendental groom, the process rebounds when a groom from the original bride's household, himself marries. When this occurs, the transcendental conqueror becomes the household itself:

> This is because submission to the conquest of native vitality, in this case represented by the young women who were born in the house, is followed by the conquest of external vitality, represented by incoming brides. This is the pattern of rebounding violence which in this case . . . creates an apparently supra-biological, transcendental and immortal existence for a human group.
>
> (Bloch 1992: 74 – 75)

This model of a universal archetype of ritual pits the official ideology of a society against people's experiences of it in everyday life, and through the act of rebounding violence ensures that the former conquers the latter. This, in turn, inhibits contestation, which means that in Bloch's formulation, rituals are essentially conservative or mystifying.

But if mystification is a function of ritual, then ritual can be argued to characterize all forms of action which mystify. This is revealed in contexts in which one might say that an activity is 'mere ritual', in comparison to more significant social action. An example is provided by Kertzer in the

form of the 'ritual elections' staged in El Salvador 'to demonstrate to the world that El Salvador was indeed ruled by the democratic masses' (Kertzer 1988: 49).

It might be argued that this example does conform to Bloch's model, in that the ritual served to demonstrate the power of transcendent democracy over the dangerous (and violent) vitality of everyday life. However, it is assumed that the 'audience' for such rituals are inevitably convinced. The continued political struggle in El Salvador would suggest otherwise.

Ritual and practice

Practice-oriented approaches to ritual focus precisely on the potential disjunction between different interpretations of ritual by different participants in particular situations. This depends in turn on the assumption that the symbols involved in ritual can be read and interpreted in a variety of different ways, depending on one's point of view. Rather than determining the ritual experience, the symbols of a ritual become the media through which participants themselves define their own experiences of the ritual. Reading different meanings into the symbols of ritual can entail the modification of that ritual, because different interpretations suggest possible alternatives for the structuring of ritual. These in turn suggest alternatives for the structuring of society.

The focus on practice, and the power of different interpretations of rituals, has been developed particularly through anthropological approaches to carnival. Rather than seeing the chaos of the carnival atmosphere as a moment of confirming *communitas*, or a part of a process whereby vitality is conquered by transcendence to maintain the status quo, such approaches see carnival as a moment of genuine potential dissent with very real political consequences.

Abner Cohen (1993) has investigated these consequences in the Notting Hill carnival in London. In this context, carnival became the means by which different constituencies involved in the ritual became agents in its restructuring. Carnival came to represent different ethnic groups, with different political agendas. Over time, this affected the form the carnival took, as it changed with the political agendas of different groups. But the political agendas themselves were changed, as the carnival became not only the medium, but also the object of political, ethnic and racial conflict. It was a means of expressing these differences, but also the means by which these differences were constructed.

This approach sees ritual and social structure as part of the same process, mutually informing each other. Ritual does not merely represent social structure, nor conceal it, but acts upon it, as social structure acts upon ritual. Put this way, rituals can be seen as the significant sites of political contest between different social groups. Because they involve symbols, rituals are particularly evocative, but they are also particularly malleable. They can therefore lead to change, as much as they evoke tradition and continuity. As Kelly and Kaplan put it, 'rituals in ongoing practice are a principal site of new history being made, and [the] study of the plural formal potentialities of rituals could be basic to efforts to imagine possibilities for real political change' (Kelly and Kaplan 1990: 141).

JON P. MITCHELL

See also: play, belief, religion, rite of passage

Further reading

Bloch, M. (1989) *Ritual, History and Power: Selected Papers in Social Anthropology*, London: The Athlone Press
—— (1992) *Prey into Hunter: The Politics of Religious Experience*, Cambridge: Cambridge University Press
Cohen, A. (1993) *Masquerade Politics: Explorations in the Structure of Urban Cultural Movements*, Oxford: Berg
Durkheim, É. (1915) *Elementary Forms of the Religious Life*, London: Hollen Street Press
Gluckman, M. (1963) *Order and Rebellion in Tribal Africa*, London: Cohen and West
Kelly, J.D. and M. Kaplan (1990) 'History, Structure and Ritual', *Annual Review of Anthropology* 19: 119–150
Kertzer, D.I. (1988) *Ritual, Politics and Power*, London: Yale University Press
Schechner, R. (1993) *The Future of Ritual: Writings on Culture and Performance*, London: Routledge
Turner, V. (1969) *The Ritual Process*, Harmondsworth: Penguin
van Gennep, A. (1960) *The Rites of Passage*, London: Routledge and Kegan Paul

Russian and Soviet anthropology

The history of Russian anthropology can be divided into three neat phases. The first was the documentation of the peoples and cultures of the pre-revolutionary Russian state, which started in the eighteenth century and reached its climax with institutionalization in ethnographic journals and museums in the nineteenth century. The second was the Soviet period when ethnographic research was subservient to Marxist theory and the requirements of Leninist policy on the national question. The third, which is even now only emerging, is the post-Marxist anthropology which has emerged since the end of communist rule.

Russian ethnography goes back to the eighteenth century – the time of extensive colonization and the formation of the centralized Russian state. Early descriptions and atlases of Siberia included information on local tribal groups. The Great Northern Expedition (1733–43) resulted in the *History of Siberia* by G. Miller, who made the first linguistic classification of the aboriginal population. A member of the expedition, S. Krasheninnikov, published his *Description of the Kamchatka Land* in 1775. As a result of an expedition organized by the Russian Academy of Sciences (1768–74), I. Georgi published the four-volume *Description of all Peoples Living in the Russian State* (1776-80).

At the end of the eighteenth century the first publication on Russian *folklore appeared, starting a long tradition of research in the field of Russian *mythology and †folk culture (V. Dahl, A. Afanasyev, O. Miller in the nineteenth century). Remarkable contributions to Russian ethnography emerged from round-the-world naval expeditions (I. Kruzenshtern, Y. Lisyanski, O. Kozebu), which conducted research among Pacific islanders, as well as from the expeditions of Langsdorf to Brazil, Bichurin to China, Veniaminov and Wrangel to the Aleutian Islands and Alaska. N. Miklukho-Maclay was the first European anthropologist to work in Oceania and Australia between 1870 and 1880, and is one of very few Russian anthropologists whose work has been analysed by Western historians of the discipline (Stocking 1991).

In 1845 the Russian Geographical Society was founded in Saint Petersburg, with an ethnographic division which published material on different regions, including studies of ethnography and languages in Central Asia, Siberia and the Far East (M. Kastren, A. Middendorf, V. Radlov). In 1867 the All-Russian Ethnographic Exhibition was organized in Moscow, and after it the Rumyantzev Museum was established. A strong *evolutionist school emerged in the 1880s, introducing methods of historical reconstruction on archaeological, physical anthropological and ethnographic materials (M. Kovalevski, D. Anuchin, L. Sternberg). V. Bogoraz and V. Iochelson were organizers of the Jessup Expedition to Chukotka and Kamchatka (1901–2). Around this time the first ethnographic journals appeared as well as many popular works on the cultures of the world.

The Bolshevik revolution of 1917 and the creation of the Soviet state, with territorial autonomy based on ethnic principles, as well as the rise of ethnic movements on the periphery, caused extensive studies of all groups, particularly for drawing borders between ethno-territorial units. Ethnographers were deeply involved in developing written alphabets and school systems for many small ethnic groups. In 1933 the Institute of Anthropology, Archaeology and Ethnography was established in Leningrad and in 1937, the Institute of Ethnography in Moscow. At this time Marxist-Leninist doctrine started to completely dominate all theoretical approaches, with its emphasis on stages in the evolution of society and *class struggle as the major force of historical changes. †Ethnology was proclaimed a 'bourgeois science', many scholars were persecuted and the department of ethnology in Moscow was closed in 1931. Soviet anthropologists concentrated on the study of primitive societies, prehistoric stages of evolution, and early forms of social organization (S. Tolstov, M. Kosven, A. Zolotarev).

From the 1950s to the 1970s the major priorities were still the study of ethnogenesis, †material culture, ethnic histories and cartography, initiated mainly from the central institutions in Moscow and Leningrad, but with active training and participation of scholars from centres in the regions and republics. It resulted in prestigious projects like historical-ethnographic atlases (*Peoples of Siberia* 1961; *Russians* 1967–70; *Peoples of the World* 1964) and a multi-volume series *The Peoples of the World*. Because of limited contacts and resources very few studies were conducted on the outside world (D. Olderogge and I. Potekhin on Africa; N. Cheboksarov, R. Its and M. Krukov on China; A. Efimov and Y. Averkieva on America). The most remarkable results were achieved in Siberian and Arctic anthropology (L. Potapov, V. Dolgikh, D. Sergeev, S. Arutunov) and in *biological anthropology and *race studies (G. Debetz, M. Levin, M. Gerasimov, V. Alexeev).

In the 1970s and 1980s there was a strong shift of interest to contemporary ethnic issues with more use of *sociological surveys; extensive research was done in Central Asia, the Baltic republics and the Volga area (Y. Arutunyan, L. Drobizheva, V. Pimenov, M. Guboglo). Y. Bromley, the director of the Institute in Moscow, with other colleagues (V. Kozlov, P. Puchkov, S. Arutunov)

developed a primordialist theory of the †ethnos, which partly reflected the existing political hierarchy of status and non-status Soviet nationalities. This theory goes back to S. Shirokogorov's writings of the 1920s and corresponds to the so-called Leninist theory of the national question, in which the 'nation' is defined as the highest type of ethnic community, and treated as an archetype and major form of social grouping, legitimizing a state and its economy and culture. Alongside this, a superficial but attractive interpretation of the ethnos as a 'socio-biological organism' (Gumilev 1989) has acquired a growing popularity. At the same time historical ethnography and ethnogenesis studies still dominated the research agenda and resulted in solid publication on the history of primeval societies and the early stages of human evolution (Y. Semenov, A. Pershitz, V. Shnirelman), on early forms of *religion like *shamanism (E. Novik, L. Potapov, V. Basilov), on linguistic reconstructions (V. Starostin, E. Khelimski, I. Peiros, A. Militarev), and on *myths and iconography (E. Meletinski, V. Ivanov, Y. Knorozov). Unfortunately, the outstanding theoretical innovations of Russian scholars like †V. Propp, †M. Bakhtin and V. Chayanov were not properly developed by academic practitioners.

Political liberalization after the late 1980s, and the rise of ethnic *nationalism and conflict, have brought radical changes to Russian anthropology. Marxism ceased to be the only paradigm for the social sciences, and political change inspired a growing interest in other *methodologies and multidisciplinary approaches, as well as broadening the thematic scope and field areas of the discipline. Studies of *identity, nationalism and conflict, *status and the rights of minorities, *ethnicity and *power, and a number of other issues, became the focus of research and lively debates on holistic theories like Marxism, *structuralism and *postmodernism are now taking place in the post-Soviet anthropological community. Another serious challenge is the growing self-assurance and alienation from the 'centre', of some anthropologists of the former 'periphery', demonstrating a strong degree of ethno-nationalistic commitment and using ethnic studies as a resource for healing collective trauma and for political mobilization. As a response, 'central' anthropology demonstrates a new interest in the problems of the 'new minorities' like Russians, and in Russian nationalism and identity, while still mainly keeping good and friendly relations and academic contacts with former compatriots. Russian anthropology, like the rest of Russian society, is going through a process of deep transformation, but its strong intellectual roots provide hope for the future.

VALERY TISHKOV

See also: Europe: Central and East, Marxism and anthropology, ethnicity

Further reading

Bromley, Y.V. (1981) *Sovremennye Problemy Ethnografii*, Moscow: Nauka

Gellner, E. (1988) *State and Society in Soviet Thought*, London: Basil Blackwell

Gumilev, L.N. (1989) *Etnogenez i Biosfera Zemli*, Leningrad: Leningrad State University

—— (1990) 'Regards sur l'anthropologie sovietique', *Cahiers du Monde Russe et Sovietique* 31: 2–3

Shanin, T. (1989) 'Ethnicity in the Soviet Union: Analytical perceptions and political strategies', *Comparative Studies in Society and History* 31 (3)

Shirokogorov, S. (1923) *Etnos. Issledovanie osnovnykh printsipov etnicheskikh i etnograficheskikh yavlenii*, Shanghai

Slezkin, Y. (1991) 'The Fall of Soviet Ethnography, 1928–38', *Current Anthropology* 32: 476–84

Stocking, G.W. (1991) 'Maclay, Kubary, Malinowski: Archetypes from the Dreamtime of Anthropology', in G.W. Stocking (ed.) *Colonial Situations: Essays on the Contextualization of Ethnographic Knowledge* (History of Anthropology 7), Madison: University of Wisconsin Press

Tishkov, V. (1992) 'The Crises in Soviet Ethnography', *Current Anthropology* 33 (4): 371–82

S

sacred and profane

Because 'sacred' and 'profane', like 'holy' and 'common', are words of ordinary language it is not surprising that they are often used without definition by writers on *religion. 'Sacred' frequently seems to be nothing more than a solemn synonym for 'religious'; when this is the case the word has no theoretical value. †Émile Durkheim gave it a more definite and restricted sense in his classic *Elementary Forms of the Religious Life* ([1912] 1915); sacred things, in contrast to profane, are set apart and forbidden, hedged with prohibitions. He conceived of sacred and profane as mutually exclusive categories, so opposed to each other as to be separated by a logical abyss, which between them comprise everything in the known world. The two categories and their implacable opposition to each other are among the universals of human thought, but what in particular is sacred and what profane can differ greatly from one society to another, as may be seen by comparing an other-worldly religion such as *Christianity with the locally focused *totemic cults of *Aboriginal Australia.

According to †Mircea Eliade, who also makes a rigid and exhaustive dichotomy, 'Man becomes aware of the sacred because it manifests itself, shows itself, as something wholly different from the profane.' He uses the term 'hierophanies' for these acts of self-manifestation by the sacred. This 'reality that does not belong to our world' can appear before us in the most varied guises, e.g. in a stone or tree, the person of a holy man or, no doubt, in earthquakes and epidemics.

Few anthropologists would agree that the wholehearted dualism posited by a Durkheim or an Eliade is universally part of human experience. Indeed, †E.E. Evans-Pritchard doubted that it could be seen among the Nuer even in ritual performances. †W.E.H. Stanner ignored it in his remarkable monograph *On Aboriginal Religion.* Elsewhere he argued that the dichotomy could be made to fit Aboriginal conduct only by adding a third category, the mundane (thereby abolishing the dualism), and making other adjustments. As for what lies behind the sacred, anthropologists are too nervous or too sceptical of ultimates to be attracted by Eliade's mysticism. There remains, however, considerable sympathy for the Durkheimian doctrine that the sacred order is a symbolic representation of the social order.

Stanner notwithstanding, it is especially in the study of Aboriginal Australia that the opposition of sacred and profane has found regular employment. †W. Lloyd Warner followed Durkheim closely, though his insistence that the sacred is peculiarly the realm of men is not necessarily implied by the master's treatment and was disputed on factual grounds by †Phyllis Kaberry. After World War II †Ronald Berndt and T.G.H. Strehlow laid great stress on the sacred. Berndt's usage, which is regrettably loose, has been influential in giving rise to the widespread opinion in Australian law and politics that any place of significance to Aborigines is sacred.

KENNETH MADDOCK

See also: religion, ritual, Aboriginal Australia

Further reading

Durkheim, É. ([1912] 1915) *The Elementary Forms of the Religious Life*, trans. by J. W. Swain, London: George Allen & Unwin

Eade, J. and M.J. Sallnow (eds) (1991) *Contesting the Sacred: The Anthropology of Christian Pilgrimage*, London: Routledge

Eliade, M. (1959) *The Sacred and the Profane*, trans. by W. R. Trask, New York: Harcourt, Brace

Spencer, B. and F. J. Gillen (1899) *The Native Tribes of Central Australia*, London: Macmillan

Stanner, W.E.H. (1967) 'Reflections on Durkheim and Aboriginal Religion' , in M. Freedman (ed.) *Social Organisation: Essays Presented to Raymond Firth*, London: Cass

sacrifice

Robertson Smith and the origins of Christian sacrifice

†William Robertson Smith placed sacrifice at the centre of anthropological theories of *religion, morality and *kinship in 1886. Defining 'sacrifice' in the *Encyclopedia Brittanica* (9th edn), he wrote that the Latin word *sacrificium*, from which we have the English 'sacrifice', 'properly means an action within the sphere of things sacred to the gods ... and strictly speaking cover[s] the whole field of sacred ritual' (1886: 132). He went on to claim, however, that the central feature of every act of ordinary worship is an offering of human comestibles to the gods, and that a 'sacrifice, therefore, is primarily a meal offered to the deity'. Replacing his initial over-broad definition with this over-narrow one begs the question. It builds his conclusions regarding the 'origins' of sacrifice in the *totemic identification of a †clan with an animal god into his premises.

Smith was an ordained minister of the Church of Scotland and professor of Hebrew and Old Testament Exegesis at the Free Church College of Aberdeen from 1870 until his removal in 1887 for the dubious orthodoxy of his views. He accepted the chair of Arabic at Cambridge in 1889 and died in 1894 (Peters 1968). Smith argued that the essence of religion was contained in collective, obligatory and fixed *rituals, and not in individual, freely chosen and unstable beliefs. Following Fustel de Coulanges, he drew a direct link between units of social or political structure and the collectivity that carried out religious worship, so that the two had evolved in tandem (Smith 1927 [1889]). In the earliest stage of human society, the unit of worship was the totemic clan which thought of its members as sharing 'a common mass of flesh, blood and bones' with one another and with their animal totem. Ties of moral solidarity needed to be periodically revivified by collectively consuming the flesh of the animal totem, which was, in a sense, already the flesh of those consuming it. Totemic sacrifice was thus both a self-sacrifice and the sacrifice of a god, whose body and blood were solemnly consumed by the congregation. Although

he did not spell it out in these terms, his analysis makes primitive sacrifice appear to be but a cruder and more materialistic form of the *Christian Eucharist.

As Detienne has recently argued, Smith saw the central rite of *Christianity, the spiritualized self-sacrifice of the Eucharist, as the goal and essence of all 'primitive' religion. He thus cleared a path for a teleological approach to non-Christian religions that was followed by later writers such as †Mauss, †Durkheim and Cassirer. The latter authors went further towards the official Christian model of sacrifice by discounting the *physical* acts of killing, butchering and consuming the sacrificial victims. They discovered in even the most exotic forms of the ritual manipulation of animals in 'totemic' societies an essentially *spiritual* self-abnegation. This spirit of self-denial was then held to form the basis of morality in every stage of social evolution. Durkheim was clearest in claiming that the god worshipped in a group ritual was nothing but a simplified mental representation of the group itself (Durkheim 1976; Detienne and Vernant 1989: 12-20).

While †Evans-Pritchard (1956) deliberately set out to challenge Smith's stress on the practical, collective side of religion and sacrifice, as well as what had become the orthodox sociological position following Durkheim, he continued to be deeply affected by Christian theology, with its concepts of 'sin', 'pollution' and 'remorse'. He defined religion strictly in terms of the individual's intentions towards a God standing outside the social structure, and interpreted sacrifice as the communication of the individual's inner spiritual state to God by means of material symbols. His approach is thus another example of Christian teleology, only now the claim is made that sacrifice is *already* an essentially spiritual phenomenon among the Nuer, despite all the blood and flesh.

Using Evans-Pritchard's own data de Heusch has shown instead that Nuer sacrifice is better understood in terms not of individual guilt and redemption, but of the restoration of the cosmic order following the transgression of its boundaries.

[Nuer] social order is one with the cosmic order. The rules of respect (*thek*) keep men and things that should be separated well apart; in the global system the celestial divinity and the spirits of the air, or the ancestors, are separated from men. Everyone is in his own place when all goes well, but when an offense has been committed, deliberately or accidentally, this symbolic order is threatened at a precise point. The sacrificial debt must then be paid to put the system back in place – God or spirits in the sky, men, defined by their network of prohibitions, on earth.

(de Heusch 1985: 13–14)

Sacrifice as practice

In order to avoid prejudicing the discussion of sacrifice by what it has come to mean in Christian theology, we will do better to use a concrete definition focusing on ritual practices rather than on exegesis. In his ethnography of a tribal religion in the Philippines, Gibson grouped a set of rituals under the heading of 'sacrifice' defined as 'the ritual manipulation, killing and commensal consumption of a sacred animal' (1986: 151). When we turn to comparative ethnography, we find that a culture may emphasize one part of this sequence more than another. Thus the Nuer described by Evans-Pritchard elaborate the acts preliminary to the killing, such as the consecration of the animal by rubbing ashes on its back, whereby the sacrificer identitifes himself with the victim, and the invocation, whereby the sacrificer further identifies himself with the victim, through his speech, his right arm, and his spear. For the Nuer, sacrifice is thus a rich source of metaphors for expressing inner mental dispositions towards God by projecting the self into the victim (Evans-Pritchard 1956).

The Muslim Moroccans described by Combs-Schilling (1989), on the other hand, play up the act of killing itself, accomplished by piercing the animal's (white) flesh, causing (red) blood to flow. This places it in the same field of meaning as other practices involving violence and blood, such as the defloration of a virgin bride and childbirth. For Moroccans, animal sacrifice is a rich source of metaphors for linking creation to patriarchal *violence and authority.

The Buid of Mindoro described by Gibson (1986) play down the consecration and slaughter of the animal and play up the different ways the cooked flesh can be surrendered to, exchanged with or shared with various human and spirit types. For the Buid, animal sacrifice is a rich source of metaphors for conceptualizing different forms of transaction. From the analyses of Greek sacrifice presented in the volume edited by Detienne and Vernant (1989), it would seem that the Greeks also preferred to focus on what

happened to the cadaver rather than on the preparation and execution of the victim.

Animal sacrifice is, in short, a complex symbolic practice, different aspects of which may be elaborated in different social settings. Rather than recognizing that there may be no more than 'family resemblances' between sacrifice in different cultures, however, many authors have attempted to identify the 'essential' features of sacrifice, and to formulate general 'theories' to explain it. What pass as different 'theories' of sacrifice are often no more than differences in the degree to which different elements of this definition are elaborated in the culture studied by the 'theorist'. The situation remains similar to the one surrounding the concept of totemism before *Lévi-Strauss's critiques in the early 1960s. Sacrifice has continued in many quarters to be viewed as an identifiable phenomenon compounded of the elements of self-abnegation and victimization (cf. Girard 1972).

Bloch (1992) has recently attempted to overcome these difficulties by showing how many different instances of 'animal sacrifice' in the ethnographic literature share a common symbolic structure with a wide variety of other ritual practices such as initiations, *marriages and even *millenarian movements. In other words, he dissolves the category into a larger problematic concerning the the the nature of *ideology and traditional authority.

*Nature, culture and *classification

Another way to approach sacrifice in comparative terms without immediately jumping to the level of universal theory is to ask what it is about domesticated animals that makes them so well suited to act as symbolic mediators, just as Lévi-Strauss found the rational kernel of the idea of totemism in the suitablity of animal and plant species to stand as a model for a class and to serve as mythological operators. In *The Savage Mind* Lévi-Strauss argued that (wild) animals provide two possible models for thinking about the social order: one focuses on the discrete boundaries separating whole species from one another and on the identity of features within species. This provides a template for †mechanical solidarity and social equivalence and is characteristic of *Australian Aborigines. The other one focuses on the internal structure of individual beasts and sees them as a template for †organic solidarity and social hierarchy. While he cites the division of the meat of a game animal by the hunting and gathering Bushmen as an example of the 'organic' model of animality (1966: 103), it is the (agrarian) Hindu *caste system that he discusses most extensively as possessing an 'anti-totemic' or 'organic' approach to social organization.

Significantly, Lévi-Strauss tends to restrict himself to societies predominantly devoted to hunting, gathering and horticulture as opposed to mixed animal husbandry and agriculture. Thus he does not consider the implications of domestication for animal symbolism in any detail. This issue was most extensively addressed by British authors inspired (or provoked) by Lévi-Strauss such as †Leach (1964), †Douglas (1966) and †Fortes (1967). They argued that the consumption of animal flesh is everywhere (at least in the pastoral or agricultural societies they discuss) subject to varying degrees of ritual regulation and emotional *taboo. Domesticated animals tend to be subject to the greatest amount of regulation and emotion. They occupy a place on the boundary between the human and non-human worlds, and between 'culture' and 'nature', in a way that wild animals do not. More generally, Leach claimed that there was a continuum between the self and the other that culture needed to break down into discontinuous units. It did so by applying behavioural and linguistic 'taboos' to certain portions of various continuous series, such as self-kinsman-stranger, domestic-field-forest and pet-farm animal-wild animal. Persons, places or animals occupying a tabooed zone, or prone to transgressing boundaries between zones, would be subject to special horror, awe or other emotion and to special rules of marriageability or edibility as the case might be. Perhaps the most successful analyses of this kind were those of Bulmer writing on the Karam of the New Guinea Highlands (1967) and Tambiah on the Thai (1969).

If one thinks about animal sacrifice in relation to this body of material, one can see that it is only a special case of a much more general set of practices relating to the classification, ritual manipulation and consumption of living creatures. The use of domestic animals as substitutes for the sacrificer in an effort to appease an angry God, and the self-sacrifice of a man-god are only two possible ways of conceiving the repair or the dissolution of boundaries between the human and non-human worlds. What Jesus and the lamb have in common is their interstitiality, their ability to open and close channels of communication between worlds. At this level of abstraction, one might almost say that animal sacrifice is to the husbandry of domesticated animals as animal totemism is to the hunting of wild animals.

THOMAS GIBSON

See also: ritual, religion, violence

Further reading

Bloch, M. (1992) *Prey into Hunter*, Cambridge: Cambridge University Press
Bulmer, R. (1967) 'Why is the Cassowary not a Bird?', *Man* 2: 5-25
Combs-Schilling, E. (1989) *Sacred Performances*, New York: Columbia University Press
Detienne, M. and J.-P. Vernant (1989 [1979]) *The Cuisine of Sacrifice among the Greeks*, Chicago: University of Chicago Press
Douglas, M. (1966) *Purity and Danger*, London: Routledge and Kegan Paul
—— (1972) 'Self-evidence', *Proceedings of the RAI for 1972*
Durkheim, É. (1976 [1912]) *Elementary Forms of the Religious Life*, London: George Allen and Unwin
Evans-Pritchard, E.E. (1956) *Nuer Religion*, Oxford: Clarendon
Fortes, M. (1967) 'Totem and Taboo', *Proceedings of the RAI for 1966* pp. 5–22
Gibson, T. (1986) *Sacrifice and Sharing in the Philippine Highlands*, London: Athlone Press
Girard, R. (1972) *La Violence et la sacré*, Paris: Gallimard
Heusch, Luc de (1985) *Sacrifice in Africa*, Manchester: Manchester University Press
Hubert, H. and M. Mauss. (1964 [1899]) *Sacrifice: Its Nature and Function*, Chicago: University of Chicago Press
Leach, E. (1964) 'Anthropological Aspects of Language: Animal Categories and Verbal Abuse', in E.J. Lenneberg (ed.) *New Directions in the Study of Language*, Cambridge
Lévi-Strauss, C. (1966 [1962]) *The Savage Mind*, London: Weidenfeld and Nicolson
Peters, E. (1968) 'Smith, William Robertson' in David L. Sills (ed.) *International Encyclopedia of the Social Sciences*, New York: Macmillan.
Smith, William Robertson (1927 [1889]) *Lectures on the Religion of the Semites* (3rd edn), New York: Macmillan
Tambiah, S. (1969) 'Animals are Good to Think and Good to Prohibit', *Ethnology* 8: 423–59

Sapir–Whorf hypothesis

The 'Sapir–Whorf hypothesis' or 'Whorfian hypothesis', in its simplest form, proposes that the structure of a given language will affect the way in which speakers of that language think. The implication of this is that people who speak different languages will think differently. Strict adherence to the Sapir–Whorf hypothesis is thus an example of extreme *relativism.

The phrase itself is derived from the names †Edward Sapir and †Benjamin Lee Whorf. In fact, Sapir wrote little of explicit relevance on the subject, but Whorf, who invented the phrase, incorporated his mentor's name in order to make it clear that, at least in Whorf's view, Sapir was the first to suggest the hypothesis. There are hints of it in Sapir's paper 'Language and Environment' (Sapir [1912] 1985: 89–103), for example, but only hints. The sharpest expression of the hypothesis comes in papers such as Whorf's 'An American Indian Model of the Universe', 'Science and Linguistics', 'Languages and Logic', and above all in 'The Relation of Habitual Thought and Behaviour to Language', which was written in 1939 for Sapir's *Festschrift*. All of these papers were published or reprinted in Whorf's collected writings (1956).

The simplest examples of the Sapir–Whorf hypothesis are those dealing with lexical distinctions. Whorf tells us that Hopi has two words for 'water'. One word is *keyi*, which means water in a container. The other is *pahe*, which means water in the sea, water in a pond, water flowing over a waterfall, water in a fountain, etc. (Whorf [1940] 1956: 210). The more complex, and therefore more intriguing, examples are those in which the purported thought processes of Native Americans are illustrated by Whorf through phrases or whole sentences, and in which grammatical features of the language appear to structure people's understanding of situations and processes. In order to help his readers follow the alien train of thought and compare it to their own, Whorf frequently *illustrated* his discussion literally, with pictures of Native North American and English thought. The complexity Whorf was trying to show is exemplified, for example, by his comparison between the English, 'He invites people to a feast', and the Nootka equivalent, 'Boiled-eaters-go-for-he-does'. The English is a sentence, with a subject and predicate, whereas the Nootka is a single word consisting of a root ('to boil') and five suffixes.

Perhaps the most vivid statement of the hypothesis comes in Whorf's conclusion to his posthumously-published paper 'A Linguistic Consideration of Thinking in Primitive Communities':

Does the Hopi language show here a higher plane of thinking, a more rational analysis of situations,

than our vaunted English? Of course it does. In this field and various others, English compared to Hopi is like a bludgeon compared to a rapier.

(Whorf 1956 [c. 1936]: 85)

The example at issue here is whether Hopi or English is more accurate in its reflection of the reality behind consciousness. English says 'I see that it is red' and 'I see that it is new', whereas Hopi expresses the former 'seeing that' through words which describe sensation, and the latter through words which describe evidence and inference. Ironically, this example belies Whorf's alleged relativism, in that it imputes a superiority to the speakers of Hopi.

Even more ironically, some of Whorf's ideas bear close, or at least interesting, relation to those of arch-antirelativist †Lucien Lévy-Bruhl (e.g. [1910] 1926: 139–80). Their ideas converge in that they both recognized the concrete complexity of grammar in the languages of so-called 'primitive' peoples. Where they differed was in their deeper interpretation of that phenomenon. To Lévy-Bruhl, the concrete expression of 'primitives' reflected an inability, or at least a reluctance, to put together abstract expressions. To Whorf, it marked an ability to think more precisely than those who speak languages prone to abstraction. Whorf envied the Hopi, the Navajo, and other Amerindian peoples for their abilities to think in ways more logical than the speakers of English. Whorf and Lévy-Bruhl also differed on the directionality of the relation between language and thought. For Lévy-Bruhl, language reflected thought. Grammatical categories are built up on the basis of 'primitive' thinking. To Whorf, the reverse was true. Thought reflected pre-existing linguistic categories. People think only through these categories, and not independently of them.

Whorf died in 1941 at the age of 44. Sadly, he did not live long enough to combat his staunchest critics, who began to appear in the following decade (e.g. Feuer 1953, Lenneberg 1953). Soon the study of *language and linguistics would change out of all recognition, as from the late 1950s, followers of †Noam Chomsky emphasized linguistic universals rather than what he regarded as the relatively insignificant syntactical differences between languages, thereby rendering Whorf's relativism as blunt as an English bludgeon.

The Sapir–Whorf hypothesis represents a particularly uncompromising version of a much more widespread anthropological tendency to attribute to language the potential to structure our perception of the world. This linguistic relativism can be found in aspects of *Boas's work, and can be traced back to the work of the German comparative linguist, †Wilhelm von Humboldt ([1836] 1988). Since the 1950s, weaker versions can be found in much *symbolic anthropology, in work on the relationship between metaphors and our perception of the world (Lakoff and Johnson 1980), and in work on the relation between language and 'cultural models' in *psychological anthropology (Holland and Quinn 1987).

Nevertheless, critical research on Whorf's central argument remains relatively scant. Partly this is because the argument itself poses grave difficulties for cross-cultural analysis. Can we meaningfully separate 'language' from 'thought', and if we can, what counts as non-linguistic evidence of mental processes? How can we describe those features of different languages which are responsible for different ways of thinking, except in terms of our own language and its grammatical and semantic distinctions? The most significant recent attempt to assess the Sapir-Whorf hypothesis (Lucy 1992) starts from questions like these, and attempts to answer them, for example, by developing a descriptive 'metalanguage' which is independent of the two languages – English and Yucatec Maya – being compared. Lucy employed a number of tests, involving both linguistic and non-linguistic procedures, on a group of Yucatec men and on a group of American students. His results show important differences between the two groups in the relative weighting given to properties such as 'shape' and 'material' in tasks involving sorting and comparing, differences which would seem to follow from differences in the way in which *number is marked in the two languages.

Lucy's study represents the most rigorous attempt to assess the Sapir–Whorf hypothesis; if nothing else demonstrating that while the hypothesis can be tested empirically, such tests require a rare combination of technical linguistic expertise and intellectual ingenuity. For most anthropologists, though, lacking either expertise or ingenuity, the significance of Whorf's hypothesis lies less in its possible truth, and more in its continuing ability to generate thought and discussion on a problem which is central to the whole anthropological project.

ALAN BARNARD and JONATHAN SPENCER

See also: classification, cognition, language and linguistics, belief, time and space, translation

Further reading

Feuer, L.S. (1953) 'Sociological Aspects of the Relation between Language and Philosophy', *Philosophy of Science* 20: 85–100

Holland, D. and N. Quinn (eds) (1987) *Cultural Models in Language and Thought*, Cambridge: Cambridge University Press

Humboldt, W. von ([1836] 1988) *On Language: The Diversity of Human Language-Structure and its Influence on the Mental Development of Mankind*, trans. by H. Aarsleff, Cambridge: Cambridge University Press

Lakoff, G. and M. Johnson (1980) *Metaphors We Live By*, Chicago: University of Chicago Press

Lenneberg, E.H. (1953) 'Cognition in Ethnolinguistics', *Language* 29: 463–71

Lévy-Bruhl, L. ([1910] 1926) *How Natives Think*, London: Allen & Unwin

Lucy, J. (1992) *Grammatical Categories and Cognition: A Case Study of the Linguistic Relativity Hypothesis*, Cambridge: Cambridge Unversity Press

Sapir, E. ([1912] 1985) *Selected Writings in Language, Culture, and Personality*, D.G. Mandelbaum (ed.) Berkeley: University of California Press.

Whorf, B.L. ([1940] 1956) *Language, Thought and Reality: Selected Writings of Benjamin Lee Whorf*, J.B. Carroll (ed.) Cambridge, MA: MIT Press

scandals, anthropological

What counts as a disciplinary scandal usually exposes revealing fault-lines in its sense of collective *identity. So it is with anthropological scandals which periodically bring the discipline's collective anxieties to the attention of a wider audience. A number of recurring themes can be drawn out from these. One is anxiety over the integrity of an individual's *fieldwork, often as revealed by discrepancies between a celebrated *ethnography and a subsequent restudy. A second is anxiety over the ethical implications of a piece of anthropological work. A third is anxiety over anthropology's uneasy interaction with wider cultural expectations and fantasies about †primitivism and the †noble savage.

A classic example is †Derek Freeman's attack on †Mead's early work in Samoa (Mead 1928; Freeman 1983). Mead used her evidence on the apparently relaxed sexual and social mores of Samoan adolescents to advance a critique of American attitudes to *education and sexuality. Freeman's counter-evidence of a profoundly hierarchical society, with high levels of rape and suicide, was ultimately intended to refute Mead's version of †cultural determinism, which he traced back to the influence of her teacher, *Franz Boas. Popular reaction to Freeman's book, especially in the American mass media, concentrated as much on the damage it caused to the paradisal vision of a South Seas primitive utopia which casual readers had taken from Mead's book. Professional anthropologists were less impressed than might be expected by Freeman's empirical onslaught. Some detected a hidden political agenda in this attack on one of America's most famous liberal intellectuals, while others pointed out the inevitable difficulties in comparing the experience of different fieldworkers, of different ages and genders, working at different times in the same cultural setting (Brady 1983; *Canberra Anthropology* 1983).

Much of the public interest generated by Freeman's critique must be due to the fact that it impinged so directly on popular ideas about the primitive, which themselves form part of a wider public critique of industrial society. The continuing controversy over the Tasaday (Headland 1992) illustrates this further. A supposedly untouched society living a stone-age existence in a remote area of the Philippines, the Tasaday were the subject of popular magazine articles, a film, and a journalistic ethnography when they were 'discovered' in the early 1970s; their subsequent 'exposure' as a hoax was itself the subject of television documentaries and newspaper articles. Nevertheless, there is still an embarrassing lack of consensus within the discipline over the exact status of the Tasaday.

The Tasaday, as originally presented, and Mead's Samoa can both be seen as examples of the use of accounts of other cultures to compose allegorical statements about Western society. Both these examples were more or less utopian, but much of the celebrity of †Colin Turnbull's account of the Ik in *The Mountain People* (1973) is due to its bleakly dystopian vision (which contrasts with the romantic view of the Mbuti in Turnbull's earlier work). This portrait of a hunting people reduced by starvation to a †Hobbesian state of nature was criticized on both ethical and empirical grounds at the time of publication. In the mid-1980s it became clear that at least some of the Ik were as suspicious of Turnbull's account as were some of Turnbull's fellow anthropologists (Heine 1985).

What particularly alarmed Turnbull's critics was his revelation that he had concluded his fieldwork by recommending that the authorities in the area should disperse the remaining Ik as far as possible from each other. As †applied

anthropology has grown, and anthropologists have presented themselves more and more as professional experts, able to speak with authority to governments and judges, so the potential for ethical scandals has increased. This is an area in which the discipline's sense of what is scandalous has probably changed most. †Evans-Pritchard's work for the colonial government of the Sudan in the 1930s was not, on the whole, seen as scandalous at the time, whereas the US government's attempts to use anthropologists in counter-insurgency work in Southeast Asia in the 1960s was. Even the apparently morally unimpeachable desire to speak for an embattled minority group has become a focus of controversy: in Australia one anthropologist has claimed that liberal colleagues have compromised their professional authority by adopting too partisan a position in land-rights cases (Brunton 1992; cf. Keen 1992).

The anthropologists of the postcolonial world are easily embarrassed by the sometimes scandalous language of their colonial predecessors, as the enduring unease about *Malinowski's field diary makes clear. In this respect, every generation is likely to discover new scandals in the work of its predecessors. But there are enduring themes which can be discerned in anthropological scandals: the anxious authority of the lone fieldworker who attempts to speak for a whole group of people on the basis of her solitary, and sometimes difficult experience; and the anxious authority of a whole discipline which is at once rooted in, but wants to distance itself from, popular images of the primitive and pre-industrial.

JONATHAN SPENCER

See also: colonialism

Further reading

Brady, I. (ed.) (1983) 'Speaking in the Name of the Real: Freeman and Mead on Samoa', *American Anthropologist* 85 (4): 908–47

Brunton, R. (1992) 'Mining Credibility: Coronation Hill and the Anthropologists', *Anthropology Today* 8 (2): 2–5

Canberra Anthropology (1983) 'Fact and Context in Ethnography: The Samoa Controversy', (Special Volume) 6 (1–2)

Freeman, D. (1983) *Margaret Mead and Samoa: The Making and Unmaking of an Anthropological Myth*, Cambridge, MA: Harvard University Press

Headland, T. (ed.) (1992) *The Tasaday Controversy: Assessing the Evidence*, Washington, DC: American Anthropological Association

Heine, B. (1985) 'The Mountain People: Some Notes

on the Ik of North-Eastern Uganda', *Africa* 55 (1): 3–16

Keen, I. (1992) 'Undermining Credibility: Advocacy and Objectivity in the Coronation Hill Debate', *Anthropology Today* 8 (2): 6–9

Mead, M. (1928) *Coming of Age in Samoa: A Psychological Study of Primitive Youth for Western Civilisation*, New York: Morrow

Turnbull, C. (1973) *The Mountain People*, London: Jonathan Cape

science

In part because anthropology describes itself as a science, and perhaps because it has in the past struggled to maintain its scientific credentials, science has itself remained largely outside the anthropological lens. Instead, a guiding presumption of much early anthropology was the belief that European anthropologists possessed a superior *rationality which differentiated them from the peoples they studied (most notably Lévy-Bruhl). Even those, such as *Malinowski, who argued for the universal presence of scientific rationality, or its prototype, among the most 'primitive' peoples did so on the assumption that it had reached its highest expression among civilized European societies. Well into mid-century, modern anthropologists were more concerned to become properly scientific than to examine the unique cultural formation of science.

Early investigations of science as a social phenomenon emerged out of history and philosophy from investigators such as Ludwig Fleck, †Thomas Kuhn, and †Karl Popper, who were largely concerned with rationality and scientific knowledge. Robert Merton inaugurated the sociology of science through studies investigating its institutionalization and professionalization. This division, between the social institutionalization of science and its status as a form of rational knowledge, has continued within science studies and is evident in contemporary feminist and sociological literatures. From the historical tradition have emerged both approaches which seek rationally to explain the history of scientific achievement and discovery, and more radical approaches which seek to explore science as an emergent cultural phenomenon, examining, for example, its popular representation, visual dimensions and symbolic resources.

By the mid-1980s, important works in the area of science studies began to bridge this divide (see especially Haraway 1989), opening the way for a greater diversity of approaches and challenging the equation of science with rational knowledge. As the definition of 'science' has begun to become more diffuse, anthropologists have played an increasing role in its analysis as a *cultural field. Recent science studies projects within anthropology, therefore, have examined a range of topics; from techniques such as Polymerase Chain Reaction, to concepts such as immunity or heredity. Communities of scientists have been studied in laboratory-based ethnographies, such as Traweek's account of high-energy physicists in Japan and the US (1988), and through more multi-sited approaches which follow the cultural production of science across a range of sites and locations.

Following the examples set by Robin Horton and Joseph Needham, important recent studies have begun to address 'science' in cross-cultural perspective (Marcus 1995). This approach complements both critical accounts of Western science produced by non-Western scholars such as Susantha Goonitilake (1984) and debates over the uses of scientific knowledge in the context of *development studies. Key to both areas are also concerns about the appropriation of †indigenous knowledges by Western scientists and their elimination in the name of scientific progress.

Decreases of public funding for research science in many Western nations have contributed to the emergence of renewed dispute over the status of scientific truth claims, and their corresponding importance to matters of local, national and global advancement. Such debates in turn invoke questions about a *postmodern readjustment to conventional definitions of scientific progress, including a greater awareness of its risks and its effect on definitions of the natural and the environment.

SARAH FRANKLIN

See also: modernism, rationality, relativism, technology

Further reading

Franklin, Sarah (1995) 'Science as Culture, Cultures of Science', *Annual Reviews in Anthropology* 24: 163–84

Goonatilake, Susantha (1984) *Aborted Discovery: Science and Creativity in the Third World*, London: Zed Books

Haraway, Donna (1989) *Primate Visions: Gender, Race and Nature in the World of Modern Science*, New York: Routledge

Heath, Deborah and Paul Rabinow (eds) (1993) 'Bio-Politics: The Anthropology of the New Genetics and

Immunology', *Journal of Culture, Medicine and Psychiatry* 17 (special issue)

Hess, David and Lina Layne (eds) (1992) 'The Anthropology of Science and Technology', *Knowledge and Society* 9 (special issue)

Marcus, George (ed.) (1995) *Technoscientific Imaginaries: Conversations, Profiles, Memoirs*, Chicago: University of Chicago Press

Traweek, Sharon (1988) *Beamtimes and Lifetimes: The World of High Energy Physicists*, Cambridge, MA: Harvard University Press

settlement patterns

Settlement patterns comprise the means by which humans place themselves and their dwellings in relation to the land, and the patterns of *migration, aggregation and dispersal which give rise to their distribution on the land. The comparative study of settlement patterns is not highly developed in social or cultural anthropology. Although *ad hoc* studies of the phenomenon are common with regard to *hunter-gatherers and *pastoralists, the ethnographic study of settlement patterns has never become a sub-discipline quite comparable to settlement geography or settlement archaeology.

Hunter-gatherers are well suited to studies of settlement precisely because they exhibit variations which are related to the availability of resources. Factors affecting *transhumance may include the availability of water, the seasonal availability of plant foods, the migration of game, or simply custom. In desert areas of Australia and Southern Africa, hunter-gatherers move seasonally or more often, and disperse to utilize outlying water resources. Great variation exists, and this is to some extent determined by local environmental conditions (Barnard 1979).

Dichotomous patterns such as upland versus lowland, coastal areas versus interior riverine ones, etc., are readily apparent among *fishing peoples as well. Native peoples of the northwest coast of North America, for example, have seasonal cycles of settlement which are partly based on the exploitation of migratory fish, such as salmon. Traditional land ownership, political allegiance, and ceremonial *exchange are all, in turn, related to the exploitation of seasonal resources and consequent patterns of migration and settlement.

The situation among pastoralists is quite similar in that transhumant settlement is common. The Nuer of the Southern Sudan spend the wet season in upland villages and the dry season in cattle camps along the rivers. In the former they live mainly from meat and grain, and in the latter from fish and milk (Evans-Pritchard 1940). In southern Africa, traditional economies based on cattle and agriculture sometimes create more complex patterns. Tswana families in rural Botswana, for example, typically have three places of residence: a village, one or more cattle posts (where boys and elders often live), and 'lands' (where crops are grown, mainly by the women). Tswana villages are complex in structure and divided into wards, each with its own headman.

An important aspect of the study of settlements in geography is central place theory. This was developed in the 1930s when German geographer Walter Christaller noticed that Southern German settlements of similar function and size were located approximately equal distances from one another, and that a hierarchy of such equally-spaced settlements, from cities to towns to villages, formed a pattern in the landscape. Christaller ([1933] 1966) hypothesized that such distributions should occur elsewhere and explained the pattern by way of the necessities of trade networks of differing scale. This geographical theory (sometimes said to be geography's *only* theory) has had some impact in social anthropology among those who practise on the fringes of geography.

ALAN BARNARD

See also: archaeology, environment, hunting and gathering, nomadism

Further reading

Barnard, A. (1979) 'Kalahari Bushman Settlement Patterns', in P.C. Burnham and R.F. Ellen (eds) *Social and Ecological Systems* (ASA Monographs 18), London: Academic Press

Christaller, W. ([1933] 1966) *The Central Places of Southern Germany*, Engelwood Cliffs, NJ: Prentice Hall

Evans-Pritchard, E.E. (1940) *The Nuer: A Description of the Modes of Livelihood and Political Institutions of a Nilotic People*, Oxford: The Clarendon Press

Ingold, Tim (1986) *The Appropriation of Nature: Essays on Human Ecology and Social Relations*, Manchester: Manchester University Press

shamanism

The term 'shaman' was taken from Russian sources in the seventeenth century, the word itself coming from the language of the Evenks

(Tungus), an eastern Siberian people. A century later the derivative term 'shamanism' was coined. Among the Evenks the 'shaman' (man or woman) occupies a central position in *ritual and *religious practices. He or she is the mediator between the human world and the world of spirits, between the living and the dead, and between animals and human society. Endowed with clairvoyance and assisted by helper spirits, a shaman fills many social and religious roles including those of sooth-sayer, therapist and interpreter of dreams. He or she also plays an offensive and defensive role in the protection of his or her group against the aggressive actions of other shamans or displeased spirits. During public seances, he or she is able to cross profane (see *sacred and profane) frontiers of *time and space, and of surface reality, and has the power to journey into the beyond and make contact with spirits. At major transitions in the life cycle and in the cycle of seasonal activity, as at times of crisis, disorder, war, famine or illness, the shaman give services to the group (freely), and to individuals (with some expectation of return).

Individuals with analogous attributes, roles and functions were described in many other groups by travellers, explorers and missionaries, especially in the Americas. These individuals were designated in the latters' accounts by various names: 'curan-dero' in Spanish, 'wizard', 'medicine man' in English, 'jongleur', 'sorcier' or 'magicien' in French, 'giocolare' in Italian and 'Gaulker' in German (Eliade [1951] 1964, Flaherty 1992). From the beginning of the nineteenth century however, 'shaman' and 'shamanism' gradually replaced the others and became generic terms applicable in other regions of the world such as the *Pacific, *Africa, *South, *East and *Southeast Asia and Australia, in addition to the Americas and Siberia, without the previous terms disappearing altogether.

Romanticism and evolutionism

During the next two centuries interest in shamanism increased to an astonishing extent, although this varied with shifts in ideas and customs. With its roots in the Enlightenment, this interest manifested itself first among early Romantic intellectuals and artists, then in certain currents in medicine. Shamanism was seen as the expression of irrationalism, the source of art, esotericism, religion, and medicine. It was thus opposed to the scientific *rationality which dominated the Enlightenment. Diderot, †Herder and Goethe were fascinated by Siberian shamanism (Flaherty 1992). We could speak of a 'demonization' of shamanism during this period, although with one qualification: for the authors mentioned above this was part of a re-evaluation of the importance of the 'devil' and occult forces; for Christian missionaries of the period, on the other hand, confronted by shamans on the ground as it were, it was more a process of devaluation, in which shamanism was assimilated to the forces of evil.

In the social *evolutionism which prevailed in the social sciences and religious studies in the second half of the nineteenth century, shamanism was held to be an intermediary stage between *magic and *religion. By stressing the importance of its collective and symbolic aspects evolutionists considered it as a socio-religious system. This was notably the case for the French sociological school which viewed shamanism as deriving from *totemism. Another perspective, tinged with psychologism, preferred to focus on the individual aspects of shamanism, linking these to the person-ality of the shaman which was described either as charismatic and 'ecstatic', or as psycho-pathological.

These diverse aproaches were taken up, with more or less success, in twentieth-century anthro-pology as well as other disciplines such as religious studies, medicine and psychology. However, this increased interest in shamanism resulted in a loss of conceptual clarity. Each author would propose a different definition of shamanism, one which emphasized the aspect of the phenomenon most compatible with their particular theoretical and disciplinary interests.

From ethnographic regionalism to psychological reductionism

With the increase in ethnographic research in the field, well-documented monographs have been produced which provide new data on shamanism. All of these, however, focus on a particular region and, while they enable us to gain a better under-standing of the diverse social contexts in which shamanism is found, such monographs have shifted attention away from an interest in the comparative work required to formulate a general theory of the collective (social and symbolic) dimensions of the phenomenon. The great evolu-tionist and comparativist essays of the beginning of the century soon went out of fashion and their conclusions were strongly contested. Psychological approaches which focus on the personality of the shaman came to dominate research and scientific debates, both in *Russian and Soviet anthropology (Shirikogorov 1935) and in American cultural anthropology (such as the *culture and personality school), as well as the history of religions.

It was the historian of religion †Mircéa Eliade who, in 1951, revived the comparative analysis of shamanism in his work *Shamanism: Archaic Techniques of Ecstasy*, first published in French (a revised and enlarged English edition was published in 1964). For the first time, an author attempted to pull together the results of research on shamanism from all over the world. Eliade presented a comprehensive account from an historical perspective, based on a compilation of sources published in the major European languages. Using an approach influenced by religious psychology, he emphasized the mystical aspect of shamanic practices, in particular that of the 'trance' which he assimilated to the notion of 'ecstasy'.

As an historian of religions, Eliade regarded himself as the best placed to produce this work of synthesis. He thought anthropology to be limited by its monographic approach, social anthropology to be too concerned with the social functions of the shaman, and psychology as interested exclusively in the consequences of the shaman's break with reality (Eliade [1951] 1964). In spite of the numerous reservations which are now made about this imposing work, it remains the best introduction to shamanism, from the point of view both of the themes covered and of the diverse cultural traditions it describes. Eliade can be criticized for reducing shamanism to trance. The latter is in fact only one aspect of shamanism as it can also be found in *possession (Rouget [1980] 1985). In emphasizing trance, he reduces a symbolic system to a psychological state. He can also be criticized firstly for having minimized – or even ignored – the importance of certain forms of shamanism which are now generally recognized but which do not fit into his narrow definition, and secondly for having been too selective in his choice of sources.

Shamanism and postmodernism

Several anthropologists have even objected to the concept of shamanism itself. In 1966 †Clifford Geertz asserted that shamanism was a dry and insipid category with which ethnographers of religion had devitalized their data. A few years later Robert Spencer described it as a residual category of the discipline. Finally Michael Taussig

has attempted more recently, from a *post-modernist perspective, to carry out a radical †deconstruction of it (as *Lévi-Strauss had done for totemism) in seeing it as a modern construct created in the West which brings together otherwise diverse practices (Atkinson 1992).

Other anthropologists such as Andreas Lommel (1967) have included aspects or groups neglected by Eliade in the field of shamanism, seeing in it the origin of art or theatre. By the end of the 1960s, shamanism had aroused new interest in the West, both among the general public and in several disciplines outside anthropology. This coincided with a questioning of industrial development and its logic, the emergence of environmentalism, the return to alternative medicines, the development of religious sects and psychedelic experiences associated with drugs. All these movements and currents sought in shamanism their truth or justification.

In this connection, it should be noted that *psychological anthropology has investigated altered states of consciousness and studied hallucinogens, a number of which are used by shamans in the Americas (Harner 1973). *Ethnopsychiatry also rediscovered shamanism, although it no longer considered it an expression of psychopathology, but instead reconsidered from the psychoanalytic viewpoint, as a therapeutic cure. The shaman was now looked upon as a 'cured madman' who could heal those around him or her; and his or her initiatory experience compared to the training analysis of psychoanalysts. In 1963 Lévi-Strauss had started to compare certain aspects of the shamanic cure and psychoanalysis by drawing attention to their symbolic effectiveness. On the fringe of this research, certain anthropologists, fascinated by their object of study and responding to the demands of their milieu, set up (originally in California), schools of shamanic training and presented themselves and their students as neo-shamans.

The revival of shamanic studies

The Ninth International Congress of Anthropological and Ethnological Sciences (held in Chicago in 1973) reflected these new tendencies in a publication entitled *Spirits, Shamans and Stars* (Browman and Schwartz 1979). Its three sections provide a good indication of contemporary preoccupations: the magico-religious use of psychotropic drugs, shamanic therapies and the analysis of religious structures and shamanic symbols. These three directions of research continued to develop throughout the following two decades, with a marked increase at the beginning of the 1980s. Contrary to the pessimistic prognosis of the preceding period, shamanism was not dead. It has even gone through a revival in numerous regions of the world, such as Siberia and Amazonia, where it had been considered doomed as a result of persecution and major socio-economic changes. In these regions an urban form of shamanism is even emerging.

Certain traditionally shamanic groups, which have long been dominated by imported ideologies and religions, have also rediscovered their roots. This phenomenon is discernible in countries as dissimilar as South Korea, Finland and Hungary. These countries have actively participated in the promotion of research on shamanism, notably by hosting scientific conferences on this theme. Research is generally on the increase. The relaxing of political constraints in the Soviet Union has allowed ethnologists to study shamanism among Siberian peoples once again (Basilov 1984). In Scandinavia, on the instigation of Äke Hultkrantz, a young generation of historians of religion has re-examined shamanism. In France and in anglo-phone countries Lévi-Straussian *structuralism has led to the detailed holistic study of several Asian (Hamayon 1990) and American (Crocker 1985) shamanic systems. This research has brought out their collective and symbolic dimensions and the ways in which they relate to representations, practices, rites, myths, and political and social organization.

Conferences on shamanism are on the increase in Eastern Europe (on Eurasia with M. Hoppal and V.N. Basilov, 1981), in France (with R. Hamayon, 1981), in Britain (on *Lowland South America, with J. Kaplan, 1982), in the United States (with R.I. Heinz, from 1984); from which many important publications have been produced. Finally, during the International Congress of Anthropological and Ethnological Sciences which took place at Zagreb in 1988, there was a very successful session on 'Shamanism: Past and Present'. The participants even decided to form an International Society for Shamanic Studies in order to promote and coordinate research. Its first congress was held in Seoul in 1991, and a second in Budapest in 1993, at which was launched the first issue of the journal *Shaman* which brings together theoretical debates, ethnographic documents and thematic studies of shamanism.

New areas of research are emerging such as the political dimensions of shamanic power (Thomas and Humphrey 1994), and *gender relations as expressed in transgression and in the sexual distribution of shamanic roles (Saladin d'Anglure 1994). There is also new interest in dream activities (B. Tedlock 1991), and shamanic texts and performances (Atkinson 1992).

Far from being being an outdated Western category, as certain postmodern anthropologists would have it, shamanism – both as a system of thought, rites and relations with the world, and as an object of study – is not, at the end of the twentieth century, situated before postmodernism but rather beyond it. It shows an astonishing capacity to adapt to new urban contexts, to be able to exist side by side with major religions, and to resist all attempts at institutionalization and reduction to one or other of its aspects.

The meaning of shamanism as a total social phenomenon and as the point of articulation of the three levels – psychological, sociological and religious – in which it is expressed, is undoubtedly best revealed by a symbolic anthropological approach. The shaman appears, from this perspective, as a mediator who transcends these levels in a complex and dynamic fusion. The shaman is able to overcome the contradictions between binary oppositions (man/woman, humans/animals, humans/spirits, living/dead) through playing with ambiguity, paradox and transgression, in order to manage crises, disorder and change. Shamanic time and space, as that of myths, dreams and spirits, holds out against rationalism, as those early Romantics understood well. It has affinities with pre-Socratic thought, irrationalism, esotericism and the great systems of non-Western thought such as Daoism. Is it not rooted in an immemorial prehistory which, by way of the ideology of hunting, was directly attuned to nature and the cosmos?

BERNARD SALADIN D'ANGLURE

See also: Asia: East, possession, ritual

Further reading

Atkinson, J.M. (1992) 'Shamanism Today', *Annual Review of Anthropology* 21: 307–30

Basilov, V.N. (1984) 'The Study of Shamanism in Soviet Ethnography', in M. Hoppal (ed.) *Shamanism in Eurasia*, Göttingen: Herodot

Browman, D. and R. Schwartz (eds) (1979) *Spirits, Shamans and Stars*, The Hague: Mouton

Crocker, J.C. (1985) *Vital Souls: Bororo Cosmology, Natural Symbolism and Shamanism*, Tucson: University of Arizona Press

Eliade, M. ([1951] 1964) *Shamanism: Archaic Techniques of Ecstasy*, Princeton: Princeton University Press

Flaherty, G. (1992) *Shamanism and the Eighteenth Century*, Princeton: Princeton University Press

Hamayon, R. (1990) *La Chasse à l'âme: Esquisse d'une Théorie du Chamanisme Sibérien*, Nanterre: Société d'Ethnologie

Harner, M. (ed.) (1973) *Hallucinogens and Shamanism*, New York: Oxford University Press

Hoppal, M. (ed.) (1984) *Shamanism in Eurasia*, Göttingen: Herodot

Lommel, A. (1967) *Shamanism: The Beginning of Art*, New York: McGraw Hill

Rouget, G. ([1980] 1985) *Music and Trance: A Theory of the Relations between Music and Possession*, Chicago: University of Chicago Press

Saladin d'Anglure, B. (1994) 'From Foetus to Shaman: The Construction of an Inuit Third Sex', in A. Mills and R. Slobodin (eds), *Amerindian Rebirth*, Toronto: University of Toronto Press

Shirokogorov, S.M. (1935) *Psychomental Complex of the Tungus*, London: Kegan Paul

Tedlock, B. (1991) 'The New Anthropology of Dreaming' *Dreaming* 1: 161–78

Thomas, N. and C. Humphrey (eds) (1994) *Shamanism, History and the State*, Ann Arbor: University of Michigan Press

sharecropping

Sharecropping involves contractual agreement to combine productive resources and share output in agreed proportions. In stereotypical representations (to which novelists and other writers have perhaps contributed more than social scientists) such contracts are extremely unequal, enabling powerful landowners to extract high profits from the vulnerable *peasants they exploit. Sharecroppers are therefore readily presented as a thinly disguised proletariat in the Marxist tradition (Byres 1983), while mainstream bourgeois economics has historically viewed share contracts as inefficient in comparison with alternative systems of fixed rents and wage labour.

In anthropology, sharecropping has provided the economic background to a considerable number of studies of peasant societies, notably in *Southern Europe, *South America and *South Asia. However, comparatively few studies have placed sharecropping at the centre of the enquiry, and it is still unusual for the details of the contracts to be subjected to close scrutiny. For example, the pioneering work of S. Silverman and D. Kertzer in Italy pays as much attention to the co-residential group and other social factors as to the economic practices of sharecropping. In this case, as elsewhere, foreign anthropologists can learn much from historical research into sharecropping undertaken by indigenous scholars. There is scope for combining resources in ways analogous to sharecropping contracts, provided that the local researchers are not treated as unsuspecting peasants to be exploited.

Only in the outstanding monograph of Robertson (1987) has the case been clearly made for the importance of a comparative anthropological focus on sharecropping itself. Building in part on the pioneering work of Hill in Ghana (e.g. 1963) and adding other African case studies, Robertson shows that the enormous variation and flexibility of sharecropping practices are what commend them to farming households. It persists in all parts of the world, under very different economic regimes, socialist and capitalist as well as peasant, and can be conducive not only to high yields and innovation, but also to high rates of social mobility. Such 'revisionist' views should not blind us to the occurrence and persistence in many parts of the world of highly exploitative forms; but through opening up the discussion with his African materials, Robertson succeeded in exposing the simplistic notions underpinning the treatment of sharecropping in other subjects, as well as uncovering important new fields of enquiry for *development and *economic anthropology.

C.M. HANN

See also: land tenure, peasant

Further reading

Byres, T.J. (ed.) (1983) *Sharecropping and Sharecroppers*, London: Frank Cass

Hill, P. (1963) *The Migrant Cocoa Farmers of Southern Ghana; A Study in Rural Capitalism*, Cambridge: Cambridge University Press

Kertzer, D.I. (1984) *Family Life in Central Italy 1880-1910: Sharecropping, Wage-labour, and Co-residence*, New Brunswick: Rutgers University Press

Robertson, A.F. (1987) *The Dynamics of Productive Relationships; African Share Contracts in Comparative Perspective*, Cambridge: Cambridge University Press

slavery

Despite the historical importance of slavery in many parts of the world anthropologists study, the subject remains somewhat marginal within the discipline. Much more has been written by historians, most of this dealing with the trans-Atlantic trade during which more than nine million Africans were transported to the New World, principally to work on European and American-owned plantations. Much of this historical work has dealt with the political and economic dimensions of the supply-side of the trade and its effects on coastal and interior populations of Africa (see also Wolf 1982: 195–231), whilst more recent studies have added to our knowledge with some particularly fine social histories of slavery in the Caribbean and Southern United States. The subject was however largely ignored in modern anthropology until it received both ethnographic and theoretical attention in the 1970s from French Africanists working within a Marxist framework, and British and American scholars drawing on ethnohistorical data (see e.g. Meillassoux 1975; Miers and Kopytoff 1977).

Given the historical significance of the Atlantic trade it is not surprising that the dominant stereotype of slavery is that of the New World Afro-American plantation system, a stereotype in which 'slavery is monolithic, invariant, servile, chattel-like, focused on compulsory labour, maintained by violence, and suffused with brute sexuality' (Kopytoff 1982: 214). Yet examples from different times and places of what is usually taken to be slavery reveal a great variation in both the type of servitude slaves experienced (a common difference often being noted between domestic and chattel slaves), and the political and economic systems in which the institution existed. There are cases of slaves owning *property (even other slaves), occupying important offices, and selling their product. And as an institution slavery was to be found among peoples with polities and economies as diverse as those of the American Northwest Coast, Borneo, and sub-Saharan Africa.

Theories seeking an economic explanation of slavery have frequently dwelled on the land-labour-capital triad, attempting to account for the incidence or type of slavery in terms of the relative availability of each in any given case. However, a central problem for recent anthropological discussions of slavery has been one of definition. Most authors abjure legalistic and economistic definitions which they see as rooted in *capitalist notions of property, although there is disagreement as to who has been successful in this regard. Legal definitions of slaves as property come up against the predictable problem of what is to be defined as property? The common distinction made between slavery and freedom also raises problems, given differing notions of social belonging in the societies that anthropologists study. Finally, the varieties of work performed by slaves in different societies also makes an economistic definition of slavery based on labour (compulsory or otherwise) similarly problematic.

Another common theme in recent discussions has been the relationship between slavery and *kinship. In the introduction to a collection on African slavery, Miers and Kopytoff (1977) for example discuss slavery in terms of transfers in 'rights-in-persons' within kinship systems open to absorbing outsiders, thereby making them quasi-kin. Thus whilst starting off as outsiders, slaves are subsequently absorbed by a kinship group, an argument which proposes that slavery must be looked at as a process rather than as a state of being. In a comparison of African and Asian systems of slavery, Watson (1980) contrasts the 'open' system described by Miers and Kopytoff with 'closed' systems where kin groups tend to be exclusive, and where slaves remain outsiders rather than being incorporated. This difference Watson links to land, arguing that in 'closed' systems land is a scarce valuable, whereas in 'open' systems land is plentiful and wealth resides in people. The status of slaves as outsiders is similarly central to Meillassoux's (1991) Marxist analysis of African slavery, although he is at pains to point out the radical differences between his own model and that of Miers and Kopytoff. For Meillassoux slaves are and remain 'aliens' *par excellence*, and he suggests that a fundamental characteristic of slavery is 'the social incapacity of the slave to reproduce socially – that is, the slave's juridical inability to become "kin"' (1991: 35). Thus for Meillassoux there is no 'slavery-kinship continuum' as Miers and Kopytoff suggest, for slavery is the antithesis of kinship.

Despite their various differences, the issue of *identity is implicit in the theories of both Kopytoff and Meillassoux. The incorporation of outsiders as kin and the incapacity to reproduce socially are both arguments about personhood and identity, issues which may prove central to further developments in the anthropology of slavery as it begins to draw on recent anthropological discussions of the *person and gift and commodity exchange. Kopytoff himself suggests that 'The sociological issue in slavery is ... not the dehumanization of the person but rather [their] rehumanization in a new setting' (1982: 222). However whilst one may agree that slaves are not dehumanized (i.e. reduced from persons to things), neither are they fully rehumanized in their new setting, and we find that systems of slavery exhibit great variation in the ways that the status of slaves is marked out in terms of their personhood. On the New World plantations we perhaps find the system in which the reduction of persons to things was most marked; elsewhere, however, we find the personhood of slaves marked differently – sometimes slaves were sacrificed, their tombs were symbolically devalued through their positioning and construction, and they were prevented from having descendants or achieving ancestorhood. In short their status as slaves was marked out by their inability to fully realize their personhood in various ways, an issue touched on in a recent paper by Guyer (1993). Thus whilst slaves are not wholly reduced to the status of things, they are always to be found as persons of a different order.

It has been the case up till now that anthropological studies of slavery have relied on archives and oral history for their data. But as anthropological interest in slavery grows, so too does its incidence in the contemporary world, with cases reported for places as different as Eastern Europe and Eastern Indonesia. Although cultural analyses of slavery may extend 'our understanding [of slavery] ... in the very process of dismantling the concept' (Kopytoff 1982: 227), some people now find themselves faced with economic conditions under which the institution thrives.

PHILIP THOMAS

See also: colonialism, identity, Marxism and anthropology, person, property

Further reading

Guyer, J. (1993) 'Wealth in People and Self-realization in Equatorial Africa', *Man* (n.s.) 28 (2): 243–66

Kopytoff, I. (1982) 'Slavery', *Annual Review of Anthropology* 11: 207–30

Meillassoux, C. (ed.) (1975) *L'Esclavage en Afrique Précoloniale*, Paris: Maspero

—— ([1986] 1991) *The Anthropology of Slavery: The Womb of Iron and Gold*, trans. by A. Dasnois, Chicago: University of Chicago Press

Miers, S. and Kopytoff, I. (eds) (1977) *Slavery in Africa*, Madison: University of Wisconsin Press

Watson, J. (1980) 'Slavery as an Institution: Open and Closed Systems', in J. Watson (ed.) *Asian and African Systems of Slavery*, Oxford: Blackwell

Wolf, E.R. (1982) *Europe and the People without History*, Berkeley: University of California Press

social structure and social organization

The terms 'social structure' and 'social organization' have long had slightly different implications, although the distinction between them has not always been as clear-cut as some commentators would have preferred. 'Social organization' has tended to be used loosely to refer to the sum total of activities performed in a given social context. 'Social structure' has usually been employed for the social context itself, or more precisely for the set of social relations which link individuals in a society. Yet the definition of 'social structure' varies according to the theoretical perspective of the writer and the degree of precision required by his or her perspective.

Writers who are mainly concerned with social action tend to concentrate on *social organization*, which defines the †roles individuals play in relation to one another. Those who are concerned more with the formal relations between people tend to concentrate on *social structure*, which defines the †statuses of actors performing such roles. Thus, social organization is of greater interest to Malinowskian functionalists, and to some extent processualists, notably †Raymond Firth (1951). Social structure is of greater interest to those whose approaches are descended from classic †structural-functionalist and *structuralist traditions.

The clearest distinction between the concepts occurs in the introduction to *Radcliffe-Brown's *Structure and Function in Primitive Society* (1952: 9–11) and in his essay 'On Social Structure' (1952 [1940]: 188–204). In the latter, he further distinguished social structure from structural form – a distinction which caused some problems for his readers, not least *Lévi-Strauss. A celebrated debate (or rather, misunderstanding) between them occurred in 1953, when Lévi-Strauss published his own essay on the subject.

For Radcliffe-Brown, 'social structure' includes the relations between individual people – he uses the example of a hypothetical Tom, Dick and

Harry. Structural form, in contrast, is at a higher level of abstraction – the positions Tom, Dick or Harry occupy in relation to one another. Tom may be Dick's father-in-law, and thus the structural form defines relations between father-in-law and sons-in-law in general, for a particular society. Essentially, Radcliffe-Brown saw social structure as a network of real people in a real society. Structural form entailed the cultural constants which enabled one to say that the grandchildren of these people would live in a society with a *similar* social structure, albeit one in which social processes had left changes to be understood and analysed in terms of an evolving structural form. In his 1953 letter to Lévi-Strauss, illustrating the difference between social structure and structural form, he used the analogy of sea shells: each individual shell has its own structure, but shells of the same species will share a structural form. Radcliffe-Brown was consciously constructing an anthropology analogous to biology, with its like concerns of structure and function. Functional (as opposed to structural) relations were more part of the social organization through which social structure was played out.

Lévi-Strauss, and many other anthropologists, have consistently employed the term 'social structure' for what Radcliffe-Brown called 'structural form'. Lévi-Strauss even uses 'social structure' to refer to a still higher degree of abstraction – the structure of social relations in all societies, as well as that within a particular society (Radcliffe-Brown's 'structural form'). In fact, Lévi-Strauss was simply doing the kind of universal cross-cultural comparison Radcliffe-Brown had long advocated but never practised, and indeed Radcliffe-Brown himself frequently slipped and used the term 'social structure' to refer to what he said *should* be called 'structural form'. Where they truly differed was in their respective understandings of the locus of structure (or structural form). Lévi-Strauss's conception of it is at the level of the mind, even the human mind in general. His concern is often with the structure of all possible structures, e.g. in the study of *kinship. Radcliffe-Brown, on the other hand, always regarded structures and forms as accessible only empirically, from Tom, Dick and Harry upwards to generalizations based on the comparison of their statuses to those of other individuals, in the same society, or ultimately in diverse societies.

In *sociology, the term 'social structure' has been around at least since †Herbert Spencer, and 'social organization' at least since †Comte. In that discipline, social structure and social organization have sometimes been defined even more formally than is generally the case in anthropology. †Parsons' view of the relation between social organization and social structure (e.g. 1951) was essentially the same as that of Radcliffe-Brown, but in addition he posited the idea of the *social system*, which comprises both. Parsons distinguished four levels of this system: social values, institutional patterns, specialized collectivities (groups), and roles performed by individuals in these collectivities or groups.

To complicate things further, †Murdock's (1949) famous book by the title seems to suggest a very wide meaning of 'social structure', one which bears little relation to the more precise formulations of other theorists, though it probably comes closer to the usual meaning of 'social organization'. Many anthropologists since have happily employed 'social structure' and 'social organization' synonymously, to refer to either of the concepts Radcliffe-Brown distinguished, or to both, as in Parsons' formulation.

In the Marxist era of the 1970s and 1980s, these concepts gave way to that of †social formation – itself a dynamic notion which hints at the action-centred idea of social organization as well as the concern with status and hierarchy which comprises classic notions of social structure. Of course, postmodernist thinkers have little use for any of these concepts, and the nuances of their meanings are no longer debated. Yet in that they define useful, even central, aspects of society, *social organization* and *social structure* remain part of the common vocabulary of the disciplines of both sociology and social anthropology – albeit with meanings which Radcliffe-Brown would have regarded as hopelessly imprecise.

ALAN BARNARD

See also: society, Radcliffe-Brown

Further reading

Firth, R. (1951) *Elements of Social Organization*, London: Watts

Lévi-Strauss, C. (1953) 'Social structure', in A.L. Kroeber (ed.) *Anthropology Today: An Encyclopedic Inventory*, Chicago: University of Chicago Press

Murdock, G.P. (1949) *Social Structure*, New York: The Free Press

Parsons, T. (1951) *The Social System*, New York: The Free Press

Radcliffe-Brown, A.R. (1952) *Structure and Function in Primitive Society*, London: Cohen & West

—— ([1953] 1977) 'Letter to Lévi-Strauss', in A. Kuper (ed.) *The Social Anthropology of Radcliffe-Brown*, London: Routledge & Kegan Paul

socialization

Socialization describes the process through which people and especially children are made to take on the ideas and behaviour appropriate to life in a particular society. As such it describes an essentially passive process and takes for granted a theory of the *person as 'an individual in society'. Here *'society' and 'the *individual' are conceived of as phenomena of different orders; society as a phenomenon of collective life is understood to precede and to encompass the individual.

Anthropologists' traditional concern was to analyse and compare the ideas and practices that informed daily life among the different peoples of the world. For the purposes of analysis, they identified relatively discrete domains of collective phenomena such as *kinship, *political economy and *religion. And because 'the individual' was understood to be a product of 'society', socialization could properly be studied only when these collective phenomena were understood. This perspective meant that studies of socialization were accorded a marginal position with respect to mainstream anthropology.

Learning culture

As a theory of 'the learning of culture', socialization has to be differentiated from the theory of cultural conditioning that was assumed by *'culture and personality' studies in early cultural anthropology. These studies were informed by *psychoanalytic theory on the one hand and, on the other, by †behaviourist explanations of learning; they focused on emotional rather than *cognitive development. Socialization as informal *education was more prominent in early studies in social anthropology. It figures in the work of *Malinowski's followers; so, for example, in *We, the Tikopia*, †Raymond Firth included data on interaction between children and their senior kin, and on the care of young children and their education especially with respect to learning the ideas and behaviour proper to kinship. Firth's account is sensitive to the quality of relationships, and his brief but evocative descriptions of interactions between particular persons allow the reader to gain a sense of what it is to become a Tikopian (1957 [1936]: 125–96).

†Meyer Fortes's (1970 [1938]) account of education in Taleland (Ghana) is perhaps the most systematic early study of socialization. Tale children, he said, are:

> actively and responsibly part of the social structure, of the economic system, the ritual and ideological system . . . the child is from the beginning oriented towards the same reality as its parents and has the same physical and social material upon which to direct its cognitive and instinctual endowment.
>
> (1970 [1938]: 18–19)

He described the attitudes of Tale adults and children to the learning process and showed how the child learns the 'categories of social behaviour . . . as patterns in which interests, elements of skill, and observances are combined'. Fortes described learning as a process of increasing differentiation of patterns of behaviour that 'are present as schemas from the beginning'. A child's kinship †schema, for example, was said to 'evolve' out of an initial discrimination (at the age of 3–4) of kin from non-kin, followed by continuing discriminations of appropriate distinctions and differential behaviour within the category of kin until (at the age of 10–12) a mature grasp of the kinship schema was attained (1970 [1938]: 53–4). (Note that Fortes's schema should not be confused with the psychologist †Piaget's idea of the schema as a self-regulating cognitive *structure*.)

This view of socialization as learning assumed that *what* was learned were the categories and behaviours given in adult behaviour; in other words, 'learning' was not understood to entail any transformation of the ideas encountered; rather the ideas and practices of the senior generation were by implication transmitted unchanged to the junior generation and informal education was analysed in terms of 'modes of transmission'.

Ethnographies published during the 1950s and 1960s often included information on 'the life cycle' *conception, birth, child-rearing practices and informal education but only rarely did they make socialization the focus of study. However, social anthropologists analysing *rituals especially those surrounding †circumcision, *menstruation and other early initiations often emphasized their didactic function. In 1970, edited collections of papers by Middleton and Mayer were published, concerning, respectively, 'education' and 'socialization' in a wide range of culture areas, including

New Guinea, China, Africa and the Pacific. Both collections include excellent descriptions of children's behaviour, but the emphasis is on child-training by adults rather than on the child's perspective.

During the 1970s an explicitly cognitive orientation began to appear in socialization studies. However, by and large, cultural anthropologists continued to focus on the socialization of emotion, the child's *understanding* being taken for granted. An excellent example is Jean Briggs's fascinating study of how Inuit children 'internalised' Inuit values; she analysed specific playful and joking interactions between particular children and adults to show how 'play expresses and controls disapproved feelings and . . . negative values. It also expresses . . . maintains and . . . creates positive values . . . [so] playfulness is highly valued in itself' (1979: 10). Social anthropologists remained concerned with kinship and the socializing force of ritual, both of which figure largely in Jacqueline Rabain's (1979) *L'Enfant du Lignage: du sevrage à la classe d'age*. This is perhaps the most detailed anthropological work of this period to be concerned explicitly with socialization.

Socialization and subjectivity

Rabain's study was the result of close participant observation of twenty-five children in two Wolof (Senegal) villages over a period of eighteen months; it focused on children aged 22 months to five years. Rabain's recognition that subjectivity is constituted in social relations made her analysis a particularly sensitive one. Her account showed how the child comes to understand itself in relation to others, to realize its place in its natal †lineage according to its birth position, age and sex. She analysed exchanges of food, talk, physical contact and objects to show how, in the course of such interactions, the child could constitute an understanding of self and others. She showed too how all these interactions between children and their seniors, and between children and their peers, related to an implicit Wolof theory concerning the nature of heredity, i.e. that the child incarnated a specific *ancestor.

Rabain paid special attention to the way that social relations are embodied in action, by contrast to explicit concepts. In so doing she described and analysed the kind of behaviour that was to prove so important for †Bourdieu's (1977) theory of †practice. Bourdieu argued cogently against the notion that cultural knowledge could be described

as a 'code' or a set of 'rules' that one learned in the course of growing up. The †'*habitus*' described as systems of durable, transposable dispositions inculcated in children by virtue of their observation and imitation of others was Bourdieu's answer to the problem of how to fill the theoretical gap between analytical models of behaviour and the actual practice of cultural actors. He wanted to understand how people come to be coerced or, as he would have it, 'enchanted', by their own cultural practice. His account of how the *habitus* is formed is a theory of socialization that implicitly combines the behaviourism of the American sociologist †G.H. Mead with an idea of embodied cognitive structures that recalls the work of Piaget. However, Bourdieu's work with the Kabyle of Algeria has more to do with continuity and change in the concepts and behaviour of adults than it does with how the *habitus* is formed in the process of socialization from child to adult. It is perhaps because of his lack of attention to the *details* of cognitive developmental processes in particular children that Bourdieu characterized the *habitus* as virtually impervious to change that is, to any change except that generated by forces external to the group within which the *habitus* is formed.

During the 1970s and 1980s the distinctions between cultural and social anthropology became increasingly blurred as did the research problems denoted by terms such as 'socialization', 'enculturation', 'acquisition', etc. In recognition of the fact that these terms always implicated historically specific ideas of person and mind, and could only denote inherently dynamic processes which were still far from understood, ethnographic researches became more complex and theoretical formulations at once more sophisticated and more tentative. So Jahoda and Lewis (1987) identified a need for:

> more sensitive and subtle cross-cultural research on the means by which cultures are reproduced . . . we may thus hope to gain additional and often novel insight into the meaning of childhood, parenthood and gender in particular societies. Through examining the earliest contexts in which they are produced and reproduced in a person's life, we are also provided with a new point of entry . . . to understanding dominant cultural symbols.

Agency and the history of social relations

Bourdieu's theory of practice has proved influential in research broadly concerned with 'socialization'. His work, and that of the sociologist Giddens, informs various studies that have reformulated the 'socialization' problem into one concerned with how the history of social relations enters into people's understandings of themselves and of the world they live in. Cognitive developmental theories of how meaning is constituted by children over time (especially those of Piaget and †Vygotsky) have been crucial to these ethnographic studies, as have findings from experimental cognitive psychology.

In the domain of 'language socialization' the work of Ochs with Samoan children and Schieffelin with Kaluli children has shown how, in learning to speak its native language, a child is also learning how *to be* in relation to others. In other words, the child's cognitive constitution of the categories of its native language is mediated by a complex array of social relations (see Ochs 1988, Schieffelin 1990). Lave's (1988) study of arithmetic as a cognitive practice in everyday contexts develops a theory of how 'the person acting' and the social world are mutually constituted; this perspective has important implications for theories of how people become who they are and in so doing constitute the social relations of which they appear to be the product. Toren (1990) analyses how everyday ritual activities inform the process whereby Fijian children cognitively construct over time the concepts that adults use to denote the hierarchical relations which implicate chiefship as a particular form of political economy; this work shows how cognition may be understood as a microhistorical process, one that inevitably transforms concepts and practices by virtue of constituting them.

Contemporary anthropologists recognize that 'the individual in society' is an historically specific idea of the person; it implicates a particular form of *rationality, one that informs and is informed by the politico-economic processes denoted by *'capitalism'. This understanding poses a considerable problem to those theories in the social sciences that depend upon 'the individual in society' formulation. People have to constitute the ideas and practices of which they appear to be the product. This new perspective means that 'socialization' is beginning to give way to a more complex understanding of persons as historical agents, actively engaged in constituting their relations with others and, in so doing, subtly transforming the concepts that denote these relations.

Nevertheless, the idea of socialization is still prevalent in anthropology.

CHRISTINA TOREN

See also: childhood, culture and personality

Further reading

Bourdieu, Pierre (1977) *Outline of a Theory of Practice*, London, New York: Cambridge University Press

Briggs, Jean (1979) *Aspects of Inuit Value Socialization*, Ottowa: National Museum of Man, Mercury Series

Firth, Raymond (1957 [1936]) *We, the Tikopia*, Boston: Beacon Press

Fortes, Meyer (1970 [1938]) 'Social and Psychological Aspects of Education in Taleland' in J. Middleton (ed.) *From Child to Adult. Studies in the Anthropology of Education*, New York: Natural History Press

Jahoda, G. and I.M. Lewis (eds) (1987) *Acquiring Culture: Cross Cultural Studies in Child Development*, London, New York: Croom Helm

Lave, Jean (1988) *Cognition in Practice*, Cambridge, New York: Cambridge University Press

Mayer, P. (ed.) (1970) *Socialization: The Approach from Social Anthropology*, London: Tavistock Publications

Middleton, John (1970) *From Child to Adult. Studies in the Anthropology of Education*, New York, Natural History Press

Ochs, Elinor (1988) *Culture and Language Development*, Cambridge & New York: Cambridge University Press

Rabain, Jacqueline (1979) *L'Enfant du Lignage: du sevrage à la classe d'age*, Paris: Payot

Schieffelin, Bambi (1990) *The Give and Take of Everyday Life*, Cambridge & New York: Cambridge University Press

Toren, Christina (1990) *Making Sense of Hierarchy. Cognition as Social Process in Fiji*, London School of Economics Monographs on Social Anthropology No 61, Athlone Press

society

The term 'society' refers both to a general aspect of the human condition – we are all necessarily *social* creatures, and therefore depend on society in order to live as humans – and to specific groups of people living together in particular ways, different *societies*. Society has been the central theoretical object of much European anthropology, especially *British social anthropology, so that any history of the theoretical use of the term swiftly becomes a history of anthropological theory. In that history, various tensions and oppositions appear and reappear: society and the *state, society and the *individual, society and *culture, society and nature, primitive society and modern society. In recent years, as the particular use of the term to denote a specific group of people and their way of life has grown ever more problematic, while some of these tensions have approached breaking-point, anthropologists have started to suggest abandoning the very idea of society as a theoretical construct.

Two senses: society and societies

In a general sense, 'society' is a universal condition of human life. This can be put in either biological or symbolic and moral terms. Society can be seen as a basic, but not exclusive, attribute of human *nature*: we are genetically predisposed to social life. Becoming fully human depends on interaction with our fellow creatures; the phylogenesis of our species runs parallel to the development of *language and labour, social abilities without which the organism's needs cannot be met.

But society can also be seen as constituting one particular, exclusive dimension of *human* nature (Ingold 1994), our dependence on the rules of our particular society. The very idea of social †agency is revealed in behaviour which is not founded in instincts, selected by *evolution, but instead in rules which have their origins in history rather than in the requirements of the human organism. The notion of †'rule' may be taken in different senses: in †structural-functionalism it is moral and prescriptive; in *structuralism or in *symbolic anthropology it is cognitive and descriptive. Despite this important difference, in both cases an emphasis on rules expresses the institutional nature of the principles of social action and organization. The rules of different human societies vary in time and space, but there are rules of some sort everywhere (Lévi-Strauss 1969 [1949] , Fortes 1983). The social condition is no longer seen as one of the attributes of *Homo sapiens*, but instead defines the very idea of 'humanity' as a unique entity, made up not of individuals but of 'subjects' who are both creators and creatures of the world of rules.

'Society' is also used to refer to more specific entities: different *societies*. In this specific sense, the idea of *a* 'society' is applicable to a human group having some of the following properties: territoriality; recruitment primarily by sexual reproduction of its members; an institutional organization that is relatively self-sufficient and capable of enduring beyond the life-span of an individual; and cultural distinctiveness.

In this sense, society may denote the group's population, its institutions and relations, or its culture and *ideology. In the first case, society is used as a synonym for '(a) people', or a particular type of humanity. In the second sense, in which society is equivalent to †'social system' or *'social organization', the socio-political framework of the group is important: its morphology (composition, distribution and relations between the subgroups of society), its body of †jural norms (ideas of authority and citizenship, conflict regulation, status and role systems), and its characteristic patterns of social relations (relations of *power and exploitation, forms of co-operation, modes of *exchange). In the third case, in which 'society' is interchangeable with *'culture', what is emphasized is the affective and cognitive content of group life: the set of dispositions and abilities inculcated in its members by various symbolic means, as well as the concepts and practices that confer order, meaning and value upon reality.

One of the ways to handle the relation between the two senses of 'society' has been to divide anthropology into 'ethnographic' description and interpretation, focusing on the analysis of the particular and emphasizing the differences between societies; and 'theoretical' comparison and explanation, which attempts to formulate synthetic propositions valid for all human societies. In spite of efforts to define the two activities as methodologically complementary 'stages', anthropology has tended to polarize between *'ethnography', which deals with specific societies, and 'theory', which deal with society in its abstract and general sense. The universalist perspective predominated in the early years of anthropology, with an emphasis on the *'comparative method' and on the definition of major *types* of society. The golden age of the ethnographic method was the period of †culturalism and *functionalism, in which ethnography was used polemically to demolish speculative typologies (by *Boas) or as the royal road to the universal (for *Malinowski). The structuralisms of *Radcliffe-Brown and *Lévi-Strauss, and American †neo-evolutionism (†White, †Steward), in turn shifted back to comparison and generalization.

Since the 1960s this polarization has intensified. On the one hand, the interest in meaning and interpretation has restored ethnography to a pre-eminent position, privileging the actor's perspective and seeking a critique of the anthropologist's concepts in the different *emic views of society. Society in the general sense came to be subordinated to society in the specific, plural sense. On the other hand, developments in *sociobiology, the psychological study of *cognition, and cultural ecology have led to ambitious hypotheses concerning 'sociality' as a genetic property of the human species, along with behavioural and cognitive universals (eventually attributing the 'phenotypic' diversity of the human ethogram to such extrinsic variables as the *environment). This polarization between ever more specific culturalist interpretation and ever more grandiose naturalist explanation has ultimately emptied the concept of society of any significance, reducing it either to particular representations or to universal behaviour.

Two genealogies: individualism and holism

Two contrasting images of society can be discerned in the history of Western thought, which combine and recombine at different moments, and in which the specific and the general senses of society meet. To use †Louis Dumont's distinction, we may speak of 'individualistic' and 'holistic' views of the social; and we may call these images *societas* and *universitas* (Dumont 1986 [1965]). The individualist version is based on the idea of partnership between ontologically independent individual atoms: society is an artifice resulting from the consensual adhesion of individuals, rationally guided by interest, to a set of conventional norms; social life negates and transcends a pre-political 'state of nature'. The key metaphor for this view is the constitutional and territorial state, and its central problem is the foundation of political order. The holistic version rests on the idea of society as an organic whole which pre-exists its members. Society is a corporate unit guided by a transcendent value, a 'concrete universal' in which human nature is actualized. The key metaphor in this view is *kinship, as a natural principle for the constitution of collective moral *persons, and its central problem is the cultural integration of a people as a 'nation'. The most frequent modern images associated with these two views of society are the †contract (or its opposite, conflict) and the organism, both of which have persisted in twentieth-century anthropology in many forms, most recently as the contrast between †'action' and 'structure'.

Universitas is associated with the premodern world dominated by Aristotelian thought, *societas* with early modern 'Natural Law' thinkers from †Hobbes to †Hegel. The holistic organic model of *universitas* resurfaced in the Romantic reaction to the *Enlightenment, playing a key role in the development of the anthropological image of a society as an ethnically-based community sharing a universe of traditional meanings legitimated by *religion. On the other hand, much of Victorian anthropology and its progeny may be seen as a continuation of the Enlightenment version of *societas*.

The competition between 'society' and 'culture' as comprehensive labels for the object of anthropology can also be interpreted in terms of the opposition between *societas* and *universitas*, individualism and holism. The notion of society in British *social* anthropology is derived from the 'civil society' of Natural Law theorists, from French and Scottish rationalist thinkers of the eighteenth century and, more directly, from the sociologies of †Comte, †Herbert Spencer and †Durkheim. The notion of culture in American *cultural* anthropology comes from German Romanticism, the 'historico-ethnological' schools of the first half of the nineteenth century, and directly from the work of Boas.

This does not mean, however, that it is possible to derive social anthropology directly from the individualism of *societas* and cultural anthropology equally directly from the †holism of *universitas*. In certain respects, the situation is quite the opposite. For instance, Durkheim and †Maine assimilated the progressive schemes of the eighteenth-century rationalists, but at the same time reacted against their artificial and †utilitarian aspects in the name of *essentialist and organic conceptions of society like those that would later inspire the anthropology of Radcliffe-Brown and his followers. And Boas, though a descendant of German idealism and historicism, defended a view of culture in which the individual was the only real locus of cultural integration. But there are unmistakable marks of rationalist utilitarianism in several tendencies of social anthropology, particularly Malinowski's functionalism and the Spencerian element in Radcliffe-Brown's thought. And it is equally clear that the 'configurational' concerns of such American anthropologists as †Kroeber, †Benedict, or †C. Geertz derive from the Romantic paradigm of society as a spiritual organism.

Two oppositions: nature/culture and individual/society

The division between 'society' and 'culture' is further complicated by each term's relationship with the central oppositions of the social sciences: *'nature'/'culture' and 'individual/society'. In both cases there is the same theoretical dilemma: whether the relationship between individual and society, or between nature and culture, is one of continuity or one of discontinuity. Is culture an outgrowth of human nature that can be exhaustively analysed in terms of the biology of the human species, or is it something of a quite different order which transcends any basis in the human organism? And is society merely the sum of the interactions and representations of the individuals that make it up, or is it too a specific level of reality, of a different order to its individual components?

The overlap between these two polarities is complex: often one is subsumed into another, as when society or culture is opposed to individual and nature. Moreover, both 'individual' and 'nature' are †polysemic notions with several meanings. 'Individual' has at least two: a universal empirical sense (the individual representatives of the species, the human component of any society) and a particular cultural sense (the individual as the ultimate value, origin and finality of social institutions). 'Nature', in turn, may signify: the material world as opposed to its conceptual representations, the sphere of 'facts' versus that of 'values', the 'innate' or 'constant' component of human behaviour as opposed to its 'acquired' or 'variable' component, the 'spontaneous' and 'necessary' versus the 'artificial' and the 'conventional', 'animality' in contrast with 'humanity', and so on.

The idea that the society and culture stand 'above' the individual and/or nature is found in all the most influential anthropological authors, but with important differences (Ingold 1986). Herbert Spencer saw society as the end-product of the interactive association of individuals, and as an instrument for the attainment of their goals; it was a supra-individual (but not a supra-biological) sphere of reality. Society was a natural phenomenon (which does not distinguish man from other animals), the †superorganic phase of a universal evolutionary process that encompasses the inorganic and organic spheres. Durkheim's position was precisely the opposite: for him, society was an exclusively human phenomenon, a unique supra-individual and supra-biological reality of a moral and symbolic nature. It was a totality greater than the sum of its parts and endowed with a purpose of its own, a †collective conscious-ness higher than and external to individual consciousnesses, produced by the 'fusion' of the latter. Finally, Boas proposed a third solution: culture was an extra-somatic and ideational reality, but it did not make up a distinct ontological realm. Because it exists in human minds, it is individual and suprabiological, a nominal entity (similar to the Darwinian species) somehow reducible to the individuals who bear it.

Later anthropological theories present combinations of these three paradigms. Kroeber's theory of culture, for instance, oscillates between Boasian and Durkheimian positions, whereas his concept of society is similar to Spencer's. In general, *American anthropology has tended to concentrate on the nature/culture pair. Sometimes this has meant nature in the sense of 'human nature', which lead to analyses of the affective and cognitive moulding of individuals by culture, or alternatively to attempts to establish transcultural psychological constants. Sometimes it has meant non-human nature, as in the kind of †materialism that treats culture as an instrument of adaptation to the environment.

*British anthropology, on the other hand, has tended to focus on the 'individual/society' polarity and the associated concepts of 'structure' and 'function'. For Malinowski, the idea of function referred to the role played by social institutions in the satisfaction of the basic needs of individual organisms. For Radcliffe-Brown, function meant the contribution of these institutions to the maintenance of the conditions of existence of the collective organism. Radcliffe-Brown's definition provided an answer to the central problem of structural-functionalist theory: elucidating the foundations and modes of permanence of a given social form. Modishly rephrased as 'reproduction', the same issue was taken up again in the *Marxist anthropology of the 1970s.

Radcliffe-Brown proposed definitions of *'social structure' in terms of both natural interaction and moral regulation, hesitating between the image of a network of relationships between individuals and that of a structure of normative relations between groups. The prevailing image, however, was that of structure as a jural codex, or body of rules, in which individuals or collectives have social personalities and define their relative positions in terms of rights and duties. This idea, as developed by †Fortes, was dominant for a while. But the individualistic and utilitarian position, first championed in anthropology by

Malinowski, made a comeback with †Edmund Leach's reaction against structural-functionalism, and then flourished in various †transactionalist alternatives to the Durkheimian paradigm, all of them emphasizing the difference between what was normative and 'ideal' and what was empirical and 'actual', and favouring 'strategies' or 'processes' over 'rules' and 'structures', 'action' over 'representation', and 'power' over 'order'. These opposed concepts express the classical dilemma of British anthropology, the disjunction between 'norms' and 'practices', which reflects the persistence of the society/individual antinomy in this tradition.

Lévi-Strauss, in turn, inherited from the Boasians the issue of the relation between psychological universals and cultural determinism, the interest in the unconscious dimension of social phenomena, and the 'nature/culture' dichotomy. But his treatment of nature and culture evokes classical attempts to derive an ideal genesis of 'society' from a 'state of nature'; and Lévi-Strauss's idea of 'culture' is in many ways analogous to the notion of †'civil society'. Defining the *incest taboo and *marriage exchange as universal conditions of collective life, Lévi-Strauss described the transition from nature to culture in sociopolitical terms directly influenced by †Mauss's theory of *exchange and reciprocity. Mauss's theory has itself been interpreted as an alternative response to the Hobbesian problem of the emergence of the social order from the natural state of *war, with the gift and exchange as the primitive analogues of the state and the contract (Sahlins 1972). But Lévi-Strauss also drew from Boas and †Saussure to explore a new analogy for socio-cultural phenomena, *language. And, by countering Durkheim's thesis on the social origins of symbolism with the theme of the symbolic foundations of the social, Lévi-Strauss derived both culture and society from the same substratum, the unconscious, the place where the oppositions between nature and culture, and between individual and society, are resolved.

The linguistic model underlies Lévi-Strauss's concept of structure as a code; that is, as a system of signs with positional values. The problem of function is here replaced by the problem of meaning, a move which, among other things, explains structuralism's relative indifference to the notion of *social* structure. After his book on kinship, in which 'structure' is still sometimes used in a way that remains close to the concept's traditional morphological interpretation, Lévi-Strauss concentrated on *classification and *mythology – that is, on 'cultural' structures. His famous definition of ethnology as a kind of psychology finally abolished the distinction between society and culture, and in this way structuralism indirectly contributed to the predominance of culture over society in recent anthropology. This very emphasis on the taxonomic and cognitive aspects of social life has been frequently pointed out as a symptom of one of structuralism's most serious limitations: its difficulty in accounting for the 'passage' from meaning to action, from the order of ideas to the order of experience, or from structure to history.

Two types of society: primitive and civilized

The main problem associated with the idea of different *societies* has been the establishment of historical and morphological *types* of society, and the ways in which one type relates to another.

The distinction between social types has a long intellectual history. The three-part Enlightenment division between †'savagery', †'barbarism' and †'civilization' was especially important. For †Montesquieu this scheme was more geographical than historical. The classification was temporalized by such thinkers as Turgot, †Adam Smith, †Ferguson and †Condorcet, and it also generated †Comte's 'law of the three states', which was of great importance for Victorian theories of religion. This scheme acquired full anthropological citizenship with *Morgan's division into *hunter-gatherer societies (savagery), †agricultural societies (barbarism) and *complex societies (civilization), which was subsequently incorporated into Marxist thought and developed by neo-evolutionary theories.

But the most productive scheme in Western thought has been the dichotomy, which is best suited to describe strong discontinuities. The conceptual polarity between *universitas* and *societas*, holism and individualism, has been treated as a real opposition, emphasizing various differences that are all ultimately reducible to the contrast between 'us' and 'them', thus providing the nucleus for those †'great divide' theories that make the modern West unique among human societies. All the most famous dichotomies contain some allusion to the pairs 'primitive/civilized' or 'traditional/modern'. Among the best known are:

kinship/territory (Morgan)
status/contract (Maine)
†mechanical/organic solidarity (Durkheim)
*community (*Gemeinschaft*)/association (*Gesellschaft*)
(Tönnies)
simple/complex societies (Spencer)
gift/commodity or gift/contract (Mauss)
traditional/rational (Weber)
holism/individualism (Dumont)
cold/hot (Lévi-Strauss)

These dichotomies draw on the nature/culture opposition, the first term generally representing a more 'natural' state. They also draw on the individual/society opposition – here the first term denotes social forms in which the group prevails as the basic unit, whereas the second term points to a social form where the individual is pre-eminent. Finally, they echo the traditional division of theoretical labour, according to which anthropology is concerned with simple, kinship-based, stateless societies with a gift economy, while *sociology deals with modern, industrial, and (originally) Western societies.

These dichotomies may be interpreted either in terms of absolute and irreducible differences, or more heuristically as expressing the relative dominance of one pole over the other within each social type. Anthropologists have recently become sceptical of any formulation which suggests a 'great divide', especially if it reinforces the image of 'primitive society' established by Victorian thinkers and employed as a basic model for anthropology ever since. This, it has been argued, is no more than an inverted projection of the self-image of modern bourgeois society as it has been envisaged from the eighteenth century on (Kuper 1988). But it seems that anthropology cannot easily do without such dichotomies. Though they carry with them a cumbersome ideological burden, they do point to a substantive difference between most of the societies that have traditionally been the object of anthropology and modern *capitalist society. The theoretical productivity of this difference may be gauged by the recent revival of certain classical contrasts, like the gift–commodity distinction (Gregory 1982), and theoretical attempts to relativize and redefine the great divide (Latour 1993 [1991]).

There have been different ways of conceiving the relation between the terms in these dichotomies. Evolutionists interpreted it as an objective historical succession: 'modern' society is a *societas*

which emerged from the *universitas* of 'primitive', 'ancient', or 'traditional' society. In this solution what prevails is the viewpoint of *societas*, seen as the final cause of a progressive movement in which all societies are caught up, and thus as the latent truth of the world of *universitas*.

Echoes of this model, shorn of its teleological connotations, can be found in those theories which privilege alleged formal action universals (such as maximization of value, for instance) and that see the sociological categories generated by and for modern society (such as 'individual', 'power', 'interest', 'economy', and 'politics') as applicable to any society, since the opposition between types of society is one of degree rather than one of kind.

The alternative position, which stresses the qualitative difference between the terms, tends to treat *universitas* as the normal form of society, while *societas* is conceived as a historical oddity or an ideological illusion. Here the opposition between the two types of society reflects above all the difference between two global socio-*cosmological views, one of which, the holistic, reveals the true nature of the social. This idea, the immediate roots of which are in Durkheim's sociology of religion and in the Boasians' 'cultural determinism', has led to quite different developments in the hands of such authors as Dumont, †Sahlins, or †Schneider. To the extent that many anthropologists conceive their task as above all that of undertaking a political and epistemological critique of Western sociological reason, this position occupies a central place in the discipline. *Universitas* is valued even by those who point to the deep connection between holistic and individualistic views, refusing both as 'Western' in favour of emic, reflexive views of the social condition entertained by other societies.

With primitive society as its traditional object, anthropology has virtually identified its concept of society with the theme of kinship. By taking kinship as the constitutive link of primitive social units, anthropology revived the Aristotelian concept of a natural continuity between the family and the *polis* that had been rejected by the Natural Law thinkers. Maine's and Durkheim's critiques of Bentham's and Spencer's utilitarianism, Morgan's discovery of Amerindian classificatory terminologies and his attempt to fit them into a scheme that singled out the kinship group as the original political unit of human society, †McLenann's and †Bachofen's speculations on primeval †matriarchy – not to mention the impact of the earliest Australian ethnographies on the Victorian intellectual world – led the fledgling discipline of anthropology to explore a dimension of the social that had been neglected by the social contract tradition in favour of the immediate opposition between the individual and the state.

The dichotomies internalized

To contrast anthropological traditions on the basis of these oppositions and dichotomies is no more than a simplification for didactic purposes. The tension between 'Hobbesians' and 'Aristotelians', or 'Malinowskians' and 'Durkheimians' (Kuper 1992), to use more recent totemic ancestors, re-appears within the major theoretical strands. Evolutionism already showed a conceptual com-promise; it projected the opposition between primitive collectivism (founded on group kinship and normative status relationships), and modern individualism (organized on the basis of local contiguity, the individual contract and freedom of association), onto the diachronic plane. It served as a critical foil for almost all later social anthro-pology, which attempted to show the simultaneous workings of both orientations within 'primitive' societies. A very common solution here was to divide the social sphere into two complementary aspects, one more 'social' and the other more 'individual'. This division is apparent in several famous analyses, from the contrast in Trobriand society between 'mother-right' and 'father-love' (Malinowski), through the role of the mother's brother in †patrilineal societies (Radcliffe-Brown), to such contrasts as *descent versus *complemen-tary filiation (Fortes), descent versus kinship (†Evans-Pritchard), *social structure versus social organization (†Firth), and structure versus *commu-nitas* (†Victor Turner). Once one of these polarities was established, much analytical effort was dedicated to the task of transcending it – that is, determining the institutional mechanisms which mediate between intergroup links and inter-personal links, the political order of global society and the domestic order of kinship, the obligatory or normative component of social relationships and their optional or strategic component.

In short, one may say that the image of 'primitive society' in classical social anthropology 'internalized' the contrast previously established between global societies or global views of society. And though it owes much of its inspiration to the 'Aristotelian' tradition, there is one aspect of 'Hobbesian' modernity to which anthropology has

not remained immune (Verdon 1989): it is the idea that society (even if it is a 'natural' state because it is equivalent to humanity) is a problematic condition – that is, something that must be explained. This, in turn, derives from the idea that society is made up of *asocial* individuals who require *socialization (that is, constraint by the inculcation of normative representations to behave in a given way), and who resist such constraint by means of a selfish manipulation of norms or by an imaginary regression to an original condi-tion of freedom. This idea can be found in various forms in Durkheim as in †Freud, in Lévi-Strauss as in Fortes or Leach. *Homo sapiens* may well be a social animal, but to modern thought this phrase suggests a contradiction in terms, and the unease it inspires is what motivates anthropology's unceasing search for solutions that transcend the oppositions and dichotomies implicit in it.

Criticism and crisis

The standard anthropological representation of 'a society' in the functionalist and culturalist traditions is that of an ethnically distinct people, living in accordance with specific institutions and having a particular culture. The ideal coincidence of the three components is seen as making up an individual totality, with its own internal organiza-tion and purpose. The functionalist emphasis is on the 'total' and systemic aspect; the culturalist emphasis is on the 'individual' and expressive aspect.

This image has been questioned for a long time. Theoretically, Lévi-Strauss (1987[1950], 1963 [1958]) insisted that structuralism was not a method for the analysis of 'global societies'. He suggested that a society is a contradictory mani-fold in which structures of different orders co-exist, and that the 'order of orders' is a problem more for cultural self-consciousness than for analysis. Ethnographically, Leach (1965 [1954]) demon-strated the foolishness of epistemologically 'well-behaved' models that fail to take into account the historical and political contexts in which social structures are set.

More recently, it has been observed that the specific sense of *a* society as a self-contained whole relies on categories and institutions that are characteristic of the modern West. Thus it is argued, for instance, that the idea of mankind as divided into discrete, socially and culturally unique ethnic units derives from the ideology of the nation-state, imposed on non-Western peoples

by *colonialism, the great inventor, both conceptually and practically, of †'tribes' and 'societies'.
This criticism has led to an emphasis on the interdependence of actual social systems (seen as the
coalescence of heterogeneous, open-ended social
*networks). The relations making up wider
*regional configurations determine the internal
processes of local units – a view which ultimately
breaks up different societies into increasingly
global systems, up to the level of the planet. And
it has lead to a predilection for processual, action-
centred approaches at the expense of structural,
regulative approaches, resolving society into a web
of atomic interactions and representations.

In its general sense, the notion of society has
also been losing ground; contemporary anthropology tends to reject *essentialist or teleological
views of society as an agency that transcends
individuals. The notion of society as an instinctual
or normative order, endowed with the objective
status of a thing, is giving way to ideas such as
†'sociality', which supposedly are better at conveying a sense of social life as an intersubjectively
constituted process. In this way, social realism is
being replaced by a view that extends to society
the same constructivism that the sociology of
knowledge applied successfully to nature.

If it makes sense to speak of a dominant
tendency in contemporary anthropology, it is the
rejection of structural views of society in favour of
a †pragmatics of social agency that seeks 'to
promote a recovery of the subject without lapsing
into subjectivism' (Giddens 1979: 44). Intentionality and conscience, hitherto explained away
as mere epiphenomena of structures, or even
denounced as epistemological obstacles to the
determination of these explanatory principles,
have become not only what must urgently be
explained, but possibly the very essence (if not the
true explanation) of sociality. This can be seen in
different theoretical manifestations: the dissatisfaction with the alternative between interactive or
naturalistic and regulative or culturalist views
of society (Ingold 1986); the various theories of
†'practice', of 'communicative action', and 'structuration' (Bourdieu 1977 [1972]; Habermas 1984
[1981]; Giddens 1984); or, the unanimous criticism of the 'Saussurean' paradigm of action as the
passive actualization of a set of rules to be found
in some collective counsciousness or in the mental
apparatus of the species. In a nutshell: crisis of the
structure, return of the subject. This return may
be theoretically sophisticated, as in the proposals

to overcome the antinomies of Western social
thought, especially that between individual and
society, which is what is at stake in this idea of a
nonvoluntaristic view of social action. But it may
also mean a straightforward revival of concepts
that were rightly rejected by structuralists: philosophy of consciousness, celebration of the infinite
creativity of human action, instrumentalist rationalism (or its reciprocal, romantic irrationalism),
retranscendentalization of the individual, and
so on. As every social theory at some point
believed it held the key to the resolution of
the classic dichotomies and oppositions, only
to be later accused of favouring one of them in
the most scandalous manner, one wonders
whether these developments have indeed broken
free of the perennial oscillation between *societas*
and *universitas*.

Contemporary criticism has thus undermined
the anthropological view of society from all sides:
'primitive society' as a real type; society as an
empirically delimited object; society as an objective basis for collective representations, an entity
endowed with structural coherence and functional
purpose. This conceptual crisis is, firstly the consequence of a historical crisis. The end of political
colonialism, and the accelerated †globalization of
economic and cultural flows, have highlighted
the ideological and artificial character of some of
anthropology's ideas: the isolated primitive was
never primitive and was never isolated. But such
a historical crisis also reflects a change in Western
social apperception – in other words, a cultural
crisis. The ideal object of anthropology, 'primitive
society', was dissolved, not so much because of the
objective globalization of local 'primitive' worlds,
or as a result of the progress of anthropological
enlightenment, but rather because of the demise
of the notion of 'modern society' that was its
obverse. There seems to be a growing conviction
that the West has left behind its 'modern' period,
predicated upon the absolute separation between
the realm of facts and that of values, between
nature and culture, the private and the public
sphere, and finally between the 'West' and the
'rest'. It remains to be seen whether we (and this
'we' includes every society on Earth) have indeed
entered a *postmodern phase in which such
contrasts are no longer operative or, contrary to
the assumptions of the great divide cosmology
that has made anthropology possible, 'we have
never been modern' (Latour 1993 [1991]) except
in the imagination. We do know, however – and

this much we have been taught by anthropology itself – that imaginary conceptions may produce quite real effects. If this is indeed the case, then we must continue searching for concepts that can illuminate the differences between societies, there being no other way for anthropology effectively to view the social condition from a standpoint that is truly universal – that is, one that can generate and acknowledge difference.

EDUARDO VIVEIROS DE CASTRO
(translated by Paulo Enriques Britto)

See also: culture, nature and culture, social structure, individualism, Enlightenment anthropology, socialization

Further reading

Bourdieu, P. (1977 [1972]) *Outline of a Theory of Practice*, Cambridge: Cambridge University Press
Dumont, L. (1986 [1965]) 'The Political Category and the State from the Thirteenth Century Onward' in L. Dumont, *Essays on Individualism*, Chicago: University of Chicago Press
Fortes, M. (1983) *Rules and the Emergence of Society*, London: Royal Anthropological Institute of Great Britain and Ireland
Giddens, A. (1979) *Central Problems in Social Theory: Action, Structure and Contradiction in Social Analysis*, Berkeley: University of California Press
—— (1984) *The Constitution of Society: Outline of the Theory of Structuration*, Cambridge: Polity Press
Gregory, C. (1982) *Gifts and Commodities*, London: Academic Press
Habermas, J. (1984, 1987 [1981]) *The Theory of Communicative Action. I: Reason and the Rationalization of Society. II: Lifeworld and System: A Critique of Functionalist Reason*, Boston: Beacon Press
Ingold, T. (1986) *Evolution and Social Life*, Cambridge: Cambridge University Press
—— (1994) 'Humanity and Animality', in T. Ingold (ed.) *Companion Encyclopedia of Anthropology: Humanity, Culture and Social Life*, London: Routledge
Kuper, A. (1988) *The Invention of Primitive Society: Transformations of an Illusion*, London: Routledge
—— (ed.) (1992) *Conceptualizing Society*, London: Routledge.
Latour, B. (1993 [1991]) *We have Never Been Modern*, Cambridge, MA: Harvard University Press
Leach, E. (1965 [1954]) *Political Systems of Highland Burma: A Study of Kachin Social Structure*, Boston: Beacon Press
Lévi-Strauss, C. (1963 [1958]) *Structural Anthropology*, New York: Basic Books
—— (1969 [1949]) *The Elementary Structures of Kinship* 2nd ed., Boston: Beacon Press
—— (1987 [1950]) *Introduction to the Work of Marcel Mauss* London: Routledge

Sahlins, M. (1972) *Stone Age Economics*, New York: Aldine
Verdon, M. (1991) *Contre la culture: fondement d'une anthropologie sociale operationnelle*, Paris: Éditions des Archives Contemporaines

sociobiology

Evolutionary origins

In its widest sense sociobiology is the science that deals with the social behaviour of organisms in the light of *evolution. This would include all disciplines that accept the neo-Darwinian mandate. In the narrow sense, following the coinage of E.O. Wilson (1975), it refers to the application of specific theories of evolutionary genetics to animal (including human) behaviour. Here we shall explore both senses of the word.

All the sociobiological disciplines derive ultimately from †Darwin's (1861 [1859]) theory of natural selection (as modified by later discoveries in genetics), differing only in their interpretations. Thus they should not be confused with so-called Social Darwinism, which was in fact derived more from †Herbert Spencer's developmental and progressive theories than from Darwin's essentially non-progressive theory of 'descent by modification'.

Social anthropology had its origins in the social evolutionary school, and for various reasons, including the rise of *functionalism in England under *Malinowski and *Radcliffe-Brown and the rise of †culturalism in the USA under *Boas and †Kroeber, it has tended to repudiate these origins. In doing so it has often confused Darwinian theory with the Spencerian version and felt obliged to repudiate any general theories of human behaviour that are grounded in man's evolution and animality (e.g. Sahlins 1976). This has cut it off from many interesting hypotheses regarding classical anthropological problems. Such issues as the *incest taboo, the *avunculate, †polygamy, *exchange, †cross-cousin marriage, †hypergamy, *taboo, social categories and initiation are open to Darwinian examination, and there are now heartening signs that the initial rejection is being replaced by a greater openness to such explorations.

Strands of sociobiology

There are several strands or traditions that follow in the Darwinian tradition. One is the *natural history* tradition. During the 1930s, this observational tradition developed an academic base under Heinroth and Lorenz in Germany, Tinbergen in Holland, Huxley in England and Allee in the USA. The academic development came to be known as †*ethology*. Its general principle was that behaviour throughout the life-cycle of an organism emerged according to an evolved programme, but a programme that needs releasers or stimuli from the environment for its completion, as in the classic case of 'imprinting'. The main stress was on the *communication mechanisms* that evolved to make social interaction possible. After World War II it was joined by remarkable developments in primatology stemming from both zoology and anthropology.

The involvement of anthropologists as well as the growing interest in human behaviour among the ethologists proper, led to various attempts to apply principles derived from animal behaviour studies to human behaviour ('comparative ethology'). These involved such areas as territorialism, dominance hierarchies, mother-infant bonding, male bonding, female hierarchies, optimism, aggression, ritualization, attention structure, kinship, incest avoidance, social categories, attachment, facial expression, art, fathering and politics, to name but a few. The first general attempt at synthesis for social scientists came with Tiger and Fox's *The Imperial Animal* (1971). The general attempt to use theories and methods of ethology to study human behaviour came to be known as *human ethology* (see Fox and Fleising 1976; and Eibl-Eibesfeldt's definitive *Human Ethology* 1989) and continues as a lively tradition, especially in Europe. A direct attempt to address social anthropologists was Fox's *Biosocial Anthropology* (1975).

Another major tradition stems from the rediscovery of Mendel and the growth of genetics. This was an independent development in its origins, but once married to Darwin's theory of natural selection it developed an impressive field of *evolutionary population genetics* which was concerned with the causes of the shifting of gene frequencies in populations over time. There was a remarkable convergence of these ideas in the 1930s which, following the title of a book by Julian Huxley, has come to be known as the 'modern synthesis'.

Either explicitly or implicitly much of this thinking operated under the idea of 'group selection' – that traits were selected for the good of the group or species. During the 1960s a reaction set in to this form of thinking. Williams (1966) produced an elegant series of arguments

insisting that natural selection could only work on individual organisms, not groups, and Hamilton (1963, 1964), in an attempt to produce an answer to Darwin's unsolved puzzle of the existence of sterile castes in insects, demonstrated that such 'altruism' (i.e. sacrifice of one's own reproductive fitness to further that of others) could spear in populations if certain conditions were met. This was the concept of 'inclusive fitness'.

Largely under the influence of Alexander (1974), a school of sociobiological thought emerged which took as its central precept the *maximization of reproductive success*. Its main assumption is that such maximization is a basic motive and can explain a whole range of human mating and kin-related behaviours. Thus organisms would strive to maximize reproductive success through inclusive fitness, and attempt to ensure (largely in the case of males) that the genes they 'invested' in were their own; i.e. ensure the certainty of paternity. Thus the problem of the avunculate (the special relationship between mother's brother and sister's son) and hence the origins of †matrilineal descent were attributed to 'low paternity certainty' in promiscuous societies where males would prefer to invest in sisters' sons with a low but definite degree of genetic relationship, rather than their own sons whose degree of relationship could be zero (for a critique see Fox 1993). The logic of this general position has been applied to hypergamy, despotic †polygyny, child abuse, legal decisions, kin support in illness, family structure, cross-cousin marriage, mate competition, kin-term manipulation, polyandry, bridewealth, morality, parental care, among many others. (See, e.g. Chagnon and Irons 1979; Betzig *et al.* 1988.)

Another tradition, however, rejects the primacy of reproductive fitness maximizing. It argues that while differential reproductive success *in the past*, and particularly in the species' *environment of evolutionary adaptation* (EEA), certainly led to specific adaptations, no such generalized motive can explain ongoing behaviour. Such a motive, it is argued, does not give specific enough instructions to the organism, which is more likely to act on proximate motives like desire for sex, avoidance of cheaters, accrual of resources, achievement of status etc. These may well lead to reproductive success, but they are not based on any general desire for its maximization.

Many sociobiologists then reject the 'adaptation agnostic' stance of their other brethren and look for specific adaptational mechanisms in human perception and cognition ('information processing mechanisms') whether or not these lead to *current* reproductive success. This school of *evolutionary psychology* has attempted to devise means of testing for 'domain specific algorithms' in the human mind, and is firmly opposed to 'domain general mechanisms' such as are proposed, for example, by many artificial intelligence theorists. They have looked, for example, at cognitive mechanisms for social exchange and the detection of cheating, mate-preference mechanisms, male propriety behaviour, sex differences in spatial ability, pregnancy sickness as an adaptive response to teratogens, and evolved responses to landscape. Linguists, like Pinker, adhering to this approach, take issue with †Chomsky and others who while seeing linguistic competence as innate do not see it as a product of natural selection. Evolutionary linguists see language, on the contrary, as having all the design hallmarks of an evolved adaptation.

Sociobiology, both broadly and narrowly speaking, shows then a continuing vigorous development with influences in all the social sciences as well as philosophy and literature. The future holds promise for the development of a normal science paradigm within which constructive disputes will be possible and cumulative progress made. The big question for social anthropology is the degree of its willingness to end its flirtation with anti-scientific trends in the social sciences and to enter into a constructive debate with the sociobiologists.

ROBIN FOX

See also: biological anthropology, ecological anthropology, environment

Further reading

Alexander, R.D. (1974) 'The Evolution of Social Behavior', *Annual Review of Ecology and Systematics* 5: 325-83
Betzig, L., M.B. Mulder and P. Turke (1988) *Human Reproductive Behavior: A Darwinian Perspective*, Cambridge: Cambridge University Press
Chagnon, N. and W. Irons (1979) *Evolutionary Biology and Human Social Behavior*, North Scituate, MA: Duxbury
Darwin, C. (1861) *On the Origin of Species by Means of Natural Selection*, London: John Murray
Eibl-Eibesfeldt, I. (1989) *Human Ethology*, New York: Aldine de Gruyter
Fox, R. (ed.) (1975) *Biosocial Anthropology*, London/New York: Malaby Press
—— (1993) *Reproduction and Succession*, New Brunswick, NJ: Transaction Publishers
Fox, R. and U. Fleising (1976) 'Human Ethology', *Annual Review of Anthropology* 5: 265-88
Hamilton, W.D. (1963) 'The Evolution of Altruistic Behavior', *American Naturalist* 97: 354-6
—— (1964) 'The Genetical Evolution of Social Behavior', *Journal of Theoretical Biology* 7: 1-89
Sahlins, M. (1976) *The Use and Abuse of Biology: An Anthropological Critique of Sociobiology*, London: Tavistock
Tiger, L. and R. Fox (1971) *The Imperial Animal*, New York: Secker and Warburg
Williams, G.C. (1966) *Adaptation and Natural Selection*, Princeton: Princeton University Press
Wilson, E.O. (1975) *Sociobiology: The New Synthesis*, Cambridge, MA: Belknap Press of Harvard University Press

sociology

Sociology is so varied a discipline that it can be identified only very loosely as the study of social relationships, institutions and structures. Not only is this definition loose, it is also negative, for 'social' often means, in effect, not distinctly economic, not distinctly political, not distinctly religious and so forth. Although sociologists can trace their intellectual origins back to the Scottish *Enlightenment and beyond, the discipline did not begin to become established until the last quarter of the nineteenth century. Although sociology is concerned with the study of social relationships, institutions and structures, the discipline is a child of industrial *capitalism and its predominant field of study is modern Western societies.

There are differences in style among the sociologies of various countries. However, the predominant sociology worldwide is that of the United States, despite the fact that the word 'sociology' was invented by a French philosopher, †Auguste Comte, early in the nineteenth century (Coser 1971). This does not reflect just the country's general power and influence, but also the fact that it was in the US that the discipline first established a strong institutional base, though sociology appeared fairly early in France as well. For instance, the two leading American sociology journals, the *American Journal of Sociology* and the *American Sociological Review*, were founded in 1895 and 1936. Contrast this with the two leading British sociology journals, the *British Journal of Sociology* and *Sociology*, which were founded only in 1950 and 1967. (†Durkheim founded †*L'Année Sociologique* in 1898.)

Sociology's focus

Even though sociology is a varied discipline, there are some general intellectual attributes that distinguish it from anthropology. I have already noted one, its concern with the nature of modern societies. Also striking are its social meliorism and its tendency to scientific generalization. Briefly put, sociology much more than anthropology seeks to identify *modernity and the problems associated with it by producing valid empirical generalizations about its subject matter.

From the establishment of their discipline late in the nineteenth century, sociologists have attempted to map the nature of modernity in general. Such a grand project led sociologists to subordinate their descriptions of specific times and places to the larger and more abstract question that concerned them. In consequence, sociology did not develop a valued body of specific case studies that parallel anthropology's *ethnography. Instead, it has concentrated on what *Radcliffe-Brown (1952: 2) calls 'comparative sociology', an area that is much less important in anthropology.

Meliorism, too, has been important from the earliest sociological works; the discipline has been concerned not just to study modern society but also to alleviate the problems associated with modernity. If Comte is the first sociologist by virtue of his invention of the word, it is pertinent that one issue that concerned him was the decay of social cohesion associated with modernity. Further, of the three leading nineteenth-century thinkers who are taken as the substantive founders of sociology, †Marx, †Weber and Durkheim, all but Weber wrote extensively about the problems of modernity and their solution. This melioristic tendency continues to the present, as sociologists describe the nature and consequences of specific social inequalities and injustices, as well as the problems that many see as systematic features of modern capitalist society.

Likewise, from the early decades of the twentieth century sociologists have been concerned to pursue their enquires scientifically. While this manifested itself in a concern for theoretical and analytical rigour, its more striking form has been a concern for empirical and particularly quantitative analysis, though this tendency is more pronounced in the United States than elsewhere. Thus, sociology embraced 'hard data', quantitative series and social surveys. This is reflected in postgraduate education. Many sociology departments urge or require their students to study statistics and quantitative methods. Similarly, many students organize their doctoral research in the classic framework of the formulation and empirical testing of hypotheses, and base their work solely on the secondary statistical analysis of national surveys and government statistics. This tendency has never been overwhelming, however, partly because of the influence of the more interpretative German †verstehende sociology, particularly embodied in Max Weber's *The Protestant Ethic and the Spirit of Capitalism* (1958 [1904]); and partly because of the influence of the more qualitative *political economy, particularly embodied in the work of Karl Marx (though this influence was much weaker in the United States than elsewhere). In spite of these qualifications, sociologists are much more likely than anthropologists to present their findings in numerical terms and to make their arguments in statistical terms.

This tendency to scientific generalization about modernity and its problems is rooted deeply in the discipline. In Britain, for instance, late nineteenth-century social reformers like Rowntree and Booth surveyed the populations of York and London to assess the empirical degree and distribution of poverty, much as sociologists late in the twentieth century surveyed the cities of the United States to assess the empirical degree and distribution of homelessness. More striking is Durkheim's *Suicide* (1951 [1897]). Not only was his topic considered a social problem, but his method was the investigation of a succession of hypotheses about the causes of suicide, which he tested quantitatively using an extensive body of statistics over a number of years from several European countries. Although the quality of Durkheim's data and his statistical techniques would not satisfy modern sociologists, his overall approach is indistinguishable from attempts a century later to investigate, for instance, the causes of differences in pay between men and women.

Sociology and anthropology

Sociology and anthropology share a number of common intellectual forebears, notably Marx, Weber and Durkheim. Equally, they can be said to share a common historical origin: the growing conception in the nineteenth century that modern (which is to say industrial capitalist) societies are unique. In spite of these commonalities, however, the two disciplines have developed in different ways and there has been less communication between the two sciences of society than one might have thought likely.

The most obvious reason for this lack of communication is that the disciplines addressed opposed faces of the question of modern society: while sociology was concerned with the world that the modern West had gained, anthropology was concerned with the world that it had lost – what early scholars called communal and, ultimately, primitive society (Kuper 1988). Equally, as I have already noted, the research strategies of the two disciplines have been very different, with sociologists oriented more towards quantitative generalization and anthropologists oriented more toward qualitative description.

This concern with different faces of the question of modernity leads to a more subtle difference between the two disciplines that also hinders communication between them. Each tends to embrace a stylized distortion of the concerns of the other discipline that makes its theories and findings appear fairly irrelevant. Anthropologists, then, tend not only to be ignorant of the nature of modern societies, but tend also to have a stereotyped view of such societies that exaggerates the difference between them and the societies that anthropologists normally study. Some call this stereotyping *Occidentalism. Equally, sociologists tend not only to be ignorant of the nature of societies outside the modern sphere, but also to have a stereotyped view of such societies that exaggerates the difference between them and the modern societies they conventionally study. Some call this stereotyping *Orientalism.

This misperception of each other's subject matter means that people tend to ignore the possibility that the information, interests and ideas found in one discipline are pertinent to the concerns of the other. What have models of bureaucratic organization and capitalism to do with studies of villages in Melanesia? What have models of kinship and exchange to do with studies of factory workers in Leeds? While the connections certainly exist, there is little pressure to discern and describe them.

The intellectual barriers between the two disciplines, however, are not absolute. For example, some anthropologists have studied under and been influenced by sociologists, as †David Schneider studied under and was influenced by †Talcott Parsons. Likewise, there is a tradition of community studies in sociology, exemplified by the Lynds' classic description of *Middletown* (1929); a tradition

that extended by the 1970s to include studies that were more narrowly focused but that used ethnographic techniques (e.g. Willis 1977). While the authors of these studies may have been concerned with the sociological question of modernity and its discontents, many of the results resemble conventional ethnography.

The barriers between the two disciplines are generally weakest when scholars in one discipline become dissatisfied with conventional approaches to problems and seek new ones. Thus, for instance, the anthropologist Scheffler (1965), confronted with seemingly intractable theoretical problems in the study of Oceanic *kinship and social organization, went outside the discipline to draw on †Goffman's (1961) more sociological model of social groups. Similarly, sociologists dissatisfied with their own discipline's limited view of *culture draw on anthropologists like †Mary Douglas and †Clifford Geertz. In the closing decades of the twentieth century these barriers were weakened still further, in two different ways. First, they weakened with the growth of specialist areas of study (such as *gender and *consumption) that attracted members of both disciplines. Second, they weakened as a growing number of anthropologists began to study Western societies; a change that occurred without a corresponding growth in the number of sociologists studying societies outside the modern sphere.

It is important, however, not to exaggerate the weakening of the barriers between the two disciplines, for the differences between them remain strong and members of each generally remain ignorant of the issues of interest in the other. A telling example of this is the work of †Bourdieu. Sociologists are likely to be aware of his writings on French education (Bourdieu and Passeron 1977) but ignorant of more than the title of his work on the Kabyle (Bourdieu 1977), while the reverse is the case for most anthropologists. An example of the difference in orientation is the way that each discipline deals with *exchange. This has been an important topic in anthropology for several decades, as researchers have described different forms and understandings of exchange. However, the topic is much less important in sociology, where the dominant approach sees exchange as the transaction of equivalents between autonomous and self-regarding actors (Emerson 1976).

Conclusions

Since about 1960, sociology has grown rapidly and become markedly more fragmented, so that it is difficult to assess likely trends within the discipline. However, part of that fragmentation seems to involve a bifurcation into more quantitative and more qualitative approaches. This is apparent in the fact that there has been a growing interest in historical and cultural topics at the same time that the statistical techniques used in sociology have become more refined. While historical and cultural topics can be studied in a rigourously quantitative way, the growing concern with them marks a rejection by many of the established and powerful quantitative, scientific orientation within the discipline.

Further, it seems likely that the relationship between the two disciplines will become more complex as a growing number of anthropologists study modern Western societies. Probably this will bring individuals and sub-disciplines in the two fields into greater contact, as I have already mentioned with regard to the studies of gender and consumption. It is premature, however, to suggest any significant interchange between the two disciplines more generally, for their orientations and methods remain markedly distinct.

JAMES G. CARRIER

See also: complex societies, capitalism, class, functionalism, methodology

Further reading

Bottomore, Tom and Robert Nisbet (eds) (1978) *A History of Sociological Analysis*, London: Heinemann

Bourdieu, Pierre (1977) *Outline of a Theory of Practice* (trans. Richard Nice), Cambridge: Cambridge University Press

Bourdieu, Pierre and Jean-Claude Passeron (1977) *Reproduction in Education, Society, and Culture* (trans. Richard Nice), London: Sage Publications

Coser, Lewis A. (1971) *Masters of Sociological Thought: Ideas in Historical and Social Context*, New York: Harcourt Brace Jovanovich

Durkheim, Émile (1951 [1897]) *Suicide: A Study in Sociology* (trans. John A. Spaulding and George Simpson), New York: The Free Press

Emerson, Richard M. (1976) 'Social Exchange Theory', *Annual Review of Sociology* 2: 335–62

Friedrichs, Robert W. (1970) *A Sociology of Sociology*, New York: The Free Press

Goffman, Erving (1961) *Encounters*, Indianapolis: Bobbs-Merrill

Hinkle, Roscoe C. and Gisella J. Hinkle (1954) *The Development of Modern Sociology, Its Nature and Growth in the United States*, Garden City, NY: Doubleday

Kuper, Adam (1988) *The Invention of Primitive Society*, London: Routledge

Lynd, Robert S. and Helen Merrell Lynd (1929) *Middletown: A Study in American Culture*, New York: Harcourt, Brace

Madge, John (1962) *The Origins of Scientific Sociology*, New York: Free Press of Glencoe

Radcliffe-Brown, A.R. (1952) *Structure and Function in Primitive Society*, London: Routledge & Kegan Paul

Ross, Dorothy (1991) *The Origins of American Social Science*, Cambridge: Cambridge University Press

Scheffler, Harold (1965) *Choiseul Island Social Structure*, Berkeley: University of California Press

Weber, Max (1958 [1904]) *The Protestant Ethic and the Spirit of Capitalism*, New York: Scribner's

Willis, Paul (1977) *Learning to Labour*, Aldershot: Gower

state

The problem of the state runs through the history of anthropology. This is as much due to the nature of the object – the state as a mode of grouping and control of people – as to the history and presuppositions of anthropology itself. The question has a long philosophical heritage culminating in the *Enlightenment: thinkers as different as †Locke, Diderot and †Rousseau all thought that structured and centralized political organization begins from a state of nature, from an aggregate of individuals left to their own devices, good or bad, innocent or industrious, according to the particular view of each author. From these speculative reconstructions emerged the idea of a primitive contract marking the beginning, in some way, of modern political society. We can see how central the juridical paradigm was to these conceptions of the state, quite apart from the spectral notions of contract and sovereignty. It is precisely this paradigm that was questioned by the late nineteenth-century historical research – on ancient society and ancient law respectively – of *L.H. Morgan and †H.S. Maine.

It is notable that these precursors of modern anthropology, whose work has made a lasting impression on later approaches to politics, were both concerned to identify the point of transition between two great modes of organization in the *evolution of humanity: the first founded on †gens, †phratry and †tribe; the second on territory and *property (Morgan 1877). There is a move away from the idea of a state of nature being replaced by the notion of the political state, consisting of people wilfully bound together by contract. Yet an opposition remains, this time between two 'states of *society', one primitive and based on bonds of *kinship, the other with a state: the appearance of property and the significance of territoriality mark the passage from one mode of organization to the other.

Substituting an explanation which aims to expose the objective material conditions for the appearance of the state, in place of the hypothesis of a collective subjective act, nevertheless retains the philosophical presupposition of a dichotomy between two worlds. This leaves open the question deriving from this presupposition, the problem of the *origin* of the state. Thus a vast anthropological project takes form: as there is an essential difference between the state and all earlier forms of political organization, it is necessary to identify the nature of this difference in order to understand the source of this new type of political system.

Working from Morgan's data, †Engels ([1884] 1972) saw the emergence of the state as a consequence of the division of society into antagonistic *classes. The state is then defined as the instrument of the dominant class whose members ensure that it maintains order and peace and that all within the society feel secure, while at the same time perpetuating their ascendancy over the subordinate classes. This vision of a coercive apparatus that operates 'above society' in the mystified consciousness of the oppressed, and which ensures the reproduction of the phenomena of exploitation and oppression to the benefit of the dominant group, finds empirical support in the correspondence between the development of private property and the existence of state forms. Engels draws upon Greek, German and Roman examples to back up the idea of a causal sequence which links in succession private appropriation, *inequality, economic oppression and political †hegemony. Underneath this version of the genesis of the state we find the primacy of the economic †infrastructure so dear to †historical materialism. Morgan and Engels have been subjected to two types of criticism: the first questioned the universality of the causal hypothesis, the second challenged the evolutionist presuppositions of their research. These criticisms correspond to two distinctive approaches to the state in anthropology.

State formation

The neo-evolutionist approach is well illustrated by †J.H. Steward (1955), who attempted to reconstitute the different stages from *hunter-gatherer †bands to the formation of the state. The emphasis here is on the role of irrigation which allows a large concentration of population and therefore leads to more elaborate territorial organization, requiring a new division of labour and a more developed power structure. For Steward, as for the historian †K. Wittfogel (1957), the expansion of the †hydraulic economy would have been a determining factor in the invention of the state. Starting from †Marx's arguments on the †'Asiatic mode of production', Wittfogel showed that the absence of private property in *peasant societies is entirely compatible with the development of a substantial political and administrative apparatus. Morton Fried (1967) distinguished four successive stages – egalitarian societies, class societies, stratified societies and state societies. For Fried the decisive factor in the transition to stratified societies and the emergence of the state is the fact of unequal access to resources due to demographic pressure within the limits of a given territory.

However, the more we have learnt about traditional states, the more limited these different explanations appear. We cannot reduce to a single cause this process of the formation of a hierarchical and centralized apparatus, whose ascendancy spreads over a complete territory. In addition to ecological, economic, technological and sociological factors, it is necessary to account for the part played by †superstructural, religious and ideological determinants in establishing a domination which everyone regards as legitimate. Maurice Godelier (1984) has shown how the formation of the state implies the prior consent of the dominated, who accept their subservience in exchange for the protection of those who control the supernatural. The emergence of the state is thus not treated as the simple product of a situation of inequality or of relations of exploitation, but as the unique and coherent consequence of several distinct processes. While the †unilinear evolutionary hypothesis is challenged, the idea of a primitive exchange between the dominated and those who dominate is re-introduced: the asymmetry of the partners does not forbid all reciprocity. This curious oscillation between a mechanistic theory of the emergence of the state and an approach which, in aiming to recapture the complexity of the phenomenon, re-introduces the philosophical idea of the social contract, is revealing. It also marks the limits of an anthropological analysis which privileges the question of origins.

Beyond the search for origins

Anthropological studies, which have now been going on for more than fifty years, in *Africa, the *Pacific, *Southeast and *South Asia, and in Amerindian societies have considerably modified the terms of the debate. Researchers are now more interested in the form and workings of the state in apparently very different societies, than in the question of state formation. Is it appropriate to apply the modern concept of the state in socio-cultural contexts which contrast very strongly with those more familiar settings in which the concept has usually been employed? Following †S.F. Nadel the state can be defined as a form of political system which is the product of a conjunction of three factors: a unitary polity based on territorial sovereignty; a specialized governmental body with a monopoly on legitimate force; and a ruling group, distinguished from the rest of the population by training, recruitment and †status, with a monopoly on the apparatus of political control. It is in this sense that it is possible to consider as states forms of government that are far removed from the complex and highly developed hierarchical structures of modern society, and to oppose them, as did †E.E. Evans-Pritchard and †M. Fortes (1940), to other political systems that have no centralized authority, no specialized judicial institutions, no differences of rank and status, and where kinship groups provide the basis for political roles.

This definition of the state nevertheless remains somewhat abstract. As Claessen and Skalnik (1978) point out, the traditional state (or 'early state' in their terms), as studied by anthropologists, shares certain characteristics with stateless societies. Politics and kinship often overlap and ties of reciprocity and redistribution still predominate. Aidan Southall has even proposed the idea of the †'segmentary state' in order to cover states based on relatively discrete local units or segments (based on territory or descent) but with a centre which is stronger in ritual than in administrative terms. Is the classic opposition between territory and kinship valid in the traditional state? As the work of Claude Tardits on the Bamoum of Cameroon (1980) has shown, territorial organization may be a geographical working out of relations between kin groups within a single genealogy. Kinship also plays a part in the accession to office: power is a matter of competition within royal lineages, and relationships between the designated monarch and the other princes are never without tension. The king generally aims to limit the princes' influence by removing them from the administrative apparatus, while filling positions with nobles from outside his lineage, or men recruited from lower strata such as servants and even slaves.

Apart from the mode of recruitment of the ruling elite, traditional states are marked by complex *rituals and the role given to the symbolic and ideological element. Divine *kingship has been found in many very different contexts (the Inka in Highland *South America; African kingship among the Swazi, Jukun, Shilluk, Rukuba, and Moundangi, Hindu and Buddhist kingship in South and Southeast Asia), and has become the subject of debate on its origins and extensions: rites of enthronement, prohibitions connected to the royal person, representations of 'royal *incest', the tradition of ritual regicide in certain societies, which evokes the close association between political power and the practices which reveal the sovereign's special relationship with the cosmic order and the supernatural powers that participate in his reproduction. This whole set of beliefs and rituals must be treated as an integral part of the power apparatus which we call the state, rather than as a state religion employed to legitimate some pre-existing balance of political power.

The wealth of ethnographic and historical research on political organization, lineage segmentation and the representation of kingship demonstrates the specificity of a kind of state, which the labels 'lineage state', 'tributary state', 'or 'archaic state' merely simplify. Similarly we now have very precise data not only on institutions but on processes of decision-making, by the king and his counsellors, within the body of the state. The fruitfulness of anthropological methods in this context raises the possibility that a similar application to Western society might rejuvenate studies of the modern state. So investigations have rapidly developed concerning the centralization and territorial configuration of Western states, the networks of relationships which run through their institutions and apparatuses, and the rituals and symbols of power (Abélès 1990, Kertzer 1988). Such developments indicate the broad relevance of anthropological research on the state, once freed from its obsessive quest for origins.

MARC ABÉLÈS

See also: colonialism, kingship, nationalism, political anthropology

Further reading

Abélès, M. (1990) *Anthropologie de l'État*, Paris: Armand Colin

Claessen, H. and P. Skalnik (eds) (1978) *The Early State*, The Hague: Mouton

Cohen, R. and E. Service (eds) (1978) *Origins of the State: The Anthropology of Political Evolution*, Philadelphia: ISHI

Engels, F. ([1884] 1972) *The Origin of the Family, Private Property and the State*, London: Lawrence and Wishart

Evans-Pritchard, E.E. and M. Fortes (eds) (1940) *African Political Systems*, London: Oxford University Press

Fried, M. (1967) *The Evolution of Political Society*, New York: Random House

Godelier, M. (1984) *The Mental and the Material*, London: Verso

Kertzer, D. (1988) *Ritual, Politics and Power*, New Haven: Yale University Press

Morgan, L.H. (1877) *Ancient Society*, New York: Holt

Nadel, S.F. (1942) *A Black Byzantium*, London: Oxford

Southall, A. (1968) 'A Critique of the Typology of States and Political Systems', in M. Banton (ed.) *Political Systems and the Distribution of Power*, London: Tavistock

Steward, J. H.(1955) *Theory of Culture Change*, Urbana: University of Illinois Press

Tardits, C. (1980) *Le Royaume Bamoum*, Paris: Armand Colin

Wittfogel, K. (1957) *Oriental Despotism: A Comparative Study of Total Power*, New Haven: Yale University Press

structuralism

The term 'structuralism' has been used in anthropology to designate a number of quite distinct theoretical positions but recently it has normally only been used to label the theories which were originally developed from the 1940s onward by the French anthropologist *Claude Lévi-Strauss.

In the 1940s Lévi-Strauss found himself in New York as a refugee. He came with some experience of fieldwork among South American Indians and with a fascination for the great wealth of accumulated ethnographic data on the North American Indians which had been published in a largely unanalysed form by the American Smithsonian Institution. This material was mainly transcription and translation of what elderly Native Americans could remember of their youth and the myths and stories that had been told to them. The sheer volume of this data seemed to require an analytical approach and, at first, Lévi-Strauss was swayed by the *Boasian tradition

which, in its later developments, had become influenced by the psychological theory called †*Gestalt* theory (Benedict 1934). This stressed how human beings coped with information and emotions by creating encompassing configurations of knowledge. *Gestalt* theory stressed how cultures formed 'patterns'.

Lévi-Strauss was, however, searching for something more precise and he found it in a sister subject to cultural anthropology: linguistics. By the end of the war he had obtained a post at the New School for Social Research in New York and there he became closely linked with another refugee, the linguist †Roman Jakobson. Jakobson had become an advocate of a particular theory in linguistics called 'structural linguistics'. This proved to be what Lévi-Strauss was looking for.

Linguistics and anthropology

Understanding the history of structural linguistics is therefore essential to understanding the origins of structuralism in anthropology. The history of structural linguistics is the coming together of two distinct traditions, one European and the other American.

The origin of the European tradition lies in the shift of direction which the Swiss linguist †Ferdinand de Saussure brought about as a result of his lectures (which were subsequently published by his students [Saussure 1960]). Saussure redirected linguistics away from studying the history of particular languages' development (and demonstrating family links between them), and towards the study of the general principles according to which language in general worked. Saussure wanted to understand how the sounds produced by the human voice could convey the meaningful messages that were transmitted between individuals. In trying to account for this, he stressed how language worked by defining units which could be combined and recombined according to rules, such as those of syntax. His semantic theory, according to which the units were combinations of sounds (†signifier) and concepts (†signified), although naive, has often been solemnly discussed by many non-linguists including Lévi-Strauss himself. (See Sperber (1976 [1974]) for a discussion of its limitations, especially when applied to anthropology.) The significance of Saussure's work for structuralism is, however, more general: it is that he saw the task of linguistics as the study of meaningful communication, and that he suggested that the answer to the problem of how this came about lay in understanding how units are placed in structures.

In fact it was not the most general Saussurian programme which was taken up by linguists immediately following him, but a more modest part of what is usually called †phoneme theory. Phonemes are the minimal sound units which every language distinguishes in order to make lexically significant combinations. Thus, to take a simple example, the English word 'bat' consists of three phonemes which are conveniently designated by three letters (it is not always the case that letters and phonemes correspond so neatly). However, not all languages have these same phonemes. Thus, although English distinguishes between the phonemes normally indicated by the letters p and b, a distinction which enables English-speakers to distinguish between the words 'pat' and 'bat', many languages make no such distinction. In other words native speakers, in order that they may use and understand their own language, have to be trained to pay special attention to certain sound contrasts and at the same time ignore others (which in another language might have been significant, but which in their own would just muddle them by introducing irrelevant and misleading information). Phonemes are thus arbitrarily defined non-meaningful sound units which are combined and recombined in order that we can then construct higher level units (for example words) which themselves carry meaning.

The general universal aspects of phoneme theory (i.e. the definition of units by means of establishing conventional arbitrary contrasts in what would otherwise be a continuum of variation), and the fact that the units so defined have the potential to be combined according to rules in order that they may carry messages, became the basis of all forms of structuralism. Phoneme theory was originally developed by a group of Eastern European linguists to which Roman Jakobson belonged. When he moved to the USA with other colleagues, phoneme theory was extended both by linguists and by anthropologists such as Lévi-Strauss.

The linguists combined this theory with other American ones and in this way attempted to use the same model as had been used for phonemes for aspects of languages less concerned with sound and more with meaning. In this way they produced an all-embracing linguistic theory. What they retained from phoneme theory, however, was the idea that language works by: (1) defining units constructed through the emphasis of certain contrasts and the minimizing of others; and (2) combining and recombining these units according to rules of structure so that units plus structure produced the potential for meaningful communication. This general theory was 'structural linguistics'. What became crucial for anthropology, above all, was the shift from understanding phonemes (or other elements of culture) as things in themselves, to understanding them as more or less arbitrary elements which only make sense *in relationships* with other elements.

Intellectual structures

At the time when Lévi-Strauss became acquainted with structural linguistics it had also become caught up in a much more general theory of communication which went under the name of †cybernetics. Cybernetics was a science which underlay the development of early computers. At that time, these computers were being incorporated into such military technology as guided missiles, and could perform tasks which no machine and only living beings had previously been capable of; for example, adjusting the trajectory of a missile in flight to compensate for the avoiding action of its target. In being able to perform such reflexive tasks, computers could therefore be said, in some ways, 'to think'. If that were so, it was not an unreasonable supposition that at the same time as they had made computers, cyberneticians had discovered how the nervous system of animals in general, and of humans in particular, worked. Most cyberneticians did indeed make this supposition.

Because that was the way they thought their computers functioned, cyberneticians thought the brain worked by endlessly combining and recombining units defined through binary contrasts. Through these endless combinations and recombinations, messages could be encoded and problems solved. Put in this way the similarity between the way the structural linguists were arguing language worked and the way computers worked was strikingly similar. This came as no surprise to the cyberneticians because, since language was something processed by the human brain, it was inevitable that it would be structured in a way the human brain worked. Linguistics thus became, so it seemed for a time, part of the general science of cybernetics, which also took in such diverse fields as electronic engineering and neurology.

This is what Lévi-Strauss found most exciting. He put it in the following way:

> Of all the social sciences, to which it certainly belongs, linguistics is exceptional: it is not a social science like the others since it is the one which, by a long way, has achieved the most progress; it is probably the only one which can truly claim to be a science
>
> (Lévi-Strauss 1967 [1958]: 296).

With such a conclusion, it was then only a small step to decide that cultural and social anthropology should follow the lead of linguistics and show that the general principles of cybernetics operated there too. This became the aim of structural anthropology.

It seemed that the principles of structural linguistics could easily be imported into the field of *culture. Culture was, after all, most often seen, by *American anthropologists at least, as the information which individuals shared and which was contained in their minds. Thus, since culture was, like language, a mental phenomenon, it too had to be organized in structures because that was the way the mind or the brain – the two terms are interchangeable in Lévi-Strauss's writings – stored, handled and communicated information. Lévi-Strauss therefore set out to demonstrate the existence of such structures in cultural fields as diverse as *kinship terms or *mythology. In the field of the social too, mental structures were claimed to exist. This was because, even though the social was not a mental phenomenon in itself, what anthropologists inevitably have to do when studying the social is interpret it through the understandings of the people who operate it. In this way even the social is governed by psychological requirements and therefore it too must also be structured by the structures required by the human brain/mind.

'Totemism' and 'The Savage Mind'

The fullest exposition of structuralist theory is to be found in two books which Lévi-Strauss published in the 1960s – *Le totémisme aujourd'hui* (1962), translated into English as *Totemism;* and *La Pensée Sauvage* (1962) translated into English as *The Savage Mind* (1966).

The first of these books argues against *functionalist approaches to *totemism which try to explain why specific totemic animals or plants are chosen in terms of either their usefulness, or alternatively because the totemic animals and plants are scarce and therefore need preserving by totemism as most totemic species are tabooed. These arguments, Lévi-Strauss suggests, are quite unconvincing. Instead we should abandon explanations in terms of use and look into the patterns which sets of totems form, seeing these patterns as the structures imposed by human beings in order to be able to operate mentally in, and with, their *environment.

In *The Savage Mind* the argument is developed further. Not only is it shown how the kind of structures which structural linguists saw in the arrangements of phonemes is present in such things as plant and animal *classification, but Lévi-Strauss begins a discussion of the operations which can be carried out with the units of structures he isolates, in this case plant and animal species. These operations correspond to the way phonemes can be combined and recombined to create messages which can carry meaning. With a structured system of classification, both mental and practical, experiments become possible. Lévi-Strauss argues that this type of experimentation is what must have led to the first domestication of plants and animals (the †Neolithic revolution), an advance which many consider to be the most significant in the history of mankind. This use of 'concrete' (i.e. referring to classes of empirically existing objects) units such as classes of plants and animals to investigate and solve problems is what Lévi-Strauss calls 'the science of the concrete' or 'the savage mind'.

There is, however, another element to the science of the concrete which is discussed at length. This concerns analogy. Lévi-Strauss notes the frequency with which we talk of one kind of phenomenon, often abstract or difficult to grasp, in terms of quite different, more easily perceived, concrete objects (i.e. by using various types of metaphors). Totemism is a case in point. Totemism always involves social groups which may have no obvious empirical referents (like dispersed †clans) being spoken of, and thought about, as though they were animal or plant species. This means that a metaphorical 'evidence' is given to clan identity and to differences between clans. This use of one concrete phenomenon to talk about another, more abstract, realm is part of a much more widespread aspect of human thought; by means of analogy the complexity, fluidity and inaccessibility of the real world can be visualized and approached through various 'as if' devices.

These devices prove suitable for such operations because the devices themselves, unlike their targets, can easily be structured and therefore processed efficiently by the human mind or brain.

Myths and transformations

In *The Savage Mind* and *Totemism* Lévi-Strauss is principally concerned with the way structured knowledge is used for practical ends, although he is keen to emphasize that human thought is never limited to the practical. In other works, especially in the many articles and books concerned with mythology, he explores types of human intellectual activity which are, according to him, purely speculative. In this area too he attempts to isolate units which correspond to the phonemes of structural linguistics and, since he is dealing with myth, at one point he calls these units 'mythemes'. Having isolated the mythemes, he then goes on to show how, in particular myths, structures can be shown to govern the way mythemes are combined and recombined. He is, however, more interested in the way different versions of a myth represent transformations of its basic structure. What is meant by 'transformation' here is the way in which, although different versions of a myth may seem totally different, they may nonetheless have a systematic relation to one another. A simple example of this would be total rigorous inversion.

Lévi-Strauss is particularly interested in transformations because they enable him to expand his theory of structuralism into a theory of history. According to this theory, human beings are continually trying to make sense of their world and they do this by imposing structures on it because that is the only way in which the human brain can handle information. However, this structuring of the world can only be partial because the world obviously does not conform to the cognitive requirements of knowing minds. The drive towards structuring is therefore always finally incomplete and unsatisfactory. This is all the more so because the world itself is in a continual process of change as events succeed events, events which may be human in origin (e.g. the spread of a new technology), or non-human (e.g. natural disasters). Human beings therefore have to adjust their knowledge while maintaining its structured character; thus they transform it according to principles which owe something to the events which cause the change and something to the previous structures by which they had organized what they knew. This leads to a further contrast.

In some societies, because they are isolated and live in a fairly stable environment, the structures which people construct as a way of interpreting the world need little modification as events rarely challenge them. In other societies, however, where there is much external contact and internal differentiation, and where the environment is continually changing, structures have to be continually adapted and readapted, transformed, in order to catch up. But these very transformations bring about events which require further transformation, creating continual movement and innovation. The former types of societies he qualifies as †'cold societies' and the latter as 'hot societies', though these two terms are intended to mark extremes of a continuum in the middle of which most actual cases find their place.

Lévi-Strauss's theory of structuralism is unusually coherent for the discipline of anthropology. Indeed it could be said that it is the only fully-fledged theory to have been formulated in social or cultural anthropology since the demise of *evolutionism. Because of its boldness it is easy to point to its errors and limitations and these will be discussed below. However, it would be misleading to judge Lévi-Strauss's work purely in theoretical terms. Lévi-Strauss is not only interested in structuralism as such, but also in the richness and complexity of the ethnographic record and most of his work is an attempt to analyse this in a non reductionist way, nonetheless inspired by the general theory. In fact, as has been pointed out by Sperber (1982), in practice Lévi-Strauss seems to proceed as much by intuition and artistry as anything else, but his intuitions have proved amazingly suggestive. He has been able to lay bare extraordinarily important themes in human thought which had often been overlooked by anthropologists and ethnographers but which, having been pointed out, enable us to go forward in understanding.

For example, in his work on mythology he stresses the way we order food in terms of whether it is cooked or raw or rotten, and how these oppositions serve for further human speculation and attempts at organization. This is a theme which has revealed itself to be of central importance in many parts of the world which Lévi-Strauss was hardly aware of. It is never entirely clear how he uses his structuralist method but it is important to note that somehow, and often bafflingly, it has proved extraordinarily productive and suggestive.

Criticisms

The limitations as well as the strengths of structuralism are now well known. The basis of the theory rests on the two pillars of structural linguistics and cybernetics and both these have crumbled. The general theory of structural linguistics assumed that from an empirical analysis of what language was like one could discover structures which were the same as those used by the brains of speakers and hearers. This hypothesis would not now be acceptable to most linguists and psychologists because of the revolutionary change brought about by the linguistic theories of †Chomsky. Indeed, the use of the model derived from phoneme theory for other levels of language has now been abandoned, though the phoneme theory itself is still, to a certain extent, accepted.

Similarly the cybernetic model of the brain is now seen as far too simple. As Sperber notes, it is very unconvincing to argue, as did the cyberneticians by implication, that the structure of the human brain is simpler than the structure of the human hand. Information is probably not stored lineally and the binary computer is not a good model for artificial intelligence.

There are also problems about the way Lévi-Strauss deals with *ethnography. He seems to forget the process of interpretation which is inevitably involved and so he treats ethnographic accounts as though they were the actual reality to which they refer. He overemphasizes the intellectual aspect of culture, paying insufficient attention to the emotive or, indeed, the practical. His choice of source material often seems arbitrary.

All this having been said, however, Lévi-Strauss's achievement is impressive. He constructed a theory which defined the relation between the mental and the social in a way which has been the basis for all subsequent work. He moved ethnographic analysis away from the naive reductionism which characterized much earlier work to a state where the content, as well as the form, of ethnographic data was examined seriously once again. He integrated many areas of enquiry in a way which has continued to be fruitful. He generated an immense wealth of medium-level hypotheses which continue to inform and stimulate a large part of the ethnographic enterprise. Finally, the extraordinary sensitivity and personal philosophical honesty which characterizes his thought make him a writer whose work is aesthetically arousing and often very moving.

Structuralism and structuralists

The success, ambitions, and even failures of Lévi-Strauss's structuralism are perhaps now being seen in some sort of perspective, but in the period from the 1960s to the early 1980s it dominated not only anthropology but many other domains. There was a structuralist vogue in literature, in philosophy, in history, even in cinema. Such very diverse writers as †Barthes, †Foucault, †Lacan, †Althusser and many literary critics have sometimes been seen as inspired by Lévi-Strauss and described as 'structuralist', even by themselves. Now, it is very difficult to see what they have in common except that they were contemporaries and they were French. Much of what was written about structuralism in literature and the arts is ridiculous. Lévi-Strauss has for the most part denounced such enthusiasm for his work, sometimes with a good deal of irony, fuelled by his marked distaste for the intellectual fashions of the moment.

More serious have been the claims by a number of anthropologists to be following his principles. These can be divided into three groups.

The first are mainly *French anthropologists and keep closely to certain aspects of the Lévi-Straussian enterprise. Thus F. Héritier and her collaborators have developed some aspects of his earlier work on kinship (Héritier 1981). A number of writers have developed his analyses of myth and symbolism, several of whom are represented in the work edited by Izard and Smith called *Between Belief and Transgression* (1982 [1979]). It is notable, however, that these close followers seem to steer clear of the wider theoretical claims of structuralism and limit themselves to specific applications of a structuralist methodology.

Then there is the group of writers who, in the 1970s and 1980s, attempted to marry the renewed *Marxism of the time with structuralism. Lévi-Strauss himself claims that he has been much influenced by Marxism, though this is far from obvious in much of his writing. The link was, however, first emphasized by a close collaborator, L. Sebag, who stressed how the notions of †Hegelian dialectics, which so influenced Marx, are present in a similar way in Lévi-Strauss (Sebag 1964). The theme was then taken up by a number of writers, most prominent of whom is M. Godelier (1973). Godelier understood structuralism to apply to the Marxist †superstructure only, and to be quite compatible with a theory of infrastructural causation by the *modes of production.

The third group was mainly British and is associated with the names of †Edmund Leach and †Rodney Needham. Leach was an advocate as well as a critic of the theories of Lévi-Strauss and became their main exponent to the English-speaking world (Leach 1970). He also attempted a number of analyses which he himself described as 'structuralist'. In particular he published several studies of biblical texts which demonstrated structures and transformations between related texts (Leach and Aycock 1983). These studies differ from those of Lévi-Strauss in a number of ways. First of all, they are studies of written texts; something which Lévi-Strauss did not believe would be fruitful. Second, the notion of transformation is used in a simpler way than it is in Lévi-Strauss's own work. Third and most important, Leach is always eager to demonstrate the social significance of the myths he analyses in a way which is closer to functionalism than structuralism.

Needham was also an early advocate of the theories of Lévi-Strauss and defended them strongly against functionalist criticisms (Needham 1962). Later on he also attempted a number of analyses which have often been called structuralist because of similarity with some aspects of Lévi-Strauss's work. This type of analysis can be found in the work of a number of other anthropologists who were closely associated with Needham, such as D. Maybury Lewis (1967) and J. Fox (1975). In fact it is doubtful whether these types of work have any great relation to the ideas of Lévi-Strauss. They demonstrate that the symbols of certain societies can be shown to form master patterns, often of a binary character, which organize the general cognitive outlook of the people concerned. Such an approach is more †Durkheimian than structuralist in that it assumes a unified culture existing beyond the mind of individuals; while Lévi-Strauss stresses how culture never forms coherent wholes, how it is a matter of continual communication and modification between individuals which leads to endless transformation, and how its nature is a consequence of specific neurological requirements of living people.

MAURICE BLOCH

See also: Lévi-Strauss, French anthropology, kinship, language and linguistics, mythology

Further reading

Benedict, R. (1934) *Patterns of Culture*, Boston: Houghton Mifflin

Fox, J. (1975) 'On Binary Categories and Primary Symbols' in R. Willis (ed.) *The Interpretation of Symbolism*, London: Malaby Press

Godelier, M. (1978 [1973]) *Marxist Analyses in Anthropology*, Cambridge: Cambridge University Press

Hériter, F. (1981) *L'exercice de la parenté*, Paris: Gallimard Le Seuil

Izard, M. and P. Smith (eds) (1982 [1979]) *Between Belief and Transgression: Structuralist Essays in Religion, History and Myth*, Chicago: University of Chicago Press

Leach, E. (1970) *Lévi-Strauss*, London: Fontana

—— and D.A. Aycock (1983) *Structuralist Interpretations of Biblical Myth*, London: RAI

Lévi-Strauss, C. (1963 [1962]) *Totemism*, and *La Pensée Sauvage* (1962) translated into English as *The Savage Mind*, Harmondsworth: Penguin

—— (1966 [1962]) *The Savage Mind*, Chicago: University of Chicago Press

Maybury-Lewis, D. (1967) *Akwe-Shavante Society*, Oxford: Oxford University Press

Needham, R. (1962) *Structure and Sentiment*, Chicago: Chicago University Press

Saussure, F. de (1960) *Course in General Linguistics*, New York: McGraw Hill

Sebag, L. (1964) *Marxisme et Structuralisme*, Paris: Payot

Sperber, D. (1976 [1974]) *Rethinking Symbolism*, Cambridge: Cambridge University Press

symbolic anthropology

The term symbolic anthropology is usually used to cover a broad tendency in the anthropology of the late 1960s and 1970s. Symbolic anthropology involved the study of *culture as a relatively autonomous entity, a system of meaning which the anthropologist would attempt to unravel through the decoding or interpretation of key symbols and *rituals. If symbolic anthropology ever constituted a distinctive school, its home was in *American anthropology, especially in those students and colleagues who had been influenced by its three key figures – †Clifford Geertz, †Victor Turner and †David Schneider – all of whom briefly coincided at the University of Chicago around 1970. Geertz and Schneider were both products of †Talcott Parsons' Harvard Social Relations department of the early 1950s, while Turner was a genuine maverick: a Scottish protégé of †Max Gluckman whose eclecticism and intellectual ambition found a more comfortable home in American anthropology. The founding texts are Turner's analyses of the rituals and symbols of the Ndembu of Zambia (Turner 1967), Schneider's *American Kinship: A Cultural Account* ([1968] 1980), and Geertz's essays of the 1960s and early 1970s, collected in his *Interpretation of Cultures* (1973). To this trio, we should probably add the work of †Marshall Sahlins, who started the 1970s an economic anthropologist of a gently Marxist persuasion, but declared his conversion to the American cultural tradition in the highly influential *Culture and Practical Reason* (1976).

Although influenced by *Lévi-Strauss's *structuralism, most obviously in treating culture as analogous to language, symbolic anthropology departed from Lévi-Strauss in two important ways. One was a resistance to scientistic *methodology, most clearly articulated in Geertz's post-1970 writings. The other was an emphasis on cultural particularism, which had deep roots in American anthropology from the time of *Boas, and his successors like †Ruth Benedict, but which was at odds with Lévi-Strauss's concern with the pan-human roots of specific symbolic structures. Although symbolic anthropology was an American expression for a predominantly American movement, its effects were felt much more widely. In Britain, Scandinavia, Holland and France, for example, where structuralism and structural Marxism had far more impact in the late 1960s and early 1970s, by the late 1970s there was a marked shifted towards issues of culture and interpretation, and away from grand theories. This was least true in France, but even there the work of Sahlins proved influential in linking American culturalism to more characteristically European traditions of social anthropology.

Decoding symbols

If Geertz and Schneider were mainly responsible for grounding symbolic anthropology in a coherent theoretical framework, Turner probably exercised the most influence by sheer ethnographic virtuosity. He carried out fieldwork in the early 1950s as a research officer at the †Rhodes-Livingstone Institute, by then emerging as the African base of the so-called †Manchester school of anthropologists which gathered around its former director Max Gluckman. Turner's first book, *Schism and Continuity in an African Society*, was a careful analysis of the structural tensions within Ndembu society, illuminated by the use of vivid case studies. As such, it was a particularly stimulating, but nevertheless conventional, example of state-of-the-art *British anthropology of the time. Turner followed this, though, with a series of extraordinary papers exploring the ritual and symbolism of the Ndembu.

In particular, from work with one exceptionally gifted informant – Muchona – he was able to elicit extremely rich and detailed accounts of the meaning of specific symbols employed in Ndembu ritual. These decoded symbols were then placed within an analytic framework derived from †van Gennep's classic model of *rites of passage, and from Turner's own earlier sociological account of Ndembu society. So, for example, the *mudyi* tree, a dominant symbol in certain rituals, exudes a white latex: according to Turner it stands for milk, mother's breasts, the link between mother and child, the principle of †matriliny, and ultimately the endurance of Ndembu custom itself (1967: 20–1).

Such detailed †exegesis, of course, raises serious questions about the whole question of symbols and their meaning. Whose meanings are these – the ethnographer's, his gifted native informant, all the participants in the ritual? What of all those cases, numbingly familiar to fieldworkers, in which informants claim an incapacity to interpret or decode complex symbolism – 'we do it this way because the ancestors told us to', 'we don't understand these rituals ourselves, you should ask the priest or ritual specialist'? In a forensic critique of prevailing theories of symbolism, Dan Sperber (1975) argued that symbols were not simply elements in a conscious or unconscious code, and that exegesis, where it occurs, does not so much represent the 'meaning' of symbols, but rather an extension of symbolic discourse itself. Sperber's critique, based in large part on Turner's Ndembu examples, emphasized the way that symbols 'evoke' in an indeterminate manner, rather than carry fixed and unambiguous 'meanings'.

Sperber's essay on symbolism was part of a much more ambitious project to ground anthropological analysis of cultural forms in a new science of *cognition. As such, it was seriously out of step with the growing disillusion with †positivist theories in anthropology, and the resultant tendency to retreat into ethnographic particularism. Although, Turner's qualities as an ethnographer might have encouraged such a retreat, in fact he was no more comfortable with the restrictions of uncritical culturalism, than he had been with the anxious boundaries of late 1950s British social anthropology. In fact, he retained an interest in the somatic bases of symbolic efficacy throughout his life, whether this was manifest in his argument that behind the triad of colours (red-white-black) in Ndembu ritual lay a triad of primal bodily experiences (blood-semen/milk-faeces), or in his meditations in his late work on the neurobiology of ritual and symbolism.

Core symbols and cultural systems

David Schneider was in many ways the reverse of Turner. His most influential work, *American Kinship*, can be most charitably described as schematic. Instead of Turner's flesh-and-blood accounts of rituals, symbols and explanations, Schneider provides a short, highly stylized account of American ideas about *kinship, synthesized from interviews with middle-class white residents of Chicago. In this, American ideas about what constitutes a *person, about what makes a person a relative, about blood and sex and biology, nature and law, substance and code, were explored systematically. Behind Schneider's oddly deadpan prose style lay a hugely ambitious idea: that it was possible to abstract a 'cultural system' from statements and behaviour and render it in a clear, analytic way which demonstrated that culture was both systematic and autonomous. As the cultural system in question was the central area of kinship and family in Schneider's own society, his account required a heroic effort of self-abstraction.

Schneider defines a 'cultural system' as 'a system of symbols', and a 'symbol' as simply 'something which stands for something else' (Schneider [1968] 1980: 1). What interests him, though, is less the project of decoding individual symbols, and more the idea that symbols constitute an autonomous system; within this system, certain symbols are central points of orientation on which all else depends. The claim that culture is a system of meanings which cannot be reduced to accounts of individual behaviour derives from Parsons; the emphasis on the system as a set of relationships derives to some extent from Lévi-Strauss; the focus on the cultural core or distinctive essence of an apparently complex society derives from Ruth Benedict and the later work of the *culture-and-personality school on national cultures.

Although Schneider's account of American kinship is empirically weaker than the work of Geertz and Turner – almost self-evidently so in the areas of *class, *race and *ethnicity – and although his theoretical emphasis on the autonomy of culture as a system is clearly contentious and has hardly stood the test of time, nevertheless it can be argued that his work stimulated some of the most imaginative anthropology of the 1970s and 1980s. Partly this is because of his position as a teacher and supervisor of students at Chicago, some of whom were responsible for both the most penetrating critiques of Schneider's work and the most interesting developments of it. Mostly, though, it is because his example opened up important areas for ethnographic enquiry: the systematic examination of indigenous ideas (and especially *systems* of ideas) about persons and relatedness, work which has transformed research into areas as diverse as *caste in *South Asia and *gender in *Melanesia.

From reading to writing

Clifford Geertz's career has interesting parallels with Schneider's: Harvard beginnings, a short period in California and a longer one in Chicago, an attachment to a concept of culture as meaning derived in equal part from Parsons and the Boasian tradition in American anthropology, and oracular pronouncements in the 1960s on symbols and cultural systems and the idea of the person. But it also has its differences too: Geertz left Chicago for the Institute for Advanced Study at Princeton in 1970; where Schneider's influence was as much felt through his students and followers, Geertz's influence was broader (especially outside anthropology itself) but more diffuse, owing more to literary and intellectual panache and less to personal attachments. And while Geertz's influence, like Turner's, owes much to sheer ethnographic élan, it is ironic that his best-known and most apparently virtuosic work – the essays on the person and the cockfight in Bali (Geertz 1973: 360–453) – has now been almost completely rejected by many area specialists (cf. Wikan 1990).

Geertz has carried out fieldwork in Java, Morocco and Bali and published important monographs on such apparently diverse topics as agricultural development and the dual economy in Java, the rituals of the pre-modern *state in Bali, *Islam, kinship, and ethnographic writing. Despite this, his most influential work is contained in four chapters of his first collection of essays: 'Thick description', 'Religion as a cultural system', 'Person, time and conduct in Bali' and 'Deep play: notes on the Balinese cockfight' (Geertz 1973). The earliest of these, the essay on religion, reveals much of Geertz's Parsonian heritage – not least in the isolation of a cultural system, in this case *religion, as a 'system of meanings', which once it is understood in its own terms can then be related to questions of psychology and social structure. The essays on the person and the cockfight investigate the area of †ethos – the distinctive moral, aesthetic and affective 'tone' of a culture – which was a central concern of the culture-and-personality theorists of the 1930s. (Critics would claim that his essays on Bali owe as much to the study of *Balinese Character* by †Gregory Bateson and †Margaret Mead, as to anything the Balinese themselves might do or say.)

And the opening essay of the collection, †'Thick description', makes a powerful case for anthropology as an interpretive activity, concerned above all with the elucidation of local detail rather than grand comparison. The expression 'thick description' itself derives from the philosopher Gilbert Ryle, and refers to the embeddedness of the tiniest detail of human life in layers of contextual significance. Anthropologists deal above all in interpretations, and interpretations of interpretations. To employ the word which was just beginning to gain wider currency through the work of Ricoeur (who Geertz cites) and †Habermas (who he doesn't), anthropology should be concerned with †hermeneutics. Understanding another culture is like reading, and interpreting, a text. And difficulties in formulating and communicating that understanding are as much as anything problems of writing. Geertz concludes by making *ethnography, conceived as a kind of writing, central to anthropological practice.

In many ways, Geertz represents the sharpest break with earlier anthropology. His commitment to the particularity of ethnographic description sets him far apart from the grand ambitions of *structuralism or Marxism, even as it anticipated the noisily trumpeted 'decline of metanarratives' (or big stories) of the postmodern 1980s. Similarly his intellectual points of reference – Ricoeur, Kenneth Burke, the later †Wittgenstein – helped prepare the ground for the so-called 'literary turn' in anthropology, signified above all by the publication of *Writing Culture* (Clifford and Marcus 1986). Certainly when scholars from the humanities – historians and literary critics – cite an anthropologist, it is more often than not Geertz they are citing, and usually it is Geertz on thick description or Geertz on the cockfight.

After culture

Although lesser anthropologists may have described themselves as 'symbolic anthropologists' and thought of themselves as constituting a 'school', it is quite clear that the three most influential figures in the emergence of symbolic anthropology – Geertz, Turner and Schneider – differed considerably in their intentions and approaches. What they shared, and what gives retrospective coherence to the work of the 1970s in particular, is the triumph of a certain vision of culture as a set of shared meanings. Where they differed was in the extent to which they attempted to relate their vision of cultural meaning to social processes and social practices. Turner never completely lost his sociological roots in British social anthropology, and Geertz's early work makes frequent reference to issues of sociology (although he gradually distanced himself further and further from the concerns of his British and French colleagues). Schneider was most overt in his attempts to remove the study of culture from the study of *society.

This uneasiness with what was felt to be sociological or *functionalist reductionism separated American symbolic anthropologists from colleagues pursuing apparently similar goals elsewhere. In Britain †Mary Douglas, for example, saw her work on symbolic boundaries and natural symbols as a direct continuation of †Durkheim's comparative sociology, as to some extent did †Rodney Needham, who nevertheless managed to isolate a domain of symbols and symbolic exegesis every bit as isolated from social action and history as the work of his American contemporaries. The work which most explicitly confronted the European sociological tradition with the cultural concerns of American symbolic anthropology was Sahlins's *Culture and Practical Reason* (1976). As well as arguing against all those who would 'reduce' cultural phenomena to social explanations, Sahlins first confronted, then co-opted, the two main rival strains of 1970s European theory, Marxism and structuralism. Marxism, Sahlins argued, is ultimately predicated upon peculiarly Western assumptions about material needs and economic rationality; as such it can function as a compelling self-account of 'the West', but imposes one historically specific and inappropriate cultural logic on to non-Western societies. He is much more sympathetic to Lévi-Strauss's structuralism, and employs its procedures in his analyses, yet is clearly uneasy about its location of an ultimate cause in the transcultural ether of the human spirit. In the ascension of culture-as-meaning in the late 1970s, Sahlins's argument carried more weight with European anthropologists, not least because it was so palpably engaged, however critically, with their own intellectual traditions.

Intellectually, there were certain obvious problems with the symbolic anthropology of the 1970s (ably summarized by Ortner 1984). Too often symbols were abstracted from social action, resulting in an idealist and oddly conservative view of the world. Similarly, symbolic systems seemed curiously atemporal and, like structuralism, unable to deal with history. †Bourdieu's *Outline of a Theory of Practice* (1977) seemed to point the way out of the first dilemma by showing how implicit meanings were marshalled in the service of power, and how individual agents pursued strategies rather than mutely obeyed rules. Moreover, Bourdieu argued that in emphasizing problems of meaning, translation and interpretation, anthropologists unreflexively equated their problem, as academically-trained outsiders trying to make sense of an unfamiliar social landscape, with the human condition. Bourdieu's work was, nevertheless, equally open to the second criticism, that of being unable to deal with history and change. Sahlins provided the most remarkable attempt to provide a theorized account of historical change within the logic of a cultural or symbolic system in his work on first contact in Hawaii (Sahlins 1981). Many others followed, gradually shedding Sahlins' structuralism but not his attachment to symbolic analysis, in their interpretations of societies in history.

The least resilient aspect of symbolic anthropology was the notion of culture itself. Empirically, it became less and less possible for anthropologists to maintain the necessary fiction of a world made up of separate, discrete, internally homogeneous cultures. This may have been obvious in the *world-system of the 1980s, but it could be shown to have been equally dubious as a depiction of the 1880s, 1780s or even 1680s (Wolf 1982). Moreover, it could easily be shown that 'culture' was itself every bit as 'Western', and therefore culturally and historically specific, as Marxism and functionalism and any of the other forbidden reductionisms of the symbolic anthropologists. And the whole problem of 'meaning-for-whom' was reopened in the light of feminist and †poststructuralist, critiques which challenged both the view of cultures as unproblematically homogeneous, and the idea that meaning can be unequivocally fixed. Finally, Sperber's 1970s challenge to the notion of 'meaning' returned, as anthropologists interested in the cross-disciplinary study of *cognition started to argue that a great deal of cultural knowledge was not analogous to language at all.

JONATHAN SPENCER

See also: person, ritual, myth, American anthropology, structuralism

Further reading

Bourdieu, P. (1977) *Outline of a Theory of Practice*, Cambridge: Cambridge University Press

Clifford, J. and G. Marcus (eds) (1986) *Writing Culture: The Poetics and Politics of Ethnography*, Berkeley: University of California Press

Geertz, C. (1973) *The Interpretation of Cultures*, New York: Basic Books

Ortner, S. (1984) 'Theory in Anthropology since the 1960s', *Comparative Studies in Society and History* 26: 126–66

Sahlins, M. (1976) *Culture and Practical Reason*, Chicago: University of Chicago Press

—— (1981) *Historical Metaphors and Mythical Realities: Structure in the Early History of the Sandwich Islands*, Ann Arbor: University of Michigan Press

Schneider, D. ([1968] 1980) *American Kinship: A Cultural Account* (2nd edn), Chicago: University of Chicago Press

Sperber, D. (1975) *Rethinking Symbolism*, Cambridge: Cambridge University Press

Turner, V. (1967) *The Forest of Symbols: Aspects of Ndembu Ritual*, Ithaca: Cornell University Press

Wikan, U. (1990) *Managing Turbulent Hearts: A Balinese Formula for Living*, Chicago: University of Chicago Press

Wolf, E. (1982) *Europe and the People without History*, Berkeley: University of California Press

syncretism

Syncretism refers to the hybridization or amalgamation of two or more cultural traditions. However, all cultures comprise a variety of diffused and borrowed elements – a point †Ralph Linton made in his ironic piece 'One Hundred Per-Cent American' (1937). Given this, 'syncretism' loses much of its descriptive precision and many have deprecated the utility of the term. It makes best sense in the context of *functionalist theories of integrated social systems, or doctrines of cultural holism, that presuppose unified and bounded social or cultural units that, under certain conditions, can be conceived as merging to produce some novel syncretic formation. Syncretistic analysis, however, unavoidably raises problems of history and social change and thus sits uneasily alongside classic functionalist theory (see for example, *Malinowski's uncomfortable attempt to alloy functional coherence and social change in Southern Africa [1945]).

†Ethnohistorians and *diffusionists concerned with population movements, migrations, invasions and colonial empires have used 'syncretic' to describe cultural and social systems that emerge from these various sorts of historical connections among different peoples. †Melville Herskovits, for example, found the term useful to describe the culture of African Americans – a culture, he argued, that blended elements of European and African traditions: syncretism is a fundamental 'mechanism in the acculturative process undergone by New World Negroes' (1941: 184-5).

Anthropology shares the concept of syncretism with scholars of comparative religion who have used the term at least since the early 1600s (often disparagingly to condemn the adulteration of true Christian belief). Theologians continue to apply the term to religious systems (various forms of *Hinduism, Japanese *Buddhism, Santeria, Bahai'i and the like) that amalgamate several different traditions (see Hartman 1969). Within anthropology, the concept of syncretism also most commonly describes hybrid religious systems, particularly those that developed in response to the disruptions of European colonialism. Thus, the nineteenth-century North American *ghost dance movement combined certain Native American elements and Mormonism; Melanesian *cargo cults often conjoined Christian Adventist notions of the millennium with island concerns to control the production of wealth; and African Zionism 'attempts to reform the received world by means of a syncretism of images and practices, a syncretism drawn from the local and global systems whose contradictory merger it seeks to transcend' (Comaroff 1985: 250).

Other cultural or social domains, besides religion, may also conspicuously combine elements from multiple traditions. For example, †pidgin lingua francas – which commonly overlay words from one language upon a simplified grammatical substrate from a second – have been termed 'syncretic'. Art traditions (e.g. European †primitivism), nationalist political ideologies (Vanuatu's Melanesian Socialism), economic systems (Japanese capitalism) or any similarly blended formation may all be deemed syncretic.

New terminology to describe the cultural admixtures occasioned by expanding global

economic, communicative and political systems, however, is replacing an earlier language of syncretism. *Culture and *society are both late nineteenth-century anthropological terms, developed to describe human communities that were mostly localized and bounded. Over the past century, what economic, political, informational and geographic boundaries that may once have separated human societies have much decayed. Surges of people, goods, words and images wash throughout global networks. We apply the terms 'culture' and 'society' with increasing difficulty to non-localized and dispersed communities. Notions of syncretism likewise, that suggest the blending of two holistic traditions, are proving insufficiently commodious to describe the admixture of multiple cultural influences that converge at the borderlands of the *world system.

Increasing interest in cultural studies of 'diaspora' and the minglings of peoples in cultural borderlands and 'contact zones' (Rosaldo 1989) has conjured up a new descriptive language of 'ethnoscapes' (Appadurai 1991) and 'hybridity'. An ethnoscape is 'the landscape of persons who make up the shifting world in which we live: tourists, immigrants, refugees, exiles, guest-workers, and other moving groups and persons' (Appadurai 1991: 192). The ethnoscape of the borderlands breeds cultural hybridity in which multiple traditions fuse, as itinerant peoples negotiate and construct their shared and unshared *identities. Similar attempts to grasp what might be called the emerging 'hyper-syncretism' of the contemporary global ethnoscape will continue to engage anthropological attention.

LAMONT LINDSTROM

See also: complex society, great and little traditions, plural society, religion, world systems

Further reading

Appadurai, A. (1991) 'Global Ethnoscapes: Notes and Queries for a Transnational Anthropology' in R. Fox (ed.) *Recapturing Anthropology: Working in the Present*, Santa Fe: School of American Research Press

Comaroff, J. (1985) *Body of Power, Spirit of Resistance: The Culture and History of a South African People*, Chicago: University of Chicago Press

Hartman, S. (1966) *Syncretism*, Scripta Institutu Donneriani Aboensis III, Stockholm: Almqvist & Wiksell

Herskovits, M. (1941) *The Myth of the Negro Past*, New York: Harper & Brothers

Linton, R. (1937) 'One Hundred Per-Cent American', *The American Mercury* 40: 427–9

Malinowski, B. (1945) *The Dynamics of Culture Change: An Inquiry into Race Relations in Africa*, New Haven: Yale University Press

Rosaldo, R. (1989) *Culture and Truth: The Remaking of Social Analysis*, Boston: Beacon Press

Stewart, C. and R. Shaw (eds) (1994) *Syncretism/ Antisyncretism: The Politics of Religious Synthesis*, London: Routledge

T

taboo

Polynesian origins

Introduced into English by Captain Cook, 'taboo' was once central among the constructs of social anthropology. Reporting the custom of human sacrifice in Tahiti, Cook observed: 'The solemnity itself is called Poore Eree, or Chief's Prayer; and the victim, who is offered up, Tataa-taboo, or consecrated man' (III 1784, ii: 40). The natives of Atui Island asked Cook's party apprehensively whether certain objects shown them were 'taboo, or, as they pronounced the word, tafoo?' (Cook III 1784 ii: 249). Following Cook's death, his successor in maintaining the ship's journal wrote of native priests 'tabooing' a field of sweet potatoes using wands, and of women who – throughout Polynesisa – 'are always tabooed, or forbidden to eat certain kinds of meats' (Cook III 1784, iii: 10–11).

On the basis of such accounts, *taboo* – with the stress shifted from the first to the second syllable – rapidly entered the English language. In common usage throughout the nineteenth century, it was given a new lease of life in the twentieth through the writings of †Sigmund Freud (e.g. [1913] 1965), who linked it particularly with sexual prohibitions such as the **'incest taboo. †James Frazer, *Bronislaw Malinowski, *A.R. Radcliffe-Brown and many other social anthropologists used the term when referring to any strong ritual prohibition.

Etymologically, the Maori term, '*tapu*', derives from two words: '*ta*', to mark, and '*pu*', thoroughly (Steiner [1956] 1967 , citing Shortland 1854: 81). But in Polynesian usage, more than secular marking was signified. Cook and subsequent European visitors were never sure whether *tapu* meant 'sacred' or 'defiled'. They alternated

between the two ideas in their translations, noting that in either case, strict ritual avoidance was required. It may seem paradoxical to allow a single term to link, say, the 'pollution' of a woman's *menstrual flow with the 'holiness' of a priest, and although this Polynesian pattern is far from unusual, not every symbolic system would permit it. 'One has only to think of Indian caste society', comments Steiner in his classic account, '. . . to see how inapplicable the Polynesian range of taboo would be there: it would mean using the same word for Brahman and pariah, for the sacred cow and human faeces' ([1956] 1967: 35).

Returning to Polynesia, political power throughout the region was traditionally inseparable from ritual power or *mana, in turn measurable by reference to the 'taboos' a person could impose. Cook mentions the Tongan food controller, alerting people to the foods they were prohibited from eating (III 1784, i: 410–11). This official could declare any category of food taboo when it grew scarce; it was then protected from consumption until the next harvest. Local history records occasions when officials or chiefs went too far, tabooing foods to the point of provoking a revolt. To challenge a chief's right to impose food taboos was to doubt his *mana*, calling into question his whole right to rule.

The taboos imposed by a chief were conceptualized as emanating directly from his physical constitution. Thanks to his *mana*, the whole body of a chief was *tapu*, and if he wanted to extend this to certain external objects – claiming them to himself – he could do so by calling out, for example, 'Those two canoes are my two thighs!' Once the objects in question were his body – rendered, like his name, symbolically inseparable from his very flesh and blood – then for as long as his *mana* held, no-one could challenge such supernaturally sanctioned ownership. Comparable linkages of 'taboo' with the notion of bodily 'self' are to be found worldwide; such a mystical identification between persons, names and 'respected' things forms an important strand in what used to be termed *'totemic' thinking (Knight 1991: 106–21; Lévi-Strauss [1962] 1969b).

After taboo

The term 'taboo' is no longer fashionable among anthropologists. In many modern textbooks and treatises, it is missing from the index. Comparable terms thought to impute 'otherness' or 'irrationality' to non-Western cultures – such as 'totemism' – have suffered similarly. In justification it could be pointed out that Captain Cook and his crew condescendingly found the 'taboos' of the Polynesians amusing, and that in subsequent European popular usage, to refer to a 'taboo' was to question the rational basis of a prohibition or rule. Freud linked the term with sexual neurosis. A 'taboo' in psychoanalytic parlance was compulsive behaviour, perpetuated by the patient for irrational reasons. Freud equated 'savages' with neurotics, using terms such as 'taboo' to underline such parallels ([1913] 1965). Given this historical background, abandonment of the old vocabulary has recently seemed a safe way to maintain political correctness, helping to emphasize that traditionally organized peoples are not 'different' but in reality 'just like us'.

The consequent terminological impoverishment has its costs, however. Apart from 'taboo', what better word do we possess to describe a collective prohibition which is to be obeyed categorically, without question? And who is to say that unquestioning adherence to a ritually established rule – where this is found – is intrinsically less logical than a stance of sustained scepticism and challenge? A *rationality which incites the individual to weigh up the personal costs and benefits of each course of action contrasts starkly with one in which the collectivity asserts the primacy of its own interests. But to rank the former as logically superior to the latter is to slip from *science into *ideology. An alternative might be to ask why kin-coalitions and other collectivities, in traditional cultures, so insistently assert that certain things, being 'sacred', are to be respected unquestioningly.

One of the strongest of taboos, in Polynesia as elsewhere, insulates women from contact with males during their menstrual periods (Steiner

[1956] 1967). Comparable taboos cross-culturally have long been considered oppressive of women, or else without rational basis. However, recent scholarship has re-evaluated them as frequently protective and even empowering to women (Buckley and Gottlieb 1988). An early proponent of such a view was †Durkheim ([1898] 1963), according to whom female fertility was the first domain of 'the sacred' whilst menstruants (rather than priests or priestesses) were the first beings to be periodically 'set apart'.

Durkheim's model of social origins pictured menstruants as actively repulsing their spouses during each menstrual period, their 'tabooed' blood becoming equated with that of game animals killed in the hunt. Men were by such means obliged to 'respect' bloody flesh, whether menstrual or animal. In a recent reworking and updating of this theory, Knight (1991) argues that early Homo sapiens females prevented inequalities and conflicts over the distribution of meat by forming powerful kin-based coalitions. These enabled women to refuse sexual advances whenever meat was scarce, making sexual access dependent on adequate supplies being brought home to them. The signal selected to indicate 'No!' was the blood of menstruation, signifier of fertility. This was appropriated collectively by the menstruant's coalition partners and augmented as required by animal blood, red ochre or other pigments. Combined in this way as if on a picket line, women monthly declared themselves 'on strike', linking the periodicity of the hunt with that of the moon in a pattern still discernible in Southern African *hunter-gatherer and other ritual traditions worldwide.

Claude Lévi-Strauss demonstrated that so-called 'incest taboos' and elaborate rules of †exogamy in traditional cultures are not irrational phobias but intricate expressions of collective wisdom, ensuring social integration by regulating the circulation of marriageable partners between groups. The seemingly irrational food taboos of hunter-gatherer and other traditional cultures can be similarly explained. The extension of incest-taboos from human to animal flesh is the central principle of what used to be termed 'totemism'. It implies that 'one's own flesh' – whether one's own offspring, or one's own kill in the hunt – is not for selfish appropriation but for others to enjoy. If the sex-strike theory of cultural origins is accepted, men were first prevented from eating their own kills under pressure from their affines, to whom all meat supplies had to be surrendered. Asserting themselves periodically as inviolable, marriageable women drew on their male kin and offspring as coalitionary allies in asserting the force of their combined action. Insofar as they were withdrawn from sexual circulation, all members of each coalition were 'sisters' and 'brothers'. All were 'protected' by the same real or surrogate 'blood', which equally protected the raw flesh of game animals which hunters killed. Sexual taboos and 'totemic' food taboos – as Durkheim was among the first to realise – stem from the same culture-generating source.

Where menstrual taboos retain their traditional force, a woman during her periods is to be respected without question. Her 'taboo' is a part of herself. Like a Polynesian's *mana*, it is her ritual potency – inseparable from her very flesh and blood. Although scarcely modern, such a viewpoint has a parallel in at least one strand of contemporary politically correct thinking. An instructive contemporary Western example of a taboo can be found in the industrial labour movement's founding principle: the prohibition against crossing a picket line. Costs and benefits to the individual are not to be taken into account. The principle is that regardless of precise issues in the particular dispute at hand, a trades unionist simply does not cross. Adherence is bound up with the very identity of those involved, and with the perceived nature of the world they inhabit. To cross a picket line would be to abandon self-respect, denying the very existence of the social class categories out of which identity is constructed. Reserved for violators, the English abuse term 'scab' most perfectly conveys defiled flesh. Although social anthropologists have scarcely focused on such home-grown ritual, it is known that in the prevailing ethic a trades unionist respects the picket-line unquestioningly, without thinking. The 'rationality' of such behaviour can of course be contested, in accordance with the class standpoint of the observer. What is certain is that participant observation among members of a striking community would reveal a taboo maintained successfully, on grounds of collective self-interest, without appeals to mystical forces or supernatural powers.

CHRIS KNIGHT

See also: Pacific: Polynesia, *mana*, totemism, primitive mentality, ritual, incest, menstruation

Further reading

Buckley, T. and A. Gottlieb (1988) 'A Critical Appraisal of Theories of Menstrual Symbolism', in T. Buckley and A. Gottlieb (eds) *Blood Magic. The Anthropology of Menstruation*, Berkeley, Los Angeles and London: University of California Press

Cook, Capt. James (1784) *A Voyage to the Pacific Ocean...in His Majesty's Ships the Resolution and Discovery, in the Years 1776, 1777, 1779 and 1780*; 3 vols I & II by Capt. James Cook, III by Capt. James King, Dublin

Durkheim, É. ([1898]1963) 'La prohibition de l'inceste et ses origines', *L'Année Sociologique* 1: 1–70; reprinted as *Incest. The Nature and Origin of the Taboo*, trans. by E. Sagarin, New York: Stuart

Freud, S. ([1913]1965) *Totem and Taboo. Some Points of Agreement between the Mental Lives of Savages and Neurotics*, London: Routledge

Knight, C.D. (1991) *Blood Relations. Menstruation and the Origins of Culture*, New Haven and London: Yale University Press

Lévi-Strauss, C. (1969a) *The Elementary Structures of Kinship*, London: Eyre & Spottiswoode

—— ([1962] 1969b) *Totemism*, Harmondsworth: Penguin.

Radcliffe-Brown, A.R. ([1929] 1952) 'Taboo', in A.R. Radcliffe-Brown *Structure and Function in Primitive Society*, London: Routledge

Shortland, E. (1854) *Traditions and Superstitions of the New Zealanders*, London:

Steiner, F. ([1956] 1967) *Taboo*, Harmondsworth: Penguin

technology

Techniques and representations

Technology can be defined as the particular domain of human activity immediately aimed at action on matter. Since †Mauss (1935) demonstrated long ago that the most 'natural' of our technical actions – like walking, carrying a load or giving birth – vary from culture to culture, it has become clear that every technique is a social production learnt through tradition. Techniques (or material culture) are embedded with all kinds of social relations, practices and representations, but they are also of concern to anthropology in themselves, and not solely for their effect on the material life of society or for the social relations surrounding their application.

Techniques always have a systemic aspect (Gille 1978). First, any particular technique involves five kinds of element – matter, energy, artefacts, gestures and a specific knowledge (or set of representations) – and these elements interact. If one is changed, then others will change.

Secondly, if one considers all the technologies in a given society, it can easily be shown that many are interrelated. In particular, several different techniques may share some common technical knowledge; that is, *representations* concerning action on matter. For instance the way people build planes is related to the way cars are made, and the technical knowledge involved in the hafting of a stone-axe is related to that involved in the making of a trap or in the tying of some wooden part of a house. A last general characteristic is that every artefact or technical behaviour always has two dimensions or functions, which are intimately related: a physical one, and one which communicates some kind of information and plays a †symbolic role in social life (Lemonnier 1992).

The description and study of technology goes back to the very beginning of anthropological research. The 'anthropological expeditions' of the turn of the century looked closely at material culture and the description and study of technology was long a classical domain of the discipline (Forde 1939). But, besides the mere collection of artefacts and *museum work, for years most studies on the link between technology and other social behaviour have dealt either with the effects of technological systems on culture and society, or with a search for what human groups communicate when they make and use artefacts. Unfortunately, researchers interested in the effects of techniques often consider the techniques themselves as merely a set of constraints, i.e. as a black box into which no inquiry is needed. This was notably the case in *ecological and *Marxist anthropology. As for those concerned with the *cultural* aspects of material culture, they tended to limit their study to the 'style' of artefacts, thereby curiously reducing the social content of techniques to details of shape or decoration aimed at conveying a 'message', but with little or no physical function. But, in a break with most archaeological and ethnological tradition, scholars no longer study the material effects of technical systems *or* the meanings which societies impute in them. Instead, they focus on the uninterrupted process by which material culture is made part of culture; that is the way in which material culture simultaneously results from, and participates in, particular socio-cultural characteristics (Latour and Lemonnier 1994; Lechtman and Merrill 1975).

In this respect, social representations of action on the material world appear as the most important link between technology, culture and society, because any technique, be it a mere gesture or a simple artefact, is always a physical manifestation of mental †schemata of how things work, how they are to be made, and how they are to be used. Some representations of technology are related to basic, universal, and necessary principles of action or to physical laws involved in action on matter. People may, for example, have representations of the principles of gravity, the accumulation of energy and the precarious equilibrium that underlie the functioning of a dead-fall trap, or of the kinetic laws behind the functioning of the crown and pinions in a car transmission. Other such representations are mental algorithms, or a kind of mental plan of the sequence of operations involved in a given task. But members of a culture or a society also have 'ideas' about every element of a technical process: raw materials, sources of energy, tools, actors, where and when things should take place, etc. A different society may have different ideas, and the reason for this is often to be found in the symbolic values each society attributes to these elements rather than in physical necessity.

Social representations of technology are therefore embedded in a broader, symbolic system: people and societies *put* meaning into the very creation, production, and development of techniques as well as *make* meaning out of existing technical elements (Hodder 1989; Miller 1994). As a result, technologies display an irreducible element of free creativity, despite material constraints, just like other social phenomena (myths, rules of marriage, religious concepts) which are also human products mediated by social representations. The sheer diversity of the components of technical systems involved in such a creative process is puzzling. Conversely, a particular technical trait may relate to various domains of social organization and culture at the same time. For instance, the fence that protects a New Guinea garden from the pigs is certainly a physical means to separate pigs from sweet potatoes. But it is also a particular way to divide and distribute human activities between several domains: pigs could be enclosed instead of gardens, but people would then have to feed them more intensively, and they would have to work more in their gardens. Furthermore, a garden fence is at once the visible mark that distinguishes a 'private' individual domain from clan or lineage land, and also something which has been built through the cooperative work of a dozen people, especially †affines.

Technological choices

This element of free creativity in material culture explains why people and groups adopt technical behaviours which seem to have absurd material results (even though they are correct and coherent in terms of the social logic of which they are a part) or why they develop techniques that fail to achieve their material goal. Needless to say, those technologies which perfectly accomplish their physical goals are also shaped by a background of wider social relations.

This leads to a dilemma, or at least to a paradox. On the one hand, as soon as one considers a particular society in a particular time and place, it appears that many techniques are far from 'rational', 'efficient', or the 'best possible'. On the other hand, if one considers the long-term *evolution of technical systems, progress is patent, if one calls humanity's increased control over wide domains of the natural and material world, or the increased productivity of labour (Mumford 1934), 'progress'. By the same token, most unadapted or odd technical procedures drop out of sight, even though people lived with these techniques, which deeply influenced their everyday life, as well as the meaning they read into the world, for years (and sometimes for centuries). Moreover, in spite of humanity's freedom in the production of technology, we have examples of ceramics, weaving, wood-working tools, agricultural practices, hunting and fishing devices, etc. from all over the world which often show amazing similarities. This results from what †Leroi-Gourhan (1943) called '*tendance*' (tendency), that is the propensity that human groups have to perform the same technical actions and to develop very similar means of performing these actions. A recurrent – and unanswered – question in the anthropology of technology is to understand how this '*tendance*' interferes with the incredible diversity of the ways cultures co-produce techniques and meaning. Are the social relations and meanings linked to technology the decisive element in its social production, or are they such a marginal aspect of innovation that at any moment technology has only a few possible lines of evolution open?

Societies seize, adopt or develop only some technical features (principles of action, artefacts, gestures), and dismiss others, because technical actions as well as changes in technology are in part determined by, and simultaneously the basis for, social representations or relations that go far beyond mere action on matter (Lemonnier 1993).

It is as though societies choose from a whole range of possible technological avenues that their environment, their own traditions and contacts with foreigners open to their means of action on the material world. The nature and range of such technical choice has recently become the subject of research which attempts to determine how and to what extent societies play with the apparently overriding laws that govern their action on the material world. Among other results, it has been shown that technological choices may well bear on items or elements of material culture which necessarily produce real physical effects, as well as those involved in some form of communication. Conversely, non-technical representations of technology are found to participate in systems of meaning by virtue of their physical (and not only their stylistic) characteristics. For instance, the strength of a New Guinean eel-trap or a garden fence may be part of the mythical representation of eels or express the strength of affinal collaboration. It it also crucial that a given feature of a technological system (a particular stone axe, a particular hunting technique, etc.) may have meaning with respect to several sets of social relations at the same time; in politics, status, or ethnic identity, for example.

A consideration of technological choices also sheds light on the issue of change and continuity in material culture, whether this involves the invention of a new element aimed at acting on matter, or its borrowing from some external source (van der Leeuw and Torrence 1989). In both cases the social context of change, and notably the 'meaning' attributed to various elements in the technological system, are crucial factors. And both processes involve, among other things, a recombination of already existing elements. Yet, technical invention differs fundamentally from technical borrowing. Borrowing involves adapting or dismissing a technical feature that already exists as such (say a tool, or a relation between a material action and a material effect), whereas invention is, by definition, a process of discovery and creation of ideas and things which were previously unknown. Fortunately, no society lives in total isolation, so that the possibility of borrowing technical features has probably always existed, which enables scholars to escape the puzzling problem of invention in non-industrial societies.

It is noteworthy that the same expertise in the study of social representations, which is basic to the social anthropology of *classification or *cognition, can be applied to technological knowledge, particularly in order to investigate the local representations of elementary principles of action on the material world : what is cutting, pressing, squeezing, punching, drilling, etc.? How do people imagine or describe the accumulation of energy, the dilutive property of water, the use of a lever, etc. Moreover, what can be investigated in anthropological case-studies is of immediate interest to *archaeologists and scholars working in the 'new' sociology of *science and technology, with which ties have been recently re-established. The study of technology is also a bridge between anthropology and other people's lives because it documents, in a very practical way, the feasibility of inserting and adapting bits of Western technology into non-Western material cultures, a recurrent issue in the anthropology of *development.

PIERRE LEMONNIER

See also: science, environment, ecological anthropology, museums, art, archeology

Further reading

Forde, C.D. (1939) *Habitat, Economy and Society*, New York: Dutton
Gille, B. (1978) *Histoire des techniques*, Paris: Gallimard
Haudricourt, A.-G. (1987) *La Technologie Science Humaine: Recherches d'Histoire et d'Ethnologie des Techniques*, Paris: Éditions de la Maison des Sciences de l'Homme
Hodder, I. (1989) *The Meanings of Things: Material Culture as Symbolic Expression*, London: Unwin Hyman
Ingold, T. (1986) *The Appropriation of Nature: Essays on Human Ecology and Social Relations*, Manchester: Manchester University Press
Latour, B. and P. Lemonnier (eds) (1994) *De la Préhistoire aux Missiles Balistiques: l'Intelligence Sociale des Techniques*, Paris: La Découverte
Lechtman, H. and R.S. Merrill (eds) (1975) *Material Culture: Style, Organization, and Dynamics of Technology*, Proceedings of the American Ethnological Society, St Paul, New York: West Publishing Co.
Lemonnier, P. (1992) *Elements for an Anthropology of Technology*, Ann Arbor: Museum of Anthropology
—— (1993) *Technological Choices: Transformation in Material Cultures since the Neolithic*, London: Routledge
Leroi-Gourhan, A. (1943) *Evolution et Techniques*, vol. 1: *L'Homme et la Matière*, vol. 2: *Milieu et Techniques*, Paris: Albin Michel
Mauss, M. ([1935] 1979) 'Techniques of the Body' in *Sociology and Psychology*, London: Routledge and Kegan Paul
Miller, D. (1994) *Modernity – An Ethnographic Approach: Dualism and Mass Consumption in Trinidad*, Oxford: Berg
Mumford, L. (1934) *Technics and Civilization*, London: Routledge
Sillitoe, P. (1988) *Made in New Guinea: Technology in the Highlands of Papua New Guinea*, London: British Museum
van der Leeuw, S. and R. Torrence (eds) (1989) *What's New: A Closer Look at the Process of Innovation*, London: Unwin Hyman

time and space

Time and space as concerns for social anthropologists derive from the work of †Durkheim and his associates such as Hubert and †Mauss (1909). But there are also important methodological issues regarding time and social anthropology which have been raised in a particularly acute way by †Bourdieu (1990).

For Durkheim time and space can only be conceived of in so far as they are mediated by *society, or rather by the †collective representations generated by, and therefore reflecting the social structure of, particular societies. Awareness of extension as space and duration as time is only possible by distinguishing different regions and moments and by encountering their associated boundaries and intervals. These divisions and distinctions have their origins in social and collective life. 'We cannot conceive of time, except on condition of distinguishing its different moments ... It is the same thing with space' (Durkheim 1915: 10–11). This kind of thinking echoes ancient Indian traditions where the Hindu temple is a map of the cosmos and a representation of the cosmogonic processes which produced the universe. The construction of a temple is then the recreation of the universe. The *Upanishads* and the *Vedas* refer to the gods measuring time and space and as a consequence creating the cosmos. The Sanskrit term referring to the temple, *vimana*, means 'well measured', or 'well proportioned'. Given the diversity of societies, and the feeling we have that time and space are somehow of cosmic and fundamental significance, Durkheim opened up the attractive prospect of exploring and documenting by empirical field research, as opposed to metaphysical speculation in the study, a vast range of radically different space-time worlds.

Space: symbolism and phenomenology

For the people of the Guinea Coast of West Africa there is a widespread cultural distinction between the space of the settlement and the space of the forest. The latter is regarded as a vastly rich and diverse life-sustaining resource, but it is also dangerous and life threatening for it is in the forest that serious injuries are most likely to occur. The relationship between settlement and forest is also temporal, both in the sense of the origin of settlements and in the dynamics of the continuing relationship between settlement and forest. Not only were houses built by founding *ancestors in a space cut out of the forest but the settlement and its inhabitants are sustained only by re-establishing a relationship between settlement and forest. Peoples' experience of the relationship between forest and settlement lies at the heart of Guinea Coast *cosmology where the relationship is a metaphor of the more abstract relationship between the visible world of mortals and the invisible world of spiritual beings.

However, the symbolism of sacred architecture and the metaphorical appropriation of the *landscape to provide the terms of an account of the ineffable are both quite compatible with a scientific concept of space whose attributes are that it is continuous, homogeneous, isotropic, and the ultimate container of all things. Some anthropologists, by exercising restraint in the resort to symbolism and metaphor, have attempted to infer from the data of their ethnographic research a †phenomenology of space which suggests that space is actually radically different for people of other cultures. Littlejohn (1963) sought to establish that for the Temne of West Africa space was neither homogeneous nor isotropic. He concluded on the basis of what Temne say and do that space for them comprises qualitatively different yet coextensive 'regions' which are actual and objectively present. These 'regions' are not mere metaphors for modes of existence, such as the English expressions 'worldly' and 'other worldly'. Temne space is identical with dream space, and consequently for Temne happenings in the one are as objectively real as happenings in the other.

Time: relativities and constants

As with space so with time, and attempts have been made to show not only that time indications and reckonings are culturally relative but also the concept of time itself. Among Nuer, †Evans-Pritchard (1940) noted that seasonal activities were used to indicate times. The time of a notable event is referred to the activities of that time, such as the formation of the early cattle camps, the time

of weeding, the time of harvesting, and so on. Likewise daily activities are timed by what Evans-Pritchard has called the 'cattle clock'. The passage of time through the day is marked by the succession of tasks which constitute the pastoral daily regime and this is used to coordinate their actions: 'I shall return at milking', 'We shall meet when the calves come home'. The Nuer year is divided into two seasons, *tot* and *mai*, but the terms refer to the cluster of social activities characteristic of the height of the dry season and the depths of the rainy season. In this sense Nuer may use the words as verbs in utterances such as 'going to *tot* (or *mai*)' in a certain place. The times correspond to localities, to village residence and to residence in the cattle camps. So far there is nothing here that is exceptional to a commonplace understanding of time. However, it may be that the quality of time in these locations and during these different periods is rather different. For example, mortuary rites are confined to the villages, as is procreation; the rites of sacrifice are also different, so that in general the experience of the cattle camp is one of affluence, and of a proximity of Divinity, a conjunction of the celestial and terrestrial. The villages, on the other hand, are dominated by production and reproduction, they are associated with birth and *death, initiation and wedding ceremonies, and therefore by a sense of transition and change. The time of the cattle camps seems to approximate to that quality of timelessness that prevailed at the beginning of time.

Despite the immense diversity of metaphors for time and of the indicators used to tell time, in the end time generally tends to be perceived as both a linear flow and as repetitive. The former is probably based in an awareness that life irreversibly moves from birth to death, from a beginning to an end, while the latter is based in the experience of periodicities such as heart beats, *menstruation, the recurrence of days and nights, of the moon, and annual seasons. For example, in Northwest Amazonia Hugh-Jones (1979) has described how for the Barasana the †patrilineal links between men of successive generations form a continuity between ancestral times and the present. This patrilineal path removes the living progressively further from the creative powers of their ancestral origins. Women, on the other hand, are symbolically associated with alternation and repetition through their being exchanged between patrilineal †exogamous groups and the periodicity of menstruation. Barasana rituals which seek to promote change and regeneration borrow extensively from female symbolism. In Papua New Guinea for the people of Umeda on the upper Sepik river, the annual *ida* ritual of regeneration, though lasting only two weeks towards the end of the dry season, is the conclusion of a period of time which began with a day and a night playing musical instruments some nine months before. Not only has the playing of the *music to be orchestrated but villagers have also to decide who will play the ritual roles of the *ida* to come, since they will immediately have to observe restrictions on their activities up to the *ida*. The ranking of these roles from junior to senior results in a personal experience of irreversible progression through the series. So though the *ida* rite is part of a repeating annual cycle, for any individual it also marks the non-recurring stages of their own maturation (Gell 1992).

Some anthropologists have been tempted to argue that in cultures where time is represented and experienced predominantly as repetitive it is conceived of as static. According to this view the return of the rainy season is literally the return of the previous rainy season, so that life is merely an alternation between two contrasting states, and time has no depth, no beginning or end. Geertz (1973) has, for example, argued that given, among other things, their complex calendar, for the Balinese time is 'a motionless present, a vectorless now'. This view has been disputed by other ethnographers of Bali who have pointed out that Balinese frequently use their calendars to calculate the passage of time (Howe 1981). The return of, for instance, the rainy season is also the appearance of another rainy season which will in due course be succeeded by yet another rainy season, and nobody has any trouble talking about the passage of rainy seasons or years. However, calendrical rituals which seek to recover the generative and life-promoting qualities of a cosmic beginning may well attempt to articulate a sense of the rites as being not only the most recent in a series of such rites but also as representing the qualities of the original creative beginning, just as the current rainy season shares attributes with all previous rainy seasons. So Barasana dancers dance the dance performed by the anaconda ancestors when they first emerged from the river and settled the land. In short, a persisting resemblance among recurrent events does not necessarily imply a conception of time as static.

†Van Gennep's ([1909] 1960) analysis of the structure of *rituals locates them at the conjunction of the spatial and temporal dimensions of social life. The three fundamental components of what he called *rites de passage* – separation, liminality, and incorporation – appeal to both spatial and temporal metaphors. Rites bringing about a change in the social status of an individual, or group of individuals, will not only involve crossing thresholds, such as from the interior of a dwelling to the exterior, from the village into the forest, but these will also take place at dusk, or at dawn, between the dry season and the wet season, etc. In so doing these rituals also bring about the differentiation and therefore the recognition of time and space. It has been suggested that the liminal phase of *rites de passage* may be characterized by the reversal of the normal profane flow of time. The evidence for this is that normal conduct is reversed: juniors take precedence over seniors, women dress as men and vice versa, normally invisible spirits appear in the village while people disappear in the forest, and so on. But such an inference is unfounded. There is no reason to suppose that the people carrying out the rite perceive time to be flowing backwards during a period of licensed deviance. Indeed, if time were perceived to be flowing back then they would return to the first phase of the ritual rather than progress to the last, and they would never accomplish what the ritual project set out to achieve.

Time and space, practice and structure

Finally, time has become a matter of theoretical interest for social anthropologists not only as a matter to be studied in its cultural representations, but also as a methodological issue in the practice of anthropological research and in the writing of anthropological accounts. Bourdieu (1990) in his critique of, for example, the *structuralist analysis of the social significance of gift *exchange, has pointed out that the giving, receiving, and the return of gifts is not the outcome of the autonomous workings of some abstracted and synchronic 'law of reciprocity', but rather is a consequence of the political judgement of the agents involved as regards the timing of the giving of the initial gift and then of the counter gift. Without the lapse of time between the gift and the counter gift, a lapse of time which is a matter of the agents' judgement, the exchange could not function. Bourdieu's argument is part of a more general critique of the possibility of a science of social practice. Structural analysis deals with a

†synchronic virtual reality which tends to privilege spatial relations and their analogues in such forms as synoptic tables, diagrams (structures) and figures, while †practice, which includes anthropological practice, necessarily unfolds in time and has all the properties which synchronic structures cannot take into account, such as directionality and irreversibility.

M.C. JEDREJ

See also: landscape, house, history and anthropology

Further reading

Bourdieu, P. (1990) *The Logic of Practice*, Cambridge: Polity Press

Durkheim, É. (1915) *The Elementary Forms of the Religious Life*, London: George Allen and Unwin

Evans-Pritchard, E.E. (1940) *The Nuer*, Oxford: Clarendon Press

Geertz, C. (1973) *The Interpretation of Culture*, New York: Basic Books

Gell, A. (1992) *The Anthropology of Time*, Oxford: Berg

Hubert, H. and M. Mauss (1909) 'Études sommaire de la représentation du temps dans la religion et la magie', *Melanges d'histoire des religions*, Travaux del'Année Sociologique, Paris: Alcan

Hugh-Jones, C. (1979) *From the Milk River: Spatial and Temporal Processes on Northwest Amazonia*, Cambridge: Cambridge University Press

Howe, L. (1981) 'The Social Determination of Knowledge: Maurice Bloch and Balinese Time', *Man* (n.s.) 16: 220–34

Littlejohn, J. (1963) 'Temne Space', *Anthropological Quarterly* 36: 17

Munn, N. (1992) 'The Cultural Anthropology of Time', *Annual Review of Anthropology* 21: 93–123

van Gennep, A. ([1909] 1960) *The Rites of Passage*, Chicago: University of Chicago Press

totemism

The term 'totamism' first appeared in print in 1791. The trader James Long related how an Ojibwa hunter, having 'accidentally' killed a bear, was accosted by an avenging bear who demanded an explanation. Although the Indian's apology was accepted, he remained disturbed, telling Long (1791): 'Beaver, my faith is lost, my *totam* is angry, I shall never be able to hunt any more'.

On the basis of comparable reports, J.F. McLennan (1869) posited a worldwide reverence for the 'mystical power' of living things, arguing that 'there is no race of men that has not come through this primitive stage of speculative belief'.

Thinkers then developed an elaborate scheme linking descent from animal *ancestors, food-taboos, †exogamy and 'the matriarchal stage of culture' (Haddon 1902: 7n). A 'totemic' community was envisaged as divided into clans, each named after a totem or animal ancestor. Morality was reducible to two prohibitions: against eating the totem; and against marriage within the clan. For †Sigmund Freud ([1913] 1965), †Émile Durkheim ([1912] 1965) and †James Frazer (1910), this was humanity's first religion.

The topic perplexed theoreticians well into the twentieth century. *Radcliffe-Brown's first, *functionalist theory ([1929] 1952) explained totemic 'reverence as reflecting species' economic importance. His second (1951) anticipated *structuralism. Certain *Aboriginal Australian tribes, he observed, had matrimoieties called 'Eaglehawk' and 'Crow'. These species provided useful 'totems' because they were conceptualizable, like the moieties, as 'opposites', mythology making of the carrion-eating Crow a selfish meat-thief in contrast to Eaglehawk, a generous hunter.

Earlier, however, †Alexander Goldenweiser (1910) had concluded that so-called 'totemic' phenomena were 'conglomerates of independent features', associated – if at all – only by history and chance. This attack on totemism as a valid category culminated in *Claude Lévi-Strauss's *Totemism* ([1962] 1969). Whilst accepting that 'names' may be termed 'totemic', Lévi-Strauss dismissed any intrinsic link with food/sex taboos as a fantasy of nineteenth-century bigots, much like the 'hysteria' of contemporary medical prejudice.

In arguing this point *Totemism* begins with a discussion of Long's 1791 account. Lévi-Strauss asserts that 'all the food tabus reported from the Ojibwa derive from the *manido* system', which is entirely distinct from the system of totemic names (1969: 91). A 'Bear' man should therefore feel free to hunt bears. Admittedly, Long had reported the reverse. But he must have been 'confused' (p. 92). Among the Ojibwa as elsewhere, Lévi-Strauss asserts, people can be *named* after a species without feeling any guilt about *eating* it. He insisted that naming systems are purely 'mental': in them, species are chosen not because 'good to eat' or 'good to prohibit' but simply because 'good to think' – natural distinctions serving as a useful model for social ones.

We need not follow Lévi-Strauss as he surveys the world, carefully excluding peoples' food avoidances from what he defines as their 'totemism'. This is, after all, a question of personal definition. What matters is whether the earlier writers were correct in discerning some unity of principle linking (a) the identification of one's kin-group with a natural species and (b) the idea that a creature once defined as 'kin' must be 'respected' accordingly. In denying any such internal logic, Lévi-Strauss misleadingly overstated his case.

To choose a natural species as one's emblem – as Lévi-Strauss himself acknowledges – is to identify with it. Representatives of that species may then become 'kin', the corresponding rules of 'avoidance' logically applying. †Margaret Mead's (1935: 83) Arapesh informants explained incest avoidance by reciting:

> Your own mother,
> Your own sister,
> Your own pigs,
> Your own yams that you have piled up,
> You may not eat.
> Other people's mothers,
> Other people's sisters,
> Other people's pigs,
> Other people's yams that they have piled up,
> You may eat.

Recall that the Ojibwa word *ototeman* (hence 'totem') means, simply, 'uterine kin' (Hewitt in Hodge [1910: 2, 787–8]). In many traditional cultures, one's kin are one's 'flesh', just as is one another's produce. Morality is rooted in the principle that 'one's own flesh is for *others* to enjoy'. Consequently, a man may selfishly abuse neither the species he hunts, nor his female kin: the two avoidances are one. This principle is neither hallucinatory, nor a matter of mere classification. It reflects a morality acknowledged by humanity for millennia (Knight 1991). With an insistence too widespread and a simplicity too stunning to be attributed to mere historical contingency, the 'own flesh' rule links food with sex, economics with *kinship, *myth with *ritual, thought with real life. And with all the connotations and ambiguities lent it by usage over the years, the old-fashioned term 'totemism' still evokes this moral unity more tellingly than any other expression we have.

CHRIS KNIGHT

See also: evolution and evolutionism, primitive mentality, classification, myth and mythology, incest, taboo

Further reading

Durkheim, É. ([1912] 1965) *The Elementary Forms of the Religious Life*, New York: Free Press

Frazer, J.G. (1910) *Totemism and Exogamy* (4 vols), London: Macmillan

Freud, S. ([1913] 1965) *Totem and Taboo: Some Points of Agreement Between the Mental Lives of Savages and Neurotics*, London: Routledge

Goldenweiser, A.A. (1910) 'Totemism, an Analytical Study', *Journal of American Folklore* 23: 179–293

Haddon, A.C. (1902) *Presidential Address to the Anthropological Section, H, of the British Association for the Advancement of Science*, Belfast, pp. 8–11

Hodge, F.W. (ed.) (1910) *Handbook of American Indians North of Mexico*, (2 vols), Bulletin of the Bureau of American Ethnology 30, Washington DC: Smithsonian Institution

Knight, C.D. (1991) *Blood Relations: Menstruation and the Origins of Culture*, New Haven and London: Yale University Press

Lévi-Strauss, C. ([1962] 1969) *Totemism*, Harmondsworth: Penguin

Long, J. (1791) *Voyages and Travels of an Indian Interpreter and Trader*, London

McLennan, J.F. (1869) 'The Worship of Animals and Plants. Part 1' *The Fortnightly Review* (n.s.) 6: 407–27

Mead, M. (1935) *Sex and Temperament in Three Primitive Societies*, London: Routledge

Radcliffe-Brown, A.R. ([1929] 1952) 'The Sociological Theory of Totemism', in A.R. Radcliffe-Brown *Structure and Function in Primitive Society*, London: Cohen & West (reprinted from *Proceedings of the Fourth Pacific Science Congress*, Java)

—— (1951) 'The Comparative Method in Social Anthropology', *Journal of the Royal Anthropological Institute* 81: 15–22

tourism

In spite of the enormous importance of tourism in the world economy and its great significance for students of social change and culture contact, the anthropology of tourism has only really developed since the 1970s. Until that relatively recent past, tourism was not regarded as a central or even serious field in anthropology, yet it is a fascinating subject which raises a number of theoretical questions at the very heart of anthropology.

If one defines tourism simply as travelling for pleasure, certain interesting characteristics of tourism as a special form of social relations emerge:

1 Tourism implies transience. It is a form of temporary *nomadism in which tourists step out of their normal life and social setting, and interact

with natives on their home grounds. In Jafar Jafari's terms, the tourist space is the intersection of the tourist's extraordinary life with the native's ordinary one (Jafari 1987).

2 Tourism is characterized by encounters between strangers who do not expect a long-lasting relationship and whose transactions tend to be instrumental, limited in their aim, not repeated, and, hence, open to mutual attempts at manipulation for short-term gains (a situation often defined as being cheated or exploited).

3 Tourists and natives are almost always quite different from one another in culture, language, religion, social class and a variety of other social and cultural characteristics. Indeed, it is often these very differences that make natives interesting to tourists. *Ethnic* tourism especially is a search for the exotic other.

4 Because of these cultural and social differences between tourists and natives, tourism is a form of ethnic relations where communication is frequently impeded or truncated by language barriers and multiple forms of misunderstandings and breeches of normal rules of interaction. Tourist relations are thus commonly unchartered or subject to simplified or truncated codes of interaction, such as the use of pidgin or sign language. Mutual stereotypes, irritation and low expectations often result, but also pleasure and amusement at the unexpected and unfamiliar. Tourists and natives make a spectacle of themselves to each other, in ways that are often more self-conscious than in normal day-to-day interaction.

5 Tourist-native interactions are not only qualitatively truncated but spatially segregated in most cases. The vast majority of tourists concentrate in a limited number of 'points of interest' and in a small range of specialized facilities (hotels, restaurants, travel agencies, means of transport). A few tourists seek, however, to penetrate beyond this tourist frontstage.

6 Tourist-native interactions are characterized by countervailing asymmetries. Tourists almost always enjoy more leisure and discretionary income than most natives. The bulk of tourists come from the rich countries or from the privileged classes of the poorer countries (Turner and Ash 1976). Tourist wealth and high status are often resented by natives, and put tourists in an advantageous position. On the other hand, natives can take advantage of tourists through their much greater knowledge of local conditions, prices, services and the like.

7 Many tourists seek both an escape from their normal life and an authentic experience of the exotic (in such matters as climate, fauna, flora, architecture, archeology, cuisine, music, and 'local colour'). However, the presence of tourists frequently compromises the authenticity of the tourist experience (MacCannell 1989). Thus most tourists resent other tourists, and are irritated at being treated as tourists, yet also seek each other's company for security, and exchange of information and experience.

8 The tourist quest for authenticity generates what MacCannell called 'staged authenticity', that is, cultural artefacts, performances and behaviours that will be accepted by tourists as authentic or at least a reasonable facsimile of the pre-tourist situation. Sometimes, staged authenticity (e.g. theatrical performances, concerts, dances, sculptures, weavings, pottery) can lead to a cultural renaissance of native traditions, to a renewal of ethnic consciousness, and even to the invention of new traditions and new identities.

Tourism, in short, can produce extremely complex situations of culture change and shifting ethnic boundaries, both phenomena of great interest to anthropologists. In the modern world, tourism, along with permanent migration, has become one of the most dynamic sources for the destruction, blending, modification and creation of culture. Tourism is a special form of temporary migration that puts different peoples, their languages, their artefacts and their thoughts in massive contact with one another. Inevitably, tourism affects many aspects of life beyond what one usually thinks of as tourism: tastes, styles, trade, politics, gender roles, race and ethnic relations, and many other domains of daily existence. To ignore tourism in our accounts of culture contact in the twentieth century is probably as great an omission as to ignore *slavery in the eighteenth century or *colonialism in the nineteenth. Indeed, tourism can even be seen as a mirror of anthropology itself: both constitute a quest for the other. In a sense, ethnic tourism is amateur anthropology, or anthropology professional tourism. Perhaps, in the end, we all yearn to achieve better self-understanding by looking at others.

PIERRE L. VAN DEN BERGHE

See also: complex societies, world system

Further reading

MacCannell, D. (1989) *The Tourist*, New York: Schocken

Nash, D. and V. L. Smith (1991) 'Anthropology and Tourism', *Annals of Tourism Research* 18 (1): 12–25

Smith, V.L. (ed.) (1989) *Hosts and Guests: The Anthropology of Tourism,* Philadelphia: University of Pennsylvania Press

Turner, L. and J. Ash (eds) (1976) *The Golden Hordes: International Tourism and the Pleasure Periphery*, New York: St Martin's Press

transhumance

Transhumance, seasonal movement from one climatic zone to another, allows people to use beneficial aspects of their environment while avoiding some of its dangers. The word 'transhumance' is indigenous to French and Spanish and is generally applied to the movement of livestock herds of cattle, sheep, and goats to mountains in summer and to valleys or plains in winter. As livestock is a major element in the economic production of many rural communities – providing milk, cheese, butter, meat, skins, wool, and monetary income, and until the twentieth century traction and transport – measures such as transhumance to safeguard the well-being of the animals and improve their productivity are actively pursued.

The culturally established or institutionalized adaptive technique or strategy of transhumance moves livestock to avoid dangerous climatic extremes, the hot temperatures of lowland summers and the cold temperatures of highland winters. At the same time, livestock are provided with the best available pasture, the fresh grass or bushes of highland summer when lowland pasture has been grazed or has dried up, and lowland pasture or fodder when the highland pasture is frozen or under snow. The movement of the livestock allows use of a larger territory, thus providing more pasture area and nourishment per animal and a larger herd or flock than spatial stability would allow.

Transhumance is one pattern of *pastoralism, because it uses natural, unimproved pasture for raising livestock. However, many livestock breeders, such as Swiss villagers dwelling in high valleys, also provide cultivated fodder for their animals, particularly in winter. Transhumance cannot be considered *nomadism if the family residence and community remains stable, as is usually the case in Europe, only designated individuals transhuming with the livestock. Some nomadic peoples, whose entire communities and populations migrate, such as the Sarakatsani of Northern Greece and the large Bakhtiari, Qashqai and Basseri tribes of the Zagros mountains in Western Iran, regularly make seasonal changes of altitude which could be considered transhumance.

In European transhumance, the village may be in a valley and transhumance is to high summer pastures, as is often the case in Western Europe, or the village may be in the mountains and transhumance is to lowland winter pastures, as is often the case in Mediterranean Europe. In either pattern, transhumance involves extensive land use of large tracts of territory, intensive, around-the-clock labour of herding, milking and supervision, and the spatial separation, sometimes for long periods, of herders from their families and communities.

Although the availability of motorized vehicles in recent decades has, at least in Europe, made possible daily commuting to distant pastures, various other factors have led to the decline of transhumance: the intensification of agriculture and reduced relative cost of fodder; the industrialization of dairying; the loss of coastal winter pastures to agriculture and tourism; and lucrative, alternative employment possibilities outside of traditional agricultural production.

PHILIP CARL SALZMAN

See also: ecological anthropology, pastoralism

Further reading

Angioni, G. (1989) *I pascoli erranti: Antropologia del pastore in Sardegna*, Naples: Liguori

Campbell, J.K. (1964) *Honour, Family and Patronage: A Study of Institutions and Moral Values in a Greek Mountain Community*, Oxford: Clarendon Press

Galaty, J.G. and D.L. Johnson (eds) (1990) *The World of Pastoralism: Herding Systems in Comparative Perspective*, New York and London: The Guilford Press

Ravis-Giordani, G. (1983) *Bergers corses: Les communautés villageoises du Niolu*, Aix-en-Provence: Edisud

translation

The concept of translation is a long-established one across many disciplines, with the distinctive anthropological contribution being an emphasis on the *social* nature of translation and on the many-layered nature of meaning.

First, a common metaphor for the anthropologist's task has come to be that of a 'translation' from one culture to another. However it is also accepted that this is a problematic and controversial process, in philosophical, practical and ethical or political terms. Thus there have been as many explicit (and implicit) approaches to 'cultural translation' as there have been contrasting theoretical positions throughout the history of anthropology.

Second, there is the more literal sense of the translation of verbal texts from one language (or sometimes †dialect) to another – something most anthropologists in practice engage in. This is not straighforward either, and many anthropologists now explicitly recognize the complexities of translating, inspired particularly by the work of American and Scandinavian literary-linguistic anthropologists on verbal art, *oral literature, and so on (for a summary see Finnegan 1992, ch. 9). Many of the issues turn on the differing theories about the nature of *language and communication, and therefore about what it is that is being 'translated'. There is also the issue of whose voice is being represented, and for what audience. Recent approaches challenge the notion of 'literal' translation and often focus on the expressive and †performative aspects, arguing, for example, that translation should not be just into a bare verbal text, but also try to recreate some of the performance and contextual features (see Tedlock 1971 for a classic statement). There is also now increasing awareness of the ethical and political

dimensions of translation: the translators may be in a position of power or take a particular viewpoint on contested views of linguistic usage. Some translators in the past have given a very derogatory and 'primitive' impression of the original authors, particularly in cases where the multi-media channel of an oral performance is 'translated' into the single-channel medium of print.

Finally, the social process of translation can itself be the subject of anthropological study (for example Sherzer 1990: 36ff): there is a need for more ethnographic work on this intriguing subject.

RUTH FINNEGAN

See also: emic and etic, fieldwork, relativism

Further reading

Feleppa, R. (1988) *Convention, Translation, and Understanding: Philosophical Problems in the Comparative Study of Culture*, Albany: State University of New York Press

Finnegan, R. (1992) *Oral Traditions and the Verbal Arts. A Guide to Research Practices*, ASA Research Methods Series, London: Routledge

Hymes, D.H. (1981) *'In Vain I Tried to Tell You': Essays in Native American Ethnopoetics*, Philadelphia: University of Pennsylvania Press

Pálsson, G. (ed.) (1993) *Beyond Boundaries. Understanding, Translation and Anthropological Discourse*, Oxford: Berg

Sherzer, J. (1990) *Verbal Art in San Blas*, Cambridge: Cambridge University Press

Swann, B. (ed.) (1992) *On the Translation of Native American Literatures*, Washington and London: Smithsonian Institution Press

Tedlock, D. (1971) 'On the Translation of Style in Oral Narrative', *Journal of American Folklore* 84: 114–33

U

urban anthropology

Perhaps the most telling feature of anthropological studies in urban sites is the lack of precedence accorded to *kinship (e.g. Finnegan 1989; Geertz 1960; Whyte 1943). As opposed to the classic *ethnography of the Iroquois, Todas, Trobriand Islanders or Nuer – societies in which nearly all an informant's †consociates may be placed on a cognitive grid of kin, clan and affine – in urban locales it is relationships ordered in other ways that assume centrality in everyday life. This is not to say that kinship is unimportant in cities or that anthropologists do not study it there; it is, and they do. Urban anthropology, however, has foregrounded forms and principles of human organization beyond kinship in order to depict the full complexity of social life in towns and cities.

Urban anthropologists have pursued their objectives with both bottom-up and top-down approaches. Traditions of research that document the micro-terrains of daily life are well established in studies of *migration, social *networks, streetcorner cliques, neighbourhoods, political processes, traders and entrepreneurs, careers, *patron-client relations, voluntary associations, religious congregations, public ceremonies, urban festivals, bureaucratic encounters and social movements. And so are more holistic attempts to elaborate forms and qualities of urbanism, the rural-urban continuum, diverse heterogenetic and traditional orthogenetic urban centres, regional and transnational social orders, marketing networks, dimensions of scale and specialization, spatial symbolism, and the cross-cultural domains of urban life. In short, there has evolved both anthropology in the city, and of the city.

Lineages of urban anthropology

*Fieldwork by anthropologists in urban locales began in the 1930s and 1940s, with its theoretical direction set mainly by the social anthropology of *A.R. Radcliffe-Brown and *Bronislaw Malinowski. During these decades the ethnographic method of participant observation was used by †W. Lloyd Warner and his students in 'Yankee City', Chicago and Natchez, Mississippi; by †Robert Redfield and associates in Yucatan; and by William F. Whyte in Boston (1943), Edward Spicer among the Yaqui in Tucson, Arizona, Horace Miner in Timbuctoo, William Bascom in Ife, †Godfrey Wilson in Zambia, and Ellen Hellmann and †Bengt Sundkler in South Africa. This work shared inspiration with contemporaneous studies of *peasant and rural communities in Europe, North America, Japan and China, and of †acculturation to *colonialism among kin-ordered 'tribal' peoples.

This research in towns and cities (not then called or thought of as a separate 'urban anthropology') also had non-anthropological roots. The most important were in the University of Chicago sociological tradition of research into the neighbourhoods and institutions of that city initiated by Robert Park after World War I (Hannerz 1980). Drawing upon the nineteenth-century British social survey methods of Charles Booth and others, and influenced by continental European social theorists, Park and his colleagues moved in an ethnographic direction as they studied immigrant communities, neighbourhood zones and leisure life. They tied their work to an overarching theory of industrial city organization and concentric outward growth. Though never acknowledged, this theory is largely anticipated in †Frederick Engels's analysis (1969 [1892]) of the impact of capitalism on Manchester in the 1840s.

The first academic application of Booth's approach in the USA, however, was W.E.B. Du Bois's *The Philadelphia Negro* (1899). Also influenced like Park by the new settlement house movement, this study was undertaken two decades before the Chicago work was to begin. Du Bois, the first African-American Harvard PhD, was a historian and his Philadelphia study drew as much on documentary historical contextualization as on statistical analysis of his extensive interviews. Although he lived in the neighbourhood he studied, direct insights from participant observation are few; they appear mainly in passages on churches, social classes and amusements, and race prejudice. Nonetheless, in articulating the informant's point of view, and in enriching theoretical analysis of racial division (a major non-kin principle of human organization in contemporary complex societies), Du Bois's community study had lasting impact, as was evident in the Warner-sponsored studies of *race by Allison Davis and St. Clair Drake during the 1930s (see Harrison 1988).

Urban anthropology heydays and aftermath

In 1963 the phrase 'urban anthropology' appeared in print; and essay collections, textbooks and the journal *Urban Anthropology* (1972–) followed in the 1970s. During the 1960s and 1970s students could also wade into a powerful stream of new urban ethnographic monographs that sparkled with theoretical, substantive and methodological ideas. From the mid-1950s on, Africa was particularly well-represented. Most notable of all was the set of studies of urban Copperbelt and rural communities in Central Africa, the work of several Manchester anthropologists attached to the †Rhodes-Livingstone Institute in Zambia (see Hannerz 1980). Other urban ethnographies concerned neighbourhoods, social groups and cultural processes in the USA, Britain, Latin America and Asia.

The distinctive features of this body of work are discussed by Richard Fox (1977) under the topical headings of urbanism, urban subcultures and urbanization. *Urbanism* stands for the top-down approach, the investigation of city-centred societal processes, schemes of role differentiation and interpersonal relations, and historical typologies of cities (the major concern of Fox's book, which identifies regal-ritual, administrative, mercantile, colonial and industrial city types). The bottom-up focus on *urban subcultures* is applied by

Fox principally to studies in Western cities, particularly of the poor and racialized groups. Research in this category should also include ethnographic accounts of closely-knit urban neighbourhoods (see Whyte 1943), sometimes inappropriately termed 'urban villages', and of *class-linked cultures, well-exemplified in several Asian urban ethnographies (including Geertz 1960). Studies of *urbanization* deal with cityward movement and modes of settlement; those of the 1950s-1970s urban anthropology heydays concerned Third World 'peasants in cities', the 'adaptive functions' of kinship and voluntary associations, and the persistence and creation of ethnic identities and political organization.

During the 1980s, gaps in the urban anthropology agenda were filled by an efflorescence of urban ethnography (Sanjek 1990). Much of this work was responsive more to wider theoretical currents in the discipline than to themes raised in the heyday period, or in its appraisals by Fox (1977) and Hannerz (1980). Accordingly, by 1990 concern with the poor and migrants was balanced by studies of established working and middle classes, élites, and policy makers; an urban anthropology of work complemented attention to residential settings; *gender, sexuality, life cycle stages, and learning processes received ethnographic scrutiny; and urban politics, *religion, health care and popular culture became issues for intensive fieldwork. In addition, the earlier attention to urban order and connectedness was complemented in studies of ephemeral and tangential relationships, particularly in research on homeless persons, the elderly and household workers.

Theoretical accomplishments

In papers spanning the 1960s, 1970s and 1980s, Anthony Leeds (1994) offered both critique and re-orientation to the self-identified subfield of urban anthropology. Leeds insisted that urban society begins with formation of the *state, and includes all interlocked specialized sites (of food production, mining, administration, exchange, education, worship, etc.), whether located in countryside or city. He directed attention to trans-local processes like taxation and trade, and to extra-local control of *land tenure, labour markets and military force. It was to regional and transnational flows of labour, *commodities, credit, information and cash that Leeds urged scrutiny from all anthropologists working in complex societies, and which he illuminated in his own writings on Brazil and Portugal.

Leeds's approach to *power in urban social orders dissolves this unitary concept into three different forms. First he identifies the 'supralocal' power of resources (capital, credit, corporations, government institutions, police) controlled by the upper class and its élites. Against this stands the power of numbers, particularly mobilizable for voting, protest and direct action by the urban working class and poor. Mediating these forms of power is the 'lubricatory' power of middle-class bureaucratic, technical, informational and legal expertise. In contemporary states, this form of power has its own institutional bases, and while normally used to support the power of resources, it may be enlisted to support the power of numbers. Leeds sees conflict in urban society as arising repeatedly between the power of numbers (in emergent forms of cross-locality mass organization – labour unions, neighbourhood alliances, social movements) and the opposed forms of power centred in the state and the classes it serves.

As Leeds's work distills significant top-down urban anthropological theorizing, that of Ulf Hannerz (1980) presents an important bottom-up perspective. Hannerz envisions *persons as moving sequentially through situations, each of which has its interpenetrating analytic aspects of behavioural performance, consciousness and potential re-allocation of resources. The roles persons create through continuous situational involvement are assigned by Hannerz to five discrete domains: provisioning (production), *household and kinship (social reproduction), leisure, neighbouring and traffic (routine but impersonal urban contacts). The content and relative volume of situations in each domain vary from city to city, and with different forms of urbanism (Fox's five city types, for example).

An impressive application of Hannerz's viewpoint is contained in Ruth Finnegan's *The Hidden Musicians* (1989), an ethnography of the leisure domain of amateur *music-making (rock, folk, classical, etc) in a British town. Participants in musical groups travel individually to locations of practice and performance; few groups are neighbourhood-based, and only in brass bands does kinship connect any members. Interaction is limited mainly to musical activities; most musicians do not interact with others in non-musical situations, but instead have different sets of consociates. Nor do groups last forever, and persons move in and out of them while they do. As with members of many urban congregations, associations, political organizations and leisure groups, the amateur musicians are linked by practice and not by enduring multiplex relationships. Each follows their own urban pathway, moving through situations and domains that vary in intimacy, continuity, predictability and symbolic elaboration.

Depending upon the significant theories determining their research goals, urban anthropologists follow urban pathways by fieldwork at selected stopping points (as did Finnegan), through tracing individual networks (Whyte 1943), or with a combination of interviews and participant observation (Geertz 1960).

Anthropology in an urban world

By the end of the 1990s, more than half the world's six billion people will live in cities. The proportion of city dwellers will slope upward even further in the next century. Many anthropologists with no special interests in urbanism already do fieldwork in cities and more will follow. But for those committed to continuing interplay between bottom-up and top-down urban anthropological approaches, there are several important areas for research.

The Cold War cut off Western anthropologists from fieldwork in socialist cities in several world areas (Sanjek 1990). As they now enter these locales and interact with new colleagues, comparative issues of how urban life is organized and governed under planned and free-market regimes need to be addressed.

By the year 2000, six cities will contain more than fifteen million people, and scores of others will house millions. With this vast on-going expansion of urban space, countless human beings will leave or be displaced from familiar places and create attachments to new ones. The psychological, symbolic and political processes involved in this culturalization (and deculturalization) of space and place are fertile soil for urban anthropology (Rodman 1992).

Finally, the quality that Indonesians call *ramé*, 'the crowds, the helter-skelter, and the constant buzz of joking conversation' (Geertz 1960: 49) – what Brazilians term *movimento* or Americans 'streetlife' – both attracts many urban residents and repels others. This quality epitomizes the tension between vitality and order, masses and élites, creators and commercializers. It remains the quintessence of urban existence yet elusive to urban anthropology.

ROGER SANJEK

See also: community, complex society, ethnography, great and little traditions, markets, migration, network analysis, political economy, world system

Further reading

Du Bois, W.E.B. (1899) *The Philadelphia Negro: A Social Study*, New York: Schocken

Engels, Frederick (1969 [1892]) *The Condition of the Working Class in England*, London: Panther

Finnegan, R. (1989) *The Hidden Musicians: Music-Making in an English Town*, Cambridge: Cambridge University Press

Fox, R. (1977) *Urban Anthropology: Cities in their Cultural Context*, Engelwood Cliffs: Prentice-Hall

Geertz, C. (1960) *The Religion of Java*, Glencoe, IL: Free Press

Hannerz, U. (1980) *Exploring the City: Inquiries Toward an Urban Anthropology*, New York: Columbia University Press

Harrison, F.V. (1988) 'An African Diaspora Perspective for Urban Anthropology', *Urban Anthropology* 17 (2-3): 111–41

Leeds, A. (1994) *Cities, Classes, and the Social Order*, R. Sanjek (ed.), Ithaca, NY: Cornell University Press

Rodman, M. (1992) 'Empowering Place: Multilocality and Multivocality', *American Anthropologist* 94: 640–56

Sanjek, R. (1990) 'Urban Anthropology in the 1980s: A World View', *Annual Review of Anthropology* 19: 151–86

Whyte, W.F. (1943) *Street Corner Society: The Social Structure of an Italian Slum*, Chicago: University of Chicago Press

V

violence

Just as violence has long been taken to be a sign of the primitive, the savage or the uncivilized, or alternatively of the deviant, the individual and the unsocialized, so anthropology has long been concerned to show that violence obeys rules, is part of culture, and even fulfils certain social functions. Classic *functionalist accounts of institutions such as the feud (e.g. Gluckman 1956), stress that feuds bind people together, through the shared norms and expectations that participants invoke, even as they appear to divide them. But, despite this well-worn interpretive path, violence retains its capacity to unsettle and disturb.

Theoretically, violence lurks behind many important anthropological conceptions of the human and the social. Violence represents 'natural' drives which society must tame and repress if it is to survive: this broad idea can be found in Western political philosophy (classically in †Hobbes), as well as in Freudian *psychoanalysis, in †Durkheim's notion of humans as 'homo duplex', in †Mauss's implicit argument in his essay on *The Gift* that gifts are society's means of overcoming the inevitability of war. From these perspectives emerges the linked notion of *society, or most often the *state, as the monopolist of 'legitimate' violence. The place of violence as a sign of the natural and unsocialized is even more marked in its prominence in *sociobiological arguments about human nature and genetics, such as those employed by Chagnon in the complex controversy about Yanomamo violence in lowland *South America (Chagnon 1988; Lizot 1994). Not surprisingly, such emphases have generated a counter-literature in which ethnographic examples are employed to suggest that peaceful sociability is the 'natural' condition (cf. Howell and Willis 1989).

Anthropology's most useful contribution has probably been its documentation of the fact that violence is pre-eminently collective rather than individual, social rather than asocial or anti-social, usually culturally structured and always culturally interpreted. This was already implicit in functionalist interpretations of violence, but in recent years it has been greatly extended as anthropologists have reported the experience and interpretation of violence from the point of view of (among many others) paramilitaries in Northern Ireland (Feldman 1991), Indian riot victims (Das 1990), and torture survivors in Sri Lanka (Daniel 1994). Here the anthropology of violence becomes part of a new anthropology of the *body, in which the body becomes a privileged site for the inscription of signs of *power.

What is harder to escape is the assumption that questions about violence are inevitably questions about human nature. Simon Harrison (1989), writing about the Avatip of the Sepik River area of New Guinea, argues that the Avatip distinguish between two types of sociality linked to two different concepts of the *person. The unmarked type, so to speak, is one in which everyday social relations are lived in an idiom of peaceful equality; the other type of sociality, encountered in the world of men's politics and men's *warfare, is marked by assertion, aggression and potentially uncontrollable violence. This second type is not, however, treated as a natural property of men, but rather as something which has to be created and sustained in ritual action. In order to perform those acts of violence which warfare requires (and warfare itself is politically necessary if Avatip society is not to descend into entropy), Avatip men have to acquire the capacity to be violent.

Harrison's argument is an excellent example of the way in which cultural accounts of other people's ideas about violence, *gender and personhood can serve to undermine powerful Western assumptions about human nature. Such cultural accounts do not, though, clarify any of the definitional confusions in the analysis of violence. Even in societies with an explicit concept which we could translate as 'violence', not all acts involving the deliberate inflicting of physical pain, marking or damage to another's body are defined as 'violent'. Are *sacrifice, †circumcision, tattooing, fighting, and biomedical procedures ranging from appendectomy to electro-convulsive therapy, all usefully classifiable as acts of 'violence'? Do we dismiss acts of *witchcraft and sorcery which are clearly intended to cause bodily harm, even if we doubt their efficacy? What of attempts to break down such literal assessments of violence, like †Bourdieu's use of the term 'symbolic violence' to refer to acts of coercion which are usually unaccompanied by overt physical violence? One way to imagine an anthropology of violence is to see it as a kind of mapping of the different moral and aesthetic evaluations people in different contexts make of their actions on the bodies of others.

Precisely because violence has such a central position in Western theories of power and human nature, anthropological evidence has an important capacity to disturb and unsettle our received understanding of violence. It is hard, though, to imagine such disparate evidence leading to a new anthropological synthesis, in which violence remains as central and as unquestioned. Instead, the broad category of 'violence' seems to contain particularly valuable evidence which can help us to explore the links between two connected aspects of human life: what Mauss called the 'techniques of the body'; and the intersubjective world of signs and communications.

JONATHAN SPENCER

See also: body, sacrifice, war, warfare

Further reading

Chagnon, N. (1988) 'Life Histories, Blood Revenge, and Warfare in a Tribal Population', *Science* 239: 985–92

Daniel, E.V. (1994) 'The Individual in Terror' in T. Csordas (ed.) *Embodiment and Experience*, Cambridge: Cambridge University Press

Das, V. (ed.) (1990) *Mirrors of Violence: Communities, Riots and Survivors in South Asia*, Delhi: Oxford University Press

Feldman, A. (1991) *Formations of Violence: The Narrative of the Body and Political Terror in Northern Ireland*, Chicago: University of Chicago Press

Gluckman, M. (1956) *Custom and Conflict in Africa*, Oxford: Blackwell

Harrison, S. (1989) 'The Symbolic Construction of Aggression and War in a Sepik River Society', *Man* (n.s.) 24 (4): 583–99

Howell, S. and R. Willis (eds) (1989) *Societies at Peace: Anthropological Perspectives*, London: Routledge

Lizot, J. (1994) 'On Warfare: An Answer to N.A. Chagnon', *American Ethnologist* 21: 841–58

Riches, D. (ed.) (1986) *The Anthropology of Violence*, Oxford: Blackwell

war, warfare

Social scientists have proposed many different definitions of war over the years. But those definitions put forward by anthropologists usually envision war as a particular type of political relationship between groups, in which the groups use, or threaten to use, lethal force against each other in pursuit of their aims. Warfare is therefore distinct from other kinds of hostile or violent behaviour because war is made by organized collectivities rather than by individuals, and for collective ends rather than merely personal ones. To define war in this way has the very fundamental implication that the causes of war must lie in the nature of these collectivities and not in the individual.

Anthropologists have accordingly tended to reject theories based on notions of a death drive, killer instinct, or some other innate destructive or aggressive predisposition. Such theories are useless for answering the sorts of questions that anthropologists have considered central: why the frequency and intensity of war vary across time and space; why war does not occur at all in some societies; and why, where it does occur, it assumes many different forms and meanings. It is true that drive theories of aggression, implying as they do that activities such as sport, games or *rituals could function as non-violent outlets for aggression, might thereby explain the absence or low incidence of war in some societies. But the evidence seems against it: there are, for instance, clear cases of societies that practise neither warfare nor any other activity interpretable as a mechanism of catharsis (e.g. Howell 1989).

The dominant theories of war in anthropology are †materialist and view war as a type of competition for scarce resources, though opinions differ as to what these scarce resources are. To anthropologists influenced by *sociobiology, they are opportunities for mating and reproduction, and the causes of warfare lie in competition between individuals for inclusive fitness (e.g. Chagnon 1990). This approach is essentially a contemporary substitute for the older 'killer instinct' theories, and suffers from the same weaknesses which are inherent in all biologically-based explanations. Another school, the most influential and prolific, adopts a perspective from *ecological anthropology and views land, food and trade opportunities as the key scarce resources (e.g. Ferguson 1984). Some of these ecological studies are *functionalist, arguing that war may under some circumstances play a positive role by redistributing populations in relation to environmental resources.

The common element of all the resource-scarcity theories is that variations in the incidence of war are to be explained as the outcomes of rational calculations of costs and benefits by the protagonists (with some uncertainty as to whether these actors are individuals or groups). At any rate, war occurs when it 'pays' in terms of some reproductive or other material calculus, and does not occur if it does not pay. No conscious reckoning is necessary: it is enough that the actors behave 'as if' they are reckoning in this way and that they are penalized, ultimately by extinction, when they fail to act in their own interests.

Another approach to war is in terms of *social structure, and seeks explanations in the patterning of social relations. A common theme of this tradition is that cross-cutting ties – of *marriage *alliance, co-residence, trade, gift-exchange or other forms of sociability – play a crucial role in limiting the frequency and intensity of warfare (e.g. Gluckman 1955). Conversely, patterns such as the 'fraternal interest groups' of some tribal societies – tightly-knit groups of male kin, with relatively few and tenuous ties between these groups (see Ferguson 1990: 36) – seem often associated with high levels of warfare. Again, there are functionalist versions of this tradition, envisioning war as contributing to social stability by, for instance, maintaining in-group solidarity *vis-à-vis* the enemy.

A weakness of the social-structural tradition is that its basic intention has been to construct not theories of war at all but theories of social order or social control. That is to say, it has tended to treat peace as the central problem requiring explanation, and war as a residual phenomenon, merely the absence or failure of order. From the point of view of the theoretical understanding of war, this has been unfortunate.

The †phenomenological tradition in anthropology, concerned with interpreting and translating systems of meaning, has also contributed to the study of war. This approach implies that variations in the nature and incidence of war are to be explained by cultural differences in values and beliefs. But it has failed so far to deliver a general, comparative theory. Rather, it has mostly produced sensitive ethnographic accounts of the indigenous meanings of warfare in particular societies. An example is Rosaldo's (1980) attempt to explain headhunting among the Ilongot of the Philippines by reference to Ilongot concepts of the *person and †social action.

An anthropologist asked to explain war is likely to hedge his or her bets, and reply that it is a complex phenomenon having multiple causes rather than one. Ferguson (1990) has recently constructed a synthetic explanation of this sort; it is essentially a resource-scarcity theory incorporating some social-structural and ideological factors.

A problem besetting attempts to construct a theory of war is that virtually every factor that has ever been posited as a cause of war can also be interpreted as an effect of it. For instance, certain kinds of expansionist warfare have been variously suggested as a cause, and as an effect, of the emergence of the *state. These sorts of circularities seem to arise from trying to understand war without first having grounded it in its proper context: namely, in the deeper and more general phenomenon of *violence, of which war is an aspect. An adequate theory of war must await the solution of the larger problem of the theoretical understanding of violence, which is poorly developed in anthropology.

SIMON HARRISON

See also: feud, violence

Further reading

Chagnon, N. (1990) 'Reproductive and Somatic Conflicts of Interest in the Genesis of Violence and Warfare among Tribesmen', in J. Haas (ed.) *The Anthropology of War*, Cambridge: Cambridge University Press

Ferguson, R.B. (1990) 'Explaining War' in J. Haas (ed.) *The Anthropology of War*, Cambridge: Cambridge University Press

—— (ed.) (1984) *Warfare, Culture, and Environment*, Orlando: Academic Press

Foster, M.L. and R. Rubinstein (eds) (1986) *Peace and War: Cross-Cultural Perspectives*, New Brunswick: Transaction

Gluckman, M. (1955) *Custom and Conflict in Africa*, Glencoe: Free Press.

Harrison, S. (1993) *The Mask of War: Violence, Ritual and the Self in Melanesia*, Manchester: Manchester University Press

Howell, S. (1989) '"To be Angry is not to be Human, but to be Fearful is": Chewong Concepts of Human Nature', in S. Howell and R. Willis (eds) *Societies at Peace: Anthropological Perspectives*, London: Routledge

Rosaldo, M.Z. (1980) *Knowledge and Passion: Ilongot Notions of Self and Social Life*, Cambridge: Cambridge University Press

witchcraft and sorcery

The terms 'witchcraft' and 'sorcery' are words taken from pre-Enlightenment Europe and applied to reported occult agencies in, for the most part, non-European, small-scale or tribal societies. The distinction in anthropology between the two kinds of malign occult action is usually credited to †Evans-Pritchard (1937), who was translating a category difference in the thought of the Azande peoples of Central Africa.

The essence of Evans-Pritchard's (or rather the Zande's) influential distinction is that 'witchcraft' is an inherited ability to cause occult injury to others which, at least for the Zande, can be exercised unconsciously by its possessor. 'Sorcery' is a conscious activity associated with the skilled manipulation of certain substances, with the intention of causing harm, a usage that long predated Evans-Pritchard and had been employed in ethnographic accounts of Australian and Melanesian peoples. The witchcraft/sorcery distinction is widely reported in other parts of Africa and elsewhere. However, it is not always made. Over much of East-Central Africa, for example, the notion of inherited ability to cause occult damage is largely absent; instead the emphasis is on the use for malign purposes of occult techniques involving 'medicines'. Middleton and Winter (1963) have interestingly suggested an association between witchcraft in the Zande sense and the importance of *descent as a principle of social organization. They suggest that where descent is not of prime significance in social organization the occult emphasis will be on sorcery, but that where descent largely determines social †status witchcraft is likely to dominate. The distinction is obviously related to that in *sociology between †ascribed and †achieved social roles. A pioneering attempt to explain the specific forms assumed by witchcraft/sorcery beliefs is †Nadel's (1952) comparative analysis of four African cultures, including one (the Korongo of Sudan) where such beliefs are said to be absent. Nadel's explanation for this comparatively untypical situation is that Korongo social life is unusually free of conflict; and their *mythology provides a comprehensive account of causality in terms of non-human spiritual agencies.

The sociological approach to the understanding of witchcraft/sorcery was further developed by Marwick (1965) in a study of the Cewa-speaking peoples of Northeast Zambia and Malawi. In what came to be known as the 'social strain-gauge' theory, Marwick showed that in this †matrilineal society sorcery accusations were particularly likely to be levelled by a young man against an ageing or incompetent village headman who was also the accuser's maternal uncle. If the accusations 'stuck' they could be used to turn the older man out of office and to install his presumed victim. A similar process by which witchcraft accusations are used to get rid of unpopular elders has been described for the Lugbara of Northern Uganda by Middleton (1960). Although illuminating to a degree, this 'obstetric' reading of witchcraft accusations, as it was labelled by †Douglas (1963), clearly leaves many aspects of the phenomenon in obscurity. Once again it was Evans-Pritchard who identified an important function of the witchcraft concept among the Azande, and many other peoples. Witchcraft, according to Evans-Pritchard, explained otherwise inexplicable events. His famous example was the Zande granary which collapsed, killing the people who had been sheltering under it. Zande understood *how* the granary had collapsed: its supports had been eaten away by termites. The further question to which 'witch-

craft' provided the answer was *why* the collapse had occurred when it did and not at some other time when no-one would have been hurt. *Science had no explanation on why the two chains of causation had intersected at a certain time and place. But the concept of witchcraft provided that missing link (1937: 69–70). The historian Keith Thomas has similarly argued that in pre-modern English society 'witchcraft . . . served as a means of accounting for the otherwise inexplicable misfortunes of daily life' ([1971] 1978: 638).

Other studies have focused on the ideas, or constellations of ideas, present in indigenous thought in the areas of witchcraft and sorcery. Marwick maintains that the witch or sorcerer is always conceived of in terms that are antithetical to local concepts of the 'good' and socially acceptable person. Thus witches or sorcerers are often associated with murder, *incest and *cannibalism – all actions generally held to epitomize the antisocial. Frequently there are images of the witch or sorcerer as literally inverted. The Lugbara of Northern Uganda, for example, describe witches as travelling on their heads rather than their feet (Middleton 1960), as do the Kaguru of Central Tanzania (Beidelman 1963). Witches and sorcerers are also commonly associated with darkness, night, dirt and wild animals (cf. Mayer [1954] 1970).

†Kluckhohn (1944) seems to have been the first to note the socially levelling effects of witchcraft fears on the Navaho group of Native Americans. In Navaho society those who made themselves conspicuously different from their fellows by accumulating wealth were believed to be using witchcraft to gain their ends, and were liable to be persecuted and even killed. Similar observations have been made in Africa, for example by †Monica Wilson (1959) for the Nyakyusa of East-central Africa. In the different context of Tudor and Stuart England, however, MacFarlane (1970) has shown how the contemporary fear of witches was manipulated by upwardly mobile villagers to free themselves from the customary obligation to support older and poorer kinsfolk.

*Postmodern developments in anthropology have given a new twist to the tortuous semantic history of the terms 'witchcraft' and 'sorcerer'. Inaugurated with the controversial works of Castaneda (1968), who dubs his Yaqui Native American hero a 'sorcerer' (today he would probably be called a *shaman), other and more ethnographically substantial works have cast doubt on the past assumption that witchcraft and sorcery, however 'real' to indigenous peoples, were based on unfortunate delusions. Where Evans-Pritchard could declare magisterially, in the name of modern science, that such 'mystical' notions had no basis in fact (1937: 12), Favret-Saada (1980) has testified to what she sees as the objective reality of 'sorcery' among present day inhabitants of Normandy, France. In Africa, Stoller and Olkes (1989) have described their own experience of attack by sorcery among the Songhay people.

In the industrial societies of the West, feminist scholars have resuscitated the thesis of Margaret Murray (1921), according to which many of the persecuted 'witches' of medieval Europe were members of a religion of the Mother Goddess which originated in the Palaeolithic era. Under the name of *Wicca* (Anglo-Saxon for 'witchcraft') the re-emergent cult has succeeded in attracting adherents among middle-class professionals in England (Luhrmann 1989).

ROY WILLIS

Further reading

Beidelman, T.O. (1963) 'Witchcraft in Ukaguru', in J. Middleton and E.H. Winter (eds) *Witchcraft and Sorcery in East Africa*, London: Routledge and Kegan Paul

Castaneda, C. (1968) *The Teachings of Don Juan*, Berkeley: University of California Press

Douglas, M. (1963) 'Techniques of Sorcery Control', in J. Middleton and E.H. Winter (eds) *Witchcraft and Sorcery in East Africa*, London: Routledge and Kegan Paul

Evans-Pritchard, E.E. (1937) *Witchcraft, Oracles and Magic Among the Azande*, Oxford: Clarendon Press

Favret-Saada, J. ([1977] 1980) *Deadly Words*, Cambridge: Cambridge University Press

Kluckhohn, C. (1944) *Navaho Witchcraft*, Boston: Beacon Press

Luhrmann, T. (1989) *Persuasions of the Witch's Craft*, Oxford: Blackwell

MacFarlane, A. (1970) *Witchcraft in Tudor and Stuart England*, London: Routledge and Kegan Paul

Marwick, M. (1965) *Sorcery in Its Social Setting*, Manchester: Manchester University Press

Mayer, P. ([1954] 1970) 'Witches', in M. Marwick (ed.) *Witchcraft and Sorcery*, Harmondsworth: Penguin Books

Middleton, J. (1960) *Lugbara Religion*, London: Routledge and Kegan Paul

Middleton, J. and E.H. Winter (eds) (1963) *Witchcraft and Sorcery in East Africa*, London: Routledge and Kegan Paul

Murray, M.A. (1921) *The Witch-cult in Western Europe*, Oxford: Oxford University Press

Nadel, S.F. (1952) 'Witchcraft in Four African Societies', *American Anthropologist* 54: 18–29

Stoller, P. and C. Olkes (1989) *In Sorcery's Shadow*, Chicago: University of Chicago Press

Thomas, K. ([1971] 1978) *Religion and the Decline of Magic*, London: Penguin Books

Wilson, M. (1959) *Communal Rituals of the Nyakyusa*, London: Oxford University Press

work

Whether seen as drudgery and humiliation or as honoured art, the work that humans do is a key site for understanding both material and cultural reproduction: how we survive and what it means to persist. The transformations which humans produce through work are read by anthropologists as distinct cultural markers, e.g. as *archaeologists identify a stone adze of a specific period or cultural anthropologists distinguish Mayan from Maori carving. Humans not only transform †material culture through work, but we can also believe ourselves to be transformed through the work we do, or work to demonstrate our transformation, as †Max Weber pointed out so well in *The Protestant Ethic and the Spirit of Capitalism* (1930). Anthropologists of work have endeavoured to understand not only the basic needs humans work to accommodate in any culture, following *Malinowski's *functionalism, but also the inequalities that are reproduced through the organization of work, following †Marx, and the relationship between work, *identity, and value in various cultural settings.

While most early *ethnographies mentioned the kinds of work done by the people studied, work did not receive major theoretical and methodological attention from anthropologists until the latter half of the twentieth century. Attention to work in anthropology has been diverse. †Physical or *biological anthropologists interested in human †adaptation have measured the calories humans have expended in working to transform items from their *environments for human use. *Economic anthropologists have used caloric expenditure to argue that, for example, *hunting and gathering provides more leisure time than industrial organization of a society's work activities (Sahlins 1972), making ultimately, of course, the argument that a shift from egalitarian hunting and gathering work to industrial capitalist work is not necessarily an improvement. *Psychological anthropologists have, like *sociologists and applied economists, studied perceptions of work and the significance of employment for self-worth, especially in industrial societies. Work has been an area for the convergence of historical materialist and symbolic approaches. Paul Willis (1977), for example, studied how, through training for work while in schools, young men learned to valorize tasks differently and reproduce *class identities. Foley (1990), reproducing Willis's study in a US context, looked at the way young people learned to manage *gender, class, and *ethnic identity, as well as conflicts, in their work at school and their training for future work. Kondo (1990) looked at the powerful formation of social identity through workplace relations in *Japan, and the relationship between work and identity has been one focus for the wide-ranging discussions of identity by cultural anthropologists in the 1990s.

The valorization of work and workplaces has been the topic of several lively debates in anthropology in the late twentieth century, most notably: the comparison of non-industrial with industrial forms of work; the issue of whether theories of economic rationality could explain all work, including *ritual work; and the questioning of whether women's work – from domestic to ceremonial – has been attended to properly in anthropological analyses and how it is organized and attributed value across cultures. Discussion of gender divisions of labour and their relative valorization was related to attention in anthropology from the 1970s through the 1990s to other historical divisions of labour and the relationship between forms of work – e.g. slavery and child labour – and forms of *power. Anthropologists of work have been influenced by historians of labour and by human geographers as they study changes in the marking of work time and the spatial aspects of production, and the inequalities embedded in the control of those changes.

Sociology, with its attention to industrial societies and Marxist theorizing of the organization of production, has most greatly influenced the anthropology of work, especially as anthropologists look at how local labour (whether industrial or non-industrial) is related to global production, distribution, and consumption patterns and how they are controlled. Studies of the global factory by anthropologists (cf. Nash 1989; Ong 1987; Rothstein and Blim 1992; and Ward 1990) have focused on workplaces to describe the ambiguous relationships between local and global organization of production; workplace discipline and other forms of discipline – e.g. through religious fundamentalism – and classifications of kinds of work such as agricultural and industrial, in an increasingly interconnected and transnational marketplace. Migrant work has drawn anthropologists' attention to neocolonial labour relations and questions of transnational identities and policies.

Ethnographic attention to the specifics of consumption and distribution, as well as to (more traditionally) production, has yielded such interesting insights as Néstor Garcia Canclini's (1993: 63) finding that international tourist consumers of Mexican crafts valued individualism in purchasing artisans' work, while the producers in a crafts collective saw their work as interchangeable, using one another's unique seals freely. Late capitalism affords many opportunities to study cultural values through the cross-cultural valorization of work and worker identity, and categories of work studied by sociologists and anthropologists have shifted. Service sector work, for example, has been increasing, and so, increasingly studied. The anthropological, sociological and labour studies literatures have merged in discussions of *technology and the labour process; unionization; and workplace discrimination by race, ethnicity, gender, and age. Anthropologists studying work in the 1990s (cf. Calagione et al. 1992) have challenged their discipline to reconceptualize work and the expressive culture of those defined as workers.

It is only fitting that anthropologists of work have organized themselves professionally. In Britain, the Association of Social Anthropologists held a conference in 1979 on the anthropology of work, well-documented by Wallman (1979). In the US, the Society for the Anthropology of Work, a unit of the American Anthropological Association, has published the *Anthropology of Work Review* since 1979.

ANN E. KINGSOLVER

See also: economic anthropology, Marxism and anthropology

Further reading

Calagione, J., D. Francis and D. Nugent (eds) (1992) *Workers' Expressions: Beyond Accommodation and Resistance*, Albany: State University of New York Press

Canclini, N.G. (1993) *Transforming Modernity: Popular Culture in Mexico*, Austin: University of Texas Press

Foley, D.E. (1990) *Learning Capitalist Culture: Deep in the Heart of Tejas*, Philadelphia: University of Pennsylvania Press

Kondo, D.K. (1990) *Crafting Selves: Power, Gender, and Discourses of Identity in a Japanese Workplace*, Chicago: University of Chicago Press

Lamphere, L., A. Stepick and G. Grenier (eds) (1994) *Newcomers in the Workplace: Immigrants and the Restructuring of the US Economy*, Philadelphia: Temple University Press

Nash, J.C. (1989) *From Tank Town to High Tech: The Clash of Community and Industrial Cycles*, Albany: State University of New York Press

Ong, A. (1987) *Spirits of Resistance and Capitalist Discipline: Factory Women in Malaysia*, Albany: State University of New York Press

Rothstein, F.A. and M.L. Blim (eds) (1992) *Anthropology and the Global Factory: Studies of the New Industrialization in the Late Twentieth Century*, New York: Bergin & Garvey

Sahlins, M. (1972) *Stone Age Economics*, New York: Aldine Publishing Company

Wallman, S. (ed.) (1979) *Social Anthropology of Work*, London: Academic Press

Ward, K. (ed.) (1990) *Women Workers and Global Restructuring*, Ithaca, NY: ILR Press

Weber, M. (1930) *The Protestant Ethic and the Spirit of Capitalism*, trans. by Talcott Parsons, London: G. Allen & Unwin Ltd

Willis, P. (1977) *Learning to Labour: How Working Class Kids Get Working Class Jobs*, Farnborough: Saxon House

world system

World systems theory was an important influence in the anthropology of *development and *political economy in the 1970s and 1980s. Drawing on the writings of André Gundar Frank and Fernand Braudel, world systems theory is most clearly laid out in the work of the economic historian Immanuel Wallerstein. In brief, Wallerstein's (1974, 1980) thesis is that the *capitalist world system originated in the late fifteenth and early sixteenth centuries, leading to the creation of a global market and global division of labour divided between 'core' and 'periphery' zones, each characterized by their own form of labour organization. Relations between these zones are marked by unequal *exchange, with capital intensive goods produced at the core being indirectly exchanged for labour intensive goods produced at the periphery. Capitalism itself has expanded on the basis of this unequal exchange, which has led to the underdevelopment of periphery zones.

The tendency to gloss over historical and cultural variation within these zones has been the main thrust of anthropological critiques of

Wallerstein. Rather than elaborating on the system itself, anthropologists have tended to look at the impact of the system on peripheral and semi-peripheral peoples, and how their situation has been transformed through their relation with the core. In doing so they have criticized another aspect of Wallerstein's argument, his tendency to see peripheral peoples as passive in the face of the expansion of capitalism. Ethnographic work suggests that rather than being passive, peoples on the periphery have offered their own forms of *resistance, as well as appropriated goods from the core frequently in novel and imaginative ways. Thus whilst peripheral peoples have been transformed by the world system, it is also the case that certain aspects of the world system have been transformed by its encounter with peripheral peoples.

Although anthropological critiques of Wallerstein's thesis are various, its influence is to be found in a number of works ranging in scale from Eric Wolf's monumental *Europe and the People Without History* (1982) to more micro-focused ethnographic studies on places as different as Sicily and Sumatra. Whilst many of these studies grew out of Marxist-inspired analyses of political economy in the 1970s, anthropological interest in the effects of externally introduced economic processes goes back at least to the work of the †Manchester school in the Central African copperbelt. The tendency of some studies in the 1970s to become mired in arguments about multiple versus unitary *modes of production and their articulation has been avoided by the more historically attuned anthropology that emerged in the 1980s. This covered similar ground; most notably Mintz's (1985) history of sugar, along with various studies focusing on the expansion of colonialism in the Pacific (Sahlins 1988; Thomas 1991).

In all this work there has been an attempt to understand the effects of global processes on local cultural systems, an inquiry which has taken a new tack in the 1990s with the study of †globalization (Featherstone 1990). Transnational corporations and digital communications systems are seen to be part of a process of global homogenization where 'third cultures' transcending local boundaries are emerging in this postmodern period of late capitalism. Whereas relations of production and exchange were often the focus of anthropological analyses of political economy and the world system, studies of global culture focus mainly on *consumption, whether of such goods as Coca

Cola and Macdonalds or images and information on the internet. Yet it can be argued that whilst Wallerstein's world systems theory ignored variation within core and periphery zones, global culture studies sometimes overlook inequalities in wealth among consumers, and unequal access to the communications systems said to be revolutionizing everyone's life. Whilst some may argue for the globalization of culture and global homogenization, few would argue for the homogenization of wealth; for every person creatively 'appropriating' soft drinks and hamburgers there are countless others for whom globalization means the thwarted desires of window shopping.

PHILIP THOMAS

See also: capitalism, colonialism, history and anthropology, political economy

Further reading

Featherstone, M. (ed.) (1990) *Global Culture: Nationalism, Globalization and Modernity*, London: Sage

Mintz, S.W. (1985) *Sweetness and Power: The Place of Sugar in Modern History*, New York: Viking Penguin

Nash, J. (1981) 'Ethnographic Aspects of the World Capitalist System', *Annual Review of Anthropology* 10: 393–423

Sahlins, M. (1988) 'Cosmologies of Capitalism: The Trans-Pacific Sector of "the World System"', *Proceedings of the British Academy* 74: 1–51

Thomas, N. (1991) *Entangled Objects: Exchange, Material Culture and Colonialism in the Pacific*, Cambridge, MA: Harvard University Press

Wallerstein, I. (1974, 1980) *The Modern World-System* (2 vols), New York: Academic Press

Wolf, E.R. (1982) *Europe and the People Without History*, Berkeley: University of California Press

Biographical appendix

Adam, Leonhard (1891–1960) A jurist and anthropologist, Adam is perhaps best remembered for his invention of the words †'virilocal' and †'uxorilocal', to replace †'patrilocal' and †'matrilocal' ('"Virilocal" and "uxorilocal",' *Man* 1948). His works include *Primitive Art* (1940) and books on anthropological theory.

Althusser, Louis (1918–90) French Marxist philosopher whose reinterpretations of Marx emphasized the anti-humanism in Marx's later works, and were highly influential in the development of †structural Marxism in the 1960s and 1970s. Works include *Pour Marx* (1965; *For Marx*, 1969) and, with Etienne Balibar, *Lire Le Capital* (1965; *Reading 'Capital'*, 1970). See *Marxism and anthropology.

Ardener, Edwin (1927–87) British anthropologist who made contributions to the relation between social anthropology and linguistics and to the introduction of *postmodernist ideas into British anthropology. His major essays are included in *The Voice of Prophecy and Other Essays* (1989), and *Kingdom on Mount Cameroon* (1996).

Arensberg, Conrad M. (1910–) American anthropologist, associated in *economic anthropology with the †substantivist school. He conducted pioneering fieldwork in North America, Ireland, and India and became noted in the field of *community studies. His most important monograph in this tradition is *Family and Community in Ireland* (with Solon T. Kimball, 1940).

Avebury, Lord See †Lubbock, Sir John

Bachofen, J.J. (1815–77) A Swiss jurist who practised in Basel. As an anthropologist, he is most famous for his *Das Mutterrecht* (1861) in which he propounded his theory of †mother-right, or ancient †matriarchy as the earliest form of society. This idea was later to take prominence, especially through the work of *Lewis Henry Morgan.

Bakhtin, Mikhail M. (1895–1975) Russian literary critic whose work has become increasingly important since his death. Bakhtin criticized the static and formal ideas of structural linguistics, emphasizing instead the fluidity and contingency of language in use. Key concepts such as the idea of the †dialogical, and the notion of †heteroglossia, have been taken up in post-1970s anthropology. Works include *Rabelais and his World* (1965; English translation 1968) and *The Dialogic Imagination: Four Essays* (1934–5; English translation, 1981).

Balandier, Georges (1920–) French anthropologist known for his work on social change in Central Africa and on *political anthropology, as well as for his efforts in fostering Africanist research in France. His works include *Sociologie actuelle de l'Afrique noire* (1955), *Sociologie des Brazzavilles noires* (1955), *Anthropologie politique* (1967; *Political Anthropology*, 1970) and *Anthropo-logiques* (1974).

Barth, Fredrik (1928–) Leading Norwegian anthropologist. Barth has carried out fieldwork in the Middle East and South Asia, most notably the North West Frontier of Pakistan, Iran and Oman, and more recently in Melanesia and Bali. He has made numerous notable contributions to anthropological theory from his early monograph *Political Leadership among Swat Pathans* (1959), his edited volume *Ethnic Groups and Boundaries* (1969), and his later monographs *Cosmologies in the Making* (1987) and *Balinese Worlds* (1994), tracking a path from the study of transactions and the emergent nature of social structure, to the study of cosmologies and the processes of knowledge transmission. See *ethnicity.

Barthes, Roland (1915–80) French literary critic whose work in †semiotics has been influential for *structuralist and †poststructuralist anthropology. Works include *Mythologies* (1957).

Bastian, Adolph (1826–1905) Influential German anthropologist of the late nineteenth century. He wrote a number of texts, but these have mainly appeared only in German, largely because of their obscure and virtually untranslatable style. His most significant was *Ethnische Elementargedanken in der Lehre vom Menschen* (1895), in which he propounded his theory of the relation between 'elementary thoughts' (*Elementargedanken*) and 'folk thoughts' (*Völkergedanken*). The former were defined as those ideas which were universal, and the latter were defined as those peculiar to specific cultures. This distinction made explicit the †psychic unity of humankind and foreshadowed much later *structuralist theories, such as those of *Lévi-Strauss. See *German and Austrian anthropology.

Bateson, Gregory (1904–80) Bateson was, by common consent, a maverick and much under-rated by his own generation. He conducted fieldwork in New Guinea, Bali, and the United States, and practised as a psychologist and zoologist. In the former capacity, he treated victims of schizophrenia and alcoholism and came up with the famous double bind theory. In the latter, he spent many years in Hawaii studying dolphins. As an anthropologist, his contributions were mainly early in his career, beginning with *Naven* (1936). This extraordinary work details the initiation ceremonies of the Iatmul of the New Guinea Highlands and analyses them through the concepts of †eidos, †ethos and †schismogenesis. Bateson went on to do research with his then wife †Margaret Mead in Bali, producing a remarkable photographic ethnography *Balinese Character* (1942) with her. The latter part of his career was spent largely outside anthropology, and towards the end of his life he made important contributions to educational theory and the politics of environmentalism.

Beattie, John H.M. (1915–90) Oxford-trained anthropologist who published widely on the Bunyoro kingdom of Uganda and wrote a popular textbook in the British tradition, *Other Cultures* (1964).

Benedict, Ruth Fulton (1887–1948) Student and close associate of *Franz Boas, Benedict is most remembered as the foremost proponent of the *culture and personality school in the United States. Her version of *psychological anthropology was based on the notion that cultures were characterizable by standardized personality types. These ideas were widely propagated in the popular *Patterns of Culture* (1934), while her remarkable study of Japanese character, *The Chrysanthemum and the Sword* (1946) remains influential despite the fact that it was composed with no first-hand ethnographic experience of Japan itself. In the 1930s she was active in the intellectual battle against scientific racism. See *culture, *race.

Berndt, Catherine (1918–94) New Zealand-born ethnographer of Aboriginal Australia. Her first major study was *Women's Changing Ceremonies in Northern Australia* (1950). With her husband Ronald M. Berndt, she subsequently published much on social change. See *Aboriginal Australia.

Berndt, Ronald M. (1916–1990) Australian anthropologist, who with Catherine Berndt published much on social change in *Aboriginal Australia. Their joint writings include *The World of the First Australians* (1964), as well as several edited volumes. Berndt's single-authored works include *Australian Aboriginal Religion* (1974) and *Excess and Restraint* (1962), the latter based on his early fieldwork in Papua New Guinea.

Binford, Lewis R. (1930–) American archaeologist long associated with the University of New Mexico. He was instrumental in the development of †'processual archaeology' (also called 'the new archaeology') which applied notions of cultural anthropology, and in particular, ethnographic analogy, to the interpretation of archaeological data. Key works include 'Archaeology as anthropology' (*American Antiquity*, 1962) and *Nunamiut Ethnoarchaeology* (1978). See *archaeology.

Birket-Smith, Kaj (1893–1977) Danish ethnographer of the Inuit (Eskimo). He was influenced by the †*Kulturkreis* school and was critical of the lack of historical interest among social anthropologists of his generation. He wrote many volumes on material culture and other aspects of life in Greenland and Alaska. These include his Danish monograph *Eskimoerne* (1927), and *The Caribou Eskimos* (2 vols, 1929).

Bloomfield, Leonard (1887–1949) American linguist credited with being one of the leaders of the structural school in North America. In his most important work *Language* (1933) he broke away from earlier psychological influences and took a behaviourist approach under the influence of A.P. Weiss.

Boas, Franz (1858–1942) German-born anthropologist who emigrated to the United States in 1887. There he developed his own school of anthropology which advocated a rejection of conjectural history, especially *evolutionism, in favour of empirical research into the detail of *culture and the variation between cultures. His work was of paramount importance in developing the *relativist tradition which has dominated *American anthropology through much of its history. His teaching at Columbia University became the basis for that tradition. Fieldwork among Inuit and Kwakiutl. Works include *Anthropology* (1907), *Race, Language and Culture* (1948), and *Kwakiutl Ethnography* (1967). For further details, see main entry.

Bopp, Franz (1791–1867) German linguist and founder of Indo-European comparative philology. Through systematic work on Sanskrit, Greek, Latin, Gothic, and Lithuanian, he produced the first comparative grammar of the Indo-European languages.

Bose, Nirmal Kumar (1901–72) Indian anthropologist who wrote extensively on Indian society and on Ghandism and edited the journal *Man in India* for over twenty years. Among his important works is *The Structure of Indian Society* (1949). See *Indian anthropology.

Bourdieu, Pierre (1930–) French sociologist who did fieldwork with the Kabyle and has published extensively on Algeria and France. His prominence in anthropology rests on his *Esquisse d'une théorie de la pratique* (1972; *Outline of a Theory of Practice*, 1977; reworked as *La logique de la pratique*, 1980; *The Logic of Practice*, 1990), in which he developed a critique of *structuralism, from the point of view of practice and strategy, introducing the notion of †habitus to an anthropological audience. His work on France has been more obviously sociological, but his study of class and *consumption *La distinction* (1979; *Distinction* 1984) has been highly influential in the anthropology of consumption. See also *education.

Burnett, James See †Monboddo, Lord

Burton, Sir Richard Francis (1821–90) British soldier, traveller, linguist and ethnographer. He was a founding member and vice-president of the Anthropological Society of London, but he spent most of his adult life abroad. Among the most significant of his forty published volumes are *Personal Narratives of a Pilgrimage to El-Medinah and Meccah* (3 vols, 1855-1856) and *The Lake Regions of Central Africa* (2 vols, 1860).

Childe, V. Gordon (1892–1957) Australian archaeologist who taught at Edinburgh and London. Important within social anthropology for his development of the theory of †universal evolution and advocacy of archaeology as a branch of the social sciences. His many works include *Man Makes Himself* (1936). See *archaeology.

Chomsky, Noam (1928–) American linguist and political activist. Although his linguistic theories have developed through the years, his work has consistently emphasized the innateness of linguistic ability. Many anthropologists have sought inspiration in his work, with reference to both universal grammar and the †deep structures of particular languages. However, Chomsky has distanced himself from these attempts, on the grounds that language and culture are not really analogous. Among his most important works for anthropologists is *Language and Mind* (1968), while his most enduring theoretical treatise in linguistics is *Aspects of a Theory of Syntax* (1965).

Clastres, Pierre (1934–77) French Amazonianist. Famous for his anarchist politics and his ethnography of the Guayaki Indians, Clastres put these two interests together in his *La société contre l'état* (1974; *Society against the State*, 1977). In it he argues that the major enemy of society for small-scale indigenous cultures is the *state.

Colson, Elizabeth (1917–) American anthropologist who has carried out fieldwork in Southern Africa, North America and Australia. Trained in the United States and Britain, she has carried out long-term fieldwork among the Plateau Tonga and Gwembe Tonga of Zambia, initially as a researcher with the †Rhodes-Livingstone Institute. Her publications have focused on change and dislocation, especially the effects of *migration and *colonialism.

Comte, Auguste (1798–1857) French philosopher and naturalist and one of the founders of sociology (a term he invented), a sociology which included what would now be considered social anthropology. He advocated an approach characterized by †positivism (also his term) and was among the earliest to advocate a notion of social *evolution as a phenomenon analogous to biological evolution. His positivist sociology was an influence on, among others, †Durkheim and †Tylor. Works include the *Cours de philosophie positive*, (6 vols, 1830–42), of which the fourth volume (1839) deals with sociology.

Condorcet, Jean-Antoine-Nicolas de Caritat, Marquis de (1743–94) French philosopher whose understanding of progress influenced †Comte and others. His key work was the *Esquisse d'un tableau historique des progrès de l'esprit humain* (1795; *Sketch of a Historical Picture of the Progress of the Human Mind*, 1955).

Conklin, Harold C. (1926–) A major proponent of *ethnoscience or †cognitive anthropology based on understanding the linguistic categories of the people under study. Conklin worked in the Philippines and taught for many years at Yale. Among his more distinctive publications is 'Lexicographical treatment of folk taxonomies' (1962), which is reprinted in Stephen A. Tyler's *Cognitive Anthropology* (1969). See *classification.

Coon, Carlton S. (1904–81) Highly prolific writer of texts in archaeology, ethnology and biological anthropology, as well as travel narrative and fiction. In *The Origin of Races* (1962), he put forward the controversial view, now discredited, that human races evolved in parallel. Other well-known works include *Principles of Anthropology* (1942), *The Story of Man* (1954), and *The Hunting Peoples* (1971).

Cushing, Frank (1857–1900) Early ethnographer of the Zuñi, among whom he spent several years. His intensive fieldwork, which included initiation as Priest of the Bow, was too much for his employer, the Smithsonian Institution, and he was eventually transferred to the †Bureau of American Ethnology. Selected writings published as *Zuñi* (1979). See *ethnography.

Dart, Raymond (1893–1988) Australian anatomist and paleoanthropologist. Most associated with the discovery of the Taung skull in Africa and the recognition of its significance as belonging to a higher primate which showed signs of developing in a human direction. It was considered one of the most important breakthroughs in paleoanthropology in the twentieth century. Dart is also remembered as a great teacher and brilliant researcher.

Darwin, Charles (1809–82) Perhaps the greatest naturalist of all time, Darwin also made a small mark within anthropology. Although *Origin of Species* (1865) only hinted at human *evolution, *The Descent of Man* (1871) made the implications of evolution and of natural selection explicit for the human species. Darwin was also a contributor to †*Notes and Queries on Anthropology* (first edition, 1874).

Derrida, Jacques (1930–) French literary theorist and philosopher. His *De la grammatologie* (1976; *Of Grammatology*, 1976) represents an important attack on the foundations of *structuralism, and his strategy of †deconstruction has been important in destabilizing anthropological (and other) assumptions about language and meaning. See *postmodernism.

Dévereux, Georges (1908–85) Psychoanalyist and anthropologist, born in Hungary, he was educated in France and practised for many years in the United States before returning to France in the early 1960s. His field research among the Mohave provoked a long and fruitful reflection on the application of Freudian notions of transference and counter-transference to the anthropological field situation. Works include *From Anxiety to Method in the Behavioral Sciences* (1967) and *Essais d'ethnopsychiatrie générale* (1970). See *psychoanalysis.

Dieterlen, Germaine (1903–) French ethnographer of the Dogon and other West African peoples. From the late 1940s she collaborated with †Marcel Griaule in the study of the Dogon of Mali. She continued this research, producing the first volume of the co-authored *Le renard pâle* (1965) almost a decade after his death in 1956. A key figure in the development of Africanist ethnography in France, she also edited an important symposium on the concept of the *person (*La notion de personne en Afrique noire*, 1973). See *French anthropology.

Douglas, Mary (1921–) British anthropologist whose original fieldwork in Zaire was influenced by her teacher †Evans-Pritchard. Her most influential book among anthropologists is still probably her comparative analysis of ideas of *pollution and purity, *Purity and Danger* (1966). Her theoretical ideas about 'grid' and 'group', expounded in *Natural Symbols* (1970), have had less impact in anthropology, but have been widely employed by sociologists of science and technology. More recently she has written widely on the sociology of risk and attitudes to the environment (*Risk and Culture*, 1982), while returning regularly to classic themes from the sociology and anthropology of religion and *classification.

Driver, Harold E. (1907–) American anthropologist important for his comparative work on North American Indians (e.g. *Indians of North America*, 1961).

Du Bois, Cora (1903–) A leading figure in the *culture and personality school who sought to objectify it through statistical methods. Her most important work was *The Peoples of Alor* (1944).

Dumézil, Georges (1898–1986) French philologist and historian of religions. He was first influenced by the sociology of †Durkheim which he was introduced to by †Granet. He is mainly remembered for developing a comparative mythology to establish a model of the common roots of Indo-European ideology. His works include *Les dieux des Germains* (1959), *Mythe et épopée*, (3 vols, 1968–73) and *Heur et malheur de guerrier* (1969).

Dumont, Louis (1911–) French anthropologist and historian of ideas best known for his synthetic account of Indian *caste, his ideas on †hierarchy, and his intellectual history of the Western concern with equality and *individualism. A student of †Mauss, he initially conducted research in southern France, before carrying out fieldwork in southern India in the late 1940s (*Une sous-caste de l'Inde du Sud*, 1957; *A South Indian Sub-caste*, 198?). As a lecturer in Oxford in the 1950s he was influenced by †Evans-Pritchard, and started his collaboration with D. Pocock which led to the founding of the journal *Contributions to Indian Sociology* in 1957. After further fieldwork in north India, he published *Homo hierarchicus* (1967; English translation 1970), a book which set the agenda for

a generation's worth of anthropological research on *South Asia. Since then he has concentrated on the intellectual genealogy of modern individualism, work which has gained him unexpected celebrity among political philosophers in France.

Durkheim, Émile (1858–1917) The founder of modern French anthropology and *sociology, influenced by †Comte and †Spencer, and himself an influence especially in the French and British traditions. He sought to establish sociology as a distinct field of enquiry and consistently argued against the reduction of †'social facts' to non-social explanations. His early works, such as *De la division du travail social* (1893; *The Division of Labour in Society*, 1933), *Les règles de la méthode sociologique* (1895; *The Rules of the Sociological Method*, 1938) and *Le suicide* (1897; *Suicide*, 1951), introduced the notions of †collective consciousness and †collective representation, as well as the distinction between †mechanical and organic solidarity. His later works, such as *Les formes élémentaires de la vie religieuse* (1912; *The Elementary Forms of the Religious Life*, 1915), were more concerned with problems of religion and the sociology of knowledge, and drew much more heavily on recognizably anthropological sources. He gathered a group of dedicated students around him, including his nephew †Marcel Mauss, publishing the results of their work in the journal †*Année sociologique*. This collective body of work set the intellectual agenda for much of what was to follow in *French anthropology, as well as in *British anthropology, where it was particularly important in the work of †Evans-Pritchard and his associates in Oxford. Steven Lukes's *Émile Durkheim* (1973) is an excellent guide to Durkheim's ideas and their influence.

Eggan, Fred (1906–91) American anthropologist, trained and taught at the University of Chicago, where he was strongly influenced by *Radcliffe-Brown during his period there. A key representative of the British 'social' tradition in American anthropology, he published widely on *Native North America, advocating controlled *regional comparison with both historical and sociological dimensions. Most important works include *Social Organization of the Western Pueblos* (1950) and the edited volume *Social Anthropology of North American Tribes* (1937).

Eliade, Mircea (1907–86) Romanian-born historian and theorist of comparative religion, Eliade taught for many years at the University of Chicago. Among his many publications *Le chamanisme et les techniques archaïques de 'extase'* (1951; *Shamanism*, 1964), has probably had the greatest anthropological impact, especially on studies of *possession and *shamanism.

Elkin, A.P. (1891–1979) Elkin was perhaps Australia's foremost anthropologist. He wrote widely on Aboriginal culture and edited the journal *Oceania* from 1933 to 1979. Before taking up anthropology he became an Anglican priest, and he maintained a lifelong interest in Aboriginal religion and in Aboriginal welfare. He was also involved in the post-war reconstruction of Papua New Guinea. His major publications include *Studies in Australian Totemism* (1933), *The Australian Aborigines* (1938), *Aboriginal Men of High Degree* (1946), and *Social Anthropology in Melanesia* (1953). See *Aboriginal Australia.

Elliot Smith, Sir Grafton (1871–1937) Australian anatomist based at Manchester and London. The leading figure of the British *diffusionist school, he held the eccentric belief that virtually all high culture the world over diffused from ancient Egypt. Works include *The Migrations of Early Culture* (1915), *The Search for Man's Ancestors* (1931), *The Evolution of Man* (1927) and *The Diffusion of Culture* (1933).

Engels, Friedrich (1820–95) German businessman and revolutionary who spent most of his working life in England. Although more generally known for his political and intellectual collaboration with †Karl Marx, Engels's importance in anthropology is based on his influence on the Marxist and feminist traditions through his *Der Ursprung der Familie, des Privateigentums und des Staates* (1884; *The Origin of the Family, Private Property and the State*, 1902), essentially an elaboration on *L.H. Morgan's *Ancient Society*. See *family, *gender, *Marxism and anthropology.

Evans-Pritchard, E.E. (1902–73) British anthropologist who conducted fieldwork in East Africa in the 1920s and 1930s and later, as professor of social anthropology at Oxford, became the foremost British anthropologist of his generation. In his first major work, *Witchcraft, Oracles and Magic among the Azande* (1937), made a powerful case for the internal coherence and rationality of apparently alien modes of thought; the book is still a primary point of reference in philosophical arguments about *rationality and *relativism. In *The Nuer* (1940), he pioneered an ecological, as well as a structural, approach though the former was largely ignored by subsequent generations of his followers. This book and his subsequent *Kinship and Marriage among the Nuer* (1951) could be seen as developments within the *functionalist tradition, as well as anticipating aspects of *structuralism, but from his appointment to the chair in Oxford onwards, he displayed growing disenchantment with *Radcliffe-Brown's project for a scientific anthropology, preferring instead the model provided by humanities disciplines like history. With the series of articles that culminated in *Nuer Religion* (1956), he demonstrated his concern with what he described as the 'translation of culture'. Evans-Pritchard was knighted in 1971, and in his last years he advocated a return to diffusionism, much to the chagrin of his closest colleagues. Among Evans-Pritchard's other important works are *The Sanussi of Cyrenaica* (1951), *The Comparative Method in Social Anthropology* (1963), *Theories of Primitive Religion* (1965), *The Position of Women in Primitive Societies and Other Essays* (1965), *The Azande* (1971) and *Man and Woman among the Azande* (1974). See *British anthropology.

Fei Xiao-tong (Fei Hsiao-T'ung) (1910–) Greatest of Chinese social anthropologists, Fei was educated in Western schools in China and wrote his PhD thesis, under *Malinowski's supervision, at the London School of Economics in 1938. He did extensive fieldwork in China and advocated the development of light industry to ease China's rural poverty. Although never a Communist and often branded a counter-revolutionary, he was eventually able to get sociology re-established in Beijing after Mao's death. Works include *Peasant Life in China* (1939) and many subsequent writings, in Chinese and English, on Chinese village life. See *Chinese anthropology.

Ferguson, Adam (1723–1816) Scottish military chaplain, librarian, and professor of natural philosophy and, subsequently, of moral philosophy at Edinburgh. In his *Essay on the History of Civil Society* (1767), he traced the progress of humankind from the 'rude' to the 'polished' state, but argued against the corruption inherent in the latter. His theory of society emphasized the rise in importance of private property and the harmful effects of excessive individualism. See *Enlightenment anthropology.

Firth, Sir Raymond (1902–) New Zealand-born anthropologist who has made important contributions in economic anthropology, action theory, and the ethnography of *Polynesia. One of Malinowski's first students, he held the chair in anthropology at the London School of Economics from 1944 to 1968, and has continued to write and publish into the 1990s. During this time he developed the Malinowskian interest in †social organization (rather than *social structure) and encouraged fieldwork in many areas, including notably East London. As an economic anthropologist, he has advocated an essentially †formalist approach and criticized †substantivists and *Marxists alike. He has also made important contributions to *kinship theory, but his reputation rests above all on his work as an ethnographer – possibly the most gifted of his generation – especially his many works on the Tikopia, including *We, the Tikopia* (1936), *The Work of the Gods in Tikopia* (1940), *Social Change in Tikopia* (1959), and *Tikopia-English Dictionary* (1985), among others. Other works include *Primitive Economics of the New Zealand Maori* (1929), *Malay Fishermen* (1946), *Elements of Social Organization* (1951), *Essays on Social Organization and Values* (1964), *Symbols: Public and Private* (1973) and *Religion* (1996).

Fison, Lorimer (1832–1907) Missionary-ethnographer and one of the first to record details on Aboriginal kinship systems, which he did mainly through correspondence with white settlers rather than intensive study with Aborigines. His most famous work, with A.W. Howitt, was *Kamilaroi and Kurnai* (1880). See *Aboriginal Australia.

Forde, Daryll (1902–73) For many years editor of *Africa* and leading Africanist anthropologist in the United Kingdom. Trained originally as a geographer, Forde tried to introduce ideas from this field into social anthropology. His *Habitat, Economy and Society* (1934), was one of the first major works to review the relation between *environment and *social structure. Among his ethnographic contributions were *Marriage and the Family among the Yakö* (1941) and *Yakö Studies* (1964). With *A.R. Radcliffe-Brown, he edited *African Systems of Kinship and Marriage* (1950).

Fortes, Meyer (1906–83) One of several South African-born anthropologists who emigrated to Britain and helped to establish anthropology in that country. After giving up psychology for social anthropology, Fortes became one of the foremost exponents of †structural-functionalism and †descent theory, and at Cambridge he trained two generations of fieldworkers in the functionalist tradition. Despite this, he never renounced his original psychological background, publishing important esays on *religion, the *person and the emotions. His major fieldwork was in the Gold Coast (now Ghana). Books include *The Dynamics of Clanship among the Tallensi* (1945), *The Web of Kinship among the Tallensi* (1949), and *Kinship and the Social Order* (1969). With †E.E. Evans-Pritchard, Fortes also edited *African Political Systems* (1940). See *British anthropology, *family, *kinship.

Fortune, Reo F. (1903–79) New Zealand-born anthropologist best known for his ethnographic work on the island of Dobu and for his brief marriage to †Margaret Mead. His major work was *Sorcerers of Dobu* (1932).

Foucault, Michel (1926–84) French philosopher and historian. His work on topics such as the history of psychology, medicine, penology, and sexuality has been enormously influential across the human sciences, encouraging critical attention to the genealogy of modern humanism, and a deep suspicion of liberal assumptions. In particular, his arguments about power and knowledge, and the production of modern subjects, have been used in feminist anthropology, *medical anthropology, in the critique of *Orientalism, and in the emerging anthropology of *resistance. Works include *Les mots et les choses* (1966; *The Order of Things*, 1970) *Surveiller et punir* (1975; *Discipline and Punish* 1978), and *Histoire de la sexualité* (3 vols, 1976–84; *The History of Sexuality*, 1979–90). See *postmodernism, *power.

Frazer, Sir James (1854–1941) A classicist who wrote sublimely and extensively on early religion and kinship. In a sense his work represents a survival from the nineteenth century, the product of the last great 'armchair' evolutionist. Although popular in many quarters it was attacked by new generations of fieldworking social anthropologists. Ironically, it is partly to Frazer that we owe the label 'social anthropology', as this was the title of the honorary professorship bestowed on him by the University of Liverpool. His style was much praised, and it is said that Malinowski took up anthropology after turning to *The Golden Bough* (originally 2 vols, 1890, later expanded to 12 vols) to improve his English. It is also said that the fieldwork revolution initiated by Malinowski, consigned Frazer and his works to anthropological oblivion. Yet *The Golden Bough* has remained in print for over a century, and has exerted real influence over literary figures like T.S. Eliot. Other works include *Totemism and Exogamy*, (4 vols, 1910) and *The Belief in Immortality and the Worship of the Dead*, (2 vols, 1911–13). See *classical studies, *kingship, *magic.

Freeman, J. Derek (1916–) New Zealand-born anthropologist and psychoanalyst, for many years best known for his ethnographic work in *Southeast Asia and his contribution to the study of *cognatic societies. In 1983 his *Margaret Mead and Samoa*, with its biting criticisms of †Margaret Mead's work on adolescent Samoan sexuality and of cultural *relativism generally, propelled him to much wider fame. The book was intended to convince anthropologists of the error of their non-scientific ways and bring them to the truth of broadly *sociobiological approaches to anthropological problems. In fact, Freeman's polemical style was counter-productive within the discipline, even as it convinced many general readers of the validity of his case against Mead. See *scandals.

Freud, Sigmund (1856–1939) Austrian physician and the founder of psychoanalysis. Most anthropologists associate him with his *Totem und Tabu* (1913; *Totem and Taboo*, 1950). In its closing pages he suggests, somewhat polemically, that human society began with the overthrow of 'father right' by a primeval band of brothers who sought to commit *incest with their mother. His argument is significant for its insistence that the desire to commit incest is natural, and its prohibition a major determinant of culture. Freud's more general arguments have influenced the development of *Lévi-Straussian *structuralism, and American *symbolic anthropology, as well as the relatively small number of psychoanalytic anthropologists like †Devereux and †Roheim. See *psychoanalysis.

Frobenius, Leo (1873–1938) A highly prolific member of the *diffusionist school and originator of the concepts of the †*Kulturkreis* (culture-circle) and of the *Paideuma* (or 'soul' of a culture). Although he had no academic training, he did extensive research in Africa financed by donors and by his own income from books and lectures.

Major works include *Der Ursprung der afrikanischen Kulturen* (1898; *The Voice of Africa*, 2 vols, 1968), *Und Afrika sprach*, 3 vols. (1912-13), *Atlantis* (12 vols (1921-30), *Erlebte Erdteile*, 7 vols. (1925-30) and *Kulturgeschichte Afrikas* (1933). See *German and Austrian anthropology.

Fürer-Haimendorf, Christoph von See †Haimendorf, Christoph von Fürer.

Fustel de Coulanges, Numa-Denys (1830–89) French sociologist who influenced †Durkheim. His major work was *The Ancient City* (1864).

Gadamer, Hans-Georg (1900–) German philosopher especially influential among anthropologists who see the discipline as essentially †hermeneutic in method. He and his followers see hermeneutics as not merely concerned with passive interpretation, but with the culturally-influenced recreation of knowledge. Works include *Wahrheit und Methode* (1960; *Truth and Method* 1984).

Geertz, Clifford (1926–) Highly influential American cultural anthropologist. After graduate school at Harvard, he taught at Berkeley and the University of Chicago, before becoming the first (and only) anthropologist at Princeton's Institute for Advanced Study. He has carried out fieldwork in Java, Bali and Morocco, and published important studies of *religion (*The Religion of Java*, 1961), *cultural ecology (*Agricultural Involution*, 1963), *Islam (*Islam Observed*, 1968), and the fictions of *ethnographic writing (*Works and Lives*, 1988). But it is for his essays, especially those collected in *The Interpretation of Cultures* (1973) that he is best known. His theoretical position derives from †Max Weber, or that version of Weber promulgated by †Talcott Parsons, with additional influences from American *culture and personality anthropologists, literary theorists like Kenneth Burke, and philosophers such as †Ricoeur and the later †Wittgenstein, all melded in a baroquely inimitable prose style. Above all Geertz is credited with advancing the idea of anthropology as a kind of †interpretive or hermeneutic practice, concerned to elicit what he calls ††thick description. See *symbolic anthropology.

Gellner, Ernest (1925–95) A philosopher and social theorist as much as an anthropologist, Gellner conducted fieldwork in North Africa and wrote extensively on *Islamic society, but is at least as well known for his work in the philosophy of the social sciences. Before his retirement he held chairs in philosophy (at the London School of Economics) and social anthropology (at Cambridge). A genuine cosmopolitan, Gellner was among the first anthropologists to establish relations with colleagues in the former Eastern bloc, and did much to encourage anthropology in *Eastern and Central Europe. A formidable polemicist, never afraid to attack what he thought was a bad idea, his numerous publications include *Words and Things* (1959), *Saints of the Atlas* (1969), *The Devil in Modern Philosophy* (1974), *Nations and Nationalism* (1983), and *Relativism and the Social Sciences* (1985). See *nationalism, *rationality.

Gifford, Edward W. (1887–1959) Long curator of the University of California Museum of Anthropology, Gifford is perhaps best remembered for his work in Californian archaeology and for his 'discovery' of the †segmentary lineage system, a notion later borrowed by †E.E. Evans-Pritchard. His famous paper, 'Miwok Lineages and the Political Unit in Aboriginal California', was published in *American Anthropologist* in 1926.

Gillen, F.J. See †Spencer, Sir Baldwin.

Gluckman, Max (1911–75) South African anthropologist who settled in Britain and became prominent through his work on the anthropology of *law, on conflict, and on *ritual, especially in the context of Southern and Central African ethnography. Professor at Manchester, and leading figure in the †Manchester school of anthropologists, he lead anthropology there away from simplistic functionalist models towards ones more concerned with social dynamics. Among his major books are *Custom and Conflict in Africa* (1955), *Order and Rebellion in Tribal Africa* (1963), and *Politics, Law and Ritual in Tribal Society* (1965).

Goffman, Erving (1922–82) Canadian-born sociologist who emphasized the analysis of everyday events. He did fieldwork in the Shetland Islands and in a mental hospital in Washington, DC. His most important works are *The Presentation of Self in Everyday Life* (1959) and *Asylums* (1961).

Goldenweiser, Alexander A. (1880–1940) Ukrainian-born anthropologist and philosopher who studied under *F. Boas and wrote widely on education, morality, and immigration. However,

his fame today rests on his 'Totemism, an analytical study', *Journal of American Folk-Lore* (1910), which anticipated *Lévi-Strauss's argument that totemism is but a figment of the Western mind. Other works include *Early Civilization* (1923), *History, Psychology and Culture* (1933), and *Anthropology* (1937). See *totemism.

Goodenough, Ward H. (1919–) American anthropologist who came to prominence through his work on *kinship, and especially through his development of *componential analysis. His works include 'Componential analysis and the study of meaning', *Language* (1956), *Description and Comparison in Cultural Anthropology* (1970) and *Culture, Language and Society* (1971).

Goody, Jack (1919–) British anthropologist whose early work was associated with the Cambridge functionalist tradition of †M. Fortes. Goody has conducted extensive fieldwork in West Africa and published ethnographic analyses of *kinship, *ritual and *ancestors. Since the early 1970s, though, he has almost single-handedly maintained the tradition of grand comparison, returning repeatedly to the broad contrast between Africa and Asia. He is particularly noted for his work on kinship and the *family (e.g. *Production and Reproduction*, 1976; *The Development of the Family and Marriage in Europe*, 1983) and the implications of *literacy (e.g. *The Domestication of the Savage Mind*, 1977; *The Logic of Writing and the Organization of Society*, 1986).

Graebner, Fritz (1877–1934) Leading *diffusionist thinker, who took up †Frobenius's notion of 'culture circles' (†*Kulturkreise*) and in 1904 founded a 'school' (the *Kulturkreislehre*) around the idea. Like Malinowski, he happened to be in Australia at the outbreak of World War I. He was interned there for five years, and unlike Malinowski never got the chance to engage in fieldwork despite his wide knowledge and interest in the cultures and culture circles of Oceania. He became director of the Cologne Museum in 1925, but within three years mental illness forced him into retirement and he returned to his native Berlin. Among his works are 'Kulturkreise und Kulturschichten in Ozeanien', *Zeitschrift für Ethnologie* (1905), *Methode der Ethnologie* (1911) and *Das Weltbild der Primitiven* (1924). See *German and Austrian anthropology.

Gramsci, Antonio (1891–1937) Italian Marxist theorist and political activist, who died as a prisoner of Mussolini's fascist regime. In his *Prison Notebooks* (published in English in 1971) he developed a version of Marxist theory which emphasized the cultural mechanisms of *class domination, through an analysis of processes of †hegemony within †civil society. His ideas were important in the development of *cultural studies, and have been widely employed by anthropologists interested in issues of *power and *resistance.

Granet, Marcel (1884–1940) French sociologist and sinologist, influenced by †Durkheim and a close associate of †Marcel Mauss, whose many publications include *La religion des Chinois* (1922; *The Religion of the Chinese People*, 1975), *La civilisation chinoise* (1923; *Chinese Civilization*, 1930) and 'Catégories matrimoniales et relations de proximité dans la Chine ancienne' (*Année sociologique*, 1939). The last was a major influence in the development of *Lévi-Strauss's theory of kinship. See *Chinese anthropology.

Greenberg, Joseph (1915–) One of the great anthropological linguists in the tradition of *Boas and †Sapir. Although he wrote his PhD dissertation on the influence of Islam on Sudanese religions, almost all of his subsequent work has been in descriptive linguistics and language classification. His major works include *The Languages of Africa* (1963), *Universals of Language* (1963) and editing the four-volume *Universals of Human Language* (1978).

Griaule, Marcel (1898–1956) French anthropologist best known for his rich ethnography of the Dogon of Mali. He first encountered the Dogon in 1931 during the Dakar-Djibouti Mission (whose members included †Michel Leiris), and returned repeatedly in subsequent years, culminating in his intense work on Dogon *cosmology with an old informant called Ogotommêli. His writings include *Méthode de l'ethnographie* (1937), *Masques Dogon* (1938), *Arts de l'Afrique noire* (1947) and *Dieu d'eau, entretiens avec Ogotemmêli* (1948; *Conversations with Ogotemmeli*, 1965), and with †G. Dieterlen *Le renard pâle* (1965). See *French anthropology.

Grottanelli, Vinigi (1912–) Foremost Italian ethnologist. Grottanelli did fieldwork in Ethiopia, Somalia, Kenya, and Ghana, among other places, and his work has been influenced by the †*Kulturkreis* school. Among his more general works is *Storia universale dell'arte: Australia, Oceania, Africa nera* (1987).

Gusinde, Martin (1886–1969) Missionary-ethnographer who wrote *Die Feuerlandindianer*, (3 vols, 1931–39), *Die Kongo-Pygmäen in Geschichte und Gegenwart* (1942) and *Von gelben und schwarzen Buschmännern* (1966). See *German and Austrian anthropology.

Habermas, Jürgen (1929–) German philosopher and social theorist whose critique of technological rationality, championing of †hermeneutics, and grand theory of communicative action have all had an impact across the human sciences. His writings are, however, relentlessly Eurocentric, which probably explains their muted reception by anthropologists, although in recent years his critique of *postmodernism has attracted anthropological attention, as has his interest in the sociology of criticism in the public sphere.

Haddon, Alfred Cort (1855–1940) Cambridge zoologist and anthropologist. Leader of the Cambridge Expedition to the †Torres Straits in 1898–9 and father-figure of Cambridge anthropology. His works include *Evolution in Art* (1895) and *A Short History of Anthropology* (1910). The latter remains one of the finest histories of anthropology ever written.

Haimendorf, Christoph von Fürer (1909–95) Austrian-born anthropologist who taught for many years at the School of Oriental and African Studies, University of London. His extensive field research, especially among so-called 'tribals', in India and Nepal led to a great number of publications, including ethnographic studies such as *The Chenchus* (1943) and *The Sherpas of Nepal* (1964), comparative works such as *Morals and Merit* (1967), and studies of social change such as *A Himalayan Tribe* (1980).

Harris, Marvin (1929–) American anthropologist whose materialist approach has been both influential and controversial. Characteristic publications include *Cannibals and Kings* (1977) and *Cultural Materialism* (1979). He is also the author of a major history of the discipline, *The Rise of Anthropological Theory* (1968). See *cultural materialism.

Hegel, Georg Wilhelm F. (1770–1831) German philosopher whose philosophy of history and dialectical method had a profound impact on †Marx and ultimately upon Marxism. The Hegelian dialectic is commonly phrased simplistically as 'thesis, antithesis, synthesis', a rational process through which history, among other things, unfolds. In his philosophy of history Hegel employed comparative examples, particularly from Asian history, but his impact on anthropology has generally been mediated through other thinkers he influenced, mostly, but not exclusively, Marxists.

Herder, Johann Gottfried (1744–1803) German philosopher and early anthropological thinker. A critic of aspects of *Enlightenment thought, he is often seen as an early champion of German nationalism. Most importantly for anthropologists, he argued for a strong version of linguistic and cultural relativism, criticized European *colonialism, and started to use the word 'culture' in its modern, plural sense. See *culture.

Herskovits, Melville J. (1895–1963) American anthropologist, influenced above all by his teacher *F. Boas. Herskovits made important contributions to *economic anthropology and the theory of †acculturation, but is best known for his pioneering ethnographic research on African Americans, including the black population of *Central America and the *Caribbean, and his championing of Africanist research in the United States. Major works include *The American Negro* (1928), *Man and His Works* (1948), *Economic Anthropology* (1952), *The Human Factor in Changing Africa* (1962). See *Caribbean.

Hertz, Robert (1881–1915) Sociologist of religion. One of the most brilliant and promising of †Durkheim's students, he was tragically killed in World War I. Little known outside France until the publication of a translation of his essays on *death and right-left symbolism in *Death and the Right Hand* (1960). See *body, *death.

Heyerdahl, Thor (1914–) Norwegian adventurer, known for his attempts to prove the possibility of migration and *diffusion across the oceans by sailing in replica boats and rafts. Among his many popular books are *Kon-Tiki* (1950), *Aku-Aku* (1958), *The Ra Expeditions* (1971), and *The Tigris Expedition* (1981).

Hobbes, Thomas (1588–1679) English philosopher whose classic description of the state of nature as 'solitary, poore, nasty, brutish and short' came to be contrasted with the *Enlightenment notion of the †'noble savage'. His famous statement comes from *Leviathan* (1651), which depicts the origin and growth of the *state.

Hocart, A.M. (1883–1939) British anthropologist of French descent. Carried out fieldwork in the Solomon Islands with Rivers as part of the Percy Sladen Trust Expedition. Worked also in Fiji, Tonga and Samoa where he followed his chief interest in the history of culture, before taking up a position as Archaeological Commissioner in Ceylon from 1921 to 1928. In 1934 he took up †Evans-Pritchard's chair in Cairo, where he died in 1939. Hocart's combination of *diffusionism, *evolutionism, and †conjectural history, was at odds with the prevailing mood of British anthropology in the 1930s, and his work drifted out of fashion until first †Louis Dumont, and then †Rodney Needham, championed it in the 1950s and 1960s. Since then, his ideas have provoked fresh analyses of topics like *caste and *kingship. His works include *Kingship* (1927), *The Progress of Man* (1933), *Kings and Councillors* (1936), *Les Castes* (1938; *Caste* 1950), *The Life-Giving Myth* (1952) and *Social Origins* (1954).

Hodgkin, Thomas (1798–1866) English anatomist and leading figure in early eighteenth-century ethnology. He is best known for his discovery in 1832 of the disease of the lymph nodes which bears his name. Less well-known is the fact that, shortly after, he was denied promotion because of his outspoken championship of the rights of North American Indians. He campaigned for the abolition of slavery, for the recognition of socio-economic causes of poor health, and for the reconciliation of religion and evolutionary theory. He was also instrumental in setting up the Aborigines Protection Society (in 1837) and the Ethnological Society of London (in 1844), each in their different ways dedicated to the essential unity of the human species.

Hoebel, E. Adamson (1906–93) American anthropologist of *law. Well known both for his ethnographic work among *Native North Americans and for his collaborative work with lawyers such as Karl Llewellyn, most notably in *The Cheyenne Way* (1941). His other works include

The Law of Primitive Man (1954), *Man in the Primitive World* (1949) and with T. Weaver, *Anthropology and the Human Experience* (1979).

Hoernlé Agnes Winifred (née Tucker) (1885–1960) Called by †M. Gluckman the 'mother' of South African anthropology, Hoernlé trained a generation including †Eileen and †Jack Krige, †Hilda Kuper, Ellen Hellmann, and Gluckman himself, at the University of the Witwatersrand. She herself had studied under †Haddon and †Rivers at Cambridge and †Durkheim at the Sorbonne. Like many of her successors in South African anthropology, she was active in social causes, particularly in the improvement of black education and in penal reform. A collection of her writings, *The Social Organization of the Nama, and Other Essays*, appeared in her centennial year (1985).

Honigmann, John Joseph (1914–77) American anthropologist known for his work on personality and on †acculturation. He did extensive fieldwork in the Canadian Subarctic and *Arctic, and shorter studies in Pakistan and Austria. His more general works include *Culture and Personality* (1954), *The World of Man* (1959), *Personality in Culture* (1967), *Handbook of Social and Cultural Anthropology* (1973) and *The Development of Anthropological Ideas* (1976).

Howitt, A.W. See †Fison, Lorimer

Hsu, Francis L.K. (1909–) Chinese-born American anthropologist. Hsu has carried out fieldwork in China, Japan, India and the United States and written extensively on *culture and personality. Works on Chinese society include *Under the Ancestors' Shadow* (1948). Other major works include his edited volume *Kinship and Culture* (1971), which explores his 1965 hypothesis that culture-specific dyadic relationships in *kinship determine attitudes and behaviour within wider social relations later in life.

Humboldt, Alexander von (1769–1859) Traveller-naturalist and ethnographer, and younger brother of the philosopher-linguist †Wilhelm von Humboldt. He travelled and wrote widely on the peoples of the Americas, especially Mexico. Among his many works is *Reisen in Amerika und Asien*, (4 vols, 1842). See *Enlightenment anthropology.

Humboldt, Wilhelm von (1767–1835) Philosopher and linguist, best known for his work in establishing the modern German university system, but also a formidable comparative linguist. In his posthumous *Über die Verschiedenheit des menschlichen Sprachbaues* (1836; English translation *On Language: The Diversity of Human Language-Structure and its Influence on the Mental Development of Mankind*, 1988) he attempted one of the first systematic explorations of the relation between language structure, †world-view and *cognition, thus initiating the line of enquiry which was to culminate in the so-called *Sapir–Whorf hypothesis.

Hunter, Monica See †Wilson, Monica

Husserl, Edmund (1859–1938) Austro-German mathematician and philosopher. The founder of †phenomenology.

Huxley, Thomas Henry (1825–95) English biologist who became the foremost proponent of †Darwin's theory of *evolution by natural selection. Anthropological works include *Evidence as to Man's Place in Nature* (1863), 'Essay on the Methods and Results of Ethnology' (*Fortnightly Review* 1865).

Ishi (c. 1862–1916) A Yahi who became known as the last 'wild Indian' of North America. He escaped from genocidal attacks on the Yahi by settlers but was eventually captured and turned over to †A.L. Kroeber and Thomas Waterman. He spent his last years living in the Anthropology Museum of the University of California at San Francisco and his biography was recorded by Theodora Kroeber, in *Ishi in Two Worlds* (1961).

Jakobson, Roman (1896–1982) Russian-American linguist, associated with the Prague school, whose work in phonology greatly influenced *Lévi-Strauss's structural anthropology. The two met in New York in the early 1940s, when both were in exile from German-occupied Europe. Lévi-Strauss applied Jakobson's methods of linguistic analysis to the study of culture, particularly his use of †distinctive features to analyse †binary oppositions. Of his many publications, *Fundamentals of Language* (with M. Halle, 1956) has been most often quoted by structural anthropologists.

Jenness, Diamond (1886–1969) New Zealand-born anthropologist who worked for many years at the National Museum of Canada. His fame rests on his classic ethography, *The Life of the Copper Eskimo* (1923), and his encyclopedic *The Indians of Canada* (1932). The latter has gone through many editions and remains the standard work on its subject.

Jones, Sir William (1746–94) British lawyer and Orientalist. He published on Persian grammar and Arabic poetry, but his importance rests on his discovery, in 1787, of the similarities between Sanskrit, Greek and Latin.

Jones, William (1871–1909) Born on the Sauk and Fox Reservation in Oklahoma, Jones became probably the first anthropologist of Indian descent to work with his own people. He studied anthropology at Columbia under *F. Boas and did fieldwork both in Oklahoma and on the Great Lakes. In 1907 he began research with the Ilongot of the Philippines and was killed there in 1909.

Josselin de Jong, J.P.B. de (1886–1964) One of the founders of the Leiden structuralist school. Important also for bringing *Lévi-Strauss's theory of kinship to the attention of anglophone anthropologists. His works include *De Maleische Archipel als ethnologisch studieveld* (1935; 'The Malay Archipelago as a Field of Ethnological Study', in P.E. de Josselin de Jong, ed., *Structural Anthropology in the Netherlands*, 1977) and *Lévi-Strauss's Theory of Kinship and Marriage* (1952). See *Dutch anthropology.

Junod, Henri (1863–1934) Swiss missionary in Mozambique. His writings on the Tsonga (Ba-Thonga) sparked *Radcliffe-Brown's early critique of *evolutionism, with reference to the *avunculate. Works include *La tribu et la langue Thonga* (1896) and *The Life of a South African Tribe*, (2 vols, 1912–13). See *German and Austrian anthropology.

Kaberry, Phyllis M. (1910–77) American-born British anthropologist who studied at Sydney and with *Malinowski at the London School of Economics. She did fieldwork in Western Australia, Papua New Guinea, and Cameroon. With books such as *Aboriginal Women* (1939) and *Women of the Grassfields* (1951) she pioneered the anthropological study of women, and she took great pride in her title Queen Mother of Nso, conferred upon her by the Fon (king of Nso) in appreciation of her work with his people. See *Aboriginal Australia.

Kardiner, Abram (1891–1981) American psychoanalyst who made major contributions in *psychological anthropology. His 1930s seminar on *culture and personality in New York included †Sapir, †Benedict, †Cora Du Bois, and †Ralph Linton. In *The Individual and His Society* (1939) he developed a distinction between †primary and secondary institutions and the concept of a basic personality structure in any given society. A pupil and analysand of †Freud, he spent much of his career as a clinical analyst.

Kenyatta, Jomo (Johnstone Kemau) (1889–1978) Kenyatta is best known as leader of the Mau Mau rebellion and subsequent Prime Minister and President of Kenya. However, he was also a member of *Malinowski's seminar at the London School of Economics and wrote his ethnography of the Kikuyu, *Facing Mount Kenya* (1938), under Malinowski's influence.

Kirchhof, Paul (1900–72) German anthropologist perhaps best known for his 1927 classification of *relationship terminologies (published in various journals in the late 1920s and early 1930s), which anticipated later work by both †Lowie and †Murdock. Deprived of his German nationality in 1939, Kirchhof became a Mexican citizen and spent most of his career in that country. In 1955 he helped to establish the Escula Nacional de Antropología e Historia. See *German and Austrian anthropology.

Klemm, Gustav (1802–67) German social philosopher who wrote extensively on the concept of *culture, thus providing an intellectual link between early Romantic writers like †Herder, and *Boas's development of the full-blown anthropological concept of culture. His major work was *Kulturgeschichte der Menschheit*, 10 vols (1843–52).

Kluckhohn, Clyde (1905–60) American anthropologist best known for his work on Navaho culture, and more generally on *culture and personality, on religion, and on cultural values. He created the Harvard Department of Social Relations, with †Talcott Parsons, whose students included †Clifford Geertz and †David Schneider. His works include *Navaho Witchcraft* (1944), *Mirror for Man* (1947), and *Culture and Behavior* (1961), and with †A.L. Kroeber *Culture: A Critical Review of Concepts and Definitions* (1952).

Knox, Robert (1641–1720) British seaman who spent many years as a captive of the King of Kandy in what is now Sri Lanka and wrote an important early ethnography, *An Historical Relation of the Island Ceylon* (1681).

Knox, Robert (1791–1862) Scottish anatomist famed for his involvement with the murderers Burke and Hare. His importance to anthropology rests on the theory of †polygenesis propounded in *Races of Men: A Fragment* (1850).

Kohler, Josef (1849–1919) Jurist from Heidelberg and an early theorist on primitive *marriage. Works include *Zur Lehre von der Blutrache* (1885), *Recht der Azteken* (1892) and *Zur Urgeschicht der Ehe* (1897; *On the Prehistory of Marriage*, 1975).

Krige, Eileen Jensen (1904–95) South African anthropologist trained by †Hoernlé and influential as first professor of social anthropology at the University of Natal, Durban. Contributions include *The Social System of the Zulus* (1937) and, with Jack Krige, *The Realm of the Rain Queen* (1943).

Krige, J.D. (Jack) (1896–1959) South African anthropologist. His interest in anthropology came in part from his uncle, the soldier-politician Jan Smuts, who was instrumental in bringing *Radcliffe-Brown to South Africa. E. Jensen Krige and J.D. Krige's romantic and functionalist account of Lovedu social structure (*The Realm of the Rain Queen*, 1943) became a classic.

Kroeber, Alfred Louis (1876–1960) Along with †Lowie, Kroeber was one of *Boas's early students. With Lowie he helped to establish the anthropology department at Berkeley and bring it to prominence. He carried out ethnographic research among California Indians and made major contributions in a variety of theoretical areas within the broad Boasian tradition, including *cultural ecology, historical anthropology, and culture patterns and processes. His important works include *The Superorganic* (1917), *Anthropology* (1923), *Handbook of the Indians of California* (ed., 1925) and *Configurations of Culture Growth* (1944). See *culture.

Kropotkin, Peter (1842–1921) Russian geographer, anarchist philosopher and (at least according to tradition) early mentor of *Radcliffe-Brown. In *Mutual Aid* (1902) Kropotkin described the evolution of society as one in which co-operation proved persistent and functional.

Kuhn, Thomas (1922–) American philosopher of science. In *The Structure of Scientific Revolutions* (1962), Kuhn described science in terms of communities of scientists, whose activities are constrained by sets of shared assumptions which he termed †paradigms. In periods of 'normal science' these paradigms effectively guide and limit research, but when they fail, the ensuing crisis can lead to a 'revolution' and replacement of an old paradigm with a new one. Although Kuhn has claimed that his work describes only the workings of physical science, and that he actually borrowed his ideas from social science (which conspicuously lacks the kind of implicit agreement on basic assumptions characteristic of the 'hard' sciences), nevertheless his work has had great impact in the social sciences, not least in anthropology. See *rationality, *science.

Kuper, Hilda Beemer (1911–92) Distinguished British ethnographer of Southern Africa. She was one of *Malinowski's students and went on to do fieldwork in Southern Africa, especially in Swaziland, producing works such as *An African Aristocracy* (1947) and *Indian People of Natal* (1960). She was also active in politics and together with her husband, Leo Kuper, was a founder member of the Liberal Party in South Africa.

Lacan, Jacques (1901–83) French psychoanalyst who argued against many of his contemporaries that Freudian, and especially early Freudian theory (e.g. in dream analysis), ought to remain the basis of psychoanalysis. He also famously argued that the unconscious is structured like a language, thus replacing the mechanical elements in Freud's metapsychology with rhetorical figures and endlessly slippery acts of signification. Despite his fiercely difficult writing style, he has become increasingly influential, especially in feminist theories of the gendered subject. His collected *Écrits* (writings) were published in French in 1966 and in English in 1977. See *psychoanalysis.

Lafitau, Joseph-François (1681–1740) Missionary and ethnographer of the Iroquois. He anticipated *Morgan in his discovery of †classificatory kinship terminology in *Les moeurs des sauvages américains comparées aux moeurs des premiers temps* (2 vols, 1724; *Customs of the American*

Indians Compared with the Customs of Primitive Times, 1974–77).

Lane, Edward William (1801–1876) Early Orientalist and author of *Manners and Customs of the Modern Egyptians* (1836) and *Arabic Lexicon* (1863–90).

Lang, Andrew (1844–1912) Scottish folklorist who made a name for himself in attacks on the work of †F. Max Müller, †J.G. Frazer, and †E.B. Tylor, among others. His central contentions were that myth represents true history and that primitive monotheism predates the technological advances other writers believed led to it. Lang also wrote on psychic phenomena and collaborated with H. Rider Haggard in *The World's Desire* (1890), a fantasy set in Ancient Egypt. His more important works include *Custom and Myth* (1884), *Myth, Ritual and Religion* (1887), *The Making of Religion* (1898), *Magic and Religion* (1901), and *The Secret of the Totem* (1905).

Layard, John (1891–1972) Layard was trained at Cambridge by †W.H.R. Rivers and did fieldwork in the New Hebrides (now Vanuatu) in 1914–15. He was later a patient, then a disciple, of Carl Jung, and incorporated Jungian psychology into his Melanesian ethnography. His best-known work is *Stone Men of Malekula* (1942).

Leach, Sir Edmund R. (1910–89) One of the greatest of British anthropologists. Trained originally as an engineer, Leach later worked with *Malinowski and †Firth. His field research in Burma was famously interrupted by World War II, but was used as the basis of *Political Systems of Highland Burma* (1954), his account of the oscillating equilibrium between two models of social structure he called †*gumsa* and *gumlao*. This extraordinarily imaginative analysis explicitly challenged the reigning assumptions of British *functionalism, as did the work of *Lévi-Strauss, which he championed during the 1950s and 1960s. Leach moved from the London School of Economics to Cambridge, where his combative intellectual style was pitted against the arguments of colleagues like †M. Fortes and †J. Goody, and he gathered around him a cohort of highly gifted students. Further fieldwork in Sri Lanka lead to the sternly materialist and empiricist *Pul Eliya* (1961), while his brilliant critical essays of the

1950s and early 1960s are collected in *Rethinking Anthropology* (1962).

Leakey, L.S.B. (1903–72) British paleontologist, archaeologist and anthropologist. He was a pioneer in uncovering the human past in Africa through his numerous expeditions in the east of the continent. He set up the highly successful Centre for Prehistory and Palaeontology as part of the Kenya National Museums. He published a wide range of works, from *Stone Age Africa* (1936) and *The Progress and Evolution of Man in Africa* (1961), to *Kenya: Contrasts and Problems* (1936) and his autobiography, *White African* (1937).

Leenhardt, Maurice (1878–1954) French missionary and ethnographer. After more than twenty years in New Caledonia, he returned to Paris where in 1941 he inherited †Mauss's chair in primitive religion. Although many of his writings are relatively unstructured compilations of ethnographic data, his final work *Do Kamo* (1947; English translation, 1979) is an extraordinary synthetic account of *myth and *personhood in *Melanesia. Its English translation in 1979, and the publication of James Clifford's excellent biography *Person and Myth: Maurice Leenhardt in the Melanesian World* (1982), successfully turned this occasionally rather nineteenth-century figure into a model for the *postmodern future of anthropology.

Leiris, Michel (1901–90) French anthropologist and poet. He used his participation in the Mission Dakar-Djibouti of the early 1930s as the basis for his *L'Afrique fantôme* (1934), an early exercise in francophone *reflexivity. His literary activities, membership with Bataille of the surrealist 'Collège de sociologie', and early anti-colonial arguments brought him late celebrity in United States in the postmodern 1980s.

Leroi-Gourhan, André (1911–86) French biological anthropologist, prehistorian and ethnologist. His major contributions were in the the methodology and theory of prehistoric art and technology. Works include *Archaeologie du Pacifique Nord*, 2 vols (1964–5). See *technology.

Lesser, Alexander (1902–82) American anthropologist who studied under *Boas, conducted fieldwork in several Plains Indians cultures and became an ardent critic of *Radcliffe-Brownian *functionalism. His collected papers were published as *History, Evolution and the Concept of Culture* in 1985. See *American anthropology.

Lévi-Strauss, Claude (1908–) Belgian-born French anthropologist and the founder of anthropological *structuralism. His work has been highly influential, not only in anthropology but also in other social sciences and in literary theory. See main entry and *structuralism.

Lévy-Bruhl, Lucien (1857–1939) French philosopher whose evolutionist ideas of primitive thought influenced not only his contemporaries but later thinkers such as †Evans-Pritchard, whose study of *witchcraft among the Azande was intended as a refutation of Lévy-Bruhl's central claims. The most important of his six monographs on the subject was *La mentalité primitive* (1922; *Primitive Mentality*, 1923). After his death his notebooks were published, and these indicate a change in his thinking with a recognition that the characteristics he had isolated for primitive thought were in fact encountered in certain contexts in all societies. See *primitive mentality, *rationality.

Lewis, Oscar (1914–70) American anthropologist famous for his controversial notion of the †culture of poverty and for his restudy of †Robert Redfield's field area. Whereas Redfield had emphasized normative rules, Lewis concentrated on behaviour and came to rather different conclusions about life in the Mexican village. Works include *Life in a Mexican Village* (1951), *La Vida: A Puerto Rican Family in the Culture of Poverty* (1966) and *The Children of Sanchez* (1961).

Lienhardt, Godfrey (1921–93) British anthropologist who carried out fieldwork among the Dinka and Anuak in Southern Sudan and taught for many years with †E.E. Evans-Pritchard at Oxford. One of the most brilliant, but relatively reticent, anthropologists of his generation, his monograph on Dinka religion *Divinity and Experience* (1961) is at once a classic ethnography and a subtle meditation on the necessary limits of ethnography.

Linton, Ralph (1883–1953) American anthropologist of the *culture and personality school. He began his career as an archaeologist of Native North America and Polynesia. In 1925 he began ethnographic fieldwork in Madagascar, but his ethnography (e.g. *The Tanala*, 1933) was weak by modern standards. Important general works include *The Study of Man* (1936), *The Cultural Background of Personality* (1945), *The Tree of Culture* (1955).

Locke, John (1632–1704) British moral philosopher whose methodology stressed careful observation of people in daily life. He is most famous for the notion of the person as a †*tabula rasa*, an idea which anticipates the twentieth-century relativistic anthropology of *F. Boas. His works dealt with a theory of learning in *Essay Concerning Human Understanding* (1690), the process of socialization in *Some Thoughts Concerning Education* (1693), and political society in *Two Treatises on Government* (1690).

Lorenz, Konrad (1903–89) Austrian scientist who founded the discipline of †ethology. His works on aggression and other aspects of animal behaviour have also been influential in the later development of *sociobiology.

Lounsbury, Floyd G. (1914–) Linguist and anthropologist who, with †Goodenough, introduced *componential analysis in the study of *relationship terminologies in 1956. His later work on kinship terminology, however, focused on the formal logic behind the 'reduction' of kinship terms to their primary genealogical foci. Among his significant works is *A Study in Structural Semantics* (co-authored with Harold Scheffler, 1971), which applies his formal methods to the analysis of the *'Crow'-type kinship terminology of the Siriono of Venezuela.

Lowie, Robert H. (1883–1957) Lowie was *Boas's first PhD student and an advocate of †historical particularism, who went on to become one of the most important anthropologists of his day. He contributed greatly to the development of theoretical ideas in American anthropology by fostering systematic enquiries in kinship, culture history, and cross-cultural comparison. His major fieldwork was among Plains Indians, and he also maintained ethnographic interests in South American and European culture. His many works include *Primitive Society* (1920), *Primitive Religion* (1924), *The Origin of the State* (1927), *The Crow Indians* (1935), *The History of Ethnological Theory* (1937), *The German People* (1945), *Social Organization* (1948) and *Indians of the Plains* (1954). See *culture.

Lubbock, Sir John (Lord Avebury) (1834–1913)
Banker, politician, entomologist, prehistorian, and
anthropologist, who was very active in the early
days of the Anthropological Institute. His major
contribution as an anthropologist was in popular-
izing evolutionary theory, which he did with a
style unequalled among his contemporaries. Works
include *The Origin of Civilization and the Primitive
Condition of Man* (1870) and *Prehistoric Times* (1872).

Lyotard, Jean-François (1924–) French philosopher. In his influential *La condition postmoderne:
rapport sur le savoir* (1979; *The Postmodern Condition*,
1984) he characterized the *postmodern in terms
of the decline of grand theory (or †metanarratives
as his translators would have it), and its replacement by any number of incommensurable
language-games.

McLennan, John Ferguson (1827–81) Edinburgh jurist. Disputed with *Morgan over the
relative importance of †exogamy (McLennan's
term) and *relationship terminologies as clues to
the past. Works include *Primitive Marriage* (1865)
and *Studies in Ancient History* (1876).

Maine, Sir Henry Sumner (1822–88) Legal
historian whose early academic career culminated
in the publication of *Ancient Law* (1861), which
famously posited a general evolutionary movement from †status to †contract. He then spent
seven years in India, overseeing legislation and
legal reform, and continuing his work on comparative social institutions, some of which was
published in *Village Communities in the East and West*
(1871), before returning to an academic career in
Oxford and Cambridge.

Mair, Lucy (1901–86) British anthropologist
trained by Malinowski. She worked extensively
in East Africa and contributed to the growth of
†applied anthropology, first in colonial administration and later in social *development. Works
include *An African People in the Twentieth Century*
(1934), *Studies in Applied Anthropology* (1957) and
Anthropology and Development (1984).

Malinowski, Bronislaw (1884–1942) Polish
anthropologist who moved to England in 1910.
At the start of World War I he was in Australia
and chose to spend his 'internment' (he was
then an Austrian citizen and enemy alien) on the
Trobriand Islands, where, anthropological tradi-

tion has it, he developed the methodology of
†participant observation which became characteristic of the British school he later led. Upon his
return to England, he taught at the London School
of Economics and trained a generation in his
methods and theoretical stance. He called his
perspective *functionalist, and although he battled
with *Radcliffe-Brown over the locus and nature
of social functions, the two became twin pillars of
the British tradition which emerged. His major
publications include *Argonauts of the Western Pacific*
(1922), *Crime and Custom in Savage Society* (1926), *Sex
and Repression in Savage Society* (1927), *The Sexual Life
of Savages in North-Western Melanesia* (1929) and *Coral
Gardens and Their Magic* (1935). For further details,
see main entry, and *British anthropology, *fieldwork, *ethnography, *kula.

Mannheim, Karl (1893–1947) Hungarian sociologist and founder of the field which came to be
known as the sociology of knowledge. He taught
at Heidelberg, Frankfurt, and London.

Marett, R.R. (1866–1943) English barrister who
was influential in establishing social anthropology
at Oxford. In *The Threshold of Religion* (1909), he
speculated on 'pre-animist religion'. He also wrote
a popular introduction, *Anthropology* (1912).

Marshall, Lorna (1898–) An amateur anthropologist whose extensive ethnography of the
!Kung Bushmen provided much material for
evolutionist and ecological theorists. Her most
important work was published in the journal *Africa*
in the 1950s and 1960s.

Marx, Karl (1818–83) German political philosopher and revolutionary. See *Marxism and
anthropology.

Mauss, Marcel (1872–1950) Mauss provides the
intellectual and personal link between the work
of his uncle, †Émile Durkheim, and the French
anthropologists of the generation of *Lévi-Strauss
and †Louis Dumont. He published important
essays, alone or in collaboration, on *magic, *sacrifice and *classification. After the First World War,
he devoted much of his time to rescuing the work
of his many close colleagues who had died, but
also published his immensely influential essay on
*exchange (*The Gift*, [1925] 1952), which still
provides ideas and problems in *economic anthropology. In the 1930s he taught ethnographic

method to the first generation of French field-workers, and published characteristically short but fruitful essays on the category of the *person and techniques of the *body.

Mead, George Herbert (1863–1931) American sociologist and philosopher, influential in the development of †symbolic interactionism, and best known for his *Mind, Self and Society* (1934). His account of the emergence of 'self' from the encounter with the social world provides *inter alia* one source for the vocabulary of 'self' and 'other' in 1980s anthropology.

Mead, Margaret (1901–78) Probably the most famous anthropologist of the twentieth century, Mead studied under *Boas, and was greatly influenced by †Ruth Benedict. Her early study of adolescence, *Coming of Age in Samoa* (1928), was self-consciously aimed at a popular market and became a huge best-seller, at least as much for what it told its audience about America as for the quality (now hotly disputed) of its ethnography. She carried out fieldwork in New Guinea and Bali, making important contributions to the study of *socialization, *childhood and *gender, but never lost sight of her popular readers. Her very popularity made her an object of professional suspicion, especially in *British anthropology, and a predictable target for critics. See *scandals.

Monboddo, Lord (James Burnett) (1714–99) Eccentric Scottish judge, famous for his theory that the 'Orang Outang' (including chimpanzees) is a speechless branch of the human species. Works include *Of the Origin and Progress of Language* (6 vols, 1773–92) and *Ancient Metaphysics* (6 vols, 1779–99).

Montaigne, Michel Eyquem de (1533–92) French courtier and essayist. His *Essais* (first edition, 2 vols, 1580) include comments on the supposedly utopian lifestyle of American Indians, thus beginning the European myth of the virtues of 'savage life' (see †noble savage). Most famous among these writings is his essay 'On Cannibals', an eloquent early defence of cultural *relativism.

Montesquieu (Charles-Louis de Secondat, Baron de la Brède et de Montesquieu) (1689–1755) French nobleman and political philosopher. He studied law and the natural

sciences at Bordeaux, but became well known in his lifetime for works such as the *Lettres persanes* (1721; *Persian Letters*, 1722), a satirical account of French life through the eyes of two fictitious Persian travellers; and *De l'esprit des loix* (1748; *The Spirit of the Laws*, 1750), a monumental ethnographic survey of political systems. The latter anticipated *evolutionist, *ecological and *functionalist anthropology in many ways and was said by *Radcliffe-Brown to mark the beginning of anthropological enquiry. See *Enlightenment anthropology.

Morgan, Lewis Henry (1818–1881) American lawyer, politician, businessman, naturalist and anthropologist, widely regarded as the founder of the modern study of *kinship. For further details, see main entry.

Müller, F. Max (1823–1900) Orientalist and authority on mythology. Works include *Introduction to the Science of Religion* (1873), *Contributions to the Science of Mythology*, (2 vols, 1897), *Comparative Mythology* (1956).

Murdock, George Peter (1897–1985) American anthropologist best known for his massive cross-cultural surveys, and his typologies of *relationship terminologies. In 1949 he set up the †Human Relations Area Files, first at Yale then at Pittsburgh. He established the journal *Ethnology* in 1962 to promote the publication of ethnographic data. He also encouraged ethnographic research in the Pacific and set up a programme funded by the Office of Naval Research. His works include *Social Structure* (1949), *Outline of South American Cultures* (1951), *Outline of World Cultures* (1954) and *Africa: Its People and their Cultural History* (1959).

Nadel, S.F. (1903–1954) Nadel was born in Vienna but spent most of his academic career in England, where he studied with *Malinowski, and Australia. He was trained in psychology and music, but made his main contributions in Sudanese ethnography. His works in this field include *A Black Byzantium* (1942) and *The Nuba* (1947). He also brought an uncharacteristic concern for theoretical rigour to the resolutely empiricist tradition of *British anthropology, particularly in his two last books, *The Foundations of Social Anthropology* (1951), and the posthumous *Theory of Social Structure* (1957).

Needham, Rodney (1923–) Highly prolific British anthropologist and former professor of social anthropology at Oxford. Needham was an early champion of *Lévi-Strauss's theory of *kinship, and when Lévi-Strauss claimed Needham had misunderstood him (in *Structure and Sentiment*, 1962), an equally early critic. He has also published prolifically on issues of *belief and *classification.

Nimuendajú, Curt (Kurt Un[c]kel) (1883–1945) German ethnologist who settled in Brazil and took his Indian name Nimuendajú as his surname. He was a major contributor to †Julian Steward's *Handbook of South American Indians* (vol. 3, 1948) and also wrote *The Apinayé* (1939) and *The Eastern Timbira* (1946). See *Americas: Native South America (Lowland).

Oliver, Douglas (1913–) American anthropologist and historian of the Pacific. His *A Solomon Island Society* (1955) has become the classic study of *Big Man politics. Other major works in anthropology include his early ethnography, *Studies in the Anthropology of Bougainville, Solomon Islands* (1949), and general works such as *The Pacific Islands* (1951) and *Oceania* (1988). See *Pacific: Polynesia.

Opler, Morris E. (1907–) Opler wrote extensively on many subjects but is best known for his early work on the Apache (an interest he returned to later in his career) and his work on North India. Major works include *An Apache Life-Way* (1941) and *Apache Odyssey* (1969).

Pareto, Vilfredo (1848–1923) Italian economist and social theorist whose ideas have made occasional appearances in anthropology; †Edmund Leach, for example, claimed Pareto as the source of his idea of oscillating equilibrium in *Political Systems of Highland Burma* (1954). His major work was *Trattato di sociologia generale* (4 vols, 1916).

Parsons, Talcott (1902–79) The dominant theoretical figure in modern American *sociology, Parsons's first book, *The Structure of Social Action* (1937), introduced both †Durkheim and †Weber to American audiences. His version of *functionalism allowed space for *culture as a relatively autonomous domain of meaning, and Parsons's view of culture provides the link between the work of Weber himself and the *symbolic anthropology of †Clifford Geertz and †David Schneider.

Peirce, Charles Sanders (1839–1914) American scientist and pragmatic philosopher. He wrote extensively on the concept of the †sign, and his terminology of †symbol, †icon, and †index is used by some semiotically inclined anthropologists.

Peristiany, Jean George (1911–87) Greek-born, Oxford-trained anthropologist who wrote on both East African and Mediterranean societies – editing a classic symposium on *Honour and Shame* (1965) – and contributed to the international organization of anthropology through his post (from 1960 to 1978) as UNESCO Professor of Sociology. He later served as Cypriot Ambassador to France, Spain and Portugal.

Peter, H.R.H. Prince of Greece and Denmark (1908–80) Studied with *Malinowski and conducted fieldwork in the Himalayas and in South India. In spite of his royal background (which he admitted was a help in fieldwork), he spent his last twenty years working as a banker in the mornings and as an anthropologist in the afternoons. His most significant book was *A Study of Polyandry* (1963).

Piaget, Jean (1896–1980) Swiss psychologist whose studies of children's cognitive development transformed psychology. Although his general account of the interaction between innate schemas and the environment, which he called his 'genetic epistemology', provides a potentially powerful model for the anthropology of *childhood and learning, he is usually only known by anthropologists for his much less interesting system of developmental stages, which has been rather crudely and controversially applied to the modes of thought of non-Western cultures.

Pike, Kenneth L. (1912–) Anthropologist, linguist and evangelical missionary. Working with the Summer Institute of Linguistics, Pike developed techniques for language-learning for use in Bible-translation. Pike's fame, however, rests on distinction between *emic and etic, discussed at length in *Language in Relation to a Unified Theory of the Structure of Human Behavior* (1954).

Pitt Rivers, A.L (A.H. Lane Fox) (1827–1900) Soldier and founder of one of the world's most extraordinary ethnographic museums, the Pitt Rivers Museum, first established in London and later moved to Oxford. His publications include

Primitive Warfare (1868), *The Evolution of Culture and Other Essays* (1906).

Polanyi, Karl (1886–1964) Economic historian, born in Vienna, grew up in Hungary and moved first to Britain and then the United States, where at Columbia University in the late 1940s and early 1950s he presided over a highly influential seminar. One product of this was *Trade and Market in the Early Empires* (with C. Arensberg and H. Pearson, 1957) in which he published his essay on 'The Economy as Instituted Process', the seminal document in the emerging dispute between *formalists and substantivists.

Polanyi, Michael (1891–1976) Hungarian chemist and philosopher, and brother of †Karl Polanyi, who emigrated to Britain in the 1930s. In his *Personal Knowledge* (1958) Polanyi drew explicit parallels between the ideas and actions of communities of scientists to which he had belonged, and the closed but coherent world of Azande *witchcraft as described by †Evans-Pritchard – a crucial link in the emerging sociology of *science, as well as an important contribution to the philosophical argument on *rationality.

Popper, Sir Karl (1902–94) Philosopher of science. In *The Logic of Scientific Discovery* (1934), he argued that scientific knowledge is based upon the possibility of falsification, rather than upon certain verification. This 'falsification principle' is widely accepted today, and the question of whether ethnography or social anthropology is a science by Popper's definition has been much debated.

Powell, John Wesley (1834–1902) Founder of the †Bureau of American Ethnology, which he served as director between 1879 and 1902, and ethnographer of Shoshone, Ute and Paiute Indians. In his time he contributed much to the popularization of evolutionist theory, but he is remembered today more for establishing government-sponsored research among Native American peoples.

Prichard, James Cowels (1786–1865) British medical doctor who trained at Edinburgh and later practised in England. With fellow Quaker †Thomas Hodgkin he helped establish the Ethnological Society of London in 1843. His *Researches into the Physical History of Man* (1813) went into five editions and stood as a †monogenic,

evolutionist tract for that society, against the mainly †polygenist Anthropological Society of London.

Propp, Vladimir (1895–1970) Russian *folklorist who introduced a formalist approach to the structure and content of folk-tales. He is best known for his *Morfologiia skazki* (1928; *Morphology of the Folktale*, 1958).

Quatrefages, Armand de (1810–92) Influential French anatomist and anthropologist. He strongly supported †monogenism but opposed the idea of the primate origins of humankind.

Radcliffe-Brown, A.R. (1881–1955) British anthropologist who, with *Malinowski, oversaw the professional consolidation of British social anthropology. For further details, see main entry.

Radin, Paul (1883–1953) One of several anthropologists of Central European origin who were trained by *Franz Boas at Columbia University in New York. He was most active as an anthropologist of religion, but is probably most remembered for his classic ethnography of the Winnebago, and for his collaborative work (with C.G. Jung) on the †trickster figure in Native North American mythology. Works include *Crashing Thunder: The Autobiography of an American Indian* (1926), *Primitive Man as Philosopher* (1927), *Social Anthropology* (1932) and *Primitive Religion* (1937).

Raglan, Lord (Fitzroy Richard Somerset, Third Baron Raglan) (1885–1964) Soldier, traveller, folklorist, and anthropologist, much influenced by †A.M. Hocart. He held the unusual view, consistent with his *diffusionist ideology, that mythological heroes resulted from the secularization of former gods rather than the deification of historical heroes. Major works include *Jocasta's Crime* (1933), *The Hero* (1936), and *The Origins of Religion* (1949).

Rasmussen, Knud (1879–1933) Arctic explorer and ethnographer of the Inuit. Rasmussen was of part-Inuit descent himself and born and raised in Greenland. He participated in the famous Fifth Thule Expedition (1921–4), and his sections of the reports of that expedition, e.g. *The Netsilik Eskimos: Social Life and Spiritual Culture* (1931), have become ethnographic classics. See *Arctic.

Rassers, W.H. (1877–1973) Dutch Orientalist. In spite of the fact that he never visited any part of the East Indies, he taught Javanese, Malay, and ethnology at a mission school in the Netherlands and was instrumental in the development of the Leiden school of structuralist anthropology. A collection of his works was published in English under the title *Pañji, the Culture Hero* (1959). See *Dutch anthropology.

Rattray, R.S. (1881–1938) Barrister and colonial administrator in the Gold Coast (now Ghana), Rattray produced extensive ethnographic studies of the Asante and other groups. Among his major works were *Ashanti* (1923), *Religion and Art in Ashanti* (1927), and *Ashanti Law and Constitution* (1929). See *Africa: West.

Ratzel, Friedrich (1844–1904) German 'anthropo-geographer' (as he defined himself), who contributed significantly to the late nineteenth-century development of theories of *diffusion and migration. He sought historical connection through the 'criterion of form' (*Formengedanke*), or formal, non-functional characteristics of objects, which are unlikely to be simultaneously invented. Works include *Anthropogeographie*, (2 vols, 1882–91), *Völkerkunde*, (3 vols, 1885–88) and *Politische Geographie* (1891). See *German and Austrian anthropology.

Redfield, Robert (1897–1958) American anthropologist based at the University of Chicago, and influenced by Chicago sociologists like Robert Park. His account of a Mexican village, *Tepoztlan* (1930) more or less launched the study of *peasant culture in anglophone anthropology, and the ideas developed in later works like *The Primitive World and Its Transformations* (1953), *The Little Community* (1955), and *Peasant Society and Culture* (1956), have been the source of endless argument in subsequent peasant studies. See *great and little traditions.

Reichel-Dolmatoff, Gerardo (1912–94) Colombian anthropologist noted for his structural analyses of society and thought in *Lowland South America, e.g. *Amazonian Cosmos: The Sexual and Religious Symbolism of the Tukano Indians* (1971).

Richards, Audrey (1899–1984) British social anthropologist and one of *Malinowski's first students at the London School of Economics. She carried out fieldwork in different parts of Africa, but is best known for her work on the Bemba of Zambia. Her *Hunger and Work in a Savage Tribe* (1932), and *Land, Labour and Diet in Northern Rhodesia* (1939) were important, not least for their empirical quality, in the emerging fields of *economic anthropology and the anthropology of *food and *nutrition, while *Chisungu* (1956) remains a classic account of a woman's *rite of passage.

Rivers, W.H.R. (1864–1922) British doctor and psychiatrist whose interest in ethnology came from his role in the Cambridge expedition to the †Torres Straits in 1898. He carried out further research in India and Melanesia. His interests lay in areas as diverse as *kinship – in which he pioneered the *genealogical method – and sensory perception and he taught both psychology and anthropology at Cambridge. He is as well remembered in literary history – as Siegfried Sassoon's doctor during World War I, and as the subject of a remarkable trilogy of novels by the British writer Pat Barker – as in anthropology. His premature death in 1922 left the field open for the new orthodoxies of *Radcliffe-Brown and *Malinowski, and Rivers's pioneering efforts to bring together anthropology and psychology more or less died with him. His anthropological works include *The Todas* (1908), *Kinship and Social Organization* (1913), *The History of Melanesian Society*, (2 vols, 1914) and *History and Ethnology* (1922).

Roheim, Géza (1891–1953) Hungarian-born psychoanalyst and anthropologist, who carried out field research in North America and Australia. He published both general works on psychoanalytic anthropology, like *The Riddle of the Sphinx* (1934), and specific studies like his psychoanalytic account of Australian Aborginal mythology, *The Eternal Ones of the Dream* (1945). See *psychoanalysis.

Rousseau, Jean-Jacques (1712–78) Genevan-French social philosopher whose work is still highly influential. His best known works are the two 'Discourses' (1750 and 1775), *Émile, ou de l'education* (1762) and *Du contrat social* (1762). In his Second Discourse (*Discourse on the Origins and Foundations of Inequality among Men*), Rousseau extols the virtues of an imaginary, short-lived 'nascent' society in which all human beings were equal. This characterization became associated with the view of 'primitive man' as †'noble savage'. See *Enlightenment anthropology.

Sahlins, Marshall (1930–) One of the most influential and original American anthropologists of his generation, Sahlins's early work, such as *Social Stratification in Polynesia* (1958) was influenced by the materialist *evolutionism of †Leslie White, but during the 1960s he moved closer to the British and French traditions. His classic *Stone Age Economics* (1972) is at once a vindication of †K. Polanyi's substantivist approach to *economic anthropology and an important exploration of *Marxist ideas. He followed this with *Culture and Practical Reason* (1976), which synthesized Lévi-Straussian structuralism and Boasian culturalism in a powerful critique of Marxist anthropology. His most recent work, like *Islands of History* (1985), has been both influential and controversial in the arguments about *history and anthropology.

Said, Edward W. (1935–) Literary critic and political commentator, born in Palestine but long resident in the United States. His most influential book is *Orientalism* (1978), in which he provides a powerful polemic against Western stereotypical writing about 'the East'. See *Orientalism, *Occidentalism.

Sapir, Edward (1884–1939) Linguist and anthropologist trained by *Franz Boas at Columbia, and subsequently based at Chicago and Yale. Although his name is most often asociated with the so-called *Sapir–Whorf hypothesis, he made important contributions to linguistic theory, to the emerging field of *culture and personality studies, and to the general theory of *culture. Many of these are to be found in the collection of his lapidary essays, posthumously edited by David Mandelbaum (*Selected Writings in Language, Culture and Personality*, 1949).

Saussure, Ferdinand de (1857–1913) Swiss linguist regarded as the founder of modern theoretical linguistics. The influential *Cours de linguistique générale* (1916, *Course in General Linguistics* 1959) was assembled from the notes of his students after his death. The distinctions made in this work – between †langue and parole, †synchronic and diachronic, †signifier and signified – have become part of the standard vocabulary not just of structural linguistics, but of anthropological and literary *structuralism.

Schapera, I. (1905–) South African anthropologist who was a student of *Radcliffe-Brown in Cape Town and *Malinowski in London, and was for many years professor of anthropology at the London School of Economics. He carried out fieldwork in Southern Africa among the Bushmen, in *The Khoisan Peoples* (1930) and the Tswana, in *A Handbook of Tswana Law and Custom* (1938) and *Migrant Labour and Tribal Life* (1956).

Schmidt, Pater Wilhelm (1868–1954) Catholic priest and ethnologist who explored the nature of 'primitive monotheism' and wrote extensively on the relationship between the world's religions. Schmidt also founded the journal *Anthropos* in 1906 and developed, within the *diffusionist school, the idea of 'culture circles' (†*Kulturkreise*). Major works include *Der Ursprung der Gottesidee* (12 vols, 1912–55), *Handbuch der vergleichenden Religionsgeschichte* (1930; *The Origin and Growth of Religion*, 1931) and *Handbuch der Methode der kulturhistorischen Ethnologie* (1937; *The Culture Historical Method of Ethnology* 1939). See *German and Austrian anthropology.

Schneider, David M. (1918–95) American anthropologist, best known for his work on *kinship, and his pivotal role in the development of *symbolic anthropology. His *American Kinship: A Cultural Account* (1968) was an immensely influential analysis of kinship as a set of symbols and meanings in American culture, and led the way to his more fundamental assault on the very idea of kinship as a coherent field of study in *A Critique of the Study of Kinship* (1984). For many years an inspirational teacher at the University of Chicago, Schneider published a characteristically pungent memoir just before his death, *Schneider on Schneider: The Conversion of the Jews and Other Anthropological Stories*, with R. Handler, 1995.

Seligman, Brenda Z. (1882–1965) British anthropologist who conducted fieldwork, with her husband C.G. Seligman, in Ceylon (now Sri Lanka) and East Africa. With C.G. Seligman she wrote *The Veddas* (1911), *Pagan Tribes of the Nilotic Sudan* (1932), and other works.

Seligman, C.G. (1873–1940) British physician and anthropologist who worked in the Torres Straits, Ceylon and East Africa. He taught social anthropology at the London School of Economics from 1910 to 1934, where his students included *Malinowski, †Schapera, and †Evans-Pritchard.

Service, Elman R. (1915–) American anthropologist who was influential in the revival of *evolutionist thinking in the 1960s, especially in relation to political structures and *hunter-gatherer society. Later works concern mainly the history of anthropology. Important books include *Primitive Social Organization* (1962), *Origins of the State and Civilization* (1975) and *A Century of Controversy* (1985).

Simmel, Georg (1858–1918) German sociologist and social philosopher whose work on *money and *exchange (e.g. in his *Philosophie des Geldes*, 1900; *The Philosophy of Money*, 1978) has been used by some economic anthropologists. An often brilliant writer, his essays on topics like lying and the stranger have also been used to great effect by anthropologists.

Smith, Adam (1723–90) Scottish moral philosopher and economist. His early work was written while teaching at Glasgow University, most importantly *Theory of Moral Sentiments* (1759). His most famous and influential work remains *An Inquiry into the Nature and Causes of the Wealth of Nations* (1776), which developed a model of the modern economy which called for economic liberty and non-intervention.

Smith, William Robertson (1846–1894) Biblical scholar and historian of religion. Appointed professor of Oriental languages at Aberdeen in his early twenties, Smith soon encountered difficulties with the authorities over his historical and theological speculations. He was dismissed in 1881, then took over the editorship of the *Encyclopaedia Britannica* and subsequently a chair in Arabic at Cambridge. His important works include *Kinship and Marriage in Early Arabia* (1885) and *Lectures on the Religion of the Semites* (1899), in which he advanced the view, later developed by †Durkheim, that religious practice – i.e. *ritual – should take analytic precedence over religious *belief. See *sacrifice.

Speck, Frank G. (1881–1950) Ethnographer and folklorist who worked with many Native North American peoples. Works include *Family Hunting Territories and Social Life of Various Algonkian Bands of the Ottawa Valley* (1915), *Beothuk and Micmac* (1922) and *Naskapi* (1935).

Spencer, Sir Baldwin (1860–1929) British-born biologist and ethnographer renowned for his

pioneering Australian Aboriginal fieldwork with local postmaster F.J. Gillen. Together they wrote *The Native Tribes of Central Australia* (1899) and three subsequent volumes on central and northern Aboriginal peoples, most significantly the Aranda. Their rich ethnography was both influenced by and contributed to the ideas of †James Frazer on *totemism, and was the source for the explosion of interest in that topic in the first two decades of the twentieth century. See *Aboriginal Australia.

Spencer, Herbert (1820–1903) British sociologist who developed the ideas of 'Social Darwinism' into a major theory of social *evolution. His *System of Synthetic Philosophy* (1862–96) developed his ideas on general evolutionary principles. His ideas of evolutionary sociology were highly influential in their time but fell out of favour after 1900. However, his works such as *Descriptive Sociology* (1874–81) and *The Principles of Sociology* (1880–96) made important contributions to the methodology and concepts of *sociology.

Spier, Leslie (1893–1961) Important ethnographer of Native North Americans, famed for his dissertation and subsequent publications on the Sun Dance rituals of the Plains Indians. He served as editor of a number of series of publications, including the *American Anthropologist*, and the *Southwestern Journal of Anthropology*, which he founded in 1944. His own publications include *The Sun Dance of the Plains Indians* (1921), *Yuman Tribes of the Gila River* (1933) and *The Prophet Dance in the Northwest* (1935).

Srinivas, M.N. (1916–) Indian anthropologist, trained by *Radcliffe-Brown at Oxford, where he briefly taught, before returning to India, where he has been a pivotal figure in the emergence of a distictively Indian anthropology. His South Indian ethnography *Religion and Society among the Coorgs* (1952) was an early classic, while *The Remembered Village* (1976) is a reflexive and affectionate return to his original fieldwork. See *Indian anthropology.

Stanner, W.E.H. (1906–81) Australian anthropologist trained by *Radcliffe-Brown, †Elkin and *Malinowski. He sought to redefine †Durkheim's notion of *sacred and profane, to develop a more action-oriented approach than his teachers had given him, and to gain recognition for Aboriginal land rights in the Northern Territory.

Among his significant works is *On Aboriginal Religion* (1963). See *Aboriginal Australia.

Steiner, Franz (1909–52) Czech-born anthropologist trained at Oxford. He achieved posthumous fame in anthropology for his monograph *Taboo* (1956), and has gradually acquired a formidable literary reputation for his poetry.

Steward, Julian H. (1902–72) American cultural anthropologist credited with founding the method of cultural ecology. His work among the Shoshoni produced the theory which explained social systems in terms of their accommodations to environmental and technological circumstances. His works include *Basin-Plateau Aboriginal Sociopolitical Groups* (1938), *Handbook of the South American Indians*, (6 vols, 1946–50), *Area Research: Theory and Practice* (1950) and *Theory of Culture Change* (1955). See *evolution and evolutionism.

Sundkler, Bengt (1909–) Lutheran theologian and church historian who wrote important ethnographic works on independent churches in Africa, notably *Bantu Prophets in South Africa* (1948), as well as books on church history.

Swadesh, Morris (1909–67) American linguist. In the early part of his career he worked with Nootka and other Amerindian languages, but his fame rests on his development of †lexicostatistics and his concern, in later years, with the origin of language. Publications include 'Time depths of American linguistic groupings' (*American Anthropologist*, 1962) and *The Origin and Diversification of Language* (1972).

Tax, Sol (1907–95) Chicago-based anthropologist who strongly advocated self-determination for American Indians. His work among the Mesquakie Indians in the 1940s led him to place his knowledge and influence at their service. This formed the basis of a philosophy of applied anthropology which came to be known as †action anthropology. An indefatigable organizer and proselyte for anthropology in the international arena, his numerous edited volumes include *Heritage of Conquest* (1952), *An Appraisal of Anthropology Today* (1953) and *The People vs The System* (1968).

Thurnwald, Richard (1869–1954) Leading German *functionalist of his generation. Although he was an outspoken opponent of the Nazis, he

returned to Germany from the United States in 1936 and, with his wife Hilde, later founded the post-war Institute of Ethnology at the Free University of Berlin. Works include *Die Gemeinde der Bánaro* (1921), *Die menschliche Gesellschaft in ihren ethnosoziologischen Grundlagen* (5 vols, 1931–35), *Economics in Primitive Communities* (1932) and *Koloniale Gestaltung* (1939). See *German and Austrian anthropology.

Tönnies, Ferdinand (1855–1936) German social theorist and philosopher. In his best remembered work, *Gemeinschaft und Gesellschaft* (1887; *Community and Association*, 1957), he characterized †*Gemeinschaft* as the family and small community where cooperation and custom expressed an intense emotional spirit. This he contrasted with *Gesellschaft*, the large-scale organization based on convention, law and public opinion. A selection of his major writings, in English, may be found in *Ferdinand Tönnies on Sociology* (1971).

Turnbull, Colin (1924–94) British-born anthropologist well known for his publications on the Mbuti of Zaire, including the popular and somewhat romanticized *The Forest People* (1961), and for his controversial depiction of social disintegration among the Ik of Uganda in *The Mountain People* (1972).

Turner, Victor W. (1920–83) Scottish anthropologist, who emerged from the †Manchester school of †Max Gluckman with a set of extraordinarily rich ethnographies of the Ndembu of Northern Rhodesia (later Zambia). *Schism and Continuity in an African Society* (1957) was a state-of-the-art contribution to 1950s *political anthropology, but his 1960s essays on *ritual and symbols, collected in *The Forest of Symbols* (1967) broke quite new ground and became essential points of reference in *symbolic anthropology. He moved to America in the early 1960s, where he developed his ideas about ritual, *pilgrimage and social drama.

Tylor, Sir Edward Burnett (1832–1917) British anthropologist whose main interest was in the *evolution of society and its institutions. He developed these themes in *Researches into the Early History of Mankind and the Development of Civilization* (1865) and *Primitive Culture* (2 vols, 1871). He is also credited with introducing the German idea of *culture as a particular way of life into British anthropology. He was an influential figure in British anthropology and his other works include *Anthropology* (1881).

van Gennep, Arnold (1873–1957) French linguist and ethnographer. He is best known in anthropology for *Les rites de passage* (1909; *The Rites of Passage*, 1960) which demonstrated that *rituals in the life cycle were based on a three-part structure of separation, transition and incorporation. In the second half of his life he concentrated on the ethnography and *folklore of France, publishing the huge *Manuel de folklore français contemporain* (1937–58). See *rite of passage.

Veblen, Thorstin B. (1857–1929) American sociologist, best known for his *Theory of the Leisure Class* (1899), in which he introduced the idea of 'conspicuous consumption'. See *consumption.

Vico, Giambattista (1668–1744) Italian philosopher whose *Scienza nuova* (*New Science*) became a classic precursor of anthropology. The first, short unsuccessful edition of *Scienza nuova* was published in 1725, but the essence of his ideas appeared with greater coherence and success in the definitive edition of 1744. Despite this, his arguments were neglected at the time, but have been the subject of growing interest in the twentieth century. He argued that we can only know with confidence those things made by humans, thus marking off the area and methods of the human sciences from the new physical sciences of his day (which attempted to know things made by God). His schema of historical cycles anticipated the great evolutionist theories of the nineteenth century, while his emphasis on the interconnectedness of social and cultural institutions is an early argument for what came to be anthropological †holism.

Vygotsky, Lev Semionovich (1896–1934) Russian psychologist whose posthumous *Thought and Language* (1937; English translation, 1962) develops a model of human psychology which emphasizes the role of *culture and †sociality in child development. Since his early death, and the proscription of his works under Stalin, his ideas have become steadily more important, both for a genuinely cultural psychology, and for a properly *psychological anthropology. See *socialization.

Wallace, Alfred Russel (1823–1913) Naturalist and traveller whose work anticipated Darwin's theory of *evolution by natural selection. Works include *Travels on the Amazon and Rio Negro* (1853) and *The Malay Archipelago* (2 vols, 1869).

Warner, W. Lloyd (1898–1970) American anthropologist who was a student of †Kroeber, †Lowie, *Malinowski and *Radcliffe-Brown. He did fieldwork in *Aboriginal Australia but is equally remembered for his research on communities and institutions in the United States. Characteristic publications include *A Black Civilization* (1937) and *The Emergent American Society* (1967).

Weber, Max (1864–1920) German scholar regarded as one of the founders of modern *sociology, whose great work in comparative historical sociology was published, uncompleted, after his death (*Wirtschaft und Gesellschaft*, 1922; *Economy and Society*, 1968). He is best known for his argument linking European Protestantism to the emergence of *capitalism, an argument frequently misrepresented as a simple refutation of the theories of †Marx and †Engels, but his comparative sociology (based on the principle of †*Verstehen* or understanding) has provided both technical concepts (†charisma, †ideal type) and intellectual inspiration to anthropologists as well as sociologists, particularly those concerned with the problem of social change and the analysis of *modernity.

Westermann, Diedrich Hermann (1875–1956) Missionary anthropologist and long-time editor of the journal *Africa*. Among his many publications are *The Shilluk People* (1912), *Die Kpelle* (1921), *Die westlichen Sudansprachen* (1927), *The African Today* (1934), *Afrikaner erzählen ihr Leben* (1938), *Die Zukunft der Naturvölker* (1939), *Geschichte Afrikas* (1952).

Westermarck, Edward (1862–1939) Finnish anthropologist who wrote extensively on sexual *taboos and *marriage. Against the spirit of his time, he held the view that 'primitives' were not promiscuous and formulated the notion that 'familiarity breeds contempt'; thus the *incest taboo is an extension of the abhorrence of mating between people who are closely related. Works included *Origin and Development of Moral Ideas* (2 vols, 1906–08), *The History of Human Marriage* (3 vols, 1921), *Ritual and Belief in Morocco* (2 vols, 1926) and *Wit and Wisdom in Morocco* (1930). See *incest.

White, Leslie A. (1900–75) American anthropologist who combined a materialist theory of *evolution, based on technological determinism, with a paradoxical concern with *culture as a system of meaning. His works include *The Pueblo of Santa Ana* (1942), *The Science of Culture* (1949), *The Evolution of Culture* (1959) and *The Concept of Cultural Systems* (1975).

Whorf, Benjamin Lee (1897–1941) Chemical engineer who studied linguistics with †Sapir at Yale. He spent most of his life as a fire-prevention expert for an insurance company. It is said that, noticing that workers happily smoked near fuel cans they described as 'empty' (but which in fact contained inflammable fumes), led him to the idea that linguistic categories determine thought. He developed this notion in several essays post-humously collected as *Language, Thought, and Reality* (1956). See *Sapir–Whorf hypothesis.

Williams, Raymond (1921–88) British Marxist literary critic and historian. His particular version of cultural Marxism was mostly ignored by British anthropologists of his generation, but has become extremely influential in *cultural studies, and for anthropologists interested in *resistance and †hegemony, who draw mostly on the rather arid theorizing of his *Marxism and Literature* (1977), rather than the more culturally and historically specific analyses of *Culture and Society* (1958) and *The Country and the City* (1973).

Wilson, Monica (Monica Hunter) (1908–82) South African anthropologist trained by *Malinowski, she was noted for her work on African religion and social change and for her stand against apartheid. As Monica Hunter, she wrote *Reaction to Conquest* (1936), based on early fieldwork in South Africa. Later she did fieldwork with the Nyakyusa of Tanganyika (now Tanzania) with her husband Godfrey Wilson, who died during World War II. Other works include *Rituals of Kinship among the Nyakyusa* (1957) and *Religion and the Transformation of Society* (1975).

Wissler, Clark (1870–1947) Anthropologist at the American Museum of Natural History in New York. Not having a university department in which to train students, his direct influence was less than many of his contemporaries, but his writings were significant for inspiring others in his time, especially with reference to the †culture-area approach. His publications included *The American Indian* (1917), *Man and Culture* (1923), *Introduction to Social Anthropology* (1929), *The Indians of the United States* (1940). See *culture.

Wittfogel, Karl (1896–1987) Sociologist and economic historian whose most famous works were based on his studies of China and his development of Marx's ideas about Asiatic societies. In his major work *Oriental Despotism* (1957) he elucidated his concept of the †Asiatic mode of production, depicting a kind of domination based on a bureaucratic state, a model which could also be read as an allegory of Soviet communism.

Wittgenstein, Ludwig (1889–1951) One of the greatest philosophers of the twentieth century. His early work, exemplified by the *Tractatus Logico-philosophicus* (1921), held that ordinary language can be reduced to a logically perfect system. His later philosophy, expounded in the posthumous *Philosophical Investigations* (1953), emphasizes language use, particularly in language games or forms of life, and is openly critical of his early work. The later Wittgenstein has inspired quite different anthropologists from †Rodney Needham to †Bourdieu and †Clifford Geertz.

Wundt, Wilhelm (1832–1920) German philosopher widely regarded as the founder of experimental psychology. In the later part of his career he published extensively on the relationship between *culture and psychology (e.g. *Völkerpsychologie*, 10 vols, 1900–20) although very little of this work has been translated. His anthropological significance is heightened by the fact that he either taught or influenced – at different times and before either would consider himself an anthropologist – both *Malinowski and *Boas. See *psychological anthropology.

Glossary

ablineal A consanguineal relative who is neither a †lineal nor a co-lineal.

aboriginal, Aboriginal Indigenous to a given place. The term is always spelled with upper case 'A' when used in reference to the Aborigines of Australia. See also †indigenous.

acculturation The process of acquiring culture traits as a result of contact. The term was common, especially in American anthropology, until fairly recently.

acephalous Literally 'without a head'. Acephalous societies are those in which groups operate without formally recognized leaders. They include †foraging and *pastoralist societies where political control is vested in collective †bands, other local groups, or †unilineal kin groups.

achievement and ascription Achieved status or authority is that which is earned, while ascribed status authority automatically derives from a person's inherited social position. The distinction is common in *political anthropology.

action, actor Theories which stress **social action** view social life from the point of view of individual actors (or agents) engaged in social processes, rather than emphasizing the persisting structural features which may be thought to exist and endure irrespective of the actions of particular men and women.

action anthropology The branch of †applied anthropology, or branch of anthropology allied to applied anthropology, which seeks to combat immediate threats to population groups. Action anthropologists thus seek to use their anthropological knowledge for political goals deriving from moral commitment. Promoted originally by †Sol Tax, the field is especially prominent in Germany.

action group, action set An action group is a group of †actors united in common purpose. An action set is a group of actors who operate for political purpose, but without a unified, corporate identity. Both terms were defined in 1960s *political anthropology, as part of a broader concern with the classification of different sorts of group and leadership.

adaptation The process of accommodating to the natural or social *environment. The term is common in *ecological anthropology and *evolutionary theory.

adelphic polyandry The *marriage of two or more brothers to the same woman. See †polyandry.

adhesion †E.B. Tylor's term for elements of *culture which are usually found together. The idea anticipated notions in the †Kulturkreis school, as well as cross-cultural comparisons as understood by †G.P. Murdock.

affine, affinity Relationship through *marriage. Usually opposed to †consanguine (related through blood).

agamy *Marriage in the absence of a rule of †exogamy or †endogamy.

age-area hypothesis The idea fostered by †Clark Wissler that †culture traits are spread from the centre to the periphery of a †culture area, and therefore that at any given time those at the periphery are older than those in the centre.

age-class systems, age grades, age sets Age-class systems are societies in which formal age grades or age sets are crucial to the *social structure. These are especially common in *East Africa. Age grades are stages through which individuals pass; e.g. upon initiation or upon being made an elder. Age sets are categories of persons united by age. Often members of an age set are defined as those initiated at the same time. See main entry on *age.

agency, agent An agent is a person who is the subject of †action. Agency, then suggests intention or consciousness of action, sometimes with the implication of possible choices between different actions. The concept of agency has been employed by anthropologists and social theorists, especially those influenced by †Max Weber, in contrast to †structure, which implies constraint on action.

agnate, agnatic An agnate is someone related through the male line. Agnatic is the adjectival form, often used as a synonym of †patrilineal. See main entries on *descent and *kinship; cf. †cognate (sense 1), †uterine.

agriculture In its widest sense, the production of food, as opposed to the procurement of food from the wild. In a narrower sense, agriculture is often distinguished from †horticulture as a more labour-intensive, literally 'field' (as opposed to garden) based system found in technologically sophisticated and socially complex societies.

alliance theory In *kinship, the perspective which emphasizes ties between groups through *marriage, rather than ties within a group through *descent. Contrast †descent theory. See main entry on *alliance.

alter In *kinship, the person or *genealogical status to which relationship is traced. Cf. †ego.

alterity Literally 'otherness'. Variously used in recent anthropology to describe and comment on the construction and experience of cultural difference.

ambilineal Used to describe a *kinship system in which membership of a group may be acquired through either †patrilineal or †matrilineal ties. In the ethnography of *Polynesia, ambilineal groups are sometimes called †ramages.

ambilocal A form of *marriage in which post-marital residence can be in either the husband's or the wife's place.

amoral familism Term first employed by E. Banfield to describe a characteristic †ethos of Mediterranean societies in which loyalties to immediate family take precedence over corporate obligations. See *Europe: South.

animism
The belief in spirits which inhabit or are identified with parts of the natural world, such as rocks, trees, rivers and mountains. In the nineteenth century, writers such as †Sir Edward Tylor argued that animism represented an early form of *religion, one

which preceded theistic religions in the evolution of 'primitive thought'. The term is sometimes used loosely to cover religious beliefs of indigenous population groups, e.g. in Africa and North America, prior to the introduction of Christianity, and is still widely used to describe the religious practice of so-called †tribal or †indigenous groups in areas like *Southeast Asia.

anisogamy *Marriage between partners of unequal status, i.e. either †hypogamy (in which the bride is higher than the groom), or †hypergamy (in which the groom is higher than the bride). The opposite is †isogamy.

***Annales* school** The school of French historians originally associated with the journal *Annales d'histoire économique et social* (now *Annales: économies, sociétés, civilsations*), founded in 1929, which has been especially important in the interdisciplinary development of *history and anthropology. After World War II, the school became associated with the idea of a history of †'mentalities', and with F. Braudel's project for a structural history of the '*longue durée*'.

Année sociologique The name of a journal (literally, the 'sociological year') founded by †Émile Durkheim in 1898 and, by extension, the theoretical persuasion of those who published in it in the early twentieth century. The *Année* school included Durkheim, †Mauss and other French sociologists whose concern with issues of comparative anthropology ultimately precipitated the development of †structural-functionalism in Britain and *structuralism in France.

anomie †É. Durkheim's term for a condition of normlessness, often confused with Marxist uses of the word 'alienation'.

anthropometry The comparative study of human body measurements, e.g. to determine relationships between different population groups. *Biological anthropologists working with living and recent populations (as opposed to ancient fossil populations), have largely replaced anthropometry with genetic studies.

anthropomorphism The attribution of human-like characteristics to non-human things.

apical ancestor The *ancestor at the top of a *genealogical table.

applied anthropology Term used to cover the use of anthropological methods and ideas in a variety of practical or policy-related contexts. Applied anthropology has its roots in work on behalf of *colonial administrations, but is now firmly established in contexts as diverse as development agencies, health education and social work as well as work for private-sector corporations. See *colonialism, *development, *ethnopsychiatry, *medical anthropology.

appropriate technology In *development studies, *technology (usually low rather than high-technology) which is designed to be appropriate to the socio-economic, environmental and cultural needs of the communities under consideration.

archetype C.G. Jung's term for symbols which are common to all humanity. The notion has found little support among anthropologists.

armchair anthropology An often disparaging description of anthropological research carried out without original fieldwork, but rather through reading the product of the fieldwork of others. Typically, twentieth-century anthropololgists have characterized their nineteenth-century predecessors (and sometimes their contemporaries) with this term.

articulation of modes of production In *Marxist analysis, the interaction between different *modes of production in the same †social formation.

ascribed status See †achievement and ascription.

Asiatic mode of production Marx's term for a *mode of production in which villages are relatively self-sufficient, but surpluses are drawn off by a despotic state. In †K. Wittfogel's *Oriental Despotism* (1957), this was used for a grand model of Asian †hydraulic civilizations, which also served as a thinly-disguised critique of Soviet state power. The concept received further theoretical attention in French Marxist anthropology in the 1960s and 1970s.

associative See †paradigmatic.

atom of kinship *Lévi-Strauss's term for the unit of kinship consisting of the relations husband/wife and brother/sister, and father/son and mother's brother/sister's son.

avunculocal *Marriage involving postmarital residence with the husband's mother's brother. This form of residence is common in strongly †matrilineal societies in which men control the affairs of each matrilineal group. When repeated throughout society, it has the effect of uniting men of each matrilineal group and dispersing the women through whom they are related. See also *avunculate.

ayllu Term used in Andean societies to describe a form of kinship- and territory-based social grouping. See: *Americas: Native South America (Highland).

B In *kinship studies, the symbol for the genealogical position of the brother.

balanced reciprocity See †reciprocity.

band The basic unit of *hunter-gatherer social organization. Typically bands number from twenty or thirty (often erroneously called the †patrilocal or †patrilineal band) to over 300 (the composite band). Hunting and gathering societies are often described as band societies, i.e. societies whose primary political unit is the band.

barbarism In nineteenth-century *evolutionary theory, the stage of development between †savage and civilized. It is characterized by agriculture and the use of pottery.

barter *Exchange of goods without the use of money.

base and superstructure In Marxist theory, the base (or infrastructure) is the material basis of society (technology, resources, economic relations) which is held ultimately to determine the superstructure, or ideological levels of society (law, religion, etc.).

behavioural level Especially in *kinship studies, the level of analysis which describes people's actions, in contrast to the †jural and †categorical levels.

behaviourism, behaviourist The school of psychology which emphasizes learned behaviour over innate cognitive propensities.

bifurcation, bifurcate collateral, bifurcate merging In *kinship, bifurcation refers to the terminological distinction of father's and mother's sides, relatives on each side being called by different terms. For example, one's MB would be distinguished from one's FB. Bifurcate collateral refers to the terminological distinction between both father's and mother's sides and between †lineals and †collaterals. Bifurcate merging refers to the terminological distinction between father's and mother's sides where the same-sex siblings of lineals are equated with lineals themselves.

bilateral Relations on both the mother's and father's sides.

bilineal A synonym for †duolineal or †double descent.

binary opposition In *structuralist anthropology, an opposition between two paired terms (e.g. *nature and culture, †right and left, male and female); more formally a distinction marked by the presence or absence of a single †distinctive feature.

biomedicine Term used in *medical anthropology for conventional Western medicine.

blood feud A †feud carried through generations on the basis of family or †lineage membership.

bricolage, bricoleur A *bricoleur* is a kind of French handyman who improvises technical solutions to all manner of minor repairs. In *The Savage Mind* (1962) *Lévi-Strauss used this image to illustrate the way in which societies combine and recombine different symbols and cultural elements in order to come up with recurring structures. Subsequently *bricolage* has become a familiar term to describe various processes of structured improvisation.

bride capture *Marriage in which the groom or his kin forcibly take the bride from her family. Nineteenth-century scholars (notably †McLennan) assumed real bride capture as a norm at certain stages of *evolution. The fiction of bride capture is enacted in many societies.

brideprice, bride-service, bridewealth Terms for various sorts of *marriage payment. Brideprice is an alternative, and generally old-fashioned, term for bridewealth. Bride-service is labour performed by a groom or recently-married man for his wife's parents; it is common among *hunter-gatherers and can last ten years or more. Bridewealth is a marriage payment from the groom or his kin to the kin of the bride, usually to legitimate children of the marriage as members of the groom's †lineage; it is common among *pastoralists. Cf. †dowry.

Bureau of American Ethnology A government bureau established by Congress in 1879, after †John Wesley Powell successfully argued that such an institution would be useful in the government's dealings with Native peoples. A central institution in the developing anthropology of *Native North America, it is perhaps best known for its illustrious researchers (including †F. Cushing and *F. Boas) and its annual reports and other publications.

carrying capacity A term used in *ecological anthropology to describe the maximum potential population which can be supported from a given resource base.

carrying mother The woman in whose womb a foetus develops. The term is employed especially in reference to a woman who is neither the genetic mother nor the future social mother of the child. See *conception, *reproductive technologies and cf. †genetrix, †mater.

case study A detailed ethnographic example which focuses on specific individuals or incidents. In the 1950s and 1960s, the use of extended case studies was characteristic of the †Manchester school of †Max Gluckman and his students.

cash crops Crops grown for the *market rather than for subsistence or internal redistribution.

categorical level Especially in *kinship, the level of analysis which focuses on classifactory structures as revealed in indigenous categories (e.g. in prescriptive *relationship terminologies). See †jural level and †behavioural level.

centre (or core) and periphery A construct which depends on the opposition between a socio-economic centre, wherein activities dominate peripheral areas. The opposition has been important in social geography and Marxist anthropology, especially in approaches influenced by *world-systems theory.

charisma In †Max Weber's terms, authority based on the personal characteristics of the leader.

chiefdom A unit or level of social organization in which chiefs govern. Chiefs can be elected or, more commonly, given their status through descent.

choreometry The measurement or formal recording of *dance and movement.

circulating connubium The term invented by *Dutch anthropologists to characterize a *marriage system in which groups are linked by †affinal ties and women circulate in †generalized exchange. In such systems, common in *Southeast Asia, no one group has predominance over the others, though an ideology of †hypogamy is usually found.

circumcision In males, the removal of the foreskin of the penis. Circumcision is practised in many cultures throughout the world as part of male initiation. Female circumcision, or removal of part of the clitoris (clitoridectomy), is rare except in parts of Africa, where it has become the focus of intense controversy. Cf. †subincision.

civil society Term widely employed in eighteenth-century political philosophy to describe the *state, or political society in its broadest sense. The term lapsed into disuse until the early twentieth century. In †Gramsci's usage, civil society became that area of society (churches, schools, etc.) within which the powers-that-be create and maintain consent. In Eastern Europe under Communist rule, the term came to refer to a broad sphere of potential opposition to the totalizing claims of the state.

civilization In nineteenth-century *evolutionary theory, the level of society more advanced than †barbarism. It is characterized by factors such as irrigated agriculture, writing, complex organization, and cities.

clan Usually defined as a †lineage or cluster of lineages in which the exact genealogical connections between all members cannot be traced. The term is generally applied to a †corporate group with a strong identity. Although the term comes from a Gaelic word which designated a †bilateral kin group, in anthropology it is usually applied to †unilineal kin groups. In †G.P. Murdock's usage, it designated specifically †matrilineal kin groups (patrilineal ones being called *gentes*). See also †gens, †sib.

classificatory kinship. See †descriptive and classificatory kinship.

clitoridectomy See †circumcision.

code, code-switching A code is a particular level or style of speech determined by social factors such as degree of formality. Code-switching is the process of changing from one linguistic code to another, according to social circumstances.

cognate (1) In *kinship, a †consanguine related through either the mother's or father's side (i.e. †bilaterally). The term is derived from Latin *cognatus* (a consanguineal relative who is not a member of one's own †patrilineal group), as distinct from *agnatus* (English †agnate, being a member of one's †gens.). See *cognatic societies. (2) In linguistics, a word which has the same origin as another word, to which it is being compared, e.g. German *Hund* and English hound. The term may be used as either a noun or an adjective. Contrast †loan word.

cognitive anthropology In general, any anthropological approach to the study of *cognition. In particular, it refers to a specific subdiscipline or theoretical perspective which emphasized the formation of cultural categories through semantic distinctions. It was popular in the 1960s in the study of colour and *relationship terminologies, and its premises remain prominent in †ethnozoology and †ethnobotany. See *componential analysis, ethnoscience.

cohort A group of people involved in the same action, e.g. an age cohort who are all initiated into adulthood at the same time. The term, originally from the Latin for a Roman military unit, is also used in biology and *biological anthropology for a subdivision of a phylogenic class.

cold society See †hot and cold societies.

co-lineal A †consanguineal relative who is the same-sex sibling of either an ancestor or a descendant of a given person. Cf. †collateral, †lineal, †direct relatives.

collateral A *consanguineal relative who is neither an ancestor nor a descendant of a given person. Contrast †direct relatives.

collective   consciousness †Durkheim's   term (*conscience collective*) for the common consciousness shared by individuals belonging to the same *society or social group. The French *conscience* may be translated as either 'conscience' or 'consciousness'; thus the *conscience collective* is at once both cognitive and moral.

collective representation Any †representation held in common: †Durkheim's term for the specific components which make up the †collective consciousness of a society or social group.

commensality Eating together. Rules of commensality may imply social status or relations of *exchange. See also *food, *pollution and purity.

commodity Any object which has a value in relation to other goods, and can therefore be the object of economic *exchange. Sometimes commodities are distinguished from gifts, whose value lies in the social relations created between giver and receiver, rather than in the †exchange value of the goods themselves. See also †fetishism.

communalism The term has various meanings, all relating to communities or communal living. It is most often used in modern anthropology to refer to what is called communalism in South Asia: attachment to a particular religious or caste community, to the detriment of the nation or the broader society (e.g. as in the use of 'communal violence' to refer to Hindu–Muslim violence in India).

communitas †Victor Turner's term for the experience of heightened †sociality which occurs in certain *ritual contexts, such as the †liminal phase of *rites of passage or during *pilgrimage.

comparative religion The academic discipline which examines different religions in comparative perspective.

complementary dualism A pervasive division into two opposing parts in a social or symbolic order. †Moiety systems and symbolic classes such as Chinese Yin and Yang are examples.

complex structure †Lévi-Strauss's term for a structure of *alliance characterized by negative *marriage rules. Cf. †elementary structure.

component Within *componential analysis, a unit of meaning. The term is synonymous with †significatum.

concubinage The institutionalized taking of a sexual partner in addition to one's spouse or spouses.

conjectural history The reconstruction of *evolutionary development through logical speculation. The term was invented by Dugald Stewart to describe favourably the methodology of many eighteenth-century writers, but it came to prominence in anthropology through *Radcliffe-Brown's attack on the method as it was employed by late nineteenth-century evolutionist and *diffusionist writers.

connotatum Within *componential analysis, a feature which has meaning but whose meaning is literally not significant (see †significatum) for definition, i.e. which connotes rather than signifies. For example, avuncular behaviour might be a connotatum of the English word 'uncle', but it is not a distinguishing feature in the same sense as the significata male, collateral and first-ascending generation.

consanguine, consanguineal, consanguinity Literally, somone who is related through shared 'blood'; usually opposed to †affines and affinity, which refer to relations through *marriage.

consociate A term, used by the social †phenomenologist Alfred Schutz and later by †Clifford Geertz, to describe any individual with whom a person has actual social relations.

contagious magic †J. Frazer's term for *magic based on the notion that things which were once in contact can have an influence over each other. Frazer considered this an advance over †sympathetic magic.

contract An agreement between two parties. One half of †Sir Henry Maine's vision of a world which has progressed from †status to contract. See also †social contract.

controlled comparison Comparison of specific features of two or more societies, where the range of variables is narrowed by the choice of societies which are similar. Often controlled comparison is regional, i.e. based on comparison of societies which are culturally related and geographically contiguous. See *comparative method.

core See †centre and periphery, †culture core, *world system.

corporate group A group, e.g. a †lineage, which possesses a recognized identity. The term was of great importance in the hey-day of British †structural-functionalism, when some anthropologists, drawing on the ideas of †Maine (corporations aggregate) and †Weber, restricted the term to a group with a single legal personality, e.g. a lineage which holds property in common.

cosmogony A theory of the origin of the universe. See *cosmology.

counter-hegemony Opposition to hegemonic modes of cultural domination. The term was popularized through †Raymond Williams's reworking of concepts from †Gramsci.

couvade So-called 'false pregnancy', institutionalized for men in some cultures while their wives are bearing a child.

creole A language which originates from extended contact between two linguistic communities, one of which is usually dominant. Creoles generally begin as †pidgins, but the defining feature of a creole which distinguishes it from a pidgin is that a creole is spoken as a native language by at least some individuals. Thus it takes at least one generation to produce a creole.

creolization The process of forming a †creole language. In recent anthropology the term has been widely used (especially following the Swedish anthropologist Ulf Hannerz) to refer to the creation of inter-cultural hybrids as a result of processes of †globalization. See *complex society, *world system.

cross-aunt An aunt related through an opposite-sex sibling link, i.e. a FZ or MBW.

cross-cousin, cross-cousin marriage A cousin related through an opposite-sex sibling link. In other words, a father's sister's child or mother's brother's child, in contrast to a †parallel cousin (cousin by same-sex sibling link). 'Classificatory cross-cousins' are those classified by the same term as first cross-cousins. The practice of cross-cousin marriage (marriage, usually with a classificatory cross-cousin) forms the basis of *alliance theory and *Lévi-Strauss's theory of †elementary structures.

cross-cutting ties Ties between individuals which cross-cut each other: e.g. two people may live in the same village but belong to different *descent groups and different †age grades.

cross-relative Any relative whose relationship is traced through an opposite-sex sibling link, e.g. a †cross-cousin. Contrast †parallel relative.

cross-uncle An uncle related through an opposite-sex sibling link, i.e. a MB or FZH.

Crow terminology In †G.P. Murdock's classification of *relationship terminologies, one otherwise like †Iroquois but in which FZD is called by the same term as FZ. Often such terminologies are found in strongly †matrilineal societies, the principle being that female members of one's father's matrilineage are all called by a single term. See *Crow–Omaha systems.

cultural anthropology One of the †four fields (with linguistics, archaeology and physical anthropology) which combine to make up North American anthropology. Broadly comparable to European *social anthropology, although the use of 'cultural' indicates significant historical differences in their intellectual genealogies. In the 1950s and 1960s the differences between social and cultural anthropology were the stuff of fraught controversy within anglophone anthropology; since the 1970s these differences have become less and less important (as the title of this *Encyclopedia* makes clear). See *culture.

cultural determinism Any perspective which treats culture itself as determining the differences between peoples, e.g. in personality type. It is associated especially with *relativism of various kinds.

culturalism, culturalist Any anthropological approach which gives first priority to explaining a culture in its own terms; employed as a term of mild abuse by British anthropologists of the 1950s. See *culture.

culture area A geographical region whose inhabitants share similar or related culture. The concept was of theoretical importance in early twentieth-century studies of *Native North Americans and in subsequent work in *ecological anthropology.

culture bearer A person who possesses and transmits a given culture.

culture-bound syndrome Term used in *medical anthropology for certain conditions which, it can be argued, are only experienced by people from certain, specific cultures (e.g. depression for Euro-Americans, *amok* for Malays). See *ethnopsychiatry.

culture circle See †*Kulturkreis*.

culture complex Especially in early twentieth-century American anthropology, a cluster of †culture traits functionally related to each other. For example, the East African *cattle complex includes not only cattle but also nomadism, bridewealth, patrilineal kinship, acephalous politics, etc.

culture contact The meeting of two cultures, especially where one becomes culturally dominant over the other; the term was popular in the 1930s as a euphemism for colonial domination.

culture core In †Julian Steward's terminology, those aspects of a given culture which are most strongly influenced by environmental and sometimes technological factors.

culture history The history of a culture reconstructed through comparison with closely-related cultures. The idea was prominent among *diffusionists and students of *Franz Boas, as a reaction against †conjectural history.

culture of poverty A term first used by †Oscar Lewis to suggest that poverty is not simply a lack of material resources, but entails in addition a set of associated cultural values which drastically limit the capacity of the poor to change their own circumstances. The concept has come in for much criticism, particularly through its application to problems of race and poverty in the United States.

culture trait A single cultural attribute. In the early twentieth century, the idea that such traits were linked in larger complexes became prominent.

customary law Indigenous legal rules and practices, usually as codified (and thus transformed) by colonial governments. See *law.

cybernetics A field which stresses the relation between elements in a system of interrelated actions. It is used in engineering, computer technology, psychology, and education, but its significance in anthropology comes largely through the work of †Gregory Bateson who helped develop the field in the 1940s.

cyborg A hybrid, part human and part machine. The idea has been explored by feminist anthropologists (most notably Donna Haraway) and those working in the new field of the anthropology of *science.

D In *kinship, the symbol for daughter.

deconstruction †Jacques Derrida's term for a strategy of critical analysis which serves to expose underlying metaphysical assumptions in a particular text, in particular assumptions which would appear to contradict the surface argument of the text itself. The term has become synonymous with *postmodern theory of various sorts and is often applied much more loosely to refer to the taking apart, or unpacking, of a particular term or concept.

deep and surface structure In linguistics, where the distinction was introduced by †Chomsky, the deep structure of a particular language contains the rules for generating the surface structure, i.e. the structure of what is actually said. At its most abstract, deep structure is common to all human languages.

deictic, deixis In linguistics, deixis is the aspect of language which relates the speaker, the hearer and their spatio-temporal context. A deictic is a word which specifies in the context of deixis, such as a personal pronoun (e.g. 'I', 'you') or an adverb indicating place or time (e.g. 'here', 'now'). Deixis is especially important in recent work in †pragmatics.

delayed return See †immediate and delayed return.

deme An ancient Greek word for 'people'. It was introduced into anthropology by †G.P. Murdock to describe social units which are based on both common *descent and locality and which are essentially †endogamous. Demes have been found not only in ancient Greece, but more particularly in *Southeast Asia and Madagascar.

denotatum Within *componential analysis, a member of a given category. For example, father's mother and mother's mother (more properly in kinship notation, FM and MM respectively) are the denotata making up the category designated by the English word 'grandmother'. See also †designatum.

dependency theory A theory of *development, in which underdevelopment is analysed as part of broader relations of domination and dependency operating at the level of world capitalism.

descent theory In *kinship, the perspective which emphasizes ties within descent groups, rather than between groups through marriage. Contrast †alliance theory. See main entry on *descent.

descriptive and classificatory kinship In the study of *relationship terminologies, descriptive ones are those in which specific terms represent specific genealogical positions and classificatory ones are those in which a large number of genealogical positions are labelled with the same term. *L.H. Morgan coined the term 'descriptive' specifically for those systems in which †direct relatives and †collaterals are classified by different terms, and 'classificatory' for those which classify any collateral by the same term as a lineal, e.g. when a single term is employed for siblings and †parallel cousins alike. Later writers made finer distinctions between different terminology structures and thereby rendered Morgan's distinction obsolete.

designatum Within *componential analysis, a term which designates a category, e.g. the English word 'grandmother' for the category which includes an English-speaker's father's mother and mother's mother. See also †denotatum.

developmental cycle More fully, the developmental cycle of domestic groups, this term describes the culture-specific pattern of *household or hamlet composition as it changes in respect of *age structure. It came to prominence through the work of †Meyer Fortes and others working in West Africa, where domestic units expand through marriage but contract through death and division, e.g. when brothers previously occupying the same unit move apart to head new units when their parents die. See *family, *household.

diachronic Literally, 'through time'. Diachronic perspectives include *evolutionist and *diffusionist ones, in which time depth is the significant factor. The opposite is †synchronic.

dialect Any variety of speech or language in reference to a larger linguistic unit. In a more restrictive sense, the term very often refers to a regional or class-determined variety of a given language. Many linguists would now argue that the real distinction between a dialect and a language is political: i.e., a language is a dialect formalized and institutionalized by a state. Cf. †speech community.

dialectical materialism Another term, like †historical materialism, for the theoretical approach of †Marx and his followers in which †Hegel's dialectical style is married to a materialist concern with the production of human needs.

dialogic, dialogical Terms employed by the Russian literary theorist †Mikhail Bakhtin to indicate that language and meaning are never fixed in themselves, but only work in situations of dialogue, where meanings and understandings are contingent on other meanings and understandings. In this context, dialogue refers to a broader idea of language in use than simply conversation between two people.

diaspora A group of people dispersed from their original place. The term was originally applied to Jews living outside Palestine, but in recent years has been applied to African Americans and members of many other ethnic minorities.

différance In *postmodern terminology, *différance* is †Derrida's punning term (combining the French for 'differ' and 'defer') for the endless slippage of meaning from sign to sign, such that any appeal to some real, foundational meaning is always 'deferred'.

difference In feminist theory, the word difference has been used to challenge the self-evidence of *gender differences; instead differences of gender are but one case of more pervasive structures of difference, some marked some unmarked, which together make up the *identity, or †subject-position, of particular gendered persons.

diglossia The presence of two ways of speaking, often one 'high' and the other 'low', in the same *language. Each is appropriate to a different set of social conditions.

direct exchange In *kinship, the exchange in marriage of members of one's own group with those of another. The notion is central to *Lévi-Strauss's theory of †elementary structures. Also called 'restricted exchange', in opposition to †generalized exchange.

direct relatives In kinship, †lineal relatives plus †co-lineals. Contrast †collateral.

disembedded †Karl Polanyi's term for economies which have been institutionally separated from other areas of social life, and thus may be analysed independently of their social context (e.g. through the formal procedures of Western economics). Premodern economies, in contrast, are said to be embedded in other social relations, such that religion or kinship may play the part taken by abstract, impersonal market transactions in the modern West. See *formalism and substantivism.

disharmonic regimes In *Lévi-Strauss's theory of †elementary structures, those *kinship systems which possess one rule of *descent and a contradictory rule of residence, i.e. †patrilineal descent with †uxorilocal residence, or †matrilineal descent with †virilocal residence. The assumption is that both descent lines and residential groups are †exogamous, thereby creating a minimum of four intermarrying 'sections' such as those found among the Kariera of Western Australia. Cf. †harmonic regimes.

disposition In the works of †Bourdieu, a propensity for some specific action. The culturally-determined set of dispositions available to any particular actor is called the †habitus.

distinctive feature In linguistics (especially phonology), a feature whose presence or absence distinguishes between otherwise identical forms. For example, the distinction between the bilabial stops /p/ and /b/ is that /p/ is unvoiced and /b/ is voiced. Thus the distinctive feature of 'voicing' defines both /p/ (which lacks it) and /b/ (which possesses it). *Lévi-Strauss was influenced by †Jakobson's account of distinctive features, and employed analogous devices in his early structural analyses. See *structuralism.

domestic mode of production †Marshall Sahlins's term for a *mode of production, supposedly characteristic of a broad range of kinship-based societies, in which both production and *consumption are exclusively or mainly oriented to the requirements of the *household or domestic sphere. See *peasants.

double descent A *descent system which has both *patrilineal and *matrilineal groups. Each member of the society belongs to one such patrilineal group and one such matrilineal group. The classic examples are mainly in West Africa (e.g. the Yakö of Nigeria) and, disputably, in Aboriginal Australia. Also known as 'double unilineal descent' and 'dual descent'.

dowry A *marriage payment from the bride's family to the groom or his family. In some societies it represents the woman's inheritance, taken with her to her marital home. Common in the Mediterranean and South Asia. Cf. †bridewealth.

Dravidian kinship The Dravidian languages are those (such as Tamil, Malayalam, and Kannada) spoken in the southern part of India. Their *relationship terminologies imply prescriptive bilateral †cross-cousin marriage, and apparently similar 'Dravidian systems' have been identified in *Lowland South America and among some *Australian Aborigines. See *preference and prescription, †sister's daughter marriage.

duolineal Literally, 'having two lines'. In the study of *descent systems, a synonym for †double descent.

duolocal Residing in both places, i.e. *marriage in which the bride maintains residence in her natal home, and the groom in his. This form of residence is rare, but does occur in a significant minority of families, in some West African societies.

dysfunction A function which is not adaptive and which may contribute to disequilibrium. The term is more common in sociology than in functional anthropology.

E   In kinship, the symbol for spouse (from French *épouse*).

e   In kinship, the symbol for older (elder), e.g. FBDe means 'father's brother's daughter, who is older than †ego'.

economic man   In economic theory, a hypothetical individual (*Homo economicus*) who always acts in an economically rational way, i.e. to secure the most benefit in any given economic context. Since *Malinowski's assault on the idea of 'primitive economic man', the concept has been much criticized by economic anthropologists.

ecosystem   A theoretically 'closed' system embracing interrelated parts of the *environment. In *ecological anthropology, the term often describes the relation between a particular people and their environment.

egalitarianism   Equality between individuals in a social system. This ideal is often ascribed to *hunting-and-gathering communities. It is theoretically important as a baseline for the comparison of societies on the basis of social hierarchy, including those 'advanced' hunting-and-gathering societies whose subsistence pursuits (e.g. intensive fishing) have led to the development of hierarchical systems. In a rather different context, †Louis Dumont has systematically explored the intellectual roots of the modern Western ideology of egalitarianism.

ego   In *kinship, the person (who may be real or hypothetical) from whom relationship is traced. The term is from the Latin for 'I'; its opposite is †alter (meaning 'other').

eidos   †Gregory Bateson's term for the distinctive cognitive or intellectual pattern of a *culture, as opposed to the †ethos, which refers to the emotional tone of a culture.

elderhood   The status of being an elder, which is important especially in societies which recognize formal †age grades and †age sets. See *age.

elementary structure   *Lévi-Strauss's term for a *kinship system based on positive *marriage rules, e.g. one must marry someone of the category †'cross-cousin'. Lévi-Strauss classifies elementary structures into †direct (or restricted) and †generalized. The contrast is a †complex structure, and Lévi-Strauss also identifies an in-between type, a *Crow–Omaha structure, which is a form of complex structure where the choice of spouse is so narrow that the system functions in a similar manner to an elementary structure.

embedded   See †disembedded and main entry on *formalism and substantivism.

empiricism   In philosophy, the doctrine that knowledge depends on experience, in contrast to *rationalism which posits that knowledge is structured by mind. More broadly in anthropology and the other human sciences, empiricism is used (often pejoratively) to characterize any approach which places the collection of empirical evidence before the construction of theoretical schemes.

enculturation   The process of acquiring a culture. The term is more-or-less synonymous with *socialization.

endogamy   *Marriage within a given group or category. The opposite is †exogamy.

entitlement theory   In economics, the theory which explains the distribution of goods and services, not so much in terms of supply and demand, but in terms of the 'entitlements' which people bring to a situation. So, for example, Amartya Sen has argued that many famines are less the product of an absolute shortage of food (because food is available but is too expensive for people to obtain) but have to be explained as a failure of entitlements. See *food.

environmental determinism   The view that the *environment determines aspects of culture or social organization. Absolute environmental determinism is generally rejected by *ecological anthropologists in favour of the more moderate view that the environment limits or constrains aspects of culture and social organization.

eschatology   The branch of theology which deals with the 'last things', death and the end of the world.

Eskimo terminology   In †G.P. Murdock's classification of *relationship terminologies, one (such as English) in which siblings are distinguished from cousins and no distinction is made between †parallel and †cross-cousins.

ethnic group, minority   Any group of people, or minority within a nation-state (ethnic minority), who define themselves as a group by reference to claims of common descent, language, religion or race. See *ethnicity.

ethno-   A prefix which usually (but not always) treats the substantive concept in light of indigenous explanations. See †ethnobotany, †ethnomedicine.

ethnobiology   A broad term for any culture's indigenous knowledge of 'biology', which may cover

†ethnobotany, †ethnomedicine and †ethnozoology. See *ethnoscience.

ethnobotany The study of the indigenous botanical knowledge of a given people. See *ethnoscience.

ethnocentrism The tendency to view the world from the perspective of one's own culture, or the inability to understand cultures which are different from one's own. The accusation of ethnocentrism is a severe one when levelled at anthropologists, as ethnocentrism is seen, especially among exponents of *relativism, as the antithesis of anthropology itself. See also †secondary ethnocentrism.

ethnocide Systematic destuction of the culture (or the members themselves) of a particular ethnic group. Cf. †genocide.

ethnographic present A hypothetical time frame, characterized by the use of the present tense, employed in *ethnographic writing. Normally it coincides with the time of *fieldwork, which is not necessarily the time of writing, or indeed of reading.

ethnohistory The field which comprises the boundary area between *ethnography and *history. In some usages, it implies the use of indigenously-defined historical data, whereas in others it implies documentary evidence relating to marginal, often illiterate, peoples.

ethnology Broadly, a synonym for †social or †cultural anthropology. In early nineteenth-century Britain, the term often implied a †monogenic theory of humankind, whereas 'anthropology' implied a †polygenic theory. Often in Continental usage, 'ethnology' means social anthropology and 'anthropology' means physical anthropology. In yet another usage, *Radcliffe-Brown distinguished ethnology (the study of culture history and relationships) from social anthropology (the study of society).

ethnomedicine The study of indigenous healing systems. See *medical anthropology.

ethnomethodology A style of analysis developed by the sociologist Harold Garfinkel, in which the purpose is to construct models of the knowledge, or methods, which particular actors bring to bear in everyday social situations. The prefix 'ethno-' is intended to suggest its similarity to anthropological approaches to the collection of indigenous knowledge (e.g. *ethnoscience), although in practice it has had surprisingly little impact outside sociology.

ethnomusicology The study of indigenous musical systems. See *music.

ethnos Literally a 'people', the term is applied in some Continental traditions to a set of culture traits which make up a given cultural tradition.

ethnosociology (By analogy with *ethnoscience) the system of sociological knowledge possessed by a given people, or (by analogy with †ethnohistory) the study of a cultural group in light of its own sociological knowledge and the unique aspects of its social structure. The term has been most systematically used in the anthropology of *South Asia, to describe the attempt, by McKim Marriott and his associates, to construct an account of South Asian societies in South Asian terms.

ethnozoology A given culture's indigenous knowledge of zoology. See *ethnoscience.

ethology The study of behaviour. Ethology is variously a part of zoology and psychology, and human ethology seeks to differentiate universals from cultural peculiarities by the comparative study of behaviour in different cultures. Human ethologists may also compare the behaviour of humans to non-humans in order to find universals wider than the human species, e.g. †territoriality.

ethos In anthropology, the emotional tone or 'feel' of a particular culture. The term was popularized by *culture and personality theorists like †Gregory Bateson, who drew a contrast between the ethos (the emotional tone) and the †eidos (the intellectual style) of a culture, and revived by *symbolic anthropologists like †Clifford Geertz, who contrasted ethos and †worldview.

eugenics The doctrine or practice of selective breeding in order to 'improve' the human genetic pool.

evil eye A supposed power or capacity to harm others, deriving from envy or other wicked thoughts. The idea is found in many *peasant societies, where it is believed that an individual's wicked thoughts can cause harm to others, often involuntarily.

exchange value In economics and *economic anthropology, the value of something as defined by what it can be exchanged for. It is distinguished from †use value, which measures the utilitarian purpose of something. Marx's labour theory of value was largely an attack on the notion of exchange value.

exegesis A term common in theology to mean explanation. In anthropology, it maybe used to describe an indigenous exegesis, or informant's explanation or interpretation of something.

exogamy *Marriage outside a given group or category (the opposite of †endogamy). The term was coined by †J.F. McLennan as part of his theory of social evolution to explain the phase of †bride-capture and what came after, when groups developed rules against taking mates from within. It is commonly used today to designate any kind of out-marriage, including both rules and practice.

extended family Loosely, any *family unit beyond the †nuclear family (e.g. including grandparents, cousins, etc.). The term can be used in either an ego-centric or a sociocentric sense, depending on context.

extension, terminological In *kinship theory, the classification of a distant relative as equivalent to a nearer relative. For example, the usage for a Trobriand father's sister's son may be described as an 'extension' of the genealogical position 'father' since both FBS and F are termed *tama* and F is the closest representative of this category. However, the notion of terminological extension has come under much criticism, since it privileges some genealogical positions over others on the basis of distinctions which are formal and not necessarily of any cultural significance.

F In kinship, the symbol for the genealogical position of the father.

feedback In †systems theory, a mechanism which results from some action within a †cybernetic system, usually when an effect returns to the point in the system from which it originally emanated. The term is commonly used in *ecological anthropology to describe the results of environmental or socially-induced change.

female circumcision See †circumcision.

fetish, fetishism, fetishization A fetish is an object which is believed to have spiritual power, such as a magical charm. The concept was used especially in late nineteenth-century anthropology to describe ritual objects used in supposedly 'primitive' societies. (For the history of the concept see main entry on *religion.) Fetishization is the act of treating something as if it were a fetish. The term is often used to describe a process by which a culture or a social group irrationally overrates something (that which it fetishizes). In this sense, the object does not have to be material but may be, for example, a theoretical idea in anthropology. In this sense, the term becomes an accusation which is levelled against theoretical opponents. In a famous passage in *Capital*, Marx used the image of the fetish to illustrate the way in which people misapprehend the true nature of †commodities by treating them as persons, thus attributing power and agency to things, while treating people (who really do have agency) as things, mere repositories of labour power for sale in the market.

feud A long-running, structured dispute between groups. In the ethnographic record, feuds are often violent and involve raiding or warfare between two groups who see themselves in opposition, or even define their *identity as groups in terms of their place in a system of feuding kinship or local groups. The Nuer of southern Sudan, studied by †Evans-Pritchard, are the classic example in the anthropological literature. See *violence, *war.

fictive kinship Social relations which are perceived as analogous to *kinship, but which are based on some other criterion, e.g. godparenthood, blood-brotherhood, or 'fraternal' solidarity in the trade union movement. See *adoption and fostering, *compadrazgo.

filiation In English usage, relation to a given side of the family (mother's or father's) or to kin groups of that side (not necessarily one's own †unilineal group). The term was coined by †Meyer Fortes, who used it especially in reference to *complementary filiation. However, in French, *filiation* is simply the word for *'descent'.

fission and fusion Splitting and coming together. In anthropology the terms are used in reference to †lineages in those †segmentary societies, such as the Nuer, in which political alliances are so formed and dissolved.

folk culture A term sometimes applied to traditional, especially rural, aspects of culture which have escaped changes taking place in urban centres. The concept is associated with European *folklore studies, and in America, with the work of †Robert Redfield. Its critics, however, argue that it is value-laden in its apparent assumption that folk culture is inferior to cosmopolitan forms. See † *Volkskunde*.

folk-urban continuum †Robert Redfield's term for the range of cultural variation within a given society between rural *peasants and the urban bearers of the *great tradition.

foraging society An alternative term for *hunting-and-gathering society. Many anthropologists employ this term in reference to the 'hand-to-mouth' ideology often found in foraging societies. However, others prefer to see 'foraging' as an essentially animal activity (in contrast to humans, who 'gather' food).

forces of production In Marxist theory, the material forces (technology, raw materials) which combine with the social †relations of production to form the economic †base, or infrastructure of a particular society.˙ See *mode of production; cf. †means of production, †relations of production.

form That which is defined by relations rather than essences. Loosely, it is often equated with structure (see *structuralism), although sometimes distinguished as being more abstract (see †structural form). The opposite is †substance.

formal analysis The methods, popular in American anthropology especially in the 1960s, through which given cultural items were described according to their formal, non-culture-specific features. Methods of formal analysis include *componential analysis and †transformational analysis, as well as the use of classical economic modelling by the so-called *formalists in *economic anthropology.

four-field approach The idea of anthropology as consisting of four interrelated subject areas, namely †cultural anthropology, *biological anthropology (or physical anthropology), anthropological linguistics, and prehistoric archaeology. The four-field approach is the basis of the organization of most anthropology departments in North America.

Fourth World A term employed to characterize either (a) the extremely impoverished members of Third World societies, or (b) highly marginalized minority groups such as *hunter-gatherers or †indigenous peoples, who are dominated by other groups or by state bureaucracies.

function This is a commonly-used term of no agreed definition. As a verb, it has been applied in its mathematical sense (by *A.R. Radcliffe-Brown), in the sense of a part fitting the whole (by †Herbert Spencer), and in the sense of elements of social structure interrelating with each other. As a noun, it commonly means 'purpose', but generally connotes also the idea of interrelationship, which is crucial to most functionalist theory in anthropology. See *functionalism, †manifest and latent functions, †structural-functionalism.

fundamentalism Any doctrine, especially a religious one, marked by a putative return to basics. The concept has special meaning within American anthropology, where anthropology itself was pitted against fundamentalist Christianity in the 1980s over the issue of contradictions between *evolutionary theory and the biblical creation story.

funeral rites Rites involving the disposal of the physical remains of a dead person and often the transition of that person's spirit from one culturally-defined realm to another. Funeral rites may include burial, reburial, cremation, or other means of disposal. See *death.

game theory By analogy with competitive games, the notion that in political or economic activities individuals calculate the advantages they may have by making certain 'moves', and likewise the probable consequences of their opponents' 'moves'. While game theory has been widely applied in other areas of the human sciences, from economics to *sociobiology, it has had very little impact on anthropology, apart from some 1960s work in *political anthropology.

Gemeinschaft* and *Gesellschaft One of the most enduring of many nineteenth-century characterizations of the so-called †great divide, †F. Tönnies's distinction between the traditional kinship-based world of 'community' (*Gemeinschaft*), and the modern, impersonal world of 'association' (*Gesellschaft*).

generalized exchange In *kinship, *Lévi-Strauss's term for a form of †elementary structure in which women are 'exchanged' in one direction only. For example, group A gives its women as wives to group B, who give their women to group C, etc. A man is not allowed to marry someone from a group into which his female kin marry. These systems are common in Asia, where a hierarchy (either 'wife-givers' or 'wife-takers' being designated as superior) is often established or maintained through such marital links. See also †hypergamy, †hypogamy.

generalized reciprocity See †reciprocity.

generation A group of related people who occupy the same genealogical level. More loosely, any group of people of roughly the same age.

generational terminology In *kinship, a *relationship terminology which distinguishes neither †parallel from †cross-uncles and aunts, nor †lineal from †collateral relatives. In other words, the term for M, MZ and FZ will be the same, and the term for F, FB and MB will be the same.

generative Having rules which determine either an outcome or a more visible form in the social structure. The term, borrowed from linguistics, has been commonly used by *structuralist anthropologists, as when †deep structures generate surface structures.

genetrix The presumed 'genetic' or 'biological' (as opposed to a social or †carrying) mother. Cf. †genitor.

genitor The presumed 'genetic' or 'biological' father (as apart from the legal or social father or

†pater). Most kinship specialists use the term as a cultural description. Thus the true genetic father is irrelevant, and indeed a given culture may have a notion that more than one male can contribute to the physical substance of a given child.

genocide Systematic killing of people because of the ethnic or racial group to which they belong. Cf. †ethnocide.

genotype The genetic make-up of an organism. Contrast †phenotype.

gens The Latin term for †'clan' (i.e. the Roman †patrilineal kin group). It was used by *L.H. Morgan in reference to the †matrilineal clans of the Iroquois, and has at times since been used by American anthropologists as an alternative term for 'clan', especially a patrilineal clan. The plural is *gentes*.

Gesellschaft See †*Gemeinschaft* and *Gesellschaft*.

***Gestalt* theory** In psychology, the approach which argues that phenomena should be studied as wholes, through their configuration or internal relations, rather than merely in part. This idea influenced the *culture and personality school in American anthropology.

ghost marriage The practice, described by †Evans-Pritchard for the Nuer, of a woman marrying a dead man so that he becomes genealogical †pater to her children.

gift See †commodity, *exchange.

globalization The tendency towards increasing global interconnections in culture, economy and social life. Belatedly noticed by sociologists and social theorists in the 1980s. See *complex society, *world system.

glottochronology See †lexicostatistics.

godparenthood A ritual relation common in some Christian communities, in which an often unrelated adult sponsors a child at baptism. This †fictive kinship relation may continue through life, and may involve *compadrazgo* between the child's godparents and its real parents.

great divide Mildly disparaging term for the pervasive theoretical postulate of a qualitative division in human history between the *modern (or civilized or simply 'us') and the traditional (or premodern or primitive or simply 'them'), a division often said to be accompanied by different modes of thought. See *primitive mentality.

green revolution The introduction since the 1960s of new, more productive strains of rice, wheat, etc., especially in Asia. While these new †high yielding varieties have greatly increased overall productivity in many Asian agricultural systems, critics have argued that this has been at the expense of widening inequalities, increased landlessness, and environmental degradation.

group marriage In *kinship theory, the notion of a group of men all being married collectively to a group of women. The idea was common in the nineteenth century but has little basis in ethnographic fact.

gumsa* and *gumlao Two forms of social organization described by †Edmund Leach in his *Political Systems of Highland Burma* (1954). The *gumsa* Kachin are hierarchical, and their high-ranking lineages are believed to have close association with the ancestors of all of them. The *gumlao* Kachin are egalitarian, and each lineage is believed to have equal access to the ancestors. Leach's analysis showed how two very different forms of social organization could be viewed as poles in a single system of oscillating equilibrium. Leach's argument was formulated while he worked at the London School of Economics, where it so impressed his colleagues that for many years it served as an unacknowledged model for the Department of Anthropology's internal administrative structure.

H In kinship, the abbreviation for the genealogical position of the husband.

habitus A term taken by †Bourdieu from the work of †Mauss, to denote the total set of †dispositions which shape and constrain social practices. Habitus is Bourdieu's central notion, and he uses it to acknowledge the appearance of structures in the social world, while allowing the reality of individual strategy.

harmonic regimes In *kinship, *Lévi-Strauss's term for †elementary structures in which the rule of *descent coincides with the rule of residence. In other words, these systems have †patrilineal descent and †virilocal residence, or †matrilineal descent and †uxorilocal residence. In Lévi-Strauss's theory, harmonic regimes entail †generalized exchange. Cf. †disharmonic regimes.

Hawaiian terminology In †G.P. Murdock's classification of *relationship terminologies, one in which cousins are called by the same terms as siblings. This structure is common in *Polynesia and in parts of Africa.

headman A term for many kinds of local leader recognized by colonial authorities. More technically, in chiefly societies, a leader of lower rank than a chief. In other societies, especially †foraging and *pastoral societies, any recognized leader.

hegemony Domination or power of one person or group over another. The term was used by †Gramsci to describe the cultural processes through which the ruling classes maintain their power, and has been widely employed in ethnographic studies of domination and *resistance. Cf. †counter-hegemony.

heliocentrism Literally, belief in the centrality of the sun. In anthropology, it usually refers to the British *diffusionist school of †G. Elliot Smith and W.J. Perry, who believed that significant features of nearly all of the world's cultures are derived from those of the sun-worshipping ancient Egyptians.

hermeneutics The practice of interpretation. In anthropology, it refers to the theoretical position which sees ethnographic practice as one of interpreting, or 'reading', cultures as if they were texts. See *symbolic anthropology.

heteroglossia †Bakhtin's term for the variety of different 'languages' at work in any given social context. In opposition to structural linguistics, Bakhtin argued that the idea of a single linguistic system (†*langue* in †Saussure's terms) is a political project, which is always resisted by the tendency for languages to fragment into new multiplicities. See †dialogue, dialogical.

hierarchy A system of individuals, social classes or groups ranked from high to low in status. Hierarchy has been important in many areas of anthropology, especially for *Marxists and other *evolutionists and for those who have carried out field research in highly stratified societies. On the basis of his work in *South Asia, †Louis Dumont has suggested a more specific definition of hierarchy as characterized by a holistic relationship of encompassing to encompassed. His argument has been more widely applied, especially in *French anthropology, in a range of ethnographic contexts.

high yielding varieties (HYV) General term for a range of new crop strains introduced as part of the so-called †green revolution in the 1960s and 1970s.

historical materialism †Marx's theory of society and social change, based on the analysis of the material forces at work in the unfolding of human history.

historical particularism The work of *Boas and his followers who emphasized the need to reconstruct the particular histories of different cultural items, rather than attempt to place them in grand, usually *evolutionary or *diffusionist, theoretical frameworks.

historicism In general, a term which indicates a need to be sensitive to the historical dimension of society and culture. More specifically it can either refer to any †diachronic approach, which emphasizes the unfolding of processes in time (however broad), or to the need to attend to the particular historical context of social and cultural practices.

holism Any approach which treats the whole as greater than the sum of its parts. In anthropology, this includes perspectives such as *functionalism and *structuralism. In contrast, non-holistic approaches such as *transactionalism emphasize the role of the individual rather than the total social or cultural system in which he or she operates.

Homo oeconomicus, Homo economicus See †economic man.

homology Similarity of structure or appearance (but not necessarily of function or purpose).

horticulture Gardening, as opposed to growing crops in fields (†agriculture). The distinction is not a precise one, but generally horticultural societies are taken as those whose efforts at food production are on a small scale, and whose social organization is, in evolutionary terms, at a lower level of complexity.

hot and cold societies *Lévi-Strauss's distinction between those (hot) societies in which social differentiation and social change are taken for granted – which explain themselves through their history – and those (cold) ones which are relatively undifferentiated and static, and which explain themselves through their myths. Lévi-Strauss's distinction was not intended to deny the reality of change and historical transformation in so-called 'cold' societies, but only to suggest that history and change had a more limited place in their self-understandings.

Human Relations Area Files (HRAF) A massive database of ethnographic information, orginally appearing on index cards housed at the University of Yale. Their founder, †George Peter Murdock, devised the HRAF as an aid to statistical cross-cultural *comparison.

hydraulic civilization †K. Wittfogel's term for societies, such as ancient Egypt, dependent on irrigated agriculture. Cf. †Asiatic mode of production, †Oriental despotism.

hypergamy Marriage of a woman to a man of higher status (e.g. in North India, where 'wife-takers' are often considered superior to 'wife-givers'). Cf. †anisogamy, †hypogamy, †isogamy.

hypogamy Marriage of a woman to a man of lower status (e.g. in *Southeast Asia, where 'wife-givers' are often considered superior to 'wife-takers'). Cf. †anisogamy, †hypogamy, †isogamy.

hypostasis The true, underlying nature of something as distinct from its surface characteristics.

hysteria A term used in the past in Western medicine for a variety of supposedly 'feminine' emotional conditions. Rarely used in clinical contexts now, it may be thought a good example of a †culture-bound syndrome.

icon, iconicity In †semiotics, an icon is a †sign whose physical form in some way resembles that which is being signified. Iconicity refers to non-arbitrary, or motivated, signification in general.

ideal type †Max Weber's term for a deliberately simplified and abstract representation employed for heuristic purposes. The term is sometimes used synonymously with †model.

illocutionary A †speech act in which the utterance is equivalent to an action. For example, 'I *order* you to go', 'I apologize'. Cf. †locutionary, †performative, †perlocutionary.

immediate and delayed return A distinction first made by James Woodburn in the late 1970s and which is important in *hunter-gatherer studies. Immediate-return economies are those in which investment in work effort yields an immediate result, e.g. food-gathering. Delayed-return economies are those in which time must be spent in order to yield subsistence later, e.g. through making complex fishing nets or through investing in livestock production or agriculture. The overwhelming number of the world's societies are delayed-return.

imperialism Literally, the seeking or propagation of empire. In †postcolonial times, the term often connotes a reputed residual domination over a country or people by economic or cultural forces (e.g. anthropology) from Europe or North America.

index, indexical The word index has a range of meanings in anthropology, philosophy, †semiotics and linguistics, all based on some idea of an index as something which stands for or indicates something else. So, in linguistics, an indexical feature of someone's language use is something (accent, into-

nation, etc.) which marks them as belonging to a particular social class or occupational category. In semiotics an index may be something associated through 'natural' properties (e.g. a flower as an 'index' of spring). And in philosophy indexicals are terms whose purpose is to pick out a particular thing – obviously personal names, but also words like 'this', 'here' and 'today' – but which nevertheless also apply to other things when the same word is used in a different context.

indigenous knowledge systems The systems of thought analogous to scientific understanding within traditional cultures. The notion implies that such knowledge is indeed systematic in a similar way to modern science. In recent years, a strong case has been made for development projects to be at the very least compatible with – if not informed by – indigenous technical knowledge or ITK. See also *ethnoscience.

indigenous peoples A term which tends to refer to peoples who were present in a given territory before the arrival of larger, usually European population groups. The meaning of the term is clear in some geographical regions, such as *South America (where it refers to Indians as opposed to those of European or African ancestry), but its usage is problematic in others, such as much of Africa, Asia, and especially Europe. See also †aboriginal.

indirect rule In British *colonialism, the policy of ruling through indigenous or pseudo-indigenous political structures, rather than directly.

Indo-European language family The family of languages which includes Indic, Slavic, Italic, and Germanic languages, i.e. the languages of the northern Indian peninsula and most of Europe which share a putative common ancestor known as Proto-Indo-European.

infanticide The killing of small children, usually at birth. In many parts of the world, infanticide (especially female infanticide) is either culturally sanctioned, tolerated or ignored.

informal economy The term coined by Keith Hart to describe those economic activities which take part outside official or recognized arenas and therefore usually escape both regulation and the official record. Sometimes referred to as the 'informal sector'.

informant A person who gives information to an ethnographer. Some ethnographers utilize the services of a great many informants, e.g. in census work. Others rely on just a few, e.g. individuals who are singled out as experts in some aspect of their own culture, such as ritual, herbal medicine, or oral history. See *ethnography, *fieldwork, *methodology.

infrastructure In Marxist writings, a synonym for 'base'. See †base and superstructure.

inheritance *Property transferred from one generation to the next, usually upon the death of its owner. The term is sometimes used in a loose sense to include †succession, but since †Rivers, *kinship specialists have generally distinguished between the two.

initiation A *ritual which marks the transition from one status to another. For example, initiation often marks the passage from childhood to adulthood, and the term is most often used in this sense. Another common example is initiation into a secret society. See *rite of passage.

institution In †structural-functionalist theory, an element of a social system. Institutions (e.g. bridewealth, marriage, the family) are said to make up systems (e.g. kinship), which in turn make up society.

internal colonialism Colonialist-like tendencies *within* a given nation-state. For example, the elite of some newly-independent nation states have been likened to former colonial oppressors. The term has gained widest currency, though, in discussions of minorities, *nationalisms and proto-nationalist movements, such as those of the Bretons and Basques, within European nation-states.

International African Institute Originally the International Institute of African Languages and Culture, it was founded in 1926. It has fostered both pure and applied studies, especially in the colonial period, and published the quarterly journal *Africa*. In particular, *Malinowski's successful bid for funding from the Rockefeller Foundation in the 1920s cemented British social anthropology's relations with the Colonial Office as well as reinforcing his growing intellectual domination in British anthropology. See *British anthropology, *Malinowski.

interpretive anthropology Anthropology which is informed by a concern with problems of interpretation. The term usually applies to that kind of *symbolic anthropology practised by †Clifford Geertz.

intersubjective In philosophy, that which occurs between subjects, in other words all that makes the communication of subjective meanings possible between people.

intertextuality In †literary criticism, the relations between texts. A term widely used in *postmodern and †poststructural criticism, as part of a general tendency to avoid questions of authorial intention by treating texts as relatively autonomous.

involution Term employed metaphorically in †Clifford Geertz's *Agricultural Involution* (1963), a classic early study in *ecological anthropology, to characterize a situation of socio-economic stagnation accompanied by increasingly baroque cultural elaboration.

Iroquois terminology In †G.P. Murdock's classification a *relationship terminology in which a distinction is made between †parallel and †cross-cousins. In these terminologies, parallel cousins are usually termed as siblings.

isogamy Marriage between people of the same social status. Cf. †anisogamy, †hypergamy and †hypogamy.

jajmani system The traditional system of labour obligations and *caste services said to obtain between the different castes in traditional *South Asian villages. Early accounts stressed the harmonious and integrated nature of these obligations and services, and from the 1960s a revisionist literature developed stressing instead the degree of exploitation and coercion involved. Most recently, C.J. Fuller has argued that the very appearance of a closed system is an artefact of colonial history, rather than an aspect of traditional Indian society.

joint family A type of *family composed of two or more †nuclear families linked by ties of siblingship.

jural and moral domains The word 'jural' refers to the legal world of rights and obligations and was widely used in mid-century British †structural-functionalism. In †Meyer Fortes's usage, the jural domain relates to obligations according to status, e.g. obligations within a †lineage. The moral domain is that which transcends the structural principles of the jural domain, e.g. obligations towards one's family, irrespective of lineage membership.

jural level Especially in *kinship, the level of analysis which entails consideration of the rules. In contrast, the †behavioural level is that of what people actually do, and the †categorical level is that implied by the structural constraints, e.g. of a *relationship terminology. In studies of prescriptive kinship systems, distinctions between these three levels, behaviour, jural, and categorical, have been likened respectively to the distinction between practice, preference, and prescription. See also *preference and prescription.

karma In *South Asian religions such as *Hinduism and *Buddhism, the law of moral causality in which a person's past actions determine his or her future state.

kin group Any group of people related through real or putative ties of *kinship. The term implies no specific means of acquiring such membership, and thus includes †lineal and †collateral groupings alike.

kindred The culturally-recognized category to which an individual may trace kin relationship. It is, by definition, egocentric and †bilateral. In other words, each individual has his or her own kindred, and this kindred includes relatives on both the mother's and the father's sides. See *cognatic society.

kinship terminology See *relationship terminology.

Kulturkreis Literally, 'culture circle'. The concept was employed by the German-Austrian *diffusionists in reference to a cluster of functionally-related †culture traits specific to a historical time and geographical area. See *diffusionism, *German and Austrian anthropology.

langue* and *parole †Ferdinand de Saussure's analytic distinction between the level of language (*langue*) and the level of speech (*parole*). Language is the abstract system which is the proper object of analysis for structural linguistics; speech is the infinite variety of things people actually say. The use of the analogy in anthropological *structuralism has two important implications: that we are concerned with whole systems, and these systems are necessarily abstracted from the more confusing and messy world of empirical data.

latent functions See †manifest and latent functions.

legal pluralism Term widely employed in both the anthropology of *law and comparative jurisprudence to indicate that formal courtroom-based procedures are usually only one of a variety of more or less formal systems people employ in order to seek justice or retribution. The term also applied to situations in which two or more formal legal systems co-exist, e.g. in colonial societies or with family law in India.

levirate The *marriage or 'inheritance' of a woman as a wife by her late husband's brother. In many African societies, leviratic marriage is either preferred or assumed. It often reflects the fact that a woman is perceived as marrying into a kin group, not merely to an individual member of that group. Cf. †sororate.

lexicostatistics A statistical method for measuring the distance between related languages by the number of †cognates within a set vocabulary. When applied to a presumed time scale (as it usually is), this method is called †glottochronology. The presuppositions of lexicostatistics or glottochronology are that vocabulary is lost at a common rate and that it is possible to distinguish cognates from †loan words.

liminality A phase within *ritual, especially within *rites of passage, in which participants are regarded as being betwixt and between their former social position and the new position to which they are moving. The phase is often accompanied by either the suspension, or reversal, of everyday social values. The term derives from the Latin for 'threshold' and was highly elaborated by †Victor Turner in his reworking of †A. van Gennep's classic formulation.

limited good The belief, said to be held in *peasant societies, that the good things in life are limited in quantity and thus that any improvement in social conditions will have to be at the expense of one's neighbours. Like the related notion of the †culture of poverty, this concept has had much criticism from those who see it as an argument against the potential for social development.

lineage In *kinship theory, a *descent group formed on the basis of †unilineal descent; lineages may be either †patrilineal (†patrilineages) or †matrilineal (†matrilineages).

lineage theory Another name for *descent theory.

lineal A †consanguineal relative who is either an ancestor or a descendant of a given person. Sometimes the term is used loosely as a synonym for †direct relative, i.e. to include †co-lineals as well as lineals proper. Cf. †collateral.

linguistic relativism The notion that each language possesses its own characteristic mode of thought or perception of the world. Thus, people who speak different languages will think differently. The idea is most strongly associated with the work of †B.L. Whorf. See *Sapir–Whorf hypothesis.

Linnaean taxonomy The *classification system for plants and animals which was devised by Carl von Linné (Carolus Linnaeus) in the eighteenth century, and which forms the basis of modern botanical and zoological classification.

literary criticism The discipline which concerns the analysis and interpretation of literature. Literary criticism has been influenced by anthropological theory, in the case of *structuralism, and more recently, has left its own influence in anthropological theory, in the case of *postmodernism. See *ethnography, *poetics.

little tradition See *great and little traditions.

loan word In linguistics, a word which is 'borrowed' from one language to another. For example, *totem is borrowed from Ojibwa into English.

locutionary In †speech-act theory, any act of meaningful communication. Cf. †illocutionary, †perlocutionary.

M In kinship, the symbol for the genealogical position of the mother.

Manchester School In anthropology, the group of anthropologists (including †Victor Turner and Clyde Mitchell) associated with the Manchester department chaired by †Max Gluckman in the 1950s and 1960s. The department had strong links with the †Rhodes-Livingstone Institute, through which it developed a distinctive empirical and analytic style, predominantly concerned with African material, usually acknowledging change in the broader society and process in local social life, and pioneering research in areas like *urban anthropology and *ethnicity.

manifest and latent functions Manifest functions are those which are recognized by individual †actors, and latent functions are those which are not. The terms were first employed by the sociologist R.K. Merton in a critique of earlier *functionalist theory, e.g. in anthropology, which fails to make this distinction.

marker In linguistics, a feature which distinguishes one word from another within the same semantic system. The term is essentially synonymous with a †component or †significatum in *componential analyis.

marriage classes In Australian Aboriginal *kinship, the †exogamous social categories, whether they be †moieties, sections, or subsections.

mater The Latin for 'mother'. In anthropology the term designates the social mother, in contrast to the †genetrix or the †carrying mother. Cf. †pater.

material culture The material aspects of culture – artefacts, clothing, *houses, *technology. Long regarded as a distinctive subdiscipline in anthropology, as well as the inescapable basis of most *archaeology, from the 1980s onward material culture studies expanded enormously as anthropologists started to investigate areas like *consumption. See also *art, *museums.

materialism Broadly, any approach which emphasizes matter over mind (e.g. materialism in opposition to idealism in philosophy). Within anthropology, the term tends to refer to approaches – like *Marxism or *cultural materialism – which see the *environment, the means of production or other material aspects of society as determining other aspects of society, such as religion.

matriarchy This term refers to domination by female members of society. In the nineteenth century, matriarchy or †'mother right' was thought to be representative of an early stage of social evolution, and †matrilineal descent was seen as a vestige of such a stage. However, most anthropologists today would sharply distinguish matrilineal descent (in which property and positions are transmitted *through* female links, but by no means necessarily *to* women) from matriarchy (in which women hold power).

matricide See †parricide.

matrifocal Mother-centred, in reference to the *family. Matrifocal families are reported ethnographically especially in the *Caribbean, but also in Europe and North America.

matrilateral On the mother's side of the family. Matrilaterality is properly distinguished from †matrilineality, which implies a line of descent through females across generations. All people have matrilateral kin, whereas only people in specifically matrilineal societies have kin recognized as matrilineal.

matrilateral cross-cousin marriage *Marriage of a man to his mother's brother's daughter or another person belonging to the same relationship category as his mother's brother's daughter. Thus, for a woman, marriage is to her father's sister's son. By convention, the term 'matrilateral' is always taken from the male point of view. See *kinship.

matrilineage A †lineage formed on the basis of †matrilineal *descent.

matrilineal In *kinship, through the mother's line. The term implies a recognition of a category of *descent inherited by both females and males but transmitted to offspring only by females. Cf. †matrilateral, †patrilineal.

matrilocal Literally, in the mother's place of residence. In a loose sense, the term is sometimes used as a synonym for †uxorilocal residence. In the stricter sense, 'matrilocal' may be taken to imply residence in a matrilineal group generated by uxorilocality repeated through the generations.

means of production In Marxist theory, that part of the economic †base made up of natural resources and *technology, as apart from the social †relations of production. See *mode of production; cf. †forces of production.

mechanical and statistical models In the first volume of *Structural Anthropology* (1958) *Lévi-Strauss made a distinction between two kinds of models which may be used in structural analysis. Mechanical models are based on phenomena of 'the same scale' as whatever it is that is being modelled; statistical models involve differences of scale. He provides two explanatory examples: suicide, in which a mechanical model would be based on the individual circumstances – psychological type, family history – of particular suicides, while a statistical model would look at different rates of suicide in different social contexts; and marriage rules, which in some societies may be coherently expressed in terms of particular kin groups in a mechanical model, and in other cases (like modern Western societies), can only be expressed through complex statistical models.

mechanical solidarity One half of †Durkheim's version of the †great divide between the traditional and the modern. Societies based on mechanical solidarity have no great internal complexity and little division of labour, but a relatively strong †collective consciousness: they are held together by their uniformity. Modern societies, in contrast, are characterized by †organic solidarity, and are held together by their interdependence.

medical pluralism The idea, common in *medical anthropology, of different modes of healing (e.g. Western †biomedicine as well as various indigenous practices) being simultaneously available to people in the same socio-cultural circumstances.

men's house A *house used by men for sleeping, eating or social activities. These houses are a common feature in societies in *Melanesia and *Lowland South America, where there is sharp segregation on the basis of *gender and strong single-sex solidarity. They are often associated with *age groups.

mentality The supposed mental condition of human beings as members of their societies. The term has two different connotations in anthropology. On the one hand it is still strongly associated with †Lévy-Bruhl's arguments about the supposed *'primitive mentality', but it is also used by historically-minded anthropologists in the broader sense employed by

the French †*Annales* school of historians, for whom the 'history of mentalities' referred to an anthropological style of history concerned to recover the distinctive cultural perspective of people in the past.

mercantile capitalism A social system based on competition for control of natural resources and trade in external markets. A mercantile system was significant in the development of European *colonialism in the seventeenth and eighteenth centuries. See *world system.

merging In *kinship, the terminological equation of people in the same generation by virtue of same-sex sibling links. For example, a Trobriander calls his father, father's brother, and mother's sister's husband by the same term (*tama*). Cf. †bifurcate merging, †parallel relative, †skewing.

Mesolithic The 'stone age' period between the †Palaeolithic and the †Neolithic. It began in Europe at the end of the last glaciation and is characterized by †microlithic industries.

mestizo In *Latin America, a person of 'mixed' Indian and Spanish parentage. Originally, the term referred to individuals whose respective parents included one of Indian and one of Spanish origin. Today it is generally employed for anyone whose ancestors include both Indian and Spanish people.

meta- A prefix widely used in anthropological and other social scientific neologisms, usually with the meaning of 'about' or 'at a higher (or more fundamental) level'. So, for example, in problems of translation, a 'metalanguage' is a language into which two natural languages can be translated.

metacommunication Communicating about communication. The term was introduced by †G. Bateson to describe the complex process through which humans communicate.

metadescription Describing the act of description. The term is employed by some anthropologists to refer to the practice of *ethnography, especially where that practice is regarded as theoretically problematic.

metanarrative A story about stories. The term was employed by the translator of Lyotard's *The Postmodern Condition* (1984) for the French *grandes histoires* (or 'big stories'), which Lyotard used to describe the grand post-Enlightenment intellectual schemes of Kant, Hegel and Marx. This is what commentators are referring to when *postmodernism is said to be characterized by the 'decline of metanarratives'.

metaphor In rhetoric, a figure of speech based on analogy: e.g. 'the tide has turned in our favour' to mean that events are beginning to develop in the way we want. The linguist †R. Jakobson distinguished between metaphor (based on similarity of relationships) and †metonym (based on contiguity or common substance), a distinction which mapped onto other key pairs in structural linguistics such as †paradigmatic and †syntagmatic. *Lévi-Strauss has made frequent use of Jakobson's distinction, as have other *structuralists. Other anthropologists have sought to explain apparently bizarre or irrational beliefs in terms of metaphor. More recently *psychological anthropologists, influenced by the work of George Lakoff and Mark Johnson, have explored the way in which metaphors structure the acquisition of cultural knowledge. See *rationality *cognition.

methodological individualism and methodological holism Methodological individualism is the position (advanced, for example, by the philosopher †Karl Popper) that the individual is the basic and irreducible unit of explanation in social analysis. It is sometimes contrasted to methodological holism, which aims at understanding through social or symbolic structures. Examples of methodological individualism in anthropology would include certain kinds of †transactionalism and †game theory. See *individualism.

metonym In rhetoric, a figure of speech based on the substitution of either a part for a whole, or an associated thing for the thing itself: e.g. talking of 'the crown' or 'the throne' to refer either to a particular monarch or to monarchy in general. Often contrasted with †metaphor, in which something of radically different substance is used to suggest the properties of whatever it is that is being discussed.

microlithic industries Stone-tool traditions utilizing sophisticated techniques to produce small, accurate implements.

mimesis Literally, imitation or representation. The term has a philosophical history going back to Plato, and has come into anthropology by way of †literary criticism, and is now used in theories and critiques of the nature of †representation.

model A simplified or consciously artificial representation of reality. All social and cultural anthropology is based on the use of models. However, the meaning of models and their relation to reality has been the subject of much debate, especially in the 1960s. See *mechanical and statistical models.

moiety Literally, a half. In parts of *Lowland South America and *Aboriginal Australia, societies typically divide into two moieties which are recruited through a principle of †unilineal descent (either †matrilineal or †patrilineal). Such moieties are generally †exogamous, which means that an individual always marries into the opposite (and not his or her own) moiety. In the classic theoretical explanation of four-section systems in Aboriginal Australia, both matrilineal and patrilineal moieties are present at the same time, and each individual belongs to one of each. Their intersection thus generates the four sections. However, ethnographic evidence for recognition of both patrilineal and matrilineal moieties at the same time is weak.

monogamy *Marriage of one man to one woman at a time. Cf. †polygamy.

monogenism The doctrine that all humankind has the same origin. All modern anthropology (at least from *evolutionism to *structuralism) depends on this notion, which became widely accepted in the middle of the nineteenth century along with Darwinian evolution. The opposite is †polygenism.

monotheism Belief in one god. The concept is not as unproblematic as it may seem, since many religions (notably *Hinduism) have an ambiguous distinction between a single divine principal and a multifaceted divinity. Cf. †polytheism.

moral domain See †jural and moral domains.

moral economy A concept widely used in *peasant studies and *economic anthropology. In an influential article, the historian E.P. Thompson argued that participants in so-called food riots in early modern Britain were animated by a coherent economic ideal – based on ideas of a just price and resistance to naked *market principles – which he called the 'moral economy of the crowd'. The idea was developed, and to some extent transformed, by James Scott in his *Moral Economy of the Peasant* (1976), a book which argued that peasant economies are based on mutual institutions designed to insure against risk, rather than on principles of individual maximization.

mores Customs and conventions, especially those which reveal the value system as a whole in any given culture.

mortuary rites Rites involving the disposal of the dead. Disposal can include burial, reburial, cremation, or exposure, and the rites which involve such procedures are equally varied in their symbolic meaning. Such rites may, for example, involve the reincorporation of a spirit with its ancestral lineage or the rebirth of a spirit in another world. See *death.

mother-right From the German *Mutterrecht*, the notion of †matriarchy as the first phase, or an early phase, in human society. It is especially associated with the nineteenth-century Swiss jurist †J. Bachofen, who introduced the concept.

multilinear evolutionism The theory of *evolution associated with †J. Steward and his followers. It posits a distinct evolutionary trajectory, contingent on environmental and historical variables, for each society or group of related societies. Steward invented the term in order to distinguish his approach from those of nineteenth-century †unilinear evolutionism and early twentieth-century †universal evolutionism.

Mutterrecht See †mother-right.

negative reciprocity See †reciprocity.

neo-classical economic theory The dominant theory in twentieth-century economics, based on 'classical' assumptions about rational individuals exercising choice on the basis of means-ends calculations.

neocolonialism A relation between former colonial power and former colonies which in some way or another perpetuates the domination which had existed under *colonialism.

neo-evolutionism Twentieth century theoretical perspectives (e.g. those of †J. Steward and L. White) which revived interest in *evolutionism rather than *functionalist or *relativist positions. See also †universal evolutionism, †multilinear evolutionism.

Neolithic Literally, of the 'New Stone Age'. Within social and cultural anthropology, the term tends to refer much more to the subsistence methods and social organizational features thought to be typical of a Neolithic period, rather than to any particular stone tool tradition. Thus the Neolithic is associated with the early development of †agriculture or *pastoralism and the formation of social groups to accomplish these tasks efficiently.

neolocal †Marriage involving a new place of residence. Neolocality involves a couple moving to a place which is the previous home of neither party.

New Ethnography Another term for the sub-discipline or theoretical perspective developed in *American anthropology in the 1960s to focus on the formal relations between cultural categories.

More-or-less synonymous with †cognitive anthropology, at least as that term was then employed. See *componential analysis, *ethnoscience.

NGO (Non-governmental organization) Term used to refer to a range of organizations working in the field of *development, from tiny grassroots co-operatives to multinational charities like Oxfam.

noble savage The romantic ideal of 'savage' or 'natural' humankind, represented by societies which supposedly lack the unsavoury trappings of advanced civilization. The phrase originated in John Dryden's play *The Conquest of Granada*, Part I (1692) but is usually associated with the views of †J.J. Rousseau. In the eighteenth century, the image of the noble savage was attributed especially to aboriginal inhabitants of North America. See also *Enlightenment anthropology.

nodal kindred A †kindred whose focus is a set of core siblings. The term was coined by †W. Goodenough to describe ethnographic cases such as the Saami, for whom this type of organization is common.

non-unilineal descent *Descent based neither on †patrilineal nor on †matrilineal ties. Approximately synonymous with †cognatic or †bilateral descent.

norm Usually, in any given culture the established mode of behaviour to which conformity is expected. Sometimes the term refers to the average or typical behaviour, referred to as the statistical norm, rather than the expected behaviour, or ideal norm.

Notes and Queries on Anthropology A hand-book for ethnographers, originally intended to prompt travellers (missionaries, colonial officials, etc.) to collect theoretically useful data. Published in six editions between 1874 and 1951, its definitions and guidance served as a point of reference (and a source of dispute) in *British anthropology well into the 1960s.

nuclear family A *family group consisting of one set of parents and their children but excluding more distant relatives. Cf. †extended family.

objectivism Any approach in social theory which regards its subject-matter as in some sense made up of 'objects', things which can be objectively observed and assessed, rather than 'subjects' which require some special empathetic attention. Another term for various †scientistic or †positivistic approaches to anthropology (e.g. *Radcliffe-Brown's version of *functionalism, or American *ethnoscience in the 1960s).

oligarchy Rule by a small number of people.

Omaha terminology In †G.P. Murdock's classification, a *relationship terminology similar to †Iroquois but in which MBS is called by the same term as MB. Often such terminologies are found in strongly †patrilineal societies, the principle being that male members of one's mother's patrilineage are all called by a single term. See *Crow–Omaha systems.

orality An emphasis on the spoken over the written, especially in reference to the notion of writing as being dependent on speech.

organic analogy The idea that 'society is like an organism', e.g. in the sense that just as an organism is made up of systems (nervous, circulatory, etc.), so too is society (kinship, politics, economics and religion). This is the best known version of the organic analogy, as found in *Radcliffe-Brown's *functionalism, but †A. Comte, †H. Spencer, and †É. Durkheim formulated earlier versions.

organic solidarity The modern pole in †Durkheim's contrast between traditional and modern sources of solidarity, organic solidarity is characterized by a relatively complex division of labour, in which each social unit functions as an 'organ' within a larger 'organic' whole, allowing for greater diversity in individual consciousness. Contrasted to †mechanical solidarity.

Oriental despotism According to †K. Wittfogel, the form of political organization characteristic of societies based on irrigated agriculture with the centralized control of water resources. See also †Asiatic mode of production, †hydraulic civilization.

Palaeolithic Literally, the 'old stone age', characterized archaeologically by crude tools and palaeontologically by premodern as well as modern forms of humanity. The period includes, for example, australopithecines and early forms of the genus *Homo*. The precise definition and delineation of palaeolithic sites has changed since †Lubbock invented the term in 1865, but today it is usually equated with the period ending in Europe with the last glaciation. The following period is known as the †mesolithic.

palaeontology The study of fossils. The boundary between palaeontology and prehistoric *archaeology is not precise, and most work on early human sites falls within the bounds of palaeontology.

paradigm, paradigmatic Paradigm is a term with a variety of meanings, depending on context. In common English, it often refers simply to an example.

It was given a fuller and more technical meaning by the philosopher of science †Thomas Kuhn who used it to refer to a set of common assumptions, shared by members of a particular scientific community at any one time, which serve to structure and restrict the questions asked by those scientists during periods of what he called 'normal science'. Kuhn's sense was swiftly taken up by social scientists to refer loosely to any theoretical tendency. In linguistics, on the other hand, linguists influenced by †Saussure contrast †syntagmatic relations which link successive words or sounds in the chain of spoken language, with paradigmatic (or associative) relations which link together all the words or sounds which might potentially occupy a particular position in the syntagmatic chain.

parallel In *kinship, a parallel relative is any relative (e.g. a parallel uncle or aunt) whose relationship is traced through a same-sex sibling link (e.g. FB or MZ, but not MB or FZ); the contrast is with †cross-.

parallel cousin A cousin related through a same-sex sibling link. In other words, a father's brother's child or mother's sister's child. In many societies, parallel cousins are classified in the same way as siblings. Cf. †cross-cousin, †patrilateral parallel cousin marriage.

parallel descent A very rare form of *descent in which a man takes membership in the †patrilineal group of his father and the woman takes membership in the †matrilineal group of her mother. It is reported in Lowland South America, e.g. among the Apinayé.

parole See †*langue* and *parole*.

parricide The killing of a parent. The killing of a father is known as patricide, and the killing of a mother, matricide.

participant observation Term used for the most basic technique of anthropological *fieldwork, participation in everyday activities, working in the native language and observing events in their everyday context. See *ethnography, *methodology.

pater The Latin for 'father'. In anthropology the term designates the person socially recognized as the father, in contrast to the term †genitor, which designates the presumed biological father. Cf. †mater, †genetrix.

paternity Fatherhood. The term usually refers to presumed biological fatherhood.

patriarchy Rule by the father, and by extension, rule in the hands of men. Cf. †matriarchy.

patricide See †parricide.

patrilateral In *kinship, relations on the father's side. To be distinguished from †patrilineal, which refers to relations of descent traced through fathers.

patrilateral cross-cousin marriage *Marriage of a man to his father's sister's daughter or another person belonging to the same relationship category as his father's sister's daughter. Thus, for a woman, marriage is to her mother's brother's son. Cf. †matrilateral cross-cousin marriage. See *kinship.

patrilateral parallel-cousin marriage *Marriage of a man to his father's brother's daughter, or a woman to her father's brother's son. The practice is common in Arab societies, where it serves to keep property within the †patrilineage.

patrilineage A †lineage formed on the basis of †patrilineal *descent.

patrilineal In *kinship, through the father's line. The term implies a recognition of a category of *descent inherited by both males and females but transmitted to offspring only by males. Cf. †matrilineal, †patrilateral, †unilineal.

patrilocal *Marriage in the father's place of residence. In a loose sense, the term is sometimes used as a synonym for †virilocal residence. In the stricter sense, 'patrilocal' is often taken to imply residence in a patrilineal group generated by virilocality repeated through the generations.

performative In †speech-act theory, any utterance which is in some way equivalent to an action: e.g. 'I name this ship . . .', 'I promise you . . .'. Cf. †illocutionary, †perlocutionary.

periphery See †centre and periphery.

perlocutionary In †speech-act theory, the effects of an utterance on the feelings or behaviour of the hearer. For example, a perlocutionary act may be one which amuses or frightens the hearer. See also †locutionary, †illocutionary.

petty commodity production Small-scale, often *household-based, production for the *market, often by rural people also engaged in †subsistence agriculture. Petty commodity production was much debated in †structural Marxism and *peasant studies in the 1970s.

peyote A small cactus or the drug (mescaline) made from it. A *millenarian peyote cult developed among *Native North Americans over a wide area in the late nineteenth century.

phatic communion Malinowski's term for conversation whose purpose is the establishment or maintenance of social relations, rather than the seeking or imparting of information. Talking about the weather or the prices of goods are examples common in Western societies, as are expressions like 'hello' or 'how do you do?'.

phenomenology A term with varied but related meanings in philosophy, psychology, and sociology. In anthropology, it tends to take its sociological meaning: the study of the ways in which people experience and understand everyday life. As a theoretical perspective, it is closely allied to †ethnomethodology.

phenotype The physical nature of an organism, determined by its †genotype and its *environment.

phone In linguistics, a sound, i.e. a unit at the †phonetic level of language. Contrast †phoneme.

phoneme, phonemic In linguistics, a phoneme is a meaningful unit of sound peculiar to a particular language. A given phoneme is necessarily an abstraction from the patterns of actual speech: it may, for example, be realized in one, two or more allophones, or sounds which vary according to dialect or appearance in relation to other phonemes (e.g. in English the phoneme /p/ at the beginning of a word is pronounced with breath, whereas it is not if preceeded by an /s/). Phonemes occur within a system unique to a particular language or dialect, namely the phonemic or †phonological system. See also *emic and etic.

phonetic In linguistics, the study of, or the theoretical level of, the objective auditory or acoustic nature of sounds, independent of their place in the sound system of a given language (the phonology or phonemic system). See also *emic and etic.

phonology In linguistics, the study of speech sounds as part of a system of such sounds in a given language. Phonology is important in anthropology because *structuralist anthropologists, notably *Lévi-Strauss, have borrowed theoretical ideas from the field.

phratry In *kinship, a group of †clans related by common †unilineal *descent. The term comes from the Greek word for patrilineal clan (and ultimately from that for brother), but it is most often used in reference to large, often exogamous, *Native North American groupings which are larger than the clan but smaller than the indigenous society as a whole.

physical anthropology The branch of anthropology which includes the study of physical difference both in living populations and through human evolution. It is one of the †four fields of anthropology in North America. The term 'physical anthropology' has tended to fall into disuse in recent years, and *biological anthropology' has been taken as a more accurate description of the field which has developed from it.

pidgin A new language which contains elements from different natural languages. Often pidgins are used in contact situations, then develop into †creoles as individuals grow up speaking them as natural languages.

pluralism See †legal pluralism, †medical pluralism, *plural societies.

polyandry In *kinship, the *marriage of one woman to more than one man. Adelphic polyandry is the marriage of one woman to a group of brothers. Cf. †polygamy, †polygyny.

polygamy *Marriage of one man to more than one woman or one woman to more than one man. Thus it includes both †polygyny and †polyandry. Cf. †monogamy.

polygenism The doctrine that humankind has more than one origin, and by implication that each branch of humankind has a separate origin. Members of the Anthropological Society of London were prominent in its support, against those of the rival Ethnological Society of London who supported †monogenism. Polygenism was commonly accepted in the early nineteenth century but challenged with the coming of Darwinian *evolution. See also *anthropological societies.

polygyny The *marriage of one man to more than one woman. †Sororal polygyny is the marriage of one man to a group of sisters. Cf. †polyandry, †polygamy.

polysemy The characteristic of having more than one meaning.

polytheism Belief in more than one god. Cf. †monotheism.

positivism This term has varied but related meanings. In anthropology, it tends to refer to any approach which treats anthropology as a science concerned with the pursuit of objective knowledge through the collection of facts and the formulation of laws. In its strictest sense, it refers to the scientific methodology of †A. Comte, who in the early nineteenth century sought to place social science on the same philosophical footing as the natural sciences. Cf. †objectivism, †scientism.

postcolonial Referring to the period which begins with the withdrawal of Western colonial rule. In literary criticism, the term has come to be used for a body of radical work on the persistence of colonial representations of the non-European 'other', influenced by †E. Said's *Orientalism* as well as various strands of †poststructural theory. See colonialism.

post-processual archaeology Any approach in *archaeology which goes beyond the mere establishment of a chronological record. Post-processual archaeologists (e.g. Ian Hodder) tend to be interested in some of the same phenomena as social and cultural anthropologists, e.g. *ritual and *belief. Cf. †processual archaeology.

poststructuralism A broad tendency within †literary criticism and other fields, poststructuralism developed out of *structuralist theory in France in the 1970s, and was identified above all with the work of †Jacques Derrida, †Michel Foucault and †Jacques Lacan. See also *postmodernism.

practice What people do, as opposed to what they say. The concept is central to †P. Bourdieu's notion of †habitus. Cf. *preference and prescription.

pragmatics In linguistics, the study of how language is *used* and what it *does,* through the interpretation of utterances and their implications in social contexts, rather than what it *means,* through the †semantic analysis of sentences and their referents. See also †deixis, †speech-act.

praxis In Marxist social theory, †practice or practical action, especially that which is directed to fostering radical change.

preference See *preference and prescription.

presentism In historiography, an overly present-focused analysis which sees the past in terms of its anticipation of more recent developments. This approach has been criticized, e.g. by George Stocking, writing about anthropologists' own accounts of the *history of anthropology.

prestation Term used by †Mauss in his essay on *The Gift* (and retained in the otherwise flawed first English translation), meaning those gifts and services which make up what Mauss called a 'total social phenomenon'. See *exchange.

primary and secondary institutions In the *culture and personality school, primary institutions are those which define the 'personality' of a group, while secondary institutions are those which are derived from this. The distinction was first drawn by †A. Kardiner.

primitive, primitivism Always an ambiguous term in anthropology, primitive is no longer in general use. Prior to the 1970s, it was employed in opposition to 'civilized' to refer to peoples who were the subject of most anthropological enquiry. The term was widely and loosely used in a non-pejorative sense through the twentieth century, whereas nineteenth-century *evolutionary writers tended to make a more precise distinction between †savagery, †barbarism, and †civilization. Primitivism is the ascription of virtue to what is often a romanticized or idealized version of the primitive. The term is widely used, especially in art historical writing on those *modernist artists (some influenced by contemporary anthropology) who self-consciously borrowed motifs and formal elements from so-called primitive *art.

primitive promiscuity The notion that humanity once engaged in promiscuous sexual behaviour, prior to the development of the *family and †matrilineal and †patrilineal kinship institutions. The notion was common in nineteenth-century discourse on the origins of society, e.g. in the works of *Lewis Henry Morgan.

primogeniture Inheritance or succession by the first-born child, or more usually, by the first-born son. Cf. †ultimogeniture.

processual archaeology The approach in *archaeology which emphasizes chronology, historical development, or *evolution, rather than the understanding of a single given period (e.g. the work of †Lewis Binford). Cf. †post-processual archaeology.

profane See *sacred and profane.

prophet In general terms, either a person who speaks with knowledge on the future or with divine inspiration. Anthropologists have used †Max Weber's distinction between priests (whose authority derives from their office) and prophets (whose authority derives from their personal qualities or †charisma).

Protestant ethic †Max Weber's characterization of those qualities of the early Protestant worldview, specifically the ethic of this-worldly asceticism, which he claimed played a crucial part in the emergence of *capitalism in Europe.

prototype theory The theory which holds that humans classify their world, not in terms of criteria which must apply to all items in a particular category, but through the recognition of best-cases, or prototypes, which become the model to which other items in the category approximate. The theory originates in Berlin and Kay's work on colour categories, but has been developed in other areas of cognitive science. See *classification.

proxemics The field which examines the social use of space. It is associated especially with the work of E.T. Hall.

psychic unity The notion that all humankind shares the same essential †mentality. This nineteenth-century idea underlies diverse perspectives in anthropology, but in more recent times is most strongly associated with Lévi-Straussian *structuralism. See also †A. Bastian.

puberty Biologically, the phase in early adolescence when the sex glands become functional. Many societies mark this phase by *rituals which symbolically transform a child into an adult. See *rite of passage.

ramage In *Polynesian ethnography, a †cognatic †descent group, or in some usage a system of ranked descent groups.

rationalism In philosophy, the doctrine that knowledge depends on reason rather than on experience, i.e. it is actively structured by the mind. In anthropology, this doctrine is characteristic of approaches such as *structuralism. Contrast †empiricism.

reciprocity Mutual *exchange or obligation. More generally, the relation between people in an economic system, the obligations they have towards each other in such a system, or the practices they engage in in relation to one another. In *Stone Age Economics* (1972), †M. Sahlins distinguishes three types of 'reciprocity' in the widest sense. **Generalized reciprocity** involves giving without the expectation of return, and is associated with the family. **Balanced reciprocity** involves exchanges of equal value between people, and is associated with the community. **Negative reciprocity** involves economic activities in which people seek to gain at the expense of others (e.g. barter, theft), and is associated with dealings with strangers or people outside the community.

reflexive anthropology See *reflexivity.

relations of production In *Marxist theory, the social relations (e.g. between employer and employee or master and slave) within any given *mode of production.

relative deprivation A term common in social psychology and sociology to refer to a situation in which people feel themselves deprived, either in comparison to other people, or in comparison to their own previous condition. Analyses of rebellions, and other overt acts of political *resistance, often show that participants are suffering from relative (rather than absolute) deprivation.

representation Anything which stands for, or takes the place of, something else. In philosophy, the idea that our perception of the world is composed of mental representations lies behind †Durkheim's idea of the †collective representation. In politics, we typically delegate our part in active political life to someone who promises to represent our interests. And anthropological writing, of course, involves the attempted representation of other people and their way of life. From the 1980s onward, these meanings have grown increasingly tangled, not least as proponents of multiculturalism and the politics of *identity have raised the question of who, if anyone, has the right to represent, or speak for, anyone else.

reproduction Literally the producing of offspring in each succeeding generation, but more generally can refer to the reproduction of society and culture as in the *Marxist concern for †social reproduction.

restricted exchange In *kinship, *Lévi-Strauss's term for †direct exchange.

revitalization A process of conscious cultural, and especially religious, change. Revitalization movements are characterized by the emergence of a †charismatic leader with ideas which overthrow the established order.

Rhodes-Livingstone Institute Now the Zambian National Research Institute, this former colonial foundation was instrumental in setting up ethnographic research in Central Africa and in the development of theoretical models based on †action rather than social structure. Associated with it were †M. Gluckman, J.C. Mitchell, †M. Wilson, and others. See †Manchester school.

right and left In many cultures, the right hand or right side of the *body is symbolically associated with good and the left hand or left side with evil. Right may also symbolize male, and left, female, etc. The study of right/left symbolism became prominent through the work of †Robert Hertz.

ritual kinship Fictive kin relations which come into being in a ritual context. †Godparenthood and *compadrazgo* are the classic examples. Cf. †fictive kinship.

ritual of rebellion A form of *ritual in which roles are reversed and junior members of society act out roles associated with senior members (e.g. initiates, those of their elders, or commoners, those of their king). Using examples from Southern Africa, †M. Gluckman argued that such rituals serve the function of renewing the existing social order, while appearing to overthrow it. Historians of early modern Europe have examined the extent to which annual rituals like carnival expressed real social protest. See *rite of passage.

role According to †R. Linton's classic definition, role is the dynamic aspect of †status. Roles imply activities associated with particular statuses in society.

routinization †Max Weber's notion of the process by which †charisma develops into routine; i.e. charismatic leaders become established as part of a new social order. In †revitalization movements, routinization is often the outcome.

S In *kinship, the symbol for the genealogical position of the son.

salvage archaeology Any archaeological study which is carried out on a site soon to be lost, e.g. through destruction caused by modern building or roadworks.

salvage ethnography Any ethnographic study which is carried out in order to document cultures or institutions which are disappearing or expected to disappear in the near future.

sanction A reward for socially correct behaviour or, more commonly, a punishment for socially incorrect behaviour. See also †social control.

Saussurean With reference to the linguistic theories of †Ferdinand de Saussure. See also †*langue* and *parole*.

savage, savagery Although today generally a term of abuse, savage has not always had such connotations in anthropological writings. In the eighteenth century 'savages' could be noble as well as ignoble, and 'savage society' was regarded by some philosophers as superior to 'polished society'. In nineteenth-century *evolutionary theory, 'savagery' was the lowest level of human society, below †barbarism and †civilization. However, in the early twentieth century the terms came into disfavour, replaced at first by †'primitive', which, some felt, had fewer negative connotations. Today, both terms are best avoided.

scarification The ritual marking of the *body, often in the context of a *rite of passage.

schema The idea that our knowledge of the world is structured in terms of mental models, or schemas, is common in many areas of cognitive science, and has recently been applied in *psychological anthropology in work on cultural models.

schismogenesis †Gregory Bateson's term for a process of structured interaction in which two opposed entities produce a situation of increased differentiation. Bateson (in *Naven* [1936]) originally located these processes at the level of the individual, but the term can be extended to collective agents like clans or nation-states. **Complementary schismogenesis** describes a situation where one party's behaviour reinforces the other party's different reaction (e.g. the more one party is assertive, the more the other party is submissive). **Symmetrical schismogenesis** describes the interaction of two parties who react in the same way to each other (e.g. boasting on one side producing intensified boasting on the other).

scientism Adhering to the procedures or appearance of ('hard') science; an alternative to †positivism as a term of anthropological abuse.

secondary ethnocentrism A form of †ethnocentrism in which an anthropologist sees the world not through the lens of his or her own *culture, but through that of the culture in which he or she has done fieldwork. *Lewis Henry Morgan, for example, was accused of seeing 'primitive society' in general as being much like Iroquois society.

secret societies Social groups which are formed for purposes of engaging in secret ritual activities to the exclusion of people of opposite *gender (especially men excluding women) and of minors and people who belong to other secret societies. They are common in *West Africa, among other places.

sedentarism Staying in one place, i.e. living in a non-nomadic community. The concept is applicable especially to comparisons between nomads and settled (sedentary) groups. See *nomadism, *pastoralism.

segmentary lineage system A system of *descent groups (†lineages) organized around a principle of opposition to one another. According to †Evans-Pritchard's classic account of Nuer lineage segmentation, if a man is involved in a dispute with a member of a closely related lineage, members of each lineage are brought into the dispute as well. If, however, the dispute is with a man from a very distantly-related lineage, then larger lineages, i.e. all those tracing descent back to the disputants' common ancestors, may be involved. The elegance of Evans-

Pritchard's model, which has been applied with modifications elsewhere in Africa and the *Middle East, has now been superseded by the ever more inelegant and intractible ethnographic evidence it has generated. See *descent.

semantics The branch of linguistics concerned with the study of meaning. Semantics is traditionally taken as the highest level of linguistic analysis (above †phonetics, †phonology, and †syntax), and therefore the one which marks the bridge between language and the rest of culture.

semiology Another name for †semiotics in Saussure's sense.

semiotics The general science of †signs. The field was instituted through the work of †Ferdinand de Saussure and has developed, especially in literary and film criticism. There is a second tradition of semiotics which stems from the work of the American philosopher †C.S. Peirce. This tradition emphasizes the connection between 'natural' and 'artificial' signs. This latter tradition distinguishes signs as †symbols (purely conventional signs such as words), †indexes (natural signs such as smoke as a sign of fire) and †icons (which stand in between, such as maps).

seriation Especially in *archaeology, the classification of objects by their sequence; e.g. in evolutionary terms.

shifting cultivation An alternative term for †swidden agriculture, in reference to the fact that such agricultural practices involve regularly moving the cultivated area in order to allow the regeneration of soil and forest cover.

sib In *kinship, an alternative term for †clan. †G.P. Murdock employed the term to include both †patrilineal clans (which he called gentes, singular †gens) and †matrilineal ones (which he called clans).

sign, signified, signifier At the most general, something (like a †symbol or a †representation) which stands for, or indicates something else. †Saussure spoke of linguistic signs as made up of a concept (*signifié*, that which is signified) and a sound-image (*signifiant*, or signifier). Saussure insisted on the fundamentally arbitrary, or unmotivated, relationship between signifier and signified in the case of the linguistic sign. For †Peirce, on the other hand, signs, which usually share some property with that which is being signified, can be distinguished from symbols, which are wholly conventional.

significatum Within *componential analysis, a unit of meaning which distinguishes one term or concept from another. For example, the significatum male (as opposed to female) distinguishes 'father' from 'mother'. See also †connotatum, †marker.

sister's daughter marriage Marriage of a man to his elder sister's daughter or a woman to her mother's brother. This form of *marriage is practised in parts of South India and *Lowland South America where sisters' daughters are terminologically equivalent to †cross-cousins.

skewing In *kinship, the terminological equation of people in different generations, usually because they belong to the same †lineage. For example, a Trobriander calls his father's sister's daughter by the same term as his father's sister (*tabu*), both being members of his father's matrilineal group. The notion is found especially within †transformational analysis, where it defines the rule which generates *Crow–Omaha terminology structures. Cf. †merging.

slash and burn agriculture See †swidden agriculture.

social action See †action.

social anthropology In its literal sense, this term tends to refer to the branch of anthropology which emphasizes *society over *culture (cf. †cultural anthropology). 'Social anthropology' is historically the preferred term in British anthropology and is now widely used throughout Europe, whereas 'cultural anthropology' tends to be the favoured term in North America. There the term 'social anthropology' can have the connotation of a specifically British type of anthropological theory (e.g. some forms of *functionalism and *structuralism). The differences between the two traditions were probably at their greatest from the 1940s to the 1960s, since when their interests have increasingly merged, as demonstrated by some anthropologists' use of hybrids like 'socio-cultural anthropology' to describe their interests.

social charter A culturally-understood justification for an action, a social institution, or a set of beliefs. In a classic statement, *Malinowski referred to *myth as 'a charter for social action'.

social contract Most literally, an (imaginary) agreement between individuals who decide to give up their complete, natural liberty in order to form a *society. By extension, the act of consent on the part of individuals who accept †sociality and the protection afforded by government. The concept was prominent in the seventeenth and eighteenth centuries, e.g. in the works of †Hobbes and †Rousseau. See *Enlightenment anthropology.

social control Any constraint, institution or practice which maintains order in social life. See also †sanction.

social fact †Durkheim's term for the fundamental subject matter of sociology, as expressed in his famous †positivist aphorism that 'social facts must be studied as things', in other words as 'realities external to the individual'. See *functionalism.

social formation A term commonly employed by †structural Marxists to mean *society. See *Marxism and anthropology.

social history The discipline, closely allied to economic history, which emphasizes the social, cultural, and technological, rather than the political factors of historical periods or in historical change.

social institution See †institution.

sociality The human capacity for the social. The concept was first prominent in seventeenth and eighteenth-century political philosophy but has earned renewed interest in †ethology and anthropology in the late twentieth century, where some prefer it to the implicit dualism (individual v. society) in the more common term *society.

social organization The activities of members of a society as these relate to the *social structure. Since *Malinowski's time, the term 'social organization' has been the preferred description of society by those who favour approaches focused on social †action (e.g. †R. Firth), whereas 'social structure' has been preferred by those (e.g. *structuralists and †structural-functionalists) who see society as consisting more of relational elements than activities. See also main entry on *social structure and social organization.

social reproduction The renewal of the socio-economic order through processes involving labour, technology, etc. The concept was prominent in Marxist anthropology in the 1970s and 1980s.

social stratification The division of society by 'vertical' elements in a hierarchy. Forms of social stratification can include those by *class, by *caste, and by †achieved status. See *inequality.

social system A broad-ranging term which sometimes refers to *society as a whole, sometimes to its inner workings (in reference to its 'systematic' nature), and sometimes to specific 'systems', such as the *kinship system or the political system.

sororal polygyny *Marriage of one man to two or more sisters. In many †polygynous societies it is the preferred form of marriage because, it is felt, sisters are likely to be better co-wives than unrelated women. See †polygamy, †polygyny; cf. †adelphic polyandry.

sororate The *marriage or acquisition of a woman as a wife by her late sister's husband. In many African societies, sororate is either preferred or assumed. It often reflects the fact that †bridewealth paid for at marriage needs to be reciprocated by the gift of a woman from one kin group to another, and that that reciprocity is not fulfilled if she dies, especially if she dies before bearing children. See also †levirate.

soul The spirit, moral aspect or non-material part of a human being. In many religions, souls are believed to survive the death of the physical *body. In some religions, it is believed that souls may travel during the lifetime of an individual or otherwise be temporarily removed from the body, e.g. when a person is in a trance state during ritual activity. As a term with a very specific history in the Christian tradition, it may now be felt problematic to apply to other religious traditions. See *religion.

speech-act theory Speech-act theory refers to a body of work in philosophy and linguistics, drawing upon the work of J.L. Austin and John Searle, which concentrates on what words *do* in ordinary linguistic interaction. Closely related to †pragmatics, it has produced a set of technical distinctions (†performative, †illocutionary, †perlocutionary, etc.) which have been widely employed by linguistic anthropologists, for example in the analysis of *ritual.

speech community Any group of people who speak the same form of speech, or †dialect.

speech event Any act of speech and its associated non-linguistic aspects.

sphere of exchange In all societies different goods (objects, services, persons) are subject to conventional constraints on their *exchange. For example, in Euro-American society it is quite acceptable to exchange *money for subsistence food, possible but disreputable to exchange money for sex, and quite unacceptable to exchange money for permanent possession of another *person. Among the Tiv of West Africa, as described by Paul Bohannon, different commodities were exchanged within what he called different spheres of exchange: subsistence goods by market transactions, prestige goods in which brass rods served as a medium of exchange, and marriageable women. In this case virtually all exchanges were confined to their appropriate sphere, although it was possible (if morally dangerous) to

'convert' goods from one sphere to another. See *consumption, *exchange, *money.

state formation The economic and political process by which pre-state societies evolve into states. See *evolution and evolutionism, *state.

statistical models See †mechanical and statistical models.

status The term status has two different usages in anthropology. For *functionalists following †Ralph Linton, status refers to a position within a social order, e.g. king (as opposed to commoner), worker (as opposed to boss), or mother (as opposed to child). The term is often seen in reference to †role. In classic functionalist theory, statuses are seen as part of †social structure whereas the roles they imply are part of †social organization. Other anthropologists have followed †Max Weber in isolating status as one of three factors (with power and wealth) which combine in determining †social stratification. So, in †Louis Dumont's account of †hierarchy in *South Asia, power (as embodied in the figure of the king) is encompassed by status (as embodied in the Brahman or priest). See †achievement and ascription.

stem family A *family consisting of a †nuclear family plus one married son (who would usually inherit). The term has been much debated in recent studies of the history of the European family.

stratification See †social stratification.

structural adjustment In *development, a term used from the 1980s onward for a range of policies, strongly favoured (some would say imposed) by international agencies such as the World Bank and the International Monetary Fund, usually involving drastic reductions in state activity (e.g. welfare payments or subsidies on foodstuffs) and so-called 'liberalization' of free market activity.

structural form *Radcliffe-Brown's term for the theoretical abstraction which described a social phenomenon in a generalized way. For example, if one observes the relationship between a number of fathers and their respective sons in a given society (these making up *social structure), one can come up with a general description of the typical father/son relationship in this society (an aspect of structural form). However, later writers, including many of Radcliffe-Brown's followers, have tended not to make this distinction, and rather, describe both simply as manifestations of the social structure. See *social structure and social organization.

structural-functionalism The theoretical perspective associated with *A.R. Radcliffe-Brown (though he rejected the term) and his followers. It involved the emphasis on †synchronic analysis of societies as isolated wholes. Each society was conceived as a set of systems related to each other analogously to the systems of a biological organism (cf. †organic analogy). The approach dominated *British anthropology from the 1940s to the 1960s. See *functionalism.

structural Marxism General term for a range of theoretical positions in Marxist anthropology in the 1960s and 1970s, influenced by the French *structuralism of †Louis Althusser and, in some cases, *Lévi-Strauss. See *Marxism and anthropology.

subaltern Translation of †Gramsci's term for 'subordinate' (as in 'subaltern classes'), subaltern has taken on a slightly different meaning, mostly from the work of the radical South Asian historians associated with the series *Subaltern Studies*. In their usage, subaltern refers to the position of any dominated group, whether this be on grounds of *class, *gender, *age, *ethnicity or *religion.

subincision An extreme form of mutilation involving cutting along the length of the penis. The practice is found among Aboriginal Australians, who perform it as part of male †initiation rituals. Cf. †circumcision.

subjectivism Any approach in social theory which emphasizes that its proper subject-matter is subjects (with consciousness, †agency, etc.) rather than objects (which can be objectively observed, counted, measured, etc.). Contrast †objectivism.

subject-position Term favoured by seriously *postmodern anthropologists, influenced by the theoretical critique of the subject (in French writers like †Foucault): if subjectivity is less a self-evident foundation for knowledge, but instead a product of external *discourses and practices, it is more appropriate to designate different kinds of subjectivity as so many subject positions.

subsistence agriculture Agriculture directed to the maintenance of basic subsistence (the provision of food, clothing, shelter) rather than to the *market. Cf. †cash-crops.

substance The opposite of †form. In linguistics, the term is employed for those things with which language is constructed, including speech (the phonic substance). In cultural approaches to *kinship, indigenous notions of bodily substance are (after †David Schneider) often seen as crucial to understanding local idioms of relatedness.

substantivism See *formalism and substantivism.

succession The passing of rank or office, e.g. kingship, from a senior person to a junior person, usually upon the death of the former. Cf. †inheritance.

Sudanese terminology In †G.P. Murdock's classification of *relationship terminologies, one in which siblings are distinguished from cousins and †parallel-cousins are distinguished from †cross-cousins.

supernatural That which cannot be explained with reference to 'nature', as this concept is socially constructed. Important in some nineteenth-century definitions of *religion, the term is now usually avoided by modern anthropologists, except in the context of indigenous ideas about the natural.

superorganic Above the level of the physical (human) organism. Now usually used in reference to *culture, the term means definable in terms of culture itself, i.e. not reducible to psychological or other non-cultural phenomena. The concept was introduced by †Herbert Spencer but came to prominence in anthropology through †A.L. Kroeber in the early twentieth century. See *culture.

superstition Any belief or action which is thought to be irrational. Anthropologists today do not generally impute superstition on the basis of their own system of rationality, but leave it to be defined in indigenous contexts. See *rationality, *relativism.

superstructure See †base and superstructure.

surface structure See †deep and surface structure.

swidden agriculture A system of agriculture, widely practised on tropical soils, in which fields are temporarily cleared, usually from primary or secondary forest, burnt in order to transfer nutrients from cleared growth into the soil, cultivated for a limited period, then allowed to return to forest. The subject of much abuse from colonial administrators and ill-informed environmentalists, it is often a perfectly stable and sensible regime for the soil and climatic conditions in which it is usually practised. If, however, the fallow period is reduced, either due to population pressure or the lure of †cash-cropping, long-term soil degradation may set in. Also known as †shifting cultivation or (often pejoratively) slash-and-burn agriculture.

symbol A thing which stands for something else. Cf. †icon, †index, †sign. See also main entry on *symbolic anthropology.

symbolic interactionism In sociology and social psychology, the perspective based on the work of †G.H. Mead and sociologist Herbert Bulmer which stresses the emergent nature of social interaction, social knowledge and self-knowledge. It is related to †transactionalism in social anthropology, and is one source of the recent vocabulary of 'self' and 'other'.

symmetric alliance In *kinship, a system of *marriage alliance in which groups exchange members as spouses, and where such exchanges may go in either direction. See *alliance.

sympathetic magic †J. Frazer's term for magical practice in which like is believed to influence like, e.g. sticking pins in a doll to cause harm to the individual whom the doll depicts. Cf. †contagious magic.

synchronic Synchronic perspectives, such as *structuralism and *functionalism, emphasize the relation of things in the present or at some specific time. In contrast †diachronic approaches, such as *evolutionism, emphasize relations through time.

syntagm, syntagmatic, syntax A syntagm is literally, a 'sentence'. Syntax refers to the grammatical relations which hold between the elements within a sentence. †Saussure distinguished between two levels of linguistic analysis: the syntagmatic and the associative (renamed the †paradigmatic by his followers). The syntagmatic refers to the succession of linguistic items through time in an utterance, and the relations between those items. The paradigmatic refers to the relations between any one item in a particular syntagmatic position and all other items (not actually present) which may occupy that position. See †metaphor, †metonymy, †paradigm.

system In †structural-functionalist theory, a major social division, such as economics, kinship, politics, religion, and sometimes law. Each of these may be said to be made up of various †institutions which are functionally related within the system.

systems theory An approach applied in many different disciplines, related to †cybernetics and drawing on computer analogies, which emphasizes relations between elements within a dynamic system, such that if one element changes it affects others within the system. It has been particularly important in *ecological anthropology.

tabula rasa Literally, in Latin, a blank slate. The term is used especially in reference to †John Locke's theory that human behaviour and understanding are derived from learning, and are not innate. Boasian anthropologists were influenced by this notion, whereas *Lévi-Strauss and his followers, for example, have maintained that there are human cognitive universals.

taxonomy *Classification, especially within a formal system such as the classification of plants by a Western botanist or the classification of birds in a society in which birds are culturally important. Such a classification may be referred to as *a* taxonomy.

technological determinism The explanation of social or cultural phenomena as the product of specific technologies or a specific level of *technology. For example, the use of iron tools may be said to determine certain aspects of social organization not found among peoples who use stone tools.

teknonymy System of personal naming, common for example in *Southeast Asia, in which the term of reference for a particular person incorporates that person's relationship to another person. For example, an adult may be referred to as 'the father of X' or 'the mother of Y'. See *names and naming.

territoriality A slightly ambiguous term which may refer either to cultural mechanisms to define or defend territory or to observed behaviour indicating a preference for remaining within a given territory. The term is in common use in *archaeology and †social anthropology (especially in reference to *hunter-gatherers), but often has †ethological connotations.

theodicy The attempt to understand or explain evil in the world.

thick description The term introduced by †Clifford Geertz in *The Interpretation of Cultures* (1973) as a description of what good *ethnography, and by implication good anthropology, is. What makes an ethnographic description 'thick' rather than 'thin' is the layering of interpretation of all sorts: ethnographer's interpretations, informant's interpretations, people's own interpretations. See *symbolic anthropology.

Third World Broadly, that part of the world which is neither First World (the industrialized West) or Second World (the former Soviet block). The term, always contentious, is current in anthropology, politics, development studies, etc., for poorer regions of the world, especially former colonies of Western states.

Torres Straits Expedition A Cambridge expedition of 1898–9, led by †Haddon, to the Torres Straits between New Guinea and Australia. The expedition was important for its extensive documentation of local custom, for its opportunity to test then current theoretical ideas, and for the invention and extensive use of the *genealogical method by †W.H.R. Rivers, and has acquired semi-mythological status as one of the founding moments of the *fieldwork tradition in *British anthropology.

totem See *totemism.

trance An altered state of consciousness. It can be induced by any number of means, including drugs, hyperventilation, music, or spirit possession. See *possession, *shamanism.

transactionalism An action-oriented approach which sees *society as the product of interactions between individual actors. The classic example is †Fredrik Barth's *Political Leadership among Swat Pathans* (1959), which argues that relations between leaders and their clients make up the social order, and further that this order can be manipulated by the †actors themselves in the pursuit of their goals. Transactionalism was popular in the 1970s, but met with criticism from those (including Marxists) who saw the model as based too much on the assumptions of †methodological individualism, and allowing too little space for cultural difference.

transformational analysis In *kinship, the formal method developed by †Floyd Lounsbury to account for the apparent †extension of *relationship terms. In transformational analysis, terms for closer genealogical positions are said to be 'extended' to more distant genealogical positions. Therefore rules can be described in order to 'reduce' these distant positions to closer ones. For example, if father and father's brother are called by the same term, this can be accounted for by a specific 'reduction rule', which itself is generated by a deeper '(same-sex) merging rule'. See *relationship terminology.

transformational-generative grammar In linguistics, a theory of grammar developed by †Chomsky since the late 1950s. The idea is to account for all sentences which a native speaker would regard as grammatical, something previous descriptive grammars failed to do. Transformational-generative grammars are constructed through levels of linguistic structure, with †deep structures linked to surface structure by rules which generate elements of the surface structure. Parallels have been drawn between this approach and those of some anthropologists, e.g. *Claude Lévi-Strauss and †Floyd Lounsbury, though Chomsky has distanced himself from such comparisons.

tribe, tribal The terms 'tribe' and 'tribal' (from Latin *tribus*) have a variety of meanings, some of which are taboo in modern anthropology. The accepted usage of 'tribe' is as a political unit larger than a †clan and smaller than a *nation or people, especially when indigenous populations themselves use the term. This is the case especially among *Native North Americans and in some parts of Africa. 'Tribal' is less politically correct in some quarters, but is accepted by *evolutionists (e.g. in the work of †Elman Service) in discussions of a level of political development which lies between †band societies and chiefly ones. The use of 'tribal' to refer to aspects of culture other than politics is generally discouraged in contemporary anthropology, although current fashions for green †primitivism have given the term a new lease of politically acceptable life in Euro-American youth culture. See †indigenous peoples, †primitive.

trickster In *folklore and *mythology, a character who plays clever tricks on other characters. Often taking the form of an animal such as a fox or coyote, the trickster can represent downtrodden elements of a community or the triumph of good over evil.

trope In rhetoric, any figure of speech. The term has been widely used in anthropology as *postmodern and †poststructural theorists have drawn attention to the non-referential, or creative, aspects of language.

twins Two children from the same pregnancy. In many cultures, twins are either considered 'unnatural' or are associated with extraordinary phenomena such as supernatural power. In some cultures, the birth of twins is a sign of ill luck and one or both might be put to death.

two-line prescription In *alliance theory, a notion developed by †Rodney Needham and others to analyse relations between intermarrying †moieties or lines. For example, in some *Lowland South American societies, members of one †matrilineage must marry members of the opposite matrilineage, there being only two such †exogamous descent 'lines' in the society.

ultimogeniture Inheritance or succession by the youngest child. Cf. †primogeniture.

underdevelopment See *development.

unilineal, unilinear Unilineal is a blanket term which covers both †patrilineal and †matrilineal (but not †bilateral) *descent. Unilinear is a synonym, although unilineal is most common in discussions of *kinship, while unilinear is more often used in other contexts (e.g. *evolution).

unilinear evolutionism The theory of evolution associated with late nineteenth-century anthropologists such as *L.H. Morgan and †Tylor. Its distinguishing feature is the emphasis on all societies passing through the same precise stages of evolution, each of which has characteristic features in terms of kinship, political structure, etc. Contrast †multilinear evolutionism, †universal evolutionism. See *evolution and evolutionism.

universal evolutionism The theory of evolution associated with mid twentieth-century anthropologists and archaeologists, such as †L. White and †V.G. Childe. It emphasizes broad evolutionary phases rather than the more specific evolutionary schema of the †unilinear evolutionists. Cf. †multilinear evolutionism. See *evolution and evolutionism.

universal kinship A *kinship system in which all members of society stand in relationships of kinship or †affinity to each other. In other words, no-one is defined as non-kin in relation to anyone else. Such systems are common among *hunter-gatherers, and in small scale agricultural societies practising prescriptive marriage.

Untouchables One of a number of terms for the lowest *castes in Indian society, so called because of the belief in their 'polluting' character. Untouchables are also known as *harijan* (Gandhi's preferred term, meaning children of God) and Scheduled Castes. See *South Asia, *pollution and purity.

use value In *economic anthropology (especially in *Marxist theory) the practical value of something as opposed to its †exchange value in the *market place.

usufruct The right to use resources or goods belonging to another person, e.g. a waterhole open to non-owners.

uterine A synonym for †matrilineal or maternal. Cf. †agnatic.

utilitarianism The moral and philosophical doctrine that the most just action is the one which creates 'the greatest good for the greatest number', especially associated with Jeremy Bentham. In recent anthropology, any argument which can be seen as based on assumptions of individual calculating *rationality might be (pejoratively) described as 'utilitarian'.

uxorilocal The form of postmarital residence in which a couple move to the home of the woman. Repeated uxorilocal residence (sometimes called †matrilocal residence) has the effect of uniting women of a given †matrilineal group. See *marriage. Cf. †avunculocal; †virilocal.

Verstehen German for 'understanding'. It is used broadly in the human sciences to characterize those, including Dilthey and †Max Weber, who have argued that because of their subject-matter, the human sciences must differ qualitatively from the natural sciences. As such, it forms a link between early proponents of this view, like †Vico, and modern anti-positivist anthropologists like †Evans-Pritchard and †Clifford Geertz. See *symbolic anthropology.

virilocal The form of postmarital residence in which a couple move to the home of the man. Repeated virilocal residence (sometimes called †patrilocal residence) has the effect of uniting men of a given †patrilineal group. Sometimes called **viri-avunculocal** in order to make it clear that a couple move to the man's (rather than the woman's) mother's brother's home upon *marriage. Cf. †uxorilocal.

Völkerkunde, Volkskunde *Völkerkunde* is German for 'folks-study' (as opposed to 'folk-study'). The term is synonymous with †ethnology (German *Ethnologie*) or †cultural anthropology, but sharply distinguished from *Volkskunde*, 'folk-study', the field which is broadly associated with the study of the folk customs of one's own country. The distinction between *Völkerkunde* and *Volkskunde* can be roughly equated with that between cultural anthropology and *folklore studies, and the German terms are in common use in English and other languages to make this distinction, which occurs throughout much of Central Europe and Scandinavia, as well as in German-speaking countries. See *German and Austrian anthropology.

W In kinship the symbol for wife or wife's.

Weltanschauung German for †worldview.

widow inheritance, widow marriage The inheritance by a man of the wife of one of his deceased kinsmen.

wizard A synonym for medicine man, †shaman, witchdoctor, etc. This term, with its European connotations, is often preferred by those European or Euro-American anthropologists who wish to avoid the terms more commonly associated with alien cultures and which, by implication, connote strangeness in ritual medical practices.

woman marriage The practice, described by †Evans-Pritchard for the Nuer, of a woman marrying another woman in order to perpetuate her own †lineage by acting as a social or genealogical †pater to the woman's children.

worldview A loan translation of the German *Weltanschauung*. The term was common especially in the *culture-and-personality school, but it remains in use in American anthropology where it characterizes the understanding of the world which is unique to a given culture. Cf. †ethos.

Writing Culture A book edited by James Clifford and George E. Marcus and published in 1986, which has become the standard point of reference in discussions of *postmodernism and *ethnography in anthropology. See *poetics.

y In *kinship, the symbol for younger, e.g. FBDy means 'father's brother's daughter, who is younger than †ego'.

Z In kinship, the symbol for sister or sister's.

Name index

Page-spans highlighted in bold indicate the position of either a main entry on the headword subject or an entry in the Biographical appendix. Authors treated in the Biographical appendix are highlighted in bold.

Abdullah, M., 240
Abélès, M., 529
Aberle, D.F, 35, 323
Abraham, R.C., 19
Abrahams, R.G., 209
Abu-Lughod, L., 163, 358, 369, 471
Acheson, J.M., 236, 323
Ackerknecht, E., 121, 199, 358
Adair, J., 234
Adam, L., **568**
Adas, M., 419
Adams, R.N., 446
Adler, G., 384
Adorno, T. 354
Afanasyev, A., 493
Agar, M., 196
Agassi, J., 469, 470
Aguirre-Beltran, G., 29
Aiello, L.C., 67–8
Ajayi, J.F.A., 20
Akinnaso, F., 179
Alavi, H., 58
Alexander, J., 348
Alexander, P, 348
Alexander, R.D., 523
Alexeev, V., 494
Alford, R., 391
Algarra, B., 5
Allen, C., 40
Almagor, U., 10, 167
Althusser, L., 26, 134–5, 274, 294, 353, 354, 370, 376, 435, 534, **568**
Altman, J.C., 3
Amin, S., 434
Anderson, B., 116, 208, 310–11, 392
Anderson, M., 226
Anderson, R., 208
Angioni, G., 553
Ankermann, B., 264

Anthony, A., 144
Anuchin, D., 493
Appadurai, A., 47, 238, 275, 349, 540
Appiah, K.A., 21
Appleby, R.S., 305
Archetti, E.P., 34
Ardener, E., 126, 328, **568**
Arens, W., 82, 296
Arensberg, C.M., 208, **568**
Aristotle, 67, 165, 174, 177, 516, 519–20
Armah, A., 85
Arnold, M., 137
Arnould, E.J., 288
Aron, R., 304
Artemidorus, 165–6
Arutunov, S., 494
Arutuntunyan, Y., 494
Asad, T., 64, 79, 97, 111–12, 369, 432, 433, 435, 446, 471, 483
Asch, T., 233, 234
Ash, J., 552
Atkinson, M., 406
Atkinson, P., 427
Atran, S., 106, 203
Austen, J., 323
Austin, D.J., 89
Austin, J.L., 326, 329
Avebury, Lord, *see* **Lubbock, Sir J.**
Aycock, D., 535

Babb, L.A., 272, 437
Bachofen, J.J., 48, 126, 213, 519–20, **568**
Backer, B., 206
Bahn, P., 45
Bailey, F.G., 26, 301, 303, 431–2
Bakel, M. van, 66
Baker, P.T., 70

Bakhtin, M., 490, 494, **568**
Balandier, G., 245, **568**
Balikci, A., 397–8
Banfield, E., 212, 419
Banton, M., 106, 124, 464, 530
Barber, K., 404
Barnard, A., 5, 15, 184, 262, 288, 311, 450, 451, 476, 478, 504
Barnes, J.A., 208, 257, 301, 312, 313, 370, 431
Barnes, R.H., 133
Barnicot, N.A., 66–8
Barrett, J., 324
Barth, F., 115, 131, 154, 170, 192, 208, 251, 301, 362, 367, 369, 397, 415, **568**
Barthes, R., 245, 534, **569**
Bartlett, F.C., 108, 362
Bartok, B., 385
Barton, R.F., 60, 429–30
Bascom, W.R., 20, 163, 555
Basilov, V.N., 494, 507
Basso, K.H., 339
Bastian, A., 161, 264, **569**
Bastide, R., 200
Bates, D., 2
Bateson, G., 92, 108, 115, 232–3, 301, 301, 362, 388, 538, **569**
Baudrillard, J., 6
Bauman, R., 163, 237, 404
Baumann, H., 264
Baxter, P.T.W., 10
Beals, R.L., 379
Beattie, J.H.M., 342, **569**
Beauvoir, S. de, 253
Beck, L., 397
Beckwith, M., 87
Behnke, R., 416
Beidelman, T.O., 374, 563
Bell, D., 5

Bellah, R., 486
Belmont, N, 243
Ben-Ari, E., 56
Bender, B., 324
Benedict, R.F., 25, 35–6, 74, 109,
    138–9, 143, 155, 155, 292, 394,
    455, 479, 516, 530, 535, 536,
    537, **569**
Benesh, 147
Benjamin, W., 354
Benson, S., 464
Benthall, J., 76
Bentham, J., 519
Berger, P., 301
Berkes, F., 188
Berlin, B., 104–5, 110, 202–3
Berlin, I., 184
Berman, H.J., 84
Bernardi, B., 9, 22
Berndt, C., **569**
Berndt, R.M., 3, 496, **569**
Bernstein, B., 75
Bernstein, H., 241
Berreman, G., 286, 303
Besnier, N., 441
Besson, J., 88
Béteille, A., 58, 91, 303, 304
Betzig, L., 523
Beuchat, H., 52
Bieder, R.E., 382
Biersack, A., 414
Binford, L.R., 48, **569**
Bird, N.M., 86
Bird-David, N., 187, 289–90
Birdwhistell, R.L., 75
Birket-Smith, K., 52, **569**
Black, M., 119
Black M.B., 202
Blacking, J., 76, 385
Blanton, R., 349
Blau, P.M., 220, 303
Blaxter, K.L., 400
Blier, S.P., 284
Blim, M.L., 565
Bloch, J.H., 255
Bloch, Marc, 228–9, 452
Bloch, Maurice, 99, 109, 149, 150,
    221, 255, 293–4, 328–9, 354,
    362, 376, 380, 406, 453, 482,
    491–2, 498
Bloch, J. 255
Blok, A., 211, 280, 417
Blom, J.P., 327, 329
Bloomfield, L., **570**
Bloor, D., 470
Blum, E., 101
Blum, R., 101
Blumenbach, J.F., 184, 463

Blumer, H., 301
Boas, F., 25, 35–6, 52–3, 54,
    67–8, **71–4**, 87, 92, 95, 109–10,
    136–40, 155, 161, 169, 206,
    183, 194, 195, 214, 244–5, 264,
    272, 277, 278, 282, 299, 325,
    333, 353, 366, 378, 385, 387,
    391, 394, 395, 430, 445, 456,
    463–4, 479, 501, 502, 515, 516,
    517, 518, 519, 522, 530, 536,
    537, **570**
Bock, P.K., 144, 457
Boddy, J., 261, 369, 441–2
Bogoraz, V., 52, 493
Bohannan, L., 19
Bohannan, P., 19, 218–19, 221, 349,
    362, 430
Boiles, C., 385
Boissevain, J., 208, 222, 246, 301,
    365, 431
Bolton, R., 39, 361
Bond, G.C., 464
Bonte, P., 245
Boon, J., 336
Boone, E.H., 337
Booth, C., 525, 555
Bopp, F., **570**
Borofsky, R., 179, 367, 414
Bose, N.K., 297–8, **570**
Boserup, E., 215
Bossy, J., 97
Bott, E., 208
Bottomore, T., 527
Bourdieu, P., 26, 76, 128, 178–9,
    220, 301, 304, 316, 324, 354,
    432, 447–8, 450, 459, 489, 471,
    513–14, 521, 526, 539, 547, 549,
    560, **570**
Bowen, J., 189
Bowerman, M., 460
Bowler, P.J., 278
Bowra, M., 100
Boyarin, J., 339
Brady, I., 427, 502
Brailoui, C., 385
Braithwaite, L., 89
Brandes, S., 30
Brantlinger, P., 136
Brass, P.R., 191
Braudel, F., 26, 46, 83, 210–11,
    212, 566
Brenneis, D.,406
Brewer, J., 128
Briggs, C., 163
Briggs, J., 229, 231, 513
Bringa, T., 206
Broca, P., 66
Brockington, J.L., 272

Bromley, Y.N., 191, 494
Brown, D., 191
Brown, P., 98
Bruner, E., 301, 406
Bruno, G., 340
Brunton, R., 502
Buckley, T., 363, 543
Buffon, G.L.L., Comte de, 183, 184
Bujra, J., 222
Bulmer, R., 499
Bunzel, R., 74
Burghart, R., 311
Burke, K., 538
Burling, R., 68, 242
Burnett, J., see **Monboddo, Lord**
Burnham, P.C., 504
Burridge, K., 85, 300–1, 374, 388
Burrows, J.W., 278
Burton, Sir R.F., **570**
Buxton, W., 251
Byres, T.J., 508

Cabrera, L., 87
Cai Yuan-pei, 95
Caillois, R., 425
Calagione, J., 565
Calame-Griaule, G., 244
Calder III, W.M., 100
Calverton, V.F., 345
Cameron, D., 328
Campbell, C., 128
Campbell, I.C., 412, 414
Campbell, J.K., 101, 210, 417, 553
Camper, P., 184
Cancian, F., 30, 248, 380
Canclini, N.G., 565
Cannadine, D., 311
Carby, H., 134
Carman, J.B., 438
Carneiro, R.L., 171, 215, 216
Carneiro da Cunha, M., 41
Carrier, J.G., 76, 84, 128, 189,
    403, 407
Carrithers, M., 230, 231, 390, 396,
    420, 421, 422·
Carsten, J., 60, 93, 282–4
Cartledge,P., 101
Casagrande, J., 230
Casimir, M.J., 269
Cassirer, E., 497
Castaneda, C., 342, 563
Castro, F., 434
Catédra, M., 150
Caton, S.C., 369, 396
Chadwick, H.M. and N.K., 404
Chagnon, N., 233, 234, 523, 559,
    561
Chanock, M., 331

Charbonnier, G., 333
Chateaubriand, F.R., Vicomte de, 183
Chatterjee, P., 392
Chattopadhyay, K.P., 297
Chavannes, A.C., 185
Chavunduka, G.L., 9
Chayanov, A.V., 205, 418–19, 494
Chevalier, J., 436
Child, F., 237
Child, I.L., 93
Childe, V.G., 48, **570**
Chisholm, J.S., 458
Chomsky, N., 203, 325, 362, 385, 500, 524, 534, **570**
Christaller, W., 504
Christian, W.A., 97, 210
Cicero, 164
Cissé, Y., 76
Claessen, H.J.M., 167, 215, 216, 217, 529
Clammer, J., 99
Clarke, D., 48
Clarke, E., 88
Clastres, P., **570**
Clendinnen, I., 274
Cleuziou, S., 49
Clifford, J., 142, 198, 244, 279, 371, 373, 388, 408, 427, 442–3, 470, 471, 538
Clutton-Brock, J., 415
Cobbett, W., 323
Cock, J., 464
Codrington, R., 346
Coedès, G., 61–2
Cohen, Abner, 492
Cohen, Anthony, 115–16, 209, 301
Cohen, C., 28
Cohen, D., 101–2
Cohen, R., 190, 192, 217, 530
Cohn, B.S., 59, 112, 274, 275, 432
Cohn, N., 372
Cole, J.W., 205
Cole, M., 108
Cole, S., 236
Colen, S., 287
Coleridge, S.T., 137
Collier, J., 255, 260, 261, 331, 351
Collins, S., 391, 423
Colson, E., 266, 474, **571**
Comaroff, J., 14, 97, 113, 354, 371, 374, 433, 440, 447, 484, 489, 540
Comaroff, J.L., 14, 113, 332, 351, 371, 374, 433, 484
Combs-Schilling, E., 498
Comte, A., 511, 516, 518, 524, 525, **571**
Condominas, G., 245

Condorcet, J.-A.-N. de C., Marquis de, 518, **571**
Conklin, H.C., 60, 105, 181–2, 390, **571**
Connerton, P., 362
Constant, A.L., 340
Conte, E., 265
Cook, Capt. J., 263, 412, 414, 542, 543
Cook, S., 242, 375
Coon, C.S., 368–9, **571**
Cooper, F., 156, 432
Coote, J., 6
Copans, J., 185, 246
Copet-Rougier, E., 133
Coppet, D. de, 380
Coquery-Vidrovitch, C., 435
Cornford, F.M., 100
Cornwall, A., 261
Coser, L.A., 524
Cosgrove, D., 324
Coudart, A., 49
Coward, R., 126
Coy, M., 179
Cranston, M., 117
Crapanzano, V., 301, 441, 443, 471
Crawford, P., 7
Crittenden, R., 411
Crocker, J.C., 390, 507
Croll, E., 187
Crowder, M., 21
Crump, T., 30, 307, 379–80
Cruz, J., 358
Csordas, T.J., 76, 459
Curtis, E.S., 273
Cushing, F., 194, 195, **571**
Cushman, D., 198
Cuvier, L.C.F.D., 184

Dahl, G., 415
Dahl, V., 493
Dakhila, J., 362
Dalrymple, Sir D. (Lord Hailes), 183
Dalton, G., 242, 349
Damas, D., 53
Damon, F.H., 150
D'Andrade, R.G., 145
Daniel, E.V., 315, 559
Daniels, S., 324
Daniels, T., 372
Darnton, R., 274
Dart, R., **571**
Darwin, C., 67, 76–9, 161, 214, 217, 247, 468, 469, 522, 523, **571**
Das, V., 59, 559
David, K., 317
Davis, A., 464, 556

Davis, D., 55
Davis, J., 209, 211–12, 220, 321, 369, 416
Davis, K., 248
Davis, N.Z., 274
De Heusch, L., 245, 311, 497–8
Debetz, G., 494
Debray, R., 434
Dee, J., 340
Deere, C.D., 33
Delaney, C., 127
Deluz, A., 455
Demoule, J.P., 49
Deng, 6
Deng Xiaoping, 55
Dening, G., 274
Derrida, J., 112, 141, 301, **571**
Descartes, R., 165, 456, 458
Deshen, S., 368, 424
Despres, L.A., 190
Detienne, M., 497, 498
Deutsch, G., 164
Dévereux, G., 199–200, 201–2, 454, 455, **571**
Dévisch, R., 456
DeVore, I., 15
DeWalt, B.R., 364, 365
Di Donato, R., 100
Di Leonardo, M., 261
Diamond, S., 353
Dickey, S., 357
Diderot, D., 183, 505, 527
Dieterlen, G., 20, 76, 244, **571**
Digard, J.P., 415
Dighe, A., 358
Dilly, R., 348
Dirks, N., 112, 275, 276, 433
Ditton, P., 5
Dodds, E.R., 100
Dolgikh, V., 494
Donham, D.L., 375
Dorsey, J.O., 134
Dostal, W., 265
Doughty, P.L., 240
Douglas, M., 26, 75, 99, 105, 128, 131, 154, 437, 438, 439, 455, 489, 499, 526, 538, 563, **572**
Dove, M., 61
Drake, St C., 463, 464, 556
Dresch, P., 369
Dressler, W.W., 364, 365
Driver, H.E., **572**
Drobizheva, L., 494
Drucker, P., 445
D'Souza, F., 238, 240
Du Bois, C., 144, **572**
Du Bois, W.E.B., 556
Du Boulay, J., 267

Duchet, M., 183
Duguid, P., 252
Dumézil, G., 100, 245, 310–11, **572**
Dumont, L., 24–5, 57–9, 79, 90, 243, 268, 275, 293, 299, 300, 303, 310, 314, 352, 392, 421, 438, 475, 485, 516, 519, **572**
Dunbar, R.I.M., 68
Duncan, O.D., 303
Dundes, A., 237
Dunlop, I., 234
Dupire, M., 20
Duranti, A., 406
Durham, W.H., 68
Durkheim, É., 1, 3, 61, 64, 75, 79, 95,99, 100, 103, 105, 116, 130, 131, 132, 183, 194, 243, 244, 249–50, 292, 299–300, 341, 346, 362, 366, 367, 368, 377, 388, 420–2, 433, 437, 446, 451–2, 456, 466, 482, 490, 496, 497, 516, 517–18, 519–20, 524–5, 535, 538, 543, 547, 550, 559, **572**
Durrenberger, P., 209
Dwyer, K., 471

Eade, J., 496
Eades, J., 370–1
Easton, D., 428
Edgerton, R., 398, 415
Edholm, F., 254–5
Edwards, C.P., 3, 7, 93
Edwards, J., 488
Eggan, D., 145
Eggan, F., 35, 121, 308, 466, **572**
Ehrmann, T.F., 184
Eibl-Eibesfeldt, I., 523
Eickelman, D.F., 179–80, 369, 423
Eisenberg, L., 360
Ekeh, P., 319
Ekman, P., 75
Elboudradi, H., 369
Eley, G., 433
Eliade, M., 75, 496, 505, 506, **572–3**
Elkin, A.P., **573**
Ellen, R., 106, 172, 188, 231, 504
Elliot Smith, Sir G., 161, **573**
Ellis, A.J., 384
Ellis, H., 466
Emeneau, M.B., 74
Emerson, R.M., 220, 526
Engels, F., 98, 126, 215–16, 223, 253, 254, 264, 302, 370, 352–4, 374, 381, 434, 453, 451, 477, 528, 555, **573**

Ennew, J., 93
Epstein, A.L., 367, 455
Erasmus, 485
Eribon, D., 333
Erikson, E., 93, 292
Errington, S., 60, 62
Escobar, A., 156, 158–9
Evans-Pritchard, E.E., 8–9, 13, 19, 21–2, 109, 118, 140, 141, 152, 163–4, 183, 210, 247–8, 273, 277, 303, 314, 317, 329, 335, 341–2, 358–9, 366, 368, 351, 428, 431, 465, 468, 480, 482, 496, 499, 502, 520, 529, 548, 562, **573**

Fabian, J., 97, 155, 157, 274, 407, 443
Fairbairn, R., 455
Fairhead, J., 239, 240
Fallers, L., 330–1, 377
Fanon, F., 434
Fardon, R., 474
Farias, P.F. de M., 404
Faris, J., 111
Farmer, B.H., 241
Farmer, P., 361
Farris, J., 236
Favret-Saada, J., 231, 342, 563, 564
Featherstone, M., 124, 566
Febvre, L., 452
Feeley-Harnik, G., 97, 310–11
Fei Xiao-tong (Fei Hsiao-T'ung), 95, **573**
Feld, S., 385, 426
Feldman, A., 559
Feleppa, R., 554
Fenner, F., 70
Ferguson, A., 183–4, 518, **573**
Ferguson, C.A., 327
Ferguson, J., 159, 433
Ferguson, R.B., 561–2
Fernandez, J., 452
Fernandez, N., 252
Feuchtwang, S., 96
Feuer, L.S., 500
Ficino, M., 340
Finley, M., 100–1
Finnegan, R., 337, 338, 404–5, 428, 554, 555, 557
Firth, Sir R., 54, 107, 112, 118–19, 208, 236, 262, 333, 343, 375, 414, 467, 512, 510, 520, **574**
Fischer, M.M.J., 89, 471
Fisher, M., 443
Fishman, J.A., 327

Fison, L., **574**
Flaherty, G., 505
Flaherty, R., 232
Fleck, L., 503
Fleising, U., 523
Fletcher, La F., 133
Fogelson, R.D., 446
Foley, D.E., 565
Foley, R.A., 67
Forbes S., 474
Forde, D., 19, 88, 153, 169, 317, 466, 545, **574**
Forge, A., 54, 410
Forster, G., 263
Forster, J.R., 263, 264
Fortes, M., 8–9, 13, 19–20, 43, 60, 121–2, 154, 199, 200, 205, 224–5, 262, 308, 313, 335, 419, 431, 455, 466, 499, 512, 515, 517, 520, 529, **574**
Fortune, R.F., 95, **574**
Foster, G., 32–3
Foster, M.L., 562
Foster, R.J., 129, 392
Foucault, M., 26–7, 76, 112, 141, 163, 201, 245, 261, 278–9, 301, 331, 408, 433, 447, 468, 489, 534, **574**
Fox, J., 105, 274, 284, 535
Fox, Richard, 556, 557
Fox, Robin, 154, 262, 311, 478
Frake, C.O., 125, 183, 203
France, P., 112, 275
Francis, D., 565
Frank, A.G., 46, 370, 566
Frankenberg, R., 114, 117, 122, 208, 353, 431
Franklin, S., 127, 136, 488, 503
Frazer, Sir J.G., 1, 3, 100, 126, 194, 310, 341, 344, 386, 437, 451, 542, 550, **574–5**
Frazier, E.F., 87
Freedman, M., 95, 154, 426, 497
Freedman, R.L., 400
Freeman, (J.) D., 60, 106–7, 396, 414, 501, **575**
Freire-Marreco, B., 343
Freud, S., 3, 121, 127, 143, 166, 194, 199, 294, 333, 341, 454–6, 520, 542, 543, 550, **575**
Fried, M., 98, 215, 528
Friedl, E., 254
Friedland, R., 348
Friedman, J., 133, 169, 215
Friedrichs, R.W., 527
Frobenius, L., 264, **575**
Fry, C.L., 23
Fuller, C.J., 58, 153, 272

Fürer-Haimendorf, C. von, *see*
   Haimendorf, C. von F.
Furnivall, J.S., 88, 425–6
Fustel de Coulanges, N.-D., 43,
   100, 497, **575**
Fyfe, C., 19

Gable, E., 190
Gadamer, H.-G., **575**
Gaines, A.D., 202
Galaty, J.G., 415
Galey, J.-C., 310
Galton, F., 79, 121
Gamio, M., 32
Ganshof, F.L., 228
Gardner, B.B., 465
Gardner, K., 370–1
Gardner, M., 465
Gardner, R., 27, 232, 233
Garine, I. de, 241
Garrett, W., 53
Garrison, V., 441
Gathercole, P., 49
Gearing, F.O., 398
Geertz, C., 60–2, 101, 115, 130,
   141, 157, 169, 189, 198, 203,
   273, 293, 305, 330, 366, 367,
   377, 388, 390, 392, 407, 418–19,
   422, 432, 442, 472, 478, 481,
   482–3, 490, 506, 516, 526, 535,
   536, 537–8, 549, 555, 557, **575**
Geertz, H., 145, 326, 390
Geiger, R.L., 251
Gell, A.F., 410, 549
Gellner, D.N., 80
Gellner, E., 180, 204, 206, 353,
   392, 417, 469, 483, 495, **575–6**
Georgi, I., 493
Gerasimov, M., 494
Gerholm, L, 208
Gerholm, T., 208
Gerndt, H., 265
Gernet, L., 100
Getz, L., 296
Ghurye, G.S., 297
Gibson, T., 60, 498
Giddens, A., 292, 301, 324, 446,
   514, 521
Gifford, E.W., **576**
Gilad, L., 473
Gille, B., 544
Gillen, F.J., 1–2, 4, 126, 194, 496,
   590 (Spencer, Sir Baldwin)
Gillison, G., 150
Gillison, R., 456
Gilmore, D., 211, 246, 280
Gilroy, P., 134
Gilsenan, M., 305, 369, 417

Ginsberg, F., 233, 488
Ginsberg, M., 429
Girard, R., 499
Gittens, D., 228
Gjessing, G., 208
Glazer, N., 193
Gluckman, M., 13–14, 157, 266,
   321–2, 327, 330, 353, 431, 453,
   489, 490, 491, 535–6, 559, 561,
   576
Glucksberg, S., 109
Goddard, V., 204, 281
Godelier, M., 26, 66, 177, 178,
   245, 294, 353, 410, 435, 528,
   534
Goethe, J.W. von, 505
Goffman, E., 324, 526, 576
Goldenweiser, A.A., 550, 576
Goldfrank, E., 74
Goldman, I., 413, 414
Goldschmidt, W., 72
Goldthorpe, J.H., 303
Gombrich, R.F., 80
Good, A., 5, 262, 311, 449–50
Good, B., 200, 201
Goodall, J., 140
Goodenough, W.H., 125, 182,
   301, **576**
Goody, E.N., 5
Goody, J.R., 18–19, 6, 101, 121,
   150, 223, 227, 286–7, 313, 322,
   337, 338, 351, 375, 453, 475, **576**
Goonitilake, S., 503
Gordon, R., 467
Gordon-Grube, K., 82
Görög-Karady, V., 404
Gossen, G.H., 29
Gottlieb, A., 363, 543
Gough, K., 111, 153, 225, 432, 435
Gould, S.J., 463
Gouldner, A. 220
Gow, P, 93
Graburn, N., 53
Graebner, F., 161, 264, **576**
Graff, H.J., 338
Gramsci, A., 134, 354, 433, 435,
   447, 488, **577**
Granet, M., 95, 130, 577
Gray, J.N., 285, 286, 287
Greenberg, J., **577**
Greenwood, D., 189
Greer, S., 114, 117
Gregory, C.A., 220, 320, 411, 519
Gregory, S., 288, 463, 464
Grenier, G., 566
Griaule, M., 20, 130, 243, 244,
   245, 308, **577**
Grice, H.P., 326

Grieco, M., 226
Grillo, R., 156–7
Grønhaug, R., 15
Grosz, E., 190
Grottanelli, V., **577**
Groves, C.P., 67
Guasti, L., 223
Guboglo, M., 494
Gudeman, S., 29, 117, 177, 285,
   348
Guevara, C., 434
Guha, Ramachandra, 171, 353
Guha, Ranajit, 294, 447
Guiart, J., 86
Gulbrandsen, Ø., 14
Gullestad, M., 4,9–10
Gullick, J., 62
Gulliver, P., 331
Gumilev, L.N., 191, 494
Gumperz, J.J., 327
Gupta, A., 417
Gusfield, J., 117
Gusinde, M., 265, **577**
Guthrie, W.K.C., 130
Guy, M., 85
Guyer, J., 510

Haas, J.D., 400–1
Habermas, J., 455, 521, 538, **577**
Hackenberg, R., 263
Haddon, A.C., 161, 232, 277, 297,
   409, 465–6, 550, **577**
Haekel, J., 265
Hagesteign, R., 66
Haimendorf, C. von F., **577**
Halbwachs, M., 362
Hall, S., 134
Hallowell, A.I., 28, 278
Hallpike, C.R., 215–17, 452, 468
Hamayon, R., 507
Hamilton, W.D., 523
Hammel, E.A., 286
Hammoudi, A., 369
Handler, R., 142, 190, 392–3
Hann, C.M., 206, 269
Hannerz, U., 85, 124, 129, 339,
   555, 557
Hansen, A., 474
Hansen, E., 34
Hanson, A, 275, 414
Haraway, D., 279, 472, 481, 503
Hardiman, D., 222
Hardin, G., 236
Harding, S., 98
Härke, H., 49, 50
Harkness, S., 458
Harner, M., 82, 342, 506
Harrell, S., 55, 96

Harrell-Bond, B.E., 473
Harriss, B., 401
Harris, G.G., 9, 423
Harris, M., 73, 82, 98, 133–4, 157,
    170, 171, 180, 182, 186, 216,
    277, 366, 376, 395, 464, **577**
Harris, O., 39, 261
Harris, P., 106
Harris, R., 208
Harrison, F.V., 556
Harrison, G.A., 67–8, 241
Harrison, G.G., 400–1
Harrison, J.E., 100
Harrison, S., 65–6, 453, 559, 562
Harriss, J., 58, 239
Hart, K., 20, 435
Hartley, E., 145
Hartman, S., 540
Hartmann, P., 355, 356
Hastrup, K., 209
Hathaway, J., 473
Haudricourt, A.-G., 47, **547**
Haugen, E., 327
Haviland, J., 267
Hayes, E.N., 336
Hayes, T., 336
Headland, T., 180, 502
Heald, S., 455, 456
Heath, D., 503
Heath, H.B., 338
Heberstein, 51
Hebdige, D., 444
Hechter, M., 192
Heelas, P., 106
Hefner, R.W., 97
Hegel, G.W.F., 516, **578**
Heidegger, M., 112
Heider, K., 232, 234, 358
Heilman, S., 267
Heine, B., 502
Heine-Geldern, R., 61, 118, 264–5
Heinz, R.I., 507
Heizer, R., 445
Helander, B., 152
Hellmann, E., 555
Helvétius, C.A., 183
Hemming, J., 41
Hénaff, M., 336
Hendry, J., 55
Herder, J.G., 183, 191, 236,
    136–8, 142, 263, 391, 505, **578**
Herdt, G.H., 410, 458
Héritier-Augé, F., 133, 245, 352,
    478, 534
Hersh, R., 399
Herskovits, M.J., 20, 73, 87,
    91–2, 119, 266, 464, 479, 480,
    540, **578**

Hertz, R., 75, 149, 167, **578**
Herzfeld, M., 7, 101, 190, 211,
    212, 280
Hess, D., 504
Hewitt de Alcántara, C., 32
Heyerdahl, T., **578**
Hiatt, L.R., 2
Hildebrandt, H.-J., 265
Hill, J.H., 328
Hill, K.C., 328
Hill, P., 508
Hillery, G., 114
Hinkle, G.J., 527
Hinkle, R.C., 527
Hinsley, C.M. Jr, 278, 383
Hirsch, E., 129, 324, 488
Hirschberg, W., 265
Hirschon, R., 474
Hjort, A., 415
Ho Chi Minh, 434
Hobbes, T., 218, 502, 516, 518,
    520, 559, **578**
Hoben, A., 154, 158
Hobhouse, L.T., 429
Hobsbawm, E., 275, 372, 392
Hocart, A.M., 130, 310, 414, **578**
Hockings, P., 233,
Hodder, I., 51, 545
Hodgen, M.T., 237, 278
Hodgkin, T., **578**
Hoebel, E.A., 330, **578–9**
Hoernlé, A.W. (née Tucker), 15,
    579
Hoggart, R., 134
Holland, D., 110, 501
Hollis, M., 109, 470
Holston, J., 378
Holy, L., 11, 118
Holm, G., 52
Homans, G.C., 63, 220, 448
Home, H., see Kames, Lord
Honigmann, J.J., 217, 263, **579**
Hope, K., 303
Hoppal, M., 507
Hornbostel, E. von, 384
Horne, D., 383
Horowitz, D., 192
Horrigan, S., 396
Horton, R., 20, 485, 503
Hoskins, W.G., 323
Howard, A., 414
Howard-Malverde, R., 40
Howe, L, 549
Howell, P.P.
Howell, S., 317, 404, 559, 561
Howitt, A.W., **574** (Fison, Lorimer)
Hsu, Francis L.K., 43, 95, 457,
    579

Huang Chieh-shan, 96, 295
Huber, M., 374
Hubert, H., 466, 499, 547
Hudson, K., 383
Hugh-Jones, C., 131, 363, 548
Hugh Jones, S., 60, 281, 283, 284,
    388
Huizinga, J., 424
Hultkrantz, A., 52, 507
Humboldt, A. von, 263, **579**
Humboldt, W. von, 184, 263,
    501, **579**
Hume, D., 183
Humphrey, C., 205, 322, 507
Hunt, G., 72, 387
Hunter, J., 184
Hunter, M., see **Wilson, M.**
Huntingford, G.W.B.
Husken, F., 107
Husserl, E., 264, **579**
Huxley, J., 523
Huxley, T.H., 67, **579**
Hyatt, M., 72
Hymes, D., 28, 124, 325–6, 404,
    426, 444, 447, 471, 554

Ileto, R., 61–2
Impey, O., 382
Inden, R.B., 275, 315, 407
Ingold, T., 213, 217, 290, 302, 396,
    504, 515, 517, 521, 547
Iochelson, V., 493
Irimoto, T., 53
Irons, W., 398, 523
Isaac, R., 274
Isaacman, A., 433
Isherwood, B., 128
Ishi, **579**
Ivanov, V., 494
Izard, M., 245, 534

Jackson, A., 124, 209
Jackson, J., 41
Jackson, M., 20, 76, 301, 342
Jacobson-Widding, A., 75, 292
Jafari, J., 552
Jahoda, G., 94, 513
Jakobson, R., 245, 334, 530,
    531, **579**
James, W., 111
Jamin, J., 185, 242
Janet, P., 200
Janzen, K., 82
Jarvie, I., 85, 469, 470
Jedrej, M.C., 166
Jenness, D., 52, **579–80**
Jennings, J.D., 413
Jensen, A.E., 264, 265

Jerome, N.W., 400
Johnson, A.W., 33, 364
Johnson, D., 11
Johnson, D.L., 415, 553
Johnson, M., 110, 501
Johnson, R., 136
Johnson, T.M., 361
Jolly, M., 113, 320, 411
Jones, E., 127, 455
Jones, Sir W. (1746–94), **580**
Jones, W. (1871–1909), **580**
Jordan, D., 96
Jordanova, L.J., 255–6
Jorion, P., 183
Josephides, L., 411
Josselin de Jong, J.P.B. de, 167, 475, **580**
Josselin de Jong, P.E. de, 131, 167
Jung, C.G., 164, 454
Junod, H.A., 8, 63, **580**
Justice, J., 360

Kaberry, P.M., 3, 154, 496, **580**
Kahn, J., 376, 435, 474
Kames, Lord, 183–4
Kaminski, I.-M., 269
Kandel, R.F., 402
Kant, I., 6, 184
Kapferer, B., 441, 459
Kaplan, J., 507
Kaplan, M., 414, 490, 493
Kardiner, A., 143–4, 454, **580**
Karp, I., 383
Karve, I., 297
Kastren, M., 493
Kay, D., 474
Kay, P., 110, 202–3
Kearney, M., 371
Keen, I., 3, 502
Keenan, E., 406
Keesing, R.M., 203, 346, 411
Kehoe, A., 266
Keith, J., 23
Keller, J.D., 458
Keller-Cohen, D., 339
Kelly, J.D., 414, 490, 493
Kelly, W., 56
Kemau, J., see **Kenyatta, J.**
Kemp, J., 107
Kemper, R.V., 279
Kendall, L., 55
Kent, S., 289
Kenyatta, J., 8, **580**
Kertzer, D.I., 21, 448, 490, 492, 508, 529
Keur, D., 208
Keur, J., 208
Keyes, C.F., 80

Khare, R.S., 438
Khatib-Chahidi, J., 179
Khelimski, E., 494
Kidd, D., 92
Kieckhefer, R., 424
Kilani, M., 362
Kilborne, B., 461
Kildea, G., 234
Kimball, S., 208
King, V.T., 107
Kirch, P.V., 46, 412
Kirchof, P., 264, **580**
Kirkpatrick, J., 422
Kitajoi, H., 285
Kleinman, A, 200–1,
Klemm, G., **580**
Kligman, G., 206
Kloos, P., 167
Kluckhohn, C., 100, 136–7, 139–40, 155, 183, 325,.563, **580–1**
Kluckhohn, R., 144
Knight, C.D., 140, 363, 543, 551
Knorozov, Y., 494
Knox, R. (1641–1720), **581**
Knox, R. (1791–1862), **581**
Knudsen, J., 474
Kobben, A.J., 121
Koch, K., 82
Kohlberg, L., 480
Kohler, J., 132, **581**
Kolinski, M., 384
Kollár, A.F., 184
Kondo, D.K., 447, 565
Koppers, P.W., 265
Kopytoff, I., 509–10
Koskoff, E., 385
Kossima, G., 48
Kosven, M., 494
Kottak, C.P., 216, 357
Kovalevski, M., 493
Kozebu, O., 493
Kozlov, V., 494
Kraepelin, E., 198, 200
Kramer, C., 47
Kramer, F., 441
Krasheninnikov, S., 493
Krauss, W., 183
Kretchmer, N., 401
Krige, E., 13, **581**
Krige, J.D. (Jack), 13, **581**
Kroeber, A.L., 25, 72, 74, 95, 118, 119, 120, 123, 136–7, 139–40, 167, 184, 188, 277, 282, 299, 325, 341, 394, 477, 516, 517, 522, **581**
Kropotkin, P., 451, 466, **581**
Kruzenshtern, I., 493

Küchler, S., 363
Kuhn, T.S., 77, 248, 468, 470, 503, **581**
Kuklick, H., 77, 161, 248, 250, 345
Kulick, D., 339
Kulp, D., 95
Kumar, N., 231
Kunst, J., 384
Kuper, A., 154, 277, 278, 281, 475, 512, 519, 526
Kuper, H.B., **581**
Kuper, L., 193, 426

La Fontaine, J.S., 259
Labouret, H., 308
Labov, W., 327–8
Lacan, J., 245, 455, 534, **581**
Ladurie, E. Le Roy, 490
Lafitau, J.-F., 35, 183, 243, 476, **581–2**
Lakoff, G., 110, 501
Lambek, M., 441
Lamphere, L., 254, 566
Lan, D., 14, 85
Lancaster, W., 397
Lande, C., 223
Lane, E.W., **582**
Lane Fox, A.H., see **Pitt Rivers, A.L.**
Lang, A., **582**
Langmore, D., 374
Langness, L.L., 461
Langton, M., 5
Lansing, J.S., 171
Lanternari, V., 372
Lantis, M., 52
Larsen, M.T., 338
Larson, B., 39
Larson, W.D., 337
Lasker, G.W., 70
Laslett, P., 226, 286
Last, M., 9
Latour, B., 379, 481, 519, 521, 545
Lattas. A., 190
Lave, J., 179, 251, 459, 514
Lavine, S., 383
Lawrence, P., 85
Lawson, A., 190
Lawson, J.C., 101
Layard, J., **582**
Layne, L., 504
Layton, R., 5, 54
Le Goff, J., 165
Leach, E.R., 2, 24, 60, 77, 105, 119, 122, 127, 129, 140, 154, 183, 262, 283–4, 301, 313, 314, 320, 333, 351, 363, 431, 453, 455, 489–90, 499, 518, 520, 535, **582**

Leach J.W., 234, 320
Leach, M., 238
Leacock, E.B., 123, 253, 303, 464
Leakey, L.S.B., 140, **582**
Lechtman, H., 545
Leclair, E., 242
Lee, R.B., 15, 170, 397
Leeds, A., 556–7
Leenhardt, M., 243, 244, 373, 388, **582**
Legesse, A., 22
Leiris, M., 244, **582**
Lemoine, J., 96
Lemonnier, P., 47, 545, 546
Lenin, V.I., 149, 205, 435
Lenneberg, E.H., 500
León, M., 33
Leroi-Gourhan, A., 47, 546, **582**
Lesser, A., 26, 266, **582–3**
Levi, E., 340
Levin, M., 494
LeVine, R.A., 144–5, 461
Lévi-Strauss, C., 20, 23–5, 26, 41, 53, 54, 60, 63, 73, 79, 94, 105, 122, 109–10, 130–1, 133, 140–1, 182, 201, 218–19, 239, 243, 244–5, 254, 262–3, 281–3, 294, 319, 312, 314–15, 324–5, 333–6, 350, 353, 354, 363, 379, 381, 385, 387–8, 390–1, 394–5, 410, 440, 443, 448–9, 466–7, 468, 475, 484–5, 498–9, 506, 507, 510–11, 515, 518, 520, 530–5, 535–6, 537, 538, 543, 550–1, **583**
Lévy-Bruhl, L., 109, 166, 243, 244, 451–2, 468, 480, 500, 503, **583**
Lewin, E., 287
Lewin, R., 67
Lewis, G.A., 401
Lewis, I.M., 83, 94, 152, 154, 201, 397, 440, 513
Lewis, J., 358
Lewis, N., 165
Lewis, O., 31, 32–3, 58, 121, 370, **583**
Lewis-Williams, J.D., 363
LiCausi, L., 417
Lienhardt, G., 300, 420, 441, **583**
Lier, R.A.J. van, 88
Lin Huixiang, 95
Lin Yao-hua, 95
Lincoln, J.S., 166
Lindblom, G., 8
Lindenbaum, S., 97
Lindisfarne, N., 261, 280–1
Lindstrom, L., 1, 4, 65–6, 86

Ling Chun-sheng, 95
Linton, R., 143–4, 195, 372, 539, **583**
Lipsedge, M., 199, 201
Lisyanski, Y., 493
Little, K., 19
Littlejohn, J., 19, 208, 548
Littlewood, R., 198, 200, 201
Lizot, J., 559
Llewellyn, K., 330, 331
Llewelyn-Davies, M., 258–9
Llobera, J., 207, 376
Lloyd, G.E.R., 452, 470
Lloyd, P., 99
Locher, G.W., 167
Locke, J., 527, **583**
Loescher, G., 474
Loizos, P., 233, 261
Lomax, A., 233, 384
Lommel, A., 506
Long, J., 550
Lönrott, E., 236
Lord, A.B., 404
Lorenz, K., 523, **583**
Lounsbury, F.G., 132, **583**
Lowen, A., 76
Lowenthal, D., 49
Lowie, R.H., 25, 52–3, 74, 132, 139, 161, 214, 243, 299, 302, 333, 334, 341, 453, 477, **583**
Lubbock, Sir J., 77, **584**
Lucy, J., 501
Luhrmann, T., 342, 564
Lukes, S., 109, 298, 391, 423, 470
Lull, J., 358
Lumière, L., 232
Lury, C., 136
Lutz, C., 163, 457–8
Lynd, H.M., 526
Lynd, R.S., 526
Lyotard, J.-F., 378, 443, **584**

Maalki, L., 473
McCabe, J., 295
MacCannell, D., 552
McCay, B.M., 236, 323
McCloskey, D.N., 348
Maccoby, E., 145
MacCormack, C.P., 255, 395
Macdonald, C., 281, 282
McDonald, M., 392
McDonogh, G.W., 85
MacDougall, D., 233, 234
MacDougall, J., 233, 234
Macfarlane, A., 209, 226, 300, 563
MacGaffey, J., 84, 241
Macgregor, A., 382
McGrew, W.C., 140

McGuire, M., 296
McGuire, R.H., 446
Macintyre, M., 113, 320
McKendrick, N., 128
McKinley, R., 60
McKinnon, S., 131
McKitterick, R., 228
McLennan, J.F., 126, 312, 477, 519, 550, **584**
MacLeod, W.C., 430
McLuhan, M., 338, 358
McMillan, D., 241
MacNamara, R., 158
Maddock, K., 167, 467
Madge, J., 527
Magocsi, P.R., 204
Mahapatra, M., 480
Mahoney, M., 455
Maine, Sir H.S., 100, 116, 213, 330, 428–9, 451, 453, 516, 519, 527, **584**
Mair, L., 91, 156, **584**
Majumdar, D.N., 297
Malinowski, B., 8, 26, 28, 73, 79, 88, 92, 95, 100, 126–7, 153, 154, 155, 156, 161, 169, 172, 195, 197, 206, 207–8, 214, 217, 218, 220, 224, 225, 230–1, 232, 249–50, 266, 267, 277, 278, 299, 312, 318–19, 321, 325, 329, 330, 335, 341, **343–6**, 353, 362, 364, 375, 378, 386, 390, 410, 430, 453, 454–5, 456, 468, 502, 503, 512–13, 510, 515, 516, 517, 520, 522, 540, 542, 555, 564, **584**
Mallon, F., 433
Malm, K., 385
Manganaro, M., 25, 378
Manker, E., 53
Manners, R., 89
Mannheim, K., **584**
Manuel, P., 385–6
Mao Tse-tung, 99, 434
Maquet, J., 54
Marcus, G.E., 84, 89, 198, 427, 442, 443–4, 470, 471, 503, 538
Marett, R.R., 100, 346, **584**
Marglin, F.A., 438
Marquardt, W., 34
Marriott, M., 58, 267, 315, 421, 438
Mars, L., 199
Marsella, A.J., 201
Marshall, L., 15, 584
Marshall, M., 62
Marshall, P.J., 185
Martel, C., 228
Martin, E., 76, 261, 361, 448

Martin, R.D., 67
Martin-Barbero, J., 358
Martinez, W., 234
Martínez-Alier, V., 88
Marty, M.E., 305
Marx, K., 116, 215, 216, 242, 254, 264, 300, 302, 352–4, 366, 370, 377, 391, 477, 485, 528, **584**
Marwick, M.G., 365, 563
Maryanski, A., 295
Mascia-Lees, F., 28
Mascie-Taylor, C.G.N., 70
Maslow, A., 76
Mason, J.A., 74
Mathiasen, T., 52
Matthews, H.F., 19
Mauss, M., 47, 52–3, 75, 83, 100, 103, 105, 130, 131, 132, 172, 199, 218, 219–21, 243, 244, 245, 299, 308, 318–19, 333, 334, 341, 390, 392, 420–1, 422, 445, 466, 485, 497, 518, 519, 544, 547, 559–60, **584–5**
Maybury-Lewis, D.H.P., 41, 167, 426, 450, 535
Mayer, A.C., 58
Mayer, P., 14, 514, 563
Ma Yin, 96
Mbiti, J.S., 9
Mead, G.H., 292, 513, **585**
Mead, M., 25, 73–4, 85, 92, 122, 143, 157, 195, 197, 232–3, 255, 279, 292, 330, 394, 395, 410, 414, 501–2, 538, 551, **585**
Mearns, D.J., 285, 286, 287
Meehan, B., 3
Meek, C.K., 19, 321,
Meek, R.L., 183
Meggers, B.J., 41
Meggitt, M.J., 5, 410
Meillassoux, C., 20, 26, 245, 353, 370, 435, 509–10
Meiners, C., 264
Meletinski, E., 494
Melhuus, M., 34, 317, 353
Melion, W., 363
Mendel, G., 161, 523
Menget, P., 243
Menninger, K., 399
Merleau-Ponty, M., 76, 460
Merriam, A., 384, 385
Merrill, R.S., 545
Merry, S., 332
Merton, R.K., 250, 503
Merton, T., 85
Messenger, J., 208
Messer, E., 238
Métraux, R., 122

Meyer, E., 39
Middendorf, A., 493
Middleton, J., 9, 43, 514, 563
Miers, S., 509
Migdon, J., 435
Miklukho-Maclay, N., 493
Militarev, A., 494
Mills, A., 390
Miller, D., 47, 128, 379, 545
Miller, G., 493
Miller, J.G., 480
Miller, O., 493
Mills, C.W., 446
Mimica, J., 399, 459–60
Minar, D., 114, 117
Miner, H., 555
Mintz, S.W., 33, 87, 90, 117, 566
Mirandola, P. della, 340
Mirga, A., 269
Mitchell, J.C. 14, 301, 371, 431
Modell, J., 6
Moeran, B., 56
Moerman, M., 162, 326
Monboddo, Lord, 183–4, **585**
Montagu, A., 127, 464
Montaigne, M.E. de, 243, **585**
Montesquieu, C.-L. de S., 183, 429, 479, 518, **585**
Mooney, J., 35, 265–6, 429
Moore, J., 434
Moore, S., 124, 332
Moore, W.F., 121
Moreau, R.E., 308
Morgan L.H., 25, 28, 35–6, 48, 53, 78, 95, 126, 154–6, 193–4, 213–14, 235, 264, 265, 294, 299, 312, 350, 352, 375, **381–2**, 390, 428–9, 434, 451, 453, 476–7, 518, 519, 527–8, **585**
Morgan, S., 474
Morgen, S., 28
Morin, E., 235
Morley, D., 135
Morphy, H., 3, 6, 54
Morris, B., 302
Morton, S., 463
Moser, B., 234
Mowaljazlai, D., 5
Moynihan, D., 193, 227
Mühlmann, W.E., 185, 264
Mulder, M.B., 524
Müller, F.M., **585**
Muller, J.-C., 351
Mumford, L., 546
Mumford, S.R., 80
Munn, N., 5, 54, 320, 363
Murdock, G.P., 53, 60, 106, 120, 224, 390–1, 475, 477–8, 511, **585**

Murdock, J., 52
Murphy, H.B.M., 200
Murphy, R., 28
Murra, J.V., 38–9
Murray, C., 14
Murray, M., 564
Myerhoff, B., 21, 471
Myers, F., 5, 288, 406, 422
Myres, J.L., 343

Nadel, S.F., 19, 111, 206, 264, 364, 475, 529, 563, **585**
Nader, L., 123, 403, 447
Naipaul, V.S., 324
Nash, D., 553
Nash, J.C., 30–1, 33, 565, 567
Nash, M., 80
Needham, R., 24–5, 63, 64, 105, 107, 164, 167, 311, 314, 448–9, 484, 503, 535, **586**
Nelson, E., 52
Netting, R. McC., 171, 205, 285–7
Nettl, B., 385
Neu, J., 456
Neville, G.K., 424
Newcomb, H., 358
Newcomb, T., 145
Ngugi wa Thiongo, 327
Nichter, M., 361
Nimuendajú, C., 41, **586**
Nisbet, R., 154, 527
Nissan, E., 423
Novik, E., 494
Nugent, D., 565
Nugent, S., 436

O'Barr, W., 406
O'Hanlon, M., 6, 324
Obeyesekere, G., 80 , 414, 440, 441, 454, 455
Ochs, E., 94, 514
Ohnuki-Tierney, E., 55, 103, 307
Okamura, J.Y., 192
Okely, J., 269
Olkes, C., 342, 562
Oliver, D., **586**
Omori, Y., 234
Ong, A., 489, 565
Ong, W., 338
Opler, M.E., **586**
Oppong, C., 18, 288
Orbach, M., 236
Ortiz, F., 87
Ortiz, S., 349
Ortner, S., 254, 257–8, 433, 539
Ottenberg, S., 197
Ottino, P., 413

Padilla, E., 89
Paine, R., 208, 246, 266–7, 301, 406
Pálsson, G., 209, 554
Papataxiarchis, E., 261
Paracelcus, 340
Pareto, V., **586**
Park, R., 96, 555–6
Parker, E.S., 194, 381
Parkin, D.J., 9, 187, 328–9
Parry. J., 149, 150, 220, 221, 379–80, 439
Parsons, E.C., 74
Parsons, T., 98, 141, 224, 226, 247, 251, 301, 511, 526, 535, 537, **586**
Passeron, J.-C., 179, 304, 526
Pasternak, B., 96
Patil, B., 358
Paul, B., 359
Paul, R., 454
Paulme, D., 308
Paynter, R., 446
Peacock, J.L., 355
Pearce, S., 383
Peck, P.M., 164
Pedler, F.J., 308
Pedreira, A.S., 87
Peel, J.D.Y., 20
Pehrson, R., 53
Peirce, C., **586**
Peiros, I., 494
Pelletier, D.L., 400
Pels, P., 111, 274
Pelto, G.H., 364, 402
Pelto, P.J., 364
Pena, M., 385
Perry, W.J., 161
Peristiany, J.G., 8, 211, **586**
Peshitz, A., 494
Peter, HRH Prince of Greece & Denmark, **586**
Peters, E.L., 369
Peterson, N., 4
Phillips, A., 158
Phinney, J.F.S., 279
Piaget, J., 93, 452, 512, 513–14, **586**
Pianka, E.R., 67
Piasere, L., 269
Piddington, R., 451
Pigg, S., 159
Pike, K.L., 180–1, **586**
Pilbeam, D.R., 70
Pimenov, V., 494
Piña-Cabral, J. de, 150
Pinney, C., 112
Piscatori, J.P., 306, 423
Pitt Rivers, A.L., **586**

Pitt Rivers, G.H.L.-F., 451
Pitt-Rivers, J., 116, 213, 280
Plato, 468
Platt, J., 249
Plattner, S., 177, 347
Plumb, H.H., 128
Pocock, D., 268
Poggie, Jr, J.J., 364, 365
Polanyi, K., 173, 177, 206, 242, 349, 353, 468, **587**
Polanyi, M., **587**
Polhemus, T., 76
Polier, N., 444
Politis, N.G., 236
Poole, D.A., 38
Popper, Sir K.R., 468–9, 503, **587**
Porter, R., 185
Posey, D.A., 326
Pospisil, L., 330, 380
Potapov, L., 494
Potter, J., 55, 99
Potter, S., 55, 99
Pottier, J., 239, 240
Powdermaker, H., 230
Powell, J.W., **587**
Pratt, M.L., 324, 443
Price, F., 488
Price, R., 89
Price, S., 89, 311
Price-Mars, J., 87
Prichard, J.C., **587**
Propp, V., 237, 426, 494, **587**
Prout, A., 94
Puchkov, P., 494

Quatrefages, A. de, **587**
Quiggin, A.H., 279
Quine, W.V.O., 480
Quinn, N., 110, 501

Rabain, J., 513
Rabelais, F., 243
Rabinow, P., 27, 232, 378, 443, 471, 503
Radcliffe-Brown, A.R., 1–2, 8, 26, 28, 35, 60, 63, 64, 79, 95, 106–7, 132, 140–1, 153, 161, 169, 183, 195, 214, 232, 247, 250, 272, 277, 299, 308–9, 312–13, 333, 335, 343, 345, 362, 366, 433, 451, **465–7**, 478, 510–12, 515, 516, 517, 520, 522, 525, 542, 550, 555, 587
Radin, P., 266, 277, **587**
Radlov, V., 493
Raglan, Lord, **587**
Ragone, H., 127, 488

Raheja, G.G., 58, 310
Ranger, T., 275, 393
Rao, A., 269, 397
Rapp, R., 488
Rappaport, J., 40
Rappaport, R., 169, 186, 395
Rapport, N.J., 301
Rasmussen, K., 52, **587**
Rassers, W.H., **588**
Rattray, R.S., 19, **588**
Ratzel, F., 264, **588**
Ravis-Giorani, G., 553
Rawski, E.S., 55
Ray, S.K., 298
Read, K., 230
Read, M., 92
Reader, I., 308
Redfield, R., 33, 114, 116, 123, 119, 208, 267–8, 370, 418, 430, 555, **588**
Reich, W., 76
Reichard, G.A., 74
Reichel-Dolmatoff, G., **588**
Reina, R., 246
Reiter, R., 253
Renfrew, C., 45
Resek, C., 382
Reuter, T., 228
Revel, J., 40
Rew, A., 5
Rey, P.P., 245
Rezende, C.B., 246
Ricard, R., 30
Ricardo, D., 174
Rice, T., 385
Richards, A., 178, 196, 238, 322, 370, 400, 489, **588**
Richards, P., 18, 20
Riches, D., 34, 291, 560
Ricoeur, P., 455, 471, 538
Rivera, A. 285
Rivers, W.H.R., 79, 108, 161, 195, 199, 232, 262–3, 297, 313, 343, 358, 362, 409–10, 451, 465–6, **588**
Rivet, P., 244
Rivière, P.G., 41, 487
Robbens, A., 236
Robertson, A.F., 159, 348, 508
Robertson, W., 183–4
Robillard, A.B., 412
Rodman, M., 557
Roff, W.R., 306
Roheim, G., 454, **588**
Roney-Dougal, S., 343
Roniger, L., 417
Roosevelt, A., 41, 42
Rorty, R., 481

Rosaldo, M., 60–1, 254, 351, 422, 562
Rosaldo, R., 274, 480, 540
Rosch, E., 106
Roscoe, P.B., 296
Rose, D., 85
Roseberry, W., 433, 434, 444
Rosman, A., 36, 445
Ross, D., 27
Rostow, W.W., 157
Rothstein, F.A., 565
Rouch, J., 20, 233, 244
Rouget, G., 385, 506
Rousseau, G.S., 185
Rousseau, J.-J., 1, 41, 183–4, 255, 527, **588**
Rowlands, M., 215
Rowley, C.D., 4
Rowntree, J., 525
Roy, S.C., 297
Rubel, P., 36, 445
Rubinstein, R., 562
Ruby, J., 234
Ruey Yih-Fu, 95
Russell, B., 465
Russell, S.D., 239
Ryle, G., 538

Sabloff, J.A., 47
Sacks, K.B., 99, 253
Safa, H., 33
Sahlins, M., 3, 46, 65–6, 128, 140, 141, 157, 178, 186, 205, 214–15, 217, 219–20, 242, 274, 276, 311, 354, 376, 418–19, 413, 414, 433, 460, 518, 519, 536, 538–9, 564, 566, **589**
Said, E., 142, 189, 278, 280, 3323–4, 403, 407–8, 433, 472, 483, **589**
Saladin d'Anglure, B., 390, 507
Salemink, O., 111, 274
Sallnow, M.J., 39, 423, 496
Salmond, A., 406
Salo, M.T., 269
Salomon, F., 38
Salzman, P.C., 365, 397, 416
Sampson, S.L., 206
Samuel, G., 81
Sandelowski, M., 488
Sandford, S., 416
Sangren, S., 444
Sanjek, R., 72, 194–5, 197–8, 285, 286–7, 396, 428, 462, 463, 464, 556, 557
Sansom, B., 13
Sapir, E., 25, 74, 109, 139, 143, 145, 325, 394, 480, 499–501, **589**

Sarana, G., 121
Sargent, C.F., 361
Saul, M., 281
Saussure, F. de, 3, 26, 244, 245, 324–5, 518, 521, 530, **589**
Saville, W.J., 344
Schama, S., 274
Schapera, I., 9, 13, 15, 330, 370, **589**
Schebesta, P., 265
Schechner, R., 491
Scheele, R., 89
Scheffler, H.W., 154, 313, 526
Scheper-Hughes, N., 93, 150, 361
Schieffauer, W., 204
Schieffelin, B., 94, 514
Schieffelin, E.L., 411
Schmalhausen, S.D., 345
Schmidt, P.W., 161, 264–5, **589**
Schmidt, S., 223
Schnapp, A., 47
Schneider, D.M., 63, 127, 140–1, 153, 281, 315, 392, 442, 448, 487, 519, 526, 535–6, 537, 538, **589**
Schneider, H., 242
Schneider, J., 97, 435
Schnirelman, V., 494
Schoepf, B.G., 240
Scholte, B., 471
Schousboe, K., 338
Schulte Nordholt, H., 275
Schutz, A., 292
Schwartz, R., 507
Schwartz, T., 457
Schweder, R.A., 452, 480
Schwidetzky, I., 66
Scott, J., 62, 223, 396–7, 419, 489
Scribner, S., 108
Searle, J.R., 326
Sebag, L., 534
Seddons, D., 376
Seeger, A., 385
Segal, D.A., 89
Segalen, M., 209
Seligman, B.Z., 589
Seligman, C.G., 10, 199, 200, 345, 344, 409, **589**
Semenov, Y., 494
Sen, A., 240
Sergeev, D., 494
Service, E.R., 157, 186, 214–15, 530, **590**
Shanin, T., 205, 418, 495
Sharpe, P., 28
Shaw, B., 296
Shaw, P., 191
Shaw, R., 541

Shelton, A., 7, 54
Shephard, R.J., 69
Shepherd, J.R., 56
Sherper, J., 295
Sherzer, J., 330, 426–7, 554
Shils, E., 193, 251
Shirokogorov, S.M., 96, 191, 494, 506
Shokeid, M., 368, 424
Shore, C., 207,
Shweder, R.A., 458
Siikala, J., 413
Silberbauer, G.B., 15
Sillitoe, P., 547
Sills, D.L., 499
Silverblatt, I., 37
Silverman, S., 25, 27, 508
Simmel, G., 292, 377, **590**
Singer, M., 361
Skalník, P., 215, 216, 343, 529
Skinner, G.W., 347, 396
Sklenár, K., 47
Slezkin, Y., 495
Slobodin, R., 390
Smart, C., 332
Smelser, N., 372–3
Smith, Adam, 174, 183, 218, 242, 349, 375, 518, **590**
Smith, Andrew, 415
Smith, Anthony D., 193
Smith, A.O., 474
Smith, C., 347
Smith, G., 435
Smith, G.E., *see* **Elliot Smith, Sir G.**
Smith, M.F., 97
Smith, M.G., 19–20, 88, 123, 191, 425
Smith, P., 245, 534
Smith, R.J., 43
Smith, R.T., 88, 225, 226–7
Smith, V.L., 553
Smith, W.R., 368, 437, 497, **590**
Somerset, F.R., 3rd Baron Raglan, *see* **Raglan, Lord**
Southall, A., 26, 529
Speck, F.G., **590**
Spencer, Sir B., 1–2, 4, 126, 194, 232, 496, **590**
Spencer, H., 1, 25, 77, 139, 214, 217, 299, 428–9, 511, 516, 517, 519, 522, **590**
Spencer, J., 428, 444
Spencer, P., 9, 21
Spencer, R., 506
Sperber, D., 64, 110, 198, 336, 362, 530, 533, 536, 539

Sperling, L., 240
Sperry, R.W., 164
Spicer, E., 555
Spier, L., 53, 74, 118, **590**
Spindler, G.D., 178
Spiro, M.E., 80, 145, 295, 454, 457, 460
Spivak, G.C., 189, 447
Springer, S.P., 164
Srinivas, M.N., 58, 92, **590**
Stacey, J., 135
Stack, C., 227
Stahl, A.B., 162
Stanner, W.E.H., 2, 467, 497, **590–1**
Starostin, V., 494
Starr, J., 331
Stavenhagen, R., 32
Stefansson, W., 52
Steiner, F., 437, **591**
Steiner, G., 265
Stepick, A., 566
Stern, S., 433
Sternberg, L., 493
Steuart, J., 434
Steward, J.H., 26, 33, 40–1, 48, 74, 89, 119–20, 123, 162, 214, 217, 515, 528, **591**
Stewart, C., 268, 541, **591**
Stewart, F., 23
Stewart, M., 206, 269
Stigler, J.W., 458
Stocking, Jr, G.W., 28, 72, 77, 111, 137–8, 145, 161, 230, 243, 278, 344, 383, 396, 454–5, 493
Stoler, A., 62, 113, 239
Stoller, P., 342, 564
Stow, R., 85
Strathern, A.J., 6, 410
Strathern, M., 6, 66, 127, 209, 220, 255, 256–7, 259–60, 317, 395, 411, 421, 487–8
Strauss, C., 110
Street, B., 179, 338, 339
Strehlow, T.G.H., 1, 496
Strickland, S.S., 67, 400
Strong, B., 53
Stross, B., 326
Stroud, C., 339
Stubel, H., 95
Stumpf, C., 384
Sumption, J., 424
Sundkler, B., 555, **591**
Sutherland, A., 269
Swadesh, M., **591**
Swann, B., 554
Swartz, M., 145 , 431

Takado, Y., 53
Tambiah, S.J., 61, 80–1, 268, 275, 499
Tandeter, E., 39
Tanner, A., 291
Tanner, J.M., 70
Tao Yunkui, 95
Tapper, R., 369
Tardits, C., 20, 529
Taussig, M., 354, 436, 440, 443, 485, 506
Tawney, R.H., 250
Tax, S., **591**
Taylor, C., 141–2
Tedlock, B., 166, 507
Tedlock, D., 426, 554
Terray, E., 99, 245, 293, 353, 435
Thapar, R., 272
Thomas, K., 563
Thomas, N., 54, 112, 273, 403, 411, 414, 507, 566
Thomas, W.I., 206
Thompson, E.P., 273, 354, 432, 488
Thompson, Evan, 461
Thompson, R.H., 191
Thompson, S., 237
Thomsen, C.J., 48
Thornton, R., 343
Thrupp, S., 372
Thurnwald, R., 263, 264, **591**
Tien Ru-kang, 95
Tiger, L., 523
Tinbergen, N., 523
Tishkov, V., 495
Tollefson, J., 474
Tonkin, E., 404
Tonkinson, R., 234, 411
Tönnies, F., 116–17, 451, **591**
Tooker, E., 390
Toren, C., 94, 179, 461, 514
Torgovnick, M., 378
Tornay, S., 23
Torrence, R., 546
Traweek, S., 503
Traube, E.G., 131
Trautmann, T.R., 382
Treiman, D.J., 4,9
Trevarthen, C., 94
Trigger, B.G., 45, 47, 49
Trimestigus, H., 340
Trouillot, M-R., 89, 462
Trudgill, P., 327
Tucker, A.W., *see* **Hoernlé, A.W.**
Tuden, A., 434
Tunstall, J., 236
Turgot, A.R.J. (Baron), 183
Turke, P., 524
Turnbull, C.M., 397, 502, **591**

Turner, E., 97, 342
Turner, J., 295
Turner, L., 52, 552
Turner, T., 141, 233, 436
Turner, V.W., 14, 26, 97, 106, 163–4, 201, 262, 273, 358, 392, 423, 425, 428, 431, 461, 489–90, 491, 520, 535–7, **591**
Turton, D., 234
Tyler, S.A., 126, 180, 443
Tylor, Sir E.B., 48, 109, 126, 137–9, 154–5, 161, 164, DR,3, 194, 212, 213, 217, 248, 294–5, 340–1, 346, 451–2, **591–2**

Uberoi, J.P.S., 319
Uexküll, J. von, 75
Uhl, S., 246
Ulijaszek, S.J., 67, 400
Umbagai, E., 5
Un(c)kel, K., *see* **Nimuendajú, C.**
Urry, J., 274, 278
d'Urville, D., 414
Uttemorrah, D., 5

Vakhtin, N., 53
Valentine, J., 56
Valle, T. del, 317 ,
Van Bakel, M.A., 413
van de Velde, P., 66, 215, 217
van der Berghe, G., 117
van der Berghe, P.L., 117, 191
van der Leeuw, S., 546
van der Veer, P., 306, 486
van Gennep, A., 126, 244, 423, 489, 491, 492, 536, 549, **592**
Van Maanen, J., 427
Van Parijs, P., 215–16
Van Velsen, J., 364
van Wouden, F.A.E., 24, 60, 167, 131
Varela, F.J., 459
Vatin, J.-C., 368
Vatuk, S., 287
Vayda, A.P., 16
Veblen, T.B., 128, 174, **592**
Verdery, K., 192, 206, 393
Verdon, M., 520
Vermeulen, H.F., 184
Vernant, J.-P., 100, 150, 497, 498
Verrips, J., 208
Viazzo, P.P., 205
Vico, G., 183, 236, 452, **592**
Vidal-Naquet, P., 100
Vincent, J., 428, 434, 448
Viveiros de Castro, E., 246
Voget, F., 25
Vogt, E.Z., 399

Voloshinov, V., 325
Voltaire, F.M.A. de, 183–4
Vorozheikinal, T., 417
Vorren, Ø., 53
Vossen, R., 269
Vygotsky, L.S., 93, 108, 514, **592**

Wachtel, N., 40
Wacquant, L., 471
Wagner, R., 150, 219, 388, 389
Walcher, D.N., 401
Walens, S., 388
Wall, R., 226
Wallace, A.F.C.,109, 266, 301, 372–3
Wallace, A.R., **592**
Wallerstein, I., 46, 192, 370, 432, 434, 566
Wallis, R., 385
Wallman, S., 209, 563
Walu, E., 240, 241
Wang Ming-ming, 96
Ward, K., 565
Warman, A., 33
Warner, W.L., 2–3, 115, 117, 166, 200, 392, 496, 555, **592**
Warren, N., 106
Waterlow, J.C., 400
Waters, F., 76
Watson, J.L., 55, 95, 99, 370–1, 509
Watson, R., 149
Watson, W., 149
Webber, J., 423
Weber, M., 13, 57, 61, 83, 97, 99, 119, 128, 141, 242, 299, 300, 354, 366, 367, 370, 377, 378, 391, 446, 482, 519, 525, 564, **592**
Wedel, J.R., 206
Weiner, A., 220, 319
Weiner, J., 6, 387
Weiner, M., 274
Wenger, E., 179
Werbner, R.P., 13–14, 163

West, I., 5
Westermann, D.H., **592**
Westermarck, E.A., 95, 295, 126, 343, 350, **592**
Wheeler, E., 240, 241, 401
Wheeler, G.C., 429
White, G.M., 201, 422, 457–8
White, H., 361
White, L.A., 26, 28, 48, 73, 141, 157, 166, 214, 217, 186, 353, 393, 394, 515, **592–3**
Whitehead, A., 239
Whitehead, H., 257, 258–9
Whiteley, P.M., 323
Whiting, B.B., 93
Whiting, J.W.M., 93, 121, 144
Whorf, B.L., 109, 480, 499–501, **593**
Whyte, W.F., 246, 555, 556, 557
Wikan, U., 422, 537
Wildavsky, A., 439
Wilk, R., 129, 288
Willey, G.R., 47
Williams, B.F., 89, 287
Williams, F.E., 86
Williams, G., 158
Williams, G.C., 523
Williams, N., 5
Williams, R., 133, 134–5, 136, 137, 154, 323, 354, 433, 488, **593**
Williams, R.H., 129
Willis, P., 179–80, 444, 526, 565
Willis, R., 106, 559
Wilmott, P., 226
Wilmsen, E., 15, 27, 289, 474
Wilson, B., 372, 470
Wilson, E.O., 522
Wilson, G., 555
Wilson, M., 9, 563, **593**
Wilson, P.J., 88
Winch, P., 480–1
Winkelman, M., 342
Winkler, J.J., 100
Winnicott, D., 455

Winter, E.H., 563
Wissler, C., 74, 91, 139, 474–5, **593**
Wittfogel, K., 61, 215, 528, **593**
Wittgenstein, L., 201, 538, **593**
Wokler, R., 184
Wolf, A., 96, 295
Wolf, E.R., 27, 32–3, 72, 117, 123, 205, 229, 345, 353, 376, 419, 432, 434, 509, 539, 566
Wolf, M., 55
Wolf, R., 89
Wood, D., 324
Wood, G., 241
Woodburn, J., 290
Worsley, P., 85, 353, 435
Worth, S., 234
Worthman, C.M., 458
Wrong, D., 247, 251
Wu Wenzao, 95
Wundt, W., 343, 456, 593
Wungunyet, J., 5

Xiaoping, Deng, *see* Deng Xiaoping

Yalcin-Heckmann, L., 204
Yanagisako, S.J., 255, 260–1, 285
Yan Fuli, 95
Yang Kun, 96
Yang, Martin C.K., 96
Yankah, K., 406
Yelvington, K.A., 88
Yngvesson, B., 455
Yoshino, K., 307
Young, J.C., 31
Young, K., 261
Young, M., 226, 229, 319

Zaslavsky, C., 425
el-Zein, A.H., 305
Zemp, H., 385
Znaniecki, F., 206
Zolotarev, A., 494
Zuidema, R.T., 38

Peoples and places index

Headwords in bold are the subject of entries in the main text of the encyclopedia; page-spans highlighted in bold indicate the position of the main entry on the headword subject.

Aboriginal Australia, **1–5**, 24, 43, 54, 127, 135, 109, 153, 166–7, 194, 232, 288–91, 303, 309, 312, 322–3, 323, 381, 389, 422, 466, 496, 498, 502, 550; Gunabibi cult, 3, 166; Wawilak cult, 3; Yabuduruwa cult, 166
Abron, 293
Accra, 285, 286–7
Afghanistan, 367–9
Afikpo, 23
Africa:
Central, 8, 9, 16, 24, 75, 92, 163–4, 178, 239, 241, 288–91, 302, 322, 329, 331, 341, 370, 463, 490–1, 555, 556, 562–3
East, **7–9**, 10, 21–3, 63, 91, 153, 164, 170, 240, 258, 289, 302, 322, 327, 415, 502, 562–3
Nilotic, 6–7, 8, **10–12**, 91, 22–3, 152, 154, 164, 397, 420, 463, *see also* Nuer
North, *see* **Middle East and North Africa**
Southern, 7, 8, **13–16**, 23, 91, 92, 149, 150–1, 216, 283, 288–91, 322, 328, 362, 363, 370, 372, 397, 406, 426, 475–6, 482, 484, 488, 491, 496, 504, 535–6, 540, 555
West, **16–21**, 23, 43, 76, 84, 87, 92, 121, 130, 146, 153, 163, 175, 179, 199, 218–19, 225, 238, 244, 282, 283, 286–7, 283, 293, 313, 322, 370, 397, 415, 425, 439, 452, 475, 508, 512, 513, 529, 547–8, 555, 564
Afrique Occidentale Française, 17
Alaska, 52, 493
Albania, 205, 210

Aleutian Islands, 493
Algeria, 367–9, 513
Amazon, 171–2, 217, 334, 359, 363, 388–9, 390–1, 452, 507, 548–9, 559; *see also* **Americas: Native South America (Lowland)**
Americas:
Central, **28–31**, 34, 96–8, 163, 483, 492, 501
Latin America, 29–30, 240, 31–4, 286, 326, 329, 334, 342, 378, 380, 399, 416–18, 464, 473, 483, 485, 489, 555, 557, 563, 565; Cartagena; Declaration, 473
Native North America, 25, 34–7, 52, 54, 71–4, 75–6, 132–3, 138, 143, 164, 184, 193–4, 216, 222, 234, 235–6, 258–9, 265–6, 282, 288–91, 381–2, 384, 387, 388, 424–5, 428–9, 430, 445, 463, 475, 476, 477–8, 500, 504, 540, 555, 563
Native South America (highland), 34, **37–40**, 131, 171, 177, 256, 310, 415, 424, 529
Native South America (lowland), **40–3**, 131, 171–2, 217, 246, 281, 334, 342, 363, 372, 385, 388–9, 390–1, 439, 452, 507, 548–9, 559
USA and Canada, 26, 52, 66, 74, 135, 171, 227, 232, 260–1, 263, 286, 287, 303–4, 328, 370, 377, 381, 394, 421, 448, 463, 493, 502, 524, 525, 537, 555, 556,
Amhara, 154
Anangu, 1–5
Ancient Polynesian Culture (APC), 412–13
Andalusia, 246

Andaman Islands, 343, 465–6
Andes, 31–4
Angola, 91
Ankole, 8
Aranda, 2
Arapaho, 35, 74
Arawate, 246
Arctic (incl. Siberia), 24, 34, 36, **51–3**, 71–4, 170, 229, 231, 269, 288–91, 390–1, 398, 493–4, 505, 507, 513, 504,
'Aré 'Aré, 380
Argentina, 31–4
Asante, Ashanti, 19, 225, 452
Asia:
Central, 80, 84, 150, 271–2, 305–6, 310, 359, 407–8, 415, 492
East, 26, 43, 52, **54–7**, 60, 80, 95, 99, 130, 163–4, 167, 372, 282, 285–6, 307–9, 407–8, 421, 447, 485, 507, 565
South, 24, **57–9**, 80–1, 149, 153, 163, 171, 195, 219, 222, 225, 239, 245, 267–8, 271–2, 286, 289, 297, 299–300, 303, 310, 315–16, 321, 343, 351, 355, 357, 359, 392, 407–8, 415, 421, 432, 438–9, 449, 463, 465–6, 483, 485, 492, 508, 537, 555
Southeast, 5–6, 24, 26, 50, **59–62**, 80, 92, 95, 101, 103, 105, 131, 149, 167, 168, 171, 174, 181–2, 198–9, 230, 239, 245, 275, 281, 282, 283–4, 288, 302, 305–6, 310, 314, 326, 343, 348, 384, 390, 392, 407–8, 419, 422, 423, 425, 426, 429–30, 441, 455, 459, 463, 475, 483, 498, 499, 502, 537, 538, 549, 562
Atlanta University, 74, 463

Atui Island, 542
Austronesian languages, 319, 346–7
Avatip, 559
Aymara language, 39
Azande (Zande), 8, 164, 329, 341, 562–3

Bacwezi, 8
Baganda, 7–9, 425
Bahamas Islands, 87
Bakhtiari, 170, 553
Bali, 61, 92, 101, 171, 275, 422, 425, 537, 538, 549
Bambarra, 76
Bamoum, 20, 529
Banaras, 149
Bangladesh, 13–16
Bantu, 13–14, 92, 475–6
Barasana, 363, 388–9, 548–9
Bari, 10–12
Barotse, 24
Baruya, 178
Basongye, 384
Basque country, 392
Basseri, 553
Batek Negritos, 302
BaThonga, 7–9, 63; see Thonga, Tsonga
Bedouin, 170, 324, 369, 397–9, 489
Belize, 87
Bella Coola, 72–3
Bemba, 178, 322
Bénin, 17–19, 20
Berber, 170, 324, 367, 368
Bermuda, 87
Betsileo, 216
Bihar, 297
Blackfoot, 74
Bokmal, 327
Bolivia, 31–4, 37–40, 40–2, 256, 485, 489
Boran Dromo, 22–3
Borana, 9
Bororo, 334, 452
Bosnia, 204
Boston, 555
Botswana, 13, 23; see also Kalahari
Bougainville Island, 65, 86
Brazil, 31–4, 40–2, 372, 378, 385, 439, 557; see also Amazon,
    Americas: Native South America (Lowland)
Brittany, 392
Brunei, 59
Budal, 166
Buganda, 8
Bugis, 62
Bulgaria, 28–31

Burkina Faso, 17
Burma, 24, 59–60, 80, 283, 314, 425
Burundi, 7–9
Bushmen, 15, 288–91, 451; see also Kalahari, !Kung, San

Caduveo, 334
Calusa, 34
Cambodia, 60, 80
Cameroon, 16–18, 529
Canada, 135, 171, 232, 394;
    'Indians', see **Americas: Native North America**
Cape Verde Islands, 17
Caribbean, 10, 40, **86–90**, 148, 171, 226, 286, 372, 425, 426, 439, 464
Cathay, see China
Ceylon, see Sri Lanka
Cewa-speakers, 563
Chad, 16–17
Cheyenne, 35
Chile, 31–4, 37
China, 43, 52, 80, 95–6, 99, 130, 163–4, 167, 372, 421; see also
    Asia: East
Chinook, 445
Chotanagpur, 297
Chukchi, 51–2
Chukota, 52
Cochin, 297
Colombia, 31–4, 37, 40–2, 485
Conibo, 342
Cook Islands, 413
Coorgs, 58
Copper, 52
Corsica, 149
Costa Rica, 28–31, 31–4
Côte d'Ivoire, 17, 20
Cree, 289, 291
Crow, 74, 132–3
Cuba, 31–4, 87, 88, 90, 372
Cushitic, 10–12
Cuzco, 38

Dakota, see Plains Indians
Dahomey, 20
Daribi, 219, 389
Denmark, 51, 208
Detroit, 227
Dinka, 6–7, 11–12, 164, 420
Dobu, 43
Dogon, 130, 244
Dolgans, 51
Duwa, 166–7

Easter Islands, 216, 412, 413
Ecuador, 31–4, 40–2

Egypt, 367–9
El Salvador, 28–31, 31–4, 492
England, 134–5, 342, 564; see also
    Europe: North
Eskhol, 147
Eskimo, see **Arctic**, Inuit
Ethiopia, 10, 22–3, 154, 463
Europe:
    Central & Eastern, 203–7, 279, 286, 372, 392, 435, 507
    North, 51, 134–5, 171, 183–5, 203–4, 208–9, **207–10**, 237, 265, 286, 327–8, 342, 371, 384, 392, 415, 463, 507, 535, 553, 557, 559, 564
    South, 31, 37–40, 51, 100–2, 117–18, 149, 163–4, **210–13**, 222, 246, 257, 261, 280–1, 296, 321, 327, 340, 342, 382, 384, 392, 396, 415, 416–17, 419, 435, 462–3, 467, 468, 498, 508, 557
Evenks, 51, 504
Evens, 51

Far East, see **Asia: East**
Fiji, 66, 112, 179, 274, 275, 346, 412, 414, 514
Finland, 51, 208, 209, 507
Flathead, 384
Foi, 6–7, 388
France, 183–5, 149, 209–13, 242–6, 327, 392, 486, 524, 564;
    see also **Europe: North, Europe: South**
French Guiana, 31–4, 40–2, 87
French Polynesia, 412
Fulani, 18, 20, 415

Gahuku-Gama, 300
Gambia, 16–17
Germany, 183–5, 203–4, 209, 237, 263–5, 384, 463; see also
    Europe: North
Ghana, 16–19, 20, 92, 43, 121, 283, 285–7, 313, 322, 397, 425, 452, 475, 508, 512
Gimi, 150
Great Britain, 76–9, 134–5, 183–4, 207–8, 209, 286, 328, 342, 371, 392, 535, 557, 559, 564; see also
    Europe: North
Greece, 261, 280, 382; ancient, 51, 100–2, 163, 213, 296, 462–3, 467, 468, 498; Sarakatsani, 210, 416–17
Greenland, 51
Guatemala, 28–31, 31–4

Guinea Bissau, 16–17
Guinea Coast, 547–8
Gulf states, 367–9
Guyana, 31–4, 40–2, 87, 89,
    117–18, 226
Gwiyal, 166
Gypsies, 164, 204, **269–70**, 322

Hadza, 3, 7–9, 289, 302
Hagen, 256–7, 259–60
Haida, 35–6, 445
Haiti, 87, 148, 439
Hanunoo, 181–2
Hauka, 84
Hausa, 17–18, 20, 175, 439
Havasupai, 74
Hawaii, 46, 274, 412–13, 539
Honduras, 28–31, 31–4
Hong Kong, 95
Hopi, 35, 75–6, 500
Hungary, 205–6, 507

Iban, 59–62, 106–7
Iceland, 209
Ife, 18–19, 555
Ifugao, 60, 429–30
Igloolik, 51
Ik, 502
Ilongot, 60–1, 562
Inca, *see* Inka
India, 24, 80–1, 149, 153, 163, 195,
    222, 225, 239, 267–8, 271–2,
    286, 289, 297–8, 299–300, 303,
    343, 351, 355, 357, 359, 392,
    421, 438–9, 449, 465–6, 483,
    492, 555; *see also* **Asia: South**
Indonesia, 59–60, 62, 131, 168, 282,
    305, 419, 425; *see also* **Asia:
    Southeast**
Inka, 37–40, 171, 529
Inuit, 24, 34, 36, 51–3, 71–4, 170,
    229, 231, 269, 288–91, 390–1,
    398, 513; *see also* **Arctic**
Iqwaye, 399, 460
Iran, 170, 179, 340, 367–9, 397–8,
    553
Iraq, 367–9
Ireland, 208–9, 286; *see also*
    Europe: North, Northern
    Ireland
Irian Jaya, 232
Iroquois, 35, 193–4, 381–2, 476,
    477, 555
Israel, 367–9; ancient, 175
Italy, 210, 212, 321, 508; ancient
    Rome, 100–2, 163–4, 213;
    Renaissance, 340, 342, 384
Ivory Coast, *see* Côte d'Ivoire

Jamaica, 10, 88–90
Japan, 43, 80, 282, 285–6, **307–9**,
    447, 463, 485, 565; *see also*
    Asia: East
Java, 59, 60–2, 103, 105, 131,
    198–9, 239, 310, 348, 384,
    537
Jivaro, 342
Ju/'hoansi, 170

Kabyle, 513
Kachin, 283–4, 314
Kaguru, 7–9, 563
Kalahari, 3, 13–16, 27, 63, 170,
    288–91, 302, 363, 397, 451, 476,
    504; *see also* Bushmen, Khoisan,
    !Kung, San
Kalanga, 13
Kale, *see* **Gypsies**
Kalinga, 60
Kaluli, 385, 514
Kamba, 8
Kapauku, 380
Karam, 499
Kariera, 2
Kanem, 18
Kathmandu, 84
Kenya, 7–9, 10, 91, 240, 327
Kerala, 297
Kerema, 86
Kgalagadi, 13
Khanti, 51
Khoekhoe, 14–15
Khoisan, 15, 476, *see also* Bushmen,
    Kalahari
Kikuyu, 8
Kipingamarangi, 412
Kipsigi, 8
Korea, 80, 372, 507; minority in
    Japan, 307–8
Korongo, 563
Koryaks, 51–2
Kosova, 204
!Kung, 15, 27, 302; *see also*
    Bushmen, Kalahari, Khoisan
Kurds, 367–9
Kwakiutl, 34, 36, 72–3, 143, 235,
    282, 388, 445
Kwoma, 93

Ladakh, 492
Lakota, 425
Lamuts, *see* Evens
Langkawi Island, 5–6
Laos, 59, 80
Lapita, 412, 413
Lapps, *see* Saami
Laymi, 256

Lebanon, 367–9
Lesotho, 13
Liberia, 17
Libya, 367–9
LoDaggaa, 19, 475
Lotuko, 10–12
Lovedu, 283, 476
LoWiili, 475
Lozi, 322
Lugbara, 9, 563
Luo, 10–12
Luyia, 8
Luzon, 61

Maasai, 9, 10, 22, 170, 258, 415
Macedonia, 203–7
Madagascar, 149, 150–1, 216, 328,
    362, 406, 482
Magdalenians, 53
Malaita Island, 85, 380
Malawi, 7, 563
Malay Archipelago, 167, 475
Malaysia, 5–6, 50, 59, 62, 167, 302,
    419, 426, 463, 475
Mali, 17–18, 130, 555
Malta, 222, 396
Mande, 20
Mangareva, 413
Mansis, 51
Manus Island, 85, 92, 143
Maori, 75, 107, 219–20, 372, 405,
    412, 414, 485, 542
Marakwet, 10–12
Maravars, 449
Marawar, 166
Marquesas Islands, 412, 413
Mauritania, 17
Maya, 29, 501
Mbuti, 302
Mediterranean, *see* **Europe:
    South, Middle East and
    North Africa**
Mekeo Islands, 66
Melanesia, *see* **Pacific:
    Melanesia**
Merina, 149, 328
Mexico, 28–31, 31–4, 326, 329,
    342, 380, 399, 555, 563, 565
Micronesia, *see* **Pacific:
    Micronesia**
Middle East and North Africa,
    170, 175, 180, 305–6, 340,
    367–70, 378, 384, 397–9,
    407–8, 415, 423–4, 439 485–6,
    489, 498, 553
Morocco, 305, 367–9, 378, 498
Mossi, 18
Mozambique, 7–9, 63

Murinbata, 3
Murngin, *see* Yolngu

Nahuatl, 329
Nama, 63
Nambikwara, 334
Namibia, 13–16, *see also* Kalahari
Nandi, 10–12
Navajo, 35, 234, 500, 563
Nayaka, 289
Nayars, 153, 225, 351
Ndebele, 13
Ndembu, 164, 491, 535–6
Nenets, 51–2
Nepal, 80, 271–2, 310, 359
Netherlands, 208
New Caledonia, 66, 244
New Guinea, 6, 54, 63, 65–6, 82,
    85, 86, 92, 93, 126–7, 131, 143,
    150, 151, 153, 178, 186, 195,
    218, 219, 224, 230, 232, 256–7,
    259–60, 263, 300, 312–14 319,
    330, 341, 343–4, 380, 388, 389,
    390, 399, 409–12, 445, 453, 454,
    460, 499, 520, 545, 546, 549,
    555, 559
New Zealand, *see* Maori
Nganasans, 51
Ngoni, 13, 92
Nicaragua, 28–31, 31–4
Niger, 17–18, 84, 282, 564
Nigeria, 17–19, 23, 146, 153, 175,
    218–19,
Nilo-Hamites, 10–12
Nilotes, 10–12
Nootka, 235–6, 500
North Africa, *see* **Middle East and
    North Africa**
Northern Ireland, 559; *see also*
    Europe: North, Ireland
Northwest Coast Indians
    (N. America), 34–6, 54, 72–3,
    138, 143, 216, 235–6, 282, 388,
    445, 500, 504
Norway, 51, 208, 209, 327
Nuer, 8, 10–12, 22, 64, 109, 195,
    225, 235–6, 283, 314, 351, 415,
    484, 497, 498, 504, 548, 555
Nupe, 19
Nyakyusa, 9, 23, 563
Nyoro, 7–9, 164

Oaxaca, 380
Occitanie, 327
Ojibwa, 550–1
Omaha, 132–3
Oman, 367–9
Oyo, 19

Paama, 65
Pacific:
    Melanesia, 6–7, 43, 46, 54, 63,
        65–6, 82, 85–6, 92, 93, 100,
        126–7, 131, 143, 150, 151, 153,
        175, 178, 186, 194–5, 218–20,
        224, 230, 232, 244, 256–7,
        259–60, 262, 263, 279, 282, 300,
        312, 318–20, 330, 341, 343–4,
        346–7, 372, 380, 388, 388, 389,
        390, 399, 403, **409–12**, 412, 421,
        431, 445, 453, 454, 460, 499,
        520, 537, 540, 545–6, 555, 559
    Micronesia, 346–7
    Polynesia, 63, 65, 66, 69, 75,
        92, 107, 112, 143, 179, 184,
        219–20, 216, 257–8, 274, 283,
        286, 310, 319, 346–7, 372, 405,
        406, 410, **412–14**, 485, 501–2,
        514, 539, 542; Ancient
        Polynesian Culture (APC),
        412–13; Austronesian
        languages, 319, 346–7
Pahari, 286
Pakistan, 57–9, 170, 367–9
Panama, 28–31, 31–4
Papua New Guinea, *see* New
    Guinea
Persia, 340, *see also* Iran
Peru, 31–4, 37–40, 40–2, 240
Philadelphia, 556
Philippines, 59, 60–2, 181–2, 425,
    429–30, 498, 502, 562
Pintupi, 4, 422
Plains Indians, 35, 74, 118, 130,
    265–6, 398
Plateau-Basin, 74
Pokot, 10–12
Poland, 205, 257
Polynesia, *see* **Pacific: Polynesia**
Portugal, 31, 257, 557
Pueblo Indians, 34–7, 75–6, 194,
    234, 425, 500, 563
Puerto Rico, 31–4, 87, 89
Pukapuka, 179
Pygmies, 288–91, 302

Qashqai, 553
Québec, 394
Quechua language, 39

Ranamal, 327
Rerwondji, 166
Rom, *see* **Gypsies**
Rome, *see* Italy
Romania, 204, 205–6, 392
Rossel Island, 319
Rwanda, 8, 91 463

Saami, 51
Samoa, 92, 143, 406, 412, 414,
    501–2, 514
Samoyeds, *see* Nenets
San, 3, 15, 27, 288–91, 363, 397
Sarakatsani, 210, 416–17
Sarawak, *see* Iban
Saudi Arabia, 367–9
Scotland, 183–4, 207, 392, 535
Seneca, 381–2
Senegal, 17, 513
Siberia, 51–2, 493–4, 505, 507
Sierra Leone, 17, 19, 238
Singapore, 60, 95
Sinhalas, Sinhalese, 59, *see also* Sri
    Lanka
Sinti, *see* **Gypsies**
Sioux (Dakota), 35, 130, 265–6
Society Islands, 412
Solomon Islands, 65–6, 85, 86,
    194–5, 232, 262, 319, 343,
    346–7, 380, 409–10, 540
Somalia, 10–12, 152, 397
Songhay, 84, 564
Sotho, 476
Sotho-Tswana, 13
South Africa, Rep. of, 8, 14, 426,
    488, 555
Spain, 31, 37–40, 117–18, 210
Sri Lanka, 24, 57–9, 61, 80, 230,
    392, 423, 441, 455, 459
Sri Vijaya (empire of), 61–2
Sudan, 6–8, 10–12, 164, 261, 269,
    329, 341, 367–9, 420, 441, 502,
    562–3; *see also* Nuer
Sulawesi, 59–62
Sumatra, 62
Surinam, Suriname, 31–4, 40–2,
    86–90, 425
Suya, 385.
Swazi, 13, 476, 491
Sweden, 51, 208, 209
Switzerland, 171, 553
Syria, 367–9

Tahiti, 184, 413, 542
Taiwan, 95
Tale, 19, 512
Tallensi, 19, 43, 121, 283, 313
Tamils, 59, 315–16; *see also* Sri
    Lanka
Tanga, 413
Tangu, 388
Tanna, 85
Tanzania, 7–9, 10, 23, 289, 302,
    322, 425, 563,
Tasaday, 502
Temne, 548

Thailand, 59, 61, 80, 174, 310, 326, 499
Thonga, 8; *see also* BaThonga, Tsonga
Tibet, *see* Asia: Central
Tikopia, 283, 412, 414
Timbuctoo, 555
Tiv, 19, 218–19
Tlinglit, 35–6, 445
Toda, 195, 555
Togo, 17
Tonga Islands, 63, 412, 542
Torres Straits Islands, 232, 194–5, 262, 343, 409–10
Toulon Island, 343
Transylvania, 204
Travancore, 297
Trinidad and Tobago, 87, 89
Trobriand Islands, 63, 66, 85, 126–7, 153, 195, 218, 224, 230, 312, 319, 330, 341, 343–4, 390, 453, 454, 520, 555
Tsembaga, 186
Tsimshian, 235, 387
Tsonga, 7–9, 63, 476; *see also* BaThonga, Thonga
Tswana, 13, 23, 476, 484, 504
Tswapong, 13
Tuarej, 170
Tungus, *see* Evenks

Tunisia, 367–9
Turkana, 10–12
Turkey, 367–9, 424
Turkmen, 170, 398
Tzeltal, 326
Tzintzuntzan, 33

Ubakala Igbo, 146
Uganda, 7–9, 10, 164, 425, 502, 563
Umbanda, 372, 439
Umeda, 549
USA, 26, 52, 66, 74, 135, 227, 260–1, 263, 286, 287, 303–4, 328, 370, 377, 381, 421, 448, 463, 493, 502, 524, 525, 537, 555, 556; Hawaii, 46, 274, 412–13, 539; 'Indians', *see* **Americas: Native North America**

Vanuatu, 65, 85, 346
Venezuala, 31–4, 40–2
Vietnam, 60, 62, 80, 355–6
Voguls, *see* Mansis

Walbiri, Warlpiri, 3, 54
Wales, 207
Warlpiri, Walbiri, 3, 54
Winnebago, 74
Wolof, 513

Xhosa, 13
Xingu, 42

Yakö, 19, 153
Yakuts, 51–2
Yanomamö, 217, 559
Yaqui, 342, 555, 563
Yemen, 367–9
Yiridja, 1–5, 166–7
Yolngu, 2–4
Yoruba, 20, 163, 179, 199
Yucatan, 555
Yucatec, 29, 501
Yugakirs, 51–2
Yugoslavia, 204, 210, 286, 392
Yurok, 36, 282

Zaire, 7, 75, 239, 241, 302
Zambia, 8, 164, 178, 322, 491, 535–6, 555, 556, 563
Zambian National Research Institute, 14, 157, 370, 431, 536, 556
Zande (Azande), 8, 164, 329, 341, 562–3
Zimbabwe, 8, 13
Zinacantan, 399
Zulu, 13, 23
Zuni, 194

Subject index

Words in bold are either the subject of main entries or of entries in the glossary. Page-spans highlighted in bold indicate the position of either a main entry on the headword subject or an entry in the glossary.

ablineal, 594
Academy of Social Science
  [China], 95
acculturation, 39, 87, 112, 147,
  156, 188, 194, 273, 372, 381,
  463, 555, **594**
acephalous societies, 19, 269, 322,
  431, **594**
achievement and ascription,
  65, 414, 452, 564, **594**
action anthropology, 26, 64, 123,
  516, **594**
action group, set, 107, 222,
  396, **594**
action theory, 431–2
adaptation, 169, 170, 564, **594**
address, terms of, 285
adelphic polyandry, 594
adhesion, 594
adolescence, 92, 143
adoption and fostering, 5–6, 23,
  152, 285, 487
aesthetics, 6–7, 54, 237, 383–4,
  426
affine, affinity, 23, 24, 60, 122,
  125, 223, 313, 476, 545, **594**
agamy, 594
age, 10–11, 18, **21–3,** 41, 70, 246,
  256, 257, 258, 323, 337, 353,
  475, 489; see also **childhood**
age-area hypothesis, 594
age-class systems, 21–3, 594
age grades, 9, 21, 22, 23, 431, **594**
age sets, 9, 10–11, 21, 101, 115,
  258, **594**
agency, agent, 24, 245, 254, 260,
  262–3, 298, 300–1, 348, 349–50,
  367, 407, 420, 422, 431, 439,
  441, 446, 513–14, 515, 521, **595**
agnate, agnatic, 313, **595**
agon, 425
agriculture, 20, 172, 173, 196,

238–41, 288–9, 321–3, 360,
  381, 418, 429, 499, 518, **595;**
  subsistence, 624; swidden,
  41, 171, **624–5**
alcoholism, 31, 201, 401
alea, 425
alliance, 20, **23–5,** 60, 132–3, 150,
  153, 245, 282, 283, 284, 289,
  313, 314, 334–5, 350–1, 410,
  449–50, 475, 478, 561, **595**
allometry, 67
All-Russian Ethnographic
  Exhibition, 493
alter, 595
alterity, 595
ambilineal, 154, **595**
ambilocal, 595
American Anthropological
  Association, 25, 44, 74, 393
American anthropology, 13,
  25–8, 38, 52, 54, 71–4, 125, 130,
  132, 136–41, 155–7, 161, 191,
  193–4, 214, 234, 277–9, 326,
  334, 343, 345, 353, 354, 370,
  381–2, 392, 421–2, 429–30, 443,
  455, 456, 470–2, 474–5, 479–80,
  516, 517, 532, 535–6, 537
American Ethnological Society, 44
American Folklore Society, 44
American Museum of Natural
  History, 74
amoral familism, 212, 419, **595**
ancestors, 1, 4, **43,** 55, 85, 95,
  131, 151–4, 173, 175, 286, 299,
  307, 313, 362, 411, 420, 439,
  482, 513, 548, 549, 550
ancient history, 302; see also
  classical studies
ancient Greek anthropology, 467,
  468
Ancient Polynesian Culture (APC),
  412, 413

animism, 61, 165, 346, **595**
anisogamy, 595
Annales **school,** 273, 452, **595**
Année sociologique, 244, 341,
  524, **595**
anomie, 595
anthropocentrism, 185, 187
Anthropological Association of
  Washington, 44
Anthropological Institute of Great
  Britain and Ireland, 76
Anthropological Society of London,
  44
anthropological societies, 44–5,
  74, 184–5, 278
Anthropological Survey of India,
  297
anthropometry, 72, 463, **595**
anthropomorphism, 595
anti-structure, 491; see also
  communitas
apical ancestor, 595
applied anthropology, 168,
  187–8, 321, 322, 359, 502,
  595
appropriate technology, 596
archaeology, 4, 25, **45–51,** 67, 73,
  77, 78, 162, 169, 265, 289, 324,
  353, 381, 429, 446, 547
archetype, 596
architecture, 36, 47, 281, 283–4,
  378, 547–8
Archiv für Anthropologie, 66
area studies, 407–8
armchair anthropology, 596
art, 3, 6, 20, **54,** 72, 232, 382, 392,
  404, 465, 505, 506, 507
**articulation of modes of
  production,** 14, 158, 353, **596;**
  see also **mode of production**
ascribed status, see **achievement
  and ascription**

Asiatic mode of production,
  215, 353, 375, 528, **596**
Association of Social
  Anthropologists (ASA), 44
Association of Social
  Anthropologists in Oceania
  (ASAO), 45
atom of kinship, 63, **596**
attribution theory, 201
Australian Anthropological
  Association, 45
Australian anthropology, 1–5, 194,
  520
Australian Social Science Research
  Council, 4
auxology, 69–70
avoidance, *see* **joking and
  avoidance**
avunculate, **63**, 309, 313, 475, 523
avunculocal, 313, 522, **596**
ayllu, 39, 177, **596**
Ayurveda, 359

Bahai'i, 540
band, 214, 431, 528, **596**
barbarism, 154–5, 383, 429,
  518, 596
barter, 347
base and superstructure, 52,
  134, 352–4, 534, **596**
behavioural level, **596**
behaviourism, 64, 92, 143, 512,
  513, **596**
belief, **64**, 97, 475
berdache, 258–9
Berlin school, 384
bifurcation, 132, 477, **596**
Big Man, 65–6, 86, 175, 219, 256,
  313, 410, 430
bilateral, 2, 53, 106–7, 153–4,
  225, 313, 351, **596**
bilateral cross-cousin marriage, 314
bilateral descent, 153
bilineal, **596**
binary opposition, 105, 245, 254,
  438, 507, **596**
biological anthropology, 25, 27,
  45, **66–71**, 72, 77, 78, 265, 279,
  312, 400, 494, 564
biological determinism, 391–6
biology, 393–6, 456–61
biomedicine, 181, 358–61, **596**
Birmingham Centre for Cultural
  Studies, 134, 136, 444
birth, *see* childbirth
birth control, 23
blood feud, 152, **597**
body, 6–7, **75–6**, 104, 146, 149,
  173, 178, 253, 259, 261, 361,
  385, 399, 437, 441, 456, 459,
  461, 560

Branch Davidian movement, 373
bricolage, bricoleur, **597**
bride capture, **597**
brideprice, 65, **597**
bride-service, 351, **597**
bridewealth, 14, 91, 225, 258,
  351, 409, 410, **597**
British anthropology, 19–20, 24,
  26, 54, **76–9**, 130, 132, 155–7,
  161, 194–5, 214, 247, 249–50,
  278–9, 310, 319, 335, 353, 354,
  343, 345, 370–1, 392, 395, 443,
  455, 471, 478–9, 490–1, 514,
  516, 517–18, 536, 538, 556
brokerage, 123, 417
Buddhism, 54–6, 57–9, **80–1**,
  149, 373, 407–8, 437, 482–6;
  Japanese, 308, 540; and
  kingship, 310; Mahayana, 61,
  80–1; Tantric, 80; Theravada,
  59, 61, 80–1, 485
**Bureau of American
  Ethnology**, 25, 72, 222, 381,
  428–9, **597**
bureaucracy, 8, 171, 189, 326, 338,
  416, 467
burial, *see* **death**

Cambridge Group for Population
  Studies, 226
Cambridge 'Ritualists', 100
Canadian Arctic Expedition, 52
Canadian Ethnology Society, 44
Canberra Anthropology, 502
cannibalism, **82–3**, 150, 199,
  263, 563
capitalism, 29–30, 46, 53, **83–5**,
  101, 86–90, 116, 128, 158, 172,
  205, 227, 229, 236, 242, 253,
  260, 322, 349, 350, 352–4, 360,
  370–1, 375, 377, 378, 432, 434,
  435–6, 484–5, 509, 514, 519,
  524, 525, 540, 565, 566
cargo cult, **85–6**, 354, 372, 411,
  432, 540
carnival, 490, 492–3
carrying capacity, 67, 235, 397,
  597
carrying mother, **597**
case-study, 364, **597**
cash crops, 239, 368, **597**
caste, 24, 57–9, **90–1**, 112, 187,
  222, 272, 275, 293, 303, 437–9,
  462, 463, 499, 537, 542
categorical level, **597**
cattle complex, **91–2**
Central Minorities Institute
  [China], 95
central place theory, 347, 504
Central Research Institute
  [Beijing], 95

centre and periphery, **597**; *see
  also* world system
Centre for Contemporary Cultural
  Studies (CCCS), 134, 136, 444
change theory, 85, 272–7, 371–3,
  539; *see also* **colonialism,
  diffusion, evolution**
charisma, 346, **597**
Chicago school, 95, 370, 555
Chicago, University of, 377, 537,
  555
chief, 65–6, 175, 217; talking, 406
chiefdom, **597**
childbirth, 254, 258, 261, 359,
  395, 498, 512
childhood, 21, **92–4**, 121, 178,
  286, 395, 410, 455
Chinese Anthropological
  Association, 95
Chinese anthropology, **95–6**,
  352, 353, 375
Chinese Ethnological Society, 95
choreometry, 233, **597**
Christianity, 14, 64, 90–1, **96–8**,
  153, 201, 203, 290, 299, 414,
  437, 482–6, 496; Adventism,
  540; Bible, 355; dreams in, 165;
  Evangelical, 38, 39, 40, 482–6;
  kingship, 310; magic, 340;
  missionaries, *see* **missionaries**;
  Mormonism, 540; person, 421;
  Protestantism, 483–4; Roman
  Catholicism, 30, 32, 39, 59, 61,
  117, 483–4; sacrifice, 497–8
circulating connubium, 60, 167,
  475, **597**
circumcision, 10, 144, 258, 512,
  560, **597**
civil rights movement, 372
civil society, 417, 447, 486, 516,
  518, **597**
civilization, 37–8, 126, 381, 429,
  484, 518, **597**
clan, 4, 22, 43, 132, 150, 152, 214,
  283–4, 299, 387, 390, 421, 429,
  497, 532, 550, **598**
class, 33–4, 58, 88, 89, 96, **98–9**,
  123, 107, 117, 128, 134–5, 146,
  179, 198, 205, 207, 222, 227,
  238–9, 246, 251, 287, 302, 325,
  328, 352–4, 360, 367, 375–6,
  383, 385, 391–2, 417, 423, 426,
  435, 436, 445–6, 453, 488, 488,
  494, 528, 537, 556, 565
classical studies, **100–2**
classification, **103–6**, 110, 125,
  130, 166–7, 202, 245, 255, 304,
  312, 333, 335, 353, 358, 387,
  430, 448, 449, 518, 519, 532, 546
classificatory kinship, 1, 35,
  381, **598**

clients, *see* **patrons and clients**

clitoridectomy, *see* **circumcision**

clothing, 84, 85, 130, 169, 258, 440

code and substance, 58, 315–6, 438, 537

code-switching, 598; *see* **language and linguistics**

cognate, 598

cognatic society, descent, 53, **106–8**, 133, 153–4, 313

cognition, 27, 105, **108–11**, 134, 178–9, 245, 292, 393, 400, 420, 456–61, 514, 516, 517, 518, 535, 536, 539, 547

cognitive anthropology, 103, 125, 167, 180, 200, **598**

cohort, 21, **598**

cold society, 377, 533; *see* **hot and cold societies**

Cold War, 206, 222, 428, 557

collateral, **598**

collective consciousness, 299, 517, **598**

collective representation, 244, 299, 341, 452, 460, 547, **598**

colonialism, 1, 4, 7, 9, 10, 16–20, 29–30, 31–2, 38–40, 42, 46, 50, 54, 57, 62, 79, 82, 83, 86–90, 97, **111–14**, 123, 142, 153, 155, 156, 167, 171, 178, 189, 196, 207–8, 218–19, 243–4, 250, 253, 271, 273, 274–5, 277, 279, 291, 306, 321, 324, 327, 359, 370, 373–5, 372, 382, 403, 407–8, 409, 412, 414, 425–6, 429–30, 432, 435, 439, 443, 445, 446–7, 453, 462–3, 470–1, 472, 474, 479, 483–4, 486, 521, 552, 556; **internal**, 192, **598**

colour terminology, 110, 125–6

Columbia University, 74, 194

commensality, 175, **598**; *see also* **food**

commodity, 318, 348, 415, 484, 556, **598**

commons, 175, 235

communalism, 59, 321–2, **598**

communism, 204, 222, 372; *see also* **Chinese anthropology, Marxism, Russian and Soviet anthropology**

communitas, 423, 490, 491, **598**

community, 39, **114–17**, 171, 194, 208, 359, 415, 418, 426, 451, 486

community economy, 173

compadrazgo, 5, 30, 33, 39, **117–18**, 211, 417

comparative analysis, 364, 505, 563

comparative method, **118–21**, 272, 304, 306, 364, 429, 466, 515

comparative religion, 185, **598**

complementary dualism, 38–9, **598**

complementary filiation, **121–2**, 313, 520

complete-universe comparison, 119–20

complex society, 42, 116, **122–3**, 171, 339, 436, 518, 556–7

complex structure, 24, 334–5, 429, **598**

complex system, 281–2

component, **599**

componential analysis, 109, **125–6**, 180, 202

computers, 49, 531, 534

conception, **126–8**, 312, 315–16, 480, 512; *see also* **reproductive technologies**

conceptual aggregate, 118

concubinage, **599**

configurationalism, 143

Confucianism, 55, 60, 421

conjectural history, **599**

conjugal family, 223, 224–6, 227

conjugality, 60

connectionism, 110

connotatum, **599**

consanguine, consanguinity, 125, 477, **599**

consociate, 287, 555, 557, **599**

constructivism, 521

consumption, 47, **128–9**, 154, 170, 172, 220, 224, 238, 255, 256, 287, 377, 392, 418, 434, 526, 566

contagious magic, **599**

contract, 377, 451, 516, 518, 519, 520, **599**

controlled comparison, 26, 429, **599**

conversational analysis, 162–3

conversion, 20

core, *see* **centre and periphery**, world system

corporate group, 21, 106–7, 282, **599**

Corpus Hermeticum, 340

cosmogony, 129, **599**

cosmology, 9, 20, 41, 105, 127, 118, **129–32**, 148, 194, 244, 264, 346, 359, 386, 390, 466, 485, 492

costume, 148

counter-hegemony, 432, **599**

couvade, **599**

cremation, *see* **death**

creole, 17, 86, 328, 485, **599**

creolization, **599**

Critique of Anthropology, 273

cross-cousin marriage, 2, 63, 132–3, 309, 314, 448–9, 477, 522, 523, **599**; *see also* **marriage**

cross-cutting ties, 153, **599**

cross-relative, 125, 477, **599**

Crow–Omaha systems, **132–3**, 477–8, **599**

cultural analysis, 134–6

cultural anthropology, 25, 108, 138–40, 141–2, 162, 393–4, 530, 565, **600**

Cultural Anthropology, 444

cultural change, 85, 112, 371–3, 539

cultural determinism, 186–7, 391–6, 501, 519, **600**

cultural ecology, 27, 33, 53, 186, 516

cultural holism, 516, 519, 539

cultural materialism, 83, 98, **133–4**, 169, 180, 186–7, 277, 376, 433

cultural particularism, 536

cultural pattern, 74, 143

cultural pluralism, 426

cultural psychology, 458–9

cultural studies, 124, **134–6**, 141, 146, 162–3, 234, 353, 386, 443–4, 472

culturalism, 140, 515, 520, 521, 522, **600**

culture, 25, 36, 47–8, 64, 68, 72–3, 75–6, 85, 86–7, 96, 123, 124, 125, 108, 110, 133–4, 134–6, **136–43**, 146, 161, 163, 169, 179, 182, 190–3, 209, 213, 214–15, 231, 253, 255, 256–7, 289–90, 292, 293, 299, 304, 311, 326, 335–6, 336–7, 353–4, 361–3, 370,356–7, 378, 379, 387, 391–2, 391–6, 407–8, 426, 433, 456–61, 463, 481, 490, 498–9, 503, 514, 515, 517, 518, 520, 526, 531–2, 535–9, 540, 551–3; *see also* **nature and culture**

culture and personality, 26, 32, 53, 92–3, 122, 130, 139, **143–5**, 232–3, 292, 301, 360, 410, 455, 456–7, 506, 512–14

culture area, 72–3, 167, 210–11, 474–5, **600**

culture bearer, **600**

culture-bound syndrome, 199, 200, **600**

culture circle, *see* **Kulturkreis**

culture complex, 139, **600**

culture contact, 156–7, 161, 382, 430, 551–3, **600**

culture core, **600**

culture history, 264, 265, **600**

Culture, Medicine and Psychiatry, 202
culture of poverty, 31, 33, 123, **600**
culture trait, 91, 139, 475, **600**
customary law, 331, **600**
cybernetics, 186, 531–2, **600**
cyborg, **600**

Dakar-Djibouti Expedition, 244
dance, 85, **146–9**, 232, 233, 383, 385, 404, 427; *see also* **ghost dance**
Daoism, 55
death, **149–51**, 311, 438, 489, 492, 548
deconstruction, 135, 259–61, 335, 506, **600**
deep and surface structure, **601**
deictics, deixis, 104, **601**
deme, **601**
demography, 70, 193, 198, 262–3
denotatum, **601**
dependency, 32–3, 157, 353, **601**
descent, 1, 11, 18, 20, 21, 23–4, 35, 43, 39, 60, 121, 132–3, **151–4**, 173, 191, 192, 195, 245, 262, 281–4, 288, 312–14, 334, 351, 410, 413, 430, 477–8, 520, 563, **601**
descent group, 4, 151–4, 288, 290
descriptive kinship, 1, 35, 381,477, **601**
designatum, **601**
development, 83,92, 85, 96, **154–60**, 168, 183, 188, 205, 208, 222, 238, 240–1, 253, 261, 265, 321, 323, 326, 338, 349, 357, 358, 372, 376, 377, 416, 434, 503, 508, 547, 566
developmental cycle, 205, 224–6, 419, **601**
diachronic, 119, 272, 335, 390, 490, **601**
dialect, 327, 554, **601**
dialectical materialism, 134, **601**; *see* **Marxism**
dialogic, dialogical, 427, 441, **601**
diaspora, 20, 371, **601**
diet, 400–1
différance, **601**
diffusion, 26, 48, 73, 78, 95, 118, 156, **160–2**, 194, 232, 264, 272, 384, 409, 430, 474, 479, 540
diglossia, 327, 328, **601**
direct relative, 125, **601**
discourse, 6–7, 115, 119–20, 141, **162–4**, 326, 328, 331, 348, 373, 387–8, 405, 408, 482–3, 486
disease, 360

disembedded economy, 173, 242, **602**
disharmonic regimes, *see* **harmonic regimes**
disposition, **602**
disputes, 85, 151, 197; *see* **law**
distinctive feature, **602**
divination, 105, **163–4**, 179, 341–2
divorce, 286, 312; *see* **marriage**
domestic mode of production, 3, 205, 255, 376, 418, **602**
double descent, 153, **602**
dowry, 351, 435, **602**
drama, 232, 404
Dravidian kinship, 133, **602**
dreams, **165–6**, 199, 440
drive theories of aggression, 561
drugs, 85
dual organization, 39, **166–7**, 314
duolineal, **602**
duolocal, **602**
Dutch anthropology, 24, 130, 131, **167–8**, 353, 475
dysfunction, **602**

Eastern Anthropologist, 297
ecological anthropology, 3–4, 70, 133, **169–72**, 185–8, 359–60, 545, 561; *see also* **cultural materialism**, **environment**
ecology, 195
economic anthropology, 83, **172–8**, 205, 242, 245, 321, 322, 347, 375–6, 453, 508, 564
economic man, 347–8, **603**
Economy and Society, 273
ecosystem, **603**
education, 38, 124, **178–80**, 308, 325, 328, 356, 369, 377–8, 392, 447, 486, 501, 512
egalitarianism, 288–9, 290, **603**
ego, **603**
eidos, **603**
elderhood, **603**
elementary structure, 2–3, 24, 122, 334–5, 412, **603**
embedded, 173, 176, 353; *see* **formalism and substantivism**
emic and etic, 104, 125, 134, 145, **180–3**, 199, 203, 285, 312, 313, 315, 358, 360, 515
empiricism, 57, **603**
enculturation, **603**
endogamy, 134, 269, 282, 350, 366, 413, 476, **603**
Enlightenment, 47, **183–5**, 222, 243, 255, 263, 277, 340, 346, 384, 435, 442, 481, 505, 516, 524, 527

entitlement theory, 240, **603**
environment, 1, 4, 144, 151, 169–72, **185–8**, 216, 245, 289, 381, 445, 460, 476, 516, 532, 564; *see* **ecological anthropology**, **landscape**
environmental determinism, 41–2, 185–8, **603**
environmentalism, 186
episteme, 468
epistemological relativism, 480–1
equality, *see* **inequality**
eschatology, **603**
Eskimo terminology, 477, **603**
essentialism, 50, 111, 112, 142, **188–90**, 201, 255, 305, 403, 407, 462, 516, 521
ethical relativism, 479–80
ethics, 209, 433
ethnicity, 16, 18, 39, 49, 87, 89, 116, 123, 146, **190–3**, 195, 204, 251, 326, 383, 392, 409, 423, 426, 431, 464, 488, 494, 537, 565
ethnoarchaeology, 47
ethnobiology, 41, 42, 104–5, **603**
etnobotany, 125, 199, 359, **603**
ethnocentrism, 6, 155, 194, 301, 338, 341, 404, 422, 457, 462–3, 479, 481, **603–4**; **secondary**, **621**
secondary, 621
ethnocide, **604**
ethnogenesis, 53, 191, 494
ethnographic film, *see* **film**
ethnographic present, **604**
ethnography, 19–20, 27, 41, 47, 57, 64, 65–6, 66, 72–3, 85–6, 120, 128, 162, 172, 204, **193–8**, 208–7, 222, 228–32, 232–3, 237, 243–4, 305, 317, 319, 326, 329, 331, 359, 364–7, 373–4, 375, 378, 381, 382, 404, 411, 427, 443–4, 467–8, 469, 488, 471–2, 474–5, 493, 494, 501, 513–14, 515, 525, 526, 534, 538, 555, 556, 564, 565; of speaking, 426
ethnohistory, 26–7, 37–40, 59, 266, 540, **604**
Ethnological Society of London, 44, 76
ethnology, 10, 95–6, 207–8, 466, 494, **604**
ethnomedicine, 358–9, 360, **604**
ethnomethodology, 162, 604
ethnomusicology, 237, 383–6, **604**
ethnopoetics, 427
ethnopsychiatry, **198–202**, 359, 457, 506
ethnos, 191, 494, **604**

ethnoscience, 105, 125, 168, 180, 199, 200, 202, **202–3**, 326, 442–3

ethnosemantics, 457

ethnosociology, 58, **604**

ethnozoology, 125, **604**

ethogram, 516

ethology, 68, 395, 523, **604**

ethos, 139, 212, 289, 419, 482, 538, **604**

etic, *see* **emic and etic**

eugenics, 74, 189, 463, **604**

European Association of Social Anthropologists, 44, 209

evil eye, **604**

evolution and evolutionism, 1, 15, 21, 32, 35–6, 37–8, 48, 49, 54, 57, 66–71, 73, 77, 95, 98, 116, 126, 118, 130, 138–41, 154–7, 165, 167, 189, 190–1, 194, **213–18**, 223, 225–6, 232, 236–7, 247, 248, 254, 264, 265, 272, 282, 288, 335, 341, 352, 377, 381, 384, 394, 395, 429, 437, 453, 454, 477, 482, 483, 493–4, 505, 515–16, 517, 519, 520, 522–4, 527–8, 533, 546; multilinear, **615**; **unilinear**, 528, **627**; **universal**, **627**

exchange, 36, 38, 46, 65–6, 83–4, 86, 91, 150, 172, **218–21**, 223, 225, 244, 245, 255, 259, 283, 314–15, 319, 334, 347, 349, 350–1, 379–80, 400, 409, 415, 416, 421, 485, 504, 510, 515, 518, 522, 526, 549, 561, 566; **direct**, 24, **602**; **exchange value**, **604**; **generalized**, 60, **606**; indirect, 24; **restricted**, **620**; **sphere of**, 218, 435, **623**

exegesis, 536, 538, **604**

exogamy, 132, 152–3, 166, 250, 282, 295, 314, 350, 366, 476, 543, 548, 550, **604**

exorcism rites, 460

extended family, 205, 223–4, 226, 286, **604–5**

factions, **222**, 419, 446

false consciousness, 367

family, 20, 84, 87–8, 101, 127, 115–16, 173, **223–8**, 260–1, 285–6, 294, 300, 316–17, 350, 374, 381, 398, 415, 419, 450, 477

famine, 240

feedback, 216–17, **605**

female circumcision, *see* **circumcision**

feminism, 27, 59, 76, 99, 112, 113, 134, 189, 227, 253–61, 278,

280–1, 287, 325, 361, 381, 366–7, 404, 428, 433, 434, 442, 447, 453, 488, 472, 481, 503, 539, 564

fetish, fetishism, 173, 219, 349, 484–5, **605**

feud, 409, 559, **605**; **blood feud, 597**

feudalism, 96, 175, **228–9**, 353, 372, 430

fieldnotes, 73, 197–8

fieldwork, 25–6, 46, 55–6, 87, 92, 193–8, 207–9, 214, **229–32**, 233, 253, 278, 303, 321, 326, 343–5, 364–7, 390, 409–10, 422, 429, 433, 438, 444, 454, 501, 556, 557; *see also* **ethnography**, **methodology**

fictive kinship, **605**

fiesta, 30, 31

filiation, 282, 313, **605**

film, 20, 147, 206, **232–35**, 244, 356–7

fishing, 34, 41, 172, 175, **235–6**, 418, 504

fission and fusion, **605**

folk culture, 25, 50, 103, 105, 204, 243, 493, **605**

folk-urban continuum, 33, 370, 418, **605**

folklore, 72–3, 87, 96, 138, 196, 199, 205, 207, 233, **236–8**, 244, 245, 263, 279, 385, 392, 404, 426, 435, 493

food, 27, 172, **238–41**, 360, 361, 437, 533; taboos, 133, 171, 439, 542, 543–4, 550–1; *see also* **nutrition**

foraging, 3, 15, 68, **605**; *see also* **hunting and gathering**

forces of production, **605**

forensic anthropology, 69

formal analysis, 125, 132, 478, **606**

formalism and substantivism, 132, 203, 206, **242**, 347, 349, 427, 434, 445

fostering, *see* **adoption and fostering**

four-field anthropology, 25–7, 45, 73, **606**

four-stage theory, 183

Fourth World, **606**

Frankfurt school, 354

French anthropology, 20, 118, 130, 132, 140, 167, **242–6**, 273, 333–6, 443, 466, 475, 505, 534

friendship, 116, 123, **246**, 267, 417

functionalism, 2, 4, 7, 12, 13, 19–20, 33, 54, 62, 64, 68, 78, 79, 95, 98, 112, 115, 118, 119, 130,

132, 146, 155–6, 158, 161, 191–2, 195, 206, 214, 232, 234, 240, 241, **246–52**, 264, 266, 273, 282, 295, 319, 325, 343, 344–5, 358, 375, 385, 386, 388, 404, 410, 429, 453, 466, 468, 469, 470, 477, 479, 482, 490, 490–1, 510, 515, 516, 517, 520, 522, 532, 534–5, 538, 539, 550, 559, 561, 564

fundamentalism, 300, 485–6, **606**

funeral rites, 91, 307, 380, 425, **606**; *see also* **death**

Galton's problem, 121

gambling, 425

game theory, 431, **606**

Gemeinschaft and *Gesellschaft*, 116, 377, 451, **606**

gender, 18, 20, 21, 33–4, 41, 54, 57, 55, 84, 87, 88, 93, 99, 101–2, 127, 113, 134, 143, 146–7, 172, 178–9, 196, 198, 200–1, 222, 223, 224, 227, 238–9, 246, **253–62**, 269, 279, 280, 281, 303–4, 317, 323, 324, 325, 328, 337, 361, 369, 374, 383, 385, 351, 353, 388, 395, 403, 419, 409, 411, 423, 432, 435, 446, 475, 488, 482, 487, 489, 507, 526, 537, 556, 559, 565

genealogy, **genealogical method**, 65, 181, 195, **262–3**, 316, 390, 410, 494

generalized exchange, *see* **exchange**

generational terminology, 477, **606**

genetrix, 312, **606**

genitor, 312, 317, **606**

genocide, 332, 426, **607**

genotype, **607**

gens, 527, **607**

geology, 333

German and Austrian anthropology, 26, 233, **263–5**, 474

gerontocracy, 23

Gesellschaft, *see* *Gemeinschaft* **and** *Gesellschaft*

Gestalt **theory**, 143, 530, **607**

ghost dance, 35, 265–6, 372, 429, **540**

ghost marriage, 351, **607**

gift, *see* **exchange**

globalization, 339, 521, 567, **607**

glottochronology, *see* **lexicostatistics**

godparenthood, 117–18, **607**

gossip, 123, 197, 246, **266–7**, 280, 398

great and little traditions, 33, 39, 81, 123, 208, **267–9**, 407, 418
'Great Chain of Being', 184
great divide, 369, 518–20, 521, **607**
green revolution, 239, **607**
group marriage, *see* **marriage**
gumsa and *gumlao*, **607**

habitus, 178–9, 316, 459, 513, **607**
harmonic regimes, **607**
haruspicy, 163
Harvard Kalahari Project, 15
Harvard University, 537
Hawaiian terminology, 477, **607**
head-hunting, 60–1
headman, **607**; *see also* **Big Man**
health and healing, *see* **medical anthropology**
hegemony, 89, 124, 134, 332, 386, 417, 428, 432, 440, 447, 488, 528, **608**
heliocentrism, **608**
herders, *see* **pastoralists, transhumance**
hermeneutics, 26, 324, 455, 538, **608**
heteroglossia, 441, **608**
hierarchy, 57–8, 88, 179, 438, 446, 482, 485, **608**
high yield varieties (HYV), **608**
Hinduism, 57–9, 61, 149, 199, 238, 267–8, **271–2**, 286, 299–300, 407–8, 437, 438, 463, 482–6, 499, 540; Brahmans, 57, 80, 90–1, 310; and Buddhism, 80; caste, *see* **caste**; cattle, 171; kingship, 310–11; pilgrimage, 423–4; pollution, 187, 438–9; Saivite, 61; temple, 547
historical linguistics, 185
historical materialism, 528, **608**; *see* **Marxism**
historical particularism, 36, 54, **608**
history, 45, 87, 124, 195, 208–9, 244, 245, 266, **272–7**, 460; conjectural, **599**; inferential, 118, 119; **of anthropology**, 27–8, 35, 274, **277–9**, 381–2
holism, 185, 188, 214, **608**; **methodological**, **614**
hologeistic sampled comparison, 120, 500–1, 511
hominid, 67
Homo economicus, oeconomicus, see **economic man**
homicide, 66; *see also* murder
homosexuality, 199

honour and shame, 34, 101, 211, **280–1**, 416, 419
horticulture, 65, 196, 499, **608**
hot and cold societies, 377, 533, **608**
house, 60, 104, 131, 257, 280, **281–5**, 285, 287, 324, 335; **men's**, **613**
house societies, 281–2, 335
household, 3, 11, 70, 88, 107, 123, 171, 172, 196, 205, 223–8, 238, 239–41, 254, 256, 257, 280, 281, **285–8**, 307, 316–17, 321, 397–8, 401, 415, 418–19, 432, 492, 557
Human Relations Area Files (HRAF), 93, 120, 393, **608**
human rights, 29, 300, 332, 473, 480
hunger, 240; *see also* **food, nutrition**
hunting and gathering, 3, 15, 27, 34, 41, 75, 170, 172, 187, 196, 216, 235, 254, 286, 287, **288–91**, 302, 303, 304, 322, 351, 381, 363, 397, 429, 476, 499, 504, 518, 528, 543, 564
hydraulic civilization, 171, 528, **608**
hypergamy, 62, 282, 476, 522, 523, **608**
hypogamy, 167, 282, 314, 476, **609**
hysteria, **609**

icon, iconicity, **609**
ideal type, 119, 186, **609**
identity, 20, 33, 39, 57, 116, 152, 154, 175, 190, 190–3, 204, 209, 225, 261, 269, 286, **292**, 311, 329, 371, 357, 386, 392, 415, 464, 486, 494, 501, 509–10, 540, 564
ideology, 27, 99, 124, 134, 216, **293–4**, 223, 227, 255, 260, 328, 349–50, 352–3, 417, 435, 482, 491, 498, 515, 543
illness, 360
illocutionary, **609**
illustrative comparison, 119
imagined community, 392, 423
immediate and delayed return, 290, 302, 303, **609**
imperialism, 134, **609**
incest, 140, 153, **294–7**, 314, 334, 350, 454–5, 518, 522, 523, 529, 542, 543, 550–1
inclusive fitness, 191, 523, 561
increase rites, 1
indeginismo, 32

index, indexical, 442, **609**
Indian anthropology, 57–9, **297–8**, 353
indigenous knowledge systems, 322, 326, 503, **609**
indigenous peoples, 266, 322, 382, 426, **609**
indirect rule, 19–20, 321, 431, **609**
individualism, 27, 80–1, 92, 128, 226, 247, **298–302**, 321–2, 338, 347, 376, 411, 419–21, 430, 445, 451, 456, 512, 514, 516–18; **methodological**, 185, 188, 301, **614**
Indo-European language family, **609**
industry, industrialization, 32, 83, 151, 172, 196, 254, 348, 378, 446, 519, 564, 565
inequality, 99, 122, 135, 217, 253–4, 257–9, **302–5**, 418, 446, 462, 528
infant mortality, 158
infanticide, 23, 150, 170, **609**
informal economy, 20, **609**
infrastructure, 352–4, 528, **610**
inheritance, 19, 122, 175, 195, 262, 286, 313, 401, 475, **610**
initiation, 22, 290, **610**; *see also* **rite of passage**
institution, 118, 121, **610**; **primary and secondary institutions**, 144, **610**
institutional comparison, 118
internal colonialism, 32, 192, **598**
International African Institute (IAI), 19, 45, 345, **610**
International Congress of Anthropological and Ethnographical Sciences, 45
International Institute of African Languages and Culture, *see* International School of American Archaeology and Ethnology
International School of American Archaeology and Ethnology, 73
International Société Americanistes, 45
interpretive anthropology, 26, 203, 410, 432, 436, 489, **610**
intertextuality, 427, **610**
involution, **610**
Iroquois terminology, 35, 477, **610**
Islam, 16–18, 20, 59, **305–6**, 368–9, 407–8, 429, 437, 482–6, 537; and caste, 90; fundamentalist, 300, 485–6;

Koran, 355; law, 331; missionaries, 373–4; pilgrimage, 423; sacrifice, 498
isogamy, 610

Jainism, 80
jajmani system, 219, 610
Japanese Society for Ethnology, 45
Jesup North Pacific Expedition, 52, 493
John Frum movement, 85
joint family, 286, 610
joking and avoidance, 35, 63, 308–9, 387, 551
Journal of the Anthropological Institute, 194
Judaism, 131, 204, 437; dietary laws, 105; Old Testament, 355; pilgrimage, 424; Quabalah, 340
jural and moral domains, 312, 450, 515, 517, 610
jural level, 312, 610

karma, 271, 272, 463, 611
kava (*Piper methysticum*), 85
key informant, 230
kindred, 39, 107, 154, 211, 269, 611; nodal, 615
kingship, 59, 60, 81, 151, 274, 275, 310–11, 321, 491–2, 529
kinship, 1–4, 11–12, 18–20, 24–5, 26, 30, 43, 35, 37–9, 41, 53, 55, 57, 60, 63, 72, 78, 88, 92, 95, 99, 104, 106–7, 115, 116, 117, 118, 121, 123, 125, 127, 131, 132, 143, 151–4, 173, 181, 191, 192, 195, 211, 213, 219, 223–8, 232, 242, 245, 246, 256, 257–8, 262, 269, 280, 281–5, 285, 298, 308–9, 311–18, 330, 333, 334–5, 344, 350, 353, 362, 368, 369, 381, 392 , 401 ,410, 412–14, 416–17, 418, 435, 440, 453, 460, 464, 466, 475–6, 476–8, 487–8, 497, 509, 511, 512, 513, 516, 518–20, 526, 528, 529, 532, 534, 537, 543, 550–1, 555, 557; atom of, 63, 596; descriptive and classificatory, 1, 35, 381, 477, 598; Dravidian, 133, 602; fictive, 605; ritual, 117, 211, 620; terminology, *see* relationship terminology; universal, 627
kula, 46, 218, 318–19, 341, 410
Kulturkreis, 48, 118, 161, 264–5, 474, 611

Labanotation, 147
land claims, 3–4

land tenure, 4, 196, 238–9, 290, 322–4, 453, 466, 556
landscape, 43, 39–40, 321–2, 333, 548
language and linguistics, 17, 67–8, 72, 73, 87, 109, 125–6, 162–3, 179, 244, 324–30, 387, 391, 423, 458, 461, 463, 499–501, 515, 518, 536, 553–4
langue and *parole*, 325, 611
Latin American anthropology, 31–4
law, 242, 330–3, 325, 429, 446, 447; customary, 331, 600
left, *see* right and left
legal anthropology, *see* law
legal pluralism, 332, 611
legitimation, 228
leopard-skin chief, 11
levirate, 351, 487, 611
lexicostatistics, 611
life-crisis ritual, *see* rite of passage
life-history, 364, 366
liminality, 97, 489–90, 490–5, 549
limited good, 33, 212, 611
lineage, 5, 11–12, 19, 22, 35, 95, 121, 132, 149, 151–4, 223–8, 283, 284, 313–14, 445–6, 513, 611
Linguistic Minorities Project, 328, 329
linguistic relativism, 611; *see also* Sapir–Whorf hypothesis
linguistics, 25, 45, 72, 109, 162–3, 180–2, 245, 324–60, 362, 499–501, 530–1
Linnaean taxonomy, 103, 181, 611
literacy, 37, 101, 122, 152, 178–9, 209, 268, 308, 325, 336–9, 356, 369
literary criticism, 27, 134, 612
little tradition, *see* great and little traditions
loan word, 612
locutionary, 612
logical positivism, 469
London Missionary Society, 412
longue durée, 46
ludus, 425

Maasina Rule, 85
magic, 9, 65, 76, 195, 340–3, 410, 437, 483, 505
Magdalenians, 53
Mahayana, *see* Buddhism
malnutrition, 401
Man in India, 297
mana, 346–7, 413, 542, 544
Manchester School, 14, 370, 566, 612

manifest function, 612
marker, 612
market, 29–30, 83–5, 173–7, 221, 236, 238, 239, 241, 242, 293, 298, 347–50, 379, 396, 415, 434; economy, 153, 173–7, 242
marriage, 1–2, 14, 18–20, 23–5, 35, 60, 69, 88, 90, 91, 126–7, 117, 131, 132–3, 150, 151–4, 166, 195, 205, 210, 217, 223, 219, 254, 257, 260, 283–4, 285, 295, 311–18, 350–2, 360, 369, 415, 448–50, 460, 464, 476, 478, 489, 518, 561; bilateral cross-cousin, 314; classes, 612; cross-cousin, 2, 63, 132–3, 309, 314, 448–9, 477, 522, 523, 599; exchange, *see* alliance; ghost, 351, 607; group, 132, 477, 607; matrilateral cross-cousin, 60, 132–3, 283, 315, 449, 612; parallel cousin, 314, 369; patrilateral cross-cousin, 132–3, 449, 617; patrilateral parallel-cousin, 617; payments, 150, 258, 351; sister's daughter, 622; widow, 627; woman, 351, 628
Marxism, 3, 20, 33–4, 38, 49, 58, 79, 83, 98–9, 123, 134, 134, 157–8, 168, 173, 174, 177, 206, 219, 224, 229, 235, 242, 245, 253, 254–5, 265, 273–4, 293–4, 302, 321, 325, 333, 347, 352–5, 366–7, 370, 372, 375–6, 377–8, 381, 385–6, 404, 417, 418, 410, 432, 434, 435, 442, 445–6, 453, 488–9, 472, 474, 491–2, 494, 508, 509, 517, 518, 525, 534, 538, 539, 545, 564, 565, 566; in archaeology, 49, 352; structural, 169, 353, 442, 536, 624
mass media, 123, 134–5, 355–8, 377, 385–6; *see also* film
mater, 311–12
material culture, 26, 45, 47, 54, 139–40, 194, 233, 264–5, 279, 281, 302, 362, 494, 544–7, 564, 612
materialism, 64, 186–7, 517, 561, 612
matriarchy, 35, 153, 313, 519, 550, 612
matricide, *see* parricide
matrifocal family, 88, 226–7, 612
matrilateral cross-cousin marriage, 60, 132–3, 283, 315, 449, 612
matrilineage, 43, 77, 121, 194, 283, 284, 313, 381, 612

matrilineal belt, 153
matrilineal descent, 35, 63, 126, 152–3, 166, 224–5, 282, 351, 454, 478, 523, 536, 563, **613**
mechanical and organic solidarity, 377, 451, 499, 519, **613**
mechanical and statistical models, 449, **613**
medical anthropology, 27, 31, 199–200, 245, 263, **358–61**, 447
medical pluralism, 359, **613**
memory, 361–3, 355
men's house, 613
menstruation, 261, **363–4,** 411, 512, 543–4, 548
mentality, 468, **613**; *see also* **primitive mentality**
mercantile capitalism, 436, **613**
Mesolithic, 235, **613**
messianic movement, 372
mestisaje, 32
mestizo, 29–30, 31, 39, **613**
metacommunication, 613
metadescription, 613
metanarrative, 378, 435, 443, 472, 538, **614**
metaphor, 148, **614**
methodological individualism, holism 185, 188, 301, **614**
methodology, 26, 118–21, 209, 239–40, 318, 326, **364–7**, 390, 535
metics (Greece), 175
metonym, 148, **614**
migration, 28, 33, 40, 86, 149, 161, 261, 263, 264, 274, 287, 360, 368, **370–1**, 462, 473–4, 474, 486, 504, 555, 556
millennial movements, millenarianism, 35, 40, 199, 85–6, 265–6, 374, **371–3**, 411, 540
mimesis, 440, **614**
mind, *see* **cognition, psychological anthropology**
Minority Rights Group, 53
missionaries, 373–5, 477, 483–4, 485, 486; Buddhist, 80, 373; Christian, 9, 16, 19, 85, 113, 178, 193, 243, 245, 344–5, 373–5, 412, 429; Islamic, 373
modal personality, 144
mode of production, 20, 37, 157–8, 173, 215, 229, 245, 254–5, 273, 347, 352–3, **375–6**, 418, 436, 488, 534, 566
modernism, 305, **378**, 435

modernity, 14, 25–6, 33, 40, 191, 225, **378–9**, 392, 428, 441, 483, 525
modernization, 32, 39, 85, 96, 156–8, 191, 212, 305, 370, 372, **377–8**, 419, 434
moiety, 2, 39, 166–7, 550, **614**
moksa, 271
Mondo Cane, 85–6
money, 65, 85, 175, 218, 347, **379–80**
monogenism, 76, 194, 382, 463, **614**
monotheism, 104, **614**
moral domain, *see* **jural and moral domains**
moral economy, 349, 419, **614**
mortuary rites, 307, 548, **615**; *see also* **death**
Moscow Company, 51
mother-right, 615
multiculturalism, 300, 306
multiplex relations, 114, 327, 557
multi-resource economy, 397
murder, 319, 563; *see also* homicide
museums, 25, 50, 54, 184, 207, 264, 278, **382–3**, 429, 545
music, 146, **383–4**, 387–8, 404, 427, 549, 557
mutilation, 480
Mutterrecht, see **mother-right**
myth and mythology, 41, 65, 72–3, 94, 101, 130, 138, 148, 194, 213, 227, 245, 274, 283, 324–5, 333, 335–6, 363, 366, **386–9**, 404, 426, 440, 466, 468, 493, 494, 518, 532, 533–4, 563
mythemes, 533

names and naming, 390–1
narratology, 427
nation-state, 31–3, 191, 192, 204, 306, 327, 331–2, 434
national character studies, 133, 144
nationalism, 37, 40, 49–50, 62, 73, 81, 87, 89, 99, 123, 142, 149, 152, 180, 188, 204, 236, 263, 300, 307, 377, **391–3**, 432, 463, 486, 494, 496
Nationality Affairs Commission [China], 96
nativistic movements, 372
nature and culture, 140, 185, 187, 253–61, 294, 315, 323, 361, **393–6**, 440, 487, 516–18
Naturvölker, 263
Nazism, 265, 463
negative reciprocity, *see* **reciprocity**
neo-classical economics, 173, 176, **615**
neo-colonialism, 615

neo-evolutionism, 515, 519, **615**
Neolithic, 235, 532, **615**
network analysis, 123, 208, 217, 246, 263, 301, 365, 375, **396–7**, 555
New Archaeology, 48–9
New Ethnography, 615
New School for Social Research (New York), 26, 530
New Zealand Association of Social Anthropologists, 45
NGO (Non-governmental organization), **615**
nicknames, 391
Nigerian Association of Social Anthropologists, 45
Nine Nationalities College [China], 95
noble savage, 41, 183, 501, **615**
nodal kindred, 615
nomadism, 170, 216, 269, 289, 367, **397–9**, 415, 550, 553
non-verbal communication, 68, 147, 355
non-unilineal descent, 106–7, **615**
norm, 115, 355, **615**
normalization, 331
North American Society for the Study of Culture and Psychiatry, 200
Notes and Queries on Anthropology, 194, 195, 262, 350, 351, 429, 453, **615**
Nouvelle Revue d'Ethnopsychiatrie, 202
nuclear family, 223, 224, 225–6, 300, **615**
number, **399–400**, 452, 460, 501
nutrition, 70, 395, **400–2**

objectivism, 188, 190, 366, **615–6**
Occidentalism, 189, 379, **403**, 407, 526
Oedipus complex, 127, 144, 454–5
Omaha terminology, 477–8, **616**; *see also* **Crow–Omaha systems**
oral literature, 21, 245, 325, **404–5**, 426, 554
orality, 268, 338
oratory, 65, 232, 233, 329, **405–7**, 404
Order of the Golden Dawn, 340
organic analogy, 616
organic solidarity, *see* **mechanical and organic solidarity**
Organization of African Unity (OAU), 473

Oriental despotism, 61, 215,
616; *see also* Asiatic mode of
production, hydraulic
civilization
Orientalism, 57, 111–12, 189,
271, 278–9, 280, 305–6, 324,
403, 407–8, 433, 443, 472, 483,
526

paida, 425
Palaeolithic, 289, 616
palaeontology, 616
Paliau movement, 85
paradigm (Kuhnian), 26, 248,
468, 616
paradigmatic (relations), 335, 616
parallel cousin, marriage, 314,
369, 477, 616
parallel descent, 39, 616
parole, see langue *and* parole
parricide, 616
participant observation, 194,
196, 209, 230, 305, 364, 365,
384, 461, 616
pastoralists, 10–12, 17, 21–2,
170, 172, 196, 238–41, 258, 287,
288–9, 322, 397–8, 415–6, 429,
504, 553
pater, 311–12, 616
patriarchy, 313, 331, 363, 617
patrilateral cross-cousin
marriage, 132–3, 449, 617
patrilateral parallel-cousin
marriage, 314, 369, 617
patrilineage, 11, 21, 43, 77, 121,
152–3, 280, 282, 309, 313–14,
410, 520, 617
patrilineal descent, 2, 63, 132,
152–3, 166–7, 262, 366, 478,
548, 617
patrons and clients, 33, 99, 123,
117, 211, 246, 280, 416–18,
419, 555
peasants, 32–3, 38, 61–2, 83, 87,
98, 122, 158, 171, 173, 205, 207
212, 229, 236, 254, 255, 310,
347, 353, 368, 370, 418–19, 430,
434, 508, 528, 555
performance, 20, 175, 304, 329,
346, 404, 405, 426–7, 459, 491,
554
performative, 617
periphery, *see* centre and
periphery
perlocutionary, 617
person, 5–6, 20, 21, 93, 97, 127,
110, 144, 146, 149, 225, 244,
259, 261, 292, 311, 315, 316,
311, 319, 361, 362, 369, 390,
411, 419–23, 454, 456–61, 487,
510, 512, 516, 537, 557, 559, 561

petty commodity production,
236, 353, 376, 418, 435, 617
peyote, 35, 617
phatic communion, 329,
617
phenomenology, 12, 76, 264,
459–60, 548, 561, 617
phenotype, 617
phoneme, 180, 182, 324, 531,
617
phonetic, 337, 617
phonology, 180, 182, 617
photography, 232; *see also* film
phratry, 527, 617–8
physical anthropology, 66, 564,
618; *see also* biological
anthropology
pidgin, 540, 618
pilgrimage, 39, 97, 369, 423–4,
484, 490
plantations, 29, 81–90, 274
play, 424–5, 491
plural society, 33, 88, 123,
425–6, 464
pluralism, 474; *see also* legal
pluralism, medical
pluralism
poetics, 7, 426–8, 433
political anthropology, 19, 26,
146, 222, 229, 310–11, 325, 381,
417, 428–34, 445–6
political economy, 26–7, 37–8,
55, 58, 87, 93, 98, 128, 157, 169,
206, 216, 254, 305–6, 347,
352–4, 360, 375, 426, 431, 432,
434–7, 512, 566
pollution and purity, 57, 105,
151, 187, 268, 269, 272, 293,
303, 361, 363–4, 411, 435,
437–9
polyandry, 286, 351, 618
polygamy, 351, 522, 618
polygenism, 76, 161, 382, 463,
618
polygyny, 152, 351, 523, 618
polysemy, 323, 517, 618
polytheism, 104, 311, 618
positivism, 141, 191, 203, 207,
384, 391, 455, 536, 618
possession, 75, 84, 146, 163, 199,
200–1, 268, 358, 420, 439–42,
489, 506
postcolonialism, 112, 135, 171,
190, 392, 407, 419, 439, 485,
618
postmodernism, 25, 27, 49, 87,
89, 135, 182, 183, 192, 198, 223,
255, 259, 279, 325, 342, 366,
377, 378–9, 392, 407, 428, 432,
436, 442–5, 472, 494, 503,
506–7, 521, 563

post-processual archaeology,
49, 618
poststructuralism, 112, 134–5,
141, 182, 354, 404, 427, 539,
618
potlatch, 34, 36, 100, 143, 290,
319, 445
power, 23, 27, 33, 65, 89, 93, 134,
135, 163, 179, 241, 254, 260,
267, 279, 304, 310–11, 328, 346,
349–50, 354, 386, 428, 436,
440–1, 445–8, 453, 480, 494,
515, 557, 559, 565
practice, 64, 293, 316, 431, 490,
492–3, 513, 521, 550, 618
pragmatics, 618
praxis, 316, 618
preference and prescription,
24–5, 153, 448–50, 478
prelogical mentality, 109, 451–2
presentism, 277, 618
prestation, 173, 351, 411, 619
primary and secondary
institutions, 144, 619
primatology, 68, 523
primitive, primitivism, 126,
264–5, 302, 340–1, 376–7, 378,
429, 450–1, 468–9, 500, 501,
540, 619
primitive communism, 3, 53,
302, 321, 375, 450–1
primitive mentality, 244, 338,
451–2, 468
primitive promiscuity, 450, 619
primogeniture, 619
processual archaeology, 49,
619
processualism, 510
profane, *see* sacred and profane
property, 5, 11, 63,122, 126,
151, 151–3, 174, 223, 226, 227,
253, 254–5, 258, 259, 265, 302,
311, 330, 381, 415, 433, 434,
453–4, 466, 477, 509, 527–8
prophets, 11–12, 85, 371–3, 619
Protestant ethic, 83, 97, 525,
564, 619
prototype theory, 104, 105,
619
proxemics, 619
psychic unity, 109, 161, 264,
456, 619
psychoanalysis, 93, 127, 134,
143, 245, 292, 333, 341, 360,
410, 441–2, 454–6, 512, 559
psychological anthropology, 27,
108–11, 143, 292, 404, 421,
451–2, 456–61, 501, 505–6, 564
psychology, 361–3; cultural, 458–9
puberty, 619
purity, *see* pollution and purity

quantitative methods, 365, 525
questionnaires, 197, 200, 477

race, 38–40, 73, 77, 87, 89, 99,
    114, 134–5, 138, 161, 190–3,
    198, 213, 227, 278, 300, 303,
    391, 394, 395, 407, 425–6, 435,
    436, 446, 462–5, 479, 494, 537,
    556
racism, 14, 31–2, 38, 49, 73–4, 127,
    134, 139, 462–4, 479, 556, 565
ramage, 413, 619
ranching, 415
rank, see inequality
rationality, 64, 109, 173, 176,
    298, 301, 333, 338, 348, 442–3,
    456, 467–70, 480–1, 503, 505,
    514, 543
reading, see literacy
rebellion, ritual of, 13, 387, 620
reciprocity, 66, 173, 219, 319,
    410, 619
reflexivity, 27, 182, 209, 234, 273,
    385, 443, 455, 470–3, 480
refugees, 464, 473–4
regional analysis, comparison,
    119, 123, 182, 195, 474–6
reincarnation, 80, 391, 420
relations of production, 620
relationship terminology, 63,
    103, 125, 132–3, 161, 181, 312,
    448, 476, 476–8; Choctaw, see
    Crow–Omaha; Crow, 477–8,
    600; Crow–Omaha, 132–3,
    477–8; Eskimo, 53, 269, 477,
    603; Hawaiian, 477, 607;
    Iroquois, 35, 477–8, 610;
    Omaha, 477–8, 616;
    Sudanese, 269, 477, 624;
    terminological extension, 132
relative deprivation, 372, 620
relativism, 64, 116, 136, 138,
    155–7, 188, 191, 196, 393, 399,
    470, 478–82, 499–501
religion, 3, 9, 11–12, 20, 39–40,
    52, 55, 58, 59–61, 64, 73, 80–1,
    85–6,91–2, 87, 89–90, 93, 95,
    96–8, 99, 101, 127, 116, 118,
    129, 143, 146–7, 173, 186, 189,
    194, 198, 213, 267–8, 290, 294,
    299, 335, 341, 346–7, 353, 354,
    358–9, 368–9, 371–3, 381, 391,
    392, 410–11, 423–4, 426, 456,
    482–7, 490–1, 494, 496, 497–9,
    504–7, 512, 516, 519, 528, 529,
    537, 540, 550, 556; see also
    individual religions by name
remote sensing, 49
Renaissance anthropology, 468
reproductive technologies, 127,
    317, 351, 361, 487–8

resistance, 4, 14, 42, 83–4, 85, 99,
    113, 124, 171–2, 173, 206, 212,
    265, 274, 322, 332, 446, 447,
    354, 374, 419, 432, 436, 440,
    462, 464, 486, 488–9, 490, 566
revitalization movements, 372,
    620
Rhodes-Livingstone Institute,
    14, 157, 370, 431, 536, 556, 620
right and left, 75, 105, 620
rite of passage, 21–2, 101, 105,
    244, 286, 423, 489–90, 491,
    536, 549
ritual, 1, 3, 9, 13, 22, 41, 64, 85,
    92, 94, 97, 103, 105, 131, 144,
    148, 150, 166, 170, 178, 194,
    196, 206, 233, 244–5, 258, 266,
    294, 303, 310, 341, 351, 372,
    358, 362, 366, 387, 388, 392,
    393, 409, 410, 440, 460, 489,
    475, 482, 489–90, 490–3, 496,
    497–9, 504–7, 512, 529, 535–7,
    549, 561, 565; of rebellion,
    620
ritual kinship, 117, 211, 620
Rockefeller Foundation, 345
role, 510–11, 620
Romanticism, 505, 507
routinization, 620
Royal Anthropological Institute, 44,
    76, 279
Rumyantzev Museum, 493
Russian Academy of Sciences, 493
Russian and Soviet
    anthropology, 52–3, 191, 229,
    265, 302, 352, 375, 381, 493–5,
    506
Russian Geographical Society, 493

sacred and profane, 167, 171,
    437, 496, 505
sacrifice, 12, 39, 43, 97, 163, 413,
    420, 485, 497–9, 560
salvage anthropology, 25
salvage archaeology, 620
salvage ethnography, 194, 620
sampling, 365
Sapir–Whorf hypothesis, 109,
    234, 325, 480, 499–501
Saussurean
savage, savagery, 37, 154–5, 159,
    183, 184, 381, 429, 484, 518,
    620–1; see also noble savage
scandals, 501–3
Scandinavian anthropology, 353
Scandinavian school, 52
scapulimancy, 163
scarification, 621
schema, schemata, 106, 108, 110,
    145, 512, 545, 621
schismogenesis, 621

science, 101, 118, 184, 338, 341,
    342, 366, 377, 378, 468, 469,
    481, 482, 487–8, 503–4, 543,
    544–7, 563
scientific materialism, 340
scientism, 26, 621
seasonal cycle, 11, 18, 52, 170,
    187, 235, 240, 269, 367, 398,
    401, 476, 504, 548–9, 553
secret societies, 36, 73, 410,
    431, 621
section systems, 1–2, 105, 312
sedentarism, 216, 397, 621
segmentary lineage, 11, 22, 24,
    152, 154, 313, 368, 410, 529,
    621
segmentary society, 24, 529
semantic domain, 125
semantic parallelism, 105
semantics, 104–5, 621; see also
    componential analysis,
    ethnoscience
semiology, 3, 324–5, 621
semiotics, 54, 135, 237, 410, 621
Sendero Luminoso, 40
seriation, 48, 621
settlement patterns, 476, 504
sex and sexuality, 101–2, 257–9,
    261, 395, 410, 501, 556
sex roles, see gender
sexual communism, 53
sexual division of labour, see
    gender
shamanism, 52, 55–6, 75, 100,
    178, 199, 201, 290, 342, 359,
    413, 439, 489, 494, 504–8, 563
shame, see honour and shame
shanty town, 99
sharecropping, 508
Shi'a, see Islam
shifting cultivation, 60, 287,
    621; see also swidden
    agriculture
Shining Path movement, 40
Shintoism, 55, 308
sib, 621
siblingship, 60
signified and signifier, 530,
    621–2
Sikhism, 59
sister's daughter marriage, 622
slash and burn, see swidden
    agriculture
slavery, 16, 18–19, 76, 86, 101–2,
    218, 225, 375, 463, 509–10,
    552, 565
social action, 431–2, 562, 594
social anthropology, 26, 67, 79,
    262, 421, 622
social charter, 622
social class, see class

social construction theory, 458–9, 460
social contract, **622**
social control, 65, 410, 430, **622**
social Darwinism, 522
social fact, 26, 126, 232, 249, 299, **622**
social formation, **622**
social movements, 85–6, 207, 371–3, 431, 446
social network, 267, 521; *see* network analysis
social organization, 26, 410, **510–12**, 515, 520, **622**; *see also* social structure
social reproduction, 410, 436, **622**
social strain-gauge theory, 563
social stratification, **622**; *see also* class, inequality
social structure, 57, 86, 115, 140, 223, 232, 254, 255, 260, 263, 290–1, 313, 368, 371, 410, 419, 429, 453, 490, **510–12**, 517, 520, 561; *see also* social organization
social system, 515, **622**
socialism, 205–6, 322, 453; African, 322
sociality, 323, 514–21, **622**
socialization, 55, 93, 147, 178, 206, 224, 254, 287, 292, 299, 355, 457, **512–14**, 520
societas, 516–21
Société d'Anthropologie, 66
Société des Observateurs de l'Homme, 44, 184
Société Oceanistes, 45
sociétés à maison, *see* house societies
society, 25, 47, 110, 116, 137, 140–1, 183, 190–3, 231, 298–9, 302–4, 318, 326, 370, 429, 456, 471, 476, 489–90, 512, **514–22**, 527–9, 538, 540, 547, 559
Society for Applied Anthropology, 44
sociobiology, 68, 139–41, 191, 255, **522–4**, 561
sociocentrism, 186
sociology, 26, 79, 96, 134, 135, 157, 207, 210, 247, 251, 265, 295, 298, 299, 303–4, 362, 392, 394, 396, 418, 437, 446, 471, 474, 494, 503, 511, **524–7**, 538, 559, 565
solidarity, *see* mechanical and organic solidarity
sorcery, *see* witchcraft and sorcery
sororal polygyny, **623**
sororate, **623**

soteriology, 271
soul, 150, **623**
Soviet anthropology, *see* **Russian and Soviet anthropology**
space, *see* time and space
speech act, 237, 326, **623**
speech community, 237, 326, 405, 427, **623**
speech event, 162, 196, 326, 328–9, **623**
spirit possession, *see* **possession**
spheres of exchange, 218, 435, **623**
sport, 400, 561; *see also* play
state, 50, 61–2, 81, 113, 116, 123, 134, 188, 193, 215–16, 224, 227, 228–9, 260–1, 302, 310, 381, 391, 392, 416–17, 419, 429, 434, 445–6, 447, 453, 463, 482–4, 486, 494, 514, 516, 518, 520, **527–30**, 537, 556, 559, 562; formation, 123, 215–16, 375, 446, 511, 528–9, **623**
statistical models, *see* **mechanical and statistical models**
status, 36, 115, 253–61, 290, 362, 357, 377, 413, 494, 510–11, 529, 563, **623**
stem family, 223, 224, 286, **623**
structural adjustment, 239, **623**
structural amnesia, 362
structural anthropology, 530–5; *see also* structuralism
structural distance, 22–3
structural form, **623–4**
structural-functionalism, 13, 26, 35, 47, 88, 210, 214, 385, 431, 510, 515, 517–18, **624**
structural linguistics, 333, 334–5, 530–2, 534
structural Marxism, *see* **Marxism**
structuralism, 26–7, 36, 38, 47, 49, 54, 73, 79, 115, 118, 119, 130–1, 167, 237, 245, 319, 326, 353, 376, 386, 404, 410, 426, 432, 443, 475–6, 477, 494, 507, 510, 515, 518, 520, 530–5, 536, 539, 549, 550; Dutch, 167–8, 475
structuration, 521
Subaltern Studies, 27, 59, 294, 432, 433, 435, 439, 488, **624**
subculture, 124, 139, 556
subincision, 363, **624**
subject position, **624**
subjectivism, **624**
subsistence agriculture, **624**
substance, *see* code and substance
substantivism, *see* **formalism and substantivism**
succession, 311, 313, **624**

Sudanese terminology, 269, 477, **624**
suicide, 150
Sunni, *see* Islam
superorganic, 517, **624**
superstructure, *see* **base and superstructure**
surface structure, *see* **deep and surface structure**
survey methods, 365
survival, 63, 468
survivalism, 236–7
swidden agriculture, 41, 171, **624–5**
symbol, 2–3, 41, 47, 49, 54, 60, 97, 105, 115–16, 173, 194, 245, 316, 336, 342, 351, 361, 355, 357, 482, 490–3, 497–9, 505, 507, 518, 545, **625**
symbolic anthropology, 26, 53, 103, 141, 169, 301, 392–3, 455, 480, 481, 488, 501, 515, **535–9**, 565
symbolic capital, 316, 433
symbolic interactionism, 266–7, 431, **625**
symbolic system, 253, 256–7, 258, 259, 260, 261, 506
symmetric alliance, **625**
sympathetic magic, **625**
syncretism, 32, 55, 61, 81, 90, 97, 485, **539–41**
syntagmatic, syntax, 335, **625**
systems theory, 201, **625**

taboo, 52, 104, 131, 133, 144, 151, 171, 341, 346, 363, 413, 437–9, 440, 499, 518, 522, **542–4**, 550
tabula rasa, **625**
taxonomy, **625**; *see also* classification
Techniques et Culture, 47
technological determism, 338
technology, 47, 53, 134, 144, 169, 186, 216, 288, 336, 386, 398, 460, 487–8, **544–7**, 565; appropriate, **625**
teknonymy, 390, **625**
terminological extension, 132
terminology, *see* **relationship terminology**
territoriality, **625**
text, 72, 163, 194
theism, 12
theodicy, 272, **625**
Theravada, *see* **Buddhism**
thick description, 101, 273, 326, 538, **625**
Third World, 154–60, **625–6**
time and space, 9, 103, 179, 390, 400, 420, 452, 505, **547–50**

tools, 48, 85, 169, 175, 186, 544–7
Torres Straits Expedition, 409–10, **626**
totemism, 1, 3, 105, 118, 166, 290, 335, 440, 496, 505, 507, 532–3, 543–4, **550–1**
tourism, 412, **551–3**
trade, 27, 61–2, 65, 172, 216, 556, 561
tradition, 26, 57–9, 85, 113, 143, 158–60, 179, 272, 275, 321, 409, 491
traditional society, 151, 300, 527–30
trait, 118, 121, 475
trance, 202, 385, 506, **626**; *see also* **possession**, **shamanism**
transactionalism, 58, 123, 168, 266–7, 301, 410, 431, 518, **626**
Transcultural Psychiatric Research Review, 200
transformational analysis, 626
transformational-generative grammar, 626
transhumance, 235, 367, 416, 504, **553**
translation, 255, 259, 480, **553–4**
transmigration, 271, 272
transvestism, 164
tribe, tribal, 18, 521, 527, **626**
trickster, 626
trope, 452, **626**
two-line prescription, 626

ultimogeniture, 626
underdevelopment, 434; *see also* **development**

unilinear evolutionism, *see* **evolution and evolutionism**
United Nations Convention on the Status of Refugees, 473
United Nations High Commissioner for Refugees, 473
Universal Declaration of Human Rights, 300, 473
uniliversal evolutionism, *see* **evolution and evolutionism**
universal kinship, 627
universitas, 516–21
Untouchables, 627
urban anthropology, 27, 122, 263, 381, **555–8**
Urban Anthropology, 556
use value, 627
usufruct, 238–9, **627**
utilitarianism, 192, 483, 516, 517, 519, **627**

Vailala Madness, 86
Vienna school, 263, 264
Vietnam War, 418–19
Viking Fund, *see* Wenner-Gren Foundation
village studies, 39, 57–8
violence, 81, 211, 432, 498, **559–60**, 562
visual anthropology, 27, 232, 404, 427; *see also* **film**
Volk, 191
Völkerkunde, Volkskunde, 184, 263–4, **627**

war, warfare, 2, 4, 216, 409,

410, 429, 448, 518, 559, **561–2**
Wenner-Gren Foundation for Anthropological Research, 45
Whorfian hypothesis, *see* **Sapir–Whorf hypothesis**
widow inheritance, widow marriage, 627
wife-giver, -taker, 284
witchcraft and sorcery, 85, 341, 475, 560, **562–4**
woman marriage, 351, **628**
women, *see* **gender**
work, 173, 260–1, **564–5**
World Bank, 158, 322
world system, 32, 46, 87, 123, 157, 169, 192, 193, 195, 273, 347, 353, 370, 376, 378, 419, 428, 434, 436, 462, 485, 488, 539, 540, **566–7**
worldview, 342, 388, 468, 482, **628**
writing, *see* **literacy**
Writing Culture, 427, 443, 471, 538, **628**

Yali movement, 85
Yanjing-Yunnan Station for Sociological Research, 95
youth movement, 372
yurt, 397–8

Zambian National Research Institute, *see* **Rhodes-Livingstone Institute**